# THE
# COLLECTOR'S
# ENCYCLOPEDIA
# OF DOLLS

*By the Authors*

DOLLS, MAKERS AND MARKS
THE AGE OF DOLLS

# THE
# COLLECTOR'S
# ENCYCLOPEDIA
# OF DOLLS

by dorothy s.,
elizabeth a.,
and
evelyn j.
COLEMAN

CROWN PUBLISHERS, INC.   NEW YORK

Library of Congress Catalog Card Number: 68-9101
ISBN: 0-517-00059-8
Printed in the United States of America
Published simultaneously in Canada by
General Publishing Company Limited
20   19   18   17

# CONTENTS

A LA GALERIE VIVIENNE
Mᵒⁿ· GUILLARD
JEUX & JOUETS
REMOND Sᵘᶜᶜ·
4 Rue des Petit Champs 4
PARIS

A la Galerie Vivienne

E Z
Fabrik Marks

Emil Zitzmann

# ACKNOWLEDGMENTS

A book of this magnitude requires the assistance of a great many people. We have been most fortunate in the tremendous response from various museums, private collectors, and dealers who have offered to help us in our search for rare dolls as well as those that the beginning collector may readily find. We are extremely grateful to Mr. Voorhees and the McCready Publishing Co. staff of PLAYTHINGS, who permitted us free access to all their issues. We thank the following for permitting us to take or use pictures of their dolls: Chester County Historical Society (Maxine Waldron); FitzWilliam Museum, Cambridge; Germanisches National - Museum, Nürnberg; International Doll Library Foundation, where both Samuel Pryor and June Douglass allowed us many privileges; Museum of the City of New York (John Noble); Newark Museum, Newark, N.J.; Smithsonian Institution (Rodris Roth); Sonneberg Museum (Emmy Lehmann); Stadtbibliothek, Nürnberg; Franz Weber Museum (Marg. Weber-Beck); Western Reserve Historical Society (Florence Dawley); Helen Ackert; Eunice Althouse; Dorothy Annunziato; Mrs. Charles Axelrod; Evelyn Barrows; Madame Alexander (Beatrice Behrman); Cherry Bou; Hildred Brinkley; Grace Brockman; Sylvia Brockmon; Rosemarye Bunting; Eleanor Jean Carter; Alberta Darby; Mary Dawson; Virginia Dilliplane; Diane Domroe; Mary E. Edwards; Sally Euchner; Lottie Fahrenbruch; Helen Fish; Miss Fulmer; Josephine Garrison; Theodora Gearhart; Bess Goldfinger; Edna Greehy; Peg Gregory; Lester and Alice Grinnings; Freda Hawkins; Gladyse Hilsdorf; Marion Holt; Eva M. Horváth; Flora Gill Jacobs; June Jeffcott; Winnie Langley; Mrs. Latimer; Ollie Leavister; Winifred Leese; Fidelia Lence; Louise Lund; Ruth and R. C. Mathes; May Maurer; Marie McCollom; Edith Meggers; Frances Miller; Ruth Noden; Jessica Norman; Helen Jo Payne; Marian Pickup; Maurine Popp; Bernard Ravca; Kit Robbins; Mary Roberson; Pat Robinson; Pat Schoonmaker; Laura Treskow; Hazel Ulseth; Frances Walker; Betty Lou Weicksel; May Wenzel; and Margaret Whitton. Besides the above, we wish to express our gratitude to: Genevieve Angione; Thelma Bateman; Mrs. D. E. Corder; Dorothy Cook; Marjorie Darrah of Mary Merritt Doll Museum; Jo Elizabeth Gerken; Mary Kahler of the Library of Congress; Joseph L. Kallus of Cameo Doll Co.; Benjamin Michtom of Ideal Novelty & Toy Co.; Herman Reinhardt; Frances Smith; Kitty Smith; Joyce Alexander; Mrs. J. R. Latimer; Florence McCarter, and all others who gave us generous assistance.

A special word of gratitude goes to H. C. Smith, Dorothy Coleman's father, who spent endless hours in the tedious task of carding and filing data, and to Alberta Darby for helping in all phases of this book.

This book would not have been possible without the tremendous aid given by many members of the doll world. One of the great attractions of doll collecting is the spirit of cooperation and friendship among those who share this hobby. Having lavishly enjoyed these benefits, we hope that this volume will in turn pass some of them on to our readers.

# INTRODUCTION

"A doll is one of the most imperious wants, and at the same time one of the most delicious instincts, of feminine childhood."—*Godey's Lady's Book and Magazine,* October, 1869.

Many people never outgrow their love of dolls and never lose the ability to appreciate and enjoy the artistic beauty of dolls. However, as in nearly everything, enjoyment increases with knowledge, and this volume is written especially to bring added knowledge — and, therefore, pleasure — to doll collectors and to students of antique dolls.

The word "doll" is relatively new, but it has had a variety of meanings. In attempting to prepare an encyclopedic volume about dolls, it was first necessary to evolve a limited definition of the word itself. For the purposes of this book, "doll" is defined as "a child's plaything in human form." Our definition excludes all religious, fetish, pincushion, candy-box, and other purely decorative "dolls," as well as figurines. Some imaginary creatures in semihuman form are included, such as Kewpies, Billikens, and Happifats, for example. Two-dimensional dolls of paper, wood, metal, or other materials are excluded, but three-dimensional dolls, even those made of paper, are included. Strictly oriental dolls and dolls made by native Indians, Eskimos, and various other peoples are excluded, though dolls made in Europe with oriental features or dolls made in the Orient with occidental features are included. The same is true for Indian and other types of dolls, especially those made by large commercial firms. Although souvenir "dolls" produced entirely by natives are excluded, some foreign costume dolls are included. These dolls were often manufactured in Germany and France, and are no different from ordinary play dolls, except that they were dressed in native costumes before or after distribution to other countries.

For our definition, it was also assumed that mechanical "dolls"—especially clockwork "dolls" that play music and/or perform feats—are toys rather than dolls. But dolls that perform simple human functions such as walking, talking, and nursing are included.

This book does not pretend to cover all dolls as defined, or even all doll makers, before 1925. It is hoped, however, that the principal documented ones are included; and collectors will no doubt be amazed at both the vast number of these that are known and also the number that need further exploration.

Dolls are made primarily as playthings for children, but the successful maker has a dual purpose—he must please not only the child but also the adult who purchases the doll. Penny dolls were more likely to be purchased to fill the wants of a child; luxury dolls, on the other hand, had to please adults as well as children, and sometimes may even have served as status symbols.

Competition forced doll makers to change their dolls continually. Each year new models were added and slight changes were made in the old ones—different wigs, clothes, or sizes—even in trivial things, in order to tempt the buyer to get the latest doll for his child. A new and successful doll was immediately copied by other makers. This fact must be kept in mind when studying dolls that closely resemble each other. In many cases, they may merely have originated in the same period rather than have been made by the same maker.

It is sometimes said that the dolls that have survived for collectors are the failures of the doll world—the ones that did not perish from overloving in the nursery; but this does not appear to be true in many instances. Even children tend to guard and protect the dolls they love the most. Many of the best dolls that find their way into collections have been carefully cherished in a family through the years and may have survived the affection of several generations of children. After all, it is not necessary for well-behaved children to destroy their beloved dolls—most Victorian youngsters were taught to care for and appreciate their possessions. Actually, the ravages of time and insects have played the greatest havoc with dolls, followed closely by the efforts of overzealous collectors who attempt to restore and redress their acquisitions.

A collector is fortunate indeed when he can obtain a doll directly from the family of the original owner. Doll collectors are most grateful for the information provided by descendants and successors of early doll makers or original owners, though if the descendants or successors were small children or not even born when the events described took place, caution must be used in accepting their hearsay evidence. When such evidence is presented in this volume, it has generally been verified (or refuted) by contemporary records.

The purpose of this book is to identify dolls through descriptive materials, photographs, and marks. The written entries attempt to provide documented data on who, when, where, and what. The "who" covers manufacturers, distributors, designers, and patentees. The "when" covers contemporary documentation from the ancient world through 1925.

The "where" includes Western Europe and America,

with a few entries for other parts of the world, especially countries producing commercial dolls for the markets of the Western World.

The "what" covers the names of dolls; the materials used for dolls; the methods of manufacturing both entire dolls and parts of dolls; descriptions of types of dolls and their parts, including marks, clothing, sizes, and relative prices.

The names of dolls are those actually given to them by their manufacturers or distributors. Those included here have a documentary basis; we do not include the multiplicity of names bestowed by individual collectors. Often, a name was used by several manufacturers, and sometimes one manufacturer would use the same given name for dolls that appeared totally different. This is generally the case when a name applied to a line of dolls rather than to a specific doll. An attempt has been made to indicate that fact when a name applied to a line of dolls, but records do not always provide this information.

Names sometimes vary slightly for the same type of doll by the same maker: "Baby" or "Bébé" sometimes is included as part of a given name and sometimes omitted. "Baby Darling" and "My Darling," both made by Morimura Bros. at the same time, were probably the same doll. Often, the name on the copyright is not the same as that of the actual doll when it was marketed; for example, "Gamine" on the copyright became "Little Annie Rooney." The name "Frozen Charlotte" has been used in this volume because the trade names for this type of doll varied so considerably during the 19th century. They appear to have been known as China Babies, Bisque Babies, Bathing Dolls, and—after 1880—as Solid Chinas, Solid Bisques, and so on.

Individuals often gave names to the dolls in their collections, and these may appear in publications with pictures of the dolls. Thus, a given type of doll may have numerous names, all of which are simply personal nomenclature and are unrelated to trade names—and are therefore not included in this volume.

The principal manufacturers are generally listed under their original names in this book, and the names of successors are cross referenced. In a few instances where the original name was used for a very brief period and is relatively unknown, the entry is listed under the familiar name. The names in italics denote separate entries that, in many cases, provide additional information. Names of makers, distributors, and the like are entered under the surnames, but names of portrait dolls are entered under the given names. The spelling variants of names are usually cross referenced.

Names not having entries, but appearing in the index, include partners, nontrade names such as the name of a person who carried on business under a pseudonym, and artists from whose works dolls were copied. Large companies that produced many dolls have references to these dolls listed under the company name in the index.

The dates given are not necessarily terminal dates. Dolls were often made for longer periods than indicated by the sources we were able to consult. The dates given for most European trademarks represent only the spread between the application for and registration of these marks. A mark could have been used for some time prior to its registration and, no doubt, was often used for some years after its registration. Even in a United States trademark, the earliest date applies only to its use in interstate commerce. The plus sign after a date indicates a continuation for an unknown period. Since data after 1925 were not searched thoroughly, many names may, or may not, have continued after that date. Some of these companies may still be in operation; others may have ceased as soon as 1926. The 1925 cut off date was an arbitrary one necessitated by the magnitude of the doll industry and the fact that most dolls of interest to collectors precede this date.

Many dolls were assembled from parts made in several different countries. Often, dolls designed in the United States and distributed worldwide might have heads made in Germany, mohair wigs produced in England, and Parisian clothes. The changing boundaries also make geographical identification difficult. The Grödner Tal area that produced "Dutch" wooden dolls was located in both Austria and Italy, at various times. A border alteration changed Neustadt and Coburg from Thüringia to Bavaria after World War I. ("Thüringia" generally appears in the text simply as "Thür.") Usually, places mentioned in the text are designated by town and state or province, in abbreviated form, except for New York City and similar well-known cities.

Source material on dolls is somewhat meager prior to 1850. Since wooden dolls and wax dolls were the principal early dolls, the information on them is less complete than on the china, bisque, and composition dolls of the later period. The meaning of words varies sometimes with different periods and different areas. It should also be kept in mind that advertisements tend to exaggerate. This characteristic becomes a factor in the 20th century especially, where advertisements formed a considerable portion of the source material. The documents consulted were often in French or German, and sometimes precise translations were difficult, as for example "Bébé Incassable" in French and "Täuflinge" in German. In such instances, the original word is generally used to prevent a misleading translation. The family relationship terms such as "Gebrüder" and "Frère" are usually kept in the original language, since the initials for these words are often valuable for identification. There is also spelling variation in names from one country to another. For example, "John" in England, "Jean" in France, and "Johannes" in Germany could all refer to the same person. The spelling in the country where the doll maker resided has been used wherever possible. Labels in French or French names such as "Bébé Elite" may appear on dolls produced entirely in Germany. Labels in English are found occasionally on dolls made in France for the English trade. The umlaut over a vowel in German can be replaced by an "e" following the vowel. Thus Bähr & Pröschild can also be written "Baehr

& Proeschild." The spelling with the umlaut has been used almost entirely in this volume. The letters "K" and "C" are often interchangeable, as are "I" and "J," and occasionally "D" and "T," or "B" and "V," or "I" and "Y." A name can appear as Carl or Karl, for instance. These variations are especially important in locating initials.

The names of dolls frequently appear in both singular and plural forms. If a name is not found in the singular form, the reader should seek the plural form, and vice versa. English and French names usually add an "s," but occasionally the word changes—as, for example, "Baby" and "Babies." The plural for most German names is made by adding an "e." The words "Le," "La," "Les," "De," "Des," "Der" are usually alphabetized and not ignored as "The" usually is.

It should be emphasized that the PRICES QUOTED IN THIS BOOK ARE THE PRICES FOR WHICH DOLLS WERE ORIGINALLY OFFERED FOR SALE AND NOT THE PRICES FOR WHICH THEY CAN BE PURCHASED AT THE PRESENT TIME.

The prices given are for a single doll unless noted as for a dozen or gross. Prices for individual dolls are usually retail list prices. These do not allow for discounts. However, it was not always discernible whether the prices quoted in our sources were retail, wholesale, or for jobbers. Where possible, original prices have been included to provide the reader with some indication of the relative quality of various dolls and of their value when they were new, but contemporary prices often have little relationship to current collectors' prices. There is a separate entry on Prices, which attempts to indicate the relative values of antique dolls to collectors and the factors that account for the variations in these values.

The sizes given should be considered as approximate, since there seems to be considerable variation due to stretching, shrinking, settling, the type of hairdo, and other factors. Often additional sizes were made in some years, and this may help to date a particular doll. Dolls made in many different sizes were usually dolls that enjoyed a wide popularity. The heights given with the pictures are for the entire doll unless otherwise designated.

A *double* slant line (//) is used to indicate the beginning of a new line in a mark, since a *single* slant line (/) sometimes occurs as part of a mark.

In addition to the alphabetical entries, bibliography, and general index, this book contains a special index covering the initials and symbols found on dolls, and also numbers other than size numbers. Many symbols and initials still remain unidentified, or there is confusion about them because more than one maker used the same symbol or initials. In these cases, the collector must study all the available information about a doll and then decide which is the most probable identification. The numbers can be mold numbers, dates, account numbers, and so on. The marks shown herein are those actually found on dolls, for the most part. It is sometimes difficult to decipher such marks, especially those incised on bisque heads. Because of this fact, and because a maker might use many variations of his mark, the reader should not be concerned with slight differences. Note that in the mark shown in Ill. 1694 the maker corrected one of his numbers but left traces of the erroneous digit. It is important to study types of marks and their characteristics. Often, part of a mark is obliterated or illegible and the mark can be identified only through knowledge of similar marks. The special index should help in many of these instances.

---

The prices given for dolls are those for which the dolls were originally offered for sale. They are *not* today's prices.

# HOW TO USE THIS BOOK

Trace a marked or labeled doll simply by looking up the name (or initials) in the entries or indexes; also read any suggested cross references (indicated by italicized words). Further useful information appears in the entries on the materials of which a doll is made, and in those on doll parts (Eyes, Hands, Cloth Bodies, for instance).

Helpful entries in tracing an unmarked doll are those on the different types of dolls (Walking Dolls, Talking Dolls, Baby Dolls, Lady Dolls, etc.); on the manufacture of various types of dolls (Manufacture of Bisque Heads, Manufacture of Composition Heads, for example); and on special characteristics such as Flirting Eyes, Multi-Face, and so on. Other pertinent information appears in general entries like Age of Dolls, Chronology, Clothes, Custodianship, Patents, etc. Data on trends in the types of dolls at various periods can be found in the entries for large distributors—Borgfeldt, Ehrich Bros., Horsman, Samstag & Hilder, Louis Wolf, and numerous others.

The many illustrations provide opportunities for comparing an unknown doll with similar ones that have been identified.

# A

**A B C Bodies.** See **Pet Names.**

**A. F. & C.** Found on papier-mâché heads with *Superior* labels.

**A la Clinique des Poupées.** 1920. Trademark registered in France by *Fernand Paulin Olivier.*

**A la Galerie Vivienne.** See **Guillard.**

**A la Grande Duchesse.** 1877. Paris. Doll shop of *M. Vulquin, Jne.*

**A la Maison Bleue.** 1925. Paris. Doll repair shop.

**A la Poupée de Nuremberg.** 1865–70. Paris shop of Mme. Lavallée-*Peronne,* who specialized in dolls' trousseaux. Name of shop appears on label on chest of wooden and/or kid-bodied lady dolls.

**A la Tentation.** 1889–1900. Paris. Trademark of *Maison Guyot* for dolls and bébés, dressed and undressed.

**A. Marque.** See **Marque, A.**

**A. P. W. Paper Co.** 1924. Albany, N.Y. Advertised 3-colored rag dolls to be cut out and stuffed; dolls' dresses had large checks; size 12 inches.

**Abe Kabibble.** 1915. *Bleier Bros.* doll based on cartoon character created by H. Hershfield for Hearst papers; sizes 16 and 18 inches.

1. Guillard mark for A la Galerie Vivienne.

2. A la Poupée de Nuremberg, mark of Mme. Lavallée-Peronne.

**Abicht & Co.** 1897–1914. Ilmenau, Thür. Manufactured earthen and terra-cotta dolls.

**Abraham & Straus.** 1903–25+. Brooklyn, N.Y. Distributors. Trademark *Baby Violet,* used for dolls since 1903, registered 1906 in U.S. by L. Abraham, assigned to firm of Abraham & Straus. Trademark renewed 1926.

**Abt & Franke.** 1895–1909. Hannover, Prussia. Made dressed dolls.

**Aceedeecee Doll.** 1920. *American Character Doll Co.* Wood-fiber composition dolls, sixteen styles, with painted hair or wigs.

**Achard, Mme.** (Also Widow Achard.) 1851–76. Paris. Listed in directories under Dolls.

**Ackley, Clara.** 1917. Philadelphia, Pa. Listed in directory under Dolls.

**Acme Toy Manufacturing Co.** 1908–25+. New York City. Made Acme line of dolls.

1914–15: Advertised unbreakable character baby dolls.

1920: *Davis & Voetsch,* distributors of cork-stuffed and dressed dolls made by Acme.

1922: "Mama" and "Papa" voice dolls, walking and talking dolls, advertised for $1.50 up.

1925: *Kaufman, Levenson & Co.* distributed Acme's *Peek-A-Boo* infant doll. Acme made a composition baby head with a grumpy-type face; on a cloth body with celluloid hands; size 13½ inches.

**Acorn Doll Co.** 1919–20. Brooklyn, N.Y. Produced unbreakable character dolls with sleeping eyes, fully jointed composition dolls with sleeping eyes and mohair wigs, and stuffed dolls.

**Acrobat.** See **Gent Acrobat.**

**Ada May.** 1924. Trade name of a *Celebrity Doll* originated by *Margaret Vale* and produced by *Jane Gray.*

**Adamich, Joseph.** 1924–25. San Francisco, Calif. Secured a U.S. design patent for a baby in swaddling clothes and a baby on a pillow.

**Adams, Emma E.** 1891–1900. Oswego, N.Y. Made rag dolls with the aid of her sister, Marietta, and her parents, Mr. and Mrs. William Adams. To meet the demand, these dolls were sold commercially through Marshall Field & Co. of Chicago. At the Chicago World's Fair in 1893, they received a diploma of merit and were honored with the name *The Columbian Doll.* Miss Adams painted the features and hair of every one of her dolls until she died in 1900. After her death, her sister Marietta carried on the doll-making business for at least a decade. In 1906, Marietta became Mrs. Ruttan. Emma Adams had studied art and was also noted for her crayon portraits.

**3.** Contemporary studio picture of a doll made by Emma E. Adams; doll was purchased at the 1893 Columbian Exposition. *Courtesy of Helen Fish.*

COLUMBIAN DOLL
EMMA E. ADAMS
OSWEGO
N.Y.

4

THE COLUMBIAN DOLL
MANUFACTURED    BY
MARIETTA ADAMS RUTTAN
OSWEGO, N.Y.

5

**4 & 5.** Columbian dolls' marks used by Emma Adams and Marietta Adams.

**Ade, W.** 1909. Frankfurt am Main, Hesse-Nassau. Manufactured dolls.

**Adèle.** 1886. Doll distributed by YOUTH'S COMPANION. Had "French Bisque" head, shoulder plate and hands, swivel neck, blue glass eyes, blonde Rembrandt-style hairdo; jointed kid body, lace stockings, and slippers with buckles; size 15½ inches; price ($1.50) included paper patterns for trousseau.

**Adeline.** 1916. Baby doll with composition head and hands, distributed by *Montgomery Ward & Co.* It had painted hair, open mouth with a pacifier, and wore a lace-trimmed white dress; size 21 inches; price $3.05.

**Adler, Stella.** 1919–25. St. Louis, Mo. Registered trademark *Baby Love* in U.S.

**Admiral Dewey.** Ca. 1898. Portrait doll made by *Cuno & Otto Dressel,* 15½ inches tall.

**Admiral Dot.** 1914. Portrait doll of the sailor boy made famous by Barnum and Bailey circus; manufactured by *Ideal Novelty & Toy Co.*

**Admiral Sampson.** Ca. 1898–1903. Portrait doll made by *Cuno & Otto Dressel,* 15½ inches tall.

**Admiration (Babies).** 1917–23. Line of dolls made by *Progressive Toy Co.*

1917: Fully jointed lightweight wood-fiber composition dolls, in sizes 16 and 24 inches.

1918: All-composition dolls made of wood fiber, jointed at the neck, shoulder, and hips; stationary or sleeping eyes; molded hair or wigs; sizes 14 and 16 inches.

1920: Bent-limb character baby dolls.

1923: All-composition walking and talking dolls, and walking dolls with cotton-floss-stuffed bodies. Slogan for this line of dolls in 1923: "Admiration—Dolls of the Better Grade."

**Adrian, Elizabeth G.** 1925. New York City. Registered *Jim-in-ee* as a trademark in U.S.; it was applied to the doll on a woven label.

**Adt, Société Nouvelle des Etablissements.** 1925+. Factories at Pont à Mousson, M. & M. and Forbach, Moselle; made dolls and character bébés with unbreakable heads of *fibrolaque.* Their dolls had sleeping or stationary eyes, were dressed or undressed, and some of them walked and talked.

**Adtocolite.** 1917–19. Trade name of a material used by *Aetna Doll & Toy Co.* to make composition dolls, which were distributed by *E. I. Horsman Co.* Advertisements claimed this material was light, smooth, and tough. It was used for bent-limb character babies and fully jointed composition dolls with diagonal hip joints, so that the dolls could stand alone. Ball joints of wood were used with some of the adtocolite bodies. The dolls had either adtocolite heads or bisque heads made by *Fulper. Peterkin* was one of the all-adtocolite dolls. Since adtocolite tends to crack into circular bands, it can readily be dis-

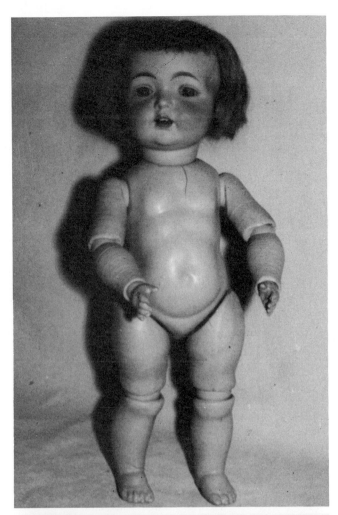

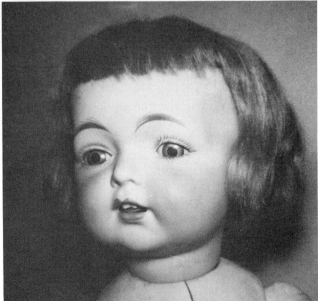

**6A & B.** Doll with bisque head made by Fulper Pottery Co. for Horsman, on a Horsman Adtocolite body made of a material used at the end of World War I. Doll has celluloid-over-metal eyes, an open mouth with tongue and teeth. Head mark: Ill. **612.** Body mark: Ill. **844.** H. 16 in. *Coleman Collection.*

tinguished from the earlier *Can't Break 'Em* materials made by Aetna. The 13-inch size had a fixed head and painted eyes; the 16-inch size came in two models: painted or glass eyes with pasted mohair wigs; or sleeping eyes and a sewed mohair wig.

**Aetna Doll & Toy Co.** 1909–19. Brooklyn, N.Y. Purchased the *Hoffmann* factory, which consisted of a loft and three sewing machines, and the secret process for making *Can't Break 'Em* dolls' heads. *Borgfeldt* was a distributor of their dolls.

1910–18: New York City. *Benjamin Goldenberg*, president of Aetna; *Horsman*, sole distributor. Aetna made Can't Break 'Em heads for Horsman's *Campbell Kids, Baby Bumps,* and many other dolls. In 1912 Aetna was producing over 4,000 dolls' heads a day for Horsman.

1917–19: They made *Adtocolite* dolls and dolls' heads for Horsman.

1919–25: Aetna merged with Horsman to form E. I. Horsman & Aetna Doll & Toy Co.

**Aetna Novelty Co.** 1901–15. New York City. Made dressed dolls and doll outfits.

**Age of Dolls.** Very few dolls can be dated precisely, but there are many clues to the age of an old doll. Early catalogs are one of the best sources for comparison and determining a doll's age. Many popular dolls were made over a long period of time and can be later or earlier than indicated by a catalog, advertisement, or other contemporary illustration. Patents, copyrights, and trademarks provide official data that often tell the approximate age of a doll. When a trademark is registered in the U.S., the date of its first use must be given, but this is not true for European trademarks. A patented doll could not have been produced more than a year or so before it was patented, but if it was successful, it might be produced for many years thereafter. All the many *Autoperipatetikos* dolls found in collections were certainly not made in 1862; probably some were produced decades later, as indicated by the type of hairdos.

Molded hair styles and molded shoes often provide clues to the age of a doll. It is fairly certain that a doll with a datable hair style or shoe style was not made prior to the period when the particular style was in fashion, although it could have been made either a short time or many years later. In determining the date of a given hair style, detailed study is required. For example, wind-blown short hair was worn by women in the time of Napoleon I. Dolls representing children have this type of hairdo around the mid-nineteenth century, and dolls representing boys or men have the same style at the end of the nineteenth century.

Often, several different clues must be put together to determine the age. A doll may bear a stamp showing that that line of dolls won a medal in a particular international exhibition, or it may bear a trademark date. Both of these might indicate the earliest possible date for the doll, but other clues would be needed to arrive at a close approximation of its age. For example, a collector may have a *Bébé Jumeau* on the body of which is a stamp MEDAILLE D'OR, which refers to the gold medal won in 1878. According to the trademark papers, Bébé Jumeau has been used as a trade name since 1840, and advertisements show that it was still in use as late as World War II. Examination indicates that the doll's head was poured, and it is known that Jumeau pressed his doll heads in 1885 or even later (see **Manufacture of Bisque Heads**), but was pouring them in 1894. Using these facts, the most important of which is the evidence of how the head was made, the collector is forced to conclude that the doll should be dated in the 1890's or later. Of secondary importance is the stamp, which indicates that the doll was made after 1878. This type of stamp was used by Jumeau over a period of years to advertise the excellence of its products.

In general, poured heads are likely to be later than pressed heads, though this is not always true. The hairdo and style of molded shoes have already been discussed, but the body itself can often provide a clue. If an original body is machine sewn, it is almost certain to have been made after 1860.

In a few cases, it is possible to date dolls fairly precisely. The *All Steel Doll* of the *Metal Doll Co.* was made in 1903. That is the only year in which it was advertised, and records show the factory was used for other purposes in 1900 and 1905. *Gie-Fa* was first used as a trademark for a doll in 1919. In January, 1919, the doll was advertised as having a bisque head on an all-wood body; in February and thereafter, it was advertised as having an aluminum head. Therefore, a bisque head Gie-Fa doll can be dated precisely as at the beginning of 1919.

Many dolls come with carefully written family histories and the dates of birth of their former owners. This information is of interest, but it should not be accepted as fact without verification. Experience has shown that in the majority of such cases the original owner either would have had to be playing with the doll as a grown woman, or that she must have bought it for her child or grandchild. When a doll can be documented—and several of the dolls sold at the Civil War Sanitary Fairs do fall into this category—it helps to date other similar dolls. The dates given in museums for dolls sometimes must be questioned, but when proved accurate they can help to date more obscure dolls of a similar type.

Seldom should a doll be dated by its clothes, although collectors often try to do so. Even when it can be proved that the clothes were made for the original owner of the doll, there was often a time lag in styles. Records show that colonial-type clothes were still worn by some people as late as the 1840's, and dolls were usually dressed similarly to the owner if the clothes were made at home. Commercially made clothes, especially when a doll has an original trunk of clothes, all of approximately the same period, can indicate the age of the doll.

In 1891, the United States passed a tariff act requiring that imports should have the country of origin indicated. A study of this act, of the 1909 act that strengthened it, and of subsequent acts, shows that dolls were not required to have a permanent mark of their native country on them, and therefore it is erroneous to assume that dolls without the name of a country are prior to 1891 and that all those with the name of a country were made subsequent to this date. In 1922, *Horsman* lost a copyright case because of the fact that they had failed to put their full name on their dolls as required by copyright law. They had used only the initials "E.I.H." Other companies had done the same thing, and it is probable that dolls that are marked with initials only were made prior to this 1922 decision.

The principal types of dolls down through the years are shown in the entry titled *Chronology of Dolls*, and a study of this, together with changes in manufacturing techniques, patents, and other factors should provide the collector with a comparative basis for approximating the age of most dolls.

**Agnes.** See **Pet Name.**

**Ahler, Edwin Arthur.** 1920–21. Chester, Pa. Obtained a U.S. patent for a *multi-face doll,* the faces having different expressions and turning on a vertical axis when a button at the shoulder is pressed.

**Ai-Ai.** 1923. Trademark for dolls registered in Germany by *Arno Lützelberger & Co.*

7. Peg wooden doll with painted features, dressed in original dress of pink silk with wide collar and yellow silk apron; sloping shoulders of the 1830's. H. ca. 3 inches. *Courtesy of the Newark Museum, Newark, N.J.*

**8A, B, & C.** Talking "Bébé Jumeau," bisque head, glass eyes wig, jointed composition body with torso slit in half for insertion of the voice mechanism. Pull-cords at waist regulate the voice. Marks: head, Ill. **924;** body, Ill. **918.** Probably made some years after winning a gold medal in 1878, as indicated on the body. H. 19 inches. *Courtesy of Virginia Dilliplane.*

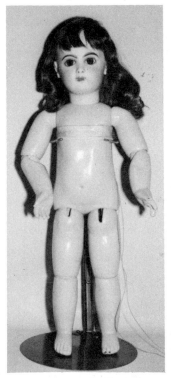
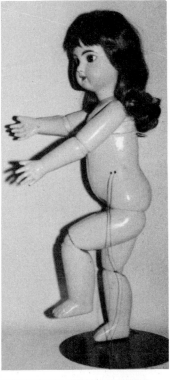

A              B

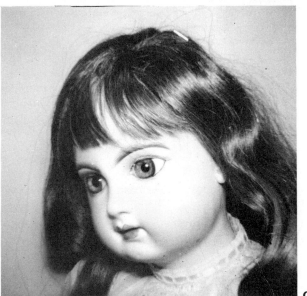

C

9. Mark used by Frederic Aldis.

**Aimée.** 1921–22. *Amy M. Eshleman* registered this trademark in U.S.

**Akiyama, T.** 1880. Japan. Showed dolls at the Melbourne International Exhibition.

**Alabama Indestructible Doll.** See **Smith, Ella.**

**Alabaster.** Material of ancient Babylonian doll with movable arms in the British Museum. There was also an 18th-century four-foot-high alabaster doll, called "le grand Courrier de la Mode," which was sent from Paris to London even in wartime. *Poupards* were sometimes made of alabaster.

**Aladin & Lam.** 1925. Paris. Created *Art Dolls.*

**Alah.** 1923–24. Trademark registered in Germany by *Anni Lonz* for dolls.

**Albert, J. V., Jr.** 1851–1909. Frankfurt am Main, Hesse-Nassau. Displayed dolls at London Exhibition of 1851; his London agent was A. Pritchard.

1909: Successors of the son of Albert manufactured dolls.

**Alderson, Matthew W.** 1890. Bozeman, Mont. Was issued a U.S. patent for a doll with jointed or movable fingers; patent assigned to *American Doll Co.*

**Aldis, Frederic.** 1878–1901. London. Doll maker and doll importer; used *Pierotti* wax heads for some of his dolls.

**Aldred, Thomas.** 1881–1903. London. Manufacturer and importer of dolls; used *Pierotti* wax heads for some of his dolls.

**Alexander, Madame (Beatrice Behrman, née Alexander),** 1917–25+. New York City. Designed and produced dolls. Maurice Alexander went from Odessa, Russia, to Germany as a young boy. There he became interested in toys. In 1891 he moved to New York City, where he was befriended by *Foulds & Freure.* Alexander established his own shop and doll hospital, and married a girl from Austria. Their eldest daughter, Beatrice, showed considerable artistic talent. During World War I she designed and helped to make *Red Cross Nurse* dolls, which her father sold. In 1923, after becoming Mrs. Behrman, she founded the Alexander Doll Co. and started manufacturing dolls. One of the first was called *Alice-in-Wonderland.* Madame Alexander, as she was henceforth known in the doll world, herself the eldest of four sisters, was an admirer of the four sisters in Louisa Alcott's book, LITTLE WOMEN. There were no illustrations to follow in the LITTLE WOMEN books as there had been for Alice-in-Wonderland, and so Madame Alexander had to make her own interpretation of *Meg, Jo, Beth,* and *Amy* in doll form. They were soon joined by dolls representing characters in the books of Charles Dickens, among them *David Copperfield, Tiny Tim, Little Nell, Little Emily,* and *Oliver Twist.* These were rag dolls with mask-type faces and pressed features that were hand-painted by Madame Alexander.

**11.** Henri Alexandre mark.  HⱭA

**Alexandre, Henri.** 1889–91. Paris. In 1892 was succeeded by Tourrel; 1895, Tourrel merged with the *Jules Steiner* firm. Alexandre was the designer and one of the above three manufacturers of *Bébé Phénix* dolls, which came in thirty models. In 1889, Alexandre displayed dolls at the Paris Exposition.

**Alice.** 1909–12. Doll made by *F. Kaempff*, distributed by *Strobel & Wilken, Butler Bros.*, and *A. S. Ferguson*. It had a cloth body with printed or lithographed cloth face or a celluloid face, and was dressed as a Quakeress. Available in four sizes priced at 25¢, 50¢, 75¢, and $1.00.

**Alice in Wonderland.** 1915. Doll made by *Horsman*, taken from the John Tenniel illustrations of the Carroll book; golden hair; dressed in a blue frock and white pinafore.

**10.** Rag doll named "Tippy Toe," made by Madame Alexander shortly after 1925. H. ca. 18 inches. *Courtesy of Alexander Doll Co. and Kathryn DeFilippo.*

**12.** Rag dolls made by Martha J. Chase; represented the Tenniel drawings of the characters in *Alice-in-Wonderland*. From left to right: the Frog Footman, Alice, the Duchess, Tweedle Dum, the Mad Hatter, and Tweedle Dee. The names are on the collars of Tweedle Dum and Tweedle Dee. *Photograph by Winnie Langley.*

**13.** Alice-in-Wonderland, an all-rag doll, one of the first dolls made by Madame Alexander; 1923. H. 14 inches. *Courtesy of Alexander Doll Co. and Kathryn DeFilippo.*

**Alice-in-Wonderland.** 1905–21. According to the family of *Martha J. Chase*, she designed this doll in 1905. The doll was advertised in PLAYTHINGS in 1921. This stockinet-faced doll resembles the John Tenniel illustrations; it has blonde hair and is dressed in blue with a white apron.

**Alice-in-Wonderland.** 1923–25+. One of the first dolls made by *Madame Alexander*. The faces at first were flat, but later these cloth dolls had mask faces with raised features, which were hand-painted by Madame Alexander. The hair was made of yarn. The body was of pink muslin with cloth hands and feet. The doll was 14 inches high and cost $2.00.

**Alice Lee.** 1924. Made by *EFFanBEE*. Had composition head and limbs, blue sleep eyes and hair eyelashes, curly hair; a soft body, dressed in organdy and Irish lace, and wore a golden heart necklace; 23 inches tall; cost $10.00.

**14.** All-bisque doll with molded café-au-lait hair, painted features, socket head; jointed at shoulders; well-modeled body. H. 7 inches. *Courtesy of Ollie Leavister.*

**Alida.** 1909. Cloth doll made by *Steiff,* distributed by *Borgfeldt;* dressed as a Dutch girl; sizes 11 and 20 inches.

**Alisto Manufacturing Co.** 1920. Cincinnati, Ohio. Advertised *American Doll, Esther Doll,* and *Cupid Doll,* all 12 inches high.

**Alkay Doll & Toy Co.** 1919–22. New York City. Made dolls' heads in various sizes.

**All-Bisque Dolls.** Generally these are small dolls. They have been made for many years, but were especially popular in the 1880's; in 1906 they were used as decorations for birthday cakes; their greatest popularity came in the 20th-century *Kewpie* era. Most all-bisque dolls have shoulder joints; many are jointed at both hip and shoulder, and a few are fully jointed like a ball-jointed composition doll.

**All-in-One Dolls.** See **Frozen Charlottes.**

**All Steel Doll.** 1902–3. Invented by Vincent Lake; made by Vincent Lake and Isaac Risley operating as the *Metal Doll Co.;* distributed by *Borgfeldt.* Entire doll made of thin sheet steel with fully ball-jointed limbs; hand-painted; strung with steel springs and even jointed at the wrists and ankles; constructed so that it would stand upright alone. Its several removable wigs could be interchanged by merely snapping them off and on with three snaps. Glass or painted eyes. The dolls came in sizes 12 and 18 inches.

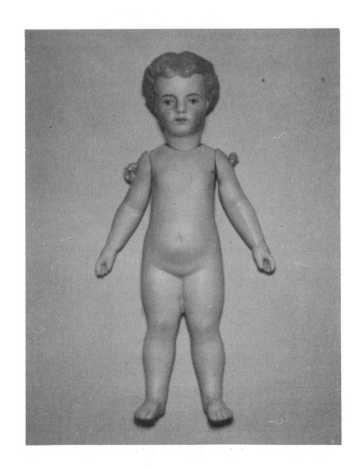

A

A

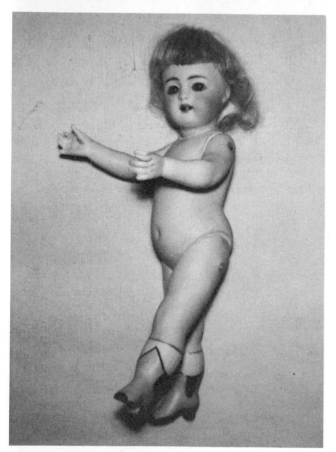

B

B

**15A & B.** All-bisque doll; Rembrandt hairdo wig; stationary brown glass eyes; open mouth with one lower and two upper teeth; molded yellow boots. Note the kid at neck and shoulder joints. H. 8 inches. *Courtesy of Ollie Leavister.*

**16A & B.** Thinly poured all-bisque doll with molded and painted features, hair, shoes, and socks; jointed at the hips and shoulders, with kid washers for protection of the bisque; original lace clothes. H. 9 inches. *Coleman Collection.*

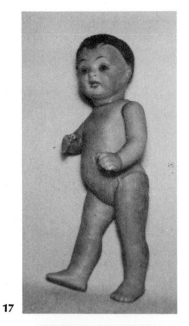

**17.** All-bisque doll with socket head; joints at shoulders and hips; glass eyes, open-closed mouth; fur wig on a solid crown. H. 5½ inches. *Courtesy of May Maurer.*

**18.** All-bisque doll with ears of exaggerated size; marked "Déposé"; painted blue eyes, brown hair. *Courtesy of Fidelia Lence; photograph by Winnie Langley.*

**19.** All-bisque baby doll with character face; painted features; bent, jointed limbs. H. 5½ inches. *Courtesy of Mrs. Edgar Dawson.*

**20.** All-bisque girl with molded hair having blue enameled ribbon across the back and bows at the top and both sides; molded shoes and socks. Body marked "10490." H. 6 inches. *Courtesy of Ollie Leavister.*

**21.** All-bisque doll with head resembling a boy's; molded hair, eyes, shoes, and socks. Marked on body: "790/92 6." H. 6½ inches. *Courtesy of Lester & Alice Grinnings.*

17                                                          18

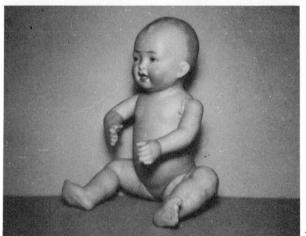

19

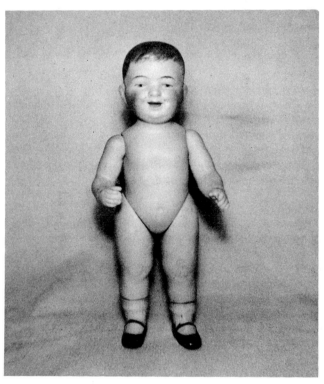

21

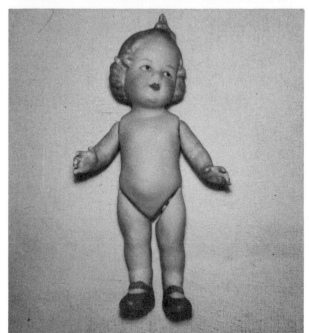

20

**All Wood Perfection Art Doll. See Schoenhut, A., & Co.**

**Allen, C. W., & Co.** 1921. American doll manufacturer.

**Allen, Jennie L.** 1918. Long Beach, Calif. Obtained U.S. patent for a rag doll; head, torso, legs, and arms each made and stuffed separately, then stitched together; features and hair embroidered on head in different colors.

**Alliance de la Fabrication Française des Jouets Comptoir d'Echantillons.** 1889. Paris. Handled dolls.

**Allied Doll Co.** 1919. New York City. Produced dolls whose cloth bodies were stuffed with ground cork.

A

**23.** Mark found on "Alma" dolls.　　　**24.** Alt, Beck & Gottschalck mark.

**Alma.** 1900–1901. Doll made in Germany; trademark registered in Germany by *Borgfeldt*. Doll marked "Alma" has a bisque shoulder-head, swivel neck, kid body, bisque hands, heavy eyebrows, open mouth with upper teeth; size 25½ inches, marked "4."

**Almost Human.** 1916. Doll advertised by *Capo*.

**Alphonse & Gaston.** 1903. Dolls sold in America.

**Alt, Beck & Gottschalck.** 1854–1925+. Nauendorf, Thür. Water-operated porcelain factory; founded in 1854 as Porzellanfabrik von Alt. Among the bisque dolls' heads made for *Borgfeldt* were the *Bye-Lo* and Bonnie Babe.

1893: They showed products at the Chicago Exhibition.

1907–11: Advertised nanking (*nankeen*) dolls. These were probably dolls with china or bisque heads and cloth bodies.

**Althof, Bergmann & Co.** 1848–81. New York City. Louis and Frederick Althof were listed in the New York City Directories at different addresses but both in the toy business. Frederick Althof was the successor to the widow of Gustavus F. Meyers. Directories as early as 1839 listed Gustavus F. Meyers. By 1858 Louis Althof was a member of the firm Althof, Bergmann & Co., which also included Charles Althof, Frederick Althof, and Hermann Bergmann. Frederick Althof lived in Europe at that time. The New York City Directory of 1860 listed Althof, Bergmann & Co. as toy importers, and in 1867 Augustus Bergmann, toyman, was listed at the same address as Althof, Bergmann & Co. HARPER'S BAZAR, January, 1868, shows a picture drawn from the actual Christmas doll display of Althof, Bergmann & Co. In 1874 Louis Althof with Hermann Thomass of Brooklyn, N.Y., obtained a U.S. patent for a mechanical doll with a bell and hoop. The 1874 catalog of Althof, Bergmann & Co. shows this patented mechanical doll as well as others, including the 1868 walking girl patented by *William Farr Goodwin*, which usually has the rag head patented by *George Hawkins* in 1868. Althof, Bergmann & Co. displayed

B

**25.** Dolls drawn for the Christmas advertisement of Althof, Bergmann & Co. in 1867, *Harper's Bazar*. Note the variety of dolls and the bizarre clothing on some of them.

chiefly mechanical dolls in the Philadelphia Exhibition of 1876. Their products were commended for imitating very naturally the motions of the human body, for their originality and cheapness. In 1881 they registered their "A.B.C." trademark in the United States and stated that they were engaged in trade with France, Great Britain, Germany, and China. They were one of the largest toy jobbers of that era and 95 percent of their toys were imports. *A. S. Ferguson,* Geo. *Riemann,* and many other well-known toy men started their careers with Althof, Bergmann & Co.

**Aluminia.** 1913. Trade name of dolls' heads distributed by *Strobel & Wilken.*

**Aluminum.** This material was used for dolls from 1898 until 1921, and probably thereafter.

1898: *Sommereisen* obtained French patent for aluminum dolls' heads.

1903: New doll of aluminum, colored and floatable, came in various sizes.

1919–21: Several companies used aluminum heads and limbs on their dolls; *Aluminum Doll Head Works* made heads and hands; *Giebeler-Falk Doll Corp.* made entire dolls of aluminum as well as those partly of aluminum; *New England Doll Co.* used aluminum hands.

**Aluminum Doll Head Works.** 1919–20. New York City. Made aluminum doll heads and hands for ball-jointed composition-body dolls or stuffed-body dolls.

**Amana Colonies.** Iowa. Made papier-mâché dolls.

**Amberg, Louis, & Son.** 1878–1925+. Cincinnati, Ohio, and New York City. 1878–81, doll importer; 1881–90, Fechheimer & Amberg, Cincinnati, doll importers and dealers; 1890–94, Louis Amberg & Co., Cincinnati, one of the largest toy jobbers and importers in the Middle West; 1894–98, Louis Amberg, Brill & Co., Cincinnati, toy import and commission house; 1899–1907, Louis Amberg, Brill & Co., New York City; 1907–10, Hahn & Amberg, New York City, doll and toy manufacturers; 1911–25+, Louis Amberg & Son, New York City, doll manufacturers.

1903: The Amberg firm controlled the entire output of two doll factories, one of their orders alone being for 16,000 dolls. They produced a doll that "walked" on

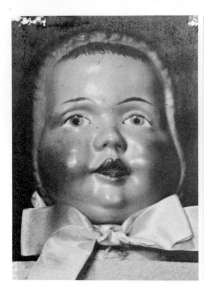

**& B.** "Girl with Baby Cap" copyrighted by Louis Amberg & Son in 1911. This is a copy of the original pictures filed with the copyright application. The doll's head had a molded cap with a cloth ribbon attached at the sides and tied under the chin.

**27.** "New Born Babe," copyrighted by Louis Amberg & Son in 1914 and reissued at the time of the Bye-Lo success. The doll has a bisque flange-necked head with glass sleep eyes and an open mouth. The body is cloth with composition arms. Mark: Ill. **29.** H. 8½ inches. *Coleman Collection.*

three wheels by a clockwork mechanism and had two strings for saying "Mama" and "Papa." The doll had sleeping eyes, was 18 inches tall, and sold wholesale for $12.00 a dozen.

1905: Amberg made a doll with eyes that could be made to open and shut in any position by means of a button. When this doll was raised from a horizontal position, it would automatically say "Mama."

1909: Louis Amberg was listed as the artist and owner of *Lucky Bill,* the first-known American-copyrighted doll head. *Sunny Jim* was Amberg's first unbreakable composition head.

Amberg made *Samson,* "Uncle Sam's first born," which he claimed was the first complete wire-jointed composition doll made in America. It was not a success, and by the beginning of 1912 a few broken molds were all that was left of it.

1910: The trade name *Baby Beautiful Dolls* was first used by Amberg for a line of dolls.

1911: There were 75 new style models of Baby Beautiful designed by American artists and sculptors, including Grace G. Wiederseim (*Drayton*) and *Jeno Juszko.* It required two new factories to supply the demand, and Amberg advertised that they were the "largest makers of doll babies in the world." Innovations included piercing the composition heads so that real ribbons could be inserted in the hair.

1912: The improved finish of the faces was advertised as "look like bisque, feel like bisque." Pink sateen bodies were stuffed with cork and had steel joints. Some of the heads were movable. The unbreakable composition dolls' heads were made by a secret formula "very carefully guarded . . . unknown even to the employees," according to a contemporary article. Amberg began to use the slogans, "American Dolls for Americans" and "The American Standard."

1913: Amberg had one hundred new models ranging in price from $2.00 to $96.00 a doz. wholesale, including the *Tiny Tots.*

**28–30.** Marks found on dolls made by Louis Amberg & Son. Mark No. **28** has the copyright symbol and 1911 date.

L.A.S. ©
414
1911

28

LA & S
RA 241 ⁵⁄₀
GERMANY

29

GERMANY
A-R
LA&S 886.2

30

1914: One of the most important Amberg dolls is the infant *New Born Babe,* designed by the artist Jeno Juszko, and described in their 1914 copyright.

1915: New *Ambisc* all-composition dolls appeared. Two important portrait dolls were produced, the famous *Charlie Chaplin* doll and *Oo-Guk-Luk,* a portrait of a Zulu and the last doll's head sculptured by Juszko for Amberg. A *multi-face doll* was also made.

1917: Amberg advertised that their sleeping-eye dolls had the only one-piece head with glass eyes then made in America. They were still advertising cork-stuffed, steel-jointed, cloth-body dolls and all-composition Ambisc dolls, but some of their dolls of the war era are stuffed with straw, perhaps because of material shortages. *Reinhold Beck* designed *Fine Baby* for Amberg.

1918: Fool-Proof Eyes and *Amkid* shoulder-head dolls were introduced.

1919: Real kid was used for the Amkid dolls, and a new walking doll was advertised. Soon after the war, Amberg used bisque heads made by *Fulper Pottery Co.* and labeled "The World Standard."

1921: His factory having burned down, Amberg was forced to seek dolls abroad. Nevertheless, he brought out two dolls, one designed by *Julio Kilenyi,* and *Mibs* created by *Hazel Drukker.* Joshua Amberg, son of Louis, who died in 1915, patented a soft stuffed walking doll in both England and Germany.

1924: PLAYTHINGS for April contains a *Borgfeldt* advertisement for the *Bye-lo* doll, which closely resembles Amberg's New Born Babe copyrighted in 1914. Before the end of 1924, Amberg reissued his New Born Babes with heads made by *Armand Marseille.* The ensuing battle over alleged copyright infringements was lost by Amberg because they had not complied with Section 18 of the Copyright Act requiring the full name (and not merely the initials) of the copyright owner on the doll. Some versions of the Amberg New Born Babe have been found with the mark of *Hermann Steiner* or with the initials "R A," which may stand for *Recknagel* of Alexandrinenthal.

**Ambisc.** 1915–20. All-composition jointed baby character dolls made by *Louis Amberg & Son.*

1916: Molded-hair dolls, 25¢ and 50¢; wig dolls in forty styles, 59¢ to $8.00.

1919: Ten sizes.

**American.** Name found over profile of an Indian head as a mark on celluloid dolls. (See Ills. 278 and 280.)

**American Art Dolls.** 1916–17. Distributed by *Strobel & Wilken.*

**American Baby.** 1915. Made by *Petri & Blum;* jointed all-composition character babies with either painted eyes and molded hair or wigs of short hair, or sleeping eyes with short hair wigs. Prices 50¢ to $6.00.

31                               32

33

31. "American Baby" mark of Petri & Blum.

32. "American Beauty" mark of Strobel & Wilken.

33. Mark used by American Bisque Doll Co.

**American Beauty.** 1895–1924. Trademark for a line of dolls registered in the U.S. in 1905, used since 1895 by *Strobel & Wilken,* who advertised dolls with this trademark as late as 1924.

1906: Rag dolls with highly colored photographic faces; prices 25¢ to $3.00.

1914–15: Kid-body dolls. Other companies appear also to have used this registered trademark.

**American Beauty.** 1919. *American Ocarina & Toy Co.* manufactured fully jointed composition dolls; 30 styles, with or without sleeping eyes, with or without curly wigs; sizes 16, 17, 18, and 19 inches.

**American Beauty.** 1919. *Seamless Toy Corp.* manufactured wood-fiber, jointed composition dolls with composition heads.

**American Beauty Doll.** 1913. Cutout rag doll. One large and two small dolls were on a single cloth sheet. Made by *Empire Art Co.*

**American Beauty Doll.** 1919–21. Trademark used by the *American Bisque Doll Co.* employing a rose as a ground for the trademark. Dolls bearing this trademark walk, talk, and sleep.

**American Beauty Doll Co.** 1923–25. Los Angeles, Calif. Doll manufacturer.

**American Bisque Doll Co.** 1919. Chicago, Ill. Copyrighted Babbie and *Toodles,* both by the artist *Ernesto Peruggi.* Babbie is a figurine type rather than a doll.

**American Bisque Doll Co.** 1919–21. Newark and Hoboken, N.J. Trademark a rose with the words *American Beauty Doll* on it. By arrangement with the manufacturers and designers of *Madame Hendren Life-Like Dolls,* license was secured to manufacture soft-body toddler dolls under the *Georgene Averill* doll patent of 1918. Made American Beauty Dolls and *Romper Boy*.

**American Character Doll Co.** 1919–25+. New York City.

1919: Made jointed all-composition character babies of wood-fiber mixture with molded hair or wigs and with or without sleeping eyes; sizes 13, 14, and 16 inches.

1920: Used trade name *Aceedeecee*, for 16 styles of wood-fiber composition dolls.

1921: Dolls called *Baby's Pal, Baby's Joy, Baby's Playmate*.

1922: Used trade name *Baby Petite* for Mama dolls with soft bodies and composition heads; sizes 12, 16, 17, 20, and 22 inches; 12-inch size with voice in the head of the doll priced at 98¢.

1923: Registered *Petite* as trademark in U.S.

1925: Baby Petite line of dolls priced $1.00 to $25.00.

**American Doll.** 1920. Trade name of dolls produced by *Alisto Manufacturing Co.;* size 12 inches.

**American Doll & Toy Co.** 1892–1909. Brooklyn, N.Y. Until 1895 known as the First American Doll Factory; 1896–99, also known as Goldstein & Hoffmann; 1905–6, also known as Hoffmann & Co. Founder and proprietor was *Solomon D. Hoffmann,* a subject of the Czar of Russia, who obtained a U.S. patent in 1892 for making composition dolls called *Can't Break 'Em;* advertised in 1907 that they were the only makers of composition head dolls in America and that their sales were three times as large as in 1906. They made *Fluffy Ruffles* in 1907 and 1908.

1908: Formerly imported bodies from Germany, but now made their own stuffed, sitting bodies, which they claimed allowed freedom of motion to the limbs.

1909: Hoffmann having died, the company and the rights to Can't Break 'Em patents were sold to *Aetna Doll and Toy Co.*

**American Doll Co.** 1890. New York City. Assigned patent for dolls' hands by *Matthew Alderson.*

**American Doll Co.** 1893–1904. Philadelphia, Pa. Listed in directories under Doll Heads and Doll Bodies.

**American Doll Manufacturing Co. (American Doll Co.)** 1912–25+. New York City. Made composition doll heads and parts.

1912: Advertised that they were the largest maker of doll babies in America.

**American Doll Toy Co.** U.S. Made plaster dolls and plaster casts for dolls; advertised baby dolls with or without human-hair wigs; size 15 inches.

**American Dolls. (U.S. Dolls.)** Few commercial dolls were produced in America until after the Civil War. Philadelphia, New England, Cincinnati, and New York were the principal doll-making centers during the 19th century.

Just before the turn of the century, New York City began to attract doll makers in large numbers, and together with neighboring New Jersey and Long Island became the heart of the industry in America. New York's pre-

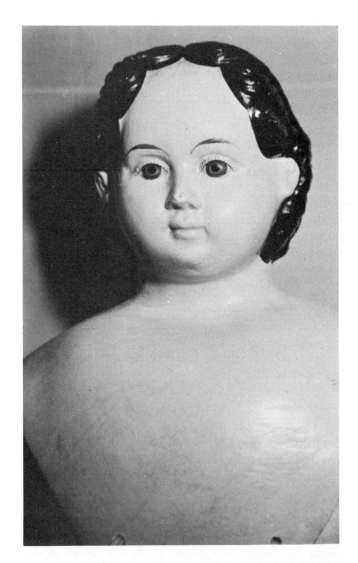

**34.** Mark used by American Character Doll Co.

**35.** Papier-mâché head made by Ludwig Greiner using his 1858 patent, and so labeled. (See Ill. **695.**) Molded black hair, exposed ears, painted eyes. Note depth of the shoulder plate. *Courtesy of Winnie Langley; photograph by Winnie Langley.*

eminence grew rapidly until it became an important international doll center when World War I increased the demand for American-made dolls. Many of the early American doll makers had brought their skills and knowledge from Europe, but the wooden dolls made by the *Cooperative Doll Co.* and the *Jointed Doll Co.*, in Springfield, Vt., in the 1870's and 1880's were distinctly the product of American ingenuity. Often dolls' heads were imported from Europe and used on bodies made commercially here in America. Some of the outstanding dolls' bodies of the 19th century were made by *Lacmann* of Philadelphia, *Steuber* of Philadelphia, *Gibson* of Boston, *Braitling* of Bridgeport, Conn., *Robinson* of Chicago, and *Goldsmith* of Cincinnati. American-made dolls' heads were usually of composition or rag. Solomon Hoffmann started to make *Can't Break 'Em* composition dolls' heads in 1892. Goldsmith had experimented unsuccessfully with making bisque dolls' heads in the 1880's, but *Ernst Reinhardt* is believed to have made the first commercial American bisque dolls' heads in Philadelphia just prior to World War I. *Ludwig Greiner* of Philadelphia obtained the first U.S. patent for a doll's head in 1858; *Edward Peck* obtained the first U.S. design patent for a doll (other than mechanical) in 1886. The *All Steel Doll* of 1902–3 was probably the first ball-jointed doll made in America. *Louis Amberg* obtained the first known copyright for a doll's head in 1909. Many of the dolls' heads manufactured in Germany in the 20th century were designed in America. The total value of dolls made and sold here in America in 1923 was considerably larger than the total value of all toys, including dolls, that were imported.

**American Dolls for Americans.** 1914. Slogan used by *Louis Amberg & Son.*

**American Fashion.** 1905. Trade name used by *Strobel & Wilken* for a dressed doll they distributed.

**American Girl.** 1907–12. Trade name used by *B. Illfelder & Co.* for a dressed doll line.

**American Glueless Doll Co.** 1918. Brooklyn, N.Y. Manufactured character dolls and dolls' heads made entirely without glue. These dolls were washable in hot water, did not shrink, and were guaranteed not to crack or peel. No elastic was used; arms, legs, and head were attached by socket joints. Covered by four patents; came in four sizes: 12, 14, 16, and 18 inches.

**American Kids in Toyland.** 1911–12. Line of dolls with one hundred numbers, headed by the *Campbell Kids*; made by *Horsman*; came with *Can't Break 'Em* heads and sateen-covered bodies.

**American Lady.** 1901–4. Rag doll with lithographed washable face and hair bangs, jointed limbs; dressed in removable underwear, shoes, stockings, dress, and sunbonnet; distributed by *Montgomery Ward & Co.*

1904: Size 14 inches, price 75¢.

**American Limb Doll Co.** 1918–19. New York City. Manufactured dolls.

**American Maid.** 1900–1910. Trade name for rag dolls handled by *Horsman, Montgomery Ward & Co.*, and *Sears, Roebuck & Co.*

1900: Sizes 11½, 16, and 17½ inches; price 25¢ to 95¢.

1910: Came in six different styles; can be undressed. Size 13 inches; price 50¢ each.

**American Ocarina & Toy Co.** 1919–21. Newark, N.J. Advertised that they made only dolls but might make ocarinas later. Dolls were jointed wood-fiber composition and included *American Beauty* line, *Snookums*, and Karo Princess. The latter had a representation of an ear of corn as a body.

1920: Assignee of U.S. design patents for dolls by Eduardo Malavarco, president of the company.

**American Produced Stuffed Toy Co.** 1917–18. New York City. Made composition heads with molded hair or wigs, in forty styles, and composition hands; heads priced 50¢ to $2.00.

**American Queen.** 1905. Trademark registered in Germany by the *Otto Morgenroth* firm.

**American Rose Bud.** 1921. Trade name used by *Sophia E. Delavan* for rag dolls; price $18.00 doz. wholesale.

**American Standard, The.** 1914. Slogan of *Louis Amberg & Son.*

**American Stuffed Novelty Co.** 1924–25+. New York City. Made hand-painted, pressed-cloth-face dolls called *Life Like Line*, including *Trilby, Pierrot, Pierrette, Co-Ed Flapper*, etc.

1924: Trilby, size 16 inches.

1925: Trilby in six styles, 16 and 19 inches; Pierrot and Pierrette, 20 inches; Co-Ed Flapper, 26 inches.

　　Distributors: *Edwin A. Besser, Borgfeldt*, and *Louis Wolf & Co.*

**American Style Doll Manufacturing Co.** 1924. New York City. Manufactured dolls.

**American Tissue Mills.** See **New England Doll Co.**

**American Toy & Doll Manufacturing Co.** 1917. Chicago, Ill. Made all-composition dolls and composition-head dolls with stuffed bodies. Both types had sleeping or stationary eyes and mohair wigs, and were dressed by *Katherine A. Rauser.* Dolls priced 59¢ to $2.50.

**American Toy & Manufacturing Co.** 1917–18. Kansas City, Mo. Made *Snow White*, a portrait doll of Marguerite Clark; distributed by *Strobel & Wilken, Borgfeldt*, and *Owens-Kreiser Co.*

**American Toy & Novelty Co.** 1917–25+. New York City. Distributed composition dolls with wigs; priced 50¢ and $1.00.

**American Toy Co.** 1867–74. New York City. George W. Brown and J. E. Stevens, proprietors. Made mechanical toys, including the walking doll based on the *William Farr Goodwin* patent of 1868.

**American Toy Co.** 1880–94. Covington, Ky. *Philip Goldsmith,* proprietor. Made composition dolls' heads and cloth dolls' bodies with leather arms.

**American Unbreakable Doll Corp.** 1923–25. New York City. Made character *Mama Dolls* as well as heads and arms of composition for other doll manufacturers.

1923: 12-inch doll priced at 49¢ and 16-inch doll priced at 98¢.

1925: *Princess* line of stuffed and composition character dolls.

**Ames, Edward Remington.** 1923. Los Angeles, Calif. Copyrighted *Doll,* a girl doll with eyes glancing to the side.

**Amis de l'Enfance.** See **Aux Amis de l'Enfance.**

**Amkid.** 1918–19. Trade name for real or imitation kid-body dolls made by *Louis Amberg & Son.*

1918: Imitation kid bodies only; had composition shoulder-heads and forearms, painted features, open mouths, and wigs; they had swing, sewed joints at hips and knees. Sizes 17 and 20 inches came with painted eyes at $17.20 and $21.00 doz. wholesale; sizes 17, 20, 24, and 28 inches came with moving eyes; wholesale price was $21.00, $27.00, $36.00, and $54.00.

1919: Both real kid and imitation kid were used for the dolls' bodies, which came with ball-jointed arms and composition lower legs; in thirty-five styles and 12 sizes.

**Ammer, Louis.** 1890's–1918. Eisenberg, Thür. Doll manufacturer.

**Amor Metal Toy Stamping Co.** 1922. Bayonne, N.J. Made metal heads for Amor dolls with painted or sleeping eyes and mohair wigs; used fully jointed bodies or jointed sanitary stuffed bodies. Also made walking dolls. Dolls came in 14, 16, 18, and 22 inches.

**Amour Bébé.** 1896. Trademark registered in France by *Louis Guillet.*

**Amphibious Clown, The.** 1921. Soft doll made by the *Giftoy Co.,* designed by *Gertrude Stacy.*

**Amstea Co.** 1924–25. Berlin. Produced dolls.

**Amuso.** Name found as a mark on doll made in Germany.

**Amy.** 1912. Trade name for doll from LITTLE WOMEN made by *Elektra Toy & Novelty Co.* Had a ribbon band in molded hair, and eyes glancing to side (*Coquette* type); dressed in school clothes; mate for *Laurie.*

**Amy.** 1923–25+. Rag doll designed and made by *Madame Alexander.* It had a mask face with raised features, which were hand-painted by Madame Alexander. Came with wig of mohair, imported from England; pink muslin body. Size 14 inches; price $1.20.

**Anchor Toy Corp.** 1924. New York City. Imported dolls and toys from sixty-five European factories.

**Anderson, Eva M.** 1921–24. Waterloo, Iowa. Secured U.S. patent for producing a doll from two socks.

**Anderson, William H.** 1884–85, Brooklyn, N.Y. Obtained patent in U.S. for a doll with spiral wire legs.

**Andy Gump.** 1924. Doll made by *Fleming Doll Co.,* representing comic-strip character of that name.

**Anel & Fraisse.** 1914–ca. 20. Anel & Fils, 1921. Doll factory at Muzy, France; salesroom in Paris; made celluloid dolls.

**Anfray.** 1925. Paris. Made stuffed dolls.

**Anker, H.** 1914. Paris. Specialized in dolls for export.

**Anners, Thomas S.** 1822. Philadelphia, Pa. Distributed leather dolls with composition heads.

**Annette.** 1912–14. Trade name for girl doll made by *Horsman* with a *Can't Break 'Em* composition head and soft body; dressed in white lawn with apron.

**Annie.** 1911. Name of a character doll that was named for the little girl who posed for it. Made by *Kämmer & Reinhardt* as one of their *Royal* line.

**Annie Rooney.** See **Little Annie Rooney.**

**Anniversary Baby.** 1924. Trade name for doll made by *Louis Amberg & Son,* a *Mama Doll* with sleeping eyes, soft body, and composition legs. Wholesale price $18.00 doz. and up.

**Anniversary Dolls.** 1914. Line of dolls made by *C. M. Bergmann,* to celebrate their twenty-fifth anniversary.

**Anqueulle, Albert, & Anqueulle, Marie.** 1865. Paris. Secured a French patent for dolls with circular swivels as joints, which were covered with pink or white kid. Ingredients given for composition were glue, plaster, whiting, and alkaline stone, molded together with linen.

**Anschütz, Hugo.** 1895–98. Sonneberg and Oberlind, Thür. Made flannel dolls in *Flanell-Puppenfabrik;* specialized in export items.

**Anschütz & Weber.** 1915. Eisfeld, Thür. Doll manufacturers.

**Antenori, Natale.** 1917. Rome. Obtained a French patent for a doll made of separate pieces of leaf metal joined by soldering or other processes.

**AMOUR-BÉBÉ**

**36**

A MUSO
100
Made in Germany.

**37**

**38**

36. "Amour Bébé" mark.

37. Mark found on "Amuso" dolls.

38. Anchor Toy Corp. mark.

**Anthony.** 1909+. Trade name for a felt doll made by *Margarete Steiff;* dressed as a Bavarian boy with short trousers, leather buttons on jacket, and rucksack on back; 20 inches; later made in smaller (10-inch) size.

**Anton-Russell.** 1924–25. Bremen, Germany. Made baby dolls and other types of dolls.

**Apfelbaum, Lothar.** 1925. Fürth, Bavaria. Made dolls' house dolls of porcelain and of celluloid.

**Apples, Dried.** 19th century–1925+. Used as a material for making dolls' heads, hands, and feet in the late 19th century by people in the North Carolina mountain area. These dolls represented the sang diggers (sang = a root), and portrayed men and women. A woman doll in the collection of Maud Brewer, mentioned in the Laura Starr book of 1908, had in her mouth a stick that was called a "dip," used to rub snuff on the gums according to the custom in that area. *Mrs. Mary McAboy* of Montana and her mother made dried apple dolls representing Indians. They sold these at church socials for many years prior to 1913, when Mary McAboy began to make her *Skookum* dried apple dolls commercially. In 1911, *Isabel Million* of Tennessee began to make dried apple dolls depicting the Tennessee mountain folk. She made men, women, and even babies. She also tried making Indian dolls, but was not successful with them; apparently hers never competed with the fine Indian dolls of Mary McAboy. By 1916, the demand for the Skookum Indian dolls was so great that it required the *H. H. Tammen Co.* of Denver and Los Angeles to produce the McAboy-designed dried apple dolls. These dolls continued to be made for many years.

**Arabesque.** 1914–23. Line of kid-body dolls distributed by *Strobel & Wilken.*

**Araki, Hikozo.** 1915–16. Resided Brooklyn, N.Y. Subject of the Emperor of Japan. Obtained U.S. design patent for *Queue San Baby,* which he assigned to *Morimura Bros.*

**Arcade Toy Manufacturing Co.** 1913. New York City. Made thirty models of composition character dolls; price 25¢ to $1.00.

**Arctic Boy.** 1913. Trade name used by *Ideal Novelty & Toy Co.* for a washable, composition-head doll dressed in knitted coat, hat, and leggings.

**Arcy Toy Manufacturing Co.** 1912–25+. New York City.

1915: Advertised unbreakable, unpeelable, composition dolls in forty styles, among them the *Daddy Long Legs Doll.*

1920: *Bell Toy Co.* was listed as their successor, but by 1924 the name appeared again as Arcy Manufacturing Co. Made stuffed dolls.

1924: Made *Blue Bird* doll.

**Arena, Félix.** 1918–20. Paris. Registered in France trademark *Mignon* for use on doll heads and doll articles. Joined by Michel Lafond in 1920.

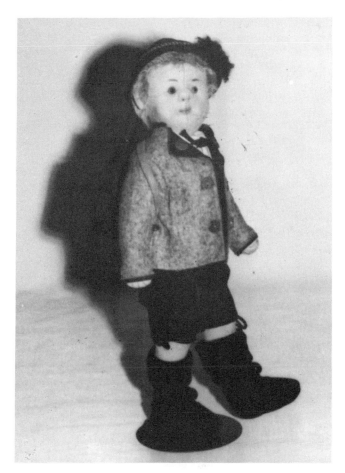

39. Steiff doll known as "Anthony"; made of felt with plush hair; ca. 1910. He is dressed as a Bavarian hiker, including a cloth knapsack. H. 10½ inches. *Coleman Collection.*

**Arhelger, Liddy (née Riedel), & Gummersbach, Franz.** 1912–13. Olpe, Germany. Obtained patents in Germany and England for attaching wigs to dolls' heads with elastic.

**Arkadelphia Milling Co.** 1914–15. Arkadelphia, Ark. Obtained U.S. trademark for *Dolly Dimple,* a rag doll.

**Arles, Dufour & Co.** 1880. Agent for *Bru* firm of Paris at the Melbourne, Australia, Exhibition.

**Armand Marseille.** See **Marseille, Armand.**

**Army Nurse.** 1917. Trade name of a doll made by *Horsman.*

**Arnaud, Jean Louis Hubert.** 1852–79. Paris. Obtained four French patents, 1852, 1855, 1857, and 1864, for jointed kid-body dolls with rubber joints or wooden bodies covered with vulcanized rubber. He showed dolls at the 1855 Paris Exposition.

1879: Widow Arnaud was head of the firm.

**Arnold, Max Oscar.** 1878–1925+. Neustadt near Coburg, Thür. Doll and toy manufacturer; used the initials "MOA" in an eight-pointed star as the firm's mark.

Arnold exhibited dolls at the International Exhibition in Melbourne, 1888, and in Chicago, 1893. He was listed as making dressed dolls in 1898, and specialized in patented mechanical dolls between 1904 and 1914. The first doll patented by Arnold moved on wheels, alternately saying "Mama" and "Papa," turning its head to the right and left, opening and closing its eyes, and swinging its arms forward and backward. Arnold obtained a British and French patent for this doll in 1904 and a U.S. patent in 1906 under the name Oscar Arnold. He then became interested in phonograph dolls, and obtained a German and a British patent in 1906 and a French patent in 1907 for a jointed composition-body doll with a talking machine in its body, which was separated above the hips so that the phonograph could be placed inside. Further improvements, such as making a metal front on the body for a speaker, were patented in Great Britain and Germany in 1908. According to PLAY-THINGS, May, 1909, Arnold's patented talking dolls were to be manufactured by the *International Talking Doll Co., Inc.*

Although specializing in mechanical dolls, Arnold was listed from 1907 through 1914 as a manufacturer of dressed and jointed dolls of every description, including unbreakable jointed dolls that were especially light for export. In 1909 Arnold obtained a German patent for a *bathing* doll, and was listed in a directory under both Doll Manufacturers and Dolls' Clothing.

1918: Firm became a joint stock company and specialized in papier-mâché products.

1920's: Listed as a porcelain factory. The heads marked with "MOA" and "Welsch" were probably made during this period. It is likely that the heads were made by MOA and the dolls assembled by Welsch.

**Arnold Print Works.** 1876–1925+. North Adams, Mass. Manufactured printed fabric for making cutout dolls, which was sold by the yard or half-yard. The fabric cost 12¢ to 20¢ a yard and provided from two to eight dolls per yard depending on their size. The dolls, printed in color, were to be cut out and sewed together, then stuffed. A piece of pasteboard had to be inserted in the bottom to make the dolls stand erect. Arnold used the design patents obtained by *Celia M. Smith* in 1892 and *Palmer Cox* in 1893. *Charity Smith,* sister-in-law of Celia Smith, obtained patents in 1893 in the U.S. and in England for a jointed rag doll that was manufactured by the Arnold firm. *Selchow & Righter* were Arnold's distributing agents.

**Arnoldi, H. & A.** 1898–1909. Hüttensteinach, Thür. Manufactured dolls.

**Arnoldt.** 1880–1925+. Cincinnati, Ohio. Otto Arnoldt founded Arnoldt's Doll Manufactory in 1880. Beginning in 1886 and for several years thereafter, he advertised all kinds of domestic and imported dolls as well as doll parts. He also repaired dolls. Mrs. Mary Arnoldt, probably his wife, made dolls' clothing and won a first prize

**40.** Max Oscar Arnold (MOA) doll with bisque head, composition body; purchased in Cologne, Germany, for Christmas, 1894. Mark: Ill. **41.** *Courtesy of Marian Pickup.*

**41.** Mark used by Max Oscar Arnold.

**42.** Mark of Arnold Print Works.

at the Cincinnati Centennial Exhibition of 1888. Beginning in 1894, the advertisement was listed under M. Arnoldt. In 1914, the Arnoldt Doll Dress Co. of Cincinnati manufactured Blue Bird Doll Clothes, which were distributed by *Borgfeldt*. Later, the Arnoldt firm dropped the "t" at the end of the name.

**Arnoult.** 1882. Listed in Paris Directory under Dolls.

**Aronson, Louis V.** 1914–25+. Newark, N.J. Obtained several U.S. patents in 1915; one was for a talking mechanism with bellows and a reed device; the voices were made by the *Art Metal Works*, and were called Ronson Voices. Another patent was for a doll whose head and arms moved when the sound mechanism was actuated. Aronson obtained many other patents for *Mama Doll* voices and was president of Voices, Inc., in 1924.

**Arranbee Doll Co.** 1922–25+. New York City. Imported dolls' heads, dolls, and doll hospital supplies and assembled dolls.

1923: Advertised imported dolls 12 to 40 inches, including a doll with a turning bisque head and flirting eyes that rolled as the doll walked. This doll was 24 inches tall. *Mama Dolls* in four sizes, including one of 22 inches, were made.

1924: Advertised Mama dolls with eyelashes, price $1.45 to $5.00; bisque novelty dolls with painted hair or wigs, with or without sleeping eyes; fully jointed dolls; character baby dolls with bisque heads. (The most famous of these was *My Dream Baby,* an infant whose head was made by *Armand Marseille* and is sometimes called Dream Baby.)

1925: Arranbee registered My Dream Baby in the U.S. as a trademark, made flirting eye Mama dolls whose head and eyes moved when they walked. These Mama dolls had imported composition heads, both white and Negro, with sleeping crystal eyes and hair eyelashes; 9 to 26 inches tall. "R & B Doll Co." found on later dolls probably was an Arranbee mark.

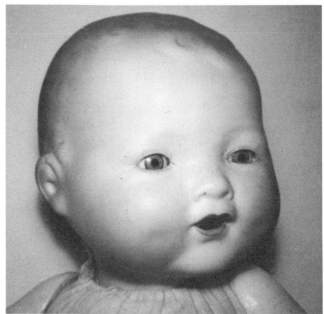

44 A

B

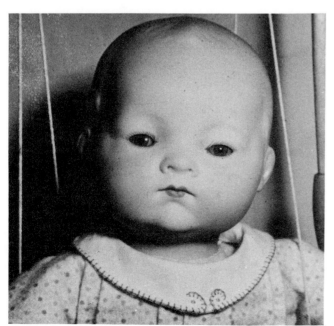

43

Germany
ARRANBEE
45

(R&B)
46

**43.** A bisque-headed infant doll with sleep eyes assembled by Arranbee; molded blond hair, glass eyes, closed mouth. *Courtesy of Winnie Langley; photograph by Winnie Langley.*

**44A & B.** Arranbee infant doll with bisque head marked as in Ill. **45**; molded and painted hair, glass eyes, open mouth, stuffed body, composition arms. *Courtesy of Dorothy Annunziato.*

**45 & 46.** Marks found on Arranbee dolls.

**Arrenberg, Else (née Liedtke).** 1920. Berlin. Registered "Arrenberg" in Germany as a trademark for dolls.

**Arrow Doll Wig Co.** 1924–25. New York City. Advertised *Mama Dolls* in a variety of sizes and prices, including some 28 inches tall.

**Arrow Novelty Co.** 1920. New York City. Advertised *Skookum* Indian dolls designed by *Mary McAboy.*

**Art Doll & Novelty Co.** 1920. Brooklyn, N.Y. Made cork and excelsior for stuffing dolls.

**Art Doll & Toy Co.** 1916. New York City. Made *Nevva-brake dolls,* using a patented process to give a bisque-like finish; over one hundred character models shown at 50¢, $1.00, and up.

**Art Dolls.** Dolls designed by well-known artists or inspired by famous works of art and created by the hands of skilled craftsmen. Among the many artists who have designed dolls are *Paul Vogelsanger,* a German sculptor; *Jeno Juszko,* a Hungarian sculptor; *Julio Kilenyi; Ernesto Peruggi; Rose O'Neill;* and *Laura Gardin.* Some dolls were inspired by Donatello's babies, others by children's' heads sculptured by artists in the 18th and 19th centuries. *Käthe Kruse* used the Luca della Robbia Bambini as her models. In 1921 Miss *Marcelle Giblet* made dolls "à la Gauguin." One of the functions of dolls as an educational toy is to teach children to know and appreciate beauty. Unfortunately, commercialism has sometimes thwarted this function and some dolls of poor artistic taste have been produced.

Besides the fine arts, dolls have a relationship to other forms of art. Many dolls are created as portraits of popular personalities on the stage or screen—*Lillian Russell, Marguerite Clark, Charlie Chaplin,* etc. Dolls have also been made to portray Queen Victoria, *Princess Angeline, Admiral Dewey,* and other famous personages. And they have actually been used in the performing arts. Fourteen-inch dolls costing $100 each portrayed the characters in a five-reel photoplay entitled THE DREAM DOLL produced by Howard S. Moss in 1917. A *Bye-Lo Baby* took the part of the baby in NEW TOYS, a motion picture starring Richard Barthelmess in 1925.

Dolls are an important part of folk art, and many of them represent folklore characters. Such dolls were usually first produced to please neighboring children, and met with such success that they were later made commercially; the dolls of *Margarete Steiff,* Käthe Kruse, and *Mary McAboy* are examples.

**Art Dolls.** 1910–25+. Line of dolls produced by *Horsman,* the dolls' heads modeled from life by famous sculptors and made of *Can't Break 'Em* composition. Prior to World War I, these dolls had cloth bodies; forty models were shown in 1910, with additional models in later years.

**Art Dolls.** See **Schoenhut, A., & Co.** (All-Wood Perfection Art Dolls).

**Art Fabric Mills.** 1899–1910. New York City. *Selchow & Righter* were the sole distributors, and in 1911 they were the successors.

1900: Edgar G. Newell, president of the company, obtained a U.S. patent for a rag doll the size of an infant or a child of two or three years, which he called a *Life Size Doll.* The picture of this doll and the words "Life Size" were registered by Newell in the U.S. as a trademark with the assertion that the words "Life Size" might or might not be used with it. The February 13, 1900 patent date generally appears on the foot of these dolls,

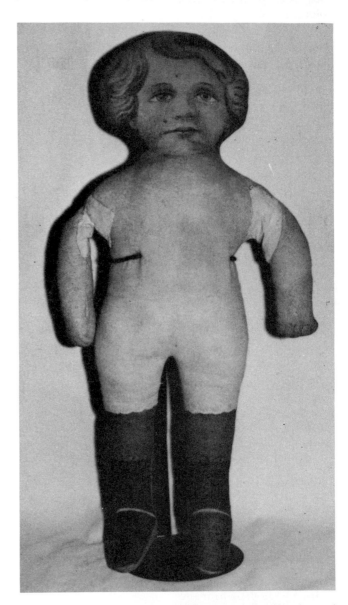

**47.** Cutout printed rag doll made by Art Fabric Mills; has red hair-ribbon and stockings; high black laced boots are printed on the feet. The sole of one foot reads "Art Fabric Mills, New York"; the other sole reads "Pat. Feb. 13th, 1900," the date of Edgar Newell's patent. H. 19 inches. (Doll has been patched under the arms.) *Courtesy of Lester & Alice Grinnings.*

**48.** Mark of Art Fabric Mills. PAT. FEB. 13, 1900

which were made 30 inches tall so that they could be dressed in a real baby's cast-off clothes. Also made a smaller size, both white and Negro, called *Topsy Dolls* and a Cry Baby Pin Cushion, which, although made for a pincushion, was often used as a doll. It depicted a crying baby dressed in shirt and breech clout, and sold for 15¢.

1904: Advertised *Foxy Grandpa, Buster Brown,* etc., full-color rag dolls.

Ca. 1907: Made rag dolls named *Diana, Bridget, Uncle, Baby, Billy,* and the *Newly Wed Kid.*

**Art Fabric Mills.** 1913–16. London. Made rag dolls.

**Art Metal Works, The.** 1914–23. Newark, N.J. 1924, merged with other companies to form Voices, Inc.; made metal dolls and dolls' voices.

1914: Made *Mama Doll* named *I Talk.*

1915: New Mama doll; arms could be placed in any position; 9 inches tall.

1918: Factory employed six hundred persons.

1919: Made the *Treat 'Em Rough Kiddie,* of stamped brass from head to toe, enameled and with movable joints.

**Art Toy Manufacturing Co.** 1919–21. London. Made rag *Misska* dolls; registered *Bathing Jeff* as a trademark in Britain for dolls.

**Artcraft Toy Products Co.** 1918–20, New York City; 1920–21, successor, Artcraft Playthings Corp., Brooklyn, N.Y.

1918: Made all-composition, jointed-limb dolls with human hair wigs, sleeping eyes; sizes 10 to 32 inches.

1919: Made washable *bisquette* heads with human hair wigs and sleeping eyes; ball-jointed wood-pulp composition bodies for 20- and 23-inch dolls; papier-mâché ball-jointed bodies for 26-inch dolls to lighten weight. A sample of one of each size sold for $11.84.

1920: Fully jointed dolls with sewed mohair wig or human hair in long curls; sizes 19, 21, 24, and 26 inches. Character baby dolls with sewed bob or ringlet mohair wigs; sizes 13, 15, 20, and 22 inches.

**Article Français.** 1890's. Mark of the *Chambre Syndicale des Fabricants de Jouets Français,* probably the Articles of Paris founded in 1883.

**Articulé.** See **Bébé Articulé.**

**Artistic Doll Co.** 1918–22. New York City. Made dolls.

**Artola Brothers.** 1878. Cobija, Bolivia. Exhibited dolls in Indian costumes at the Paris Exposition.

**Asador.** 1922–25+. Trademark registered in Germany by *Bauer & Richter,* Rodaer Puppenfabrik.

**Aschard.** 1839–45. Paris. Doll maker.

**Aschenbach, Eduard.** 1925. Sonneberg, Thür. Doll manufacturer.

**Ascher, Adolf.** 1892–93. Berlin. Obtained French and German patents for making hollow bodies in one piece by pressing. Bodies used on *Linon dolls* with *Kestner* heads. Also secured another French patent for making parts of jointed dolls. (See also *Landshut.*)

**Asco.** See **Strauss, A., & Co.**

**Asiatic Import Co.** 1924. Showed dolls at a U.S. toy fair.

**Assael, Gabriel Mentech.** 1919–25+. London. Doll maker.

**Asselot.** 1869–71. Paris. Made dolls, including jointed dolls.

**Association des Petits Fabricants.** 1914. Engaged some master porcelain makers to manufacture bisque heads.

**Assortments.** 1920's. Doll manufacturers, especially in Germany, offered assortments of dolls to distributors and retailers that included a wide range of models and prices. This arrangement was designed to promote business by easing buyers' choices yet presenting appealing and salable selections priced around $100, $500, and $1,000.

**Assuérus.** See **Desrosiers.**

**Ateliers Artistiques.** 1921–25+. Paris. Rag character dolls made by *Madame T. Lazarski,* exhibited at Salon National des Beaux-Arts and at Musée des Arts Décoratifs (Louvre) and all over the world; shown in moving pictures by Pathé and others both in France and abroad.

**Atlantic Rubber Co., Ltd.** 1923. London. Manufacturers; British trademark, *Toggy.*

**Atlantic Toy and Manufacturing Co.** 1922–25. New York City. Walking and talking dolls; connected with *P G & Atlantic Toy Manufacturing Co.* in 1922.

**Atlas Doll & Toy Co.** 1917–19, New York City; 1920–25+, Baltimore, Md. Made all-metal dolls of stamped metal, and dolls with metal heads and arms and soft cork-stuffed bodies; heads have wigs and sleeping eyes. Used trade names *Hug Me Kid* and *A.D.T. Co.*

**Atlas Doll Co.** 1921–22. Chicago, Ill. Registered in U.S. the trademark *Toddles,* which was molded into dolls.

49                              50

49. "Article Française" mark of the Chambre Syndicale des Fabricants de Jouets Français.

50. "Asco" mark of A. Strauss & Co.

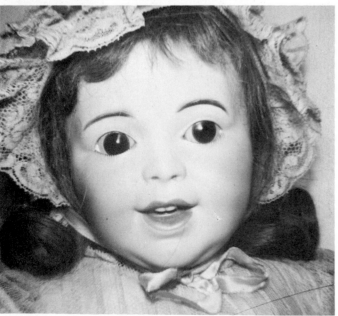

**Atlas Toy Manufacturing Co.** 1923. Moderately priced, walking and talking dolls.

**Atterholt, Susie M.** 1923–24. West Albany, N.Y. Secured a U.S. design patent for stockinet rag doll with embroidered features.

**Attimont, Madame.** 1882. Listed under Dolls in Paris Directory.

**Atwood, Kimball C.** 1877. New York City. Obtained U.S. patent for a metal doll.

**Au B B Rose.** 1910. French trademark of *Société Au Bébé Rose.*

**Au Bébé Incassable.** 1914–21. Paris. Made all-composition bébés and trousseaux for bébés.

**Au Nain Bleu.** Before 1890–1925+. Paris. Early dolls marked "Au Nain Bleu, E. Chauvière" usually have bisque heads and kid or cloth bodies. In the 1920's under Fauvet they specialized in jointed bébés, dressed and undressed, and distributed *S.F.B.J.* dolls marked *"Unis France."* (See **Chauvière** for possible earlier history.)

**Au Paradis des Enfants.** 1873–1925+. Paris. Proprietors were *Perreau Fils* (Sons), *Edme Louis Rémond,* Mons. Ouachée (1890), E. P. Malaret (1921). (See **Guillard.**) This was a large store that handled both French and German toys.

**51A & B.** Original clothes; label in bonnet reads "Au Nain Bleu // 406, 408, 410 rue St. Honoré // Paris," their address in the 20th century. Bisque head is labeled "SFBJ // 236." Open-closed mouth. Dress has numerous tucks and much lace, including epaulets at the shoulders. Pink silk bonnet is covered with lace and has a bow on each side. Mark: Ill. **1563.** H. 20 inches. *Courtesy of Lester & Alice Grinnings.* (See color photograph C24.)

1ᴱᴿ CHOIX

52

53

**52 & 53.** Marks found on dolls of Au Paradis des Enfants.

**54A & B.** "Augusta," name on doll's head manufactured by Ernst Reinhardt in Perth Amboy, N. J. The head has his patented celluloid eyes. The doll has a jointed composition baby's body. Mark: Ill. **55.** H. 24 inches. *Coleman Collection.*

U. S. A.
Augusta
Perth Amboy. N. J.
15. 8.

**55.** Mark used on "Augusta" dolls.

**Au Perroquet Cie.** 1924. Paris. Registered in France the trademark *La Négresse Blonde.*

**Au Petit Noël.** 1879. Paris. Proprietor was *Pnèau (Pineau),* doll maker.

**Aubeaux, M.** 1876. Listed under Dolls in Paris Directory.

**Aubin.** 1890. Paris. Dressed dolls in provincial costumes of Normandy, Brittany, and Auvergne.

**Augusta.** Ca. 1920. Name incised on bisque heads made by *Ernst Reinhardt* in New Jersey; named after Reinhardt's sister, Augusta.

**Augustin, Frau.** 1909. Mügeln near Dresden, Saxony. Made dressed dolls.

**Aunt Dinah.** 1900–1901. Distributed by *Nugent.* Came with black composition head, gray hair, cotton-stuffed body, and held a tiny doll in long dress. Size 13 inches; price dressed, $1.00.

**Aunt Jemima.** 1923–25. Made by the *Toy Shop* of a material previously unknown and by a special process; came in sizes 14, 20, and 24 inches. Obtained permission from the successors of *Aunt Jemima Mills Co.* to make these dolls.

**Aunt Jemima Mills Co.** 1908–25+. St. Joseph, Mo. Registered in U.S. as trademarks Aunt Jemima, *Uncle Mose,* and *Wade Davis.* By 1910 it was the Davis Milling Co., and the cutout rag dolls included Aunt Jemima and Uncle Mose, both 15 inches, and Wade and *Diana,* both 12 inches. A revised version of these rag dolls was made in 1924, lithographed on cloth by the Grinnell Lithograph Co. The dolls represented the same characters and were the same sizes as the earlier version. These were sold for 25¢ plus a box top.

**Auntie Blossom.** See **Mrs. Blossom.**

**Auntie Jo's Own Rag Babies.** 1920. Unique rag doll made by Miss *Josephine L. Malone,* 12 inches tall.

**Aurora.** 1902–9. Trade name for a line of kid-bodied dolls produced by *Friedrich Richter* and distributed by *Borgfeldt.*

**Austrian Dolls.** Many dolls were probably made in Austria, especially pre-World War I Austria, which encompassed the Grödner Tal where numerous jointed, peg wooden dolls were carved during the entire 19th century. Several small (about one inch) Viennese china baby dolls have been identified as having been made around 1800. The fine porcelain heads with wax crowns and inserted hair were based on an 1884 patent by Viennese *Josef Kubelka.* Other Austrian doll makers include *Heinrich Dehler, Franz Frankl, D. Freud, Haller, Auguste Gottfried, Leo Katz, Carl Knabe, Emil Pfeiffer,* and *Friedrich Seeber.* PLAYTHINGS, 1915, reported that an ample supply of Austrian bisque dolls was on hand at the outbreak of World War I. (See also **Czechoslovakian Dolls.**)

**56.** Bisque-headed doll made in Austria. Glass eyes; open mouth with four teeth; wig. Head is on a jointed composition body with molded shoes. Mark: Ill. **57.** H. 8¼ inches. *Courtesy of Eunice Althouse.*

**Auto Dolls.** 1909. Trade name for blonde boy and girl character dolls, dressed in yellow cravenettes and goggles; girls wear dust-proof veils; price 50¢, 75¢, and $1.00.

**Autoperipatetikos.** 1862. Walking doll patented in England and America by *Enoch Rice Morrison;* doll made and/or distributed by *Daniel S. Cohen* and *Joseph Lyon & Co.* of New York City, *Martin & Runyon* of London, and others. The walking mechanism operated by clockworks. The doll came with a rag, papier-mâché, china, or untinted bisque head; height around 10 inches depending on hair style.

At least two types of marks are found printed on the disk at the bottom of the doll's skirt:

"Patented July 15th, 1862; also, in England."

or

"Patented July 15th, 1862; also, in Europe, 20 Dec. 1862."

A & M
Made in Austria

**57.** Mark on doll made in Austria.

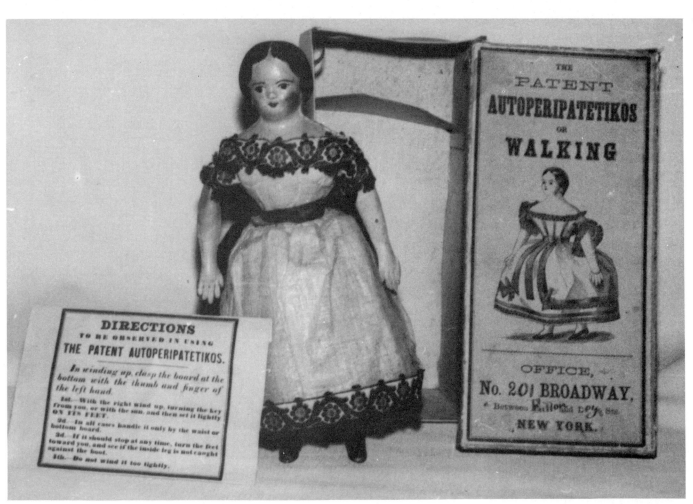

A

DIRECTIONS
TO BE OBSERVED IN USING
THE PATENT AUTOPERIPATETIKOS.

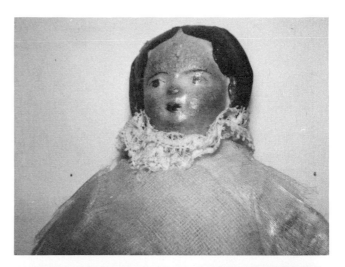

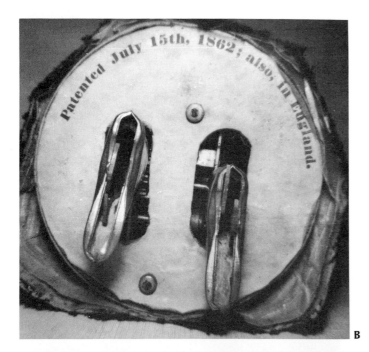

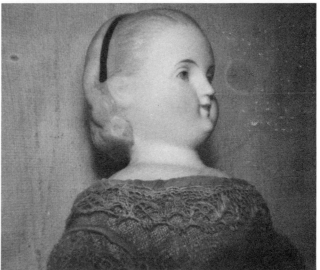

**60.** Bisque head with Alice-in-Wonderland type of molded hairdo on an Autoperipatetikos, patented in 1862. H. 10 inches. *Courtesy of the Newark Museum, Newark, N. J.*

**61.** Patented Autoperipatetikos doll with china head. The curls are held in place by a semicircular comb resting on the top of them. Note brush marks. H. 10½ inches. *Coleman Collection.*

**58A, B, C** (left and above). Autoperipatetikos with cloth head, shown with the original dress, box, and directions. Patent date 1862 appears on bottom board. H. 10 inches. *Courtesy of the International Doll Library Foundation.*

**59** (at top, right). Cloth head on an Autoperipatetikos. Note that on both Autoperipatetikos cloth heads, the eyes are painted to glance to the side. It seems unlikely that this would happen accidentally in both cases. H. 10 inches. *Courtesy of the Newark Museum, Newark, N J.*

**Aux Amis de l'Enfance.** 1870–75. Paris. *E. Cousin*, proprietor; made jointed dolls.

**Aux Bébés Sages.** 1863–79. Paris. *Marchal & Buffard,* proprietors and doll makers.

**Aux Enfants de France.** 1869+. Paris. *Alice Couterier,* proprietor; made jointed dolls, small dolls, and doll clothes.

**Aux Enfants Sages.** 1870's. Paris. Proprietors were Benon & Cie. and *Guiton* at different times; distributed and exported lady dolls and their trousseaux. The name Aux Enfants Sages is found both on dolls and on a metal plate attached to a doll's trunk.

**Aux Rêves de l'Enfance.** 1870's. Paris. Distributor of fine dolls with bisque heads and kid bodies, many of them kid over wood with bisque forearms. On some of their dolls the same type of bisque head was used as found on *Jacob Lacmann's* doll bodies. Probably parts were bought elsewhere and the dolls assembled in this establishment.

**Avenir, L'.** See **Bébé l'Avenir.**

**Averill, Madame Georgene (née Hopf).** 1913-14, Portland, Ore.; 1915–16, Los Angeles, Calif.; 1916–25+, New York City. Wife of (James) Paul Averill of *Averill Manufacturing Co.*

1913: First creation was a Dutch boy, which became popular in the U.S. and Canada. This was in a line of felt-dressed character dolls that later included cowboys, Indians, etc.

1915: Used trade name *Madame Hendren;* designed and patented dolls for Averill Manufacturing Co.

1916: Obtained four U.S. design patents for dressing dolls as a Dutch girl, an Indian papoose, an Indian girl, and a cowboy. Georgene Averill resided in Los Angeles at that time, but assigned these patents to the Averill Manufacturing Co. of New York City. A cowboy with composition head and hands, dressed in yellow felt, has a cloth attached at the rear waist; it reads: "Madame Hendren // Character Doll // Costume Pat. May 9th 1916."

1917: Designed American babies and little girls dressed in the latest styles. New line trade-named *Lyf-Lyk* (Life-Like) included one hundred and fifty numbers dressed in long and short dresses of lawn, dimity, dotted swiss, voile, and silk.

1918: Patented famous Madame Hendren walking *Mama Doll,* one of the first American Mama dolls. This doll had movable arms, legs, and head (without mechanical joints such as ball-and-socket joints), flange neck, body made of stuffed fabric with two front and two rear sections stitched at hips and shoulders to make them movable.

**62A & B.** Bisque head with swivel neck on shoulder plate; kid-covered wooden body with mortise-and-tenon joints. Bisque lower arms. Mark of Aux Rêves de l'Enfance stamped in turquoise on the chest: Ill. **65.** H. 17½ inches. *Courtesy of Sylvia Brockman.*

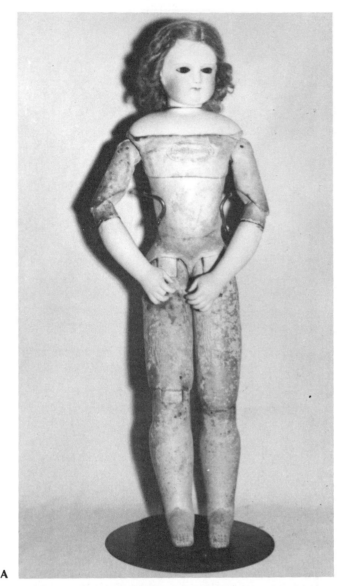

A

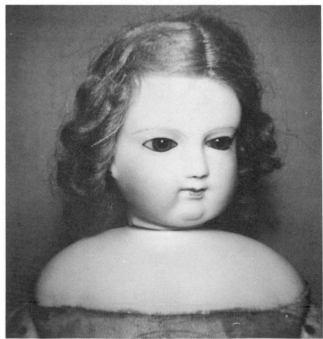

B

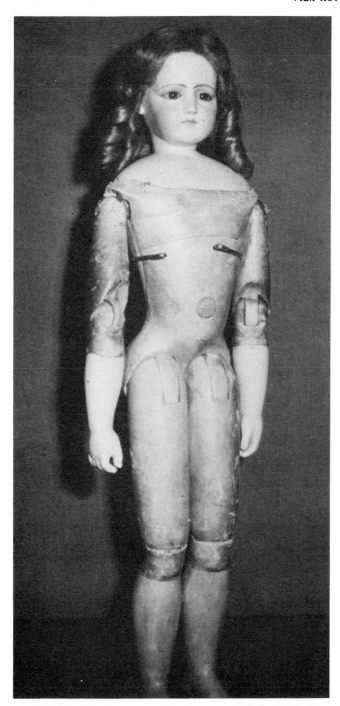

A

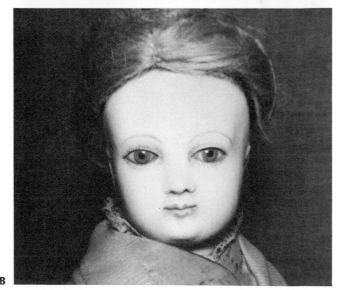

B

**63.** Doll distributed by the shop Aux Rêves de l'Enfance. It has a bisque head and shoulder plate, glass eyes, a kid-covered body with lower arms of bisque and legs of wood. Black and white sticker mark on stomach: Ill. **66.** H. 26 inches. *Courtesy of Margaret Whitton; photograph by Winnie Langley.*

**64A & B.** Lady doll from Aux Rêves de l'Enfance; has bisque swivel head, gusseted kid body, glass eyes, wig. Original tan silk and wool dress. Mark in turquoise on stomach: Ill. **65.** H. 18 inches. *Courtesy of Hildred Brinkley.*

**65 & 66.** Marks found on dolls of Aux Rêves de l'Enfance.

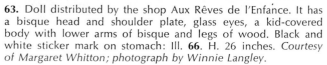

65

66

Hands were connected to arms by wires that forced fabric into recess; foot had projecting heel to hold shoe in place.

1923: Georgene Averill no longer with Averill Manufacturing Co., but with *Madame Georgene, Inc.,* whose president was her husband, James Paul Averill. Probably J(ames) Paul Averill and the I. Paul Averill who witnessed many of Georgene Averill's patents and I. P. Averill, a toy buyer for Meier & French of New York City in 1905, were all the same person, since I & J were often used interchangeably. The trade names Madame Hendren, Life-Like, and many others remained with the Averill Manufacturing Co., but the name *Wonder,* used since 1920, was trademarked by Madame Georgene, Inc. *Borgfeldt* had the exclusive distribution of the Wonder dolls, which were made in the *K & K Toy Co.* factory.

1924: Georgene Averill created a doll for *Pinky Winky Products Co.*

1925: Georgene Averill continued to create many dolls for Borgfeldt.

**Averill, Paul, Inc.** 1920–24. New York City. Manufactured and distributed dolls designed by *Madame Georgene Averill.* The Averills appear to have left the *Averill Manufacturing Co.* in the early 1920's and worked closely with *Borgfeldt.*

**Averill Manufacturing Co.** 1915–25+. New York City. Firm members in 1917 were Rudolph A. Hopf, brother of Georgene Averill, and (James) Paul Averill; in 1923, Rudolph Hopf was president, and Mr. and Mrs. James Paul Averill no longer seemed to be connected with the company.

1916: They made a Dutch girl named *Gretchen, Indian Maid, Cowboy,* etc., all designed and patented by Georgene Averill.

1917: Employed one hundred and twenty-five people, and made thirty styles of baby dolls and two hundred and fifty styles of character dolls; and used trade names *Madame Hendren* and *Lyf-Lyk* (Life-Like).

1920: *Wonder Walking Dolls, Madame Hendren's Life-Like Mama Dolls, Rock-a-Bye Baby,* and other dolls priced up to $50.00 each.

1922: *Wonder Baby* used in musical comedy on Broadway and in five road companies. A soft-body doll called *Dolly Dingle* was designed for the firm by *Grace G. Drayton.*

1923: *Dolly Rekord,* a phonograph doll, *Gold Medal Baby,* and *U-Shab-Ti* were among the new dolls; *Lloyd* voices were used in the Mama dolls.

1924: Made *Chocolate Drop* and other dolls designed by Grace G. Drayton, and an infant doll named *Lullabye.*

**Avery, Claire.** 1914–15. New York City. Secured U.S. patent for a rag doll with eyes glancing to side.

**Avinein, Mme.** 1890. Listed in Paris Directory under Dolls.

**Axthelm (Axhelm), Ernst.** 1897–1918. Neustadt near Coburg, Thür. Doll manufacturer, specialized in dressed dolls.

**Ayrand, A.** See **Prieur, C.**

# B

**Baba.** 1918. Trademark registered in France by *Mme. Poulbot.*

**Babbitt at Your Service Cleanser Boy.** 1916. Doll made by *Modern Toy Co.,* representing the trademark of the B. T. Babbitt Co., holds a can of cleanser; 15 inches tall, price $1.00.

**Babee.** 1914. Cherub-type doll made by the *Fair Amusement Co.*

**Babes in the Woods.** 1925. *Story Book Doll,* manufactured by *Sol Bergfeld & Son,* distributed by *Borgfeldt;* composition heads, 15 inches tall.

**Babet.** 1921. Trademark registered in France by Mlle. Cécile Lambert, doing business as *Edmée Rozier.*

**Babette.** See **Mlle. Babette.**

**Babette.** 1924. Trade name of *Century Doll Co.*

**Babies.** 1909–25+. With bent limbs; also called sitting or position babies. One of the first dolls of this type found in advertisements appears to have had the head mold #100 made by *Kämmer & Reinhardt.*

**Babies Grumpy.** 1924. Later version of *Baby Grumpy,* made by *EFFanBEE;* includes dolls named *Joan, Billie, Gladys,* and *Peter.*

**Babs.** 1914. Imported all-bisque boy doll, standing, naked with jointed arms, eyes glancing to the side, mouth slightly open, chubby body. Made in eight sizes from 3 to 10 inches, priced 10¢ to $1.50.

**Babs Manufacturing Corp.** 1917–20. Philadelphia, Pa. Trademark Babs registered in U.S., the name of a non-mechanical walking doll with flexible steel springs. Doll could walk, kneel, sit down, or take fancy steps; 28 inches tall.

**Baby.** 1907. Trade name for a rag doll made by *Art Fabric Mills.*

**Baby.** 1909+. Trade name of character baby made by *Kämmer & Reinhardt;* distributed by *Strobel & Wilken* and *Borgfeldt;* head mold #100 is usually bisque and on a bent-limb composition body.

**Baby Beatrice.** Early 20th century. Imported dolls, advertised as popular priced and of a grade of bisque below standard.

**Baby Beautiful.** 1910–12. Line of composition character baby dolls made by *Louis Amberg & Son.*

**Baby Beautiful.** Ca. 1920. Composition-headed doll made by the *Putnam D. Smith* family.

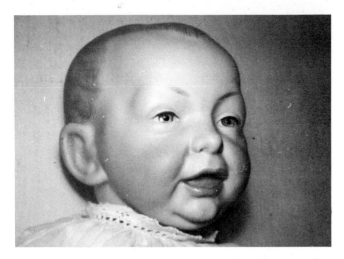

67. "Baby," a Kämmer & Reinhardt doll, marked on the bisque head as shown in Ill. **69.** Hair and eyes are molded and painted. Doll has open-closed mouth, bent-limb composition body. H. 15 inches. *Courtesy of the International Doll Library Foundation.*

68. All-composition baby with bent limbs. Resembles the K [star] R, mold 100, "Baby." Ca. 1910. *Courtesy of Maurine Popp; photograph by Winnie Langley.*

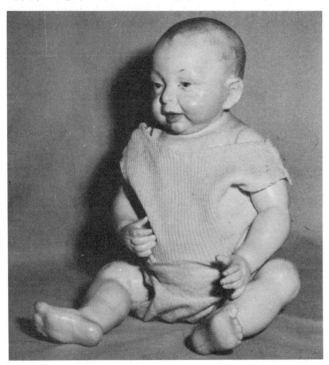

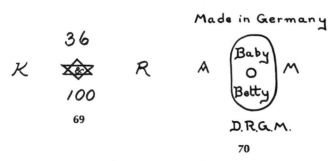

69. Mark found on Kämmer & Reinhardt's "Baby."

70. "Baby Betty" mark.

**Baby Belle.** 1906–10. Trademark registered in U.S. by *Bawo & Dotter* for a line of dolls made in Waltershausen, Thür., including kid-body dolls, jointed composition-body dolls with wigs and a newly patented eye device that prevented the eyes from dropping into the head; dolls were dressed in American-style dresses.

**Baby Belle.** 1908. Trademark registered in Germany by *Borgfeldt;* used for some of the dolls in their *Celebrate* line.

**Baby Belle.** 1913–15. *Louis Wolf & Co.* used this trade name for a line of character dolls made by *C. M. Bergmann;* advertised as finest quality dolls; made with wigs or with painted hair.

**Baby Bettie.** 1913–14. Trade name for a bent-limb baby doll made by *Ideal Novelty & Toy Co.* Doll's head made of "unbreakable, washable composition."

**Baby Betty.** 1912. German trademark registered by *Butler Bros.* Bisque doll's heads were inscribed "Baby Betty"; were made by *Armand Marseille.*

**Baby Betty.** 1917. Trade name of a doll made by *Ideal Novelty & Toy Co.;* this could be a later version of their *Baby Bettie.*

**Baby Betty.** 1919. Trade name for dolls made by the *Perfect Toy Manufacturing Co.* in various sizes.

**Baby Betty.** 1924. Trade name for a *Mama Doll* made by the *Uneeda Doll Co.*

**Baby Bi-Face.** 1916–17. Trade name for two-faced dolls made by *Ideal Novelty & Toy Co.;* by twisting the head, a tearful face was replaced by a smiling face.

**Baby Bill.** 1911–12. Copyright by *Horsman;* designed by *Helen Trowbridge.* This doll may have been sold by Horsman under the trade name of *Gold Medal Prize Baby.* Dolls had *Can't Break 'Em* composition heads and arms and were dressed in white; five sizes; life-size model added in 1912; price 50¢ to $5.00.

**Baby Blanche.** Name incised on bisque heads made by *Simon & Halbig.* Heads had sleeping eyes, molded eyebrows, and open mouths; found on jointed composition bodies, sometimes on walking bodies where the head turned as the doll walked; sizes 21 and 23½ inches, and probably others.

**Baby Blossom.** 1913–14. Trade name for *Horsman* doll with *Can't Break 'Em* head, lips parted to hold a pacifier; three sizes.

1914: Painted hair and eyes, cork-stuffed cloth body; five sizes, 10½, 13½, 15, 19, and 21½ inches; prices 59¢ to $3.98.

**Baby Blue.** 1910. Copyrighted by *Hahn & Amberg.* Girl's head with blue eyes, blue velvet body; 12 inches. Price $8.75 doz. wholesale.

1913–14: Probably the *Baby Blue Eyes* offered as a subscription premium, with other Amberg dolls; had molded hair, long dress. Size 12 inches, price 50¢

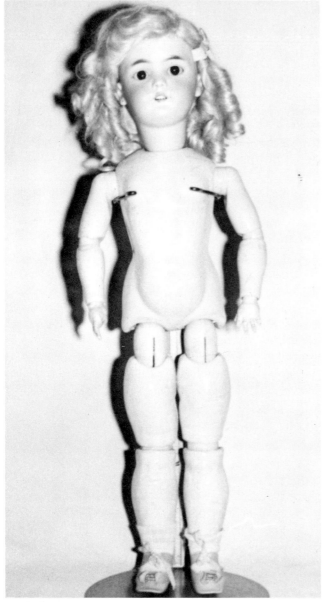

**71A & B.** "Baby Blanche" bisque head made by Simon & Halbig. Mark: Ill. **72.** Body is composition and wood. Doll walks and talks; head turns as she walks. H. 23½ inches. *Courtesy of Helen Jo Payne.*

**72.** Mark on "Baby Blanche" dolls.

# S & H
# Baby Blanche

**Baby Blue Eyes.** 1909. Cutout rag doll made by *Saalfield Publishing Co.*

**Baby Bo Kaye.** Ca. 1925+. Head made by *Cameo Doll Co.* in composition and by *Kestner* in bisque; designed by *Joseph L. Kallus* and copyrighted in 1926; assembled by *K & K Toy Co.*, who probably made bodies; distributed by *Borgfeldt.* Head and limbs of wood-pulp composition; cloth body stuffed with cotton wadding; voice box; molded hair; two lower teeth; 18 inches tall and possibly other sizes; named *"Bo"* for *Borgfeldt* and *"Kaye"* for *Kallus.* In all, about 50,000 Baby Bo Kayes were produced.

**Baby Bobby.** 1911–13. Trade name for one of the *Horsman* infant *Nature Babies* with a serious-looking face; head and hands of *Can't Break 'Em* composition, molded hair, cloth body; wore long dress; nearly 12 inches tall, price $1.00.

A
B

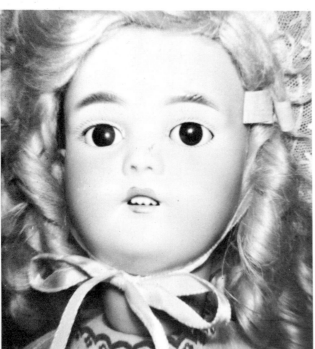

**73.** "Baby Bo Kaye"; bisque head marked "J. L. Kallus: Copr. Germany // 1394/30." Head has flange neck and molded hair. *Courtesy of Margaret Whitton; photograph by Winnie Langley.*

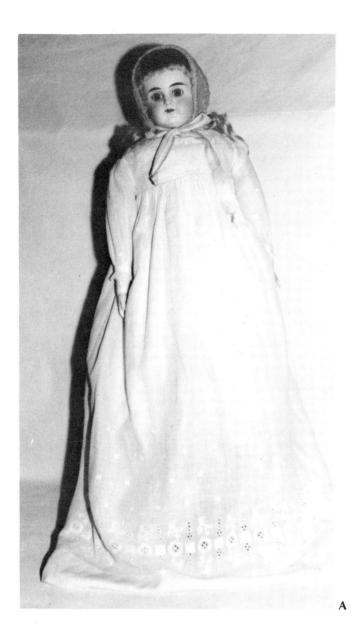

A

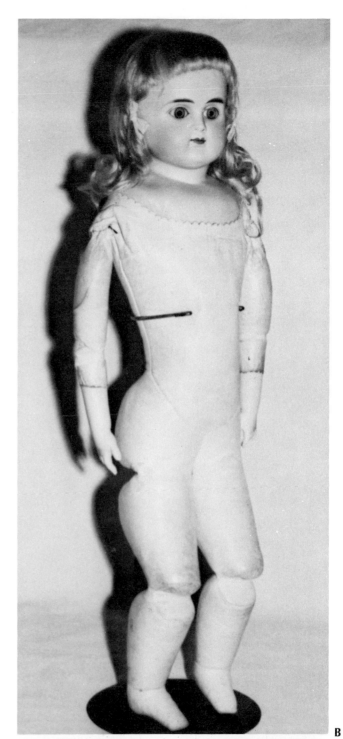

B

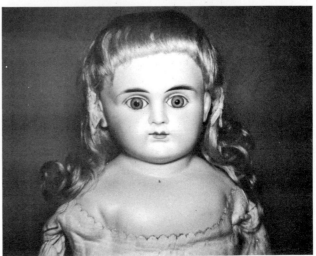

C

**Baby Bodies.** Usually these were chubbier and had shorter limbs and necks proportionately to the head than children or adult dolls' bodies. The word "baby" referred to dolls representing all ages until about the beginning of the 19th century; during most of that century, "baby" and "child" were synonymous. Wooden and wax dolls of the 18th and early 19th centuries, which were dressed as babies, usually had very short arms. Queen Victoria, as a princess in the 1830's, dressed small cloth dolls as babies; the dolls representing older ages were peg-jointed wooden dolls. At the 1851 London Exhibition, *Mme. Montanari* showed dolls representing all ages beginning with infancy, and varied the faces and bodies according to their ages. *Ch. Motschmann* of Son-

**74A, B, & C.** Bisque head is slightly turned; short neck; kid body has relatively short limbs. Dolls of this type appear to have represented babies in the 1880's, and were generally dressed in long baby dresses. Marked "1127 #10" on shoulder. H. 22½ inches. *Coleman Collection.*

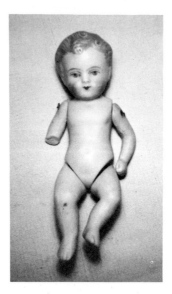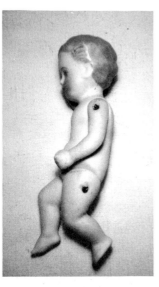

**75A & B.** All-bisque baby with molded and painted features and hair with brush marks. Note the curvature of the torso. The asymmetrical shape and decorative techniques suggest that this doll may have preceded the bent-limb babies of ca. 1909. H. 4½ inches. *Coleman Collection.*

**76.** Character baby. Bisque head has painted and molded features, and is on a composition bent-limb baby body. Mark on head: Ill. **77.** *Courtesy of Margaret Whitton; photograph by Winnie Langley.*

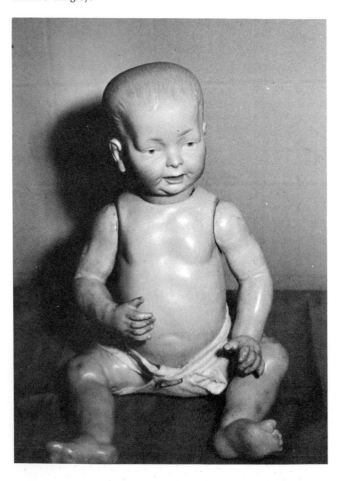

neberg in 1857 patented a new type of baby body that appears to have been popular for at least a decade. These bodies were inspired by some oriental baby dolls, and the papier-mâché ones often have a slightly oriental look. They were made in nearly all types of material—papier-mâché, china, wood, wax, and stiffened rag. They had shoulder heads with cloth mid-torso. The lower torso was made of the same material as the shoulder head. The upper arm and leg parts were usually of cloth. The legs and arms frequently were constructed with wooden tubes and floating joints for hands and feet. The cloth mid-torso nearly always contained a squeak box that operated by pressing the head and lower torso portions together. The cloth was generally twill, but in the cheaper versions sometimes cheesecloth.

Also in the mid-19th century, the unjointed so-called *Frozen Charlottes* or pillar dolls began to appear, and many of these had the chubby bodies we associate with babies. This type has even been found with the cloth mid-torso and squeak box for a crying baby. In the 1870's and 1880's, small dolls, frequently Frozen Charlottes, in long dresses were often carried in the arms of larger dolls. Most of the early kid bodies appear to have been used on lady or children dolls, but by the 1880's the kid bodies were made with the proportions of younger children and were attired in long dresses. This trend seems to have reached almost ridiculous proportions in the 1890's, as shown by the short, dumpy, almost dwarflike body made by *Kestner,* but having the *Dolly Doll* face found on many other dolls.

One of the greatest improvements in the making of baby bodies occurred around 1909, when *Kämmer & Reinhardt* brought out their bent-limb composition baby bodies, also known as *Next to Nature* jointed bodies. In 1909 *Louis Amberg & Son* made a similar composition baby body for a doll named *Samson,* but the body was jointed with wire instead of elastic. Some all-bisque and wax babies have similar bent-limb bodies. These appear to be earlier, and may have inspired the bent-limb composition bodies, which were part of the trend toward making lifelike character dolls. At last, the bodies really resembled a chubby baby. The hands were usually molded in baby-like poses—one hand with the fingers curved in, the other with the fingers stretching out. The big toe was usually turned up slightly. Many of the character dolls of this era, especially those made in America, had cloth bodies of somewhat similar shape. In 1918 *Georgene Averill* introduced the *Mama Doll,* which had the squeaking voice of the early Motschmann baby plus a soft, cuddly body shaped like a real baby but without the detail obtainable with composition. The infant *Bye-*

F 1 B
Germany

**77.** Mark found on bent-limb baby body. The letters suggest a possible relationship to EFFanBEE.

*Lo Baby* body in 1924 was also a modified version of the character baby body.

**Baby Bo-Kaye.** See **Baby Bo Kaye.**

**Baby Booful.** 1920. Trade name for doll of *Averill Manufacturing Corp.;* four styles of bent-limb babies, sleeping or stationary eyes; with wig.

**Baby Boy, Model Number 1.** 1911. Copyrighted and made by *Louis Amberg & Son.*

**Baby Bright.** 1912. Distributed by *Montgomery Ward & Co.* Bisque head and hands; teeth; sleeping eyes and wig; kid body with swivel hip-joint; mechanism in head caused doll to say "Mama" when raised from a reclining position or when walking. Size 19 inches; price $1.25.

**Baby Bright Eyes.** 1911. Copyrighted and made by *Louis Amberg & Son;* designed by *Jeno Juszko.* Young baby with big, wide-open eyes; big forehead and cheeks; configuration for a little hair.

**Baby Bright Eyes.** 1918–19. Distributed by *T. Eaton.* Came with bisque head, composition baby body, sleeping eyes, and wig. Size 12 inches; price $1.75.

**Baby Brite.** 1924. One of the *Lyf-Lyk* dolls in the *Mme. Hendren* line of dolls made by *Averill Manufacturing Co.*

**Baby Bud.** 1915. Trademark registered in Germany by *Butler Bros.* for dolls. All-bisque versions of Baby Bud were made later in Japan. These dolls had molded clothes on the upper torso, painted eyes glancing to the side, and parted lips. They closely resembled the dolls designed by *Langfelder* for *Morimura Bros.,* except for the clothes. Came in 3½- and 4½-inch sizes. A similar all-composition doll marked "(??)arbee" is 7 inches tall. (See color photograph C12.)

**Baby Bumps.** 1910–12. *Horsman's* second successful doll (first one was *Billiken*). Character doll with painted face modeled by an American sculptor. It was a *Can't Break 'Em* composition head version of the *Kämmer & Reinhardt* bisque model #100 *(Baby);* advertised as an *Art Doll* taken from life.

**78A, B, & C.** "Baby Bumps," White and Negro versions, made by Horsman ca. 1912. Label was originally sewed on the rompers; see Ill. **79.** H. 12 inches. Larger doll (next page) may be a "Big Baby Bumps"; it has composition head and arms on a sateen body, and allegedly came in a Horsman box. H. 18 inches. (See also "Smiling Sue.") *Two smaller dolls (below) courtesy of Patricia Schoonmaker; photograph by John Schoonmaker. Larger doll (next page), courtesy of Lester & Alice Grinnings.*

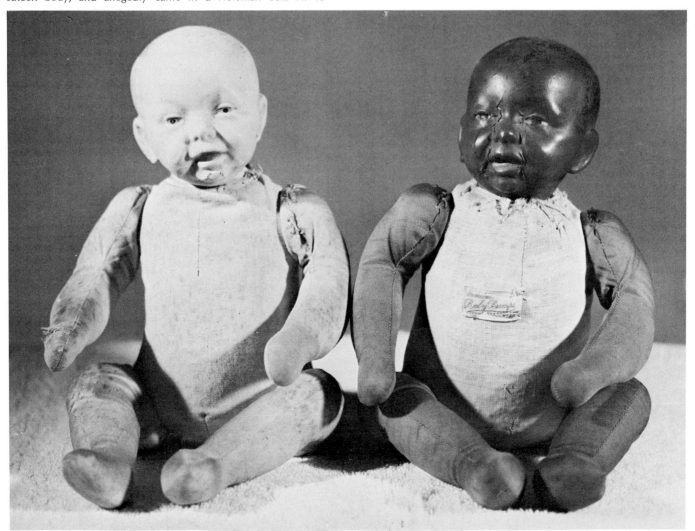

A

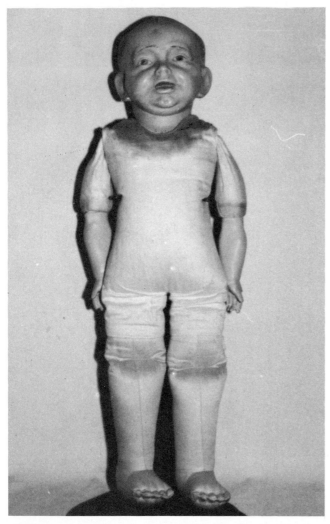

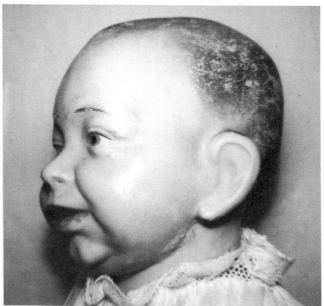

**78B & C.** See caption on preceding page.

1910: Carne with velvet, cork-stuffed body; dressed in rompers; price $9.00 doz. wholesale.

1911: Registered as a trademark by Horsman in the U.S. and Germany. Came with salmon-pink face, brownish-red molded hair, dressed in a one-piece garment called a "jumper" made of blue and white cotton trimmed with bands of plain blue; possibly also dressed in other colors.

1912: Came with flesh-colored sateen, cork-filled body, jointed at shoulders and hips; dressed in rompers; advertised by *Montgomery Ward & Co.* 11-inch size cost 98¢. (See also **Big Baby Bumps.**)

**Baby Bundie (Bundie).** 1918, made by *Rex Doll Co.;* 1919–21, *Mutual Doll Co.;* 1922–25+, *Cameo Doll Co.* Designed by *Joseph L. Kallus* and copyrighted in 1918 and again in 1919 by Joseph L. Kallus.

1918-25+: Distributed by *Borgfeldt;* character baby of wood-pulp composition; 12-inch size—shoulder joints only; 16-inch size—movable shoulder and hips with coiled spring joints. Came with eyes glancing to one side, long upper lashes, and painted hair or wig.

**Baby Bunting.** 1903. Advertised in PLAYTHINGS as a small, new, and expensive doll, dressed all in white fur with a fur hood.

**Baby Bunting.** 1914. Trade name of *Ideal Novelty & Toy Co.* for a doll as large as a live baby; price $5.00.

**Baby Bunting.** 1917. Doll held can of Colgate talcum powder.

**Baby Bunting.** 1917–18. Design for a rag doll patented in U.S. by *Lelia Fellom.*

**Baby Bunting.** 1922–23. Trademark registered in the U.S. by the *Flexie Toy Co.* for dolls. Baby Bunting was a walking *Mama Doll* 19 inches tall.

**Baby Bunting.** 1925. Trade name for an infant doll of the *Bye-Lo* type, made by *J. Bouton & Co.*

**Baby Butterfly.** 1913–14. Trademark registered in U.S. by *Horsman.* Doll had *Can't Break 'Em* head made by *Aetna Doll & Toy Co.;* was designed by a Japanese artist and represented the Japanese baby in the opera MME. BUTTERFLY; it was olive-skinned and chubby, dressed in a brilliant-colored Japanese kimono; the manufacturers of Babcock's Corylopsis placed some of the oil of their perfume on every Baby Butterfly.

*Genuine*
*Baby Bumps*
TRADEMARK

**79.** Mark on Horsman's "Baby Bumps."

**Baby Catherine.** 1918. Doll with composition head and hands distributed by *Butler Bros.* It had moving eyes, a bobbed mohair wig, and a cork-stuffed body; sizes 13, 14½, 18, and 21 inches; priced from $22.50 to $60.00 doz. wholesale.

**Baby Cuddles.** 1920. Produced by *Colonial Toy Manufacturing Co.*, distributed by *Samstag & Hilder Bros.* Came with composition head, hands, and feet, smiling face, cork-stuffed body; three sizes, twelve dress styles.

**Baby Dainty.** 1912–25+. Trade name used by *EFFanBEE* for a line of girl dolls with stuffed bodies.

1912–14: Name used for a toddler with unbreakable composition legs that enabled the doll to stand alone.

1918: Doll came with composition breastplate head, painted features, open mouth with a pacifier, mohair wig, composition hands, cork-stuffed body with concealed shoulder and hip joints. Dressed in long or short dress of white lawn; sizes 15, 18½, 21½, and 24 inches; prices $14.40 to $43.80 doz. wholesale.

1925: Name used for a newborn infant doll. Price $15.00 doz. wholesale, including the blanket in which the doll was wrapped.

**Baby Darling.** 1915. Trade name used by *Horsman* for a little girl doll with *Can't Break 'Em* composition head; six sizes, 50¢ and up.

**Baby Darling.** 1918. Trade name for a *Madame Hendren Mama Doll* made by *Averill Manufacturing Corp.* Fully jointed, sleeping eyes; sizes 17, 20, and 24 inches.

**Baby Darling.** 1919. Trade name used by *Morimura Bros.* for an all-bisque doll with molded hair, ribbon in her hair, and jointed shoulders. The name Baby Darling was printed on a shield-shaped sticker on the stomach of the doll, but it seems likely this was the doll that Morimura Bros. advertised as *My Darling*.

**Baby Darling.** 1925. Trade name for a character doll distributed by *Bing Corp.*

**Baby Dingle.** 1924–25. One of the *Madame Hendren* line made by *Averill Manufacturing Corp.* Designed by *Grace G. Drayton* and based on the Drayton drawings of *Dolly Dingle* in PICTORIAL REVIEW. Composition head, painted hair, painted or moving roguish eyes; dressed as a baby.

**Baby Dolls.** The word "baby" was used for all types of dolls until the 19th century. The French word *bébé* usually indicated a young child doll. Throughout history, babies have been one of the most popular types of dolls. The 19th-century descriptions of baby dolls generally mentioned only their clothes. PLAYTHINGS, January, 1904, states, "Baby dolls with proportions of a baby are now on the market. They have typical baby faces with lips parted slightly for insertion of a nipple of a nursing bottle. These dolls have celluloid heads. They are a vast improvement over old style baby dolls that resembled nothing except a baby doll of the same kind."

EFFANBEE
BABY DAINTY
81

**80A & B.** "Baby Dainty" made by Fleischaker & Baum 1920's See Ill. 81 for mark. Arms, legs, and head are made of composition; stuffed cloth torso. H. 14 inches. *Coleman Collection.*

**81.** EFFanBEE's "Baby Dainty" mark.

**82.** "Baby Darling," all-bisque doll, made in Japan for Morimura Bros. Jointed arms, painted features. Mark: label on stomach, Ill. 83. H. 4¾ inches. *Courtesy of Dorothy Annunziato.*

**83.** "Baby Darling" mark of Morimura Bros.

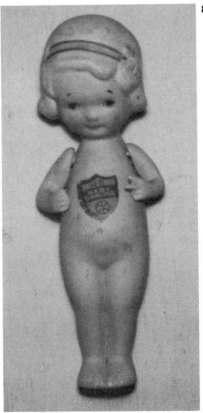

83

The character baby dolls modeled from life are chiefly 20th century, but many of the 19th-century dolls were supposed to represent small children or babies. Dolls with very short hair are often dressed as men when, frequently, they were originally intended to be babies. The dolls with short necks and round faces are actually baby or child dolls, although many collectors dress them as ladies. In 1910 baby dolls were preferred, especially by children under five years of age, according to PLAY-THINGS. (See also **Baby Bodies**.)

**Baby Dumpling.** See **Dolly Dumpling.**

**Baby EFFanBEE.** 1925. Newborn infant made by *EFFanBEE*.

**Baby Ella.** 1916. Composition head, bent-limb baby distributed by *Montgomery Ward & Co*. It came with a mohair wig and a chemise. Sizes 9½, 12, 14½, 17½, and 19½ inches; price from 61¢ to $4.10.

**Baby Ella.** 1918–21. Produced by *Morimura Bros.*, distributed in U.S. and Canada. Bisque head made in Japan; fully jointed body, French glass moving eyes with or without eyelashes; "bald" head or with mohair or natural hair wig. Sizes 6½, 8, 9, 11, 13, 14½, 16, 19, and 23 inches; 8-inch size cost 75¢, 13-inch size cost $3.00, 16-inch size cost $4.70.

**Baby Glee.** 1915. Copyrighted by *Louis Amberg & Son*, designed by *Jeno Juszko*. A young child with a dash of hair painted on the forehead, a gleeful expression, broad smile, open-closed mouth with molded two upper teeth and tongue; eyes glance to the side.

**Baby Gloria.** Ca. 1920. Name incised on bisque head made in Germany, probably by *Armand Marseille*. Came with sleeping glass eyes, open mouth with two upper teeth; composition arms and legs on soft Mama body with squeak box.

**Baby Grumpy (Baby Grumpy Jr.).** 1914–25+. *EFFanBEE* boy or girl doll, molded hair.

1915: Twelve new models of Baby Grumpies plus Baby Grumpy Jr.; price 50¢ and up.

1916: Distributed by *Butler Bros*. Boy dressed in rompers and girl in a dress to match the rompers. Made in two sizes—11½ inches for $4.50 doz. wholesale; 14½ inches for $8.75 doz. wholesale, dressed in piqué clothes.

1920: Reissue of Baby Grumpy.

1921: Advertised as waterproof and unbreakable; size 14 inches.

1923: Copyrighted by *Hugo Baum*, designed by *Ernesto Peruggi*. Doll had "baby's head in a petulant mood."

1924: Price $1.00 and up. (See also **Babies Grumpy**.)

**Baby Helen.** 1905–6. Trademark registered in U.S. by *Strawbridge & Clothier* for dolls.

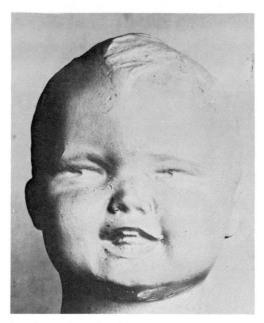

84. "Baby Glee," copyrighted by Louis Amberg & Son in 1915, designed by Jeno Juszko. This is a copy of the original picture of the plaster model, filed with the copyright application. The molds for the doll's head were made from this casting. (The hole on the left is for the Copyright Office filing rod.)

85. "Baby Gloria" has a bisque head with sleeping glass eyes, open mouth with two upper teeth, dimples in her cheeks; composition arms and legs. Cloth "Mama" body has a squeak box. Mark: Ill. 86. H. 18 inches. *Courtesy of Dorothy Annunziato.*

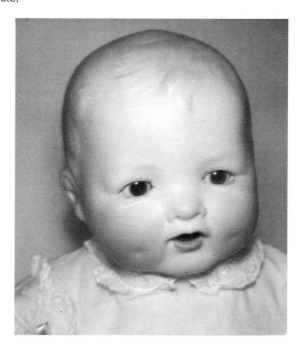

Baby Gloria
Germany

**86.** Mark on "Baby Gloria" dolls.

**Baby Hilda.** 1916. Baby doll with a pacifier; distributed by *Montgomery Ward & Co.* Size 13½ inches, cost 99¢.

**Baby Horsman.** 1923. Copyrighted by *Horsman*; designed by Edith Hitchcock. Represented the head of a child.

**Baby Irene.** 1913–14. Trade name used by *Louis Wolf & Co.* for a child doll modeled from life, mate to *Little Jimmy.* Price $1.00 and up.

**Baby Lolo.** 1914. Trade name used by *Ideal Novelty & Toy Co.*

**87A & B.** "Baby Grumpy" has molded composition head and limbs, cloth Mama Doll type of body. Mark on shoulder plate: see Ill. **88.** H. 18 inches. *Courtesy of Jessica R. Norman.*

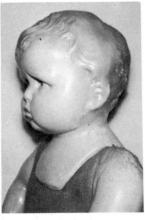

**88.** EFFanBEE's "Baby Grumpy" mark.

The prices given for dolls are those for which the dolls were originally offered for sale. They are *not* today's prices.

**Baby Love.** 1919–20. Trademark registered in U.S. by *Stella Adler*; distributed by *R. F. Novelty Co.* Handmade and hand-painted three-dimensional paper dolls with movable arms, legs, and head.

**Baby Lucy.** 1918, *Tajimi Co.*; 1919–21, *Taiyo Trading Co.*; producers. Made in Japan; bisque-head character baby doll with sleeping eyes, mohair wig; sizes 10, 12, 14, 16, and 18 inches.

**Baby Luxe.** 1919. Made by *Deluxe Doll & Toy Co.*; sizes 13 to 20 inches; prices $1.00 to $10.00.

**Baby Marion.** 1913. Made by *Ideal Novelty & Toy Co.* Washable composition head, knitted clothes.

**Baby Marion.** 1917–18. *Emkay Doll Manufacturing Co.*, manufacturer; distributors, *Louis Wolf & Co.* and *Riemann, Seabrey Co.* Fully jointed composition dolls, made in America; sleeping eyes; natural hair or mohair wigs.

**Baby Mine.** 1911–25. Character doll produced by *Ideal Novelty & Toy Co.* with special permission of Margaret Mayo, playwright of the comedy BABY MINE.

1911: Stuffed bodies made by patented "Skeleton Process" and covered with blue cloth; dressed in white cloak and baby bonnet; price 25¢ to $1.50.

1921: Sleeping eyes; price $1.00 to $30.00.

Benjamin Michtom, son of the founder of Ideal, commented, "Baby Mine was indeed a most important doll in the early Ideal line. It was virtually the trademark for the infant type dolls which Ideal made in those years. Dolls changed somewhat from year to year and heads were constantly being remade, although they were always an infant doll. If I remember correctly, they generally wore long swaddling dresses, although a great many were made with shorter baby dresses."

**Baby O'Mine.** 1920. Made by *Morimura Bros.* Japanese doll.

**Baby Outfitters, The.** 1917–18, New York City. Made dressed character dolls of celluloid and composition; used brand name *Bo-Peep.*

**Baby Paula.** 1914. Made by *Ideal Novelty & Toy Co.*

**Baby Peggy (Baby Peggy, the Nation's Darling).** 1923–24. Portrait doll of Baby Peggy made by *Louis Amberg & Son* by arrangement with Baby Peggy and the Century Film Corp. Tiny bisque models, 10¢, 15¢, and 25¢; or made with porcelain heads, sewn wigs, dressed in foreign costume, price $5.00 to $6.00.

**Baby Peterkin.** 1911–13. One of *Horsman's Nature Babies,* with *Can't Break 'Em* composition head modeled from life. Had laughing face, molded hair, cloth body, long infant's dress; 11-inch size cost $3.90 doz. wholesale.

**Baby Petite.** 1916–18. Bent-limb baby doll made by *Jessie M. Raleigh,* distributed by *Butler Bros.* Came with painted hair, a white lawn dress and bonnet. Sizes 10½, 12½, and 18 inches; prices $2.40, $3.10, $4.30.

**Baby Petite.** 1922–25. *Mama Doll* line of *American Character Doll Co.;* sizes 17 and 21 inches.

**Baby Phyllis Doll Co.** 1919–25. Brooklyn, N. Y. *Joseph G. Kaempfer,* manager; *J. Bouton & Co.* (Jay Bee), distributors. Baby Phyllis *Mama Doll* line from tiniest infant to "grown-up," sizes 14 to 26 inches.

1925: New bisque-head babies with sleeping eyes, price 50¢ to $5.00; bisque heads supplied in various sizes. These may be the Baby Phyllis bisque heads made by *Armand Marseille.*

**Baby Pierrot.** See **Carnival Baby.**

**Baby Rose.** 1919–21. Produced and distributed by *Morimura Bros.;* bisque doll or bisque head made in Japan. All-bisque doll with "Baby Rose" sticker on stomach, made in Germany, may have been handled by Morimura Bros.' successor.

**Baby Rosebud.** 1914–22. Copyrighted in 1914 by *Horsman,* designed by *Helen Trowbridge;* head of a laughing child made of *Can't Break 'Em* composition.

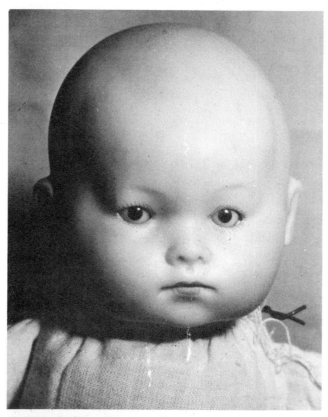

89. "Baby Phyllis," bisque-headed infant doll on a cloth body. Doll has glass eyes. Mark: Ill. **90.** *Courtesy of Margaret Whitton; photograph by Winnie Langley.*

BABY PHYLLIS
Made in Germany
2 4014

**90.** Mark used by Baby Phyllis Doll Co.

1915: Dressed in fashionable frock, six sizes, 50¢ and up.

1918: Soft body or new *Adtocolite* body, sleeping eyes; long dress all hand worked.

1922: Horsman sued *Gem Toy Co.* for infringement of their copyright on Baby Rosebud, but lost the case because they had failed to deposit two copies with the copyright office and had placed only their initials on the doll instead of the full name as required by law. After this date, the full names of doll companies usually appeared on dolls rather than just initials.

**Baby Ruth.** 1893–1907. Trademark registered in U.S. by *Crämer & Héron,* manufacturer; *Ehrich Bros.,* American distributor.

**Baby Ruth.** Ca. 1914–19. Distributed by *Sears, Roebuck & Co.* and *T. Eaton Co.* Came with bisque head, composition baby body, sleeping eyes, and wig; sizes 7 ³/₄, 9, 10, 12¹/₄, 14, 18, and 20 inches. In 1918, the 18-inch size cost $4.95.

**Baby Shirley.** 1918. Line made by *Century Doll Co.* Character baby heads made with a glue process composition; sleeping glass eyes, open mouth for pacifier; wig; six styles of dresses, both long and short; six sizes.

**Baby Sister.** 1919. Made by *Jessie McCutcheon Raleigh;* distributed by *Butler Bros.* Came with wig and white dress; 11¹/₂ inches tall; price $2.40.

**Baby Sister.** 1925. Infant-type doll made by *Roth, Baitz & Lipsitz, Inc.; John Bing,* distributor. Modeled from a baby in a New York maternity hospital.

**Baby Stuart.** 1900–11. Rag doll patented in U.S. by Madge Lansing Mead on November 6, 1900, and made by *Mother's Congress Doll Co.* Head was from a single piece of a seven-piece pattern; doll was stuffed with a soft substance.

**Baby Stuart.** 1919. Made by *Jessie McCutcheon Raleigh;* distributed by *Butler Bros.* Came with painted hair and white lawn dress; sizes 11¹/₂ and 13¹/₂ inches; prices $2.25 and $2.85.

**Baby Sunshine.** 1925. Distributed by *Louis Wolf & Co.;* one of the *Happiness Doll* line.

**Baby Surprize.** 1923–25. Made in America. Jointed at shoulders and hips; size 16 inches.

**Baby Talc.** 1915. Made by *Ideal Novelty & Toy Co.*

**Baby Violet.** 1903–25. Trademark registered in U.S. by *Abraham & Straus,* used for dolls.

**Baby Virginia.** 1917–18. Made by *Averill Manufacturing Corp.; Madame Hendren* line. It had a soft, chubby, infant-type body.

**Baby-Gelenkpuppen (Baby-Jointed Dolls).** 1911. Trade name for dolls with wooden shoulder joints made by *P. M. Schilling.*

**Babykins.** 1910. Produced by the *Dolly Co.;* one of the rag dolls in the *Dolly Dollykins* series.

**Babyland Rag.** 1904–20. Made by *Horsman.* Rag dolls with painted faces until 1907, when new *Life Like* faces printed in colors were introduced with nine designs.

1907: Topsy Turvy doll with one end smiling and one end crying.

1909: R. H. Macy & Co. advertised Babyland Rag dolls dressed in pink or blue lawn with lawn underwear; shoes and stockings. Sizes 12, 14, 15, and 18 inches; prices 24¢, 49¢, 98¢, and $1.78.

1910–11: Dolls advertised with both painted and printed faces, the latter in fifteen colors. The 14-inch dolls included Babyland Rag, Babyland Baby, Babyland Topsy, Babyland Topsy Baby, Topsy Turvy (Topsy at one end and Betty at the other end), Babyland Fancy, and Babyland Boy; price $1.00 to $1.25. The white and colored babies wore long dresses; all wore bonnets or hats. Faces could be cleaned with soap and water; bodies were stuffed with cotton. Larger sizes included 16½-inch Babyland Beauty for $2.00; 20-inch Babyland Dinah for $2.50; 20-inch Babyland Lady (little girl doll) and Babyland Big Baby for $3.00 each; 30-inch Babyland Dorothy and Babyland Jack Robinson, $5.00 each. Fingers on largest size were stitched, but not on smaller ones. (See color photograph C8.)

1913: Advertised by F. A. O. *Schwarz* in sizes 13 to 30 inches; price 60¢ to $5.00.

**91A & B.** Babyland rag doll made by Horsman has lithographed face, original Dutch costume except for the pants, which were copied from 1905 picture of a corresponding doll. *Courtesy of Dorothy Annunziato.*

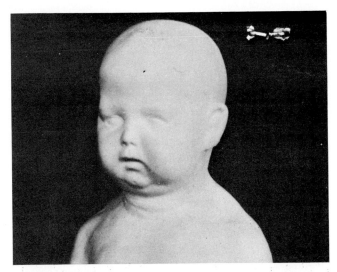

**92.** Copy of the original picture of the model of the Schoenhut Baby's head filed with the copyright application by Harry Edison Schoenhut in 1913. Many subsequent Schoenhut dolls had wooden heads molded after this model.

**Babys.** 1925. Trade name for porcelain-headed doll made by *Karl Müller & Co.*

**Baby's Head.** 1913–25. Copyrighted 1913 by Harry Edison Schoenhut of *A. Schoenhut & Co.*, one of the Schoenhut All-Wood Perfection Art Doll heads; used on bent-limb and fully-jointed-limb, wooden bodies; also used on walking body and on cloth body, which was new in 1924.

**Baby's Joy.** 1921. Made by *American Character Doll Co.*

**Baby's Pal.** 1921. *American Character Doll Co.* advertised that they made Baby's Pal doll in regular and indestructible styles.

**Baby's Playmate.** 1921. Doll made by *American Character Doll Co.*

**Baby's Voice, Mother's Choice.** 1924. Walking and talking doll made by *Gem Toy Co.*, price 50¢ to $10.00.

**Bach Bros.** 1908–9. New York City. Registered in U.S. as a trademark *The Bye Bye Kids,* rag dolls, including Sunbonnet Baby, Topsy, etc.; exported particularly to England.

**Backhausen, R.** 1891–97. Berlin. Manufacturer of dressed dolls and doll articles.

**Baculard (Favier & Baculard).** 1860–76. Paris. Obtained a patent in France in 1860 for the use of gutta-percha in making dolls' heads; Favier joined Baculard in the 1870's.

**Baer & Strasburger.** 1922–25. New York City. Importer and factory agent for dolls.

**Baehr & Proeschild.** See **Bähr & Pröschild.**

**Baffert, A.** 1925. Paris. Made rag dolls and wax dolls.

**Bagge & Hanck.** 1920. Coburg, Bavaria. Doll manufacturer.

**Bahn (Bohne), A. E.** 1851. Berlin. Showed various types of dolls at the London Exhibition.

**Bahner, Doscher Co.** 1921–25. New York City. Doll importer.

**Bähr & Co.** 1891. Hamburg, Germany. Doll distributor.

**Bähr & Pröschild.** 1871–1925+. Ohrdruf, Thür. Porcelain factory; made china dolls, dolls' heads, and bathing children.

1910: Registered a trademark in Germany. Also made celluloid dolls and doll parts.

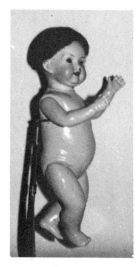
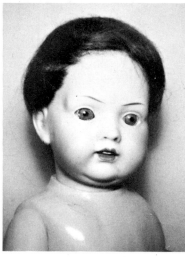

**93A & B.** Bähr & Pröschild bisque head with mark as seen in Ill **95**, except for "604" instead of "624" and "3/0" instead of "6." Sleeping eyes, open-closed mouth; rotund bent-limb composition baby body. Note the ridge at the top of the socket neck. H. 10 inches. *Courtesy of Eleanor Jean Carter.*

**94A & B.** Bähr & Pröschild mark appears on the bisque head (see Ill. **96**). Sleeping eyes, open mouth with two teeth, bent-limb baby body. Note the slant and shape of the eyebrows, which appear to be typical of this company. H. 10 inches. *Courtesy of Dorothy Annunziato.*

**95–97.** Marks used by Bähr & Pröschild. Nos. **95** and **96** were found on dolls. No. **97** was a trademark registered in 1910.

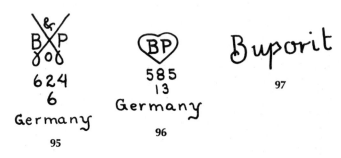

**Bailey, Doris Sylvia, & Baxter, Sarah Jane.** 1916. Longton, Staffs. Obtained a British patent for coating doll parts with wax. Busts, bodies, arms, and legs were first fired and painted; then the unglazed porcelain, earthenware, or plaster of Paris was dipped in transparent wax heated to 250°. After draining and cooling, it was dipped again for a second coat. In order to produce a glossy appearance, it was then dipped into cold water.

**Baird, Edna, & Alig, Cannie May.** 1919–21. Des Moines, Iowa. Secured U.S. design patent for a boy doll.

**Baker, Marie K.** 1912. Houston, Tex. Obtained U.S. patent for a doll with fabric continuous from head to feet and fingertips, in order to eliminate seams at points of stress; celluloid or metal face and neckpiece clamped onto the head of the doll.

**Baker & Bennett Co.** 1902–25+. New York City. Dewitt C. Baker started working for *Horsman* in 1886; later went with *Borgfeldt,* then with *Amberg,* and in 1902 he formed his own company with John Bigler, then with C. H. Bennett; distributors at first, later both distributors and manufacturers.

1910: Registered *Killiblues* as trademark in U.S.; also used initials "B. & B."

1911: Distributed dolls made by *Ideal Novelty & Toy Co.*

1915: Advertised *The Spearmint Kid* with Wrigley eyes, and with voice, by permission of the Wm. Wrigley Co.; size 12½ inches; price 50¢, later $1.00.

1916: Distributor of *Zaiden dolls.*

1917: Distributor for dolls manufactured by *Wigwam Co.* Wartime catalog shows only dolls with composition heads; many of these were priced over $100 doz. wholesale. The highest price was $132 doz. wholesale for a 26-inch doll with ball-jointed composition body.

1922–25: Baker Dolls made under their own supervision, walking and talking dolls, with or without wigs. Sizes 14, 16, 22, 27, and 28 inches; prices $8.00 to $36.00 doz. wholesale.

**Bald Heads.** A term which, in the 19th century, seems to have applied to dolls' heads whose crowns were not cut off, but may or may not have a few small holes.

"Bald heads" are found in practically all types of material. They were often used for infant dolls. In the 1870's there are references to both bald heads of wax and bald heads of bisque. In the doll trade of the early 20th century, "baldhead" referred to dolls with molded and painted hair. Bald china heads with wigs were advertised as late as the 20th century. Some collectors use the term "Belton-type" for dolls with bald heads of bisque.

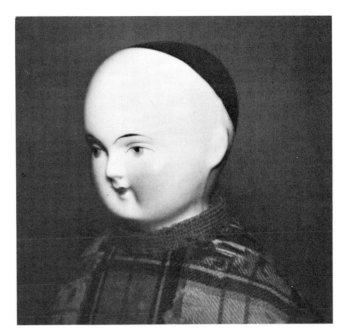

**98.** Bald china-headed doll with large black pate; painted features; original woolen plaid dress. H. 16 inches. *Coleman Collection.*

**99.** Bald china head with small black pate; painted features. H. of shoulder head, 4 inches. *Courtesy of Alberta Darby.*

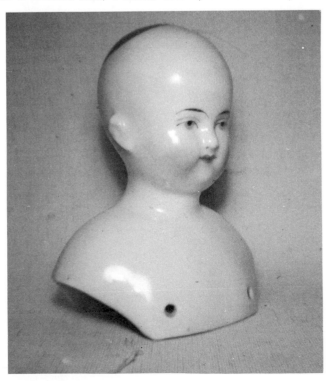

**100A & B.** China-headed doll with no black on its pate, which is unglazed and covered with a red wig; head, made in a three-part mold, is on a cloth body with china limbs and shoes with heels. H. 25½ inches. H. of shoulder head, 7 inches. *Coleman Collection.*

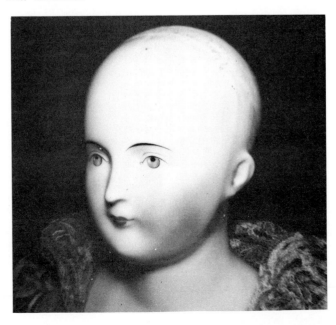

**101.** Bald china head with four holes but no black on the pate; painted features. The molded shoulder plate includes a portion of the upper arms; lower arms are china. Kid body is stamped in turquoise blue: "BREVETE . . ." in an ellipse. Dress is old. H. 21 inches. H. of shoulder head, 6 inches. *Courtesy of Sylvia Brockmon.*

**102.** Bald head of untinted bisque has glass eyes, wig, deeply molded chest. H. of shoulder head, 3¼ inches. *Coleman Collection.*

**Ball Joints.** A ball joint was composed of a ball (usually wooden) and two adjacent sockets strung with elastic or a metal spring to permit the doll joint to move in all directions. Frequently neck joints and sometimes other joints were made of a hemisphere with only one socket. Wooden-body dolls with ball joints are known to have been made at least as early as the eighteenth century. The wooden bodies often had a ball joint at the waist as well as hips, knees, shoulders, etc. Around 1870 both Casimir *Bru* and *Charles Parent* were experimenting with ball-jointed composition bodies. By the 1880's, this type of body proved to be a universal favorite in France under the name *Bébé Incassable* (unbreakable baby). The early French bébés do not usually have jointed wrists. Competition soon forced the German doll manufacturers to adopt this method of making doll bodies. By 1909 Germany had invented the bent-limb baby body that did not use ball joints. However, ball joints continued to be most popular; a doll with them was generally referred to in the doll trade as "fully jointed." When World War I cut off German dolls, American doll manufacturers began to make ball-jointed dolls. In the 1920's efforts were made to modify the hip joints so that otherwise-ball-jointed dolls could stand alone. Ball joints usually are found on composition bodies, but they were also used on bodies of wood, metal, bisque, stiffened fabric, celluloid, and various other man-made materials. Except for a few companies such as *Jumeau*, *Kester*, etc., the manufacturers of ball-jointed bodies purchased the bisque heads from large porcelain factories.

**Balland, E., Fils (Son).** 1882. Paris toymaker. Used "E. B." as mark. Dolls marked "E. B." may have been made by Balland, but there were other doll makers with those initials, and dolls so marked appear to have been made earlier than 1882.

**Ballard, E.** 1840–90. Clinton, Mass. Produced dolls, according to TOYS IN AMERICA by McClintock.

**Ballu, Ernst.** 1890–1914. Paris. Distributor. Successor was *Gerbaulet Frères* in 1914.

1890: Ballu was agent for *Ch. Rossignol*.

1896 and 1911: Registered *Bébé Olga* as a trademark in France.

1898: Advertised Bébé Olga as an indestructible bébé dressed in wool and satin.

**Balsam Dolls.** 1917. *Moore & Gibson Corp.* Dolls made of leather or fabric.

**Baltimore Bargain House.** Early 20th century. Baltimore, Md. Distributed dolls.

**Bamba, Ysaekiti.** 1900. Japan. Won Honorable Mention at Paris Exposition for dolls.

**Bamberger.** 1892–1925+. Newark, N.J. Distributor. Bamberger mark found on doll's body of early 20th century.

**Bambin.** See **Le Bambin.**

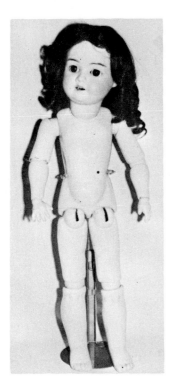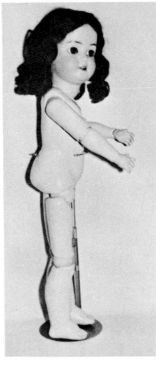

**103A & B.** Ball-jointed composition body strung with elastic; balls at shoulders, elbows, hips, and knees are made of wood. Anatomical details are molded in the composition. Bisque head made by Schoenau & Hoffmeister in the 20th century. Mark: Ill. **1465.** H. 22 inches. *Courtesy of Alberta Darby.*

BAMBINA

**104**

**104.** "Bambina" trademark of Cuno & Otto Dressel.

**Bambina.** 1909. *Cuno & Otto Dressel.* Trademark registered in Germany for dolls.

**Bambini.** 1910. *Käthe Kruse* line of *Art Dolls,* some taken from works of Luca della Robbia.

**Bambolificio Italiano (di Rizza, Giovanni).** 1920–21. Milan, Italy. Listed in directory under Dolls.

**Bamboo Teeth.** See **Teeth.**

**Bandeau Sales Co., The.** 1920. Philadelphia, Pa. Distributor *Louis Wolf & Co.* Made hand-painted *Mickey* dolls.

**Banigan, Joseph.** 1875. New York City. Assignee of *Wesley Miller's* U.S. patent for making a rubber doll with a flexible framework.

**Banker's Daughter.** 1893. Trade name used by *Butler Bros.* for a dressed doll with bisque head, glass eyes, open mouth, and teeth; 21 inches tall, price $2.37.

**Bankograph Co.** 1921. New York City. Distributed dolls.

**Bannawitz, Albert.** 1925. Schalkau, Thür. Manufactured stiff-jointed and double-jointed dolls, walking dolls, talking dolls, baby dolls, and dressed dolls only of their own make.

**Banner Kid Dolls.** 1893. Trade name of line of dolls with half-kid, half-muslin, bodies; distributed by *Butler Bros.* Came with bisque heads and hands, glass eyes, open mouth, and teeth. Size 13 inches, with knee joint only; 16½ inches, with knee and hip joint; 18 inches, with elbow, knee, and hip joint; 22 inches, fully jointed. Prices 25¢ to $1.00; with moving eyes, curly wig, and kid calves, the 22½-inch size cost $2.50.

**Bannon, Winifred.** 1921–22. Joliet, Ill. Secured a U.S. design patent for a clothespin-shaped doll.

**Barbara.** 1924. Used by *Century Doll Co.* as a trade name.

**Barbara Lee.** 1924. *EFFanBEE* doll with composition head and limbs, eyelashes, blue sleeping eyes, curly hair, soft body; dressed in organdy and Irish lace and wore a golden heart necklace; 29 inches tall, price $15.00.

**Bärbel-Puppe.** 1922. Trademark registered in Germany by *Bärbel Wichmann* for dolls.

**Barclay Baby Belle.** 1908–10. *Bawo & Dotter.* Trademark registered in U.S. in 1910 for dressed dolls. (See also **Baby Belle.**)

**Bare Kid.** 1910. *The Dolly Co.* Rag doll in the *Dolly Dollykins* series. Bare Kid represented a dusky child with wide eyes and a broad toothy grin, dressed only in a string of beads.

**Barfuss, Witwe (Widow) Carl.** 1909. Gotha, Thür. Made dolls.

**Barker, Florence Annie (née Rees).** 1906. Mirfield, Yorkshire. Registered trademark in Great Britain; secured British and French patents for a doll with head, body, and limbs made of fabric stuffed with hops, rose leaves, lavender, or other flowers; features marked or woven on face; eyes of stones or glass. Dress represented the flower with which the doll was stuffed.

**Barker Bros.** See **Hamilton, Ellen.**

**Barnard, Frank.** 1920–22. Louisville, Ky. Obtained U.S. design patent for a stockinet rag doll dressed as a Negro minstrel.

**Barney, Cecilia R.** 1923–24. Obtained U.S. design patent for a rag doll that looked Spanish.

**Barnicol, Carl.** 1921–25. Sonneberg, Thür. Doll manufacturer.

**Barreck, Eugene.** 1904–14. Philadelphia, Pa. Listed in directory under Dolls.

**Barrois.** 1846–52, Madame Barrois was listed on rue St. Martin, Paris, under Dolls; 1858–77, E. Barrois, also on rue St. Martin at a different number, distributed French and German dolls' heads of porcelain and of paste. It should be noted that the initials "E. B." are sometimes found on front shoulders of early-type bisque heads.

One of the "Barclay Baby Belle" Dressed Dolls

**B & D** NOW READY

**B & D** NOW READY

# B & D Import Lines, 1908
# Doll, Toy and Novelty Departments

Greatly enlarged displays, affording wider variety than ever before, will greet the visitor to the B & D establishment during the coming import season. A wondrous line of Imported Toys—wood, tin and mechanical; a surpassing line of Toy Tea Sets—china and enamel; an incomparable line of Dolls—kid body, jointed and dressed, including the famous

**"Barclay Baby Belle Line"** :: and :: **Special Value Jointed Dolls**

Don't neglect the opportunity to secure a line of

**"MUNICH BUILDING BRICKS."—The Greatest Building Block Ever Invented**

Made of hardwood, enameled. Washable, and will not chip or break.
We are the sole agents for the United States.

**Bawo & Dotter,** 26 TO 34 BARCLAY STREET, **New York**

105. One of the "Barclay Baby Belle" dressed dolls in the B & D import lines as advertised by Bawo & Dotter in 1908 in *Playthings. Courtesy of McCready Publishing Co.*

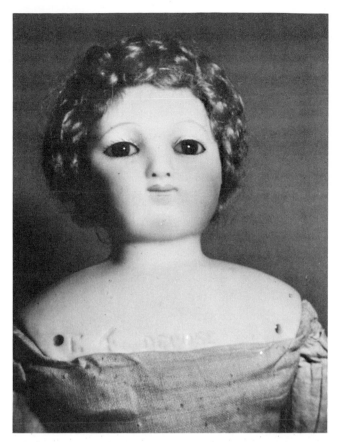

**106.** Bisque shoulder-headed doll (for mark, see Ill. **107**); possibly marked for E. Barrois. *Courtesy of Margaret Whitton; photograph by Winnie Langley.*

**108A & B.** Two-faced doll patented by Bartenstein; waxed-over-composition head. The faces revolve horizontally under a metal cap. Name "Bartenstein" is stamped in purple ink on the stomach of the cylindrical body. H. 20 inches. *Courtesy of the Chester County Historical Society.*

# E J. DEPOSE B

**107.** Possible mark of E. Barrois.

**Barry, Elizabeth.** 1921–22. Portland, Ore. Obtained U.S. patent for a rubber ball covered with fabric having embroidered features for a doll's head.

**Bartenstein, Fritz.** 1880–98. Hüttensteinach, Thür. Jointed-doll factory.

1880–81: Obtained three German patents and one U.S. patent for double-faced doll heads, usually with one face laughing and one face crying. Movable double face turned on vertical axis by pulling string. April, 1880 patent, string came out the front of the chest; December, 1880, patent, string came out the top of the head; September, 1881, patent, string came out the side of the body. The doll's head might be of wax, composition, or bisque, and one face was hidden by a hood.

**Barth, Pierre Joseph.** 1857. Paris. Secured French patent for making molded dolls.

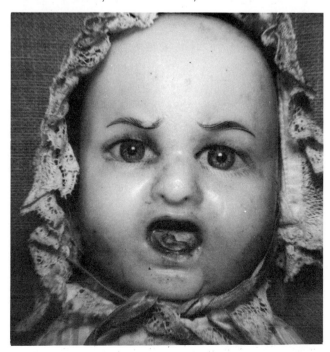

**Bartholomew, Mrs.** 1919. Portland, Ore. Made dolls entirely of kid except for the hair; painted in natural colors and stuffed with silk floss.

**Bartholomew's Babies.** 17th–18th century. England. Name given to dolls sold at the St. Bartholomew Fair.

1695: POOR ROBIN'S ALMANACK refers to a Bartholomew's Baby tricked up with ribbons and knots.

**Barton, John.** 1847–56. London. Wax doll maker.

**Base Ball Boy.** 1912. Made by *Ideal Novelty & Toy Co.*

**Baseball Boy.** 1913–14. Subscription premium doll with composition head and hands on stuffed body. Probably *Louis Amberg's Swat Mulligan,* since the other premium dolls in the group appear to have been made by Amberg; wore baseball outfit including cap; size 12 inches, price 50¢.

**Baseball Fan.** 1913–14. Trademark registered in Germany by *Max Fr. Schelhorn* firm for dolls and doll parts.

**Basté, H.** 1909. Hannover, Prussia. Made dolls.

**Basté, Marie.** 1895–1909. Hannover, Prussia. Made dressed dolls.

**Basté & Co.** 1909–25+. Berlin. Manufactured dolls.

**Bastier, François Félix.** 1800–81. Paris. Doll manufacturer. Secured British and German patents for mechanically molding dolls from paper pulp or plastic material.

**Bataille, Madame.** 1855–56. Paris. Handled undressed dolls and dolls dressed in provincial and foreign costumes.

**Bates, Reuben Harlow Neal.** Mid-19th century. Providence, R.I. Made an iron two-piece mold for a doll's head. Both the mold and the rag doll made from it are pictured in Johl, YOUR DOLL AND MINE. Bates may have worked with *Izannah Walker.*

**Bather.** 1860's–1925+. Small porcelain dolls, made first in Germany; also made in France by 1878. (See **Bathing Dolls; Frozen Charlottes.**)

**Bathing Beauty.** 1922–23. *Capital Doll Corp.* Lady doll of wood-pulp composition; 19 inches tall; had movable arms.

**Bathing Dolls (Bathing Children).** 1870's–90's. Made by *Kestner, Kling, Bähr & Pröschild,* etc.

Ca. 1876: *Strasburger, Pfeiffer & Co.* advertised both china and bisque bathing dolls. The china ones were white or Negro, came with black or yellow hair, plain feet, or painted boots or gilt boots. About twenty sizes from 1 to 6½ inches; prices 8¢ to $2.75 doz. wholesale. The bisque ones were white, came chiefly with yellow hair, plain feet, or painted boots or gilt boots; not quite as many sizes as the china bathing dolls, but they ranged from 1 to 7½ inches; prices 9¢ to $4.75 doz. wholesale. (See color photograph C12.)

1886: RIDLEYS' FASHION MAGAZINE advertised "Small Bisque Bathing Dolls, finest quality, with moving eyes

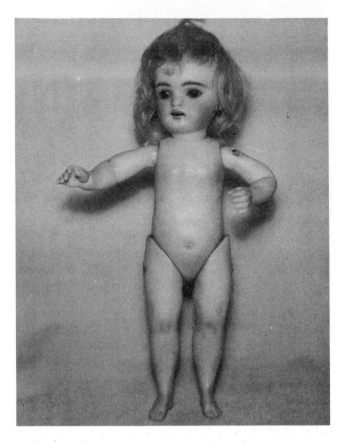

**109.** All-bisque jointed doll with wig and glass sleep eyes. H. 7¾ inches. *Courtesy of Lester & Alice Grinnings.*

and head to turn, jointed arms and limbs, with long flowing hair, at $1.00, $1.15, $1.35 and up.

"Same, without moving eyes, in smaller sizes, at 25¢, 38¢, 50¢, 65¢, 75¢.

"Bisque Bathing Dolls, without hair, jointed arms only, 10¢, 13¢, 17¢, 22¢, 30¢, 45¢."

1888: RIDLEYS' FASHION MAGAZINE advertised "Chubby Bisque Bathing Dolls, painted hair. Sizes 3¼, 4¼, 5, 6¼, 8 inches. Prices, 6¢, 10¢, 15¢, 22¢, 33¢.

"Same as above, with hair, glass eyes, and turning head. Sizes 4¼, 5, 5¾, 6¼ inches. Prices, 24¢, 29¢, 33¢, 39¢.

"Bisque Bathing Doll, in bathing clothes with oil silk cap. Sizes 5, 5¾, 6¼ inches. Prices 25¢, 35¢, 40¢.

"Fine Bisque Bathing Baby, in fancy costume. Size 5 inches, price 35¢.

"China Bathing Dolls at 2¢, 3¢, 5¢, 7¢, and 10¢."

**(See Bather; Frozen Charlottes.)**

**Bathing Jeff.** 1919. Trademark registered in Britain by the *Art Toy Manufacturing Co.* for dolls.

**Bätz, K.** 1909–18. Wildenheid near Sonneberg, Thür. Made dolls' bodies.

**Baube, Mme.** 1870–72. Paris. Handled dolls.

**Baudich.** Ca. 1890. Name reported as stamped on sole of foot of a *Steiner, le Petit Parisien.*

**Baudry, Charles Louis.** 1920. Paris. Obtained German patent for a jointed doll.

**Bauer, Armin.** 1909–18. Bettelhecken, Thür. Made dolls and *Täuflinge*.

**Bauer, Aug., Jün.** 1918–25+. Neustadt near Coburg, Thür. Made jointed dolls.

**Bauer, B. (G.).** 1907–9. Neustadt near Coburg, Thür. Made dolls.

**Bauer, Curt.** 1924. Sonneberg, Thür. Made and exported dolls.

**Bauer, Edm.** 1909. Hönbach, Thür. Made dolls' heads.

**Bauer, M.** 1909. Neustadt near Coburg, Thür. Made dolls.

**Bauer, Th.** 1899. Vienna. Manufactured dolls and dolls' heads.

**Bauer & Richter, Inc. (Rodaer Puppen und Spielwaren-fabrik).** 1922–25+. Roda near Jena, Thür. Registered in Germany the following trademarks: *Herzkäferchen* (Lady Bug), *Mein Kleiner Schlingel* (My Little Rascal), and *Asador*. They made "Rodaer" dolls, including ball-jointed dolls, character sitting and standing dolls, walking *Mama Dolls*, porcelain children, celluloid babies, and celluloid heads.

**Bauernkinder:** 1914. Made by *Horsman*. Boy and girl dolls with olive-tinted faces; dressed as European peasants.

**Bauersachs, Emil.** 1882–1911. Sonneberg, Thür.; 1911–25+ Victor Roth, successor. Made bisque-head ball-jointed dolls, and character babies.

1893: Won silver medal at Erfurt Exhibition.

1895: Won bronze medal at Dresden Exhibition. Registered in Germany a picture of a doll in a wreath as a trademark for dressed dolls.

1900: One of the Grand Prize winners at the Paris Exposition.

1904: Showed dolls with Sonneberg group at the St. Louis Exposition.

1907–11: Advertised dressed dolls.

1914: Had Berlin and Paris agents.

1921: Registered in Germany *Caprice* as a trademark.

**110.** Trademark of Emil Bauersachs.

**Bauersachs & Henninger.** See **Schönau, Arthur.**

**Baum, Hugo.** 1910–25+. New York City. Member of the firm of *Fleischaker & Baum*, also known as *EFFanBEE;* obtained two U.S. design patents, one in 1921 for a cloth body, and one in 1924 for a Negro boy playing a harmonica. He copyrighted two dolls: *Baby Grumpy* in 1923; *Contented Baby* in 1925.

**Baumann, Karl.** 1922. Überlingen, Germany. Secured German patent for sleeping eyes in dolls' heads.

**Baumann, Victor.** 1897–1925+. London and Nürnberg, Bavaria. Manufacturers' agent and maker of composition dolls.

1921: Successor to *British Toy Agency*.

**Baumann Rubber Co.** 1903. Made crying baby of soft rubber with two faces, one laughing and one crying. When body was pressed and released, it made a crying noise that could be varied in intensity. Doll was dressed in cloth garment; price 10¢.

**Bautler & Scheller.** 1891–1925+. Sonneberg, Thür. Doll manufacturer; specialized in jointed dolls and dressed dolls.

**Bawo & Dotter.** 1838–1913. Bavaria; New York City; Limoges, France, etc. According to Jervis, A BOOK OF POTTERY MARKS, Bawo & Dotter began to make fine porcelain in 1838. The New York importing firm of Bawo & Dotter was established in 1864 by Francis H. Bawo and Charles T. Dotter.

1872: They established the *Elite* porcelain factory in Limoges, France. On December 7, 1880, Charles T. Dotter obtained a U.S. patent for "the body of a doll, consisting of a woven fabric suitably cut to form a front and back piece, which are sewed together at the sides to form an outer casing and stuffed with sawdust or other suitable material. On the front of this outer casing is printed in ink, or otherwise delineated, a representation of the front portion of a corset, and on the back there may be similarly delineated a representation of the back portion of a corset . . .

"The bust and head of the doll are . . . made in one piece, of china or like material, and affixed to the body in the usual manner by an adhesive substance, such as a suitable glue or cement.

"The arms may consist of stuffed upper sections united to lower sections of china or like material."

Most of the china heads found on the Dotter patented bodies bore the inscription "Pat. Dec. 7/80" on the back of the shoulders. Inscribed marks were rather rare on china heads, and it is possible that these heads were made in Limoges or one of the other porcelain factories controlled by Bawo and Dotter.

1883: They established a porcelain factory at Fischern near Carlsbad, Austria (now Czechoslovakia).

1888: Charles T. Dotter of Brooklyn and New York City retired and was succeeded by C. F. W. Bawo.

**111.** China head used on the Dotter patented corset body. Head is marked with patent date (see Ill. **113**). The corset was printed on the fabric of the body. H. 18½ inches. H. of shoulder head, 4 inches. *Coleman Collection.*

**112.** China head, flesh-tinted; painted features; made by Bawo & Dotter. Mark on back shoulder: Ill. **114**. H. 14 inches. H. of shoulder head, 3⅛ inches. *Coleman Collection.*

**113–115.** Bawo & Dotter marks found on dolls: No. **113** on back of china shoulders; **114** on back of china shoulders; **115** on back of bisque heads.

1893: Bawo & Dotter exhibited porcelain ware at the Chicago World's Fair.

1896: Established a white china factory at Limoges, and in 1897 Bawo & Dotter were listed in Directories as of New York, Limoges, and Fischern (Karlsbad).

1906: Opened new department devoted entirely to dolls: china, bisque, celluloid, metal, rag, and composition dolls and dolls' heads; kid-body dolls, jointed dolls, walking and talking dolls, dressed dolls; the cream of the lines of some of the best German doll makers, including fine Waltershausen dolls.

1907: Advertised *Baby Belle,* kid-body or jointed composition-body dolls of Waltershausen make, with new patented moving eye device so eyes could not drop into head; dolls dressed in latest American styles; *Old Glory* jointed dolls with A1 *Simon & Halbig* heads; new model heads with lifelike expression, moving eyes, auburn, brown, or blond parted wigs, fully ball-jointed bodies with moving wrists; dressed in trimmed chemise, shoes, and stockings; sizes 16 to 35 inches; price 5¢ to $10.00; also china-limb, celluloid, patent rag, wool, and unbreakable dolls; bisque, china, wool, and celluloid babies; china, bisque, metal, celluloid, patent, and wood dolls' heads.

1908: Advertised *Barclay Baby Belle* and kid-body dolls; dolls with bisque, metal, and celluloid (turtle brand) heads.

1910: Advertised character dolls.

1912: Advertised doll department bigger than ever before.

Both china-head and bisque-head dolls have been found with the B. & D. mark of Bawo & Dotter incised on them. Both *Strobel & Wilken Co.* and *Hamburger & Co.* used "Carlsbad" as part of their marks, which suggests a connection with the Carlsbad factory of Bawo & Dotter. Bawo & Dotter were agents for the English porcelain makers *W. H. Goss,* who made dolls, and W. T. Copeland, who originated Parian ware in the 1840's.

**Baxmann, Witwe (Widow) A.** 1918. Altona, a. d. Elbe, Schleswig-Holstein. Made dolls' heads.

**Bay Ridge Toy Co.** 1913. Brooklyn, N.Y. Manufactured Esquimaux, satin-bodied romper and baby dolls; *Borgfeldt,* distributor; specialized in 10¢ dolls.

**Bayer, J.** 1925. Paris. Made cloth dolls' heads.

**Bayersche Celluloid Warenfabrik.** See **Wacker, Albert.**

**Bayeux (Bayeaux), A., & Mothereau, F.** See **Mothereau.**

**Bazet, Mme.** 1879. Paris. Doll maker.

**Bazzoni, Anthony.** 1843–78. London. Made wax dolls, composition dolls, and "speaking" dolls.

**Beach, James E., Jr.** 1923–24. Fair Oaks, Calif. Secured U.S. design patent for a doll dressed like *Jackie Coogan* as he appeared in THE KID, with cap visor on the side, long trousers held up by one suspender, and a turtle-neck sweater.

**Beach Baby.** 1923. Trade name used by *EFFanBEE.*

**Beach Boy and Beach Girl.** 1915. Made by *Louis Amberg & Son.* Dolls dressed in blue and white bathing suits.

**Beaky-Ba.** 1912. Trademark registered in Britain by *Eisenmann & Co.* (Einco) for dolls.

**Beam, John & Louisa.** 1884–1903. Philadelphia, Pa. Produced dolls and doll materials.

**Beau Brummel.** 1924. Made by *Ideal Novelty & Toy Co.* Came with sleeping eyes and a wig or painted hair.

**Beauchamp, J. E., Co.** 1918. Montreal. Canadian agents for *Century Doll Co.*

**Beaumont, Iris (née Nordmark).** 1922. Berlin. Registered initials I.B., superimposed, as a trademark in Germany for artist dolls, character dolls, and play dolls.

**Beaussillon, A.** 1889–90. Paris. Specialized in jointed French dolls.

**Beauty.** 1898. Trade name used by *W. A. Cissna & Co.* for dolls with bisque heads and arms, sleeping eyes, woven wigs, kid bodies with gusset joints; size 16 inches, undressed, $5.90 doz. wholesale; size 19, dressed in silk with ostrich-trimmed bonnet, $11.50 doz. wholesale. It is possible that these dolls had bisque heads made by *Armand Marseille,* since he incised the name "Beauty" on some of his heads.

**Beauty Doll.** 1915. Made by *Joseph Roth Co.* with heads of patented pressed composition, cork-stuffed cloth bodies, 25 inches tall.

**Beauty Kist.** 1920. Copyrighted by *Manhattan Toy & Doll Manufacturing Co.* A cherub-type doll that closely resembled *Kewpies Model,* copyrighted the previous year. The use of the word "Kewpie" in the name may have necessitated the second copyright; both dolls were designed by *Ernesto Peruggi.*

**Beaver Co., The.** 1916–17. Beaver Falls, N.Y.; Buffalo, N.Y.; Ottawa, Ontario; London, England; etc. Made wooden dolls. Trademarks registered in U.S.: *Beaverbilt, Beaverbeasts.*

**Beaverbeasts.** 1916–17. Trademark registered in U.S. by *The Beaver Co.*

**Beaverbilt.** 1916–17. Trademark registered in U.S. by *The Beaver Co.*

**Bébé.** Name applied to a doll representing a small child, ranging in age from infancy to about six or seven years. Name used by both French and German manufacturers. (See also **Bébé Incassable.**)

**Bébé.** 1915–16. Trademark registered in Germany by *Emil Pfeiffer* firm.

**Bébé, Le.** See **Le Bébé.**

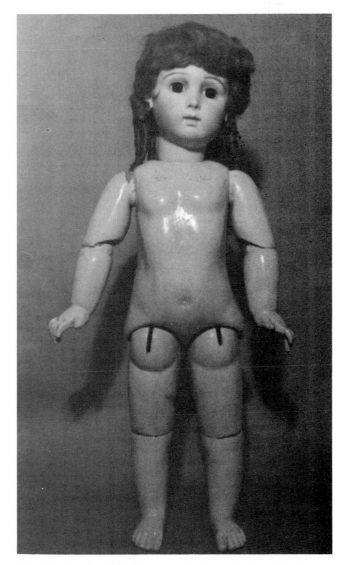

**116.** This Jumeau bébé is typical of the dolls referred to as "bébés." They have bisque heads and jointed composition bodies with childlike proportions. Bébés may also have kid or wooden bodies. H. 29 inches. *Courtesy of Hazel Ulseth.*

**Bébé A. L.** 1912–21. *Alexandre Lefebvre & Cie.* made a character bébé of this name with head and body of washable papier-mâché. The doll had patented joints made so that it could sit or kneel naturally.

1919: Bébé A. L. was awarded a gold medal.

1921: This name was part of a trademark registered in France by Alexandre Lefebvre, Aîné (Sr.). Bébé A. L. advertised as having an unbreakable and washable head, and joints that enabled it to sit or kneel.

**Bébé Articulé.** 1899. Trademark registered in Germany by *Friedrich Edmund Winkler* and used for jointed dolls.

**Bébé Bijou.** 1887–90. Doll line of *M. Grandjean.*

1889–90: Advertised that Grandjean was the inventor and first maker in France of jointed bébés in competition with German inventors; dolls superior in lightness and finish to the German dolls; non-toxic colors used on them. New models each season. Over a million dolls a year produced in this line in both 1888 and 1889.

**Bébé Bijou.** 1919. Trademark registered in France by *Pierre Levy & Cie.*

117. "Bébé Bijou" mark of Pierre Levy & Cie.

118. "Bébé Breveté" with bisque head and shoulder plate, kid gusseted body, lower arms of bisque, glass eyes, wig. Mark: Ill. **119.** H. 13 inches. *Courtesy of the International Doll Library Foundation.*

119. "Bébé Breveté" mark as it appears on dolls.

**Bébé Breveté.** Name could refer to any patented bébé, but is found especially on dolls with bisque heads and forearms, kid bodies, made in Paris; usually with paper label on chest. Face and hands resemble *Bru* dolls, but the hands are larger proportionately than the marked Brus, and the kid around the shoulder plate is cut with straight edges instead of scallops as found on marked Bru dolls.

**Bébé Bru.** Ca. 1866–ca. 1883, line of dolls made by *Bru*; ca. 1883–89, made by H. Chevrot; 1889–99, made by

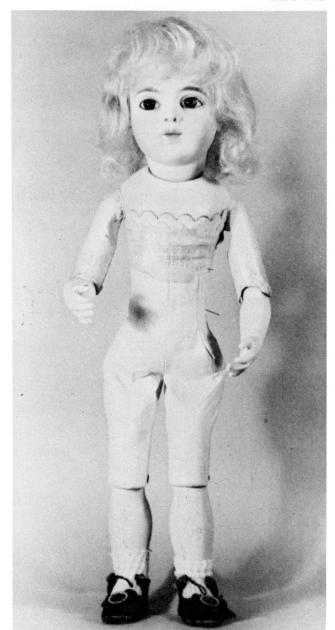

120. "Bébé Bru" with bisque head and shoulder plate, bisque forearms, wooden lower legs, size 4. Mark: Ill. **250.** H. 15¹⁄₂ inches. *Courtesy of Hazel Ulseth.*

Paul Girard; 1899–1925+, made by *Société Française de Fabrication de Bébés et Jouets.* Name registered in France in 1891 and as late as 1954.

1866: Dressed dolls made especially for the American trade; price $1.00 to $6.00 doz. wholesale.

1868: Dolls' heads of bisque, rubber, or hardened paste; bodies of pink or white kid, with or without joints, or bodies of carved wood with joints; specialized in stylishly dressed dolls and dolls' trousseaux.

1869: Leon Casimir Bru obtained a French patent for a ball-jointed composition-type doll body, held together with pegs or pins and not elastic; it was jointed at the waist, wrists, and ankles.

1873: Advertised bisque doll heads, stationary or swivel; rubber doll heads, stationary or swivel; double-faced dolls with one face asleep and one awake; doll bodies of carved wood or rubber or kid with wooden hands and feet; dressed in the latest fashion with clothes that could easily be put on and taken off.

1879: Jointed hard-rubber dolls were new, as well as talking bébés.

1881: The new dolls were *Bébé Teteur* (nursing Bru) and *Bébé Gourmand* (eating Bru); continued to advertise kid-body dolls, carved jointed wood-body dolls, and hard-rubber dolls.

All the gold medals won by Bébé Bru were during the period when H. Chevrot was in charge of the business.

1885: Advertised that the words "Bébé Bru" were to be seen on each bébé; *Le Dormeur* (the sleeper) was the new doll, but Bébé Teteur and Bébé Gourmand were still being shown.

1890: Advertised bébés made with hollowed wooden bodies; composition heads were new, and Bébés Bru were the only bébés having natural eyelashes.

1891: Walking and talking bébés.

1892: Advertised bébé that said "Mama" or "Papa" while simultaneously the chest expanded and contracted and the eyes opened and shut; Bébé Teteur and hard-rubber bébés were still being advertised.

1895: Kiss-throwing Bébé Bru was patented. After the merger into the Société Française de Fabrication de Bébés et Jouets in 1899, Bébés Bru continued to be made.

1921: *Arthur Geoffroy* was the sole distributor in the U.S.

**Bébé Caoutchouc.** 1900–1904. Rubber doll made by *L. Delachal.*

**Bébé Carmencita.** 1912–25+. Line made by *Arthur Schönau;* name registered as a trademark in Germany in 1913; distributed by *Butler Bros.*

1913: Advertised as having bisque head, curly wig, sleeping eyes, real eyebrows and eyelashes; jointed composition body; size 20 inches; price dressed, $2.00.

**Bébé Caro.** 1910. Jointed composition bébé made by *F. Ch. Rivaillon.*

**Bébé Charmant.** 1892–98. Jointed composition bébé made by *Pintel & Godchaux;* wholesale price, 30¢ doz.

**Bébé Coiffure.** 1911. Trademark registered in Germany by Société *Gutmann & Schiffnie* for a bébé with hair that a child could arrange.

**121.** "Bébé Coiffure" trademark of Gutmann & Schiffnie.

## BÉBÉ-COIFFURE

**Bébé Colosse.** 1898. Made by *A. Gobert.*

**Bébé Cosmopolite (Handwerck's Bébé Cosmopolite).** 1895–1902. Trademark registered in Germany in various forms by *Heinrich Handwerck* and used for ball-jointed dolls. Some of these dolls had bisque heads made by *Simon & Halbig.*

BÉBÉ DE PARIS

## R. D.

**122.** "Bébé de Paris" mark.

**Bébé de Paris.** 1890–98. Bisque heads; fully jointed, composition bodies; "undressed" but wearing a muslin chemise trimmed with lace and ribbons, and also shoes and stockings. Sizes 11, 12½, 13½, 14½, 16, 18, 20, 23, 26, 29, and 32 inches; prices 75¢, 90¢, $1.15, $1.38, $1.75, $1.95, $2.50, $3.50, $4.30, $6.60, and $9.80. Completely dressed in various silks: sizes 11, 12½, 13½, 14½, 16, 18, 20, 23, 26, 29, and 32; prices $1.70, $2.10, $2.50, $2.90, $3.30, $3.90, $4.50, and $7.00—no price was given for the three largest sizes. These dolls were probably made by *Rabery & Delphieu,* since in 1898 the trade name "Bébé de Paris" was used by Genty, successor of Rabery & Delphieu.

**Bébé de Réclame.** 1898. Trademark registered in Germany by *Heinrich Handwerck.*

**Bébé Dormeur.** 1898. Sleeping bébé made by *Ad. Bouchet* in various sizes. (See also **Le Dormeur.**)

**Bébé E. Gesland.** Mark stamped on stockinet body. (See also **Gaultier.**)

**Bébé Elite.** 1900–1901. Trademark registered in Germany by *Max Handwerck. William Goebel* made bisque socket heads marked "Bébé Elite" and "Max Handwerck."

**Bébé Eureka.** 1911. Trademark registered in France by *Société La Parisienne.*

**Bébé Excelsior V. G.** 1899. Trademark registered in France by Verdier & Cie., the makers. (See also **Verdier & Gutmacher.**)

**Bébé Favori.** 1892. Trademark registered in France by *Cosman Frères,* makers of this doll.

**Bébé Favori.** 1893–95. Trademark registered in France by *Clément Gatusse* for a line of dolls he made, including fully jointed dolls, baby dolls, and a French walking doll; came dressed and undressed.

**Bébé Français.** 1891, trademark registered in France by *Danel & Cie.;* 1896, trademark registered in France by *Jumeau;* 1911, trademark registered in France by *Société Française de Fabrication de Bébés et Jouets.* Jumeau probably took over the Danel Company and their rights to this trademark.

**123A & B.** "Bébé E. Gesland" with a Gaultier-marked bisque head and a child's proportioned stockinet-covered body; composition lower arms and legs; original dress. Mark on head: see Ill. **625.** Mark on body: see Ill. **124.** H. 13½ inches. H. of shoulder head, 3¼ inches. *Courtesy of Bess Goldfinger.*

BEBE E.GESLAND
BTE. SGDG
5, RUE BERANGER. 5
PARIS

**124.** "Bébé E. Gesland"; mark on body.

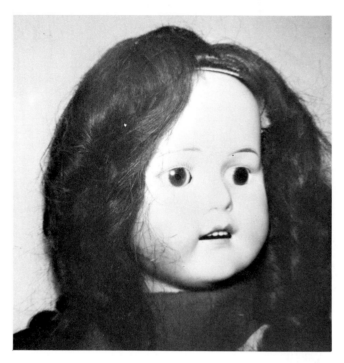

**125.** Bisque head made by William Goebel for Max Handwerck, using the latter's trademark "Bébé Elite." The head has open mouth, teeth, and glass sleep eyes. Mark: Ill. **126.** *Coleman Collection.*

Max Handwerk
Bebe Elite
286/3
Germany

**126**

**126.** "Bébé Elite" mark found on heads.

**127.** "Bébé Excelsior" trademark of Verdier & Cie.

**128 & 129.** "Bébé Favori" trademarks; No. **128** registered by Cosman Frères and No. **129** registered by Clément Gatusse.

BÉBÉ EXCELSIOR
**127**

Bébé Favori      BÉBÉ FAVORI
**128**                      **129**

# BÉBÉ FRANÇAIS
### 130
# BÉBÉ FRANÇAIS   BĒBĒ LE GLORIEUX
### 131                                   132

**130 & 131.** "Bébé Français" trademarks: No. **130** registered by Danel & Cie. and No. **131** registered by Jumeau.

**132.** "Bébé Le Glorieux," trademark of Claude Bonnal.

**Bébé Géant.** 1889–98. Trade name of doll line made by *Ad. Bouchet.* Bébé Géant won a silver medal at the 1889 Paris Exposition.

1895: Priced at 2¢ to 29¢.

**Bébé Gentil.** See **Gentil Bébé.**

**Bébé Gesland.** See **Gesland.**

**Bébé Gloria.** 1915. Trademark registered in France by *J. Cesar Koch* for doll made in Paris.

**Bébé Gourmand.** 1881–85. Trade name for a doll that could eat and digest food by itself, according to the advertisement of the *Bru* firm. Leon Casimir Bru was a remarkable inventor, and this doll was made while he was still head of the firm. It continued to be made under H. Chevrot, and probably was one of the Bru dolls in the 1885 Paris Exposition where the Bru firm won their first gold medal in an international exposition.

**Bébé Habillé.** 1900. Trademark registered in Germany by *Carl Geyer* for dressed dolls.

**Bébé Hamac.** 1898. Trade name for doll in a hammock made by *Ad. Bouchet* and priced at 29¢ and up.

**Bébé Incassable.** Literally, this means unbreakable or indestructible baby. It was a term usually applied by the French doll makers to their bisque-head, jointed composition-bodied dolls representing infants and children. It first appeared in advertisements in the 1870's, and by the 1880's the majority of the French dolls were bébés incassables. In 1885 *Jumeau* made almost entirely this type of doll, and its popularity continued into the 20th century. The French distinguished between bébés and poupées. The "Report of the Jury" at the 1878 Paris Exposition reads, "We are happy to affirm that no other country is able to rival France in the skill of imitating nature so perfectly. We congratulate our principal manufacturers who with their great care have brought this industry to perfection. The bébé which best suits the taste of children tends to supersede the poupée [doll] and it appears to us indubitable that if the bébé had been produced as inexpensively as the poupée the sales would have increased considerably."

**Bébé Jeannette.** 1917. Trademark registered in France by *J. Cortot.*

**Bébé Jumeau.** Ca. 1840–99, line of dolls made by *Jumeau;* 1899-1925+, line of dolls made by *Société*

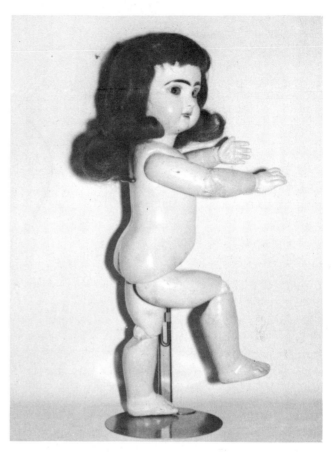

**133A & B.** Bébé incassable made by Jumeau; bisque head is incised "Tête Jumeau//S.G.D.G.//6" and "vx" in red. The jointed composition body represents that of a small child. Body mark: Ill. **918.** H. 15 inches. *Courtesy of Virginia Dilliplane.*

*Française de Fabrication de Bébés et Jouets*, successors to Jumeau. Bébé Jumeau was registered as a trademark in France many times. It was registered as a trademark in the U.S. in 1888, and at that time Emile Jumeau, head of the Jumeau firm, stated that the trade name had been used since about 1840. However, Jumeau in his 1885 advertisement stated that Bébé Jumeau had been on the market only since 1879.

1879: Advertisement stated, "makes jointed kid body dolls; jointed wood body dolls; indestructible jointed bébés of a unique model. The dolls and bébés are dressed in wool foulard or silk. Special doll heads in porcelain are manufactured at the factory in Montreuil-sous-Bois."

1881: Jumeau made the statement, "Tous marques à son nom" (all marked with his name). This is very important for doll collectors who are trying to date a Bébé Jumeau. Note that it states that the name—not just the initials—is on ALL dolls.

1882: Advertised that Bébés Jumeau had "human" eyes, applied ears, wore a pearl necklace and a comb in their hair; sizes from #9 to #16 (size 10 was 22 inches tall).

1885: Advertisement was still headed "Tous marques à son nom," and it added a "new creation, talking Bébé Jumeau." (Talking bébés had been advertised by Jumeau as early as 1865; he made his own voice mechanism, which was usually marked "Jumeau.") Jumeau also advertised, "Bébés with kid bodies. These bébés are of a fabrication exactly equal to that of the dolls [lady dolls as opposed to bébés] and consequently have all their defects and are not recommended by my firm which only makes them on order." The description of these doll bodies in the 1885 account of a visit to the Jumeau factory is almost identical with the 1897 description of kid bodies filled with sawdust that Jumeau made when he started in 1843.

1892: Advertisement stated: "NOTICE OF CHANGE: The Maison makes two new models of indestructible jointed bébés undressed and dressed with some differences of 20% and 40% but with the same irreproachable quality remaining and NOT CARRYING THE JUMEAU NAME. Complete change of articles in the Maison Jumeau. . . .

"Large production of bébés known throughout the entire world by the name 'Bébé Jumeau.'

"Races—French, Mulatto or Negro."

1895: Further reductions in price were advertised: "The Maison makes three new models of indestructible jointed bébés, dressed and undressed; WITHOUT MARK with a difference of 40% to 60%."

1897: Counterweight sleeping eyes were used in Bébés Jumeau; it was also stated, "The most expensive dolls including those sent to England, Spain and Germany every year as fashion models are fully dressed at the Jumeau warehouse on the rue Pastourelle." This suggests that as late as 1897 Bébés Jumeau were still being used as couriers of fashion.

**134A & B.** "Bébé Jumeau" with stationary glass eyes and closed mouth. Bisque head mark: same as in Ill. **919**, except that this doll is size 12 instead of size 6. Composition body; contemporary dress. H. 28 inches. *Courtesy of Helen Jo Payne.*

## BÉBÉ JUMEAU    BÉBÉ JUMEAU
**135**                 **136**

**135 & 136.** Marks found on "Bébé Jumeau" dolls. (See also Jumeau marks.)

## Bébé l'Avenir
**137**

**137.** "Bébé L'Avenir" mark of Gutmann & Schiffnie.

**138.** "Bébé Le Favori," mark of Cosman Frères.

## Bébé le Favori
**138**

## BÉBÉ LE PETIT FRANÇAIS
**139**

## BÉBÉ LE RADIEUX
**140**

**139.** "Bébé Le Petit Français," trademark of Claude Bonnal.

**140.** "Bébé Le Radieux," trademark of Claude Bonnal.

## BÉBÉ LE SELECT
**141**

## BEBE LE SPECIAL
**142**

**141.** "Bébé Le Select," trademark of Verdier & Cie.

**142.** "Bébé Le Special," trademark of Claude Bonnal.

## BEBE-LIÈGE
**143**

## BÉBÉ L'UNIQUE
**144**

**143.** "Bébé Liège," trademark of Jules Mettais.

**144.** "Bébé L'Unique," trademark of Claude Bonnal.

1917: *Grey & Grey* imported Bébés Jumeau into the U.S.

1921: *Arthur Geoffroy* was the sole distributor of Bébé Jumeau in America. Several hundred thousand Bébés Jumeau were made each year in the 1880's; in the 1890's the figure rose to two or three million a year, and in the early years of the 20th century, five or six million were made annually. Bébé Jumeau won high awards at nearly all the expositions; for details of these awards and additional information, see **Jumeau.**

**Bébé l'Avenir.** 1907–21. Trademark registered in France by *Société Guttmann & Schiffnie.*

**Bébé le Favori.** 1892. Trademark registered in France by *Cosman Frères,* maker of this doll.

**Bébé le Glorieux.** 1904. Trademark registered in France by *Claude Valéry Bonnal.*

**Bébé le Parisien.** See **Le Parisien.**

**Bébé le Petit Français.** 1900–1906. Made by *Claude Valéry Bonnal,* who registered the name as a trademark in France.

**Bébé le Préféré.** 1898. Made by *A. Gobert.*

**Bébé le Radieux.** 1904. Trademark registered in France by *Claude Valéry Bonnal.*

**Bébé le Rêve.** 1911. Trademark registered in France by *Société La Parisienne.*

**Bébé le Select. V. G.** 1899. Trademark registered in France by the maker, Verdier & Cie. (See **Verdier & Gutmacher.)**

**Bébé le Spécial.** 1904. Trademark registered in France by *Claude Valéry Bonnal.*

**Bébé le Splendide (Bébé Prime).** 1892. Bébé made by *Cosman Frères.* It was advertised as having a bisque head, blonde wig, fully jointed composition body with jointed wrists; dressed in chemise trimmed with lace and ribbons. Came with patterns for a complete trousseau. Doll was 20 inches tall; price $1.60.

**Bébé Liège.** 1899–1900. Trademark registered in France by Jules Mettais, successor of *Jules Nicholas Steiner;* dolls made by Mettais.

**Bébé Linon.** 1900. Trade name for doll (*Bébé Incassable*) made by *B. Brun;* not to be confused with the *Landshut* doll named "Linon."

**Bébé Loulou.** 1891. Trade name for bébé handled by *Wannez & Rayer.*

**Bébé Louvre.** 1922. Doll distributed by the Paris store named *Louvre,* and marked "B. L."

**Bébé l'Unique.** 1904. Trademark registered in France by *Claude Valéry Bonnal.*

**Bébé Lux.** 1911. Trademark registered in France by *Société La Parisienne.*

**Bébé Marcheur.** 1890. Walking doll patented by *Jules Nicholas Steiner.*

**Bébé Marcheur.** 1895–98. Trade name for walking doll made by *Jumeau.*

**Bébé Mascotte.** 1890–1901. Trademark registered in France in 1890 by *May Frères Cie.,* who later became part of the Société Steiner.

1892: Trademark used by May & Bertin for a doll with wooden joints that could kneel and take all of the positions of the human body.

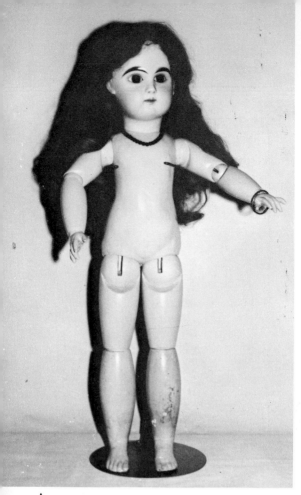
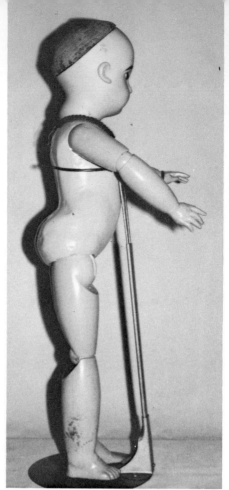

A

B

C

**145A, B, & C.** "Bébé Mascotte" has bisque head (note the heavy eyebrows) on composition body (note the sway-back style of the 1890's). Mark on head: Ill. **146.** Mark on body: Ill. **147.** *Courtesy of Helen Jo Payne.*

**146–148.** "Bébé Mascotte" marks: Nos. **146** and **147** found on dolls; No **148** trademark registered by May Frères Cie.

**149.** "Bébé Metropole," trademark registered by Verdier & Cie.

1901: Jules Mettais, successor of *Jules Nicholas Steiner,* used the trade name Mascotte.

**Bébé Merveilleux.** 1890. Trade name of doll made by *Henry Ulhenhuth & Cie.*

**Bébé Métropole. V. G.** 1899. Trademark registered in France by the makers, Verdier & Cie. (See **Verdier & Gutmacher.)**

**Bébé Mignon.** 1880–1902. Line of dolls made by *Falck & Roussel.*

1880: Won silver medal at Melbourne Exhibition.

1885: Trademark registered in France by Falck & Roussel for jointed dolls.

1886: Bébé Mignon advertised with sleeping eyes; price 58¢.

1889: Over a half-million of these dolls produced in a year.

1890: Advertised dolls and bébés guaranteed to be strong and well made; jointed at arms and legs.

1895-1902: Advertised that they were the only bébés that could not be taken to pieces, and were very light in weight.

**Bébé Mignon.** 1911–14. Trade name for doll made by *Dammerval Frères & Laffranchy.*

**Bébé Modèle.** 1900–1901. Trademark registered in France by Jules Mettais, successor of *Jules Steiner.* This doll was made by Mettais.

**Bébé Moderne.** 1893. Trademark registered in France by *P. H. Schmitz.*

**Bébé Moderne.** 1903–20. Trademark registered in France by *Société Française de Fabrication de Bébés et Jouets.*

**Bébé Mon Trésor.** 1914. Trademark registered in France by *Henry Rostal.*

150

# BÉBÉ MODERNE
151

**BÉBÉ MONDAIN**     **BÉBÉ MONOPOLE**
152             153

**150.** "Bébé Mignon," trademark registered by Falck & Roussel.

**151.** "Bébé Moderne," trademark of Société Française de Fabrication de Bébés et Jouets.

**152.** "Bébé Mondain," trademark of Bernheim & Kahn.

**153.** "Bébé Monopole," trademark of Verdier & Cie.

**Bébé Mondain.** 1906. Trademark registered in France by Société *Bernheim & Kahn,* who made this doll.

**Bébé Monopole. V. G.** 1899. Trademark registered in France by Verdier & Cie., the makers (see **Verdier & Gutmacher).**

**Bébé Mothereau.** 1880–95. Line of dolls made by (Alexandre Célestin Tiburée) *Mothereau,* who patented in France the joints for this type of doll in 1880. The patent drawing shows ball joints and wrists without joints. "B. M." was the trademark used for this line of dolls. They received silver and bronze medals. A 17½-inch doll has size 6 bisque socket-head with large French-type glass eyes and fully jointed composition body, including jointed wrists and tiny feet. Size 10 is 29 inches.

**Bébé Moujik.** 1888. Trademark registered in France by *Jacques Berner.*

**Bébé Olga.** 1896–1925+. Trademark registered, 1911, in France by *Ernst* (Ernest) *Ballu,* distributor; doll dressed in wool or satin.

1914–20: Advertised by *Gerbaulet Frères* (Bros.), doll manufacturers.

1921–25: Advertised by Etablissements Gerbaulet Frères.

1926: Trademark registered in France by Gerbaulet Frères.

**Bébé Oracle.** 1909. Trademark registered in France by *Mme. E. Cayette,* née Marie Mommessin.

**Bébé Parfait.** 1920. Trademark registered in France by *Société Française de Fabrication de Bébés et Jouets.*

**154A & B.** "Bébé Mothereau" bisque head (mark: Ill. **155**) has a cork pate, stationary eyes, tinting above the eyes, closed mouth; composition body with wood upper arms and legs; small extremities. H. 17½ inches. *Coleman Collection.*

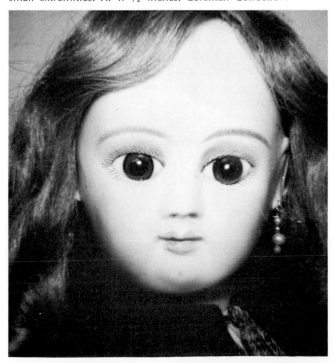

**6.**
**B. M.**
155

**155.** "Bébé Mothereau" mark found on dolls.
**156.** "Bébé Olga," trademark of Ernst Ballu.

*BÉBÉ-OLGA*
156

**Bébé Parisiana.** 1902–20. Trademark registered in France by *Société Française de Fabrication de Bébés et Jouets.*

**Bébé Parisiana.** 1905. Trademark registered in France by *Société Anonyme de Comptoir General de la Bimbeloterie.*

## "BEBE PARISIANA"

**157.** "Bébé Parisiana," trademark of Société Française de Fabrication de Bébés et Jouets.

**Bébé Parlant (Talking).** 1898. Doll made by *Ad. Bouchet;* said "Mama" and "Papa."

**Bébé Petit Pas (Baby Small Step).** 1891. Walking and talking doll with clockwork mechanism, patented in France by Paul Eugène Girard of the *Bru* firm.

**Bébé Phénix.** 1889–1900. Line of dolls.

1889: Advertised by *Henri Alexandre,* designer and manufacturer, as being patented and registered.

1890: Advertised by Alexandre as a series of thirty models with jointed composition bodies, notable for their lightness, elegance, and excellent build; came dressed and undressed.

1892: Tourrel, successor to Alexandre, used same advertisement as appeared in 1890.

1895: Trademark registered in France by Mme. Marie Lafosse of Maison *Jules Steiner,* manufacturer.

1900: Advertised by Jules Mettais, successor of Jules Steiner. See also **Phénix-Baby.**

**Bébé Phonographe.** 1893–98. Doll with phonograph inside its torso, made by *Jumeau.*

1893: Advertised as a talking, singing doll that could hold a conversation of thirty-five words; size 25 inches; price $9.80.

1894: Same advertisement as 1893, with the addition of a cylinder for changing the conversation into French, English, or Spanish at an additional cost of 70¢.

Removable metal chest plate gave access to the mechanism, and a winding key projected from the center of the back, together with a plunger, to operate the sound. The phonographic parts carried the trademark of Lioret; the cylinders were of white wax. The dolls were generally open-mouthed Jumeaus with ball-jointed composition bodies.

**Bébé Premier.** 1911–13. Doll made by *Horsman;* had oil-painted head and hair.

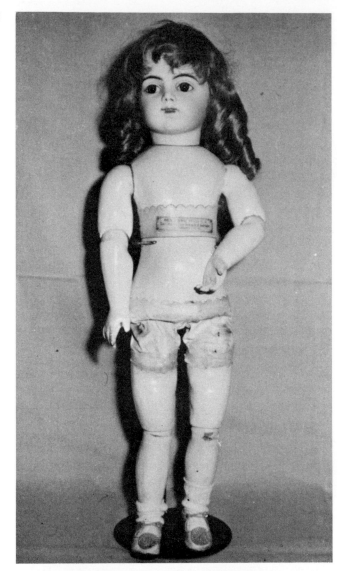

**158A & B.** "Bébé Petit Pas," a walking and talking Bru, has bisque head with glass eyes; the composition body holds the voice mechanism. The swinging hip joints and the voice-box openings are concealed by a piece of flexible material. *Courtesy of Margaret Whitton; photograph by Winnie Langley.*

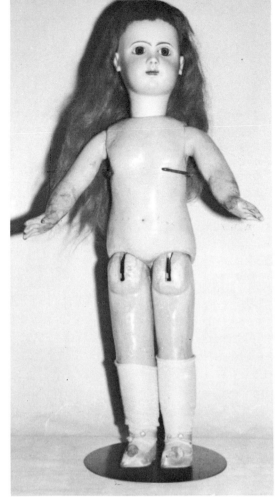

**159A, B, & C.** "Bébé Phénix," bisque-headed, composition-bodied doll. Mark on head: Ill. **160.** The word "Phénix" is in red, the rest incised. The nostrils are indented and painted inside. One-piece arms and legs. H. 25 inches. *Courtesy of Helen Jo Payne.*

**Bébé Premier Pas (Baby First Step).** 1890–92. Walking doll made by *Jules Nicholas Steiner,* based on one of the last French patents obtained by Steiner.

1892: Advertised by *Amédée Lafosse,* Steiner's successor, as having "unbreakable" heavy bisque heads.

**Bébé Prime.** See **Bébé le Splendide.**

**Bébé Prodige.** 1896–1911. Trademark registered in France by *Jumeau* in 1896 and by *Société Française de Fabrication de Bébés et Jouets* in 1911.

**Bébé Prophète.** 1909. Trademark registered in France by *Mme. E. Cayette,* née Marie Mommessin.

**Bébé Rabery.** Mark found on jointed composition body. (See also **Rabery & Delphieu.**)

PHÉNIX
★ 95

**160**

BÉBÉ PHÉNIX

**161**

MARQUE DÉPOSÉE
ARTICLE FRANÇAISE N° 13
BEBE "PHÉNIX"
ARTICULE BREVETE S.G.D.G.
NO.

**162**

PHÉNIX-BABY

**163**

BÉBÉ PRODIGE

**164**

BÉBÉRABERY
Sc

**165**

**160–163.** "Bébe Phénix" marks. No. **160** found on dolls' heads. No. **161** registered by Mme. Lafosse and No. **163** registered by Jules Mettais.

**164.** "Bébé Prodige," trademark of Société Française de Fabrication de Bébés et Jouets.

**165.** "Bébé Rabery" mark on body of Rabery & Delphieu doll.

**Bébé Réclame.** 1898. Trademark registered in Germany by *Heinrich Handwerck*.

**Bébé Schmitt.** 1879–90. Line of dolls made by Schmitt & Fils (Sons); these were jointed composition bébés, usually with bisque heads, jointed composition bodies with long feet and flat-bottom torso on which the same mark is generally stamped as found on the head.

**Bébé Soleil.** 1891. Trademark registered in France by (Jean Marie) *Guépratte*. This name is found on the hip of a jointed composition-bodied doll.

**Bébé Steiner.** 1855–ca. 1908. Line of bébés made by *Jules Nicholas Steiner* and his successors. Bébé Steiner won a silver medal at the 1878 Paris Exposition and a gold medal at the 1889 Paris Exposition. The dolls had bisque heads on jointed composition or kid bodies; some were made of rubber.

**Bébé Stella.** 1911. Trademark registered in France by *Société la Parisienne*.

**Bébé Sublime.** 1898. Trade name for doll made by *A. Gobert*.

**Bébé Superior.** 1912–13. Trademark registered in Germany by *Heinrich Handwerck*.

**Bébé Tanagra.** See **Tanagra**.

**Bébé Tentation.** 1900. Trademark registered in France by *Sylvain Thalheimer & Cie*. Fully jointed bébé; it won a silver medal.

**Bébé Tête Mobile.** 1895. Trade name used by *Ad. Bouchet* for dolls with interchangeable heads and fingers.

**Bébé Teteur.** 1878–98. Nursing or sucking bébé made by *Bru* and patented in Germany and in France in 1879, when it was described as equipped with a feeding bottle. This doll's head held a container for liquid; the feeding process worked by suction and gravity.

The patent papers showed the body as a ball-jointed composition type, but most of these Bébés Teteurs are found with kid bodies; an 1881 advertisement described them as "a new and ravishing bébé of kid, except for the head." Bébé Teteur had been shown for the first time at the Paris Exposition of 1878. The following instructions came with this doll: "To cause this new Baby to suck, the key placed behind the head should first be caught hold of and turned to right hand.

"Then turn the top of the nursing bottle into the Baby's mouth and turn the key to the left hand. Immediately the Baby sucks up by himself.

"On turning anew the key to right hand the liquid comes back into the bottle.

"This may be done as many times as wanted. NOTE—To obtain a white liquid some drops of Cologne-Water should be put into the nursing bottle."

1890: It was advertised as having an unbreakable head and being the only drinking bébé.

169. "Bébé Steiner" mark found on bodies.

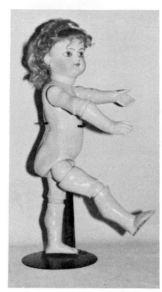

**166A & B.** "Bébé Schmitt" with bisque head, glass eyes, pierced ears, ball-jointed composition body. Note the flat bottom of the torso, large balls at elbow and shoulder, and characteristic long feet. Marks: head, Ill. **167**; body, Ill. **1452**. The paper sticker on the stomach is undecipherable, except that it is the name and address of a Paris distributor; "16" appears on the sole of foot. H. 22½ inches. *Courtesy of Virginia Dilliplane*.

**167.** "Bébé Schmitt" mark found on dolls. B☩ SG DG
o

**168.** "Bébé Steiner," bisque head, glass eyes, original wig; jointed composition body. Original peasant dress in black and red. Marks: head, "Steiner, Paris, FIᴬᴱ A 11"; body, Ill. **169**. H. 19 inches. *Courtesy of the International Doll Library Foundation*.

*Le Petit Parisien*
**BEBE STEINER**

**170A & B.** "Bébé Teteur," the nursing doll, made by the Bru firm. Bisque shoulder head, glass eyes, original sheepskin wig. Leather body with bisque lower arms. In original white lawn dress and on original couch and pillow. H. 15 inches. *Courtesy of the International Doll Library Foundation.*

**Bébé Tout en Bois.** 1914. Trademark registered in Germany by *Rudolf Schneider* for a fully jointed bébé.

**Bébé Triomphe.** 1898–1913.

1898: Trademark registered in France by the makers, *Fleischmann & Blödel Cie.*

1913: Registered as a trademark by *Société Française de Fabrication de Bébés et Jouets.*

**171.** "Bébé Triomphe," trademark of Fleischmann & Blödel.

# BÉBÉ TRIOMPHE

**Bébés Incassables.** See **Bébé Incassable.**

**Bechmann, Christ.** 1898–1925+. Neustadt near Coburg, Thür. Manufactured little or baby dolls and *Täuflinge.*

**Beck, Adelbert.** 1911–25+. Königsee, Thür. Porcelain manufacturer; made dolls' house dolls.

**Beck, Carl, & Schulze, Alfred.** 1925. Ohrdruf, Thür. Doll manufacturer.

**Beck Manufacturing Co.** 1888–1920. Brooklyn, N.Y., and New York City. Doll manufacturer.

1918: Advertised composition "Beck Dolls" with glass eyes, human or mohair wigs; sizes 13, 18, and 20 inches.

1919: New French baby-doll line with straight limbs or jointed character babies.

1920: Dolls with *Porcelainette* unbreakable heads or with bisque heads, sleeping eyes, with or without eyelashes, human hair or mohair wigs; fully jointed bodies; sizes 2 to 27 inches.

**Beck, Reinhold.** 1917. German citizen, residing in U.S. Artist for *Fine Baby,* copyrighted by *Louis Amberg & Son.*

**Becker, Frz.** 1902. Kreis, Braunschweig. Cloth doll factory.

**Becker, Otto.** 1923. Babenhausen, Hesse. Secured a German patent for stringing jointed celluloid dolls with knotted elastic.

**Becq, Mme. Victor.** 1900. Paris. Exhibited dolls at the Paris Exposition for Maison *André Duclos.*

**Beddy-Bye.** 1920–21. Trademark registered in U.S. for rag dolls made by *Julia E. Greene.*

**Bedella.** 1904. Name of a rubber doll that cried when squeezed.

**Bedtime.** 1917. Rag dolls made by *Richard G. Krueger, Inc.* Hand-painted, filled with kapok; 10 inches high. Wholesale price, $4.25 doz.

**Bedtime.** 1917. Leather or fabric dolls made by *Moore & Gibson Corp.*

**Bedtime.** 1923. Registered as a French trademark by *Borgfeldt.*

**Bedtime Baby.** 1916–18. Made by *Jessie McCutcheon Raleigh;* distributed by *Butler Bros.* This was a bent-limb baby with painted hair; wore flannelette sleeping garment. Size 12½ inches; price $2.85.

**Bee Bee Brands.** 1915. Character dolls made by *Bleier Bros.,* New York City; including *Abe Kabibble.*

**Beecher, Mrs. Thomas K. (née Jones, Julia).** 1893–1910. Elmira, N.Y. Made *Missionary Ragbabies* of old silk-jersey underwear; flat hand-painted and sewn features; yarn hair; Negro and white babies. Sizes 16 to 18 inches, 19 to 20 inches, 21 to 23 inches, and larger sizes; prices $2.00, $3.00, $5.00, $6.00, $7.00, and $8.00, with 50¢ off when material was sent. Money from the sale of these

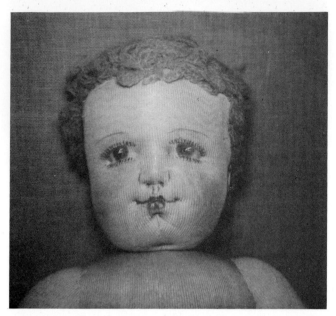

**172.** Pink stockinet rag doll made by Beecher; features were molded by sewing, and painted; hair is wool loops. *Courtesy of the Chester County Historical Society.*

dolls was used as a missionary fund by the Park Congregational Church of Elmira.

**Beedle, Claude de Witt.** 1912–13. Leominster, Mass. Obtained U.S. patent for stringing a doll with a spring holding the head and legs together.

**Beers-Keeler-Bowman Co.** 1922–23. U.S. doll manufacturer.

**Beers, William P.** 1924–25. Norwalk, Conn. Doll manufacturer.

**Behu.** 1892. Obtained French patent for stringing dolls with removable elastic spheres.

**Beinroth, Geschw. (Bros. & Sisters).** 1909–18. Hamburg, Germany. Made dolls.

**Belaunsaran, Isabel.** 1914. Cuernavaca, Mexico. Made dolls ³/₄ inch tall with wire framework wound with silk thread. The dolls were dressed in embroidered clothes with ornaments in their hair; flower girls carried baskets made of woven hair. Two hours were required to make a doll; price 25¢ each.

**Belgian Doll & Toy Co.** 1918–22. New York City. Manufactured dolls.

**Bell.** 1898. Trade name used by *W. A. Cissna & Co.* for dolls with bisque heads, teeth, woven wigs, kid bodies scalloped at the bust; size 20¹/₂ inches; price $7.25 doz. wholesale. It is possible that these dolls were named for the bell mark that *Kling* put on their bisque dolls' heads.

**Bell, Elizabeth W.** 1908–11. Norwood, Pa. Obtained U.S. patent for a stuffed doll with a wire frame made so that the doll could sit or stand unsupported; patent assigned to *Belle Novelty Co.*

**Bell, James.** 1921. Newark, N.J. Distributed dolls.

**Bell, Mary E.** 1921–22. Redondo Beach, Cal. Secured U.S. design patent for a doll.

**Bell, W.** 1917. Secured a British patent for dolls' eyes moving from side to side by gravity.

**Bell & Francis.** 1911–23. London. Doll makers.

**Bell Brand.** 1920. Bell Toy Co. Line of dolls that included *Maybelle* and *Florabelle;* these were stuffed dolls. Price 50¢ to $2.00.

**Bell Toy Co.** See **Arcy Toy Co.;** also **Bell Brand.**

**Bella Puppen (Beautiful Doll).** 1923–24. Trademark registered in Germany by *Leo Nordschild* for dolls, dolls' heads, dolls' wigs, and dolls' clothing.

**Bella Veneziana.** 1919. Doll copyrighted by *Voccia Guglielmo.*

**Belle Novelty Co.** 1908–11. A Delaware corporation, assignee of U.S. patent of *Elizabeth W. Bell.*

**Bellet, Henri.** 1919–21. Paris. Trademark *Poupard Art,* registered in France; specialized in making papier-mâché *poupards.*

**Belleville & Co.** 1920. Paris. Trademark *Mystère,* registered in France, used for dolls, dolls' heads, and mechanism for dolls' movable eyes.

**Belton.** 1842–57. Paris. 1842–46, Belton & *Jumeau;* 1847–52, Belton; 1855, Widow Belton; 1856–57, F. Pottier, successor. Made dressed and undressed dolls with kid bodies.

1844: Belton & Jumeau exhibited dolls at the Paris Exposition and received Honorable Mention for the clothing of the dolls but not for the dolls themselves.

1855: Widow Belton dressed dolls in foreign and provincial costumes for export. DOLL NEWS, August, 1962, notes a "fashion"-type doll with the word "Belton" written in heavy black letters across the chest, but it is not known when the word was written.

**Ben-Arthur Studios.** 1919. Copyrighted *Impie* for *Borgfeldt,* a cherub-like doll designed by *Bertha Oscher,* 8¹/₂ inches tall.

**Benda, Anton.** 1858. London. Importer, agent for a foreign patentee of stringing a doll with elastic cord.

**Benda, David.** 1896–1902. Fürth, Bavaria. Exporter of dolls.

**Benda, Gabriel. L., & Co.** 1855–73. London, Paris, and Coburg, Thür. Distributor; displayed dolls at the London Exhibition in 1862; listed with Marc Wemschenk Sons in 1867 and with P. Guénot in 1873. Gabriel Benda obtained an English patent in 1871 and French and U.S. patents in 1872 for a doll with a detachable masklike face so that faces with various expressions could be fitted onto the head and into the neck.

**Benda & Hipauf.** 1909–12. London. Doll makers and importers.

**Benedictus, Edouard & Mme.** 1919. France. Obtained

French patent for a doll's body of flexible metal, covered with kapok or similar material, and bound together with wire.

**Benjamin, Henry Solomon.** 1887–1924. London. Agent for *Gebrüder Krauss* of Eisfeld, Thür., *Société Française de Fabrication de Bébés et Jouets* of Paris, and *Société Industrielle de Celluloid* of Paris.

1917: Registered in Britain as a trademark for dolls the word *Victory* under a figure of Victory.

**Benoist.** Ca. 1850-70. Paris. Mlle. Benoist was succeeded by *G. H. Most* in 1852, but the name Benoist appears in the Paris Directories in the 1860's under Dolls.

**Benoliel, Mrs. William A.** 1923–24. Wife of the supervisor of the *Live Long Toy Co.*, Chicago, Ill.; she conceived and executed the idea of putting *Frank King's Gasoline Alley* figures into doll form.

**Benon & Cie.**  See **Aux Enfants Sages.**

**Bensinger & Co.** 1897. Mannheim, Germany. Made dolls of rubberized linen; used turtle mark of *Rheinische Gummi und Celluloid Fabrik Co.*

**Bently-Franklin Co.** 1916. New York City. Produced *Hug-Me-Tight* line of cotton-stuffed rag dolls designed by *Grace G. Drayton.*

**Benvenuti, Julius Desire.** 1919–20. San Francisco. Obtained a design patent for a winking cherub-type doll that was copyrighted by May *Moran* under the name Blynke *(Blynkie)*, with Benvenuti named as the artist; Benvenuti copyrighted a molded-hair doll named the *Girl of the Golden West.*

**Bercovitch, L. W., & S., and Annison, J. H.** 1923. Manchester, England. Doll manufacturers; trademark *Bersonian* registered in Britain.

**Bereux, Mlle. J. L.** 1865–78. Paris. Showed dolls at the 1867 and 1878 Paris expositions.

**Berg (Von Berg), Hermann.** 1904–25. Köppelsdorf, Thür. Manufactured dolls and dolls' heads.

**Berg Brothers, Inc.** 1914–25+. New York City. Handled composition-head character dolls.

1914: Sizes 8, 11, 13, and 18 inches; wholesale price per gross, $10.50 to $54.00.

1917: Advertised composition-head character dolls dressed in rompers, overalls, etc.; sizes 12, 13, 16, 20, and 25 inches. Retail prices 25¢, 50¢, and $1.00. Babies with open mouth and pacifier, dressed in white lawn dress and cap; sizes 12, 15, and 28 inches; wholesale price $2.25 to $9.00 doz.

1923: Distributors of the *Change-O-Doll Co.* dolls with several heads that could be interchanged by screwing the neck on and off.

1924: Trademark *Famlee* registered in U.S. for multi-headed dolls.

**Bergeson, Lenna.** 1923–24. Los Angeles, Calif. Obtained design patent for a stockinet rag doll.

**Bergfeld, Sol, & Son.** 1923-25. New York City. Doll manufacturer; *Borgfeldt* distributor.

1923: Advertised *Mama Dolls.*

1924: Advertised the *Charlotte Doll.*

1925: *Story Book Dolls,* including *Little Red Riding Hood, Little Bo-Peep,* etc.

**Bergler, Ludwig.** 1899–1907. Vienna. Successors, 1908–21, kept the name Ludwig Bergler. Manufactured dolls and dolls' heads.

**Bergman, Fritz, & Co.** 1903–11, London, distributors. 1912–13, Bergman, Kleemann & Co., London, doll manufacturers and distributors, probably successors to Fritz Bergman & Co.

**Bergman, Henry.**  See **Borcherdt, Richard.**

**Bergmann, Charles M.** 1877–89, Waltershausen, Thür., employee in doll factories. 1889–1925+, doll manufacturer; *Louis Wolf & Co.* was distributor of Bergmann's dolls.

Bergmann, a native German, fought Indians as a cowboy in the American West of the 1870's. He returned to Germany in 1877 and began work as an apprentice in a doll factory at Waltershausen. After gaining experience under several manufacturers, he started his own doll factory in 1889, the year in which he obtained a French patent for the mechanism to move a doll's head in any direction. By 1909 the business had grown so that he had a factory at Friedrichroda as well as at Waltershausen, and he claimed that he was one of the largest makers of "papier-mâché dolls" in Germany. He pro-

**173.** Head made by Simon & Halbig for C. M. Bergmann. The doll has glass sleep eyes, open mouth with teeth, a jointed composition body. Mark: Ill. **175.** H. 12½ inches. *Courtesy of Ollie Leavister.*

**174.** Bergmann doll with bisque head on a jointed composition body; the head bears the mark shown in Ill. **176.** Doll has sleep eyes, open mouth with four teeth, and "Rembrandt" style wig. H. 22 inches. *Courtesy of May Maurer.*

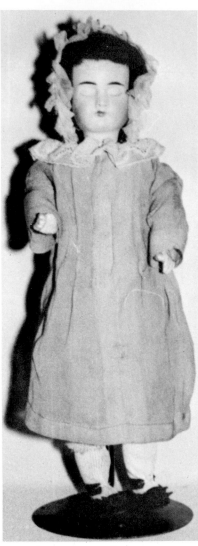

**178A, B, & C.** A three-faced doll. For stamp on back shoulder, see Ill. **179.** This may be a Carl Bergner doll. The white bisque face sleeps, the mulatto smiles, and the Negro cries. Note the molded tears. H. 13 inches. *Courtesy of Sylvia Brockmon.*

S & H
C.M.B
3

175

G. M. Bergmann
Waltershausen
Germany
1916
6½ a

176

C.M. BERGMANN
4/0

177

**175–177.** Charles Bergmann marks found on dolls.

 **179.** Mark on dolls probably made by Carl Bergner.

duced chiefly what is now known as ball-jointed composition-body dolls. In 1897, C. M. Bergmann registered his trademark *Cinderella Baby* in Germany. This same trademark was registered in the U.S. by Louis Wolf & Co. in 1897, but had been used since 1892. The U.S. trademark was renewed in 1917.

Another well-known Bergmann line was named *Columbia*. A 1904 advertisement relates to Columbia kid-body dolls, but by 1915 the Columbia line included both kid-body and jointed composition dolls. A third line, *Baby Belle* character babies, appeared in 1913. Louis Wolf & Co. was the American agent for all these doll lines. In 1914, Bergmann brought out the *Anniversary* doll line in celebration of their twenty-fifth anniversary. In 1910, the name C. M. Bergmann was registered in Germany as a trademark. Bergmann did not make the bisque heads used on his dolls, but purchased them from *Simon & Halbig, Armand Marseille,* and probably others.

**Bergmann, Geschw. (Bros. & Sisters).** 1909–25+. Berlin and Leipzig, Saxony. Manufactured dolls.

**Bergner, Carl.** 1890–1909. Sonneberg, Thür. Successors to Carl Bergner, 1910–25+. Doll manufacturer.

1890: Obtained German patent for a doll's head turning with a spring.

1904–5: German and British patents for dolls with faces or face parts made so that different facial expressions could be attached at will—the doll's face could be either laughing, crying, or sleeping, and either white or Negro. The body was made of cheaper and stronger material than the face, which was important to exporters; the German patent mentioned a removable wig. Many multi-face dolls have "C. B." stamped on them, and it is possible that this stands for Carl Bergner since it is evident he was interested in multi-face dolls.

1910–25: Carl Bergner advertised high-class jointed dolls and babies.

**Bergner & Brandweiner.** 1923–25. Vienna. Doll maker.

**Berkander, George F.** 1920–22. Providence, R.I. Trademark *Shimmikins* registered in U.S.

**Berlin.** See **Königliche Porzellan Manufaktur.**

**Berlin, J., Sr.** See **Fleischmann & Blödel.**

**Berliner Puppenfabrik.** See **C. M. Schmalfuss.**

**Berlizheimer, Mrs. Herminia (Hermona).** 1880–83. Philadelphia, Pa. Made dolls' bodies.

**Berman.** 1847. Paris. Doll maker.

**Bernard.** 1885. Paris. Made dolls.

**Bernard, E.** 1873. Paris. Distributed and exported dolls from France and Germany.

**Berner, Jacques.** 1888. Paris. Made *Bébé Moujik.*

**Bernhard, Adam.** 1925. New York City. Distributed *Turtle Brand* celluloid dolls.

**Bernhard & Co.** See **Fabriken Bernhard & Co.**

**Bernhardt, B., Fiai (Sons).** 1896–1925+. Budapest. Hungarian dummy and doll factory.

**Bernheim & Kahn (Société Bernheim & Kahn).** 1904–6. Paris. Made Parisienne bébés named *Etoile Bébé* and *Bébé Mondain.*

1905: Obtained French patent for a method of molding dolls and bébés.

**Bernhold, Julius.** 1912. Paris. Trademark *Nini Kaspa* registered in France for a jointed composition bébé.

**Berry, Long.** 1867. Providence, R.I. Doll maker.

**Berryman, Rozel.** See **Meier, Harry.**

**Bersonian.** 1923. Trademark registered in Britain for dolls made by *L. W. & S. Bercovitch* and J. H. Annison.

**180.** China-head doll made for Butler Bros., with embossed name "Bertha"; known as a "Pet Name" doll. Mark on back of shoulder: Ill. **181.** Note that the gilt on the collar does not extend to the back. H. 9¾ inches. H. of shoulder head, 3 inches. *Coleman Collection.*

## PATENT APP'D FOR
### GERMANY

**181.** Mark on "Pet Name" dolls produced by Butler Bros.

**Bertal & Taffe.** 1861. France. Doll makers.

**Bertha.** 1905–25+ and possibly earlier. China dolls' heads made with this name in gold letters on the chest. (See also **Pet Name.**)

**Berthe.** 1890's. Name on a tambourine belonging to a closed-mouth bisque-head doll made by *Jules Steiner,* which was found in its original clothes and box. Mark on doll is "J. Steiner//Bte. S.G.D.G.//Paris//A3." Size, 11 inches.

**Berthoyette.** 1924–25. Trademark registered in France and U. S. by *Adolphe Schloss Fils & Cie.*

**Bertie.** 1911–12. Import line of felt-faced character dolls, distributed by *Strobel & Wilken;* advertised as having large protruding eyes. In some dolls the eyes themselves could be moved; in others, there was a knob at the back of the head whereby the eyes could be moved in any direction; natural eyebrows, hair was "wildly riotous"; mate of doll named *Gertie.*

**Bertie.** 1913. American doll made by *Tip Top Toy Co.;* dressed as a sailor, mate of doll named *Gertie.*

**Bertoli, Frères (Bros.).** 1895. Marseilles, France. Trademark *Idéal Bébé,* registered in France.

**Bertolini, Louis.** 1922. Detroit, Mich. An Italian citizen. He copyrighted a cherub-like doll named *Kiss Me Quick.*

**Bertram, An.** 1897. Berlin. Doll exporter.

**Bertram, S.** 1891–1918. Berlin. Doll manufacturer; specialized in Parisian-type dressed dolls.

**Bertrand, René.** 1921–25. Paris. Registered in France as a trademark the name *Gaby,* for a doll, in 1923.

**Berwick Doll Co.** 1918–25. New York City. Handled the *Famlee* dolls with changeable heads, patented by *David Wiener.* The dolls came with from three to twelve different heads that could be screwed off and on; appropriate costumes to match the various heads; height 16 inches; price $6.00 to $20.00 a set, depending on the number of heads in the set.

1924: Heads included Little-Sweet-Face, Black-Boy-Sam, Funny-Face-Clown, Miss-from-Holland, and Ching-Ching-Chinaman. (See also **Change-O-Doll Co.**)

**Besnard, Mme. A.** 1869–79. Paris. Advertised jointed dolls, dressed and undressed, and doll repairs.

**Bess.** 1910. Trade name of a *Neverbreak* doll handled by *A. Steinhardt & Bro.*

**Bess Darling.** 1921–22. Sleeping-eyed doll made by *National Manufacturing Co.,* over 12 inches tall.

**Besser, Edwin, Co.** 1925. New York City. Importer and manufacturers' agent for dolls. They handled dolls of the *American Stuffed Novelty Co.*

**Bessy Brooks.** 1921. Trade name for a *Chase* stockinet rag doll.

**Best & Co.** 1902–25+. New York City. Distributed dolls.

1902: Advertised dolls with jointed composition bodies, sizes 12 to 32 inches; bisque heads on kid bodies, sizes 15 to 25 inches; all-celluloid dolls, sizes 3½ to 16½ inches; American "Unbreakable" dolls (probably made by *Hoffmann*), sizes 13, 16, 18, 19, and 23 inches, price 50¢ to $1.50; dressed rag dolls, including a girl, a boy, and Topsy (probably produced by *Horsman*), sizes 14, 20, and 30 inches, price $1.00 to $4.85; oil-painted stockinet baby dolls (probably made by *Martha Chase),* sizes 16 and 19 inches, price $3.75 and $4.50 undressed and $5.50 and $7.50 dressed; baby dolls with jointed bodies, short hair, baby-like expression, showing two teeth, sizes 9 to 25 inches. Dressed dolls with jointed bodies and movable eyes were priced up to $15.00 each.

1917: Registered in U.S. *Snuggles* as a trademark to be used on dolls of glass, wood, metal, celluloid, cotton, wool, wax, bisque, china, rubber, or composition. This probably does not mean that Snuggles was made in all these various materials but that it could be.

**Best Baby.** 1920. Made in Japan for *Haber Bros.* Injunction to stop production issued November 11, 1920, because the doll looked too much like a *Kewpie.*

**Bestelmeier, Georg Hieronymus.** 1793–1808. Nürnberg, Bavaria. Published catalogs containing dolls. The dolls appeared to have been primarily of wood and generally attached to a wooden base. Bestelmeier claimed that all his dolls were made in Nürnberg, but many of the pic-

tures appear to be the same cuts found in contemporary catalogs of Sonneberg and the Grödner Tal.

**Bester Doll, The.** 1918. American-made doll distributed by *Morimura Bros.* Later, the *Bester Doll Manufacturing Co.* sold dolls directly to the trade. These dolls came with or without eyelashes and had ball-jointed bodies; sizes 16, 18, 20, 22, 24, and 26 inches.

## BESTER DOLL C?
## BLOOMFIELD

**182.** Mark of Bester Doll Manufacturing Co.

**Bester Doll Manufacturing Co.** 1919–21. Bloomfield and Newark, N.J. Doll manufacturers who sold their dolls direct to the trade. Probably in 1918 made the Bester Doll distributed by *Morimura Bros.*

**Beth.** 1923–25. Rag doll designed and made by *Madame Alexander.* It had a mask face with raised features, which were hand-painted by Madame Alexander. Came with wig of mohair imported from England; pink muslin body; size 14 inches; price $1.20.

**Betsy.** 1922–23. Trademark registered in Germany by *Borgfeldt* for dolls.

**Betsy Bobbitt.** 1899. Name of rag doll to be made at home using patterns as given in pattern and fashion books, especially BICYCLE FASHIONS; seven sizes, 12 to 24 inches.

**Betsy Ross.** 1924. Name of a *Mama Doll* distributed by *Borgfeldt* and known to the trade as #1217. Made with or without composition legs and in five sizes.

**Bettijak.** 1914. Trademark registered in U.S. by *Borgfeldt* for a doll.

**Betts, Thomas.** 1879–1905, London; 1907–12, successor was Mrs. Marion Betts. They made wax and/or composition dolls.

1881: Miss H. Spratt, doll maker, was listed at the same address.

**Betty.** 1909. Name of a *Horsman* doll with celluloid face, 14½ inches tall, price 25¢. In 1911, Horsman copyrighted a bust of a child and named it Betty; *Helen Trowbridge* was the artist.

**Betty.** 1920–24. *Madame Georgene Averill* was the originator and designer; *Paul Averill, Inc.* was the manufacturer and distributor. It was a walking-talking doll with composition arms and legs and soft body. It came with either painted hair or natural blond or tosca ringlet wig, and wore a lace-trimmed organdy dress with bonnet and bloomers to match. Its mate was *Billy (Billie) Boy.*

1920: Size 26 inches.

1922: Sizes 20, 23, 25½, and 28 inches.

1924: Little Betty dressed in gingham and wore a cap. Price $1.75.

**Betty Blazer.** 1912. Character doll made by *Horsman*. It had a composition head and a pink sateen body stuffed with cork.

**Betty Bonnet.** 1918. Doll made by *Jessie McCutcheon Raleigh* and distributed by *Butler Bros.* It had a wig and came in two sizes; 11½ inches cost $2.90; 13½ inches cost $3.60.

**Betty Bounce.** 1913–14. Line of dolls made by *EFFanBEE*.

**Betty Bright.** 1916. Doll made by *Horsman* and distributed by *Montgomery Ward & Co.* It had composition head and hands, bobbed wig, cork-stuffed body, and wore a cloak and cap. Size 18 inches cost $4.43.

**Betty Bright.** 1920. Rag doll with yellow hair and a red ribbon; 22 inches tall.

**Betty Lee.** 1924. Made by *EFFanBEE*. The doll had composition head and limbs, blue sleep eyes, eyelashes, curly hair, a soft body, and was dressed in organdy and Irish lace. It wore a golden heart necklace, was 20 inches tall, and cost $7.50.

**Betty Lou.** 1923. Advertised as talking, walking, and sleeping; 18 inches tall.

**Betty Walker.** 1922. Walking-talking line of dolls made by *Du Bois Manufacturing Co.* Faces were hand-painted, and no two were alike. Dolls were made of a material more resilient than cotton but not of composition. Bodies were stuffed. Sizes 15, 18, and 21 inches; price less than $5.00.

**Beuchin, Barbara.** Ca. 1600. Nürnberg, Bavaria. Made and distributed dolls.

**Beug, Glee.** 1922. Sturgis, S. Dak. Secured U.S. design patent for a rag doll.

**Bevan, William.** 1894. Auckland, N.Z. Obtained British patent for a walking doll with heavy feet that could be pulled along by a string. His London agent was Francis Graham Lloyd.

**Beygrau, Paul.** 1918. Paris. Sculptor and artist who created dolls for *Pacific Coast Doll Manufacturing Co.*, Seattle, Wash. (Pronounced "bay grow.")

**Bianchi, P.** 1855. London. Wax doll maker.

**Bi-Ba-Bo.** 1908. Trademark registered in Germany by *Julius Jeidel*, doll distributor.

**Biedermeier.** Second quarter 19th century. Term used to describe German interpretations of the French Empire styles. Some doll collectors use this term for bald china heads, especially those with a black pate. Probably most of the china heads of this type were made in the decades after 1850; advertisements for bald china-head dolls appear as late as the early part of the 20th century. (See also **Bald Heads.**)

**Bien.** 1889. France. Obtained French patent for improving doll joints.

**Bierer, L.** 1851–1920. Sonneberg, Thür., and Fürth, Bavaria. Doll and toy firm and exporters.

1908–10: The American partner was Strauss, Haas & Co. of New York City.

1911: London agent was J. L. Morison Son & Jones.

**Bierschenk, Fritz.** 1907–25+. Sonneberg, Thür. Made jointed dolls and felt dolls. They came undressed or dressed "from the simplest to the most elegant." (See also **Escher, E.**)

**Big Baby Bumps.** Made by *Horsman*. Dressed in rompers; wholesale price $15.00 doz. (See also **Baby Bumps.**)

**Big Bertha or German Vampire.** Before World War I, names given to large (21-inch), cheap (price $1.00) dolls made in Germany; names reported in 1919.

**Big Candy Kid.** 1911. *Art Doll* made by *Horsman*. Had *Can't Break 'Em* head with molded hair; cloth body; dressed in rompers. (See also **Candy Kid.**)

**Big Shaver.** 1915. All-composition, jointed character doll.

**Big Sister.** 1916. Composition doll made by *Horsman* and distributed by *Montgomery Ward & Co.* It had a bobbed mohair wig and wore a cloak trimmed with imitation fur. Height 15½ inches; cost $2.80.

**Bijard.** See **Borreau.**

**Bijou Bébé.** See **Bébé Bijou.**

**Bijou Doll Co., The.** 1915–17. New York City. Manufactured inexpensive dolls priced at 25¢, 50¢, and $1.00.

**Billard, A.** 1880. Paris. Listed under doll makers.

**Billie.** 1924. One of the *Baby Grumpy* line made by *EFFanBEE*.

**Billie Boy.** See **Billy (Billie) Boy.**

**Billie Button.** 1921–23. Trademark registered in U.S. by *Alma P. Hickman* for cloth and stockinet dolls.

**Billiken.** 1909–12. Copyrighted doll made by *Horsman*, had *Can't Break 'Em* composition head and plush body, which later was changed to pink sateen.

Early in 1909 Horsman entered into agreement with Billiken Sales Co. for sole right to manufacture and sell Billiken dolls in the U.S. and Canada. This was one of the first copyrighted dolls; it is described on the copyright as "having a head with a broad smile on the face, outstanding ears and hair brought to a peak on top and having the body clothed in somewhat loose-fitting drapery, wide loose sleeves on arms and legs in loose raiment." In the first six months 200,000 Billikens were sold.

These were 12 inches tall and cost $1.00 each. At the peak of their popularity over half a million were sold in a year.

1910: *Butler Bros.* advertised Billikens with pink or white velvet bodies, 13 inches.

**Billy.** 1907. Rag doll made by *Art Fabric Mills.*

**Billy Blink.** 1912. Made by *Horsman*. Represented a two-year-old toddler. Had *Can't Break 'Em* composition head and cork-stuffed pink sateen body.

183. Billiken, made by Horsman, has composition head, cloth body, white outfit trimmed with blue and white checked material. H. 13 inches. *Courtesy of The Smithsonian Institution.*

**Billy Boy.** 1912. Trade name of doll made by *Elektra Toy & Novelty Co.*

**Billy Boy.** 1918. Trade name of all-rubber doll made by *Faultless Rubber Co.* Had molded clothes and was made in either tan or red color.

**Billy (Billie) Boy.** 1920–24. *Madame Georgene Averill* was the originator and designer; *Paul Averill, Inc.* (a firm separate from the *Averill Manufacturing Co.*) was the manufacturer and distributor. It was a walking-talking doll with composition arms and legs and a soft body. It came with painted hair and wore gingham rompers and a sunbonnet. Its mate was *Betty.*

1920: Size 26 inches.

1922: Sizes 20, 23, 25½, and 28 inches.

1924: Billy Boy cost $3.75.

**Billy Doll.** 1909. Trademark registered in Germany by *Steiff.*

**Billy Possum.** 1909. Trademark registered in Germany by

*Max Illfelder,* exporter, for dolls' heads, dolls' bodies, wool dolls, and dolls of all kinds.

**Bimco Doll Co.** 1918. New York City. Made dolls priced from 50¢ to $5.00.

**Binder & Cie. (Société).** 1918–21. Paris. Registered French trademark of "B K" in a shield for use with rag dolls.

 **184.** Mark used by Gebrüder Bing.

**Bing, Gebrüder (Brothers), A. G. (Joint Stock Co.)** 1882–1919, Nürnberg, Bavaria, plus branches all over the world; used "G. B. N." as a trademark; 1920–25+, successor of Gebr. Bing was Bing Werke, which used "B W" for a trademark. Bing, one of the largest German toy manufacturers, made and distributed all kinds of dolls. Before World War I they had as many as 4,000 employees.

1900: Bing won a gold medal at the Paris Exposition. *John Bing & Co.* was their sole representative in the U.S. and Canada.

1912: Bing registered in Britain the trademarks *Sunshine Girl* and *Sunshine Kid.*

1922: Registered *Pitti-Bum* as a trademark in Germany for dolls.

1923: Registered "B.W." in Britain as a trademark, which they had used since 1920.

1925: Bing Künstlerpuppen *(art dolls)* & Stoffspielwaren Gesellschaft registered "BIN" in Germany as a trademark for dolls. G

**Bing, John, Co.** 1910–25. New York City. Sole representative in U.S. and Canada of *Gebr. Bing.*

1911: Represented Gebr. Bing, *Louis Lindner & Sons,* and the United Toy Factories of Waltershausen.

1915: Placed orders amounting to about one million dollars with Gebr. Bing.

1922: Sole American agent for *Kämmer & Reinhardt* and *Heinrich Handwerck.*

1923: Sole American agent for Kämmer & Reinhardt and *Welsch.*

1925: Advertised K & R dolls, S & Q bisque babies, K–F dolls, R. B. & L. dolls, and "Bing" dolls, including American-made Regal dolls (see **German American Doll Co.**).

**Bing, Jr., & Co.** 1890. Frankfurt am Main, Germany. Listed under Dolls in Paris Directory; Emile Gerson was Paris agent.

**Bingo.** 1911. *Art Doll* made by *Horsman.* Had *Can't Break 'Em* composition head, molded hair, Negro features and color, cloth body; dressed in rompers.

301

Germany

**186.** Mark found on dolls handled by John Bing.

**Binkie Doll.** 1921. Trademark registered in U.S. by *Notaseme Hosiery Co.* for dolls.

**Birthday.** 1923–24. Trademark registered in U.S. by *Stella N. Webster* for dolls.

**Bisaccia, Nicola.** 1919. Brooklyn, N.Y. Copyrighted a doll named *Little Beauty.*

**Bisc Novelty Manufacturing Co.** 1917. East Liverpool, Ohio. Genuine bisque dolls' heads were made by *Ernst Reinhardt* entirely from American materials. These may have been the first successful porcelain bisque dolls' heads made commercially in America. Shoulder heads, socket heads, *Dolly Doll*-type heads, character-type heads, and heads with molded hair or with cardboard pates were all made in this factory. Most of the heads had sleeping eyes of celluloid, but a few had painted eyes.

**187.** Original bisque model for a doll's head, from which master molds were made. Created and used by Ernst Reinhardt for the Bisc Novelty Manufacturing Co. Mark: Ill. **188.** H. 8½ inches. *Coleman Collection.*

**188.** Mark on dolls of the Bisc Novelty Manufacturing Co.

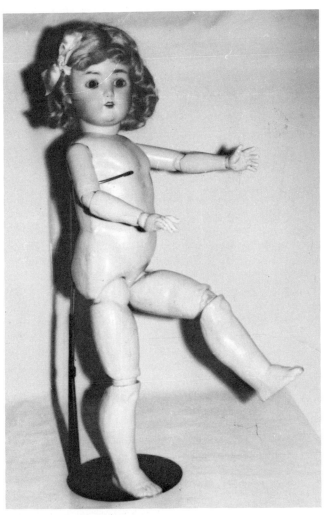

**185A & B.** John Bing handled S & Q dolls in 1925. See Ill. **186** for the mark. Doll has bisque head, open mouth and teeth, ball-jointed composition body H. 22 inches. *Courtesy of Cherry Bou.*

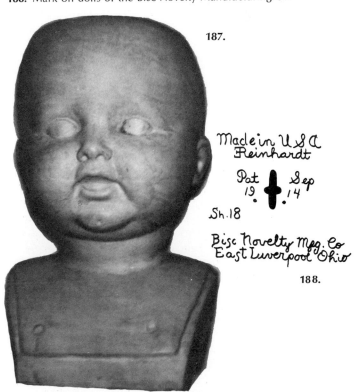

187.

Made in USA
Reinhardt
Pat 19 ✝ Sep 14
Sh. 18
Bisc Novelty Mfg. Co
East Liverpool Ohio

188.

**Bischoff, Charles.** 1863–74. Sonneberg, Thür. Made doll heads. *Gottschalk & Co.* was his Paris agent.

**Bischoff, Christian, & Co. (Bischoff & Co.).** 1863–1902. Sonneburg, Thür. Made doll heads that were displayed at the 1873 Vienna Exhibition. *Gottschalk & Co.* was their Paris agent. *Charles* and *Emil Bischoff* may have belonged to this company.

**Bischoff, Emil.** 1863–74. Sonneberg, Thür. Made doll heads that he displayed at the 1873 Vienna Exhibition. *Gottschalk & Co.* was his Paris agent. It should be noted that the initials "E.B." are sometimes found on the front shoulders of early-type bisque heads.

**Bischoff, L. M.** 1896–98. Sonneberg, Thür. Doll manufacturer; produced dressed dolls.

**Bischoff, Peter.** 1909–15. Sonneberg, Thür. Made dolls.

**Biskoline.** 1910–18. Material used by *Parsons-Jackson Co.* for making dolls. It was similar to celluloid, and they advertised that it had "no surface color to wear off, will never crack, break, surface chip or peel, 1 year guarantee." However, the test of time has proven the material far from durable.

**Biskoline Nature Dolls.** 1911–13. Line of dolls made of *Biskoline* by *Parsons-Jackson Co.* In 1912, two sizes were made, priced at $1.50 and $2.50.

**Biskuit-Imitation.** 1886. Was registered as a trademark in Germany by *Gebrüder Haag*.

**Bisque (Biscuit, Bisc, Bisk).** A ceramic material with a hard mat or nonglossy surface that, in the better grades, is translucent. Some bisque heads have glossy parts as decoration. Bisque heads may be pressed or poured into a mold. The pressed ones are usually rough on the inside and not of uniform thickness. These are generally earlier than the poured heads, most of them having been made prior to 1890. Bisque dolls' heads were often produced in factories that manufactured various ceramic products. However, doll parts had to be fired in kilns devoted exclusively to this type of goods. If the kilns were also used for articles requiring other grades of ceramics, the doll items would absorb the dust from these other products. The tremendous heat required for firing and the amount of equipment necessary to produce bisque articles made it difficult for small operators to compete with large potteries before the introduction of the electric kiln. But large potteries often sold dolls' heads "in the white" for smaller companies to decorate.

Bisque dolls' heads were popular as early as the 1860's, and no doubt some were made before then. They were produced primarily in Europe, especially in Thür., Bavaria, and Bohemia, the environs of Paris, and Limoges. Some were made in England and America around the time of World War I, and Japan produced many bisque dolls during and after World War I. Unsuccessful attempts had been made in America as early as the 1880's to produce bisque heads commercially. In 1899 *Montgomery Ward & Co.* advertised dolls with "American Bisque Heads." This confusing phrase is an example of the impression advertisements gave that American composition heads resembled "bisque" or "bisc."

Before 1880, most bisque heads were the shoulder type, with or without a swivel neck. Many of these had molded hair and sometimes molded bonnets or hats. Occasionally, dolls with such heads were given bisque arms and/or legs. Bisque was used for the hip section as well as head and limbs for the type of doll patented by *Motschmann* in 1857. Ca. 1876, *Strasburger, Pfeiffer & Co.* advertised the following bisque dolls and dolls' heads:

Bisque Babies: These included *bathing dolls,* and dolls with natural hair; the molded-hair dolls were predominantly blonde; a few of them were boys; they came with plain feet or painted or gilded boots; sizes 1 to 8 inches; price 9¢ to $9.00 doz. wholesale. (These were probably all-bisque dolls.)

Bisque Limb Dolls: These came with bisque heads and limbs on cloth bodies; blonde molded hair; stationary necks; painted or gilt boots; sizes 6 to 20¾ inches; price 75¢ to $9.00 doz. wholesale. Bisque Limb Dolls also came with swivel necks and natural flowing curly hair, stationary glass eyes, painted shoes and stockings; sizes 11 to 22½ inches; price $9.00 to $30.00 doz. wholesale. The higher prices included an embroidered chemise and velvet necklace.

Bisque Dolls on jointed French kid bodies: The heads were jointed at the neck; velvet bands, natural hair; kid limbs; eleven sizes, $2.00 to $12.00 each; with bisque hands, five sizes, $3.75 to $6.50 each.

Bisque, heads only: With molded blonde hair, painted or glass eyes; some boys had gilt collars and neckties; some girls had earrings and/or fancy painted chests; sizes 2¼ to 6½ inches; price 75¢ to $10.50 doz. wholesale. With natural braided hair, glass eyes, stationary necks; seven sizes starting with 3 inches; price $3.00 to $8.50 doz. wholesale. French bisque, heads only, with swivel necks, glass eyes, fancy coiffures of natural hair, earrings, and necklaces; eight sizes, $1.50 to $4.00 each.

According to the 1879 French patent of *Schmitt & Fils,* all-bisque dolls had not been made prior to that date. However, Schmitt was a doll manufacturer and not a doll historian. It seems more likely that the Bisque Babies advertised by Strasburger, Pfeiffer & Co., ca. 1876, were all-bisque. All-bisque dolls were usually small, and might be jointed or stiff (the latter are called *Frozen Charlottes* or pillar dolls by many collectors). The innovation of the late 1870's was a doll with a jointed composition body that required a bisque socket head. In the 20th century, a number of bisque heads with flange necks were made; these could be easily attached to cloth bodies.

Bisque dolls' heads vary in grade according to the ingredients, the firing techniques, the polishing, and the painting. Most bisque heads are fired both before and

**189A & B.** Doll dressed in a handmade provincial costume of France. She has an untinted bisque shoulder head with a solid crown, painted features, a blonde wig; body is cloth with bisque lower arms. H. 16 inches. H. of shoulder head, 4 inches. *Courtesy of Jessica Norman.*

**190A & B.** Untinted bisque head has black and gold hair bands, molded glazed earrings, painted features; doll wears original dress. H. 8½ inches. H. of shoulder head, 2¼ inches. *Coleman Collection.*

BISQUE

192

193

194

195 A

B

191

**191.** Untinted bisque shoulder head has glass eyes; full-chested; head is on cloth body with leather forearms. Contemporary sprigged dress. H. 19 inches. H. of shoulder head, 4³/₄ inches. *Courtesy of Eunice Althouse.*

**192.** Untinted bisque shoulder head, glass eyes, wig. Mark: Ill. 204. H. of shoulder head, 4¹/₂ inches. *Courtesy of Ollie Leavister.*

**193.** Bisque socket head on shoulder plate has tinting above the glass eyes, and a wig. Head is on a kid gusseted body. Lac-

mann used similar heads in the 1870's. H. 22 inches. H. of shoulder head, 6¹/₂ inches. *Courtesy of Alberta Darby.*

**194.** Smiling bisque socket head on a shoulder plate has tinting above the glass eyes; wig. Kid body. Head marked, at top of forehead: "DEPOSE K." On back, "K." H. 22¹/₂ inches H. of shoulder head, 6 inches. *Courtesy of Eunice Althouse.*

**195. A, B, C, & D.** Pair of swivel-necked bisque-headed dolls on twill-covered, articulated wooden bodies. Bisque forearms,

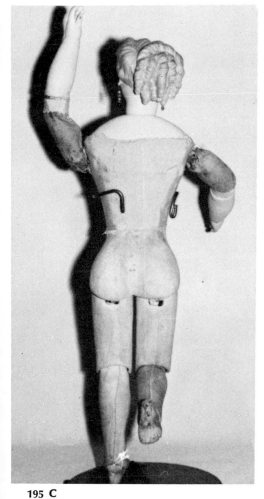

195 C
D

196 A

B

197 A

B

198

glass eyes. Man wears original suit. H. 17 inches. (See also Ill. 227.) *Courtesy of Sylvia Brockman.*

**196A & B.** Untinted bisque head with pink roses, cluster of curls; has teeth, pierced ears, blue glass eyes. A comparison with the lady doll in Ill. **195** shows interesting similarities and differences. *Courtesy of Margaret Whitton; photograph by Winnie Langley.*

**197A & B.** Untinted bisque head of the same mold as Ill. **198.**

Note differences in the trim—i.e., molded pendant and chain, "embroidered" foliate bodice. Also note similarity of ruching. H. 19½ inches. H. of shoulder head, 4½ inches. *Courtesy of Alberta Darby.*

**198.** Bisque head, untinted, with molded and applied glazed yoke, hair of café-au-lait color with rosettes. Doll has pierced ears, painted features, cloth body, and bisque lower limbs. H. 17 inches. H. of shoulder head, 4½ inches. *Courtesy of the Chester County Historical Society.*

**199 A**

**B**

**200 A**

**B**

after the color is applied, but *Otto Zeh* in 1898 obtained a patent for painting the heads and then covering them with transparent lac in order to eliminate the second firing. A *Lenox* doll's head of beautiful-quality bisque is made mediocre by lack of artistry in the painting, whereas rather ordinary-quality bisque can produce a beautiful doll's head when it is painted by an artist. Some collectors believe that the earlier bisque heads can be identified by their lighter-colored complexion. This may be true in some cases. However, the color of a finished bisque head is dependent on many factors and on each step of its production. Applied ears are also considered to be an indication of an early doll, but evidence shows that they are more likely to be a function of size than of period. Applied ears are seldom found on bisque dolls made in Germany. Most bisque heads with glass eyes have the crown sliced off and usually replaced with a cork pate on dolls made in France, and a cardboard or plaster pate on dolls made in Germany.

Bisque dolls made from the same mold can appear quite dissimilar if one has a closed mouth and another an open mouth with teeth, or if their eye sockets are cut out in different sizes. The decoration also can make them look very different.

**199A & B.** Untinted bisque shoulder head with painted features, molded blonde hair, cloth body, with sewed-on stockings and kid boots. H. 23 inches. H. of shoulder head, 6¼ inches. *Courtesy of Dorothy Annunziato.*

**200A & B.** Untinted bisque, turned shoulder head with glass eyes, pierced ears, blonde molded hair; full-chested; kid body. H. 20 inches. H. of shoulder head, 5 inches. *Courtesy of Virginia Dilliplane.*

**201.** Untinted bisque, turned shoulder head with blond hair and painted features. Cloth body has kid arms. H. 13 inches. H. of shoulder head, 3 inches. *Courtesy of Ollie Leavister.*

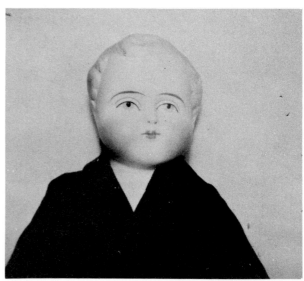

**201**

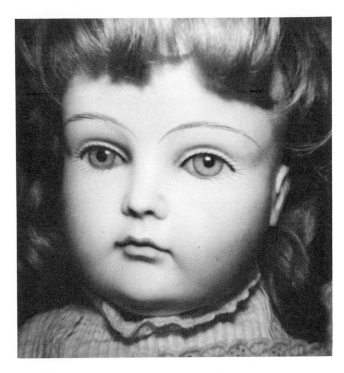

**202.** Bisque head marked "XI" just under crown rim at the back; has stationary glass eyes, closed mouth with heavy red line between the lips. Head is on a composition body. H. 16 inches. *Courtesy of the Chester County Historical Society.*

**203.** Bisque head marked only with "196//15"; has stationary brown glass eyes and closed mouth. Body is composition. H. 25 inches. *Courtesy of Theodora Gearhart.*

$\varepsilon\,4\,S$

**204.** Bisque doll's head mark. (See Ill. **192.**)

**Bisque Babies.** 1910. Trade name of all-bisque character-face boy dolls. Some of the faces were smiling and some crying; bodies jointed at neck, shoulder, and hips; 5 inches tall, price 25¢.

**Bisquette.** 1919. A "washable" composition used for dolls' heads by *Artcraft Toy Products Co.*

**Black, Arthur.** 1921–22. Toledo, Ohio. Registered *Koaster Kid* in U.S. as a trademark for dolls.

**Blake Bros.** 1918–21. London. Doll maker.

**Blakslee, Charles F.** 1865. New York City. Obtained a U.S. patent for making leather dolls' arms by using two layers of unsplit leather, gluing the cut fingers of the layers together, and stuffing only the hand and arm. There were several Blakeslees in Connecticut who were in the toy business. In 1866 Leonard Blakeslee witnessed the *Darrow* patent for making leather dolls.

**Blampoix, Aîné (Senior).** 1840–70. Paris doll maker; 1871–85, successor was Dalloz; Duval-Denis was listed as a successor in the early 1860's; then Blampoix returned.

1855: Blampoix, Sr., obtained a French patent for the application of glass or enamel eyes to porcelain dolls. This is probably the beginning of porcelain dolls' heads with glass eyes in France.

1863–70: Advertised that they made kid dolls, but specialized in applying enamel eyes to porcelain heads. This was done at a large factory where the porcelain heads were made and dolls were dressed in the latest and most elegant style.

1873: Dalloz advertised that the Blampoix firm specialized in jointed dolls, and bisque and china dolls' heads, as well as talking dolls.

**205.** China head with blue glass or enamel eyes, the type advertised by Blampoix, Sr., in the 1860's. H. 26 inches. H. of shoulder head, 7½ inches. *Courtesy of Eleanor Jean Carter.*

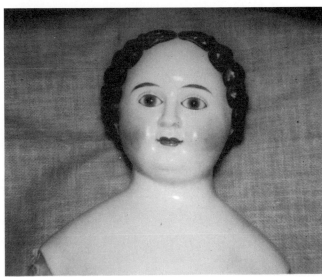

1876–78: Widow Blampoix was also listed in directories as a doll maker; she exhibited dressed and undressed dolls in the Paris Exposition of 1878 and won a bronze medal.

1879: Dalloz advertised swivel-neck porcelain dolls' heads and talking bisque dolls.

1885: Dalloz advertised bébés with kid bodies, composition-bodied bébés, and dolls' heads.

**Blampoix, Jeune (Junior).** 1856–81. Paris. A doll maker like *Blampoix, Aîné,* but at a different address.

1860–64: Blampoix, Jne., advertised that he made dolls in rose kid; specialized in porcelain dolls; porcelain bébés; all-porcelain dolls and German articles.

1881: He advertised that he made jointed bébés and dolls that came dressed in trousseaux of the latest fashion, or undressed; he also sold "swimmers," dolls' heads, and "coiffures."

**Blanche.** 1916. *Art Doll* distributed by *Strobel & Wilken.* It was a lifelike, indestructible character doll with painted hair and eyes; wore a mobcap and resembled *Käthe Kruse* dolls.

**Bland & Hawkes, M. J.** 1918. Surrey, England. Obtained a British patent for the articulation of the limbs on soft-bodied dolls.

**Blaurock, Ernst.** 1896–1925+. Neustadt, near Coburg, Thür. Made dolls of various types, including dressed dolls.

**Blay.** 1888. Obtained French patent for doll with movable head, arms, and legs.

**Blaydes, William Franklin J.** 1921–22. Assigned half of his U.S. design patent to *Lester H. Jacobson,* for a long-limbed doll representing a man with center-parted hair and ears that stuck out.

**Bleier Bros.** 1915. New York City. Made *Bee Bee* brand character dolls, including *Abe Kabibble.*

**Blink.** 1915–16. Made by *Horsman.* Represented one of the Gene Carr Kids in the Lady Bountiful cartoon series published in the NEW YORK WORLD.

1916: Horsman copyrighted the doll, naming the artist as *Bernard Lipfert,* and describing the doll as a boy laughing, with his eyes closed.

**Blinkie.** See **Blynkie.**

**Block Frères (Bros.).** 1862. Paris. Made bébés, dressed dolls, and trousseaux.

**Bloedel.** See **Fleischmann & Blödel.**

**Blondel Fils (Sons).** 1829–52. Paris. Made shoulder heads for dolls.

**Bloom, Charles, Inc.** 1919–25+. New York City. Registered *Emmylou* as his trademark in U.S. in 1921.

1925: Charles Bloom secured a patent for a rag-doll head made by superimposing a layer of cotton sheeting,

which constituted the face cloth, over two layers of buckram, which contained sizing for binding and stiffening when moisture, heat, and pressure between dies were applied. The resultant mask had features painted on it and a filling of cotton was added.

**Blue Bird Doll.** 1920–21. Made by *Horsman.* Represented a character in THE BLUE BIRD by Maurice Maeterlinck. Doll came in various sizes; price $2.50 up.

**Blue Bird Doll.** 1924. Made by *Arcy Toy Manufacturing Co.*

**Blue Eyes.** 1921. Rag dolls with bobbing heads made by *Century Doll Co.,* designed by *Grace Corry.*

**Blue Ribbon.** 1914–17. Line of jointed dolls made by *Carl Silverman*

1917: Blue Ribbon Baby was a character doll with bisque head; had sleeping eyes and either a light or dark hair wig. Came in five sizes, prices $1.00 to $6.00.

**Bluestocking Dolls, The.** 1917. Trademark, including a picture, was registered in Britain by John Green Hamley of *Hamley Bros.*

**Bluett, Thomas.** 1856. London. Made wax and composition dolls.

**Bluine Manufacturing Co.** 1921. Concord, Mass. Made walking and sleeping dolls.

**Blum, Charles B.** 1888–1925+. New York City. Was associated with various doll-making companies.

1917: He was with *Federal Doll Manufacturing Co.*

1919: He had his own company and made *Cee Bee* dolls of composition; then briefly he formed the partnership of Blum and Bates, which handled exclusively dolls of their own manufacture.

1924: Blum's company appears to have been the *Cee Bee Manufacturing Co.*

**Blum & Bates.** See **Blum, Charles B.**

**Blumenthal, C. L.** 1897. Berlin. Doll exporter.

**Blumhardt, Heinrich & Co.** 1891. Stuttgart, Württemberg. Made wooden dolls; had agents in most European capitals.

**Blum-Lustig Toy Co.** 1924–25. New York City. Doll manufacturers. It is not known whether or not this was one of the *Charles Blum* companies.

**Blynkie (Blinkie, Blynke).** 1919–20. Copyrighted by May B. Moran of the *Moran Doll Manufacturing Co.* Its successor in 1920 was the Western Doll Co. The artists are named in the copyright as A. Brymcardi and *Julius Benvenuti.* In 1920, Julius Benvenuti obtained a design patent for this doll, which had one eye almost closed and glanced to the side with the other eye. It was an all-composition doll of a cherub type, and came dressed or undressed.

**Bo Peep.** 1909. One of the dolls with *Life Like* (char-

BO-PEEP

AMERICAN

207

206. "Bo-Peep" all-celluloid molded doll with painted features. Mark: Ill. 207. H. 6½ inches. *Coleman Collection.*

207. Bo-Peep brand mark found on dolls.

acter) faces and *Can't Break 'Em* heads made by *Horsman;* price $1.25.

**Bo Peep.** 1909. *Art Fabric* cutout doll distributed by *Selchow & Righter;* size 20 by 27 inches.

**Bo Peep Brand.** 1917. Celluloid and composition, character dressed dolls made by the *Baby Outfitters.*

**Boase, Elizabeth.** 1914. London. Registered *The Soldier's Baby* as a trademark in Britain.

**Boatright, Lenore.** 1922–23. San Francisco, Cal. Registered *Goo-Goo* as a trademark in U.S.

**Bobbie Burns Lassies.** 1918. Dolls made by *Jessie McCutcheon Raleigh* and distributed by *Butler Bros.* They wore Scottish-type dresses, had wigs, and came in sizes 13½ inches costing $3.65 and 18½ inches costing $5.00.

**Bobbikins.** 1920. Advertised by *S. K. Novelty Co.;* height 6½ inches.

**Bobby.** 1910. Copyrighted by *Louis Amberg & Son.* The artist was said to be anonymous, but this doll was probably the one sold under the name *Bobby Blake,* by special arrangement with Grace G. Wiederseim (*Drayton*).

**Bobby.** 1910. Copyrighted by *Horsman.* Artist was *Helen Trowbridge.* It had painted hair and open mouth.

**Bobby Blake.** 1911. Line of dolls made by *Louis Amberg & Son,* by special arrangement, after designs by the artist and originator G. G. Wiederseim (*Drayton*). Came with unbreakable heads, face slightly wider than high, round Drayton-type eyes; in some dolls the tongue curled up from one corner of the mouth; with or without unbreakable hands; cork-stuffed pink sateen bodies. Retail price $1.00 up. (See also **Bobby.**)

**Bobby Bobbykins.** 1909–11. Trademark registered in U.S. by *Frank A. Hays* for a line of rag dolls that looked like the *Drayton* drawings.

1910: *Strawbridge & Clothier* was the exclusive wholesale distributor.

1911: Distributor was *The Dolly Co.,* which advertised that these dolls were "designed, made and patented by the author of the famous 'Bobby and Dolly' series"; probably one of the earliest dolls with eyes glancing to the side, except for *Brownies.* Price was 25¢, 50¢, and $1.00.

**Bobby Bright.** 1906. Cloth doll to be cut out and stuffed; made by *Horsman.* It came in three sizes, priced at 5¢, 10¢, and 25¢.

**Bobêche.** Empire period. Name of a doll dressed as a a clown.

**Bobette.** 1920. Copyrighted by May B. *Moran.* Cherub-type doll with wig, open mouth, and teeth.

**Boccheciampe.** 1925. Paris. Made cloth Art Dolls under the trade name *Maguy.*

**Bochet, Mlle.** 1914. Paris. Made dolls.

**Bochet, Mme.** 1920–21. Paris. Made dolls.

**Bodies of Dolls.** In the first half of the 19th century, most dolls' bodies were peg wooden, kid with wooden limbs, or cloth. A new type of body was introduced in the 1850's when *Motschmann* patented a doll with a firm hip section, cloth upper torso, and sometimes "floating" joints. This type of body, popular in the 1860's, was soon superseded by the many inventions relating to wooden and/or composition dolls' bodies, especially those of *Briens* in 1860, *Benoit Martin* in 1863, *Anqueulle* in 1865, *Lemonnier* in 1866, *Chevallier & Brasseur* in 1868, *Bru* in 1869, and *Charles Parent* in 1871. Some of these patents related not only to the type of joints but also to the composition of which the body was made. Great interest continued to focus on the construction of doll bodies during the 1870's and 1880's, both in Europe and America. In America patents were obtained by *Joel Ellis,* 1873; *Lacmann,* 1874; *Wesley Miller,* 1875; *Kimball Atwood,* 1877; *George Sanders,* 1880; *Lefferts & Carpenter,* 1881; *Lucinda Wishard* and *Sarah Robinson,* 1883; etc.

By the 1880's jointed composition bodies had begun to attain wide popularity, although many dolls through the 1920's continued to be made with kid and/or cloth bodies. Rivet joints for kid bodies were patented in the 1890's. During the first decade of the 20th century, bodies similar to those on Teddy bears and the bent-limb character baby body were introduced. The latter rivaled the ball-jointed composition body for many years. Later, attempts were made to combine the attributes of these two popular types into a body representing a toddler. During World War I the cloth body of the "walking" *Mama Doll* was introduced. When infant-type dolls came on the market, many of them had specially shaped cloth bodies.

It should be pointed out to collectors that it is often very difficult to detect whether the components of a doll as currently seen were originally together. A description by an author of her childhood rag doll, published in CHILDREN'S FRIEND of June, 1868, illustrates this problem: "At first Polly was a big rag-baby of plain linen with black marks for nose, eyes and mouth, then somebody cut her head off and replaced it with a plaster head which had bright rosy cheeks, dark eyes and

**208A & B.** Turned wooden, jointed body with bisque head and shoulder plate, flange swivel neck, glass eyes, and wig. Kid covers the chest area where the head joins the body. H. 14 inches. *Courtesy of Sylvia Brockmon.*

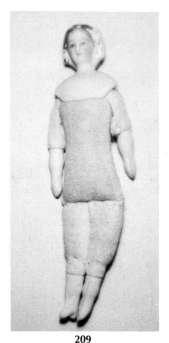 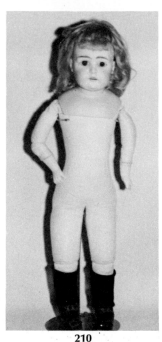

209                                    210

**209.** Untinted bisque head; hair is decorated with snood and feather. Cloth body and bisque arms typical of factory-made bodies. H. 4 inches. H. of shoulder head, 1 inch. *Courtesy of Dorothy Annunziato.*

**210.** Gusseted kid body with cloth lower legs and bisque lower arms; bisque shoulder head with teeth. H. 18 inches. H. of shoulder head, 5 inches. *Courtesy of Miss Fulmer.*

**211.** Doll with wooden torso and legs, composition arms, bisque head with black pupil-less glass eyes, open mouth with five upper teeth. Head mark: Ill. **212** incised; a raised "V" is at the base of the neck in the back. H. 9 inches. *Coleman Collection.*

211

**212.** Bisque doll's head mark.

1907
R/A   DEP
I 12/o

curling hair. One day a friend offered to make her some new shoes and stockings, but said her feet were too clumsy to fit nicely; so poor Polly's legs were amputated just above the knees. When the new limbs were added and the new shoes and stockings put on, her arms and hands did not seem to match; so off they came, and new arms, with hands in little kid gloves took their place. . . . She has had several heads in the course of her life, and her body has been newly covered once or twice." (See also **Baby Bodies; Cloth Bodies; Kid Bodies.**)

**Bo-Fair.** 1920–21, *Mutual Doll Co.*; 1921, *Metro Doll Co.*; 1922–25, *Cameo Doll Co.*

1920: Designed and copyrighted by *Joseph L. Kallus*; design of socket joints mentioned on the copyright.

1920–25: Distributed by *Borgfeldt*; named by Kallus after a character in a popular musical play. Kallus considered it to be one of his most artistic dolls. Bo-Fair represented a five-year-old girl; had molded hair or wig; 16 inches tall. Wigs and shoes were made by *Braitling*.

**Bogie Man.** 1902–3. Indestructible type of doll.

**Bohemia.** See **Czechoslovakia.**

**Böhm, Anton.** 1920–21. Nürnberg, Bavaria. Secured two German patents for doll wigs.

**Bohne.** See **Bahn, A. E.**

**Bohne, Ernst.** 1854+. Rudolstadt, Thür. Porcelain factory; one of the most likely candidates for the "E.B." marks found on bisque dolls' heads.

**Böhnke, Clara, & Zimmermann, Helene.** 1921–22. Königsberg, Prussia. Doll manufacturers; registered *Henny* as a trademark in Germany for dolls, dolls' bodies, dolls' wigs, and dolls' clothes.

**Boitel, Valmore.** 1887. France. Obtained a French patent for celluloid doll heads. He claimed that until then dolls' heads had been made of wood, papier-mâché, rubber, or bisque.

**Bollag, Léon.** 1923. Zurich, Switz. Registered *Goolagool* as a trademark in Britain for dolls.

**Bolshevik Doll.** 1922. Made in Russia and Paris, fabricated mostly of rubber with yellow stripes showing where the ribs would be. When a hidden spring was pressed, the doll curled up into a knot of about one-quarter its original size.

**Bonafé (Bonafie).** See **Bonnafé, P.**

**Bonin & Lefort (Société).** 1923. Paris. Registered trademarks *Ninon, Select,* and *Gaby* in France for dolls and dolls' heads.

**Bonnafé (Bonafé, Bonafie, Bonaffé), P.** 1876–84, Paris; 1885–95, successor was J. Cros.

1879: Bonnafé advertised that he made rose-cloth and kid-body dolls of all kinds.

**213.** Mark used by Ernst Bohne on bisque heads.

1885–90: Cros advertised that he made kid or cloth-body dolls, which had heads of bisque, porcelain, composition, rubber, or wood, and enamel eyes. His products were for domestic or export purposes. In 1890 he also advertised that he handled *Paris Bébé* made by *Danel & Cie.*

1892: Cros advertised kid-body dolls, rigid and jointed, "turning" heads, rose- and white-cloth bodies, *Parisienne Heads*, glazed china heads, and wigs. He also performed repairs.

1895: Cros advertised that he sold dolls with rose- or white-cloth bodies, as well as kid-body dolls; bébés with composition and bisque heads and enamel eyes.

**Bonnal, Claude Valéry.** 1898–1906. Factory at Vincennes, Seine; shop in Paris. Made indestructible bébés.

1904: He registered as trademarks in France *Bébé l'Unique, Bébé le Radieux, Bébé le Spécial, Bébé le Petit Français,* and *Bébé le Glorieux.*

**Bonneaud, Mme.** 1922. Paris. According to a contemporary account, she was the "Premier Artiste" of the *Société Française de Fabrication de Bébés et Jouets* at their factory on the rue de Picpus, with a score of assistants in her charge. Mme. Bonneaud was the creator and adapter of fashions for the dolls. She made the patterns out of buckram, and each pattern was given a number. Each model was scrutinized and, if approved, was then sent to the production department, where it was turned out in quantity. The dolls' wardrobes were made of the finest silks, linens, and laces, and in styles that would arouse the envy of any woman. The machinery used to make the clothes was almost identical with that found in clothing factories in America.

**Bonnefond, Claude.** 1921. France. Secured a French patent for a two-faced doll with one face smiling and one face sad.

**Bonnet Dolls (Dolls With Hoods).** These were dolls with molded bonnets or hats, usually made of *stone bisque*. In 1860, *Danjard* was granted a French patent for the decoration of dolls' heads with bonnets.

1890: Dolls with bisque hats were advertised in sizes 8 and 11 inches, costing 43¢ and 85¢ doz. wholesale.

1894: Dolls with fancy hoods were advertised in sizes 8½ and 12 inches, costing 39¢ doz. and up, wholesale.

1901: *Marguerite Dolls* were advertised having bisque heads with butterfly, cloverleaf, and flower-design headdresses.

1905: *Butler Bros.* advertised fancy bonnet dolls with bisque heads, china limbs, and cloth bodies; size 7¾ inches; priced 37¢ doz. wholesale.

1911: *Louis Amberg & Son* made a composition-headed baby with a molded bonnet.

1912: *Schoenhut* in wood and *Gebrüder Heubach* in bisque made dolls with similar type of bonnets.

1915–16: *Morimura Bros.* made bonnet dolls.

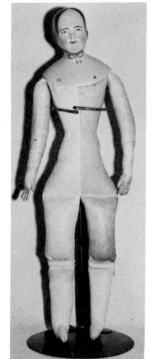

I H

O

214C. Mark appearing on head of doll in 214A & B.

215

216

**214A & B.** Deeply flesh-tinted china head with brick-red bonnet trimmed with green; leather body has one leg and half the torso in one piece. Note the shape of shoulder piece. H. 13½ inches. H. of shoulder head, 3¼ inches. *Courtesy of Sylvia Brockmon.*

**215.** China head with molded white cap decorated in red and blue, blond hair, brown mustache, blue eyes. *Photograph by Winnie Langley.*

**216.** Untinted bisque head with molded yellow "straw" hat trimmed with a pink feather and blue and gold rosette. Molded brown hair and blue eyes. *Courtesy of Peg Gregory; photograph by Winnie Langley.*

217

218

219

**217.** Wax bonnet head with mohair under the brim of the hat; black glass eyes. *Courtesy of Gladyse Hilsdorf; photograph by Winnie Langley.*

**218.** Wax-over-composition head wearing blue wax bonnet with white plume; hair is glued to the wax beneath the hat.

Glass eyes, hand-sewn cloth body, wooden upper arms and legs. H. 21 inches. *Courtesy of Josephine Garrison.*

**219.** Wax-over-papier-mâché head has molded bonnet with blonde lace; glass eyes; pierced ears. *Courtesy of Gladyse Hilsdorf; photograph by Winnie Langley.*

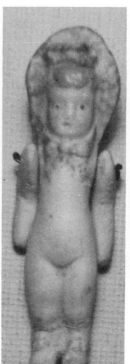

222

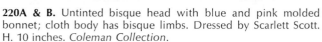

**220A & B.** Untinted bisque head with blue and pink molded bonnet; cloth body has bisque limbs. Dressed by Scarlett Scott. H. 10 inches. *Coleman Collection.*

**221.** Small all-bisque bonneted doll with jointed arms. Pink bonnet, painted features. H. 1³/₄ inches. *Coleman Collection.*

**222.** Untinted bisque bonnet doll with molded yoke and painted features; cloth body. H. 12 inches. H. of shoulder head, 3 inches. *Courtesy of Edith Meggers.*

221

**223A & B.** Untinted bisque shoulder head with painted features and molded cap, yoke, and cross on chain. Black hair, blue cap. Contemporary provincial costume to go with cap. H. 8 inches. H. of shoulder head, 1³/₄ inches. *Courtesy of Josephine Garrison.*

223 A

B

**224.** Bisque head with molded tam-o'-shanter and yoke, painted features. Body is cloth, lower limbs china. Ca. 1893. H. 15 inches. H. of shoulder head, 4 inches. *Courtesy of Edith Meggers.*

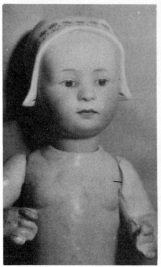
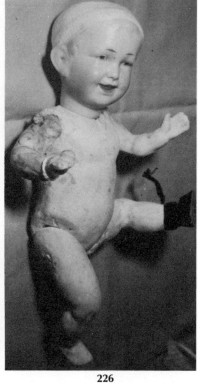

225 226

**225.** Gebrüder Heubach bisque head with molded bonnet that has holes for tying ribbons; intaglio painted eyes. Jointed composition baby body. *Courtesy of Margaret Whitton; photograph by Winnie Langley.*

**226.** Bisque-headed character baby with molded white cap, blue intaglio eyes. Marked "RA." Composition baby body. *Courtesy of Margaret Whitton; photograph by Winnie Langley.*

**Bonvoisin, Louis Herman.** 1907–8. Berviers, Belgium. Obtained three German patents for jointed dolls.

**Bonwit, Carol, & Bonwit, Lester R.** 1920. Baltimore, Md. Were granted a design patent for an all-bisque doll that looked like *Tiss Me*.

**Boobrig Co.** 1924. New York City. Displayed dolls at the Toy Fair.

**Bo-Peep.** See **Bo Peep.**

**Bo-Peep Brand.** See **Bo Peep Brand.**

**Borcherdt, Richard, & Bergman, Henry.** 1865. Thompkinsville, N.Y. Obtained a U.S. patent for a composition to be used in making bodies for little dolls. The ingredients were sugar or honey, glycerine, and powdered chalk.

**Borel & Soeur (Sister).** See **Botel & Soeur.**

**Borgfeldt, Geo., & Co.** 1881–1925+. New York City, 1881+; Toronto, 1882+; Hannover, Germany, 1882; London, 1886+; Paris, 1886+; Berlin, 1886+; Fürth, Bavaria, 1886+; Sonneberg, Thür. 1887+; Vienna, etc. Doll importer and manufacturer. It is not known whether the "G. B." found on bisque heads stands for George Borgfeldt or not.

George Borgfeldt began working in the commission business in New York City in 1865, and rose to be a managing partner in the firm *Strasburger, Pfeiffer & Co.* by 1880. He conceived the idea of assembling in New York examples of the best European dolls manufactured, and booking orders through the display of these samples. With Marcell and Joseph L. Kahle, also of Strasburger, Pfeiffer & Co., a co-partnership was formed January 1, 1881, and named Geo. Borgfeldt & Co. The business grew rapidly, and soon branch offices were opened in Canada and all over Europe. George Borgfeldt resigned from the presidency of the company in 1900 and was succeeded by Marcell Kahle, who died in 1909. Before he died, George Kolb was the vice president and *Fred Kolb* was the manager of the doll department, a job he had held for some years. Later Fred Kolb became president.

There seems to be little doubt about Borgfeldt's having fulfilled his aim of handling many of the finest dolls manufactured abroad. Before World War I the firm had exclusive American and Canadian rights on *Kestner* dolls, *Kämmer & Reinhardt, Handwerck, Steiff, Käthe Kruse, Bushow & Beck,* and *Karl Standfuss,* and the dolls of many other German manufacturers were handled by Borgfeldt. The name Geo. Borgfeldt & Co. was included in the list of Sonneberg doll manufacturers who won a Grand Prize at the St. Louis Exposition in 1904. The bisque heads on their dolls were made by such famous factories as *Simon & Halbig, Armand Marseille, Kling,* and *Alt, Beck & Gottschalck.* Geo. Borgfeldt & Co. did not neglect American-made dolls. They were distributors for the following companies:

1903: *Metal Doll Co., All Steel* doll.
1903+: *Mary Foote: Fairyland Rag Doll.*
1905: *Dreamland Doll Co.: Dreamland Rag Doll.*
1909–10: *Aetna Doll & Toy Co.: Can't Break 'Em dolls.* (This was before the company merged with *Horsman.*)
1913: *Bay Ridge Toy Co.*
1913+: *Tip Top Toy Co.: Kewpies.*
1914: *Arnoldt Doll Dress Co.: Blue Bird Doll Clothes.*
1916–18: *Rex Doll Co.: Kewpies, Bundie Dolls.*
1916–25+: *K & K Toy Co.;* owned and controlled by Borgfeldt.
1918: *American Toy & Manufacturing Co.: Snow White.*
1920: *Mutual Doll Co.: Kewpies, Bundie, Bo-Fair.*
1921: *Metro Doll Co.: Kewpies, Bo-Fair, Vanitie Doll.*
1922–25+: *Cameo Doll Co.: Kewpies, Bye-Lo Baby, Baby Bo-Kaye.*
1925: *American Stuffed Novelty Co.*
1925: *Sol Bergfeld & Son: Story Book Dolls.*

In 1916 and during World War I, Borgfeldt distributed dolls made in Japan.

The designs for dolls were often made and owned by distributors, who then engaged manufacturers. Fred Kolb designed several dolls, but Geo. Borgfeldt & Co. also used the services of many fine artists for designing their dolls, as shown in the following list:

1912–25: *Joseph L. Kallus:* numerous designs.

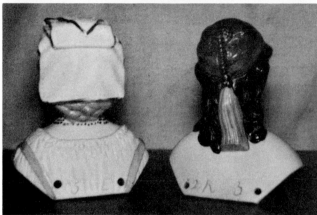

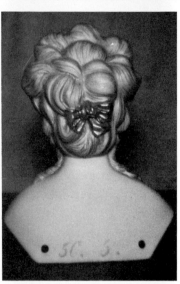

**227.** Two groups of dolls handled by Borgfeldt. The earlier group of bisque heads, shown in the small photographs here, was given to the Museum of the City of New York by Fred Kolb of Borgfeldt. All these heads have molded hair and decorations; some have painted eyes and some have glass; some have pierced ears and some do not. The letters and numbers on the back of the shoulders appear to indicate the mold identification. In the photograph showing two heads, from left to right the marks read: "5E," "2K3." The head with the molded collar and tie is marked "5M5." The doll with the comb across the front of the head is marked "G." The one with the bow in back is marked "5C5." The first two are 4 inches; the "5M5" is 4½ inches, and the last three are 5 inches high.

The later group (see top of page 88) shows dolls advertised in *Playthings,* January 1908. *Heads, courtesy of the Museum of the City of New York. Advertisement, courtesy of McCready Publishing Co.*

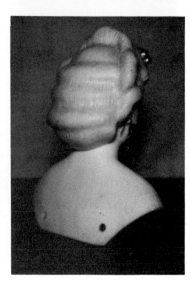

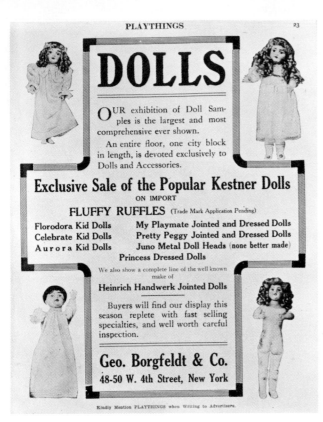

(See caption **227**.)

**228**                                    **229**

**230**                                    **231**

**228–231.** Marks probably belonging to George Borgfeldt. No. **228** is the Borgfeldt trademark. Nos. **229, 230,** and **231** are found on Armand Marseille heads that were probably made for Borgfeldt.

1912–25: *Rose O'Neill:* Kewpie, *Scootles.*

1914: *Kate Jordan: Happifats.*

1914: *Grace G. Drayton: September Morn.*

1916: Helen Nyce: *Flossie Fisher.*

1918–19: *Genevieve Pfeffer: Splashme, Com-A-Long.*

1918–19: Henry Mayer: Tiss-Me, Tumble-Bo.

1919: *Bertha Oscher: Impie.*

1919–20: *Jeno Juszko:* Tiss-Me, Lotta Sun, Poutie (these were figurines rather than dolls); *Winkie.*

1922–23: *Grace Storey Putnam:* Bye-Lo Baby.

1923: *Gene Byrnes: Reg'lar Fellers.*

1923–25: *Madame Georgene Averill: Mme. Georgene line,* many creations.

1925: *Joseph Kallus* and *Jack Collins: Little Annie Rooney.*

All the above except Flossie Fisher were copyrighted as dolls unless otherwise specified.

Borgfeldt was the assignee of two United States patents, both taken out by members of the Steiner family of Sonneberg. The first was the fur eyebrow patent of *Louis Steiner* in 1910. These were used on dolls made by Kestner. The second was *Albin Steiner's* 1914 patent on a crying doll that would emit a long slow cry.

The Borgfeldt firm seems to have been engaged in many lawsuits. In 1905 they won a libel case against the American Protective Tariff League. In 1911 they were sued by *Elizabeth Lesser* for an alleged copyright infringement; Borgfeldt won the suit. There were at least three suits over alleged copying of Kewpies. Rose O'Neill lost the case to *Hecht,* but won against *Cinquini* in *1918* and *Haber Bros.* in 1921. Borgfeldt owned exclusive rights to Kewpies. Although there appear to have been no actual court cases involving the Bye-Lo Baby, there was strong feeling expressed in advertisements regarding the similarity between the Bye-Lo and *Amberg's New Born Babe* copyrighted in 1914.

Some of the best-known dolls distributed by Borgfeldt have been named above, but there were also the *Minerva* line in 1894 and *Alma* in 1900, as well as the following dolls' names registered as trademarks. The dates given are the earliest known for each country.

**Born, Jean & Co.** See **Thieck, Francis.**

**Börner, Martin.** 1898. Oberneubrunn, Thür. Manufactured dolls.

**Börner, Reinhardt.** 1918. Oberneubrunn, Thür. Manufactured dolls.

**Börner, Richard.** 1909. Oberneubrunn, Thür. Manufactured dolls.

**Börner, Rud.** 1898. Oberneubrunn, Thür. Manufactured dolls.

**Bornoz, Léon.** 1895–ca. 1903, Paris; ca. 1904–ca. 1907, successor was Lucas; ca. 1907–10, successor was *P. Brunet.* They made indestructible bébés, dolls, dolls' heads, wigs, and footwear for dolls, and did repairs.

**Borreau.** 1878–1925+. Paris. 1878–ca. 1889, J. (I. or G.) Borreau; ca. 1890, Widow Borreau was the successor; ca.

# Trademarks Registered by Borgfeldt

| DATE* | GERMANY | UNITED STATES | ENGLAND | FRANCE |
|---|---|---|---|---|
| 1895 | | Celebrate | | |
| 1897 | Princess<br>Elsie | | | |
| 1898 | The International Doll | | | |
| 1899 | Uwanta | Uwanta | | |
| 1900 | Alma | | | |
| 1901 | Florodora | | | |
| 1903 | My Playmate | | | |
| 1904 | | Juno | | |
| 1905 | Tootsie | Florodora | | |
| 1906 | | Kidlyne | | |
| 1907 | Celebrate, Baby Belle | My Playmate | | |
| 1908 | | My Dearie | | |
| 1909 | Irvington | | | |
| 1910 | | Pansy Doll | | |
| 1911 | Little Bright Eyes | | | |
| 1912 | My Girlie | Little Bright Eyes | | |
| 1913 | Dotty<br>Happifat<br>Prize Baby | My Girlie<br>Happifat<br>Cubist<br>Peero<br>Butterfly | Kewpie | Kewpie |
| 1914 | Nobbikid | Prize Baby<br>September Morn Doll<br>Mamma's Angel Child<br>Bettijak | | |
| 1915 | | Nobbikid<br>Rastus<br>Skating Charlotte | | |
| 1917 | | Preshus<br>Em-Boss-O<br>Hollikid | | |
| 1918 | | | | Kewpie |
| 1919 | | | Winkie | |
| 1920 | Flossie Fisher's<br>Own Doll | Com-A-Long | | Winkie<br>Hollikid |
| 1921 | Com-A-Long<br>Pansy<br>Teenie Weenie | | | |
| 1922 | Mimi<br>Daisy<br>Betsy<br>Reg'lar Fellers<br>The Skipper | | | |
| 1923 | Happy Hooligan | Bye-Lo Baby<br>Daisy Doll<br>Rosemarie | | Bedtime<br>Nifty<br>Happy Hooligan |
| 1924 | | Felix<br>Bringing Up Father<br>Whatsamatter | | |
| 1925 | Ko-Ko<br>Little Annie Rooney | Ko-Ko<br>Little Annie Rooney | Little Annie Rooney | |

* Date when *trademark* first appeared in the records that have been found.

1895, Bijard was the successor; ca. 1900–ca. 1920, Paillard was the successor and called the firm Borreau-Paillard; 1921–25, G. Velter was the successor.

1880's: Borreau advertised jointed *bather* dolls, as well as dressed *bébés incassables* and "unbreakable" Russian heads for bébés. He specialized in dolls' clothes for domestic consumption and export. He received an Honorable Mention for his dolls at the Paris Exposition of 1878. Bijard and Paillard advertised dressed *mignonettes* as well as dolls.

1925: Velter advertised mignonettes.

**Borthwick, Jessica.** 1917. London. Registered in Britain the trademark *Nellfoy* for dolls and dolls' dresses.

**Bortnik, Jacob.** 1915–17. Philadelphia. Listed under dolls.

**Bortnik, Etienne.** 1883–1925+. Factory at Avon, S. et M.; shop in Paris. He specialized in natural hair wigs for dolls and bébés, made fixed or sleeping eyes, with or without eyelashes, as well as other articles for repairing dolls.

1924: Registered his eight-pointed star trademark in France.

**Boston Pottery Co.** 1920–25+. Boston, Mass. Bisque dolls' heads marked with initials "B. P. D. Co." and "Made in Boston, Mass.//U.S.A." were probably made by this factory.

**Botel (Borel) & Soeur (Sister).** 1855–58. Paris. Made dolls in wood, papier-mâché, kid, or linen.

**Böttcher, Frau H.** 1909. Berlin. Made dolls.

**Boucher.** 1860–89. Paris. 1885–89, Widow Boucher was listed. In the early years Boucher advertised dolls' bodies, and later only dolls.

**Bouchet, A.** 1851. London. Was awarded an Honorable Mention at the London Exhibition for "Her Majesty's representation of the Great Exhibition with moving figures and various dolls."

**Bouchet, Ad.** 1889–98. Paris. Won a silver medal at the 1889 Paris Exposition, and gold medals at Paris in 1895, Rouen in 1896, and Brussels in 1897. The trade names of some of his dolls were *Bébé Géant, Gentil Bébé, Bébé Tête Mobile, Bébé Parlant, Bébé Dormeur, Le Séduisant,* etc.

1894: Obtained a French patent for a new method of mounting dolls' heads and limbs.

In 1903 the *Société Française de ·Fabrication de Bébés et Jouets* registered in France Le Séduisant as one of their trademarks. This fact suggests that Ad. Bouchet probably had become a member of the S. F. B. J. by 1903.

A small bisque socket head with black pupil-less glass eyes, open mouth, and four upper teeth has the following incised on the back of the neck:

A·D
BOUCHET
O

**Bouffard.** See **Marchal, Ed.**

**Bouis, Mme.** 1866–70. Paris. Made dolls.

**Boulouch (Bouloch), Mme., & LaPorte.** 1934–90's, Paris; 1876–81, Deltour, successor; 1882–90's, A. Cassanet & Cie., successor. Made dolls.

1847: Mme. Boulouch & Widow LaPorte advertised, "Dolls made with rose kid bodies and either French or German heads. Assorted dolls' heads and French or German dressed dolls." After 1847, the Widow LaPorte appears to have carried on the business alone for some years.

1880: Deltour made dolls of fine kid and dressed dolls.

1882: Cassanet advertised dolls and bébés dressed in the costumes of provincial peasants.

1889: Advertised dressed dolls and bébés.

**Boult, Wade & Tennant.** 1913–24. London. Agents for *Horsman, Hermann Steiner,* and others.

**Bound, Harry Joseph.** 1895–99. London. Distributed dolls.

**Bour.** 1892. Obtained French patent for improvements in making dolls.

**Bourgoin (Bourgoine).** Ca. 1880's–90's. Name found on bisque heads, especially the wire-eyed Steiner and other *Jules Steiner* heads. Name also found on bisque heads of lady dolls, among them a painted-eye bisque head on a wooden body.

**Bouton, Dewitt C.** 1899. Ithaca, N.Y. Obtained a design patent for a *topsy turvy* doll with one head white and one Negro.

**Bouton, J., & Co.** 1919–25. New York City. Distributed Jay-Bee brand of dolls, which included *Baby Phyllis, Bouton's Dancing Girls, Peter Pan Doll, Baby Bunting,* etc. They imported fully jointed and character dolls from France, Germany, and other countries.

**Bouton's Dancing Girls.** 1923. Handled by *J. Bouton & Co.* They were not mechanical dolls but were dressed in Follies-type costumes. They had bisque heads and sleeping eyes.

**Boutons dans l'Oreille.** See **Button in Ear.**

**Bouvet, Simonne.** 1922–23. New York City. Registered *Dad's Doll* as a trademark in U.S.

**Bouvier.** 1889–90. Paris. Doll maker.

**Bowden, Junius Powell.** See **Rouech-Bowden Co.**

AB
232

ᶜ STEINER    BSGDG
ᶜ BOURGOIN
233

**232.** A. Bouchet mark; it should be noted that several porcelain manufacturers used similar marks.

**233.** "Bourgoin" mark found on dolls.

**Bowden, Louise M.** 1893. Newark, N.J. Secured U.S. patent for a rag doll pattern blank. The rounded head was made in four pieces of stamped flesh-colored fabric with features and hair marked on it.

**Bowie, Harold D.** 1921–25. Mahwah, N.J. Assigner to *Horsman* of a U.S. patent that he secured for a walking toddler's body jointed at shoulder and hips.

**Bowman, Geo. H., Co.**  See **Hamburger & Co.**

**Boxwood.** Ca. 1900. Material of which some Parisian dolls were made.

**Boy Blue.** 1909. *Art Fabric* cutout rag doll distributed by *Selchow & Righter;* size 20 by 27 inches.

**Boy Scout.** 1913. Made by *Horsman,* mate of *Camp Fire Girl.*

**Boy Scout.** 1916. *Art Doll;* distributed by *Strobel & Wilken.* It was a character-type doll with painted hair and eyes.

**Boy Scout.** 1918. Made by *Faultless Rubber Co.* All-rubber doll with molded clothes; came in tan or red.

**Boy Scout Doll.** 1918. Made by *Wigwam Co.* Had painted hair and eyes, 16 inches tall; price $12.00 doz. wholesale.

**Boy with Cap, Model No. 12.** 1911. Copyrighted by *Louis Amberg & Son* and advertised in PLAYTHINGS.

**Boyd, Leora.** 1917. Los Angeles, Calif. Secured a U.S. design patent for a crying papoose with tears on cheeks.

**Bradley & Galzenati.** 1913–17. London. Made dolls' heads.

**Braitling, Charles F.** 1869–1900, Bridgeport, Conn.; 1900–25+, Frederick K. Braitling succeeded his father. They were one of the largest manufacturers of dolls' bodies and dolls' shoes in the world. Later they made wigs and other dolls' articles. The kid or muslin bodies were stuffed with Sea Island cotton, which was noted for its cleanliness; its long fibers helped the body retain its shape. The muslin bodies were made of Dwight Anchor Brand muslin and came in various sizes. The dolls' shoes came in many styles and in twenty-two different sizes from less than a half-inch to nearly 5 inches long.

1902: Kid bodies were made in sizes 1 to 20 and measured 8 to 28 inches in height. The Braitling bodies of this era were made with two rows of stitching where the legs joined the torso, and there was also a row of stitching across the top of the foot.

1916: By this time Braitling had discontinued the manufacture of doll bodies. As the demand for his kid and cloth bodies diminished, he had begun to make other doll accessories such as stockings, and in 1909 had begun to make real hair wigs in blond, brown, tosca, and auburn.

1918: By this time, he had purchased the patent rights and machinery for making *Dolly Dimples Doll Elastic,* used for stringing jointed composition-body dolls. *Cameo*

*Doll Co.* used wigs and shoes made by Braitling on many of their dolls.

**Brandenstein, Benjamin.** 1867. New York City. Made dolls.

**Brandes, E. L.** 1895. Hannover, Prussia. Made dressed dolls.

**Brandl, Resi.** 1923–24. Berlin. Registered *Bufli* as a trademark in Germany for dolls. Also used the initials "R.B."

**Brandner, Hermann & Co.** 1922–25. Sonneberg, Thür. Manufactured dolls; distributor in New York was *Roth, Baitz & Lipsitz.* Specialized in baby dolls that moved their heads, eyes, and arms, and said "Mama" and "Papa."

**Brasch, H.** 1918–25+. Berlin. Manufactured dolls.

**Brass.** 1888–1901+. Material used by *Buschow & Beck* for dolls' heads.

1919: Material used by *Art Metal Works* to make *Treat 'Em Rough Kiddies.* The stamped brass was enameled, and the dolls had movable joints.

**Brasseur & Videlier.** 1865–82. Paris. Made dolls. (An earlier *Videlier* was listed as making dolls in 1829.)

1867: They advertised dressed and undressed bébés, as well as ordinary, fine, and jointed dolls.

1868: Brasseur & Chevallier (his position in the firm is not known) obtained a French patent for a composition-bodied doll made of sawdust and glue as an imitation of wood. The body was to be painted or varnished or covered with linen; the legs and arms were to be made of the above composition or of bisque or porcelain.

1879–82: Brasseur & Videlier specialized in fine jointed dolls and dolls of carved wood.

**Brauer, Justus, & Son, Co.** 1922–23. Philadelphia, Pa. Registered *Flo-To* in U.S. as a trademark for dolls.

**Braun, Hugo.**  See **Cellulobrin.**

**Braun, Ludwig.** 1905. Leipzig, Saxony. Obtained German patent for neck joint on dolls.

**Braun, W.** 1918. Nürnberg, Bavaria. Manufactured dolls.

**Braune & Breitenfeld.** 1882. Waltershausen, Thür. Made papier-mâché dolls.

**Brauner, Gustav.** 1899–1921. Vienna. Made dolls and dolls' heads.

**Brauner, Therese.** 1899. Vienna. Made dolls and dolls' heads.

**Braunschmidt, Max.** 1895–1909. Neustadt near Coburg, Thür. Made dressed dolls.

**Breadcrumbs.** Material used for making dolls.

1860: Widow *Poncet & Mlle.* Poncet obtained a French patent for making dolls of breadcrumbs.

1907: Breadcrumb dolls made in Ecuador.

*Bernard Ravca* later made dolls of breadcrumbs.

**Breast Plate Dolls' Heads.** Term used by American manufacturers for a head with shoulders attached. (See also **Bust Heads.**)

**Breiner Doll & Toy Co. (Breiner Doll Heads Inc.).** 1923–24. New York City. Made dolls' heads for *Mama Dolls*, as well as arms and legs. The heads came in sizes for dolls of 10 to 30 inches.

**Brelaz, F.** 1865–84. Paris. In 1885, Lanée was successor; made kid-body dolls and bébés.

**Brenner, M. & H.** 1898. Leipzig, Saxony. Distributed dolls.

**Breslaur, Louis.** 1918. Berlin. Manufactured dolls.

**Bretschneider, G.** 1909–25+. Neustadt near Coburg, Thür. Manufactured dolls and *Täuflinge.*

**Breveté (Bté.).** French word for "patented (patentee)." Bté. is the abbreviated form of the word.

**Briaux, G.** 1889. Paris. Made dolls.

**Brick Top Twins.** 1912. Had unbreakable composition heads. Red-haired character dolls with large stationary eyes, wide apart, called "Wall-Eyed Dolls," which cost 50¢.

**Bride.** 1919. Doll made by *New Toy Co.*, handled by *Hitz, Jacobs.* It came with a human hair wig and had a bridesmaid doll to go with it.

**Bridget.** 1907. Name of a rag doll made by *Art Fabric Mills.*

**Bridget.** 1911. Name of doll made by *Seligman and Braun.*

**Brieger & Co.** 1895. Breslau, Silesia. Made doll bodies of leather and of cloth. Specialized in ball-jointed bodies in leather.

**Briegleb, Adolf.** 1909–18. Nürnberg, Bavaria. Handled dolls.

**Briens.** 1860–62. Paris. Was granted two French patents for dolls' joints. The 1860 patent was for a rubber doll head with enamel eyes and invisible joints. The arms were joined to the papier-mâché body with wooden rings.

1862: Patent was for a doll's head that rolled on a hemisphere inside the neck so that the head could move in all directions. The heads were to be made of varnished or enameled metal with enamel eyes. Mlle. *Huret* had patented a swivel neck for porcelain dolls in 1861.

**Bright Baby Doll.** 1918. Distributed by *Robert Simpson Co.;* had composition baby body; 15-inch size cost $2.29.

**Bright Eyes.** 1898. Distributed by *W. A. Cissna & Co.* Had bisque head, teeth, kid body with scalloped edge; size 12½ inches cost $2.00 doz. wholesale.

**Bright Eyes.** 1912. Laughing baby doll made by *Louis Amberg & Son;* had short baby hair painted by an airbrush.

**Brighto.** 1914. Trademark registered in U.S. by *Strobel & Wilken;* used for "bisque china" dolls.

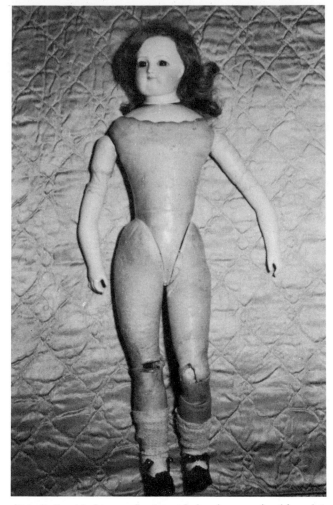

**234.** Doll with bisque flange-neck head on a shoulder plate, and a body that in construction seems to follow the Briens patent of 1860. *Courtesy of Gladyse Hilsdorf; photograph by Winnie Langley.*

**Bringing Up Father.** 1924. Trademark registered in U.S. by *Borgfeldt* and used on dolls of wood, stuffed textile fabrics, oilcloth, etc. Probably used for *Maggie and Jiggs* made by *Schoenhut.*

**Bringlee Doll.** 1919. Trademark registered in Britain by *Models (Leicester) Ltd.,* who made "unbreakable" dolls.

**Brinsley, W. H., & Brinsley, E. R.** 1920. Obtained a British patent for doll joints.

**Brintnall, Leslie Clark.** 1919–20. Los Angeles, Calif. Registered *Sunny-Twin* as a trademark in U.S.

**Bristol, Emma L.** 1886–1900. Providence, R.I. Made composition dolls' heads with real hair. "Bristol's Unbreakable Doll" appears on a label on the front of shoulder head dolls. PLAYTHINGS, July, 1903, mentioned a doll maker in Rhode Island who had made dolls for forty years, which they described as "aristocrats in pink silk, with blue eyes and real hair, sailor boys and red coated soldiers." There was a very large wig factory in Providence, and Emma Bristol was the only doll maker in the area who has

BRISTOL'S UNBREAKABLE DOLL
273 HIGH St. PROVIDENCE, R.I.

235. Label on Emma Bristol's dolls.

been found as yet to fit the description. If this did refer to her, she was engaged in making dolls for a longer period than the directories indicate.

**Britannia Toy Co.** 1921–25. London. Made dolls.

**British Dolls.** See **English Dolls.**

**British Novelty Works, Ltd.** 1915. London. Registered as a trademark in Britain a picture of a bulldog's head with the initials "B.N.W." to be used for dolls.

**British Products Manufacturing Co.** 1919-21. London. Made composition and other types of dolls.

**British Rag Doll Co.** 1913. London. Made rag dolls.

**British Textile Novelty Co.** 1917–25. London. Made rag dolls.

**British Tommy.** 1917–18. Doll made by *Horsman*.

**British Toy Agency.** 1916–ca. 1920, London; 1921–25+, *Victor Baumann* was successor. They distributed dolls.

**Brix, Mlle.** 1878. Copenhagen, Denmark. Exhibited dolls in national costume at the Paris Exposition.

**Brock, William.** 1873–74. New York City. Obtained a patent relating to the use of fabrics for the manufacture of hollow dolls' heads by pressing leather into molds and stiffening it with a backing of woven fabric saturated with glue.

**Brodbeck, Heppet.** 1873. Paris. Distributor for dolls made by *Louis Lindner & Son*.

**Brogden, James.** 1843–48. London. Made composition dolls.

**Broncho Bill (Billy).** 1914–15. Western cowboy-type doll made by *Ideal Novelty & Toy Co.*

**Bronx Doll Manufacturing Co.** 1920. New York City. Made hands for dolls in fourteen sizes.

**Brooman, Richard Archibald.** 1848–58. London. Secured U.S. patent (1848) and British patent (1858) for making doll heads from gutta-percha by molding, stamping, or embossing.

**Brophey Doll Co.** 1917. Toronto, Canada. Made *Madame Hendren* dolls in Canada.

**Brother.** 1912. Composition-head doll made by *Gund Manufacturing Co.*

**Brother, Model No. 2.** 1911. Doll copyrighted by *Louis Amberg & Son.*

**Brotteig (Taig).** German name for a malleable mixture of rye flour, glue, and water from which dolls were molded. The mixture had the consistency of dough and was pressed into molds. Its use at the end of the 18th century for dolls' bodies revolutionized the industry, according to PLAYTHINGS, February, 1908. It was still used in the 20th century.

**Brouillet (Broullet) & Cacheleux.** 1842–56. Paris. Made and distributed dressed and undressed dolls. Cacheleux was listed as a toy merchant as early as 1811. In 1842, Brouillet & Cacheleux distributed French and German toys, especially rubber goods.

1844: Brouillet exhibited dolls at the Paris Exposition and received an Honorable Mention award. The report of the exposition stated that Brouillet made dolls so well constructed that they could stand upright without support of sticks; these dolls could easily be dressed and undressed so that little girls could learn to cut out and sew dolls' clothes.

1856: Brouillet obtained a French patent for making dolls of a mixture of papier-mâché and resins or oils to form a plastic and resistant substance.

**Brown, Daisy G.** 1913. Challis, Idaho. Obtained a U.S. patent for the neck joining of a shoulder-type doll head.

**Brown, Edward C.** 1921. Cincinnati, Ohio. (He was a British subject.) Copyrighted a cherub-type doll with real hair named *Girlie.*

**Brown Skin Dolls.** 1922. Trade name used by *Century Doll Co.*

**Browne, Mayotta.** 1922–24. San Francisco, Calif. Registered trademark in U.S. of a doll holding streamers on which was printed *Otsy-Totsy-Dolls*. Initials "M. B." also on trademark. Browne obtained a design patent for a rag doll with yarn hair.

**Browne, Thomas.** 1899. London. Secured a British patent for a rag doll. The head, torso, and limbs were of sateen, calico, or other textile, stuffed with disinfected flock or wool. The eyes were made of earthenware upholstery buttons, sewed through white linen disks. The lips and teeth were made with woolen stitches. A strip of fur formed the hair.

**Brownie.** 1920–22. U.S. design patent obtained by *Frae C. Hamill.*

**Brownie Policeman.** 1905. Fully jointed doll covered with wool and silk plush and stuffed with cork. Distributed by *Hamburger & Co.*

**Brownies.** 1892–1907. Dolls based on the copyrighted figures of *Palmer Cox*. The words "Copyright 1892 by Palmer Cox" appear on the rear of the right foot of each of the cutout rag Brownie dolls. There were twelve different dolls to a yard of goods, made in colors by the *Arnold Print Works*, which sold for 20¢. They were *Chinaman, Dude, German, Highlander, Indian, Irishman, Soldier, Sailor, John Bull, Uncle Sam, Canadian*, and *Policeman*. Each doll was about 7 inches tall and had a front and back to be cut out, sewed together, and stuffed with cotton, bran, or sawdust. Brownies were also made in bisque, composition, cloth and chamois on a wire base, and other materials.

1895: Both men and lady Brownies manufactured by several firms; had heads of brown, undressed kid, wire arms and legs covered with stockinet; sometimes dressed in silk, satin, calico, or crepe paper.

1897: Brownie dolls of papier-mâché were distributed by the *John D. Zernitz Co.* These were jointed at the shoulders and hips, and the two larger sizes also had turning heads; sizes 5, 9¼, and 12 inches; prices $1.90, $4.00, and $8.00 doz. wholesale.

1902–3: Two girls brought from London the idea of having Brownies' arms and legs wired so they would stay in any position in which they were placed.

1907: New-type Brownies were made in Chicago with metal legs and arms that could be bent into innumerable positions; retail price $3.00 doz. When *Kewpies* appeared in 1913, they were advertised as having a meaning to children similar to the meaning Brownies had had years ago.

 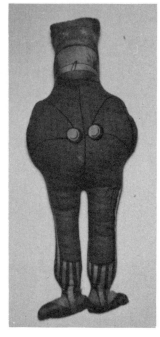

**236A & B.** A Palmer Cox Brownie doll representing "Uncle Sam." Front and back views of the two-piece rag doll. Copyright date 1892 is on the sole of the foot. Mark III. **237.** H. 7½ inches. *Courtesy of Ollie Leavister.*

Copyrighted. 1892
by PALMER COX

**237.** Mark used on foot of cloth Brownies.

**Bru (Bru Jne. & Cie).** 1866–99, Paris and Montreuil-sous-Bois, France. 1866–83, Casimir Bru Jeune; 1883–89, H. Chevrot; 1890–99, Paul Eugène Girard; 1899–1925+, *Société Française de Fabrication de Bébés et Jouets,* the successor. Made dolls and bébés. Edouard Fournier, in HISTOIRE DES JOUETS ET DES JEUX D'ENFANTS, written around 1866, states, "Some establishments with over thirty employees are occupied exclusively in the making of dresses, pinafores, etc., for dolls. One of these establishments located on the rue Saint Denis [Bru was listed on the rue Saint Denis in the 1868 Paris Directory] works especially for the American trade and sells these emigrants all decked out for from 5 to 30 francs a dozen [1 franc then equaled about 20¢]. One other establishment, even larger, is located on the rue Mauconseil [*Jumeau* was listed on rue Mauconseil from 1848 to 1866. In 1867 Jumeau had moved to the rue Anjou-Marais]. . . . Occasionally one of the great Parisian Couturiers will stoop to compete with the dressmakers of dolls but the prices that they charge are exorbitant—nearly $100 in one instance."

Luella Hart, in COMPLETE FRENCH DOLL DIRECTORY, quotes the 1868 Paris Directory, which is the earliest listing in Paris found for Bru: "Bru Junior, and Co., b.s.g.d.g. Maker of dolls of all kinds in pink or white kid, straight or jointed, crying or talking. New doll in rubber. New doll in porcelain. New doll in hardened paste. (It's pate in the French.) New doll in carved wood with joints (such as those at feet and hands) giving it specially graceful look. Big workshops for making dressed dolls made always with new materials and in new styles; trousseaux. Maker of dolls' heads in bisque, rubber, or hardened paste. Commission agent. Exporter. 374, rue St. Denis."

During the years 1867 to 1869, several French patents were obtained by Leon Casimir Bru. Included among these were the following two—one for a crying doll and one for a double-faced *Surprise Doll.* The crying doll had a rubber ball fitted with a reed, placed inside its body; this produced a crying sound. The Surprise Doll worked on a rod mechanism imbedded in the chest that allowed the head to turn without disarranging the doll's hair. In 1869 Leon Casimir Bru patented a doll's body, which he claimed was more durable. Made of papier-mâché, the body had ball joints, including joints at the wrists, ankles, and waist, but it was held together with pegs or pins and not elastic. Madame Bru obtained a patent for another Surprise Doll in 1872, this one having a body of wood, metal, or any other substance that would allow the torso to contain a multi-disk music box.

Casimir Bru, Jeune, founder of the doll firm Bru Jne. & Cie., continued the family's experiments in creating doll innovations. Between 1873 and 1882, he took out several patents among which were a French patent (1878) for a jointed rubber bébé, a bébé of India rubber with the rubber built over wire frame as a skin, and both a French and German patent (1879) for a nursing bébé that was called *Bébé Teteur.* Also in 1879, Bru obtained a patent for a doll with a kid body. The 1882 doll patent was for the improved making of dolls. This was to simulate the natural action of the eyelids, the arms, legs, hands, and fingers, so that they would take any desired position and hold it naturally. The eyelids were to be fixed so that they would move while the eyeballs remained stationary. Also in 1882, Bru and Jumeau took out a patent for a mechanical boat.

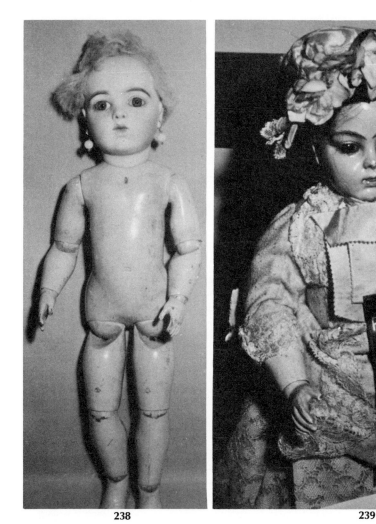

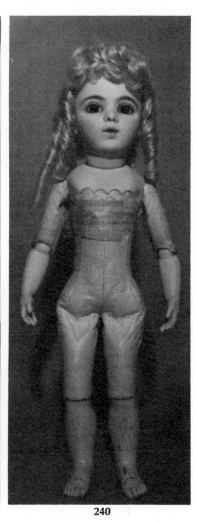

238.                                                     239                                                     240

**238.** Bru bisque head with a blonde skin wig and glass eyes on an articulated wooden body. *Photograph by Winnie Langley.*

**239.** Rubber and/or gutta-percha marked "Bru" doll. This might be the patented hard-rubber bébé, entirely jointed, that

Bru advertised ca. 1880. *Photograph by Winnie Langley.*

**240.** Bru bisque head and arms, kid body, wooden legs. Size 4. Mark on body: Ill. **250.** H. 15½ inches. *Courtesy of Hazel Ulseth.*

1873: Bru Jne. & Cie. advertised that they were large makers of dressed and undressed dolls of all kinds. They specialized in dolls of the latest models and inventions that were entirely new and exclusive: dolls with music (called magic); dolls in carved wood (compared to other known articulations, these possessed a shape, hands, and feet that gave them the most perfect grace); dolls in ordinary wood with simple joints; dolls entirely of rubber costumed as a boy or girl bather; dolls in kid of new form with arms and hands in jointed wood; double-faced dolls, one face asleep, one awake; and kid-body dolls with rubber heads. All these different models were patented or trademarked. The firm also carried bisque dolls' heads, stationary or swivel; rubber dolls' heads, stationary or swivel, on dolls that could be dressed and undressed. The doll clothes were of luxurious materials and in the latest fashion. These dolls were both marketed in France and exported.

1879: New items appearing in the Bru advertisement were patented bébés entirely jointed in hard India rubber, the only ones guaranteed absolutely unbreakable; dolls and bébés in carved wood, completely jointed; and mechanical talking dolls and bébés.

1881: Bru Jne. & Cie. had patented twenty-one inventions according to their advertisement. The Bru line included bébés in kid; an unbreakable doll of greatest perfection, this bébé was supple, light, and firm, and was offered at a very low price. The advertisement stated that by all reports it was the most complete doll. Again mentioned was the patented bébé in hard India rubber, guaranteed absolutely unbreakable; the completely jointed carved wood bébé, and the bébé with music. The sucking Bébé Teteur and *Bébé Gourmand* also appeared. The advertisement went on to state that the Bru firm manufactured bisque heads and made rubber dolls for

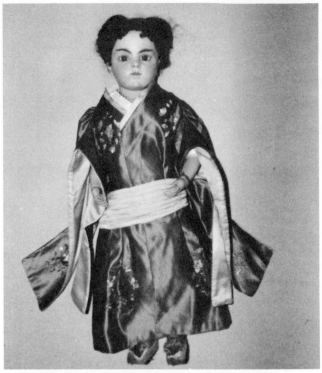

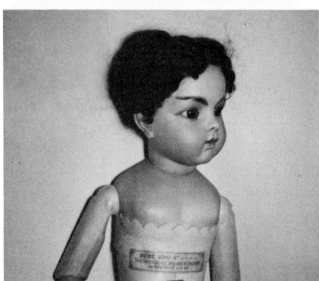

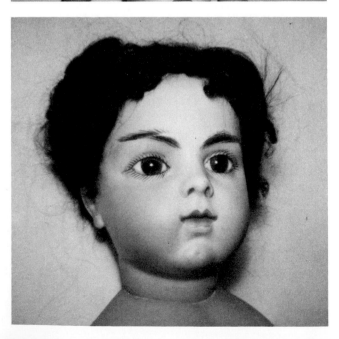

French and export consumption and that always the latest novelties were being made.

Bru, like other leading doll makers of his day, showed his products in international exhibits. While he was head of the firm, dolls (rather than bébés) were exhibited at Paris in 1878. The dolls were awarded a silver medal. In 1880 Bru dolls and bébés were displayed at Melbourne, again meriting a silver medal. At this exhibition Bru also received a certificate for mechanical toys. The Bru agent in Melbourne in 1880 was Arles, Dufour & Co.

By 1883 the firm of Bru Jne. & Cie. had passed to H. Chevrot, but the Bru name remained. (An 1883 French patent for organic substance appears to be the last record of Bru's activities.) It is possible that Chevrot was related to the Chevrot of Limoges, France, who was succeeded by *Lebon* & Cie. before 1863. In 1874 Lebon & Cie. made porcelain articles and toys for export. From 1880 to 1883 Chevrot was listed as a Paris toymaker. Chevrot took out a patent in 1883 for a jointed kid-body doll in which the system of joints was manipulated from the interior of the doll.

1885: The Bru advertisement under Chevrot reads: "Bru factory at Montreuil-sous-Bois; 25 patent inventions. The Bébés Bru, with new patented joints, are the newest, prettiest, the best built, the best jointed, and the most luxurious of all Parisian dolls. The words 'Bébé Bru' can be examined on each bébé. The darling patented Bébé Le Teteur, that sucks all by herself is still being shown, as is Bébé Gourmand [see 1881 advertisement]. The new bébé is *Le Dormeur*; a patented bébé, this one opens and closes its eyes naturally by means of its eyelids." The bisque heads were manufactured at the factory in Montreuil-sous-Bois.

All the gold medals won by the Bru firm at exhibitions were received under Chevrot's management. The exhibitions and awards were: Paris, 1885, gold medal; Antwerp, 1885, gold medal; Liverpool, 1886, gold medal; Paris, 1886, gold medal; Le Havre, 1887, gold medal; Toulouse, 1887, gold medal; Barcelona, 1888, gold medal; Melbourne, 1888, gold medal; Paris, 1888, gold medal; Paris, 1889, silver medal. At Melbourne, Chevrot had an exhibit in his own name as well as the Bru Jne. exhibit.

Chevrot's successor as head of Bru Jne. & Cie. was Paul Eugène Girard. While Girard was head of the company, he took out at least five French patents on dolls. In 1891 a patent was obtained for the combined movement of the eyes and eyelids of dolls, and another for a walking and talking bébé with a key-winding mechanism, known as *Bébé Petit Pas*. The patent for eye movement was also secured in Germany in 1891. The

**241A, B, & C.** Unusual oriental Bru. The oriental features have been adapted to a stock face. Note how the eyebrows transverse the molded eyebrow line. The doll has a bisque socket head with glass eyes, shoulder plate; kid torso, bisque lower arms, wooden lower legs. Original outfit of blue and gold embroidered satin. Head and shoulder mark: Ill. **248.** Body label: Ill. **250.** H. 20½ inches. *Courtesy of the Newark Museum, Newark, N.J.*

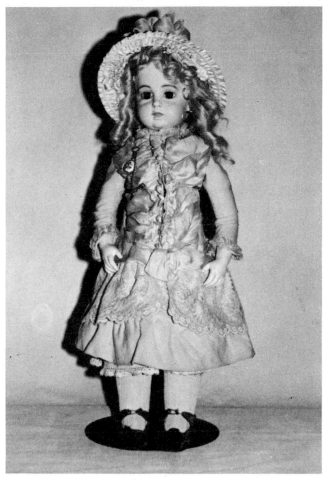

242. Bru doll with bisque head, molded shoulder plate and lower arms, kid gusseted body. Dressed in pink silk. Mark on head: Ill. 244. H. 22 inches. *Courtesy of Helen Jo Payne.*

243A & B. Doll wearing original green satin dress and hat. Shoes are marked "Bru," as is the box she came in. Sheepskin wig, glass eyes, kid body; unmarked bisque head and bisque forearms. H. 11½ inches. *Courtesy of the International Doll Library Foundation.*

The prices given for dolls are those for which the dolls were originally offered for sale. They are *not* today's prices.

244–250. Marks used on Bru dolls. No. 250 is a paper label found on bodies. Nos. 244 and 245 are incised symbols that probably were used by the Bru firm.

244          245          246

BRU. JNE R
11

247

BRU·JNE

248

BRU JNE R
BREVETE S.G.D.G.
Y 8 M

249

BÉBÉ BRU BTE    S.G.D.G.
Tout Contrefacteur sera saisi et poursuivi
conformement a la Loi

250

year 1892 was the one in which the Mama-Papa doll with an expanding chest was patented. In 1895 and 1897, varieties of kissing dolls were patented. The 1897 patent was taken out by Eugène Frederick Girard. The kissing doll of the first patent threw kisses when a string was pulled, but the second one performed by leg movement and also walked and talked.

1889–92: Bru advertisements announced new and unbreakable bébés with hollowed wooden bodies, which were more solid and lighter than those of composition. Also mentioned were composition heads, the latest novelty, which Girard claimed to be as pretty and as well molded and decorated as bisque heads. The advertisement also stated that the bébés Bru were the only bébés having natural eyelashes. The bébés were distinguishable by the fineness of their hands and feet as well as by the beauty and good taste of their clothes. As late as 1892, the Bru firm was still advertising India rubber bébés, and as late as 1898, Bébé Teteur.

Girard showed his products in one exhibition (Chicago, 1893) where his display won a silver medal.

1899: The Bru company became part of the Société Française de Fabrication de Bébés et Jouets (S. F. B. J.).

**Bruchet, Marie.** 1852. Paris. Secured a French patent for a jointed doll.

**Bruchlos, Ernst.** 1894–1925+. Eisfeld, Thür. Made dressed dolls.

1914: Dolls dressed in modern styles and in national costumes; also made hats for dolls. Doll prices ranged from 8¢ to $2.50.

**Bruchlos, Georg.** 1883–1925+. Eisfeld, Thür. Had steam factory where he made dressed dolls especially for export.

1911: Employed three hundred workers.

**Bruchlos, Valentine M.** 1907–25+. Eisfeld, Thür. Made dolls, including dressed dolls and dancing dolls.

**Bruckmann, Hattie (née Ross).** 1917+. Portland, Ore. Made dolls of various materials such as paper pulp, cornstarch, and plaster, which she pressed into a mold; face was covered with a chamois skin and given a thin glaze; then features were painted; natural hair wigs. During World War I, made all-kid dolls for Meier & Franke Co. Also papier-mâché heads covered with kid and given glass eyes; waxed dolls and dolls of cloth. Used *Delavan* wigs.

**Brückner, Albert.** 1901–ca. 1922. Jersey City, N.J.; ca. 1922–25+, successors were Albert Brückner's Sons.

1901: Albert Brückner and Rudolph Gruss obtained a U.S. patent for making a doll face, described as follows: ". . . to cover the front part of a stuffed doll-head. The face is composed of two or more layers of suitable material the outer layer being preferably of suitable textile fabric, while the inner layer or layers are made of paper or other suitable material. The outer layer in flat con-

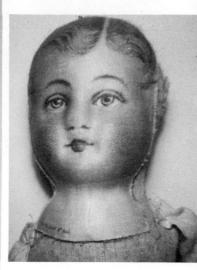

**251A & B.** Rag doll with stiffened mask face patented by Albert Brückner; for mark on right front shoulder edge; see Ill. **253.** H. 13½ inches. *Courtesy of Dorothy Annunziato.*

dition is first printed in suitable colors in imitation of the colors of a natural face and cemented to the inner layer, which also is flat, and the two are then molded together into shape. The printing on the outer layer is so arranged that an attractive face is obtained when the two cemented layers are completely molded into shape. Below the face is an extension forming the neck. . . . The completed face is glued or otherwise securely attached to the stuffed dummy-head of the doll." Evidence suggests that these dolls that Albert Brückner made were distributed by *Horsman.* The words "Pat'd July 9th 1901" (Brückner's patent date) appear on the right front side of the neck of the dolls, which resemble pictures of dolls advertised by Horsman. Brückner was the first American doll manufacturer to have his name in Kelly's Directory, which suggests British distribution also. (See color photograph C7.)

1918: Advertised rag dolls with embossed faces, and composition dolls' heads and arms.

1921–25: Applied for another rag doll patent in 1921, which was granted in 1925. This was for a papier-mâché or other fibrous composition material stamped or embossed and the outer surface painted and glazed or given a polish to resemble bisque or china. At the bottom of the head there was a circular disk connected to the shoulder with a bolt and wing-nut so that the head could turn. This doll was provided with a wig.

1925: Albert Brückner's sons, Elliott and Henry Brückner, registered *Dollypop Dolls* as a trademark in U.S. These dolls had hand-painted faces, cotton-stuffed bodies with voices, and were 13 inches tall.

**252A & B.** Two-headed lithographed rag doll distributed by Horsman, made by Albert Brückner. Wears original clothes, white aprons, blue checked dress on white girl, red dress on Negro. Mark on shoulder: Ill. **253.** H. 14½ inches. *Courtesy of the International Doll Library Foundation.*

## PAT'D. JULY 8ᵀᴴ 1901

**253.** Albert Brückner's mark on rag dolls.

**Brückner, Arno.** 1925. Oeslau, Thür. Doll maker.

**Brückner & Och.** 1923–25. Stockheim, Bavaria. Doll maker.

**Brüderchen (Little Brother).** 1923. Trademark registered in Germany by *Friedrichrodaer Puppenfabrik* for ball-jointed dolls, standing and sitting baby dolls.

**Bruguier, Charles Abram.** 1815–21. London. Made mechanical walking dolls.

**Bruin Manufacturing Co.** 1907–8. New York City. Made the *Vivian* line of *Wide Awake* rag dolls with two faces on a turning head, as patented by *Lillian A. Sackman.*

**Brun, B.** 1900. Paris. Made an indestructible bébé named *Bébé Linon,* which he claimed was patented.

**Brunessaux, J.** 1881–85, Paris; 1889–90, Les Fils [Sons] de J. Brunessaux, successors; 1895–98, H. Brunessaux, successor; made rubber dolls.

1895: Advertised India rubber bébés dressed in latest fashion and jointed bébés with enamel eyes and with fine wigs.

**Brunet & Pajean.** Before 1921, Paris; 1921, successor was Mme. A. Jomin. They specialized in doll repair articles, dolls' heads, wigs, etc. This was probably the P. Brunet who was a successor of *Léon Bornoz* around 1910.

**Brunot, Mlle. Marguerite.** 1918. Algiers, No. Africa. Registered in France as a trademark the intertwined initials "M. B.," for dolls.

**Brunswick & Cie.** 1912–19. Paris. Used the name *Les Parisiennes à la Mode* for their dolls.

1919: They used the initials "R. F." for dolls with interchangeable parts.

**Bté.** See **Breveté.**

**Bubbles.** 1920. Baby doll with teeth, tongue, and wig, made by the *Republic Doll & Toy Co.*

**Bubbles.** 1925+. Made by *EFFanBEE.*

**Bubbles.** See **Master Bubbles.**

**Bubenheim, Lenore.** 1924. New York City. Obtained five design patents, which she assigned to the *Mme. Lenore Art Doll Co.* These were long-limbed character dolls: two were Pierrette-type dolls, one was an Indian, one was Chinese, and one was a girl wearing shirtwaist and knickers.

**Bucherer, A. (Firm).** 1921. Amriswil, Switz. Obtained German and British patents for metal ball-jointed dolls. (See Ill. 254.)

**Buchhold, Max.** 1895. Lauscha, Thür. Had porcelain factory that specialized in dolls' heads.

**Büchner, Anton.** 1918. Neustadt near Coburg, Thür. Made jointed dolls.

**Büchner, Oskar.** 1923–25. Neustadt near Coburg, Thür. Made dolls; used initials "O. B." as mark.

**Buck.** 1919. Indian-type doll made by *J. R. Miranda & Co.* It had painted features and was dressed in Indian blanket; 12 inches high.

**Buckland, Edmund.** 1843. London. Doll maker.

**Buckler, Mary M.** 1921–23. Springfield, Mass. Obtained U.S. patent for a doll's eye, which was made circular with a bead inside it.

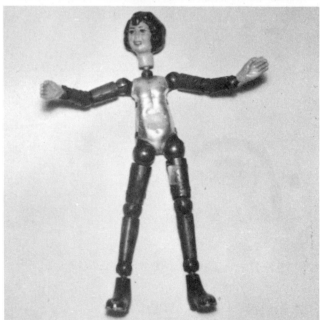

**254A & B.** Metal dolls patented by A. Bucherer in 1921; completely ball-jointed, including wrists and ankles; heads, hands, and feet of molded composition. Pressed on the stomach is the mark shown in Ill. **255.** One wears her original red-print dress. H. 7½ inches. *Courtesy of Winnie Langley and Dorothy Annunziato; photographs by Winnie Langley.*

MADE IN
SWITZERLAND
PATENTS
APPLIED FOR

**255.** A. Bucherer's mark on metal bodies.

**Buddie.** 1921. Rag doll made by *Sophia Delavan*; clothes designed by *Katherine A. Rauser* and Queen G. Thomas. Price $12.50 doz. wholesale.

**Buddie Clown.** 1921. Rag doll made by *Sophia Delavan*; price $12.50 doz. wholesale.

**Buddie Toy & Novelty Co.** 1919. Chicago, Ill. Proprietor was *Katherine A. Rauser;* made doll named *Mlle. Babette.*

**Buddies.** 1921. Rag dolls made by *Sophia Delavan;* dresses designed by *Katherine A. Rauser.*

**Buddy.** 1916. Distributed by *Strobel & Wilken.* It was an *American Art Doll* representing a farmer boy, and had painted eyes and hair.

**Buddy.** 1918. Doll copyrighted by *Marguerite Rogers;* had large round eyes, and the corners of the mouth turned down.

**Buddy Boy.** 1920–21. Made by *Averill Manufacturing Co.* It walked and cried at each faltering step; was dressed in rompers.

**Buddy Bud.** 1916–17. Trademark registered in U.S. by *Robert Lindsay* for dolls.

**Buddy Lee.** Ca. 1920–25+. All-composition doll dressed in denim overalls to advertise the H. D. Lee Mercantile Co., manufacturer of overalls. Doll had molded hair, painted eyes glancing to the side; jointed at shoulders; size 13 inches. Each year Buddy Lee was dressed in a new suit of clothes; sold to dealers for window display and then sold as a doll after its use in the window.

1923–24: Thousands of these dolls were dressed in playsuits and sold to feature the company's playsuit line.

**Buds.** 1921. Rag dolls made by *Sophia Delavan;* dresses designed by *Katherine A. Rauser* and Queen G. Thomas; price $18.00 doz. wholesale.

**Buemon, Iwasa.** 1893. Japan. Exhibited dolls at the Chicago World's Fair.

**Buffaut.** 1874. Paris. Made dolls.

**Bufli.** 1923–24. Trademark registered in Germany by *Resi Brandl* for dolls.

**Bühl (Bühle), H., & Söhne.** 1869–98+. Grossbreitenbach, Thür. Dolls' heads have been found with the mark of this porcelain factory. (See also **Greiner.**)

256

257

**256 & 257.** Marks used by H. Bühl & Söhne.

**Bühl, Paul & Tannewitz.** 1911–1925. Gotha, Germany. Made dolls with celluloid heads and *Tago* stuffed dolls.

**Buisson, Mme. (née Charot, Adrienne Lucie).** 1922. France. Obtained a French patent for dolls made with enameled metals.

**Bulgarian Princess.** 1914. Doll dressed in vivid Bulgarian colors, made by *Ideal Novelty & Toy Co.*

**Bully Boy Brewster.** 1921. Soft doll made by the *Giftoy Co.*, designed by *Gertrude Stacy.*

**Bumble Puppy.** 1909. Trademark registered in Germany by *Max Illfelder* to be used for dolls of all kinds, dolls' heads, dolls' bodies, and wool dolls.

**Bundie.** See **Baby Bundie.**

**Bunny Hug.** 1913. Trademark registered in Britain by *Eisenmann & Co.* for dolls.

**Bunsel, E.** 1909. Hamburg, Germany. Made dolls' heads and leather bodies for dolls.

**Buonocore (Buonocove), Louis, & Son.** 1918. Garfield, N.J. Made composition dolls' heads and arms. Factory employed ten people.

**Bürckner, Elisabeth.** 1925. Elsterwerda, Germany. Made dolls' house dolls.

**Burd, Clara M.** 1917–18. New York City. Secured two U.S. design patents for rubber dolls that were dressed as a boy and as a girl. These patents were assigned to the *Faultless Rubber Co.*

**Burger & Bentum.** 1897–1925+. Prague, Bohemia. Made dolls; specialized in papier-mâché and wax dolls.

**Burgess & Bowes.** 1925. London. Doll importers.

**Burke, Alfred.** 1914. New York City. Imported pyroxylin dolls and bébés; sole American agent of *Société Industrielle de Celluloid.*

**Burley, George.** 1862. Southwark, Surrey. Displayed dolls at the London Exhibition.

**Burmester, C.** 1895. Hamburg, Germany. Made dolls.

**Burnbaum, Paul.** 1914–15. Cologne, Germany. Obtained a German patent for moving eyes in dolls' heads.

**Burnell & Hockey.** 1906–7. Crouch End, Middlesex. Obtained a British patent for rag dolls made of printed or painted fabric patterns, to be sewed together and stuffed. Patterns were made so that, stitched at the hips, the doll could sit down; had defined fingers and feet, natural looking from both front and back.

**Busch & Co.** 1925. Coburg, Thür. Doll maker.

**Buschbaum, Th.** 1902–18. Wallendorf, Thür. Made and exported dolls, especially dressed dolls.

**Buschow & Beck.** 1888–1925+. Reichenbach, Silesia, and Nossen, Saxony. Made metal dolls' heads and celluloid dolls' heads.

1894–1906: *Alfred Vischer & Co.* of New York City was their distributor. They made dolls' heads of sheet metal,

especially brass plate, for which they won prizes at the Brussels Exhibition of 1888 and the Barcelona Exhibition of 1889.

1900: They registered *Minerva* as a trademark in Germany for dolls' heads, dressed and undressed dolls, and parts of dolls. Vischer & Co. registered Minerva as a trademark in the U.S. in 1901. This trademark is found on both metal and celluloid dolls; it had been in use since 1894.

1903: Obtained two German patents for sleeping eyes.

1904: They obtained another patent for sleeping dolls' eyes, a patent for metal dolls' joints, and a patent for ball-jointed celluloid dolls, all German patents.

1907: Advertised Minerva metal dolls' heads and Minerva celluloid dolls' heads and dressed dolls. Specialized in unbreakable stuffed and woolen dolls with Minerva heads; unbreakable patent ball-jointed celluloid dolls without rubber cords.

1910: Obtained another German patent for sleeping dolls' eyes.

1911: Advertised unbreakable stuffed dolls, wool and felt dolls with Minerva heads, patent ball-jointed dolls of celluloid without rubber cords; dolls' parts.

1925: Used name "Hansa Haus."
(See also **Schön, Joseph.**)

**Bussi.** 1925+. Trade name for rag dolls made by *Willi Steiner.*

**Bust Heads.** Term used especially in France, for shoulder heads or heads having a shoulder piece attached to them. (See also **Breast Plate Dolls' Heads.**)

**Buste Richard.** 1853. Name of doll head made of a composition produced from malleable paste of lime, plaster, stearic wax, tallow, and whiting. The composition was patented by *Monsieur Richard.*

**Buster Boy.** 1911. Composition doll made by *Louis Amberg & Son.*

**Buster Brown.** 1902–5. In 1902 Richard Felton Outcault originated "Buster Brown" as a cartoon for the NEW YORK HERALD.

1904: *Hamley Bros.* registered "Buster Brown" in Britain as a trademark. Both *Art Fabric Mills* and *Knickerbocker Specialty Co.* advertised Buster Brown cutout rag dolls.

1905: Rag doll advertised by Art Fabric Mills as 16 inches tall, priced 25¢.

**Buster Brown.** 1910. Distributed by *Butler Bros.* Came with composition head; when body was pressed, the mouth opened and a bellows sounded the voice. Size 11½ inches; price dressed, $2.00 doz. wholesale.

**Buster Brown.** 1915. This doll and his sister were made by *Ideal Novelty & Toy Co.;* came with human hair wigs.

**Buster Brown.** 1915. One of the *Jam Kiddos* made by *Non-Breakable Doll Co.* Came with molded hair; cost $1.00.

**Buth, Belle & Lachmann.** 1897. Berlin. Doll exporters.

**Butler, Alice Harding.** 1910–15. Evanston, Ill. Produced dolls.

1913: Obtained a U.S. patent for a cloth-body doll that was rotund and natural in shape. The joints connecting the lower limbs to the torso were made with two circular cardboard disks covered with cloth and connected with a cotter pin.

1915: Obtained a German patent for fastening the hair of dolls' wigs.

**Butler, Charles.** 1843–48. London. Doll maker.

**Butler Bros.** 1877–1925+. Sonneberg, Thür.; New York City, and elsewhere. Made and distributed dolls. They registered the following trademarks in Germany: 1912, *Baby Betty;* 1913, *Miss Millionaire* and *Dolly Dimple;* 1914, *Wide-Awake Doll;* 1915, *Baby Bud.* They used the initials "B. B." (See color photograph C12.)

1905–7, and probably longer: Butler Bros. advertised that they owned the molds for making the china heads with *Pet Name* in raised gold letters. They sold both the heads separately and on "A B C" body educational dolls.

Butler Bros. used the trade name *Marvel,* which was stamped under the *Kestner* crown and streamers on kid-bodied dolls.

**Buttercup.** 1924–25. Soft rag doll made by *Modern Toy Co.,* Brooklyn, N.Y. Doll represented the baby created by Jimmy Murphy in his TOOTS AND CASPER comic series for King Features Syndicate and was copied with their permission. The doll was 18 inches tall.

**Butterfield, Louis M.** 1923–24. Raymond, N.H. Obtained U.S. patent for a walking doll that moved on wheels. He assigned half to Hermann Gove Sumner.

**Butterfly Doll.** 1901. A *Marguerite* or bonnet-type doll with molded butterfly headdress. It came with pink muslin body and porcelain limbs. Sizes were 8, 9, 12½, and 15 inches. The 9-inch size retailed for 10¢ and the 12½-inch size for 15¢ or 20¢.

**Butterfly Series.** 1908. Trademark registered in Britain by *Eisenmann & Co.* for dolls.

**Butterick Publishing Co.** 1908. New York City. Produced the "Butterick Rag Doll." This was a cutout doll, printed on a sheet of cloth in eight colors; the price of 25¢ included patterns for clothes for the doll.

**Button in Ear (Knopf im Ohr).** 1904–25+. Trademark registered in Germany and U.S. by *Margarete Steiff.*

**Buttons.** 1911. Character doll made by *A. Steinhardt & Bro.;* represented a messenger boy.

**Buttons.** See **EFFanBEE "Buttons" Monk.**

**Bwporit.** 1909–10. Trademark registered in Germany by *Bähr & Pröschild* for celluloid dolls and doll parts. The "W" shown here as the second letter in the trademark replaces what, in the actual trademark, is a "symbol" having a shape quite similar to a "W."

**Bye Bye Baby.** 1918. Bent-limb baby doll made by *Jessie McCutcheon Raleigh.* It came with painted hair and was dressed in a white corded coat and bonnet. Size 18 inches sold for $5.50.

**Bye Bye Kiddies.** 1917. Deluxe rag dolls made by *Horsman.* Their faces were hand-painted, and they were made of the finest materials.

**Bye Bye Kids.** 1908–9. Trademark registered in U.S. by *Bach Bros.* & Katzenstein. These rag dolls representing chiefly soldiers and sailors were made by Bach Bros. Katzenstein was a member of the firm.

**Bye-Lo Baby.** 1922–25+. Doll designed and copyrighted by *Grace Storey Putnam.* She obtained four copyrights on it—one in 1922, two in 1923, and one in 1925. The 1922 copyright described the doll's head as "life-sized modeled from a baby three days old, eyes slightly narrowed, mouth closed, fat rolls at back of neck, neck constructed to fit a socket." Very soon thereafter, it was decided to give the doll a soft body instead of the jointed composition one for which the socket head was designed, and the head was made with a flange. PLAYTHINGS, January, 1925, reported that Grace Storey Putnam "hunted all through the great hospitals in Los Angeles, Calif., to find the most perfect baby she could find. After weeks of search and after examining hundreds of little babies, she found this baby, who was only three days old, in one of the smallest hospitals. To her artistic eye here was the most perfect baby she had ever seen. Then she went to work with her deft fingers and creative brain, using this perfect baby as a model, carefully copying every little feature. When she had finished she laid her model doll of wax alongside the real live baby model, and she and the others who looked at these two babies could hardly tell which was the live* baby and which was the doll baby.

"Then she worked for weeks and weeks perfecting the model, and when she had it just as perfect as it was humanly possible for her to make it, she brought it to New York and showed it to one of the officials of Geo. Borgfeldt & Co. He was taken with it at once and with the wonderful possibilities it afforded. He put their best men to work to exactly reproduce this wax doll in bisque in order to bring out the features and the many fine and delicate lines necessary to make this a most lifelike doll.

"Other problems came up. Three-day-old babies do not talk, but they do cry, so they worked another long time so that they could make this doll baby cry just like a three-day-old baby. Next they had to give this tiny baby doll eyes that would open and close and look like a real live baby's eyes . . . besides opening and closing. In dressing this baby doll they put real babies' underwear on and a little baby's dress and knit booties."

---

* Unconfirmed rumors claim the model was a dead baby.

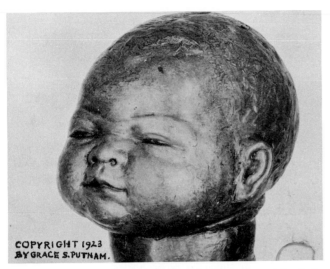

**258.** Copy of the original picture of the wax model of the "Bye-Lo Baby" filed in the copyright office by Grace S. Putnam in 1923. Note the rolls of fat and other details not found in the bisque heads used on dolls.

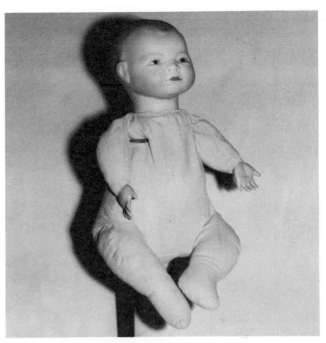

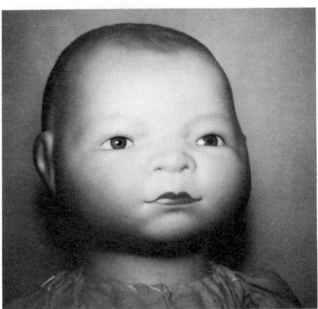

*Borgfeldt* distributed the Bye-Lo Babies. *K & K Toy Co.* assembled them and made their bodies; the bisque heads were made by *Kestner; Kling; Hertel, Schwab & Co.; Alt, Beck and Gottschalck,* etc., in Germany; wood-pulp composition heads were made by *Cameo Doll Co.* beginning in 1924, and *Karl Standfuss* was the sole manufacturer of celluloid heads for Bye-Lo Babies in 1925. *Schoenhut,* for whom Borgfeldt was a distributor, made wooden Bye-Lo Baby heads. Borgfeldt registered the name Bye-Lo Baby as a trademark in the U.S. and in France in 1925, stating that he had used this name since 1923. The first advertisement for the Bye-Lo Baby did not appear in PLAYTHINGS until April, 1924. Each Bye-Lo Baby had a tag on it with a facsimile signature of Grace Storey Putnam.

According to Luella Hart, Milio of New York City cast two hundred wax Bye-Lo Babies that were life-sized and cost $25.00 each. One of these wax Bye-Los is in the collection of the Museum of the City of New York.

In 1924 the Bye-Lo Baby doll was used as the baby in Inspiration's moving picture NEW TOYS, which starred Richard Barthelmess and Mary Hay.

At the beginning of 1925 there were five sizes ranging from 13 to 20 inches. During 1925, two sizes were added, making the range from 9 to 20 inches, selling for $3.00 to $14.95. *Foulds & Freure* sold the flange neck heads alone; these came in nine sizes for dolls ranging from 8 to 20½ inches and sold for $8.00 to $36.00 doz. wholesale. Socket-type heads were also sold separately. One of these bisque heads purchased ca. 1924 is marked "Copr. by// Grace S. Putnam// Made in Germany// 136(??) 3/0." The indentation in the socket eliminated the incised numbers, if any, between the "6" and the following "3." A few of the Bye-Lo Baby bisque flange heads have "© 1923" on them as well as "Grace S.

**259A & B.** "Bye-Lo," the "Million Dollar Baby" designed by Grace Putnam, has bisque head with flange neck, molded hair, glass sleeping eyes, cloth body, and celluloid hands. Mark: Ill. **261.** H. 14 inches. *Coleman Collection.*

Putnam," etc. These heads usually have longer necks than the ones without the date, and the shape of the head is slightly different. It is possible that they were made in a different porcelain factory than those without the date.

In 1925 or soon thereafter, the all-bisque Bye-Lo Babies made by Kestner appeared on the market. These did not have the date on them, as found so far. They came with molded pink or blue shoes—brown eyes with the pink shoes and blue eyes with the blue shoes—in

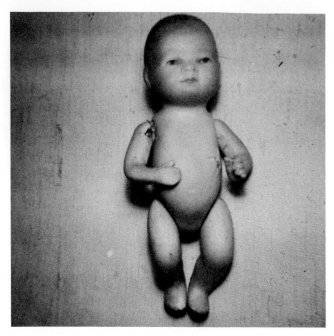

260. All-bisque "Bye-Lo Baby" with painted features, jointed limbs. Mark: Ill. 263. H. 4 inches. *Courtesy of Jessica Norman.*

© 1923 *by*
*Grace S. Putnam*
*MADE IN GERMANY*
261

262

20 – 10
Copr. by
GRACE S. PUTNAM
Germany
263

261–263. "Bye-Lo Baby" marks. No. 262 is a tag label; No. 263 is found on all-bisque versions. (See also Putnam, Grace.)

various sizes. Size 6 inches cost 67¢. Other bisque Bye-Los and those made of rubber were made after 1925. It is not known when the all-celluloid Bye-Lo Babies were first made. (See also **Louis Sametz.**)

**Byrnes, Gene.** 1922–23. Carmel, Calif. Secured four copyrights for dolls representing *Reg'lar Fellers* in the comics. These dolls were handled by *Borgfeldt.* There was the head of a laughing boy with and without his cap, representing *Jimmie Dugan,* and the head of a laughing fat boy, also with and without his hat, representing *Puddin' Head.*

# C

**Cábaña, Charles.** 1920–23. Buffalo, N.Y. Obtained U.S. patent for a type of ball-and-socket joint, which was stamped out of sheet metal or other material.

**Cabbagerino.** 1923. Trademark registered in Britain by *Margaret Ann Dakin* for dolls.

**Caccialanza, Romeo.** 1918–19. An Italian subject residing in Los Angeles. Obtained a U.S. patent, which he assigned to *Western Doll & Toy Manufacturing Co.* The patent was to make dolls more durable by enclosing the bottom of the shoulders.

**Cadet, Mlle. Elisa.** 1873. Won a medal of cooperation at the Vienna Exhibition as an agent of *Jumeau.*

**Caho.** 1925. Trademark registered in Germany by *Canzler & Hoffmann* for dolls and dressed dolls.

**Caillard, Varenne.** 1890. Obtained a French patent for the use of plastic paste (composition) in making dolls' heads.

**Callaz, J.** See **Derolland.**

**Callot.** 1918. Exhibited two dressed wax dolls in the Galleries of the Art Alliance.

**Calots.** 1855. Paris. Specialized in making fashion dolls' heads. Note use of word "fashion."

**Calumet Manufacturing Co.** 1919–25. New York City. Made dolls.

**Calvé, Mme. Emma.** 1907. Noted opera singer whose real name was Emma de Roquer. She made rag dolls, which were sold for charity. One of her dolls with the diva's own hair sold for $265 to a Philadelphia woman.

**Calvert Tot.** 1916–17. Distributed by *Katherine A. Rauser;* resembled *Käthe Kruse* dolls. These comparatively expensive rag dolls were made with formed faces.

**Cameo Doll Company.** 1922–25+. New York City. Moved to Port Allegany, Pennsylvania, in 1930; made composition dolls of a wood pulp, rosin, and starch mixture in a hot press. Some of the dolls had composition heads and bodies; others had cloth bodies stuffed with cotton wadding. Some of the wigs and shoes were made by *Braitling,* and some of the clothes were made by Blanche Cromien. Cameo dolls, distributed by *Borgfeldt,* included: *Kewpies,* 1922–25+; *Bye-Lo,* 1924–25+; *Baby Bo Kaye,* 1925+; *Little Annie Roonie,* 1925+.

**264.** Kewpie made by Cameo. The doll is all-composition and has painted features. H. 11½ inches. *Coleman Collection.*

**Camp Fire Girl.** 1913. Doll made by *Horsman;* mate to *Boy Scout.*

**Campbell Kids.** Portrait dolls handled by *Frederick Devoll.*

**Campbell Kids.** 1910–14. Made by *Horsman* under license of Joseph Campbell Co. The dolls are marked "© 1910," but there is no record in the copyright office of this doll under either Horsman or Campbell, unless it is the *Bobby* copyrighted by Horsman and designed by *Helen Trowbridge.* However, Joseph Campbell Co. did copyright numerous drawings by *Grace Drayton,* which the Campbell Kids resemble. They came with cork-stuffed bodies, jointed at shoulder and hip; in assorted costumes; price $1.00.

**265.** Indian Campbell Kid has molded composition head, painted brown; cloth body, original clothes. H. 12 inches. (See Ill. 267.) *Courtesy of Dorothy Annunziato.*

1911: The trademark "The Campbell Kids" was registered in Britain. Boys and girls were made in sizes 10½, 13, and 15½ inches.

1912: Horsman secured two U.S. design patents for clothes for the Campbell Kids. One was for a girl and one for a boy; both had yokes with doll figures on them. These dolls came with *Can't Break 'Em* heads, painted features, pink sateen bodies stuffed with cork, and swinging joints. *Montgomery Ward & Co.* advertised that the boy and girl were usually bought as a pair. Size 11 inches cost 98¢ (other sources seem always to refer to the size as 12 inches), and size 8½ inches cost 48¢. New features were a Campbell Kid Baby with a ribbon in its hair; Campbell Kids dressed in the design-patent clothes and also in various college colors. *Butler Bros.* advertised 9½- and 11¾-inch sizes.

1913: Campbell Kids wore wigs, both boys and girls.

1914: The dolls had hair painted red, blue, green, etc.; size 12 inches cost 75¢. A 16-inch doll came with composition legs and knee joint similar to the *universal* type.

**266.** Campbell Kid. Composition head and hands, cloth body, painted features. Wears red jacket, white skirt, plaid tie, stockings, and brown felt shoes. Cloth label is sewed to the left sleeve. H. 15½ inches. *Courtesy of The Smithsonian Institution.*

E.I.H. © 1910

**267.** "Campbell Kids" mark used by Horsman.

A 16-inch Campbell Kid with cloth legs wears a cloth tag on its arm that reads: "The Campbell Kids// Trademark// Lic'd by Joseph Campbell Company// Reg'd by E. I. Horsman Co.// name Gesetzlich Geschützt in Deutschland."

(See Ill. 266.)

**Canadian.** 1892. One of the *Brownies* designed by *Palmer Cox.*

**Canadian Dolls.** 1914–25. The outbreak of World War I started the manufacture of dolls in Canada. There was a 100 percent increase in the manufacturing of dolls in 1918 over 1917. In 1919 it was reported, "The industry has been confronted with many difficulties in its comparatively brief existence. In some other toy-producing countries, such as Great Britain or Germany, the manufacture of dolls, for example, is greatly simplified by parts being secured from makers who specialize in a single phase of the industry. Doll-makers have been assemblers rather than manufacturers . . .

"Such developments have not been entered upon fully in Canada yet. Eyes for dolls, for instance, are not made in the Dominion, but have to be secured from outside. Bisque sand has been discovered recently in Hastings county [Ontario], and bisque dolls' heads are now being manufactured that are stated to be of fine quality. Similarly hair and other parts are now produced within the country.

"The making of dolls' clothing has been another problem for toy-makers to solve. The manufacture of stockings, shoes, etc., demands special equipment, and these articles have not been easily secured in the past. . . .

"One German-made doll that formerly retailed in Canada at about $5.50 now is quoted by its manufacturers at about $12.00. . . .

"The manufacture of wooden toys has been a field in which Canadians say they have excelled . . . Fibre dolls, made of wood pulp, are proving to be quite attractive.

"About one-third of the toys now being shown in the Dominion are made in Canada."
Canadian doll manufacturers include:
*Brophey Doll Co.*
*Reliable Toy Co.*
Canadian doll distributors include:
The *J. E. Beauchamp Co.,* agent for *Century Doll Co.*
*T. Eaton Co.,* who handled the same doll lines as *Sears, Roebuck & Co.*

**Candia, Lillian S.** 1924. New York City. Obtained U.S. design patent for a two-piece rag doll with African features and fuzzy hair.

**Candy Kid, The.** 1911–1912. One of the *Horsman Art Dolls* made with *Can't Break 'Em* composition head and hands on a cloth body. It had molded hair and was dressed in rompers.

1912: Advertised by *Montgomery Ward & Co.* as wearing a playsuit, 11 inches tall, price 98¢, and as a

YOUTH'S COMPANION premium with size nearly 12 inches, price $1.00.

**Cannon, James.** 1852–55. London. Made dolls.

**Can't Break 'Em Dolls.** 1892–ca. 1917. Made of a composition patented by *Solomon D. Hoffmann* in 1892.

1895–1909: These dolls were made by *The American Doll & Toy Co.* Stuffed bodies, jointed for sitting, were used with "Can't Break 'Em" heads. At first these bodies were imported from Germany, but by 1908 they were made by the American Doll & Toy Manufacturing Co.

1909–ca. 1917: Made by *Aetna Doll & Toy Co.* and distributed by *Horsman.* For description of the ingredients and method of manufacture in 1892, 1903, and 1912, see **Manufacture of Composition Heads.** Although these heads had a reputation for durability, they did not stand the test of time; most of the ones surviving are badly cracked and peeling.

1908: According to advertisements, a nail was hammered with one of the dolls' heads by a salesman in St. Louis in order to prove its toughness. Dolls came with painted hair or wigs, and some had glass eyes. One of the new dolls was named *Fluffy Ruffles.*

1909: *Borgfeldt* was distributor of these dolls for a short time.

1910: Horsman sole distributor; produced *Campbell Kids, Baby Bumps, Peterkin,* etc. They advertised that faces were hand-painted by trained artists and included character faces and "doll type of beauty." Light gray eyes were used extensively. *Butler Bros.,* secondary distributor, advertised Can't Break 'Em dolls with glass eyes, mohair wigs, and composition hands; size 17 inches; price 75¢.

1911: There were fifty different numbers made in various sizes; these included two new jointed baby-body dolls. A girl character doll with wig cost $2.00, and a boy character doll cost $3.00. Among the new dolls were *Chinkee, Fairy, Jap Rose Kids,* etc.

1912: Over a million Can't Break 'Em dolls were being produced each year. *Gee Gee* designed by *Grace Drayton* and *Little Billy* were among the dolls that were new. Dolls of this material were probably made for several more years; it is not known when they were finally superseded, but it may have been with the introduction of *Adtocolite* by Horsman in 1917.

**Canton Kids.** 1915. Dolls copied after two Chinese children in San Francisco by *Horsman.*

**Canzler & Hoffmann.** 1906–25+. Berlin and Sonneberg, Thür. Doll manufacturer and exporter.

1925: Registered *Caho* as their trademark in Germany for dolls and dressed dolls.

**268.** Trademark of Canzler & Hoffmann.

**Caoutchouc.** See **Rubber Dolls.**

**Capital Doll Corp.** 1922–24. New York City. Made all wood-pulp dolls; among them was *Bathing Beauty,* a lady doll.

**Capital Toy Co.** 1923–25. New York City. Made Capital *Mama Dolls* in sizes 13 to 27 inches.

**Capo.** 1916–17. Line of dolls made by *Non-Breakable Toy Co.* Some have composition heads with stuffed bodies; others are all-composition and made to stand alone. A molded-hair baby was 24 inches tall; a clown was 36 inches tall. Nearly a million of these dolls were advertised to have been made in a year. "Capo" was a shortened form of the name Joseph Capuano. (See Ill. 1727.)

**Capo Di Monte.** 1736–1925+. Environs of Naples, Italy. Dolls have been found with marks that resemble those of this famous porcelain factory, but identification should be authenticated by experts as this factory, like *Meissen,* has been imitated and copied.

**269.** Capo Di Monte mark.

**Caprice.** 1921. Trademark registered in Germany by *Emil Bauersachs* for character dolls.

**Captain Jinks.** 1912. Made by *Ideal Novelty & Toy Co.;* came dressed in khaki uniform, trimmed with red.

**Card, Edson B.** 1921–22. White Plains, N.Y. Obtained two U.S. design patents for men dolls with elongated limbs and a copyright for the *Daddy Doll.*

**Cardarelli.** 1869–75. Paris. Made dolls and dolls trousseaux.

**Cardon, Mme. Augustine (Andrée Vassor née Cardon).** 1921. France. Obtained a French patent for a doll's head with two faces and a reversible wig.

**Care of Dolls.** See **Custodianship.**

**Carette.** See **Huret.**

**Carette.** 1921. Paris. Distributor and exporter of dolls' heads, eyes, wigs, and Tibetan mohair.

**Caretto, Mary.** 1922. Bisbee, Ariz. Obtained U.S. design patent for a rag doll.

**Carey, Lawrence F.** 1919–20. Philadelphia, Pa. Registered *Babs* as a U.S. trademark.

**Carey, Patricia M.** 1919–20. Los Angeles. Designed dolls that were made by the *Sunny Twin Dolly Co.* She obtained two U.S. design patents, one for a girl and the other for a boy, both bent-limb babies. These she assigned to *Leslie C. Brintnall.*

**Carl.** 1910. Trade name for a boy character doll made by *Kämmer & Reinhardt* and distributed by *Strobel & Wilken* and *Borgfeldt.*

**Carl.** 1911. Character child doll designed by *Helen Trowbridge* and made by *Horsman.*

**Carl, August Friedrich.** 1923–25. Sonneberg, Thür. Made dolls.

**Carl, Max, & Co.** 1891. Neustadt near Coburg, Thür. Specialized in dolls.

**270.** Mark used by Max Carl & Co.

# R.C. DEPOSE

**271.** Robert Carl's mark for dolls.

**Carl, Robert.** 1895–1910, Köppelsdorf Thür.; 1910–25+ *Frickmann & Robert A. Lindner,* successor of Robert Carl. They produced and distributed dolls and doll parts, especially dolls with porcelain heads. (See Ill. 1617.)

1908: Robert Carl registered *Mausi* (Mousie) as a trademark in Germany.

**Carlier, Fournelle & Gibon.** 1925. Paris. Listed with a doll named *La Parisienne* created by *Maurice Millière.*

**Carmencita.** See **Bébé Carmencita.**

**Carnival Baby.** 1912–14. Clown doll made by *Horsman.* Also named "Baby Pierrot." Came with *Can't Break 'Em* head, soft body, white satin dress, white face with red and blue spots; size 13 inches; price $1.00.

**Caro.** See **Bébé Caro.**

**Caron.** 1855–90. Paris. Made dolls. J. Caron was listed in directories from 1855 to 1860.

1867: He displayed mechanical dolls at the Paris Exposition.

1868: Won a silver medal for dolls at the Paris Exposition.

1878: A. J. Caron showed clowns, dressed toys, and mechanical dolls at the Paris Exposition.

1882: J. Caron, toymaker, was listed as using the initials "J.C."

1885–90: A. Caron was listed in directories as a doll maker.

**Carpenter, William B.** 1880–81. Newark, N.J. Obtained two U.S. patents and one British patent, all relating to the manufacture of celluloid dolls. His U.S. patents he assigned to the *Celluloid Novelty Co.* His British patent pertained to the manufacture of molded hollow articles out of celluloid, especially dolls' heads, by means of a screw press and heating arrangement that rendered the celluloid plastic by heat.

**Carriage Dolls.** 1917. Trade name of leather or fabric dolls made by *Moore & Gibson.*

**Carrie.** 1913. Doll distributed by *Borgfeldt;* had eyes glancing to the side; was mate to *Harry.*

**Carrie Joy.** 1924–25. Trademark registered in U.S. by *Ideal Novelty & Toy Co.*

**Carrier Belleuse.** Up to 1887, Sèvres, France. Artist for porcelain products made at *Sèvres;* he is believed to have designed some of the *Jumeau* bébés.

**Carroll McComas.** 1924. *Celebrity Doll* originated by *Margaret Vale,* designed and made by *Jane Gray.* The doll represents Carroll McComas as the *Jolly Roger* in Walter Hampden's vehicle THE JOLLY ROGER. It has a hand-painted face and bears a tag with a facsimile autograph of Carroll McComas.

**Carson, Pirie, Scott & Co.** 1911–14. Chicago, Ill. Registered *Dolly Mine* as a U.S. trademark.

**Carton Moulé, Carton Pâté, Carton Pierre.** French terms for various types of composition out of which dolls were made, excluding wood pulp composition.

**Carvaillo, Adrien.** 1923–25. Paris. Made rag dolls called *La Vénus,* a name that he registered as a trademark in France.

**Casadora.** 1920–25. Trademark registered in Germany by *Hüttinger & Buschor* for a walking and talking doll, which they also patented in Germany. They advertised that the doll walked in a natural manner when led by its hand, and moved its eyes in all directions.

**Case, Minnie E.** 1925. Pratt, Kans. Secured a U.S. design patent for a rag doll dressed as an Arabian.

**Cassanet, A., & Cie.** See **Boulouch & Laporte**

**Casseler Puppenfabrik.** 1909–18. Kassel, Hesse-Nassau. Doll factory operated by *M. R. Rosenstein, Jr.*

**Cassia.** 1867. Type of tree or shrub used to make dolls' heads.

**Cassidy, Alice.** 1916–17. Hubbard, Ore. Was granted a U.S. design patent for a doll dressed as Santa Claus.

**Catterfelder Puppenfabrik.** 1902–25+. Catterfeld near Waltershausen, Thür. Also known as the doll factory of Carl Trautmann (Trautwein) and of his successors, Hugo & Richard Gross, and later Franz Kundy. They specialized in jointed dolls and baby dolls, and advertised their products as being in hand-made and machine-made qualities. They also made doll parts.

1905: Meffert & Co. of New York City was the sole U.S. distributor of the *Waltershauser* dolls manufactured by Carl Trautmann; they advertised dolls that walked, talked, saluted, turned their heads, slept, and could sit down.

1910: Catterfelder Puppenfabrik registered two trademarks in Germany. One was a picture of two dolls with the initials "C. P.," and the other was *Mein Sonnesschein* (My Sunshine).

1922: Franz Kundy registered in Germany two trademarks for Catterfelder Puppenfabrik. They were *Kleiner Sonnenschein* and its English version, *Little Sunshine.*

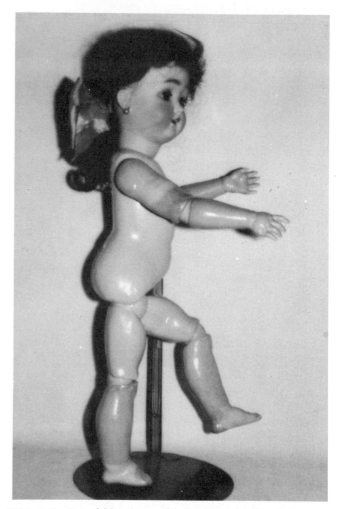

**272A & B.** Catterfelder Puppenfabrik produced this doll using Kestner bisque head No. 264. Mark: Ill. **274.** Sleeping eyes with eyelashes, open mouth with four teeth, ball-jointed composition body. H. 19 inches. *Courtesy of Dorothy Annunziato.*

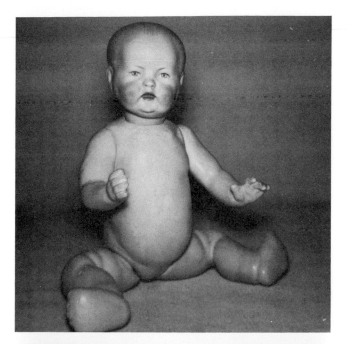

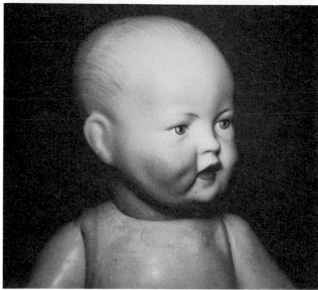

273A & B. Catterfelder Puppenfabrik mark: Ill. 275. Wire-strung composition bent-limb baby body. Bisque head has painted eyes and hair. H. 11 inches. *Coleman Collection.*

274 & 275. Marks found on dolls made by Catterfelder Puppenfabrik.

1923: Registered Little Sunshine as a trademark in Britain.

The fact that "Catterfelder Puppenfabrik" and "K & Co.," the *Kestner* mark, both appear on a bisque head seems to indicate that Kestner supplied some of the heads used on dolls made by Catterfelder Puppenfabrik.

**Catusse.** 1904–19. Paris. Made dolls. The listing was Catusse Père (Sr.) in 1910–19.

**Cauldon Potteries.** 1774–1925+. Cauldon, Staffordshire. Fragments of dolls' heads have been found on the Cauldon premises, but the marks—if any—that were used on the dolls' heads have not been identified. These heads were probably made in the late 19th or early 20th century. (See also **Ridgeway.**)

**Caussin.** 1879. Paris. Doll maker.

**Cawood Novelty Manufacturing Co.** Ca. 1920. Danville, Ill. Made "Cutie," a cherub-type doll, priced 25¢.

276 & 277. Trademarks of Mme. Cayette.

276        277

**Cayette, Mme. E. (née Mommessin, Marie).** 1909. Paris. Registered in France the following trademarks: *Bébé Prophéte, Bébé Oracle, La Fée au Gui, La Fée au Trèfle, La Fée aux Trèfles, La Fée Bonheur,* a four-leaf clover, and a five-pointed star.

**Cayuga Felt Products Co.** 1923. Union Springs, N.Y. Made hand-tinted rag dolls, 13 inches tall, price 50¢.

**Cecily Doll, The.** 1918. Trademark registered in Britain by Edward Joseph Revill of *Edwards and Pamflett,* a firm specializing in dolls.

**Cee Bee Doll Manufacturing Co.** 1919–24. New York City. Proprietor was *Charles B. Blum;* his initials were used for the company name. They made composition dolls of the cherub type, which came with or without wigs.

1919: Four sizes, priced $1.00 and up.

**Celebrate.** 1895–1925+. Trademark registered in the U.S. and in Germany by *Borgfeldt.* The label on an original box containing a doll whose head has the sunburst mark of *Gebr. Heubach* reads "Celebrate Dressed Dolls."

1909: "Celebrate" trademark used by Borgfeldt for a line of kid-body dolls.

**Celebrity Dolls.** 1924. *Margaret Vale's* Celebrity Creations, Inc., selected celebrities and obtained rights from them; then *Jane Gray* produced the dolls, which were hand-painted likenesses of stage or screen celebrities with costumes copied from those worn by them. Each doll bore a tag with the facsimile autograph of the celebrity it represented, the name of the character portrayed, and the most appropriate line from the play.

**Cellaline Co.** 1919–21. London. Made dolls.

**Cellulobrin.** 1909–12. Patented material used by *Hugo*

*Braun* and *Franz Schmidt* in their Cellulobrinwerke Inc., Georgenthal, Thür., to make doll bodies. The name was registered as a German trademark in 1909 by Franz Schmidt & Co.

**Cellulobrinwerke Inc.** See **Cellulobrin.**

**Celluloid Dolls.** Ca. 1869–1925+. Originally, the trade name for dolls made by the Hyatt Brothers of a synthetic material composed of cellulose nitrate (pyroxylin), camphor, pigments, fillers, and alcohol. In 1869, John Wesley Hyatt and his brother Isaiah Smith Hyatt began to manufacture celluloid products in Newark, N.J., under the name *Celluloid Novelty Co.* The material had been discovered earlier in England, and later the name "celluloid" was applied to pyroxylin plastics made by other manufacturers.

The Hyatts had started to experiment with celluloid products as early as 1863, and it is not known when they produced the first celluloid dolls. A celluloid doll is made by blowing steam or hot air into molds. (See **Manufacture of Celluloid Dolls.**)

1880: *William B. Carpenter* obtained a U.S. patent for improving celluloid dolls' heads. He claimed that up to that time celluloid heads had a glazed or glossy look. This patent was assigned to the Celluloid Novelty Co.

1881: Carpenter and M. C. Lefferts obtained another U.S. patent on celluloid dolls, which they likewise assigned to the Celluloid Novelty Co. (*Rheinische Gummi & Celluloid Fabrik Co.* of Bavaria had been founded in 1873, but it is not known when they started making celluloid dolls.)

1887: *Valmore Boitel* obtained a French patent to make celluloid dolls, which he claimed were new in France.

During the first decade of the 20th century, celluloid dolls were still expensive, but were coming more and more into favor. They were made by *Cuno and Otto Dressel, Kämmer & Reinhardt* (who obtained a German patent for a sleeping-eyed celluloid doll in 1903), *Buschow & Beck, Kestner,* and other firms.

1903: A new bisque finish for celluloid dolls was advertised as making them resemble wax dolls.

1906: Celluloid hands with cloth bodies were a new feature. Kestner advertised that their celluloid heads would not fade, as had happened heretofore when aniline colors were used. Italian girls brought to Germany painted celluloid dolls' heads.

1907: A New Jersey manufacturing company (possibly Celluloid Novelty Co. or its successor) patented fireproof celluloid. Since celluloid's basic ingredient is gunpowder cotton, the dolls heretofore had been highly inflammable.

1907–10: *Minerva* metal heads were coated with a combination of celluloid and washable enamel to prevent their cracking and chipping (but, alas, not successfully).

1909: *Horsman* advertised dolls with celluloid faces for 25¢ and 50¢. Other firms advertised similar celluloid-faced dolls.

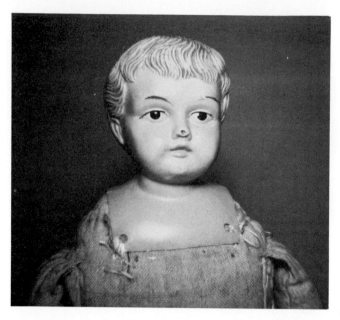

278. Celluloid head of a child, with painted and molded features. Mark: Ill. **280.** H. of shoulder head, 3 inches. *Coleman Collection.*

279. All-celluloid baby with bent limbs, painted features. Marked only "2" on the body. H. 8 inches. *Courtesy of Theodora Gearhart.*

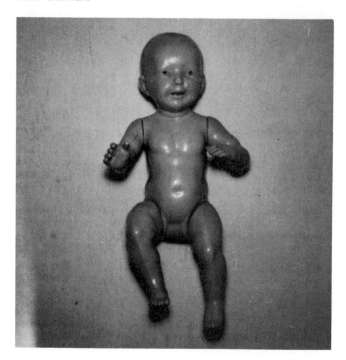

280 281

**280 & 281.** Marks found on celluloid dolls. (See Ill. **278.**)

1910: *Butler Bros.* advertised celluloid heads on kid bodies. These dolls had painted features, molded hair, bisque hands; all except the smallest size had patent rivet hip joints; sizes 9¾, 12, 14½, and 16¼ inches; prices $2.10 to $9.00 doz. wholesale.

Celluloid was used for dolls' heads, faces (masks), entire dolls' bodies, and hands. *Parsons-Jackson Co.* made all-celluloid type baby dolls before World War I. During World War I celluloid was used for dolls' eyes, and celluloid dolls were imported from Japan. After the war, celluloid continued to be used for dolls, but it does not appear to have had the popularity it had prior to the war.

**Celluloid Novelty Co.** 1869–81. Newark, N.J. The original company of the Hyatt brothers. Manufactured celluloid dolls.

1880–81: Assignee of two U.S. patents for celluloid dolls and/or dolls' heads by *William B. Carpenter.*

**Cellulosine.** See **La Cellulosine.**

**Cellunova.** 1913. Trademark registered in Germany by *Kley & Hahn* for dolls and dolls' heads.

**Central Doll Manufacturing Co.** 1917–21. New York City. Made stuffed character baby dolls.

1917: Advertised baby dressed in white lawn, 26 inches tall.

1921: There were 144 numbers; babies came in four sizes up to 30 inches; prices 25¢ to $5.00.

**282.** Mama Doll with bisque head, made by Kestner for Century Doll Co., has cloth body, composition limbs. Mark: Ill. **284.** H. 19 inches. *Courtesy of Jessica R. Norman.*

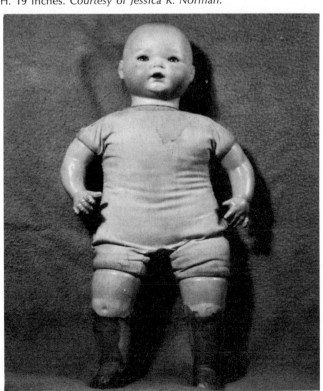

**Century Doll Co.** 1909–25. New York City. Doll distributors. Made "Century Dolls."

1916: Advertised one hundred new numbers; came with wigs, painted eyes, etc.

1917: Advertised *Breast Plate dolls' heads,* and that

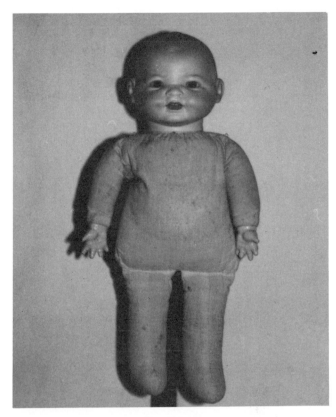

**283A & B.** Bisque flanged-neck baby head with sleeping eyes. Cotton body with composition hands. Voice box. Mark: Ill. **285.** H. 15 inches. *Courtesy of Lester & Alice Grinnings.*

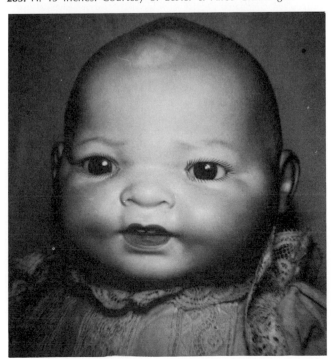

**284**

Germanÿ.
℃ENTURY DOLL &.℮·

**285**

Germany
Century Doll Co.

**286**

CENTURY DOLL C℃.
Kestner Germany

**287**

**288**

**284–288.** Marks used by Century Doll Co.; Nos. **284–287** found on dolls' heads.

every pair of hands would match head in flesh tint; moving glass eyes or stationary glass eyes; real curly-hair wigs. Century Doll Co. was distributor for Follender Co. wigs.

1918: Advertised *Quality Bilt* line of American dolls and *Baby Shirley* line of glue-process-composition shoulder heads. The heads came plain or wigged. Century claimed that glue process was superior to brittle wood-pulp composition. They had a Canadian agent, *J. E. Beauchamp Co.*, in Montreal, and were still handling Follender wigs.

1920: Advertised 250 new numbers of cork-stuffed dressed dolls and eight new models of dolls' heads; five numbers of jointed composition dolls with glass moving eyes and eyelashes. Dolls could sit or stand; came in sizes 7 to 32 inches.

1921: Advertised genuine bisque or "Wood-Bisk" heads; baby dolls came in four sizes; straight jointed-limb dolls had sleeping glass eyes and came in four sizes; eight new styles of stuffed dolls. Century also advertised the *Fiji Wiji* line of rag dolls created by *Grace Corry*, including Fiji Wiji, *Blue Eyes, Romper Boy,* and *Clown*.

1922: Advertised *Mama Dolls* that would walk, talk, and sleep. They had Grubman voices and wood-fiber heads,

with no rubber or glue used. The new trade names included *Brown Skin Dolls* and *Kuddle Kiddies*.

1924: They had agents in Britain and South America. Among their new dolls were *Babette* and *Barbara*.

1925: Obtained exclusive U.S. use of the *Kestner* crown trademark. They advertised a new series of "unbreakable" bisque heads made by Kestner with glass sleeping eyes. One of these was a swivel socket head on a soft body, made so that the head could turn up or down. It had sleeping eyes, eyelashes, movable arms and legs, and a Mama-Papa voice. At the beginning of 1925 they made *Sweetums,* their version of the *Bye-Lo Baby.* It came in two sizes, and by the end of the year it was called *Clap Hands* because it could do so.

**Century Toy & Novelty Co.** 1912. Brooklyn, N.Y. They made dolls with "plastic" (composition) heads, the models of which were advertised as exclusive designs by doll artists. Company merged with *Ideal Novelty & Toy Co.*

**Ceramic Furga.** See **Furga.**

**Ceresota.** After 1895. Trademark found on a rag doll representing a farmer boy, with high boots and hat. The Northwestern Consolidated Milling Co. began using the trademark Ceresota in 1891, but they did not use the farmer boy as a trademark until 1895. This cutout-type

**289.** Doll distributed as an advertisement by the North Western Consolidated Milling Co. with their trademark "Ceresota" across the chest. Design is lithographed on the fabric, which is sewed together and stuffed. Mark: Ill. **290.** H. 15½ inches. *Coleman Collection.*

290. Mark found on Ceresota rag doll.

rag doll was a form of advertisement for the milling company, and may have been made out of a flour sack. The date of the doll and how long it was made are unknown.

**Cervenka, Emanuel.** 1918. France. Obtained a French patent for a doll with an elastic material for its face so that it could change expression.

**Cetand Co.** Name reported found on bisque head of a bent-limb baby doll.

**Chad Valley Co.** See **Johnson Bros., Ltd.**

**Chalory, Vve. (Widow).** 1893. Paris. Obtained a French patent for a lightweight bébé.

**Chalté & Leborgne.** 1861–68. Paris. Made dolls.

1861: Advertised small, flexible dolls without clothes; porcelain heads and dolls' trousseaux.

1867: Specialized in little dolls that were flexible and undressable, dressed and undressed bisque dolls, clothes for bébés, and a patented doll that walked alone.

**Chalureau, Mme.** 1902–6. Paris. Made dolls.

**Chambre Syndicale des Fabricants de Jouets Français (Chambre Syndicale des Fabricants de Jouets et Jeux et Engins Sportifs).** 1886–1921. Paris. Trade organization composed of a group of French toy manufacturers. *Péan (Frères)* was #1, G. Vichy (maker of mechanical dolls) was #5, *Henri Alexandre* was #13, and *Falck & Roussel* was #31. *Dehais* used the mark of this organization, but his number is not known. All these companies were members before 1890. Number 84 has been found on dolls, but has not been identified with a member.

**Chamson, Mlle.** 1868. Paris. Secured a French patent for a type of composition to be used in making dolls.

**Change-O-Doll Co.** 1923. U.S. Made Change-O-Dolls based on the patent of *David Wiener*. These dolls were distributed by *Berg Bros.* and *Berwick Doll Co.* Dolls came with six different heads, including a clown and a Negro, some with eyes glancing to the side and others looking straight ahead. They had stuffed bodies and were 15½ inches tall; priced $9.00 to $21.00 doz. wholesale depending on the number of heads, the wig and the Mama voice. Heads alone cost $2.75 doz. wholesale with painted hair and $4.25 doz. wholesale with wigs.

**Chantilly, Cie. (Société Anonyme).** 1924–25. Paris. Registered in France their trademark "Chantilly" over a coat of arms. They specialized in "unbreakable" dolls' heads, and had factories at Montreuil and at Lilas, Seine.

**Character Dolls.** Lifelike representations of real people, especially babies and children.

During the 19th century, a few portrait-type dolls were made representing famous personages and were called character dolls, but the great period of the character doll was after 1900. In the 1890's there were *Brownies, Steiff,* and a few other character dolls. As early as February, 1903, *Edmund Ulrich Steiner,* then with *Samstag and Hilder,* predicted: "The dolls whose faces are copied from American baby models will attract universal attention." It should be noted that Samstag and Hilder in 1903 were advertising *Duchess (Armand Marseille)* and *Royal (Kämmer & Reinhardt)* doll lines. In 1904 the models of actual American baby faces reached greater perfection and received more notice. The following statements appeared in January and February, 1904: "Faces now made to coincide with the apparent age of the doll. The baby in long dress does not have the same head as a young lady in the latest Parisian gown. . . . Chubby faced baby dolls, dolls in which the faces are real baby faces and little baby faces at that are popular. More and more reality and life-likeness are given to dolls each year, the last year or two having brought forth marked advances in this direction."

*Bawo & Dotter* advertised "Character Dolls" in January, 1906. *Dolly Dimples,* a doll with a real baby face, was described in February, 1907 as follows: " 'Dolly Dimples' doll head was modeled after that of a real baby. Manufacturers went to a famous artist for their model. He was a man who had never modeled a doll before. He was a maker of portrait busts. The new model was to be entirely different from anything that had been seen before. . . . With these baby faces a separate model must be used for each size, as it will not do to enlarge or diminish from the same model to produce larger or smaller heads. The delicate curves of the ears, standing rather far away from the head; the dainty, bumpy forehead with that characteristic depression just over the eyebrow; the perky little nose as unlike a grown-up nose as anything can be; the chubby cheeks with the chubbiness rather low as it is seen in the youngest children; a photograph of this doll is really a photograph of a baby." Also in 1907, Edmund Ulrich Steiner advertised *Human Face Dolls.* Laura Starr, in THE DOLL BOOK published in 1908, described the character-type dolls made by *Orwell Art Industries* in Dublin, Ireland.

The popularity of character dolls swept through the industry; it has accounted for a large percentage, if not the majority, of the dolls produced in the 20th century. Among the early character dolls were the *Munich Art Dolls* of *Marion Kaulitz* and sculptor *Paul Vogelsanger,* the "Character Brand" dolls of Kämmer & Reinhardt, and dolls made by Steiff, *Kestner, Gebrüder Heubach,* and *Käthe Kruse.* Some of these dolls were shown in the 1909 Berlin Exhibition, and were noted for their lifelike appearance and the fact that they were specially designed by artists, sculptors, and painters with national reputations.

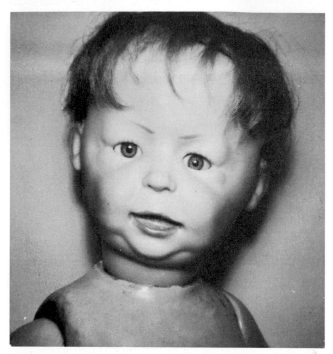

**291.** Character-faced doll, bisque head marked "1428//6," glass sleep eyes, wig, jointed bent-limb baby body. H. 14 inches. *Courtesy of Jessica Norman.*

**292.** Character-faced doll with pensive look, made by Gebrüder Heubach; has blue glass eyes, closed mouth, brown hair wig. *Courtesy of Margaret Whitton; photograph by Winnie Langley.*

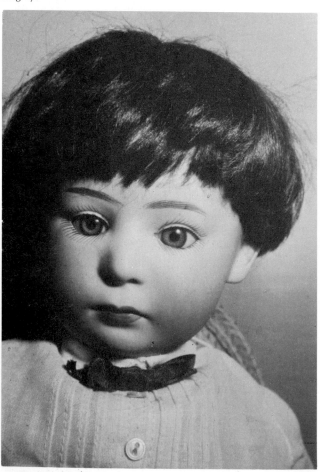

In 1904, *Carl Bergner* of Sonneberg had applied for a British patent for a multi-face doll with laughing, crying, and sleeping faces. By 1912, other moods besides laughing and crying were portrayed in character dolls.

The prices of character dolls were high at first, and complaints were made that the heads were too large. The German character dolls resemble German children and the French character dolls resemble French children.

**Charakterpuppe.** 1909. Trademark registered in Germany by *Kämmer & Reinhardt* for dolls and parts of dolls.

**Charity Girl.** 1881–82. Trade name for a doll dressed in the uniform of an orphanage; distributed by *Millikin & Lawley*; price 37¢ to $2.62.

**Charlie Chaplin.** 1915. Doll representing the actor was made by *Louis Amberg & Son.* A portrait doll, it came with composition head and hands, molded hair and mustache, stuffed body, characteristic suit, hat, and cane. Cloth label on sleeve has profile of an Indian chief and the following words printed in green:

CHARLIE CHAPLIN DOLL
WORLD'S GREATEST COMEDIAN
MADE EXCLUSIVELY BY LOUIS AMBERG & SON, N.Y.
BY SPECIAL ARRANGEMENT WITH ESSANAY FILM CO.

The doll sold for 65¢ and $1.00.

**Charlie Chaplin.** 1917. Advertised by *Baltimore Bargain House* as having composition head and hands; size 36 inches; price $1.45.

**Charlier.** 1925. Paris. Made artistically dressed dolls for wholesale and export trade.

**Charlot.** 1922. French dolls representing *Charlie Chaplin.* These dolls were made after he visited Paris and the French gave him the name of "Charlot."

**Charlotte Doll.** 1925. Made by *Sol Bergfeld & Son*; distributed by *Borgfeldt.*

**Charlotte-Louise, The.** 1919–22. Trademark registered in the U.S. by *Charlotte L. Glosbrenner.*

**Charmant.** See **Bébé Charmant.**

**Charpentier, Charles (G).** 1885–95. Paris. Made dressed bébés with composition heads that are either fixed or swivel. Trademark is the words "Fabrique Française du Lion, Marque Déposée" in an oval around "C." and a picture of a lion couchant.

**Chase, Martha Jenks.** Ca. 1880's–1925+. Pawtucket, R.I. Made dolls with heads of stockinet fabric. The stockinet material was stretched over a mask with raised features. Then the head and limbs were sized with a coating of glue and/or paste, dried, and painted with oils, so that they could be washed. The features were hand-painted, the rough brush strokes of the hair providing a realistic texture. The eyes were blue or brown, and the hair was usually blonde. The ears and thumbs were applied separately.

The earliest Chase dolls had pink sateen bodies, but later bodies were heavy white cotton cloth, stuffed

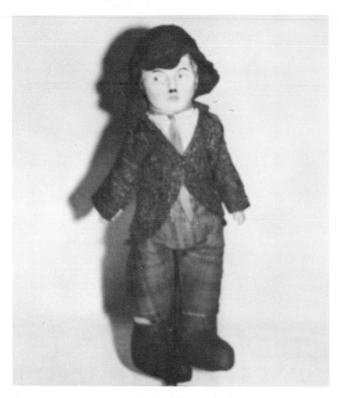

**293A & B.** "Charlie Chaplin" doll, made by Louis Amberg & Son in 1915, has molded composition head and hands, straw-filled body with pin and disk joints. Original clothes include black felt hat. Mark is sewed on right sleeve: Ill. **294.** H. 14½ inches. *Coleman Collection.*

CHARLIE CHAPLIN DOLL
WORLD'S GREATEST COMEDIAN
MADE EXCLUSIVELY BY LOUIS AMBERG & SON, N.Y.
by SPECIAL ARRANGEMENT WITH ESSANAY FILM CO.

**294.** Mark on Amberg's "Charlie Chaplin" doll.

with cotton batting. Legs and arms were painted to above the knees and above the elbows, and an unstuffed area was left at each joint to facilitate movement. Many of the Chase dolls were jointed at the shoulder, elbow, hip, and knee, but later ones were jointed only at the hips and shoulders (probably those made in the 1920's). Dolls came in sizes 00 to that of a year-old child. They have been found as small as 9 inches. Baby dolls had fatter faces and bodies and slightly different eyes from those of the children dolls.

1909: R. H. Macy & Co. advertised Chase stockinet dolls in sizes 16, 17, 21, and 24 inches; prices $2.49 to $4.96.

1910: Advertised dolls that could be washed in warm water, which suggests that by this time they were painted all over with waterproof paint; also advertised that all dolls carried the Chase trademark. This was either on the thigh or under the arm, but often it has been rubbed off. Dolls came in six sizes, 12, 16, 20 24 27, and 30 inches.

1913: F. A. O. *Schwarz* advertised Chase dolls in sizes 12 to 30 inches; prices $2.50 to $7.50.

1921: Chase advertised characters from ALICE IN WONDERLAND, including *Alice,* Tweedle-dee and Tweedle-dum, the Mad-Hatter, the *Duchess,* and the Frog-footman; characters from books of Joel Chandler Harris, including *Mammy Nurse* and two *Pickaninnies* (see color photograph C9); also *George Washington.* The characters from Dickens, Mrs. Gamp, Little Nell, etc., probably were made about this same time. Mrs. Chase may have developed all these character dolls at an earlier date—a descendant states as early as 1905.

1922: Advertised nineteen numbers, including dolls with molded Dutch-cut bobbed hair. A bow of ribbon was attached to the heads of these dolls, which came in six sizes.

**295.** Chase stockinet doll with face and lower limbs painted in oils; hair defined by paints in impasto; cloth body. H. 12 inches. *Coleman Collection.*

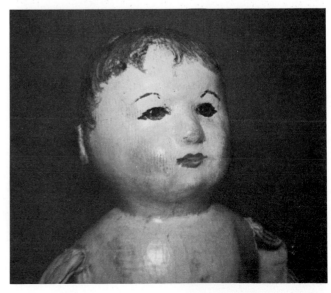

**296.** Three rag dolls made by Martha Chase representing characters in books by Charles Dickens; original clothes. *Photograph by Winnie Langley.*

M.U.C.
Stockinet Doll
Patent Applied For
297

PAWTUCKET, R.I
MADE IN U.S.A.
298

**297 & 298.** Martha Chase marks; No. **297** is an early mark, and No. **298** is her trademark.

Special clothing for the Chase dolls was designed by Mrs. Gretchen Murray.

In 1911, Mrs. Chase developed a hospital doll, but it was life size and not a play doll.

**Chassoux.** 1900–1902. Paris. Made dolls.

**Chattanooga Medicine Co.** 1909–10. Chattanooga, Tenn. Registered *Velvokin* as a trademark for dolls in the U.S.

**Chatterbox.** 1923. Talking doll made by the *Progressive Toy Co.*; talks when wound; size 25 inches.

**Chaufour.** 1871–75. Paris. Made dressed and undressed dolls, including *La Poupée Merveilleuse.*

**Chautard.** 1852. Paris. Handled dolls.

**Chauvière.** 1848–90 or later. Paris. Jacques Chauvière was in the doll business from 1848 to 1852, or longer.

1861: Mlle. Chauvière obtained a French patent for improvements in making a jointed, stuffed, kid-body doll.

1870: She secured a French patent for an automatic talking bébé made in a lighter and more resistant composition and with better articulation in the arms and legs. She claimed it had a better talking and crying mechanism. The bébés (bodies) were to be covered with cloth or kid, which was glued or stitched on. Mlle. Chauvière & Cie. appeared in Paris Directories under Dolls from 1863 through 1877.

1890's: Chauvière was listed as specializing in jointed bébés at *Au Nain Bleu*. Several dolls have been found with the body marked "Au Nain Bleu, E. Chauvière." There was an Edouard Chauvière at Au Nain Bleu, and the "E" may stand for Edouard. According to A HISTORY OF TOYS by Antonio Fraser, Au Nain Bleu was founded in 1836 by Jean-Baptiste Chauvière, and Edouard Chauvière was his son.

**Checalier & Venard.** 1850. Paris. Secured a French patent for a doll jointed so that it could be put into any desired position.

**Checkeni (Cheeckeni), Dominico.** 1866–85. Marion, Conn., Brooklyn, N.Y., and New Haven, Conn. Obtained a U.S. patent in 1866 for a doll with a wax face, which revolved vertically, displaying four different expressions. In 1867 he patented a toy rope-dancing doll. The 1866 patent was assigned in part to *George Thompson*. The New Haven Directories, 1883–85, list both Dominico Checkeni, toymaker, and Ozias Morse; see Ill. 303.

**Chemise.** The garment often found on "undressed" dolls. It usually had sleeves and covered the doll from the neck to mid-calf. It could be of fine muslin or printed batiste with lace, ribbons, and ruffles; or it might be made of the cheapest cheesecloth.

**Chéret & Moreau.** 1879–85. Paris. From 1889–92, E. Chéret distributed dolls.

1881–92: Advertised *nankeen*-bodied dolls, swimmers, bathers, jointed dolls with hair, as well as German bébés and patented walking bébés. Chéret was an agent in Paris for doll makers of Saxony, Bavaria, and Austria.

**Chéri Bébé.** 1914. Trademark registered in France by *Rehbock & Loewenthal;* used for dolls with bisque heads and ball-jointed composition bodies.

**Chérie.** Name on bisque head made in Limoges by *Lanternier;* came with open mouth, pierced ears, glass eyes, and wig.

**Cherie.** 1921. Trade name for a doll made by the *New Era Toy & Novelty Co.* Came in sizes 14 and 16 inches; priced $8.75 and $10.00 doz. wholesale.

**Cherub Doll, The.** 1886–87. Trademark registered in Britain by A. & J. *Isaacs,* doll importers and doll dressers.

S&H 1079-6
DEP.
Germany

300                                    301

**300 & 301.** Marks on dolls handled by Chauvière.

**299A & B.** One of a pair of dolls with Simon & Halbig bisque heads; marked "Au Nain Bleu, E. Chauvière." Have composition bodies, original dress, glass sleep eyes, and wig. Marks: head, Ill. **300;** body, Ill. **301.** H. 15 inches. *Courtesy of Mary Wenzel.*

**302.** Four-faced doll patented by Dominico Checkeni in 1866; wax over composition; long corkscrew curls; hat trimmed with a green feather. The sleeping face is shown in the photograph. Mark: Ill. **303.** *Photograph by Winnie Langley.*

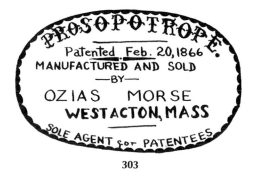

303                                    304

**303.** Mark on dolls patented by Dominico Checkeni.

**304.** The "Cherub Doll" trademark.

**Cherub-Type Doll.** After 1910, various dolls were made with puckish expressions and features resembling those of *Kewpies*.

**Chessler Co., The.** 1921–22. Baltimore, Md. Made a stuffed doll named *Flo* that walked and talked.

**Chester Gump.** 1924. Represented cartoon character; made by *Fleming Doll Co.*

**Chevallier.** See **Brasseur.**

**Chevrot, H.** See **Bru.**

**Chicago Novelty Co.** 1921. Made dolls.

**Chicin.** 1919–20. Trademark registered in U.S. by *Magic Novelty Co.*, for dolls. Some of these composition dolls had eyes glancing to the side and movable arms.

**Chief.** 1919. Trade name for an Indian-type doll made by *J. R. Miranda & Co.*; 14-inch doll was dressed in an Indian blanket.

**Chief Wolf Robe.** 1915. Copyrighted by *Mary Frances Woods*. It was an Indian-type doll with head modeled in composition and painted; came with braids of hair, a war bonnet and feathers, and was wrapped in a woolen Indian blanket.

**Childhood Character Dolls.** 1912. Line of "unbreakable" character dolls made by *Gund Manufacturing Co.* The line included *The Little Rogues, Marion, Wally,* etc.; price 25¢ to $2.00.

**Children, Well and Happy.** 1917–22. Trademark registered in U.S. by *May Bliss Dickinson* for dolls. The words were printed on a banner, carried by a toddler.

**Chilian, H.** 1909. Neustadt near Coburg, Thür. Made dolls' bodies.

**Chime Dolls.** 1911–22. When the doll is shaken up and down, a musical chime inside the doll can be heard.

1911: Came as Negro or character dolls, 8 inches high; price $1.00 and up.

1922: Distributed by *Sears, Roebuck & Co.*; came with composition heads and wigs; sizes 14, 16, and 17½ inches; price 48¢ to $1.19.

**Chin Chin Baby.** Germany. All-bisque doll with its name on a triangular sticker on its stomach; reported by Genevieve Angione.

**China Head Dolls.** Made of glazed porcelain, although some early advertisements refer to "unglazed china." However, collectors distinguish between unglazed ceramics, which they call "bisque," and the glazed ceramics, which are called "china." Generally it is only the head or head and limbs that are made of china. An article in HARPER'S BAZAR, November, 1884, states, "China dolls are more exclusively the product of the factory. . . . A single oven contains 5,000 dolls, and thirty ovens are often full at once in the one factory. . . . One German factory has been running about one hundred and thirty years, and has produced about one billion dolls."

Although the making of china dolls began around 1750, they did not reach great popularity until the 1840's. A few china heads have the Apollo's knot hairdo, popular in the 1830's, but the hairdos of most of the more elaborate china heads reflect the fashions of the 1840's, 1850's, and 1860's. It *must* be remembered that a popular style of doll often continued to be made many years after it first appeared. For example, the flat top with short curls all around the head was shown at the 1862 London Exhibition, but it was still being advertised as late as 1884. Many of the early china heads have long necks with adult-type hairdos, which identifies them as lady dolls. Dolls representing children have shorter necks and short hair styles; some of these windblown types are found advertised, especially in the 1850's. Another child type has corkscrew curls all around the head. This was an extremely popular china head, and appears to have been made from the 1840's to the 1870's. Many of this type have a pink tint, which makes them more realistic. This was an additional feature that the stress of competition later seems to have eliminated. The pink or flesh tint is usually uneven in coloring—some parts will be darker than others, and sometimes the pink appears only down to the neck.

The pressed china heads are usually older than the poured ones, but this is not always true. Some companies started to make poured heads at an earlier date than others. (See color photograph C10 and C11.)

In the mid-19th century, china heads and limbs were made to go on peg wooden bodies. The heads often had a flat bottom with a hole, which fitted over a dowel on top of the wooden body. One of these china heads on a wooden body was suggested for use in making a worktable companion in the GODEY'S LADY'S BOOK AND MAGAZINE of 1866. Small-size heads are sometimes solid porcelain rather than hollow.

The following features represent rarity in old china heads: glass eyes, swivel neck, painted brown eyes, pierced ears, and a bald head made for a wig. The bald heads are sometimes called *Biedermeier*, but evidence suggests that most of them were made after 1850. A fine china head is distinguished by its detailed modeling and artistic painting, such as the brush marks at the hairline, and the eye and nostril detail. The cheaper-type china heads usually lack the red dot in the corner of the eye and the red line over the eye.

Nearly all early china heads have black hair. During the 1880's blondes became more prevalent (some of the china heads with bangs are blondes), and by 1900 one out of three of the common-type china heads with wavy hair was blonde.

Some recent china heads marked "F.G." have rare features such as glass eyes, but they can easily be distinguished from early china heads. The old ones usually have imperfections, kiln dirt, and so on, which the perfected 20th-century dolls lack; and later china heads also lack some of the artistic charm of the early ones.

As early as 1873, HARPER'S BAZAR referred to china dolls as being "old fashioned."

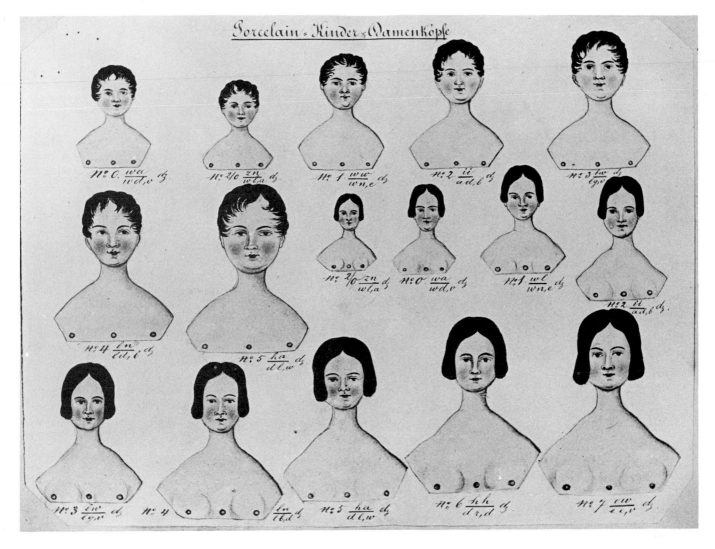

In 1862, dolls with porcelain heads cost from $1.90 to $3.40. Around 1876, *Strasburger & Pfeiffer* advertised china heads in eighteen different sizes ranging from 2³/₄ to 8³/₄ inches for the heads alone, and costing 63¢ to $15.00 doz. wholesale. Nearly all these had black hair; a few had gilt combs, and a few others were boys' heads with gilt and colored neckties. In 1893, *Butler Bros.* advertised glazed china heads, with the blondes outnumbering the brunettes two to one. The shoulder heads came 2³/₈, 3¹/₂, 3³/₈, and 4¹/₈ inches high; prices were 42¢ to $1.87 doz. wholesale. As the popularity of china heads declined, so did the price and quality. And, as time passed, fewer heads were sold separately from the bodies.

China heads with names stamped in gold letters on a molded yoke were called *Pet Name* heads.

Some of the factories known to have made china dolls' heads are *Kestner, Kling, Hertwig, Closter Veilsdorf,* and *Bähr & Pröschild.* (During World War I, china heads were made in Japan.) Many companies distributed dolls with china heads; among them were Strasburger & Pfeiffer, *Bawo & Dotter, Borgfeldt,* Butler Bros., and *Morimura Bros.* No doubt most of these companies assembled as well as distributed dolls with china heads, which were known to the trade as *China Limb Dolls.* (See also **Manufacture of China Heads.**)

## CHINA HEADS

**305A & B.** Two pages showing porcelain heads for child and lady dolls, reproduced from a Swiss catalog of German toys dated between 1845 and 1860. These catalog drawings resemble the china heads shown in Ills. **306** and **307.** *Courtesy of Marg. Weber-Beck from Franz Carl Weber, Zurich.*

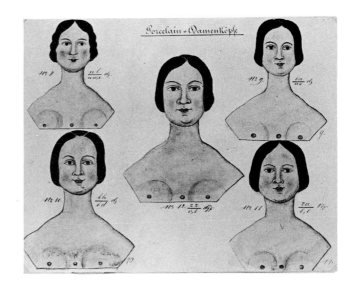

**306A & B.** Flesh-tinted china head with dark brown hair and eyes. Note how the chest is formed and how the hair divides into three sections in the same manner as on the china lady dolls' heads shown, particularly in Nos. 8–12, in the catalog pages from Franz Carl Weber, Zurich (Ills. **305A & B**). H. 4½ inches. *Courtesy of Sylvia Brockmon.*

**308.** China head with anatomical detail in the molding of the chest. The hair is drawn back into a bun with a hair ornament piercing it. Head belongs on a cotton body with blue kid arms. *Courtesy of Laura Treskow.*

**307A & B.** Pink-tinted china head, with the hair in the fashion of the 1840's, has ears exposed and a braided bun. Marked "10" on the inside. This head resembles some of the heads pictured in the Swiss catalog (Ills. **305A & B**). *Courtesy of Laura Treskow.*

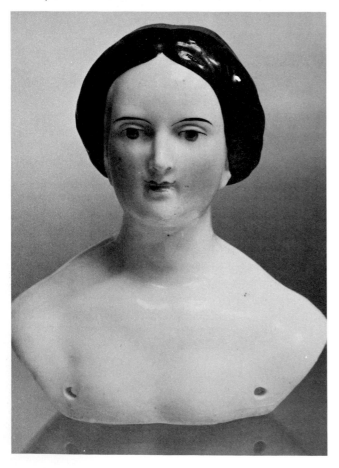

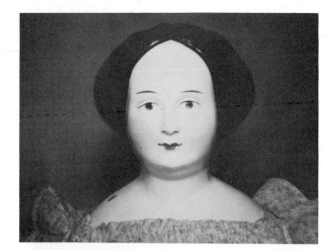

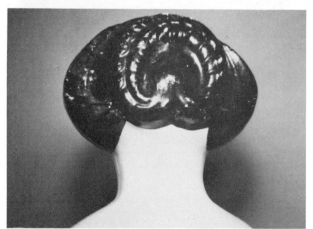

**309A, B, & C.** Soft-paste porcelain doll's head with black hair puffed at the sides and twisted into a braided wreath in back; indigo blue eyes. Doll wears contemporary rose-sprigged dress. H. 20 inches. H. of shoulder head, 5 inches. *Coleman Collection.*

**310A & B.** China head, flesh-tinted, has painted features. Note the comb in the center of the braided bun. H. 24 inches. H. of shoulder head, 6½ inches. *Courtesy of Dorothy Annunziato.*

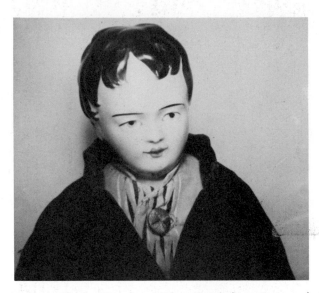

**313.** Flesh-tinted china boy with painted features, rounded shoulder piece, and kid body identical to doll shown in Ill. **214.** *Courtesy of Sylvia Brockmon.*

**311A & B.** Two pink-tinted china heads, probably made in Bohemia, with brownish black hair, dark red lip line. H. of shoulder head at left, 7 inches. *Courtesy of Eva M. Horváth and Margaret Whitton; photograph on right by Winnie Langley.*

**314A & B.** China-headed doll with cloth body, leather arms, and contemporary brick-red and black checked dress. Painted features include brown eyes and lower eyelashes. H. 18 inches. *Coleman Collection.*

**312A & B.** Pressed china head with boyish hairdo, and brush marks; cloth body. H. 17 inches. H. of shoulder head, 4 inches. *Coleman Collection.*

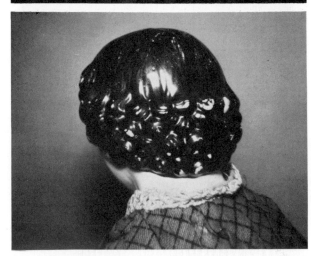

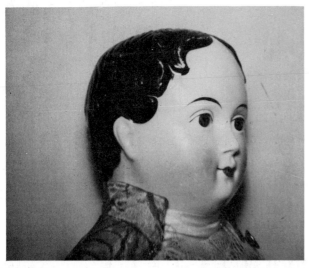

**315.** Poured, tinted china head with short hair and painted features, including large brown eyes. H. 23 inches. H. of shoulder head, 6 inches. *Courtesy of Alberta Darby.*

**316.** Poured china head; painted features include lower eyelashes and unusually large brown eyes. Hair is in ringlets conforming to the shape of the head. H. 20 inches. H. of shoulder head, 5 inches. *Courtesy of Alberta Darby.*

**318.** Unusual china head with brown glass sleep eyes, open crown with plaster pate, human hair wig. Cloth body has leather lower arms. H. 20 inches. H. of shoulder head, 5 inches. *Coleman Collection.*

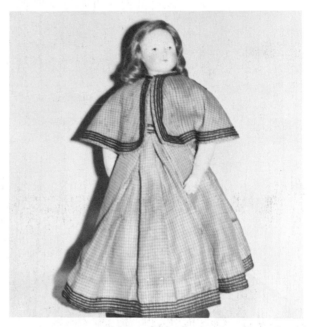

**317.** China head similar to the one in Ill. **316,** except that it has glass eyes and both upper and lower eyelashes. H. 19 inches. H. of shoulder head, 4½ inches. *Courtesy of Sylvia Brockmon.*

**319A & B.** Swivel-neck pink-tinted china head on china shoulder plate, gusseted kid body. Painted features include deeply shadowed eyes and eyelashes. Wig is set over cork pate. Doll wears contemporary brown and black checked dress and cape. H. 16 inches. *Coleman Collection.*

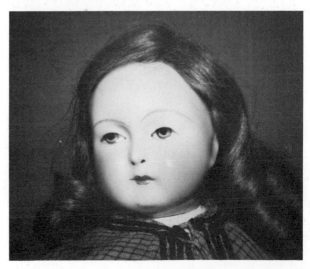

**322A & B.** China head with snood, brush marks, and comb marks. H. 23 inches. H. of shoulder head, 5¹/₂ inches. *Coleman Collection.*

**320.** Swivel-neck china heads. Girl has brown hair; boy has black hair and china limbs. *Courtesy of Gladyse Hilsdorf; photograph by Winnie Langley.*

**321.** Swivel-neck china head on china shoulder plate; brown hair with a white band across the top of the head. *Courtesy of Marion Holt; photograph by Winnie Langley.*

**323.** China head with painted features is attached to a cloth body and legs; leather arms. Printed red dress is contemporary. Note that her lips are painted as if she were smiling. H. 22 inches. H. of shoulder head, 5¼ inches. *Coleman Collection.*

**325A & B.** China head with hair caught in a snood, which is held in place by a white frill trimmed in the center with a cluster of grapes. The body and china limbs are original, as is the dress of trimmed net. H. 20 inches. H. of shoulder head, 5¼ inches. *Courtesy of the Chester County Historical Society.*

**324A & B.** Two identical china heads with painted features, nineteen ringlets; mark is incised on the back. Front-view doll bears an "F." Side-view doll has a "G." H. of shoulder heads, 4 and 4½ inches respectively. (A similar head marked "D" is 3¼ inches.) *Courtesy of Edith R. Meggers; Coleman Collection.*

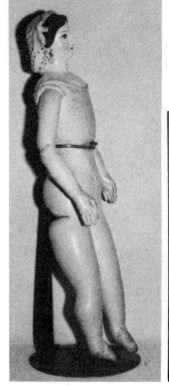

**326A & B.** Pink snood with blue beads, trimmed with a yellow and gold twisted band and bow, is molded into this china head. The painted features include eyelashes and shadowed eyes, pierced ears. Head is attached to a gusseted kid body. H. 14 inches. H. of shoulder head, 3½ inches. *Courtesy of Sylvia Brockmon.*

**327A & B.** China head with hair caught in a snood at the neckline, painted features; molded disk earrings were once gilded. H. of shoulder head, 3 inches. *Coleman Collection.*

**328A & B.** China head with snood, a plume on one side, and a ribbon on the other. Similar but not identical heads were frequently made in bisque. H. 16 inches. H. of shoulder head, 5 inches. *Courtesy of Western Reserve Historical Society.*

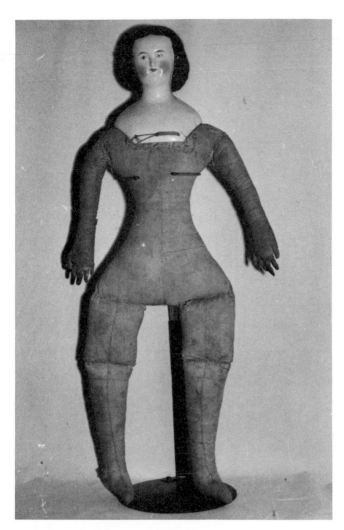

**330.** China head with (originally gilded) snood attached to a raised headband and with bows at the ears. Note the differences between this head and the one in Ill. **329**, which has the same type of hairdo. H. 14 inches. H. of shoulder head, 3½ inches. *Courtesy of Alberta Darby.*

**329A & B.** China head with snood similar to, but not the same as, that seen in Ill. **330.** Note how the hair projects in back. Crude contemporary cotton body is made of many-sized patches. H. 23 inches. H. of shoulder head, 5½ inches. *Coleman Collection.*

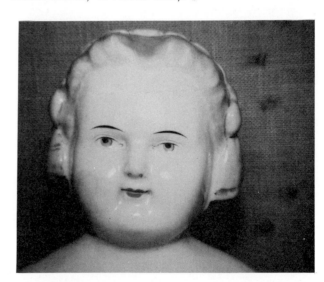

**331A & B.** China head with black snood over its yellow hair. The snood is trimmed with blue bows at the sides and ribbon across the top. H. 20½ inches. H. of shoulder head, 5½ inches. *Courtesy of the Chester County Historical Society.*

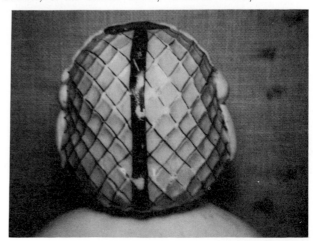

**332.** Swivel-neck china head with blue eyes; flowers are affixed to either side of a popular type of doll's hairdo of the 1860's. *Courtesy of Gladyse Hilsdorf; photograph by Winnie Langley.*

**333.** China head with gold comb across the top supporting a gold snood; doll has a cloth body. H. 17 inches. H. of shoulder head, 4½ inches. *Courtesy of Edith R. Meggers.*

**334A, B, & C.** Three views of cream-tinted, pressed china head with flower decoration, brownish hair, brush marks; incised on back: "P" and "2a"; on front, "15" and "L(?)." H. of shoulder head, 3½ inches. *Courtesy of Margaret Whitton; photographs by Winnie Langley.*

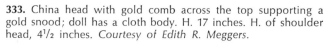

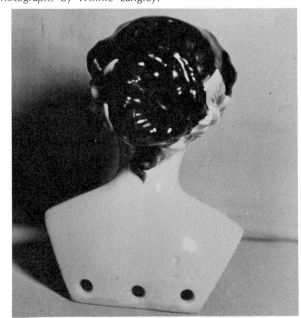

**335A & B.** Flesh-tinted poured china head has aquamarine-color eyes; brush marks. Hair is puffed out at the sides and has a loop in back. H. 13 inches. H. of shoulder head, 3½ inches. *Courtesy of Alberta Darby.*

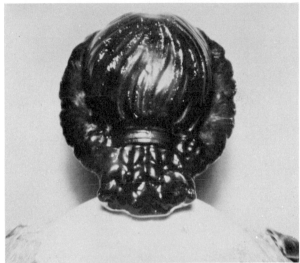

**336A, B, & C.** The pressed china head has hair puffed at the sides and three braids held by floral comb as a chignon in the back; three-piece mold. H. of shoulder head, 6 inches. The doll at bottom is only 7 inches tall. She has a head of the same mold, but it is poured and lacks detail because of its small size. The body is cloth with kid arms and plaster legs. *Coleman Collection.*

The prices given for dolls are those for which the dolls were originally offered for sale. They are *not* today's prices.

**339.** A small cluster of unpainted flowers forms a coronet among the curls of this china head. H. 18 inches. H. of shoulder head, 4³/₄ inches. *Coleman Collection.*

**337.** China head with brush marks, elaborate hairdo, and blue eyes. *Photograph by Winnie Langley.*

**338.** Blonde china head with short curls, ears showing; arms are china too. H. 17 inches. H. of shoulder head, 4¹/₂ inches. *Courtesy of Western Reserve Historical Society.*

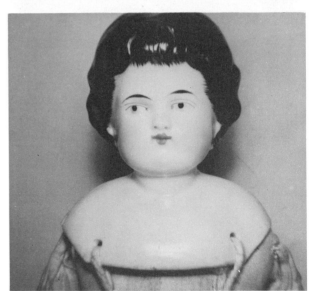

**340.** China head with bangs and brush marks on commercially made cotton body with Steuber-type feet. H. 15 inches. H. of shoulder head, 3¹/₂ inches. *Coleman Collection.*

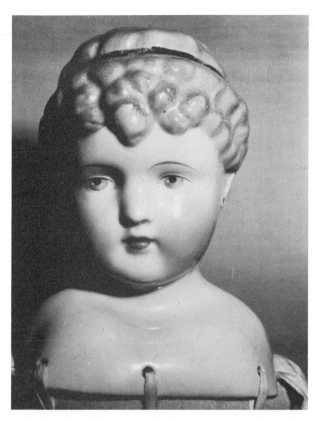

**341A & B.** Pink-tinted china head with "137//10" incised on back shoulder; has blonde hair with black ribbon, blue eyes, pierced ears. *Photographs by Winnie Langley.*

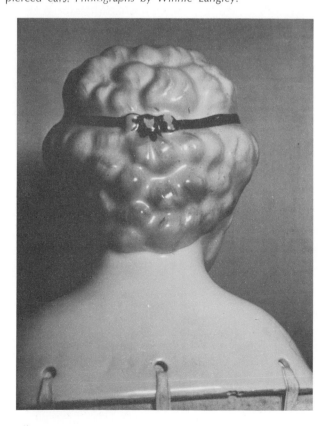

**342A & B.** China head, painted features, blonde hair with molded black ribbon. H. 18 inches. H. of shoulder head, 5 inches. *Courtesy of Alberta Darby.*

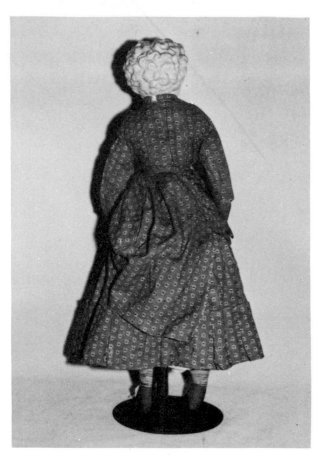

**344.** Blond china head that could represent either a boy or girl. H. 21 inches. H. of shoulder head, 5¾ inches. *Courtesy of Alberta Darby.*

**343A & B.** Blonde china head on cloth body; printed stockings and sewn-on leather shoes. Contemporary printed red dress. H. 20 inches. H. of shoulder head, 5 inches. *Courtesy of Edith R. Meggers.*

**345.** China head has painted features and a hair style appropriate for either a young boy or girl. H. of shoulder head, 6½ inches. *Courtesy of Alberta Darby.*

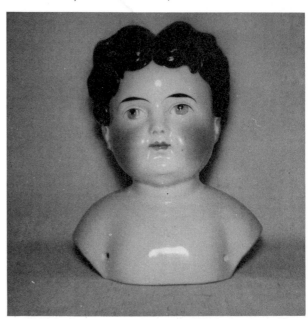

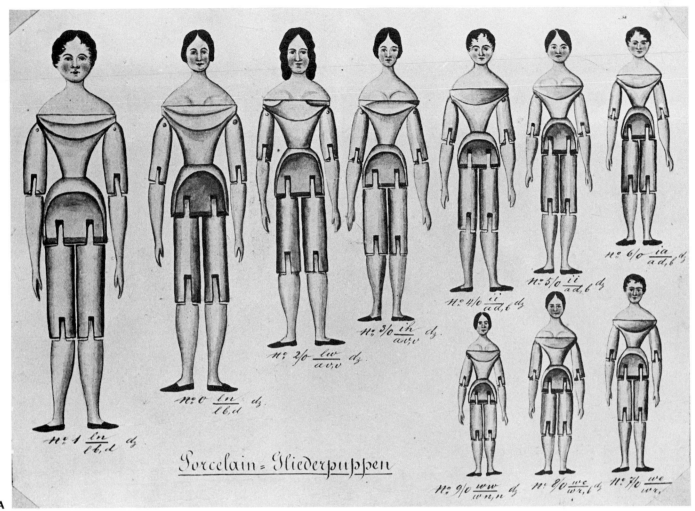

A

## CHINA LIMB DOLLS

**346A, B, C, & D.** Comparison study of turned wooden, peg-jointed china-headed and china-limbed dolls. Note that the head on one of the single dolls is secured by use of a dowel up into neck, and on the other doll shown in the two single pictures by pegs in the chest and a single hole in back. The catalog page is for porcelain-jointed dolls similar to the boy with dowel construction. It is dated between 1845 and 1860. *Courtesy of Mrs. Marg. Weber-Beck, from Franz Carl Weber, Zurich; the Chester County Historical Society; the Newark Museum, Newark, N.J.*

B

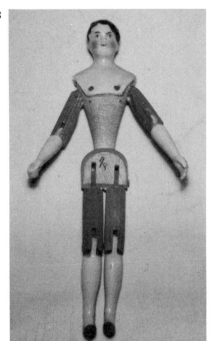

C

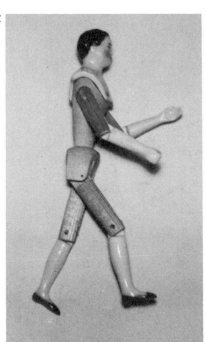

D

**China Limb Dolls.** Trade name for dolls with china heads and china limbs. Around the middle of the 19th century, these dolls had jointed wooden bodies; later, cloth or other material was used for the bodies. The cloth bodies came without joints or with swinging-type joints. The legs usually had molded and painted shoes and stockings. The china legs on wooden bodies generally have red or orange slippers, but later the shoes were made with heels, and fancy garters were painted on the stockings.

Ca. 1876: *Strasburger & Pfeiffer* advertised over thirty different sizes of china limb dolls ranging from 2⅛ to 30 inches, with molded hair or with natural hair, price 38¢ to $13.50 doz. wholesale.

1893: *Butler Bros.* advertised eight different sizes of china limb dolls ranging from 7½ to 20½ inches and priced 4¢ to 50¢ each; the more expensive ones had either a red or blue insertion down the front.

1902: Ten sizes were advertised ranging from 4 to 18 inches and priced 30¢ to $4.00 doz. wholesale. (See also **Regulation China Limb Dolls.**)

**347.** China head on jointed peg wooden body; features are painted on a flesh-tinted ground. China lower limbs. H. 12 inches. H. of shoulder head, 3 inches. *Courtesy of the Chester County Historical Society.*

**348A & B.** China head and china limbs on cloth body. Head has bun in back. Note the breadth of the neck in relation to the head. H. 18 inches. *Courtesy of Western Reserve Historical Society.*

A          B

A

**350A, B, & C.** Swivel-necked china-headed baby doll with squeak box and lower china limbs. Body is cloth-covered; wooden shoulder piece. The doll is dressed in its original infant's dress and petticoats. It is documented as having been won at the Baltimore, Md., Sanitary Fair of 1861. H. 13 inches. *Coleman Collection.*

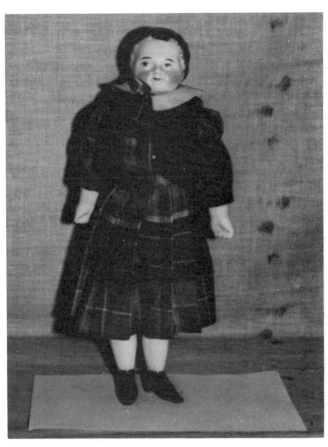

**349.** Boy; his china head pivots on a china shoulder plate; has painted features. Cloth joins the ceramic sections of a body of the type patented by Motschmann in 1857. Original dress is red plaid with Eton-type jacket and collar. H. 11½ inches. H. of shoulder head, 3½ inches. *Courtesy of the Chester County Historical Society.*

B

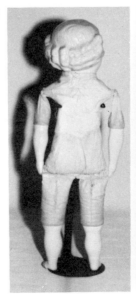

C

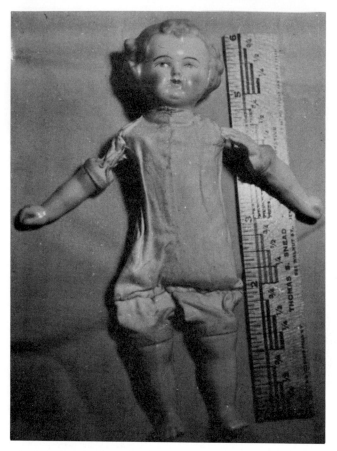

**351.** Swivel-neck china head with blonde hair and blue eyes; china limbs on a cloth body. H. 6¼ inches. *Courtesy of Peg Gregory; photograph by Winnie Langley.*

**352.** Doll with china head, arms, and legs; sawdust-stuffed cloth body. Painted features compare with those of smaller doll of similar mold shown in Ill. **353.** H. 25 inches. H. of shoulder head, 6¾ inches. *Coleman Collection.*

**353.** China shoulder head and limbs on a cloth body. Original dress from the 1880's. Note the elaborate tasseled boots, cobalt blue trim, with slate-blue uppers, black heels and toes. H. 10 inches. *Courtesy of The Smithsonian Institution.*

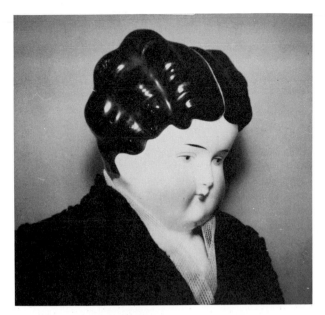

**354.** China head and limbs; painted features; cloth body. H. 21 inches. H. of shoulder head, 5 inches. *Coleman Collection.*

**355.** China-headed doll in original Near-Eastern dress with burnoose. This head is tinted a light brown flesh color and has brown eyes suitable to her nationality. Most of her dowry coins have Arabic writing on them, but two are marked "Nürnberg." H. 12¼ inches. H. of shoulder head, 3 inches. *Coleman Collection.*

**356.** China head and limbs on a cloth body. The shoes are brown with blue bows. The doll is typical of late products of this type. Mark: "GERMANY." H. 12¼ inches. *Coleman Collection.*

**357.** China head, probably 20th-century. Sawdust-stuffed silesia body; china limbs. *Courtesy of Edith R. Meggers.*

**Chinaman.** 1892. One of the cutout cloth *Brownies* designed by *Palmer Cox.*

**Chinaman Acrobat.** Ca. 1906. Wooden doll, rubber jointed, made by *Schoenhut* for *Humpty Dumpty Circus.*

**Chinese Dolls.** Made in abundance by home industry, but not many were exported to the Occident. Kauchau was the doll-making center of China. *Knight & Co.* of Newchwang exported dolls to Europe. *Door of Hope Mission* produced dressed dolls.

**Chinese Dolls.** 1897. Made in Europe; distributed by *John D. Zernitz Co.* Had bisque heads, glass eyes, black wigs, swivel necks, jointed wooden bodies; dressed in Chinese-style clothes; sizes 10 and 12 inches; price $8.00 and $17.00 doz. wholesale.

**Chinkee (Chin Kie).** 1911–12. Made and copyrighted by *Horsman. Helen Trowbridge* painted a portrait of an oriental child from which she designed this doll. It came with a *Can't Break 'Em* head, soft body, and was dressed in sateen clothes consisting of a pink hat, green and pink blouse, black trousers, and black slippers.

**Chinn, Howard Thomas.** 1923–24. Inglewood, Calif. Obtained U.S., French, and British patents for the articulation of a doll.

**Chipps, Mary Alice.** See **Mary Alice.**

**Chiquet, F.** 1871–85. Paris. Made talking bébés and *bébés incassables.*

**Chitian, Heinrich.** 1895. Neustadt near Coburg, Thür. Made leather dolls' bodies.

**Chocolate Drop.** 1923–24. Trademark registered by *Averill Manufacturing Co.* in the U.S. for rag doll designed by *Grace Drayton.*

**Choiseul.** 1870. Paris. Made dolls.

**Choumer & Collet.** 1878–90. Paris. Made dolls; won a silver medal for their doll display at the Paris Exposition in 1878.

**Christening Babies.** 1919. Made by *EFFanBEE.*

**Christening Baby.** 1913. Made by *Horsman.*

358. "Chocolate Drop" rag doll designed by Grace Drayton and made by Averill Manufacturing Co. Original dress and tag stating that it is a "Madame Hendren Doll." Ribbons on the pigtails are multi-colored. *Courtesy of Rosemarye Bunting; photograph by Winnie Langley.*

**Christiansen, Mlle. Kristine.** 1925. Denmark. Obtained a French patent for the limb movement of a doll.

**Christie, Walter Edward.** 1907. London. In Britain, registered a picture of a pair of gloves as a trademark for dolls.

**Christinchen.** 1916. Trade name of a girl doll made by *Käthe Kruse;* doll cost $15.00.

**Christophle (Christophe, Christophie), Mme.** 1865–67. Paris. Made doils.

**Chronology.** ANCIENT EGYPTIAN. Dolls have been found in some of the earliest Egyptian tombs. Some of these were probably used for religious purposes rather than for play; this is certainly true of the Ushabti. By 2000 B.C., there seems to be evidence of dolls as children's playthings. The cruder dolls of the ancients were of clay, wood, or bone, but the fine dolls for rich children were of ivory, wax, fabric, or terra cotta. An Egyptian doll with wooden head, rag body, and movable arms was found in excavations near the city of Antenore.

GREEK AND ROMAN: Dolls had movable limbs and garments that could be taken off and put on again. Plutarch told of his two-year-old daughter playing with a doll. The tomb of a Roman girl who died in the first century B.C. contained a box filled with her dolls and cosmetics for them. Carved wooden dolls of this period sometimes had mortise and tenon joints at elbows, shoulders, hips, and knees.

MEDIEVAL: Legends about dolls at the various courts are practically all that has survived of dolls in the Middle Ages. According to undocumented stories, dolls came into widespread use in Europe in the 14th century. This theory appears to be based on the discovery, under Nürnberg paving stones, of some clay women and baby dolls in 14th-century costumes. Allegedly, dolls of wood, wax, and papier-mâché were shown at the annual fairs in Venice and Florence during the 14th century. Tradition puts the rise of Nürnberg and Sonneberg as toy and doll centers in the 14th century. Augsburg and Judenberg were also mentioned as doll-making areas.

15TH CENTURY: Documents on doll makers as well as dolls have been found. These include the records of "Dockenmachers" (doll makers) in Nürnberg, as well as the "Hortus Sanitatis" woodcuts showing doll makers at work. (See Ill. 360.)

16TH CENTURY: With the flowering of the arts in Northern Europe during the Renaissance, contemporary pictures of dolls provide documented data on their development. Numerous dolls were shown in 16th-century paintings, among them the doll of Lady Arabella Stuart, a cousin of Queen Elizabeth I; and the several pictures with dolls in them painted by Lucas Cranach (of Kronach in the doll-making area near Sonneberg), including one of Princess Marie of Saxony holding a doll. In a painting by John White, an Indian girl is shown holding a doll that, in 1585, had been brought to Roanoke from England. A silver vessel of the 16th century shows a

**359.** Etruscan jointed doll of terra-cotta. Tightly curled hair was the fashion, and the crisscross lines on the crown of the head suggest the net worn by patrician ladies. Dated ca. 700–600 B.C. H. 9¾ inches. *Courtesy of the Newark Museum, Newark, N.J.*

**360.** Late 15th-century doll maker of Nürnberg, as shown in a woodcut from the *Hortus Sanitatis.*

girl with a doll dressed in Spanish garb. A woodcut of a doll in this period was probably part of the evidence used in dating the Nürnberg doll in Ill. 361.

Wooden dolls from Bavaria were marketed in Venice. A Vienna museum dated a doll with movable head and limbs as of the 16th century.

17TH CENTURY: Dolls were made primarily of wood or wax; some dolls' heads were made of glazed stoneware. Christoph Weigel in 1698 referred to dolls made partly of gold or silver, and to *alabaster* dolls. He also pictured the making of pulp dolls (composition) and *gum tragacanth* dolls. The supremacy of Sonneberg, Thür., in making dolls began with granting the makers an exemption from taxes and duties equal to that accorded the merchants of Nürnberg at public markets, especially in Frankfurt am Main. In 1695 Higginson wrote from Massachusetts to England for dolls that he wished to sell in America.

18TH CENTURY: The distribution of dolls became a large industry, as did the making of dolls. An organized system of agents distributed German dolls all over the world. Distributors of the wooden dolls made in the Austrian Grödner Tal came as far as America to sell their wares. The SPECTATOR, Vol. 3, reports a letter by Betty Crosstich saying she had received "a French baby for the year 1712. I have taken the utmost care to have her dressed by the most famous tire-women and mantua-makers in Paris. . . . The puppet was dressed in a cherry-coloured gown and petticoat, with a short working apron over it which discovered her shape to the greatest advantage." She describes its hair, patches on the breast, and its curious necklace.

**361.** This doll is believed to be one of the oldest Northern European play-dolls to be preserved; it was probably made in Thüringia about 1530. The doll is carved wood painted with a red and white striped skirt and outlines of lace on the bodice and cap. H. 8½ inches. *Courtesy of Germanisches National-museum, Nürnberg.*

**362.** Doll in a painting by Jan de Meyer, ca. 1730. It belonged to the little daughters of Sir Matthew Decker. The doll's dress is of crimson with brown inserts, and she wears a crimson and white cap. *Reproduced by permission of the Syndics of the FitzWilliam Museum, Cambridge, England.*

Dolls became more plentiful and were improved in many respects. The poisonous bismuth paint formerly used on dolls was discontinued. In 1700 a wax baby with an invention to make it cry and turn its eyes was purchased in England for five shillings. In 1737 walking dolls were made in Paris. The Dressels of Sonneberg were making dolls in the 18th century. A 1781 document describes the turning of wooden bodies in Neuenbau, a village near Sonneberg. These wooden bodies were then embossed with dough (probably rye flour mixed with lime water and glue) by embossers in Sonneberg. Some of these dolls probably had the form of a skittle. Wooden and wax dolls were produced in London and Paris. Wooden dolls attributed to England had dots around the eyes and at the top of the eyebrows. The *Greiner* porcelain factories were in operation in Thür., but it is not known when they began to make porcelain dolls.

1800–24: Revolutions of the preceding century had changed many things, but the industrial revolution wrought the greatest change in the making of dolls. Methods were discovered to mass-produce papier-mâché dolls in Sonneberg. The toy catalogs of *Georg Bestel-meier* of Nürnberg, in the collection of Arthur Maury of France, and the sample books of Sonneberg show a wide variety of dolls. Wood seems to have been the

**363.** Doll with wooden head, stuffed body with kid arms; early 19th century. H. 10 inches. *Courtesy of the Newark Museum, Newark, N. J.*

**364A & B.** Wax-over-composition head on a one-piece hand-sewn body; black, pupil-less glass eyes. The hair is inserted in a slit at the top of the head. The tan leather arms end in a three-fingered hand. Note the length of the body relative to the head size, and the inward-turned toes. Contemporary blue silk dress. H. 22½ inches. *Coleman Collection.*

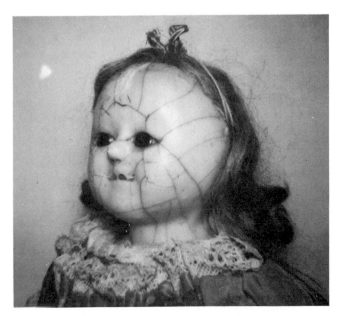

most popular material still, and many exquisite examples with delicate painting, highly varnished, are extant. Papier-mâché heads on stuffed kid bodies appeared in large numbers. Earthenware dolls were also made, but few have survived.

1825–49:The popular dolls of this era were the wooden dolls made in the Grödner Tal, dolls with heads of poured wax or wax over other materials, especially papier-mâché. Papier-mâché heads on kid bodies with wooden limbs were made chiefly in Germany (see color photograph C4), as were most of the early china heads, although some were also made in Austria, Denmark, France, and other European countries. Most of these china heads had a bun in the back if they represented an adult, and short hair if a child. A few bald china heads date back to this period, which probably accounts for the fact that some collectors call them *Biedermeier*. The wooden dolls' heads of this period usually had less carving and more molded plaster or gesso than earlier. Machines for sewing leather had been in use for some time, but several patents were obtained to sew cloth by machine. The clothes for dolls still were generally handmade—either in Paris for the well-to-do, or by seamstresses in the home. The Jury of the 1849 Paris Exposition wrote:

"The doll is composed of ten pieces:

1. A bust of wax or composition
2. A body, sometimes of cardboard, sometimes stuffed with sawdust and covered with a kid skin
3. Teeth of straw or enamel
4. Eyes, painted, or of glass or enamel
5. Hands of wood, or composition, or yellow skin
6. Hair curled and coiffed
7. Stockings and underwear
8. Complete toilette
9. A hat
10. Shoes

"Each of these detailed items is entrusted to the hands of a specialist, which makes for perfection.

"Wax busts have for a long time been brought from England; those that are made in Paris are less delicate, but modeled more truly. The cardboard bodies are put together by the thousands of grosses at the price of 5¢ a dozen; this price is, one says, higher than in Saxony whence we formerly obtained them. We have the milliners, the wigmakers, the artificial flower makers for dolls.

"It is partly through dolls that most people of the two hemispheres know France and are familiar with her customs, her ideas and her costumes. If one opened a case destined for Valparaiso, Mexico, Smyrna, etc., one would find an assortment there that would include some girls of the lower classes, some peasants, some sutlers, some rabble-rousers, some grand ladies in wedding outfits, in town clothes or in ball gowns, some queens, some marquises of the last century, etc."

**365.** German catalog page from a volume dated 1830–40. The hand-drawn illustrations are tinted. The dolls' heads include a mask and a head with natural hair. The line chart at the bottom was possibly used to indicate the sizes in which the dolls were available. *Courtesy of Stadtbibliothek, Nürnberg—Nor. K.*

**366.** Doll with papier-mâché head, glass eyes, real hair styled as in ca. 1830's, leather arms, and a contemporary printed dress. *Photograph by Winnie Langley.*

**367.** Papier-mâché head of this doll has molded and painted hair in the style of ca. 1830's. Body is kid with wooden limbs; contemporary pink dress. *Courtesy of Marion Holt; photograph by Winnie Langley.*

The most popular dolls at the 1849 Exposition were the Queen Victorias, the Quakeresses, and the Chinese.

1850's: The first international exhibition held in London in 1851 brought together various types of dolls from all over the world. Edouard Fournier, a Frenchman, wrote that at the London Exhibition the "English wax dolls were more brilliant than ever. The doll with the well-made body was indeed French, but the doll with the elegant head and with the pretty face was certainly English. Ours could not compete with them, and often a London head was discreetly borrowed or one of the new porcelain heads made for them at Coburg or at Sonneberg. It must be said that the Paris dolls, whether girls of the lower classes or great ladies, must have a head that has been imported."

Up to this time, very little distinction had been made between dolls representing babies and dolls representing adults. But at the 1851 London Exhibition, *Mme. Montanari* displayed dolls representing all ages from infancy to womanhood. Then, at the 1855 Paris

Exposition, *Françoise Greffier* displayed some Japanese bébés that appear to have been the inspiration for the 1857 *Motschmann* patent. New materials as well as new designs were used for dolls, including gutta-percha and rubber. Rag was used to reinforce papier-mâché. A patent was obtained for stringing dolls with elastic. Many of the elaborately coiffured porcelain dolls' heads no doubt were made in this decade, and a patent was obtained in 1855 for putting glass eyes in porcelain heads. The all-china doll without joints, frequently called a *Frozen Charlotte*, probably came on the market in the 1850's.

1860's: The beginning of a golden era for dolls. Beautiful bisque heads both tinted and untinted became popular. The untinted heads, sometimes called "parian" by collectors, usually had molded hair and were often placed on cloth bodies. The tinted heads, which usually had wigs, were at first used largely on wooden and/or kid-bodied lady dolls. Many of the Thomas Nast pictures of Santa Claus in the early 1860's show one of the Motschmann-type babies. A variety of materials—

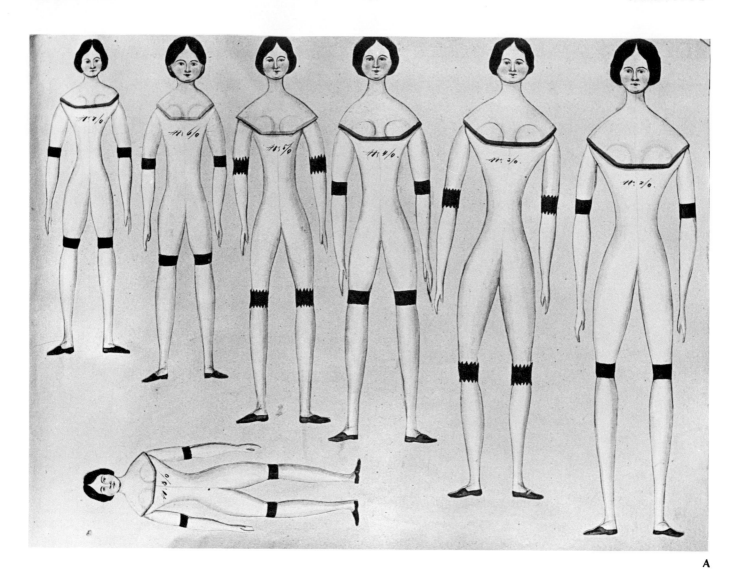

A

papier-mâché, china, wood, wax over papier-mâché, and rag—was used to make this type of baby doll. It seems to have been one of the first attempts to differentiate between the bodies of baby dolls and lady dolls. Most Motschmann-type dolls were originally dressed in long baby clothes, but the bisque lady dolls enjoyed Parisian trousseaux. Mons. Natalis Rondot, a Frenchman, wrote about the dolls as follows:

"Most dolls' heads are of papier-mâché. Saxony furnishes them, but we get our wax heads from England. We have had the idea of making porcelain heads in France and this manufacture, neglected by us, has been introduced in Bavaria, Prussia and Austria; it has developed greatly in Coburg, Sonneberg and Nürnberg. The heads that come from these places are very well executed. The back of the head is hollowed out, because this kind of porcelain has to pay customs duties of 75¢ per kilogram, so we are obliged to reduce the weight of these objects as much as possible. Heads of Size No.

4 cost in Coburg $2.00 a dozen, and the dozen weigh about 2 kilograms. The cost of transportation is about 60¢ a dozen. In France good painters of porcelain consider it degrading to paint dolls' heads, and this is the reason we have to go to Coburg and Sonneberg, which have a customs rate of 7 per cent. . . .

"In order to compete with the English, we have tried to make wax figures in France that could also be used for dolls. Long ago we originated true colored wax dolls that imitated nature. The English copied us, and we have been dependent on them for a long time. We have always excelled our neighbors in the production of layettes and dolls' clothes. The layettes comprise ten pieces, a bib, a baby cap, corset, gown, baby blanket, diaper, pad, etc. The trousseaux are composed of 16 pieces, 3 dresses, shoes, stockings, hat, bag, gloves, etc. . . .

"French dolls vary from 6 inches to 40 inches in height. The two most common heights are 10 inches and

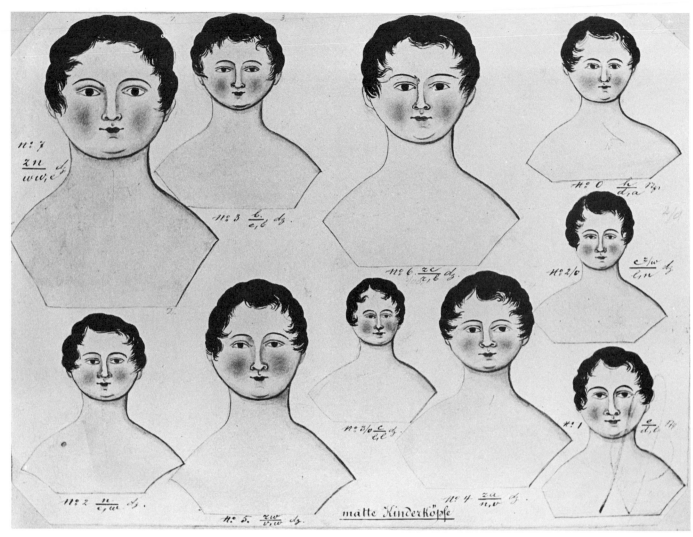

B

**368A, B, & C.** Three toy catalog pages, probably of Swiss origin, from a volume used in business by F. E. Holzach and dated between 1845 and 1860. The illustrations are nearly all hand-colored and hand-drawn. One page shows what appears to be papier-mâché heads on kid bodies with wooden limbs; the other two pages show dolls' heads representing children. *Courtesy of Marg. Weber-Beck, from Franz Carl Weber, Zurich.*

C

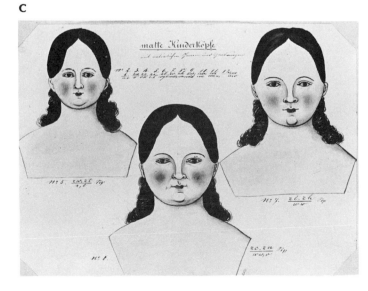

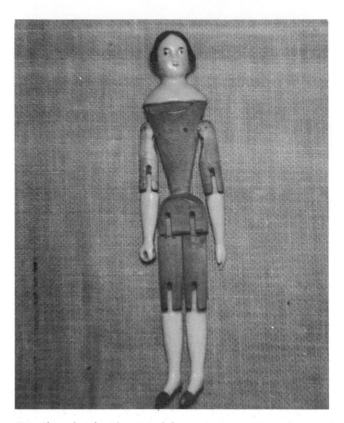

**370.** China head with painted features, on peg-jointed, turned wooden body with china lower arms and legs. H. 6 inches. H. of shoulder head, 1¼ inches. *Courtesy of the Chester County Historical Society.*

**369.** Doll of ca. 1850's with papier-mâché head, kid body, wooden limbs, contemporary clothes similar to those shown in the Swiss catalog (see #6/0). H. 19 inches. *Courtesy of the Newark Museum, Newark, N. J.*

**371.** Doll with papier-mâché head and cloth body. It belonged to Mary Louisa Adams, granddaughter of President John Quincy Adams. The head is probably a replacement for Mary Louisa's daughters, who were born in the 1850's. *Courtesy of The Smithsonian Institution.*

A | B

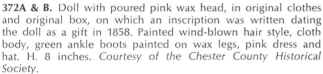

**372A & B.** Doll with poured pink wax head, in original clothes and original box, on which an inscription was written dating the doll as a gift in 1858. Painted wind-blown hair style, cloth body, green ankle boots painted on wax legs, pink dress and hat. H. 8 inches. *Courtesy of the Chester County Historical Society.*

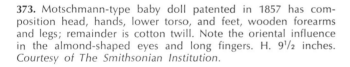

**373.** Motschmann-type baby doll patented in 1857 has composition head, hands, lower torso, and feet, wooden forearms and legs; remainder is cotton twill. Note the oriental influence in the almond-shaped eyes and long fingers. H. 9½ inches. *Courtesy of The Smithsonian Institution.*

18 inches. More dolls are made in these sizes than all the other sizes put together."

In America, dolls were sold at various Sanitary Fairs to raise money for the Civil War. A considerable number of Negro dolls appeared at this time.

Many patents were obtained in the 1860's for improving dolls. *Mlle. Huret* in 1861 patented a swivel, socket-type neck. The walking *Autoperipatetikos* was patented in 1862. *David Lee* in 1866 patented a ball-jointed doll strung with either metal or rubber. *Bru* and others helped to develop the ball-jointed composition body, but it does not appear to have been made in quantities until later. Dolls prior to 1860 usually were not able to sit down. Heels came into fashion in this decade, as well as pierced ears, for dolls.

**374**

**375**

**376**

**374.** China head, cloth body. This doll belonged to Mary Ella Slade, born 1856, granddaughter of Governor Slade of Vermont. H. 20 inches. *Courtesy of The Smithsonian Institution.*

**375.** China Frozen Charlotte. From the Slade family of Vermont. H. 5 inches. *Courtesy of The Smithsonian Institution.*

**376.** Boy doll with papier-mâché head and glass eyes was purchased about 1862 at a church fair in Rahway, N. J., which was held to raise funds for the Union soldiers. H. 19 inches. *Courtesy of the Newark Museum, Newark, N. J.*

**377.** "General Audrey W. Arlington" and his bride, "Harriet St. John Simpson," were 1867 Christmas presents for Marybelle Simpson of Baltimore, Md. The two-star general, dressed in a Union uniform, boasts an applied mustache. The bride, with glass eyes, had a thirteen-gown trousseau, plus accessories. Both have china heads, cloth bodies, and leather arms. H. 21 inches and 17½ inches respectively. *Courtesy of the Newark Museum, Newark, N. J.*

1870's: The Report of the International Jury at the 1878 Paris Exposition gives the following account of contemporary dolls:

"The making of dolls is essentially Parisian. It is one of the most important branches of the toy industry and has accomplished the greatest progress since 1867. There are 21 exhibits representing 57 doll makers and they comprise:

Undressed dolls and bébés, in leather, linen, wood, papier-mâché, porcelain, bisque, wax, etc.

Dressed dolls and bébés of all kinds

*Mignonettes* in porcelain, in bisque, dressed and undressed

Trousseaux of dolls and of bébés in all varieties

Accessories of dolls, wigs, hats, shoes, jewelry, etc.

"The once common doll in papier-mâché and the old-fashioned poupard, although it is true that these articles had a very modest price, are now forsaken because people prefer others that are better made and not very much more expensive. The linen doll was considered a medium-price doll, but the doll in rose linen once very common, which sold quite easily because of its low price, has entirely disappeared.

"Many doll makers have shown us in their fine dolls the most beautiful specimens known. The finished article shows the great effort required to maintain the place they now occupy. It is necessary to add that for the making of these toys the best French taste must be used to reproduce as exactly as possible both the lady and the child to the point of perfection of modeling of body, facial expression and movement.

"We are happy to affirm that no other country is able to rival France in the skill of imitating nature so perfectly. We congratulate our principal manufacturers

who with their great care have brought this industry to perfection. The bébé which best suits the taste of children tends to supersede the doll, and it appears certain to us without doubt that if the bébé had been produced as inexpensively as the doll, the sales would have increased considerably. [The 'doll' appears to refer to lady dolls as opposed to bébés.]

"Although there are some quite important manufacturers specializing in undressed bébés, these are only to take care of the demand.

"Some models of bébés in composition have also been presented; they were tentative and cheap products. We regret that thus far these efforts have not produced the best results. We heartily encourage our manufacturers to exert themselves to fill this gap as promptly as possible with attention to this everyday item, for a large number of which we are dependent on foreign manufacturers. . . .

"We must not forget to cite the talking bébé. The manufacturer [probably *Jules Steiner*] who is almost the only one in France to produce this toy has turned out bébés perfectly made and amazingly lifelike.

"We notice also among the products of this manufacturer of dolls and bébés some made chiefly of rubber. We are persuaded that there would be in this case a great improvement if they were able to apply hard rubber to a certain extent and thus produce dolls having the advantage of being solid.

**378.** Doll with untinted bisque shoulder head, blonde hair, painted features, original body (except the hands) and clothes, given to a child in 1872. H. 24 inches. H. of shoulder head, 7 inches. *Coleman Collection.*

**379A, B, & C.** Lady doll with bisque head and forearms, kid-covered wooden body, wooden legs. Her trunk of clothes has her name, "Daisy Paris," on it. Miss McLaren, to whom the doll was originally given, was born in 1869. H. 18 inches. *Courtesy of Hazel Ulseth.*

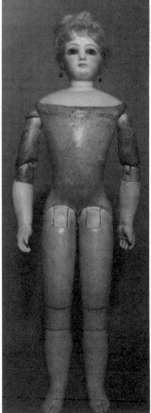

A          B          C

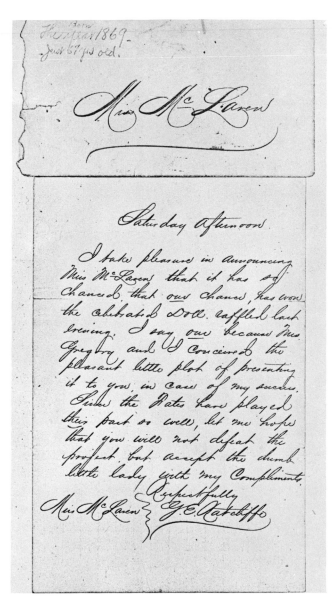

*Born 1869.*
*Just 6 yrs old!*

*Mrs McLaren*

*Saturday Afternoon*

*I take pleasure in announcing Miss McLaren that it has so chanced that our chance has won the celebrated Doll raffled last evening. I say our because Mrs Gregory and I conceived the pleasant little plot of presenting it to you in case of my success. Since the Fates have played their part so well, let me hope that you will not defeat the project but accept the dumb little lady with my Compliments.*

*Respectfully*
*Miss McLaren G.E. Ratcliffe*

**380.** Facsimile copy of the original letter of transmittal written when the "Daisy Paris" doll was given to Miss McLaren (born 1869). See Ill. **379.** *Courtesy of Hazel Ulseth.*

**381.** Doll in peasant costume, ca. 1875, has bisque swivel head, kid body, wig, blue glass eyes, and pierced ears. She is dressed in her original red wool dress with black velvet trim, black silk apron, net lace kerchief, wooden sabots, cotton stockings, lace cap, and black silk bonnet. H. 18½ inches. *Courtesy of The Smithsonian Institution.*

"We have not enlarged on the merits of the clothing of the dolls and bébés. The makers who specialize in this must follow the prevailing styles exactly and portray also the dress of the couturiers for the socially élite. We have been able to satisfy ourselves with the pretty styles shown at the Exhibition and are assured that they will meet the demands of the foreign dressmakers, who use these little models which are so easy to transport elsewhere, in order to spread the latest French fashion. Moreover, these dolls have sufficient articulation to take and keep any desired pose.

"We have seen also a great variety of costumes on dolls and bébés including the most luxurious and the most current; but we regret that these collections are not complete, because they do not include the inexpensive.

"Dolls in wax were represented by some models but the price of these toys, which are perishable, is too high. The several specimens of muslin dolls [probably *London Rag Dolls* of muslin over wax] that we have seen, although well made, have not been successful in France. This toy is expensive and becomes worn quite rapidly. If these dolls could be manufactured more cheaply, we believe they would find a ready market.

"One manufacturer who has shown some heads and dolls of porcelain [probably refers to *Jullien*] merits special mention. He is the first to establish in our country the doll *mignonette* in porcelain called 'The Bather.' Thanks to the precision of form and finish of these dolls, which heretofore we have been buying abroad, this industry has expanded and is struggling to gain an advantage over its competitors.

"In speaking of the mignonette, it should be recalled that many more companies have dressed these toys. Their coquettishness and attractiveness show all the care and taste that have been expended on them. . . .

"Austria: mechanical dolls, wooden dolls and manni-kins from Grödner Tal.

"Japan: papier-mâché dolls satisfactorily made. The costumes are luxurious. However, the examples which we have seen are expensive. . . .

"The principal toys imported into France are Sonneberg bébés of all kinds."

Very elaborate coiffures, some with flowers, were made in untinted bisque. Wigged dolls' heads were made chiefly in tinted bisque and used principally for lady dolls. (See color photograph C14.) Among the popular baby dolls were the London Rag Dolls. All-bisque bébés were patented in 1878; these may be the dolls called *Bathers*. Jointed wrists were advertised in 1879.

1880's: This decade marked the big change from lady dolls (see color photograph C14) to dolls representing babies and children. Up to this time, lady dolls had predominated, but around 1880 they were swept aside by the baby, infants in long clothes, or child dolls. These were made largely in France and Germany, and had bisque or composition heads and composition, kid, wood, cloth, or combinations of these materials for bodies. The production of French bébés numbered in the thousands at the beginning of the decade and in the millions at its end. Although not new, the revival of sleeping eyes made dolls more realistic. Jointed all-bisque dolls began to appear in quantity as did celluloid dolls. *Rembrandt Hair* style started a fashion that continued its popularity into the 20th century. Flat-top china heads on china limb dolls with cloth bodies had scarcely changed for thirty years, and china-headed dolls were referred to in advertisements as "the dolls of our grandmothers."

**382A & B.** Papier-mâché head of this doll has black pupil-less glass eyes. Body is cloth, the arms wooden. The doll was purchased in Amsterdam, Holland, on Monday, November 7, 1880. She wears the original Dutch costume, straw and cloth hat, toeless stockings, and cloth slippers. *Coleman Collection.*

**383.** China head, covered with corkscrew curls of café-au-lait molded hair, has painted features. This type was advertised in 1884 on a nankeen body with china limbs, but in smaller sizes. H. 15½ inches. H. of shoulder head, 4¾ inches. *Courtesy of Dorothy Annunziato.*

**384A & B.** Millikin & Lawley advertised a doll with this type of hairdo in 1881. The doll has an untinted bisque head and limbs on a cloth body, pierced ears, contemporary dark brown velvet and silk dress with train, paper collar. H. 7½ inches. *Coleman Collection.*

1890's: Bisque heads, mostly *Doll-Face* types on jointed composition or kid bodies representing children, continued their tremendous popularity. *Jumeau* alone made millions of these each year. Bisque shoulder heads with faces turned slightly to the side, as well as china heads with bangs, were shown widely. Both these types had the round face and short neck of a young child. Oriental,

American Indian, and Negro dolls, all made in Europe, were popular types, as were *Kiss Babies* or kiss-throwing dolls. *Bonnet* (or hooded) *Dolls* of bisque were made in the 1890's. *Flirting eye* dolls made their debut. The round-eyed *Brownies* ushered in the era of the "grotesque" character doll, although there had been *polichinelles* and similar dolls earlier. Numerous commercial dolls with rag heads were made. China limb dolls with colored insertions down the front of the body were new in the 1890's. Spring joints on jointed composition bodies replaced rubber cords on some dolls, but the rubber elastic continued to predominate.

387

388

385

386

**385.** Boy shoulder head of bisque with glass eyes, blond molded hair, on a cloth body with composition lower limbs. A similar type of doll was shown in a catalog of 1893. H. 17 inches H. of shoulder head, 4³/₄ inches. *Courtesy of Edith Meggers.*

**386.** Wax-over-composition head is shaped to include form for pompadour hair style. Doll has short wooden arms, composition legs. Original brown silk dress. A similar doll was shown in an 1893 catalog. H. 7³/₄ inches. *Coleman Collection.*

1900's: Very little change occurred at the beginning of the century. The introduction of *Pet Name* chinas and printed cloth bodies gave a last spurt to china-headed dolls. Then the introduction of character dolls that resembled real children began a trend lasting for decades. At first these dolls were not received with much enthusiasm, but soon after 1910 they swept the market. As soon

**387.** China head of ca. 1905 with the name "Ethel" in gold on the chest. Mold owned by Butler Bros. On the back of the shoulders are the words "Patent App'd for Germany." H. 17¹/₂ inches. H. of shoulder head, 4 inches. *Coleman Collection.*

**388.** Lady doll of 1911, elaborately dressed and expensively priced, as pictured in *Playthings* magazine of that year. Note the lorgnette and earrings. *Courtesy of McCready Publishing Co.*

as a new model came out, everyone rushed to imitate it; but the Doll-Faced Doll also continued to be popular. About 1905 long hair began to be parted on the side instead of in the middle.

Pierced ears began to decline in popularity soon after the turn of the century and almost disappeared from use by the 1920's. Ball joints, formerly at the knee, were raised above the knee in the 1920's so that the dolls could wear the fashionable short skirts without displaying their joints.

Each year brought forth some novelties in dolls, but the old favorites often lasted for generations. PLAYTHINGS magazine, started in 1903, shows year-by-year trends in the doll world as follows:

1903: Photographs of actual people used for making dolls.

1904: Dolls glancing to the side with flirting eyes. The Boer, Spanish-American, and Russo-Japanese wars caused an interest in dolls dressed in military costumes.

1905: Rag dolls with faces photographed from life.

1906: Celluloid or pressed felt heads on cloth bodies.

1907: Faces of real babies; flirting eyes still popular.

1908: All-felt dolls popular; new type of crying doll.

1909: Bent-limb, composition-bodied character babies introduced. *Peary's* discovery of the North Pole and similar events brought forth dolls to represent personages in the limelight.

1910: A revival of interest in lady dolls occurred, and many of these, such as *Kestner's Gibson Girl*, reflected the influence of the character dolls. Round-eyed dolls inspired by Grace Wiederseim's *(Drayton)* drawings evoked interest. Unsuccessful attempts were made to produce bent-limb composition baby bodies in America. However, cloth bodies with similar shapes were made in the U.S. Hair eyebrows were a popular but short-lived innovation.

1911: Sleeping-eyed character dolls were introduced; dolls representing teen-age girls were popular. The *Louis Lindner* advertisement (Ill. 1099) shows eight dolls; three had dolly faces and five had character faces; only one had a kid body and only one had a bent-limb baby body; all the rest had jointed composition bodies. Apparently the bent-limb baby bodies did not attain popularity as quickly as the character faces.

1912: *Coquette*-type dolls with eyes glancing to the side and roguish-eyed dolls were favorites. The first

**389.** Character baby with bisque head marked "232," sleeping eyes, painted hair, open mouth with two lower teeth and felt tongue, bent-limb composition body of a type made ca. 1910. H. 21 inches. *Courtesy of Mary Roberson.*

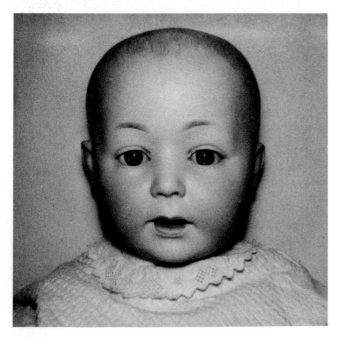

completely American ball-jointed composition-bodied dolls with composition heads were made.

1913: *Kewpies* swept the doll world.

1914: *Happifats,* whistling dolls, and Drayton-type dolls competed with Kewpies until the outbreak of hostilities in Europe caused repercussions in the doll world. Apparently production of dolls in Germany suddenly halted.

1915: The war did not affect the Thüringian area greatly, and once its initial impact was over, business seems to have resumed. However, interest turned to soldier dolls, *Red Cross Nurses,* and the like.

1916: Many new doll manufacturers started production in America, although some German dolls were still on the market and the Japanese helped to supply dolls.

1917: German dolls were cut off entirely when the U.S. declared war. Bisque heads began to be made in America and were also imported from Japan and France, but these sources were relatively insignificant; most American dolls were made of composition. Up to this time, cold-press methods had been used chiefly, but American ingenuity soon contrived the more efficient hot-press method. The better American dolls were *Art Dolls,* and commanded fairly high prices.

1918: Interest centered on the legs of the dolls. Cloth-body *Mama Dolls* were made with swinging legs so that they could "walk." Diagonal hip joints were made on ball-jointed bodies to enable them to stand alone. American character dolls grew more successful with the advent of peace.

1919: Anti-German feeling was very high, and most dolls continued to be made in America, with only a few coming from France and Japan. PLAYTHINGS, April, 1919, described the situation: "Multiplicity of French, English and American dolls, blonde of wig and gutta-percha as to body, of present-day manufacture."

1920: The great demand was still for American dolls, especially Mama-type dolls. America now made all types formerly obtained from Germany, incuding dolls with jointed composition bodies, or kid bodies with composition arms and legs, and bent-limb baby dolls. The fabric Art Dolls made by *L. R. Kampe* in the U.S. and the *Scavinis* in Italy were popular.

1921: Time began to ease the feeling against Germany and a few German dolls appeared, but American-made dolls persisted in dominating the U.S. market.

1922: Rising prices in Germany limited the demand for German dolls. American dolls continued to be in great demand and were of various types. The long-limbed French flapper doll appeared.

1923: German dolls with bisque heads once again competed with American dolls. American manufacturers turned to novel ideas such as *multi-heads,* portrait dolls, etc., in order to maintain their market.

1924: The year of the *Bye-Lo Baby.* This infant doll with bisque head made in Germany was assembled and had its body made in America. Its tremendous success caused most of the doll industry to offer similar or competitive dolls.

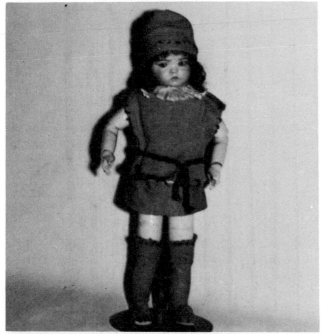

**390A & B.** Société Française de Fabrication de Bébés et Jouets character doll marked on the bisque head "SFBJ, 2LS." Doll has closed mouth, stationary eyes glancing to the side, composition body with wooden sticklike legs. Original clothes include an olive-brown cotton jersey trimmed in blue yarn, with a tan pleated silk ruffle at the neck. The leggings have thread under sole of the shoe. Ca. 1920. Mark III. **1564.** H. 13 inches. *Courtesy of Frances Miller.*

**391.** "Cinderella" trademark of C. M. Bergmann and Louis Wolf & Co.

1925: The Bye-Lo type of doll continued its popularity. Novelties such as clapping hands, twins, etc., were introduced. Rubber heads were used on dolls.

(See also **Clothes [Chronology of Clothes]; Hair Style; Wig.**)

**Chubb, Ida.** Produced Negro rag dolls, such as "Mammy" and "Mose," to represent characters in her book of Negro rhymes.

**Chubby.** 1914–16. Trademark registered in U.S. by *Louis Wolf & Co.* They advertised Chubby as an all-bisque doll with moving arms, wearing a union suit. It had eyes glancing to the side and bent arms. It may also have been the Chubby designed by *Ernesto Peruggi.*

1915–16: Came in sizes 4½, 5, and 6 inches; priced 25¢, 39¢, and 49¢.

**Chubby.** 1915. Copyrighted by *Trion Toy Co.;* designed by *Ernesto Peruggi.* It was the head of a child with hair pulled down over its forehead.

**Chubby.** 1916. Trade name for an all-composition baby doll made by *Elektra Toy & Novelty Co.* Came with jointed wrists and molded hair; 24 inches tall. Cost $21.00 doz.; with blonde or brunette wig, cost $24.00 doz. wholesale.

**Chubby Kid.** 1920–22. Cherub-type doll of wood fiber made by the *Columbia Doll & Toy Co.;* distributed by *Sears, Roebuck & Co.*

1920: Came with or without wig; size 12 inches.

1922: Came with mohair wig and veil; size 13½ inches; price 83¢.

**Churchill, James.** 1847–58. London. Made composition dolls.

**Cigarette Friend.** 1915. Indian chief with cigarette in his mouth; copyrighted by *Mary Frances Woods;* wore blanket; size 14 inches.

**Cilly Billy.** 1919. Trademark registered in Britain By John Green Hamley of *Hamley Bros.* for dolls.

**Cincinnati Doll Factory.** See **Fahlbusch, F. A.**

**Cinderella (Cinderella Baby).** 1892–1917. Trademark registered in Germany by *C. M. Bergmann* for ball-jointed dolls, which were handled by *Louis Wolf & Co.,* who also registered this trademark in 1897 in the U.S. The trademark seems to have been used for the Bergmann line of jointed dolls primarily, but Louis Wolf & Co. also used it in 1906 for a line of American-made rag dolls with faces that were reproductions of actual color photographs.

**Cinderella.** 1898. Advertised by *W. A. Cissna & Co.* as sleeping dolls with "French" bisque heads, sleeping eyes, open mouth with teeth, patent wigs, kid bodies, drop-stitch stockings; size 18½ inches; price $6.25 doz. wholesale. (See also **Columbia.**)

**Cinderella Doll.** Ca. 1910. A Naphtha Soap Powder coupon doll; came with bisque head, sewed curly wig, sleeping eyes and eyelashes, open mouth and teeth; dressed in satin; sizes 19, 21, and 26 inches.

**Cinderella Sitting Doll.** Ca. 1860–ca. 1880. Cloth body designed by *Mrs. Irene Wilkinson Gibson* with sewed swing joints at hips and knees so that doll could sit easily. Came with kid arms to elbow, kid boots with heels, striped stockings, and a circular mark on the chest reading "CINDERELLA—SITTING DOLL—PATENT—APPLD—FOR." The number appeared in the center of the circular mark.

**Cinquini.** 1918. Chicago. Made cherub-type dolls in imitation of *Rose O'Neill's Kewpies;* Rose O'Neill won an injunction.

**Cissna, W. A., & Co.** 1898. Chicago. Importers and jobbers. Distributed dolls, including "D.P." dolls of *Hamburger & Co.*

**Claflin, H. B., Co.** 1912–14. New York City, Paris, and Manchester, England. Doll distributor; represented several new factories. Registered *Konigskinder* as a trademark for dolls in the U.S.

**Clap Hands.** 1925. Infant doll made by *Century Doll Co.*

**Clark, William.** 1861. Obtained British patent for a walking doll, spring motivated, with a step by step movement.

**Clarkson, Thomas Charles.** 1849–76. Surrey, England. Obtained two British doll patents, one in 1867 for a rubber and cork doll and the other in 1876 for a cork and wood doll.

**Clay Dolls.** Dolls of this material were made in both ancient and medieval times. Roman dolls of clay were made with jointed arms and legs. Suidas, a Greek, wrote in the 10th century A.D. of "those who make little figures of clay for the beguiling of little children."

In 1859, excavations in Nürnberg unearthed clay dolls dressed in the costumes of the 14th century. At about this same time (1859), *A. Fleischmann* made dolls of burnt clay, which were painted by a terrazolite process. Clay dolls continued to be made into the 20th century, but they were usually very cheap and crude.

**Clear, Emma.** 1908–25+. Buffalo, N.Y., Cleveland, Ohio, Los Angeles, Calif. Worked for some years at home repairing dolls before opening her doll hospital in Buffalo in 1908; employed two to six helpers and bought doll parts from Germany.

1914: She left her Buffalo shop to her sister and moved to Cleveland, where she operated on a wholesale basis. War in Europe brought heavy demands for repairing irreplaceable dolls. She bought a stock of damaged dolls from a mail-order house in Buffalo and used the undamaged parts for her repair work.

1917: Mrs. Clear moved to California and opened the Humpty Dumpty Doll Hospital in Los Angeles.

1922: She bought a half interest in the patent rights of *Harry Coleman's Dolly Walker.* Later, Mrs. Clear became famous for the beautiful ceramic dolls she made.

**392A & B** (above and at right). Bisque socket-headed doll with a shoulder plate and body of pressed leather. Stamp on the torso in green (Ill. **393**) means that the doll was distributed by the Widow Clément. *Courtesy of the Museum of the City of New York; photographs by Winnie Langley.*

**Clément, F.** 1873–74. Paris. Made dressed bébés.

**Clément, Pierre Victor (V.).** 1866–75. Paris. Was issued a French patent for making dolls entirely of embossed leather in 1867; later he advertised that he made light, strong, and fine jointed dolls in natural leather.

**Clément, Vve. (Widow).** 1870's. Paris. Handled dolls. She was probably related to Pierre Clément. (See Ill. 392.)

**Clerc, Les Fils de N.** 1908–21. Paris. Successor in 1921 was M. Clerc. They made *poupards* in swaddling clothes with jointed arms and heads. In 1908, they won a medal at the London Exhibition.

**Climax Doll Co.** 1923–24. New York City. Made Climax *Mama Dolls* with composition heads; came in four sizes.

**Clinique des Poupées.** See **A la Clinique des Poupées.**

**Clinton Stoneware Co.** 1886–1907. Clinton, Mo. Made

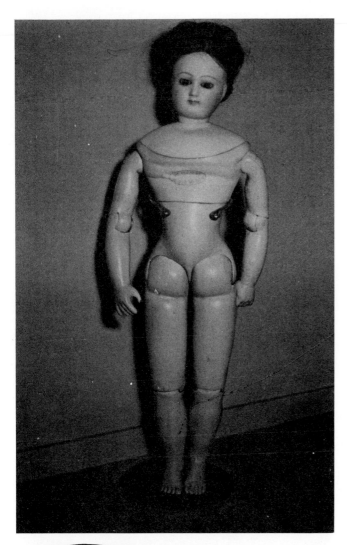

393 394 395

393. Mark stamped on bodies made by the Vve. (Widow) Clément.

394 & 395. Marks used by the Closter Veilsdorf Porzellan Fabrik Co.

stoneware dolls' heads. These were glazed and had shoulders attached; both Negro and white dolls' heads with flat-top hairdos, parted in the middle, and short curls all around the head. The unglazed part of the head was a yellowish tan in color.

**Clio Bébé.** 1917. Trademark registered in France and Britain by *Sussfeld & Cie.* for dolls.

**Closter (Kloster) Veilsdorf Porzellan Fabrik Co.** 1760–1925+. Eisfeld, Thür. One of the *Greiner* porcelain factories; used the trefoil mark from 1797.

1898: Advertised bisque and china heads, *bathing dolls, nankeen dolls.*

1905+: Made series of china heads embossed with a name (Luella Hart, SPINNING WHEEL, September, 1954). *Butler Bros.* owned molds for the *Pet Name* dolls.

**Cloth Bodies.** These are found on dolls dating back to ancient times. Cloth bodies for dolls have been popular throughout the ages because they could readily be made by a seamstress in the home, and were soft and cuddly and fairly durable. Homemade cloth bodies often reflect the skill and/or imagination of their makers. Frequently the early bodies were made of a multitude of small pieces patched together because homespun cloth was treasured by our thrifty ancestors. Several handmade jointless cloth bodies with china heads of about 1850 follow the same pattern—two-piece torsos and upper legs having seams on the sides; lower legs with front and back seams, attached at the knees; separate stub arms.

Commercial cloth bodies were made in the U.S., England, France, Germany, and other European countries. One-piece cloth bodies with little or no articulation were made in the early decades of the 19th century. *Kestner* was making dolls with muslin bodies in the 1840's. By 1860 *Fischer Naumann & Co.* patented a body that could sit easily. Shortly thereafter *Irene Gibson* made similar bodies that she called *Cinderella Sitting Dolls.* *Charles Braitling,* one of the largest manufacturers of muslin dolls' bodies, began operation in 1869. In the 1870's *Jacob Lacmann* and *Mary Steuber* patented improvements for limbs of cloth-body dolls. In the 1880's *Charles Dotter* and *Philip Goldsmith* patented cloth bodies with corsets on them. Also in the 1880's, there were several patents relating to the articulation of cloth bodies, notably those of *Lucinda Wishard, Sarah Robinson,* and *Stephan Schilling.* In 1877 Wolf Flechter obtained a patent pertaining to the stuffing of dolls' bodies. *Edward Peck* in 1886 secured a design patent for a cutout rag doll that could be put together and stuffed at home. During the 1890's this type of doll was very popular; it included those designed by *Celia and Charity Smith, Palmer Cox, Ida Gutsell, Louise Bowden,* and *Edgar Newell.* (His patent was granted in 1900, but he applied for it in 1899.) Also in the 1890's, there were knitted dolls' bodies both commercial, as shown in the patent of *Sarah Holmes,* and homemade, as seen in the HARPER'S BAZAR instructions of 1892. Some of the cloth bodies made in the 1890's had a red or blue insertion down the middle of the front of the body.

Cloth bodies with designs, such as the alphabet, flags, nursery figures, etc., on them were especially popular between 1900 and World War I. The alphabet bodies made for *Butler Bros.* were called A.B.C. bodies and usually came with *Pet Name* heads. Most of the composition-headed dolls made in America during and just prior to World War I had pink sateen bodies. In 1918, there were two important new types of cloth bodies. One was the walkable *Mama Doll* body patented by *Georgene Averill.* The other was the *Utley Company's* body formed with ball joints made of stiffened cloth. Infant dolls that appeared in 1924 nearly all had cloth bodies.

**Ca. 1876:**

| Catalog<br>Size | | Doll Bodies. | | | Price<br>per<br>Doz. |
|---|---|---|---|---|---|
| | | *Stuffed with Sawdust, Leather Hands.* | | | |
| 2/0 | 6 | inches long | ¹/₂ dozen in package. | | $ 1.12 |
| 0 | 7 | " " | ¹/₂ " " | | 1.25 |
| 1 | 8 | " " | ¹/₂ " " | | 1.38 |
| 2 | 9 | " " | ¹/₂ " " | | 1.50 |
| 3 | 10¹/₂ | " " | ¹/₂ " " | | 1.75 |
| 4 | 11¹/₂ | " " | ¹/₂ " " | | 2.00 |
| 5 | 13 | " " | ¹/₂ " " | | 2.50 |
| 6 | 14 | " " | ¹/₂ " " | | 3.00 |
| 7 | 16 | " " | ¹/₄ " " | | 3.75 |
| 8 | 17¹/₂ | " " | ¹/₄ " " | | 4.50 |
| 9 | 20 | " " | ¹/₄ " " | | 5.50 |
| 10 | 23 | " " | ¹/₄ " " | | 6.50 |
| 11 | 24 | " " | ¹/₄ " " | | 7.50 |
| 12 | 27 | " " | 1-6 " " | | 9.50 |
| | | *Hair Stuffed, Leather Arms, Closed Fingers.* | | | |
| 0 | 10 | inches long | 1 dozen in package. | | 1.75 |
| 1 | 11 | " " | 1 " " | | 2.00 |
| 2 | 11¹/₂ | " " | 1 " " | | 2.50 |
| 3 | 13 | " " | ¹/₂ " " | | 3.00 |
| 4 | 15 | " " | ¹/₂ " " | | 3.50 |
| 5 | 16¹/₂ | " " | ¹/₂ " " | | 4.00 |
| 6 | 18¹/₂ | " " | ¹/₂ " " | | 4.75 |
| 7 | 19¹/₂ | " " | ¹/₂ " " | | 5.50 |
| 8 | 20¹/₂ | " " | ¹/₂ " " | | 6.50 |
| 9 | 23 | " " | ¹/₃ " " | | 7.75 |
| 10 | | | ¹/₃ " " | | 9.00 |
| | | *Hair Stuffed, Leather Arms, Closed Fingers,*<br>*High Gaiters.* | | | |
| 0 | 10¹/₂ | inches long | 1 dozen in package. | | 2.25 |
| 1 | 11¹/₂ | " " | 1 " " | | 2.50 |
| 2 | 12¹/₂ | " " | 1 " " | | 3.00 |
| 3 | 14 | " " | ¹/₂ " " | | 3.50 |
| 4 | 15¹/₄ | " " | ¹/₂ " " | | 4.25 |
| 5 | 18 | " " | ¹/₂ " " | | 5.00 |
| 6 | 19 | " " | ¹/₂ " " | | 6.25 |
| 7 | 20 | " " | ¹/₂ " " | | 6.75 |
| 8 | 21¹/₂ | " " | ¹/₂ " " | | 7.75 |
| 9 | 22³/₄ | " " | ¹/₃ " " | | 9.00 |
| 10 | | | ¹/₃ " " | | 10.50 |
| | | *Hair Stuffed, Leather Arms, China Hands,*<br>*High Gaiters.* | | | |
| 0 | 10 | inches long | 1 dozen in package. | | 3.25 |
| 1 | 11 | " " | 1 " " | | 3.50 |
| 2 | 12 | " " | 1 " " | | 4.50 |
| 3 | 14 | " " | ¹/₂ " " | | 5.00 |
| 4 | 15 | " " | ¹/₂ " " | | 6.00 |
| 5 | 17¹/₂ | " " | ¹/₂ " " | | 7.00 |
| 6 | 19¹/₂ | " " | ¹/₂ " " | | 8.50 |
| 7 | 21 | " " | ¹/₂ " " | | 10.50 |
| 8 | 22 | " " | ¹/₂ " " | | 12.00 |
| 9 | 24 | " " | ¹/₃ " " | | 13.50 |
| 10 | | | ¹/₃ " " | | 15.00 |

*Excerpts from catalog of*
**STRASBURGER, PFEIFFER & CO.**
Note that doll bodies are often stamped with a number which corresponds with the numbers shown in these size tables.

*Courtesy of Flora Gill Jacobs*

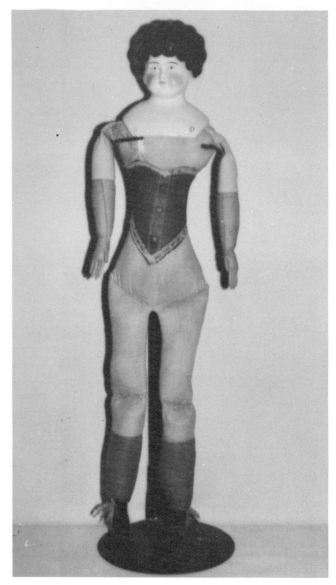

**396.** Imitation Goldsmith patented body, with red "corset" in front only; no lacings. Doll has oilcloth tasseled boots, a china head. H. 30 inches. *Coleman Collection.*

1896: Muslin doll bodies with real kid arms and patent leather shoes; sizes 11, 14¹/₂, 16, 18, and 20 inches; prices 15¢ to 40¢.

1922: Cloth doll bodies with bisque forearms; sizes 12, 15, 16, and 21 inches; prices 69¢, 85¢, 98¢, and $1.35.
(See also **Manufacture of Cloth Bodies.**)

**Clothes.** Dolls' clothes were made commercially throughout the 19th century. But it was also a popular practice to buy only a doll's head and create the body and clothes at home. Commercial dolls' clothes are often theatrical, being created primarily for the effect. This quality can readily be seen in the clothes on dolls shown by *Althof, Bergmann & Co.* in 1867. Many patterns for dolls' clothes, as given in DOLLY'S DRESSMAKER, HAR-

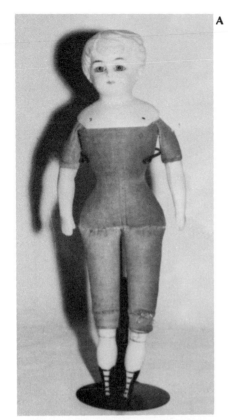

A

B

**397A & B.** Doll has cloth body with double row of stitching up the front, typical of the 1890's; flesh-tinted bisque shoulder head and bisque lower limbs, molded and painted features, blonde hair, high black boots. H. 11½ inches. H. of shoulder head, 3 inches. *Coleman Collection.*

**398.** Fashion Doll of the 18th century, a jointed wooden doll with features painted over gesso. The doll is attired in gold fabrics. Because fabrics and style were to be stressed in this pre-fashion magazine era, the gown is lined merely with a coarse paper. H. 25 inches. *Courtesy of the Newark Museum, Newark, N. J.*

PER'S BAZAR, GODEY'S, THE DELINEATOR, etc., followed the styles of the day. However, as can be seen in these publications, there was also an interest in peasant costumes and provincial clothes. Knitted and crocheted clothes too were popular for dolls.

The clothes of a doll seldom serve to tell either the exact place or the period of its origin, but sometimes they do give clues. At the time of the Centennial Exhibition in Philadelphia in 1876, colonial costumes for dolls were very popular. When Peary discovered the North Pole, many dolls were dressed as Eskimos. Dolls were often dressed in picturesque local costumes of an earlier era and a distant country. These "foreign dolls" were just as much play dolls as the doll dressed similarly to the child who owned it.

A French writer for the Association Nationale d'Expansion Economique in 1917 said that the French toy industry was practically nonexistent except for the Société Française des Bébés Jumeau (sic). This was partly the result of the fact that dressed or undressed dolls were better marketed in Germany. He also noted how little the attire of dolls changed through the years (actually, over long periods the changes were many), and he went on to say that except for *Art Dolls* changes were seldom made; as an example, he pointed out that hats "always" were raised off the face in front.

Dolls were frequently advertised as "undressed." This did not mean naked; it meant that the doll was wearing a chemise or slip, which was usually trimmed with lace, had sleeves, and covered the doll as completely as if she were dressed. A "dressed" doll usually had a silk or woolen dress and hat. In 1890, a *Bébé de Paris* was advertised either dressed in silks or undressed with a muslin chemise trimmed with lace and ribbons and with shoes and stockings. This doll sold for:

| | | |
|---|---|---|
| 11-inch size | $1.70 dressed | $ .75 undressed |
| 16-inch size | $3.30 dressed | $1.75 undressed |
| 23-inch size | $7.00 dressed | $3.50 undressed |

Thus, the fancy clothes accounted for about half the total cost of the doll. The elegantly dressed French lady dolls of the 1870's were priced as high as $25.00, and later some German dolls that were exquisitely dressed cost considerably more.

In the mid-19th century, a doll's trousseau was composed of sixteen pieces—three dresses, some shoes, stockings, a hat, bag, gloves, etc. According to PLAY-THINGS, in 1907 dolly's trousseau was more elaborate; she had a half-dozen distinctive frocks with everything to match:

1. Dainty lingerie dress of fluffy white for lawn fêtes. This was made of organdy, dotted swiss, lawn, or India linen. A lingerie hat went with it, as well as white slippers and socks.
2. A jumper frock with the waist pointed in the back and front. A guimpe of sheer lawn and lace and a straw hat.
3. A long coat with three capes for motoring, and an auto veil.
4. For a walk in the park, a long white double-breasted coat with a deep turndown collar, a Dutch cap of lawn with satin rosettes.
5. A yachting suit of white serge, made with a reefer jacket and kilted skirt, and a big straw hat.
6. Party gown with a skirt of ruffled embroidery, a satin sash ribbon, and a ribbon bow on one shoulder.

Also pajamas, night robes, corsets, and satin slippers— several pairs each of pink, blue, and white slippers.

*Jumeau* first won recognition for his dolls' clothes rather than for his dolls. Among the many other famous makers of dolls' clothes in Paris there were Mme. Lavallée-*Peronne*, Mlle. Deschamps, J. Carael (1919–25), and *Mme. Bonneaud. Georgene Averill* started by designing doll clothes; Mme. Corene Clair (1923) designed clothes for *Regal Dolls. Katherine A. Rauser* designed clothes for dolls all over America and even in England. She designed clothes worn by the dolls of *Horsman, Schoenhut,* and many other famous manufacturers. Also in America, the American Doll's Outfit Co. (1905), New York City, and the *Arnoldt* Doll Dress Co. (1914), Cincinnati, Ohio,

**399.** Wooden doll with head of gesso over wood, glass eyes with blue pupils, wig, dots around the eyes, square-bottom wooden body, white leather arms, and contemporary Empire clothes consisting of a figured lawn dress with train, silk hat, silk shoes. H. 15 inches. *Courtesy of the Chester County Historical Society.*

**400** (at top, opposite). The papier-mâché head, wooden limbs, kid body, and hair style of this doll suggest the 1830's, especially the hairdo. Contemporary dress, blue painted shoes. H. 26 inches. *Courtesy of The Smithsonian Institution.*

**402** China head and limbs on a turned wooden, peg-jointed body. Hair is pulled behind the ears and molded in corkscrew curls in the back. Doll wears original tan silk dress, pantaloons, and braided straw hat. H. 5¼ inches. H. of shoulder head, 1¼ inches. *Courtesy of the Chester County Historical Society.*

**403.** China head with sausage-curl hair style is on a cloth body. Doll is dressed in tan silk as a Quakeress. H. 9 inches. H. of shoulder head, 2¼ inches. *Courtesy of Eunice Althouse.*

**401** (at left). Peg wooden with tuck comb and original dress, which is tan printed with a red, green, and purple design; black silk apron, net around the neck and on the hood, and bloomer-type pants of pink silesia. H. 3 inches. *Courtesy of Flora Gill Jacobs.*

**404.** Vivandière of the mid-19th century. The doll has a peg-jointed body with head and lower limbs of china. The features are painted. She is dressed in original black velvet jacket, red skirt, and apron, and carries a water cask on a shoulder strap. H. 12 inches. H. of shoulder head, 3 inches. *Courtesy of the Chester County Historical Society.*

**405A & B.** The original crocheted clothes appear on this pair of dolls, Frozen Charlotte and Frozen "Charlie." The girl has luster shoes. Note the length of the boy's hair and the Alice-in-Wonderland hairdo on the girl. H. 3 inches each. *Courtesy of the Newark Museum, Newark, N. J.*

made dolls' clothes. Arnoldt used the trade name "Blue Bird Doll Clothes." Blanche Cromien (1920's) made dresses for the dolls of the *Cameo Doll Co.* Queen G. Thomas (1921) made clothes for *Sophia E. Delavan's* dolls. In Germany, C. Oesterheld of Gotha, founded in 1869, was still making dolls' dresses in 1884.

## CHRONOLOGY OF CLOTHES FOR DOLLS

The following descriptions are taken from contemporary publications or are descriptions of documented dolls:

Ca. 1810: Boy Dolls: Clothes of an aristocrat—large pleated linen collar, green waistcoat fastened by three buttons, short vest with trimming, large felt hat with two corners.

French Revolution costume—"carmagnole" jacket and "phrygien" bonnet.

1832: Babies wore long white dresses; one of a set of twins was dressed in satin, but the other twin (probably not the heir) wore humble lawn.

Ca. 1840: Of seven dressed dolls shown in a sample book, six were dressed as men; one of these was in Turkish costume, and two in clown costumes. The sole girl wore a provincial costume. In the same book, of sixty-two dolls without clothes only fourteen had short hair for boys or babies. All the rest were made to be dressed as girls or ladies.

1865: Taffetas very fashionable; next in popularity were foulards and patterned cashmeres. French antique moiré was used for dolls though not for girls.

1867: Doll dressed in the style of a French Marquise of the old "regime"—a trained skirt of cherry-colored satin open in front to disclose a white silk petticoat, ruffled with blond lace. The waist was made surplice-style with a blond chemisette. Sleeves were tight to the elbow, where they formed a ruffle lined with blond fluted lace. Cherry satin high-crowned hat with tiny tufts of white ostrich feathers at the side.

A young lady of wax wore a dress of white poplin gored "à la princesse" and braided with blue; girdle of blue silk; white felt hat with long blue veil; high Polish boots of bronze adorned with tassels and gilt buttons.

1868: Infants wore long robes and caps; dolls wore knitted and crocheted costumes.

1871: Doll had an evening dress of pink silk with overskirt of white tulle, ruched and draped with rosebuds, a train at the back.

1875: Clothes copied latest Parisian fashion; represented brides, widows, nurses carrying infants. Others dressed in national costumes or as familiar characters of the stage. (See the brides in color photograph C14.)

1880: Doll's bathing suit was made of red flannel trimmed with white lace and blue ribbon.

**406.** Bisque-head, kid-body lady doll with original clothes; late 1860's. Note that the high Congress boots have no heels. H. 17 inches. *Courtesy of the Newark Museum, Newark, N. J.*

**407A, B, & C.** Lady doll with trunk and wardrobe of clothes, including a white piqué, a blue wool, and a gold colored silk dress, all being two-piece outfits. Doll has bisque head, gusset-jointed kid body. H. 14½ inches. *Coleman Collection.*

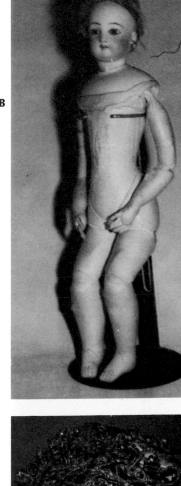

B

A

C

**408**. A French nurse or "Bonne." She has a bisque swivel head, cloth body, kid limbs, glass eyes, and a brown wig. Originally, she held a baby of bisque. She wears her original blue wool skirt and maroon headdress. Mark: "1." H. 15 inches. *Courtesy of The Smithsonian Institution.*

Boy doll's sailor suit had a plum-colored velvet blouse trimmed with narrow white braid and white pearl buttons; collar was white lace; wide ribbon sash.

1885: Newest fancy was for a walking suit with a mull poke or a plush cap and a short-waisted cloak with hood. Dolls wore a gingham slip or a Gretchen dress of cashmere or muslin.

**409A & B.** Bride wears original white satin and challis gown bedecked with orange blossoms. She has a bisque head, kid and cloth body; her hair is in long curls down her back. H. 11½ inches. (See color photograph **C14**.) *Coleman Collection.*

**410A & B.** Wax-over-composition head with sleeping glass eyes is on a cloth body with composition limbs. Doll is dressed in original Swiss provincial costume. H. 16 inches. *Courtesy of Theodora Gearhart.*

1890: Infant dolls in long clothes and cap were most in favor; their dresses were trimmed with drawn-work, feather-stitching, embroidery, and lace.

Nurse dolls wore large, round peasant cloak, and cap with streaming ribbons.

Novelty was a "double doll" with one end dressed as an infant and the other as a nurse.

Boy dolls were generally dressed in sailor suits of blue or white flannel.

1893: The Gretchen dress came with a shirred yoke and smocking.

1895: Girl doll wore white cambric chemise trimmed with narrow lace, a dress of white dotted muslin trimmed with lace and ribbon; the wide collar was separate and also trimmed with lace and ribbon.

Boy doll appeared in sailor suit of dark blue cloth, collar of blue linen with rows of narrow white braid; there was a row of buttons down each front edge.

1899: Girl doll wore satin with lace- and ribbon-trimmed yoke; hooks for fastening; feather-trimmed hat.

Dolls dressed as Rough Riders were popular.

1903: Wash materials such as organdy and dotted swiss were preferred to silks and satins. About 50 percent of the newest dolls wore military uniforms. One new line of dolls was dressed in automobile costumes. French dolls wore costumes this year that provincial Americans would not wear until next year.

1904: Dolls dressed in Dutch costumes were a fad in America; Japanese, Eskimo, Russian, and Indian costumes were also popular.

Dolls in sailor costume had the name of the town in which they were to be sold (St. Louis, etc.) on their hats or caps.

First season for doll union suits.

1910: The French Doll Shop at *Gimbel's* advertised dolls dressed in hobble skirts, black velvet walking skirts, fancy earrings, and the newest headgear—Ding-a-ling toques with a feather on them.

1911: Clothes resembled children's dress rather than that of adults, and were less elaborate. Young lady dolls wore harem or hobble skirts. Baby dolls came clad only in breech clout and bonnet. Pair of dolls (male and female) dressed in Dutch costumes was popular.

1913: Harem skirt *passé;* plain red and blue colors popular.

1917: Many dolls dressed as *Red Cross Nurses.*

1922: Dolls wore gowns of the latest Paris fashion, loose and flowing.

(See the numerous illustrations of dated dolls wearing their original dresses.)

**411A & B.** Bisque-headed, kid-bodied infant doll, dressed and undressed. Doll was purchased in the late 19th century in Paris for a member of the Batchelor family. She has cobalt-blue sleep eyes, leather body stitched in red. The original dress is white with blue trim; doll came with wardrobe. H. 13½ inches. *Courtesy of The Smithsonian Institution.*

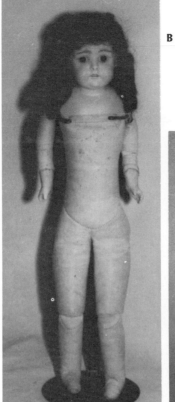

A

B

C

**412A, B, & C.** Kestner doll with bisque shoulder head, glass eyes, and an open-closed mouth with molded teeth. Kid gusseted body has bisque lower arms. Original dresses. Owned by a Kansas child in the early 1890's. Mark: Ill. **987.** H. 16½ inches. H. of shoulder head, 4½ inches. *Coleman Collection.*

**413A & B.** Bisque shoulder head on combination kid and cotton gusseted body with bisque lower arms. Original Quaker dress and bonnet. H. 23 inches. *Coleman Collection.*

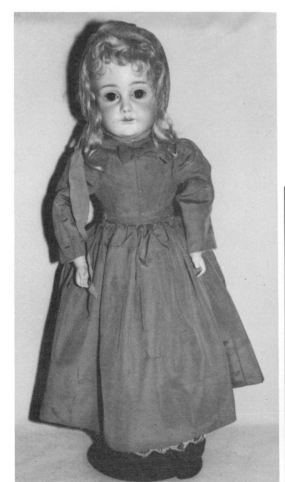

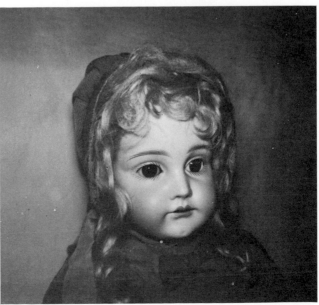

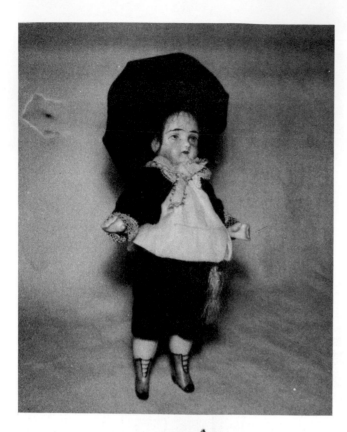

**414.** Jointed all-bisque doll with painted features and wig. He is dressed in original lace-trimmed navy velvet suit, lawn blouse, and tam-o'-shanter. Ca. 1900. H. 6 inches. *Courtesy of the Newark Museum, Newark, N. J.*

**416.** Bisque socket-headed doll with pierced ears on a jointed composition body. The doll is dressed in an outfit made to match one worn by her original owner. The hat was fashioned by a milliner. The costume is dated 1921. Mark: "SIMON & HALBIG // K.[star]R." Doll and shoes are dated 1914. H. 21½ inches. *Coleman Collection.*

**415.** Fashionably gowned lady doll, as shown in *Playthings Magazine,* 1911. Note the size of the hat, the high collar, earrings, watch, and the detail in decoration. *Courtesy of McCready Publishing Co.*

**Clover Leaf Doll.** 1901. A *Marguerite* or *bonnet*-type doll with molded headdress in the shape of a cloverleaf. It came with pink muslin body and porcelain limbs; sizes 8, 9, 12½, and 15 inches; 9-inch size priced 19¢.

**Clown.** 1903–25+. Wooden doll with rubber joints made by *Schoenhut,* patented in U.S. and Britain in 1903. Came dressed in cotton or silk clown's costume; sizes 5½, 8, and 12 inches; also 32-inch display clown.

**Clown.** 1916–17. One of the *Capo* line of dolls made by the *Non-Breakable Toy Co.;* distributed by the *Baltimore Bargain House.* Came with composition head and hands; 36 inches, priced $1.35.

**Clown.** 1920. Doll copyrighted by *Guglielmo Voccia.*

**Clown.** 1921. Trade name for a rag doll with bobbing head, designed by *Grace Corry* and made by *Century Doll Co.*

**Clown.** 1923–24. U.S. design patent obtained by *Domenic Zappia* and assigned to *Paramount Rubber Consolidated, Inc.*

**Clown With Box of Cookies.** 1916. U. S. design patent issued to Isaac Rommer for a doll that was made by *Ideal Novelty and Toy Co.* and given the trade name *Zu-Zu Kid.*

**Clownee.** 1915. One of the *Jam Kiddos* made by *Non-Breakable Doll Co.* Came with composition head, molded hair, and sleeping eyes; cost $1.00.

**Clownie.** 1911. Composition-head doll made by *Louis Amberg & Son;* had cloth body.

**Coblenz, D.** 1910–14. Paris. Handled dressed and undressed dolls, especially for export.

**Cobo-Alice and Cobo-Judy.** 1880's–1925+. Rag dolls made in Cobo, Isle of Guernsey, of heavy unbleached muslin stuffed with sawdust. Spherical heads painted with household paint, as were the hands and feet. Brows and nose needle-molded; hair and other features painted. Oval eyes had small black dots for iris and pupil; mouth was outlined in red, hair painted brown; cloth body had swing joints at hips and shoulders. Sizes 13 and 18 inches and probably others; came without clothes.

**Cocheco Manufacturing Co.** 1827–93+. Textile manufacturers.

1889–92: Made rag dolls designed by *Celia and Charity Smith.*

1893: Made rag dolls patented by *Ida Gutsell.*

**Cochet.** 1811–74. Paris. Cochet was listed as a sculptor in wood, and Cochet & Dehenne were listed as makers of masks in 1811.

1833–42: August Cochet, Jeune (Jr.), was listed as a maker of dressed dolls and kid-body dolls. He had succeeded his father by 1842.

1843: August Cochet, Jne., made undressed dolls in papier-mâché and heads with coiffures.

1847: He was listed as a maker of dressed dolls and kid-body dolls. His workshop was at Sannois, Seine-et-Oise.

1874: A. Cochet advertised that he made undressed dolls, which he packed in boxes, and dolls' heads with all types of hairdos.

**417.** Mark on rag dolls of Cocheco Manufacturing Co.

**418.** Papier-mâché head with fancy coiffure of ca. 1830's is on a kid body with wooden limbs. Doll wears a contemporary brown and beige dress. *Courtesy of Marion Holt; photograph by Winnie Langley.*

**Cochet-Verdey.** 1833–47. Paris. Workshop at Ecouen, Seine-et-Oise; made dolls of papier-mâché with kid bodies, as well as heads for milliners and hairdressers.

**Coco and Coco, L'Infernal Brise-Tout.** 1918. Two trademarks registered in France by *Mme. Poulbot.*

**Codet, Widow Jean (née Corbassière).** 1923. France. Obtained a French patent for a jointed doll.

**Co-Ed.** 1915. Character doll made by *Modern Toy Co.*

**Co-Ed Flapper, The.** 1925. Doll made by the *American Stuffed Novelty Co.* It had a hand-painted face, sewed wig, satin body stuffed with cotton, and was 26 inches tall.

**Coffield, Maude M.** 1923–24. Kansas City, Mo. Obtained a design patent for a cherub-type doll with an Egyptian headdress.

**Cohen, Adolph.** 1915. U.S. citizen; designed *Pa-na-ma* doll for *Trion Toy Co.*

**Cohen, Daniel S.** 1862–67. New York City. Distributor and possibly assembler of the *Autoperipatetikos* doll. His name appears on one of the original boxes of this doll.

**Cohen, Edward.** 1922. London. Doll importer.

**Cohen, J. G., Jr.** 1895. Hamburg, Germany. Made dolls.

**Cohen, L., & Sons.** 1923–24. New York City. Made *Elco Mama* dolls.

**Cohn (Cone), Aaron.** 1907–24. New York City. After 1912, Toronto, Ontario. Doll manufacturer. Obtained a U.S. patent for sleeping eyes in a doll's head, in 1924. He created character dolls for *Ideal Novelty & Toy Co.* until after 1912.

**Cohn, Adolf.** 1895. Breslau, Silesia. Made dolls' bodies.

**Cohn, Georg.** 1899. Breslau, Silesia. Secured a British patent for the tongue and hole type of movable doll joints.

**Cohn, Grete.** 1920. Berlin. Produced and distributed dolls. Registered *Grecon* as a trademark in Germany for a line of dolls that included fabric dolls, dolls' house dolls, etc.

**Cohn, P. (Firm).** 1898–99. Breslau, Silesia. Obtained a German patent for articulated dolls and dolls' heads. These appear to be largely two-dimensional, and made of metal or paper.

**Coiffe.** 1873–1920. Limoges, France. Porcelain manufacturer; made dolls' heads.

1882: L. Coiffe had joined with *Touron & Simon;* their Paris agent was G. Taraud.

1898: The listing was for Coiffe, Jne. (Jr.), and his Paris agent was Guindon.

1915–16: Coiffe, Couty & Cie. was one of the firms that benefited from the experiments on dolls' heads at the *Sèvres* laboratories.

419. Mark used by Coiffe.

1920: Couty, Magne & Cie. were the successors of H. Coiffe & Leon Couty, and continued to manufacture porcelain dolls' heads.

**Coiffures.** 1881. Name used by *Blampoix, Jne.* (Jr.), who made porcelain heads; appears to refer to a type of doll's head. Collectors sometimes call papier-mâché dolls' heads with fancy hairdos "coiffure dolls' heads."

**Cole, Mrs. A. R.** Before 1908. Conway, Ark. Made 2,300 dolls of various sizes, blonde and brunette. These dolls were a missionary project.

**Cole-Ackerman Co.** 1904–5. Cleveland, Ohio. The trademark *Y-Do-I* used for dolls in commerce between Canada and the U.S., registered in U.S. for them by Charles E. Cole.

**Coleman, Harry H.** 1917–23. British subject residing in U.S. and traveling around performing as a ventriloquist. Obtained British and several U.S. patents for a nonmechanical walking doll with hip and knee joints made so that the doll would walk or dance when taken by the hand and pulled forward. Doll was called *Dolly Walker,* and Coleman registered this name in the U.S. as a trademark. Dolly Walker was made by the *Wood Toy Co.* and distributed by Coleman. In 1919 one dealer sold a thousand of these dolls.

**Colgate Kid, The.** 1914. Doll made by *Horsman* and dressed all in white.

**Colin.** 1890. Obtained French patent for making bébés of wood pulp.

**Collections of Dolls.** Prior to 1900: Information on early doll collections is mostly legendary, as for example the tale that Queen Elizabeth had a passion for dolls and collected so many and with such elaborate wardrobes that the services of a maid were required to attend to the dressing and undressing of the dolls. Many collections did belong to royalty. Queen Victoria had 132 peg-jointed wooden dolls in her youth. Elizabeth, Queen of Roumania (known in literature as Carmen Silva), began to collect dolls in 1874 after she lost her only daughter. This collection eventually consisted of 1,300 dolls, and was often exhibited for charitable purposes. Princess Clementine of Belgium had an extensive collection, including many very old dolls. One of these was alleged to have been the original Poppea brought to the court of Charles VI by an Italian named *Pusmo.* Queen Wilhelmina of Holland had a large collection of dolls when she was a young princess. Some of them represented governesses and were large, adult-type dolls; others were children or baby dolls representing the governesses' charges.

Collectors interested in the history of toys have sometimes gathered together examples of old dolls, and most of these later found their way into museums. Elizabeth Lemke's dolls went to the Volkskunde Museum in Berlin, and Rodman Wanamaker's went to the Musée Carnavalet in Paris. Henri d'Allemagne had a fine collection of dolls that he used as source material for his books. Laura Starr and Annie Fields Alden also used their doll collections for writing purposes. Eugene Field, Ellen Terry, Frances Hodgson Burnett, and many other notables enjoyed collecting dolls. By 1896, Elizabeth R. Horton in Boston had what she called the International Doll Collection. *Miss Columbia*, the rag doll, was chosen from this collection to travel around the world.

Museums have always provided some of the finest collections of dolls. As well as antique examples, they have dolls used to display miniature versions of costumes representing different periods and places. Some of these may be play-type dolls dressed in costumes that are unsuitable to the doll's childish face and figure.

**College Boy.** 1915. Character doll made by *Modern Toy Co.*

**College Kids.** 1912. Line of dolls made by *Louis Amberg & Son*. They had composition heads with a molded college cap on the back of the head; cork-stuffed pink sateen bodies; were dressed in college clothes, both boys and girls, representing six colleges, and carried a college flag.

**Collet Frères (Bros.).** 1900. Paris. Listed in directory as making dolls. Ch. and H. Collet won a bronze medal for Maison *Derolland* at the 1900 Paris Exposition. Derolland made rubber dolls.

**Collins, Jack.** 1925. Los Angeles. Co-artist with *Joseph Kallus* of the copyrighted doll named "Gamine," which was called *Little Annie Roonie* when it appeared on the market. "Jack Collins" is incised on the back skirt of the bisque version of Little Annie Rooney.

**Collins & Robins.** 1916. London. Doll makers.

**Colombe.** 1834–36. Paris. Made dolls.

**Colombo, John.** 1843–48. London. Doll maker.

**Colombo, William.** 1856–68. London. Made dolls.

**Colonel Bogey.** 1924. Trademark registered in Britain by *Nunn & Smeed* for dolls.

**Colonial Dolls (Colonial Quality).** 1905–21. Trademark registered in U.S. by *Samstag & Hilder*. This mark was registered in 1921, but had been used since 1905. It is not known whether Samstag & Hilder were distributors for the *Colonial Toy Manufacturing Co.* or not.

**Colonial Toy Manufacturing Co.** 1915–20. New York City. Made all-composition Zaiden Dolls while *David Zaiden* was president (1915–18). A. E. Fountain was the president from 1918–20; the company was known as A. E. Fountain, Inc., 1920–21.

1916: The word "Zaiden" was impressed on the dolls. They advertised that there were fifty-two styles. Every head was uniform. Eyes were set by machine so accurately that if one pair of eyes in a thousand was wrong, all were wrong. Colonial produced about 300,000 dolls a year in various sizes. Dolls had to age for six weeks after being pressed before being sent to the finishing department.

1917: Advertised all-composition dolls having "Royal Colonial" finish. Fully jointed dolls came in two sizes: 13 inches with painted hair and eyes, attired in a three-piece dress; 28 inches with wig, sleeping eyes, jointed wrists, dressed in chemise. Bent-limb babies jointed at neck, shoulder, and hips came in three sizes: 14 inches, with painted eyes, molded hair or wig, dressed in chemise or three-piece white dress; 18 inches, with sleeping eyes, sewed mohair wig, dressed in chemise; 24 inches, jointed also at wrists, sleeping eyes with eyelashes, moving tongue, sewed mohair wig, dressed in silk suit and cap; clothes came in pink, blue, or white. *Snowbird* was the name of one of the Colonial dolls. They also advertised the *Mother Goose Hug-Me-Tight* dolls designed by *Grace Drayton*, which sold for 50¢.

1918: They made a line of dolls called *Miss Colonial* and the *Next-to-Nature* babies.

1919: They made a line of dolls named *Peachy Pets*. Their composition babies came in sizes 18 inches with painted hair or wig; 22 and 24 inches with wig. The prices of Colonial dolls ranged from $13.20 to $96.00 doz. wholesale.

1920: Their fully jointed dolls had mohair wigs and came in two sizes, 19 and 29 inches, priced at $61.00 and $123.00 doz. wholesale. The bent-limb babies with mohair wigs, painted or sleeping eyes, some with eyelashes, came in four sizes—14, 18, 22, and 24 inches—priced from $39.00 to $86.00 doz. wholesale.

**Columbia.** 1898. Advertised by *W. A. Cissna & Co.*; had bisque head, wig, kid body, drop-stitch-knit stockings. Size 18½ inches; price $5.75 doz. wholesale. It should be noted that both Columbia and *Cinderella*, names used by Cissna, were also used by *Louis Wolf & Co.* for dolls that they distributed, which were made by *C. M. Bergmann*.

421. "Columbia" mark on heads made by Armand Marseille.

420. Mark used by Colonial Toy Manufacturing Co.

COLONIAL
DOLL
MADE IN
U.S.A.

**Columbia.** 1904–15. Line of dolls made by *C. M. Bergmann* and distributed by *Louis Wolf & Co.* Bisque heads made by *Armand Marseille* were used for these dolls. At first the line had kid bodies, but later fully jointed composition bodies were also used.

**Columbia.** 1916. Doll with composition head, designed by *Hugo Baum* and made by *EFFanBEE;* price $1.00.

**Columbia Doll & Toy Co.** 1917–22. New York City. Made dolls with wood pulp composition heads. Among their dolls in 1920 were *Miss Columbia,* Columbia Jr., and *Chubby Kid.*

**Columbia Doll Co.** 1912. New York City. Made dolls.

**Columbia Kids.** 1917–18. Line of patriotic dolls made by *Ideal Novelty & Toy Co.* There were four styles; one of the boys wore a red, white, and blue knitted suit and a woolen cap.

**Columbian Doll, The.** 1891–1910 or later. Made by *Emma Adams* and Marietta Adams. These were rag dolls made of firm muslin stuffed with cotton around a sawdust center for the head and torso (see **Manufacture of Cloth Bodies**). The hair and features were all hand-painted by Emma Adams until her death in 1900. After that date they were painted by commercial artists, who never attained Miss Adams' skill. Sizes were 15, 19, 23, and 29 inches—girls, boys, and babies, blue eyes and brown eyes, and a few Negroes. The toes and fingers were indicated by stitches; the limbs were painted flesh color and stiffened with sizing. On the back of the cloth body, before 1900, an ink stamp appeared:

> COLUMBIAN DOLL
> EMMA E. ADAMS
> OSWEGO CENTRE
> N.Y.

After 1906, the stamp read:

> THE COLUMBIAN DOLL
> MANUFACTURED BY
> MARIETTA ADAMS RUTTAN
> OSWEGO, N.Y.

The clothes for the dolls were designed and made by Marietta Adams. They were finished with buttons, buttonholes, and trimmings. The dresses were generally pink, blue, or white and usually of cotton. Some of the dolls wore only a gown or chemise. Each doll wore a bonnet or cap, and on the feet were either stockings and hand-sewn kidskin slippers or booties. The prices ranged from $1.50 to $5.00, depending on the size of the doll and the elaborateness of the clothing. The most famous Columbian doll is Miss Columbia, who traveled around the world unaccompanied for several years. In 1902 when she arrived in the Philippines, she was greeted by William Howard Taft, who was then Governor of the Islands. Prior to her journey she had belonged to the International Doll Collection of Elizabeth R. Horton. After her return to Boston with a trunk full of trophies, she found a permanent home in the Wenham Museum.

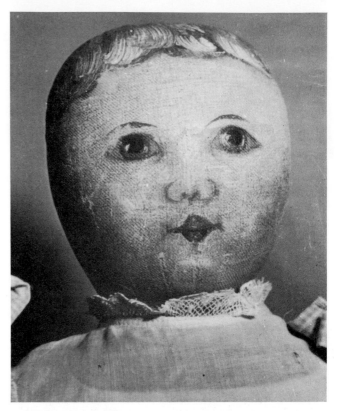

**422A & B.** Rag doll made by Emma Adams. Dolls similar to this one were sold at the 1893 Columbian Exposition in Chicago and were known as The Columbian Doll. *Courtesy of Margaret Whitton* (front view) and *Evelyn Barrows* (side view); *photographs by Winnie Langley.*

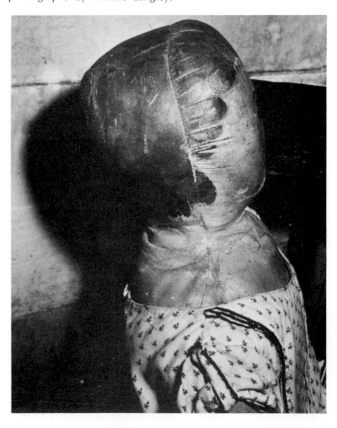

**Columbian Sailor Boy.** Ca. 1893. Cutout rag doll designed by *Celia M. Smith* and printed in colors on cloth by *Arnold Print Works*. The cloth was sold for 12¢ to 20¢ a yard, and each yard contained several dolls.

**Columbine.** 1911. Composition-head character doll made by *A. Steinhardt & Bro.* She was a mate to *Marceline;* her face was powdered white and had black beauty spots; dress was white silk with flaring skirt and three red pompoms down the front. Price $1.50.

**Com-A-Long.** 1920–21. Trademark registered in U.S. and Germany by *Borgfeldt.* Probably used on dolls of this name as designed by *Genevieve Pfeffer.*

**Comfort.** 1920. Name of an all-cloth doll made by *Jessie McCutcheon Raleigh;* size 18 inches.

**Compo Baby.** 1917–18. Trade name of all-composition baby doll made by *Ideal Novelty & Toy Co.* It came with stationary or sleeping eyes and in five sizes.

**Composition (Indestructible) Dolls.** The composition used for dolls consisted of various ingredients mixed together. Literally, composition dolls would include papier-mâché dolls, celluloid dolls, and numerous others. But collectors usually refer to dolls' heads made of a glue process or a wood pulp mixture as being composition heads. However, lacking consistency, they often call dolls' bodies "composition" that are made of papier-mâché. Another inconsistency is the use by the trade of the term "indestructible" for dolls that can in fact be damaged quite easily. In 1907, the ingredients for

some French dolls' bodies were listed as "old cardboard, old gloves, old rags and gum tragacanth."

Papier-mâché has been used for dolls for many centuries, but records of other types of composition are more recent. The ingredients of which compositions are made are often listed in the patent papers. Among papers containing such information are those granted to *Mons. Richard* (1853), *Henry Loewenberg* (1865), *Albert Anqueulle* (1865), *Henry Wurtz* (1866), *Brasseur & Chevallier* (1868), and *Solomon Hoffmann* (1892).

About 1908, one method of making composition was described as throwing sawdust into boiling water. Some 50,000 dolls a day were made by this process.

During World War I, the American composition doll swept the market because of the difficulty of importing dolls' heads of ceramics. Many of these composition dolls were more expensive than their bisque counterparts.

Around this same time (1918 and 1919), there was considerable contention as to the superiority of glue process over wood pulp composition. One doll manufacturer claimed: "Glue process full composition heads are superior to brittle inferior wood pulp heads, which when atmospheric conditions change, break or crack." Another manufacturer warned of "dolls made from some of the worst disease-breeding compositions in existence, as hide and bone glue and other waste material, to be kissed by the baby."

Each doll maker appears to have had his own "secret" formula for composition, but very few of the

**423.** Composition head marked "G L Superior" has molded and painted features and hair. *Courtesy of Margaret Whitton; photograph by Winnie Langley.* (See next page for **424.**)

**425.** Composition head marked "M & S//2015" has molded and painted features and hair. For another M&S mark see Ill. **426.** *Courtesy of Winnie Langley; photograph by Winnie Langley.*

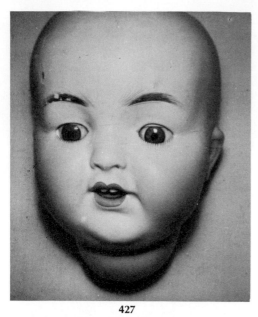

G. L
2020
Superior

424

M & S
Superior

426

M & S
50
Germany

428

427

**424, 426, 428, 430, 432, 434.** Marks found on composition heads, including "Superior" and other marks.

**427.** M & S composition head (mark: Ill. **428**) has glass sleeping eyes; crown is cut off, as on most bisque heads. H. of socket head, 7 inches. *Courtesy of Edna Greehy.*

429

**429.** Nonpareil composition head, distributed by Ridley. Mark: Ill. **430**. Has painted and molded features and hair. H. 6½ inches. *Collection of the late Sarge Kitterman; photograph by Winnie Langley.*

**431.** Composition head, marked as shown in Ill. **432**, has black molded hair, painted eyes. *Courtesy of Margaret Whitton; photograph by Winnie Langley.*

**433.** Composition head (mark: Ill. **434**) has molded and painted features and hair. *Courtesy of Mabel Quick; photograph by Winnie Langley.*

W.A.H.
nonpareil
3015

430

A F. & C.
Superior
2018

432

TRADE MARK

434

**435.** Composition shoulder head of a man has brown glass eyes, red yarn hair, molded gray mustache. Doll wears original Scottish costume. H. 12 inches. *Coleman Collection.*

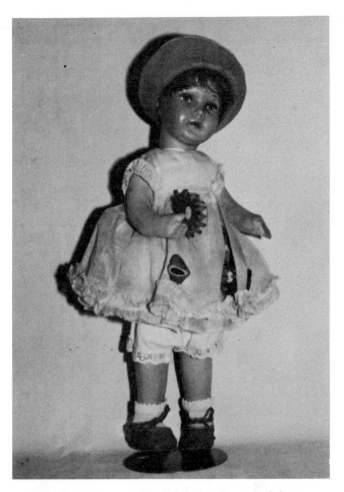

**437A & B.** Composition-headed doll with painted features, a wig, and cloth body; unmarked. Wears original clothes. H. 17 inches. *Courtesy of Dorothy J. Annunziato.*

**436A & B.** Composition doll with bent limbs, painted features. *Courtesy of Winnie Langley; photograph by Winnie Langley.*

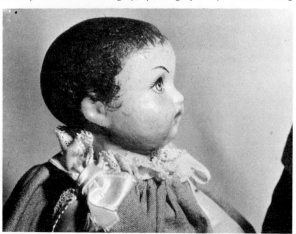

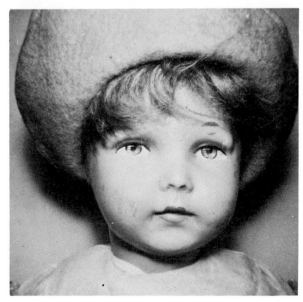

products of these recipes have successfully withstood the ravages of time—except possibly those made with papier-mâché or a rag basis.

(See **Manufacture of Composition Heads; Manufacture of Composition Bodies.**)

**Composition Novelty Co.** 1915–16. New York City. Made dolls with composition heads and papier-mâché bodies, which were fully jointed, including wrist joints. These were advertised as having real hair wigs of long curls that could be washed and also would not burn, sleeping eyes, and coming in numerous styles. Company slogans were *"Made First in America"* and *"First Made in America."*

**Comptoir de la Fantasie.** 1919–21. Paris. Directed by D. *Le Montréer.* Made dressed and undressed dolls. Their trademark *Le Victorieux* had been registered in France by Le Montréer in 1914.

**Cone, Aaron.** See **Cohn, Aaron.**

**Conrad, Paul.** 1909–18. Dresden, Saxony. Made dolls.

**Constance Binney.** 1924. *Celebrity Doll* originated by *Margaret Vale,* designed and made by *Jane Gray.* The doll represented Constance Binney as Virginia in Lawrence Schwab's play THE SWEET LITTLE DEVIL. It had a hand-painted face and bore a tag with a facsimile autograph of Constance Binney.

**Constance Talmadge.** 1924. *Celebrity Doll* originated by *Margaret Vale,* designed and produced by *Jane Gray.* It had a hand-painted face and bore a tag with a facsimile autograph of the actress, Constance Talmadge.

**Consterdine, Herbert.** 1903–4. Littleborough, Lancashire. Obtained a British patent for a pin-jointed doll with a spring wire.

**Contented Baby.** 1925. Copyrighted by *Hugo Baum;* baby has finger in its mouth.

**Convicts.** 1894–1907. French prisoners made dolls, which sold for a penny.

**Cook (Dr.).** 1909. Dolls advertised by *Borgfeldt, Theo. H. Gary & Co., Horsman,* and *Strobel & Wilken.* These dolls represented the famous Arctic explorer.

**Cook, Josephine Merwin.** 1920–21. Obtained a U.S. design patent for a rag doll.

**Cooley, Catherine C.** 1920. Omaha, Nebr. Secured a U.S. design patent for a doll.

**Cooley, Gifford W.** 1915. Plainfield, N.J. Obtained a U.S. design patent for a doll with a cylindrical-shaped face.

**Co-operative Manufacturing Co.** 1873–74. Springfield, Vt. Made mortise and tenon jointed wooden dolls with metal hands and feet. Joel Addison Hartley *Ellis,* who patented the doll in the U.S., was the president of this company; the work was believed to have been done on the premises of the Vermont Novelty Works. The dolls were made of rock maple, with the end of the grain

used for the pressed heads. Bodies and limbs were turned on a lathe. Some of the dolls were painted black to represent Negroes. Sizes were 12, 15, and 18 inches; wholesale price, $9.00, $10.50, and $13.50 doz. These dolls appear to have been displayed at the 1873 Vienna Exhibition.

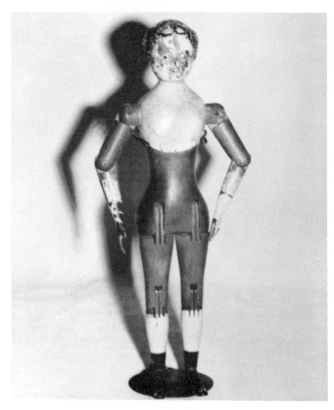

**438.** Co-operative Manufacturing Co. wooden doll, made according to the 1873 patent by Joel Ellis, has mortise-and-tenon joints, pressed and painted features and hair, metal hands and feet. H. 12 inches. *Coleman Collection.*

**Cop.** 1923. Rag doll made by *Nelke Corp.*

**Copenhagen.** See **Royal Copenhagen Manufactory.**

**Copper Dolls' Heads.** 1903. Made in U.S.

**Copyrights.** Many dolls have been copyrighted. These can usually be identified by the © symbol on them, which is recognized internationally. The American Constitution provides for copyright protection, but dolls' heads do not appear to have qualified for this protection until a major revision in the copyright law was enacted in 1909 covering Class G, Graphic Works of Art, and Class H, Reproduction of Works of Art. To qualify for Class G, "The work must embody some creative authorship in its delineation or form. The registrability of a work of art is not affected by the intention of the author as to the use of the work, the number of copies reproduced or the fact that it appears on a textile material. The potential availability of protection under the design patent law will not affect the registrability of a work of art, but a copyright claim in

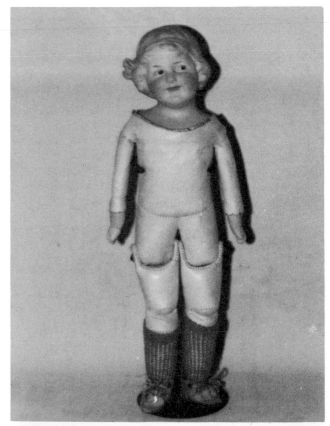

**439A & B.** Coquette doll with intaglio eyes on a bisque shoulder head with blonde hair and a molded blue ribbon. Kid body with Ne Plus Ultra hip joints, bisque lower arms, cloth lower legs. Mark: Ill. **823,** below "1 Germany" and over "7856." H. 12½ inches. H. of shoulder head, 3¾ inches. *Coleman Collection.*

a patented design or in the drawings or photographs in a patent application will not be registered after the patent has been issued."

For a copyright on a doll to be valid, the doll must have the word "copyright" or "copyr." or the symbol ©, as well as the date of the copyright and name of the copyright owner. Many doll manufacturers, not realizing that it was necessary to have their full name on the dolls, put only their initials on until an infringement case was lost by *Horsman* in 1922, partly because he had used only his initials and not his full name on the doll.

A copyright can be secured for dolls by putting them on the market for sale, providing they bear a proper copyright notice. Upon compliance with certain requirements a statutory copyright may be obtained without publicly marketing the doll, except for dolls in Class H, Reproductions of Works of Art. According to copyright law, it is permissible to use "the copyright symbol © accompanied by the initials, monogram, mark, or symbol of the copyright owner, if the owner's name appears upon some accessible portion of the work. A tag bearing a copyright notice attached to the work is not acceptable in lieu of a notice on the work itself."

The 1909 law gave protection for twenty-eight years, with the privilege of renewing the copyright for another twenty-eight years, or a total of fifty-six years. Congress is presently considering the enactment of a new copyright law that would lengthen the protection.

**Coquerie, Mme.** 1864–70. Paris. Made dolls.

**Coquet Bébé.** See **Le Coquet Bébé.**

**Coquette.** 1903–12. Trade name given to dolls with eyes that glanced to the side or *flirting eyes.*

1903: Name of a new doll with eyes that look first from one corner and then from the other corner of its eye. Doll came in various sizes priced from $2.00 to $10.00.

1907: *Kämmer & Reinhardt* registered *Die Kokette* (The Coquette) as a trademark in Germany.

1911: PLAYTHINGS reported that "Coquette" was the name given to dolls with flirting eyes.

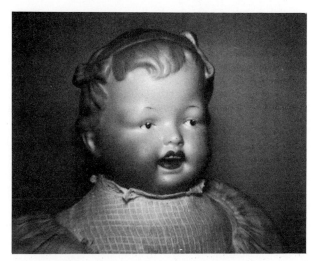

**440.** Coquette-type doll, made by Ernst Heubach, has molded bisque head with blue enameled ribbon and bows on both sides, eyes glancing to the side, and open-closed mouth with four upper teeth. Marked "E.H." and the numerals 283-1310. H. of head, 4 inches. *Courtesy of Ollie Leavister.*

1912: "Coquette" the trade name given to dolls with molded and painted ribbon in their hair and eyes glancing to the side. The heads were made of bisque, china, or composition. Different versions made by various companies were named *The Coquette, Miss Coquette, Naughty Marietta, and Amy.*

**Coquette, The.** 1912. One of the *New Toy* "Unbreakable" Character Dolls. It had a blue ribbon in the hair made of the same material as the head; dressed in a blue kimono or a white lawn frock.

**Coquillé.** 1920–21. Paris. Made dolls.

**Coquillet, Vve. (Widow).** 1918. Paris, Registered in France *La Parisette* as a trademark for dolls.

**Cordier.** 1865–70. Paris. Made dolls.

**Cordonnier, Mme. (née Palmier, Caroline).** 1922. France. Obtained French patent for dolls with heads made from molds created by professional artists and completed by purchasers. These were long-limbed dolls.

**Cork Dolls.** 1869. *Mme. Restignat* obtained a French patent for a jointed doll of cork. Later, cork was frequently used as stuffing for dolls, both as ground cork and as cork flour. Cork had the advantage of lightness in weight, and it was not as attractive to the insect world as some other types of stuffing. *Kestner, Horsman, Louis Amberg & Son,* and many other doll makers used cork for stuffing dolls well into the 20th century.

**Cork Pates.** These were primarily used on dolls' heads made in France in both the 19th and 20th centuries.

**Corker.** 1914–15. Trademark registered in U.S. by *Anna Renwick* for dolls.

**Cornet, Marius.** 1914. Lyons, France. Registered *La Poupée Française* as a trademark in France. It was used for various kinds of dolls.

**Cornhusk and Corncob Dolls.** 18th century–1925+. Made in America. Corncob was often used for the body and the husks for the head, limbs, and clothes; corn silk used for the hair. Some cornhusk dolls were displayed at the New Orleans International Exhibition in 1884.

**Cornouloid Doll.** 1913. Trademark registered by *Max Handwerck* in Germany.

**Corozo.** A vegetable ivory type of material out of which dolls were made in Ecuador.

**Corrubia, Paul E.** 1922–24. St. Louis, Mo. Obtained U.S. patent for ball-and-socket joints connected with bendable wires.

**Corry, Grace (Grace Corry Rockwell).** 1920–25+. New York City. Designed and made dolls. She obtained a U.S. design patent in 1920 for her *Fiji Wiji* dolls. She made these herself at first, but the demand was so great that *Century Doll Co.* arranged to make a complete line in 1921, including *Romper Boy, Blue Eyes,* etc. After 1925 she designed many artistic dolls.

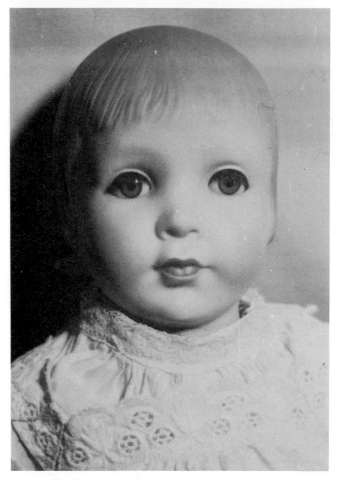

**441.** Doll's head designed and copyrighted by Grace Corry (Rockwell). The doll has a bisque head with molded blondish hair and glass sleep eyes. *Courtesy of Winnie Langley; photograph by Winnie Langley.*

**Corset on Body.** 1880's. *Charles Dotter* and *Philip Goldsmith* designed and obtained patents for doll bodies with corsets as a part of the body. Examples of other types of corset bodies have also been found, but they probably belonged to the same period. Corsets have been found on cloth bodies, kid bodies, and even ceramic torsos.

**Corso.** 1913–14. Trademark registered in Germany by *Gebrüder Grumach.*

**Cortot.** 1917–22. J. Cortot of Le Puy in 1917 registered in France as a trademark *Bébé Jeannette* with the initials "M.P.H.L." Bébé Jeannette was registered in France as a trademark in 1922 by Mlle. Jeanne Cortot of Liège, Belgium.

**Cosgrove Brothers, Inc.** 1922. Milton, Mass. Registered the name *Elizabeth* as a trademark in U.S.

**Cosman Frères (Bros.).** 1892–1925+. Paris. Made dressed bébés and dolls.

1892: They registered in France as trademarks *Bébé le Favori* and *Bébé Favori.*

1893: Registered in France as a trademark *Splendide Bébé*. This same year Clément Gatusse, doll maker, registered Bébé Favori as a trademark in France, which suggests that he must have been connected with Cosman Frères. They obtained two French patents for a bébé that could walk, talk, and turn its head as it walked.

**Cotton Joe.** 1911. *Art Doll* made by *Horsman;* came with *Can't Break 'Em* head, molded hair, cloth body. It was a Negro doll taken from life; wore a red flannel shirt and brown overalls.

**Couillard.** 1889–92. Paris. Made dolls. At other addresses in 1889, Couillard & Bienvenue, and Honoré Couillard in 1890 to 1892, were listed as doll makers.

**Couin, Mlle. Raymonde, & Camgrand, Mlle. Thérèse.** 1924. Paris. Registered in France *Kipmi* as a trademark for dolls of various kinds.

**Country Boy.** 1918. Distributed by *Gray & Dudley Co.* Had composition head and limbs; 10-inch size with wig cost 40¢; 13-inch size with embossed hair cost 48¢.

**Country Cousins.** 1913–14. Trade name for a farm boy and girl made by *Ideal Novelty & Toy Co.* The boy was called *Freddie* and the girl *Flora.*

**Couraud, E.** 1921. Paris. Made rubber dolls.

**Courtot-Lavancourt.** 1875–77. Paris. Made dolls.

**Cousin, E.** 1870–75. Paris. Operated a shop known as *Aux Amis de l'Enfance,* where jointed dolls and their trousseaux were made.

**Couterier (Couturier).** 1869–93. Paris. Alice Couterier operated a shop known as *Aux Enfants de France* in the 1870's. She made jointed dolls, small dolls, and doll clothes, and repaired dolls.

1893: Gustav Couturier exhibited toilettes for dolls at the Chicago Exhibition.

**Couty, Magne & Cie.** See **Coiffe.**

**Couzinet, Vve. (Widow).** 1889–90. Paris. Made dolls.

**Cowboy.** 1916. Made by *Averill Manufacturing Co.;* U.S. design patent obtained by *Georgene Averill.* Came dressed in felt, with gun. Three sizes; price $1.00, $1.50, and $2.00.

**Cox, Palmer.** 1892. Designed and copyrighted the *Brownies.* These Brownies were later made into dolls of various materials.

**Coxeter, Mrs.** 1865. London. Made dolls.

**Cracker Jack Boy.** 1917. Doll representing the Cracker Jack Candy Boy of Rueckheim Bros. & Eckstein; made by *Ideal Novelty & Toy Co.* Boy doll dressed in blue and white sailor suit and cap, carried a tiny replica of a Cracker Jack box under his arm.

**Cra-Doll.** 1922–23. Line of rag dolls made by *Doll-Craft Co.* in 1922 and by *Uneeda Doll Co.* in 1923. These dolls had heads of pressed buckram, but they were complete

sewed heads and not masks. A waterproof fabric covering over the head made them washable. They came as both Negro and white dolls, had bodies stuffed with silk floss. They wore checked costumes with pockets and belt, and lace-trimmed caps. There were eight numbers in 1923.

**Cramer, Albert.** 1879–84. Paris. Distributor for German doll makers.

**Crämer, Eduard.** 1896–1925+. Schalkau, Thür. Made dolls.

**Crämer & Héron (Crämer, Carl, & Héron, François Edmond).** 1893–1920. Sonneberg, Thür. Manufactured dolls.

1893: They were referred to as "late of *L. Illfelder & Co.*" Héron was a British subject. *Baby Ruth* was registered as their trademark in the U.S.

1900: They were one of the Grand Prize group of winners at the Paris Exposition.

1904: They displayed dolls at the St. Louis Exhibition.

**Cremer, Eversfield & Co.** 1923–24. New York City. Manufactured and distributed dolls.

**Cremer, Henry.** 1873–ca. 1900. London. Operated one of the finest toy shops in London. His description of his visit to the Leipzig Fair in 1873 is given in Lesley Gordon's PEEPSHOW INTO PARADISE. A rectangular paper sticker with the name "Cremer" on it has been found affixed to the bottom of a clockwork-activated walking doll made by *Jules Steiner.* (See also **Cremer & Son.**)

**Cremer & Son.** 1862–73. London. Handled dolls.

1862: Showed toys at the London Exhibition.

1867: Displayed products of William Henry Cremer, Jr., at Paris Exposition.

1873: William Henry Cremer, Jr., showed his products at the Vienna Exhibition.

Some of the Cremer dolls had wax heads made by *Pierotti.* Cremer, Jr., dressed one of his dolls in the elaborate clothes of the Watteau period (early 18th century). A colored picture was made of this doll and given to purchasers of similar dolls, together with directions for dressing the doll.

The Cremers were listed in early 19th century directories as toy distributors.

**Creole Composition.** 1924. Material of French Flapper dolls distributed by *N. V. Sales Co.*

**Crescent Toy Manufacturing Co.** 1907–20. Brooklyn, N.Y. Made stuffed dolls; one hundred numbers in 1919; prices 25¢ to $2.00 in 1920.

**Crinon.** 1860–61. Paris. Made dressed dolls.

**442.** Mark used by Cremer & Son on dolls.

**Crochot, Mme. A.** 1919–21. Paris. Made dolls.

**Croft, William, & Sons.** 1907–8. Toronto, Canada. Advertised jointed dolls with paste heads, glass eyes, flowing hair, and movable limbs; washable dolls with paste heads and limbs, hay-stuffed bodies; rubber dolls. Priced 80¢ to $21.00 doz. wholesale.

**Cronan, Joseph David.** 1919–20. Portland (state not given on registration). Doll manufacturer; registered in Germany *Mäzel-Tov* in a six-pointed star as a trademark.

**Cronnier.** 1847–51. Paris. Made dolls.

**Cros, J.** See **Bonnafé**

**Crosby, Dorothy M.** 1918–19. Duluth, Minn. Registered *Dolly Winkle* as trademark in U.S.

**Crosier, Mme. Aline.** 1917. Paris. Registered in France *Parfait Bébé* as trademark for dolls.

**Crown Doll (Kronenpuppe).** 1895–1925+. Trademark used by *Kestner;* registered in U.S. in 1896 and in Germany in 1915.

**Cry Baby Bunting (Cry Baby).** 1911–12. Crying baby doll made and copyrighted by *Louis Amberg & Son;* designed by *Jeno Juszko.* Composition head with eyes nearly closed, mouth wide open, and face screwed up as if crying. Molded hair came to a pointed twist on the forehead. Pink sateen body was stuffed with cork.

**Cry Blynkie.** 1920. All-composition doll made by *Jones-Moran Doll Manufacturing Co.* Came dressed and undressed.

**Cryer & Naylor.** 1803+. London. Made dolls.

**Crying Babies.** 1907–10. Made in Germany. Distributed by *Butler Bros.* Came with composition head, stuffed body containing a bellows so that when doll was rocked from side to side, it would cry continually.

1907: Sizes 13½ and 24½ inches.

1910: Sizes 16 and 22½ inches.

**Crying Dolls.** Dolls of this kind were available in England from as early as 1700, when a doctor bought for his three-year-old daughter a wax baby with an invention to make it cry. There have been many inventions for crying dolls through the years, most of which consist of bellows and reed pipes for producing the sound. One of the earliest recorded patents was obtained by *Johannes (Jean) Maelzel* in 1824 for a crying or talking doll operated by bellows. Probably the most famous crying voices were "Ronson Voices," named for *Louis V. Aronson* and made by *Art Metal Works* and later by *Voices, Inc.* The 1915 patent (applied for in 1914) that Aronson was granted described the sound device as "suitable bellows, and a spring attached at the sides of the top and bottom of said bellows and normally distending the same; a reed pipe or the like provided with an orifice and adapted to be operated by the said bellows." In 1922, Ronson Voices were made in two sizes. Crying devices of all periods and makes have had a tendency to get out of order, but most doll hospitals can readily

repair them. Just prior to World War I there were several such inventions alleged to be new. One was for a long, slow cry instead of the short, sharp cries previously known. Another was for a doll that squealed no matter where it was pressed. (See **Talking Dolls; Voices.**)

**Crystal Eyes.** 1925. Name used by *Arranbee* for the eyes of their dolls.

**Cubist.** 1913–14. Trademark registered by *Borgfeldt* in U.S. for dolls.

**Cuddle Kiddies, The.** 1914. Imported into U.S. Dolls squealed wherever pressed; price 50¢ and up.

**Cuddlekins.** 1917. Trade name of some of the *American Art Dolls* distributed by *Strobel & Wilken.*

**Cuillard, Honoré.** 1863–67. Paris. Made dolls.

**Cummings, Maude Abbot (M. A. Cuming & Co.).** 1920-22. New York City. Obtained a U.S. design patent for a rag doll. It is possible that the M. A. Cuming & Co., listed as making doll presses, had the name misspelled for "Cummings."

**Cunique des Poupées.** Ca. 1910. Lausanne, Switzerland. Distributed dolls. Their gold and white sticker was found on doll model No. 101 X, made by *Kämmer & Reinhardt.* Clothes marked "Kammer & Reinhardt"; silk hat marked "Carl Kellner."

**Cunning Baby.** 1918. Made by *EFFanBEE;* distributed by *Butler Bros.* Came with composition head and hands, bobbed mohair wig, sleeping eyes; wore a white organdy dress. Size 15½ inches; price $24.00 doz. wholesale.

**Cupid.** 1908–9. Registered in Germany and Britain by *M. Kohnstam & Co.* as a trademark for dolls.

**Cupid Doll.** 1920. Trade name of a doll produced by *Alisto Manufacturing Co.* Size 12 inches.

**Curly Locks.** 1911–12. Doll with baby face made and copyrighted (1911) by *Louis Amberg & Son.* Had ringlets of hair, pink sateen body; dressed in white lawn with lace and ribbons.

**Curly Locks.** 1912. Doll with a girl's face; made and copyrighted by *Louis Amberg & Son;* designed by *Jeno Juszko.* Had curls all around the head.

**Curly Locks.** 1916–18. Made by *Jessie McCutcheon Raleigh;* distributed by *Butler Bros.* Came 11½ inches tall for $2.85 and 13½ inches for $3.50.

**Curman & Steiner (Curnen & Steiner).** See **Steiner, Edmund Ulrich.**

**Curtis Product Co.** 1925. Hibbing, Minn. Made dolls' heads.

**Cussey.** 1879–85. Paris. Made dolls.

**Custodianship of Dolls.** It is essential to remember at all times that the possessor of a collection of dolls is merely their temporary custodian. Naturally it is desirable that the dolls look their best, whether in new or old garments, and that they be kept in the best possible state of repair. It is the responsibility of the custodian to main-

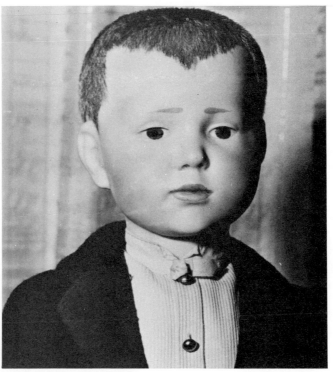

444 A

B

**443A & B.** Bridegroom with bisque socket head, painted features, and flocked hair. Head mark: Ill. **444**B. The composition body bears the Cunique label, which is lettered in gold: Ill. **444**A. His clothes are also marked "K.R." H. 15 inches. *Courtesy of Ruth Noden; photographs by George F. Nelson.*

**444 A & B.** Cunique des Poupées label found on dolls, and mark on the head of one of these dolls.

**445.** "Curly Locks" copyrighted by Louis Amberg & Son in 1912, designed by Jeno Juszko. This is a copy of the original picture of the plaster model filed with the copyright application. The molds of the doll's head were made from this casting.

tain the dolls in a healthy state: to clean them, mend "wounds" in a variety of locations, and even fashion missing appendages. However, before beginning any repair or restoration, remember that every change made on a doll alters its original state and thus detracts from its value. Repairs and restoration, when required, should be aimed at preserving originality. In other words, only

essential restoration and repair should be attempted. Do not be overzealous. Perform only such "mends" as can be removed readily if desired. It is a good idea to keep, along with the record of each doll, a list of any repairs and restorations made on it.

Suppose that at hand there is a doll with a bisque socket head, sleeping eyes, a wig, teeth, a tongue, and a ball-jointed composition body. Suppose also that a "V"-shaped piece is broken from the edge of the neck, and the eyes have fallen out. The wig is dirty and disheveled; the tongue is gone completely. The body is held together with rotted elastic, the hook from one hand is missing, paint is flaking from the forearms, mildew has gotten to the torso, a finger has been amputated, and the neck socket has fallen in on one side. All these defects, like any task involving the repair of a doll, will take time to deal with.

Begin by cleaning the doll inside and out. While the doll is in a dismembered state, such thorough cleaning is simple. Certain insects find the binders in compositions most appetizing. Even though a torso may appear to be free from such pests, it is advisable to take the precaution of using a preparation that will destroy moths and insects. Apply it directly, especially to the inside area. When cleaning the head, use cotton swabs to get into the small areas around eyes, ears, nose, and mouth. The head can be cleaned with soap and water, but do not immerse it in water if the eyes, a tongue of paper or felt, or plaster remain.

To repair the ceramic break, first make sure that both broken surfaces are as clean and dry as possible before attempting to join them. Then use an epoxy glue or a glue recommended for the mending of porcelain items. Follow the directions given on the product, being sure to hold the piece by hand until the bond is secure enough to allow the application of a more permanent force.

It is not generally advisable to use porcelain paints to cover up a repair—for several reasons. Most of them look very handsome when first applied, but in time will darken, flake, peel, or scratch easily, and if the doll is kept in a warm, moist place, they become soft. Fabrics coming into contact with these paints will either adhere or leave an impression. In addition, since a filler must usually be applied first, the area over which the paint is applied is generally considerably larger than the area of the actual break, thus making the damaged surface appear to be much worse than it really is. Should it be necessary to remove unfired porcelain paints, most will come off with a product containing acetone.

For the missing tongue, use a small piece of red felt.

Unless the collector is skilled in the setting of sleeping eyes, it is best to let an experienced person handle that task. Do not set, into a stationary position, eyes that were designed to sleep. Make sure that when the eyes *are* set, there is a piece of cork strategically placed at the point where the weight or clapper will strike the porcelain. Stationary eyes can be set with plaster of Paris.

While the eyes are being set, work can begin on the wig and body. Most old wigs are grayed with dirt, but if they have not been eaten to the extent that the hair is falling out, they can be cleaned with benzine. This will not remove the styling—just the grime. Otherwise, a wig can be washed in soap and water, but be sure any old glue has been removed first with alcohol or vinegar. Washing a wig necessitates restyling as well as much combing to remove the tangles. Work carefully, to cause the least possible loss of hair. The hair can be curled on any small curlers.

In repairing the body of this hypothetical doll, the tasks that take longest should be attempted first—the building of the finger, reinforcing the neck socket, and making and securing the hand hook. A commercial preparation of papier-mâché can be purchased and strengthened with Elmer's Glue-All or a similar preparation, or plastic wood can be used in strengthening or building up the socket area and for fashioning the finger. When dry, the area can be sanded smooth and touched up with a coat of paint as near the color and finish of the body as possible.

For the hook, use a piece of heavy-gauge wire, such as a coat hanger, bent into the shape of the complementary hand hook. Insert this into the hand with an epoxy adhesive. For the parts (usually those of turned wood) from which paint is flaking, a dab of Elmer's Glue-All inserted under the flaking surface will help to bind the paint and prevent further flaking. It is best to preserve

as much of the original paint surface as possible. Once the mildew has been removed from the torso with a lanolin-base cold cream, and the surface dried, a thin coat of varnish over the area will match it up nearly perfectly with the rest of the torso.

Now the doll is ready to assemble. Basically, what is required for this and most stringing jobs is two loops of elastic, the thickness depending on the size of the doll. First remove all old elastic; then secure the head thread through the torso to one hip joint. Secure on one side with a loop over a pencil (or something similar), and using a buttonhook or bent coat-hanger hook, pull through the various components of the legs and secure on the leg hook. Then work on the second leg.

Once the legs are connected, begin on the arms, threading through one set of component parts, through the torso, and down the other arm parts. Tension must be strong. Only when working with the elastic and the doll together will the necessary length of elastic become apparent. The doll should move easily but securely from position to position. If it snaps abruptly into one position, the elastic is too tight.

The hypothetical doll has now been repaired and restored to the extent that it retains most of its original body paint and its wig, but has a new tongue and most of its original appearance. There are a few proudly displayed scars—the piece out of its head and its new finger—which go to prove that its life has been long and not always easy. But this mending may well preserve its "health" for years.

Nine chances out of ten, the above doll should be—or was—dressed as a child. Maybe its original dress is soiled, damaged, or does not please your taste. Nonetheless, do not dispose of any of its original garments. Remember, you are only the custodian. By dispersing original garments you are devaluing the doll just as much as if you deliberately broke a limb or threw away the original body. Redress the doll if you wish—after all, she is yours to display as you please—but when it comes time to pass her along, make sure that all the old tatters go with her. To the next collector, they may be the jewel in her crown.

(See **Display; Storage.**)

## SUGGESTED MATERIALS AND EQUIPMENT

Acetone, for a paint thinner
Alcohol, for glue thinner
Ammonia, for use with water as a cleanser
Ascorbic acid, for removal of soap residue
Benzine, for cleaning fabrics and wigs
Buttonhooks, for stringing dolls
Clear shoe polish, to revitalize leathers, and as a cleaner and sealer for metals
Coat hangers, to provide stringing hooks and metal parts
Dental picks, for cleaning and poking into difficult places
Elmer's Glue-All, as a multi-purpose adhesive; also useful as a filler or coating; can be easily removed

Epoxy, as strong glue for stress points and ceramics
Insect destroyer (type that does not harm fabrics)
Lanolin cream, for cleaning compositions
Papier-mâché, commercial preparation useful as filler
Plaster of Paris, for setting eyes
Plastic wood, for filler
Soap or soap flakes, a mild pure soap, for washing
Sun (the safest bleach)
Varnish or shellac, as finish for wood or compositions
Vinegar, for glue thinner.

**Cutie.** See **Cawood Novelty Manufacturing Co.**

**Cutter, George M.** 1888. Malden, Mass. Assignee of half interest in the patent for a walking doll obtained in U.S. by *Milton Laskey.*

**Cuvillier, H.** 1904. Paris. Successor 1906, Cuvillier-Ferry. Used the trade name *Le Ravissant* for dolls and bébés of all kinds.

**Cy.** 1909. Character doll made by *Horsman;* price $1.00.

**Cy From Siwash.** 1913. Farmer boy doll made by *Tip Top Toy Co.;* price 25¢.

**Cycle Kids.** 1915. Dolls made by *Horsman.*

**Czecho-Slovak Commercial Corp.** 1921. New York City. Advertised dressed dolls of all sizes from the foremost French factories as well as Bohemian products.

**Czechoslovakian (Bohemian) Dolls.** Were produced for many centuries. They were chiefly wooden or rag dolls. On some of the 19th-century wooden dolls, leather or fabric was used to join the arms and legs to the torso. Many *poupards* of wood were made here. (For details, see FOLK TOYS by Emanuel Hercík, 1952.) Several porcelain dolls' heads have been found with the "S" mark of the *Schlaggenwald* factories. One of these appears to be dated around the 1850's. Other Czechoslovakian doll makers included *Adolf Hahn, Rudolf Heinz, Miss Marcel Giblet, F. Klemperer,* and *Gustav Kmel.* (See also **Austrian Dolls.**)

# D

**Da Da.** 1925. Name on wings of a ladybug, the trademark used by *Hermsdorfer Celluloid Warenfabrik* for celluloid dolls.

**Daddy Doll.** 1922. Copyrighted by *E. B. Card;* made by *Louis Amberg & Son.* Had long arms and legs.

**Daddy Long Legs Doll.** 1914–16. Registered in U.S. as a trademark by the *State Charities Aid Association;* doll manufactured and sold for the benefit of the Children's Department of this association.

**Daddy Long Legs Dolls.** 1915. Made by *Arcy Toy Manufacturing Co.*

**Dad's Doll.** 1922–23. Trademark registered in U.S. by *Simonne Bouvet.*

**Daffydils.** 1912–13. Copyrighted and made by *Louis Amberg & Son;* designed by *Jeno Juszko.* Boy or girl doll with smirking expression, eyes and brows arched, whites of the eyes very large, hair jerked out at odd angles.

**Dainty Doll Manufacturing Co.** 1917. New York City. Made composition dolls named "The Dainty Doll"; price 25¢ to $1.00.

446. "Dainty Dorothy" mark used by Sears, Roebuck & Co.

**Dainty Dorothy.** 1910–22. Line of dolls distributed by *Sears, Roebuck & Co.* in U.S. and *T. Eaton Co.* in Canada. Prior to World War I, these dolls were made by *Kestner,* and were described as having a bisque head, open mouth with teeth, moving eyes, hair eyelashes, long curly wig parted on the side, papier-mâché legs, bisque forearms, and a kid body with rivets at elbow, shoulder, hip, and knee joints. Later dolls came with bisque or composition head, kid or jointed composition body; usually had sleeping eyes and curly mohair wig.

1910: Five sizes, 18½ to 28 inches; price $1.75 to $4.98.

1918: 20-inch size cost $1.95.

1922: Sizes 18½, 20½, 24, and 25½ inches; cost $4.85 to $8.85.

**Dainty Marie.** 1919. Line designed by Cliff Knight (cartoonist for PLAYTHINGS magazine); made by *H. & Z. Doll Co.* Came in various styles; 9 inches tall.

**Daisy.** 1902–3. Trademark registered in Germany by *Edmund Ulrich Steiner,* who was with *Samstag & Hilder.*

**Daisy.** 1905. Doll distributed by *Samstag & Hilder;* price 25¢. *Edmund U. Steiner* was manager of the doll department of Samstag & Hilder at this time.

**Daisy.** 1905–14, and possibly earlier. China dolls' heads made with the name in gold letters on the chest. This type was produced by *Hertwig & Co.* and *Closter Veilsdorf.*

**Daisy.** 1911. Name of a premium doll offered by LADIES' HOME JOURNAL. She had a bisque head with real hair eyelashes, open mouth with teeth, blue sleeping eyes, long curls, and a ball-jointed composition body with jointed wrists. Was dressed in a white muslin slip trimmed with white lace, white slippers, and stockings; size 18 inches. Patterns for clothes were included. Price was three subscriptions, two of them new ones. It appears that premium dolls often were dolls that had been on the market for a season or so before being offered as premiums. It might be noted that Edmund U. Steiner, who registered the trademark "Daisy," was working for *Louis Wolf & Co.* in 1911; this suggests that the bisque head may have been made by *Armand Marseille.*

**Daisy.** 1922–23. Trademark registered in Germany by *Borgfeldt.*

**Daisy Anna.** 1919. Doll made by *Jessie M. Raleigh.*

**Daisy Bright Eyes.** 1893. Premium doll distributed by YOUTH'S COMPANION; shown at Chicago World's Fair. Came with bisque head, sleeping eyes, long hair in ringlets; kid body filled with cork; size 14 inches. Price of $1.40 included paper patterns for trousseau.

**Daisy Darling.** 1906. Cloth doll made by *Horsman* to be cut out and stuffed. Came in three sizes; price 5¢, 10¢, and 25¢.

**Daisy Dimple.** 1912. Composition-head, soft body doll made by *Horsman;* wore white lawn dress.

**Daisy Dolly.** 1909–11. Line of stuffed velvet dolls made by *Sackman Bros. Co.* Resembled *Grace Drayton* drawings. Dolls were printed in colors on velvet, then stuffed with hair; sewed around the edges with patent lock stitch. There were four characters in this line; 8-inch size cost 10¢, 12-inch size cost 25¢.

**Dakin, Margaret Ann.** 1923. Dunmow, Essex. Registered in Britain *Cabbagerino* as a trademark for dolls.

**Dalloz.** See **Blampoix, Aîné.**

**Dallwig Distributing Co.** 1918–22. Chicago, Ill. Registered "Dallwig Doll" as a trademark in U.S. Paul G. Dallwig, president of the company, obtained a U.S. patent for a plurality of detachable and interchangeable wigs. A crown piece came with each wig, and a painted bald crown piece that fit onto the head, which represented an infant.

**Dalsheim, Leo.** 1897–1909. Frankfurt am Main, Hesse-Nassau. Made dolls.

**Daly, Charles M., & Weidhass, Gustave A.** 1912–14. Procured U.S. and German patents for dolls' eyes with round eyeballs and pupils disposed eccentrically so that the eye could look up, down, or to either side.

**Damerval Frères & Laffranchy (Jules and Charles Damerval).** 1910–15. Paris. Factory at Montreuil, Seine; registered *Joli Bébé* as a trademark in France; also used the trade name *Bébé Mignon.*

**Dandy Doll Co.** 1918–19. New York City. Made dolls.

**Dandy Kid.** 1911. Composition-head character doll made by *Ideal Novelty & Toy Co.* using their "Skeleton Process."

**Dandyline Dolls.** 1918. Made by factory in Belgium; distributed by *E. A. Runnells & Co.* Line of dolls with one hundred numbers.

**Dane, John B., & Cannon, Charles S.** 1919–20. Elizabeth, N.J. Obtained a U.S. patent for a metal dolls' head with detachable crown and sleeping eyes with movable lids. At this same time the *Art Metal Works* of nearby Newark,

N.J., was making the *Treat 'Em Rough Kiddies* of metal.

**Danel & Cie.** 1889–95. Paris. Factory at Montreuil-sous-Bois, Seine. *J. Cros,* distributor in 1890; *Jumeau* appears to have controlled the company by 1896.

1889: Danel & Cie. registered in France *Paris Bébé* and a picture of the Eiffel Tower as their trademark, which is found on dolls' bodies.

1890: Advertised that their dolls were not strung with rubber.

1891: Registered in France *Bébé Français* as a trademark.

1892: Specialized in Negro and mulatto dolls; this was one of the earliest references in France to these types of dolls.

**Danjard.** 1860. Paris. Procured a French patent for the decoration of dolls' heads with bonnets.

**Danville Doll Co.** 1922–23. Danville, Ill. Made "Dumpie Dolls" with spring-jointed arms. Daily production was 5,000 composition cherub-type dolls with hair. Size 13 inches; price 60¢ each wholesale; size 12 inches came dressed in crepe paper.

**Darky Dolls.** 1922. Trade name of dolls made by *Century Doll Co.*

**Darling.** 1905–15. Kid-body dolls distributed by *Strobel & Wilken.*

**Darrach, Mrs. M. M.** 1884. Exhibited cornhusk dolls at the New Orleans Exposition.

**Darrow Manufacturing Co.** 1866–77. Bristol, Conn. Made leather dolls' heads, which were pressed into shape and hand-painted. One of the two patents that Franklin Elijah Darrow obtained in 1866 for making dolls of rawhide leather was in conjunction with Deon E. Peck. Darrow dolls are usually 15 or 18 inches tall and have on the chest an elliptical paper sticker in green and gold with black letters. (See Ill. 448.)

**Dars.** 1867–85. Paris. Made dolls.

**Dartheny, J.** 1855. Paris. Displayed shoulder heads molded in wax at the Paris Exposition.

**Das Süsse Trudelchen.** 1904–5. Trademark registered in Germany by *Johannes Kriege* for dolls of all kinds. The name means "Sweet Little Dancer."

**Daspres, Edmond.** 1902–8. Paris. Factory at Montreuil-sous-Bois; made bébés with the trade names of *Le Parisien* and *La Patricienne.*

1902: Procured a French patent for a walking and talking doll.

1906: Daspres was listed in the Paris Directory as successor of *Steiner.*

**Daum, Carl (Karl).** 1921–25. Sonneberg, Thür. Made dressed dolls and babies from the cheapest to the finest.

**D'Autrement (D'Autremont).** 1858. Paris. Procured a French patent for a rubber doll. The name D'Autrement has been found stamped in blue on the stomach of kid-body dolls with china heads.

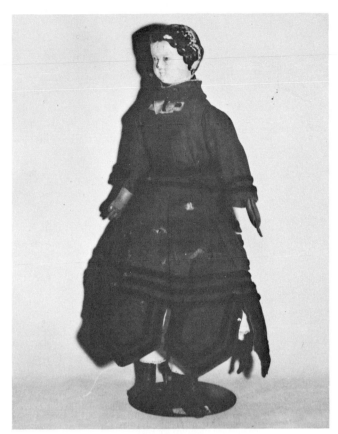

**447A & B.** Rawhide doll's head made by Darrow. Cloth body, leather arms and shoes, original red dress with black velvet trim. Sticker mark on chest in green with gold border. Mark: Ill. **448**. H. 15 inches. *Courtesy of the International Doll Library Foundation.*

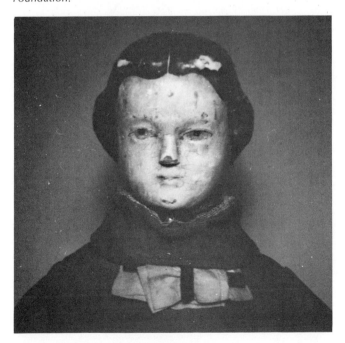

**449A & B.** Kid body marked "D'Autrement" with china head, painted features, original wool suit with blue braid trim, silk tie, leather shoes. Mark (blue stamp on stomach): Ill. **450**. *Courtesy of the International Doll Library Foundation.*

**448.** Darrow mark used on leather dolls' heads.

450. D'Autremont (D'Autrement) name stamped on kid bodies.

**David.** 1918. One of the *Madame Hendren* line of walking dolls made by *Averill Manufacturing Corp.*

**David Copperfield.** 1924–25. Rag doll designed and made by *Madame Alexander.* It had a mask face with raised features, which were hand-painted by Madame Alexander. Came with wig of mohair imported from England; pink muslin body; size 14 inches; price $1.20.

**Davile, Carmine.** 1923. Jersey City, N.J. Obtained a U.S. design patent for a doll with a face resembling the *Grace Drayton* drawings. It had stump hands and wore a long-waisted ruffly dress.

**Davis, Louisiana M.** 1920–22. Glencoe, Ill. Registered *Luzie Lovem* as a trademark in U.S. for dolls. The two words were written one under the other, sharing a single oversized capital "L."

**Davis, M. S.** 1907. Chicago, Ill. Manufactured leather dolls.

**Davis, Rees.** 1921–22. Chicago, Ill. Secured a U.S. design patent for a boy doll with eyes glancing to the side.

**Davis & Voetsch (The Dee Vee Doll Co.).** 1919–24. New York City. Distributor of *Heinrich Handwerck's* character and jointed dolls, *Acme Toy Manufacturing Co.'s* cork-stuffed dressed dolls, and dolls made by *Nelke Corp.* and by *Gund Manufacturing Co.*

1923: Registered in U.S. *Dee Vee* as a trademark; advertised scores of models of Dee Vee *Mama Dolls.*

**Day, Nellie S.** 1915–17. Springfield, Mass. Registered in U.S. *Kutie* as a trademark; obtained a U.S. design patent for a doll with a Red Riding Hood type of outfit.

**Da-Zee.** 1912. Boy and girl character dolls imported and assembled by *W. C. Horn Bro. & Co.* Had wooden bodies; molded hands, arms, and legs; hips jointed so that legs swung forward when doll was seated; feet made so that doll could stand without support; painted eyes. 6-inch size cost 25¢; larger sizes were priced up to $1.00.

**De Bezenac, Ernest.** 1919. France. Procured a French patent for a bébé with mechanism for changing its facial expressions.

**De Brzeska, Mlle. Aline.** 1924. Fontenay-sous-Bois, Seine. Registered *Lutetia* as a trademark in France.

**De Grasse, Mme. Consuelo (née Fould).** 1919. Obtained a French patent for a jointed framework of tubes and wires for dolls.

451. "D. V." incised on bisque head, probably standing for Davis & Voetsch. Head also has green stamped mark: Ill. **452**. Painted hair, sleeping eyes, indented nostrils, closed mouth, no lip line. H. 9 inches. *Coleman Collection.*

452. Mark found on dolls that may have been handled by Davis & Voetsch.

**De Kasparek (Kasparck), Mme. Jeanne.** 1922–25+. Paris. Registered in France a coat of arms with a crown for a crest, as a trademark for dolls. She made *Art Dolls* under the trade name *Sans Rival.*

**De la Fond, Léon Barjaud.** See **Lebon.**

**De la Ramée, Max Henri Marie.** 1917. Suresnes, France. Registered in France *Ma Jolie* as a trademark for dolls and dolls' heads.

**De la Thuilerie, A.** 1873–82. Paris. Operated the Grand Magasin des Jouets. The store name and "De la Thuilerie" have been found on a composition doll's body. Also on the body was the mark (See Ill. 1452) of *Schmitt & Fils.* The doll's bisque head was marked, "Bte. S.G.D.G."

**De Raphelis-Soissan, Mlle. Marguerite.** 1920. Poitiers, France. Registered in France *Jeanne d'Arc* as a trademark.

**De Roquer, Emma.** See **Calvé, Mme. Emma.**

**De Roussy de Sales, Georges.** 1917–20. Belleville and Paris. Obtained three English patents for moving doll's eyes in any direction by manipulating a device on the outside of the doll.

1918: Registered two trademarks in France, namely *Liberty* for dolls and *Expression* for dolls' heads.

1919: Registered two more trademarks in France; these were *Modestes* and *Espiègles* for movable dolls' eyes.

**De Saint Denis.** 1842–65. Paris. Made various types of dolls.

**De Toy Manufacturing Co.** 1916. Detroit, Mich. Made twenty-four models of character rag dolls stuffed with cotton, including Dutch Boy, Dinah, etc.; sizes 13 and 15 inches; price 25¢.

**De Veriane, Mlle. Renée.** 1907. France. Secured a French patent for a doll with two faces, one happy and one sad; a single bonnet served both faces.

**De Villers, Yves, & Co.** 1924–25+. New York City. Registered *Poupées Raynal* as a trademark in U.S. The mark was to be affixed to the dolls with printed or embossed labels.

**De Wart, Harry M.** 1909–11. New York City. Assignee of a U.S. patent by *Paul Charles Jacquerod* for vertical and lateral movement of glass eyeballs.

**De Wouilt, Mlle. Renée.** 1916. Paris. Registered in France a five-pointed star with rays.

**Dean's Rag Book Co.** 1903–25+. London. Henry Samuel Dean, publisher; *Horsman,* distributor in U.S.; E. Durand, distributor in France.

1903: Printed a large baby doll on a sheet of linen.

1908: Henry Samuel Dean secured a British patent for a cloth cutout doll composed of six pieces, two for the front, two for the back, and two for the feet. Doll could be painted or printed on a sheet of calico, linen, or other material. Advertised cloth dolls in sheets, lithographed in many bright colors; each doll was supplied with a variety of costumes representing several nations, including the U.S. and Japan.

1911: Registered *Dum-Tweedle* as a trademark in Britain for dolls.

1913: Registered *Fuzbuz* as a trademark in Britain for dolls.

1915–18: Secured several British and U.S. patents for rag dolls. *Arthur Leonard Wheeldon* was the assigner of most of these patents.

**Dearie.** 1916–18. Made by *Jessie McCutcheon Raleigh;* distributed by *Butler Bros.* Came with sewed mohair wig, pink or blue lawn dress, and hat with a puff crown; sizes 11½, 16½, and 18½ inches; prices $2.95, $3.60, and $4.75.

**Dearie Doll.** 1919. Handled by *Pacini & Berni* and Paris Novelty Manufacturing Co. Came with wig. Size 11 inches, priced $10.00 doz. wholesale.

**Dearman, Daisy.** 1924. Paris. Obtained U.S. design patent for a doll's head with feathers on the side of its hat and a ruff around the neck.

**Debailly.** 1846–52. Paris. Made dolls.

**Debes, Carl, & Sohn.** 1905. Hof, Bavaria. Distributor of dolls; registered *Noris* as a trademark in Germany.

**Debes, Eduard.** 1906. Blankenese near Hamburg, Germany. Obtained a U.S. patent for a ball-and-socket type of doll joint.

**Debosque, Mlle. Léontine.** 1879. Paris. Made dolls.

**Debrie.** 1889. Paris. Made dolls.

**Debutante.** 1918. Made by *Jessie McCutcheon Raleigh;* distributed by *Butler Bros.* Size 18½ inches cost $5.40.

**Decalcomania (Decal) Film.** Used for eyeballs in U.S. patent of (William G.) *Schoenhut* in 1920. The eyebrows on some bisque dolls appear to have been applied as transfer patterns before the final firing.

**Decamps.** See **Roullet & Decamps.**

**Decker, Gussie D.** 1902–3. Chicago, Ill. Procured U.S. patent for an all-leather or kid doll, stuffed and laced up the front; the features and hair were painted with waterproof paint.

**Decoeur, Alexander.** 1890. Bendlikon, Switzerland. Obtained a British patent for a talking doll operated by squeezing air in a rubber ball across a reed box.

**Decré, M.** 1885–90. Paris. Made metal bébés that were patented in 1885 in France.

**Dee Vee.** 1923–24. Trademark registered in U.S. by *Davis & Voetsch.* They were sometimes referred to as the Dee Vee Doll Co. Trademark was used especially for *Mama Dolls.*

**Defosse.** 1833–52. Paris. Made dolls of all kinds, according to his advertisement.

**Dehais.** 1836–1921. Paris. Laforest joined Dehais as a partner some time between 1847 and 1855, when they specialized in mechanical dolls and *poupards.* By 1860 Dehais had become associated with Verger, and they continued to produce mechanical dolls and poupards.

1873: Verger assumed control of Maison Dehais.

1890–1921: Louis Marie Renou was the successor; he displayed dolls at the 1900 Paris Exposition and won a bronze medal.

1905: Renou was granted a French patent for a jointed doll whose movements were actuated by a musical mechanism inside the doll.

1921: Maison Dehais specialized in *Polichinelles, Marottes,* and *Folies* with little bells and music.

**Dehler, Ad.** 1895–1914. Neustadt near Coburg, Thür. Manufactured little baby dolls.

**Dehler, E.** 1908–25+. Coburg, Thür. Made dolls.

1911: Advertised bodies with waxed heads, dressed and undressed dolls, and dolls with crocheted dresses.

1924: Advertised babies and dolls of various kinds.

**Dehler, Heinrich.** 1899. Vienna. Made dolls and dolls' heads.

**Dehler, Richard.** 1918. Coburg, Thür. Made dolls.

**Dehler, Wilhelm.** 1888–92. Neustadt near Coburg, Thür. *J. F. O. Michaelis,* distributor in Paris; also exported to America and England.

1888: Obtained a French patent for a doll using a telephone.

1889–92: Advertised jointed bébés, dressed and undressed; wax dolls and composition dolls.

**Dehors, A. & Mme.** 1860–90. Paris. Made porcelain and faïence toys.

1860: Advertised bébés, dolls, and doll dresses.

1866: Monsieur Dehors obtained a French patent for the perfection of joints for dolls and dolls' heads.

1867: Exhibited at the Paris Exposition.

1878: Both Monsieur and Mme. Dehors had displays at the Paris Exposition; he showed toys and she showed dolls and bébés.

**Dekawe Spieltiere & Puppen.** 1924. Trademark registered in Germany by *Carl Herrmann* for dolls other than rubber.

**Delachal, Louis.** 1890–1904. Paris. Successor of Maison Jung (J. F. Jung); made rubber dolls and rubber bébés that he called *Bébé Caoutchouc.* Used the initials "L.D." superimposed.
Delachal displayed his dolls at the 1893 Chicago Exposition and at the 1900 Paris Exposition. He was awarded a silver medal.

**Delacoste, B., & Cie.** See **Derolland, B.**

**Delattre.** 1921. Paris. Made bébés.

**Delaumont, Mme. la Baronne.** 1914. Paris. Created a doll.

**Delaunay, Mme.** 1839–66. Paris. Made dressed dolls.

**Delavan, Sophia E.** 1916–21. Chicago, Ill. Made dolls and wigs for dolls.

1916: Wig styles included Baby Betty with long curls and bangs, Baby Claire with long curls and center part, Victoria with hair piled on top of the head, a Buster Brown bob, Antoinette with bangs in front and curls to the shoulder, and Wilhelmina with braids around the head.

1917: Made *War Nurse* and *War Orphan* dolls with natural hair wigs representing Belgian, French, English, Italian, and Russian people.

1921: Registered War Nurse and War Orphan as trademarks in U.S.; made the *Buds* and *Buddies* rag dolls, which included *Greenwich Village Bud, American Rose Bud, Holland Bud,* and dolls of other nations. Clothes for Buds and Buddies designed by *Katherine A. Rauser* and Queen G. Thomas. Sophia Delavan obtained a U.S. patent for a doll that resembled *Grace Drayton* drawings, ex-

cept that it had angular features rather than round. The nose was indicated by two dots placed diagonally in a square; the eyes were conical shaped.

**Delbosque, Mlle. Léontine.** 1876–89. Paris. Made dressed dolls and bébés in foreign and provincial costumes, especially for export.

1889: Became Mme. Tragit-Delbosque.

**Delcourt, H.** See **Gesland.**

**Delcroix, Henri.** 1887. Factory at Montreuil, Seine. Registered four trademarks in France to be affixed by stamping them onto dolls' heads. These marks were *"PAN," "G D," "H D,"* and *"X,"* the last three with the word "Paris."
(See Ill. 668.)

**Delcros, Mlle.** 1866–73. Paris. Made dolls.

**Delero.** 1871–74. Paris. Made dolls.

**Delestaing (Delestang) A.** 1864–70. Paris. Specialized in making dolls.

**Delfour.** 1877–80. Paris. Made dolls.

**Delhaye Frères (Bros.).** 1900. France. Won a silver medal for their dolls at the Paris Exposition of 1900.

**Dell & Co.** 1918–22. London. Made dolls.

**Deller, Alf.** 1907–21. Vienna. Doll manufacturer.

**Delphieu.** See **Rabery & Delphieu.**

**Deltour.** See **Boulouch (Bouloch), Mme. & Latour.**

**Deluxe Doll & Toy Co.** 1918–21. New York City. Made "DeLuxe Dolls" with composition limbs and soft bodies, including *Baby Luxe* and *Rompy Ann.* Price $7.50 to $18.00 doz. wholesale.

**Demantin & Roy.** 1859. Paris. Made jointed dolls that stood alone.

**Demarest, Mme. (née Gosse, Marie Felicienne).** 1908. Clefs, Maine-et-Loire. Registered in France *Poupée Sanver's* as a trademark for dolls.

**Denamur, E.** 1857–98. Paris. In the later period, known as "The House of Bambin" because he made *Le Bambin* and other bébés.

1892: Advertised that the dolls had the highest notches on the legs and the best articulation, but were less expensive than other dolls of the same type. One of several French doll manufacturers having the initials "E. D.," which are sometimes found on dolls. (See also **Dumont, E.; Jumeau; Roullet & Decamps; Steiner, Jules.**)

**Denckla, Mrs.** 1919. Her rag dolls listed with *Jessie Raleigh's* dolls.

**Denivelle, Otto Ernst.** 1917–25+. Pleasantville, N.Y. Described by PLAYTHINGS as a "famous doll maker and pioneer among doll makers."

1917: He supervised the making of *Louis Amberg & Son's Victory Dolls.*

1924–25: Obtained U.S. design patent for *Sunny Orange Blossom* doll made by Louis Amberg & Son.

**453.** Mark used by Louis Delachal for rubber dolls.

454. "Belgian Milk Girl" has bisque head possibly made by E. Denamur, pupil-less glass eyes, open mouth with four teeth, wig, composition body. Original dress is a pink skirt and tan overblouse with homespun apron. Her original sabots and milkcans are lost. Mark: "E.1D." H. 10½ inches. *Courtesy of The Smithsonian Institution.*

**Dennis, Malley & Co.** 1922. London. Distributor of dolls. Registered *May Blossom* with picture of doll's head as a trademark in Britain.

**Dep.** See **Deponirt; Déposé.**

**Depiesse, Grange.** 1890–1921. Paris. Made dolls and bébés.

**Deponirt (Dep.).** Markings used on German dolls claiming registration.

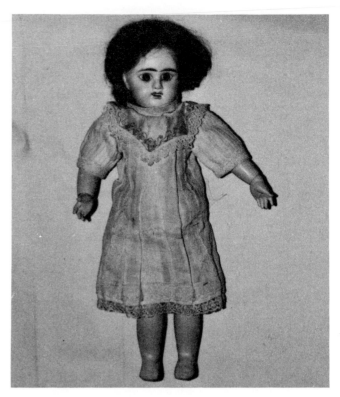

455. Bisque-head mark "E. D." may refer to E. Denamur, who made inexpensive dolls; composition body; original chemise with pink yoke and lace trim. Mark: Ill. **456.** H. 15 inches. *Courtesy of Eleanor Jean Carter.*

456. "E. D." mark, which could be Denamur, Daspres, Douillet, Decamps, or some other maker.

$$E \; 5 \; D$$
$$DÉPOSÉ$$

**Déposé (Dep.).** Markings used on French dolls claiming registration.

**Der Schelm (The Rascal).** 1908. Trademark registered in Germany by *Kämmer & Reinhardt.*

**Der Unart.** 1915. Trademark registered in Germany by *Kämmer & Reinhardt.*

**D'Erichthal, Mme. (née De Bronska, Marie Christine).** 1916. France. Procured a French patent for a doll's head made with a cloth face over a supple material, backed by a hard substance.

**Dernheim, Koch & Fischer.** 1860–ca. 1900. Gräfenroda, Germany. A porcelain factory that specialized in bisque figures with Dresden-type flowers; popular into the 1890's.

**Derolland, B.** 1878–1925+. Paris. Steam-operated factory at Asnières-sur-Oise; made rubber dolls and bébés.

1878: Basile Derolland won a silver medal at the Paris Exposition for his rubber dolls.

459          460

**459 & 460.** Marks used by Derolland firm for rubber dolls; No. 460 was used by the successor, Delacoste.

**457A & B.** Bisque head with "Dresden" flower decoration of the type made by Dernheim, Koch & Fischer; purchased in Paris. Has wreath of pink and white flowers in which each petal stands out separately. Cloth body, brown kid arms; contemporary dress. H. 20 inches. *Courtesy of the Newark Museum, Newark, N. J.*

1881: B. Derolland listed as successor of J. Callaz & B. Derolland, rubber manufacturer, who made dolls' heads, dressed and undressed dolls, and bébés.

1885: Won gold medal at Antwerp Exhibition.

1889: Derolland was a member of the jury at the Paris Exposition. U.S. report of this Exposition says of him: "Mr. Derolland, the great India rubber toy manufacturer . . . his interesting exhibit contained a number of models well known in the States. There was the greatest possible variety in the faces; there were the Punches, soldiers and little girls hanging from a thread and squeaking when squeezed . . . all tastefully colored on the dull gray India rubber, which have emigrated by thousands to the banks of the Hudson or Mississippi carefully packed in small cardboard boxes."

1900: Turburt was listed as head of the Maison Derolland. Ch. and H. Collet won a bronze medal for Maison Derolland at the Paris Exposition.

1914: B. Derolland & B. Delacoste listed as making bébés in rubber.

1921–25: B. Delacoste & Cie. were successor to B. Derolland & B. Delacoste; made rubber bébés.

**Derombies, A.** See **Dressel, Kister & Co.**

**D'Erophine, Alexandrine.** 1886. Paris. Distributor of dolls. Registered in France as a trademark a five-pointed star under a crescent.

**Derst, Edward J.** 1924. Savannah, Ga. Obtained U.S. design patent for a doll dressed as a man in overalls, gloves, and a baker's-type hat.

**Desaubliaux, Mlle..** 1915. Boulogne-sur-Seine. Registered *Gallia* as a trademark for dolls in France.

**Desbois.** See **Guerry, A.**

**Deschamps, F.** 1847–48, Paris; listed under Dolls in the directory; 1863–95, Mlle. Deschamps of Paris was listed in directories. Her mark, "Maison DESCHAMPS, 5 rue de l'Echelle," has been found on *Jumeau*'s portrait doll, Eleanor of Austria. It is believed that Mlle. Deschamps made the elaborate costume for this doll, which is copied from a famous portrait.

**Design Patents.** See **Patents.**

**Designs for Dolls.** 1904. Sonneberg, Thür. The design room of a typical factory contained from 12,000 to 18,000 designs for dolls, according to PLAYTHINGS, January, 1904.

**Desiré & Lamane.** 1893. France. Displayed dolls at the Chicago Exhibition.

**Desmee.** 1844–46. Paris. Made dolls.

**458.** Mark used by Dernheim, Koch & Fischer.

DKF

**Desportes, V.** 1876–85. Paris. Made dolls' heads, both swivel and stationary, and bisque bébés that talked or cried.

1885: It was Widow Desportes at the same address.

**Desrosiers, Th.** 1867–81. Paris. Handled wax heads portraying little children, and wax arms and legs. He also made wax crèche figures and infant Jesuses. By 1881, the firm was Assuérus & Desrosiers.

**Desty, Léon.** 1869. Paris. Made dolls.

**Detachable Heads.** See **Multi-Head Dolls.**

**Deuerlein, Josef.** Before 1910, Nürnberg; 1910–11, successor. Made character dolls of felt with celluloid heads. Won gold medal for dolls at Brussels Exhibition (1910). Used trade name "Hercules" and trademark of a teddy bear in a circle.

**Deuilly.** 1881–85. Paris. Made dolls.

**Deutsches Puppenheim.** See **Witthauer, Carl O.**

**Devanaux, Mme. L.** 1878. Paris. Exhibited dolls at the Paris Exposition.

**Devoll, Frederick.** 1865–1915. Providence, R.I. Distributed and repaired dolls. At one time he handled a line of portrait dolls called *The Campbell Kids,* named for the children of a Campbell family (not related to the Campbell Soup dolls).

**Dewey Doll.** 1899. Trademark registered in Germany by *Gebrüder Sussenguth.*

**D'Hostingue.** 1885–89. Paris. Made dolls.

**Diamond.** 1914, trade name of rubber dolls handled by *Import Sales Co.*

461. "Diamond" trademark for rubber dolls.

462. Diamond Pottery Co. mark found on dolls.

**Diamond Pottery Co.** 1908–25+. Hanley, Staffordshire. Used mark "D.P. Co.," which has been found on bisque dolls' heads and bisque dolls made in England.

**Diana.** 1902–8. Trademark registered in Germany and U.S. by *Alfred Heller* for metal dolls' heads.

463. "Diana" trademark for metal heads made by Heller.

**Diana.** 1907. Rag doll made by the *Art Fabric Mills.*

**Diana.** 1910+. One of the *Aunt Jemima* rag dolls.

**Dick, John W.** 1915. New York City. Registered in U.S. *Tipperary Kid* as a trademark for dolls.

**Dickie.** 1911. Copyrighted head of a child with hair combed down on each side of its face; made into a doll by *Louis Amberg & Son.*

**Dickie Darling.** 1916. One of the *Hug-Me-Tight* line of rag dolls designed by *Grace Drayton* and made by *Bently-Franklin Co.* Dolls were stuffed with cotton.

**Dickinson, May Bliss.** 1917–22. Boston, Mass. Registered two trademarks in U.S. for dolls and dolls' clothing. One was *Mothercraft,* and the other a picture of a toddler with a banner on which was printed "Children Well and Happy."

**Dickson, John M.** 1912. Indianapolis, Ind. Secured a U.S. patent for a doll with multiple eyes on a rotating drum, made so that when the doll was put in a horizontal position and then lifted upright, a different pair of eyes was seen.

**Dicky.** 1924. *Mama Doll* with composition head and arms; dressed in checked gingham rompers; size 14 inches; price $2.00.

**Diddums.** 1920. Trademark registered in Britain by John Green Hamley of *Hamley Bros.*

**Didi.** 1920. Copyrighted by *Jeanne I. Orsini* in U.S. The 9½-inch model had hair parted on left side, short curls, and two bows, one on each side.

**Die Kokette (The Coquette).** 1907. Trademark registered in Germany by *Kämmer & Reinhardt* for a flirting-eyed doll.

**Die Lustige Witwe.** See **Merry Widow.**

**Dies for Manufacturing Dolls.** See **Molds.**

**Diespeker, Solon.** 1876–80. Paris. Made dolls.

**Dietrich, Johannes Gotthilf.** 1915–24. Berlin. Obtained many patents for dolls. He procured about eight German patents relating to doll joints for kid-body or cloth-body dolls. These were of a construction similar to *Fausel's Universal Joint.* He also obtained over a score of German patents for joints of flat metal dolls. Some similar patents were secured in the U.S., Britain, and France.

1924: He registered *Igodi* in Germany as his trademark. Igodi was formed from his name Iohannes GOtthilf DIetrich. Dietrich used bisque heads made by *Gebrüder Heubach.*

**Dietz, Richard.** 1895. Sonneberg, Thür. Made dolls.

**Diggeldy Dan.** 1923–24. Trademark registered in U.S. by *Nelke Corp.* for a rag doll.

**Digoit.** 1869–89. Paris. Made dolls.

**Dimple.** 1914–15. Trademark for dolls, registered in U.S. by the *Japan Import & Export Commission Co.,* which had the same address as *Borgfeldt.*

**Dimples.** 1920. Trade name for doll made by *Manhattan*

*Toys & Dolls Manufacturing Co.* A cherub-type doll; came with three styles of wigs; 12½ inches tall.

**Dimples.** 1921. Trade name used by *Progressive Toy Co.* for fully jointed dolls with bisque heads; sizes 14, 16, 20, and 24 inches.

**Dinger, F.** 1909. Charlottenburg, Brandenburg. Made dolls and dolls' outfits.

**Dip Me.** 1920. Doll copyrighted by *Gordon Finlayson Gillespie;* designed by artist Fred Giorgi.

**Display.** The visual image of a doll (or dolls) is much enhanced by neatness and cleanliness. Launder and press the dolls' garments, using tissue paper and little wire hoops to give the clothes shape and help them to retain it. Lace pins should be used wherever needed, in place of the larger dressmaker's pins.

There are innumerable ways of displaying dolls. Whatever one is used, NEVER crowd them. When there are more dolls than a display area will pleasingly hold, rotate the dolls between display and storage. Also, it is a good idea to group dolls rather than line them up, and to place them at angles and on different levels. To show two views of a doll, position it in front of a mirror.

Another valuable rule is to refrain from overwhelming the dolls with accessories other than those that belong to them. Experiment with fabric to cover the base of the display area, or with a flat paint. Paint the base and support of the doll stands, blocks, or pedestals used for arranging the dolls on various levels. Fairly heavy metal stands with a circular (or nearly circular) base and adjustable height are generally preferred. The doll should be held firmly, and the upright should be attached to the base securely. Moisture may cause rust in some types of metal stands, and therefore it is usually advisable to bind the arms of the stand where they touch the body and/or garments of the doll. Should the doll be top-heavy, make sure the base is sufficiently large to support her. As much of the stand as possible should be concealed by the clothes.

Lighting is desirable, but beware of overheating dolls in a closed case with an elaborate lighting system. When dolls are displayed in a closed case, it is a good idea to set a small container of water in the case so that the area maintains a fairly constant humidity. Strong light and repeated changes in temperature and humidity can do considerable damage to dolls and their clothing. If labels are to be used to identify displayed dolls, letter and position them so that they are easily readable. (See **Custodianship of Dolls; Storage.**)

**Distribution of Dolls.** According to PLAYTHINGS (August, 1916) around the 1850's the father of *Edmund Ulrich Steiner* made dolls that were "the first prominent line to be marketed in the United States." However, as early as 1835 the *Storch Brothers* of Cincinnati, Ohio, were importing dolls; theirs was allegedly the first business of this type west of the Alleghenies.

1904: Many of the most popular dolls were completely controlled by one or another of the import commission houses in the U.S. Several of the best-known lines of dolls could not even be bought in Europe by American buyers. The dolls were designed in the U.S. by artists employed by the importers, and then produced in various European factories and distributed only in the U.S.

1912: Assortments of dolls were offered, to spare the retailers the trouble and responsibility of selecting their stock.

1920's: Distribution affiliations were broken by World War I. For example, prior to the war *Borgfeldt* had exclusive control of *Kestner* dolls, but after the war *Century* and probably others also handled Kestner dolls and dolls' heads. Both distributors and manufacturers of dolls in America increased greatly in numbers during the 1920's.

**Dittmer & Matz.** 1890's. Hamburg, Germany. 1897. Successor was August Noodt & Co. Made rubber dolls.

**Dixie Mascot.** 1911. Negro baseball doll made by *Louis Amberg & Son;* came with composition head; cost $1.00.

**Dixon, John.** 1807. London. Made dolls.

**Docken.** One of the names for wooden dolls made in Sonneberg, Thür., around 1800; used in Nürnberg for dolls as early as the 15th century.

**Dr. Dorogi Es Társa.** Ca. 1925. Albertfalva near Budapest. Made rubber dolls; employed 245 workers making dolls and other rubber products.

**Dodd, Isobel.** 1919. Dublin, Ireland. Doll manufacturer. Registered *Durax* as trademark in Britain.

**Dodo.** 1916. Copyrighted by *Jeanne I. Orsini.* Represented a doll saying its prayers.

**Doebrich, George.** 1893–1915. Philadelphia, Pa. Made and repaired dolls.

1895: Obtained U.S. patent for composition used in making dolls' hands and feet.

1906: Procured U.S. patent for flexible fingers or toes for dolls, and for attaching these appendages, especially on wax dolls.

**Doléac, L., & Cie.** 1881–1908. Paris. Made dressed and undressed dolls and bébés, *Polichinelles,* and *Marottes.* Used the initials "L. D." as their trademark.

1906–8: G. Mille was successor.

**Dolfam.** 1924. Trademark registered in Britain by *R. M. Perks* for dolls.

**Doll.** Word appeared in an English dictionary around 1700. Prior to that time, the terms "babies" and "little ladies" had been used to designate what later became known as "dolls." The word "doll" did not come into common usage in America until the mid-18th century or later. George Washington ordered a "wax baby" for his stepdaughter in 1762.

**Doll.** 1923. Indian girl doll copyrighted by *Edward Remington Ames.*

**Doll, John.** Ca. 1847–1908. Philadelphia, Pa. Father succeeded by son of the same name; both doll jobbers.

**Doll & Toy Manufacturer's Association, The.** 1922. Sonneberg, Thür. *Adolf Reisenweber* in European office; *Roth, Baitz & Lipsitz, Inc.,* New York representative.

**Doll Craft Co.** 1922. New York City. Manufactured *Cra-Doll* line of rag dolls.

**Doll O My Heart.** 1919. Made by *Jessie McCutcheon Raleigh.*

**Doll Shop, The.** 1918. New York City. Produced an "F. A. M." doll named *Dolly Dainty.*

**Doll with the Golden Heart, The.** 1923. Line of dolls wearing a golden heart necklace, made by *EFFanBEE.*

**Dollar Doll.** Pre-World War I. Large cheap dolls made in Germany; over 20 inches tall; price $1.00.

**Dollar Princess.**   See **Dolly Princess.**

**Doll-Face (Dolly) Dolls.** Created in the image of "beauty" exemplified by Lillian Russell in her era (1879–1912) and thereafter.

**Dollie.** 1893–1911. Patented in U.S. and Britain in 1893 by Charity Smith, sister-in-law of *Celia Smith;* produced by *Arnold Print Works;* distributed by *Selchow & Righter.* It was a cutout rag doll printed in colors; dart seams at neck and chin gave the doll a rounded appearance, and darts at elbows, hips, knees, heels, and ankles gave it articulation so that it could assume a sitting position. It had short hair parted in the middle; wore underclothes, a string of beads around its neck, and high button shoes; all of these were printed on the fabric. In 1911, *Elms & Sellon* advertised this jointed cloth doll 15 inches tall as the "latest thing." It should be noted that the seventeen years of the patent would have just expired. (See Ill. 1547.)

**Dollie.** 1921. *Mutual Doll Co.* and *Metro Doll Co.;* designed by *Joseph L. Kallus;* distributed by *Borgfeldt.* Bent-leg baby doll made of wood pulp composition; molded hair or wig; sleeping eyes.

**Dolling, L.** 1895. Berlin. Made doll bodies.

**Dolls' House Dolls.** Small dolls made of various materials—wood, rag, porcelain, etc.—have all been used in dolls' houses. In the late 1870's, the commercial concept of a doll family appeared in advertisements, although the ingenuity of much earlier generations had provided families of dolls that were distinguished by their clothes and relative sizes. Some of the bisque dolls' house dolls have cloth bodies and some have bisque bodies. Many of them have molded hair and shoes that help to date them, although the same molds were often used for many years. Some of the men wear mustaches or sideburns.

1893: Catalog of *Franz Carl Weber* lists "Fine dressed little dolls for doll rooms." Men, ladies, children, etc. The adults cost several times as much as the children.

1913: Flora Jacobs, in A HISTORY OF DOLLS' HOUSES, shows an F. A. O. *Schwarz* advertisement that lists, "Gentlemen and Ladies in different costumes, Maids,

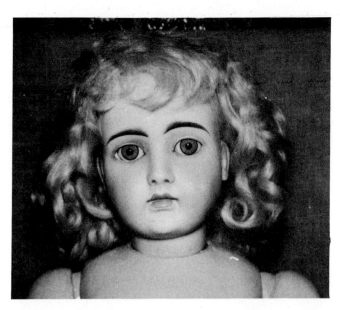

**464.** Bisque head with the "Dolly Face" inspired by Lillian Russell; has sleeping eyes, closed mouth, ball-jointed composition body. Head marked only "137." *Courtesy of Hildred Brinkley.*

Nurses, Waiters, Butlers, Cooks, etc. These dolls measure from 5 to 7 inches and range in price from 50¢ to $1.50." The author's own dolls' house family (See Ill. 465.) was purchased new after World War I, but appears to have been old stock. The family consists of a grandfather, grandmother, mother, father, boy, and girl.

Many of the dolls' house dolls have a size number on one shoulder and a mold number on the other.

Both France and Germany made dolls' house dolls, but the French ones were more expensive. *Heinrich Schmuckler* specialized in dolls' house dolls from 1895 to 1925+. *Matilde Sehm* made dressed dolls' house dolls. Other manufacturers included *Ernst Winkler, Alfred Pensky, Friedmann & Ohnstein, Elisabeth Bürckner, Grete Cohn, Schindhelm & Knauer,* and *Welsch & Co.* (See also **Bathing Dolls.**)

**Dolls of Character.** 1925. Trademark used by *Domec Toys, Inc.*

**Dolls of Quality.** 1919. Trade name for dolls made by *Qualitoy Co.* They had composition heads and soft bodies.

**Dolly.** 1910. Copyrighted by *Louis Amberg & Son.* Had the sculptured head of a little girl. The artist is given as anonymous, but probably was G. G. Wiederseim (later *Grace Drayton*) who designed *Dolly Drake,* which Amberg advertised in 1911 as a copyrighted doll.

**Dolly.** 1917. Name found on diamond-shaped paper sticker on the front of an all-bisque doll in a molded bathing suit, for which a design patent was secured by Frederick Langfelder (of *Langfelder, Homma & Heyward*). (See color photograph C 12; also **Dolly Doll.**)

**Dolly Co.** 1911. Philadelphia, Pa. Dealt in the original *Dolly Dollykins, Bobby Bobbykins,* and *Kaptin Kiddo* rag dolls.

**465.** Family group of dolls designed for use in dolls' houses. Bisque shoulder heads, cloth bodies, bisque lower limbs, painted features; probably made in Germany. H. 4 to 5½ inches. *Coleman Collection.*

**466.** All-bisque dolls'-house-size doll, jointed at neck, shoulder, and hips; painted eyes; wig; blue-painted shoes; original blue and pink dress with lace trim, blue beads at waist, gold braid; probably made in France. H. 2½ inches. *Coleman Collection.*

**Dolly Dainty.** 1910–12. Distributed by *Butler Bros.* Bisque head, fixed glass eyes, teeth, wig; jointed neck, shoulders, and hips. Sizes 11½ to 13½ inches; price 50¢.

**Dolly Dainty.** 1918. "F. A. M." doll made by *The Doll Shop.* Came with straight limbs or double jointed; human hair or mohair wigs, sleeping eyes, dressed or undressed. Sizes 14, 20, and 26 inches.

**Dolly Darling.** 1916. One of the *Hug-Me-Tight* line of cotton-stuffed rag dolls; copyrighted by *Grace G. Drayton* and handled by *Bently-Franklin Co.*

**Dolly Dear.** 1918–22. Cloth cutout doll made by *Saalfield Publishing Co.* Large girl 24 inches high and two little girls 7 inches high, all for 25¢ for uncut sheet in 1919.

**Dolly Dimple.** 1891–94. All-bisque doll distributed by YOUTH'S COMPANION. Came with blonde wig; jointed at neck, shoulders, and hips; extra dress and underclothes in Saratoga Trunk; doll size 6 inches; price including trunk and clothes, $1.15 in 1891, $1.05 in 1892.

**Dolly Dimple.** 1907–13. Character doll made by *Hamburger & Co.* and registered as a trademark in Germany by Hamburger in 1907 and by *Butler Bros.* in 1913.

**Dolly Dimple.** 1909. Lithographed rag doll made by *Art Fabric Co.;* distributed by *Selchow & Righter.* Came in cloth sheets 20 by 27 inches.

**Dolly Dimple.** 1914–15. Trademark registered in U.S. for a rag doll by *Arkadelphia Milling Co.* The doll was stamped in blue on flour sacks, and was to be cut out and stuffed; underclothes were printed on the doll; size 20 inches.

**Dolly Dimple.** 1915. One of the *Kutie Kins* line of hand-painted, felt cloth dolls produced by *A. W. Hanington & Co.*

**Dolly Dimples.** 1911. Line of character dolls with laughing faces.

**Dolly Dimples.** 1916. Distributed by *Montgomery Ward & Co.* Composition head and hands, stuffed body, mohair wig, sleep eyes; 18 inches tall; price $3.05.

**Dolly Dimples Doll Elastics.** 1906–18+. Elastics for stringing dolls, designed especially for doll hospitals; patented by *Harry W. Meier* and made by Harry W. Meier & Co. until 1918, when *Braitling* purchased the patent rights and machinery; distributed by *Strobel & Wilken.* The branched elastic device as patented in 1906 was in one piece with

**467.** Dolls' house dolls and furniture shown in Modern German Applied Arts Exhibit in 1922. *Courtesy of the Newark Museum, Newark, N. J.*

hooks that were attached to staples in the doll's extremities. Since the greatest wear came at the shoulder joints, Harry Meier obtained a second patent in 1914 for two-piece cords with the elastic cord for the arms made separately.

**Dolly Dingle.** 1923–25+. One of the *Madame Hendren* line made by *Averill Manufacturing Co.* Rag doll based on a copyright by *Grace G. Drayton.* Size 11 inches, etc.; dolls sold for $1.00 and up.

**Dolly Doll.** 1919. *Morimura Bros.,* New York City. Doll

dressed in a bathing suit. This might be the *Dolly* in a bathing suit patented in 1917 by Frederick Langfelder (See **Langfelder, Homma & Hayward, Inc.**) and assigned to Morimura Bros. (See color photograph C12.)

**Dolly Doll Co.** 1920–21. London. Made dolls.

**Dolly Dolls.** See **Doll-Face Dolls.**

**Dolly Dollykins.** 1909–11. Trademark registered in U.S. by *Frank A. Hays;* designed, made, and patented by the author (presumably Grace Wiederseim) of the famous BOBBY AND DOLLY series; distributed by *Strawbridge & Clothier;* produced by the *Dolly Co.* These were rag dolls of the type later made famous by *Grace Drayton.* Came in three sizes at 25¢, 50¢, and $1.00.

**Dolly Double and Topsy Turvy.** Cutout rag doll with two heads. Came with material for dresses.

**Dolly Drake.** 1911. Line of dolls made by *Louis Amberg & Son* and copyrighted after design by artist G. G. Wieder-seim *(Drayton)*. Unbreakable composition head with or without composition hands; cork-stuffed pink sateen bodies; in some dolls the tongue curls up from one corner of the mouth; head pierced to allow insertion of a pink or blue ribbon; price $1.00 and up.

**Dolly Drake.** 1917. Made by *Reliance Novelty Co.* with permission of Drake Bros. Co.; represented their advertisement of a girl with a cake. It is an unbreakable character doll, eyes glancing to side, teeth, curly golden wig with bangs; dressed in the Kate Greenaway manner with pantalets; big yellow baker's hat and yellow dress with drakes printed on it; 19 inches tall; price $1.00.

**Dolly Dumpling (Baby Dumpling).** 1918. Line made by *EFFanBEE;* distributed by *Butler Bros.* Composition shoulder head with painted features and hair; cork-stuffed chubby body with concealed hip and shoulder joints. There were two hundred models with twelve styles of dresses, including Little Girl and Romper Babies; 14½ inches tall; $12.00 doz. wholesale.

**Dolly Jingles.** 1923–25. Trademark registered in U.S. by *Ethel P. Westwood;* doll produced by *Horsman.* Dressed with bells on costume; 20 inches tall.

**Dolly Mine.** 1911–14. Trademark registered in U.S. by *Carson, Pirie, Scott & Co.;* registered in Germany by *Gans & Seyfarth* for jointed dolls.

**Dolly Modiste.** 1916–17. Trademark registered in U.S. by *Katherine Rauser* for dolls.

**Dolly (Dollar) Princess.** Name found on bisque heads made in Germany. The word "Special" appears on these heads, but other dolls also are marked "Special."

**Dolly Strong.** 1910. Made by *Hahn & Amberg.* Cloth-body doll; a romper-dressed version distributed with Naphtha soap coupons. Head resembled the *Kämmer & Reinhardt* #100 (Baby). Heads from the same mold on composition bodies were named *Sampson,* and Negro heads on cloth bodies were named *Sambo.*

**Dolly Twins, The.** 1922. Advertised by *Reisman, Barron & Co.*

**Dolly Varden.** 1903. Portrait doll of Lula Glaser in the part of Dolly Varden. Doll produced by *Hamburger & Co.*

**Dolly Varden.** 1906–12. Line of lithographed rag dolls advertised as having embossed linen faces; smallest size actually had embossed paper faces (see color photograph C7). Distributed by *Butler Bros.* Included Topsy and Eva double-end doll.

1906: Five types, sizes 8¾, 12, 13¾, 14, and 19 inches; price 5¢, 10¢, and 25¢.

**Dolly Varden.** 1915. Made by *Ideal Novelty & Toy Co.*

**Dolly Varden Toys.** 1925. Fresno, Calif. Made Dolly Varden dolls dressed in "colonial" costumes with real hair and sleeping eyes; 11 inches and a larger size.

**468.** Dolly Double and Topsy Turvy, a two-headed cutout rag doll with one head white and one head Negro. Came with printed red material. for doll dresses. *Courtesy of Frances Walker, photograph by Winnie Langley.*

**469.** "Dolly Princess" mark found on bisque heads.

The prices given for dolls are those for which the dolls were originally offered for sale. They are *not* today's prices.

**Dolly Walker.** 1917–23. Trademark registered in U.S. by *Harry H. Coleman,* who obtained a British and several U.S. patents for this nonmechanical doll that, according to the advertisements, could sit, kneel, dance, and sleep. The doll was made by the *Wood Toy Co.* and distributed by Coleman. It came with painted or sleeping eyes, molded hair or wig; 28 inches tall; price $10.00 to $18.50 depending on clothes, wig, etc. It was also made in sizes 18 and 24 inches in 1921. One dealer allegedly sold 1,000 of these dolls in 1919. *Emma Clear* bought a half-interest in the patent rights just before Harry Coleman died. He had bought parts for his dolls from her. The Dolly Walker bodies were primarily of wood, the torso being a wooden frame with a wire mesh. On the bottom of the torso, between the legs, some of these dolls are marked with a rubber stamp that reads: "Patented in U.S.A.// Other

Patents Pending// Patents applied for in all// Other Countries."

**Dolly Winkle.** 1918–19. Trademark registered in U.S. for dolls by *Dorothy Crosby*.

**Dollypop Dolls.** 1925. Rag dolls made by *Albert Brückner's Sons*. Face hand-painted in "oil" colors; cotton-stuffed body with patented squeeze voice; 13 inches tall.

**Dolly-Reckord.** 1922–23. *Madame Hendren* line made by *Averill Manufacturing Co.* Cylinders inserted in back to make doll recite or sing, made by Universal Talking Toys Co. and Averill Manufacturing Co. Records include "Now I Lay Me," "One Two," "Little Boy Blue," "Rock-a-Bye Baby," and "London Bridge." Composition head and limbs. Cloth body. Size 25 inches.

471 & 472. Marks used by Domec Toys Inc.

**Domec Toys Inc.** 1924–25+. New York City. Manufactured dolls; *B. Illfelder & Co.* distributed Domec Dolls. Made walking, talking, and sleeping dolls, including an infant doll named *Kradle Babe*.

1925: Lost an infringement suit to *Borgfeldt* and had to stop making Kradle Babe because it resembled the *Bye-Lo Baby* too closely.

**Donahey, William.** 1920–21. Chicago, Ill. Obtained six U.S. design patents for dolls, including such characters as a medieval craftsman, a lady doll, a boy, etc.

**Donovan, Katherine T.** 1924–25. Lynn, Mass. Procured a design patent for a Negro doll.

**Door of Hope Mission.** 1917–25+. China. A home for rescued slaves, who made dolls. Some of the wooden heads and hands were carved by *Ning-Po*. Clothes, made by girls of the Mission, were exact reproductions of the station, age, and characters the dolls represented.

470A & B. "Dolly Reckord" doll with composition head, metal sleeping eyes, and cloth body. The mechanism was in the back of the doll. Came with some cylinders made by Averill Manufacturing Co. who also made this doll, and other cylinders by Universal Talking Toys Co. H. 25 inches. *Courtesy of the Chester County Historical Society.*

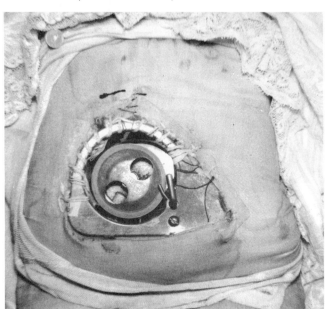

473. Doll with carved wooden head and arms on a cloth body; made at the Door of Hope Mission in China ca. 1920. Hair and eyes are painted. Original clothes, all handmade: green silk jacket trimmed with black frogs, black silk skirt over blue silk trousers. H. 10½ inches. *Coleman Collection.*

**Dora.** 1921–24. Trademark registered in U. S. by *Irokese Trading Corp.* for a *Mama Doll* with composition head and stuffed body.

1924: The 15-inch size cost $2.25, dressed.

**Dora Petzold.** 1920–25. Trademark registered in Germany by Dora Petzold. Used on dolls and baby dolls. (See **Petzold, Dora.**)

**Doremus, Schoen & Co.** 1922. New York City. Made *Mama Dolls.*

**Döring, Gebrüder (Bros.).** 1907–25+. Hüttensteinach, Thür. Manufactured dolls, specializing in stuffed dolls.

**Dormann, O.** 1918. Berlin. Made dolls.

**Dornröschen (Sleeping Beauty).** 1902. Trademark registered in Germany for sleeping dolls by *Otto Krampe.*

**Dorothy.** See **Pet Name.**

**Dorothy.** 1919. Made by *Jessie McCutcheon Raleigh;* distributed by *Butler Bros.* Dressed in figured lawn; 11½-inch size cost $2.50.

**Dorothy Dainty.** 1911–12. Copyrighted and made by *Louis Amberg & Son;* designed by *Jeno Juszko.* Represented the girl shown in the trademark of a famous brand silk-ribbon house. Doll had smiling face of a young girl with dimples; eyes glanced to the side; short brown hair in marcel waves was parted on one side and pulled over to be held by ribbon. Wore knee-length dress.

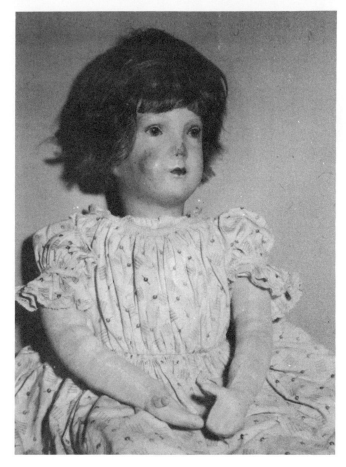

**475A & B.** "Dorothy Dainty" composition head, copyrightel by Louis Amberg & Son, 1911. Head has painted features, four upper teeth painted in the open-closed mouth. A hole is pierced through a lock of hair to receive a fabric ribbon. Mark: Ill. **476.** *Courtesy of Winnie Langley; photographs by Winnie Langley.*

**474A.** Dora Petzold, composition head on cloth body, marked with German 1920 trademark numbers: "254636." Doll has painted eyes. Mark: Ill. **474B.** *Courtesy Winnie Langley, photograph by Winnie Langley.*

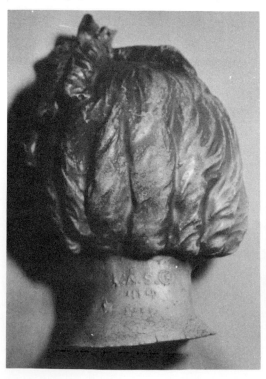

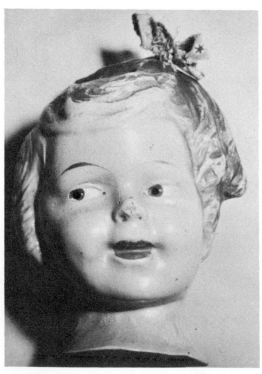

DORAPETZOLD
REGISTERED
TradeMark
DOLL
Germany

**474B.** "Dora Petzold" trademark found on dolls.

L.A.& S. ©
414

**476.** Mark found on "Dorothy Dainty" dolls made by Louis Amberg.

**Dorothy Deere.** 1912. Made by *Louis Amberg & Son.* Represented a girl about twelve years of age; *coquette* type with dimples and blue eyes; pink sateen, stuffed body; blue dress.

**Dorothy Stone.** 1924. *Celebrity Doll* originated by *Margaret Vale* and made by *Jane Gray.* Doll represented Dorothy Stone as Peter Pan in Charles Dillingham's play STEPPING STONES. It had a hand-painted face and bore a tag with a facsimile autograph of Dorothy Stone.

**Dorris & Co.** 1924–25. London. Made dolls.

**Dorst, G.** 1918. Bettelhecken, Thür. Made dolls.

477                              478

**477 & 478.** Trademarks of Julius Dorst.

**Dorst, Julius.** 1839–1925+. Sonneberg, Thür. Made wooden and wood-pulp composition dolls. Displayed dolls at Vienna Exhibition in 1873, Melbourne Exhibition in 1880, Paris in 1900, where he was one of the Sonneberg group that won the Grand Prize, and at the St. Louis Exhibition in 1904.

1895: Julius Dorst registered in Germany his trademark of an eight-pointed star, which he had used since 1879; his products included dolls, dolls' heads, and *Taüflinge* made of wood, papier-mâché, and wood-pulp composition.

1907: The Julius Dorst firm registered in Germany another trademark of the eight-pointed star.

1915–25: Georg Fr. Dorst was head of the firm, and they specialized in wooden dolls.

**Dorval.** 1867–70. Paris. Made dolls.

**Dotter, Charles T.** See **Bawo & Dotter.**

**Dottie Dimple.** 1909. Muslin cutout dolls made by *Saalfield Publishing Co.;* size 16½ by 18 inches; cost 15¢.

**Dottie Dimples (Dimple).** 1913. Baby doll advertised by *Tip Top Toy Co.*

**Dottie Dimples.** 1915. Doll made by *Ideal Novelty & Toy Co.*

**Dotty.** 1913. Trademark registered in Germany by *Borgfeldt* for dolls.

**Dotty Darling.** 1914. Doll representing a child with a bandeau of ribbon in its hair; copyrighted by *Borgfeldt.* *Fred Kolb* is listed as the artist, but he was probably assisted by *Joseph Kallus.*

**Double Face Doll.** 1912. Trade name used by *Samstag*

**479.** "Dotty Darling" copyrighted by Borgfeldt in 1914, designed by Fred Kolb. This is a copy of the original picture of the doll filed with the copyright application.

*& Hilder* for a doll with one face laughing and one face crying; cost $1.00 and up. (See also **Multi-Face Dolls.**)

**Double Joints.** 1850's–ca. 1925+. Doll joints made with twin gussets and usually used on kid-body dolls, especially the early *Lady Dolls.*

Ball-jointed composition bodies were also called double-jointed, and these were made even after 1925.

**Douglas, Anna Marie.** 1894. Leamington, Warwick. Obtained British patent for a dressed doll with a different head at each end; head could be changed by turning the doll upside down.

**Douglas & Hamer.** 1843–47. London. Succeeded by William Hamer 1848–65. Made wax and composition dolls.

**Douglas Fairbanks.** 1924. *Likeness Doll* representing Douglas Fairbanks in the film THE THIEF OF BAGDAD.

**Douillet, Emile.** See **Jumeau.**

**Downey, Clark H.** 1914–17. West Point, Ga. Secured a U.S. patent for a doll's face manufactured as follows: ". . . placing a sheet of chamois skin into a face matrix, the exposed or inner surface of the sheet being covered with shellac or other appropriate adhesive or cement, and then the mold or matrix is filled with the artificial stone producing material, which material is packed down with sufficient force to cause the leather and the stone to assume the contour of the matrix. . . . After the mold or matrix has been filled, the parts are allowed to remain until the artificial stone has set and the adhesive at the same time impregnates the pores of the chamois skin and the artificial stone, and the skin and stone are then removed and the outer surface of the chamois skin sheet is given a coating of pigment, preferably flesh color."

**Drayton, Grace Gebbie.** 1909–25+. Philadelphia, Pa. She was born Grace Gebbie in 1877, and became Grace Gebbie Wiederseim, her name when she first appeared in the doll world. Although she was three years younger than Rose O'Neill, there are striking similarities in their drawings—the round faces and eyes, the single curved line of the mouth with lines at the corners, and the starfish-shaped hands. Probably both artists reflected a trend. The Campbell Soup Co. claims that the *Campbell Kids* were first drawn in 1900. Grace drew *Bobby Blake* and *Dolly Drake* as early as 1907. The BOBBY AND DOLLY series of books had sold over 200,000 copies by 1911; the characters appear to have been made into rag dolls in 1909 under the names *Bobby Bobbykins* and *Dolly Dollykins*. In 1910, Grace gave permission to *Louis Amberg & Son* to make Bobby Blake and Dolly Drake in doll form with composition heads, which Amberg copyrighted. *Horsman* copyrighted a *Bobby* in 1910, but the artist was *Helen Trowbridge* and not Grace Wiederseim. The Drayton drawings for the Campbell Soup advertisements were copyrighted by Joseph Campbell. In 1912 Horsman copyrighted *Gee Gee,* designed by Grace Drayton (her name after her second marriage). This doll, later put on the market as *Peek-a-Boo,* had a *Can't Break 'Em* head. While Peek-a-Boos were enjoying popularity, *Borgfeldt* in 1914 produced a doll representing *September Morn* as drawn by Grace Drayton. *Bently-Franklin Co.* and *Colonial Toy Manufacturing Co.* advertised, in 1916 and 1917, the *Hug-Me-Tight* line of rag dolls designed by Grace Drayton. In 1922, Mrs. Drayton designed soft stuffed dolls for the *Madame Hendren* line made by *Averill Manufacturing Co.,* which included *Dolly Dingle, Chocolate Drop,* etc. These dolls were put on the market in 1923. Grace Drayton appears to have been one of the first artists (see **Palmer Cox**) to use round eyes in dolls, sometimes referred to as goo-goo or goggle eyes. There were many imitators of this style. (See Ill. 358.)

**Dream Baby.** See **My Dream Baby.**

**Dream Doll, The.** 1917. Five-reel photoplay by Howard S. Moss of Essanay Studio; enacted by 14-inch character dolls, specially made and costumed; dolls were as expensive as $100 each. They resemble *Schoenhut* dolls.

**Dreamland Doll Co.** 1905–8. Detroit, Mich. Made Dreamland rag dolls; distributed by *Borgfeldt.* Claimed that they originated the photograph face doll. Photographs of actual children printed on cloth face.

1905: Face on sateen; dress, bonnet, and underwear of muslin; sizes 13 and 14½ inches; prices 50¢ and $1.00.

1907: Made *Teddy-Turnover,* a doll with a teddy bear at one end and a doll at the other.

**Dreifuss, Isidore.** 1921. Strasbourg, France. Registered *Fi-Fi* as a trademark for dolls in France.

**Dress.** See **Clothes.**

**480.** Drayton face is characterized by its roundness—the roundness of the eyes, the single curved line for the mouth with the two curved lines at the corners of the mouth, round pug nose, and abbreviated eyebrows.

**Dressed Doll Manufacturing Co.** 1889–90. Their trademark, *Palais Royal,* registered in U.S. by Rosa Lisner; labels sewed or pasted on the dolls.

**Dressel, Aug.** 1909. Lengfeld, Thür. Made dolls.

**Dressel, Cuno & Otto.** 1700–1925+. Sonneberg, Thür. The oldest doll firm for which continuous records have been discovered. The firm was founded in 1700 by ancestors of Cuno and Otto Dressel; but nothing is known of the company for the first 150 years of its existence except that they specialized in wood and papier-mâché toys. Ernst Friedrich Dressel (father of Cuno and Otto) and Charles Dressel, doll manufacturers of Sonneberg, were listed in the directories from 1863–74. The company was known as Cuno & Otto Dressel as early as 1873, when Cuno Dressel, Otto Dressel, Sr., and Otto, Jr., were listed. The initials ED (with the E reversed) are found on the well-known trademark *"Holz-Masse,"* which Cuno and Otto Dressel registered in Germany in 1875.

The Cuno & Otto Dressel company had displays in the following Exhibitions: Vienna, 1873; Philadelphia, 1876; Melbourne, 1880; New Orleans, 1884; Melbourne, 1888; Chicago, 1893; Paris, 1900; and St. Louis, 1904, but no record has been found of their winning any medal except at Paris in 1900, when they were one of the Grand Prize winners. In 1876 at Philadelphia they displayed doll ladies and heads and were "commended for great variety, solid material and cheapness, especially heads with good-looking features." At Melbourne in 1888 they displayed dolls of every description. Their

A

B

CUNO & OTTO DRESSEL DOLLS

C

**481A, B, C, & D.** Two composition heads bearing the "Holz-Masse" trademark of Cuno & Otto Dressel were exhibited at the 1884 New Orleans Exposition. One head has molded hair and painted eyes; the other has a wig, glass eyes, and pierced ears. Both heads have the "Holz-Masse" mark on the back of the shoulders but the wigged head also has a paper label inside the head that includes the word "Superior." Note the difference in the two contemporary "Holz–Masse" marks. H. of molded-hair shoulder head, 5 inches; H. of wigged shoulder head, 7¼ inches. *Courtesy of The Smithsonian Institution.*

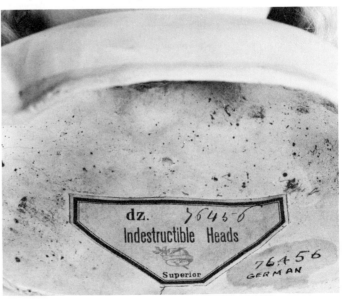

D

482. Poured wax head and arms on body with the "Holz-Masse" mark of Cuno & Otto Dressel; blue glass eyes. Mark: Ill. 485. *Courtesy of Marion Holt; photograph by Winnie Langley.*

483. Cuno & Otto Dressel marked bisque shoulder head has open mouth with teeth. Mark on shoulder: Ill. 486. H. 4 inches. *Courtesy of Dorothy Annunziato.*

484. Doll made by Cuno & Otto Dressel with bisque shoulder head, glass eyes, wig, open mouth with teeth, kid body. Mark on head: Ill. 487. H. 21 inches. H. of shoulder head, 10 inches. *Courtesy of Alberta Darby.*

marks have been found on dolls having heads of papier-mâché, wax, composition, and bisque. They purchased their bisque heads from porcelain factories such as *Simon & Halbig*, whose mark is sometimes found with a Cuno & Otto Dressel mark.

1875–95: Advertised dolls, dolls' heads, and *Täuflinge.*

Ca. 1900: Produced portrait dolls of *President McKinley, Admiral Dewey, and Admiral Sampson.* Dolls made of composition, 15½ inches high.

1906: Began to use *Jutta* as a trademark, which was registered in Germany in 1907. The trademark was to apply to double-jointed dolls of composition.

1909: Registered in Germany *Bambina* as a trademark for dolls. Advertised "leather" (kid) bodies, jointed dolls, and dressed dolls.

1911: Advertised "porcelain and celluloid heads . . . dressed dolls, jointed dolls (mark Jutta, mark Dresseldoll), character dolls and babies, leather and cloth dolls."

1912: Registered *Poppy Dolls* as a trademark in Germany for stuffed dolls.

1914: Fire destroyed much of their Sonneberg factory, but it was rebuilt and opened again in 1915.

There were three Cuno & Otto Dressel factories; the one at Sonneberg made dolls, the one at Nürnberg made metal toys, and the one at Grünhainichen made wooden toys. They had a London branch from 1894 to 1921 except for the war years. They used heads made by various companies, including *Armand Marseille.*

**Dressel, Hugo.** By 1895 the successors of Hugo Dressel were manufacturing dolls in Sonneberg, Thür. Hugo Dressel was a brother of *Wilhelm Dressel.*

**Dressel, Kister & Co.** 1840–1925+. Passau, Bavaria. Made dolls' heads and other porcelain ware. They exhibited porcelain dolls' heads at Vienna in 1873 and at Chicago in 1893.

1902: The factory had three hundred employees.

1914: They had an agent in Paris.

1925: Paris agent advertised porcelain doll busts for candy boxes, tea cosies, pin cushions, lamps, etc.

**Dressel, Wilhelm.** 1895–1920. Sonneberg, Thür. Doll manufacturer. "A. G." (joint-stock company) appears after the name from 1914 on. He displayed dolls at the Paris Exposition of 1900, where he was one of the Grand Prize group of winners; and at St. Louis in 1904. Many of his dolls were exported to England. Wilhelm Dressel was a brother of *Hugo Dressel.*

**Dressel & Koch.** 1895–98. Köppelsdorf, Thür. A porcelain factory that made dolls' heads, including bisque dolls' heads

**485 –493.** Marks found on dolls; Nos. **485–491** can be identified as handled by Cuno & Otto Dressel; Nos. **492** and **493** are questionable but their similarity to part of the No. **486** mark should be noted.

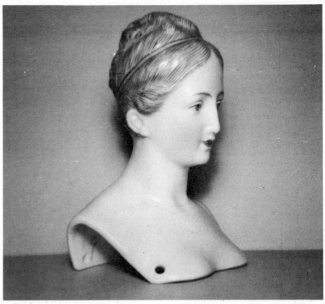

**494.** China head has painted features and brown hair with a green and gold ribbon. Mark inside the back is shown in Ill. **495.** H. of shoulder head, 3½ inches; breadth at base, 2⅝ inches; depth at base, 1⅞ inches. *Courtesy of Sylvia Brockmon.*

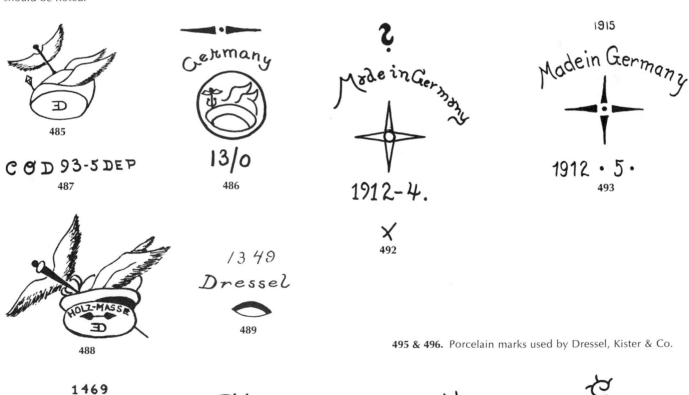

**495 & 496.** Porcelain marks used by Dressel, Kister & Co.

**Drew, Harry E., & Springsteen, Robert E.** 1883. Indianapolis, Ind. Assignees of a patent for a wire skeleton in a stuffed, flexible doll's body by *Lucinda Wishard.*

**Dreyfus, René.** 1914. Paris. Imported dolls from Germany.

**Drowsy Dick.** 1914. Child doll with eyes half closed; copyrighted by *Horsman,* designed by *Helen Trowbridge.* The head nodded to and fro when the doll was moved.

**Drücker (Drukker).** German word for presser of dolls' bodies and composition heads.

**Drukker, Hazel, Co. (Hazel Drukker Silberman).** 1919–21. New York City. Registered *Phyllis May* as a trademark for dolls in U.S. The Phyllis May doll made by the *New Toy Co.* represented the character of this name created by Hazel Drukker in the New York EVENING MAIL. In 1921, *Louis Amberg & Son* brought out *Mibs,* a Phyllis May doll created by Hazel Drukker.

**Du Bois Manufacturing Co.** 1922. New York City. Handled line of Du Bois dolls. Made dolls with unbreakable composition character heads; composition limbs, cotton- or cork-stuffed bodies with voices; sizes 12 to 28 inches. Doll with trade name, *Betty Walker,* had hand-painted face, stuffed body. Sizes 15, 18, and 21 inches; prices under $5.00.

**Du Pont de Nemours, E. I., & Co.** 1919–22. Wilmington, Del. Made enamels for spraying on dolls, including Harco Doll Finish and Pyralin, which they advertised could be blown, molded, stamped, machined, painted, embossed, engraved, or printed upon. According to *Joseph Kallus,* Du Pont made celluloid *Kewpies* for *Borgfeldt.* It is possible they were actually made of Pyralin.

**Du Serre, J.** 1904. France. Displayed jointed bébés at the St. Louis Exhibition.

**Dubois.** 1889–90. Paris. Made dolls.

**Duboulet.** 1873–74. Villers-Cotterets, near Soissons, France. Made dolls.

**Dubray.** 1839–40. Paris. Made dolls.

**Duchêne, André.** 1922. Paris. A director of *Société Française de Fabrication de Bébés et Jouets.*

**Duchess.** 1903–6. Trade name for kid-body dolls distributed by *Samstag & Hilder.*

**Duchess.** 1914. Dolls produced by *Borgfeldt* with bisque heads made by *Armand Marseille.*

**Duchess.** 1921. Rag doll made by *Martha Chase,* representing the Duchess as drawn by Tenniel for ALICE IN WONDERLAND.

**497 & 498.** "Duchess" marks on bisque heads made by Armand Marseille.

**Duchess Dressed Doll, The.** 1914–15. Trademark registered in Germany by *M. Kohnstam & Co.*

**Duckme Doll Co.** 1920. New York City. Handled cherub-type dolls.

**Duclos, André.** 1855–1921. Paris. By 1900, it was Maison André Duclos.

1855–63: Made patented gutta-percha dolls' heads.

1900: Won bronze medal for doll display at the Paris Exposition.

**Ducrey, Mme.** 1880. Paris. Made dolls.

**Dude.** 1892. One of the *Brownies* designed by *Palmer Cox;* dressed with top hat, monocle, and cane; made by *Arnold Print Works.*

**Duffner, Thérèse.** 1867. Schoenwald, Baden. Exhibited dolls dressed in national costumes at the Paris Exposition.

**Duhotoy.** 1889. France. Exhibited dolls at the Paris Exposition.

**Dulmage, Léo W.** 1920–23. Liège or Lüttich, Belgium; also resided in France. Obtained French, German, and British patents for jointed walking dolls that would walk when held by the hand.

1923: Patented in France a device for transforming a doll that could stand up, into a walking doll, by fitting a mechanism into the body and connecting it to the legs.

**Dumas, Mme. (Mme. Dumas-Bohan).** 1836-52. Paris. Made dolls.

**Dumerey.** 1848. Paris. Obtained French patent for jointed feet on a doll used to display fashions.

**Dumont (Domont), E.** Before 1843–89. Paris. Listed first as a maker of mechanical toys, and at an exposition before 1843 he had been cited with an Honorable Mention for his inventions.

1844: Received Honorable Mention for his doll display at the Paris Exposition.

1864: Advertised that he was making kid-body dolls, dressed and undressed, and dolls with porcelain heads.

1889: Displayed dolls at the Paris Exposition. He was one of several French doll manufacturers with the initials "E. D.," which are sometimes found on dolls.

**Dumontois (Dumontais).** 1865–79. Paris. Made dolls.

**Dumpie Dolls.** See **Danville Doll Co.**

**Dum-Tweedle.** 1911. Trademark registered in Britain by *Dean's Rag Book Co.* for rag dolls.

**Dunker, Henriette (née Hinzpeter).** 1923. Hamburg, Germany. Doll manufacturer. Registered in Germany *Mein Stern* (My Star) in a six-pointed star as a trademark.

**Dunne, James P.** 1916–17. Chicago, Ill. Procured a design patent for a male patriotic doll that resembled Teddy Roosevelt.

**Dupont.** 1840–68. Paris. Made dolls. In 1840 address was the same as that for *Mme. Dumas-Bohan* in 1836.

**Duran, Mme. Max.** 1915. Paris. Registered in France her trademarks "Duran Marx" and "M. D." in a circle.

**Durand, Mme. Marie Louise (née Bertaud).** 1920. France. Obtained a French patent for a doll with a flexible metal framework.

**Durand, Octave.** 1921. Colombes near Paris. Registered in France *Tanagrette* as a trademark for dolls.

**Durax.** 1919. Trademark registered in Britain by *Isobel Dodd*, doll manufacturer.

**Dusky Dude.** 1900–1904. Black-faced knock-about rag boy doll dressed in tweed or a plaid suit, sailor cap, and high shoes.

1900: Distributed by *Nugent*; size 12 inches, price 50¢.

1904: Distributed by *Montgomery Ward & Co.*; size 14 inches, price 45¢.

**Dutch Boy.** See **Neutrality Jim.**

**Dutch Boy or Dutch Girl.** 1911. Pair of dolls made by *Louis Amberg & Son.* Came with composition heads and cloth bodies; wore Dutch costumes.

**Dutch Dolls.** Late 18th century to early 20th century. Made in the Grödner Tal, Austria (now Italy). These all-wooden dolls were also known as Peg Woodens, Penny Woodens, and Nürnberg Fille. They have black painted hair, with gray wisps around the edges in the early ones, which also have a high varnish and often a tuck comb. The painted slippers are usually orange or deep pink. They were made in numerous sizes from a half-inch to over two feet. The larger ones have ball-type joints. The smaller ones have peg joints. A sample book of Nürnberg firms ca. 1840 shows one of these dolls with tuck comb and earrings. The dolls were probably painted and decorated in Nürnberg. (See also **Manufacture of Wooden Dolls.**)

**Dutch Girl.** See **Gretchen.**

**Dutch Hans or Dutch Gretchen (Gretel).** 1911. Pair of *Art Dolls* made by *Horsman.* Came with *Can't Break 'Em* heads, cloth bodies, blue eyes, blonde wigs; hat and wooden shoes. Size 14 inches; price $1.50. Hans had bobbed hair and bangs; *Gretchen* had *Rembrandt* style hair. She wore red and blue clothes with an apron.

**Dutch Man or Dutch Woman.** 1911. Pair of cloth dolls in Dutch costume made by *Steiff.* Dolls could stand by themselves. Came with blonde hair and wooden shoes. Size 16 inches. Man wore yellow coat and black knee breeches; woman wore red and blue garments.

**Dutch-He or Dutch-She.** 1911. Pair of Dutch character dolls advertised by *A. Steinhardt & Bro. David Rosenthal* obtained a U.S. design patent for these dolls, but their dress was slightly different from those in the advertisements.

**Duthiel.** 1889. France. Displayed dolls at the Paris Exposition.

**Duval-Denis.** See **Blampoix, Aîné.**

**Duveau.** 1890. Paris. Made dolls.

**Duvinage & Harinkouck.** See **Giroux, Alphonse & Cie.**

**Duyts, Abraham.** 1925. London. Imported and distributed dolls.

# E

**E. B. & E. Co.** 1907. Detroit, Mich. Made *Happyland* brand of photographic-face rag dolls.

**E. E. Houghton.** 1915. Trademark registered in Britain by *Elizabeth Ellen Houghton* for dolls.

**Eadie, Peter, Jeune (Jr.).** 1898. Obtained French patent for a doll with three faces having different features. It had a socket head on a ball-jointed composition body operated by a vertical axis, controlled by a device on the doll's stomach.

**Eagle Brand Doll.** 1925. Made by *Simplex Stuffed Toy Manufacturing Co.* under the management of *Jos. G. Kaempfer;* advertised as unique and original styles by Mrs. Kaempfer.

**Eagle Doll Co.** 1918. New York City. Manufactured dolls.

**Eagle's Head.** See **Petitcollin.**

**Ears.** Often applied on the larger-size bisque dolls' heads, especially the 19th-century French ones. *Ella Smith* of Alabama obtained a U.S. patent in 1919 for using plaster of Paris ears on her rag dolls. Many dolls of the second half of the 19th century and early 20th century had pierced ears, especially bisque-headed dolls. Ears were pierced through the lobes or directly into the heads. It is rare for glazed china heads to have pierced ears, but glazed earrings are sometimes found on un-tinted bisque heads. One exception is the glazed head made in Japan in the 20th century (See Ill. 889), which has pierced ears but is not a rare type.

Glass beads on metal wires are the usual type of earrings. Many of the earlier earrings had tiny dangles, often with colored glass beads.

**Earthen Dolls.** Some of the oldest types of dolls were made of earthenware, especially before the knowledge of making china reached Europe. Since earthenware is not fired to as high a temperature as porcelain, it is less durable and cheaper to produce. *Aug. Poppe* displayed earthenware dolls at the Berlin Exhibition of 1844. *Abicht & Co.* and *Rob. Riehm* were both making earthenware dolls in Ilmenau at the end of the 19th century.

**Eason, Gertrude.** 1917. Philadelphia, Pa. Made dolls.

**Eastern Commission & Importing Co.** 1903. U.S. Advertised dressed dolls for 25¢ to $5.00.

**Eastern Doll Manufacturing Co.** 1923–24. New York City. Made character and *Mama Dolls;* the latter were 14 to 27 inches tall and cost $1.00 and up.

A

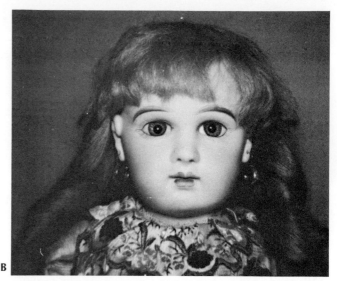

B

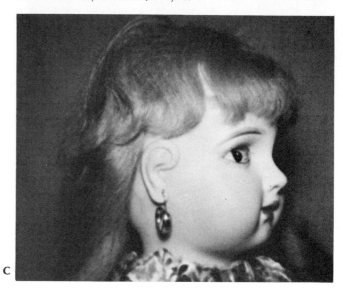

C

**499A, B, & C.** Bisque-head doll with applied ears, glass eyes, closed mouth, composition body, contemporary dress. H. 23 inches. *Courtesy of Helen Jo Payne.*

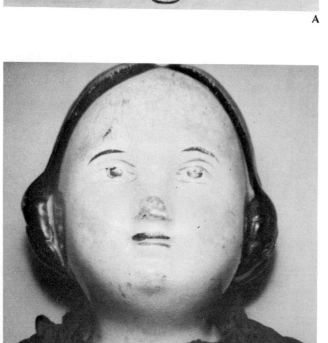

**500.** Glazed earthenware head has painted features. H. 21 inches. H. of shoulder head, 5 inches. *Courtesy of the International Doll Library Foundation.*

**Eates, Henry.** 1894. London. Manufactured dolls.

**Eaton, Florence Emily.** 1895–1904+. Tipperary and Dublin, Ireland. Obtained three British patents for making dolls' heads. Her first two patents in 1895 and 1901 used ordinary porcelain dolls' heads and covered them with dental enamel consisting of thin sheets of prepared India rubber or gutta-percha, softened in boiling water, molded over the hard face, and painted. The third patent (1904) is described as follows: "Prepare paper by boiling 24 hours and reduce it to a pulp by beating, add equal parts of dextrine or glue; this mixture is pressed into moulds, the centre being filled with cork to act as a core, both sides of the cast are then put under pressure, the figure or face is then painted with diluted celluloid and coloured with powders and paint." Laura Starr, in her 1908 book, describes these dolls as follows: "The Erin Doll Industry was started by a clever Irishwoman who has discovered a composition for making dolls that fills a long-felt want, viz., unbreakable dolls. She faithfully and artistically reproduces the features of the different types and gives great care and attention to the details of dress that each doll may be characteristic."

**Eaton, T., Co.** 1914–25+. Toronto, Canada. Distributed dolls. Handled *Dainty Dorothy* and other lines, also handled by *Sears, Roebuck & Co.*

**Eberhardt, D.** 1909–20. Coburg, Thür. Manufactured dolls.

**Eberlein, Johannes Chr.** 1853–98. Pössneck, Thür. Porcelain factory that made dolls' heads and *bathing dolls*.

**Eberwein, D., & Co.** 1923. Hamburg, Germany. Registered in Germany *Strandfee* (Sea Nymph) as a trademark for dolls.

**Eccentric Eyes.** See **Roguish Eyes.**

**Eck, Berthold.** 1876. Unterneubrunn near Eisfeld, Thür. Manufacturer of dolls and *Täuflinge*; registered in Germany his trademark of a stag's head on a shield.

**Eck, W. C., & Co.** 1919. Cincinnati, Ohio. Advertised Cupid Dolls, Kokomo Kids, and Big Tom.

**Eckardt.** See **Strauss & Eckhardt.**

**Eckardt, Rud.** 1895. Königsberg, East Prussia. Manufactured dolls.

**Eckart, Hans Englebert.** 1911. London. Doll importer. Trademark of a horse drawing a cart loaded with faggots, registered in Britain for dolls.

**Eckart, Walter, & Eckart, Ronald.** 1920–25. London. Made dolls.

**501.** Trademark of Berthold Eck.

**Eckert, Heinrich.** 1901–5. Munich, Bavaria. 1901, obtained a French patent for improvements in ball-and-socket joints for dolls. Obtained three patents in Britain and three patents plus a patent supplement in Germany for ball-and-socket joints for dolls, made of an elastic material such as rubber.

**Eckhardt, Max.** See **Strauss, Adolph, & Co.**

**Eckold, Rudolf.** 1920–21. Walterhausen, Thür. Manufactured dolls.

**Eckstein, Hermann.** 1899–1925+. Neustadt near Coburg, Thür. Manufactured dolls of various kinds. In 1909 there was an explosion at the factory, temporarily curtailing their production.

Early 1920's: Advertised dressed dolls, jointed dolls, character babies, and stuffed dolls.

1922: Registered his triangular-shaped trademark in Germany.

**Eckstein & Co.** 1924–25. Sonneberg, Thür. Belonged to German Manufacturers Association in New York City, through which their dolls were imported into U.S.

**502.** Mark used by Herman Eckstein.

**Eclipse Doll Manufacturing Co.** 1919–21. Springfield, Mass. Successor in 1921 was Worthy Doll Manufacturing Co.

1920: Advertised six models of fully jointed dolls with sleeping eyes, real hair, and teeth; eighteen models of bent-limb baby dolls; fifty models of soft body dolls.

**Ecuadorian Dolls.** Were made of pure wax, bread crumbs, or corozo, a vegetable ivory.

**Edelkind (Noble Child).** 1919. Trademark registered in Germany by *Hugo Wiegand* for dolls and dolls' bodies.

**Edelmann, Edmund.** 1921–25. Sonneberg, Thür. Made dressed dolls, jointed dolls, and baby dolls.

**Eden Bébé (Eden Puppe).** 1890–1925+. Trademark registered in France and in Germany by *Fleischmann & Blödel* and by their successor, *Société Française de Fabrication de Bébés et Jouets,* for a line of bébés.

1917: *Grey & Grey Ltd.* distributed these bisque-head dolls in the U.S.

1921: *Arthur Geoffroy* was the U.S. agent. A bisque doll's head with both "Eden Bébé" and *Simon & Halbig* on it, and a lady doll's head with both "Eden Bébé" and *"Etoile Bébé"* have been reported but not seen by the authors.

**503.** "Eden Bébé" by Fleischmann & Blödel with bisque head, glass eyes, jointed composition body; dressed in blue crocheted jumper and white guimpe. *Photograph by Winnie Langley.*

**Edison, Thomas Alva.** 1878–91+. Orange, N.J. Invented and manufactured phonograph dolls. In 1878 he obtained a British patent for a "phonographic" doll that would reproduce sound, having a "phonet" to move its lips. HARPER'S YOUNG PEOPLE, January 27, 1891, tells about Edison's first doll: "The first talking doll that Mr. Edison modelled bore as little resemblance to the doll that he now manufactures as the wood doll of the cave-dwellers bore to the dainty creature of the French court. Mr. Edison knew much more about phonographs than he did about children's nurseries, and his idea of a doll would have seemed very crude to the critical and educated mind of the present-day little girl.

"He made a tin cylinder about six inches long to hold the phonograph, with a little funnel at the upper end through which the sound was to come. It looked for all the world like a miniature stove-pipe with a letter V stuck on top of it. He then intended to have a head, arms, and legs attached to this and call it a doll. . . . The absurdity of the thing had only to be shown to Mr. Edison for that model to be promptly given up."

EDEN-BÉBÉ     EDEN-BÉRÉ
504                  505

Eden-Bébé
506

**504–506.** "Eden Bébé" marks used by Fleischmann & Blödel.

In 1887 *William White Jacques* applied for a U.S. patent for a combined doll and photograph, which he assigned to the Edison Phonograph Toy Manufacturing Company of Maine. The patent was granted in 1888, but this doll differed markedly from the doll actually produced by Edison in New Jersey. The Jacques patent drawings indicate a doll with a shoulder head on a stuffed body, and the sound funnel coming up into the head.

The improved doll actually made by Edison and begun in the fall of 1889 is described in an 1891 HARPER'S YOUNG PEOPLE article as follows: "A body of tin, shaped precisely as a human body is formed, was made. Great iron presses, some of them weighing five tons, were used, and steel dies for stamping out the different parts were constructed. Sheets of tin go into these presses, and after forty-five different operations they come out cut into half a dozen pieces, which fit together and make the cover for the phonograph.

"Next, one of the members of Mr. Edison's company went to Europe, and visited the shops in Germany where dolls' heads are made of bisque. He gave orders for all the work that two large makers could turn out for a year, in advance, and returned home. American manufacturers agreed to furnish the wooden arms and legs, and Mr. Edison proposed to make the phonographs. But all the work was not ended there. The machinery that Mr. Edison had invented to make the phonograph had to be changed to suit the new shape the talking-machine was to bear. This all took time and many thousands of dollars, but at last it was finished.

"After the tin body comes from the presses, the different parts are soldered together, except in the back, where a little door that opens and closes is left to allow the phonograph to be repaired if it should ever get out of order. In the front of the body, between the arms, there is a number of perforations, like those in the top of a pepper-box, to let the sound out.

"The phonograph consists of a small wax-covered wheel, which revolves on a little steel rod. One end of this rod sticks out of the back of the doll, and is turned by a key when the doll is made to talk. At the tip of this wheel is a tiny needle, which fits into minute grooves that are cut into the wax, as in the big phonographs. Above this needle is the artificial diaphragm, and above that the funnel through which the sound passes.

"When the key is turned, the wheel revolves, the needle follows in the grooves, moving the diaphragm up and down as the human diaphragm moved when the words were first spoken, and in a tiny Punch and

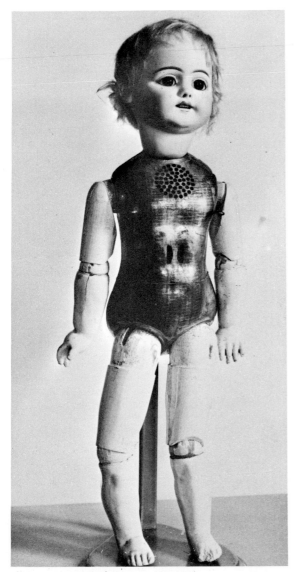

**507.** Edison phonograph doll. Metal torso contains talking mechanism with thirteen patent dates on it, ranging from 1878–89. Bisque head was made by Simon & Halbig, mold #719. Doll has wooden arms and legs, composition hands and feet. H. 22 inches. *Courtesy of Western Reserve Historical Society.*

Judy tone, the doll recites a verse from Mother Goose's rhymes. . . .

"By an ingenious mechanism a spring may be touched when the verse is ended, and the wheel is forced back to its original place, ready to go through the same performance again."

In 1890 about 500 people were engaged in the manufacture of phonographs and talking dolls at the Edison Establishment. Half were employed in the manufacture of each article. It took eighteen women just to recite the nursery rhymes for the cylinders to go into the dolls. The factory had a capacity of about 500 talking dolls a day; this would mean over 100,000 in a year.

The 1891 HARPER'S YOUNG PEOPLE's article continues: "The talking doll in its present form has proved to be such a success that Mr. Edison has thought it worth

his while to invent a new doll that will be as nearly perfect as machinery can be. The improved doll will be ready for the public in a short time. . . . In the first place all the improvements are in the internal machinery. The new phonograph will fit into the dolls' bodies which the company still has on hand. The doll phonograph will be an exact copy of the real phonograph reduced to one-fourth the size. The big phonograph contains a cylinder large enough to allow a person to talk into it for four minutes without covering the wax surface with lines. The little phonograph has a one-minute cylinder. It is about four times as big as the present doll cylinder.

"This is not the only improvement. Mr. Edison and his associates have found twenty-five different faults in the present doll. Some of these faults are grave and some are trifling. Mr. Edison has found some way of remedying each one of these faults, and the new doll will not get out of order without good cause. Its machinery will be precisely like that used in the present doll, excepting that it will be larger, heavier and more durable.

"This new doll will go all over the world. The general manager showed me letters from South Africa, China and Turkey. The last letter asked that the dolls should be 'instructed to speak' in Turkish."

The mechanism inside the doll shown in the illustration has on it "Edison Phonograph Toy//Manufacturing Co.//New York" and the patent dates Feb. 19, 1878; May 18, 1880 [appears twice, for two different patents, apparently]; May 22, 1888; Nov. 27, 1888; Dec. 4, 1888 [also twice]; Feb. 5, 1889; April 2, 1889 [four times]; July 9, 1889; and other patents applied for. (See Ill. 507.)

F. A. O. *Schwarz,* in YOUTH'S COMPANION, May 29, 1890, advertised these phonograph dolls as being "French jointed dolls," which is interesting in view of the fact that the heads were apparently made in Germany and the bodies in America. All the half dozen or so Edison dolls examined by the authors have *Simon & Halbig* heads, mold #719. These dolls were 22 inches tall and cost $10.00. An unverified source reports that they were also made in a 30-inch size. THE DOLL'S DRESSMAKER in 1891 offered these dolls as premium prizes and gave their value, dressed, as $20.00.

**Edith.** 1905–14, and possibly earlier. China dolls' heads made with this name in gold letters on the chest. This type was produced by *Hertwig & Co.* and *Closter Veilsdorf.*

**Edith Day.** 1924. *Celebrity Doll* originated by *Margaret Vale,* designed and made by *Jane Gray.* The doll represents Edith Day as Wildflower in Arthur Hammerstein's play WILDFLOWER. It had a hand-painted face and bore a tag with a facsimile autograph of Edith Day.

**Educational Doll, The.** 1916–17. Trade name for doll with letters of alphabet on its skirt, made by *Louis Amberg & Son.*

**Edwards, Charles.** 1852–65. London. Mrs. Henrietta Edwards was listed at the same address from 1878 to 1891; they made wax-over-composition dolls.

**Edwards, John.** 1856–84. London. Made wax dolls.

1868: Listed as inventor of the Exhibition wax model dolls, wax and composition dolls, also Exhibition rag dolls; dolls were dressed or undressed; sold wholesale or for export.

1871: Showed a kneeling wax doll with inserted hair at the London Exhibition. Made million dolls a year.

**Edwards, John.** 1901. Philadelphia, Pa. Made dolls.

**Edwards, T. W.** 1913. Procured a British patent for fastening the parts of a stuffed-body doll.

**Edwards & Pamflett, Mesdames.** 1918–23. London. Made dolls.

1918: Registered in Britain *The Cecily Doll* as their trademark.

**Eegee (Ee-Gee) Doll.** 1924–25. Trade name used by *E. Goldberger,* especially for *Mama Dolls.* Tag on composition-bodied Ee-Gee doll reads "I am little Miss Charming. I walk and turn my head and smile."

1925: Ee-Gee dolls priced 50¢ to $10.00.

**Eekhoff, R.** 1894. Groningen, Netherlands. Appears in Leuch's Directory under Children's Toys. Purple stamp on the upper back of a cloth-body doll with *Simon & Halbig* bisque head and hands reads: R EEKHOFF// GRONINGEN. Doll was dressed in a Groningen provincial costume with a metal helmet, lace cap under the

helmet, long green jacket, black skirt and black checked apron, black buckled slippers (not wooden shoes), and black stockings. Doll's head is bald without any hair; brown eyes are stationary. Closed mouth, shoulder head without any neck joint. The metal helmet signifies that the doll represents a married woman. When a girl received a proposal of marriage, she accepted by putting on her metal helmet, or refused by not doing so. This was an old custom in the area, and the doll could be older or younger than the 1894 date found in the directory.

**EFFanBEE.** 1913–25+. Trademark registered in U.S. in 1918 by *Fleischaker & Baum,* doll manufacturers. Name used in interstate commerce since 1914, but appeared in advertisements in 1913. (See **Fleischaker & Baum.**)

**EFFanBEE "Buttons" Monk, The.** 1923–24. Trademark registered in U.S. by *Fleischaker & Baum.* The trademark was stamped on buttons that were affixed to the doll.

**Egler, Mme.** 1919–20. Paris. Made dolls. Monsieur Egler & *Gondrand* also made dolls in Paris, 1925.

**Egret, Mme.** 1874–84. Paris. Made *nankeen* dolls.

**Ehlert, Franz, & Sohn.** 1909. Berlin. Made dolls.

**508A, B, & C.** Simon & Halbig solid-crown bisque shoulder head on cloth body marked "Eekhoff," with bisque lower arms. Doll has glass eyes; no wig. She is dressed in original clothes of the province of Groningen, Netherlands. Marks: head, Ill. **1528**; stamped on back of body in purple, Ill. **509.** H. 18 inches. H. of shoulder head, 5 inches. *Coleman Collection.*

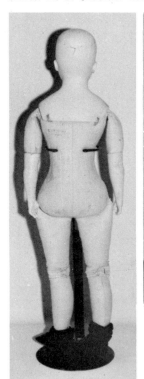

R. EEKHOFF
Groningen

**509.** Eekhoff mark stamped on dolls' bodies.

**Ehrich Bros.** 1872–1907. New York City. Distributed dolls.

1875: Their store window portrayed Barnum's circus, the seats filled with dolls of every description.

1877: Advertised:
French Lady Dolls, kid bodies, dressed—
    stationary head, painted eyes, 11 inches, $1.50
    turning head, glass eyes, 11, 12, 13, 14½ inches, $1.75 to $4.50
French Dolls, fully jointed kid bodies, bisque turning heads, glass eyes, natural hair, earrings, chemise, 12½, 14½, 16, 17½, 19, 20½, 22, 23½ inches, $2.25 to $8.00
China Head Dolls, cloth body, china limbs—
    molded hair, 5, 6, 8½, 10, 12, 14, 16 inches, 8¢ to 50¢
    bald head with hair, 11, 14, 17 inches, 55¢ to $1.00
Baby Dolls, waxed heads, hair, composition limbs, dressed, 10, 13, 14, 16 inches, 20¢ to 85¢
Waxed heads, squeak box, chemise, earrings—
    wooden arms and legs, 11½ inches, 20¢
    composition limbs, 13, 14½, 18, 21 inches, 30¢ to 75¢

1878: Advertised:
French Lady Doll, bisque turning head, glass eyes, natural hair, elegantly dressed, 15 inches, $9.00
Wax Model Doll, natural hair, "turning head which is rarely seen in a wax doll," chemise, earrings, 15½, 18, 20, 25½, 28 inches, $3.00 to $7.00
London Rag Baby Dolls with muslin-covered wax faces, dressed, 14½, 17, 20, 22 inches, 25¢ to $1.00
All-China Dolls (probably no joints), dressed—
    2½ inches, 5¢
    with gilded boots, 3¼ inches, 10¢

1879: Advertised:
French Lady Dolls, bisque turning head, real hair, fully jointed kid bodies, elegantly dressed, $2.75 to $25.00

1882: Advertised:
Bisque Head Dolls, dressed as babies—
    glass stationary eyes, 10 inches, 65¢
    sleeping eyes, 14 inches, $1.00
Composition Head Dolls, wooden arms and legs, 13½ and 18 inches, 15¢ and 25¢
Wax Head Dolls, glass eyes, wax arms and legs, dressed as babies, 16 inches, $1.00

Sheepskin wigs and patent knee joints to facilitate sitting were mentioned.

No French Lady dolls were advertised. Only the 14½-inch size of the *London Rag Baby* was listed. China-head, stuffed-body dolls were listed in the same sizes as in 1877, but the prices were lowered to 5¢ to 40¢.

1906: Advertised French dolls with fully jointed bodies and with bisque heads, sleeping eyes, flowing hair; size 22 inches; price 98¢.

1907: Advertised imported dolls, including *Baby Ruth* and rag dolls. Imported dolls priced 15¢ to $15.00.

510. Lady doll of the type sold by Ehrich's. This doll was bought in Paris in the 1870's. Her accessories included a watch and chain and a pair of gloves to cover her wooden hands. H. 18 inches. *Courtesy of The Smithsonian Institution.*

**Ehrlicher (Erlicher), Gust.** 1903–8. Neustadt near Coburg, Thür. Operated German office of *E. A. Runnells Co.*, doll distributors. Handled the *Princess* line of jointed and dressed dolls.

**Ehrlicher, Louis.** 1907–20. Sonneberg, Thür. Manufactured dressed dolls.

**Eichhorn, C. A.** 1908–14. Neustadt near Coburg, Thür. Made dressed dolls.

**Eichhorn, Christian, & Söhne (Sons).** 1909–25. Steinach, Thür. Specialized in making porcelain bathing dolls, porcelain dolls' heads, and glass eyes.

**Eichhorn, Edwin Ferdinand.** 1895–1918. Giessübel, Thür. Manufactured dolls.

**Eichhorn, Franz.** 1895–1918. Giessübel, Thür. Manufactured dolls.

**Eichhorn, Martin.** 1909–25+. Sonneberg Thür. Manufactured dolls.

**Einco.** See **Eisenmann & Co.**

**Einenkel, Brunhilde.** Made dolls that were exhibited in the Sonneberg Museum by 1926.

**Eingetragene (Eingetragen, Eingetr.).** Means "registered" in German, and is used in conjunction with *Fabrikmarke* or *Schutzmarke*.

**Eisenmann & Co. (Joseph Eisenmann).** 1905–25+. Fürth, Bavaria; London. Made and distributed dolls. Used "Einco" as trademark. Stated in British patent in 1905 that heretofore rag doll faces had generally been made with a foundation of wax molded in the required shape, with a layer of painted gauze on the outer surface. (These would be the *London Rag Dolls*.) Since wax was fragile and it often cracked, Eisenmann proposed to use cardboard molded in the desired shape, with the gauze over it, and eyesockets cut out of the cardboard and gauze. Eisenmann registered the following trademarks in Britain: 1908, *Little Pet*; 1908, figure of a butterfly; 1911, *Kiddieland*; 1912, *Hugmee*; 1912, *Toddles*; 1912, *Kwacky-Wack*; 1912, *Beaky-Ba*; 1913, *Bunny Hug*; 1914, *Floatolly*. He obtained four U.S. design patents in 1913; they all had eyes glancing to the side; one was for a girl, one a baby girl, one a boy, and one a sailor boy. In 1925 Eisenmann & Co. advertised dolls like the "Italian kind" (*Scavini?*).

**511.** Doll produced by Eisenmann & Co. (Einco), probably ca. 1912/14, has bisque head, painted hair and features, open-closed mouth, bent-limb composition baby body. Mark: Ill. **512.** *Courtesy of Grace W. Brockman; photograph by Dr. J. W. Cook, North Carolina State University.*

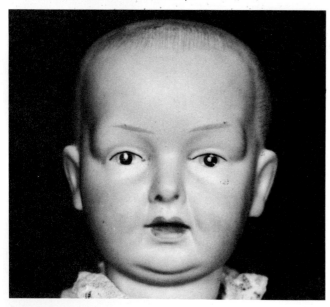

**512 & 513.** Eisenmann's "Einco" marks found on dolls' heads.

**Eisenstädt, J. (I.), & Co. (Isidor Eisenstädt).** 1895–1902. Waltershausen, Thür.; Berlin. Manufactured jointed dolls. Three German patents were obtained by members of the firm: Isidor Eisenstädt in 1899 for a walking doll; Paul Eisenstädt in 1901 for a walking doll, and Isidor Eisenstädt in 1902 for a jointed doll.

**Eisenstein & Co.** 1921. New York City. Distributed dolls.

**Eitner, Hedwig.** 1918. Leipzig, Saxony. Made dolls.

**El-Be-Co.** 1916. Trade name of dolls made by *Langrock Bros. Co.*

**Elco.** 1923–25. Trade name for *Mama Dolls* made by *L. Cohen & Son.*

**Eldridge, Stuart.** 1882–83. U.S. citizen residing in Yokohama, Japan. Obtained U.S. patent for a nursing doll with a pump in the chest and a vent at the back shoulder. The rights to this patent were assigned to *Ethel C. Hine* and *Richard W. Beyrich*.

**Elektra Toy & Novelty Co.** 1912–20. New York City. Made dolls of glue-type composition using the cold press method with collapsible molds. Used "Elektra T.N.C." as a mark on dolls.

1912: Most of their dolls had eyes glancing to the side; they included *Billy Boy*, *Jolly Jumps* (boy doll), *Goo Goo Eye Dolls*, *Laurie*, and *Amy*; the last two were a pair. Amy had a blue ribbon around her hair, as is found in the *coquette* type.

1913: There were thirty-two numbers, many of them in pairs—*Fritzi* and *Mitzi*, automobile boy and girl, *Margot* and *Frou Frou*, a Turkish boy and a Japanese girl.

1914: Copyrighted three dolls' heads, all designed by *Ferdinand Pany*. One was for a boy's head with the hair parted on the side; one was for a girl's head with a band of ribbon on her hair. The third was for a Negro doll with hair parted on the side. Advertised that their unbreakable composition was washable and sunproof. New models included *Suffragina* and *The Favorite*; prices 25¢ to $5.00.

1916: Made an all-composition doll that sold for $1.00, one of the earliest all-composition dolls made in America (see also **Sampson**). Made *Tootsie Wootsie*, price $24.00 doz. wholesale.

1917: Advertised *Chubby* with an all-composition baby body made of the same material as the heads of their stuffed-bodied dolls. They started to use the trademark *Rosy-Posy*, which they registered in the U.S. in 1918.

1920: Advertised walking dolls.

**Eléna.** 1888. Doll distributed by YOUTH'S COMPANION. Came with bisque head, open mouth, and teeth; flowing hair. Ball-jointed composition body, jointed at neck, elbows, shoulders, knees, and hips. Size 16 inches; price $1.90 including paper patterns for trousseau.

**Eleonore.** Name incised on some bisque heads made by *Simon & Halbig*. They have molded eyebrows, pierced ears, open mouth with teeth. Assembled on composition bodies by *C. M. Bergmann*.

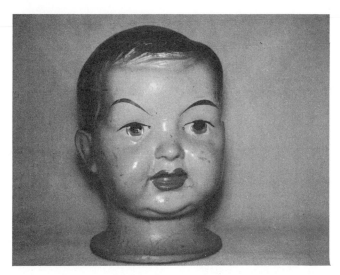

**514.** Composition head of a boy, copyrighted in 1914 and made by Elektra Toy & Novelty Co., has painted features, open-closed mouth, flange neck. Mark: Ill. **515.** H. of head, 6¾ inches. *Coleman Collection.*

## ELEKTRA T.N.C. NY
## COPYRIGHT

**515.** Mark on composition heads made by Elektra Toy & Novelty Co.

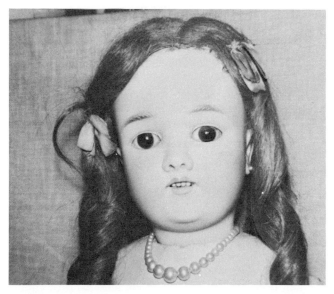

**516.** "Eleonore," name of doll made by Simon & Halbig and C. M. Bergmann; bisque head with molded eyebrows is on a jointed composition body with "Made in Germany" stamped in red on the buttocks. Mark: Ill. **517.** *Courtesy of Hildred Brinkley.*

*C.M.B.*
*SIMON & HALBIG*
*Eleonore*

**517.** "Eleonore" mark found on heads made by Simon & Halbig.

**Elfe.** 1922. Trademark registered in Germany by *Seyfarth & Reinhardt* for dolls.

**Elfie.** 1913. Trademark registered in Great Britain by John Green Hamley (See **Hamley Bros.**).

**Elfi-Kiesling-Puppe.** 1922. Trademark registered in Germany by *Kunstgewerbliche Werkstätte* for dolls.

**Eli.** Trademark of *Ernst Liebermann.*

**518.** Trademark of Ernst Liebermann.

**Elie.** 1925. Soft stuffed doll made by *Karl Müller & Co.*

**Elise.** 1910. Trade name of character girl doll made by *Kämmer & Reinhardt* as their #109; distributed by *Strobel & Wilken.* Came with bisque head and fully jointed composition body.

**Elise.** 1919. Doll made by *Jessie McCutcheon Raleigh.*

**Elite.** 1872+. Limoges, France. Name of porcelain factory established by *Bawo & Dotter.* Some of their porcelain heads were probably made at this factory.

**Elite Bébé.** See **Bébé Elite.**

**Elite Paste-Dolls.** 1902–3. Advertised by *Nerlich & Co.* Came with composition heads, painted eyelashes and teeth, glass eyes, mohair wigs, excelsior-stuffed bodies, painted shoes and stockings; wore muslin chemise trimmed with lace and ribbons. Size 23 inches; price $8.40 doz. wholesale.

**Elizabeth.** 1922. Trademark registered in U.S. by *Cosgrove Bros.* for dolls.

**Ell & Eff Doll Co.** 1917–22. New York City. Manufactured dolls.

**Ellar.** Ca. 1925. Name found on oriental infant's head made in bisque by *Armand Marseille.* Came with painted hair, closed mouth, glass eyes; cloth or composition baby body. Size "2K" was 10½ inches; size "3K" was 13½ inches.

**Ellery, Eugene, Jr.** 1922. New York City. Procured a design patent for a doll with thick lips.

**Ellis, Britton & Eaton.** 1858–69. Springfield, Vt. 1869–1925+, succeeded by Vermont Novelty Works, where the *Co-operative Manufacturing Co.* under Joel Addison Hartley Ellis made all-wooden dolls in 1873.

1858: Rodney G. Britton and Ellis M. Eaton became partners of Joel Ellis in the manufacture of children's toys.

1869: The "Price List" of Ellis, Britton & Eaton advertised that their toys were manufactured at the Vermont Novelty Works in Springfield, Vt., and distributed by Ellis & Jaquays in New York City. It is not certain that all their products were manufactured in Springfield, since their catalog includes Hill's Alphabet Blocks and Crandall's Building Blocks. Their catalog lists the following doll items:

**519.** "Ellar," oriental version of "My Dream Baby," has bisque head made by Armand Marseille. The yellow-tinted head has glass sleeping eyes and a solid crown of darkened bisque. The composition baby body has an unusual shape. Mark: Ill. **520.** *Courtesy of Ollie Leavister.*

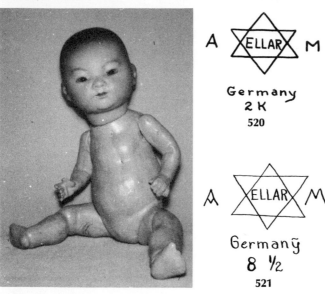

**520 & 521.** "Ellar" marks found on heads made by Armand Marseille.

China heads in eleven sizes, price 75¢ to $5.50 doz.

(These are the flat-top, high-brow type with four sew holes in the smaller sizes and six in the larger sizes.)

Dolls with linen bodies, "imitation china heads," and wooden limbs; sizes 6, 7, 8, 8½, 9½, 10½, 11, 12½, 13½, 14½, 16½, 18, 20, and 22 inches; price 50¢ to $4.20 doz.

(The imitation china heads were probably of a composition material; they resemble the later all-wood Co-operative Manufacturing Co. heads. The larger heads have six sew holes and the smaller ones four. Garters with bows were painted on the legs as well as ankle boots.)

Muslin Bodies with china limbs; eighteen sizes 3½ to 24 inches; price 40¢ to $13.50 doz.

Plain White China Dolls, eleven sizes; price 20¢ to $1.50 doz.

Wax crying dolls with fixed eyes; fourteen sizes, 7 to 28 inches; price 87¢ to $13.00 doz.

Wax dolls with moving eyes, twelve sizes 8 to 28 inches; price $1.25 to $15.00 doz.

Wax dolls with fixed eyes, curly hair and jockey hats; twelve sizes 8 to 28 inches; price $1.25 to $15.00 doz.

**Elms & Sellon.** 1910–11. New York City. Distributed rag dolls, among them the *Dollie* patented in 1893 by Char-

ity Smith, sister-in-law of *Celia Smith;* the *Life Size Doll* based on the 1900 patent of *Edgar Newell* and the 1910 patent of *Edward Gibson* for the *No-Break* rag doll. They also advertised *Foxy Grandpa.*

**Elpikbien.** 1921. Paris. Made dressed dolls. Used as their mark "C O" around a spoked wheel.

**Elsa.** 1910. Trade name for character girl doll made by *Kämmer & Reinhardt;* distributed by *Strobel & Wilken.* Came with bisque head and fully jointed composition body. (See Ill. 941.)

**Elsey, Francine.** 1925. Paris. Made dolls.

**Elsie.** 1898. Trademark registered in Germany by *Borgfeldt* for dolls.

**Elsie.** 1918. Trade name for a composition baby doll with sleeping eyes made by *Ideal Novelty & Toy Co.*

**Elsler.** See **Fanny Elsler.**

**Elsner, Emil.** 1897–1900. Berlin. Manufactured and exported dolls.

**Elsó Magyar Játékbabagyár (First Hungarian Doll Factory).** Ca. 1925. Budapest. Proprietor Gustav Ormos. Made papier-mâché dolls.

**Elwick, Mrs. Helena.** 1879. London. Made wax dolls.

**Elzer Celluloidwarenfabrik.** 1911. Wiesbaden, Germany. Made celluloid dolls and dolls' heads.

**522.** "Emaso" mark of E. Maar & Sohn.

**Emaso.** See **Maar, E., & Sohn.**

**Embossers.** Ca. 1890. Name given to highly skilled workmen who strung ball-jointed dolls with elastic.

**Em-Boss-O.** 1917. Trademark registered in U.S. by *Borgfeldt* for dolls.

**Emkay Doll Manufacturing Co.** 1917–18. Brooklyn, N.Y. Made unbreakable, fully jointed dolls, among them *Baby Marion* distributed by *Louis Wolf & Co.*

**Emma Haig.** 1924. *Celebrity Doll* originated by *Margaret Vale,* designed and made by *Jane Gray.* The doll represents Emma Haig as Cutie in George M. Cohan's play THE RISE OF ROSIE O'REILLY. It had a hand-painted face and bore a tag with a facsimile autograph of Emma Haig.

**Emmylou.** 1919–21. Trademark registered in U.S. by *Charles Bloom, Inc.* for dolls.

**Empire Art Co.** 1913. Chicago, Ill. Produced cutout rag dolls with trade name *American Beauty Doll.*

**Empire Dolhand Manufacturing Co.** 1920. New York City. Advertised that they were the world's largest manufacturer of dolls' hands.

**Empire Porcelain Pottery.** 1916–25+. Stoke-on-Trent, Staffordshire. Made dolls' heads in various sizes. Some had painted eyes and some glass eyes.

**Empress Eugenie Doll.** 1875. Name on box of doll with bisque swivel head and patented walking body marked with date of *Arthur E. Hotchkiss'* patent.

**Enamel Bisque.** 1920. Name for a type of unbreakable composition.

**Enamel Eyes.** Name given sometimes to fine eyes with parts of glass enameled together.

**Enfants de France.** See **Aux Enfants de France.**

**Engel, Robert.** 1920. Hüttensteinach near Sonneberg, Thür. Manufactured dolls.

**Engelhard, Ch.** 1885. Paris. Made dolls.

**Engelhardt (Englehardt), Hermann.** 1873–1925+. Sonneberg, Thür. Manufactured a large variety of dolls. He exhibited dolls at Vienna in 1873 and at Paris in 1900, where he was one of the Grand Prize winners.

**Engelstadt, Alexander.** 1923–25. Sonneberg, Thür., Manufactured dolls.

**English Dolls.** London, Birmingham, and Wolverhampton have been principal doll-making centers. Nearly all types of dolls have been made in England, but they are perhaps best known for fine wax dolls. *Montanari, Pierotti,* and *Bazzoni,* all with Italian-sounding surnames, lived in England in the 19th century and made some of the finest wax dolls ever produced. Jointed wooden dolls were made in England as early as the 17th century. Rag dolls of various types have also been made there for centuries. Porcelain dolls probably were made in the 19th century, but definite records have been found only for the 20th century, and most of these came from Staffordshire. Among the firms making porcelain dolls' heads were *Goss, Cauldon,* and *Empire. Meakin & Ridgeway* advertised British china, composition, kidette, and stockinet dolls in 1920. Glass eyes for dolls were made at Birmingham and Bristol, until Lauscha in Germany became the center of the industry. English mohair was used for dolls' wigs all over the world in both the 19th and 20th centuries.

Dolls representing all races were made in England, especially during the Victorian era of colonial expansion. The English particularly favored dolls dressed as brides and bridegrooms.

The 1919 PLAYTHINGS quoted the biased German viewpoint on English dolls: "England, as is her way, is attempting a huge manufacture of dolls. . . . The English doll is a piece of painted wood or a stuffed pillow enveloped in gay rags, in which one sees the painful efforts of the manufacturer to make a toy, but which must renounce its claim to any appearance of a doll. For the purchaser, such a thing is no doll. He wishes a doll, although of poor material, to be of real toy-value. The English doll has no popularity out of England. . . . Furthermore, England has always been on the lowest plane of efficiency in doll manufacture." This was written when Germany was fighting to regain her position in the doll world, which she had lost during World War I.

A few years earlier, in 1903, PLAYTHINGS reported that England spent more money on toys than all the rest of Europe put together, and that most of the toys were imported from France and Sweden.

**English Rag Doll.** See **London Rag Doll.**

**Enigma Dolls.** See **Mottschmann.**

**Eppler, Friedr.** 1895. Oberneubrunn, Germany. Manufactured dolls.

**Erhard, Stephen.** 1891. London. Made *nankeen* dolls.

**Eric.** 1913. Copyrighted by *Horsman;* artist was *Laura Gardin.* The doll had short hair.

**Erich.** See **Metzels.**

**Erika.** Name marked on *Simon & Halbig* baby doll with movable tongue; 15 inches tall.

**Erin Doll Industry.** See **Eaton, Florence Emily.**

**Erlebach, Adolph.** 1898–1904. After buying dolls in Europe for *Louis Wolf & Co.* for ten years, Erlebach established his own commission business.

**Erlicher, Gust.** See **Ehrlicher, Gust.**

**Ernst, Charles, & Hermann.** 1920–21. New York City. Sole U.S. distributor of the one hundred models of *Lenci di Scavini* character dolls.

**Ernst, Frank F., & Gorham, William H.** 1919–20. Leominster, Mass. Obtained U.S. design patent for girl doll's head with bobbed hair, side part, and bow, which they assigned to the *Yale Novelty Co.*

**Erroneous Claims.** Dolls are part of the fantasy world, and often what is written about their manufacture seems to be sheer fantasy too. It is difficult not to believe printed statements, but one must verify as much as possible the claims made in the doll world. Even primary sources are sometimes in error. This is especially true of statements regarding the "first" or "largest" one in the field. For example, *Horsman* in 1919 claimed that they were the first to produce American-made dolls commercially. Probably they had never even heard of the *Izannah Walker* dolls, the *Greiner-Lacmann* dolls, the *Joel Ellis* dolls, and the *Judge* and Early dolls. In the same year, *Isabel Million* claimed that she was the first to develop the technique for making dried-apple dolls, but *Mary McAboy*'s mother was probably making these dolls before Isabel Million was even born. Many people claimed that they made the first bisque dolls' heads in America. Such claims are further confused by the fact that an even greater number of people claimed to have made "bisque" that, in actuality, was a composition. In the 19th century there were innumerable claimants to the honor of inventing sleeping eyes for dolls, though a doll with sleeping eyes is known to have been in existence as early as 1700. The terms "French Doll" or "French Bisque" also need study. The term "French" frequently described a type rather than a geographic origin, and usually increased the price. For example, it is known that the *Edison* Phonograph dolls' heads were made by two German factories, and their bodies made in the U.S.; yet in YOUTH'S COMPANION in 1890 this doll was advertised as a "French jointed doll."

**Erste Schlesische Puppenfabrik (First Silesian Doll Factory). See Schmuckler, Heinrich.**

**Erzebirgische Spielwaren Industrie.** 1925. Schneeburg, Saxony. Made wooden dolls.

**Esanbe.** 1920. Trade name of *Schranz & Bieber Co.,* doll manufacturers.

**Escher, E., Jün. (Jr.)** 1880–1914. Sonneberg, Thür. Made and exported dolls, *Täuflinge,* dolls' heads, dolls' limbs, wool hair, and mohair for dolls.

1880: Obtained a German patent for an improved method of making papier-mâché dolls' heads.

1881: Registered in Germany his trademark of a locomotive with belching smoke, used on wooden or porcelain dolls, dolls' heads, or Täuflinge.

1891: Advertised Täuflinge.

1896: Renewed registration of his trademark in Germany.

1900: Displayed dolls at the Paris Exposition.

1908: Advertised jointed and felt dolls, dressed and undressed, from the simplest to the most elegant.

1909: Locomotive trademark used by *Fritz Bierschenk,* which suggests a connection between the two men.

**Escher, J. G., & Sohn (Son).** 1863–1925+. Sonneberg, Thür. Made dolls, dolls' heads, and dressed dolls. J. G. Escher was succeeded about 1873 by his sons, including J. G. Escher, Jr. They used "I. G. E. S." as their mark. They displayed dolls in Paris in 1900 and in St. Louis in 1904. At the former exposition, they were one of the Grand Prize group.

1924: Specialized in baby dolls and hair-stuffed dolls.

**Escher, Theodore.** 1873, Köppelsdorf, Thür. Exhibited dolls' heads at the Vienna Exhibition.

**Eshleman, Amy M.** 1921–24. Lancaster, Pa. Registered in U.S. *Aimée* as a trademark, and obtained a design patent for a barefoot toddler doll with a sunbonnet.

**Eskart, H. E., & Co.** 1908–14. London. Distributor for *Carl Max & Co.*

**Eski Dollie.** 1919–20. Trademark registered in U.S. by *Murdock MacKay Graham.* Name was affixed to the doll with a printed label.

**523.** Trademark of E. Escher.

**Eskimo.** See **Esquimo Dolls**; also **Felt Dolls**.

**Eskimo Dolls.** 1897. Distributed by *John D. Zernitz Co.* Came with bisque heads, glass eyes, jointed bodies covered with white fur. Six-inch size cost $1.50 doz. wholesale; 14-inch size cost $17.00 doz. wholesale. Similar 6-inch Eskimo dolls with painted eyes were advertised by *Butler Bros.* in 1910.

**Eskimo Dolls.** 1909–10. Made by *Aetna Doll & Toy Co.;* distributed by *Horsman,* to celebrate the discovery of the North Pole.

**Eskimo Dolls.** 1915. U.S. design patent obtained by *William Hofacker.*

**Eskridge, Belle C.** 1916. Houston, Texas. Obtained U.S. design patent for doll with eyes glancing to the side.

**Esparza, Ybo.** 1888. Madrid, Spain. Doll distributor; procured a French patent for painting papier-mâché dolls so that they resembled porcelain, by means of a combination of superimposed layers and the use of talc.

**Espiègles.** 1919. Trademark registered in France by *Georges de Roussy de Sales* for movable eyes for dolls.

**Esquimo.** See **Eskimo Dolls**.

**Esquimo Dolls.** 1904. All-bisque dolls dressed in downy white fur costumes with harpoons; size 8 inches, price 50¢.

**Esquimo Dolls.** 1918–19. Had celluloid face, jointed limbs; size 9½ inches.

**Esther.** Early 20th century. Name found on china heads.

**Esther.** 1920's. Name found on a rag doll made of oilcloth. On the back of the leg is the following mark: "ESTHER STARRING // Penny Ross" (see **Ross, Penny**).

**Esther Doll.** 1920. Trade name of doll produced by *Alisto Manufacturing Co.;* size 12 inches.

**Estivalet, Mme.** 1870–78. Paris. Made dolls. Estivalet & Martin showed "porcelain families" at the 1878 Paris Exposition.

**Esy.** 1919. Trademark of *Elise Suchetzky,* née Schmidt, registered in Germany.

**Ethel.** See **Pet Name**.

**Etoile Bébé.** 1904–6. Trademark registered in France by *Bernheim & Kahn,* manufacturers of dolls and bébés. A French lady doll has been reported as marked "*Eden Bébé,* Etoile Bébé."

**Eugenic Baby.** 1914–15. Composition-bodied doll made by *Fair Amusement Co.;* had painted hair in 1914; came in three sizes in 1915.

**Eur Dolls.** 1925. Trade name used by *European Doll Manufacturing Co.;* dolls priced 25¢, 50¢, $1.00, and $5.00.

**524 & 525.** "Etoile Bébé" marks of Bernheim & Kahn.

**Eureka Doll Co.** 1923–24. New York City. Manufactured dolls.

**Eureka Société Anonyme.** 1911–12. Paris. Manufactured bébés; capital $200,000.

**European Doll Manufacturing Co.** 1921–25. New York City. Handled unbreakable character dolls made in America. They came with or without wigs in sizes 16, 22, and 27 inches; priced 25¢ to $5.00. Used *Eur* as a trade name.

**Evaline.** 1919. Copyrighted by *F. W. Lapp.* Artist was *Jeno Juszko.* Nude cherub doll with molded hair, eyes glancing to the side, jointed at shoulders, bent arms, feet together.

**Evans, Joseph, & Sons.** 1868–81. London. Manufacturers and importers. Dolls with wax heads have been found with the mark of this company on their cloth bodies.

**Evelyn.** 1919. Trade name of doll made by *Jessie Mc-Cutcheon Raleigh;* distributed by *Butler Bros.* Came in sizes 11½ and 13½ inches; priced $2.90 and $3.70.

**Eveno, M.** 1920–25. Paris. Handled *La Parisienne* dolls in boxes and candy-box dolls made of cotton wadding.

**Everrest.** 1925. Trademark registered in Britain by *William Seelig* for dolls.

**Evers, P.** 1918. Hamburg, Germany. Made dolls.

**Eversweets.** 1921. Bisque-head, jointed composition-body dolls made by *Progressive Toy Co.* Came in sizes 14, 16, 20, and 24 inches.

**Excelcior.** 1921. Trade name for dolls with cork-stuffed bodies and with composition heads and limbs made by *E. Goldberger;* priced at 25¢ to $5.00.

**Excelsior.** 1868–70. Trade name used by *George H. Hawkins* for bonnet frames; also name found on dolls' heads. Some Hawkins' dolls' heads were marked "X.L.C.R.," which phonetically spells "Excelsior." They were of rag but resembled papier-mâché heads, and their shape duplicated some of the untinted bisque heads. In 1893 *Butler Bros.* advertised "XLCR" dolls with "patent washable heads," glass eyes, wigs; clothes included a flaring bonnet. Sizes 15, 17½, and 19 inches; prices 25¢ to 50¢.

**Excelsior.** 1892–1912. Name stamped in red on the back of jointed composition bodies, which were patented by *Kestner* in 1892 and patent amended in 1893 (patent #70685).

1905: Kestner made "Excelsior" bisque-limb dolls, distributed by *Butler Bros.* Came with flesh-tinted head and arms. Legs painted white to represent stockings and black to represent shoes. Size 6 inches; price 42¢ doz. wholesale.

526. Joseph Evans' mark stamped on dolls.

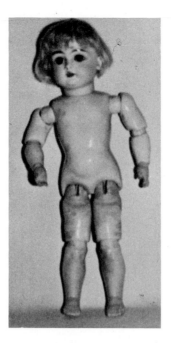

Excelsior
D.R.P. No 70686
Germany

528. "Excelsior" mark stamped in red on Kestner bodies.

**527A & B.** Kestner head on patented "Excelsior" body. Kestner secured patent in 1893 for a ball-jointed composition body. Marks: head, "B Made in Germany 6"; body III. **528.** H. 12 inches. *Courtesy of Jessica Norman.*

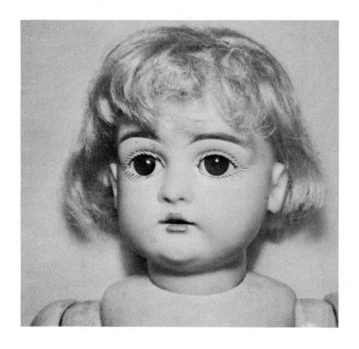

1910: Butler Bros. advertised "Excelsior" bisque-head dolls made by Kestner. Came with turning head, sleeping eyes, open mouth with teeth, sewed curly wigs; bodies were "French jointed," made of hardened layers of paper with ball joints at shoulders, elbows, wrists, hips, and knees; separated fingers. Dolls bore the Crown tag, and came in sizes 14½, 17½, 20, 21½, 24, 27, 31, 33, and 36 inches; priced 72¢ to $8.00 each. Also, sizes 22½, 25, and 29 inches came with real hair eyebrows and eyelashes; priced $2.40, $3.35, and $4.00 each. Socket heads for these dolls were sold separately for about a third of the total price of the doll.

**Excelsior.** 1911–15. Trade name of dolls distributed by *Louis Wolf & Co.* These could be the *Kestner* Excelsior dolls, but it is not known for certain that Wolf handled Kestner dolls.

**Excelsior.** 1920. Trade name of dolls made by *Gem Toy Co.*; priced at 25¢ to $1.00.

**Excelsior Bébé.** 1916–21. Handled by J. Ortiz and H. Delcourt, both successors of *Gesland.* Ortiz registered the name as a trademark in France in 1916. It was used for a line of dressed and undressed bébés and for rigid and semi-articulated dolls that were dressed or undressed. These dolls and bébés, made entirely in France, were largely for export.

**Excelsior Toy Manufacturing Co.** 1917. New York City. Made dolls.

**Export Industries.** 1924–25. Saxony. Listed in Export Directory under Doll Artists.

**Exposition Doll & Toy Manufacturing Co.** 1921–24. New York City. Specialized in *Mama Dolls.*

**Expression.** 1918. Trademark registered in France by *Georges de Roussy de Sales* for dolls' heads.

**Ey, Victor.** 1920. New York City. Secured a U.S. design patent for a cherub-type doll.

**Eye Color.** Black or very dark brown eyes predominated among early wooden and wax dolls, although a few light blue glass eyes are found on late 18th-century wooden dolls. Dolls with heads of molded cardboard and blue "enamel" eyes were advertised around 1810. Black pupilless glass eyes were used throughout the 19th century, but to a smaller extent as time progressed. Bisque dolls' heads, even those made in the 20th century, sometimes have the black pupil-less eyes. But during most of the 19th century, blue eyes predominated. On china heads, brown eyes are relatively rare and violet eyes are exceedingly scarce. Many different shades of blue eyes are found, and the variation may be attributed to different decorative techniques or to changes over the years.

There was more variation in the color of glass eyes, especially in the last few decades of the 19th century. Hazel eyes are mentioned in 1867, and in 1873 violet eyes were said to be "still the favorite." In 1877, HARPER'S BAZAR, December 29, stated: "For years blue-eyed dolls were most popular; last year gray-eyed dolls began to rival the blue-eyed blondes; and this winter some of the most popular heads have brown eyes, and there are perfect brunettes with jet black eyes." In 1880 black, brown, palest blue, and darkest violet eyes are recorded in HARPER'S BAZAR. By 1885 dark hazel eyes were most in favor, but violet eyes were also popular as well as blue and brown. YOUTH'S COMPANION chose a blue-eyed doll in 1890 and brown-eyed *Vera* in 1892 for its premium dolls. Light gray was a fashion-

**529.** Painted and molded blue eyes on a bisque bald head with wig and pierced ears. Note the highlight and the usual placing of the pupil near the top of the iris. *Collection of the late Laura Sturges; photograph by Winnie Langley.*

**530.** Papier-mâchè head with black pupil-less glass eyes, ca. 1850's, has molded hair in sausage curls like those worn by girls; cloth body. *Courtesy of Winnie Langley; photograph by Winnie Langley.*

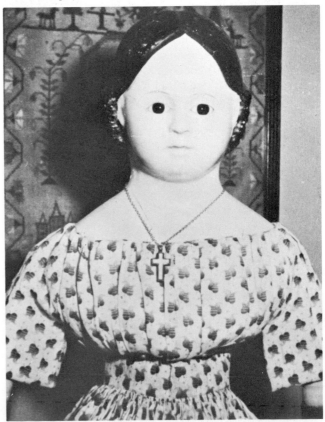

**C1.** Wooden boy made by Schoenhut. H. 19 inches. (See Ill. 1473.) *Courtesy of The Smithsonian Institution.*

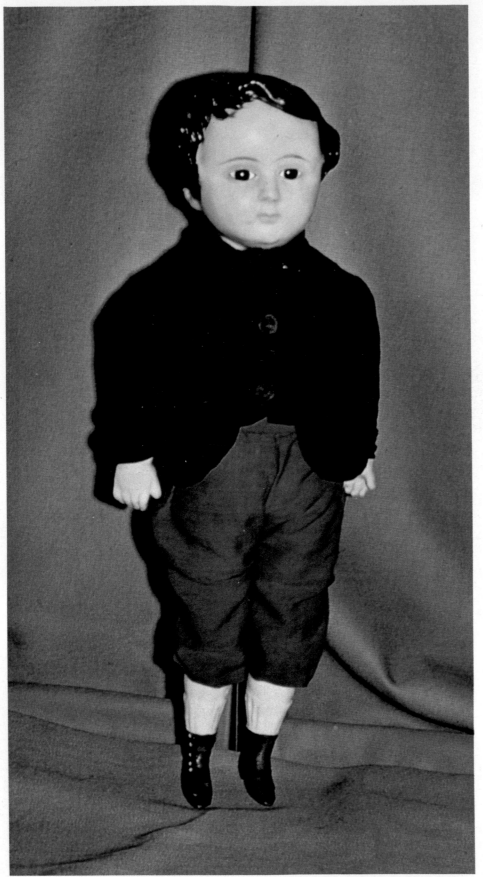

**C3.** Wax-over-composition boy. He came in a glass and wooden case similar to those of the memorial dolls found in some European churches. (See Ill. 1671.) *Coleman Collection.*

**C2.** Hand-carved wooden head and limbs on cloth body. Carved hair with bun at upper back of head. Dressed in original clothes as a 17th-century Swiss servant, but may have been made as late as the 20th century. Original tag reads "Servante // Bernoise // 17 siècle," and on other side has a printed white cross on a red shield over "S. G. F. Bern." H. 18 inches. *Courtesy of The Smithsonian Institution.*

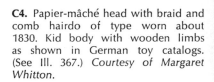

**C4.** Papier-mâché head with braid and comb hairdo of type worn about 1830. Kid body with wooden limbs as shown in German toy catalogs. (See Ill. 367.) *Courtesy of Margaret Whitton.*

**C5.** Dolls dressed as court servants, brought from Russia in 1870. Composition heads and limbs, cloth bodies, original clothes. The nurse wears a coin dowry with at least three different designs: a double eagle, "Modes // Paris" in a wreath, and a Greek woman's head. H. 12½ inches. *Courtesy of The Smithsonian Institution.*

**C6.** Dolls with composition shoulder heads. Doll with glass eyes has a rectangular paper sticker on back: "INDESTRUCTIBLE // DOLLHEAD // No. 4." H. 18½ inches. For "Gold Medal" and Greiner dolls, see Ills. 652 and 693. Boy with wig, unmarked, has features similar to those of "Gold Medal" and "Indestructible" heads. H. 14½ inches. *Courtesy of Alberta Darby and Coleman Collection.*

C7. Rag dolls of the early 1900's, in original clothes. The Brückner doll is dressed in a sailor suit. (For mark, see Ill. 253.) H. 13½ inches. Foxy Grandpa, designed by Carl Schultz, is 11½ inches. Dolly Varden has lithographed paper face and was made without arms. H. 8¾ inches. *Coleman Collection.*

C8. Babyland Rag doll made by Horsman, dressed in original Dutch costume with wooden shoes. H. 14½ inches. *Courtesy of Margaret Whitton.*

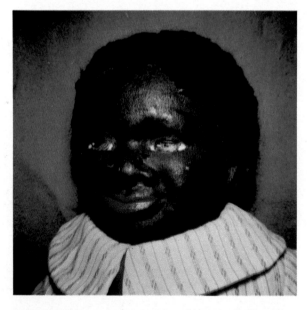

C9. Rag doll made by Martha Chase, probably one of the "Pickanninies." *Courtesy of the International Doll Library Foundation.*

**C10.** China head with long corkscrew curls at the sides and back. *Courtesy of Margaret Whitton.*

**C11.** Brown-eyed china-headed doll with fifteen corkscrew curls, cloth body, shiny bisque hands. H. 28 inches. *Courtesy of The Smithsonian Institution.*

**C12.** All-ceramic dolls ca. 1860–ca. 1920. China Frozen Charlottes are similar except for their hairdos. H. 4½ inches. All-bisque boy in center is 4½ inches. Dolls (marked "Nippon") with molded clothes are "Dolly" with the diamond-shaped paper sticker and a doll that resembles "Baby Bud" (both 3½ inches tall). *Courtesy of Alberta Darby and Coleman Collection.*

**C13.** Lady doll, with bisque shoulder head marked "4" and a kid body, has long curls in back. Dressed in original Danish costume. H. 18 inches. *Courtesy of The Smithsonian Institution.*

**C14.** Bisque-headed brides in original clothes. At left is a doll of the 1870's (see Ill. 409). H. 11½ inches. Center doll, of the 1880's, has painted eyes, bisque limbs, and a cloth body. H. 8 inches. Doll at right is early 20th century (see Ill. 1060). H. 12 inches. *Coleman Collection.*

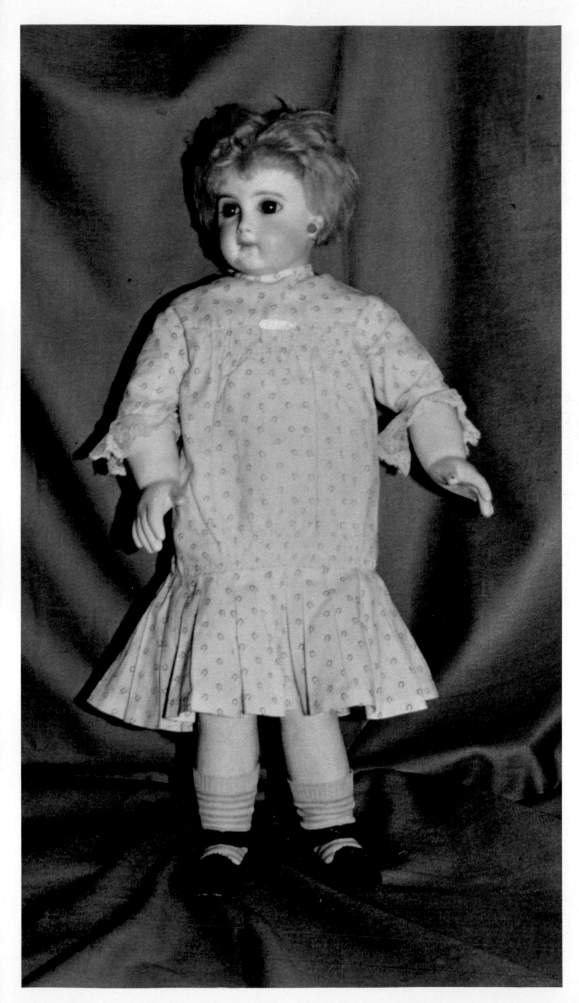

**C15.** Bébé Jumeau with original tag and clothes. This doll and its twin (Ill. 910), bought in Paris, came with matching wardrobes. The applied ears have canals impressed into the head. H. 22 inches. *Courtesy of The Smithsonian Institution.*

**C16.** Bébé Schmitt bisque head (see Ill. 1451). H. 16 inches. *Coleman Collection.*

**C18.** Bisque head is marked: "Armand Marseille // Germany // 390 // A.2¹/₂M." Label on the clothes reads "E U" Juvos E'zone Greece." H. 19 inches. *Courtesy of The Smithsonian Institution.*

**C17.** Bisque head made by Kley & Hahn in the 20th century. The socket head, without shoulder plate, is on a cloth body. Original Latvian costume is that of an unmarried girl. Mark: "Walkure // Germany // 2/0." H. 15 inches. *Courtesy of The Smithsonian Institution.*

**C19.** Bisque-headed dolls on composition bodies. Boy marked: "Made in Germany // Florodora // A 5/0 M." H. 11½ inches. Girl marked: "K[star]R // Simon & Halbig // 126 // 23." She wears original provincial costume, and is 10 inches tall. *Courtesy of Alberta Darby.*

**C23.** Dolls with bisque heads and arms on cloth bodies, dressed as Roman peasants. Both 10½ inches tall. *Courtesy of The Smithsonian Institution.*

**C20.** Bébé Jumeau on the left; in the center "Mein Liebling" (see Ill. 1241). Doll at right with metal hands is believed to have been made by Petit & Dumontier. *Courtesy of the International Doll Library Foundation.*

**C21.** Bisque heads on composition-bodied dolls dressed in original clothes. Doll at left wears a Württemberg costume. H. 12½ inches. Right doll wears Gutach costume of the Black Forest, and is marked: "269 // DEP." Paper sticker in wig reads "Made in Germany." H. 12 inches. Center doll wears costume of a Cologne peasant, and is marked: "RX-4/0." H. 13 inches. *Courtesy of The Smithsonian Institution.*

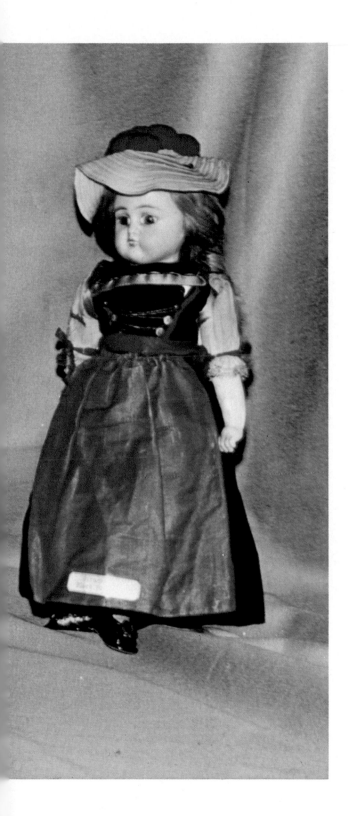

**C22.** Doll with wax head and limbs, dressed in original bridal costume, has inserted hair (see Ill. 1667). H. 23 inches. *Courtesy of Lester & Alice Grinnings.*

**C24.** Dolls with bisque heads and composition bodies. *Top:* Long type of face on Jumeau body, which also carries Simonne label. *Middle, left:* "Mein Liebling," marked as in Ill. 1241; formerly in the collection of Clara Fawcett. *Right:* S.F.B.J. #236, dressed in original clothes, marked "Au Nain Bleu." *Bottom, left:* K[star]R #126 baby in original clothes, just as received on Christmas, 1920, by Dorothy Coleman. *Right:* S.F.B.J. #227. (See Ills. 51, 946, 1540, 1555.) *Courtesy of Lester & Alice Grinnings, Alberta Darby, Coleman Collection.*

able color for dolls' eyes in 1910, but blue or brown eyes still predominated.

**Eye Makers.** Those not listed elsewhere include:
Edm. Edelmann, 1918, Neufang, Thür.
Leonh. Eichhorn, Jün., 1918, Sonneberg, Thür.
Goldmann & Cordts, 1925, Lauscha, Thür.
Gould-Baum, 1920, New York City.
A. Greiner, 1918–25+, Waltershausen, Thür.
Peter Eduard Greiner, 1909–20, Lauscha, Thür.
Harley, 1920, St. Maur, France.
E. Köhler, 1918, Waltershausen, Thür.
F. Köhler, 1918, Waltershausen, Thür.
Louis Köhler, 1897, Lauscha, Thür.
C. Laurent & Cie., 1921, Paris.
Osk. Liebermann, 1918, Sonneberg, Thür.
Josef Greiner Matzen Sohn, 1891, Lauscha, Thür.
Uri Ludwig Müller, before 1897, Lauscha, Thür.; he claimed he was the oldest maker of glass eyes in Lauscha.
Müller-Kuller, 1897–1920, Lauscha, Thür.
Overland Metal Novelty Co., 1923–25, New York City.
Pioneer Novelty Manufacturing Co., 1916–24, U.S. Made celluloid eyes.
G. Schoepfer, 1915–22, U.S.
Frederick Schumacker, 1892–1925+, Jersey City, N.J.
There were three makers in Steinheid, Germany, in 1925.

**Eye Materials.** Many dolls have painted eyes, but even more dolls have their eyes inserted as a separate part. Heads of nearly all materials can be found with painted eyes. Early clay dolls had chiefly painted eyes. Wooden dolls usually had painted or glass eyes. In the 20th century, *Schoenhut* used wooden balls decorated with decals and inserted in the eye sockets. Rag dolls usually had painted eyes, but sometimes the eyes were embroidered. For example, Queen Victoria, about 1832, had a few dolls' babies whose eyes were indicated by cross-stitches. Wax dolls generally had glass eyes, but often on early ones there were eyes made of wax beads. Fine bisque dolls of the 1870's or 1880's occasionally had the eyes painted with an enamel that made them outstanding. Glass eyes were seldom used in china heads, but were used to a large extent in bisque heads. (See Ill. 531.)

Allegedly, glass eyes for dolls originated in Birmingham, England, and large quantities were exported from there as late as the 1860's. A paperweight manufacturer of Bristol, England, also produced "paperweight" type of glass eyes for dolls. The process for this was invented about 1849; it reached its height of perfection in the French glass dolls' eyes of the late 19th century. Mons. *Blampoix* obtained a French patent in 1855 to use glass or enamel eyes in porcelain dolls' heads. French glass eyes were advertised in 1920 by *Morimura Bros.*

Although theirs were not as fine as the French glass eyes, Germany produced by far the largest number. A few glass dolls' eyes were made in America as early as 1892. *Louis Amberg* started to use glass eyes in his "unbreakable" character dolls' heads in 1911. When World War I broke out and German glass eyes were no

**531A & B.** Elaborately coiffured bisque head has convex glazed eyes, a molded yoke, café-au-lait-colored hair. Body is cloth, lower limbs china. Original dress is salmon pink silk taffeta. H. 17 inches. H. of shoulder head, 4 inches. *Courtesy of the Newark Museum, Newark, N.J.*

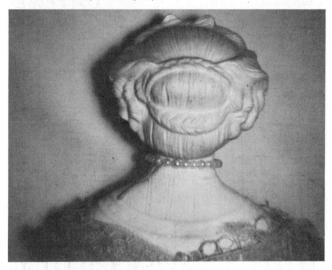

longer available, substitutes were tried. In 1915 *Ideal* advertised "imitation glass eyes." These may have been the metal and/or celluloid eyes that were used as wartime substitutes. In 1906 *Ernst Reinhardt* had obtained a German patent for sleeping dolls' eyes of celluloid, and used celluloid eyes in the bisque heads he produced here in America during World War I. Other doll manufacturers are also known to have used celluloid eyes then. The celluloid over metal eyes, patented by *Samuel Marcus* in 1918, were used in *Fulper* heads and probably in other heads handled by *Horsman*. Molded porcelain eyes were made both in France and in the U.S., probably during the period of wartime scarcity. (See also **G. D. Green.**)

The shortage of material in Germany limited the manufacture of glass dolls' eyes for several years after the end of the war. In 1919, Germany was forced to use painted cherry stones as a substitute, but toward the end of 1920 Germany was exporting glass eyes to America. Besides the many substances already enumerated, dolls' eyes have been made out of buttons, beads, tacks, patches of cloth, jewels, and other objects and materials.

**Eye Movement.** More patents have been obtained for the movement of eyes than for any other doll item. The "inventors" of movable sleep eyes are innumerable. *Kestner* claimed that he invented them about 1860. Many authorities state that *Herr Stier* invented sleeping eyes operated by a lead weight, but no date has been found as yet. The 1824 French patent drawing of *Jean Maelzel* shows a weight attached to the doll's eye, which presumably controlled movement. However, moving eyes were far earlier than any of these. In March, 1700, Dr. Claver Morris of Wells, England, wrote that he had purchased for his three-year-old daughter a wax baby with an invention to turn its eyes.

Wax dolls with eyes moved by a wire at the waist of the doll were made in the 19th century. These are referred to by collectors as "wire-eyed wax dolls." *Jules Steiner* of Paris in 1880 obtained French and German patents for moving the glass eyes of a bisque doll's head by means of a wire that protruded from the side of the doll's head—a device that he claimed was an improvement over the counterweights used up to that time. By 1885 *Jumeau* had worked out a "half spherical" eye that would enable his bébé to raise and lower its eyes at will. He patented in France in 1885 an eyelid that dropped over the eyeball, but he had trouble with the space that was left after the eyelid moved up, and in 1886 he obtained another French patent to eliminate this space.

One of the earliest known patents for eyes that move from side to side, which collectors call "flirting eyes," was obtained by *Simon and Halbig* in Germany in 1890, but papier-mâché heads with this type of eye were made much earlier. In 1903, some German dolls' eyes could be locked in either the sleeping or waking position by means of a spring in the back of the doll's head. A 1906 patent made it possible for a doll to wink its eyes when a string was pulled. The year 1907 brought two patented improvements. One was for a moving eye device made so that the eyes could not drop back into the head; the other patent was for eyelashes attached to movable lids so that when dolls closed their eyes, they did not leave the lashes on their foreheads. The 1909 invention of a fastening wire to secure the eyes to the doll's head, and thus prevent breakage in transit, probably explains some of the holes found at the back of the neck. (See Ills. 587 and 589.)

PLAYTHINGS, January, 1911, p. 128, reports: "One of the most important features of the 1911 character dolls is the excellent line of 'sleepers,' which appear for the first time in character dolls. . . . They have glass eyes of brown or blue which open and shut, thus giving the finishing touch to the natural attractiveness of the character doll." A 1911 Christmas advertisement mentions "Dolls that wink, Dolls that blink, Dolls that only stare." In 1912 a knob at the back of the doll's head made it possible to turn the eyes into any desired position, even to make the doll cross-eyed or wall-eyed.

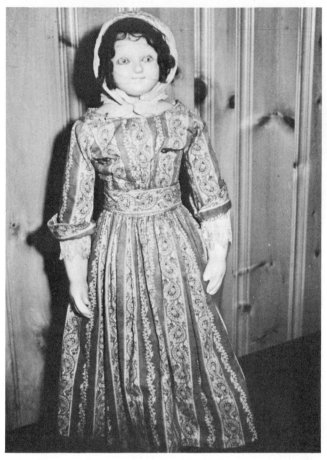

**532.** Glass eyes that open and shut by moving a wire protruding from the body; head is wax over papier-mâché. H. 29 inches. *Courtesy of Frances Walker; photograph by Winnie Langley.*

**533.** Brown-haired doll with moving glass eyes in a poured wax head; has wax arms with grommets, and wears contemporary red dress and hat. *Courtesy of Marion Holt; photograph by Winnie Langley.*

Another 1912 patent used a drum with multiple pairs of eyes. When the doll's position changed, the drum rotated and different pairs of eyes were visible. By 1913 sleeping eyes were made so that they would also turn to the right or left depending on the position in which the doll was held. The following year, 1914, brought other innovations—namely, a doll that would open and shut its eyes when its arm was moved toward or away from its head, and a U.S. patent by *Ernst Reinhardt* whereby eyes were pivoted so that the color could be changed and the eyes then locked into position.

In 1920 *Ideal* claimed that in 1914 they had made the first American moving eyes. A characteristic of the eyes used by this company was that each eye operated independently. In 1915 the *Non-Breakable Doll Company* claimed that they were pioneers in making American dolls with indestructible sleeping eyes. *Schoenhut* patented sleeping eyes for their all-wood dolls in 1921. There were many other patents for movable eyes, but either they were similar to ones listed above or there is no record found as yet of their commercial use.

**Eyebrows, Painted.** Various decorative techniques were used. Sometimes eyebrows were molded and painted; some were painted in different ways—by curved lines or dots, or were feathered, striated, two-toned, etc. It also appears that decals were occasionally used for eyebrows, especially on bisque heads.

**Eyebrows of Hair.** 1909–16. Patented in U.S. and Germany by *Louis Steiner* and assigned to *Borgfeldt.* Two long holes were made in the bisque heads, which were usually produced by *Kestner,* and the hair was positioned to protrude through these holes to represent eyebrows. Other manufacturers often glued the hair to an indentation in the bisque, in order to make hair eyebrows. These eyebrows were used on both socket-type and breastplate bisque heads, although in 1912 it was noted that the kid-body dolls with hair eyebrows were the most popular. Dolls with hair eyebrows were priced at 50¢ and up.

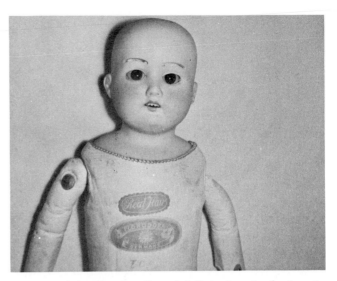

**535.** One of the Florodora line of dolls having slits for inserting hair eyebrows. Bisque shoulder head is on a kid body; two paper labels on the chest read "Real Hair" and "Florodora // Germany." Head mark: Ill. **594.** H. 18 inches. *Courtesy of Dorothy Annunziato.*

1916: Kestner shoulder heads with natural hair eyebrows came in sizes 4½, 4¾, 5, 5¾, 6¼, 7, 7½, and 8¼ inches; price was $18.00 to $84.00 doz. wholesale, including curly sewed mohair wig.

**Eyelashes, Painted.** Usually both upper and lower lashes were painted on dolls with stationary eyes, except on china dolls. These seldom had painted lashes, but when they did, generally they had only lower lashes. Sleeping-eyed dolls also usually have only lower lashes.

**Eyelashes of Hair.** 18th century–1925+. Hair eyelashes were used on wax dolls as early as the 18th century. Though early eyelashes were frequently made of silk or a bird's quill cut into two pieces, by 1900 they were largely of hair. Before 1909, a narrow eyelash ribbon was usually made and cut through the center to produce

**534.** Doll with real hair eyebrows, as patented by Louis Steiner for Borgfeldt. Bisque head, made by Kestner, is on a jointed composition body. Mark on head: Ill. **993.** H. 25½ inches. *Coleman Collection.*

**536.** Untinted bisque with painted eyelashes, blue glass eyes, molded blonde hair, and pierced ears. Note that the head is turned. *Courtesy of Freda Hawkins; photograph by Winnie Langley.*

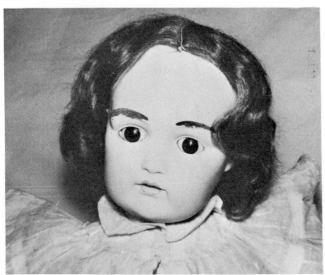

an eyelash with a braid foundation. Some dolls have the word *Wimpern* on them, which simply means "eyelashes" in German.

**Eynard.** 1864. Paris. Made dolls.

# F

**F. & M. Novelty Co.** 1920–25. New York City. Made moving glass eyes for dolls.

**F. A. O. Schwarz.** See **Schwarz.**

**Fabco Dolls.** 1917. Trade name for all-fabric jointed dolls made by *Utley Co.* Came with wigs.

**Faber, N.** 1909. Wildenheid near Sonneberg, Thür. Made dolls' bodies.

**Fabriken Bernhard & Co.** 1904. Berlin. Obtained a German patent for a metal-spring jointed doll.

**Fabrik-Marke (Fabrikmarke).** Word for "trademark" in German. (See also **Schutz Marke.**)

**Faces.** Dolls' faces are as varied as those of people. Even when dolls are made from the same mold, there are often slight differences due to the fact that each face is usually painted by hand. The faces of dolls often reflect the fashions in beauty at various periods and in various parts of the world. The most appealing faces were usually designed by people who had already achieved fame in the art world or were inspired by masterpieces of art.

As early as 1903, PLAYTHINGS stated that a line of dolls had faces modeled from those of real American babies. The women who painted dolls' faces at that time had previously gained experience by coloring photograph portraits.

The shape of the doll's face and neck usually indicates the age of the person it represents. A round chubby face with a short neck certainly indicates a baby doll; long pointed features and a long neck represent an adult doll. Similar techniques in the painting of the face may show that certain dolls were made in the same factory or in the same period. However, analysis of these techniques requires considerable study and access to large numbers of similar-type dolls. Amateurs—beware!

**Faddy Fads (Faddies).** 1914. Trade name for imported dolls that looked like meal bags tied in the middle. Came with composition heads, big blue eyes, large orange-colored feet; dressed in red and white or blue and white stripes as a girl, boy, clown, or sailor. Price 50¢, $1.00, $1.50, and $2.00.

**Fad-Ette.** 1923. Trade name of one of the fabric dolls made by *E. Scavini* and distributed in America by *Charles Ernst.*

**Fahlbusch, F. A.** 1892–98, Cincinnati; 1896–98, known as Cincinnati Doll Factory; manufactured dolls.

**Fahle, Hermann.** See **Ilgner, E.**

**Fair Amusement Co.** 1914. New York City. Advertised *Babee, Import Dolls,* which were made in the U.S., and *The Eugenic Baby,* "the first all-composition doll made in America." This last statement was erroneous, since *Louis Amberg & Son* had made an all-composition doll as early as 1909, and others had also made them before 1914.

**Fair & Carnival Trading Co.** 1914. New York City. Was assigned a design patent for a doll by *Samuel Haskell.*

**Fair Doll Manufacturing Co.** 1921. Made dolls.

**Fair Trading Co.** 1921–25. New York City. Manufactured and distributed dolls.

**Fairy.** 1911–15. Copyrighted by *Horsman,* who also registered the name as a trademark in the U.S.; designed by *Helen Trowbridge* as a doll. It represented the Fairy figure in the advertisements for Little Fairy Soap made by N. K. Fairbanks Co. and under their license. The doll had blue eyes and golden curls; wore a white cape and hood with a bunch of violets at the waist. Eyes looked straight ahead. Price $8.50 doz. wholesale.

**Fairy.** 1918. Trade name of all-rubber, undressed girl doll made by *Faultless Rubber Co.* in red and tan colors.

**Fairy Kid, The.** 1916. Trademark registered in Germany by *Peter Scherf* firm.

**Fairyland Doll Co.** 1903–9. Factory at Plainfield, N.J.; studio at Portsmouth, N.H. Made Fairyland Rag Dolls, distributed by *Borgfeldt* and *Ferguson.* "Fairyland" registered as a trademark in U.S. by *Mary Foote* in 1909.

1904: Came in seven sizes and nineteen styles.

1905: Dolls wore removable clothing to which was attached a label of the National Consumers' League. Dolls were marked with a round tag. The 15-inch size, which included a clown, cost $1.00.

1906: Sizes 15, 18, 21, 25, and 30 inches; price $1.00 to $4.00.

1907: Twenty styles.

1909: Dolls had hand-painted faces, wore fashionable dresses with a paper tag on the dresses as a label.

**Faith.** 1916. An American Art Doll representing a Quaker girl, distributed by *Strobel & Wilken;* character doll with painted hair and eyes. It resembled *Käthe Kruse* dolls.

**Falck & Roussel (Falck, Adolphe).** 1880–1902. Paris. Made dolls and composition-bodied bébés.

1880: Won a silver medal at the Melbourne Exhibition. They were No. 31 of the members of the *Chambre Syndicale des Fabricants de Jouets Français.*

1885: Registered two trademarks in France. One was

*Bébé Mignon* and the other had the letters "F. R." on it with the picture of an animal.

1886: Produced 205,000 dolls.

1887: Produced 425,000 dolls.

1888: Produced 555,000 dolls and won another silver medal at Melbourne Exhibition.

1889: Produced 643,000 dolls.

1890: Advertised Bébé Mignon and said that they were the first French maker of composition-bodied bébés; if this is true, they must have been making them before 1880.

1895–1902: Advertised Bébé Mignon as the only bébé that would not come apart; light in weight; specialized in dolls for export.

**Family of Dolls. See Dolls' House Dolls; Stair-Step Family.**

**Famlee Dolls.** 1918–25+. Trademark registered in U.S. by *Berg Bros.* in 1924; advertised by *Berwick Doll Co.* Came in four sets, each having one body with a threaded plug neck and three, five, seven, or twelve heads with sockets to fit. Heads could be interchanged with only two turns. They included such characters as a baby, Chinese boy, crying child, clown, soldier boy, Pierrette, a colored boy, Indian girl, Dutch girl, Dutch boy, French girl, sailor boy, sailor girl, Susie Bumps, Dolly Dimple, a nurse, and a commander. There were special costumes included to match each head. The dolls walked and talked, were 16 inches tall, and sold for $6.00 to $20.00 a set. Additional heads and costumes could be bought separately for $1.25 each. Dolls were based on U.S. patent granted to *David Wiener* in 1921. (See also **Change-O-Doll Co.**)

**Famous Doll Studio.** 1906–22. New York City. Manufactured dolls.

1916: Advertised *Sani-Doll*, modeled by well-known sculptor; price 50¢ to $2.00.

**Fanfois.** 1918. Trademark registered in France by *Mme. Poulbot.*

**Fanny Elsler.** 1844. Portrait doll of the famous ballet dancer, made by *Aug. Poppe* and displayed at the Berlin Exhibition.

**Fany.** Name found on some dolls made by *Armand Marseille.* The mold number is 231; the doll came in several sizes.

**Farmer.** Ca. 1908. Wooden doll with rubber joints made by *Schoenhut;* mate to the *Milk Maid.*

**Farmer Kids.** 1915. Made by *Ideal Novelty & Toy Co.*

**Fashion Dolls.** These were usually dolls distributed abroad to show current fashions in European capitals. Having the latest fashion from Paris (or Dijon when Burgundy was powerful) was of the utmost importance to the European nobility. Fashion dolls were permitted to pass from court to court even when the sovereigns

537. Mark used by Falck-Roussel.

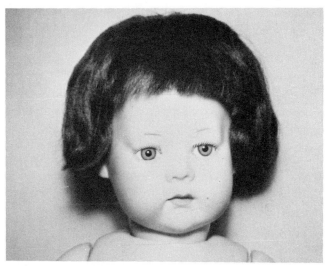

**538A & B.** "Fany," a bisque character-faced doll. The head, made by Armand Marseille, has sleeping eyes, closed mouth. Mark: Ill. **539.** H. 13 inches. *Coleman Collection.*

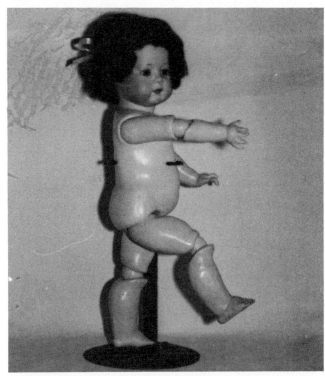

539. "Fany" mark found on heads made by Armand Marseille.

were at war, until the time of Napoleon I. The use of dolls to show fashions actually dates back many centuries. They were used especially before the advent of fashion magazines. Around 1850, Mons. Natalis Rondot wrote: "The cloak and the dress of a little doll costing but 20 cents are perfectly correct reproductions of our newest fashions. . . . The doll is hurried off to the provinces and often to foreign lands as patron of the fashions; she has even become an indispensable accessory for all the latest novelties and it is now the case that without a doll, merchants would find it difficult to sell their wares. The first cloaks that were sent to India were worn by the ladies of Calcutta on their heads, like mantillas, until the doll-models arrived to show the fashion."

In 1897 *Jumeau* advertised: "The most expensive dolls including those sent to England, Spain and Germany every year as fashion models are fully dressed at the Jumeau warehouse in the rue Pastourelle." As late as 1910, PLAYTHINGS reported that an "old fashion was revived last winter of sending dainty dolls to show latest Paris fashion." In the 19th and early 20th centuries fashion dolls were made by Jumeau, *Calots, Roch,* and various others. Although most of these were lady dolls, they also could be bébés used to show the latest children's fashions in France.

Fashion dolls were frequently mentioned in writings, but there was seldom any indication that they were a particular type of doll. They were not necessarily life-size, and more often than not were probably quite small. Nor did they necessarily have bisque heads. At the Musée des Arts Décoratifs there are eight dolls of this type with china heads made by *Sèvres,* dressed by the famous couturier Lanvin. Some of these were dressed as little girls. The same type of doll could be used either for displaying fashions or as a play doll; in fact, the same doll often served both purposes when a fashion doll was later used as a play doll.

Some collectors use the terms, "Fashion Doll" or "French Fashion" for certain types of lady dolls with fashionably formed kid and/or wooden bodies. There is ample evidence that these dolls were play dolls and seldom used merely to display fashionable attire. There are many pictures of such dolls in books and periodicals showing them in the arms of little girls who are obviously playing with them. When found in their original boxes, these dolls usually have no clothes except perhaps a string of beads as a necklace and a ribbon in the hair. Serious students of dolls have rejected having the term "Fashion" applied to this type of doll, although many dealers and collectors still use it.

Actually, a "Fashion Doll" is not a type of doll but rather a functional use of dolls. Nearly any type of doll could be dressed in the latest adult or children's fashions and be sent out to show current styles. (See **Lady Dolls;** also **Terminology.**)

**Fauche, Mlle. M.** 1916. Paris. Registered *Manos* as a trademark in France for dolls.

**Faugier, Mlle. Eugénie.** 1909. Belgium. Procured French

patent for a transformable doll that had two heads, two upper-torso parts, and two skirts.

**Faultless Rubber Co.** 1916–22. Ashland, Ohio. Made dressed and undressed molded rubber dolls.

1917: Company was assigned a U.S. design patent for a boy and a girl doll by *Clara M. Burd,* and they began to use the name *Sweetie,* which they registered as a trademark in the U.S. in 1919. (See Ill. 1609.)

1918: They made "live" rubber dolls in red and tan colors and gave them trade names such as *Fairy, Miss Sunshine, Billy Boy, Sailor Boy,* etc.

1920: They registered *Pat-Biddy* as a trademark in U.S.

**Faun, The.** 1912. Character girl doll made by *Louis Amberg & Son.* She had a composition head with classical features, and golden tresses winding around her head. Her pink sateen body was stuffed with cork, and she wore a pink dress.

**Fauré, Ph.** 1881–96. Paris. Made dressed dolls, both little girl and lady dolls, dolls dressed in provincial and foreign costumes, and dressed *bébés incassables* (unbreakable); also a large variety of *mignonettes, bathers, swimmers, follies,* and *marottes.* New models came out twice a year, winter and summer.

540 541

**540 & 541.** Marks of Faultless Rubber Co.

**542.** Charles Fausel patented a "Universal Joint" in 1895; it is used at the knees of this kid-bodied doll with composition limbs. H. 12³/₄ inches. *Courtesy of Hildred Brinkley.*

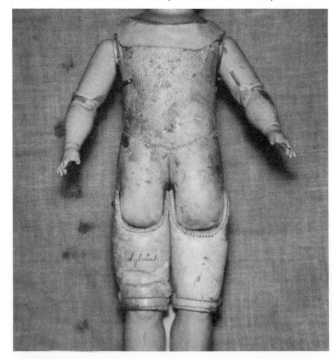

**Fauriez.** 1862–73. Paris. Made dolls' heads in imitation of those made in Germany; also made doll parts.

**Fausel, Charles.** 1895–96. Chicago, Ill. Obtained a U.S. patent for a *Universal Joint* for dolls.

**Fauvet.** See **Au Nain Bleu.**

**Favier.** See **Baculard (Favier & Baculard).**

**Favori.** See **Bébé Favori.**

**Favori-Bébé.** 1916. Trademark registered in France by *Arthur Sadin* for dolls.

**Favorite.** 1910–12. Distributed by *Butler Bros.* Came with bisque head, sleeping glass eyes, teeth, wig, soft limbs. Sizes 10½, 11¾, 13¼, 14½, 15½, 17, 18, 19, 21¾, and 24 inches; price 15¢ to $1.75.

**Favorite.** Name incised on bisque heads of some of the dolls made by *A. Lanternier & Co.*

**Favorite, The.** 1914. Trade name for composition-head doll made by *Elektra Toy & Novelty Co.* and advertised as washable and sunproof. The design patent for "The Favorite" obtained by *Ernst Karg* in 1914 appears to have been for this doll.

543. "Favorite," a bisque head made by Lanternier. Note the long face, wide eye holes, poor grade of bisque. Body is composition. Mark: Ill. **544.** H. 17 inches. *Courtesy of the Chester County Historical Society.*

544. "Favorite" mark found on dolls made by Lanternier.

> FABRICATION
> FRANÇAISE
>
> FAVORITE
>
> N° 2/0
>
> *Ed Tasson*
>
> A L & C^ie
>
> LIMOGES

**Fax.** 1925+. Trademark registered in Germany by *Gustav Wellmann Inc.* for rubber dolls.

**Fay.** See **Joanny (Jouany), J.**

**Fayaud, Mme. Alfred (née Girardin, Louise Annette Marie).** 1894. Paris. Widow; manufacturer of India rubber products. She obtained a British patent for an India rubber doll with two faces. Head was raised and twisted around by pushing on a compressed-air ball.

**Feather Light Brand.** Ca. 1914. Line of dolls distributed by *Sears, Roebuck & Co.*

**Featherstone, Charles, & Co.** 1895. London. Importer and distributor of dolls.

**Featherweight.** 1906. Line of dolls handled by *Louis Wolf & Co.* Had celluloid heads, arms, and legs on kid bodies.

**Featherweight Babies (Parcel Post Babies).** 1913. Line of imported dolls, distributed by *Samstag & Hilder.* Name later was changed to Parcel Post Babies (Parcel Post Kid). Came with celluloid heads; cloth bodies in various sizes.

**Fechheimer, J. K.** See **Amberg, Louis, & Son.**

**Fecht, M., & Co.** 1907–15. Berlin. Manufactured and exported dolls.

**Fecht & Podtnick.** 1893–1900. Berlin. Manufactured dolls.

**Federal Doll Manufacturing Co.** 1917–25. New York City. Made wood-pulp composition dolls; distributed by *Charles B. Blum.*

1917: Character dolls cost 25¢ to $3.00.

1918: Used trade name *Liberty Belle* for dolls.

1920: Registered *Roze Doll* as trademark in U.S.; name had been used in 1919 also. Roze Dolls had composition heads and arms, which were attached by rubber to the composition shoulder plates. The bodies were stuffed with cork. Came in three sizes.

1923: Advertised that the legs on their dolls looked like composition but were made of a cheaper material; among the new dolls were "Federal Follies" dolls.

1924: Over two hundred numbers, including walking and talking dolls and a 26-inch *Mama Doll.* New doll was named *Sandy*; it could be filled with sand or beans and would stand in any desired pose; price $1.00.

**Feeding Dolls.** 1866–1925+. *Lecomte & Alliot* were issued a French patent in 1866 for a doll with a food reservoir in its body that could be emptied with a tap.

1879: Probably the most famous feeding doll was *Bébé Teteur* patented by Casimir Bru, Jne. (see **Bru**).

1883: *Stuart Eldridge* patented in U.S. a nursing doll with a pump in the chest and a vent at the back of the shoulder.

1889–90: *Rudolph Steiner* patented in Germany and U.S. a feeding doll that siphoned the liquid from the bottle up into the mouth, out the back of the head, and down into a reservoir under the seat of the chair on which the doll was placed.

1894: *Theodor Liedel* patented a nursing doll in Germany.

1903: *E. A. Runnells & Co.* advertised a baby doll with a bottle as one of the latest dolls. By pressing a bulb located in the head, under the wig, the baby would slowly drink the contents of the bottle; releasing the pressure refilled the bottle.

1905: *Walter Villa Gilbert* advertised a doll that could "swallow."

1909: *Albert Schachne* patented a doll with a rubber ball in its body.

1912: Various character babies could drink liquid by pressing a bulb at the back of their necks.

**Feet.** See **Ills. 545 to 576.**

FEET

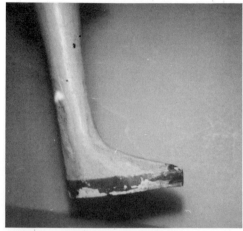
**545.** On all-wood doll with ball-jointed body.

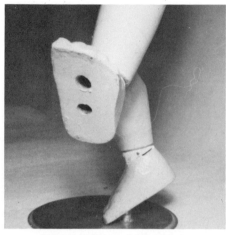
**548.** On all-wood Schoenhut.

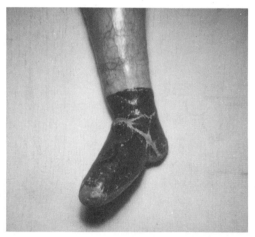
**551.** Of Izannah Walker rag doll.

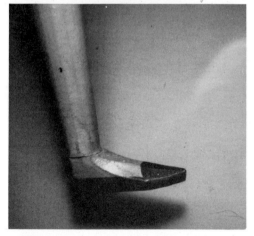
**546.** Doll has wooden limbs, papier-mâché head.
**547.** On wooden-body doll with china head.

**549.** China limbs and head on wooden body.
**550.** Of Ella Smith rag doll.

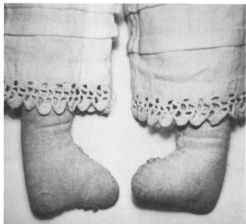
**552.** Of doll with one-piece cloth body, waxed head.
**553.** China Frozen Charlotte.

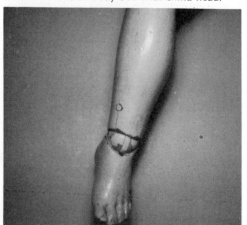

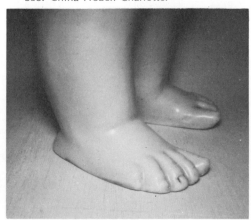

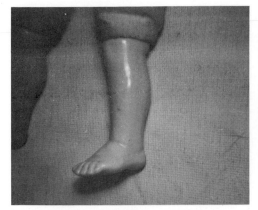

**554.** China, Motschmann type.

**555.** China-limb doll with snood head.

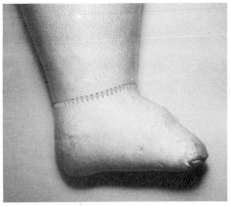

**558.** On kid body of German baby.

**559.** Cloth and leather, Steuber type.

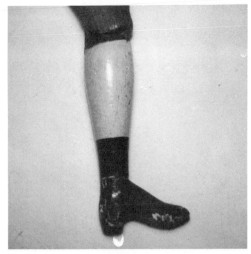

**562.** Metal foot on wooden leg, Ellis.

**563.** Aluminum foot, Giebeler-Falk.

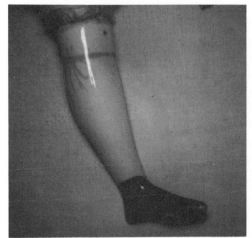

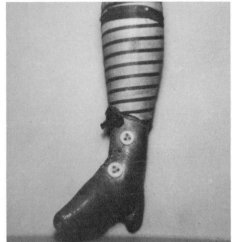

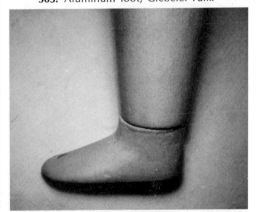

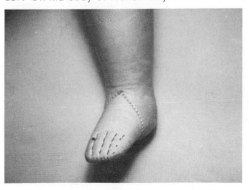

**556.** China-limb doll with molded bisque head.

**557.** On kid body of French lady.

**560.** Cloth and leather, Goldsmith.

**561.** Poured wax.

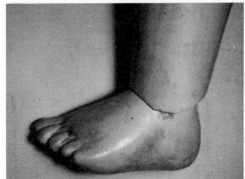

**564.** Composition foot, Motschmann type.

**565.** Composition, Jules Steiner.

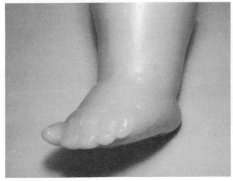

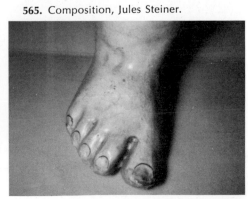

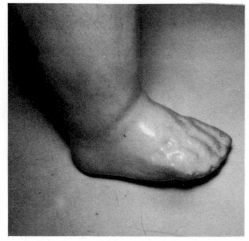

**566.** Composition, Jumeau.

**567.** Composition; Armand Marseille head.

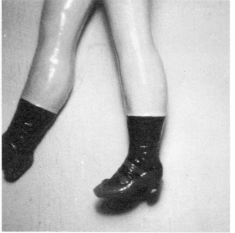

**570.** Composition, Max Schelhorn.

**571.** Bisque, Motschmann type.

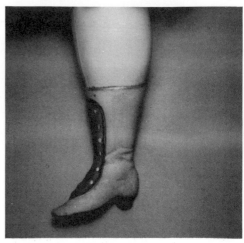

**573.** Bisque; doll has molded bisque head.

**574.** On all-bisque doll.

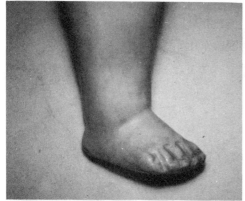

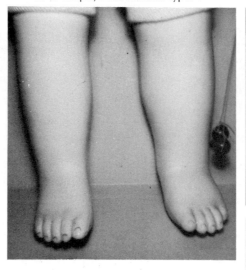

**572.** Bisque, Gesland.

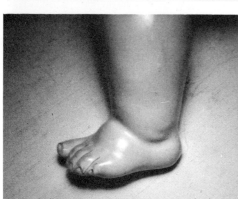

**568.** Composition, Kämmer & Reinhardt.

**569.** Composition; wax over papier-mâché head.

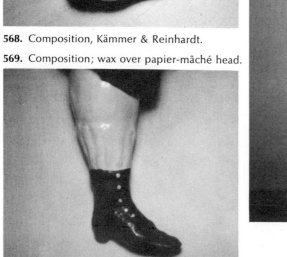

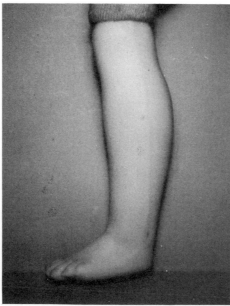

**575.** Bisque; doll has molded bisque head.

**576.** On all-bisque doll.

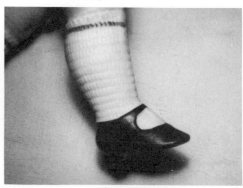

*Feet pictures courtesy of Eunice Althouse, Dorothy Annunziato, Hildred Brinkley, Sylvia Brockmon, the Chester County Historical Society, Alberta Darby, Edna Greehy, Lester & Alice Grinnings, the International Doll Library Foundation, Ollie Leavister, Helen Jo Payne, Mary Roberson.*

**Fehn, Gustav, & Co.** 1921. Köppelsdorf, Thür. Advertised dressed dolls, baby dolls, celluloid and porcelain heads, and parts for dolls, wigs, etc.

**Feiertag & Beyer.** 1925. Buchholz, Saxony. Advertised double-jointed and stiff-jointed dolls, walking dolls, baby dolls, and *Mama Dolls.*

**Feist, Bertha E.** 1921. New York City. Obtained U.S. design patent for a two-faced rag doll.

**Feldmann, Harry.** 1894–96. Sonneberg, Thür. Manufactured dolls.

**Feldmann, W.** 1915–21. Sonneberg, Thür. Manufactured dolls.

**Felice.** 1887–88. Doll distributed by YOUTH'S COMPANION. Came with bisque head, shoulder plate, and hands; swivel neck, blue glass eyes, blonde *Rembrandt* style hair; jointed kid body; blue lace stockings and kid slippers with buckles. Size 16 inches; price was $1.55 in 1887 and $1.65 in 1888, including paper patterns for her trousseau.

**Felix.** 1924. Trademark registered in U.S. by *Borgfeldt,* to be used on dolls of wood, rubber, fabrics, etc.

**Fellom, Lelia May (née Grube).** 1917–18. Los Angeles, Calif. Obtained eight U.S. design patents and one French patent for two-piece rag dolls with different faces and clothes on each side. For example, Jack was on one side, Jill on the other; Red Riding Hood was on one side and the wolf on the other side; etc. The faces were all of the *Drayton* type.

**Felt Dolls.** 1893–1925+. Felt was used for bodies and/or heads of dolls. Manufacturers of felt dolls included *Margarete Steiff, Schwerdtfeger & Co., H. Josef Leven, Mario Franco,* and *Scavini (Lenci).*

1893: *Knock About Dolls* were made in Europe with bisque heads and hands and assorted colored felt bodies.

1894: Margarete Steiff made her first felt dolls. She used felt for bodies as well as heads, but later used it for heads only.

Some *Eskimo dolls* had felt bodies made like kid bodies, with bisque heads and hands. The bisque heads had glass eyes, teeth, and natural hair. Came in sizes 11, 13, 16½, and 19 inches; price was 20¢, 25¢, 50¢, and $1.00.

1901: Felt dolls' bodies with double (gusset) joints came in red, blue, and black. They had bisque heads and hands, and the heads had sleeping eyes and wigs. Dolls came in sizes 11, 12, 13, 14, 16, and 18 inches. The three largest sizes of the felt bodies were embroidered in fancy designs on the chest. Prices were $1.95 to $6.00 doz. wholesale.

577. "Felice," a doll sold by *Youth's Companion* in 1887, for one new subscription plus 20¢, or $1.55. Has bisque head (wig not original) marked "154" or "164." H. 16 inches. *Courtesy of Mary E. Edwards.*

1912: The smallest size of the dolls with "goggle eyes" had felt faces.

**Femes Játékarugyár, R. T.** 1925. Oroshaza, Hungary. Manufactured dolls.

**Ferge, W.** 1923–25. Sonneberg, Thür. Manufactured dolls.

**Ferguson, A. S., & Co.** 1886–1925+. New York City. A. S. Ferguson started by working for *Althof, Bergmann & Co.;* then in 1886 he established his own distributing firm, which handled domestic toys only. He was the distributor for *Schoenhut, Fairyland Doll Co., Katherine Rauser, A. Rocholl, Ideal Novelty & Toy Co., F. Kaempff, J. D. Follender* wigs, etc.

**Fernand, Nathan.** 1925. Paris. Made dolls.

**Ferny, Alex.** 1925. Paris. Made *Art Dolls* with kid heads, which came dressed and undressed.

**Ferté.** 1869–90. Paris. Made dolls.

**Feuerlicht, James.** 1920. New York City. Was issued a U.S. design patent for a baby doll.

**Feuerstein, J.** 1893–1900. Berlin. Specialized in making dressed dolls.

**Fialont, Vve. (Widow).** 1867–70. Paris. Made dolls that she exhibited in the Paris Exposition of 1867.

**Fiberloid.** 1922–24. Material used for faces of *Pinky Winky* dolls.

**Fibrolaque.** 1925. Material of which *ADT, Société Nouvelle des Etablissements* made bébés.

**Fichtmüller, B.** 1909. Köppelsdorf, Thür. Made dolls.

**Fiedeler, Hermann.** 1905–8. Döhren near Hannover, Germany. Obtained one U.S. and four German patents for the movement of dolls' heads. The U.S. patent was for a device enabling the head to be turned or bowed by means of a lever projecting from the back of the doll. All the German patents related to the turning and/or nodding of dolls' heads.

**Fiegenbaum & Co.** 1884. San Francisco, Calif. Importers; distributed dolls.

**Fielder, Adolf.** 1894–1918. Sonneberg, Thür. Made leather dolls (kid body).

**Fiedler, Gottlieb.** 1918. Oberneubrunn, Thür. Made dolls.

**Fifi.** 1918. Copyrighted by *Jeanne I. Orsini*. Model of a smiling little girl, to be used as a doll. Had straight bobbed hair and bangs with a big bow on top of the head. Size of copyright model was 8½ inches.

**Fi-fi.** 1921. Trademark registered in France by *Isidore Dreifuss* for "strongly-made" dolls.

**Fifth Ave. Doll & Toy Manufacturing Co.** 1923. Advertised dolls' heads that were guaranteed not to crack or peel; price $8.00, $11.50, and $24.00 per gross wholesale.

**Fifth Ave. Dolls.** 1903. Trademark registered in Germany by *Cuno & Otto Dressel* for jointed dolls.

**Fiji Wigi.** 1921. Trade name of rag dolls made by *Century Doll Co.;* designed by *Grace Corry.* Came with chubby brown bodies and a shock of unruly hair; dressed in fringed shirt.

**Fine Baby.** 1917. Copyrighted by *Louis Amberg,* designed by *Reinhold Beck.* The doll had a slight scowl, wide forehead, small mouth with upper teeth.

**Fine Doll Manufacturing Co.** 1919. New York City. Copyrighted *Love Me,* designed by *Ernesto Peruggi.*

**Fingerhut, Jacob.** 1902–23. Kalisz, Poland. Successors of Jacob Fingerhut, 1910–23. Manufactured dolls.

**First Made in America (Made First in America).** 1915–16. Trademark of the *Composition Novelty Co.,* used for dolls.

**First Pittsburgh Commercial Corp.** 1920. Pittsburgh, Pa. Opened a new factory to make unbreakable dolls; sizes 12 to 19 inches.

**First Prize Baby.** 1919–20. Trade name for bisque dolls or bisque-headed dolls made in Japan; distributed by *Morimura Bros.*

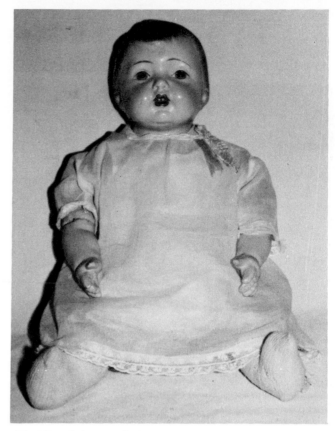

578. "Fine Baby" made by Louis Amberg & Son. Composition head mark: Ill. **579.** Doll has cloth body; original clothes bear tag reading: "Amberg's Nature Children//The Mama Doll// Spank me I cry louder." H. 23½ inches. *Courtesy of May Wenzel.*

579. Mark found on "Fine Baby" made by Louis Amberg.

580 & 581. Porcelain marks used by Arno Fischer.

| 9<br>L.A.&S·<br>1 9 ©16 | | |
|:---:|:---:|:---:|
| 579 | 580 | 581 |

**First Steps.** 1916. Feature doll made by *Louis Amberg, & Son.*

**Fischer, Albert.** 1907–11. Schalkau, Thür. Made inexpensive dressed dolls.

**Fischer, Arno.** 1907–25+. Ilmenau, Thür. Made porcelain products.

**Fischer, August Albert.** 1909–25+. Schalkau, Thür. Manufactured and exported dolls.

**Fischer, Bernhard (Berhard).** 1895–1914. Schalkau, Thür. Manufactured and exported dolls, dolls' heads, and dressed dolls; specialized in jointed wax or waxed *Täuflinge* in 1895.

**Fischer, Ernst.** 1895. Mönchröden, Thür. Manufactured dolls.

**Fischer, Johannes.** 1909. Hildburghausen, Thür. Manufactured dolls.

**Fischer, Louis.** 1866–1914. Schalkau, Thür. Made masks; in 1897 started to manufacture and export dolls.

**Fischer, Naumann & Co.** 1852–1925+. Ilmenau, Thür. Founded by Gotthold Friedrich Fischer and Leberect Naumann. Made papier-mâché dolls' heads.

1860: They were granted a patent in Britain for a doll's cloth body that was jointed so the doll could sit erect.

1875: They displayed dolls and won a prize at the Chile Exhibition.

1879: At Sydney, Australia, they were highly commended for original and well-made products.

1880: They won a bronze medal for mechanical dolls at Melbourne. Later the factory was owned by Wilhelm Fischer and the Naumann family, who had enlarged the scope of their products to include kid-body dolls, Punch and Judy, baby dolls, celluloid dolls, wigs, doll parts, and supplies for dolls' hospitals.

1891: Siebdrat & Schmidt was their London distributor; Gottschalk & Co., their Paris distributor, and Friedrich Seeber, their Vienna distributor.

1907–11: Advertised dolls' bodies.

1912: Advertised kid-bodied and character dolls.

1920's: They were advertising porcelain dolls, celluloid dolls, baby dolls, doll parts, and shoes and stockings for dolls.

**Fisher, Katherine.** 1920–22. Chicago, Ill. Registered Please and Thank-You as trademark in U.S. for dolls.

**Fisher Toy Manufacturing Co.** 1914. Made dolls.

**Fitch (Fuch), Darrell Austen.** 1909–10. Hounslow, Middlesex. Was issued a British and a German patent for dolls' eyes that moved from side to side by pull of gravity on a weight.

**Fitzpatrick, James.** 1905–13. Philadelphia, Pa. Made dolls.

**Five-in-One-Doll.** 1912. All-celluloid doll jointed at shoulders and hips, with five screw-on heads: two girls' heads, one with molded hair and one with real hair; two boys' heads, one with molded hair and one with "sandpapered" hair; and one cat's head. Size of doll, 9½ inches; price $1.00. (See Ill. 1238.)

**Flack, Alexander.** 1925. Austria. Obtained a French patent for a walking doll.

**Flag Printed Dolls' Bodies.** 1901. Flags of all nations printed on muslin dolls' bodies. Came with china head and limbs; legs had horizontal ribbing; heads had common wavy-type hairdo. There were four sizes; the doll next to the smallest size was 9 inches and sold for 10¢.

**Flanders Babies.** Early name for dolls, probably wooden dolls.

**Flanell-Puppenfabrik.** 1895. Oberlind, Thür. Hugo Anschütz, proprietor. Made and exported flannel dolls.

**Flange Necks.** 1860–1925+. Generally these are found on bisque, china, or composition heads used with cloth bodies. The cloth is sewed over the flange, thus holding the head onto the body but permitting it to rotate laterally. Some china dolls' heads of the 1860's had flange necks. Many of the 20th-century composition heads were made with flange necks. The 1914 New Born Babe and the later Bye-Lo and other infant dolls usually had this type of neck. Georgene Averill used a flange neck when she patented the Mama Doll in 1918.

**Flannel Dolls.** 1893–95. Material of which dolls were made in the Flanell-Puppenfabrik. In 1893 Knock About Dolls had Canton flannel bodies with bisque heads.

**Flantin.** 1840. Paris. Made dolls.

**Flapper.** 1922. Trademark registered in U.S. by James A. Hayes for dolls.

**Flapper.** 1925. Trade name of doll made by American Stuffed Novelty Co.; distributed by Edwin Besser, Borgfeldt, and Louis Wolf & Co.

**Flapper Dressed Dolls.** 1922–23. See **Flapper Novelty Doll Co.; George McCann; Helene Silberfeld.**

**Flapper Novelty Doll Co.** 1922–24. New York City. Lola Carrier Worrell, proprietress. Registered Floppy Flo as trademark in U.S. Made long-limbed Flapper Doll with hand-painted face.

**Flécheux.** 1904. Paris, Made bébés, bébés incassables (unbreakable), and poupards.

**Flechter, Samuel.** 1894. Cincinnati, Ohio. Made dolls.

**Flechter (Fletcher), Wolf.** See **Goldsmith, Philip.**

**Fleischaker & Baum (EFFanBEE).** 1910–25+. New York City. Made the EFFanBEE composition dolls. Bernard E. Fleischaker, a native of Kentucky, and Hugo Baum, born overseas, formed a partnership to manufacture dolls in 1910. Their first dolls, made of a concrete-type composition, were described by PLAYTHINGS in 1920 as having been " 'unbreakable American character dolls,' dolls long on strength but rather short in other respects, which fact can be frankly admitted today when American dolls are standard for doll quality throughout the world." As their dolls improved so did their business, and they continually added to the size of their factory; by 1920 they had two factories.

1912: Their dolls included Baby Dainty, Little Walter, Johnny-Tu-Face, and Naughty Marietta. Ideal brought out a doll named Naughty Marietta at the very same time, so Fleischaker & Baum immediately changed the name to Miss Coquette. It was one of the Coquette type of dolls with eyes glancing to the side and a ribbon around its head. Their dolls came with stuffed bodies and cost 50¢ to $3.50.

1913: They began to use their famous trademark, EFFanBEE. Betty Bounce, a new line of dolls, was introduced.

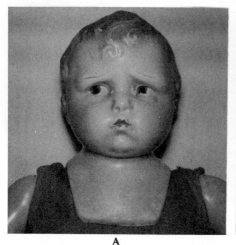
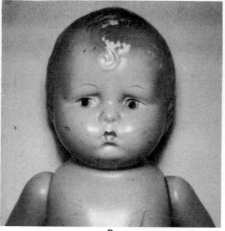
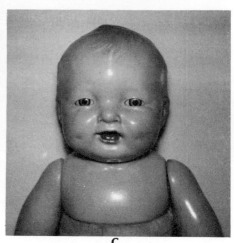

A   B   C

**582A, B, & C.** Three EFFanBEE composition heads on cloth bodies, made by Fleischaker & Baum. The doll at left is "Baby Grumpy"; note the resemblance to the center doll. The dolls at center and right have somewhat similar yokes and arm treatment. *Courtesy of Jessica Norman & Edna Greehy.*

**583A & B.** EFFanBEE bodies, made by Fleischaker & Baum. Both bodies are labeled "Walk, Talk, Sleep." They go with the two heads in *582B & C.* Body on the right is also labeled "1924," and is of the period when manufacturers were trying to combine bent-limb baby bodies and dolls that could stand upright. H. of doll at left, 11 inches. H. of doll at right, 21½ inches. *Courtesy of Jessica Norman & Edna Greehy.*

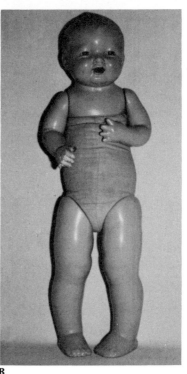

A

B

584     585     586

**584 & 585.** "EFFanBEE" marks on dolls made by Fleischaker & Baum.

**586.** Mark used by Gebrüder Fleischmann.

1914: Among their new dolls were *Baby Grumpy,* a frowning boy, Catholic Sister, and the *Jumbo* infant dolls.

1915: About one hundred babies including twelve new Baby Grumpys and Baby Grumpy Jr. were advertised. Some of the babies had real hair wigs. Price of the babies started at 25¢.

1916: *Uncle Sam* and *Columbia* designed by Hugo Baum were among the new dolls.

1917: One of the new dolls was *Mary Jane,* and a line of nurses made of wax was also advertised.

1918: They made both composition and stuffed-body

dolls. One of the new dolls was *Dolly Dumpling* (Baby Dumpling).

1919: Advertised three hundred models and used the slogan "American Dolls Are Now the World's Standard." Mary Jane was sold semiclad in a combination suit or fully dressed. A new line of Novelty Art Dolls included *Riding Hood Bud* and *Valentine Bud.* Another line, *Christening Babies,* was probably the *Mama Dolls* brought out in this year. *Butler Bros.* advertised EFFanBEE dolls with composition heads and hands, sleeping eyes, bobbed mohair wigs; dressed; size 15½ inches sold for $21.00 doz. wholesale. *Lenox Potteries* made experimental bisque dolls' heads for EFFanBEE about this time.

1920: They brought out Baby Grumpy again and advertised dolls with real kid bodies and composition arms and legs, as well as fully jointed composition bodies and dressed dolls. A new line of rag dolls, cotton stuffed, without pins in clothes; babies and children priced $10.50 doz.; Negro girl priced $12.00 doz., and a two-faced reversible doll priced $18.00 doz. wholesale.

1921: There were three hundred new numbers, including a Mama doll that said "Papa"; *Salvation Army Lass*; *Margie*, with cork-stuffed body; and *Trottie Truelife.*

1922: Three hundred numbers of walking Mama dolls with either cork- or cotton-stuffed bodies. They used the trademark *"They Walk and They Talk,"* and advertised that the voices were metal throughout and not made of rubber that would rot. Their dolls were 12, 14, and 15 inches and possibly other sizes. Some cost $18.00 doz. wholesale.

1923: Practically every doll had moving eyes, so that their trademark now read *"They Walk, They Talk, They Sleep."* A button with the name "EFFanBEE" was pinned on the dress of every doll, and in each doll box there was a folder entitled "How to Play With and Care for an EFFanBEE Doll." A new line of dolls named *"The Doll With the Golden Heart"* wore a heart-shaped pendant. Other new dolls included *Honeybunch*, *Beach Baby*, *Nancy Ann*, and *Mary Ann*. Baby Grumpy, designed by *Ernesto Peruggi*, was copyrighted by Hugo Baum.

1924: In this year there were four hundred numbers, including the four Babies Grumpy—namely, *Joan*, *Gladys*, *Billie*, and *Peter*. Two new features were real eyelashes and full composition arms jointed at the shoulder. *Joseph L. Kallus* assisted Hugo Baum in an advisory capacity. Hugo Baum obtained a design patent for *Harmonica Joe*, a little Negro boy playing a harmonica. The Lee dolls were the same model but came in three sizes: *Betty Lee*, 20 inches; *Alice Lee*, 23 inches; and *Barbara Lee*, 29 inches. Other EFFanBEE dolls cost as much as $25.00 each.

1925: Ernesto Peruggi was the artist who designed the *New Born Baby*, which Fleischaker copyrighted. Since they were late in producing their version of the *Bye-Lo Baby*, which they named *Baby Dainty*, a name previously used for one of their doll lines, they had two innovations. One was putting the dolls out as twins, and the other was *Pat-o-Pat*, an infant that clapped its hands. Other companies later imitated both of these. *Bubbles* was one of their new dolls.

The EFFanBEE trademark, "They Walk, They Talk, They Sleep," has been found on dolls that do none of these things.

**Fleischer Toy Manufacturing Co.** 1917–24. New York City. Earlier made or imported stuffed animals. New line of dolls in 1917 came with stationary or sleeping eyes, molded hair, mohair or natural hair wigs; cork-filled bodies; 12 and 16 inches tall; price $4.50 and $8.50 doz. wholesale.

1921: Known as R. Fleisher & Co.

1923: Made *Mama Dolls*, price $1.00 and up.

1924: Two members of the company left to form *Domec Toys Inc.*

**Fleischmann, Adolf.** 1844–81. Sonneberg, Thür.; 1881–1925+, A. Fleischmann & Crämer, successor, also of Neustadt near Coburg, Thür. Manufactured and distributed dolls of various kinds. He won a bronze medal at the 1844 Berlin Exhibition for his mechanical representation of Gulliver and the Lilliputians. At the London Exhibition of 1851 he won a prize medal for this display, and at the 1853 New York Exhibition he received Honorable Mention. The editor of the official New York catalog described this exhibit as "the greatest of all the toys in the Crystal Palace 'Gulliver among the Lilliputians.' This amusing work is made in papier-mâché by Fleischmann whose toys . . . [are] best of the whole collection." The Gulliver tableau, actually made partly of *brotteig* and partly of papier-mâché, was roughly four by two feet in size; after the exhibitions it was put into the Sonneberg Museum. (E. C. Spurin was the London representative of Fleischmann in 1851.)

At the command of the Duke of Saxe Meiningen in 1859, Fleischmann made some toy figures of burnt clay painted by the terrazolite process. It was A. Fleischmann & C. in 1873 and 1874. They displayed dolls at the Vienna Exhibition of 1873. It is possible that they made the composition heads marked "A. F. & Co., *Superior.*" In 1881, A. Fleischmann & Crämer registered a trademark in Germany to be used on *Täuflinge*, dolls, and dolls' heads of wood or porcelain. They exhibited dolls in 1893 at Chicago, in 1900 at Paris, and in 1904 at St. Louis. At Paris in 1900 they were one of the Grand Prize group. In 1908 they advertised wax dolls of every description, wooden, paste, leather, and mechanical toys. They had a branch in London from 1894 to 1911. It is not known whether the Fleischmann & Krämer of Neustadt near Coburg who was listed as a doll manufacturer from 1897 to 1907 was another branch or a separate firm. (*Anton Fromann* also might be A. F. & Co.)

**Fleischmann, Edm.** 1893–1905. Sonneberg, Thür. Manufactured dolls. Edm. Fleischmann & Sohn displayed dolls at the 1893 Chicago Exposition.

**Fleischmann, Julius & Paul.** 1873–92. Sonneberg, Thür. Manufactured dolls. Paris agent was *Gottschalk & Co.* In 1873, J. P. Fleischmann displayed dolls in Vienna and the following year the name appeared in a directory. Julius and Paul Fleischmann obtained U.S. and German patents in 1892 for stapling together dolls' bodies and reinforcing the apertures for head and limbs with metal eyelets; the torsos could be made in from two to four parts, and paint would conceal the metal parts.

**Fleischmann, Katherine (Kitty).** 1919–24. Previous to 1919, she was the toy buyer for *Gimbel Bros.* Then she was supervisor of a line of dolls' dresses, and from 1922 to 1924 she created the *Kay-Eff* toddle babies, distributed by *Joseph Goldstein.*

**Fleischmann & Blödel (Bloedel).** 1873–1914. Fürth, Bavaria; Paris; 1909–25+, J. Berlin, successor in Fürth. Manufactured, distributed, and exported dolls. They had a branch in Paris as early as 1890, when their advertisement read: "Office displaying samples in Paris, makes bébés incassables for France and for export. Models with stationary eyes, sleeping eyes and talking, all or partly jointed." The firm carried samples of German articles and specialized in dressed and undressed bébés. Fleischmann & Blödel obtained many patents; among them, in 1890, were three French patents for jointed dolls; in 1892, a French patent for unbreakable dolls; and also in 1892, English and German patents for a walking doll that turned its head as it walked. In 1894, they obtained seven patents: a French patent for moving eyelids, four French patents for walking dolls, a French patent for a doll that threw kisses and talked when a button was pressed, and a German patent for a kiss-throwing and talking doll. The year 1895 brought them a German patent for a moving doll, and in 1897 they secured a French patent for improvements on the kiss-throwing doll that also walked. Fleischmann & Blödel of Fürth and Paris were the assignees of a patent by *Claude Joseph Simonot* of Paris for a walking doll whose head turned as the feet moved. This patent was obtained in France, Germany, and England in 1892; in Spain, Italy, Austria, and the U.S. in 1893. They registered *Eden Bébé* as a trademark in France in 1890 and as a trademark in Germany in 1896; Eden-Puppe was registered as a trademark in Germany in 1891; *Bébé Triomphe* was registered as a trademark in France in 1898. The Paris Directory of 1898 advertised that Fleischmann & Blödel, creator of the Eden Bébé, had a steam factory and made a specialty of toy soldiers. They were one of the original members of the *Société Française de Fabrication de Bébés et Jouets* when it was formed in 1899. Fleischmann was head of this firm when World War I broke out, and since he was an alien the property was sequestered. In 1910/11, J. Berlin, successor, advertised character dolls, fabric dolls with seamless faces, and the trademark "Michu." A directory of 1914 stated that J. Berlin, Sr., a porcelain manufacturer, was the successor of Fleischmann & Blödel. In 1924 they were listed as rag doll manufacturers. (See Ill. 1013.)

**Fleischmann & Co.** 1908. Neustadt near Coburg, Thür. Manufactured dolls. Fleischmann & Krämer manufactured dolls in Neustadt also.

**Fleischmann Gebrüder (Bros.).** 1880–1925+. Sonneberg, Thür., and later of Nürnberg, Bavaria. Edmund Fleischmann was one of the brothers. They manufactured and exported various kinds of dolls. Prior to World War I their specialty was kid-body dolls. They displayed dolls at Melbourne in 1880; Chicago in 1893; Paris in 1900, and St. Louis in 1904. At Paris in 1900 they were in the group that won a Grand Prize. They advertised jointed and unjointed dolls, wholesale and for export in 1895, and dressed and undressed dolls for export in 1898.

**Fleming Doll Co.** 1922–24. Kansas City, Mo. Registered *Tum Tum* as their trademark in U.S. for dolls.

1924: Advertised *Andy Gump* and *Chester Gump*.

**Fleury.** 1873–74. Villers-Cotterets near Soissons, France. Made dolls.

**Flexie Toy Co.** 1922–23. Broadalbin, N.Y. Registered *Baby Bunting* as a trademark in U.S. for dolls.

**Flicks Kids.** 1915–16. Trade name for character dolls made by *Standard Specialty Co.* Came with composition heads in three sizes; cost $1.00, $1.25, and $2.00.

**Flintex.** 1913. Trademark registered in U.S. by *Northport Novelty Co.* for dolls.

**Flinzer, A. M. A.** 1898. Dresden, Saxony. Manufactured dolls.

**Flippety-Flop Kids.** 1913. Grotesque character dolls made by *Gund Manufacturing Co.* Came with eyes glancing to the side, swinging arms and legs, and crying voices.

**Flirt, The.** 1907–8. Trademark registered in Germany by *Kämmer & Reinhardt;* used for a doll whose eyes moved from side to side as well as slept; made by Kämmer & Reinhardt in their *Royal* line, and distributed by *Strobel*

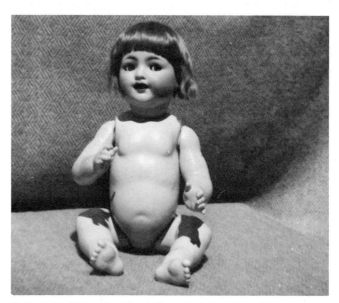

**587A & B.** "The Flirt," a doll made by Kämmer & Reinhardt. The eyes move from side to side and also open and shut; eyelids move independently of the eyeballs. The bent-limb body indicates that the doll was probably made after 1909. Mark on head: Ill. **588**, plus "Germany∥42." *Coleman Collection.*

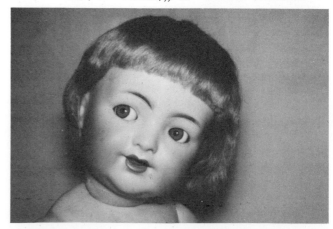

& *Wilken*. In 1925 Kämmer & Reinhardt were still making flirting eye dolls, which *Bing* was distributing.

**Flirt, The.** 1921. Trade name for cherub-type doll made by *New Era Toy & Novelty Co.*

**Flirting Eyes.** Mid-1800's–1925+. Eyes that move from side to side. In 1891 *Fouquet & Douville* obtained a French patent for the movement of eyes of dolls or bébés in any direction. Most of the flirting eyes advertised in 1903 moved from side to side instead of opening and shutting. In 1904 Carl Halbig of *Simon & Halbig* filed a patent in the U.S. for dolls' eyes that moved both laterally and vertically by means of a single weight. This patent describes previous methods as follows: "In some of the structures, where the eyes on which the eyelids are made are movable sidewise as well as vertically, there are either two or three weights to effect the movements, one weight on a horizontal pivot to open and shut the eyes and either one or two weights to move them sidewise, while in other cases the sidewise movement is accomplished by means of a cord."

PLAYTHINGS, 1904, stated that the trade called eyes that moved from side to side *Goo Goo* eyes. In 1907, PLAYTHINGS reported that one of the great attractions at the Paris Exhibition was the flirting eyes that turned from side to side and rolled under long curling eyelashes; when the eyes closed, the lashes came down too on movable lids. Numerous patents were secured for flirting eyes up until World War I. In 1924 and 1925, *Ideal Novelty & Toy Co.* and *Arranbee* advertised flirting eyes that moved from side to side.

**Flo.** 1921–22. Trade name of stuffed doll made by *The Chessler Co.* The doll could walk and talk. It was priced at $2.50 and $3.00.

**Floating Dolls.** 1917. Made by *Moore & Gibson Corp.,* of leather or fabric.

**Floatolly.** 1914. Trademark registered in Britain by *Eisenmann & Co.* for dolls.

**Flock.** 1854–1925. Hair or cloth fibers glued or pasted onto a doll for decoration, especially used for short boyish hair. In 1854, *Edouard Auguste Desiré Guichard* obtained a British patent for using flock on dolls; he proposed to use any type of powdered material—even wood, metal, or leather—as well as fabrics. In the 20th century, *Gebrüder Heubach, Kämmer & Reinhardt,* et. al., sometimes used flocked hair on their dolls' heads.

**Flo-Flo of the Follies.** 1920. Trade name of doll advertised by *S. K. Novelty Co.* It was a cherub-type doll with wig; 18 inches tall.

**Floppy Flo.** 1922–24. Trademark registered in U.S. by the *Flapper Novelty Co.* for dolls. This was probably the doll for which *Lola Worrell* obtained a U.S. design patent.

**Flopsie.** 1920. Trademark registered in Britain by *William Henry Jones* for dolls.

**Flora.** 1913. One of the *Country Cousins* made by

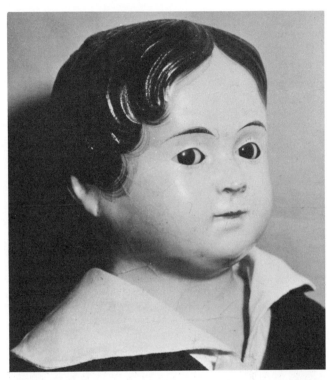

**588.** Mark found on the "Flirt" doll made by Kämmer & Reinhardt.

**589.** Papier-mâché head with flirting eyes that move from side to side. Eyes are black pupil-less glass. Molded hair has brush marks around the hairline. Doll wears a blue jacket. *Photograph courtesy of Winnie Langley.*

*Ideal Novelty & Toy Co.* Came with "washable" composition head, bow in hair, and bare feet; mate to *Freddie;* price $1.00.

**Flora McFlimsey.** 1860's. Name given to various dolls with trunks of clothes. Dolls were named for a character in the popular poem written about 1857, under the title "Nothing to Wear."

1862: A Flora McFlimsey doll was sold for $250 at the Great Central Fair in Philadelphia.

**Florabelle.** 1920. One of the *Bell Brand* dolls made by Bell Toy Co.

**Floradora.** See **Florodora.**

**Floradora Sextet.** 1912. Made by *Louis Amberg & Son.* Dolls came with imported bisque heads, teeth; they were dressed in America. Price $1.00 and up.

**Florence.** 1905–14 and possibly earlier. China dolls' heads made with this name in gold letters on the chest.

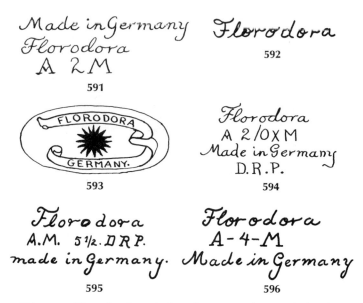

591–596. "Florodora" marks found on Armand Marseille heads.

**590A & B.** "Florodora" bisque head made by Armand Marseille has glass sleeping eyes, open mouth with teeth. Body is composition. Doll wears contemporary blue outfit. Mark: as in Ill. **591**, except for #5/0. H. 11 inches. *Courtesy of Alberta Darby.*

This type was produced by *Hertwig & Co.* and *Closter Veilsdorf.*

**Florido, José.** 1925. Spain. Was issued a French patent for a walking doll that turned its head to the right and left and said, "Mama."

**Florig & Otto.** 1920–22. Dresden, Saxony. Made jointed wooden dolls; registered "Florigotto" as trademark in Germany. They were issued three German patents for joints, especially ball joints, used on wooden dolls.

**Florodora.** 1901–9+. Trademark registered in Germany by *Borgfeldt* for a line of kid-body dolls with bisque heads usually made by *Armand Marseille.* In 1903, the name Florodora was registered again as a trademark, but with a drawing of a daisy. Later, possibly after 1909, Florodora heads made by Armand Marseille were used on jointed composition bodies. (See color photograph C19.)

**Flossie, Mme.** 1910. Paris. Made small *"fashion"* dolls with wax heads.

**Flossie Featherweight.** 1922. Stuffed dolls made by *Gem Toy Co.;* price 25¢, 50¢, and $1.00.

**Flossie Fisher's Own Doll.** 1916–21. Made by *K & K Toy Co.;* distributed by *Borgfeldt* and *Montgomery Ward & Co.;* based on the Flossie Fisher drawings by Miss Helen Nyce for LADIES' HOME JOURNAL.

1916: Came with composition head and hands, mohair wig, cork-stuffed body; wore white dress with ribbon tag at waist; about 15 inches high; price $1.70.

1921: Name registered in Germany by Borgfeldt as a trademark.

**Flossie Flirt.** 1924–25. Made by *Ideal Novelty & Toy Co.* Doll had sleeping eyes that also rolled from side to side as she walked. The name was registered as a U.S. trademark for dolls that were exported to Europe, Asia, and Australia, as well as sold in America. It came with painted hair or one of fifteen different wig types; made in seven sizes and dressed in one hundred different costumes. Some models came with flexible rubber hands.

**Flo-To.** 1922–23. Trademark registered in U.S. by *Justus Brauer & Son* for dolls.

**Flo-Vel.** 1922–23. Trade name for velvet-faced dolls made by *Master-Craft Doll Co.* Doll walked and talked; price $4.98 in 1921; in 1922, $3.00 and up.

**Flower Dolls.** Ca. 1901. *Marguerite* or *bonnet*-type dolls with flower-shaped headgear. Came with cloth bodies and ceramic heads and limbs; sizes 8 to 15 inches; 9-inch size cost 10¢.

**Fluegelman, M. F. (F. M.).** 1917–25. New York City. Manufactured dolls' heads, hands, and faces. In 1917 they manufactured dolls' hats.

**Fluffy Ruffles.** 1907–8. Trademark registered in Germany by *Max Fr. Schelhorn* firm for dolls and parts of dolls. These were probably the "Fluffy Ruffles" dolls advertised by *Borgfeldt* and *Samstag & Hilder* in 1908, and perhaps based on the cartoon character of this name in the New York HERALD.

**Fluffy Ruffles.** 1907–8. Trade name of dolls made by *American Doll & Toy Manufacturing Co.* with *Can't Break 'Em* composition heads and dressed in various styles.

**Fluteau, Auguste.** 1868–72. Paris. Made dolls.

**Follender, Wilhelm.** 1923. Düsseldorf, Germany. Registered *My Annemarie* as a trademark in Germany for dolls that they exported.

**Folly Heads (Folies).** 1890–1921. Also called *marotte* and whirling musical doll. Came with bells and played a tune when whirled around; heads usually of bisque. Maison *Dehais* made this type of doll.

**Fontaine.** 1893. France. Displayed dolls at the Chicago Exhibition.

**Foote, Mary C. W.** 1903–9. Plainfield, N.J. Registered in U.S. *Fairyland* as trademark for rag dolls.

**Foreign Dolls.** Dolls dressed in native costumes of foreign countries. These dolls have been popular for centuries, but in 1903 there was a special fad for them. They were used to teach history and geography as well as to ornament the nursery. Germany made many of these dolls, which were sent abroad to be partially or wholly dressed by the natives and then sold as foreign dolls. Many of the fine antique dolls that have been preserved were originally dressed and sold as foreign dolls. (See Ills. 508, 620, C2, C5, C8, C13, C17, C18, C19, C21, C23.)

**Forget-Me-Not.** 1918. Trademark registered in Britain by *Samuel Henry Ward* for the dolls he manufactured.

**Forster, Adolph.** 1907. Philadelphia, Pa. Doll jobber.

**Förster, Alfr.** 1925. Sonneberg, Thür. Manufactured dolls.

**Förster, Emil.** 1895–1920. Neustadt near Coburg, Thür. Manufactured dolls. In 1895 he made little or baby dolls.

**Förster, Rudolph.** See **Siebeneicher, August.**

**Forster, Thomas.** 1844. Streatham, Surrey. Secured a British patent for a composition of rubber and the coating of surfaces of leather and woven fabrics to make dolls' heads, arms, and legs by casting them in molds.

**Fortin.** 1890. Paris. Made dolls.

**Fortune Telling Doll.** 1891. Patented in Germany by *B. Voight* and called Oracle Doll. There are earlier dolls with skirts of fortune-telling slips of paper.

**Fluffy Ruffles Doll**
Registration Applied For

597. "Fluffy Ruffles" as advertised by Samstag & Hilder Bros. in 1908 appears to have a bisque head on a jointed composition body. *Courtesy of McCready Publishing Co.*

**Foskett & Edler (Eddler).** 1887–94. London. Made dolls and was manufacturers' agent for foreign dolls.

**Fouillot.** 1906–25+. Paris. Made dolls. In 1906 Mlle. Blanche Fouillot registered in France her trademark *L'Idéal*; by 1925, the listing was for Mme. Fouillot.

**Fould, Mme. Consuélo.** 1919. Paris. Registered *Les Victorieuses* as a trademark in France for dolls.

**Foulds & Freure.** 1912–25+. New York City. Doll jobber and importer of dolls and doll parts; Robert Foulds, Sr., was a toy importer in New York as early as 1842; he was succeeded by his son, Robert Foulds, Jr.

1913: Advertised socket heads of bisque with teeth.

1914: Advertised socket dolls' heads from Germany with human hair wigs instead of mohair wigs.

1915: Advertised the line #390, which included "3 socket heads." These are probably the 390's made by *Armand Marseille*, one of the most frequently found of all bisque socket heads (they were still being made in the 1930's), and are a typically dolly face. The advertisement also mentions two baby numbers, one with a wig and one with painted hair.

1916: Despite the war, they were still importing character dolls' heads and character dolls in a variety of sizes. They advertised *Handwerck* hands for jointed dolls, and character dolls' arms and bodies made by Handwerck, as well as kid-body dolls, and mohair and human hair wigs.

1917: German dolls and dolls' heads of bisque, metal, and celluloid and muslin dolls' bodies were all scarce, but they were obtaining dolls' heads from Japan. These were socket bisque character heads with sleeping glass eyes, and either wigs or painted hair.

1918: They were obtaining dolls and dolls' heads from France and Japan in both bisque and celluloid. They advertised 1,000 sample imported dolls; these were character dolls, kid-body dolls, or jointed composition-body dolls. Thirty of the large "show dolls" were in sizes from 30 to 42 inches.

1919: Still advertising French and Japanese bisque dolls and dolls' heads; also listed domestic bisque heads and imported kid dolls; celluloid doll cost 10¢ and 25¢.

1920: Specialized in celluloid dolls.

1921: Prices reduced; ten heads now cost $5.00.

1925: Advertised dolls' heads, wigs, eyes, hands, and elastic. *Bye-Lo Baby* bisque heads for dolls measuring 8 to 20½ inches cost $8.00 to $36.00 doz. wholesale.

**Fountain, A. E., Inc.** See **Colonial Toy Manufacturing Co.**

**Fouquet, Mme.** 1925. Paris. Made dolls.

**Fouquet & Douville.** 1891–93. Obtained two French patents and a German patent for eye movements; the 1891 patent related to eye movement in any direction for bébés and dolls. Fouquet alone obtained the 1893 patent for eye movement.

**Fournier, Jules.** 1900. France. Exhibited dolls at the Paris Exposition and was awarded a bronze medal.

**Foxton's Manufacturing Co.** 1918–21. London. Made dolls.

**Foxy Grandpa.** 1903–7. Rag doll with face and clothes like the character drawn by *Carl Schultze* in the Sunday supplements. U.S. design patent for doll obtained by Carl Schultze. Foxy Grandpa with his two grandsons came in a set, priced variously from 75¢ to $1.25. Grandpa was 12 inches and the boys 9 inches in height. Probably also made in other materials, especially as part of various metal toys.

1905: *Art Fabric Mills* made Foxy Grandpa as a rag doll; size 20 inches; price 25¢. (See color photograph C7.)

**Foy, F., & Cie.** 1910–12. Gentilly, Seine. Made dolls' heads of molded cardboard, compressed and varnished.

**Fraenkel (Frankl) Bros.** 1899–1903. London. Made and distributed composition dolls.

**Français Bébé.** See **Bébé Français.**

**Franceschi-Porri, Antoine Dominique Napoléon.** 1921. France. Was issued a French patent for a talking doll.

**Franck, Carl, & Co.** 1867–73. Ohrdruf, Thür. Made dolls' heads.

**Franco, Mario.** 1921–22. Turin, Italy. Obtained patents in U.S. and Germany for making felt dolls with seamless heads. Dolls stamped out of molds without stitching. These patents appear to have been used for *Scavini* dolls.

**François, A.** See **Massiot.**

**François, Aîné (Sr.).** 1811–44. Paris. Made dolls, especially mechanical dolls.

1844: Displayed dolls at the Paris Exhibition.

1846–58: Mlle. François made dolls and was probably his successor.

**Frank, L.** 1867. Kloetz, Prussia. Displayed materials for making dolls at the Paris Exposition.

**Franke, Frau.** 1909–18. Dresden, Saxony. Made dolls.

**Franke, Friedrich Carl.** 1914–23. Berlin. Distributed and exported dolls.

**Frankel, G. & Co.** 1906–12. New York City. Importer and doll jobber.

**Frankenthal Porzellan Manufaktur.** 1755–99. Mannheim, Württemberg. It is doubtful if porcelain dolls were made this early, but after 1799 the Frankenthal molds were taken to *Nymphenburg* and if dolls' heads are found with the Frankenthal mark on them, they were probably made at Nymphenberg.

**Frankl.** See **Fraenkel Bros.**

**Frankl, Franz.** 1888–1925+. Vienna. Manufactured dolls. He won a silver medal at the 1888 Melbourne Exhibition, a gold medal at the 1889 Linz Exhibition, a silver medal at the 1894 Vienna Exhibition, and a gold medal at the 1897 Vienna Exhibition.

1899: Advertised patent dolls, bébés, ball-jointed dolls, and dolls' heads.

**Franklin, J. G., & Sons.** 1921. London. Used the trademark *Rubbadubdub* for their rubber dolls.

**Franklin, Jacob.** 1895–1909. Neustadt near Coburg, Thür. Manufactured little or baby dolls.

**Franz, J.** 1871–1913. Sonneberg, Thür. Manufactured and exported dressed dolls of various kinds and articles for dolls. In 1891 exported to North, Central, and South America and Australia.

1898: Registered in Germany a trademark of two figures holding hands.

1909–13: London agent was *Walter Zimmer*.

**Franz, Otto.** 1899. Vienna. Made dolls and dolls' heads; used slogan, "zur Puppenfee" (at the fairy doll).

**Fred Stone.** 1924. *Celebrity Doll* conceived by *Margaret Vale;* designed and made by *Jane Gray.* The doll represented Fred Stone as Peter Plug in Charles Dillingham's play STEPPING STONES. It had a hand-painted face and bore a tag with a facsimile autograph of Fred Stone.

**Freddie.** 1913. One of the *Country Cousins* made by *Ideal Novelty & Toy Co.* Came with washable composition head; dressed in overalls; mate to *Flora.* Price $1.00.

**Freidank, Anna.** 1909. Charlottenburg, Brandenburg. Made dolls.

**French Baby.** 1918. Made by *EFFanBEE,* distributed by *Butler Bros.* Came with bobbed mohair wig; size 15½ inches, $21.00 doz. wholesale.

**French Bisque.** Appears to be a fine grade of bisque; not necessarily bisque made in France. Dolls' heads made by *Simon & Halbig* and other German manufacturers were sometimes described as "French Bisque."

**French Dolls.** French dolls are among the most artistic ever created. France gained an early reputation for fine dolls, even in the 17th and 18th centuries. After the fall of the First Empire, competition sprang up with the beautiful wax dolls made in England and the lovely porcelain dolls made at *Konigliche Porzellan Manufaktur, Royal Copenhagen,* etc. Although France found it necessary to purchase many dolls' heads in Germany and England, French clothes for dolls and fine French kid bodies remained unexcelled. After the Prussian War, thanks to *Jumeau, Bru,* etc., France regained pre-eminence with the exquisite French bébés. Then competition once more affected the French dolls. In 1903, PLAYTHINGS wrote, "In dolls Germany rules the world, having wrested supremacy from France. Years ago we heard a great deal about the beauties of French dolls and even to-day the phrase is much used. As a matter of fact, many people have an idea that the beautiful dolls they give their children are designed and made in France when in truth they were made in Germany and very likely designed right here in New York."

In the last six months of 1906, New York imported over $100,000 worth of dolls from Paris. When World War I began, *Fleischmann,* a German, was head of the largest doll-making group *(Société Française de Fabrication de Bébés et Jouets)* in France and his property was sequestered. After the end of the war, there was a resurgence in demand for French dolls before the German doll factories could resume competitive operations.

One of the reasons for the beautiful French clothes was the fact that fashion experts dressed French dolls, and prizes were offered each year for improvements. Women all over the world helped to design the French dolls' clothes. In 1915 the "S.S. Rochambeau" brought six hundred dolls to America; these, 14 inches high, were gowned in Paris by otherwise unemployed dressmakers and sold by *Wanamaker's* in New York City for $2.00 to $4.00 a doll. The very first day, 250 dolls were sold.

**598.** Bébé with cork pate, paperweight stationary eyes, closed mouth, pierced ears, ball-jointed composition body (wrists not jointed)—characteristics of French bébés. Mark on head: "9." H. 20 inches. *Courtesy of Hazel Ulseth.*

Wanamaker's then ordered one hundred similar dolls per week.

Another feature of French dolls is their large glass eyes made similar to paperweights. French dolls of the 19th century usually have cork pates to which their wigs were nailed. A detailed study of numerous French bébés reveals certain characteristics in design and decorating techniques, but caution should be used in attributing dolls to France on the basis of their appearance alone.

French dolls have usually been more expensive than

those made elsewhere. In 1919 the cheapest French doll cost $20.00, according to PLAYTHINGS.

**French Fashion Dolls. See Fashion Dolls; also Lady Dolls.**

**French Jointed Dolls.** So-called French Jointed Dolls were not necessarily made in France. The term appears to refer to dolls with ball-jointed papier-mâché bodies, a type believed to have originated in France.

**French Soldiers.** 1922. Disabled veterans made dolls with faces delineated with pen and brush, and bodies of a canvas frame stuffed with cotton. They came with clothes crocheted of wool; 2 inches tall.

**French Zouave.** 1917. Made by *Standard Doll Co.*, size 16 inches.

**Freshie.** 1921. Trade name for one of the *Happifat* line of dolls made by *Louis Amberg & Son*.

**Freud, D.** 1899. Vienna. Manufactured dolls and dolls' heads.

**Freundlich (Freudlich), Ralph A.** 1923–25. Brooklyn, N.Y. Obtained three U.S. design patents and registered *Little Red Riding Hood* as a trademark in U.S. for the *Jeanette Doll Co.*, of which he was an officer.

**Frickmann & Lindner, Robert A.** 1915–20. Köppelsdorf, Thür. Obtained a German patent for a voice in doll's head as "proprietors of Carl, Robert" in 1916, but listed in directories from 1915 to 1920 as doll manufacturers.

**Friedel.** 1916. Trademark registered in Germany by *E. W. Matthes* for dolls.

**Friedel, A.** 1918. Bettelhecken, Thür. Made dolls and *Täuflinge*.

**Friedel, Ed.** 1918. Bettelhecken, Thür. Made dolls and *Täuflinge*.

**Friedel, H.** 1918–25+. Sonneberg, Thür. Made *Täuflinge*.

**Friedel, L.** 1918. Bettelhecken, Thür. Handled dolls and *Täuflinge*.

**Friedel, Th.** 1909. Bettelhecken, Thür. Made dolls and *Täuflinge*.

**Friedmann & Ohnstein.** 1925. Breslau, Germany. Made and exported miniature dressed dolls of porcelain and celluloid.

**Friedrich, Adam.** 1895. Neustadt near Coburg, Thür. Manufactured little or baby dolls.

**Friedrich, Albert.** 1924. Chemnitz, Saxony. Made dolls.

**Friedrichrodaer Puppenfabrik.** 1902–25+. Friedrichroda near Waltershausen, Thür. Operated by Jäger family; also known as *Jäger & Co.* and Puppenfabrik Thüringia. Used initials "F. P." Manufactured ball-jointed dolls, standing and sitting babies.

1923: Registered *Brüderchen* (Little Brother) as a trademark in Germany for dolls. A bisque head has been found marked "Otto Jäger, Friedrichroda."

**Frisch, Arthur, & Frisch, Morris A.** 1921–25. Brooklyn, N.Y. Obtained U.S. patent for movable eyes.

**Frisch, E. Gregor.** 1924. Nürnberg, Bavaria. Made and exported dolls.

**Fritz.** 1911. Doll made by *Steiff*; 11 inches tall.

**Fritz.** 1916. Trade name of boy doll made by *Käthe Kruse*; price $15.00.

**Fritz.** 1917. Trademark registered in Germany by *Emil Pfeiffer* for dolls.

**Fritzi.** 1913. Dutch boy doll made by *Elektra Toy & Novelty Co.*; mate to *Mitzi*.

**Fritzsche, Gust.** 1918. Altenburg, Silesia. Made dolls.

**Fritzsche & Hand.** 1914–15, Berlin; 1920–23, B. Fritzsche, successor. Manufactured and exported dolls.

**Frivona.** 1879–1925+. Trademark used by *Friedrich Voight* and his successors for dolls. (See Ill. 1650.)

**Fröbel.** 1900–1920. Sonneberg, Thür. Manufactured dolls. *Müller & Fröbel* displayed dolls at the 1900 Paris Exposition and the 1904 St. Louis Exposition. Fröbel alone was listed in directories from 1915 to 1920.

**Frobenius, Lilian (Lilli).** 1909–18. Won awards for her "life-like" Art Dolls exhibited in Munich.

**Fröber, B.** 1915–23. Sonneberg, Thür. Manufactured dolls.

**Fröber, Richard.** 1895–1918. Hüttensteinach, near Sonneberg, Thür. Manufactured dolls.

**Froebel-Kan.** Tokyo, Japan. Made dolls with bisque heads.

**Froehlich, Hugo, & Frank, Max.** 1920. New York City. Procured a German patent for moving dolls' eyes.

**Frog Skins.** 1920. Material used by peasants in Brittany to make commercial dolls.

**Fromann (Frommann), Anton.** 1862–73. Neustadt near Coburg, Thür. Won a prize medal for his papier-mâché dolls at the London Exhibition in 1862. *Le Montréer* was his representative in Paris. (See **Superior.**)

**Frou Frou.** 1913. Trade name of doll representing a chorus girl; made by *Elektra Toy & Novelty Co.*

**Frou-Frou.** 1920. Cherub-type doll made by *S. K. Novelty Co.*; 10 inches high.

**Frozen Charlottes.** 1850's–ca. 1914. Also called pillar dolls, solid china or bathing babies. Made in glazed and unglazed porcelain. Came with molded hair, bonnets, or wigs; pink, white, or black china; usually represented a baby and often were carried in the arms of a larger doll. Came in sizes 1 to 18 inches or more. The slightly over 4-inch size sold for 39¢ doz. in 1886; 75¢ doz. in 1894 dressed; 38¢ doz. in 1913. The tiny one-inch size was often used as favors in cakes. An 1850's catalog advertised them with clenched fists, bent elbows, lying in a bathtub; sizes one to 8 inches. Larger sizes were probably made later. (See color photograph C12.)

**Fry, Roger.** 1914. London. Artist who designed dolls for a London Child's Welfare Exhibit.

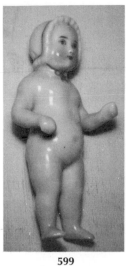

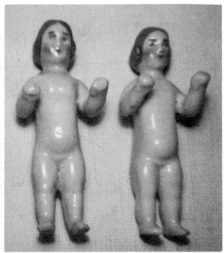

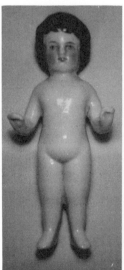

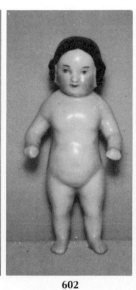

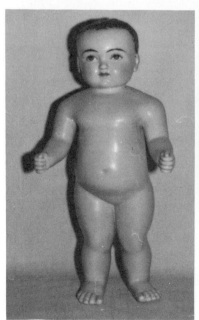

## FROZEN CHARLOTTES

**599.** Bonnet Frozen Charlotte. H. 3 inches. *Courtesy of the Newark Museum, Newark, N.J.*

**600.** Two identical Frozen Charlottes with blonde hair. H. 2¼ inches. *Courtesy of the Newark Museum, Newark, N.J.*

**601.** Frozen Charlotte. H. 4 inches. *Courtesy of Edith R. Meggers.*

**602.** Frozen Charlotte of flesh-tinted china. Note long torso and short neck. H. 5 inches. *Courtesy of Ollie Leavister.*

**603.** Bisque Frozen Charlotte with molded hair in Alice-in-Wonderland hair style; gilded boots, molded socks; original net dress H. 6¼ inches. *Courtesy of Mrs. Edgar Dawson.*

599

600

601

602

603

605

**604.** Large, all flesh-tinted Frozen Charlotte has brown eyes, brush marks around the hairline. Note the short neck and chubbiness of a baby. H. 15 inches. *Courtesy of Dorothy Annunziato.*

**605.** Large china Frozen Charlotte with head and neck flesh tinted; remainder of the body is white; brown eyes; dark line between the lips. H. 14 inches. *Coleman Collection.*

604

**Fryer, Thomas.** 1915–16. London. Distributed and repaired dolls.

**Fuch, Darrell Austen.** See **Fitch, Darrell Austen.**

**Fuchs, Paul.** 1903–4. Berlin. Procured a U.S. and a German patent for a walking doll on rollers, which he assigned to the firm of *Treude & Metz.*

**Fulper Pottery Co.** 1918–21. Flemington, N.J. Made bisque heads for dolls and a few all-bisque dolls. The pottery was established in 1805, but appears to have made dolls' heads only in the 20th century. The manufacture of bisque heads began in 1918, but apparently they were not on the market until 1919. *Horsman, Harold Bowie,* and *Benjamin Goldenberg,* all of the Horsman Co., helped with the production of the bisque heads; Benjamin Goldenberg was the expert on the coloring of the bisque. The first report in PLAYTHINGS on these heads, in June, 1919, listed two baby-face models in two sizes each, and two girl-face models in two sizes each.

1920: Advertised ten girl models of socket heads, eight baby models of socket heads, six breastplate models; all of these were made to fit dolls in sizes from 13 to 22 inches; came with sleeping glass eyes but without wigs, which had to be purchased separately. All twenty-four heads cost $35.00. They also listed bisque-head dolls, fully jointed standing ones, sizes 14, 21, and 26 inches; baby sitting dolls, sizes 14, 16, 20, and 24 inches; prices $42.00 to $93.00 doz. wholesale.

1921: Advertised twenty-two varieties of bisque dolls' heads; came in six sizes of socket heads for straight-limb dolls, five sizes for sitting babies, and seven sizes of breastplate models, as well as several other models.

A few of their heads have molded hair and intaglio eyes. The celluloid and metal sleeping eyes patented by *Samuel Marcus* in 1918 are often found in Fulper heads. Some Fulper heads also have marks of Horsman or *Amberg.*

## FULPER DOLLS

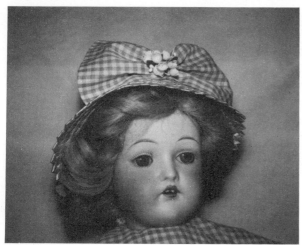

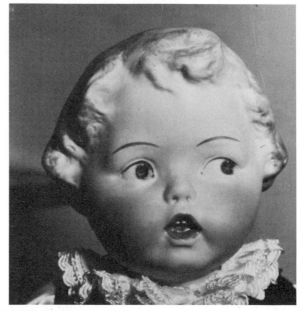

**606.** Bisque head made by Fulper Pottery for Louis Amberg & Son, ca. 1920. Mark: Ill. **610.** H. of doll 23 inches. *Coleman Collection.*

**608A & B.** All-bisque Kewpie made by Fulper Pottery has painted features; 1920. H. 11 inches. *Courtesy of the Newark Museum, Newark, N.J.*

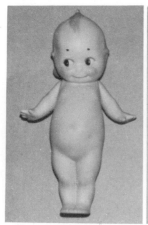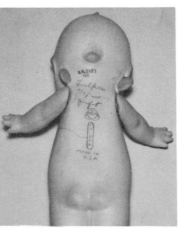

**607.** Bisque head made by Fulper Pottery has intaglio eyes, open-closed mouth, molded hair. Mark: Ill. **611.** H. 20 inches. *Courtesy of Mrs. Allen Seward; photograph by Winnie Langley.*

**609.** All bisque "Peterkin" doll made by Fulper Pottery has painted features; 1919. H. 11 inches. *Courtesy of the Newark Museum, Newark, N. J.*

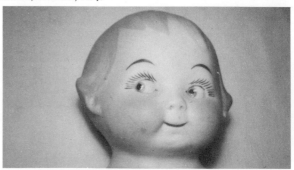

**Fumsup (Fums Up or Thumbs Up).** 1914–20. Trademark registered in Britain and in France by John Green Hamley of *Hamley Bros.* for dolls.

**Fumsup.** 1921. Registered in France as a trademark by *Gourdel Vales & Co.*

**Fur Eyebrows. See Eyebrows of Hair.**

**Furga.** 1872–1925+. Mark used by the Ceramica Furga of Canneto sull' Oglio, Mantua, Italy, a porcelain factory. This mark has been found on the head of dolls (see Ill. 1728).

**Furukawa.** 1900. Japan. Displayed dolls at the Paris Exposition and received Honorable Mention.

**Fuzbuz.** 1913. Trademark registered in Britain by *Dean's Rag Book Co.* for rag dolls.

**Fynn, Penelope.** 1921. Denver, Colo. Secured U.S. design patent for a fat boy doll.

# G

**G. & G. Doll Co.** 1921–22. New York City. Made dolls.

**Gabriel, Saml., Sons & Co.** 1916–17. New York City. Made dolls with trade name *Mother Goose.*

**Gaby.** 1923. Trademark registered in France by both *René Bertrand* and *Société Bonin & Lefort.*

**Gaby.** 1925. Doll made by *Harva Cie.*

**Gaffney, James C.** 1922. New York City. Secured U.S. design patent for doll dressed in long skirt, coat, and hat.

**Galabert, Mme.** 1925. Paris. Made richly dressed *mignonettes.*

**Galilé, B.** 1921. Paris. Made dolls.

**Galindo, Trinidad.** 1893. Puebla, Mexico. Displayed dolls at the Chicago Exposition.

**Gallais, P. J., & Co.** 1921–25. Paris. Made dolls.

**Gallia.** 1915. Trademark registered in France by *Mlle. Desaubliaux.*

**Galluba & Hofmann. See Ilmenau.**

**Gamine. See Little Annie Roonie.**

**Gans, Otto.** 1908–25+. Waltershausen, Thür. Made and exported dolls and baby dolls; claimed to have invented *roguish eyes.*

1909: Obtained German patent for jointed dolls.

1912–18: Procured five German patents for dolls with moving eyes.

1923: Obtained four German and two British patents for

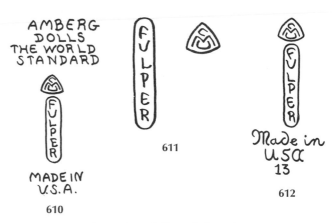

**610–612.** Marks used on dolls made by Fulper Pottery Co.

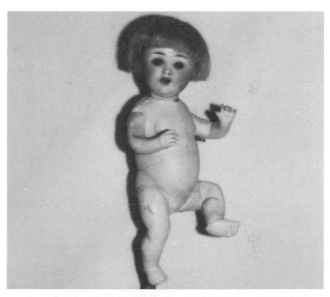

**613A & B.** Otto Gans' doll with bisque head, sleeping eyes, open mouth with two teeth, composition body with one leg bent more than the other. Mark on head: Ill. **614.** H. 12½ inches. *Courtesy of Dorothy Annunziato.*

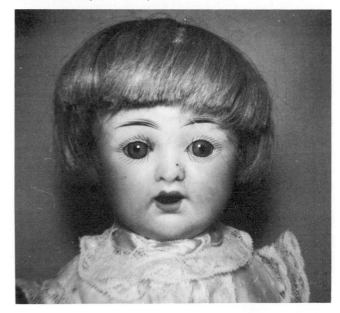

walking dolls. Some of these pertained to dolls in which the walking action caused the voice to sound; in others, it made the head turn.

1924: Obtained a German and a British patent for voice-producing devices. Registered a trademark in Germany of a bird in a shield.

1925: Member of the German Manufacturers Association in New York City (see Ill. 1738).

614

615

614 & 615. Otto Gans' marks found on dolls.

616. Mark used by Gans & Seyfarth on dolls.

616

**Gans & Seyfarth.** 1909–25+. Waltershausen, Thür. Manufactured dolls, dolls' heads, and parts of dolls.

1909: Made dolls' heads with stiffening material on the eyes and neck.

1910: Registered in Germany the initials "G. S." for jointed dolls.

1911: Registered *Dolly Mine* in Germany as a trademark for jointed dolls.

1919: Registered *Racker* (Rascal) and *Schalk* (Rogue) in Germany as trademarks for dolls' heads.

**Gardin, Laura.** 1912–13. New York City. Designed three dolls that *Horsman* copyrighted, namely *Merry Max, Eric,* and *Peter Pan.* Laura Gardin was an artist; appeared in WHO'S WHO IN AMERICAN ART. Her teacher and husband was James Earl Fraser, who designed the U.S. Indian head nickel, which came into use in 1913.

**Gardineer, Marian F.** 1920–21. Seattle, Wash. Registered in U.S. *The Peggy Doll* as a trademark for dolls.

**Garfield, James, & Co.** 1920–23. London. Made dolls.

**Gary, Theo. H., & Co.** 1909. Hoboken, N.J. Made dolls, including ones representing Dr. *Cook* and Commander *Peary.*

**Gasoline Alley.** 1923–25+. Dolls made in several materials, including all-bisque, oilcloth, etc. (See also **Benoliel.**)

**Gasparez.** 1925. Paris. Made dolls.

**Gatget, Mme.** 1885. Paris. Made dolls.

**Gatter, Edward.** 1884–87. London. Made gutta-percha dolls.

**Gatusse, Clément.** See **Cosman Frères.**

**Gaudinot, Mlle.** 1865–70. Paris. Made dolls. Merged with *Popineau.*

**Gault, André.** 1914–23. Paris. Distributor for dressed and undressed dolls and *mignonettes.*

**Gault, J. Roger.** 1917. Paris. Registered in France *Plastolite* as a trademark for a plastic paste and articles molded with this paste, such as the heads and bodies of dolls.

**Gaultier (Gautier).** 1860–1916+. St. Maurice, Charenton, Seine, and Paris. Made porcelain dolls' heads and doll parts. In 1863 it was A. Gautier.

1878: F. (Fernand?) Gaultier was awarded a silver medal for his dolls' heads at the Paris Exposition.

1880: Gaultier & Fils (Sons) won a bronze medal at the Brussels Exhibition for their entry.

1883: Exhibited at Amsterdam and won a silver medal.

1884: Exhibited at Nice and won a silver medal.

1885: Exhibited at Antwerp and won a silver medal; advertised that they were making dolls and bébés of porcelain.

DOLLS WITH BISQUE HEADS, PROBABLY MADE BY GAULTIER

**617.** Lady doll with bisque socket head on bisque shoulder plate, wooden articulated body. Marked "FG" on left shoulder and "4" on right shoulder. H. 17 inches. *Courtesy of Pat Robinson.*

**618.** Lady doll with bisque socket head on bisque shoulder plate, wooden arms, gusset-jointed kid body. Marked "FG" on shoulder. H. 13 inches. *Courtesy of Pat Robinson.*

617

618

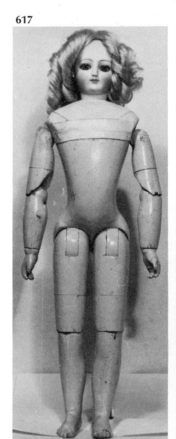

**619.** Lady doll with bisque shoulder head marked as in Ill. **624**, except #"4." She has glass eyes, pierced ears, gusset-jointed kid body. H. 18 inches. H. of shoulder head, 4 inches. *Courtesy of Virginia Dilliplane.*

**620.** Doll in a provincial costume of France, with bisque socket head on bisque shoulder plate, has glass eyes and pierced ears. Mark on shoulder: Ill. **625**. Cloth body. Note the small size of the bisque hands. H. 26 inches. H. of shoulder head, 7 inches. *Courtesy of Virginia Dilliplane.*

**621A & B.** Bébé with bisque socket head, may be Gaultier, is marked "F 9 G," has glass eyes, pierced ears, closed mouth. The jointed composition body was made and assembled by an unknown concern. The dress is probably not original. *Courtesy of Hazel Ulseth.*

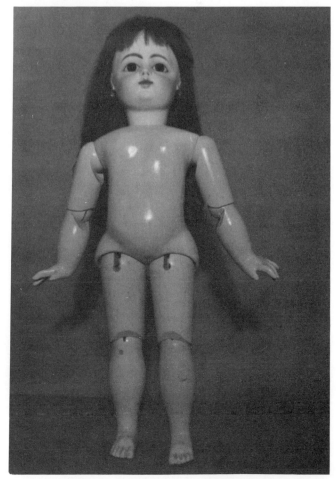

## DOLLS WITH BISQUE HEADS, PROBABLY MADE BY GAULTIER

**622.** Bisque head marked "F 3/0 G" on back of shoulder has painted features and partly painted hair. This bald head probably wore a cap or bonnet that completely covered the back portion of the head. Ears are pierced. H. of shoulder head, 2½ inches. *Coleman Collection.*

**623.** Bisque head has painted features and hair. Mark on back shoulder: Ill. **625.** Cloth body, earthenware limbs; original clothes represent a fisherwoman of Boulogne. H. 9½ inches. *Coleman Collection.*

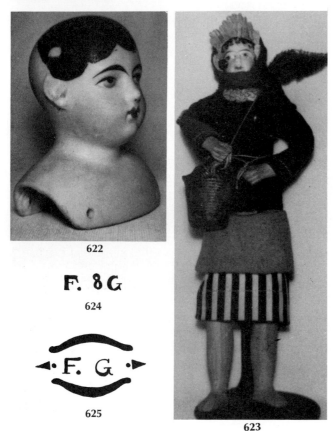

**622**

**F. 8 G**

**624**

**◄ • F. G • ►**

**625**

**623**

**624 & 625.** Marks found on bisque heads probably made by Gaultier.

1889: Received a silver medal for display at Paris Exposition. Firm became Gaultier Frères (Bros.) Advertised porcelain dolls' heads and bébés.

1900: Won a bronze medal for display at Paris Exposition.

1916: Louis Gautier registered in France *La Poupée de France* as a trademark for dolls.

It is not certain that these various Gautiers and Gaultiers belonged to the same firm, nor is it certain that the bisque dolls' heads marked "F. G." were made by these people. However, it is known that this company was making porcelain heads at an early date and that these were of a quality to win recognition at most of the International Exhibitions. The "F. G." marks appear on some dolls that seem to have been made after the 1916 date.

**Gauthier.** 1863–72. Paris. Made dolls. In 1872, obtained a French patent for an improved method of making dolls' heads.

**Gay, Benjamin.** 1843. London. Made dolls.

**Gay, William Alfred.** 1893–1903. Corry, Pa., and Litchfield, Conn. Obtained German, French, British, and U.S. patents for sound-producing dolls.

**Géant Bébé.** See **Bébé Géant.**

**Gebert, Georg.** 1891–ca. 1909, Berlin. 1909–10, successor was *Alfred Golschiner.* Manufactured and exported dressed and undressed dolls.

**Gee Gee Dolly.** 1912–14. Registered in U.S. and Germany as a trademark by *Horsman.* Copyrighted by Horsman, who named *Grace G. Drayton* as the designer.

1912: Boy- and girl-style dolls came with *Can't Break 'Em* heads; two sizes; prices $1.00 and $2.00.

1913: Name changed to *Peek-A-Boo* in U.S., but Gee Gee Dolly on the German trademark registration.

**Geffers, Carl.** 1911–15. Erfurt, Germany. Obtained two German patents for dolls' heads and/or parts. On the first patent he was joined by *Louis Schneegass.*

**Gehler, Milon.** 1925. Steinach, Thür. Made dolls.

**Geisha.** 1920. Doll dressed as a Japanese Geisha Girl, advertised by *Taiyo Trading Co.*

**Gekleidete Puppe (Dressed Doll).** 1910–11. Sonneberg, Thür. Trademark registered in Germany by *Ernst Winkler* firm.

**Gelatine Dolls' Heads.** 1909. Made by *Paul Hausmeister & Co.*

**Gem Toy Co.** 1913–25+. New York City. Made Gem character dolls of composition.

1914: Increased manufacturing facilities; made fifty models of girls, boys, and babies; priced 25¢ to $2.00.

1918: Advertised cherub-type dolls named *O-U-Kids.*

1920: Made jointed and soft-bodied dolls, including *Excelsior* dolls.

1922: Advertised *Flossie Featherweight,* as well as walking and talking dolls, 18 inches and up.

1924: Advertised a walking and talking doll named *Baby's Voice, Mother's Choice;* price 50¢ to $10.00.

1925: Registered Gem as a trademark in the U.S., and advertised an infant doll named *Just Born.*

**Gene Carr Kids.** 1916. Designed by *Bernard Lipfert* for *Horsman* from the cartoon characters created by Gene Carr.

**Gent Acrobat.** Ca. 1905. Circus doll made by *Schoenhut.* Came with wooden or bisque head, rubber jointed; sizes 6 and 8 inches.

**Gentil Bébé.** 1895–1905. Advertised by *Ad. Bouchet* as the cheapest of the standing bébés with porcelain heads, made in France. Price 15¢ in 1895. *Mons. Hippolyte*

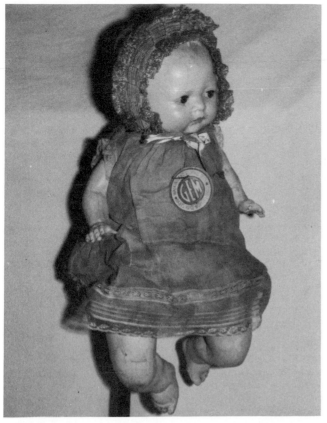

**626.** Baby doll made by Gem Toy Co. has composition head and limbs on a cloth body, celluloid and metal sleeping eyes with hair eyelashes, molded hair. Tag pinned to original dress is marked as in Ill. **627.** H. 20 inches. *Courtesy of Eleanor Jean Carter.*

**627.** Gem Toy Co.'s mark found on dolls.

**628.** Gent Acrobat made by Schoenhut; has bisque head with painted eyes, molded hair, and mustache; wooden body jointed with elastic cord; red and green felt costume with gold braid trim. H. 8 inches. *Coleman Collection.*

*Naneau* registered Gentil Bébé as a trademark in France for dolls.

**Genty.** See **Rabery & Delphieu.**

**Geoffroy, Arthur.** 1921. New York City. Sole U.S. representative of *Société Française de Fabrication de Bébés et Jouets;* advertised *Bébé Jumeau, Eden Bébé,* and *Bébé Bru,* priced up to $50.00.

**George, John.** 1891. London. Made dolls.

**George Washington.** 1905–21. Rag portrait doll made by *Martha Chase* with molded stockinet face.

**Georgi, Eleonore.** 1924. Coblenz, Germany. Made and distributed dolls; registered in Germany "Georgi" as a trademark for dolls.

**Georgia Peaches Home Grown.** 1919. Trademark registered in U.S. by *Abbie B. Stevens* for dolls.

**Georgy-Porgy.** 1915. Copyrighted by *Trion Toy Co.;* head of a young boy designed by *Ernesto Peruggi.*

**Gera.** See **Greiner.**

**Gerarbon (Girarbon).** 1874. Paris. Was issued a French patent for a multifaced doll.

**Gerardin.** 1874. Paris. Was granted a French patent for sleeping eyes adapted for rubber dolls.

**Gerbaud.** 1892. Paris. Modeler and maker of molds for dolls.

**Gerbaulet Frères (Bros.) Etablissements.** 1910–25+. Paris. Made dolls.

1910: Registered in France *Le Coquet Bébé* and the initials "G. F." as trademarks.

1914–25: Advertised *Bébé Olga,* which had been registered as a trademark by *Ernst Ballu.*

1926: Registered in France Bébé Olga as their trademark.

**Gerberg, Morris, & Hirsch, Alexander, & Morgan, Mitchel.** 1919–21. New York City. Obtained U.S. patent for a doll's body of sheet metal, jointed with spring plate, washers, flanges, and tang.

**Gerchoux.** 1847–52. Paris. Made dolls.

**Gerlet.** Before 1908. Reported by Laura Starr as a doll maker.

**Gerling Toy Co.** 1912–25+. New York City, London, Paris, and Neustadt near Coburg, Thür. Made character dolls and voices for dolls. Arthur Gerling was called "The Voice King"; he obtained a U.S. and several German patents for dolls' voices operated by reeds and bellows.

Pat Pending
GERLING

**629.** Mark of Gerling Toy Co.

1919: Advertised composition dolls, cork-stuffed dolls, excelsior-stuffed dolls, talking dolls, and crying dolls.

1925: Advertised dolls with bisque heads and glass sleeping eyes. Also, the only doll that cried when any part of its body was squeezed. About this time, made an infant doll with pierced nostrils and a bent-limb body; height of torso and head, 10¼ inches.

**Germain, M.** 1906–25+. Paris. Made indestructible bébés with either bisque heads or composition heads.

**German.** 1892. One of the *Brownies* designed by *Palmer Cox* and made by the *Arnold Print Works*.

**German American Doll Co.** Before 1918. New York City. 1919–25+, Regal Doll Manufacturing Co., successor, made "Regal" dolls.

1918–19: *Louis Amberg & Son* advertised Regal sleeping dolls in five sizes and stuffed dolls. Regal Doll Manufacturing Co. advertised a new cherub-type doll, 13½ inches tall.

1921: *Riemann, Seabrey Co.* was the distributor for Regal.

1923: Regal produced nearly 6,000 dolls a day, including heads, arms, and composition legs. Costumes for dolls created by Mme. Corrine Clair; dolls priced $1.00 to $5.00.

1924: Regal advertised dolls for 50¢ to $5.00.

1925: *John Bing* distributed Regal dolls. The trade name *Queen of Toyland* was used by Regal; also made *Kiddie Pal* line of dolls.

Later, Regal purchased the *Horsman* name.

**German-American Import Co.** 1925. New York City. Handled dolls made in Germany with bisque heads and jointed kid bodies. Came in sizes 24, 25, 26, and 28 inches.

**German Dolls.** Thüringia and Bavaria have been centers of doll-making since medieval times. Labor was cheap, most of the work being done in the homes; raw materials were readily available, as well as skills. The industry was encouraged with subsidies, and there were schools for teaching people how to design and manufacture dolls. Various grades of dolls were made and nearly all types of material were used to manufacture them. The competition between Germany and France in the manufacture of dolls was always keen, and there seems to have been a considerable amount of trade between the two countries. Many of the early records refer to the extensive use of German heads on French dolls. Mid-19th-century exhibition reports by Mons. Natalis Rondot, a Frenchman, state, "Most doll heads are made of papier-mâché. Saxony furnishes them . . . the making of porcelain heads has been introduced in Bavaria, Prussia and Austria; it has developed greatly in Coburg, Sonneberg and Nürnberg. The heads that come from these places are very well executed."

The following report on German dolls was published as part of the 1904 St. Louis Exposition reports:

**630A & B.** China head labeled by Sonneberg Museum as "Thuringian, ca. 1780, no mark; height 4 inches, breadth at shoulders 3½ inches." The hair style and decorative techniques resemble those of 19th-century dolls. *Courtesy of the Spielzeug Museum, Sonneberg, Thür.*

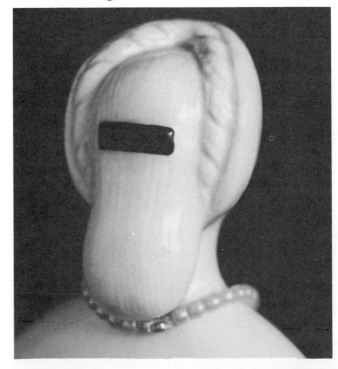

**631.** China-headed man illustrating home life in the Black Forest; has cloth body and leather hands. He is dressed in blue smock and black velvet trousers. H. 8 inches. *Courtesy of The Smithsonian Institution.*

"Sonneberg used wood from the Thüringian forests, and made dolls of wood, porcelain and papier-mâché. Papier-mâché had its origin from the art of wax modeling, which was especially popular in the 18th century, and consisted in modeling by hand portraits and little figures out of clay and wax.

"At the beginning of the nineteenth century toys were still made by hand by kneading a mixture of small pieces of paper, sand and glue together. In the following years, the price of wood went up, which made the sale of toys more and more difficult, and the industry found a quicker and ever increasing market by the introduction of an easier, more profitable and highly successful method of pressing the mixture in moulds. . . .

"Neustadt, dolls of various types made, affiliated along with Rodach, Eisfeld, Hildburghausen, etc., with Sonneberg. During the last twenty years [1884–1904] dressed dolls have become an important industry. Dolls with wax heads have gone very much out of fashion of late years, partly on account of their fragility and sensitiveness to touch and climate. To some extent they have been pushed out of the market by papier-mâché and porcelain dolls.

"The demand for dolls' heads is a very large one. In some of the establishments of Sonneberg the number manufactured every day reaches thousands of dozens. Domestic industry plays an important part in making dolls' heads of papier-mâché and wood, in making and stuffing dolls' bodies of linen and leather with hair, seaweed or wood shavings and also in making dolls' clothes."

Waltershausen, Ohrdruf, Köppelsdorf, and Ilmenau as well as other porcelain manufacturing centers in Germany made dolls and dolls' heads, but Sonneberg was the chief center. Nürnberg and Sonneberg supplied 90 percent of German toys, and three-quarters of these were exported in 1904. Some of the large German companies were *Kestner, Fleischmann & Blödel, Cuno & Otto Dressel, Kämmer & Reinhardt, Simon & Halbig,* and *Armand Marseille.*

When World War I broke out, German dolls continued to appear on American markets until 1917, but for several years after the war very few dolls were imported from Germany because of the intense feelings. Economic problems plagued Germany in the early 1920's, but nevertheless many dolls were produced and exported.

**German Novelty Co.** 1914–15. New York City. Registered in U.S. *Tipperary Tommy* and *Tipperary Mary* as trademarks for dolls. In 1915 also advertised *Laddie Boy* and *Highland Lass.*

**German Vampire.** See **Big Bertha.**

**Gérôme.** Before 1908. Laura Starr states that a doll by Gérôme was given as a prize to an inventor in Paris.

**Gertie.** 1911–12. Import line of felt-faced character dolls, distributed by *Strobel & Wilken;* large protruding eyes. In some dolls, the eyes themselves could be manipulated. In others, there was a knob at the back of the head whereby the eyes could be moved in any direction. Gertie was the mate of a doll named *Bertie.*

**Gertie.** 1913. American doll made by *Tip Top Toy Co.;* mate of doll named *Bertie.*

**Geschwister (Brother) Heinrich's Kunstlerpuppen (Art Dolls).** 1925+. Nürnberg, Bavaria. Registered in Germany the trademark *Maya* and manufactured stuffed dolls.

**Gesetzlich Geschützt (Ges. Gesch.).** Means "patented" or "registered" in German.

**Gesland.** 1860–ca. 1915, Paris; 1916–21, Joseph Ortiz, successor; 1921–24, H. Delcourt, successor. Located at 5 rue Beranger from 1877 on. Made, exported, distributed, and repaired dolls. The Gesland given-name initials

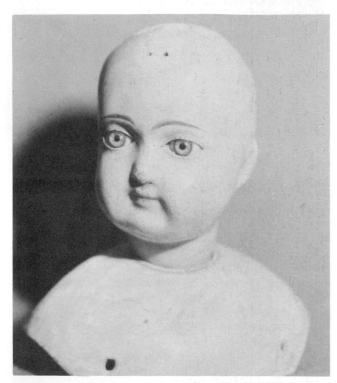

**632.** Composition head with printed paper label reading "Gesetzlich Geschützt" (patented); has swivel neck, blue glass eyes. *Courtesy of Maurine Popp; photograph by Winnie Langley.*

**633.** Label found on patented head, "Gesetzlich Geschützt," which means "patented" in German.

were E., F., and A. at various times. The name "Gesland" appears on stuffed bodies with a wire frame and stockinet covering. The heads are often bisque and marked with an "F G," which seems to represent *F. Gaultier* rather than Gesland. Gesland won a bronze medal at the 1878 Paris Exposition. Some years later, A. Gesland advertised bébés and heads "incassable" that were patented. Bébés were also made with heads, feet, and arms of hardwood. Gesland sold bébés in swaddling clothes, talking bébés, walking bébés, sleeping bébés, and Negro bébés, wigs of Thibet or of human hair, and clothes of all types for dolls.

Gesland advertised that he could repair in ten minutes bébés and dolls of all makes and replace broken heads. The shop was open from eight in the morning to eight in the evening; around Christmas and New Year's it was open on Sundays and holidays.

Undressed bébés with bisque heads came in sizes 13, 14, 15, 17, 19, 21, 23, 25, 27, 29, and 31 inches; the smallest size came with or without jointed wrists; prices were from 80¢ to $6.00. Dressed bébés with bisque heads and sleeping eyes with eyelashes came in

DOLLS WITH GESLAND-TYPE STOCKINET BODIES
(below and opposite)

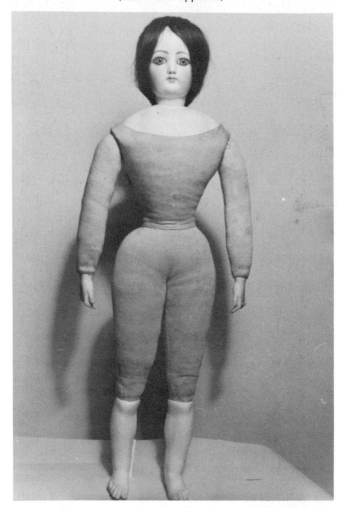

**634.** Bisque head is marked "F G" on right shoulder and "5" on back of the head. Doll has bisque limbs, tricot-covered metal-framed body. H. 19½ inches. *Courtesy of Pat Robinson.*

the same sizes as undressed bébés and cost $2.30 to $11.00. Bisque heads sold separately cost 10¢ to 90¢.

1914: Gesland advertised metal joints for bébés and repaired bébés of all makes.

1916: Registered *Excelsior Bébé* as a trademark in France.

1919: Advertised Excelsior Bébé and other dolls and bébés.

1921: Factory in Paris; sales rooms at 5 rue Beranger. Advertised dolls made entirely in France; jointed bébés dressed and undressed; rigid dolls and semi-articulated dolls. The Paris address and telephone number of *J. Verlingue* was the same as that of Gesland.

**Gesser, Gustav.** 1920–21. Waltershausen, Thür. Made dolls.

**Gessert, Schmidt & Co.** 1923–25. Engelsbach, Thür. Made standing jointed dolls and sitting baby dolls.

**Geuther, Th.** 1918–25+. Sonneberg, Thür. Made dolls.

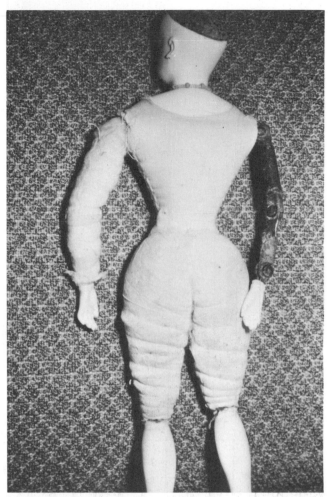

635. Arms are stripped to show the construction. The right arm is stripped down to the jointed metal framework; only the tricot is removed from the left arm, to show how the cotton wadding was bound. Doll has bisque head marked "F G," bisque hands and lower legs. *Courtesy of Margaret Whitton; photograph by Winnie Langley.*

636. Bisque head is marked "F G," probably for F. Gaultier. Stockinet-covered body is stamped "E. Gesland." Doll has glass eyes, pierced ears, bisque hands and lower legs. *Courtesy of Margaret Whitton; photograph by Winnie Langley.*

**Gewerbliche und Kunstgewerbliche Werkstauten Opifex.** 1924–25. Dresden, Saxony. Made dolls.

**Geyer, Carl (Karl), & Co.** 1885–1913, Sonneberg, Thür.; 1913–25+, Carl Geyer & Sohn (Son). Manufactured and distributed dressed dolls.

1885: Registered in Germany a trademark of two girls holding a doll.

1893: Displayed dolls at the Chicago Exposition.

1899: Had a London branch.

1900: One of the Grand Prize winners at the Paris Exposition. Registered in Germany trademarks of a cornucopia filled with dolls and *Bébé Habillé.*

1902: Registered in Germany *Liliput* as a trademark.

**Gianetto, "Dr." Fred.** 1882–1922. Boston, Mass. Repaired at least 1,000 dolls a year and advertised that he never changed a doll's features.

**Giblet, Miss Marcel.** 1921–22. Prague, Czechoslovakia. Made dolls in the imaginative style of Gauguin. One doll was a Negro made of highly decorated silks. Miss Giblet was a pupil at the School of Design and Art Applied to Industry in Paris.

**Gibson, Charles.** 1922–23. New York City. Obtained U.S. design patent for a long-limbed doll.

**Gibson, Edward Tinkham.** 1909–12. Brooklyn, N.Y. Patented in U.S. and England a rag doll with a skirt that hung free from the stuffed body, which was made from the same length of material as the skirt. Doll distributed by *Elms & Sellon* with the trade name *No-Break*, life-size doll. It was printed in colors and jointed so that it could sit.

**Gibson, Irene Wilkinson.** 1854–ca. 1875. Boston, Mass. Ca. 1875, moved to Marlboro, N.H. Made bodies for *Cinderella Sitting Dolls.* Some of these dolls had striped stockings and heeled boots. In some years, Mrs. Gibson was listed as a doll manufacturer.

**Gibson Girl.** 1910. Name stamped in blue on chest of some lady-type dolls made by *Kestner* (see Ill. 965). The number of dolls of this type suggest that they may have been made for several years. Many of these dolls have only the Kestner stamp without the name "Gibson Girl." They were pictured in the 1910 LADIES' HOME JOURNAL as "The Queen of Hearts."

**Giebeler-Falk Doll Corp.** 1918–21. New York City. Made wooden and aluminum dolls.

1919: Registered in U.S. Gie-Fa as a trademark for dolls, dolls' heads, dolls' bodies, dolls' wigs, dolls' eyes, dolls' hands and feet, and dolls' clothes. Obtained U.S. patent for improving dolls' joints and permitting them to assume "human-like" postures. January, 1919, advertised doll with bisque head, all wooden body, rubber joints, brown or blue sleeping eyes, mohair or real hair wig. Came dressed or only in chemise, shoes, and stockings; sizes, 16, 18, 20, 22, and 25 inches. The next month (February, 1919), advertised "All Wood" rubber jointed limbed doll with aluminum socket head, moving eyes, teeth, and real hair wig; same sizes as above. In April, advertised all wooden body and limbs with aluminum head and hands. In May, 1919, advertised dolls with aluminum feet as well as head and hands. June, 1919, advertised *Primadonna*, a phonograph doll with aluminum body and head; came in sizes 25 and 30 inches. Both shoulder-type metal heads and socket metal heads have been found with the five-pointed star enclosing the "G."

1920: Advertised aluminum heads, hands, and feet on jointed composition dolls in sizes as given above.

1921: Giebeler-Wanke, president of the corporation, was issued two U.S. design patents for cherub-type dolls with wigs, one a boy doll and one a girl doll.

**Gie-Fa.** See **Giebeler-Falk Doll Corp.**

**Gifford, Squire Daniel.** 1905–6. Terra Alta, W. Va. Obtained U.S. patent for mechanism to move the eyeballs and eyelids of a doll. He assigned his rights to Jacob P. Shafer.

**Giftoy Co.** 1921. Mamaroneck, N.Y. Advertised *Gertrude Stacy's* soft dolls, including *Sunbonnet Jane, Pepper-Mint Kids, Bully Boy Brewster,* and *The Amphibious Clown.*

**Giggly.** 1920. Trademark registered in Britain by *Edward Hazell Jones* for dolls.

**Gilbert, Walter Villa.** 1905–6. Port Elizabeth, So. Africa, and London. Secured a British and a U.S. patent for a doll with moving eyes, ears, tongue, etc.; doll could "swallow" food.

**Gillespie, Gordon Finlayson.** 1916–21. Los Angeles, Calif. Registered in U.S. *Vampie* as a trademark for dolls. Obtained U.S. design patent for cherub-type doll. In 1919 Gillespie copyrighted two dolls named Vampie; one was designed by Edna Berg and the other was designed by J. L. Roop. Gillespie also copyrighted *Lucky Little Devil*

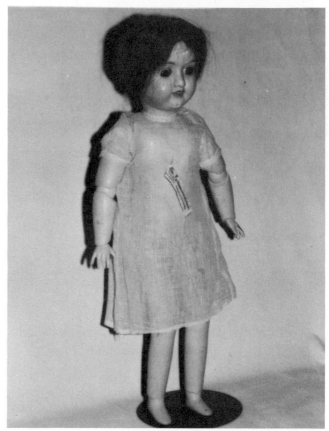

**637A & B.** Giebeler-Falk doll with aluminum head, hands, and feet; wooden torso, arms, and legs; metal sleeping eyes. She is dressed in her original chemise with ribbon label: Ill. **639**. Mark on head: Ill. **638**. H. 25 inches. *Courtesy of the International Doll Library Foundation.*

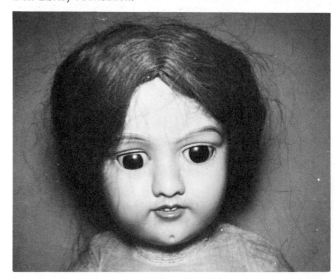

**638 & 639.** Marks on Giebeler-Falk dolls; No. **639** found on a ribbon label and **638** on the heads.

2 5

G

U.S. PAT.

638

Gie-Fa  Aluminum Heads & Hands
Trade Mark
New York, N.Y.  Guaranteed Unbreakable

639

designed by Ceseare Paoli. Previously, in 1916, Gillespie had obtained two copyrights for an Indian Doll designed by Rena Whitely.

1920: Copyrighted *Dip Me,* designed by Fred Giorgi.

**Gimbel Bros.** Ca. 1900–25+. New York City and Philadelphia, Pa. Had dolls made especially for them with heads by *Simon & Halbig.* Some of these heads are mold #550 and are also marked "G." They are found on ball-jointed composition bodies with "Gimbels" stamped in red on the back.

1910: Their doll department, where they sold dolls dressed in costumes designed and made in Gimbel's dressmaking department, was called "The French Doll Shop." The *Munich Art Dolls* of *Marion Kaulitz* were also shown in The French Doll Shop.

Before 1919 *Katherine Fleischmann,* who made the *Kay Eff* dolls, was a buyer for Gimbel's. From 1914 on, Gimbel's carried *Kewpie* dolls that *Borgfeldt* imported from Germany. Other leading suppliers of dolls were *Louis Amberg & Son, Averill Manufacturing Co., Regal Doll Co., Kestner,* and *EFFanBEE.*

**Gindelois.** 1867–70. Paris. Made dolls.

**Giotti, D. Etablissements.** 1925+. Nice, France, Made *Art Dolls* of felt; used *Magali* as a trademark.

**Girarbon.** See **Gerarbon.**

**Girard, Alexandre.** 1925. Factory at Montreuil-sous-Bois, France. Made dolls and used the trade name *Jépé.*

**Girard, C.** 1900–1908. Paris. Made dolls.

**Girard, Eugène Frederick.** Son of Paul Eugène Girard. See **Société Française de Fabrication de Bébés et Jouets.**

**Girard, Paul Eugène.** See **Bru.**

**Girl of the Golden West.** 1920. Copyrighted by *Julius D. Benvenuti.* Cherub-type doll with molded hair and lock in center of forehead; eyes centered; jointed shoulder; starfish-type hands; feet together.

**Girl with the Curl, The.** 1912. Name from a musical comedy used by *Louis Amberg & Son* for a double-faced character girl doll with a curl in the center of her forehead. Came with composition head and cork-stuffed sateen body.

**Girlie.** 1921. Cherub-type doll copyrighted by *Edward C. Brown.* Came with real hair, eyes glancing to the side, fingers apart, and legs together.

**Giroux, Alphonse, & Co.** 1839–before 1867. Paris. At some time before 1867 to 1873, successors were Duvinage & Harinkouck. Handled French, German, and English dolls. Won a silver medal for doll display at the 1839 Paris Exposition. The 1867 Paris and 1873 Vienna exhibitions both contained displays of Maison Giroux products. A doll formerly in the possession of Estrid Faurholt has a kid body and bisque head marked "B O S"; it was accompanied by a trunk of clothes. The lid of the trunk was marked: "Maison Alphonse Giroux,

**640A & B.** Bisque head was made by Simon & Halbig for Gimbel Bros. The head is marked with a "G" (see Ill. **641**), and the body has the red stamp of Gimbel Bros. on the hip (see Ill. **642**). Contemporary dress. H. 23 inches. *Coleman Collection.*

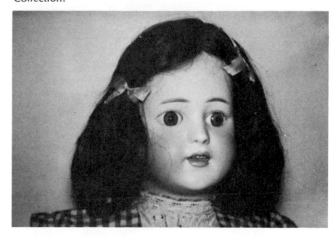

**641 & 642.** Marks on dolls handled by Gimbel Bros.; No. **641** is on the head, and No. **642** is stamped in red on the body.

550
Germany
G
SIMON & HALBIG
S & H
641

Gimbel Bros.
Germany
642

successeurs Duvinage & Harinkouck." Similar bisque heads have been found marked "B 2 S," "B 3 S," etc. Eleanor St. George, in THE DOLLS OF YESTERDAY, makes an undocumented statement that this is a *Bru* mark.

**Giroux, N.** 1881–85. Paris. Made dolls. In 1885 he was at 140 rue du Temple, an address occupied earlier by *Pannier* and *Rauch*.

**Given, John L.** See **Webber.**

**Givjoy Toys.** 1920. Trademark registered in Britain by *A. J. Holladay & Co.*

**Gladys.** 1924. A *Baby Grumpy* doll made by *EFFanBEE*.

**Glaser & Co.** 1919. Munich, Germany. Secured German patent for dolls' bodies.

**Glass Cases.** Fine dolls were sometimes placed in glass cases, in the era when playing with a doll often meant only looking at it and not handling it.

1844: Wax dolls in glass cases were shown at the Berlin Exhibition.

1862: A German doll in a glass case cost $3.75.

1878: Dolls at the Paris Exposition were "mounted in glass cases elaborately framed with gilt and lined with satin, and arranged in pretty tableaux enacted by 'life-like' dolls dressed with Parisian taste. One of these represented a garden party, and is said to have cost $700.00."

**Glass Eyes.** Glass was the principal material used for the eyes of dolls before 1926. (See the various entries under **Eye.**)

**Glass Heads.** 1888. *Parquet* obtained a French patent for making dolls' and bébés' heads of blown glass.

**Gleason Doll Co.** 1911–13. Jersey City, N.J. Made dolls with patented molded leather heads, wearing wigs; had muslin bodies stuffed with cork, and limbs joined to body with tubular connections. Albert J. Gleason and Emma Gleason obtained one German and two U.S. patents for their dolls. The molded leather face of the head was pressed and laminated with a layer of wet plaster and a layer of felt saturated with glue or shellac behind it, the layers being pressed together until dry. A layer of felt was added before the plaster of Paris on the neck portion so that it would remain soft. The ears were stiffened and sewed on. Glass eyeball hemispheres were inserted in slits made to simulate upper and lower eyelids. Eyelashes were glued over the eyes. The upper portion of the limbs consisted of a tubular member through which the unstuffed parts of the lower limbs were drawn. The stuffed and unstuffed portions of the lower limbs were defined by transverse lines of stitching.

**Gleichmann, Emil.** 1895–1909. Neustadt near Coburg, Thür. Made dressed dolls.

**Glenn Hunter.** 1924. *Celebrity Doll* originated by *Margaret Vale*, designed and made by *Jane Gray*. The doll represented Glenn Hunter as Merton in Geo. C. Tyler's play MERTON OF THE MOVIES. It had a hand-painted face and bore a tag with a facsimile autograph of Glenn Hunter.

**Globe Baby.** 1898–1925+. Line of dolls made by *Carl Hartmann;* distributed by *E. A. Runnells & Co.*

1899: Name registered in Germany by Hartmann as a trademark for dolls. The previous year the drawing of a globe had been registered also as a trademark in Germany.

**Globe Inc.** 1924–25. Berlin. Doll artists.

**Gloom.** 1912. Doll made by *Seligman & Braun,* under license of T. E. Powers, cartoonist of the NEW YORK AMERICAN. Doll had round eyes with iris in the center; wore a goatee; price $8.00 doz. wholesale.

**Gloomy Gus.** 1903–7. Doll advertised in PLAYTHINGS; represented one of the characters in HAPPY HOOLIGAN comics. Doll was dressed similarly to an undertaker with a high silk hat. Gloomy Gus was also used as part of various metal toys made in U.S.

**Gloria Swanson.** 1924. A *Likeness Doll* representing Gloria Swanson in THE HUMMING BIRD.

**Glosbrenner, Charlotte L.** 1919–22. York, Pa. Registered in U.S. *The Charlotte-Louise* as a trademark for dolls.

1920: Obtained a U.S. patent for a cloth body composed of two sections each for (a) half of the back of the torso, and the outer leg, (b) the inner half of the leg, (c) half of the front of the torso, and (d) the upper arms. Lower arms and head were to be of rigid material.

**Glue.** This was used as an adhesive agent in the manufacture of papier-mâché and composition. The pre-World War I heads of glue and flour made with cold presses often peeled and were affected by changes in temperature. The desirability of letting children kiss unsanitary glue products was questioned, but glue persisted as a popular material for making dolls. As late as 1918 it was claimed that the glue-process heads were superior to the wood-pulp heads that eventually superseded them.

**Gobelin Dolls.** 1891. Trade name of dolls made by *Adolf Wislizenus.*

**Gobert, A.** 1898. Paris. Had a steam factory and made *Bébé Colosse, Bébé Le Préféré,* and *Bébé Sublime.*

**Godfrey, Emily Dorcas, Sarah, & Catherine Maria.** 1880. Croyden, Surrey. Registered in Britain their trademark of a sheaf of wheat in a diamond, used for dolls. A doll marked "S. G." has been found, but there is no proof of a connection.

**643.** "Globe Baby" mark used by Carl Hartmann.

**644.** Trademark used by the Godfreys.

643

644

**Goebel, William.** 1879–1925+. Oeslau, Thür. Inherited porcelain factory from his father, Franz Detlev Goebel. The intertwined "W. G." mark was used from 1879 onward. Around 1900 the factory made only porcelain figures, dolls, and dolls' heads. The products were in either bisque or glazed china. Some of his bisque heads were used by *Max Handwerck*. (See **Bébé Elite.**)

**Goebel Gebrüder (Bros.).** 1921–25. Sonneberg, Thür. Made and exported dolls, especially hand-painted wooden dolls with "voices." Had an agent in Britain.

**645.** Bisque shoulder head made by William Goebel has solid bald crown, stationary eyes, closed mouth. Mark: Ill. **647.** *Coleman Collection.*

**646.** William Goebel bisque-headed doll with flower clusters molded on either side of the head. Head mark: Ill. **648**, plus "K 73/0" instead of "B5-3¾ // Germany." Composition body is jointed at shoulders and hips; shoes and socks are molded. Original gauze dress. H. 6¾ inches. *Courtesy of Edna Greehy.*

**Goerlich, Karl, & Co.** 1923. Berlin. Manufactured and exported dolls.

**Goggle Eye Doll.** 1912. Doll with eyes glancing to the side, advertised by *Samstag & Hilder*. Price $1.00 and up. (See also **Roguish Eyes.**)

**Göhring, Max.** 1918–25+. Oberlind near Sonneberg, Thür. Doll manufacturer. Registered picture of a little girl in a swing as his trademark in Germany.

**Golconda.** 1921. Trade name for a doll made by *Nordicus Inc.*

**Gold Medal.** 1870's or 1880's. Name found on papiermâché shoulder heads with molded and painted features and hair. Often came on cloth bodies with leather arms and *Steuber*-type legs. Sizes 16 and 20½ inches. Larger size sometimes had painted lower lashes. (See color photograph C6.)

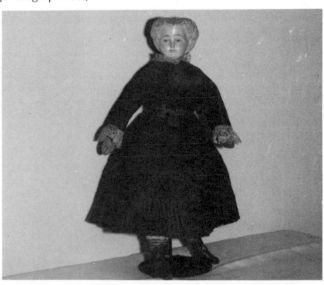

**652A & B.** Gold Medal composition shoulder head with high gloss has striated eyebrows. Sticker on back of shoulders: see Ill. **653.** Leather arms, Steuber-like legs; contemporary clothes. H. 16 inches. *Coleman Collection.*

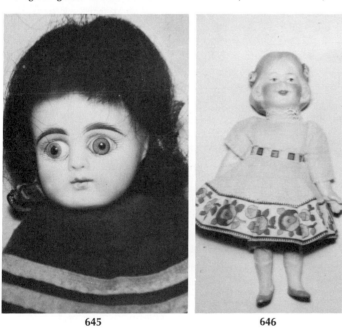

645                                646

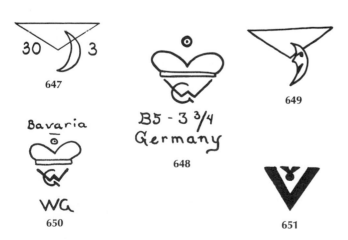

647

648

650                651

647–651. Marks found on dolls made by William Goebel; No. 651 is a trademark, used for Hummel figurines as well as dolls.

**653.** "Gold Medal" mark found on papier-mâché heads.

**Gold Medal Baby.** 1923–25. Trademark registered in U.S. by *Averill Manufacturing Corp.* Swastika design was on the medal.

**Gold Medal Prize Baby (Gold Medal Baby).** 1911–15. *Can't Break 'Em* head and arms on stuffed-bodied doll made by *Horsman*. Doll represented Adolphus Cody, a three-year-old boy who won first prize at a baby show in Georgia in 1909. The expression of the doll was advertised as suggesting delight at winning the prize. Came dressed in white; five sizes plus a life-sized doll; prices 50¢ to $5.00. In 1914, the "Prize" was dropped from the name, and the dolls had mohair wigs of red, green, blue, or yellow; still came in five sizes.

1915: Appears to have been made into a line of dolls, for new models were advertised.

**Goldberger, E.** 1917–25. New York City and Brooklyn, N.Y. Made composition character dolls.

1920: Advertised *Jollichose dolls*.

1921: Advertised *Excelcior* dolls.

1924–25: Advertised *EeGee Dolls*.

**Golden Jubilee.** 1915. Doll with *Can't Break 'Em* head and stuffed body; made by *Horsman*; price $1.00 and up.

**Goldenberg, Benjamin.** 1907–25+. New York City. Worked for *Horsman* and *Aetna Doll & Toy Co.*, to whom he assigned his two U.S. design patents and one regular U.S. patent for dolls. One of these design patents (1922) came out as the *Jackie Coogan Kid* doll. The patent was for dolls' joints comprised of a cap with a flat portion and a flange on three sides only. In 1918, Goldenberg was the expert on the desired coloring of *Fulper* bisque heads.

**Goldenlocks.** 1909–15. Life-size muslin cutout doll lithographed in color, made by *Saalfield Publishing Co.* It had light curly hair with ribbon in it, and blue eyes. The cloth came 25 by 34 inches and cost 25¢.

**Goldey Locks.** 1925+. *Story Book Doll* made by *Sol Bergfeld & Son;* distributed by *Borgfeldt.* Came with composition head; 15 inches tall.

**Goldilocks.** 1917–18. Two-piece rag doll with Goldilocks on one side and the bear on the other side; design patented in U.S. by *Mrs. Lelia Fellom;* faces were of the *Drayton* type.

**Goldilocks.** 1919–20. Trade name for doll made by *Jessie McCutcheon Raleigh.*

**Goldman, Isaac.** 1918. Obtained a British patent for attaching hair to a doll's head by using fluid adhesive for single strands or small bunches.

**Goldsmith, Philip.** 1870–94. Cincinnati, Ohio, and Covington, Ky. Made dolls' heads and cloth dolls' bodies.

1875: Exhibited at the Cincinnati Exhibition. Wolf Flechter (Fletcher) was in business with Goldsmith.

1877: Advertised dolls' bodies.

1878: Flechter sold out and went into business for himself. By 1880 he had moved to Covington; he continued to be listed as a doll maker through 1895. In 1887, he obtained a U.S. patent for a method of stuffing dolls.

1880: Goldsmith built a factory in Covington, which he called the *American Toy Co.* Here he made dolls' heads and dolls' bodies. The heads were of composition made from flour, glue, and pulp. He used three-part molds—one for the back of the head, and two for the face. The heads received two coats of varnish. Later he tried to make imitation bisque heads by using ether to give a dull finish, instead of varnish.

1885: Goldsmith was granted a U.S. patent for a doll's body with a corset made of material incorporated in the body, and outlined with an edging. These bodies were usually of muslin, with the lower part of the arms in leather. They were stuffed with sawdust except at the joints, where cattle hair was used. Across the chest in block letters was stamped: "PATD. DEC. 15, 1885."

1887: Advertised "Patent Corset bodies (no head), entirely new, with seat, kid arms, colored stockings, shoes with tassels, and adjustable lace corsets." These bodies

**654.** Goldsmith's patented corset body for dolls. Red corset, sewed into the body, back and front, has tan lacings. Red tasseled boots and stockings. Mark on top of the body, under the head: Ill. **655.** H. 18 inches. H. of shoulder head, 4¼ inches. *Coleman Collection.*

## PAT. DEC.15.1885

**655.** Mark on bodies made by Philip Goldsmith.

came with red or blue corsets, shoes, and stockings; sizes 10, 13½, and 16½ inches; prices 24¢, 32¢, and 48¢. The arms were brown leather, and the shoes were also of leather. Both corset and shoes had adjustable tan laces.

1890: The factory was destroyed by fire and the business moved to new premises. Goldsmith brought machines from Europe to make kid-body dolls, and workmen from Sonneberg to help produce wax dolls. He was half-assignee, from *Julius Wolf*, of a U.S. patent for a wax doll's head with imitation hair and glass eyes. After the death of Goldsmith in 1894, his sons carried on part of his business but discontinued making dolls.

**Goldstein, Joseph.** 1922–25. New York City. Distributed dolls, and in 1925 also manufactured dolls.

1922: Agent for the *Kay-Eff Toddle Baby*.

1925: Made *Mama Dolls*.

**Golf Boy or Golf Girl.** 1909. Dolls with *Life Like Faces* (photograph faces) made by *Horsman*, price $1.25.

**Golliwogg (Golliwog, Gollywog).** After 1895–1925+. Negro rag doll, usually with yarn hair, representing a character in the book THE ADVENTURES OF TWO DUTCH DOLLS AND A GOLLIWOGG, published in 1895.

**Gollywog.** 1917. Trademark registered in U.S. by *Etta Mansfield* and affixed to doll by a woven label.

**Golschiner, Alfred.** 1895–1910. Breslau, Germany. Made dolls. By 1909, he was the successor of *Georg Gebert* in Berlin.

**Gomptz, Willy.** 1924–25. Hamburg, Germany. Made rag dolls.

**Gondrand, E.** 1921–25, Paris; 1925+, Egler & Gondrand, successor. Made and exported dolls and bébés.

**Goo Goo Dolls.** 1904–25+. Trade name for dolls with eyes that move from side to side, also called *flirting* eye dolls. These dolls usually had real eyelashes. (See also **Roguish Eyes.**)

**Goo Goo Eye Dolls.** 1912. Trade name for composition head dolls made by *Elektra Toy & Novelty Co.*

**Gooch, C.** Late 19th century. London. Distributed wax dolls of *Charles Marsh.*

**656.** C. Gooch mark found on dolls.

**Goodie-Goodie.** 1916. Distributed by *Montgomery Ward & Co.* Came with character face, painted hair-ribbon bow; wore lace-trimmed dress. Height 14 inches; price $2.28.

**Goodman, L. & A. L. (Goodman, Louis).** 1923. London. Importer. Registered *Goody Goody Series* as trademark in Britain for dolls.

**Goodman, Samuel, & Meyers, Daniel.** 1880. Philadelphia, Pa. Assignees of U.S. patent rights obtained by *Robert Weir* for dolls.

**Goodwin, William Farr.** 1867–74. Washington, D.C. Inventor.

1867: Patented a walking toy in France.

1868: Patented in U.S. and Britain a walking doll pushing a wheeled vehicle and operated by a clockworks mechanism. (See Ill. 785.)

1874: *Althof, Bergmann & Co.* advertised this walking doll for $27.00 doz.

**Goody Goody.** 1915. Trade name for doll with Buster Brown bangs, made by *Louis Amberg & Son.*

**Goody Goody Series.** 1923. Trademark registered in Britain by *L. & A. L. Goodman* for dolls.

**Goodyear, Charles (Goodyear Rubber Co.).** 1839–90. New Haven, Conn. Invented vulcanized soft rubber or *Caoutchouc* used to make rubber dolls. In 1851, Nelson Goodyear, brother of Charles, invented hard rubber. Dolls' heads have been found labeled: "GOODYEAR'S PAT. MAY 6, 1851. EXT. 1865." Charles Goodyear obtained a U.S. patent in 1853 and a British patent in 1855 for molding toys of India rubber and gutta-percha. The U.S. patent was issued to Charles Goodyear and Robert Haering, with Charles Goodyear as assignee. The Goodyear Rubber Co. was manufacturing rubber dolls as late as 1890 and probably much later. *New York Rubber Co.* and *Benjamin Lee* both made rubber dolls under the Goodyear patents.

**Goodyear India Rubber Glove Manufacturing Co.** 1890. Naugatuck, Conn. Made rubber dolls.

**Goodyear Toy Co.** 1923–25. New York City. Made soft-body *Mama Dolls* with composition heads and arms.

1923: Dolls came in sizes 15 to 27 inches; 15-inch size cost $1.00. In 1924, sizes began at 13 inches.

1925: Used trade names *Peter Pan* and *Wendy* for their dolls.

**Goo-Goo.** 1920. Trademark registered in Britain by *Edward Hazell Jones* for dolls.

**Goo-Goo.** 1922–23. Trademark registered in U.S. by *Lenore Boatright* for dolls.

**Gooky Girl.** 1922–24. Trademark registered in U.S. by *Helen Vincent Reader* and usually stamped on the doll.

**Goolagool.** 1923. Trademark registered in Britain by *Léon Bollag* for dolls.

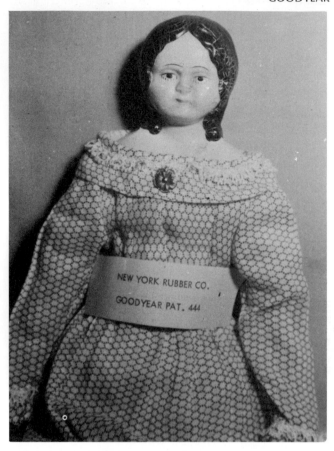

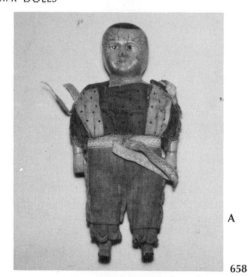

A

658

B

**657.** Rubber doll's head made by New York Rubber Co. using a Goodyear patent; painted black hair and eyes; lower lashes only. Mark on back shoulder: Ill. **1261.** *Photograph by Winnie Langley.*

**658A & B.** Goodyear rubber boy doll. Note lower lashes only; also brush marks at hairline; original clothes. Mark: Ill. **660.** H. 5 inches. *Courtesy of the Newark Museum, Newark, N.J.*

**659.** Goodyear rubber head. The rubber is dark olive color where the paint has chipped off. Mark on back of shoulder: Ill. **661.** Note similarity to the shape of the India Rubber Comb Co. doll in Ill. **877A.** H. 22½ inches. H. of shoulder head, 6 inches. *Courtesy of the Chester County Historical Society.*

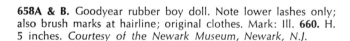

GOODYEAR   660

GOODYEAR'S PAT. MAY 6,1851 EXT. 1865   661

GOODYEAR'S
PAT. MAY 6, 1851 EXT. 1865   662

**660–662.** Marks on rubber dolls made under the Goodyear patents.

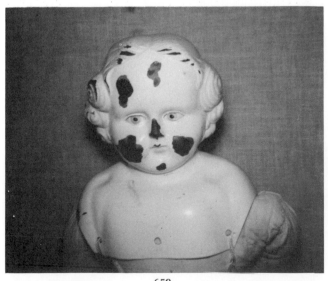

659

**Goss, Gladys.** 1920–21. Nevada, Mo. Was issued a U.S. design patent for a girl doll with bobbed hair and a bow; the eyes glanced to the side.

**Goss & Co.** 1858–1925+. Stoke-on-Trent, Staffordshire. Made "Parian" and "Ivory" porcelain busts in the 19th century and bisque dolls' heads and limbs in the 20th century. The bisque heads of the early 20th century were mostly shoulder-type heads and were marked on the back of the shoulder "GOSS." The doll parts were assembled by the *Potteries Toy Co.* The bodies were made of pink cambric and stuffed with brown wool fibers, according to the recollections of employees. An oval-shaped ink stamp has been found on the back of a body. Various types were made, including babies, in sizes up to 36 inches. The most popular size was 18 inches. The heads generally had movable eyes and the lips were usually painted a dark red. *Bawo & Dotter* were distributors for Goss products.

**Gosset, James.** 1763. London. Carved portraits in wood and modeled them in wax.

**Gossweiler, Karl.** 1913–14. Schwarenberg, Saxony. Obtained German patent for moving eyes in dolls' heads.

**Gota (Guta).** Name in blue found on inside of a china shoulder head. The bonnet molded on the head suggests the 1860's.

**Gottfried, Auguste.** 1897–1901. Vienna. Made dolls and dolls' heads.

**Gotthelf Firm.** 1873–1925+. Remscheid, Germany. Made dolls and babies. In 1915 and 1919 Johannes Gotthelf of Berlin obtained German patents for jointed dolls.

1922: Arthur Gotthelf registered in Germany *Ulla Puppe* as a trademark for dolls.

**Gottlieb, L., & Sons.** 1890–1923. New York City. Made and imported dolls.

1923: Advertised fully jointed dolls with wigs, sleeping eyes, and eyelashes; unbreakable (composition) dolls, fully jointed, with wigs and washable; *Kidalene* dolls and dressed dolls. Prices $2.25 to $66.00 doz. wholesale.

**Gottschalk, A.** 1909. Berlin. Made dolls.

**Gottschalk, H.** 1914–23. Berlin. Exported dolls.

**Gottschalk & Co.** 1863–91. Paris. Distributor. Represented German doll manufacturers, including *Fischer, Naumann & Co.; Bischoffs* of Sonneberg; *Fleischmann* of Sonneberg; *Gebrüder Heubach; J. Kirschkamp & Co.; Gebrüder Krauss; Louis Lindner & Sohn; J. F. Müller & Strassburger;* etc.

1867–73: Advertised dressed dolls.

1879–90: Advertised dressed dolls, *nankeen* dolls, washable dolls, jointed and unbreakable dolls, and multi-face talking dolls. (Multi-face dolls, 1882–90.)

**Gottwald, Johannes.** 1925. Vienna. Made dolls.

**Götz, J.** 1909. Rauenstein, Thür. Manufactured dolls.

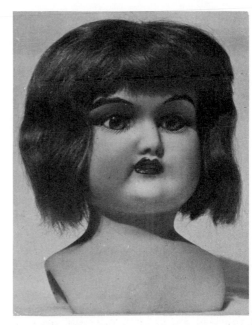

GOSS
30

664

**663.** Bisque shoulder head made by Goss has stationary blue glass eyes, dark red lips. Marked "Goss" over "20." H. of shoulder head, 5¼ inches. *Courtesy of Winifred Leese.*

**664.** Mark found on dolls made by Goss & Co.

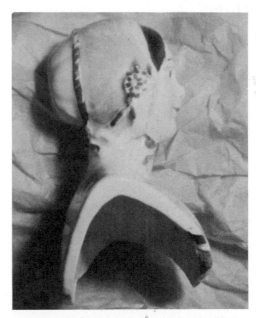

\
GOTA

666

**665.** China bonnet head marked "Gota" or "Guta" in blue inside the shoulder. Head has a molded green bonnet with pink and red trim, black hair, and blue eyes. *Courtesy of Mrs. Latimer; photograph by Winnie Langley.*

**666.** "Gota" (Guta) blue mark found inside doll's head.

**Goubeaux, M.** 1921–25+. Paris. Made and repaired dolls and bébés.

**Gould, Edward R.** 1916–20. New York City. Secured U.S. patent for friction joints to be used on composition-bodied dolls.

**Gould, Lena.** 1914–15. Rochester, Ind. Was granted two U.S. design patents for dolls—one dressed as a clown and one in rompers and hood.

**Gourdel Vales & Co.** 1921. London. *Fumsup* registered in France as a trademark.

**Gräbner, Joseph.** 1914–15. Coburg, Thür. Made dolls.

**Grabo, M.** 1909–23. Friedenau, Prussia. Made and exported dolls.

**Graefe, Otto.** 1913. New York City. Imported *Minerva* metal heads.

**Graeser, Heinrich.** 1890–91. Gotha, Germany. Successor to *May & Lindner;* made bisque dolls' heads, bathing dolls, jointed dolls, etc.

1890: He obtained U.S., French, and German patents for a doll with movable eyeballs and movable lower lips. When the doll was placed in a horizontal position, her eyes and lips closed; when she was raised to an upright position, both eyes and lips opened.

**Graham, Arthur.** 1922. London. Registered in Britain *Peebo Doll* as a trademark.

**Graham, James S.** 1921–24. San Diego, Calif. Obtained U.S. patent for a hollow doll's head with expandable and contractible mouth portion.

**Graham, Murdock Mackay.** 1919–20. Boston, Mass. Registered in U.S. *Eski Dollie* as a trademark. Name affixed to doll with a printed label.

**Gram, William.** 1876. Christiania, Norway. Showed dolls in national costumes at the Philadelphia Exhibition.

**Grammersdorf, A.** 1909–18. Hamburg, Germany. Made dolls.

**Grand Magasin des Jouets.** See **De la Thuilerie, A.**

**Grander Doll Co.** 1923–24. New York City. Made "Grander" *Mama Dolls.*

**Grandjean.** 1887–90. Paris. Made jointed bébés in competition with those made in Germany. He used the initials "G D," and the trade name *Bébé Bijou.* In 1887, he produced 140,000 dolls; in 1888 and 1889, over a million dolls were produced each year.

**Grant, John.** 1917. Philadelphia, Pa. Made dolls.

**Grant, Katherine K.** 1914. New York City. Secured U.S. design patent for a boy doll.

**Graves, Charles W.** 1892–98. Newark, N.J. Assignee of three U.S. patents obtained by *Emil Verpillier.*

1892: Patent for ball-and-socket joints.

1895: Patent for a hinge in a pierced and slotted spherical joint.

1898: Patent for joints for kid- or cloth-bodied dolls.

**667A & B.** Bisque head made by Delcroix with stationary eyes and closed mouth; no eyelashes; wig not original. Jointed composition body was made by Grandjean, who probably assembled the doll. Dressed in contemporary chemise. Mark: Ill. **668.** H. 9 inches. *Coleman Collection.*

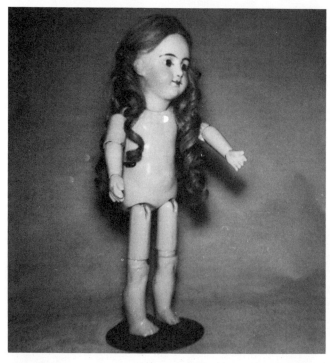

**668–670.** Marks used by Grandjean; No. **668** found on dolls.

**Gray, Jane, Co.** 1915–24. New York City. Designed and made dolls.

1917: Registered in U.S. *Kuddles* as a trademark for dolls.

1921: Advertised *Little Boy Blue* doll; price 75¢ and up.

1923: Registered *Jazz Hound* as a trademark in U.S. for dolls.

1924: Launched *Celebrity* line of dolls with *Margaret Vale,* who selected the personalities and obtained the rights. Jane Gray designed and made the dolls, which included portrait dolls of *Fred Stone, Constance Talmadge,* etc. (See also **Jane Gray Stokes.**)

**Gray & Dudley Co.** 1918. Nashville, Tenn. Distributed dolls.

**Graziella Puppen.** 1923. Trademark registered in Germany by *Max Sachs,* for stuffed dolls and wax dolls.

**Grecon.** 1920. Trademark registered in Germany by *Grete Cohn* for dolls, dolls' house dolls, and fabric dolls.

**Green, G. D.** 1916. Secured British patent for transferring design of dolls' eyes onto ceramic eyes made of china, earthenware, or parian.

**Green, S. A.** 1915. Was issued a British patent for coloring dolls' heads made of parian, pottery, or the like without firing.

**Green, Thomas.** 1855. London. Made dolls.

**Greenaway.** 1907–9. Muslin cutout dolls printed in four or five colors by *Saalfield Publishing Co.;* based on Kate Greenaway drawings. Came in sheets 17½ by 18 inches; price 25¢.

**Greene, Julia.** 1920–21. Philadelphia, Pa. Registered in U.S. *Beddy-Bye* as a trademark for rag dolls.

**Greenwich Village Bud and Student.** 1921. Rag doll mates, made by *Sophia E. Delavan;* price $18.00 doz. wholesale.

**Greenwich Village Vincent and Vivian.** 1923–24. Doll mates; made by *Ideal Novelty & Toy Co.*

**Greffier, François Alphonse.** 1844–55. Nantes, France. Displayed dolls in 1844 at the Paris Exposition and showed dolls and bébés in 1855 at the Paris Exposition. Shortly thereafter, Natalis Rondot wrote, "Fr. Greffier showed some Japanese dolls called by the names of 'bébés'; they were of good models, of excellent manufacture, and of low price." Greffier called his products *poupées genres* (natural dolls). It is possible that these dolls were the inspiration for the doll patented by *Ch. Motschmann* in 1857 and might explain the semi-oriental appearance of many of these dolls.

**Greiner.** 1760–1925+. Thür. Family owned seven porcelain factories and managed an eighth one. These factories were at Volkstedt (1760+), which they managed; Wallendorf (1764+), *Limbach* (1772+), Gera (1779+), Grossbreitenbach (1783+), Rauenstein (1783+), *Ilmenau* (1786+, founded 1777), *Closter Veilsdorf* (1789+).

**671–673.** Porcelain marks of the Gera factory, which originally belonged to the Greiner family. It has not been proved as yet that dolls were made at this factory.

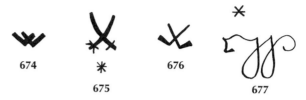

**674–677.** Porcelain marks of the Wallendorf factory, which the Greiners owned at one time; the making of dolls at this factory has not been proved.

The Greiners used the symbol of a trefoil or three-leaf clover as their mark for nearly all these factories. Dolls were probably not made at any of these factories until the 19th century and in many cases after the Greiners had relinquished their ownership, but the trefoil and other marks of these factories have been found on dolls. (See also **Greiner, Fr. Chr., & Söhne; Greiner, J. F.; Heubach; Kampe & Sontag; Schlaggenwald.**)

**Greiner, Alexander.** 1925, Steinach, Thür. Made dolls.

**Greiner, Fr. Chr., & Söhne.** 1890's, Rauenstein, Thür. Listings under Dolls have been found only in the 1890's, but this porcelain factory began in 1783 and remained in the Greiner family for over a century. In the 20th century it was known as Rauenstein Porzellanfabrik. The modern Rauenstein mark (Ill. 687) has been found on dolls' heads. Since this factory used "R" for a mark over a considerable period, it is tempting to ascribe ceramic dolls with the letter "R" to Rauenstein, but it should be noted that the Gotha Porzellanfabrik also used

**678.** Bisque head bearing the Rauenstein crossed *F*'s as well as "R" mark, stationary black pupil-less glass eyes, open mouth with six upper teeth, three stringing holes just below the crown. Pink tinting of bisque is rather splotchy. Mark: Ill. **687.** H. of socket head, 2¼ inches. *Coleman Collection.*

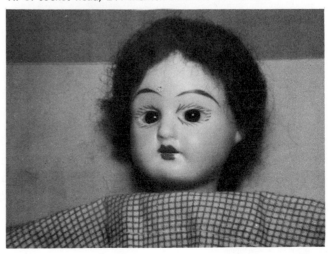

"R" as a mark for Rotberg, its founder, or the "R" could stand for *Recknagle*, Volkstedt-Rudolstadt, etc. Also, many dolls' heads have the letter "R" on them to designate their mold. (See Ill. 680.)

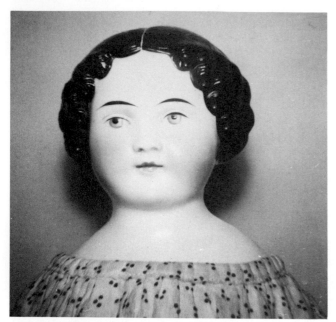

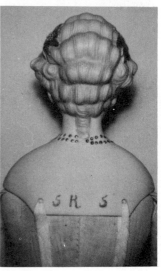

**679A & B.** China head with painted features, deeply incised comb marks. "R" is incised on center back of shoulder. This mark might stand for Rauenstein, or it could be a mold identification or a size identification. Mark: Ill. **681.** H. 18 inches. H. of shoulder head, 4 inches. *Coleman Collection.*

**680A, B, C.** Bisque shoulder head with molded and enameled lilies of the valley in the blonde hair, and beads around the neck; blue glass eyes. Head is on a cloth body with kid arms, Steuber-type legs. Original blue dress. The "R" mark on this doll closely resembles the Rauenstein "R," but a series of bisque heads in the Museum of the City of New York shows that the "R" is the mold identification. (See Ill. **227** for other heads that appear to belong to this series. These were given to the museum by Fred Kolb of Borgfeldt.) Mark: Ill. **682.** H. 17½ inches. H. of shoulder head, 5 inches. *Courtesy of Virginia Dilliplane.*

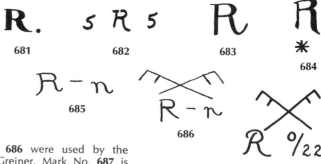

**681–687.** Marks Nos. **684, 685,** and **686** were used by the Rauenstein porcelain factory of Fr. Greiner. Mark No. **687** is found on a doll's head. The "R"'s in Nos. **681, 682,** and **683** might stand for Rauenstein or some other porcelain factory, or they may designate sizes or molds.

**Greiner, J. F.** 1855. Grossbreitenbach, Thür. Made porcelain dolls' heads.

**688**          **689**          **690**

**688–690.** Porcelain marks of the Grossbreitenbach factory owned by J. F. Greiner at one time. Dolls' heads were made by this factory.

**Greiner, Ludwig.** 1840–74. Philadelphia, Pa.; 1874–83, succeeded by Greiner Bros. (Ludwig's sons); 1890–1900, Francis B. Knell (Knell Bros.), successor. Made papier-mâché dolls' heads, in accordance with the earliest known U.S. patent for a doll's head. The ingredients in the 1858 Greiner patent were: 1 lb. white paper, 1 lb. dry Spanish whiting, 1 lb. rye flour, 1 oz. glue, and linen cloth to reinforce the head.

1872: Greiner obtained an extension of his patent rights.

1890–1900: Knell, a brother-in-law of William Greiner, after working for the Greiner firm for some years, established his own business and made not only dolls' heads but also dolls' bodies.

Greiner dolls came in a wide variety of sizes, ranging from about 13 inches to over 35 inches. Their molded hair usually had a center part, and in the 1858 versions was generally black; but in the 1872 versions there were as many blondes as black-haired dolls, if not more. A few Greiners had brown painted eyes, and a very few had glass eyes. The eyes were often of various shades of turquoise. Greiner heads are frequently found on *Lacmann* bodies. (See color photograph C6.)

## LUDWIG GREINER'S COMPOSITION HEADS

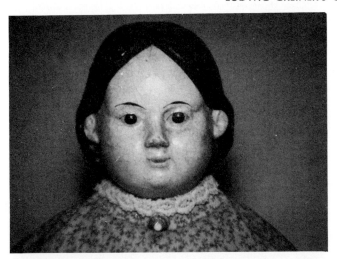

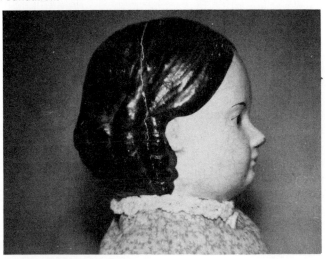

**691A & B.** Composition head with Greiner's 1858 label on back shoulder (Ill. **695**). Note painted upper eyelashes, contemporary dress. H. 23 inches. *Courtesy of the International Doll Library Foundation.*

**692.** Greiner head has 1858 paper label, size "0." H. 13 inches. *Courtesy of The Smithsonian Institution.*

LUDWIG GREINER'S COMPOSITION HEADS

**694.** Cloth reinforced composition head made by Ludwig Greiner has 1872 paper label on back shoulder: Ill. **696.** H. 26 inches. H. of shoulder head, 7½ inches. *Coleman Collection.*

**693A & B.** Greiner head has 1872 extension label on back shoulder. Mark: Ill. **696.** Cloth body, leather arms, original blue challis dress, black oilcloth boots. H. 17 inches. (See color photograph C6.) *Courtesy of Alberta Darby.*

GREINER'S
IMPROVED
PATENTHEADS
Pat. March 30th '58

695

GREINER'S
PATENTDOLLHEADS
No 7
Pat. Mar. 30'58. Ext. '72

696

**695 & 696.** Paper label marks on dolls made by Ludwig Greiner.

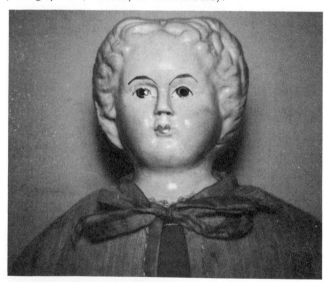

**Greiner, Peter.** 1895–1909. Neustadt near Coburg, Thür. Made little or baby dolls.

**Greiner, Reinh.** 1895. Neustadt near Coburg, Thür. Made dressed dolls.

**Greiner & Co.** 1860–1925+. Steinach, Thür. Manufactured kid-bodied dolls. After 1909 they were succeeded by Kuhnert & Egli, who made various kinds of dolls.

**Gretchen.** 1901. Trade name for character doll with two long flaxen braids; 14 inches tall, $9.00 doz. wholesale.

**Gretchen.** 1910–11. Trade name for model 114, one of the *Royal* line made by *Kämmer & Reinhardt;* distributed by *Strobel & Wilken* and *Borgfeldt. Character* girl usually came with bisque head and jointed composition body. Doll was named for the girl who posed for the model.

**Gretchen.** 1916. One of the line of *Madame Hendren* dolls manufactured by *Averill Manufacturing Co.* according to a U.S. design patent issued to *Georgene Averill.* Came dressed as a Dutch girl, in various sizes; prices $1.00 to $3.50.

**Gretchen.** 1924. Character doll; came with bisque head and body; bobbed hair, real eyelashes, sleeping eyes; price $1.69.

**Gretchen.** Rag doll representing the little Dutch girl in the advertisement of Malt Breakfast Food made by the Malted Cereals Co. of Burlington, Vt.; size 8 inches.

**Grete.** Name incised on bisque heads of character baby dolls; also have the "P M" mark of *Otto Reinecke.*

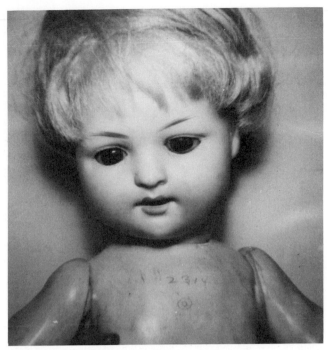

697. "Grete," bisque head with sleeping eyes, two teeth. Mark: Ill. 698. Composition baby body has one knee bent more than the other. H. 12 inches. *Courtesy Eleanor Jean Carter.*

698. "Grete" mark on head probably made by Otto Reinecke.

P. M.
Grete
2/0

**Gretel.** See **Yerri & Gretel.**

**Gretel.** 1912. Trade name of doll made by *Horsman.* Came with *Can't Break 'Em* head, stuffed body; dressed in multi-skirt Dutch costume with Dutch shoes; mate for *Hansel.*

**Gretel.** 1913. Trade name of doll in Dutch costume, handled by *Schoen & Sarkady;* mate to *Hansel.* Came with molded hair sticking out at the sides, and teeth showing.

**Grey & Grey Ltd.** 1917. New York City. Imported dolls from France and England, including *Bébés Jumeau, Eden Bébés, La Francia, Myonettes,* French dolls' heads (both socket and bust type), walking dolls, dressed and undressed dolls.

**Grimm, Frau Anna.** 1897. Joachimsthal, Bohemia. Made and exported dressed, undressed, and jointed dolls of various sizes, "after the Thüringian system."

**Grimsehl, Louise.** 1897–1918. Hamburg, Germany. Made dolls.

**Grinnell Lithographic Co.** 1924. New York City. Exhibited dolls at the Toy Fair. Secured artist to design the revised version of *Aunt Jemima* rag doll and her family.

**Grodzenskin.** 1924–25. Berlin. Listed as a doll artist.

**Groll, Carl.** 1909–20. Ilmenau, Thür. Made dolls, especially woolen dolls.

**Gropper, M., & Sons.** 1912. Doll jobbers in U.S.

**Grosjean.** 1843–50. Paris. Made dolls.

**Grosmutter.** 1915–16. Trademark registered in U.S. by *Bessie Simmons* for dolls.

**Gross, August.** 1895. Sonneberg, Thür. Made dressed dolls.

**Gross, Hugo, & Richards.** See **Catterfelder Puppenfabrik.**

**Gross & Schild.** 1924. London. Registered in Britain *Marigold* as a trademark for dolls.

**Grossman, Mme. Louise.** 1844. Hamburg, Germany. Displayed dolls in national costume at Berlin Exhibition. Dolls described as "outstandingly beautiful."

**Gruel, Adolf.** 1924–25. Leipzig, Saxony. Made dolls.

**Gruelle, John B.** 1915–25+. New York City and Norwalk, Conn. Registered in U.S. the name *Raggedy Ann* as a trademark for dolls. Also in 1915, he obtained a U.S. design patent for a Raggedy Ann doll with the name Raggedy Ann on the hat streamer. This design showed the doll dressed in a puffed peplum skirt with long pants showing below the underskirt. She wore a floppy hat with a big bow under her chin. Lower lashes were indicated under the large round shoe-button eyes. In 1920 he secured another U.S. design patent for a rag doll with sewed joints.

**Grumach, Gebrüder.** 1913–14. Berlin. Doll manufacturer. Registered in Germany *Corso* as a trademark.

**Grumeau.** 1886. Patented in France an improved method of making dolls and bébés out of unbreakable material.

**Grunhainichen School.** 1903. Grunhainichen, Germany. State school for training professional designers and modelers of dolls. There were four professors and two hundred students at the school.

**Grunty Grunts and Smiley Smiles.** 1921. Two dolls in one, produced by *Louis Wolf & Co.* Came with yarn hair, body stuffed with cotton; 20 inches tall; name tag sewed on shirt.

**Gruss, Rudolph.** See **Brückner, Albert.**

**Gudman.** 1881. Obtained French patent for a talking doll.

**Guénot, P.** See **Benda, Gabriel L., & Co.**

**Guépratte.** Before 1881–1898. Paris. Successor to Maison Renders. Jean Marie Guépratte specialized in dolls' heads. In 1898 Ch. Guépratte Fils specialized in dolls' footwear.

**Guerchoux.** 1846–52. Paris. Made dolls.

**Guerin, Mlle. Marthe.** 1915. Paris. Registered a trademark in France for dolls. The mark consisted of an "A" with the right leg extended to the right to meet a line parallel to the left leg of the "A." Before the extended right leg reaches the other line, it crosses a "C" to form "N."

**Guerry, A.** Before 1876–82. Paris. Successor to Desbois. Specialized in jointed dolls.

**Guichard, Edouard Auguste Desiré.** 1854. Paris. Was granted a British patent for ornamenting dolls by a flocked surface. This was to be done by first applying solutions of varnish, *caoutchouc,* or gutta-percha, and then covering the area with any powdered material— wood, metal, leather, cotton, etc.

**Guillard.** 1842–66, Paris; 1867–90, successor was Rémond. Made and distributed dolls. François Guillard, toymaker and dealer, located by 1847 at rue Neuve des Petits Champs, Paris; in 1853 obtained a French patent for a talking doll made of wood, which would take various natural positions.

1855: Widow Guillard displayed mechanical dolls at the Paris Exposition.

1863–67: A. T. Guillard of the above address dealt in wholesale toys and furnished toys to the Imperial Prince. In 1867, Rémond & Perreau of 156 rue de Rivoli were listed as the largest store in Paris specializing in children's toys; J. A. Rémond, successor of Maison Guillard, showed dolls and dolls' accessories at the Paris Exposition.

1873: Rémond, successor of Maison Guillard, won a medal of merit at the Vienna Exhibition. Rémond's address was the same as that given for Guillard above. However, at the same time, Perreau Fils (Sons) had retained the 156 rue de Rivoli address, where their shop was known as *Au Paradis des Enfants.*

1883: Edme Louis Rémond was issued a French patent for a puppet-type dancing doll.

1890: Rémond was selling children's toys at both the Petits Champs address and 188 rue de Rivoli. The establishment of Au Paradis des Enfants had passed to Ouachée, who advertised patented and trademarked toys. A paper sticker on a composition body gives the name of the Petits Champs shop as "A La Galerie Vivienne," with Rémond as successor of Mon. Guillard. (See Ill. 1.) A somewhat similar paper label on a kid body with bisque forearms names Rémond as successor of Guillard and *Le Maire* "A la Galerie Vivienne."

**Guillet, Louis.** 1896. Paris. Registered in France *Amour Bébé* as a trademark for dolls.

**Guillon, S.** 1925. Paris. Made *Art Dolls.*

**Guillory, G., Jeune.** 1878. Paris. Displayed dolls and pantins at the Paris Exposition.

**Guimmoneau (Guimonneau), G., Henry & Cie.** 1879–84. Paris. Awarded a bronze medal for their display of kid bodies and indestructible bébés at the 1879 Paris Exposition.

1882–84: Advertised dolls with kid bodies, indestructible bébés, dressed dolls in both the luxury and ordinary classes.

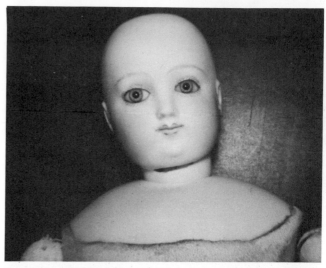

699. Doll with bisque head and forearms, kid body, has rectangular sticker on stomach that reads, "(?) plus grands Magasins //DE JOUETS DE PARIS //A LA GALERIE VIVIENNE. //Mons. GUILLARD & LEMAIRE //REMOND Succr. //Rue Nve. des Petits Champs 4." The doll has single holes into the head for earrings; fingernails are painted pink. H. 17½ inches. H. of shoulder head, 4 inches. *Courtesy of the Museum of the City of New York.*

700. Mark on doll handled by Guillard.

**Guinzburg, E. A.** 1925. New York City. Made dolls.

**Guiton.** 1870's–90. Paris. Made dolls. (See **Aux Enfants Sages.**)

**Gum Tragacanth.** Material used for making dolls, especially from the 17th to the 19th centuries. It is a white or reddish gum, which, when treated with water, forms a mucilage.

**Gummoid.** 1900–1901. Trademarked name for material used to make dolls' heads. Trademark registered in Germany by *Nöckler & Tittel.*

**Gumps.** See **Andy Gump; Chester Gump.**

**Gund Manufacturing Co.** 1898–1925+. New York City; factory later in Norwalk, Conn. Made stuffed dolls, distributed by *Owens-Kreiser Co.* and *Davis & Voetsch.*

1912: Advertised *Childhood Character Dolls,* a line with faces that were replicas of real American children. These dolls included *Tootsie, Marion, Wally, Brother, Sister,* etc. Priced 25¢ to $2.00.

1913: Advertised *Flippety-Flop-Kids,* character dolls with swinging limbs, eyes glancing to the side, crying voice.

1918: Made *Nettie Knit.*

**Gunleck.** 1866–70. Paris. Made dolls.

**Günthel, Oskar.** 1924–25. Gräfenroda, Thür. Made cellulose dolls and registered in Germany *Helgunith* as a trademark for them.

**Günther, Emil.** 1915–20, Neustadt near Coburg, Thür.; 1921–23, successor was Ferdinand Günther. Made dressed and undressed dolls.

**Günther, Emma.** 1918–25+. Berlin. Made dolls.

**Günthersfeld Porzellanfabrik.** 1884–1918+. Gehren, Thür. Made porcelain ware. It is not known for sure that dolls were made here.

1886: Registered in Germany as a trademark the initial "G" under crossed swords.

**Guschi.** 1921–22. Trademark registered in Germany by *Guttmann & Schiffnie* for dolls.

**Guta.** See **Gota**.

**Guth & Eckstein.** 1923. Prague, Czeckoslovakia. Made dolls.

**Gutsell, Ida A.** 1893. Ithaca, N.Y. Obtained a U.S. patent for a rag doll. The pattern was composed of a printed fabric blank of six pieces arranged so that it could be cut out and sewed together to form a realistic three-

**701A, B, & C.** Cut and uncut rag dolls made by Cocheco Manufacturing Co. based on Ida Gutsell patent of 1893. Dolls are shown dressed in original tan suits, and undressed with undergarments outlined in red. Uncut doll wears blue suit. H. 16 inches. *Photographs by Winnie Langley; Coleman Collection.*

A                                                                           B                                C

dimensional doll with seam down the center of the face, plus an inner and outer garment. The cotton material for these dolls was made by the *Cocheco Manufacturing Co.* and *Lawrence & Co.,* according to marks printed on the uncut cloth from which these dolls were made.

**Gutta-percha.** A material used especially in the second half of the 19th century for making dolls and parts of dolls. The substance attracted attention as early as the 1830's but was not widely used for dolls until the 1850's. It is difficult to identify dolls of gutta-percha, and often they are confused with rubber dolls, even by museums. Gutta-percha is very different from rubber, although sometimes rubber and gutta-percha were combined in the making of dolls.

In its raw state, gutta-percha is reddish white in color. It is workable by hot water alone, since it softens at 100°F. and can be molded at 190°F. It will retain its shape when cooled, but will become brittle when exposed to air. When the resins are extracted (as they are for making the white exterior for golf balls), it becomes harder and requires a much higher temperature to soften it. Gutta-percha differs from rubber in that it is fibrous, will not float, is not sticky when dry, and is not affected by atmospheric heat or by unctuous oils.

Among the doll makers who used gutta-percha were *Richard Archibald Brooman, Mlle. Calixte Huret, Lang & Co., John Edward Payne, Henry Plumb, Mlle. Marie Antoinette Léontine Rohmer, Charles Silvester Rostaing, William Scott, M. Baculard,* et al.

Lesley Gordon, in PEEPSHOW INTO PARADISE, states that the "gutta-percha heads" hawked in the streets of London contained no gutta-percha but were made of glue and molasses. Laura Starr, writing in 1908, remarked that the modern doll with its intellectual face is so different from the happy expression of the good old gutta-percha doll.

**Guttmann & Schiffnie.** 1897–1925+. Sonneberg, Thür. and Nürnberg, Bavaria. Made and distributed dolls; used the initials "G & S" and "GS."

1907: Registered in France the trademark *Bébé l'Avenir.*

1911: Registered in France and Germany *Bébé Coiffure* as a trademark for dolls; advertised that a child could comb and arrange the hair of this doll.

1914: Registered in France *Mona Lisa* as a trademark.

1922: Registered in Germany *Guschi* as a trademark. Bébé l'Avenir was still produced.

**Guyot.** 1879–1900. Paris. Specialized in indestructible bébés, dressed and undressed; also dolls, dolls' clothes, and repairs.

1888: Maison Guyot was awarded a silver medal for their display at the Paris Exposition.

In the 1890's and around 1900 they used the trade name *A La Tentation* for their dolls and bébés.

**Guzzieland Co.** 1921. Advertised as making dolls.

**702.** Head made of gutta-percha has molded and painted flowers in the hair and on the chest. This head has been chemically tested to verify that the material is actually gutta-percha. *Courtesy of Ruth E. & R. C. Mathes.*

**703.** Mark found on doll, probably made by Guttmann & Schiffnie.

# H

**H. & Z. Doll Co.** 1919. New York City. One of the *David Zaiden* companies; made *Dainty Marie* dolls.

**Haag, Gebrüder (Bros.).** 1886–1925+. Sonneberg, Thür. Manufactured dolls.

1886: Registered in Germany trademark with the words "Biskuit-Imitation" over a doll, for use with imitation bisque dolls.

1895: Specialized in washable and unbreakable dolls and dolls' heads, waxed and molded wax dolls, jointed dolls, and dressed dolls for the English and American markets.

1900: Displayed dolls at Paris Exposition and was one of the Grand Prize group.

1903: Sander & Coles was their London agent.

1911: Advertised dressed character dolls with sleep eyes, doll heads, and ball-jointed *Täuflinge.*

**Haase, Reinhold.** 1895–1909. Triptis, Thür. Made dressed dolls.

**Haber Bros.** 1917–22. New York City. Distributors; imported dolls from Japan, Germany, France, and Czechoslovakia.

1917: Advertised Japanese dressed dolls and celluloid dolls.

1919–20: Their *Best Baby,* made in Japan and shipped from Yokohama, was refused entry into the U.S. by the customs office. They were sued by *Borgfeldt,* and lost the case because these dolls looked too much like *Kewpies.*

1922: Purchased a large number of dolls in Germany when the German mark hit bottom.

1924: It is not known whether or not the M. & M. Haber listed as factory agents for toys were Haber Bros.

**Haberlandt, Franz.** 1919. Berlin. Was issued a German patent for dressed dolls.

**Habermann, Wilhelm.** 1918–20. Steinach, Thür. Manufactured leather dolls.

**Hachmeister, Hermann.** 1872–1925+. Sonneberg, Thür. (From 1921 to 1925+, it was Hachmeister & Co.) Manufactured dolls. He displayed dolls at the 1873 Vienna Exhibition, the 1893 Chicago Exhibition, and the 1900 Paris Exposition, where he was one of the group of Grand Prize winners.

1903–13: Had a London branch and made jointed dolls, babies, and dressed dolls.

1908: Registered in Germany a trademark of a dwarf with an ax, for dressed dolls.

1921–25+: Had a London branch.

**Hackmann, A.** 1891. Unterneubrunn near Eisfeld, Thür. Manufactured dolls.

**Hafraco-Puppen.** 1922. Registered as a trademark in Germany by *Schöffl & Co.,* for artistic dolls.

**Hagen, Karl.** 1779. Passau, Bavaria. Made porcelain dolls, according to Kimport's DOLL TALK.

**Hahn, Adolf.** 1897. Teplitz-Shönau, Bohemia. Made papier-mâché and wax dolls.

**Hahn, Rudolph.** 1918–19. London. Distributed dolls.

**Hahn, Simon.** 1921–22. Hamburg, Germany. Procured two German patents for moving eyes used in dolls.

**Hahn & Amberg.** See **Amberg, Louis, & Son.**

**Hahn & Co.** 1920–21. Nürnberg, Bavaria. Made stuffed and fabric dolls; registered *Hanco* as trademark in Germany for dolls.

**Hahnesand & Heiman.** 1903–8. New York City. Distributors for *E. A. Runnels Co.*

1903: Claimed they had a patent process for making real hair wigs, which eliminated the smell and were mothproof.

**Hahnesend, Joseph, & Co.** 1915–17. New York City. Specialized in handling American dolls. Joseph Hahnesend started in the toy business in 1890.

**Hail Columbia.** 1913. Trade name for "bisc finish" doll made by *Louis Amberg & Son.* Mate to *Yankee Doodle,* it came dressed in stars and stripes; 15-inch size, price $1.00.

**Hails, Daniel Troy.** 1909–10. Montgomery, Ala. Was issued a U.S. design patent for a winking doll with one eye closed and one eye round.

**Haines, Bessie A.** 1919–20. Bristol, Ind. Was granted a U.S. design patent for a doll with gauze wings and dress.

**Hair, Materials for.** Probably the most common material used on dolls to represent hair is paint. Next in importance is real hair, which may be either human hair or animal. The finest wigs are made of human hair, but mohair, the fine glossy hair of the Angora or Thibetan goat, also serves very well. Human hair was originally used in Sonneberg for dolls' wigs, until the discovery of mohair. In 1877, a single London firm supplied nearly all the mohair used by English and the best French and German doll makers. When mohair became too expensive, wool was mixed with it. Mohair dolls' wigs were one of the first casualties of World War I. By 1915, factories in America were clamoring for them.

Wool, tow, flax, cotton, silk—in fact, any fiber—could be and in general has been used for dolls' hair. Lamb's wool still attached to its original skin was frequently used as a doll's wig. Around 1867, a large factory operated by *Samuel H. Flagg* in Providence, R.I., began to make dolls' wigs largely of jute. Discarded hair switches were often put to use on dolls.

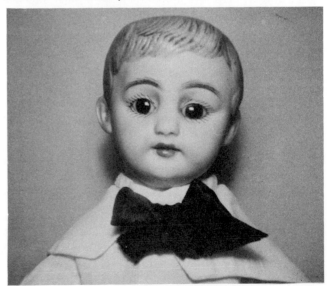

**704.** Bisque head has molded blond hair, glass eyes; jointed body is composition. H. 9½ inches. *Courtesy of Ollie Leavister.*

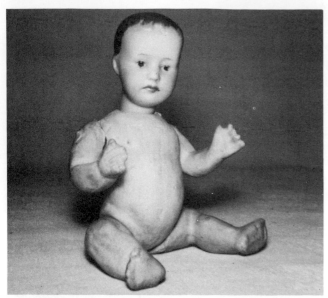

**705.** Bisque head with Heubach mark (Ill. **823**) has flocked hair. Note the crude body. H. 6¼ inches. *Coleman Collection.*

**706.** Wax-over papier-mâché head, with features painted on the wax, has pupil-less glass eyes; the hair is secured in a slit in the crown. One-piece cloth body is hand-sewn. H. 18½ inches. *Coleman Collection.*

**707.** Poured wax head with hair inserted in small groups in the front of the head and a wig on the back of the head; sleeping glass eyes; cloth body. H. 18 inches. *Courtesy of Ollie Leavister.*

**Hair, Method of Affixing.** A wig can be made by sewing, weaving, tying, glueing, or crocheting the hair together. Often, it is reinforced with a net or fabric base. When the hair is in the form of a wig, it is usually glued into place. However, short individual hairs were sometimes mixed with glue or sizing and applied directly to the doll's head. Hair applied in this way is known as flocked hair. Wooden dolls, dolls with cork pates, and a few composition or papier-mâché heads have the wigs or hair pieces tacked or pinned into place. In the case of rag-doll heads, the hair or wig is generally sewed on. Sometimes several small holes are found in the top of dolls' heads. Often these were made to permit the wig to be tied into place, frequently by means of velvet ribbons. Wooden dolls may have a hole running through the back of the head; this was also for tying on the wig. The holes around the crown of the *Ernst Reinhardt* doll are for tying on the wig, but the three holes around the crown of the *All-Steel Doll* are for attaching the wig with snaps.

Slits down the center of the top of the head or holes in the midde of the top are likely to be for the purpose of inserting tresses of hair. The slits are found most often on waxed papier-mâché dolls' heads, but they have been found on china and other types as well. HARPER'S BAZAR, August 18, 1877, described how the grooves were made: "In the less expensive [wax] or composition ones, a deep groove is cut completely through the skull, along the top of the head where the parting is to be, and the uncurled ends of the ringlets are pushed in with a blunt knife, and then fastened down with paste." The hair was sometimes inserted in the center hole and perhaps supplemented by a fringe of additional hair around the crown. This seems to have been used for short hair only.

The most realistic method of affixing hair was by inserting it singly or in groups into wax or similar-type substances. This method was used especially on poured wax-dolls' heads. *Josef Kubelka* in the 1880's patented a method whereby the top of a porcelain doll's head could be covered with wax sufficiently deep for the insertion of hair. The process of inserting hair into wax was described by Mateaux in THE WONDERLAND OF WORK, 1884, as follows: "In Sonneberg . . . Each girl holds in her left hand a bundle of soft 'hairs,' all of one length, and which have been carefully combed out like a fringe. In her right hand, which she keeps pressed on the tiny head, she holds a sort of blunt blade, with which she deftly tucks in the even roots of the hair, sending it a little way down into the wax. Then, she deftly twitches away the bundle, so that as many hairs as have remained are fixed fast. This performance has to be continued until the tresses begin to get quite thick, when she takes up a little iron roller and rubs it gently and firmly over the surface, so as to close up any gashes she may have made with the blade, begins again, and patiently repeating the whole process over and over again, until the pinky foundation is hidden and covered by soft hair."

PLAYTHINGS, 1913, reported that hair was inserted with a needle into the scalp of "unbreakable" American dolls so that it could be combed.

(See Ill. 1050.)

**Hair Color.** Painted hair was generally black on early wooden, papier-mâché, or china dolls' heads. After the mid-19th century, untinted bisque dolls' heads appeared with blonde painted hair, and blonde hair began to be used more frequently also on china, papier-mâché, composition, and rag doll heads as well as on those of other materials.

Most of the human hair used in dolls' wigs came from China (the color was extracted for blonde dolls), but the best wigs were made from the hair of Europeans, the bronze-gold color being the most expensive. The natural color of mohair wigs was blonde; mohair had to be dyed to obtain other colors.

In most years throughout the past century, blonde hair has had the greatest popularity. Dark brown or black hair was used on dolls representing Orientals, Spaniards, Italians, Negroes, Indians, and so on, and there were usually a few dolls with white hair, representing a powdered marquise or a Colonial belle.

The popular colors for dolls' hair, by years, were as follows:

1874: Titian hair.

1875: Dolls sold in pairs, one a blonde and one a brunette.

1877: Black hair seldom used on dolls.

1879: Auburn hair reported to be a favorite.

1881: Titian red again appeared.

1891: The popularity of dark hair rivaled that of blonde.

**708.** Bald pink-tinted china head with a slot for affixing the brown wig, which lies next to it. The top of the head was not glazed. The blue eyes are painted. *Courtesy of Margaret Whitton; photograph by Winnie Langley.*

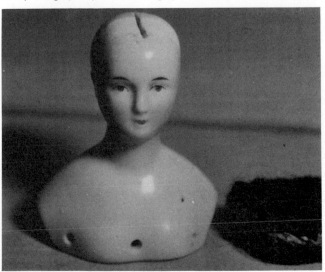

1896–99: Various shades of brown were popular, as well as blonde and auburn.

1907: A year for various shades of red hair.

1908: The new color was "tosca," a dull gold.

1909: The new blonde shade was called "chataine," but "tosca" remained a favorite for several years.

1911: The popularity of "tosca" was explained by the fact that it is similar to the color of the hair of so many children.

1913: Red hair seldom seen on dolls.

1914: Hair of every color—red, green, blue, yellow, etc.—but this craze soon passed and hair returned to blonde and brunette.

1920: Blonde, tosca, auburn, brown, and gray wigs.

1924: Chiefly brunettes; blonde dolls not in favor in Paris.

**Hair Style, Painted and/or Molded.** The styling of painted and molded hair can be very simple or extremely elaborate. Many of the so-called *Dutch Dolls* or Penny Woodens have only a black painted pate with no molding; some of the other dolls have great detail in the molding, painting, or carving of their hair, as well as fine brush marks. The hair styles on dolls are likely to follow those prevailing during the period when the doll was made, but a style may continue to be used for some time. This fact helps to date many of the elaborate papier-mâché heads, china heads, and untinted bisque heads. However, in dating dolls according to their hair style, it is necessary to have a thorough knowledge of the styles for each year for both sexes at various ages—and even then other factors may still need to be taken into consideration. Many more dolls represent children or babies than is often realized by collectors. Baby dolls that have been documented as around 1860 have been found with bald heads and mere wisps of hair or with heavily molded hair. Expense and artistic taste, no doubt, were contributing factors. The ascendancy of the character doll in the 20th century renewed the importance of molded and painted hair styles. Very little distinction seems to have been made between boys and girls, as far as hair styles were concerned, in the 19th and early 20th centuries. Catalogs indicate that some popular types of molded dolls' heads continued to be made long after the original hair style had passed out of fashion. The long corkscrew curls, the flat top with ringlets all around the head, and finally the high waves (which were often fairly flat in the back) are three hair styles that lasted for several generations.

Dolls' heads of different materials are often found with similar hair styles. Sometimes a bisque head can be identical in molding with a china, papier-mâché, or even a molded fabric head. Although there are similarities among diverse materials, there can be marked differences in what appears to a casual observer to be similar hair styles in the same material. Collectors are familiar with the hair style on china heads that has a center part, smooth hair down to eye level, then corkscrew curls to just below the ears. This relatively simple style appears with many variations—in the number of curls, the number of comb marks in the curls, the height of the forehead, and so on. The variations in other frequently found hair styles are numerous also. The likelihood of finding an exact duplicate in hair style is as small for the more common types as for the unusual hairdos prior to 1880.

Since wigs were one of the first casualties of World War I, a large percentage of the American unbreakable dolls had molded and painted hair. Sometimes a hole was made in molded hair so that a ribbon or other decoration could be inserted.

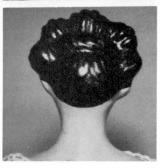

**709A & B.** Papier-mâché head with large puffs at either side and hair swept up with a comb in back. Molded breasts. There are eight sew holes, three being across front and three across the back, one on each shoulder. Doll has kid body, wooden limbs, red painted slippers; contemporary blue dress, abbreviated pantalettes. H. 10½ inches. *Coleman Collection.*

**710A, B, & C.** Papier-mâché head has diagonal curls similar to those in Ill. **711.** Kid body, turned wooden lower limbs. H. 9¼ inches. H. of shoulder head, 2½ inches. *Coleman Collection.*

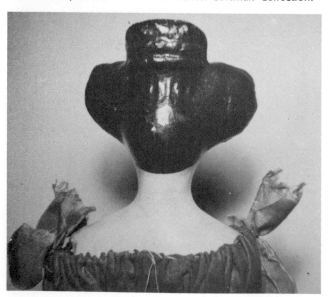

**711.** Papier-mâché head with diagonal front curls of real hair, center part and back braid of molded hair. Both kinds of hair are of a matching reddish-brown color. Hair style is that of the 1830's; see also Ill. **710.** *Courtesy of Margaret Whitton; photograph by Winnie Langley.*

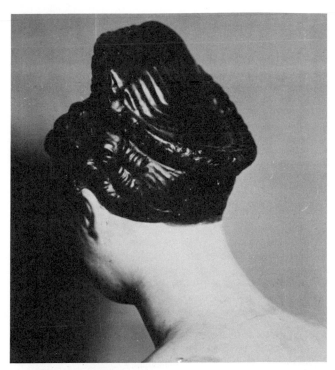

**712.** Papier-mâché head with tiers of braids held by a comb; ca. 1830's. *Courtesy of Margaret Whitton; photograph by Winnie Langley.*

**713.** Ladies' hair style of the 1840's, as shown on a papier-mâché head with glass eyes. *Courtesy of Marion Holt; photograph by Winnie Langley.*

**714.** Papier-mâché head with painted eyes, striated eyebrows; cloth body, wooden limbs; painted blue slippers. H. 36 inches. *Courtesy of the Newark Museum, Newark, N.J.*

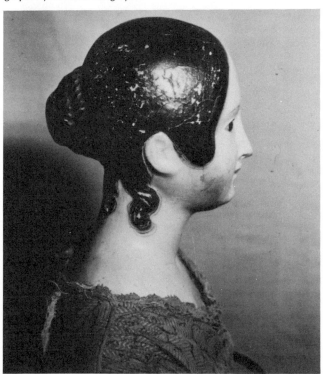

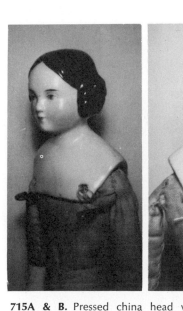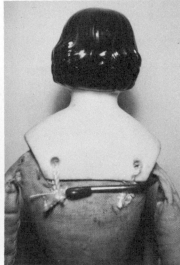

**715A & B.** Pressed china head with ten molded corkscrew curls; pink-tinted head and arms; hand-sewn cloth body. H. 11 inches H. of shoulder head, 2½ inches. *Coleman Collection.*

716 717

**716.** Flesh-tinted china head has white eyeballs, molded eyes, fourteen corkscrew curls. Note the variation in shape of face, decorating techniques, and number of curls in this photograph and in the similar hairdos shown in Ills. **715, 717,** and **718.** H. of shoulder head, 6 inches. *Coleman Collection.*

**717.** Flesh-tinted china head has a hair style popular for representing children in the mid-19th century, two-tone eyebrows, painted blue eyes; original dress is black velvet and purple silk. *Courtesy of the Newark Museum, Newark, N.J.*

**718.** Flesh-tinted china head with white eyeballs; thirteen corkscrew curls project from around the neck. Body is cloth. H. 18 inches. H. of shoulder head, 4½ inches. *Courtesy of Eunice Althouse.*

**720A & B.** Untinted bisque head with molded blonde hair with an intertwined pink and blue glazed scarf, which falls over the shoulder and terminates in a white fringe; molded gold cockade rises above the scarf on top of the head. *Courtesy of Margaret Whitton; photographs by Winnie Langley.*

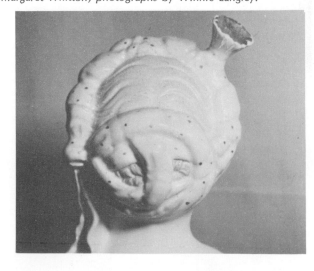

**719A & B.** Untinted bisque shoulder head has molded blonde hair, painted features, molded bodice with glazed blue tie. H. 12 inches. H. of shoulder head, 3 inches. *Courtesy of the Chester County Historical Society.*

**721A & B.** Pink-tinted china head, black hair, blue eyes, hair style of the 1870's. *Courtesy of Margaret Whitton; photographs by Winnie Langley.*

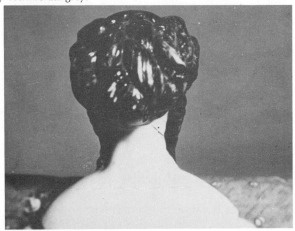

**723A & B.** Untinted bisque head, blonde molded hair, black glazed decoration, pierced ears, painted features; contemporary commercially made cloth body has kid arms. H. 20 inches. H. of shoulder head, 5½ inches. *Courtesy of Josephine Garrison.*

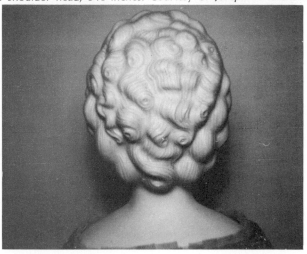

 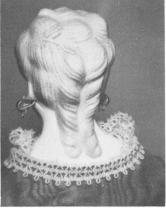

**722A & B.** Molded bisque head with pierced ears and café-au-lait-colored hair. Hair style is that of the 1870's, with curls on the forehead and down the back. H. 12½ inches. *Coleman Collection.*

**Hair Style, Wigs.** Few 18th-century wigs are extant today that show a stylish hair arrangement. Most 18th-century dolls in more or less original condition wear caps that cover most of their hair; perhaps these account for the preservation of the hair. A French doll with a wig, in the Musée des Arts Décoratifs, and a few wax dolls with high hairdos and curls on the shoulder date back to the 18th century. During the 19th and early 20th centuries, the records of coiffures found on dolls can be summarized as follows:

ca. 1810: A Swiss doll had long plaits that fell almost to her feet.

1830's: Elaborate hairdo of fashion, Apollo's knot, etc.

1840's: A German sample book with over 100 dolls shows about half with Apollo's knots, a quarter with short hair, and a quarter with corkscrew curls. Very few have bald heads or a bun.

1850's: Holzach's Swiss catalog shows children's hair parted in the middle, pulled straight back behind the ears, with shoulder length curls across the back; ladies' hair parted in middle with one piece brought down in front of each exposed ear and then caught up in a braided bun high up on the back of the head; also with a braid across the top of the head and with braids looped in front of the ears. Some of these braided buns may be earlier, as their shape suggests the 1840's; however, they were popular types carried for some years.

1867: Children's hair parted in middle with curls behind the ears, shorter than in the 1850's catalog; young ladies, short curls over the forehead and large braided chignons.

1868: Boys with hair parted on one side; young ladies' hair, frizzed and worn in chignons.

1869: Young ladies' hair arranged in chatelaines and frizzes.

1870: Babies, in short frizzed hair; children's hair flowing over the shoulders and the front section strapped across the head with a ribbon; young ladies had long braids or chatelaines.

1871: Bride had hair rolled back in pompadour style.

1873: Girls wore curls; boys had short hair parted on one side; Spanish maiden's hair braided in coronets.

1874: Girls, preferred in curls or loose waves; young ladies wore catogan, crown braids, finger puffs, chatelaine, flowing waved hair, hanging Marguerite braids (two long braids), elaborately braided.

1875: Infants with bald heads or scarcely any hair; boys wore frizzed curly hair; ladies, flowing hair with bangs on forehead (Rembrandt hairdo), Marguerite braids tied with blue ribbons, pompadour rolls, evening coiffures of puffs, braids, and curls.

1876: Babies, hair banged over the forehead; ladies, elaborate coiffures.

1877: Banged in front, falling in loose waves behind, long Marguerite braids, puffs and curls, wigs tied on with velvet ribbons.

1878: Hair banged on forehead, flowing hair in back; curly hair terminating in two long braids.

1879: Children, flowing hair with bangs most popular, then braided hair; lady dolls, puffs, loops, and braids.

1880: Infants, banged hair; girls, flowing hair with braid around crown and bangs; Marquise dolls, powdered hair in pompadour style.

1881: Bangs on forehead, flowing behind; short curly hair; short hair of sheep's wool.

1882: Little girls, bangs on forehead, flowing behind.

1883: Little girls, bangs on forehead, flowing hair behind; long Marguerite braids; short curly hair.

1884: Stylish dolls have hair "à la Rembrandt"—that is, bangs on forehead and flowing hair behind; Marguerite braids; Sonneberg plaits—twisted, braided, pinned, and tied up under a cap; switches for dolls and false hair used in coiffures. Passé now are chignons, waterfalls, and high back hair with lengthy bangs.

1885: Short bangs and short flowing locks; long Marguerite braids; curls on forehead and at nape of neck.

1886: Curled bangs and flowing hair in back.

1887: Long flowing hair; Marquise, powdered hair.

1888: Short hair, bangs and flowing.

1889: Bangs and flowing hair.

1890: Curly hair; flowing hair.

1891: French curled ends falling over the ears, and heavy bangs.

1892: Curly hair.

1893: Curls, long and short; bangs and flowing hair.

1894: Little girls, single braid down back, Psyche knot, flowing with bangs; French dolls, curls in front, plaits behind; Rembrandt style (flowing with bangs).

1895: Curly hair; flowing, with bangs.

1896: Waves; shoulder curls or long curls.

1897: Curly, with bangs.

1898: Long curls with bangs.

1899: Long and short curls.

1903: Infant, short fuzz; girls, curls with a jaunty one over the forehead, braids of straight hair, new pompadour roll.

1904: Popular style—hair parted and with side combs.

1906: Long hair parted on the side as well as in the middle.

1907: Better dolls, curls; inexpensive dolls, flowing hair.

1908: Long tresses hanging below waist; curly hair; bangs on forehead, flowing behind.

1909: Bangs or side part best; new wigs ornamented with ribbon and parted at the side.

1911: Long Marguerite braids; clusters of curls; side braids; "Buster Brown" hair style; new style "Schnecken Frisur," an elaborate knotted arrangement over each ear; Grecian effects; pompadours and chignon coiffures.

1912: Long flowing curls, side parted.

1913: Hair to waist.

1914: Flowing tresses.

1916: Long flowing curls and bangs; long flowing curls and center part; bangs and braid around crown; short "Buster Brown" hair style.

1917: Long curls.

1919: Long curls.

1922: French dolls, hair twisted and curled and puffed.

1924: Flapper wigs, short and curly all over.

It must be emphasized that the above hair styles are for dolls and do not necessarily follow the fashion trends for people, although there is often a relationship. Some interpretation is necessary in using the above information. Every type of hair style would not be reported in every year. For example the "Buster Brown" hair style that was popular in 1911 continued to be so through 1916 at least, although it was not mentioned in the intervening years. The Marguerite braids of 1911 were probably a revival of the popular old style that had not been mentioned since 1885. Special types of dolls had special hair styles—oriental dolls, for example, would have straight hair even during a period when curls were the fashion.

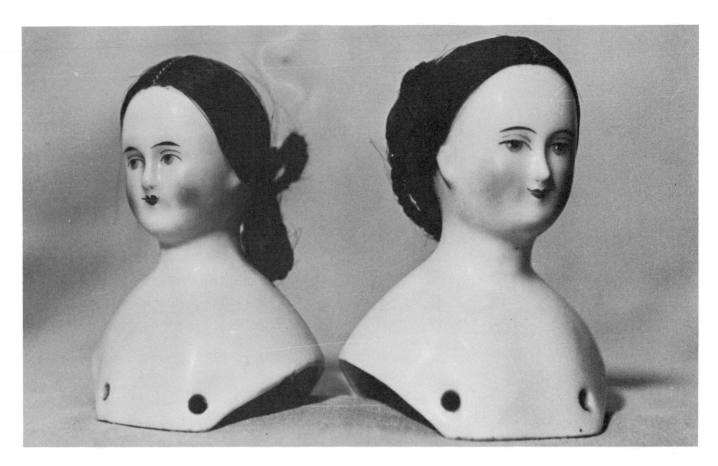

**724A & B.** China heads with coiffured wigs similar to those shown in a catalog (see Ill. **725**) have blue painted eyes, black pate under the wigs. A red ribbon embroidered with gold sequins can be seen under the braids in hair of one head. H. of shoulder heads, 3½ inches. *Courtesy of Laura Treskow.*

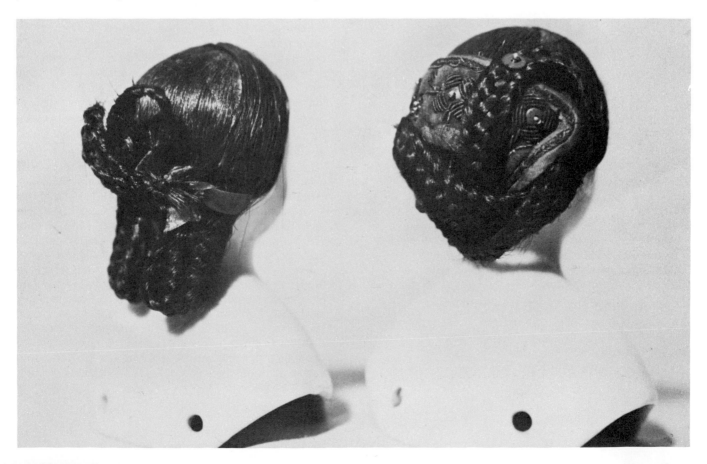

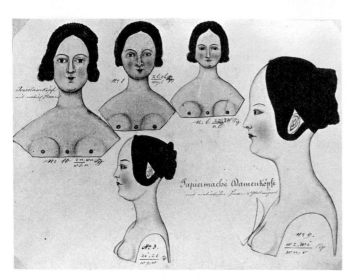

**725A & B.** Two pages from a Swiss catalog of German toys, dated 1845–60. Heads Nos. 6, 8, and 10 are china ladies' heads with real hair. Heads Nos. 3, 4, 5, 7, and 9 are papier-mâché ladies' heads with real hair and glass eyes. Note the elaborate coiffures of the wigs. *Courtesy of Marg. Weber-Beck from Franz Carl Weber, Zurich.*

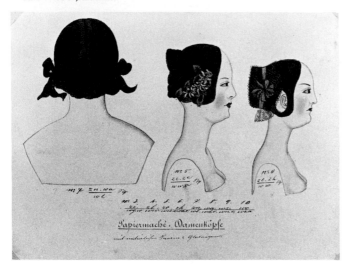

**726.** Wax-over-composition head with vertical curls in pompadour hair style held over composition form by a gold braid; curls in back fall over the shoulders. Doll has pupil-less glass eyes, a hole in the head under each ear for earrings, a cloth body, and composition limbs. Clothes are original. H. 17½ inches. *Courtesy of Lester & Alice Grinnings.*

**Halpern, J. Co.** 1923. Pittsburgh, Pa. Distributed *Waltershausen* jointed dolls, *Revalo* jointed dolls, kid and *Kidoline* dolls.

**Hamac Bébé.** See **Bébé Hamac.**

**Hamburger, Aron, & Coston, Herbert Ernest.** 1908–9. London. Photographers who obtained a British patent for distorting photographs to allow for the curvature of a dolls' face, and applying these photographs to rag, celluloid, or papier-mâché dolls' heads. Patent stated that hitherto dolls' face had had to be drawn on linen, etc. Numerous *photographic face* dolls had already been produced in America.

**Hamburger & Co.** 1889–1909. Berlin, Nürnberg, and New York City. Produced and distributed dolls and was European representative for *Strawbridge & Clothier* and other firms. Handled dolls made by *A. Wislizenus.* Hamburger & Co. used Carlsbad on one of their trademarks. They registered numerous trademarks in the U.S., including "D. P." and "H. & C" in 1895 (both used since 1893), *Imperial* in 1898, *Santa* in 1900, *Old Glory* and *Marguerite* in 1902. The two trademarks "H. & C." of Hamburger & Co. in 1895 and "H. & Co." of *Hinricks & Co.* in 1894 have caused some confusion, since Hamburger used "H. Co." on their Santa trademark. Hamburger registered in Germany as trademarks "D. P." in 1895, *Imperial H & Co.* in 1901, Santa in 1901, *Viola* in 1903, Marguerite in 1903, and *Dolly Dimple* in 1907. Advertisements of Hamburger & Co. in PLAYTHINGS as late as

**Halbeisen & Co.** 1891. Schalkau, Thür. Made jointed dolls and dressed dolls.

**Halbig, Carl.** See **Simon & Halbig.**

**Hall, Gertrude.** 1924. New York City. Obtained U.S. design patent for a rag doll with a flat face.

**Haller, J.** 1851 and before. Vienna, Austria. Made dressed and undressed dolls. His widow and son-in-law had the largest group of toys at the 1851 London Exhibition and were awarded a prize medal for dolls.

**Hallesche, Puppenklinik.** See **Petsch, Hermann.**

**Halloween Dolls.** 1916. One of the *Madame Hendren* line of dolls made by *Averill Manufacturing Co.* Came dressed in orange and black felt.

**Halopeau, A.** 1881–89. Paris. Made dolls.

1907 listed Viola, Santa jointed dolls, Imperial kid dolls, and "D. P." dressed dolls.

1898: "D. P." line of dressed dolls advertised as having bisque heads and jointed arms; some came with open mouth and teeth. They wore elaborate clothes, one style being dressed in silkaline cloth and Vandyke lace. Came in size 16 inches, price $9.80 doz. wholesale; size 18½ inches, known as the *London Belle*, price $13.50 doz. wholesale.

1903: They also produced two portrait dolls in addition to the above-named dolls; one was of *Lillian Russell* and the other of Lula Glaser as *Dolly Varden*.

1904: Won the Grand Prize, highest possible award, at the St. Louis Exposition for their group of thirty-six dolls.

1905: Advertised new *Brownie Policeman*, fully jointed, covered with wool and silk plush, stuffed with cork dust.

1907: Listed in Nürnberg as exporters of dolls and dolls' heads.

1909: Hamburger & Co. were in hands of receivers in Nürnberg.

1910: Geo. H. Bowman Co., New York City, advertised the Imperial line of dolls. They may have been a successor to Hamburger & Co.

**727.** Mark used by Hamburger & Co.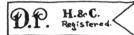

**Hamel, Fernand.** 1909. Paris. Manufactured dolls. He obtained a British patent for India rubber dolls, made by giving them first a bath of glycerized transparent gelatin, then a bath of spirit varnish, and finally another bath of gelatin.

**Hamill, Frae C.** 1921. Los Angeles, Calif. Was issued two U.S. design patents for rag dolls, one of them a *Brownie* rag doll.

**Hamilton, Ellen.** 1920. Designed dolls for Barker Bros., a Los Angeles store; dolls sold for $2.75.

**Hamilton, Eva C.** 1916. Hubbard, Ore. Secured U.S. design patent for a rag doll with sewed joints, eyes glancing to the side.

**Hamley Bros.** Mid-19th century–1925+. London. Called the "European toy warehouse"; imported dolls from Germany, France, and America, and exported dolls to India, Australia, and America. They sold *Pierotti* wax dolls in the 1880's and 1890's. John Green Hamley registered at least ten trademarks in Britain and one in France between 1904 and 1920; among these were *Buster Brown, Ni-Ni, Elfie, Pooksie, Fumsup, Lulu, Wu Wu,* etc.

**Hammerschmidt, Martin.** 1895–1909. Neufang, Thür. Manufactured dolls.

**Hammond, Thomas Rundle.** 1858. Paris. A trader; was granted a French patent for invisible joints on dolls made of flesh-colored vulcanized rubber, to prevent children

from being poisoned by the paints. He claimed that heretofore joints had been visible.

**Han, C. Dorpat.** 1862. Russia. Displayed dolls in national costumes at the London Exhibition.

**Hanco.** 1920–21. Trademark registered in Germany by *Hahn & Co.* for dolls.

**Hancock, S., & Sons.** 1891–1925+. Cauldon, Staffordshire. Porcelain factory believed to have made dolls' heads; used mark "S. H. & S.," but heads may all have been made after the pottery was known as Cauldon. This might be the maker of the Hancock "N. T. I." dolls.

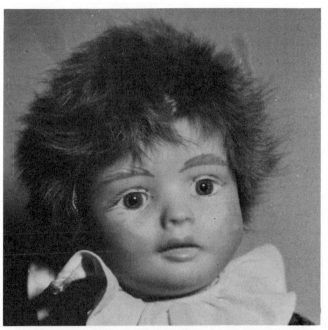

**728A & B.** N. T. I. Hancock bisque heads with wigs, glass eyes, closed mouths; made in England. *Courtesy of Marion Holt and Maurine Popp; photographs by Winnie Langley.*

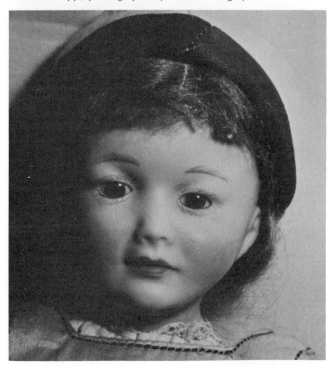

# NTI BOY ENGLISH MAKE

**729.** Mark on "N.T.I." Hancock doll.

**Händler, Fr.** 1909–18. Nürnberg, Bavaria. Manufactured dolls.

**Hands for Dolls.** 1916–20. At least three companies spe-cialized in making hands for dolls. They were *Heinrich Handwerck, Empire Dolhand Manufacturing Co.,* and *Bronx Doll Manufacturing Co.* Earlier, metal hands were used on wooden bodies marked "*Huret,*" and on wooden bodies made in Springfield, Vt., by the *Jointed Doll Co.* and the *Co-operative Doll Co.,* as well as by other com-panies. Rubber hands were used in the U.S. around 1925, especially on infant dolls. For variations in the types of hands, see Ills. 730–761.

HANDS

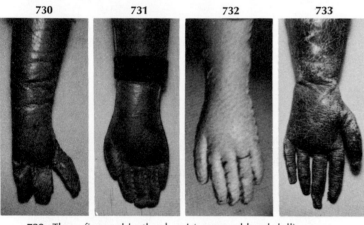

730    731    732    733

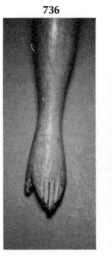  

736    737    738

**730.** Three-fingered leather hand (on waxed-head doll).

**731.** Leather; fingers indicated by stitching (rubber-head doll).

**732.** Kid; fingers wired and separate (bisque head doll).

**733.** Leather; doll has Sarah Robinson body and china head.

**736.** All-wood hand (ball-jointed body).

**737.** All-wood; Schoenhut.

**738.** Metal hand on wooden arm; Ellis.

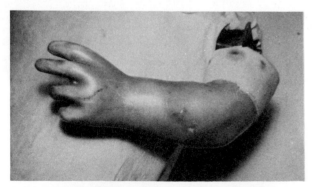

**734.** Wax-over-composition hands; Munnier (waxed-head doll).

**735.** Poured wax hand (wax head).

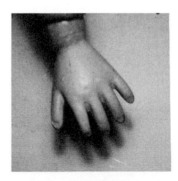

**739.** All steel; Metal Doll Co.

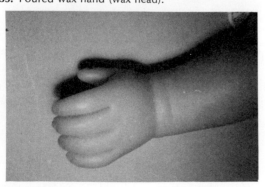

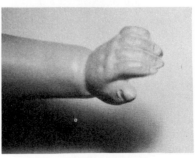

**740.** Celluloid; Kling (bisque-head doll).

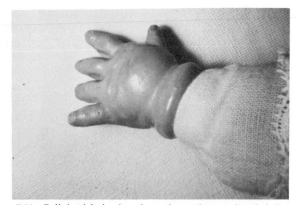

**741.** Celluloid baby hand; Amberg (bisque-head doll).

**742.** Limbs and head of china on wooden body.

**743.** China limbs and head; baby.

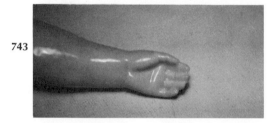

**744.** China limbs and head; lady.      **745.** China limbs and head; girl.

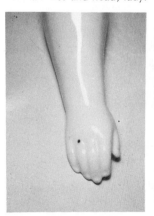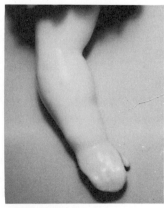

**746.** Hand of a homemade cloth body.

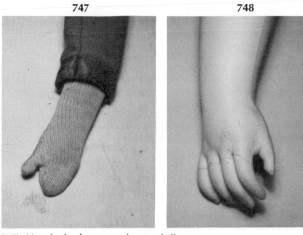

747         748

**747.** Hand of a homemade rag doll.

**748.** Bisque; Motschmann type.

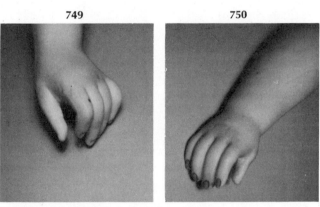

749         750

**749.** Bisque hand on Jumeau lady.

**750.** Bisque; Kubelka.

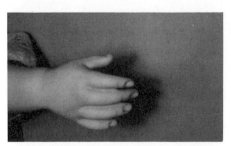

**751.** Bisque; Bru.

**752.** Bisque hand of a German baby doll.

**753.** Bisque; A. Marque.

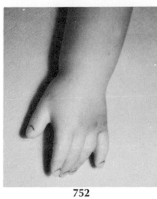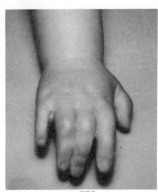

752         753

HANDS

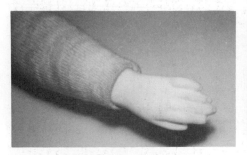

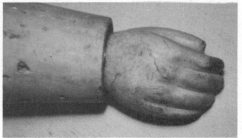

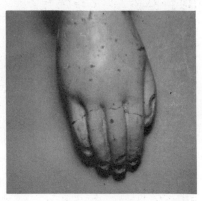

**754.** Bisque; Gesland.

**755.** Composition; Motschmann type.

**756.** Composition; uncovered Lacmann.

**757.** Composition; Jules Steiner.    **758.** Composition; Jumeau.    **759.** Composition; Mascotte.    **760.** Composition; Harmus.

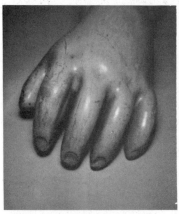

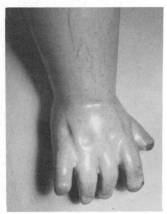

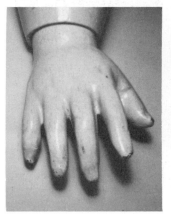

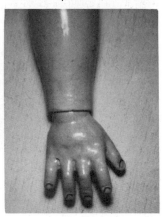

**761.** Composition; Kämmer & Reinhardt.

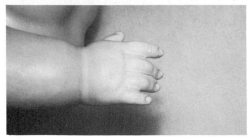

*Hand pictures, courtesy of Eunice Althouse, Dorothy Annunziato, Sylvia Brockmon, the Chester County Historical Society, Alberta Darby, Edith Meggers, the Newark Museum, Newark, N. J., Helen Jo Payne, Mary Roberson.*

**Handwerck (Handwork), Heinrich.** 1876–1902, Gotha near Waltershausen, Thür.; 1902–25+, Heinrich Handwerck firm. Manufactured ball-jointed dolls. According to Patricia Schoonmaker in RESEARCH ON KAMMER AND REINHARDT, the Handwerck factory was taken over by *Kämmer & Reinhardt* after Heinrich Handwerck died in 1902, but the firm name was carried on. Handwerck exhibited his dolls at Chicago in 1893, but his award, if any, is not known. He registered in Germany his eight-pointed star in 1891 with French wording and in 1895 with German wording. Other trademarks registered in Germany were, *Bébé Cosmopolite* in 1895, the name Heinrich Handwerck and the name *Bébé Réclame* in 1898, and the name *Bébé Superior* in 1913.

1897: Obtained German patent #100297 for a ball-jointed doll; an ink stamp on the right thigh of some dolls reads "Heinrich Handwerck D R Patent #100297."

1901: Obtained another German patent and a supplementary patent for parts of a doll's body. Handwerck dolls were advertised as having jointed papier-mâché bodies, sleeping eyes, sewed curly hair wigs. Size 18 and 20½ inches; price $12.00 and $18.00 doz. wholesale.

1902–3: Handwerck dolls distributed by *Nerlich & Co.* Advertised as having bisque head, sleeping eyes, open mouth, teeth, double-sewn mohair curly wig; body jointed at neck, shoulder, elbow, wrist, hip, and knee; came with real shoes and stockings and a chemise; sizes 19, 20, 24, 25 inches; prices $26.40 to $108.00 doz. wholesale.

1906: New York HERALD advertised Handwerck jointed-body dolls with sleeping eyes and wigs, 18 inches in size, for 98¢.

1907: Advertised jointed *Täuflinge.*

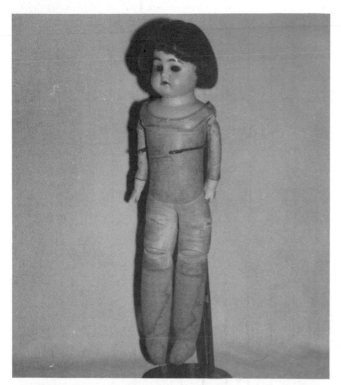

**762A & B.** This Heinrich Handwerck bisque shoulder head has glass eyes, wig, open mouth, and four teeth. Mark: Ill. **764.** Kid body; bisque forearms; lower legs of cloth. H. 16 inches. H. of shoulder head, 4½ inches. *Courtesy of Dorothy Annunziato.*

1909–10: New line of jointed Handwerck dolls with human expressions, distributed by *Borgfeldt* and *Strobel & Wilken*. The faces of these dolls were modeled by artists in Munich from living subjects; they included boys,' girls,' and women's faces in a variety of expressions. Handwerck dolls exhibited at Seattle and commended for their quality.

1911: Advertised jointed Täuflinge.

1912: Handwerck dolls included six Japanese dolls, three boys and three girls, in various sizes. They had olive complexions and were modeled from nature by doll artists; came dressed in kimonos. Regular ball-jointed doll advertised as having side-part ringlet wig, sleeping eyes, real hair eyelashes, shoes and stockings; cost $1.19.

1914: Character babies and jointed dolls distributed by Borgfeldt and *B. Illfelder*. Advertised full ball-jointed doll with bisque head, sleeping eyes, eyelashes, full sewed wig; 22½ inches tall; cost $7.50 retail.

1916: *Foulds & Freure* distributed Handwerck's dolls' hands, character dolls' arms and bodies.

1923: *Davis & Voetsch* distributed the Handwerck line of jointed and character dolls.

The fact that most mold numbers on Handwerck bisque heads end with a "9" suggests that they were made by *Simon & Halbig*. One of the Kämmer & Reinhardt mold #114's has been found on a composition body marked in purple on the thigh "Heinrich Handwerck, Germany."

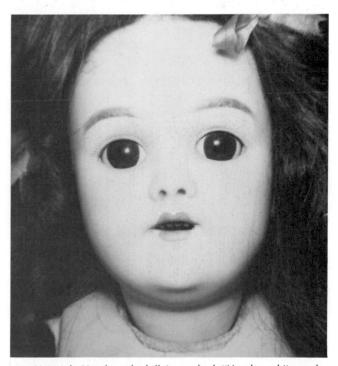

**763.** Heinrich Handwerck doll is marked "Handwerck" on the bisque head (see Ill. **765**) and on the body; doll has sleeping eyes, molded eyebrows, composition body with wooden ball joints. H. 18½ inches. *Courtesy of Hildred Brinkley.*

The prices given for dolls are those for which the dolls were originally offered for sale. They are *not* today's prices.

**764–775.** Heinrich Handwerck's marks. No. **766** is a trademark; the other marks are found on dolls. The "H" of No. **770** may or may not be a Handwerck mark.

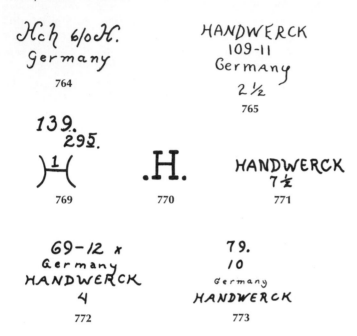

Handwerck, Max. 1900–1925+. Waltershausen, Thür. Manufactured dolls and dolls' bodies. Registered in Germany as trademarks *Bébé Elite* in 1901, *Cornouloid Doll* and *Madame Butterfly* in 1913. *William Goebel* made the bisque heads for Bébé Elite. In 1913 and 1914, Max Handwerck obtained German and U.S. patents for making hollow bodies for dolls of paper, cloth, etc. These were made by uniting two halves of thin material, securing them together by staple pins at their overlapping edges; then slightly larger halves of similar shape and thin material were united to the inner halves by sizing, cement, or brazing, completely covering the inner halves. The outer halves were united at the edges by flanges, which were so trimmed off by overlapping that they were nearly imperceptible.

**776.** Mark found on Max Handwerck doll.

Hanington, A. W., & Co. 1915. New York City. Made *Kutie Kins* dolls of stuffed felt cloth with hand-painted faces that resembled *Drayton* drawings.

Hanka. 1924–25. Trade name of dolls made by *Gebrüder Pfeiffer*. Name applied especially to *Mama Dolls*.

Hanlon. 1861. New York City. Thomas, George, William, Alfred, Edward, and Frederick Hanlon secured a British patent for a walking doll that operated by a clockwork mechanism.

Hanna. Name inscribed on back of bisque socket head made by *Schoenau & Hoffmeister*. Came in both Polynesian and Caucasian versions.

Hannoverische Gummi Kamm-Comp. Act-Ges. 1909. Hannover, Prussia. Manufactured rubber dolls.

Hans. 1910–11. Trade name for model 114 of the *Royal* line, made by *Kämmer & Reinhardt*; distributed by *Strobel & Wilken* and *Borgfeldt*. Character boy, usually came with bisque head and jointed composition body. Named for the boy who posed for the model.

Hans. See Hansel.

Hans Brinker with the Silver Skates. 1922. Trademark registered in U.S. by *Wolf Doll Co.* for dolls. Came with composition head and hands; size 15 inches, cost $1.00.

Hansa Haus. See Buschow & Beck.

Hansel. 1912. Trade name of doll made by *Horsman*. Called "Hans" in October, 1912 advertisement. Came with *Can't Break 'Em* composition head, stuffed body; dressed in multi-color Dutch costume with overalls and Dutch shoes; mate for *Gretel*.

Hansel. 1913. Trade name of doll in Dutch costume handled by *Schoen & Sarkady*; mate to *Gretel*. Came with molded hair, closed mouth.

Hansel. 1916. Line of dolls distributed by *Strobel & Wilken*.

Hansen, Karen Marie (née Petersen). 1918. Silkeborg, Denmark. Obtained Danish and German patents for dolls with standing bodies.

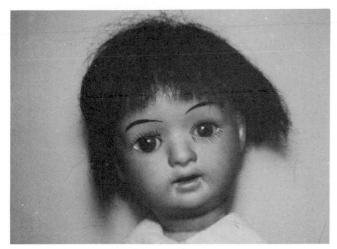

**777.** "Hanna," a Polynesian character bisque head made by Schoenau & Hoffmeister. Doll has glass sleep eyes, open mouth with two teeth, wig; jointed composition baby body. Mark: Ill. **778.** H. 9 inches. *Courtesy of Ollie Leavister.*

**778.** "Hanna" mark used by Schoenau & Hoffmeister.

**779A & B.** All-bisque "Happifats" have brown hair and eyes. The girl wears a pink dress with blue sash and shoes; boy wears green jacket and shoes, beige pants. *Courtesy of Margaret Whitton; photographs by Winnie Langley.*

**Hansen, Laurie & Co.** 1916–21. London. Made dolls.

**Hansen, Madame E.** 1878. Copenhagen, Denmark. Showed dolls at the Paris Exposition.

**Hansi (L'Oncle Hansi).** Ca. 1917. Produced small (7½- to 8½ inches) dolls, including Yerri & Gretel and character dolls with celluloid heads and cloth bodies.

**Happifat.** 1913–21. Registered as a trademark by *Borgfeldt* in U.S. and Germany in 1914. Dolls based on the drawings by *Kate Jordan,* which appeared in JOHN MARTIN'S BOOK. The rotund little boy in molded suit or underwear and little girl in molded dress both had molded hair and rubber elastic-jointed arms. They were made in 1914 in Germany of all-bisque or all-composition.

1915: Borgfeldt brought out a new version, made by *K & K Toy Co.,* with composition head and hands and stuffed bodies. These dolls were 10½ inches, priced $18.00 doz. wholesale, including clothes. All-bisque dolls were 3½ and 4½ inches high; cost $2.40 to $4.00 doz. wholesale.

1919–20: *Louis Amberg & Son* advertised the Kate Jordan Happifats with cloth bodies, composition head, painted eyes and hair, size 10 inches.

1921: Louis Amberg & Son advertised a new Happifat named *Freshie.*

An imitation or later version of the Happifat was made in Japan.

**Happiness Dolls.** 1925. Line of dolls produced by *Louis Wolf & Co.* by special arrangement with Happiness Candy Stores. Line included *Toddling Toodles,* a walking doll, and *Baby Sunshine.*

**Happy.** 1915. Doll made and copyrighted by *Trion Toy Co.* Came dressed in rompers. Head, designed by *Ernesto Peruggi,* represented a boy with a curly lock of hair hanging on his forehead.

**Happy Cry.** 1924. One of the *Madame Hendren* line of dolls made by *Averill Manufacturing Co.;* designed by *Grace Drayton;* price $1.00 and up.

**Happy Hiram.** 1912. Made by *Horsman.* Doll had *Can't Break 'Em* composition head and hands, molded hair, and soft body; teeth showed. It represented a farmer's boy dressed in blue overalls and checked shirt; size nearly 12 inches; price $1.00.

**Happy Hooligan.** 1903+. Doll reported in PLAYTHINGS. There were probably many dolls representing this hobo with his tin-can hat, as shown in the comics. Happy Hooligan was used as part of various metal toys made in U.S.

**Happy Hooligan.** 1910. Doll made by Hahn & *Amberg*, probably the one distributed by *Butler Bros.* with composition head. Pressure on the body caused the mouth to open and the voice to sound. Size 11½ inches.

**Happy Hooligan.** 1923. Trademark registered in France and Germany by *Borgfeldt* for dolls.

**Happy Jane.** 1920–22. Trademark registered in U.S. by *Harvard Garment Co.* for cloth dolls.

**Happy Rite Family.** 1916–17. Trademark registered in U.S. by *Rite Specialty Co.* for dolls.

**Happyland.** 1907. Brand name of photographic face dolls made by *E. B. & E. Co.*

**Harald.** 1915. Trademark registered in Germany by *Wagner & Zetzsche* for dolls.

**Harania, Joachim.** 1922. Frankfurt am Main, Hesse. Procured a German patent for a doll's head with changeable features.

**Harber, William Francis.** 1904. Chelsea, London. Obtained a British patent for a walking doll.

**Harburg & Vienna Rubber Co.** 1907. Hannover-Linden, Germany. Made rubber dolls, distributed by *B. Illfelder & Co.*

**Harburger Gummiwaren-Fabrik Phoenix Co.** 1924. Harburg on the Elbe, Germany. Made rubber dolls. They registered the trademark *Phoenix Quick.*

**Hardouin, H.** 1885–89. Paris. Made dolls, bébés, bathing dolls, and trousseaux.

**Harem Skirt Doll.** 1911. Doll representing a lady of about twenty-two years, made by *Louis Amberg & Son;* dressed in a type of bloomers called "Jupe-Culotte" in France.

**Harlequin.** Empire period or earlier–1925+. Dolls dressed in parti-colored costumes like clowns.

1916: Distributed by *Butler Bros.;* 13 and 15½ inches; price $4.50 and $9.60 doz. wholesale.

**Harley, Florence Deming.** 1924. San Francisco, Calif. Was issued a U.S. design patent for a rag doll representing a Chinaman with a long queue.

**Harmonica Joe.** 1924. Negro or Caucasian doll made by *EFFanBEE*, designed by Hugo Baum. Doll played harmonica when rubber ball in its stomach was pushed.

**Harmus, Carl, Jr.** 1873–1925+. Sonneberg, Thür. Manufactured dolls.

1895: Made dolls and dolls' heads for export, including "unbreakable" dolls. He displayed dolls at Paris in 1900 and at St. Louis in 1904. In Paris he was one of the group of Grand Prize winners.

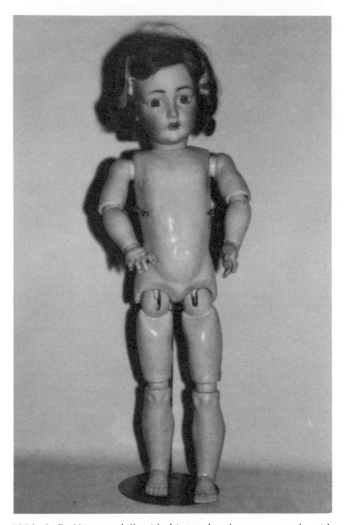

**780A & B.** Harmus doll with bisque head, open mouth with four upper teeth. Head mark: Ill. **782.** Jointed composition body. H. 20 inches. *Courtesy of Dorothy Annunziato.*

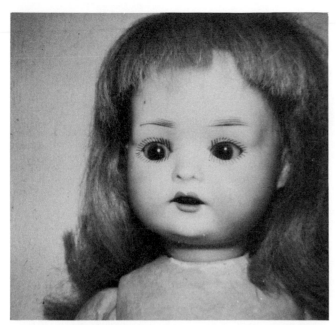

**781.** Doll produced by Carl Harmus has bisque head possibly made by Otto Reinecke. Mark: Ill. **783.** Sleeping eyes; open mouth with teeth; jointed composition toddler's body. H. 11½ inches. *Courtesy of Jessica Norman.*

**782–784.** Marks on dolls made by Carl Harmus.

PM

PM
783

Harmus
800. 0
782

Harmus
7
784

1907: Advertised dolls of all kinds.

1909: Registered in Germany a triangular trademark showing a teddy bear holding a doll; stated he was a manufacturer and exporter of dressed dolls and dolls' trousseaux.

1911: Again, he advertised dolls of all kinds.

William R. Petzsche was his London agent from 1903 to 1915. John Abraham & Co. was his agent in 1921, when he specialized in double-jointed dolls and baby dolls. The "PM" marks on dolls' heads suggest that Harmus may have used bisque heads from *Otto Reinicke's* porcelain factory.

**Harrass, Adolph.** 1861–1911. Grossbreitenbach, Thür. Specialized in jointed character dolls. Used *Unerreicht* (unrivaled) as a trademark.

**Harriet Lane.** Ca. 1860. Doll represented the popular First Lady of the White House, the niece of bachelor President James Buchanan.

**Harris, John.** 1858–60. Lambeth, England. Made dolls.

**Harrison, George.** 1856–65. London. Made dolls.

**Harrison, Martha R.** 1914–16. Jersey City, N.J. Was granted a U.S. design patent for a rotund, nude infant with bent limbs.

**Harry.** 1913. Trade name used by *Borgfeldt* for a boy doll with eyes glancing to the side; mate to *Carrie.*

**Harry Lauder Dolls.** 1909. All dolls dressed in Scottish tartans were called "Harry Lauder Dolls" because of his popularity in that year; prices 25¢ to 75¢.

**Hart, W. H., Jr.** 1874. Philadelphia, Pa. Was issued a U.S. patent for a doll.

**Hartan, Gebrüder.** 1923–25. Sonneberg, Thür. Manufactured dolls.

**Hartmann, August.** 1909. Wilhelmshaven, Germany. Obtained a German patent for wig holder for dolls' heads.

**Hartmann, Carl (Karl).** 1895–1925+, Neustadt near Coburg, Thür; also 1918–25+, Stockheim, Bavaria. Made and exported dressed dolls; jobber for German factories. Registered in Germany trademarks of a picture of a globe in 1898, the name *Globe Baby* in 1899, and *Paladin Baby* in 1904, all for dressed dolls. He made character babies at the Puppenfabrik, Stockheim. His New York agent in 1922 was *Roth, Baitz & Lipsitz.*

**Hartung, Reinhold.** 1895. Sonneberg, Thür. Made dressed, jointed dolls of medium and best kinds, according to advertisement.

**Hartwig, Albert.** 1905. Sonneberg, Thür. Made dolls.

**Hartwig, C.** 1863–74. Sonneberg, Thür. Made dolls' heads.

**Hartwig, Robert.** 1882–1925+. Sonneberg, Thür. Manufactured dolls, probably wooden. He was one of the Grand Prize group at the 1900 Paris Exposition and had a display in the 1904 St. Louis Exhibition.

**Harva Cie.** 1925. Paris. Made dolls, including *Gaby* and *Nono.*

**Harvard Garment Co.** 1920–22. Harvard, Ill. Registered *Happy Jane* as their trademark in U.S. for rag dolls, which they made.

**Harwich, Theresa.** 1922–23. Miami, Fla. Secured a U.S. design patent for a freckle-faced boy doll, dressed in overalls; feet were bare.

**Harwood, William A.** 1862–77. Brooklyn, N.Y. Secured a U.S. patent in 1877 for a crying and talking doll. This was allegedly the first American talking doll; it operated by blowing air across reeds.

**Hasckarl, Johannes.** 1895. Orlamünde, Thür. Manufactured dolls.

**Haskell, Samuel.** 1914–25. Brooklyn, N.Y. Native of Russia. Obtained three U.S. patents for dolls.

1914: He assigned his design patent for a doll with eyes glancing to the side to *Fair & Carnival Trading Co.*

1923: He patented a phonograph doll with a rotatable voice member and a horn inside the body of the doll.

1925: He assigned to *Samuel Robert* his design patent for a girl clad in pajamas; she had straight bobbed hair, and a cigarette in her mouth.

**Hassall, John.** 1914. England. Famous poster artist. Designed a series of dolls that were sent to the London Child's Welfare Exhibit.

**Hatch, Florence B.** 1919–20. St. Louis, Mo. Was issued U.S. design patent for a Negro mammy doll with buttons for its eyes.

**Hatch, Thomas.** 1848–81, London; 1884–91, appears to have been succeeded by Mrs. Sarah Hatch. Made wax and composition dolls.

**Hatsuzo, Shimizu.** 1893. Kyoto, Japan. Displayed dolls at the Chicago Exhibition.

**Haueisen, Richard.** 1908–21. Gehren, Thür. Manufactured wool dolls.

**Haupt, J.** 1921. Paris. Made *poupards*.

**Hausel, F.** 1915–20. Köppelsdorf, Thür. Manufactured dolls.

**Hausman & Zatulove.** 1919. New York City. Made cotton-stuffed, soft-body character dolls and washable cloth dolls, among them *Ku-Tee*; used "Hau-Zat" as a trade name. (See Ill. 1729.)

**Hausmeister, Paul, & Co.** 1909. Göppingen, Germany. Registered in Germany trademark of a stork on one foot, used for heads of dolls made of gelatin.

**Hau-Zat.** See **Hausman & Zatulove.**

**Havens, Clara V.** 1923–24. New York City. Secured two U.S. design patents for a boy doll and for a baby doll, which she assigned to *Karmen Corp.*

**Havens, Virginia.** 1921. Philadelphia, Pa. Made *Tubbins*.

**Hawelka, L.** See **Schünemann, L.**

**Hawkins, George H.** 1867–70. New York City. Made dolls' heads labeled on shoulder "X.L.C.R.," the phonetic equivalent of the word "Excelsior." In 1862 he was listed in a directory under Bonnets, and in 1867 as a manufacturer of "Excelsior Bonnet Frames." He obtained U.S., French, and British patents in 1868, and another U.S. patent in 1869, for making dolls' heads by saturating cloth with sizing or glue, then pressing it between dies until the glutinous material had hardened and would permanently retain its configuration. Heads made by Hawkins often carry the patent date September 8, 1868 and are sometimes found on mechanical dolls made under the patent of *William Farr Goodwin* or on the early tricycle riding dolls.

**Hawkins & Stubblefield.** 1917–20. Rogers, Ark. Registered *Sam-Me* as a trademark in U.S. for dolls.

**Hawley, Horace.** 1918–21. London. Manufactured dolls' limbs.

**Hawsky, Adalbert.** 1854–1909. Leipzig, Saxony. Won Honorable Mention for his doll displays at the 1854

**785A & B.** Walking doll with rag composition head has two stickers on the back of neck. One is a triangular label of William Goodwin, patentee of a walking doll, and one is that of George Hawkins (see Ill. **787**). Note the similarity of this head to the bisque head in Ill. **786**. H. 11 inches. *Courtesy of the Chester County Historical Society.*

Munich Exhibition and the 1862 London Exhibition. In 1862 he sold dolls in glass cases for $3.75, but puppets' heads with natural hair cost from $4.15 to $11.35. Crying dolls ranged from $3.50 to $9.40. (These may have been the *Motschmann*-type crying dolls.) Prices of dolls with porcelain heads were $1.90 to $3.40; other dolls cost 45¢ to $1.50. In the 20th century, he was listed under "Toys of All Kinds."

**Hayashi, T.** 1880. Japan. Entered dolls in the Melbourne Exhibition.

**Hayes, James A.** 1922. New York City. Registered *Flapper* as U.S. trademark for dolls. He also obtained U.S. design patent for doll with galoshes, hat, and coat.

**786.** Untinted bisque shoulder head with molded blonde hair and glazed earrings and pendant. Hawkins used a similar head as a model for some of his patented cloth heads. H. 13½ inches. H. of shoulder head, 4 inches. *Courtesy of the Chester Historical Society.*

**787.** Mark on label used for George Hawkins' dolls.

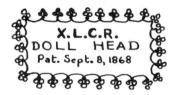

**Haynes, Rebecca.** 1884–87. London. Made rag dolls.

**Hays, Frank A.** 1909–10. Philadelphia and Overbrook, Pa. Did business under the name *Children's Novelty Co.*

1909: He registered *Bobby Bobbykins* and *Dolly Dollykins* as trademarks for dolls in U.S., having used them in trade between the several states. He also applied for a U.S. design patent for a chubby rag doll with circular face and eyes, dots for nose and for eyebrows, and mouth shaped somewhat like two parenthesis marks laid horizontally, back to back so that the curves intersect. Since *Grace Gebbie Drayton*'s sister Margaret married a Mr. Hays, and both the Gebbie girls were famous illustrators who made drawings that resembled this doll, it seems likely that the doll was a family product and one of the first of a long line of Drayton dolls. (See **Saalfield Publishing Co.**)

1910: Along with Bobby Bobbykins and Dolly Dollykins, *Strawbridge and Clothier* also advertised *Polly Pig-Tails*, *Babykins*, and *Barekid* rag dolls, all resembling the Drayton type of drawing.

**Hazel, Henry John.** 1891–1925+. London. Made dolls for the wholesale trade.

**Head of Baby.** 1921. Copyrighted by *Louis Amberg & Son*, designed by *Julio Kilenyi*; represented the head of a "pleasing" baby.

**Head of Little Girl.** Copyrighted by *Louis Amberg & Son*, designed by *Julio Kilenyi*; represented the head of a "pleasing" little girl.

**Heads of Dolls.** Dolls' heads are usually the most important part, especially the artistry of the face. In 1875, HARPER'S BAZAR noted that ". . . instead of the insipid faces of a generation ago, mothers now select for their little girls Dollies with faces of intelligence and expressive beauty, many of which are said to be copies of heads famous in painting and sculpture. Thus correct taste and an appreciation of the beautiful are taught the children of to-day." Each generation said somewhat the same thing, and it is a fact that most of the really beautiful dolls' heads appear to belong to the beginning of the use of each material. The carved wooden heads of the 18th and very early 19th centuries surpass later ones. Most of the handsome china heads appear to have belonged to the period between 1840 and 1870. There is no denying that the early French bisque-head bébés were the loveliest. Around the turn of the 20th century, dolls appear to have reached a nadir when many of them looked alike. Then the trend turned with the introduction of character dolls, which were made to resemble actual people. Doll producers found that dolls' heads needed designs made by experienced artists, and in America doll companies hired fine artists like *Laura Gardin, Jeno Juszko, Julio Kilenyi, Rose O'Neill, Ernesto Peruggi,* and others. After the molds or dies were made from the design and casting of the artist, various doll manufacturers made the dolls. One doll company in 1921 advertised, "You furnish the dies and we will make YOUR dolls." It is for this reason that the marks on a doll's head often indicate the creator rather than the manufacturer of the doll.

Fragile material was often used to make heads for dolls, and when they broke, melted, or were ruined, they were frequently replaced. This is why early dolls that are allegedly documented do not in many cases have the original head.

The head has always been one of the most valuable parts of a doll, and its proportionate value increases as it becomes an antique.

**Heath, Almon.** 1920–21. Los Angeles, Calif. Was granted a U.S. design patent for a doll representing a man with eyes looking upward and wearing a short coat and a high collar.

**Heather Belle.** 1923. Trademark registered in Britain by *Leon Rees* for dolls.

**HEbees-SHEbees.** 1925. Trademark registered in U.S. by *Horsman* for pair of dolls representing the Twelvetrees Kids drawn by Charles Twelvetrees. The dolls were dressed in various costumes; for example, there was a collegiate HEbee, a Pancho HEbee, etc. SHEbee was the mate to HEbee, and wore pink where he wore blue.

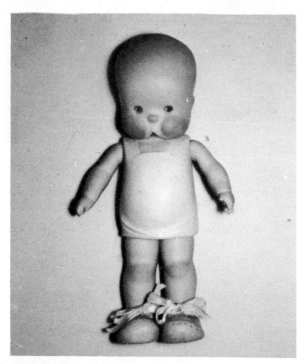

**788.** All-bisque "HEBee," jointed at shoulders and hips, has painted features, molded clothes except shoelaces, white chemise, blue shoes. H. 9 inches. *Courtesy of Dorothy Annunziato.*

Came in all-bisque or in composition; the latter were 10½ inches tall; had sticker on foot.

**Heber & Co.** 1900–1925+. Neustadt near Gotha, Thür. Hard paste porcelain factory. Made dolls' heads. They used the initials "HC" superimposed. (See Ill. 789B.)

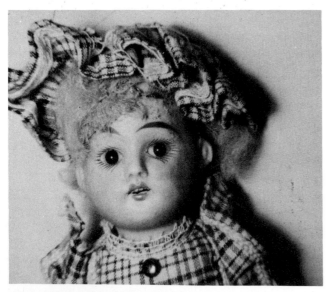

**789A.** Bisque head made by Heber & Co. has black pupil-less glass eyes with long painted eyelashes, open mouth, and teeth. Body is composition, with unpainted torso and legs; doll wears her original green, maroon, and white plaid hat and dress. Mark on head: Ill. **789B.** H. 10½ inches. *Courtesy of Eleanor Jean Carter.*

514 G 17/8

**789B.** Mark used by Heber & Co. on dolls' heads.

**Hecht.** Made cherub-type dolls and won an infringement case when sued by *Rose O'Neill.*

**Hecht, Else.** Made dolls before 1926; dolls created by her were placed in Sonneberg Museum.

**Hecquet.** 1870–78. Paris. Made dolls.

**Hedi.** 1919–24. Trademark registered in Germany by successors of *E. Schwerin.*

**Hegemann, Alice.** 1909. Displayed dolls at Munich Exhibition and won distinction.

**Hehl, Fritz.** 1891–1918. Coburg, Thür. Manufactured and exported dressed dolls; advertised that he specialized in medium and best grades of jointed dolls.

1908: Was granted a German patent for dolls' eyes that moved.

**Heibei, Wada.** 1893. Osaka, Japan. Displayed dolls at the Chicago Exhibition.

**Heico.** 1924–25. Trademark registered in Germany by *M. Heider & Co.* for dolls.

**Heider, M., & Co.** 1924–25. Nürnberg, Bavaria. Manufactured and exported baby dolls and cloth dolls.

1925: Registered the trademark *Heico* in Germany.

**Heidler, Carl.** 1895. Neustadt near Coburg, Thür. Manufactured little or baby dolls.

**Heidler, Ernst.** 1895–1909. Neustadt near Coburg, Thür. Manufactured little or baby dolls.

**Heigel, Carl.** 1899. Vienna. Manufactured dolls and dolls' heads.

**Hein, Val.** 1918–25+. Sonneberg, Thür. Made jointed dolls.

**Heincke, Hans.** 1903–25+. Waltershausen, Thür. Was the proprietor of the *A. Wislizenus* firm.

1903: Obtained a German patent for doll articles.

**Heininger, Therese.** 1925. Dresden, Saxony. Producer and distributor of dolls; registered in Germany *Original Rose Hein Puppen* as a trademark.

**Heinrich, Jules, & Co.** 1895. Paris. Distributor for German doll factories. Handled wax heads, bisque heads, *nankeen* dolls, ordinary bébés and *bébés incassables,* and porcelain bathers for export, etc.

**Heinrich & Co.** See **Hinrichs & Co.**

**Heinrich Gebrüder (Bros.).** 1893–1900. Germany. Showed dolls in 1893 at Chicago and in 1900 at Paris, where they won a bronze medal.

**Heinrich Handwerck.** 1898–1921. Trademark registered in Germany by Heinrich Handwerck in 1898 and by *Kämmer & Reinhardt* in 1921 for jointed dolls.

**Heinz, Alfred.** 1908–25+. Sonneberg, Thür. Made dressed dolls of various kinds.

**Heinz, Rudolf.** 1911–25. Prague, Czechoslovakia. Manufactured dolls.

**Heinze, Carl.** 1895. Grümpen, Thür. Manufactured dolls.

**Heinze, R.** 1880. Germany. Showed dolls at Melbourne Exhibition.

**Heithersay, E. S.** 1920. Malvern, Australia. Procured British patent for a walking doll.

**Heizer, Dorothy (née Wendell).** 1921–25+. Essex Fells, N.J. Made art rag dolls. Most of these dolls were made from contemporary portraits of the subject; flesh-colored crepe was used for the "skin." The faces were molded and painted with water colors. The bodies were built over a copper wire frame, which was padded with cotton and covered with muslin. The clothes and jewelry copied those in the portraits as closely as possible.

1921: First doll was a soft rag doll with a flat painted face.

1923: Made portrait of Irene Castle for Corticelli Silk Co.

1924: Exhibited dolls at Arts and Crafts Guild in Philadelphia; made portrait dolls of Queen Elizabeth I and Sir Walter Raleigh for Newark Museum, Newark, N.J.; size 14¼ inches.

**Helbig, George.** 1914–20. Dresden, Saxony. Secured German patent for a doll's head with elastic.

790. Fabric doll made by Dorothy Heizer, representing Queen Elizabeth I. Doll has painted features and wears original green velvet dress. H. 14¼ inches. *Courtesy of the Newark Museum, Newark, N.J.*

**Helen.** See **Pet Name.**

**Helen.** 1914. Child doll copyrighted by *Horsman*, designed by *Helen Trowbridge.*

**Helen.** 1919. Trade name for doll make by *Jessie Mc-Cutcheon Raleigh.*

**Helft, J.** 1925. Paris. Distributor for *La Cellulosine,* celluloid dolls.

**Helgünith.** 1924–25. Was registered as a trademark in Germany by *Oskar Günthel.*

**Helk, B.** 1918. Neustadt near Coburg, Thür. Made dolls' bodies.

**Hell 'N-Maria (Hellen-Maria).** 1924. Trademark registered in U.S. by *Hubert E. Leland* for dolls. Leland also obtained a U.S. design patent for this doll. It had a white lady with bobbed hair on one side and a Negro with hair in coils on the other side. Each doll had one arm on its hip and the other arm across its chest. The name was inspired by the famous "cuss words" of General Dawes, later the Vice-President. Hell 'N-Maria was advertised by *Schoen & Yondorf* as a two-faced fabric doll; Hellen on the front was Caucasian, Maria on the back was Negro. Came with yarn hair, cotton-stuffed oilcloth body; 17 inches tall, price $1.00.

**Heller, Adolf.** 1918–25+. Waltershausen, Thür. Manufactured dolls.

**Heller, Alexander.** 1919–20. New York City. Officer of the *New Toy Co.* registered in U.S. *Nutoi* and *Newbisc, The World's Doll,* as two trademarks for dolls.

**Heller, Alfred.** 1902–7. Meiningen near Coburg, Thür. Produced and distributed metal dolls' heads.

1903: Registered in Germany and U.S. *Diana* as trademark for metal dolls' heads.

**Heller & Seyfarth (Seifert).** 1909–16. Waltershausen, Thür. Manufactured dolls.

**Hellmuth, August.** 1895. Sonneberg, Thür. Manufactured dolls.

**Helm, Ottilie, & Wellhausen, Georg.** 1854–62. Friedrichroda near Gotha, Thür. Won a prize medal for their doll display at Munich in 1854 and Honorable Mention at London in 1862. Killy, Traub & Co. was their London agent.

**Hendren, Madame.** See **Madame (Mme.) Hendren.**

**Henn, Martin.** 1899. Vienna. Manufactured dolls and dolls' heads.

**Henning, M.** 1918–23. Berlin. Manufactured and exported dolls.

**Henny.** 1921–22. Königsberg, Prussia. Trademark registered in Germany by *Clara Bohnke* and Helen Zimmermann for dolls, dolls' bodies, dolls' wigs, and dolls' clothes.

**Henonin, Louis Frédéric Maurice.** 1924. France. Procured French patent for fitting moving eyes in stuffed rag dolls.

**Henry, Madame.** 1829. Paris. Handled dolls.

**Henschel, Julius.** 1909–25+. Berlin. Made dolls and dolls' articles.

**Henstes, B. L.** 1925. Assignee of a British patent for stuffing dolls with kapok so that it was packed more loosely at the shoulder and hip joints.

**Henze, Laura.** 1897–1925+. Gehren, Thür. From 1898 to 1925, known as L. Henze & Steinhäuser. Manufactured stuffed and wool dolls.

1921: Registered in Germany as a trademark a picture of a girl holding dolls.

**Herbillon.** 1858–63. Paris. Obtained a French patent for improving the making of dolls by using cork.

**Herbst, R.** 1923. Neustadt near Coburg, Thür. Also known as Herbst & Funho. Produced various kinds of dolls, especially rag and baby dolls for export.

**Herdan, Anton (H).** 1907–12. Coburg, Thür. Made dolls.

**Hering, Julius.** 1893–1923. Köpplesdorf, Thür. 1907, Julius Hering & Weithase; 1908–23, Julius Hering & Sohn. Porcelain manufacturers; made dolls' heads. They used the initials "J H & W," "J. H. S.," and "J. H. & S." These initials often appeared on a striped, unfurled flag. (See **Vililaria.**)

**791.** Mark used by Julius Hering, and found on dolls.

**Herissey, Madame.** 1829–46. Paris. Made kid-body dolls, dressed and undressed.

**Hermann, Bernhard.** 1925. Sonneberg, Thür. Manufactured dolls.

**Hermann, Carl.** 1924–25. Oeslau near Coburg, Thür. Manufactured dolls and babies in various styles, also bisque dolls' heads with or without closing eyes.

**Hermsdorfer Celluloid Warenfabrik.** 1925. Berlin-Hermsdorfer. Made celluloid dolls, including a drinking celluloid baby. Trademarks were *Marienkäffer* (ladybug) and a picture of a ladybug with *DA DA* on its wings.

**Hernandez, Natividad.** 1893. Zacatecas, Mexico. Displayed fabric dolls at the Chicago Exposition.

**Herold, Christoph.** 1909–25. Schalkau, Thür. Made dolls.

**Herold, Gottlieb.** 1909–25+. Neustadt near Coburg, Thür. Made *Täuflinge*.

**Herold, Gust.** 1895–1925+. Neustadt near Coburg, Thür. Manufactured little or baby dolls and *Täuflinge*.

**Heron, François Edmond.** See **Crämer & Héron.**

**Heront, V.** 1921–25. Prague, Czechoslovakia. Made dolls.

**Herpich, August.** 1922. Sonneberg, Thür. Made kid-body dolls, which *Roth, Baitz & Lipsitz* distributed in U.S.

**Herrera y Hoyo, Carmen.** 1893. Durango, Mexico. Showed wax dolls at the Chicago Exposition.

**Herrington, Mabelle M.** 1922–24. Mount Vernon, N.Y. Was issued a design patent for a doll with flapping galoshes, a hat, and coat; face resembles *Drayton*-type drawing.

**Herrmann, Carl.** 1924. Potsdam, Germany. Registered in Germany *Dekawe Spieltiere & Puppen* over a picture of a bulldog as a trademark for dolls other than rubber.

**Herrmann, Carl Albert Georg.** 1905–6. Dresden, Saxony. Obtained a German and a French patent for unbreakable dolls' heads and for the neck joint. The head was to be covered with kid or made of horn.

**Herrnsdorf, B.** 1918. Berlin. Made dolls.

**Hertel, Schwab & Co.** 1914–25+. Luisenthal (Stutzhaus) near Ohrdruf, Thür. Made china and bisque dolls' heads, including the *Bye-Lo Baby* bisque heads.

**Hertel, Wilhelm.** 1907–18. Coburg, Thür. Manufactured dressed dolls.

**Hertha, Albin.** 1872–1921. Sonneberg, Thür. made and exported dressed dolls.

**Hertwig & Co.** 1864–1925+. Katzhütte near Rudolstadt, Thür. Doll and porcelain steam factory; specialized in making bisque dolls, china dolls, and *nankeen* dolls. Among the latter type were the china-head dolls with names in gold on the chest such as *Daisy, Edith, Florence, Mabel, Pauline,* and the *Pet Names,* which included Agnes, Bertha, Dorothy, Ethel, Helen, and Marion. This type of doll was also made by *Closter Veilsdorf Porzellanfabrik;* it is not known which names were used by each factory.

1881–84: They had a London branch.

1911: Advertised jointed bisque dolls and dolls with bisque heads, the upper torsos having molded clothes, fabric clothes below waist.

**Hervet, Madame.** 1860–62. Paris. Made dolls.

**Herwig, Bruno.** 1920–21. Hamburg, Germany. Made dolls.

**Herz (Heart).** 1910. Trademark registered by *Bruno Schmidt* for dolls.

**Herzi.** Name found incised on bisque head with a heart mark and the initials "P.M.," which may indicate the *Otto Reinecke* porcelain factory.

**Herzkäferchen (Little Bug Heart).** 1925. Trademark used by *Bauer & Richter* for dolls.

**Herzlieb (Sweetheart).** Ca. 1925. Trademark used by *Richard Scherzer* for dolls.

**Herzog (Hertzog), G. (S.), F., & Co.** 1902–25. Berlin. Distributed and exported dolls; agent for *Heinrich Schmuckler.*

**Herzog, Hans, Inc.** 1924. Berlin. Made dolls.

**Herzpuppen-Fabrik.** 1923. Berlin. Manufactured phonograph dolls, wax dolls, and wax dolls' heads, dressed and undressed dolls. Registered three figures with the initials "H. P. F." as their trademark in Germany.

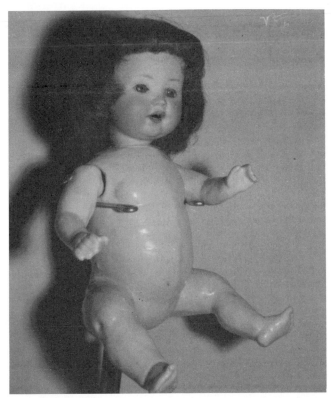

792. "Herzi" is incised on the bisque head. Doll has blue glass sleeping eyes, open mouth with two teeth; composition baby body is joined down the middle front with staples. The "P.M." on the head suggests that it may have been made by Otto Reinecke, but the heart mark was used by Gebrüder Benedikt in their porcelain factory in Mayerhöfen, Bohemia, and possibly they were the manufacturer. H. 10 inches. Mark: Ill. 793. Courtesy of Dorothy Annunziato.

793. "Herzi" mark on dolls probably made by Otto Reinecke.

**Hesli.** 1921–23. Trademark registered in Germany by *Heinrich Schmuckler* for dressed dolls made in the Erste Schlesische Puppenfabrik. "Hesli" appears on the side-view of a rabbit.

**Hess, Albin.** 1918–23. Schalkau, Thür. Made dolls.

**Hess, John.** 1909–23. Hamburg, Germany. Distributor of dolls made by *Heinrich Schmuckler.*

**Hess, Louis.** 1922. Sonneberg, Thür. Made dolls; distributed by *Roth, Baitz & Lipsitz* in America.

**Hess, Theodore, & Co.** 1919. New York City. Handled "Hessco" line of dolls, which were all-composition with sleeping eyes, curled wigs, and straight legs; 14 inches high, price $42.00 doz. wholesale.

**Hesse, A.** See **Vitu (Vittu), Madame.**

**Hetzel, L.** 1915. Sonneberg, Thür. Manufactured dolls.

**Heubach, Ernst.** 1887–1925+. Köppelsdorf, Thür. Made bisque dolls' heads in the Köppelsdorfer Porzellanfabrik.

1895: Heads only are mentioned; factory employed 260 workers.

1905: Listed as manufacturing dolls.

Ernst Heubach was allegedly a brother-in-law of *Armand Marseille.* Some dolls with pierced nostrils and some dolls with *roguish eyes* were made by Ernst Heubach.

### ERNST HEUBACH DOLLS

**794.** Character doll with bisque head has molded and painted features, including eyes glancing to the side. Mark: Ill. **798.** Note the dimples. *Collection of the late Laura Sturges; photograph by Winnie Langley.*

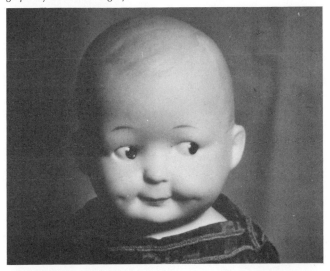

795. Bisque head has pierced nostrils, sleeping eyes, open mouth with two teeth. Mark: Ill. **799.** Composition body. H. 11 inches. *Coleman Collection.*

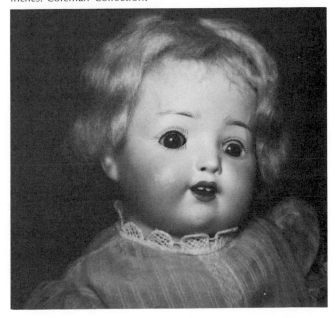

ERNST HEUBACH DOLLS

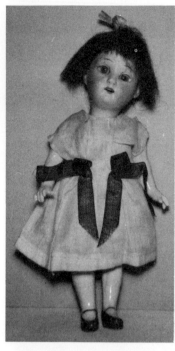

**796.** Heubach of Köppelsdorf doll with bisque head is marked with mold #250 and size "17/0." Composition body. Doll wears original white chemise with red ribbons. H. 7 inches. *Courtesy of Mary Dawson.*

**797.** Bisque head with glass eyes glancing to the side. Mark: Ill. **800.** Doll has molded shoes and socks, composition body. H. 9 inches. *Courtesy of Diane Domroe.*

271 14/0
E·H·Germany
DRGM

798

Heubach·Köppelsdorf
321·9/0
Germany

799

HEUBACH-KÖPPELSDORF
322 - 17/0
Germany

800

801

802

**798–806.** Marks found on dolls made by Ernst Heubach of Köppelsdorf. Directories and porcelain books list both Ernst Heubach and Armand Marseille as proprietors of the Köppelsdorfer Porzellanfabrik.

Germany
275.11%
Heubach·Köppelsdorf.

803

Heubach-Köppelsdorf
250·15%ª
Germany

804

Heubach
250·5
Köppelsdorf
Germany.

805

806

**Heubach, Friedrich A.** 1909–15, Sonneberg, Thür.; 1915–21, successors of Friedrich A. Heubach; 1925, successor was Frieda Heubach, wife of Friedrich A. Heubach. Manufactured dolls.

**Heubach, Gebrüder (Bros.).** 1820–63, Lichte near Wallendorf, Thür.; 1863–1925+, successors of Gebrüder Heubach; in the 20th century, Gebrüder Heubach was a joint stock company. Made bisque and probably china dolls and dolls' heads. Their trade address was in Sonneberg, where the dolls' bodies were no doubt made for the bisque heads made in the Lichte porcelain factory. *Johannes Dietrich* of Berlin used Heubach heads for some of his dolls. Heubach had agents in Paris as early as 1863.

1880: They obtained a patent in Germany for a porcelain *Polichinelle* jointed at the shoulders and hips, with wire through the arms and the body and through the legs and the body. (See Ill. 1323.)

1891: Advertised that they exported to all countries and had agents in Paris *(Gottschalk & Co.)*, Brussels, Amsterdam, Copenhagen, Vienna, and Bologne.

Ca. 1910: They made bisque-head character dolls and babies; especially notable for their intaglio eyes.

1912: They made one of the *Coquette* type of girls' heads in both socket and shoulder models.

1914: They made one of the *Whistling* boys, usually found on a cloth body.

The bodies of the dolls with Heubach heads are often of a poor quality, but the artistry of the character heads more than compensates for the inferior bodies. They have faces expressing many moods; often multi-face dolls seem to have the same expressions, but evidence has not been found as yet to prove that these were made by Heubach. Besides the round and the square marks found on Heubach heads, they are often stamped with

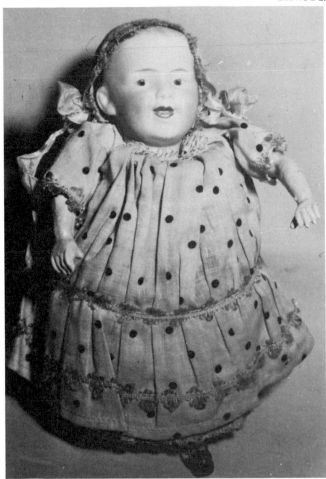

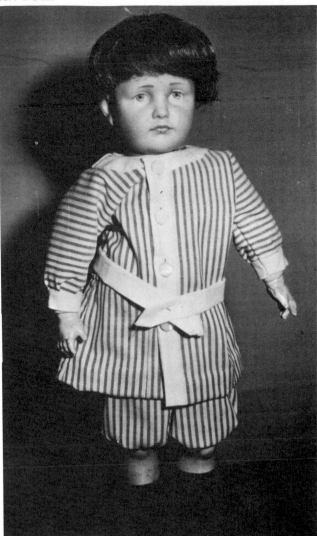

**807.** Walking doll with bisque head of Gebrüder Heubach has intaglio eyes; Izzard label on the base of the doll with London address. *Photograph by Winnie Langley.*

**808.** Bisque-head character doll with painted eyes. Mark: Ill. **822;** also green numbers. Jointed composition body. Note the similarity to Kämmer & Reinhardt's "Hans" (mold #114). *Collection of the late Martha Thompson; photograph by Winnie Langley.*

**809A & B.** Bisque head has intaglio eyes looking straight ahead; note the white highlight marks at the eyelid line; closed mouth. Mark: Ill. **822.** Bent-limb composition baby body. H. 9½ inches. *Courtesy of Alberta Darby.*

**810.** Doll with bisque character head, roguish expression, molded and painted features; composition body. *Courtesy of Gladyse Hilsdorf; photographs by Winnie Langley.*

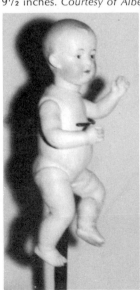

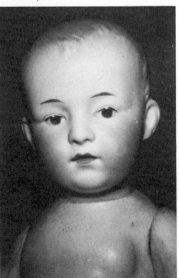

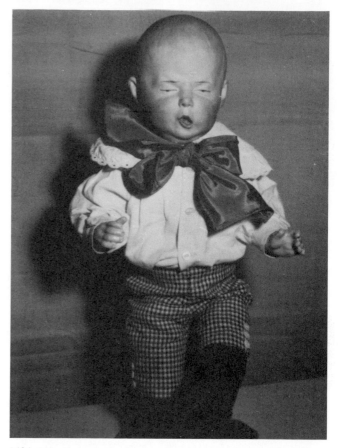

**811A & B.** Molded bisque head, intaglio gray eyes, open-closed mouth with two upper teeth; molded, brown streaked hair with pink glazed hair ribbon; bent-limb composition baby body. Square Heubach mark plus figures "77," "64," and "3." Mark: Ill. **823.** H. 11 inches. *Courtesy of Dorothy Annunziato.*

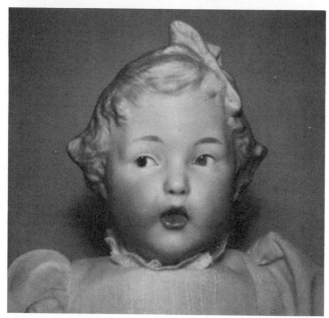

**812A & B.** Two similar bisque character heads, reddish in color, depict a child having a tantrum. Both heads have painted eyes and an open-closed mouth. One has hair partly molded under the wig, but the crown of the head was cut out before firing. The other head has molded hair, Gebrüder Heubach round mark (Ill. **822**) and mold #7761. *Photograph by Winnie Langley.* The wigged shoulder head has square mark (Ill. **823**) and mold #7843, size 2. H. of shoulder head, 4 inches. *Courtesy of Ollie Leavister.*

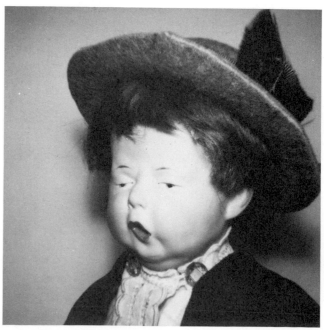

green numbers. A horizontal ellipse mark is sometimes found marked on the head with either the pressed marks or the green stamped numbers. Many of the Heubach heads have molded hair; a few have flocked hair. The dolls are generally comparatively small in size.

**Heubach, Hugo.** 1894–1925+. Sonneberg, Thür., and London. Manufactured and exported dolls. Hugo Heubach was one of the group of Grand Prize winners at the 1900 Paris Exposition, and the Maison Hugo Heubach also won a bronze medal for their doll display at the same exposition. They showed dolls in 1904 at the St. Louis Exhibition.

**813.** Bisque character head made by Gebrüder Heubach has intaglio eyes with highlight at the eyelid line, open-closed mouth with two lower teeth; appears to be same mold as doll shown in Ill. **814.** *Photograph by Winnie Langley.*

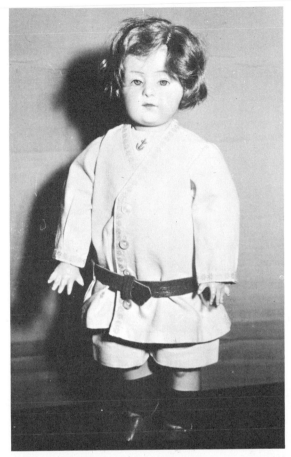

**815.** Bisque-head character doll with glass eyes, wig, jointed composition body. *Collection of the late Martha Thompson; photograph by Winnie Langley.*

**814.** Bisque character doll with glass eyes, open-closed mouth with teeth and tongue. The face is similar to those advertised by Louis Lindner in 1911 (see Ill. **1099**). Mark: Ill. **822**; mold #5636, size 3. H. 12 inches. *Courtesy of Lester & Alice Grinnings.*

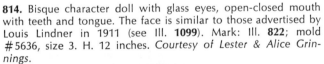

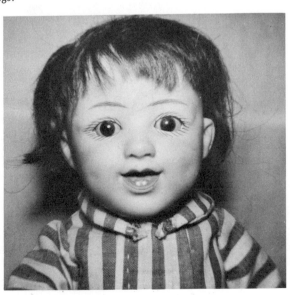

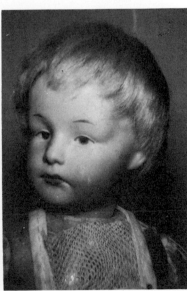

**816A & B.** Bisque heads, one with sleeping eyes, one with intaglio eyes. Both have closed mouths. Marks: Ill. **822** plus numbers 6969 and 89. H. of both, 10 inches. *Coleman Collection.*

817

818

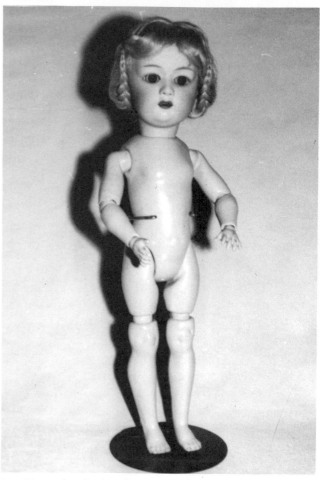

**817.** Bisque head has sleeping glass eyes, open mouth with four teeth. Body is composition. Molded slippers and socks; original costume. Mark: Ill. **824.** H. 6½ inches. *Courtesy of Mary Dawson.*

**818.** Bisque head with glass eyes, open mouth with four teeth; body is composition. Mark: Ill. **825,** except that size is "6/0." H. 11 inches. *Courtesy of Ollie Leavister.*

**820.** Bisque head, glass sleeping eyes, open mouth with four teeth, composition body with joints above knees for short skirts of the 1920's. Mark: Ill. **827.** H. 16 inches. *Courtesy of Alberta Darby.*

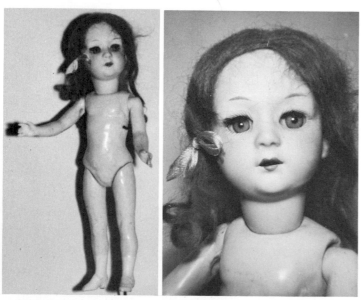

**819A & B.** Bisque head, sleeping glass eyes with hair eyelashes, composition body, molded slippers and socks. Mark: Ill. **826.** H. 11 inches. *Courtesy of Mary Dawson.*

**821.** Bisque head, glass eyes, open mouth with four teeth; composition body with wooden stick upper legs. Mark: Ill. **828.** H. 14 inches. *Courtesy of Theodora Gearhart.*

822

823

S122
Gebr. Heubach
Germany
$\frac{14}{0}$

824

8192

Germany
Gebrüder Heubach
$\frac{8}{0}$

HEU
BACH

G        H

825

8192
Germany
Gebrüder Heubach
$\frac{5}{0}$ ½
G $\frac{5}{0}$ ½ H

826

HEU
BACH

G. 2 H.

827

8192
Germany
Gebrüder Heubach

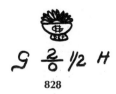

G $\frac{2}{0}$ ½ H

828

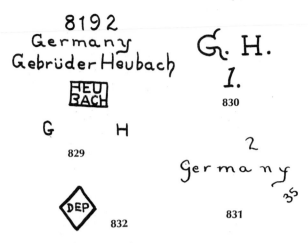

8192
Germany
Gebrüder Heubach

HEU
BACH

G        H

829

G. H.
1.

830

2

Germany

35

831

DEP

832

**822–832.** Mark Nos. **822–829** have been found on Gebrüder Heubach dolls. Nos. **830, 831,** and **832** are marks that may indicate Gebrüder Heubach.

**Heubach, Kämpfe & Sontag.** Mid-19th century–early 20th century. Wallendorf, Thür. Made porcelain dolls. They were successors to Gabriel Heubach, Friedrich Kämpfe, and Christian Hutschenreuther, an earlier porcelain factory started in 1833, but no dolls have been traced to this earlier factory. Heubach, Kämpfe & Sontag displayed porcelain dolls at the 1888 Melbourne Exhibition.

1891: Advertised they exported bisque figures and bathing children to France, England, America, and Australia. They had agents in Paris and Amsterdam.

**Heubert.** 1897. Paris. Was issued a French patent for changing eyes in a doll.

**Heublein, Bernard.** 1901. Sonneberg, Thür. Secured a German patent for sleeping eyes in a doll's head.

**Heublein, Georg.** 1915–25+. Sonneberg, Thür. Made dolls.

1925: Advertised *New Born Baby* dolls, hair stuffed dolls, dolls' heads, and wigs.

**Heublein, Louis Wilhelm.** 1908–23. Schalkau, Thür. Manufactured and exported various kinds of dressed dolls.

**Heumann, Carl.** 1918–25. Sonneberg, Thür. Made dressed dolls, jointed dolls, and babies of various kinds.

1925: Advertised "any kind of doll."

**Heurtematte (Hourtematte), Mme. Stéphanie Rosalie, & François, Mme. Stéphanie.** 1877. Obtained a French patent for a formula used to make unbreakable composition dolls.

**Hewitt Bros.** 1920. Willow Pottery at Longton, Staffordshire. Manufactured porcelain, and registered *Suner* as a trademark for dolls in Britain. Also used the initials "H. & L."

H & L

WILLOW◇ENGLAND

**833.** Mark used by Hewitt Bros.

**834A & B.** Bisque-headed witch marked "Hexe" and "15/0" has glass eyes, open-closed mouth with fanglike teeth, molded warts and wrinkles, jointed composition body. Original clothes consist of dark blue papier-mâché hat, orange felt cape, brown waist, orange skirt, white apron. H. 8 inches. *Courtesy of Ollie Leavister.*

**Hexe.** Name inscribed on bisque head representing a witch.

**Heyde, Hermann.** 1909–18. Dresden, Saxony. Manufactured dolls and dolls' trousseaux; registered the initials "H H D" as a trademark in Germany.

**835.** Trademark of Hermann Heyde.

**Heyden, Max von der.** 1922. Berlin. Obtained German patent for a wire-jointed rubber doll.

**Heymann, Armand.** 1919–25. Paris. Imported dolls from Japan, especially celluloid dolls and bébés.

1920: The name was Heymann & Dreyfus.

**Heymann, Robert.** 1914. Paris. Handled dolls known as *Lilliput.*

**Heyne, Franz.** 1911. Leipzig-Schleussig, Germany. Secured a British patent for talking dolls.

**Heyter, El.** 1909. Frankfurt am Main, Hesse-Nassau. Manufactured dolls.

**Hi Quality Doll Co.** 1918–22. New York City. Made dolls.

**Hiawatha.** 1904. Name of a rag doll.

**Hiawatha.** 1911. Indian boy doll made by *Louis Amberg & Son* with composition head and cloth body.

**Hickman, Alma P.** 1921–23. Joplin, Mo. Registered *Billie Button* as a trademark in U.S. for a cloth and stockinet doll.

**Hiecmann-Bataille.** 1857. Paris. Made dressed and undressed dolls.

**Hieulle, Edmond.** 1917. Paris. Registered in France three trademarks: *Parfait-Bébé* and *Montreuil Bébé* and a coat of arms with the intertwined initials "MSB." It is possible that he produced the dolls marked "Montreuil//s/ Bois//France//D.L.—"

**Higgs, William.** 1733. London. Made jointed wooden babies (dolls), turned on a lathe. The faces were painted by his apprentice. The dolls were dressed by his wife, then sold to shops for 5¢ each, according to ENGLISH DOLLS by Alice Early.

**Highgrade Toy Manufacturing Co.** 1916–21. New York City and Astoria, Long Island. Made dolls and dolls' heads.

1916–17: Dolls priced 50¢ to $2.50.

1918: Dolls came with or without wigs and were priced $1.00 and up.

1921: Named one of their dolls *Twolip.*

**Highland Lass (Lassie).** 1915. Name of character doll handled by *German Novelty Co.*

**Highlander.** 1892. One of the *Brownies* designed by *Palmer Cox;* dressed as a Scotsman. Made into colored cloth by *Arnold Print Works.*

**Highlander.** 1918–19. Cutout rag doll dressed as a Scotsman; distributed by *T. Eaton Co.;* 16 inches tall; price 10¢.

**Hijo, Jaime Pujole.** 1893. Spain. Showed cardboard dolls at the Chicago Exposition.

**Hilcker (Hilker).** 1829–48. Paris. Made dressed dolls.

**Hilda.** 1914. Doll's head representing a laughing baby showing two upper front teeth; copyrighted in U.S. by

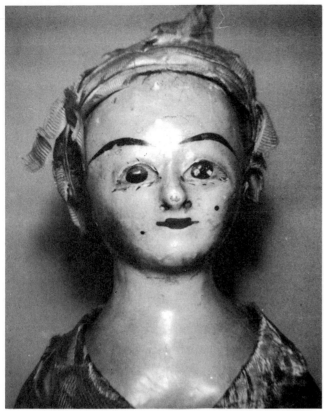

**836.** Gesso-over-wood head, the type of doll possibly made by William Higgs in the 18th century. Has molded and painted eyes, black beauty patches painted on the cheeks; peg jointed body turned on a lathe. Contemporary clothes include silk mobcap. H. 19 inches. *Courtesy of the International Doll Library Foundation.*

Hilda
©
J.D.K. Jr. 190
gesgesch 1070
made in Germany

**837.** "Hilda" mark used on Kestner dolls.

*Kestner.* It came in bisque. The several sizes included 13, 23, and 27 inches. The name "Hilda" and the © are found on the heads, but the numbers seem to differ.

**Hilda.** 1920. A *Georgene Averill* doll that wore a Dutch costume.

**Hilda Cowhan Doll, The.** 1916. Registered in Britain as a trademark of *Hilda Gertrude Lander,* designer of dolls.

**Hill, E. W., & Cushing, E. C.** 1914. London. Were granted a British patent for metal dolls' heads and limbs.

**Hiller, Robert, & Co.** 1895. Breslau, Silesia. Made dolls' bodies and dressed dolls.

**Hillmann, Friedrich Firm.** 1909. Sebnitz, Saxony. Procured a German patent for a doll; specialized in dressed dolls.

**Hindle, Thomas H., Jr.** 1915. New York City. Registered *Wot-Zat* as his trademark in U.S., and obtained a U.S. design patent for a cherub-type doll.

**Hine, Ethel C., & Beyrich, Richard W.** 1882–83. Brooklyn, N.Y. Assignees of a U.S. patent obtained by *Stuart Eldridge* for a feeding or nursing doll. This was three or four years after the *Bébé Teteur* was patented.

**Hinky Doodle Family Rag Doll.** 1920. Made by *Josephine L. Malone;* 12 inches.

**Hinrichs, Edward Augustus, & Bemis, Frederick Pomeroy.** 1896. Davenport, Iowa. Obtained U.S., French, British, and German patents for sleeping eyes, made so that when the doll was inclined to a predetermined extent, the eyes suddenly opened or closed all the way rather than gradually.

**Hinrichs (Heinrich) & Co.** 1890–1904. New York City, and Selb, Bavaria. Doll manufacturers and importers. Registered "H & Co." as a trademark in U.S. for dolls.

1894: Advertised china, bisque, patent, jointed, kid, and rubber dolls; 1,000 varieties of dressed dolls; Papa and Mama Dolls; dolls' heads.

**838.** Trademark used by Hinrichs & Co. **H & Cº**

**Hip Lung.** 1898. Doll dressed in a regulation oriental gown; price 25¢.

**Hirayama, Aijiro, Shimabara Deguchi.** 1920. Kyoto, Japan. Manufactured dolls.

**Hirsch, Martin.** 1899–1914. London, and Sonneberg, Thür. Distributed various types of dressed and undressed dolls; agent for *Carl Speyer* and *Otto Krause.*

**Hirschler, Fernand Calmon, & Hirschler, Paul Moise.** 1919. Paris. Registered *Le Jouet Artistique* as a trademark in France for dolls; also used the initials "F. P. H."

**Hitchy Koo.** 1913. Trademark registered in Britain by *Horsman.*

**Hitz, Jacobs & Kassler.** 1918–25+. New York City, and Fürth, Bavaria. Importers and factory agents. Handled the *Kiddiejoy* line.

1918–19: Known as Hitz, Jacobs & Co. Advertised *Hoopla Girl* line, *Ja Ja,* and a bride doll.

1922: Represented 182 European factories and 200 domestic factories. The 26-inch *Mama Dolls* sold for $24.00 doz. wholesale.

1925: Known as Jacobs & Kassler. Made Kiddiejoy infant dolls, which came with bisque heads made by *Armand Marseille,* glass sleeping eyes, bodies of stuffed domestic cotton, and Ronson voices (see Ill. 1737).

**839.** Mark of Hitz, Jacobs & Kassler.

**Hobbins, John.** 1856–65. London. Made wax dolls.

**Hobble Skirt Maid.** 1912. Walked by means of a metal rod in each foot; price 50¢.

**Hobo.** Ca. 1904. Wooden circus doll made by *Schoenhut;* rubber jointed.

**Hoch & Co.** 1925. Catterfeld, Thür. Made dolls.

**Hochbrunn, Dr. Paul von.** 1925. Munich, Bavaria. Specialized in jointed dolls.

**Hodgman Rubber Co.** 1890. New York City. Manufactured rubber dolls.

**Hofacker, William.** 1915. Norwood, Pa. Was granted a U.S. design patent for *Eskimo dolls* dressed in fur parkas.

**Höfer, Georg.** 1895. Eisfeld, Thür. Manufactured and exported wool dolls. Work done as a cottage industry.

**Höfer, Julius.** 1925. Nürnberg, Bavaria. Made *Norexi* standing, sitting, and walking dolls.

**Höfer, M.** 1909. Nürnberg, Bavaria. Manufactured dolls.

**Hoffmann (Hofmann), Georg.** 1895–1918. Rauenstein, Thür. Made wax dolls in 1895.

**Hoffmann, Solomon D.** 1880's–97. Moscow, and Brooklyn, N.Y. Patented in Russia and U.S. "unbreakable" composition that he called *Can't Break 'Em* composition for dolls' heads and limbs. He came to America in 1892 and established "The First American Doll Factory," which in 1895 was incorporated as *The American Doll and Toy Manufacturing Co.* After his death in 1897, his widow and son, A. A. Hoffmann, carried on the business until it was bought by *Aetna Doll & Toy Co.* For descriptions of the methods of manufacture, see **Manufacture of Composition Heads.**

**Hoffmeister, Carl.** 1894–1921. Sonneberg, Thür. Made and exported kid bodies and dolls with kid bodies. He was one of the group of Grand Prize winners at the 1900 Paris Exposition, and he also showed dolls at the St. Louis Exhibition in 1904.

**Höfler, Fritz.** 1895–1901. Neustadt near Coburg, Thür. Made little or baby dolls.

**Hofmann.** See **Hoffmann.**

**Hofmann, Carl.** 1923. Neustadt near Coburg, Thür. Specialized in making dolls and baby dolls.

**Hofmann, Johannes.** 1923–25. Neustadt near Coburg, Thür. Specialized in making stuffed dolls.

**Hofmann, M., & Co.** 1900. Sonneberg, Thür. One of the group that won a Grand Prize in Paris for their display of dolls.

**Hofmann, Witwe (Widow) J.** 1918–25+. Neustadt near Coburg, Thür. Made jointed dolls.

**Hohn, Karl.** 1909–20. Sonneberg, Thür. Made dolls with leather bodies.

**Hölbe, Richard Hugo.** 1879–1922. Oberlind near Sonneberg, Thür. Obtained four German patents for talking or singing dolls—in 1879, 1881, 1884, and 1890. In 1922

he was granted a German patent for a doll's hand with movable fingers.

**Holes in Head.** Usually the holes in a doll's head are related to either the stringing of the doll or fastening the wig. Baldheads often have from one to three small holes in the top of the crown for these purposes. Some collectors call these "*Belton*-type dolls, but no historical basis has been found for this name.

The crown of dolls' heads was sliced off for several reasons. One was the necessity of having access to the inside for setting the eyes, especially sleeping eyes. The opening in the crown also facilitated attaching the head; pates of cork, plaster, or cardboard permitted easier methods of attaching wigs. Another use for the cork pate was described in 1884: "If you examine the craniums you will find a patch of cork hiding a bit of lead. When the baby tumbles it is brought by the law of gravitation on the back of its head, and is taken up unhurt."

Dolls' heads believed to have been made in the 20th century frequently have pairs of small holes either over the ears or in the back of the head, and occasionally a small hole in the center front just below the crown opening. Dolls that have not been restrung frequently have wires hooked through these holes to hold the head onto the body. In 1921, *Schroeder & Richter* obtained a German patent for putting wire through two holes in the back of the head, hooking the wire over from the inside to the outside and fastening the other end to a rod inside the body of the doll. Another possible use for these holes may be explained by a note in PLAYTHINGS, May, 1909: "By the recent invention of a fastening wire which secures the eyes to the head in such a way that the injuries they have hitherto suffered in transit are obviated, a good deal of trouble will be in future saved. Malleable eyes have often reached foreign destinations in bad condition or cracked on account of the plaster fastening them getting loose."

**Holladay, A. J., & Co.** 1917–25+. London. Manufactured dolls and registered in Britain *Givjoy Toys* as a trademark in 1920.

**Holland, Annie J.** 1893. Boston, Mass. Secured U.S. and French patents for doll's head with stationary eyes and movable eyelids operated by a weight.

**Holland, E.** 1918. Wildenheid near Sonneberg, Thür. Made dolls' bodies.

**Holland, N.** 1909–18. Wildenheid near Sonneberg, Thür. Made dolls' bodies.

**Holland, Witwe (Widow).** 1918. Wildenheid near Sonneberg, Thür. Made dolls.

**Holland Bud.** 1921. Rag doll made by *Delavan;* cost $18.00 doz. wholesale.

**Hollikid.** 1917–20. Made by *K & K Toy Co.;* distributed by *Borgfeldt,* who registered name as a trademark for dolls in U.S. and France.

1918: Came with composition head and hands, painted hair, red-covered body with shoulder and hips jointed;

wore green flannel coat, and shoes with red-button trim; Hollikid tag on shoulder. Size 12¼ inches; price $8.75 doz. wholesale.

**Hollywood Dollies.** 1925. New York City. Firm manufactured dolls.

**Holmes, Sarah E.** 1894. Needham, Mass. Obtained U.S. patent for tubular knitted doll; features were formed by stitches; yarn hair.

**Holtermann, Kurt K., & Co.** 1925. Waltershausen, Thür., and Hamburg, Germany. Manufactured and exported dolls.

**Holton, Charles J.** See **Rouech, Bowden Co.**

**Holz-Masse.** The German word for wood-pulp composition, which appeared on the trademark registered in Germany by *Cuno & Otto Dressel* in 1875 and renewed in 1895. This trademark appears on dolls with a variety of heads—bisque, wax, etc., as well as composition. Other companies besides Cuno & Otto Dressel used the term "Holz-Masse." For example, in 1895 *Julius Dorst* said that he made dolls and dolls' heads of Holz-Masse.

**Holzschuher, Heinrich.** 1894–97. Sonneberg, Thür. Made dressed dolls.

**Homegla Inc.** 1925. Sonneberg, Thür., and Frankfurt am Main. Made dolls.

**Homer, E. B.** 1879–83. Philadelphia, Pa. Made dolls' bodies and produced dolls' materials.

**Honey Boy.** 1909. All-bisque Negro doll dressed in a large straw hat and colorful costume; size 8 inches, price 50¢.

**Honey Boy.** 1910. A mulatto *Neverbreak* doll produced by *A. Steinhardt & Bro.*; $8.50 doz. wholesale.

**Honey Boy.** 1911. Made by *Louis Amberg & Son.* Came with composition head and cloth body.

840. Papier-mâché head is impressed on the inside of the rear shoulder: "Patented // Holz-Masse"; has ribbon in the black hair and a single sewhole in front. H. of shoulder head, 2 inches. *Courtesy of Margaret Whitton; photograph by Winnie Langley.*

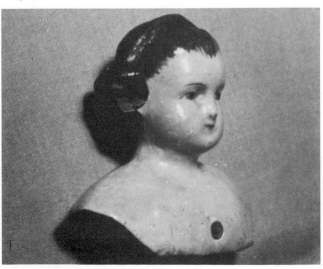

**Honey Bunch.** 1918. Doll made by *Jessie McCutcheon Raleigh;* distributed by *Butler Bros.* Came with wig and wore a lawn dress; 11½ inches, $2.80.

**Honeybunch.** 1923. Name of doll made by *EFFanBEE.*

**Honig, Fritz.** 1884. Cologne, Germany. Procured a German patent for a *Polichinelle* with jointed shoulders, elbows, hips, and knees.

**Hooded Dolls.** See **Bonnet Dolls.**

**Hooligans.** 1908. Dolls advertised by *Samstag & Hilder.*

**Hoopla Girl.** 1919. Cherub-type line of dolls produced by *Hitz, Jacobs & Co.* Came with or without real hair wigs in assorted styles and dresses.

**Hopf, Aug.** 1895–1909. Neustadt near Coburg, Thür. Manufactured little or baby dolls.

**Hopf, Christian.** 1885–1925+. Neustadt near Coburg, Thür. Made jointed dolls and dressed dolls.

**Hopf, Fritz.** 1895–1909. Neustadt near Coburg Thür. Manufactured little or baby dolls.

**Hoppe, A. W.** 1898. Meissen, Saxony. Manufactured dolls and dolls' wigs.

**Hops, B. & E.** 1909–18. Hamburg, Germany. Handled dolls.

**Horn, Carl.** Before 1918, Dresden, Saxony; 1918, successors of Carl Horn. Made miniature dolls.

**Horn, Heinrich.** 1895–1925+. Sonneberg, Thür. Manufactured dolls and dolls' bodies, especially of kid. Exhibited dolls at Chicago in 1893, Paris in 1900, and St. Louis in 1904. At Paris he was one of the group that won a Grand Prize, as he was at Brussels in 1910.

**Horn, W. C., Bro. & Co.** 1849–1914. New York City and Berlin. Imported and manufactured dolls.

1911: Distributor for *Ideal Novelty & Toy Co.*

1912: Advertised *Nonpareil* line of dolls and *Da-Zee* unbreakable character dolls.

**Horne, John Wesley.** 1906–7. Washington, D.C. Secured U.S. and German patents for a means of securing sleeping eyes in a doll's head to prevent displacement and breakage.

**Hornlein, Theodor.** 1909–25+. Sonneberg, Thür. Made dolls.

**Hornschuh, P.** 1923–25. Stadtlengsfeld, Thür. Made dolls.

**Horsman, Edward Imeson.** 1865–1901, New York City; E. I. Horsman Co., 1901–18; E. I. Horsman & Aetna Doll Co., 1918–25+. Distributed, assembled, and made dolls. During the 19th century Horsman was primarily a toy distributor, but as early as the 1870's he imported European dolls' heads and bodies, which he assembled. In 1897 Horsman began to use his famous trademark (see Ill. 846). As the business grew, so did Horsman's interest in dolls, especially the line of rag dolls. Evidence suggests that some of these were made for Horsman by *Albert Brückner.* Dolls that resemble the pictures in the

842. Bisque head made in Japan for Horsman. The socket is a wooden ring that is attached to the cloth "Mama" body; composition arms and legs. Probably ca. 1917. Mark: Ill. 843. H. 18 inches. *Courtesy of Dorothy Annunziato.*

841A & B. Doll made by Horsman has brown composition head, arms, legs; face and hair style resemble the Campbell Kids. Horsman made eyes looking straight ahead as early as 1911, but the body seems later. Cloth body has a squeak box. Mark on back of neck: "E.I.H.Co. INC." H. 13½ inches. *Coleman Collection.*

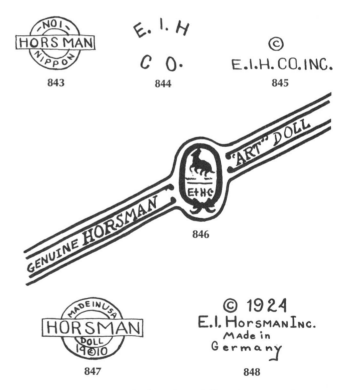

843–848. Horsman marks found on dolls; No. 846 is the Horsman trademark often found on ribbons worn by dolls.

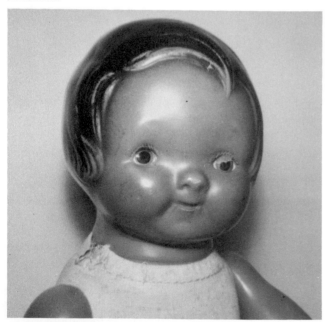

Horsman advertisements have the date of Bruckner's patent (Pat'd July 9th, 1901) printed on their necks. Among Horsman's early rag dolls were *Stella*, the *Babyland Rag Dolls* that first came with hand-painted faces and later (1907) with photographic faces printed in colors,

*American Maid Rag Dolls,* cloth cutout dolls made by Dean's Rag Book Co. of London, and in 1909 rag dolls with celluloid faces.

At the beginning of 1909, *Borgfeldt* was distributing *Can't Break 'Em* composition-head dolls made by the

*Aetna Doll and Toy Co.,* but Horsman soon secured exclusive control of the manufacture and distribution of these dolls. In response to public interest in the North Pole explorations, Horsman produced Dr. *Cook* and Lt. *Peary* dolls. Also in 1909, Horsman obtained the first known copyright on a complete doll for his *Billiken,* which was made with a Can't Break 'Em head. This was the period when character dolls were sweeping the market, and in 1910 Horsman brought out *Baby Bumps,* which closely resembles the *Kämmer & Reinhardt* doll named *Baby,* and then the *Campbell Kids,* which were inspired by the Campbell Soup drawings copyrighted by Joseph Campbell. The first advertisement for the Campbell Kids appeared in PLAYTHINGS, January, 1911, and in the same issue *Louis Amberg & Son* advertised their *Dolly Drake* and *Bobby Blake* dolls from Grace G. Wiederseim's drawings. All these dolls closely resembled the dolls in the design patent filed by *Frank Hays* in 1909. Margaret Gebbie Hays, sister of Grace Gebbie Wiederseim (later *Grace Gebbie Drayton),* also made similar-type drawings.

1910–11: Horsman copyrighted thirteen dolls that *Helen Trowbridge* designed. These included *Peterkin, Fairy* as represented in the Fairy Soap advertisements, the *Jap Rose Kids* of James S. Kirk Soap, and *Gold Medal Prize Baby.* Most Horsman dolls at this time had Can't Break 'Em composition heads and pink sateen bodies stuffed with cork. In 1911, Horsman registered Baby Bumps as a trademark in Germany for dolls.

1912: Aetna was producing over 4,000 dolls' heads a day for Horsman. The bodies of the dolls were improved so that when the doll was seated the legs would not spread far apart as they formerly did. Horsman obtained design patents for the clothes for the Campbell Kids. One of the new dolls was *Gee Gee,* designed by Grace G. Drayton.

1913: Babies appear to have been the specialty, with twenty new models, including *Our Baby, Baby Butterfly* from the opera MADAME BUTTERFLY, *Baby Blossom, Christening Baby,* and *Carnival Baby.* These babies represented boys and girls aged six months, one year, or three years. Horsman filed Gee Gee as their trademark in Germany, and registered it in U.S. as a trademark, but here they gave the former Gee Gee dolls the name *Peek-a-Boos.* Horsman registered *Hitchy Koo* as a trademark for dolls in Britain.

1914: "Baby Butterfly" was registered as a trademark in the U.S. *Drowsy Dick* and *Baby Rosebud* were new dolls copyrighted by Horsman and designed by Helen Trowbridge. Both painted hair and wigs for dolls were made in all colors—green, blue, purple, etc.

1915–16: *Bernard Lipfert* began to design dolls for Horsman; among these were the *Gene Carr Kids.* The last advertisements appeared for Can't Break 'Em composition heads made with cold presses. It is believed that Horsman and Aetna changed to the newer hot-press method soon after this. The first mention was made of litigation against

patent, trademark, and copyright infringement offenders that plagued Horsman for some years.

1917–18: Most of the dolls they made were based on wartime themes—e.g., *Army Nurse, Uncle Sam Kids, British Tommy, Middie,* etc. They handled felt character dolls made in England by Belgian refugees. One exception was the rag baby doll named *Patty-Cake.* Toward the end of 1918, Horsman and Aetna consolidated into one firm and built a large new factory that produced dolls made of a new composition, which they called *Adtocolite.* They made jointed all-Adtocolite dolls, as well as dolls with soft bodies.

1919: Horsman combined with *Fulper Pottery* to produce American-made bisque dolls' heads. *Benjamin Goldenberg,* who had managed Aetna for many years, was the expert on coloring the bisque heads. E. I. Horsman, Jr., and *Harold D. Bowie* also had much to do with the production of the bisque heads. They first brought out two baby-face models in two sizes to go on bent-limb Adtocolite bodies and two girl-face models in two sizes to go on fully jointed Adtocolite bodies. They used glass eyes made in America, which were either fixed or moving. One of their new dolls was *Little Mary Mix Up,* based on the Brinkerhoff cartoon.

1920: *Rosebud Babies* and *Blue Bird Dolls* were among the new dolls. But they still advertised Babyland Rag Dolls. They imported some French "manikin" dolls dressed in fine silk. These were play dolls dressed as little girls.

1921: Horsman began to advertise *Mama Dolls* with Lloyd's patent voices and walking dolls patented by Harold D. Bowie. One of their new dolls represented *Jackie Coogan* as THE KID.

1922: E. I. Horsman, Jr., died, and progress slowed down.

1923: Horsman copyrighted *Baby Horsman,* designed by Edith Hitchcock.

1924: The popularity of newborn baby dolls was met by Horsman with *Tynie Baby,* designed by Bernard Lipfert.

1925: Horsman brought out *HEbee-SHEbees,* based on the drawings by *Charles Twelvetrees.*

The Horsman name was later purchased by the *Regal Doll Manufacturing Co.*

**Horstmeyer, Mme. (née Burkhardt, Hedwig).** 1899. Was issued a French patent for improvements in a doll.

**Horton, Charles J.** 1906–8. Assignee of rag doll patented by *Edward R. Rouech.*

**Hospice de Pedro II.** 1867. Rio de Janeiro, Brazil. Exhibited dressed dolls at the Paris Exposition.

**Hotchkiss, Arthur E.** 1875. New Haven, Conn. Obtained a U.S. patent for walking dolls with clockwork mechanism and large metal shoes having two wooden spools under each shoe. The patent date was incised on each shoe between the spools: "Pat'd Sept. 21, 75." A bisque-head doll with the name *Empress Eugenie Doll* on its box bore this patent date on its body.

**Hottentots.** 1914–25+. Name given to Negro *Kewpies*. Name did not come into use until 1915 after the dolls had been made for a year.

**Houghton, Elizabeth Ellen.** 1915. London. An artist. Registered "E. E. Houghton" as her trademark in Britain for dolls.

**Houghton, James Albert.** 1918–25. London. Made dolls.

**Hourdeaux-Bing Inc.** 1923–25. Lichtenfels, Bavaria. Made dolls.

**House of Bambin.** See **Denamur, E.**

**House Workmen.** 1907. Name of doll makers who work in their own homes or cottages.

**Hover, Andrew C.** 1908. Paterson, N.J. Obtained U.S. patent for improving sleeping eyes so that they would not be as likely to break bisque heads as formerly.

**Howard, George H.** 1882. Washington, D.C. Procured U.S. patent for a doll with extensible joints so that arms, legs, or torso could be lengthened.

**Howard, Henry (Harry).** 1858–65. London. Made dolls.

**Howe, Margaret F.** See **Vale, Margaret.**

**Huberta.** 1917. Trademark registered in Germany by *Emil Pfeiffer* for dolls.

**Hubertus.** 1909. Name of cloth soldier doll made by *Steiff;* 20 inches tall.

**Hubner, Anton.** 1897. Waltersdorf near Zittau, Saxony. Made dolls.

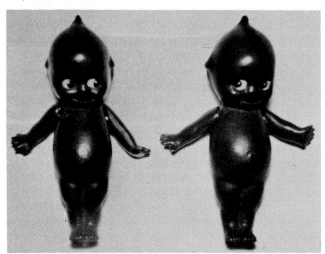

**849.** All-celluloid Negro Kewpies called "Hottentots." Wings are painted white. The dolls came as a pair in blue and white checked blanket. Their eyes glance in opposite directions. Round "Kewpie" stickers on the back differ slightly (see Ills. **850, 851**). H. 3¼ inches. *Courtesy of Jessica R. Norman.*

**850 & 851.** Marks found on labels on "Hottentot" Kewpies.

850

851

**Hubsy.** 1923. Trademark registered in Germany by *Emil Pfeiffer* for dolls and clowns.

**Huchez, Maurice.** 1925. Paris. Specialized in dolls' heads in bisque and china.

**Huck, A.** 1924. Obtained a British patent for improving the ball joints of dolls.

**Huck, H., Firm.** 1923. Nürnberg, Bavaria. Procured a German patent for jointed doll that resembled the ball-jointed metal dolls made by *Bucherer.*

**Hug Me Kid.** 1919. Trade name for a metal doll made by *Atlas Doll & Toy Co.* Came with or without wig, with sleeping or stationary eyes.

**Hug Me Kiddies (Kids).** 1912–14. Design for doll's face patented in U.S. by *Leon Rees* and assigned to *Monroe Schwarzschild.* Doll was distributed by *Samstag & Hilder,* who registered the name as a trademark in U.S. in 1912, noting on the application that the trademark was used particularly with the English trade.

1912: Factory output was completely sold out by fall. Dolls came with composition face, round eyes glancing to the side, felt body; boys and girls in assorted costumes. Four sizes; prices 50¢ to $1.50.

1913: Came with wide-open movable eyes and eyes that rolled when the doll walked; dressed in twenty costume styles, including those of American children, foreign characters, sailors, etc. Sizes 9½, 10½, 12, and 14 inches; prices 25¢ to $3.00.

1914: The line was enlarged to include imports; these were called dolls with a "Baby Stare." Each doll had a rod at the back of the head that, when moved to and fro, caused the staring eyes to move from left to right and back again. Many sizes.

**Hugele, L.** 1834. Paris. Made kid-body dolls.

**Hughes, Henry Jeffrey.** 1899–1925+. London. Henry Jeffrey Hughes & Son, 1911–20; Henry Jeffrey Hughes & Sons, 1921–25+. Made and distributed dolls; specialized in rag dolls and dressed dolls. In 1899 he was at the same address as *Henry Richard Hughes.*

**Hughes, Henry Richard.** 1891–99. London. Agent for doll manufacturers.

**Hughes, Herbert Edward.** 1895–1912. London. Distributed dolls.

**Hugmee.** 1912. Trademark registered in Britain by *Eisenmann & Co.* for dolls.

**Hug-Me-Tight.** 1915–17. Line of *Mother Goose* rag dolls designed by *Grace Drayton;* advertised by *Bently-Franklin Co.* and *Colonial Toy Manufacturing Co.;* distributed by *Montgomery Ward & Co.* They included Curly Locks, Little Red Riding Hood, Little Bo-Peep, Mary and Her Lamb, etc. The dolls were brightly colored and stuffed with cotton; sizes 10½ to 11 inches; price 50¢.

**Hugonnard, A.** 1925. Paris. Advertised dolls marked with an anchor.

**Hugot.** 1860–61. Paris. Handled dolls.

**Hula Maidens.** 1921–23. Trademark registered in U.S. by *Seamless Rubber Co.* for rubber dolls.

**Huldschinsky, Hedwig Maria (née Strasser).** 1924–25. Berlin. Made *Strasser* dolls and Strasser baby dolls at Strasser workshop.

1924: Registered "Strasser" as a trademark in Germany.

**Hülss, Adolf.** 1915–25+. Waltershausen, Thür. Made dolls and used "A H//W" as his trademark, which he registered in Germany in 1925.

**852A, B, C, & D.** Bisque head was made by Simon & Halbig for Adolf Hülss; the bisque was given a layer of flesh-colored paint. The doll has glass sleep eyes, open mouth and teeth, jointed composition body holding a voice box; original Bavarian costume. Mark: Ill. **853.** H. 15 inches. *Courtesy of Dorothy Annunziato.*

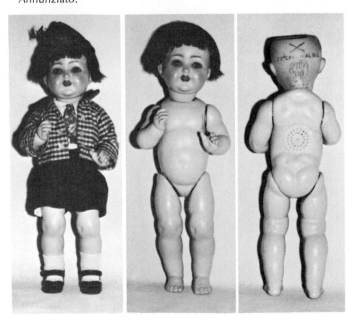

**853.** Adolf Hülss mark found on dolls.

**Hülss, V.** 1915–21. Sonneberg, Thür. Made dolls.

**Human Face Doll.** 1907–8. Name of doll produced by *Edmund Ulrich Steiner.* PLAYTHINGS, 1908, describes this doll as follows:

"Seven years ago [1901], instigated by the urgent appeals of hundreds of doll buyers who clamored for something radically new and daringly original in the doll world, E. U. Steiner, of Samstag & Hilder Bros., began experiments upon his new idea in Dolldom—the perfection of a doll which would be true to life in every possible particular, a doll whose face would have the natural babylike, expressive features which are found in little children the world over. Popular demand fairly begged for a brilliant new doll, and Mr. Steiner believed that the right thought was slowly attaining perfection in his mind. It was the 'human note' in doll making.

"From all nooks and corners where child beauty reigned supreme, photos were taken, and the children themselves posed before one of the most famous painters of children in Germany. At last, after many efforts were thrown aside as not coming up to the high ideals set for this new doll for the American market, a certain face of a favorite type was selected and molded by the most experienced doll makers in the Sonneberg factories.

"June 1907, was the month set for the launching of this Human Face Doll campaign and Mr. Steiner left for his Fatherland, where he could personally direct operations and supervise every little detail which went into the making of the new doll. Life face dolls have appeared before, but Mr. Steiner wanted to give his customers an article which would be the direct result of his own genius and long experience. He stayed in and around Sonneberg for the rest of the year, gathering his skilled workmen about him, and instilling into their minds and hearts the hopes which had so long been the very companions of his dreams.

"To more fully carry out his true-to-life doll, human hair was procured for the new line of dolls, long blonde, brunette and Titian tresses, which hung below the waist and which might be dressed simply or in any of the elaborate coiffures which the mood of Dame Fashion might dictate. The doll is made in many different styles,

every one of which portrays perfectly, a beautiful child or an age corresponding to that represented by the doll, a brilliant feature in itself. This doll was given a kid body, and the maker says that the ideal 'jointed doll' is now a reality.

". . . The work finished, Mr. Steiner and his little coterie of fellow workers took the results of their labors to the art galleries in Berlin. There they were shown for three days and elicited the most enthusiastic notes of approval that the staid old German Museum has heard for many a day. The women and children went wild over the new dolls and the artist was awarded many medals."

**Humbert.** See **Vermeiren, Maison.**

**Hume, A. E.** 1915. Obtained British patent for dolls' eyelids operated by wires or string from outside the doll.

**Humpty Dumpty Circus.** 1903–25+. Included wooden dolls made by *Schoenhut;* name was registered as trademark in U.S. by Albert Schoenhut. In 1903 the clown was the only doll advertised. Others were added later, including acrobats, ringmaster, lion tamer, etc. Most of these dolls were made in two sizes.

**Hunaeus, Dr. Paul.** 1900–25+. Linden near Hannover, Germany. Made celluloid dolls and dolls' heads. He obtained three German patents; two of them were for sleeping eyes in celluloid heads (these were granted in 1900 and 1901). The third patent, also granted in 1900, pertained to the torso and arm and leg joints on celluloid dolls. He used the intertwined initials "PH" as a mark, and in the 1920's some of his dolls were also marked *Igodi.*

**854.** Mark used by Dr. Paul Hunaeus.

**Hungarian Dolls.** These appear to include the carved wooden dolls with black painted hair, red painted torsos, and limbs jointed to the torso with leather. This conclusion is based on the fact that in 1899 Annie Fields Alden stated she had purchased this type of doll in Budapest, and in 1923 PLAYTHINGS listed under "Dolls of Yesterday" roughly carved wooden dolls of Hungary.

In 1909, Hungary went to great lengths to try to build a doll-making industry. Attempts were made to bring people from Waltershausen and other places in Thüringia. The government granted a yearly subsidy of 25 percent of the manufacturer's working capital; all materials were duty free, there was a 25 percent reduction in railroad freight costs, and free building sites and free bricks were offered for the erection of factories.

Among the doll makers in Hungary were *Pápa* Factory, Rozalia Mauks, Theodore Pohl, *Fem es Játékarugyar, B. Bernhardt, Elsó Magyar Játékbabagyár, Hunnia,* and *Our Shop.*

**"Hunnia" Dummy and Doll Factory.** 1913–25+. Budapest. Made dolls.

**Hunter, Charles A.** 1922–24. Far Hills, N.J. Procured a U.S. patent for a phonograph doll.

**Hunter, Rudolph Melville.** 1899. Philadelphia, Pa. Obtained U.S., French, German, and English patents for flirting eyes—that is, eyes that turned from side to side by gravity as well as having regular sleeping action.

**Hunter, William Crosby, & Sims, Frederick Walter.** 1922–23. Southampton, England. Secured British and German patents for dolls' eyes that would close only after the doll had been rocked.

**Huret, Maison.** 1850–1920. Paris. Mlle. Huret started making dolls ca. 1850. Léopold Huret appears at an even earlier date, but he was generally listed under Dolls' Furniture.

1850: Mlle. Calixte Huret applied for a French patent for a doll's body that was molded and articulated.

1851: Léopold Huret advertised all kinds of jointed dolls of a new type, with porcelain heads.

1855: Mlle. Huret exhibited articulated gutta-percha dolls and the molds for making these dolls at the Paris Exposition, and won a bronze medal.

1857: Léopold Huret advertised patented jointed dolls.

HURET DOLLS

**855.** China-headed doll from the Maison Huret. Stamp on the chest of the kid body: Ill. **862.** Shoulder head with painted features and wig; contemporary dress. *Courtesy of Louise Lund; photograph by Winnie Langley.*

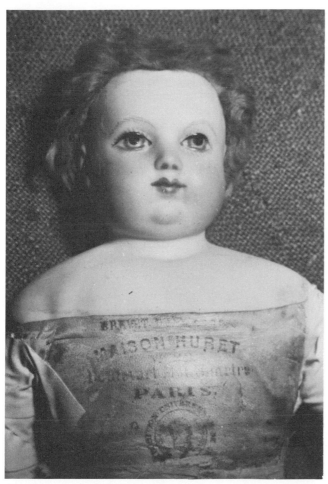

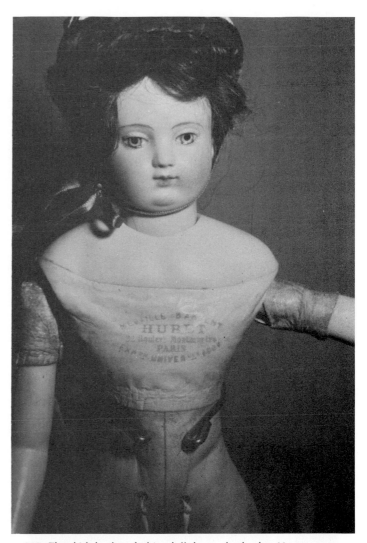

**856.** Bisque shoulder head has painted features and wig. Note the similarity to the china head in Ill. **855.** For the green stamp on the kid body, see Ill. **862.** *Courtesy of Marion Holt; photograph by Winnie Langley.*

**858.** The kid body of this doll bears both the Huret stamp on the chest (see Ill. **863**) and the green Rohmer mark (see Ill. **1399**). She has a bisque head and shoulder plate; painted eyes. Her face resembles those in Ill. **857.** The Huret-marked part of the body appears to have been added to the Rohmer body, perhaps when repairs were made. *Courtesy of Gladyse Hilsdorf; photograph by Winnie Langley.*

**857A & B.** Bisque head and shoulder plate with ridged neck joint, glass eyes, pierced ears. Body is jointed wood, spring strung, and has metal hands. *Courtesy of Margaret Whitton; photographs by Winnie Langley.*

1861: Mlle. Huret patented a porcelain doll's head that terminated in a spherical part allowing the head any desired movement. The invention of a socket swivel neck for dolls has been credited to *Jumeau* at a later date, but actually Mlle. Huret appears to deserve the credit.

1865–67: Huret & Lonchambron advertised bisque head dolls, porcelain dolls, and dressed dolls. They showed jointed gutta-percha dolls, among others, at the 1867 Paris Exposition, where they won a silver medal.

**859A & B.** The four dolls are all marked "Huret" on the body. The three standing dolls have glass eyes and pierced ears. The seated doll, shown also in close-up, has painted eyes and her ears are not pierced. Note the similarity of the faces. The seated doll wears a pink contemporary dress. *Courtesy of Marion Holt; photographs by Winnie Langley.*

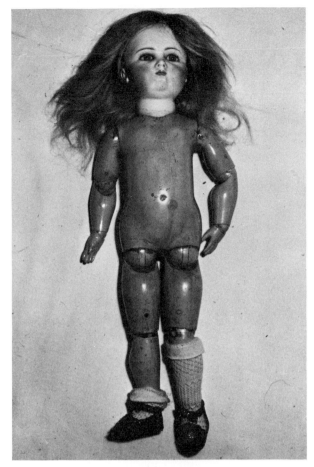

**860.** Bisque-headed Huret doll has glass eyes and a wig. The ball of the neck terminates in a ceramic rod that fits down into the body. The turned wooden body has tongue-and-groove joints. *Photograph by Winnie Langley.*

**861.** Bisque head with painted features, on a bébé-type composition body marked "Huret." *Photograph by Winnie Langley.*

Huret used metal hands on lady dolls with wooden bodies. These dolls are generally marked with an address —68 rue de la Boétie—that has not been identified as to time.

1873: Lonchambron advertised jointed gutta-percha dolls, dressed and undressed.

1879: They advertised jointed gutta-percha bébés as well as dolls.

1885: A. Lemoine, successor, advertised jointed gutta-percha dolls and bébés.

1890–1900: Carette was the successor in the Maison Huret, and advertised jointed bébés and dolls; apparently gutta-percha was no longer in use.

1902: Prevost was the successor, but the advertisements did not mention dolls.

1919–20: Maison Huret was again advertising dolls and bébés.

BREVET DEP. S.G.D.G.

MAISON HURET
N°. 22
Boulevart Montmartre
PARIS.

**862**

MEDAILLE D'ARGENT
HURET
22 Bould Montmartre
PARIS
EXP ON UNIVERLLS 1867

**863**

HURET
68 RUE DE LA BOETIE
**864**

HURET
**865**

**862–865.** Marks found on Huret dolls.

**Hush-a-Bye-Baby.** 1925+. Infant-type doll made by *Ideal Novelty & Toy Co.* Advertised as a work of art. Had composition one-piece solid head, not sliced or patched. Came with painted hair, moving eyes, cotton-stuffed body, and flexible rubber hands. Sizes 20 and 24 inches; price $2.00. Seven sizes were made in 1926.

**Hutchison, Edna A.** 1921. Independence, Mo. Was granted a U.S. design patent for doll with eyes glancing to the side.

**Hutschenreuther & Co.** 1862. Wallendorf, Thür. Displayed papier-mâché dolls at the London Exhibition. The 1833 porcelain factory of Gabriel Heubach, Friedrich Kämpfe, and Christian Hutschenreuther in Wallendorf later became *Heubach, Kämpfe & Sontag,* which made porcelain dolls.

**Hutschkau (Hutschgau), Gust.** 1895–1909. Neustadt near Coburg, Thür. Made little or baby dolls.

**Hüttinger & Buschor.** 1920–25. Nürnberg, Bavaria. Made walking and talking dolls.

1921: Registered *Casadora* as a trademark in Germany.

1923: Procured two German patents, one for a talking doll with bellows in its head, and the other for a doll that appears to have cried real tears.

1925: Advertised Casadora lifelike dolls that talk and walk when led by their hands and move their eyes in all directions.

**Hutton, George.** 1899. Philadelphia, Pa. Made dolls.

**Huyler's Inc.** 1920. New York City. Were assigned a U.S. design patent for a yarn doll by *Adelaide Porter*.

**Hyatt, Joseph.** 1891–1910. London. Imported dolls.

**Hyatt Bros.** See **Celluloid Dolls.**


# I

*(It should be noted that "I" and "J" are often interchangeable in many of the European languages.)*

**I Can Talk—I Can Walk—I Can Sleep.** 1920's. Slogan of *Ideal Novelty & Toy Co.*

**I Love You.** 1919. Doll copyrighted in U.S. by *Guglielmo Voccia,* an Italian.

**I. R. Comb Co.** See **India Rubber Comb Co.**

**I Say Papa.** 1921. *Mama Doll* made by *EFFanBEE;* also said "Papa."

**I Talk.** 1914–16. *Mama Doll* made by the *Art Metal Works.* Came with metal head and a voice that could be varied; several styles and sizes, including 17 inches. Tag on doll reads, "Fully Patented // MAMA // DOLL // I TALK ! ! ! // Squeeze me Easy! // made in America // now with arms and legs."

**I Walk—I Talk—I Sleep.** 1903. Words on ribbon worn by doll that "walked" on wheels; advertised by *Louis Amberg & Son.*

**I Wanta Doll Co.** 1916–17. New York City. Manufactured dolls.

**Iageman, Oskar.** 1912–20. Sonneberg, Thür. Made dolls.

**Idéal Bébé.** 1895. Trademark registered in France by *Bertoli Frères* (Bros.).

**Ideal Novelty & Toy Co.** 1907–25+. Brooklyn, N.Y. (Ideal Novelty Co., 1907–ca. 1912). Founded by Morris Michtom. Made composition dolls; distributed by *W. C. Horn*

Bro. & Co., Strobel & Wilken Co., Baker & Bennett Co., and *Butler Bros.* The Ideal Manufacturing Co., which handled toys, was listed in New York City Directories, 1901–1903, but no connection has been found with Ideal Novelty & Toy Co.

Morris Michtom, famous for his Teddy Bears, began to make dolls around 1906. In 1924 he advertised that he had had eighteen years' experience in making dolls.

1909: Ideal made their first unbreakable character dolls.

1911: The earliest advertisements in PLAYTHINGS for Ideal described character dolls made by a patent "Skeleton Process," of composition that was unbreakable and washable. Benjamin F. Michtom, son of the founder, described this composition as "made of flour and glue with one or two other ingredients. They were pressed on hand operated hydraulic presses, or mechanical presses. The workers would have to pull their weight down on these long extended bars for leverage. The presses were gas heated to dry the water out of the cold composition, and each time they would release the press to allow the steam to escape. Then, by pressing a little bit more, gradually the steam would be expelled from the composition. This composition was very sturdy, but it would warp under heat or excessive moisture."

Their dolls included *Baby Mine, Dandy Kid,* and *Ty Cobb;* price 25¢ and up.

1912: Ideal's character dolls were created by *Aaron Cone;* they included *Naughty Marietta* (a *coquette* type of doll), *Russian Boy,* and *Captain Jinks.*

1913: Fifty numbers with childhood character faces were made of bisque-finish composition; they included *Baby Bettie, The Country Cousins, Freddie* and *Flora, Tiny Toddler, Arctic Boy,* etc.; cost 25¢ to $3.00.

1914: They were experimenting with sleeping eyes and used imitation glass for them. There were one hundred new numbers, which included *Baby Bunting* (cost $5.00), *Baby Paula, Baby Lolo, Admiral Dot, Uneeda Kid, Little Princess,* etc.; cost 25¢ to $10.00.

1915: Factory had 200 employees and put out 150 doll numbers. These dolls were sold all around the world, even as far as Australia, Manila, and Shanghai. They advertised that one of their composition dolls was dropped eight stories to the street and the paint was scarcely scratched. The dolls could be used to drive nails without breaking. They registered *Uneeda* as a trademark in the U.S. Among the new dolls were *Farmer Kids, Baseball Kids, Dottie Dimples, Dolly Varden, Sanitary Baby,* and *Prize Baby.*

1916: The innovation was making a curved-limb baby body so that it could stand as well as sit. The limbs were less curved than previously, and when standing, the baby leaned forward slightly. Among the new dolls were *Baby Bi-Face, Zu-Zu Kid, Old Glory Kids,* and *Mabel.* A new version of Uneeda Kid came with jointed legs. Isaac Rommer, secretary of Ideal, received a U.S. design patent for a clown with a cookie box; design used for *Zu-Zu Kid.*

# IDÉAL BÉBÉ

**866.** "Idéal Bébé" mark of Bertoli Frères.

**867A & B.** Mama Doll with composition head and limbs made by Ideal Novelty & Toy Co. Head has flange neck, real hair wig, open-closed mouth with two upper teeth. The eyes of this doll move from side to side, and also open and close together or separately, thus causing the doll to wink, a special feature of Ideal dolls. The eyes appear to be the celluloid-over-metal material used at the end of World War I. Original blue cotton dress and hat. Mark: Ill. **868.** H. 21 inches. *Courtesy of Dorothy Annunziato.*

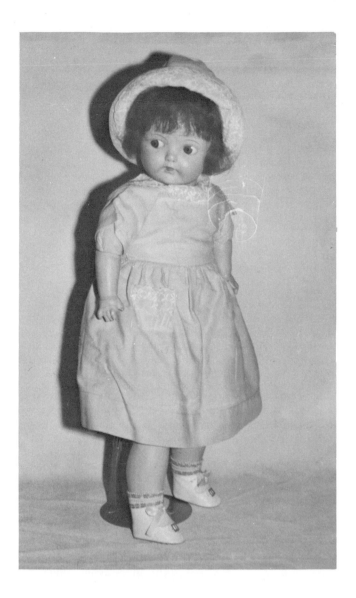

**868.** Mark found on dolls made by Ideal Novelty & Toy Co.

1917: There were two hundred numbers, one hundred varieties with sleeping eyes and one hundred without. The two hundred numbers included seventy-five different character types. Ideal made all-composition dolls with bodies of the same material as the heads. They were fully jointed so that arms and legs could be turned around and around without danger of breaking. The sleeping eyes were made so that each eye moved separately. These sleeping eyes were used on both all-composition and stuffed baby dolls. Dolls came with painted hair or wigs; the wigs were long or short curly hair, the short hair having a curl over the forehead. Dolls wore bathrobes, knitted sweaters, rompers, etc.; came in five sizes; priced $1.00 to $5.00. New dolls included *Liberty Boy, Columbian Kids* (four styles), *Cracker Jack Boy, Compo Baby,* and *Sweater Boy.*

1918: Two hundred numbers were made; dolls had sleeping eyes, even in molded-hair heads. Each eye worked independently so that the doll could close one eye and keep the other eye open. Sleeping-eye dolls came in·six sizes, 12 to 24 inches. They also made a line of socket and shoulder heads with either sleeping or stationary eyes. Dolls with composition heads and hands, sleeping eyes, painted hair, stuffed bodies, dressed in lawn, came in sizes 13½, 14½, and 16 inches and cost $8.55, $12.50, and $16.20 doz. wholesale; similar dolls with sewed mohair wigs, wearing hats and dresses with ribbons and lace, sizes 14½ and 16 inches, cost $18.00 and $24.00 doz. wholesale. Among the new dolls were *Sleeping Beauty* and *Elsie.* Dolls were priced 50¢ to $10.00 each.

1919: Ideal continued to specialize in moving-eye dolls, which were priced $1.00 to $25.00.

1920: A crying doll with the voice in its head, called *The Little Mother Teaching Dolly to Walk,* was one of Ideal's new dolls.

1921: There were 150 varieties of walking dolls, as well

as a large improved line of bent-limb babies with sleeping eyes. Non-walking dolls, priced $1.00 and up; walking dolls priced $1.50 and up.

1922: Ideal advertised "Poppa-Momma" dolls that would "sit, walk, cry, talk, smile, wink and blink." One of their new dolls was *Miss Rainshine*.

1923: There were one hundred new dolls with sleeping eyes made in three lines: (1) cotton-stuffed soft body; (2) cork-stuffed position babies; (3) cork-stuffed straight-limb dolls. Among the new dolls were *Soozie Smiles*, a name registered as a trademark in U.S. for a two-faced doll with stationary eyes. The Queen of England found this doll most amusing, according to London newspapers. Also new in 1923 were *Surprise Baby* with two faces and two voices, which was able to smile or cry real tears, *Greenwich Village Vincent,* and *Greenwich Village Vivian.* The *Mama Dolls* were priced $1.50 to $15.00.

1924: There were two hundred numbers, every one a sleeping-eye doll. Dolls were sent to Europe, Asia, and Australia. The novelty was a flirting-eyed doll named *Flossie Flirt,* whose eyes moved from side to side as she walked across the floor. Other new dolls included *Soozie Smiles Junior, Carrie Joy,* and *Beau Brummel.*

1925: They advertised one hundred numbers with the heads of the dolls made of a strong composition that could stand hard knocks, not made of wood pulp; would not fade in the sun. Ideal used "Walking, Talking, Sleeping" as a trademark for dolls. New doll named *Hush-A-Bye Baby* was an infant type made to compete with the *Bye-Lo Baby.* Flossie Flirt was made in seven sizes and with flexible rubber hands. *Sucker Thumb Baby* also had rubber hands. They were still advertising Baby Mine, one of their first dolls. Sucker Thumb (Suck-a-Thumb) was designed by *Bernard Lipfert* who also designed many dolls for other manufacturers. *Aaron Cone,* Mrs. Aaron Cone, and Mrs. Morris Michtom all designed dolls for Ideal through the years.

**Iessi, Antonio.** 1918–19. New York City. A native of Italy who procured a U.S. design patent for a girl doll with arms spread out.

**Igodi.** 1923–25+. Trademark registered in Germany by *Johannes Gotthilf Dietrich* for dolls and doll parts. This name spelled "Jgodi" has been found on bisque heads, some of which were made by *Ernst Heubach.* These heads usually have a bowl-shaped neck that fits over the hemisphere on the body part of the neck.

**Ijumi Shokai, Hichijo Omiya.** 1920. Kyoto, Japan. Made dolls.

**Ilgner, E.** Before 1909, Leipzig, Saxony; 1909–18, Hermann Fahle, successor. Manufactured dolls.

**Illfelder, B., & Co.** 1862–1925+. Fürth, Bavaria, and New York City. Exported dolls, dolls' heads, and dolls' bodies from Germany. Leopold Illfelder, with his home in Europe, was listed in New York in 1862, and with him at the same address in 1867 was Bernard Illfelder, Jr. Leopold Illfelder, senior member of the firm, died in

1901 and was apparently succeeded by Max Illfelder. No records have been found prior to the 1890's showing whether they did or did not handle dolls. By 1890 they specialized in dolls and toys. In 1896, *Carl Silverman* joined the company, and later they advertised the Carl Silverman line of dolls.

1902: Max Illfelder registered *Little Sweetheart* and *Rosebud* as trademarks in Germany for dolls.

1905: Little Sweetheart was registered as a trademark in U.S. by Max Illfelder.

1907: The firm handled jointed dolls, kid-body dolls, *American Girl* dressed dolls, and the Little Sweetheart dolls.

1908: Max Illfelder registered *Merry Widow* in Germany as a trademark for dolls and dolls' heads.

1909: Max Illfelder registered *Bumble Puppy* and *Billy Possum* in Germany as a trademark for dolls of all kinds, dolls' heads, dolls' bodies, and wool dolls.

1910: Advertised *Sweetheart* and Rosebud dolls. A doll has been found with "MY SWEETHEART" and "B. J. & Co." underneath, marked on the back of its head. This might be one of the Illfelder Sweetheart dolls (I and J being interchangeable).

1912: Advertised Rosebud jointed dolls, Sweetheart jointed dolls, American Girl dressed dolls, and the Carl Silverman doll line. This was the last year for Silverman with Illfelder, as he left and started his own business in 1913.

1914: Advertised Rosebud jointed dolls, Sweetheart jointed dolls, *Heinrich Handwerck* jointed and character dolls, kid dolls, and dressed dolls.

1915: Still advertised Rosebud, Sweetheart, and Handwerck dolls.

1918: Obtained dolls from Japan.

1925: Advertised imported dolls and *Domec* dolls. (See also **Leopold Illfelder & Co.**)

**Illfelder, Leopold, & Co.** 1882–94. Sonneberg, Thür., and London. Manufactured dolls and exported to England, South America, Central America, and other places; had an agent in Paris. They handled dressed and undressed dolls and specialized in showpieces. In 1893 when *Carl Crämer* and *François Edmond Héron* of Sonneberg registered their trademark in the U.S., they stated that they were late of L. Illfelder & Co. The relationship between this Leopold Illfelder and the one in New York with B. Illfelder & Co. has not been determined.

**Illies, Emilie.** 1909–18, Magdeburg, Saxony. Made dolls.

**Ilmenauer Porzellanfabrik A. G. (Joint Stock Co.).** 1777–1925+. Ilmenau, Thür. Made porcelain dolls and heads for dolls. This factory was one of the early *Greiner* group, which used the trefoil or three-leaf clover mark that has been found on dolls. The Ilmenau "I" mark has been reported on dolls, but without verification.

Gotthelf Greiner took charge of the Ilmenau porcelain factory around 1786. He was followed by Christian Nonne, 1792–1808; Nonne & Roesch, 1808–?; and Galluba & Hoffmann, 1888–1925+. The 1904 St. Louis Exposition Report lists Ilmenau as one of the principal manufactories of dolls and dolls' heads. It is doubtful if porcelain dolls' heads were made here before the 19th century.

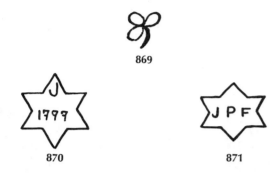

**869–871.** Porcelain marks of the Ilmenauer Porzellanfabrik.

**Imans, P.** 1920. Obtained a British patent for attaching a wax arm to a doll's torso.

**I'mere.** 1921. Trademark registered in Britain for dolls by *Polmar Perfumery Co.*

**Imex Ltd.** 1925. Sonneberg, Thür. Made dolls.

**Imhof, Ferdinand.** 1898–1909. Berlin. Made and exported dolls. He obtained three German, two British, and two French patents for dolls that "walked" on wheels. Dolls have been found with both the German and French patent numbers on the soles of their feet. (See page 316.)

**Imp.** 1923. Rag doll made by *Nelke.*

**Imperial.** 1898–1910. Line of kid-bodied dolls distributed by *Hamburger & Co.* Name Imperial registered by Hamburger in U.S. in 1898 and in Germany in 1901. (Page 316.)

1903: Advertised as having bisque head and hands, curly wig with center part, gusset-jointed kid body scalloped around the neck and arms; came in various sizes.

1904: One of the Hamburger lines of dolls that won a Grand Prize at the St. Louis Exposition.

1910: Line advertised by Geo. H. Bowman Co. following the bankruptcy of Hamburger & Co.

**Imperial Doll & Toy Co.** 1921. Made character dolls of wood fiber; sizes, 9½, 12½, 14½, and 18½ inches.

**Imperial H & Co.** See **Jmperial H & Co.**

**Impie.** 1919. One of the *Borgfeldt* cherub-type dolls; copyrighted twice; first by the *Ben-Arthur Studios,* naming the artist as *Bertha Oscher* and describing the doll as a "Figure of small child, legs apart, arms somewhat outstretched, rounded head, painted hair, oblique eyes." The doll was made of composition and was 8½ inches tall.

**Import Dolls.** 1914. Made in U.S. by *Fair Amusement Co.;* character baby dolls with or without wigs.

**Import Sales Co.** 1914. New York City. Handled *Diamond* rubber dolls.

**Imports, Dolls.** In the 18th century, imported dolls came into the U.S. chiefly by individual orders. By the mid-19th century, dolls were coming into the U.S. in large commercial quantities from France and Germany. In 1903, a New York agent declared that twenty-five years previously (1878) his customers had "objected to paying a fair price for toys that were not stamped 'Made in Germany' or 'Made in France.'"

The 1846 U.S. Tariff Act put a 30 percent duty on dolls. This was raised to 35 percent in 1862, where it remained for some years. The Tariff Acts of 1883, 1890, 1897, and 1909 all placed a 35 percent duty on dolls and dolls' heads, with some minor exceptions.

The total value of dolls imported into the U.S. was as follows:

| Year | Amount |
|------|--------|
| 1875 | $ 300,000 |
| 1881 | 800,000 |
| 1890 | 1,200,000 |
| 1900 | 1,700,000 |
| 1910 | 2,500,000 |
| 1921 | 2,600,000 |

Prior to World War I, the majority of U.S. dolls were imported from Germany; some came from Austria and a few from France and Japan. When World War I broke out in 1914, imports from Germany were immediately cut off, but after a brief time they gradually were resumed, and continued until the outbreak of hostilities between the U.S. and Germany. Following the war, anti-German sentiment prevented the resumption of importing dolls from Germany for several years. Around 1921 and 1922, dolls again began to be imported from Germany in large quantities, and fewer dolls came from Japan, which had supplied many dolls during and immediately after the war. By 1924, the majority of imported dolls were coming from Germany, though there were still some from France, Italy, and Japan.

In the case of dolls, around the turn of the century, the tariff laws harmed rather than helped the American manufacturing industry. The 1897 Tariff Act placed a 35 percent duty on dolls' heads, but the duty on wigs was over 100 percent and on glass eyes, 60 percent. Thus, in some cases, importing a doll's head with a fine wig and glass eyes could be cheaper than importing just the wig and eyes separately that would be required for the head made in America.

The 1890 Tariff Act, Section 6, contained the stipulation that "On or after March 1, 1891 all articles of foreign manufacture . . . be plainly marked . . . to indicate country of origin." On the basis of this act, some doll collectors have asserted that dolls without the country of origin marked on them must be dated prior to 1891. However, this does not seem to be correct, as indicated by an article in the New York JOURNAL OF COMMERCE in 1909, when a new tariff act was passed: "Importing merchants are expressing dissatisfaction with the marking

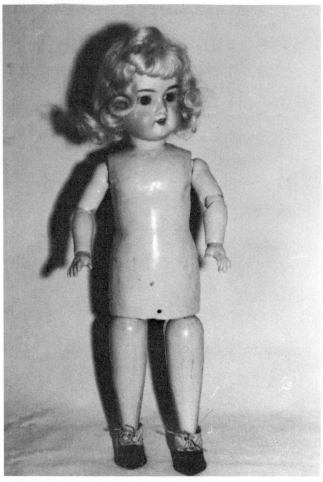

873

**872.** Imhof's walking doll with two wheels under each foot, as patented in Germany in 1900. For the mark on the sole of the foot, see Ill. **874.** The shoes are part of doll and not removable. Bisque head was made by Armand Marseille, mold #390, size 0½. See Ill. **873** for similar walking doll made under French patent. H. 16 inches. *Courtesy of Dorothy Annunziato.*

**873A & B.** Imhof's walking doll with two wheels under each foot as patented in France in 1900. Mark on the sole of the foot: "Breveté //305-269 //S.G.D.G." Composition head, which resembles celluloid, has wine-colored eyebrows. Doll wears original white chemise with red rosettes; her panties were nailed on. H. 16 inches. *Courtesy of June J. Jeffcott; photograph by June J. Jeffcott.*

**D. R. P.**
**№ 119857**
**PATENT ℓ LANDEP**

**874.** Mark found on dolls made under patent of Ferdinand Imhof.

**Jmperial H & Co.**

**875.** "Imperial" mark used by Hamburger & Co.

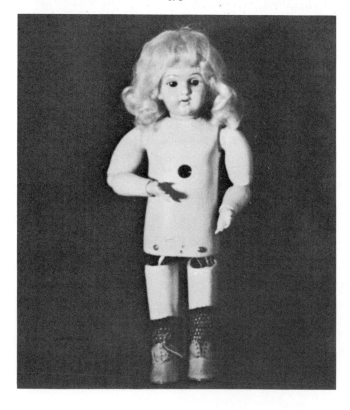

clause prescribed in the new tariff act. The change in the law affects especially the importation of toys. The protest is made on the ground that compliance with the new section will mean unnecessary expenditure of money in securing the inscriptions called for; and secondly, that importers would be giving away to their competitors the names of foreign manufacturers from whom goods are purchased. Under the new law [1909] it will be necessary to mark practically every article that enters this country.

"While the Dingley act [1897] provided that all goods of foreign manufacture, 'such as are usually or ordinarily' marked, etc., should be plainly stamped, branded or labeled in English, the Payne law [1909] is less liberal, and states that all articles of foreign manufacture or reproduction, 'which are capable of being marked, stamped, branded, or labeled, without injury,' shall bear the inscription of the country of origin. The new law goes even further, stating that the marking shall not be 'covered or obscured by any subsequent attachments or arrangements,' etc.

"Importers of toys are the principal opponents to the new marking regulation. They say that, should the appraiser choose to make a broad interpretation of the word 'capable' practically every article, no matter of what trifling value, would have to conform with these provisions in order to enter this country. . . .

"It is also said that the proviso, 'without injury,' will encounter all kinds of disputes between the importer and the appraiser."

The above suggests that prior to 1909 there were many loopholes in the law that permitted unmarked dolls to enter this country. Even after the stricter law of 1909 was passed, there seem to have been some problems of interpretation, which might have allowed merely the container in which the doll was imported to have the country of origin written on it without the inscription being actually on the doll itself. Late in 1909 there was a ruling that where the article was fragile or cost of marking would be expensive and depreciate the value of the article, its marking by a label was satisfactory and the label could be upon the package rather than the article itself. (See also **Trademarks**.)

**Incroyable.** Ca. 1800. Name of a doll according to M. Alexandre Girard, who wrote about it in 1903. Doll generally dressed as a "Dandy."

**Independent Doll Co.** 1915–22. New York City. Made composition dolls' heads in six models, one being Negro dolls' heads. Cloth bodies were filled with sawdust. Produced 7,000 heads a day.

**Independent Toy Works.** 1914. Brooklyn, N.Y. Made cloth doll named *Rosalind*.

**Indestructible.** Label on papier-mâché shoulder head.

**Indestructible (Patent Indestructible).** See **Composition Dolls**.

**Indestructible Bébé.** See **Bébé Incassable**.

No. 1879
Indestructible Head
This Composition is
perfectly harmless

**876.** "Indestructible" mark on papier-mâché heads.

**Indestructible Doll Co.** 1912. New York City. Made dolls.

**Indestructo Specialties Co.** 1915–16. New York City. Used the initials *ISCO* and registered *Sunshine Kids* as a trademark in the U.S. for dolls.

1915: Advertised that the unbreakable character heads of their dolls were modeled by some of the best-known artists in New York. Dolls came with fully jointed or baby bodies, flirting or sleeping eyes; price $1.00.

**India Rubber Comb Co.** 1851–?. New York City. Appeared in City directories for many years. Used the hard rubber formula patented by Nelson Goodyear in 1851 to make dolls' heads. These dolls were marked on the back of the shoulder "I. R. Comb Co."

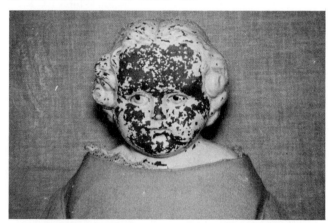

**877A & B.** Painted rubber head of the India Rubber Comb Co., marked as shown in Ill. **879**. Rubber is dark red where the paint has chipped off. Note the similarity to the shape of the Goodyear head in Ill. **659**. H. 23 inches. *Courtesy of the Chester County Historical Society.*

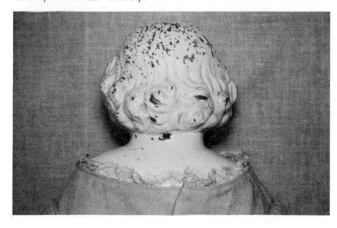

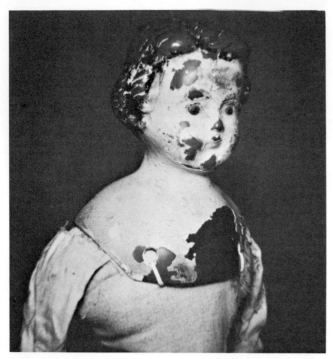

**878.** Painted head made by the India Rubber Comb Co. Mark: Ill. **879.** H. of shoulder head, 3½ inches. *Coleman Collection.*

# I.R.COMB Co.

**879.** Mark used on dolls of India Rubber Comb Co.

**Indian.** 1892. One of the *Brownies,* designed by *Palmer Cox.*

**Indian Dolls.** The many dolls created to represent members of various American Indian tribes and their folklore would require an entire volume. In this book, only play dolls sold commercially are included.

In the 1890's and early 1900's, character dolls dressed as American Indians, both squaws and chiefs, were popular. They appear to have been made in Germany, with bisque heads and jointed composition bodies, and features that were supposed to resemble those of Indians.

1895–96: Dolls with bisque heads and jointed arms and legs were distributed by YOUTH'S COMPANION (see Ill. 880). An Indian came in a set with Negro, Chinese, and Caucasian dolls; all were 9 inches tall; price for all four was $1.30. In 1895, size 7 to 11 inches for dolls of four races (plus an *Eskimo doll* in 1896) cost $1.40.

1897: *John D. Zernitz Co.* advertised Indian dolls with bisque heads, glass eyes, long black hair, swivel necks, and jointed bodies; sizes 10, 12, and 15 inches; priced at $8.00 to $24.00 doz. wholesale.

1909: Indian dolls were made in all-bisque; wore appropriate costumes of leather, beads and feathers; 8 inches tall, 50¢.

1910: *Butler Bros.* advertised Indian dolls with bisque heads, glass eyes; 8½ inches tall.

1911: Indians made of composition were introduced in two sizes and two designs; prices $1.00 and $2.00.

1913: *Mary McAboy* applied for the design patent for her famous *Skookum Indians.*

1916: An Indian Maid was one of the *Madame Hendren* line of dolls; it was dressed in bright-colored felt, with beads and feathers; various sizes; price $1.25 to $6.00.

1917: A portrait doll of the Indian Princess *Angeline,* daughter of Chief Seattle, was produced.

**Indra Kunstwerkstätten Inc.** 1922–23. Munich, Bavaria. Registered "Indra" as a trademark for dolls in Germany.

**Industrielle de Celluloid Cie.** 1909–13. France. Obtained a French patent for a celluloid doll made so that it would float upright with only its head and shoulders out of the water. They secured three other patents in France for dolls, mostly mechanical. (See also **Société Industrielle de Celluloid.**)

**Infant Dolls.** (Included here are the dolls usually dressed in long baby clothes; excluded are the infant Jesus dolls, which were partly of a religious nature.)

The wax and wooden dolls of the 18th and early 19th centuries that were dressed as infants differ very little from those dressed as babies and children. In the 1830's, Victoria (later Queen) used rag dolls for the infants in long dresses. During the 1850's and 1860's, the *Motschmann* type of crying babies often had long dresses. Some of the china-headed dolls and dolls with papier-mâché heads were dressed in long clothes as infants. The 1870's was the era of the fine French lady dolls, and about the only types of infants seem to have been the *London Rag* dolls and *Frozen Charlottes.* The 1880's was the period of the bébés. *Bru's Bébé Teteur* was patented in 1879; it generally wore long dresses. Many of the turned head, bisque shoulder-type dolls were dressed originally as infants. These dolls often had relatively short limbs compared to their torsos. Around 1900 *Kestner* brought out a dwarf kid body that was extremely short and dumpy, but the usual mold #154 was on it. This was a version of an infant doll. For the next couple of decades, infants seem to have been partially forgotten. Most of the bent-limb babies wore rompers or short dresses, and the same was true of the *Mama Dolls.* (See Ill. 963.)

1906–8: *Horsman* made infants, dressed in long clothes, with lifelike faces.

1911: PLAYTHINGS described infant dolls with the unformed heads of tiny babies and up to the actual size of young babies.

1914: *New Born Babe* was brought out by *Louis Amberg & Son.*

1923–25: New Born Babe was again brought out to compete with the tremendously popular *Bye-Lo Baby* of *Borgfeldt.* Half the dolls bought for Christmas in 1925 were infant dolls. They included, besides the two already named: *Hush-A-Bye Baby,* from *Ideal; Teenie Weenie,*

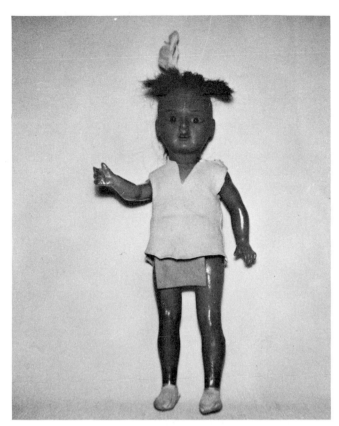

**880.** Indian doll with bisque head, glass eyes, open mouth. Marked "Germany // A. M. // 7/O." Jointed composition body; original clothes and roach (Indian)-style wig. H. 9 inches. *Courtesy of May Maurer.*

**881.** Indian doll is marked only "2" on the brown bisque head; has painted eyes, straight black-hair wig; brown composition body. Original costume includes the feather headdress. H. 7½ inches. *Courtesy of Jessica Norman.*

from *American Character Doll Co.; Lullaby Baby,* from *Averill; Baby Effanbee* and *Baby Dainty,* from *EFFanBEE; Peek-a-boo,* from *Acme; My Dream Baby,* from *Arranbee (Armand Marseille* head); *Kradle Babe,* from *Domec; Baby Phyllis* line's tiniest infant; *Tynie Babe,* from *Horsman; Just Born* from *Reisman; Baby Sister,* from *Roth, Baitz & Lipsitz Manufacturing Co.; Sweetums* from *Century; Baby Bunting,* from *J. Bouton; Kiddiejoy* line's infant, from *Jacobs & Kassler; Royal Baby Bunting; Schoenhut's* infant in wood, and many others.

**Inga.** 1924–25. Trademark registered in U.S. by *Inga Shilling-Patterson.*

**Insam & Prinoth.** 1820–1925+. St. Ulrich, Gröden Tirol; Nürnberg, Bavaria; London. Exported and distributed wooden dolls made as a cottage-type industry in the Austrian Tirol. They displayed dolls at the 1873 Vienna Exhibition and at the 1878 Paris Exposition. At that time, they had agents in both France and England; their London branch continued well into the 20th century. (See also **Chr. Prinoth.**)

**882.** Peg-jointed all-wooden dolls made in the Grödner Tal of the type handled by Insam & Prinoth. Probably made ca. 1900. Heights 13 and 12 inches. *Coleman Collection.*

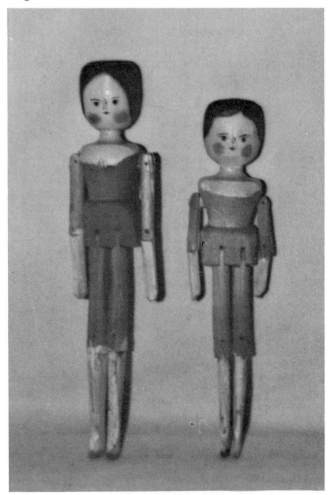

**Intaglio Eyes.** Painted eyes with the iris and pupil concave. (See Ills. 813 and 816.)

**International Doll, The.** 1898. Trademark registered in Germany by *Borgfeldt* for dolls.

**International Doll Corp.** 1920. New York City. Advertised composition character dolls.

**International Silver Co.** 1925. Meriden, Conn. Was assigned three patents by *Craig D. Munson.* One patent was for an old man with just a few tufts of hair; another, an officer; the third, a boy in overalls and wide-collar shirt.

**International Soldiers.** 1915. Character dolls handled by *German Novelty Co.*

**International Talking Doll Co.** 1909. Coburg, Thür. Incorporated to produce dolls by *Max Oskar Arnold's* patent.

**International Walking Doll Co.** New York City. Advertised a Japanese walking doll that could walk when its hand was held.

**Interwarex, Dave M. Jaskiel.** 1924. Berlin. Made dolls.

**Iona Specialty Co.** 1922. New York City. Distributed domestic and imported dolls.

**Irish Dolls.** 1895–1925. *Emily Florence Eaton* of Tipperary and Dublin started to make dolls in 1895; by 1903 there was also a doll-making industry in Stewartstown, County Tyrone. Also of Dublin, *Isobel Dodd* was making dolls in 1919.

**Irishman.** One of *Palmer Cox's Brownies.*

**Irokese Trading Corp.** 1920–21. New York City. Registered in U.S. two trademarks—one was the profile head of an Indian; the other was the name *Dora*—for dolls of celluloid, rubber, wood, paper, cloth, or metal. This might have been the Indian head found on celluloid dolls, but the feather stands up rather than points down. (See **Louis Sametz.**)

**Irvington.** 1909–10. Trademark registered in Germany by *Borgfeldt* for dolls.

**Isaacs, Abraham, & Isaacs, Henry.** 1881, London; 1884–87, successor, A. & J. Isaacs; 1891, successor, Isaac and Henry Isaacs. Made rag dolls, imported and dressed dolls.

1886: A. & J. Isaacs registered the *Cherub Doll* in Britain as a trademark for dolls.

**Isaacs, Dorothy Helen, & Smith, Lowa Belle.** 1921. Spirit Lake, Idaho. Obtained design patent for a pigeon-toed doll with eyes glancing to the side.

**Isabel.** 1912. Young woman doll copyrighted by *Elizabeth Lesser.*

**Isco.** 1915–16. Initials used by *Indestructo Specialties Co.*

**Israël, L.** 1921–24, Paris; 1925+, successor, L. Salomon. Distributed and repaired *bébés incassables,* dolls' heads, and wigs.

**Israng, Peter.** 1923. Nürnberg, Bavaria. Distributor for *Heinrich Schmuckler.*

**Italian Dolls.** Italian skill and artistry seem to have been exported to a greater extent than actual dolls. Most of the skilled wax-doll makers in England, around the middle of the 19th century, had Italian names. Later, Italian girls were brought to Sonneberg to paint dolls' faces. Many of the artists who designed early composition-head character dolls made in America around the time of World War I were natives of Italy. Cheaper dolls of papier-mâché or of wood were made in Italy for home consumption and protected by duties. Italian children liked to have their dolls dressed as famous characters such as Garibaldi, St. Francis of Assisi, etc.

By 1909, a large doll factory had been established at Milan; in other Italian provinces the manufacture of dolls was introduced as a domestic industry. Among the manufacturers of dolls in Italy after World War I were *Antenore, Mario Franco, Fels Mayer,* and *Scavini.* The Scavini dolls, known more familiarly as *Lenci,* were sought all over the world and copied in France, Germany, and the U.S.

**Italian Products Agency.** 1920-21. London. Doll distributor.

**Ives & Co.** 1868–1925+. Plymouth and Bridgeport, Conn. Made mechanical dolls. The company started out as Ives, Blakeslee & Co.; then it was Ives, Blakeslee & Williams. The members of this company obtained many U.S. patents, some of which were for dolls. They had an exhibit at Philadelphia in 1876 and at Chicago in 1893.

**Ivory.** Ivory dolls have been made since ancient times. They are usually relatively small in size. A fully jointed ivory doll a half-inch tall was shown at Cleveland in 1924.

**883.** All-bisque doll with glass eyes and wig is jointed at neck, shoulders, and hips; molded shoes; original provincial costume. Marked: "Italy//No. 1/0." 6½ inches. *Courtesy of Bess Goldfinger.*

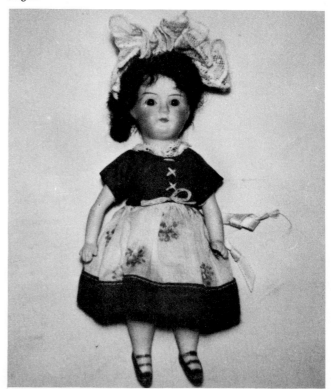

**884A & B.** Bisque head has glass eyes and open mouth with four teeth; eyebrows are a single line; painted slippers and socks. Note the unusual composition body held together with staples but not painted. Mark: Ill. 885. H. 16 inches. *Courtesy of Bess Goldfinger.*

**886.** Pair of dolls made of carved ivory have blonde wigs; their pastel-colored clothes are trimmed with gold braid. H. 5 inches. *Courtesy of Margaret Whitton; photograph by Winnie Langley.*

**Ivory Porcelain.** The name given by *Goss* to the material of which they made some of their dolls' heads.

**Ivoyette.** 1909. Line of small dolls with celluloid faces.

**Izzard.** Probably 1860's or 1870's. London. The name and address are found on a three-wheeled walking doll with *Gebrüder Heubach* head. James Izzard had a turnery and toy warehouse at another address from 1814 to 1860. From 1878 on, Frederick William Lee had a toy warehouse at 136 Regent Street, which is the address found on the doll.

**887.** Label on doll handled by Izzard.

The prices given for dolls are those for which the dolls were originally offered for sale. They are *not* today's prices.

# J

**Ja Ja Girl.** 1919. Line of cherub-type dolls made by *Hitz, Jacobs & Co.;* came with or without real hair wigs, in assorted styles and dresses.

**Jack.** 1912. Composition-head character doll with big brown eyes of glass that could be turned in any direction by a twist of the finger. Called a *Wall-Eyed Doll;* mate for *Jill.* Price 50¢ and $1.00.

**Jack.** 1925. Made by *The Toy Shop;* mate to *Jill.*

**Jack and Jill.** 1925. *Story Book Dolls.* Manufactured by *Sol Bergfeld & Son,* distributed by *Borgfeldt.* Came with composition heads; 15 inches tall.

**Jack and Jill.** 1925. Trademark registered in U.S. by Beatrice Jackson, proprietor of *Novelty Doll Co.*

**Jack Sprat.** 1923–24. Trademark registered in U.S. by *Western Grocer Co.* for dolls.

**Jack Tar.** 1911–12. *Art Doll* made by *Horsman.* Came with *Can't Break 'Em* head, molded hair, cloth body; dressed in blue and white uniform copied from the uniform worn by King George V's son (later the Duke of Windsor).

**Jack Tar.** 1914. Made by *Louis Amberg & Son.* Carried a flag.

**Jackie Coogan.** 1925. Copyrighted by Jackie Coogan Productions for *Borgfeldt;* designed by *Jeno Juszko.* Represented Jackie Coogan in the RAG MAN. Doll wore large trousers and cap; had hands in pockets.

**Jackie Coogan Kid.** 1921–22. Portrait doll of Jackie Coogan as he appeared in THE KID. Made by *Horsman,* designed by *Benjamin Goldenberg.* Came with stuffed body jointed at shoulders and hips. Wore red jersey, long overalls, and cap on sideways. Jackie Coogan button furnished with each doll. Size 13½ inches, price $1.29. (See also **Kid, The.**)

**Jacob, Louis.** 1873. Sonneberg, Thür. Showed dolls at the Vienna Exhibition.

**Jacobin.** 1848. French name for doll according to article written by Mons. Alexandre Girard in 1903.

**Jacobs & Kassler.** See **Hitz, Jacobs & Kassler.**

**Jacobson, Lester H.** 1921–22. Assignee of half the rights to the design patented by *William Blaydes* in U.S.

**Jacquerod, Paul Charles.** 1909–11. West New York, N.J. Citizen of Switzerland. Obtained U.S. patent for vertical and lateral movement of glass eyeballs, which he assigned to *Harry M. de Wart.*

**Jacques, William White.** 1887–89. Newton, Mass. Obtained two British patents, a U.S., and a French patent, all for phonograph dolls with the record-playing device inside the body of the doll, operated by a key or handle. He assigned his rights to the *Edison Phonograph Toy Manufacturing* Co. of Maine.

**Jäger, Fritz.** 1911. Bergzabern, Pfalz. Secured two German patents for dolls' wigs.

**Jäger, Gebrüder (Jäger & Co.).** See **Friedrichrodaer Puppenfabrik.**

**Jäger, Otto.** See **Friedrichrodaer Puppenfabrik.**

**Jam Kiddos.** 1915–16. Trademark registered in U.S. for composition-head character dolls made by *Non-Breakable Doll Co.* Had sleeping eyes, molded hair, cork-stuffed bodies with inside joints. Models included *Buster Brown, Sweet Lavender, Sailor Boy,* etc. Size 16 inches, price $1.00.

**Jane.** 1915. Represented one of the *Gene Carr Kids;* made by *Horsman.*

**Jane.** 1916–18. Trade name of doll made by *Jessie McCutcheon Raleigh;* distributed by *Butler Bros.* Wore striped lawn dress. Size 11½ inches; price $2.40.

**Jane & Binder Co.** 1920. Handled Parisian dolls with woolen hair; silk faces were embroidered in wool.

**Janes, Josephine, Co.** 1919–20. Lynbrook, N.Y., and New York City. Registered *Slumber Toys* as trademark in U.S. for dolls.

**Janet.** 1911. Child doll made by *Horsman;* designed by *Helen Trowbridge.*

**Janie.** 1920. Walking doll made by *Averill Manufacturing Co.* Came with composition limbs; wore colored organdy dress; 26 inches tall.

**Janus.** 1925. Trademark registered in France by *Mlle. Louise Adrienne Mabit* for dolls' heads.

**Jap Rose Kids.** 1911–12. Made by *Horsman* under license from Jas. S. Kirk & Co. (soap manufacturers), as companions to the *Campbell Kids*. Came with eyes centered, open-closed mouth, brunette molded hair. Girl wore pink, boy wore blue, kimono, both with obi sash in back. Advertised as being one of the copyrighted dolls. If so, the designer must have been *Helen Trowbridge*, since she designed all the Horsman dolls that were copyrighted around this time. The oriental-type dolls sold by *Horsman* in 1917 probably were later versions. (See also **Little San Toy.**)

**Japan Import & Export Commission Co.** 1914–23. New York City and Nagoya, Japan. New York address was the same as that for *Borgfeldt*. Registered *Dimple* as trademark in U.S. for dolls in 1915.

**Japanese Dolls.** Included herein are only those play dolls made in Japan or Europe to be exported commercially. Tokyo was the center for celluloid, metal, and rubber dolls. Osaka was the center for cotton and paper dolls, and Kyoto was the center for porcelain dolls. As in Germany, the doll industry in Japan was largely a household industry. The occasional inferior quality and oriental features were responsible for the lack of popularity of Japanese dolls in America, especially prior to World War I. *Motschmann* based the design of his patented doll on

**888.** Bisque-headed doll ca. 1925, represents a Japanese infant. Marked "Germany" under "1." *Courtesy of Ruth Noden.*

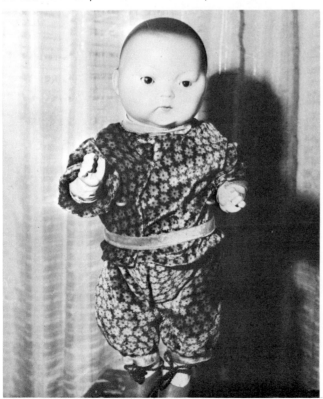

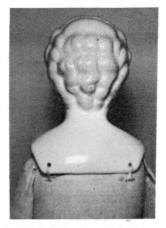 

**889A & B.** China head made in Japan for the Occidental trade. Note the variations from usual china heads—i.e., the shape of the eyes, pierced ears, size of the sewholes, and so on. This type of head came with blonde or black hair and has been seen with a paper sticker reading "Made in Japan." H. 12½ inches. H. of shoulder head, 3¼ inches. *Coleman Collection.*

Japanese dolls shown at the 1855 exhibition. Japanese dolls of the 1890's looked and dressed like Japanese people.

1894: A Japanese baby doll with open lips, teeth, natural hair, and glass eyes (16 inches tall) cost $4.05 doz. wholesale.

1901: Japanese dolls with glass eyes and paper dresses (15 inches tall) were priced at 10¢.

1904–5: Popularity of Japanese dolls increased because of the Russo-Japanese War.

1906–10: *Butler Bros.* advertised Japanese lady dolls with bisque heads, glass eyes, teeth; 16 inches tall.

1907: Japan exported dolls with enameled faces and black tufts of hair.

1912: *Heinrich Handwerck* in Germany made "Japanese" dolls with oriental complexion and features. A similar-type dolls' head was made by *Simon & Halbig* a short time earlier.

World War I period: When bisque dolls' heads were cut off from Germany on account of the war, Japan stepped in and tried to fill the demand. One rumor has it that they copied the German heads so precisely that they even included the "Made in Germany"! *Borgfeldt, Louis Wolf & Co.,* and many others obtained their dolls from Japan during this period. The bent-limb character babies made in Japan do not usually have the detail of workmanship found on their German counterparts. The hands on the German dolls are held in various positions, and the big toe is often turned up. By 1917, Japan claimed that she held first place in doll exports, and the demand so far exceeded the supply that many months were required for orders to be filled. In 1918, there was an embargo against the importation of Japanese dolls into the U.S., but they continued to flood the market. Probably the reason was that most of the big companies, such as *Morimura Bros., Yamato, Tajimi, Haber,* etc., were actually American companies that distributed and sometimes designed the dolls made in Japan. By 1925, the making of bisque dolls' heads had fallen sharply in Japan with the return of Germany to the world's markets. However, *Langfelder, Homma & Hayward* claimed that Japan still led the world in the manufacture of bisque dolls.

**Jardin, Frau L. Joh.** 1909. Dresden, Saxony. Made dolls.

**Jay Gee World Doll Co.** 1923. New York City. Made Jay Gee World *Mama Dolls.*

**Jay-Bee.** 1919–25+. Line of jointed dolls and character dolls imported by *J. Bouton & Co.*

1923: Imported from Europe boy and girl dolls with Indian features.

1924: Included *Peter Pan* dolls.

1925: Jay-Bee line included *Baby Phyllis* dolls, which had bisque heads. Price was 50¢ to $5.00.

**Jazz Hound.** 1922–23. Trademark registered in U.S. by *Jane Gray Co.* for dolls

**Jean.** 1925. Represents *Skeezix'* playmate in the Frank King cartoon. Doll made by *Live Long Toys.*

**Jeanne d'Arc.** 1920. Trademark registered in France by *Mlle. Marguerite de Raphelis-Soissan* for dolls and bébés.

**Jeannette.** 1890's. Trade name of doll handled by *Charles Auguste Wattilliaux.*

**Jeannette Doll Co.** 1919–24. New York City. Made dolls.

1919: Their cork-stuffed dolls with wigs cost $1.00.

1922: *Mama Doll* 27 inches tall; price $16.50 doz. wholesale.

1923–24: Registered *Little Red Riding Hood* as a trademark in U.S. Advertised that they sold 6,000 of these dolls the first week they went on the market.

**Jeannine.** 1924. Trademark registered in France by *Mme. Jeanne Violon.*

**Jeffreys, Edward Augustus.** 1902–3. Moseley near Birmingham, England. Secured a German patent for a crying doll.

**Jeidel, Julius.** 1908. Frankfurt am Main, Germany. Registered *Bi-Ba-Bo* as a trademark in Germany for dolls that he distributed.

**Jenny Lind Doll Co.** 1916. Chicago, Ill. Short-wind phonograph inside papier-mâché body (¼-inch thick) of the doll enabled it to sing, talk, or recite. Hair had a center part and shoulder-length curls.

**Jenny Wren.** 1915. Trade name for doll made by *Ideal Novelty & Toy Co.*

**Jépé.** 1925. Trade name for a doll by *Alexandre Girard.*

**Jeweled.** 1905–7. Trade name for china-limbed dolls distributed by *Butler Bros.* Doll had a gold necklace in front with a colored glass jewel. Came with cloth body and

china limbs. Sizes 8, 10, 11, 13, 16, and 17 inches; price 39¢ to $2.10 doz. wholesale.

**Jgodi.** See **Igodi.**

**J'Habille Mes Soldats and J'Habille Mes Poupées.** 1916. Two trademarks registered in France by Société Ch. *Ramel & Cie.* for papier-mâché dolls and toys.

**Jiggle Wiggle.** 1921–22. Trademark registered in U.S. by *Howard R. Larsen,* who stated that the mark was stamped directly on the doll.

**Jiggles the Clown.** 1923–24. Trademark registered in U.S. by *Schoen & Yondorf.*

**Jill.** 1912. Composition-head character doll with big brown eyes of glass that could be turned in any direction by a twist of the finger. Called a *Wall-Eyed Doll;* mate to *Jack.* Price 50¢ and $1.00.

**Jill.** 1925. Made by *The Toy Shop;* mate to *Jack.*

**Jim Dandy.** 1914. Trade name for a doll made by *Louis Amberg & Son;* 18 inches tall; $54.00 per gross wholesale.

**Jim-In-Ee.** 1925. Trademark registered in U.S. by *Elizabeth G. Adrian,* who stated that the mark was on a woven label on the doll.

**Jim Thorpe.** 1913. Baseball boy doll made by *Tip Top Toy Co.* and distributed by *Borgfeldt.*

**Jimmy.** 1916. Character-type *Art Doll* distributed by *Strobel & Wilken.* Came with painted hair and eyes; dressed in pajamas.

**Jimmy Boy Doll Co.** 1922–23. Sidney, Ohio. Registered "Jimmy Boy" as a trademark in U.S.

**Jimmy Dugan.** 1923. *Gene Byrnes* obtained two copyrights for dolls representing Jimmy Dugan of REG'LAR FELLERS—one doll was laughing and wearing a cap, and one came without a cap. *Borgfeldt* was listed on the copyright.

**Jing-Go-Ring Doll.** 1912–13. Trademark registered in Germany by *Fritz Lutz.*

**Jmperial H & Co.** 1900–1901. Trademark registered in Germany by *Hamburger & Co.* (See **Imperial.**)

**Jo.** 1923–25. Rag doll designed and made by *Madame Alexander* to represent the character from LITTLE WOMEN. It had a mask face with raised features that were hand-painted by Madame Alexander. Came with wig of mohair imported from England; pink muslin body; size 14 inches; price $1.20.

**Joachimstal & Wagner.** 1893–1909. Berlin. Manufactured dolls especially crocheted dressed dolls.

**Joan.** 1924. *A Baby Grumpy* made by *EFFanBEE.*

**Joanny, J.** 1884–1921. Paris. Made dolls and bébés.

1884: Secured French patent for moving eyelids in dolls' heads.

1885: Won a bronze medal for his doll display at the Paris Exposition.

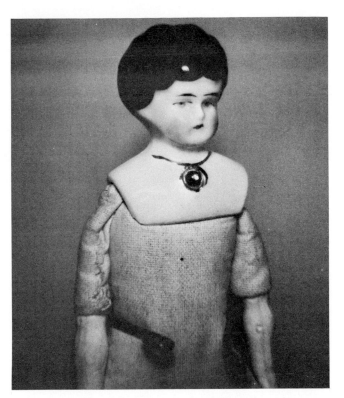

**890.** China head with jeweled green glass glued onto the chest as part of a gold necklace; the decoration appears only on the front. Ca. 1905. H. 8 inches H. of shoulder head, 2 inches. *Courtesy of Edith Meggers.*

1890: Made patented "bébé métamorphosis" (the change probably involved the face and/or head of the doll). They also made jointed bébés and "unbreakable" heads.

1921: Made jointed dolls that would take all desired positions.

**Jobard, A.** 1852–64. Paris. Made pink kid dolls, dressed dolls, and dolls' trousseaux.

**Jockey.** 1911. Character doll made by *A. Steinhardt & Bro.*

**Joffre.** 1918. Portrait felt doll representing the famous French Marshal made in England by Belgian refugees and distributed in U.S. by *Horsman.* It wore war medals that were exact reproductions of the medals won by Marshal Joffre.

**Johannes, Margaret E.** 1922–23. Kansas City, Mo. Was issued a design patent for a rag doll.

**John Bull.** 1892. One of the *Brownies* designed by *Palmer Cox* and made by *Arnold Print Works.*

**John Bunny Doll.** 1914. Portrait doll representing the moving picture star, made by *Louis Amberg & Son* in two sizes, price $4.25 and $8.25 doz. wholesale.

**John Martin's House, Inc.** 1913–22. Published the JOHN MARTIN'S BOOK, which contained the *Kate Jordan* drawings of the *Happifats.*

1922: Registered in U.S. the name "John Martin" as a trademark to be used for dolls and doll forms.

**Johnny Doll.** 1893. Name for dolls dressed like English sailors and made for baby boys.

**Johnny Jones.** 1912. Trade name for American boy doll made by *Louis Amberg & Son.* Came with pink sateen body and wore striped shirtwaist, flaring collar, large red bow tie, dark trousers, and blue silk socks.

**Johnny Jump-Up.** 1918. Doll made by *Jessie McCutcheon Raleigh,* distributed by *Butler Bros.;* size 13½ inches, price $3.15.

**Johnny-Tu-Face.** 1912. Double-faced doll with turning head, made by *EEFanBEE.* Two sizes; price 50¢ and $1.00.

**Johnson, Charles C.** See **Jointed Doll Co.**

**Johnson, Frances.** 1920–21. Chicago, Ill. Was granted a U.S. design patent for a rag doll.

**Johnson, John Henry.** 1855. Glasgow, Scotland. Obtained British patents for molding India rubber and gutta-percha to make dolls and other items.

**Johnson, Mary E.** 1924. Texarkana, Ark. Was issued a U.S. design patent for a long-limbed girl doll.

**Johnson, Rebecca E.** 1886–87. Brooklyn, N.Y. Was granted a U.S. patent for a rag doll made of open woven fabric dipped in melted wax and compressed between rollers. This was reinforced over a shell of pressed paper, buckram, etc., and stuffed with cotton, hemp, or other fibrous material.

**Johnson Bros. Ltd.** 1860–before 1923; Birmingham, England; 1923–25+, Chad Valley Co. Made cloth dolls.

1923: Registered the name *La Petite Caresse* as a trademark in Britain.

1924: Obtained two British patents for dolls' heads made of stiffened material, with glass eyes.

**Jointed Doll Co.** 1874–85. North Springfield, Vt. Made wooden dolls. Dexter Martin and his son, Frank D. Martin, were making wooden toys as early as 1874, and Martin was listed as making dolls in 1878, but the name of the company appeared in directories only from 1879–81. In 1878, Frank D. Martin applied for a U.S. patent, which was granted in 1879, for ball-and-socket joints secured by rivets. The dolls of this company had black bands around the waist often inscribed, "Improved Jointed Doll pat. April 29, '79, Dec. 7, '80, & Nov. 7, '82." The 1880 U.S. patent was obtained by George W. Sanders and the 1882 U.S. patent by Charles C. Johnson. The Johnson patent for a head of molded "plastic" (composition) material over a wooden core is similar to the 1881 patent of *Mason* and Taylor. Dolls were usually 12 inches tall, but are known to have been made as large as 18 inches. A 12-inch doll was advertised as jointed at neck, shoulders, elbows, hips, and knees. The painting on the head was "warranted" not to wash off; price $7.00 doz. wholesale. They also advertised a jointed doll with an elastic body designed to fit all heads of American manufacture.

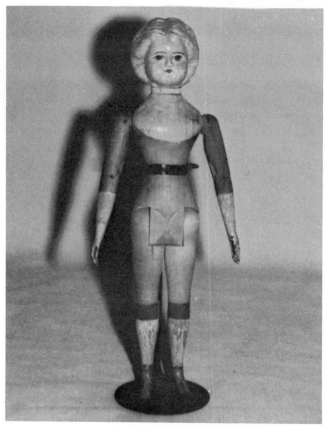

**Joints for Dolls.** Ingenious methods for making articulated dolls have existed since ancient times. Peg or pin joints were used by the ancient Greeks and Romans. Mortise-and-tenon joints were used at an early date. In 1721, Pope wrote about a little girl "gay over a jointed baby." Ball joints are found on wooden dolls at least as early as 1800. Jointed kid bodies were being made in 1842. Many patents for joints were obtained in the 1850's and 1860's. They were issued to Mlle. Calixte *Huret, Mons. Marie Bruchet,* Mlle. *Marie Rohmer,* Chr. *Motschmann, Thomas Hammond, Mons. Briens, Fischer, Nauman & Co., Mons. Reidmeister, Mons. Benoit Martin,* culminating in the patents for ball-jointed composition-type bodies issued to Leon Casimir *Bru* in 1869, et. al.

German kid bodies and cloth bodies with swinging joints often had an extra circular piece sewed across the knee joint. The sewing was frequently in red. Both *Heinrich Handwerck* and *Kestner,* two of the largest German manufacturers, obtained patents for jointed composition bodies in the 1890's.

**891A & B.** Wooden doll with patented joints, made by the Jointed Doll Co. in the 1880's. Head is composition over a wooden core and has painted features; metal hands and feet, the latter painted blue. Patent dates appear on the black band around the waist. H. 11½ inches. *Coleman Collection.*

**892.** Typical papier-mâché Motschmann-type infant, except for the three-piece neck joint, which allows the head to swivel and to nod back and forth. H. 9½ inches. *Courtesy of The Smithsonian Institution.*

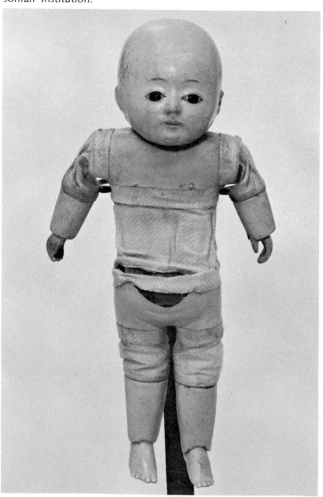

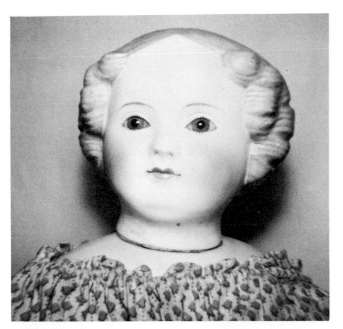

**893A & B.** Untinted bisque shoulder head has a neck joint allowing the head to turn by means of a cross bar. Doll has glass eyes, cloth body, leather hands. H. 19 inches H. of shoulder head, 4 inches. *Courtesy of Sylvia Brockmon.*

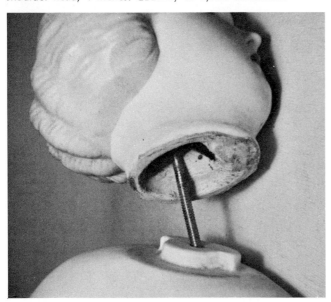

**894.** Untinted bisque shoulder head with the usual ball-and-socket type of neck joint for turning the head in any desired direction. Glass eyes, cloth body, bisque lower limbs, café-au-lait-colored molded hair. H. 18 inches. H. of shoulder head, 4 inches. *Courtesy of Jessica Norman.*

**895.** China shoulder head with glass eyes on fully articulated wooden body—jointed at wrists, ankles, and waist as well as at the usual places. H. 15 inches. *Courtesy of Sylvia Brockmon.*

The interest in dolls' joints began in America in the 1870's when *Charles Louis Parent*, Joel Ellis, *Wesley Miller*, and *Kimball Atwood* obtained U.S. patents. *Sarah Robinson* in 1883 patented a version of the pin joint to be used on cloth bodies, with thread taking the place of the pin and buttons used for the heads of the pins. (See Ill. 1392.)

The 1890's brought many refinements in making joints. Kid bodies had rivet-pin joints more often than gusset joints. Some of these were the patented *Ne Plus Ultra* type and others, after 1894, were patented *Universal Joints*. (See Ills. 542, 897.)

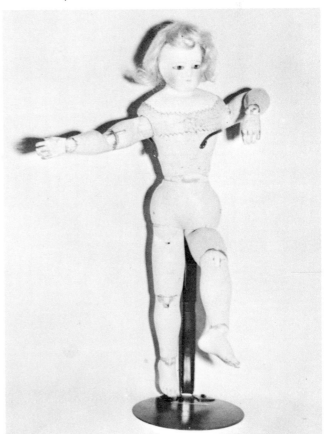

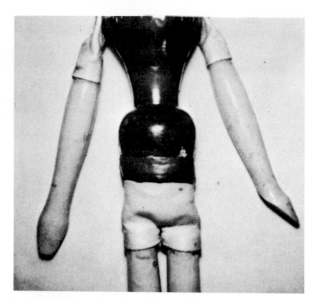

**896.** Leather-jointed red wooden torso found on dolls made in Central Europe in the late 19th century. *Courtesy of International Doll Library Foundation.*

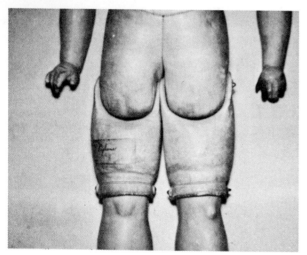

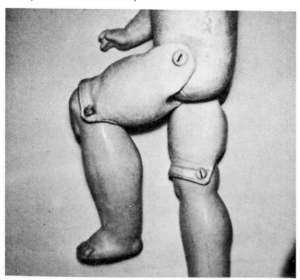

**897A & B.** "Universal" knee joints and "Ne Plus Ultra" hip joints, as used on a kid body with composition limbs. Doll has bisque head made by Armand Marseille. H. 23 inches. *Courtesy of Hildred Brinkley.*

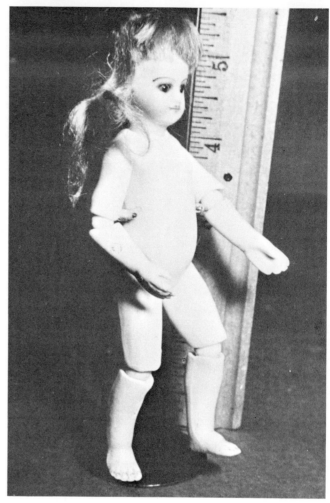

**898.** All-bisque doll with ball joints at elbows and knees. Doll has glass eyes and Rembrandt style wig. H. 5½ inches. *Courtesy of Margaret Whitton; photograph by Winnie Langley.*

**899.** Heubach bisque head with intaglio eyes and molded features. Note the molded pierced loop at the neck for stringing. Smaller heads often have a similar loop going from front to back rather than from side to side. H. of head, 3¾ inches. *Courtesy of Jessica Norman.*

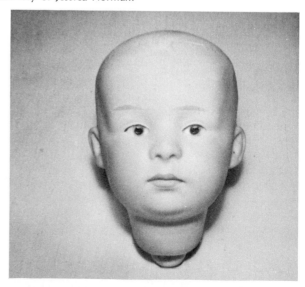

The pin and two disk-type joints were used on American cloth bodies in the 20th century. During World War I, the *Mama Dolls* achieved popularity with swinging joints on cloth bodies, which enabled them to "walk."

A detailed study of the patents for joints is beyond the scope of this work, but a few types need special mention—spring joints, wire frame joints, flange-type joints, and (most important of all) cord, especially elastic cord, to hold joints together. According to PLAYTHINGS, January, 1904, dolls with movable limbs strung together with cords drawn through the joints were first developed in Sonneberg, but the idea originally came from China. The first ones "were rough and crude but were forerunners of one of the greatest advances in the doll trade."

**Joli Bébé.** 1910–14. Trademark registered in France by Jules and Charles Damerval for doll made by *Damerval Frères & Laffranchy.*

**Joli Guy.** 1919. Trademark registered in France by *Messrs. Laquionie & Cie.,* Société des Grands Magasins du *Printemps.*

**Joliet, Nicholas.** 1867. Obtained a French patent for a doll or bébé with two faces, one of which was hidden by the adjustable hair. The limbs of the doll moved into various positions by hidden joints.

**Jollichose Dolls.** 1920. Stuffed dolls made by *E. Goldberger;* 15-inch size cost $1.00.

**Jolly Jack.** 1912–13. Character baby boy with composition head, molded hair, stuffed body, dressed in checked gingham rompers; size 8 inches.

**Jolly Jumps.** 1912. Boy doll with composition head made by *Elektra Toy & Novelty Co.*

**Jolly Kids.** 1913. Dolls with flirting eyes distributed by *Borgfeldt;* price 25¢ and up.

**Jolly Roger, The.** 1923–25. Trademark registered in U.S. by *Margaret Vale.* (See also **Carroll McComas.**)

**Jomin, Mme. A.** Before 1925, Paris; 1925, successor was J. Launay. Handled heads and wigs and repaired dolls.

**Jones, Edward Hazell.** 1920. Snaresbrook, Essex. Registered in Britain *Goo-Goo* and *Giggly* as two trademarks.

**Jones, Richard William.** 1853–65. London. Made wooden dolls.

**Jones, Robert.** 1838–48. London. Made wooden dolls. Henry Jones was listed at the same address (1852–55) as Robert Jones, and he also made wooden dolls.

**Jones, S., & Co.** 1881. London. Made dolls.

**Jones, William Henry.** 1920. London. Registered *Flopsie* as a trademark in Britain.

**Jones Manufacturing Co.** 1920–21. Attleboro, Mass. Made crying babies, sleeping dolls, and walking dolls that were 12 inches high.

**Jones-Moran Doll Manufacturing Co.** See **Moran Doll Manufacturing Co.**

**Jonnie Jingles Co., The.** 1918–20. New York City. Charles A. Goldsmith registered in the U.S. "Jonnie Jingles" as the trademark for dolls of this company.

**Jordan, Kate.** 1914–20. German citizen residing in New York City. She copyrighted the *Happifat* girl and boy, which were made into dolls. Both *Borgfeldt* and *Louis Amberg & Son* produced Happifat dolls.

**Jouany & Fay.** 1885–89. Paris. Made dolls.

**Jouet Artistique.** See **Le Jouet Artistique.**

**Joujou Pneu.** See **Le Joujou Pneu.**

**Jourlait.** 1892. Secured a French patent for making dolls' heads of celluloid without soldering them.

**Joy.** 1912. Doll made by *Seligman & Braun* under special license of T. E. Powers, cartoonist of the NEW YORK AMERICAN. Had round eyes, iris in the center; price $8.00 doz. wholesale.

**Joy Doll Corp.** 1920–21. New York City. Made wood fiber dolls, dolls' heads, and limbs. Dolls came with painted or sleeping eyes, with or without wigs.

**Joy-Toies.** 1920. Dolls with celluloid heads and cloth bodies made by *Sig. Schwartz Co.*

**Jubilee.** 1905–24. Line of jointed character babies, handled by *Strobel & Wilken.*

1909: Smiling babies with jointed composition arms, including jointed wrists; wore long dresses and baby bonnets.

1912: Bisque-head baby; head could turn in any direction, even up and down. Came with sorrowful face and crying voice, small red tongue that "wagged" whenever the doll was moved; sleeping eyes.

1914: Line included character dolls with pyroxylin heads and imported crying character dolls.

**Judge, Edward S.** 1867–78. Baltimore, Md., and Philadelphia, Pa. Made papier-mâché dolls' heads. In the 1870's, he operated as E. S. Judge & Co.

1868: He obtained a U.S. patent for producing an extra surface on papier-mâché by coating the surface of the mold with glue and whiting. Dolls' heads bear the following inscriptions:

JUDGE'S PATENT INDESTRUCTIBLE DOLL HEAD, No. 3
March 24th, 1868
and
JUDGE & EARLY, No. 5, Patd. July 27, 1875

The 1875 U.S. patent issued to Judge was for the manufacture of dolls' heads in papier-mâché.

**Jugele, Léon.** 1843–44. Paris. Made dolls.

**Jügelt, Walter.** 1924–25. Neustadt near Coburg, Thür. Manufactured dressed dolls, baby dolls, and soft-bodied dolls.

**Jullien.** 1863–1904. Paris. Prior to 1875, Jullien was listed under "Bimbeloterie" in the directories along with known doll makers.

1875: Jullien, Jeune (Jr.), advertised that he made dressed

**900.** Judge & Early papier-mâché head has molded blonde hair with long curls down onto the shoulders in back, painted eyes, pierced ears. Mark: Ill. **902.** *Courtesy of Louise Lund; photograph by Winnie Langley.*

**901.** Papier-mâché head marked "E. S. Judge // 1875"; molded black hair, painted eyes; brown kid hands. *Courtesy of Winnie Langley; photograph by Winnie Langley.*

**902.** Mark found on Edward Judge doll.

```
JUDGE & EARLY
     N. 2
Pat'd July 27, 1875
```

bébés, dolls called *Mignonettes* of *nankeen,* dolls called *Zouaves* (soldiers), and dolls called *Marottes.*

1879: Advertised dressed dolls, bébés, nankeen dolls, and bathers.

1885: Advertised dressed indestructible bébés, deluxe and ordinary; dolls included ladies, young girls, brides, and peasants with stationary or turning heads; also jointed dolls and indestructible bébés with trousseaux; bathers, swimmers, and fishermen made to bathe in the sea.

1889: Jullien was foreman of the jury at the Paris Exposition.

1892: Jullien, Jr., advertised *L'Universel,* a Paris-made indestructible bébé with the latest perfections, made in four models: No. 1, rigid; No. 2, jointed; No. 3, with jointed wrists and talking; No. 4, not described. Dolls were described as "richly dressed," "less richly dressed," and "in ordinary dress."

1895: Advertisement further described L'Universel as having limbs of hollow wood and being the lightest and most solid bébé made up to now. This bébé walked and talked, and had teeth and sleeping eyes. Mignonettes were also advertised.

**903.** Bisque head is marked "Jullien"; size "5." Glass eyes, pierced ears, open mouth with six upper teeth; jointed composition and wood body; original provincial costume. H. 18½ inches. *Courtesy of Joyce Alexander.*

**904.** Jullien's mark on dolls' heads.

JuLLieN
1 ·

1900: Jullien, Jr., won a bronze medal for his doll exhibit at the Paris Exposition, and advertised that his bébé also bowed.

Ca. 1904: Jullien became a member of the *Société Française de Fabrication de Bébés et Jouets.*

**Jumbo.** 1914. Trade name of baby doll made by *EFFanBEE*; price $5.00.

**Jumeau.** 1842–99, Paris and Montreuil-sous-Bois; 1899–1925, *Société Française de Fabrication de Bébés et Jouets;* 1842–ca. 77, Pierre François Jumeau; ca. 1877–99, Emile Jumeau. Had one of the largest doll-making establishments in the world. Statements have been made that the Jumeau firm was established earlier than 1842, but no verification has been found. In 1888, on the U.S. trademark application, Emile Jumeau stated that the trademark *Bébé Jumeau* had been in use since 1840. Although this is an official document, there is no other evidence of any French bébés being made as early as this.

In 1842 *Belton* & Jumeau were listed as makers of kid dolls and dressed dolls at 14 rue Salle au Comte in Paris. The account of the Jumeau factory given in PEARSON'S MAGAZINE, July, 1897, said that their dolls in 1843 were "all made of sheepskin stuffed with sawdust and with china heads."

At the 1844 Paris Exposition of French Industry, Belton & Jumeau received Honorable Mention for their exhibit. From 1847 to 1867, Jumeau was listed alone as a doll maker at 18 rue Mauconseil. At Paris in 1849, Jumeau won a bronze medal. In 1851 at the Great Exhibition in London, Pierre Jumeau exhibited dolls and doll's wardrobes. Here Jumeau was awarded a prize medal for dolls' dresses; the report of the Jury reads: "The dolls on which these dresses are displayed present no point worthy of commendation but the dresses themselves are very beautiful." Again Jumeau exhibited dressed and undressed dolls at the 1855 Paris Exposition and the 1862 London Exhibition, and won prize medals at both places.

Jumeau, in the 1859 Paris Directory, advertised kid-body dolls, undressed and dressed in all kinds of attire, and articulated dolls with porcelain heads. It should be noted that Jumeau did not advertise bébés, although other companies were advertising them at this time. Between 1861 and 1876 Jumeau advertisements included talking bébés. In 1865 came another new item, namely "carved dolls with porcelain heads." These were probably the wooden-bodied Jumeau dolls, which were advertised through 1885. Jumeau still made "kid body dolls dressed and undressed in all varieties and doll dresses for jointed dolls."

At the Paris Exposition of 1867, Jumeau of rue d'Anjou-Marais, where he must have recently moved, received a silver medal for his exhibition of dolls, dolls' lingerie, dolls' dresses, and dolls' heads. This is one of the first times that French dolls' heads are mentioned, but the type of material is not given. Singleton's DOLLS, pp. 58–59, quotes an undated and unnamed "French authority" as saying. "In the first models the head and bust was [sic] of a single piece. . . . One day the inventor's [Pierre Jumeau's] eldest son thought of an improvement which would give the head an ingenious articulation. By this means the head could be moved in any direction, up and down and round and round." The "one day" was in 1862 or later. However, Mademoiselle *Huret* had already applied for her patents for a swivel-neck dolls' head in 1861, which indicates that this invention has been wrongly ascribed to Jumeau's son.

This same "French authority" said, "Pink kid is used only for common dolls," but an examination of kid-bodied dolls discloses that many fine early ones had pink kid bodies; in fact, white kid bodies were usually on the more common dolls until the era of the fashionable lady dolls.

The 1873 Jumeau advertisement was the same as that carried in the last half of the 1860's, but with the important addition that their specialty was porcelain dolls' heads made at Montreuil-sous-Bois. The French Report

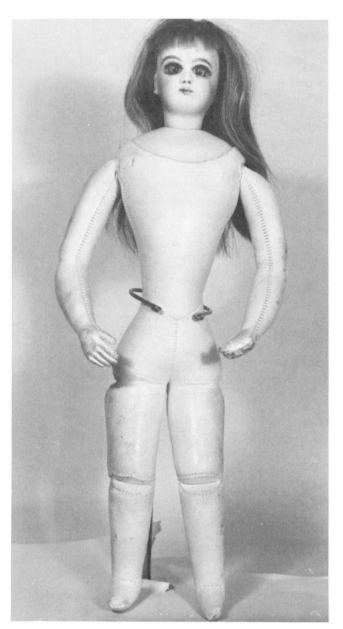

**906A & B.** Lady doll with bisque head and shoulder plate, swivel neck, glass eyes, and wig; head is marked "6" and with red symbols. Gusset-jointed kid body mark: Ill **918**. H. 16½ inches. *Courtesy of Eunice Althouse.*

**905.** Lady doll with bisque head and shoulder plate, large glass eyes. Head marked "3" and with a red "v." Kid gusset-jointed body marked JUMEAU // MEDAILLE D'OR // PARIS. The mark indicates that the doll was made in 1878 or later. H. 13 inches. *Courtesy of Pat Robinson, Lakeland, Mich.*

on the 1873 Vienna Exhibition devotes several paragraphs to Jumeau, as follows: "M. Jumeau of Paris, the first and the most important doll-making house, has freed us from our former obligation to have the foreigner furnish us with porcelain doll heads.

"M. Jumeau has established at Montreuil, near Paris, a factory where he makes doll heads of enameled porcelain with the greatest perfection. He has surpassed in beauty the products that we used to buy from Saxony.

"The Exhibit of M. Jumeau at Vienna was splendid, and Viennese merchants were impressed by the good prices at which they could purchase his products.

"They rendered justice to M. Jumeau when they congratulated him on his beautiful product and awarded him unanimously the Medal of Progress."

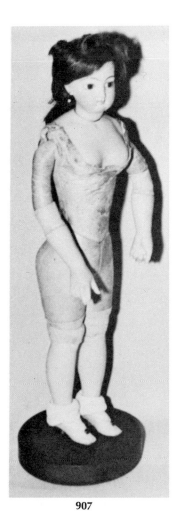

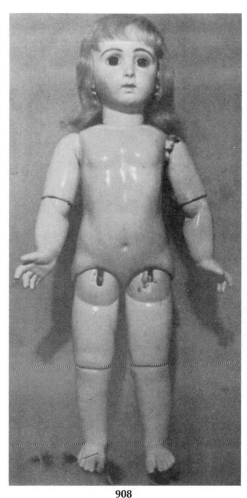

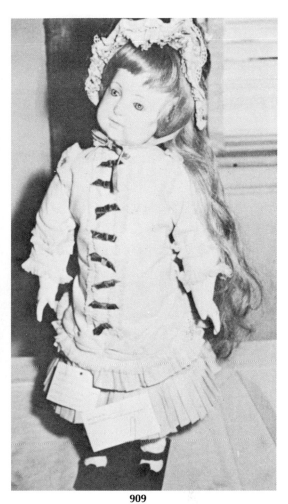

907          908          909

**907.** Lady doll with bisque head, shoulder plate, and lower limbs. Note the molded bosom and molded heeled shoes over which fabrics have been placed. Mark on body: Ill. **918.** H. 17 inches. H. of shoulder head, 5 inches. *Courtesy of Eunice Althouse.*

**908.** Bébé Jumeau with bisque head and jointed composition body. This type of doll is sometimes called a "long-faced Jumeau." The head is not marked Jumeau, but the body has the familiar JUMEAU MEDAILLE D'OR stamp. These dolls may have been among the early Bébés Jumeau. H. 32 inches. *Courtesy of Hazel Ulseth.*

**909.** Composition head on ball-jointed composition body. Longhand writing on top of the bald head reads "2nd Model // Jumeau // 1877." Since the 7's are not written 7, it is likely that the notation was made by someone outside of Continental Europe. *Photograph by Winnie Langley.*

At the Vienna Exhibition, Jumeau also won a gold medal, and a medal of cooperation went to four representatives of the Maison P. F. Jumeau, namely Emile Jumeau, Madame Blanche *Pannier*, Mademoiselle Elisa Cadet, and Oscar Rinders. This report of the 1873 exhibition suggests that few French porcelain dolls' heads were made prior to the 1870 war with Germany. The 1873 exhibition report described the Jumeau doll heads as being made of "enameled porcelain," which seems to mean glazed china rather than bisque.

At the Philadelphia Exhibition of 1876, P. F. Jumeau won a gold medal for his display of "Doll's heads and bodies. A fine collection dressed in a most fashionable style; heads of the finest imitation, superior taste and excellent workmanship in mechanical construction." Jumeau is the only French doll maker for whom a record has been found at this important American exhibition.

Between 1876 and 1878, Pierre François Jumeau retired and Emile Jumeau, whose influence had already been felt, brought the firm to its zenith. In the 1878 Paris Exposition E. L. Jumeau won the gold medal for his dolls and bébés over other French competitors such as *Bru, Steiner, Gaultier,* and *Schmitt.* It should be emphasized that dolls marked "Medaille d'Or 1878" were not necessarily made in 1878 but could have been made some years later. In 1879, in Sydney, Australia, Jumeau

## JUMEAU DOLLS

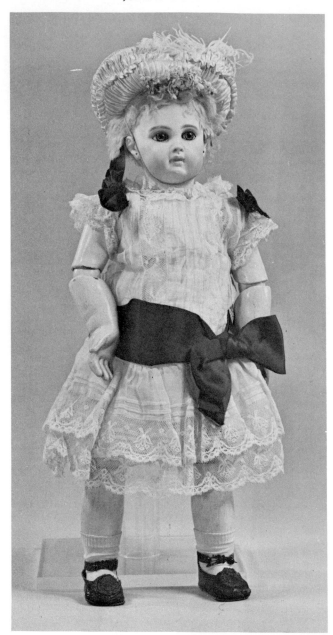

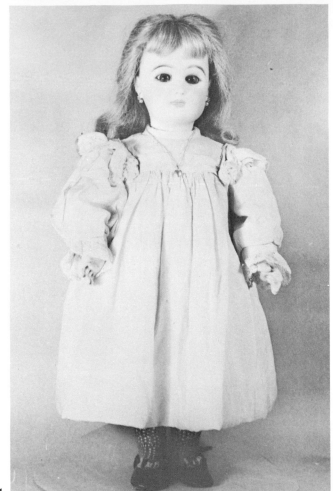

911

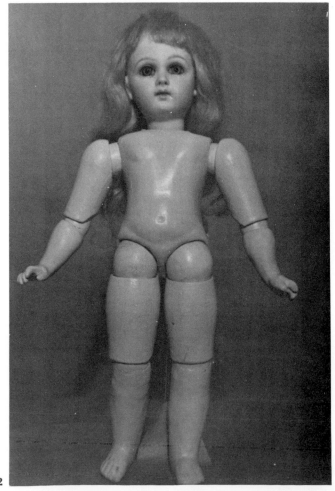

912

**910.** Bébé Jumeau purchased in Paris, with a wardrobe, in the late 19th century. Bisque head, marked "E. J." size "8," has glass eyes, pierced and applied ears; body is jointed composition. Doll wears her original outfit of white lawn dress with maroon ribbons, satin and straw hat. Shoes marked E. JUMEAU, MEDAILLE D'OR. H. 22 inches. *Courtesy of The Smithsonian Institution.*

**911.** Tête Jumeau bisque head on jointed composition body. Mark: Ill. **919,** except that the size is 8 instead of 6. H. 19½ inches. *Courtesy of Hazel Ulseth.*

**912.** Bébé Jumeau with unusual short-torso body. Shoulder and hip joints are different from those generally found on Jumeau bodies. Head is marked "Déposé" and the size "2"; body is marked "Jumeau." H. 12 inches. *Courtesy of Hazel Ulseth.*

again won the gold medal. There his dolls were described as "Artistically made and elegant in style." In 1880 at Melbourne, Jumeau won the gold medal for his dolls and bébés, and at this exhibition he also won a bronze medal for his mechanical toys. At New Orleans in 1884 and Paris in 1885, Jumeau won gold medals. At Antwerp in 1885 he was awarded the Diploma of Honor. In 1885 at Paris, Jumeau's superiority was, for the first time, challenged by Bru, who also received a gold medal.

In the Paris Directories available here in America, the term *bébé incassable* appeared for the first time in the 1879 directory. Bébé Jumeau appeared under "Bébés Incassables," and Jumeau stated in his 1885 advertisement that Bébé Jumeau was put on the market only in 1879. In 1881 Jumeau made the important statement, "Tous marques à son nom" [all marked with his name].

The London Directory of 1881 lists Jumeau as doll maker with a London address, but this is the only year when he appears to have had a branch outside France.

No patents have been found for Pierre François Jumeau, but Emile obtained several patents. In 1882 he and Bru jointly obtained a French patent for a mechanical boat. In 1885 Emile Jumeau obtained a French patent for making eyelids drop over the eyeball instead of having them move together. Apparently he had trouble with the space left after the eyelid moved up, for in 1886 he obtained another French patent to eliminate this space. In 1886 he obtained a patent for making dolls of a so-called unbreakable material. In 1887 he obtained another patent for sleeping dolls' eyes, this time including eyelashes. These eyes were patented both in France and Germany.

Emile Jumeau registered his trademark "Bébé Jumeau" in France in 1886 and in the United States in 1888. In 1886 he also registered *Bébé Prodige,* and in 1896 *Bébé Français.*

*Carrier Belleuse,* master sculptor and artist at the *Sèvres* porcelain factory, prior to his death in 1887, is believed to have designed some Jumeau bébés.

At the Paris Exposition of 1889, Jumeau was a member of the Jury and Hors Concours, but his exhibit far overshadowed that of Steiner, who won the gold medal. The official United States report on this exhibition said of the large central exhibit of Mons. Emile Jumeau: "It contained large numbers of babies (the name given to the modern doll) of the most incredible richness in every position and so intelligent. These are French dolls unmistakably. The heads are of Sèvres porcelain painted by real artists and having luxuriant and silky hair. Their hats seem worthy of Linn or Virot and their dresses are in the latest fashion and made of rich Lyons silk of the latest style. Perhaps even they have set the fashion sometimes; if so, the best dressmakers of the day need not be ashamed. Little girls could not leave the spot, they were so fascinated."

A letter from Mons. Bauduy, Director, Manufacture Nationale de Sèvres, dated November 5, 1962, reads: "It is not impossible that heads were made here at Sèvres at the time of the Universal Exposition of 1889, since, in order to render service to industry, studies of

**913A & B.** Bébé Jumeau. Mark on the head in red: Ill. **920.** Mark on the body in green: Ill. **921.** Doll has brown stationary eyes; wears a chemise of white lawn and imitation Cluny lace, which probably is original. H. 21 inches. *Courtesy of Alberta Darby.*

the best technical processes for the manufacture of doll heads were at one time made in our experimental laboratories."

According to tradition, Buffalo Bill (William Cody) purchased a Jumeau doll when he visited Europe in 1887. This was the so-called "long-face" or "Cody" Jumeau,

(See Ill. 908), a doll that came with closed mouth, stationary eyes, a face longer than that of the usual bébés; it was marked on the head with only a number and on the body with a Jumeau mark. A sufficiently large sampling of these "long face" Jumeaus has not been studied as yet to draw definite conclusions, but from the relatively few examined, the sizes seem to fit into the general Jumeau size pattern. However, it must be remembered that the dolls marked "C.P." and a few other French dolls also appear to fit into this general pattern, which is roughly as follows:

| Size No. | Height in Inches |
|----------|------------------|
| 6 | 15 |
| 7 | 17 |
| 8 | 19 |
| 9 | 20½ |
| 10 | 22 |
| 11 | 24 |
| 12 | 26 |
| 13 | 28 |
| 14 | 30 |

Not all Jumeau dolls fit this pattern.

During the 1890's, Jumeau had to seek quantity production in place of quality. His advertisement stated that in 1881 he had made 85,000 bébés; in 1883—115,000 bébés, and in 1884—220,000 bébés. In an account of an 1897 visit to the Jumeau factory the following statement appeared: "There are seventeen sizes of heads in all; from six to seven hundred of each size are manufactured every day." This would mean between three and four million dolls' heads a year, a tremendous increase but one readily explained by the Jumeau advertisement of 1892: "Notice of Change: The Maison makes two new models of indestructible jointed bébés undressed and dressed with differences in price of 20 percent and 40 percent, but with the same irreproachable quality remaining and not carrying the Jumeau name. Complete change of articles in the Maison Jumeau.

"The Maison Jumeau is not connected with any supplier and itself produces all the articles which it sells: heads, human eyes, wigs, composition bodies, lingerie, bonnets, footwear, all of superior quality and the latest style, and even their boxes and packing cases—in a word, all that comprises a complete product; this is also important in order for the dealer to obtain the highest profit."

Further reductions in price were indicated in 1895 when the advertisement read: "The Maison makes three new models of indestructible jointed bébés, dressed and undressed; without mark, with a difference of 40 to 60 percent.

"New creations, Bébé Phonographe, Bébé Marcheur [walking]. Examine the marks."

Doll collectors have often referred to so-called "early unmarked Jumeau bébés," but apparently there were a great many of these unmarked ones made during the 1890's.

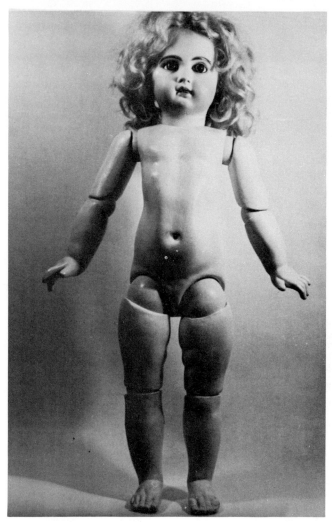

**914.** Bébé Jumeau. Note the anatomical detail in the body molding. H. 24 inches. *Courtesy of Pat Robinson, Lakeland, Mich.*

Emile Jumeau registered in 1891 a French trademark to be stamped on Jumeau shoes. This trademark was renewed by the Société Française de Fabrication de Bébés et Jouets (S. F. B. J.) in 1906. *Bébé Français* was registered in France in 1896 by Emile Jumeau.

Jumeau exhibited dolls at the World's Fair in Chicago in 1893, but it is not known what award he received there.

In 1896 Jumeau obtained a French patent for movable dolls' eyes. This seems to be the last official record, other than directories and the 1897 visit to the Jumeau factory, found for the Jumeau firm before it merged with other doll makers in the Société Française de Fabrication de Bébés et Jouets in 1899. The Paris Directory lists the S. F. B. J. at 8 rue Pastourelle, which had formerly been the Jumeau address.

In the account of the 1897 visit, Emile Douillet was

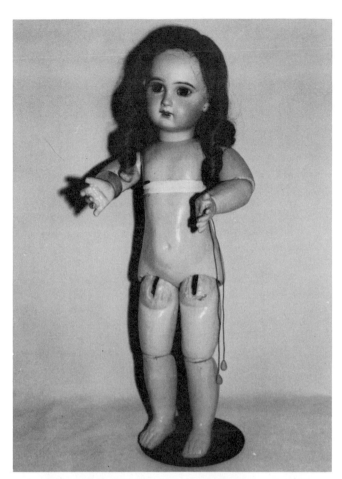

916. Jumeau bébé in original dress; original box is dated 1890, with the label written in Spanish for distribution in Spain. Mark on head: Ill. **919** except for "1" and red marks. H. 16 inches. *Courtesy of the International Doll Library Foundation.*

917. Jumeau bébé with flirting brown eyes wears contemporary printed dress. *Courtesy of Frances Walker; photograph by Winnie Langley.*

915A & B. Talking Bébé with pull-strings, one pink and one blue, to indicate "Mama" and "Papa"; voice box is marked "Jumeau." Head mark: Ill. **922** plus size "10" and some red marks. Body mark: Ill. **923**. H. 22 inches. *Coleman Collection.*

named as a partner of Emile Jumeau. Dolls resembling Jumeau bébés, with the little black check marks, have been found with the bisque head incised "E D." Thus, some of the unidentified "E D" marks might stand for Emile Douillet.

There are at least four published accounts of visits to the Jumeau factory. All mention that the larger heads had applied ears and the smaller ones molded ears. In 1885, Jumeau obtained a patent for movable eyes that could be worked by a spring so that in the future Bébé Jumeau would sleep, but by 1897 the familiar counterweight sleep eyes were being used.

In 1885 the method of making dolls' heads by applying the clay paste onto a mold is described for the Jumeau factory. This method would generally make a thicker head that was rougher on the inside than the heads made later by pouring slip—a fact that may help in the dating of dolls' heads.

Dolls have been found marked "J." According to Mons. Moynot, formerly president of the Maison Jumeau, they used the "J" mark until about 1875 (DOLL NEWS, February, 1964). Probably this "J" was used up until Emile Jumeau became head of the firm in the second half of the 1870's, but there is a question as to the authenticity of some of the dolls marked with a "J" (see SPINNING WHEEL, January–February, 1964.)

The Jumeau name was carried on by the group of doll manufacturers comprising the S. F. B. J. after 1899. No doubt in some cases they used molds created earlier by Emile Jumeau.

**Juncker, F.** 1909. Frankfurt am Main, Hesse-Nassau. Manufactured dolls.

**June Caprice.** 1921. Portrait doll representing the Pathé picture star of this name; designed by *Muriel Knight.*

**Jung, Jacob.** 1912. Mannheim, Germany. Registered in Germany his trademark of a stork carrying a baby doll; used for celluloid dolls.

JUMEAU
MEDAILLE D'OR
PARIS
918

DÉPOSÉ
TETE JUMEAU
B^TE SGDG
6
919

DÉPOSE
TÊTE JUMEAU
᪲
920

BÉBÉ JUMEAU
DIPLÔME d'HONNEUR
921

BREVETE. S.GDG
JUMEAU
922

JUMEAU
MEDAILLE D'OR
PARIS
923

DÉPOSÉ
E. 7 J.
924

∧ H₇
7
JUMEAU
PARIS
925

✓
926

918–926. Marks found on Jumeau dolls. Nos. **918, 921,** and **923** are found stamped on bodies; the other marks are found on heads. Mark No. **926** and part of **925** represent types of marks found in red or black and usually associated with Jumeau.

**Juno.** 1904–25+. Metal or celluloid dolls' heads made by *Karl Standfuss;* distributed by *Borgfeldt,* who registered the name as a trademark in the U.S.

**927A & B.** Juno metal head made by Karl Standfuss has painted and molded features. Mark on chest: Ill. **928.** H. 19 inches. H. of shoulder head, 4½ inches. *Coleman Collection.*

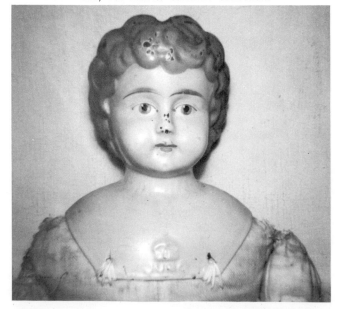

**928.** "Juno" mark found on dolls of Karl Standfuss.

**Just Born.** 1925. Infant doll made by *Gem Toy Co.;* distributed by *Reisman, Barron & Co.* Came in sizes 15, 17, and 21 inches; price $1.00 to $3.00.

**Juszko, Jeno.** 1911–20. New York City. Native of Hungary; a sculptor and medalist of note as well as a doll artist. *Louis Amberg & Son* named Juszko as the artist of sixteen of their copyrighted dolls.

1911–15: These dolls included *Baby Bright Eyes, Baby Glee, New Born Babe, Sis Hopkins,* and others.

1919–20: Juszko designed *Evaline,* copyrighted by *F. W. Lapp,* as well as several dolls for *Borgfeldt.* These included Lotta Sun, *Winkie,* and Poutie; although called dolls on the copyright papers, they were actually more like figurines.

1925: Designed *Jackie Coogan* doll for Borgfeldt.

**Jutta.** 1906–21. Line of dolls produced by *Cuno & Otto Dressel,* who registered the name in Germany as a trademark. Jutta dolls had jointed composition bodies and bisque heads. *Simon & Halbig* were among the makers of the bisque heads for Jutta dolls.

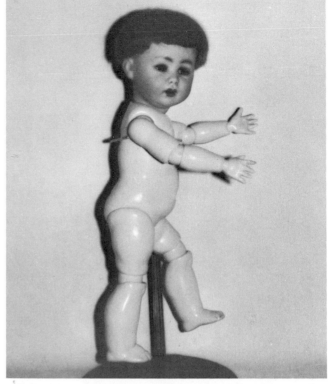

**929A & B.** "Jutta," line of dolls produced by Cuno & Otto Dressel. Doll shown has sleeping eyes, hair eyelashes, open mouth with five teeth; toddler-type jointed composition body. Mark on head: Ill. **930.** H. 16 inches. *Courtesy of Dorothy Annunziato.*

## K

**K & K Toy Co.** 1915–25+. New York City. Made dolls for *Borgfeldt;* among them were *Flossie Fisher's Own Doll, Kewpies, Hollikids, Happifats,* and *Bye-lo Baby.*

1918: Dolls advertised as having washable heads and hands, painted features, mohair wigs in blonde, tosca, or brunette, or long-curl human hair wigs; cork-stuffed bodies. Sizes 13½, 15, 17, 18, and 19 inches, prices $8.75 to $40.00 doz. wholesale.

1924: Advertised "K and K means Kept Klean." The K's probably stood for George Kolb and Fred Kolb, or Kahle and Kolb.

Soon after 1925, the *Cameo Doll Co.* took over the products formerly made by K & K Toy Co.

**K K K.** 1912–13. Trademark registered by *Parsons-Jackson Co.* in U.S. for dolls.

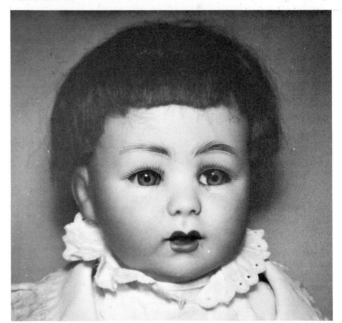

**930–932.** "Jutta" marks on dolls produced by Cuno & Otto Dressel.

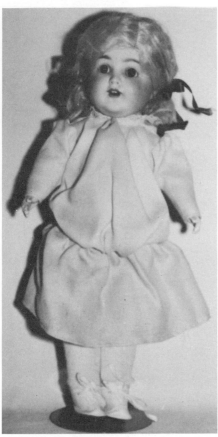

*Germany*
*K & K*
*45*
*Thuringia*

934

*K & K*
*56*
*Made in Germany*

935

*Germany*
*K & K*
*60*
*Thuringia*

936

**933.** Doll made by K & K Toy Co. has bisque head, sleeping glass eyes, open mouth with two teeth; cloth body with composition hands and leatherette legs. Mark: Ill. **934.** H. 17 inches. *Courtesy of Jessica Norman.*

**934–936.** Marks used on dolls made by K & K Toy Co.

**Kaempfer, Joseph G.** Before 1912–25+. New York City. He was associated with several doll companies; before 1912, with *New Toy Co.;* 1912–17+, with *Tip Top Toy Co.;* 1924–25, with *Baby Phyllis Doll Co.;* 1925+, *Simplex Stuffed Toy Manufacturing Co.* According to PLAYTHINGS, Mrs. Kaempfer, his wife, was famous all over the world for her unique and original styles for dolls. She designed dolls' clothes. In 1913, Kaempfer obtained a U.S. design patent for a doll's head with round eyes, open mouth, and a "look of amazement."

1925: Advertised a line of *Baby Phyllis Mama Dolls.*

**Kaempff, F.** 1911–14. Jersey City, N.J. Made rag dolls with lithographed or celluloid faces; distributed by *Strobel & Wilken* and *A. S. Ferguson Co.* Dolls included Alice, dressed as a Quaker; price 25¢ and 50¢.

**Kaeselau, Marguerite.** 1921. Provincetown, Mass. Was granted a U.S. design patent for a bald and bewhiskered rag doll with a seam down the center of the face.

**Kago Doll Co.** 1921. Maspeth, N.Y. Made wood-pulp composition dolls in sizes 9, 12½, 14, and 18 inches.

**Kahler, Edward L.** 1913–14. Milwaukee, Wis. Obtained

U.S. patent for improvement in stringing dolls by using wire hooks with several coils to distribute the tension where the hooks go over the elastic. Just above the hooks were loops to facilitate unhooking the hand or foot.

**Kahn, Albert.** 1920–24. New York City. Distributor; advertised *Kanko* dolls.

**Kahn, R.** See **Strassburger Puppen Manufaktur.**

**Kahn & Mossbacher.** 1907, New York City; 1914–21, successor, M. L. Kahn & Co., also in Philadelphia, Pa. Made dolls' outfits and distributed dolls.

**Kalbitz, Carl.** 1907–25+. Sonneberg, Thür. Made dolls, babies, *Mama Dolls,* and walking dolls.

*Copr. by*
*J. L. Kallus*
*Germany*
*1394/30*

**937.** Mark found on dolls designed by Joseph Kallus.

**Kallus, Joseph L.** 1912–25+. Designer and manufacturer. A native of Brooklyn, N.Y., he was granted an art scholarship to the Fine Arts College of Pratt Institute. One day in 1912 a notice was placed on the college bulletin board requesting interested young artists to appear for an interview with *Fred Kolb* of *Geo. Borgfeldt & Co.* They wanted an artist who could draw and sculpture children. Joseph Kallus qualified for the job, and was introduced to *Rose O'Neill.* He made some rough modeling sketches from Rose's drawings. It is the customary procedure for a designer of a prospective doll to obtain assistance in the rough casting and modeling; then the designer adds the finishing touches himself. The *Kewpie* models were handled in this manner by Kallus and Rose O'Neill working together, but with the final changes and approval made by Rose O'Neill. Fred Kolb and Rose O'Neill were delighted with Joseph Kallus' assistance on the Kewpie, and Fred Kolb kept him busy designing other dolls while he completed his studies at Pratt Institute in 1914 and also studied under the famous American painters Robert Henri, George Bridgman, William D. L. Dodge, and Frank Vincent Dumond during the years 1913 through 1916. It is believed that dolls designed by Joseph Kallus during this period prior to World War I are the bisque-head character dolls collectors find with the name "Kallus" incised on them.

Realizing the importance of art in designing dolls, and having a keen interest in the happiness of children, Joseph Kallus decided to use his talents in the designing and production of dolls. In 1916 he founded the *Rex Doll Co.,* which made composition dolls of a wood pulp, starch and rosin mixture in a hot-press process. These dolls were chiefly Kewpies made for Borgfeldt, who controlled all the Kewpie rights. With the consent of Geo. Borgfeldt & Co., some of the Kewpies made by Rex Doll Co. were distributed by *Tip Top Toy Co.* to carnivals. The Rex Company prospered, and at the beginning of 1918 Joseph Kallus obtained his first of many copyrights on doll designs. This was for the character doll named *Baby Bundie.* Shortly after this, in 1918, Joseph Kallus was inducted into the service. After the war, he returned to doll making.

1919–21: He was president of the *Mutual Doll Co.,* which made Kewpies, Baby Bundie dolls, and other dolls of the wood-pulp mixture by a hot-press process. During this time he designed *Bo-Fair,* which he considered one of his most artistic dolls. It represented a little Miss of about five. The special design of the socket joints was noted on the copyright for this doll. Joseph Kallus copyrighted two more dolls in 1921: *Dollie* and *Vanitie Doll.* For a few months in 1921, he worked with an associate in the corporation, but the arrangement did not work out and Kallus soon resigned.

1922: J. L. Kallus started the *Cameo Doll Co.,* and this company has been successfully guided by him as president ever since.

At one time Mr. Kallus helped *Hugo Baum* of *EFFanBEE* in a technical advisory capacity. Cameo made wood-pulp composition dolls, especially Kewpies for Borgfeldt to distribute, as well as introducing new dolls designed by Kallus. *Baby Bo Kaye* and *Little Annie Rooney* were made by Cameo before the end of 1925, but were not copyrighted until 1926. In 1925, Kallus obtained the first of his many U.S. patents. This pertained to the hip joints of the composition version of Little Annie Rooney. *Jack Collins* drew Little Annie Rooney for periodicals, and just as Kallus had helped Rose O'Neill in the making of a three-dimensional figure, he designed this three-dimensional doll. His name appears as the artist, together with that of Jack Collins, on the copyright paper. Two versions of Little Annie Rooney were made; one was all-bisque without leg joints, and the other was made by Cameo Doll Co. of the wood-pulp composition and had the patented leg joints.

Although absorbed in the making of dolls, Joseph Kallus still found time to paint portraits and other subjects, and to be a member of the Art League of New York. His works have been shown at various art exhibits.

**Kamkins (Kamkins Kiddies).** 1919–25+. Rag dolls made at the *Louise R. Kampes* Studios. These dolls were sold at a shop on the boardwalk and cost around $10.00 to $15.00 each. Both girl and boy dolls were made, and new outfits were designed for each season.

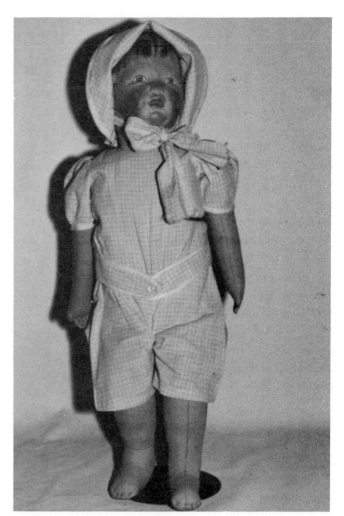

938A & B. "Kamkins," rag doll with molded mask face, made ca. 1920 by Louise Kampes. The hair is sewed in concentric circles. Mark on head: Ill. **939.** H. 19 inches. *Courtesy of Lester & Alice Grinnings.*

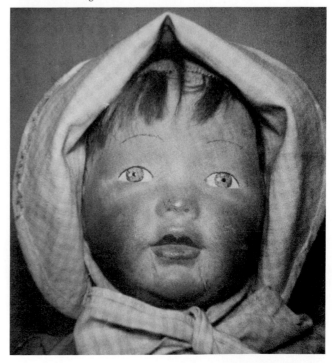

KAMKINS
A DOLLY MADE TO LOVE
PATENTED BY L.R. KAMPES
ATLANTIC CITY, N.J.

939. Mark on "Kamkin" dolls.

**Kämmer & Reinhardt.** 1886–1925+. Waltershausen, Thür. Made dolls, especially character dolls—at first probably with wooden heads and later with bisque heads usually produced by *Simon & Halbig* or celluloid heads produced by *Rheinische Gummi & Celluloid Fabrik Co.*

1893: Displayed dolls at the Chicago Exposition.

1895: Began use of the trademark "K [star] R" (see Ill. 954), which they registered later in U.S. and Germany for dolls.

1901: Applied for registration in Germany of two trademarks, *Mein Liebling (My Darling)* for dolls and dolls' heads and *Majestic Doll.* Obtained a German patent for a doll's head with moving eyes and eyelids. Ernst Kämmer, the modeler and creator of their dolls, died, and his place was taken by Karl Krauser. According to RESEARCH ON KAMMER AND REINHARDT DOLLS by Patricia Schoonmaker, "Kämmer was credited with many firsts: putting in teeth, oval wooden joints, stiff joints in which there was little separation when the doll was placed in sitting position, wooden character heads, bathing dolls with movable arms, and eyelashes."

1903: Registered in Germany two trademarks; the one for walking dolls can be translated as "My little doll can stand, can sit and walk, can hereby turn the head, a sweet thing, my darling." The other trademark, on a shield, translated, reads "My little doll is a sweet thing, My Darling." Obtained two German patents, one for moving dolls' eyes and the other for a celluloid doll's head with sleeping eyes.

1904: Obtained another German patent for moving eyes.

1906: Registered in England and in Germany the trademark of a shield with "Jointed Doll // My Darling // K [star] R" on it, to be used for dolls and doll parts of various types.

1907: Registered in Germany *Die Kokette* (The Coquette) as a trademark for dolls.

1908: Registered two trademarks in Germany, *The Flirt* and *Der Schelm* (The Rascal). *Strobel & Wilken,* distributors, advertised their *Royal Line* made by Kämmer & Reinhardt, including a new doll, The Flirt, with eyes that moved sideways as well as slept.

1909: Registered as a trademark in Germany, *Charakterpuppe* (Character Doll) for dolls and parts of dolls. Kämmer & Reinhardt stated, "We had carried on for twenty-three years and had brought out our one model and influenced the market with it." This suggests that prior to 1909 they had just used a single dolly-faced mold for most of their dolls. In 1909 they brought out the character dolls, which included *Baby* (#100), *Peter* and *Marie* (#101), and others. *Borgfeldt,* distributor, advertised Kämmer & Reinhardt's Playmate jointed dolls and the Flirt. Borgfeldt used *My Playmate* as a trademark, registered in Germany in 1903. "Baby" appears to have been one of the earliest, if not the earliest, bent-limb baby doll. It seems to be the first one advertised in PLAYTHINGS. The character dolls were allegedly

**940.** "Baby," mold #100, has painted eyes; ball-jointed composition body, which is allegedly original. The 1911 Lindner advertisement (Ill. **1099**) shows that baby heads were used on this type of body. *Courtesy of Winnie Langley; photograph by Winnie Langley.*

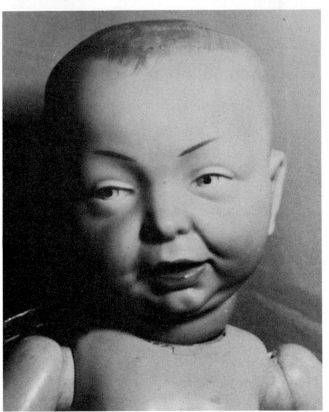

modeled from life by artists, and were generally named for the children who posed for them.

1910: Additional character dolls were produced, including *Carl* (#107), *Elsie* (#109), *Hans* and *Gretchen* (#114), *Elsa* and *Walter.* Baby (#100) was advertised by *Butler Bros.* in sizes 11 inches for 75¢ and 14½ inches for $1.50.

1911: Registered in Germany *Mein Kleines* (My Little Ones) as a trademark for dolls and doll parts.

1913: Obtained a German patent for doll's eyeballs with two pupils on them (probably to change color of the eye). Franz Reinhardt and Gottlieb Nüssle registered "K [star] R" as a trademark in U.S.

1915: Registered in Germany *Der Unart* (The Naughty One) as a trademark for dolls of all kinds. Obtained another German patent for moving eyes.

1916: Obtained a German patent for sleeping eyes.

1917: Obtained a German patent for sleeping eyes.

1920: Registered in Germany and in Britain *Naughty* as a trademark for dolls. Mold #126, one of the most frequently found character dolls made by Kämmer & Reinhardt, was on the market by 1920.

# Character Dolls

**TAKEN FROM LIFE**

**TRUE TO LIFE**

## The Strobel and Wilken Co.

**591 Broadway, NEW YORK**

Chicago Office
240 ADAMS STREET

Kindly Mention PLAYTHINGS When Writing to Advertisers.

**941.** A 1910 advertisement for dolls made by Kämmer & Reinhardt and distributed by Strobel & Wilken Co. For pictures of "Baby" and "Marie," see Ills. **940, 942.** *Courtesy of McCready Publishing Co.*

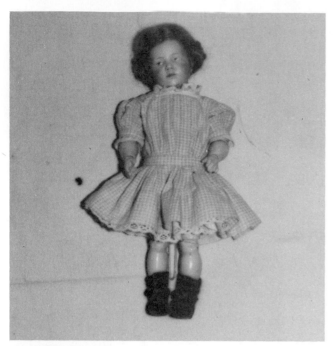

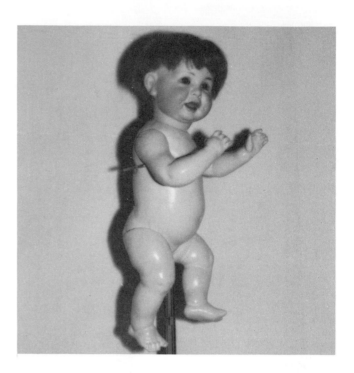

**942A & B.** "Marie," Kämmer & Reinhardt model #101: bisque head with gray-blue painted eyes, closed mouth, hair in braids around the ears; ball-jointed composition body; contemporary checked dress trimmed with lace. H. 12 inches. *Courtesy of Bess Goldfinger.*

**943A & B.** Character baby, mold #116A, has sleeping eyes, open-closed mouth, dimples. Mark: Ill. **952.** H. 13 inches. *Courtesy of Dorothy Annunziato.*

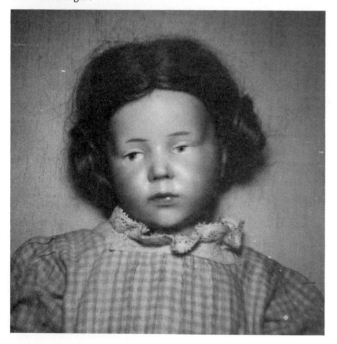

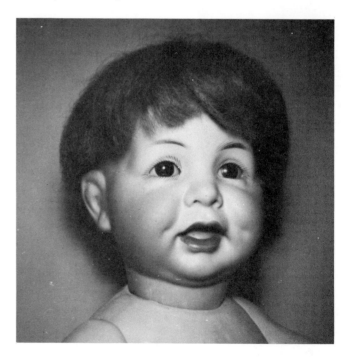

1921: Registered in Germany the trademark *Heinrich Handwerck,* to be used on dolls, dolls' heads, dolls' bodies, dolls' limbs, dolls' clothes, and dolls' wigs.

1922: Registered in U.S. "Naughty" as a trademark, used since 1919. *John Bing Co.,* distributor in America, advertised "My Darling" line of jointed dolls and character

babies with Mama voices and flirting eyes, in a range of sizes, as well as walking dolls.

1923: Bing advertised jointed dolls made by Kämmer & Reinhardt, 9 to 28 inches, price $2.00 and up.

1925: Advertised Naughty Dolly, *Mama Dolls,* walking dolls, flirting dolls.

**944.** Bisque head made by Simon & Halbig for Kämmer & Reinhardt, mold #117. Sleeping glass eyes, closed mouth, jointed composition body. H. 17 inches. *Courtesy of Bess Goldfinger.*

**946A & B.** Character baby, mold #126, has bisque head marked as in Ill. **588.** Wire-strung body. This doll, in its original dress and cap, was purchased new in 1920. H. 21½ inches. (See color photograph C24.) *Coleman Collection.*

**945.** Character baby, mold #122, has sleeping eyes, open mouth with two teeth. Bisque head mark: Ill. **953.** H. 14 inches. *Courtesy of Dorothy Annunziato.*

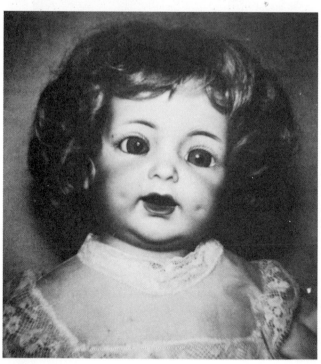

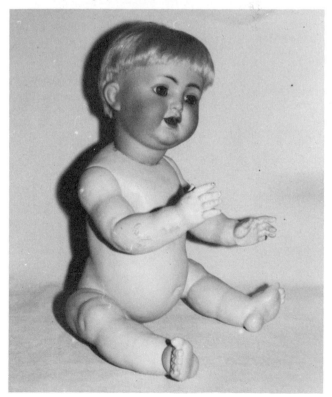

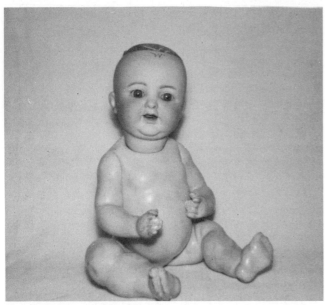

**947.** Character baby, mold #126, has glass sleeping eyes, open mouth with teeth, bisque head marked on back "K [star] R // Simon & Halbig // 126." Also, on the forehead is a script "W." H. 11 inches. *Courtesy of Jessica Norman.*

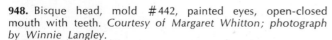

**948.** Bisque head, mold #442, painted eyes, open-closed mouth with teeth. *Courtesy of Margaret Whitton; photograph by Winnie Langley.*

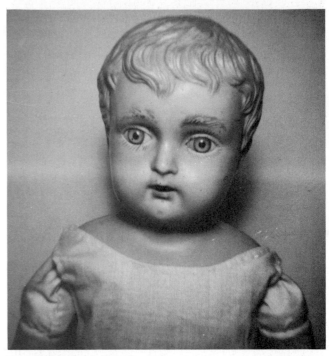

**949.** Celluloid head with stationary glass eyes, on excelsior-stuffed cloth body with composition limbs. Head marked with turtle design, "K [star] R" and "65." H. 10 inches. *Courtesy of Edith Meggers.*

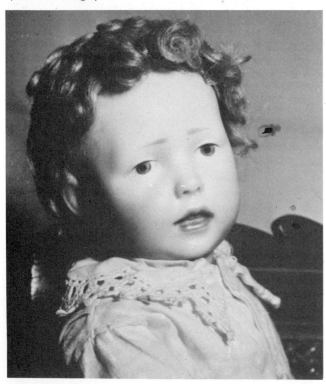

**950.** Celluloid baby produced by Kämmer & Reinhardt has molded hair, brown eyes, teeth, bent-limb baby body. *Courtesy of Peg Gregory; photograph by Winnie Langley.*

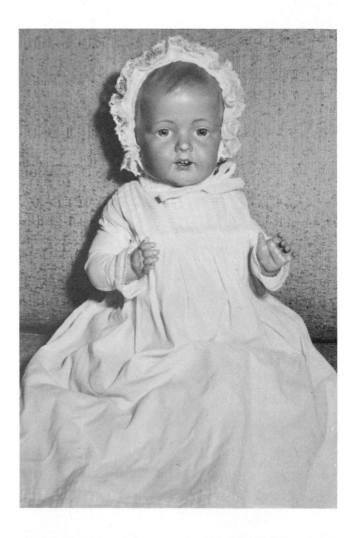

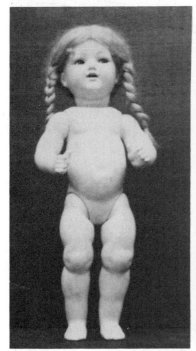

**951A & B.** Celluloid head marked "K [star] R // 728/4 // Germany." Eyes move sideways; metal eyelids move down over the eyes for sleeping. Doll has hair eyelashes, mohair wig, composition body. H. 15 inches. *Courtesy of Dorothy Annunziato.*

**952–959.** Kämmer & Reinhardt marks. No. **954** is their trademark; No. **955** is the trademark for their "Royal" line of dolls; the other marks are found incised on dolls.

*K* ✡ *R*
SIMON & HALBIG
116/A
**952**

*K* ✡ *R*
SIMON & HALBIG
122
32
**953**

K . ✡ R .
**954**

**955**

HALBIG
K ✡ R
36
**956**

HALBIG
K ✡ R
55
**957**

K ✡ R
728/4
GERMANY
**958**

191
G
B
⊙
K ✡ R
DEP.
Germany
**959**

**Kampes, Louise R.** 1919–25+. Atlantic City, N.J. Made *Kamkins* or *Kampe Art Dolls,* all handmade, with heavy canvas head and cloth body. They had real hair wigs, and the head and limbs were movable. Dolls were painted by a special process to make them sanitary. Distributor was *Riemann, Seabrey Co.*

1920: Louise Kampes obtained a U.S. patent for making dolls' heads by spreading several layers of unvulcanized rubber over a die; the fabric was applied as a cover to the rubber, and thoroughly imbedded within it. The whole was then placed in an oven or vulcanizing kiln. If desired, a plaster of Paris backing could be worked into the back before vulcanizing.

**Kämpfe & Heubach.** 1897–1918. Wallendorf, Thür. Porcelain factory, probably successors to *Heubach, Kämpfe & Sontag;* made *bathing dolls.*

**Kandy Twins.** 1911. Dolls with eyes glancing to the side, made by *Nonbreakable Toy Co.*

**Kanko Doll Co.** 1920–22. New York City. Made dolls and used "Kanko" as a trade name for dolls advertised by *Albert Kahn.*

**Kansai Trading Co.** 1893. Kyoto, Japan. Displayed dolls at the Chicago Exposition.

**Kant Krack.** 1912–13. Trade name used for material with which *Parsons-Jackson* made their baby dolls. It was a nonabsorbent material that would float in water, but time proved that it could crack. (See Ill. 1296.)

1912: Dolls came with smiling or crying faces. Sizes 10½, 13, and 14 inches.

1913: Came with either straight legs or bent legs.

**Kanwashem.** 1905. New line of dolls produced by *Strobel & Wilken.*

**Karas, Louis.** 1925. Nürnberg, Bavaria. Made dolls.

**Karg, Ernst.** 1914–20. Hoboken, N.J., and New York City. German citizen. He was issued two U.S. design patents, one for a doll dressed as a jockey with a ribbon across the chest reading *The Favorite* and the other for a doll dressed as a woman with ribbon across the chest reading *Votes for Women.*

1920: Registered *Wauketoi* as a trademark in the U.S. for the *U.S. Toy & Novelty Co.*

**Karmen Corp., The.** 1921–24. New York City. Registered *Tub* in U.S. as a trademark for washable, sanitary rag dolls, which were designed by *Clara V. Havens.*

**Karp, Leonhard.** 1891. Leipzig, Saxony. Made dolls.

**Kassel.** See **Casselaer.**

**Käthe Kruse.** 1923. Trademark registered in Germany by Käthe Kruse. (See **Kruse, Käthe.**)

**Kathrinchen.** 1916. Doll dressed as a Dutch girl, made by *Käthe Kruse.* Price $15.00.

**Katterfelder.** See **Catterfelder.**

**Katz, Leo.** 1924–25. Vienna. Made dolls, baby dolls, dolls' heads, and parts.

**Katz im Sack (Cat in Sack).** 1912. Trademark registered in Germany by *Otto May* for dolls.

**Katzenjammer.** 1908. Trade name of dolls advertised by *Samstag & Hilder.*

**Kaufman, Levenson & Co.** 1925. Distributors for *Acme Dolls;* advertised *Peek-a-boo Dolls.*

**Kaufmann & Gordon.** See **Blum, Charles B.**

**Kaulitz, Fräulein Marion Bertha.** 1908–ca. 1920. Munich, Bavaria. Produced and distributed dolls, dolls' heads, and dolls' clothes. Character dolls' heads, modeled by *Paul Vogelsanger* and painted in fast colors by Marion Kaulitz, were called *Munich Art Dolls.* These had composition heads usually on jointed composition bodies, and represented boys and girls in colorful costumes made by Marion Kaulitz. Heads from the same mold were often given different wigs and different clothes. She registered two trademarks in Germany. In 1909, one was a picture that included the words "Münchner Künstler Kaulitzpuppen." The other, in 1911, had the name "Kaulitz." By 1909 she had exhibited her dolls in Munich, Brunn, and Elberfeld, Germany. At the last-named place she was awarded a special diploma. In 1912, she exhibited her dolls in Newark, N.J. Her name was generally put on the base of the doll's neck. She also made dolls with fabric faces. In 1910, she won a gold medal at the Brussels Exhibition, and was called the instigator of the "Puppenreform."

**Kaybee Doll & Toy Co.** 1917–19. Los Angeles, Calif. Registered Kay-Bee as their trademark in U.S. for dolls. Kay-Bee stood for the initials of the proprietors, Kellow and Brown. They advertised that the dolls were made in their factory "from head to foot." They made character dolls and sleeping-eyed dolls, as well as separate heads and dresses.

**Kayborn Novelty Co.** 1924. Brooklyn, N.Y. Made dolls.

**Kay-Eff (Kay-Eff Toddle Baby).** 1922–24. Trade name used by *Katherine Fleischmann* for dolls that she created; they were distributed by *Joseph Goldstein.* Came in various sizes and prices.

**Kazarine, Serge de, & Porohovchikova, Mary de.** 1920–21. London. Russian citizens who were issued two U.S. design patents for girl dolls dressed in furs.

**Keen & Co.** 1913–18. London. Made dolls.

**Keenan, Anna.** 1921. Seattle, Wash. Secured U.S. design patent for a rag doll wearing a mob cap.

**Keep Kool.** 1920. Doll copyrighted by *Guglielmo Voccia.*

**Kelhetter Import Corp.** 1923–24. New York City. Imported dolls.

**Keller, F.** 1878. Paris. Displayed dolls at the Paris Exposition.

**Kellow and Brown.** See **Kaybee Doll & Toy Co.**

**Kenny, C. D., Co.** Prior to World War I. Baltimore, Md. Distributed all-bisque dolls with molded clothes. Dolls incised on back "C D Kenny Co.//Germany." Came

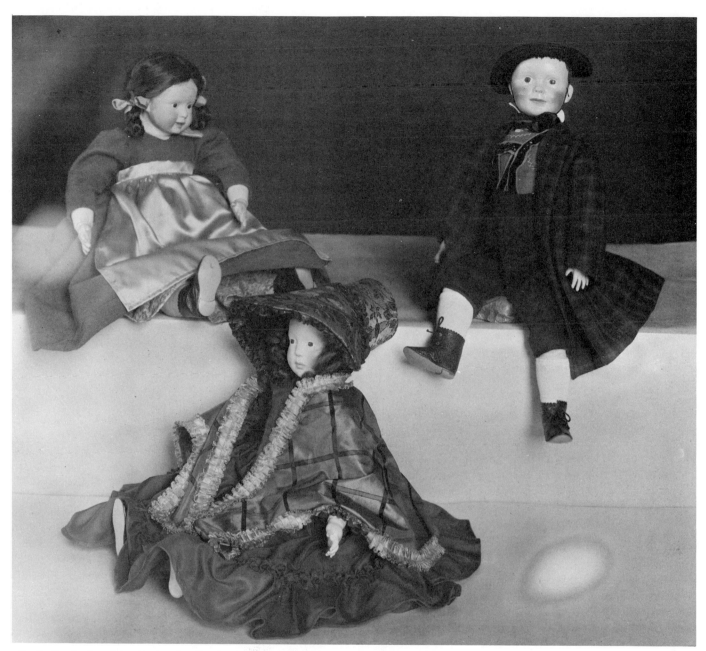

**960.** Dolls displayed by Marion Kaulitz in German Art Exhibit at Newark, N J. Dolls have composition heads and bodies. The photograph was taken in 1912 at the time of the exhibit. *Courtesy of the Newark Museum, Newark, N.J.*

with molded features and hair, molded white rompers with blue belt, tan slippers, and white socks; jointed at shoulders; size 3½ inches. These dolls were probably used as premiums and may have come in other sizes and other designs.

**Kerby, Robert E., & Kerby, Frances S.** 1923–25. Miami, Fla. Were granted two U.S. design patents for cloth-body dolls dressed as Seminole Indians.

**Kestner (Kaestner), J. D., Jr.** 1805–1925+. Waltershausen, Thür. Made complete dolls and also doll parts. *Borgfeldt* was exclusive agent in U.S. during the late 19th century and up until World War I; in 1925 *Century Doll*

Co. was also a distributor. Johannes Daniel Kestner, son of a butcher, supplied meat for the Napoleonic armies before 1802. While traveling south on this business, he became acquainted with papier-mâché fabrication. On his return home to Waltershausen, he started a factory in which he made slates of papier-mâché and wooden buttons. These products were not a success, so he tried the manufacture of dolls. The dolls' bodies were made on the lathes he had used for buttons. After being turned on a lathe, the torsos were carved and painted to make them resemble human figures. These dolls were clad in swaddling clothes and sold as *Täuflinge*, a name that continued to be used for Waltershausen babies.

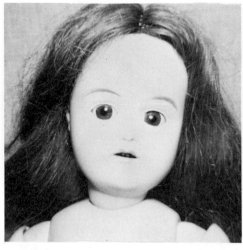

962

963

**961.** Bisque head, mold #141, has sleeping eyes. Jointed body is composition. Mark: Ill. **975.** H. 24½ inches. *Courtesy of Hildred Brinkley.*

**962.** Bisque head, mold #152, has sleeping eyes; head is on a Linon walking body. Mark on head: Ill. **976.** Probably 1890's. H. 16 inches. *Coleman Collection.*

**963.** Bisque head, mold #154, a frequently found mold number has sleeping eyes, open mouth and teeth. Mark: Ill. **977.** Dwarf baby body of gusseted kid with bisque lower arms and cloth lower legs. Ca. 1900. H. 8 inches. H. of shoulder head, 3 inches. *Coleman Collection.*

**964A & B.** Bisque head, mold #162, has sleeping eyes with hair eyelashes; face and body are longer and more mature. Mark on head: Ill. **978.** Rectangular red stamp on body, as well as paper sticker printed in black ink: Ill. **148.** H. 17 inches *Courtesy of Lester & Alice Grinnings.*

Another report says that Johannes Daniel Kestner was an official of Saxony and one of the first doll makers to have his own establishment. He was the founder of the great Waltershausen doll industry, which carried a reputation for making the finest grade of dolls; at Sonneberg, all grades of dolls were made. Johannes Daniel Kestner, Jr., succeeded his father.

Around 1845, Kestner was manufacturing dolls with either kid or muslin bodies. A history of the firm states that their dolls of this period had wooden limbs and papier-mâché heads. Dolls dressed in a chemise, shoes, stockings, and a hood were introduced by Kestner in 1845.

1860: Kestner acquired their porcelain factory in Ohrdruf, Thür., known as Kestner & Co., where the firm was able to make their own china and bisque dolls' heads. The Ohrdruf porcelain factory continued in operation after 1925, and its mark (see Ill. 984) is often found on dolls' heads. As far as is known, Kestner was the only German doll maker who made entire dolls (heads, bodies, etc.). They sold doll parts separately. They also made wax over papier-mâché heads. Some of these dolls contained a squeak box and had sleeping eyes. The Kestner kid bodies were stuffed with sawdust, cork, or hair.

1891: Kestner advertised china, bisque, and wax dolls' heads; jointed composition, kid, and *nankeen* bodied dolls.

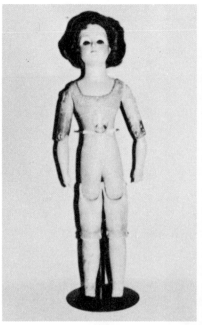

**965A, B, & C.** Lady doll, the type sometimes stamped "Gibson Girl" in blue on the chest. Bisque head and lower arms; sleeping glass eyes, hair eyelashes; kid body with rivet joints. Marked on the head "Made in Germany." Body mark: Ill. **979**, plus "½ cork stuffed." H. 16½ inches. H. of shoulder head, 5½ inches. *Courtesy of Alberta Darby.*

1892: Adolf Kestner of Waltershausen obtained two English patents for doll joints. One of them was for a doll with detachable parts so that a new limb or head could easily be substituted for a damaged one. J. D. Kestner obtained a German patent for improved doll joints.

1893: Kestner obtained the German patent #70685 for a jointed composition body. This patent number has been found stamped in red ink on the back of some doll bodies, together with the word *Excelsior,* though the heads are marked with the customary number and letter size markings (see below). At the Chicago World's Fair they exhibited dolls.

1895: Kestner began using their famous trademark of a crown and streamers, and registered it in the U.S. and Germany in 1896.

1896: Kestner made jointed dolls with composition or cloth bodies as well as dolls with kid bodies.

Ca. 1900: Kestner used slip casting for making bisque dolls' heads. It is not known how long this method had been used by Kestner.

1902: Kestner advertised dolls with bisque heads, sleeping eyes, eyelashes, flowing hair wig, teeth, kid bodies stuffed with cork, and cut (gusset) hip and knee joints; sizes 11½, 16½, 18, 20½, 22, and 23 inches; price $4.50 to $38.40 doz. wholesale.

1905–7: Kid-body dolls distributed by *Butler Bros.* were labeled *Marvel* under the regular Kestner crown on the chest.

**966.** Bisque head (Kestner mold #167) and forearms, sleeping eyes, open mouth and teeth. Mark: Ill. **980**. Muslin body with kid at the joints. H. 26 inches. H. of shoulder head, 6½ inches. *Courtesy of Dorothy Annunziato.*

1906: Kestner employed nearly one thousand workers.

1910: At the exposition in Seattle, Washington, the Kestner dolls were described as "dolls from the master hands of Kestner who produced dolls of quality." Eyebrows of natural hair were patented and used on Kestner's bisque heads. Kestner lady dolls, sometimes called *Gibson Girl,* were shown in the LADIES' HOME JOURNAL.

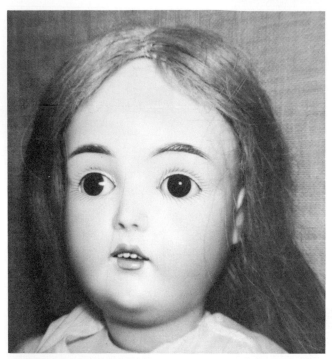

**967.** Bisque head, mold #171, has molded eyebrows. Mark: Ill. **981.** On top of plaster pate is "171" over "6¹/₂." Kestner often put numbers on the pate as well as the head. Jointed composition body is marked with "Germany" stamped in red on the back of the doll and "3¹/₂." H. 22 inches. *Courtesy of Hildred Brinkley.*

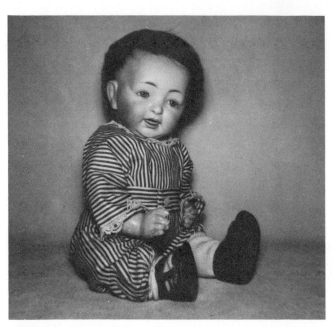

**968A & B.** Character baby, mold #211, bisque head has sleeping glass eyes, open-closed mouth. Mark: Ill. **982.** Bent-limb composition baby body. H. 12¹/₂ inches. *Coleman Collection.*

1911: Kestner advertised a blonde "beauty" with ball-and-socket joints, sewn wig, real eyelashes; size 24 inches, price $5.00. A dressed doll that wore the clothes of a five-year-old child cost $100; undressed dolls cost up to $16.00.

1912: Kestner advertised "Natural Baby" with bent limbs, two teeth, and beads around the neck (resembles mold #211). Borgfeldt was the distributor.

1913: Kestner was one of the firms that made *Kewpies.* They advertised shoulder heads sold separately; character babies with two teeth or open-closed mouth without teeth came with real skin wigs.

1914: Kestner made leather dolls, leather bodies, cloth dolls, jointed dolls of papier-mâché, cardboard or celluloid character babies, bisque bathing children, dolls' heads of porcelain, paper, or celluloid. J. D. Kestner, Jr., of Waltershausen copyrighted in the U.S. *Hilda,* the head of a child laughing and showing two front teeth. These baby dolls are marked "Hilda © J.D.K."

1915: Kestner registered two crown trademarks in Germany. On one crown there were the words "Crown Doll // Kestner // Germany"; on the other crown appeared the words *Krönen Puppe.*

1918: Advertised kid-body dolls, jointed composition dolls, bisque and celluloid heads, bathing children, and others.

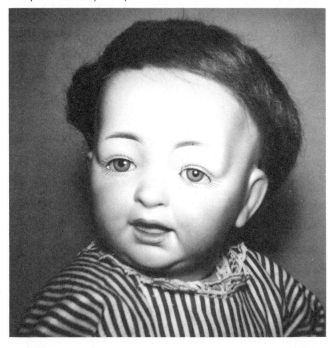

1924–25: *Bye-Lo* dolls' heads and all-bisque dolls. They also made celluloid dolls and used the celluloid *Rheinische Gummi und Celluloid Fabrik Co.,* but with their own special J. D. K. marked molds. These dolls have both the turtle and J. D. K. mark on them.

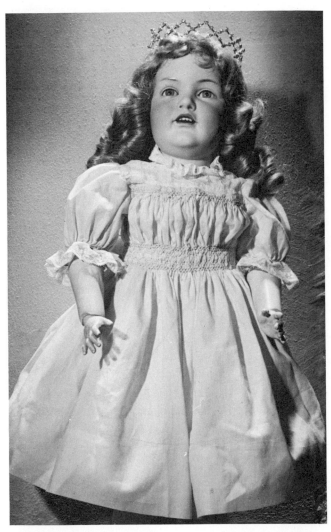

**969.** Kestner doll, mold #241; bisque head, glass eyes, open mouth with four teeth, ball-jointed composition body. H. 24 inches. *Courtesy of Sally Euchner.*

**970.** Oriental character baby, yellow tinted bisque, mold #243. Mark: Ill. **983.** Bent-limb composition baby body. *Courtesy of Winnie Langley; photograph by Winnie Langley.*

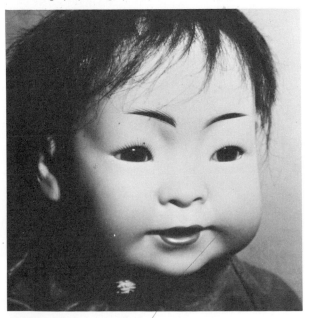

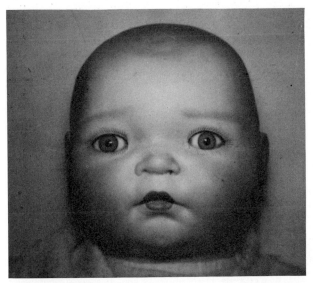

**971.** Bisque head made by Kestner for Century Doll Co. has flange neck and glass sleeping eyes. Baby body is cloth, with composition arms. Ca. 1925. H. 13 inches. *Courtesy of Mary Roberson.*

## DOLL MARK AND SIZE TABLE

| Mark on Head | | | Approx. Head Circumference (Inches) |
|---|---|---|---|
| | made in | | |
| A | Germany | 5 | 8 |
| B | " | 6 | 8½ |
| C | " | 7 | 9 |
| D | " | 8 | 9½ |
| E | " | 9 | 10 |
| F | " | 10 | 10½ |
| G | " | 11 | 11 |
| H | " | 12 | 11½ |
| J(I) | " | 13 | 12 |
| K | " | 14 | 12½ |
| L | " | 15 | 13 |
| M | " | 16 | 13½ |
| N | " | 17 | 15 |
| O | " | 18 | 16 |
| P | " | 19 | 17 |

*(handwritten notes in margin: "my doll from Olde Towne Antiques"; K row circled)*

Kestner appears to have used the above incised marks on bisque heads of dolls to indicate the size of his dolls. The average measurement applies to socket-type doll heads and is taken around the head above the ears. There is some variation in head sizes, probably due to differences in where the head is measured and the amount of shrinkage in firing. In addition to the numbers shown above, there are also half numbers, for example, D½—8½, E½—9½, Kk—14½, etc., and even quarter numbers, as well as a—4, b—3, and so on for very small sizes. Hildred Brinkley has a pair of identical twins, both mold 146; one is marked "L—15" and the other "L½—15½," with the latter about ¼ inch larger in head circumference. Shoulder heads belonging to this series appear to have the size number in the center back

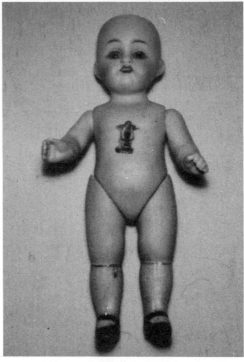

**972A & B.** Bisque head, mold #260, has glass sleeping eyes, open mouth and teeth. Mark: Ill. **984**. Compare with Ills. **985** and **973**. Marked on the composition body in red: "Made in Germany 31." H. 13½ inches. *Courtesy of Dorothy Annunziato.*

**973A & B.** Bisque head, mold #260, with glass sleeping eyes. Mark: Ill. **985**. The crown without streamers on the stickers found on the socket necks of some other 260's suggest that these were made in the 1920's. H. 13 inches. *Courtesy of Alberta Darby.*

**974.** All-bisque Kestner doll, glass eyes, open mouth with teeth, molded shoes and socks. Label sticker on the body: Ill. **986**. H. 6 inches. *Courtesy of Dorothy Annunziato.*

 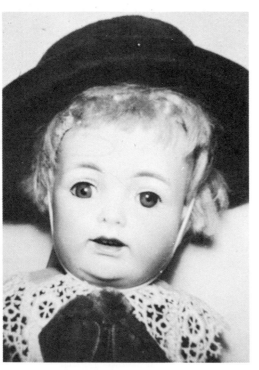

**975–997.** Marks used on dolls by J. D. Kestner. Marks Nos. **979** and **986** are used on bodies; the others are found on heads. Marks Nos. **984**, **996**, and **997** stand for Kestner & Co., the porcelain factory branch of the Kestner firm.

made in
L. Germany. 15
141
975

made in
C Germany 7
152
976

154 dep. 7/0
7/0 made in Germany
977

made in
D Germany. 8.
162.
978

979

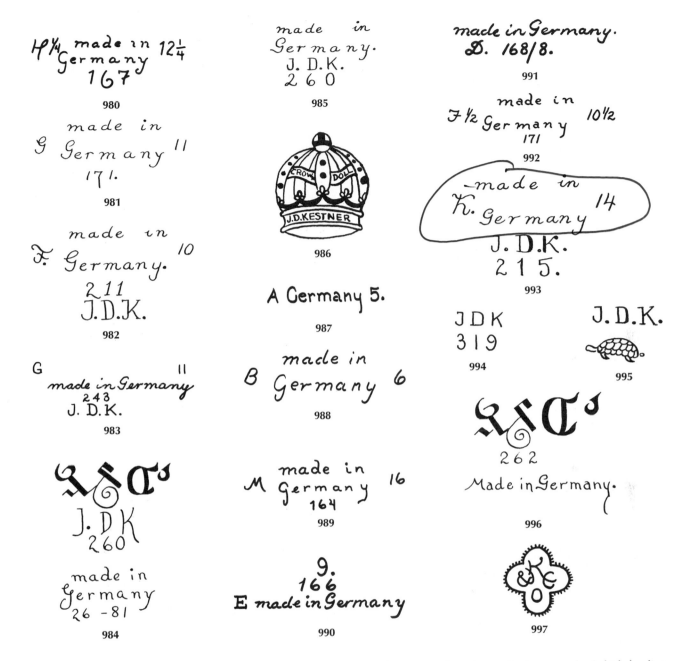

just under the crown. The letter of the alphabet and the "made in Germany" are along the edge of the back shoulder plate. The sizes of the shoulder heads seem to run slightly larger than of the socket heads, but the differentials follow the same general pattern. Appreciation goes to Genevieve Angione for introducing this study. All the sample dolls studied show plaster-like pates and heavy eyebrows.

The dolls on which these markings appear indicate that the markings were used at least from 1892 until after 1910. A jointed composition doll of 1892, mold 129, has the marking of this series without the "J.D.K." The heads in this series, which are also marked "J.D.K.," generally came from molds numbered around 200 or more. Numerous shoulder heads with mold #154 (a

dolly face) are found on Kestner marked kid bodies. Note should be made that Kestner jointed composition bodies are usually stamped on the back in red with the word "Germany" and a number probably denoting size. Sometimes the word *Excelsior* also appears.

Dolls with the numbers 171, 180, 186, 187, and 195 do not have "J.D.K." on their heads, but are known to be Kestner heads of 1910 or later. Heads with the first four of these numbers are found in an original box at the Mary Merritt Museum and were advertised in PLAY-THINGS, January, 1910. The 195 is on a fur-eyebrow head on a Kestner marked body. Fur eyebrow dolls were patented in 1910. In studying mold numbers, it should be remembered that several firms often used the same number.

**Kewpie.** 1912–25+. Designed by *Rose O'Neill* (Mrs. Rose O'Neill Wilson); *Joseph Kallus* performed the work of an assistant to Rose O'Neill. *Borgfeldt* held the rights for the Kewpie, which they produced and distributed, and for which they granted licenses to other companies. *Tip Top Toy Co.* distributed Kewpies to the carnival and amusement park trade; *Strobel & Wilken* distributed to retailers. Many companies manufactured Kewpies, among them *Kestner* (all-bisque; bisque head and composition body); *Fulper Pottery* (all-bisque); *Rex Doll Co.* (composition); *Mutual Doll Co.* (composition); *Cameo Doll Co.* (composition); *Karl Standfuss* (celluloid); and other companies in Europe.

Rose O'Neill Wilson filed for a design patent on a Kewpie in December, 1912, and was granted the patent in March, 1913. She registered Kewpie as a trademark in 1913 in the U.S., and claimed that it had been used since December 21, 1912, and obtained a copyright for Kewpie in 1913. Borgfeldt registered Kewpie as a trademark in Britain and France in 1913.

PLAYTHINGS, January, 1913, tells of Borgfeldt's arranging for Rose O'Neill to go to Europe and spend several weeks at the Kestner factory giving her personal supervision to the making of the new doll. She was received royally in Germany, and by December, 1912, the first Kewpie dolls reached America. In January, 1913, two European factories were making bisque Kewpies, and by the following January, twenty-one European factories were engaged in their manufacture.

Most of the early Kewpies were bisque or celluloid, but Kewpies with composition heads and cloth bodies were advertised as early as July, 1913, and rubber Kewpies as early as October, 1913. Kewpies were made in almost every type of merchandise and material. In dolls, there were all-bisque, bisque socket heads on composition bodies, bisque flange necks on cloth bodies, bisque shoulder heads, all-composition, and so on. Kewpies generally had molded hair and painted eyes, but some had molded hats or hair wigs and some had glass eyes. They came in sizes from 2 inches up. Ivory or bone Kewpie charms were less than an inch high.

There were Kewpies representing various occupations: farmers, firemen, policemen, cowboys, bellboys, and musicians, as well as numerous military Kewpies representing American, British, German, French, or Italian soldiers. *Tommy Atkins* and a Negro Kewpie were new in 1914. By 1915 the Negro Kewpies were named *Hottentots*.

In 1915, *Montgomery Ward & Co.* advertised bisque Kewpies 5 and 6⅞ inches tall for 25¢ and 49¢. *Sears, Roebuck & Co.*, in 1922, advertised all-composition Kewpies 8½ inches tall for 58¢.

Kewpies were made with the legs together or with the legs apart; some had jointed legs. The eyes glanced either to the right or to the left. Later Kewpies were made with jointed wooden bodies and wood pulp heads.

**Kewpies Model.** 1919. Copyrighted by *Manhattan Toy and Doll Manufacturing Co.* and designed by *Ernesto*

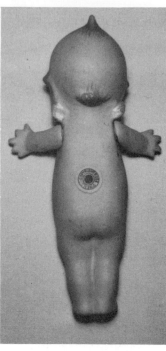
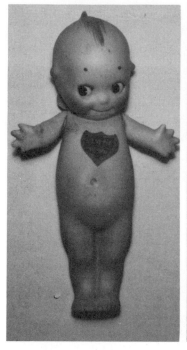

**998A & B.** All-bisque Kewpie with painted features and movable arms. Paper stickers on front and back: Ills. **1000** and **1001**. H. 5 inches. *Courtesy of Edith Meggers.*

**999.** Unauthorized "Kewpie" made in Japan. Note the distinctive eyebrow painting. For paper stickers on front and back, see Ills. **1002** and **1003**. Similar stickers may also be found on authorized versions of the Kewpie. H. 7 inches. *Courtesy of Eleanor Jean Carter.*

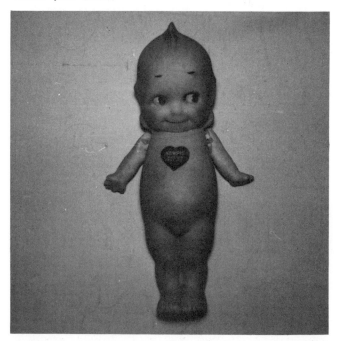

*Peruggi.* It represented a nude child with short molded hair. The eyes look upward; bent arms are jointed at the shoulders. The legs are together in this version, but apart in the similar *Beauty Kist* doll.

**1000**     **1001**     **1002**     **1003**

**1000–1003.** Kewpie marks. Nos. **1002** and **1003** were found on unauthorized versions of Kewpies.

**Kewteye Kiddies.** 1912. Clown girl and sailor boy dolls.

**Kickapoo.** 1911. Indian boy doll made by *Horsman*. One of the *Art Dolls;* came with *Can't Break 'Em* head, molded hair, copper-colored complexion, cloth body; wore feather headband and red and yellow clothes.

**Kid, The.** See **Jackie Coogan Kid.**

**Kid, The.** 1923–24. Design patent obtained by *James Beach* for a doll representing Jackie Coogan in THE KID.

**Kid Bodies.** These were popular throughout the 19th and early 20th centuries. They were made in Germany as late as the 1930's. The principal type during the first half of the 19th century was without joints and with wooden limbs, but jointed kid bodies were made as early as 1842. Gusset-type joints, also called double joints, appear to have been introduced soon after the middle of the 19th century. Pressed and sized kid was occasionally used for bodies. (See Ill. 1131 showing a doll that may be based on the 1866 patent of *Pierre Clément.)* Sometimes kid covered a wooden body, and

sometimes cloth was combined with kid for the less conspicuous portions of the body. *Kestner* stated that around 1860 their kid bodies were stuffed with sawdust, cork, or hair. (See Ills. 392, 1289, 1290.)

The fine French kid bodies were exquisitely shaped, some having the figure of an adult and others that of a child or bébé. During the 1880's baby dolls were popular, and there was competition between the kid bodies and the new ball-jointed composition bodies. In 1895 *Brieger & Co.* advertised ball-jointed bodies in leather. Some strangely shaped kid bodies were made, including the dwarflike Kestner body of around 1900. *Universal* joints, *Ne Plus Ultra* joints, and other rivet-type joints were used extensively on kid bodies in the 1890's.

In 1909 washable kid dolls were advertised. They had bisque heads; the kid was flesh-colored and could withstand scrubbing. In the 1920's fully jointed kid bodies continued to be made in sizable quantities. They came with various types of arms, including bisque, composition, celluloid, and wood. Steinach, Thür., was a center for the making of kid-body dolls.

(See **Manufacture of Kid Bodies;** also Ills. 234 and 240.)

**1005.** Kid body with toes and fingers separated; gusset joints at elbows, hips, and knees. Note the low waistline. H. 20 inches. *Courtesy of Hazel Ulseth.*

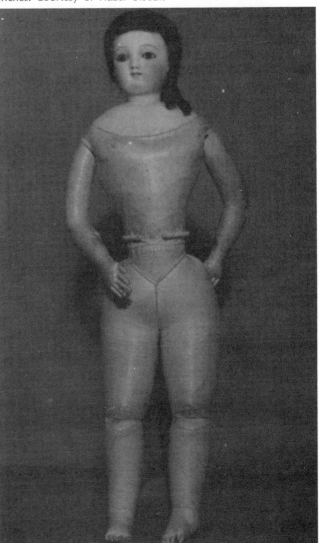

KID BODIES

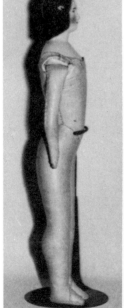

**1004A & B.** Pink kid body articulated only at the shoulders; china head. H. 10½ inches. H. of shoulder head, 2½ inches. *Courtesy of Sylvia Brockmon.*

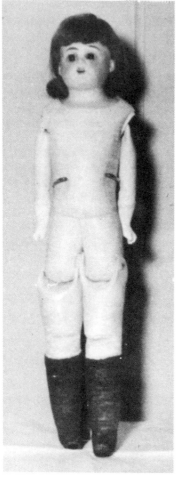

W & C 8/0

**1007**

2015 3/0

**1008**

**1006.** Kid body with Ne Plus Ultra hip joint and gusset knee joint, bisque forearms, cloth lower legs. Bisque shoulder head with glass sleeping eyes. Mark on head: Ill. **1007**. This mark may indicate that the head was made by Armand Marseille for Louis Wolf & Co. H. 15½ inches. H. of shoulder head, 4½ inches. *Courtesy of Mrs. Max Ackert.*

**1007 & 1008.** Marks found on dolls having kid bodies. These marks on the heads have not been identified.

**Kid Heads.** *Carl Albert Georg Herrmann* of Germany obtained a French patent in 1906 for making a doll's head of kid. In 1925 several Paris doll makers used kid for dolls' heads. The Victoria and Albert Museum has dolls with kid heads and wooden bodies, which they date as ca. 1830. (See **Manufacture of Leather Heads.**)

**Kidalene Dolls.** 1923. Dolls with imitation kid bodies imported by *L. Gottlieb & Sons.* They were fully jointed and had bisque heads and composition arms. Price was $11.00 to $24.00 doz. wholesale.

**Kidaline Body.** 1919–22. Advertised by *Morimura Bros.* from 1919–21. In 1922 *Langfelder, Homma & Hayward* imported these imitation kid bodies from Germany.

**Kidder, Imogene, & Melton, Lenna.** 1922. Portland, Ore. Obtained U.S. design patent for a doll in Chinese costume.

**Kiddie Kar Kiddie.** 1916–18. Doll dressed in white lawn apron; made by *Jessie McCutcheon Raleigh* and distributed by *Butler Bros.;* 18½ inches tall, price $4.50.

**Kiddie Pal Dolly.** Ca. 1925+. Line of dolls made by Regal Doll Manufacturing Co., successors of *German American Doll Co.*

**Kiddie Speciality Corp.** 1924–25. New York City. Made dolls.

**Kiddiejoy (Kiddie Joy, Kiddieioy).** 1922–25+. Line of dolls handled by *Hitz, Jacobs & Kassler.*

1922: A fifty-six-page catalog of Kiddiejoy lines covered dolls and toys made in 182 European factories and 200 U.S. factories. *Armand Marseille* made bisque heads for some of the Kiddiejoy dolls.

1925: Advertisement included infant dolls with imported bisque heads, glass sleeping eyes, molded hair; bodies were stuffed with domestic cotton and had Ronson voices. Three sizes; prices $1.50 to $3.50.

**Kiddieland.** 1911. Trademark registered in Britain by *Eisenmann & Co.* for dolls.

**Kidette.** 1917. Trademark registered in Britain by *Speights Ltd.* for dolls.

**Kidette Body.** 1922. Imitation kid body advertised by *Sears, Roebuck & Co.* Came with bisque forearms, and riveted joints at hips and knees. Sizes 12¾, 14¾, 17¾, and 19¾ inches; price 95¢ to $1.98.

**Kidiline Body.** 1925. Waterproof imitation kid body advertised by *Montgomery Ward & Co.* Came with bisque head and composition arms. Sizes of doll 16⅛, 18½, 20, and 23¼ inches; price $1.43 to $2.98.

**Kidlyn Body.** 1922. Imported by *A. Strauss & Co.*

**Kidlyne.** 1906–10. Trademark registered in U.S. by *Borgfeldt. Butler Bros.* in 1907 advertised "Kidlyne" dolls with imitation kid bodies, bisque heads and hands, glass eyes, both stationary and sleeping, teeth in open mouth. Sizes 11½, 12½, 13½, 15½, and 17¼ inches, price $1.35 to $4.00 doz. wholesale.

**Kidolene Body.** 1920. Imitation kid body produced by *Marks Bros.* Came with celluloid heads and composition hands and legs; sizes 15, 18, and 22 inches.

**Kidoline Dolls.** 1922–24. Handled by *Menco Importing Co., J. Halpern Co.,* and *Strauss*-Eckhardt Co. Probably had imitation kid bodies.

**Kidolyn.** 1918. Line of kid-bodied dolls imported from Japan by *Morimura Bros.* Came with jointed hips, knees, and arms.

**Kieffer, Valley M.** 1921–23. Obtained two U.S. design patents for rag dolls; one was a Negro wearing a bandanna and apron.

**Kiesewetter, Alwin.** 1920–21. Coburg, Thür. Advertised that he specialized in Thüringian home manufacture. He produced 1,200 different dolls and toys including bisque dolls, baby dolls, papier-mâché dolls, and celluloid dolls.

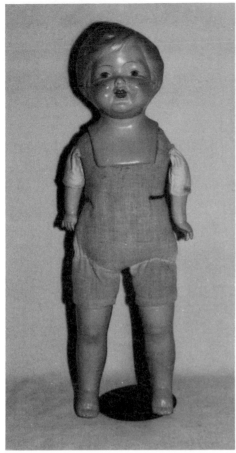

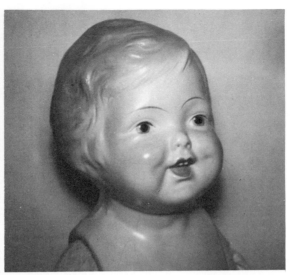

Germany
Kiddiejoy
375/6

**1011**

Germany
Kiddiejoy
372
A 1. M

**1012**

**1011 & 1012.** "Kiddiejoy" marks used by Hitz, Jacobs & Kassler.

"KIDDIE PAL DOLLY"

REGAL DOLL MFG. CO. INC.

**1010.** "Kiddie Pal" mark used by Regal Doll Manufacturing Co.

**1009A & B.** "Kiddie Pal" has composition head and lower limbs, and cloth Mama Doll body of the later type, which was slimmer; probably ca. 1925. Doll has lavender-colored eyes, painted features, two upper teeth painted in the open-closed mouth. Mark on the back of the shoulders: Ill. **1010.** H. 20½ inches. H. of shoulder head, 7 inches. *Coleman Collection.*

**Kiesewetter, M.** 1909. Neustadt near Coburg, Thür. Made dolls.

**Kiesewetter, Witwe (Widow) Anton.** 1918–25. Neustadt near Coburg, Thür. Made *Täuflinge.*

**Kihlgren, Carl Axel.** 1883–84. Boston, Mass. Procured U.S. patent for dolls' joints. On the outside the joints appeared to be gusset-type, but on the inside there were two ball joints with connecting shank and two hemispherical cups with prongs to hold the balls.

**Ki-Ki.** 1921–22. Trademark registered by *Hélène Sardeau* in U.S. for dolls.

**Kiko, Ferdinand, & Nehren, Ambros.** 1913–15. Herford, Westf., and Achern, Baden. Obtained two German patents for dolls with closing eyes.

**Kilenyi, Julio.** 1921. Native of Hungary and an Italian citizen residing in U.S. Designed *Head of Baby* and *Head of Little Girl,* which *Louis Amberg & Son* copyrighted and made into dolls. Kilenyi was a sculptor and medalist of note.

**Kilian, Emil.** 1925. Chemnitz, Germany. Registered "Kiliana" as a trademark in Germany for ball-jointed dolls, bent-limb babies, stuffed dolls, and dolls' wigs.

**Killiblues.** 1910. Trademark registered in U.S. by *Baker & Bennett Co.* for dolls.

**Kimball Girl and Kimball Boy.** 1921. Pair of cherub-type dolls made by *New Era Toy & Novelty Co.;* price $6.00 doz. wholesale.

**Kindergarten Girlie.** 1918. Doll made by *Jessie McCutcheon Raleigh,* distributed by *Butler Bros.* Wore white lawn dress. Size 11½ inches, price $2.65.

**King.** 1893. Obtained a French patent for a crying doll with reeds that vibrated when the position of the doll was changed.

**King, Frank O.** 1922–25+. Glencoe and Chicago, Ill. Registered *Uncle Walt, Skeezix, Rachel, Mrs. Blossom,* and "Puff," the kitten, as trademarks for rag dolls based on his cartoon drawings. The trademarks were affixed to the dolls as printed impressions. King obtained two design patents for rag dolls; one was for Skeezix as a baby and the other was for Mrs. Blossom dressed in an ankle-length coat, a hat, and gloves. Dolls were made of two pieces of cloth, usually oilcloth; there was a Skeezix as a child as well as a baby. His designs were also used for all-bisque dolls with swivel heads and molded clothes. *Live Long Toy Co.* handled King's dolls. (See Ills. 1544, 1636.)

**King, John Paul.** 1891–93. Philadelphia, Pa. Obtained one French, one U.S., and two German patents for a crying doll wherein reeds vibrated when the position of the doll was changed.

**King Bros.** 1918–21. London. Made dolls.

**King's Jester.** 1925. Doll made by the *American Stuffed Novelty Co.*

**Kintzback, Martin.** 1869. Philadelphia. Patented in U.S. a method for attaching a porcelain hand to a leather arm.

**Kipmi.** 1924. Trademark registered in France by *Mlle. Raymonde Couin and Mlle. Thérèse Camgrand* for dolls of all kinds.

**Kipp Bros.** 1910. Indianapolis, Ind. Produced dolls.

**Kirchner, Ida.** 1918. Nürnberg, Bavaria. Made dolls.

**Kiriu, Koshokuwaisha, & Akiyama, T.** 1880. Japan. Displayed dolls at the Melbourne International Exhibition.

**Kirk, Kittie M.** 1923–24. Minneapolis, Minn. Was issued U.S. design patent for doll in pants and conical hat.

**Kirsch, S., & Co. (S. K. Novelty Co.).** 1919–24. Brooklyn, N.Y. Handled cherub-type doll named *Million Dollar Doll* and dolls' wigs.

1920: *Flo-Flo of the Follies, Bobbikins, Frou-Frou,* and *Twinkie.*

**Kirschkamp, J., Gerpott, Fr., & Kirschkamp, I., Co. (Kirschkamp, J., & Co.).** 1867–91. Düsseldorf, Prussia. Made dolls.

1867: Displayed dolls at the Paris Exposition.

1891: *Gottschalk & Co.* were their agents in Paris.

**Kishikawa, Zensaku.** 1900. Japan. Won a bronze medal for dolls at the Paris Exposition.

**Kismi.** 1905. Trademark registered in Britain by *Stallard & Co.* for toy dolls.

**Kiss Baby (Kiss-throwing Doll).** A jointed composition-body doll whose right arm bends and right hand comes up to the doll's mouth and simulates throwing a kiss.

Early 1890's: *Fleischmann & Blödel* obtained French and German patents for a doll that threw kisses and talked when a button at the side of her bust was pressed.

1894: Paul Eugène Girard of the *Bru* firm secured a French patent for a doll that threw kisses when a cord was pulled; this was a dressed doll, 12 inches tall; retail price in U.S. was 97¢.

1895: Fleischmann & Blödel were granted a French patent for a doll that threw kisses and said "Mama" or "Papa" as it walked; the kiss-throwing was activated by leg movement.

1897: Widow Lafosse of *Société Steiner* obtained a French patent for a doll that threw kisses and said "Mama" or "Papa" when a cord was pulled.

Paul Eugène Girard of the Bru firm secured a French patent for a doll that threw kisses, talked, and turned its

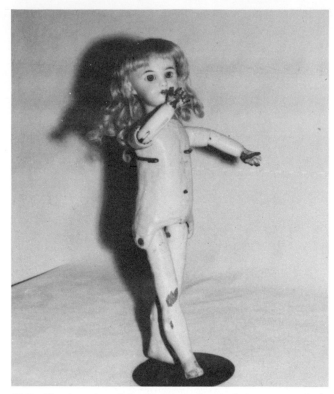

**1013.** Kiss-throwing doll with bisque head of the type made by Société Française de Fabrication de Bébés et Jouets. The doll throws a kiss as she walks. Head marked only "Dep." H. 14 inches. *Coleman Collection.*

head, all of which were activated by the leg movement when walking.

1905: *Société Française de Fabrication de Bébés et Jouets* obtained a French patent for a doll that threw kisses, walked, talked, and turned its head. They were already making dolls that threw kisses, walked, and nodded their heads, and were dressed in the latest Parisian fashion. These had human hair wigs and were 24 inches in size. By 1922, they were probably made in other sizes.

**Kiss Me Quick.** 1922. Cherub-type doll copyrighted by *Louis Bertolini,* with eyes glancing to the side and lips ready for a kiss.

**Kister, A. W. Fr., Inc.** 1898–1925+. Scheibe in Schwarzburg, Rudolstadt, Thür. Made dolls.

1898: Advertised porcelain dolls and *bathing dolls.*

1907–11: Advertised undressed jointed dolls for export.

**Kittel, Woldemar.** 1895–1908. Coburg, Thür. Made and exported dressed dolls.

**Kittleman, Eva.** 1922. Council Bluffs, Iowa. Secured U.S. design patent for a two-faced rag doll dressed as a clown.

**Klagsbrunn, Hugo.** 1914–16. Mount Vernon, N.Y., and New York City. Registered *Sunshine Kids* as a trademark in U.S. and used the initials *Isco* for *Indestructo Specialties Co.* Klagsbrunn obtained a U.S. patent for a doll with eyes that turned up and down as well as to either side.

**Kleiner Sonnenschein (Little Sunshine).** 1922. Was registered as a trademark for dolls by *Catterfelder Puppenfabrik,* for papier-mâché dolls.

**Klein's Doll Manufactory.** 1885–98. Cincinnati, Ohio. Advertised imported and domestic dolls, doll parts, and the repair of dolls.

**Klemperer, F.** 1923–25. Prague, Czechoslovakia. Made dolls.

**Kletzin, Ltd.** 1925. London. Made dolls.

**Kley & Hahn.** 1895–1925+. Ohrdruf, Thür. From 1895–1902, operated a porcelain factory that made dolls' heads and bathing dolls. From 1902–25+, they made dolls of various types.

1902: Registered *Walküre* as a trademark in Germany for dolls. (See color photograph C 17.)

KLEY & HAHN DOLLS

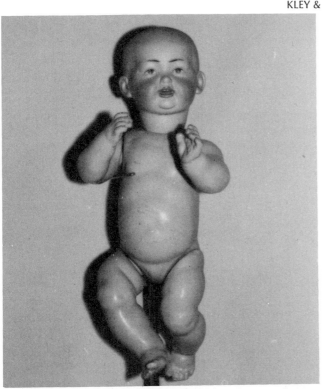

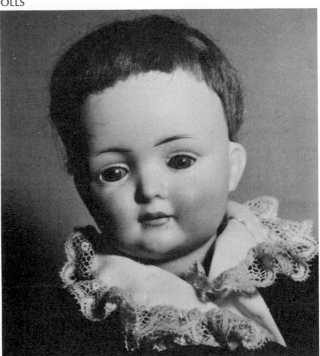

**1015.** Character baby with bisque head and glass eyes. Note the similarity between the eyebrows and those on the doll in Ill. **1014.** *Courtesy of Margaret Whitton; photograph by Winnie Langley.*

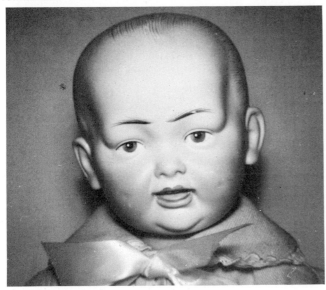

**1014A & B.** Character baby with bisque head, painted eyes, open-closed mouth with two upper teeth. Mark: Ill. **1017.** Bent-limb composition baby body. H. 16 inches. *Courtesy of Dorothy Annunziato.*

1909: Registered "K" in a keystone as a trademark in Germany for ball-jointed and leather dolls.

1910: Registered *Schneewittchen* (Snow White) in Germany as a trademark for ball-jointed dolls, character dolls, and leather dolls.

1911: Registered in Germany *Meine Einzige* (My Only One) in a six-pointed star as a trademark for ball-jointed dolls, character dolls, and leather dolls. Advertised dolls' heads with sleeping eyes.

1913: Registered in Germany *Cellunova* as a trademark for dolls and dolls' heads.

Kley & Hahn advertised that they made jointed dolls and character babies in all qualities from the cheapest to the finest. Dolls were often marked with "K & H" in a streamer and with numbers. Mold #158 has molded hair, open-closed mouth with two upper teeth and tongue; mold #167 has open mouth with two teeth, and a wig; both these are character babies with eyebrows shaped like a partially flattened, horizontal question mark.

KLEY & HAHN DOLL

**1016.** Bisque head, glass eyes, closed mouth; ball-jointed composition body with the diagonal hip joints usually found after World War I. H. 20 inches. *Courtesy of Hazel Ulseth.*

**1017–1021.** Marks found on dolls made by Kley & Hahn.

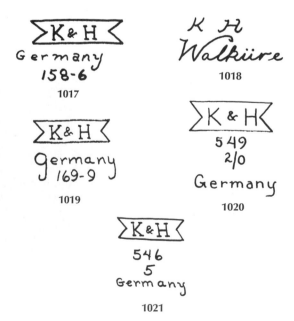

**Kling, C. F., & Co. (Kling & Co.).** 1836–1925+. Ohrdruf, Thür. A porcelain factory that produced dolls' heads and dolls. Christian Friedrich Kling founded this factory, and it remained in the Kling family until toward the end of the 19th century, when Lewis Ortlepp and others succeeded the Klings. Besides dolls' heads they made all-porcelain dolls, both the so-called *Frozen Charlotte* type and jointed all-porcelain dolls, especially in smaller sizes. They also made bathing children. In 1891, they advertised that they had won many prizes but no record has been found as yet of these prizes. They exported to all countries, and were one of the several firms that made heads for *Bye-Lo* dolls. Their mark, "K" in a bell, has been found on both china heads and bisque heads. Bisque turned shoulder heads with molded hair, generally in short curls, have been found with the Kling mark. These are highly colored and have full lips. The Museum of the City of New York has several bisque heads as well as a few china heads with Kling marks given them by *Fred Kolb* of *Borgfeldt*. A bald tinted bisque shoulder head bearing the Kling mark is on a pink cloth body with celluloid forearms made by *Rheinische Gummi & Celluloid Fabrik Co.* This combination was popular around 1912. (See Ill. 1024.)

**Klondike Doll.** 1901. Doll dressed as a Klondike miner with fur parka, picks and knives in its belt, and a gun on its shoulder. Price $2.00 doz. wholesale.

**Klooss & Bothfeld.** 1909. Halle, Saxony. Made dolls.

**Kloster Veilsdorf.** See **Closter Veilsdorf.**

**Klosterle.** 1790–1890+. Porcelain factory at Klosterle, Austria, now Czechoslovakia. Output was controlled by *Bawo & Dotter* in the late 19th century.

**Klötzer, Eduard.** 1925. Sonneberg, Thür. Made dolls.

**Klousnitzer, Frank.** 1923–24. Crafton, Pa. Secured U.S. design patent for a doll's head that resembled Nefertiti, the Egyptian queen.

**Kluge, Joh. Ernst.** 1909. Berlin. Wholesale distributor of dolls.

**Kmel, Gustav.** 1906. Fischern near Carlsbad, Bohemia. Producer of dolls' heads; obtained a German patent for improving dolls. *Bawo & Dotter, Hamburger & Co.,* and *Strobel & Wilken* all used "Carlsbad" in some of their marks.

**Knabe, Carl Heinrich.** 1897–1903. Vienna. Made dolls, dolls' heads, and cloth dolls.

**Knauer, Ernst.** 1918. Waltershausen, Thür. Made dolls.

**Knauth, Edm., & Knauth, Guido.** 1895. Orlamünde, Thür. Made dolls. A doll marked "Knauth" has brown-colored bisque head, jointed composition and wood body without knee joints, sleeping eyes, open mouth with teeth, pierced ears; doll is 16 inches tall.

**Knell Bros. (Knell, Francis P.).** See **Greiner, Ludwig.**

**Knepfer, Ada.** 1917–18. Yonkers, N.Y. Was granted a U. S. design patent for a doll with rings and bells.

**Knickerbocker Doll (Toy) Co.** 1924–25. New York City. Made dolls.

KLING DOLLS

**1022A, B, C, & D.** Three heads marked with the Kling bell, part of a group given by Fred Kolb of Borgfeldt to the Museum of the City of New York. The head on the left is of bisque and has the longer face and neck of an older child. It has "148 0" as well as the bell on the back of the shoulders. The

turned baby head of bisque in the center has the numbers "186.5." The head on the right is of glazed china and has the numbers "189 3." H. 3¾ inches. *Courtesy of the Museum of the City of New York.*

1023

**1023A & B.** China head and limb doll; china is flesh tinted. Black painted high boots. This is a black-haired version of the blonde china head in Ill. 1022. Kling mark on back shoulders: Ill. 1025. H. 10½ inches. H. of shoulder head, 3 inches. *Coleman Collection.*

**1025 & 1026.** Kling marks used on dolls.

**1024A, B, C, & D.** Two Kling dolls with highly colored bisque heads. One has molded hair, painted eyes, bisque limbs, and a cloth body with two rows of blue stitching down the front. It is marked on the back of the shoulder with the Kling bell and No. "7" H. 6½ inches. H. of shoulder head, 1¾ inches.

Other doll has a bald pate without holes, stationary glass eyes, closed mouth, celluloid forearms with turtle mark, pink cloth body. Mark: Ill. 1026. H. 16 inches. *Courtesy of Kit Robbins and Coleman Collection.*

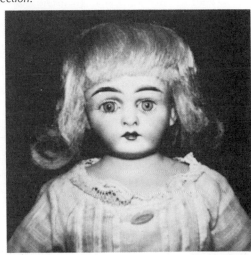

# Knauth

**1027.** Mark found on Knauth dolls.

**1028.** Edmund Knoch's mark.

**Knickerbocker Specialty Co.** Ca. 1904. Made a cutout rag doll representing *Buster Brown.*

**Knight, Cliff B.** 1919. New York City. Cartoonist for PLAYTHINGS; created *Dainty Marie* for the *H. & Z. Doll Co.*

**Knight, Muriel.** 1921. Designed a portrait doll representing *June Caprice,* the Pathé picture star.

**Knight & Co.** 1878. Newchwang, China. Displayed dolls in silk at the Paris Exposition.

**Knights, E. G., & Co.** 1894. London. Made dolls.

**Knitted Dolls.** 1881–92, and probably in many other years, dolls were knitted.

1881: *Millikin & Lawley* advertised knitted dolls made by inmates of foreign nunneries. These came in sailor or soldier costumes in six sizes; price 38¢ to $2.62.

1892: HARPER'S BAZAR published directions for knitting a boy doll and suggested using golden brown and yellow Germantown wool.

**Knoch, Edmund.** 1896–1925+. Mönchröden near Coburg, Thür. Made soft stuffed dolls and babies.

**Knoch, Gebrüder.** 1887–1918. Neustadt near Coburg, Thür. Porcelain factory; specialized in dolls' heads.

**Knoch, J. G.** 1909. Hönbach, Thür. Made dolls' heads.

**Knock About Dolls.** 1893–1913. Imported dolls, distributed by *Butler Bros.* and *Sears, Roebuck & Co.* They were made of Canton felt or flannel in a variety of colors, with gusset-jointed bodies similar to kid bodies.

1893: Advertised with bisque heads and hands, glass eyes, open mouth and teeth, wigs with *Rembrandt Hair* style; black, red, and white bodies, jointed at hips and knees with gussets. Sizes 12½, 16½, and 21½ inches; price $2.23 to $8.25 doz. wholesale.

1894: Came with bisque head and hands, and body of red, green, or blue felt; size 16 inches, price 45¢.

1901: A similar type of doll was advertised with red, blue, or black felt body; sizes 11, 12, 13, 14, 16, and 18 inches.

Ca. 1913: Dolls with felt bodies came with celluloid heads and *Minerva* metal heads.

Knock About Dolls with Minerva metal heads were advertised by *Montgomery Ward & Co.* as early as 1904 and by *Alfred Vischer & Co.* in 1905. It is not known what type of body these dolls had, except that they were advertised as being "extra strong."

**Knock-About Character Dolls.** 1917. Distributed by the *Baltimore Bargain House.* Came in pink or blue costumes; 11 inches tall, $1.20 doz. wholesale.

**1029A & B.** Pair of dolls with bisque heads made by Gebrüder Knoch; both heads are marked as in Ill. **1030,** except that the numbers are "192–14/0" instead of "201–6/0." These same dolls were pictured in *The Doll Book* by Laura Starr in 1908. She purchased them from a wholesale doll house in New York and described them as "very good specimens of American dolls." Uncle Sam has lost his mustache and hat. Their clothes are original: red and white striped skirt and pants, white blouse and vest, blue dotted coat and scarf. H. 11 inches. *Courtesy of the International Doll Library Foundation.*

**1030 & 1031.** Marks used on dolls by Gebrüder Knoch.

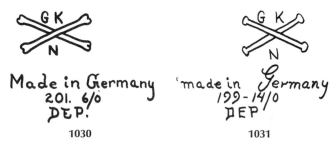

**1030**          **1031**

**Knockabout Worsted Dolls.** 1901. Came with gauze heads, cotton-stuffed bodies, worsted suits of clothing. Sizes 8½, 12, and 14 inches, prices 77¢ to $4.00 doz. wholesale.

**Knockout Grade.** 1916–22. Dolls with *Minerva* metal heads, distributed by *Sears, Roebuck & Co.* Came with painted hair and eyes, pink silesia-cloth bodies, forearms and hands of carved wood. Sizes were 11¾, 13¾, 15¾, and 17½ inches. The 17½-inch size was deleted by 1922. The price range in 1916 was 25¢ to 50¢; in 1922 it was 45¢ to 79¢, for comparable size dolls.

**Knopf im Ohr.** See **Button in Ear.**

**Knoxall Doll Co.** 1922–24. New York City. Handled various types of dolls, including Knoxall flapper dolls, sizes 20 and 26 inches; Knoxall Babies and *Mama Dolls,* sizes 15 to 27 inches.

**Knuepfer, Arno.** 1924. Leipzig, Saxony. Made dolls.

**Koaster Kid.** 1921–22. Trademark registered in U.S. by *Arthur Black* for dolls.

**Koch, J. César.** 1915. Paris. Registered in France *Lutecia Baby* and *Bébé Gloria* as trademarks for dolls.

**Koch, Paul.** 1915–25+. Neustadt near Coburg, Thür. Made dolls.

**Koch & Weithase.** 1902. Köpplesdorf, Thür. Porcelain factory; made dolls' heads. Note that the initials of this firm are "K & W." It is not known whether they ever put these initials on their dolls' heads.

**Kochendörfer, Fritz.** 1891–1921. Sonneberg, Thür. Made dolls.

1891: Obtained German patent for a method of using interchangeable parts for dolls.

**Kochendörfer, M.** 1909. Sonneberg, Thür. Made dolls.

**Kochniss, Carl.** 1888–1925+. Sonneberg, Thür. Made dolls.

**Kock, W.** 1915–23. Köppelsdorf, Thür. Made dolls.

**Koenig, Andreas.** See **König, Andreas.**

**Koenig, Mlle. Marie.** 1890–1914. Paris. Created a doll display for the state-owned Musée Pédagogique, as part of the permanent exhibit of sewing arts. Mlle. Koenig was Inspector of Education. She wrote several books about this doll display, which was also shown at the 1896 Rouen Exposition and the 1900 Paris Exposition. One book titled POUPEES ET LEGENDES DE FRANCE contains drawings of dolls in various provincial costumes and descriptions of their costumes, but no descriptions of the dolls themselves. Another book, MUSEE DES POUPEES, written by Mlle. Koenig was published in 1909. By 1914, the display was known as the Musée des Poupées in the Trocadéro, Paris. In August, 1914, PLAYTHINGS described it as follows: "They stand for national and provincial types. This one wears the costume of Alsace, that of Brittany or Lorraine. Here is a Siamese doll, there an Egyptian. . . . In one corner of the museum is a collection of Balkan dolls. Last year a young and pretty Parisienne, who had married a Bulgarian, brought to the museum a number of dolls that she had snatched, as it were, from the battlefield. . . . Fleeing the country that had now become unbearable, the widow arrived in Paris, and carried to Mlle. Marie Koenig, who is the founder of the Musée des Poupées, a number of beautiful dolls in Balkan costumes. . . . Dancers from Seville, Venetians, cowboys, Argentines, redskins, braves and their squaws, Auvergates and Paris Belles in 'hobble skirts.' It is a strange and motley crew drawn from all the ages, representing all the races. Some dwarfs, others are giants, some beautiful, others astonishingly ugly."

**Koenig, Mary.** 1921–22. New York City. Was issued a U.S. design patent for a doll with eyes glancing to the side and a wig.

**Koenig & Rudolph.** See **König & Rudolph.**

**Koenig & Wernicke.** See **König & Wernicke.**

**Koenigliche Porzellan Manufaktur.** See **Königliche Porzellan Manufaktur.**

**Koerner, O.** 1900. Berlin. Made dolls.

**Kohl & Wengenroth.** 1912. Offenbach am Main. Produced dolls and heads; *bathing dolls* and celluloid babies.

**Kohler, L. G.** 1862. Neustadt, Bavaria. Won a prize medal for his papier-mâché dolls at the 1862 London Exhibition.

**Köhler & Bovenkamp, R.** 1909. Barmen, Prussia. Made dolls.

**Kohnstam, J.** 1913–25+. London. Obtained a British patent for molding a hollow doll's body in one piece, including the sockets for the limbs.

**Kohnstam, M., & Co.** 1902–25+. Fürth, Bavaria, and London. Manufactured and exported dolls, especially composition dolls. Used initials *Moko.*

1909: Registered *Cupid* as a trademark in Britain and Germany for dolls.

1910: Registered in Britain and Germany as a trademark for dolls a picture of a baby's bottle with the words: "Mother's Darling // quiet and good // requires no nursing // attention or food."

1915: Registered *The Duchess Dressed Doll* with the initials "D D D" in a triangle as a trademark in Germany. The letters "Moko" on a flag appeared on the last two trademarks as well as on later marks.

**Kokette.** See **Die Kokette.**

**Ko-ko.** 1925. Trademark registered in Germany and U.S. by *Borgfeldt.*

**Kokomo Kids.** See **Eck, W. C., & Co.**

**Kolb, Fred.** 1892–1925+. New York City. Managed *Borgfeldt*'s doll department; later became president of Borgfeldt. He copyrighted *O-U-Kid* and *Dotty Darling* in 1914.

**Köllner, M.** 1923–25. Luisenthal near Ohrdruf, Thür. Made dolls' heads, *bathing dolls,* dressed and undressed dolls, and dolls' clothing.

**König, Andreas.** Ca. 1890–1909. Sonneberg, Thür. Manufactured and exported dolls, especially Santa Claus dolls and babies in bags. In 1900 and 1904, displayed dolls and was in the Grand Prize winning group at the Paris Exposition and at the St. Louis Exposition.

**König & Rudolph.** 1912–14. Waltershausen, Thür. Doll manufacturers; registered in Germany *Königskinder* (King's Children) as a trademark.

**König & Wernicke.** 1912–25+. Waltershausen, Thür. Made jointed dolls and character babies; sometimes used *Simon & Halbig* bisque heads. Trademarks were "K & W"

**1032.** König & Wernicke mark found on dolls.

and *Mein Stolz* (My Pride). They made composition baby bodies for socket-head *Bye-Lo Babies*.

**Königliche Porzellan Manufaktur.** 1761–1925+. Berlin. The state-owned porcelain factory. They used the initials "K. P. M." Earlier the *Meissen* factory had used the same name and initials, but it is doubtful if any dolls were made at that early time. Several of the marks of this factory have been found on the inside of the shoulders of china dolls' heads. These marks are usually the ones used from ca. 1840 to 1870.

**Königliche Sächsische Porzellan Manufaktur.** See **Meissen.**

**Königskinder (King's Children).** 1912–14. Trademark registered in Germany by *Koenig & Rudolph* and registered in U.S. by *H. B. Claflin Co.*

**Konroe Merchants.** 1921–24. New York City. Sole importers of *My Honey* dolls, registered "My Honey" as a trademark in the U.S. in 1923. These dolls came with bisque heads and roguish sleeping eyes.

1924: Advertised *The Parisienne* with real hair bobbed wig, a "cigarette" in the mouth; wore trousers and high heels.

**Konstructo Co.** 1920. New York City. Sole distributor of Indian dolls made by *M. F. Woods Co.*

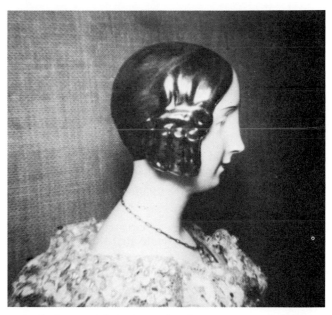

**1034.** Finely modeled china head with painted features. Streaked brown hair has center part; five curls are on the side not shown; molded bosom. Inside of the head was not examined, but the head was probably made by Königliche Porzellan Manufaktur. Base of the shoulder head, 2 inches in depth and 2³⁄₄ inches in width. These heads are deeper than the usual china heads. (See also Ill. **494.**) *Courtesy of the Chester County Historical Society.*

**1035–1039.** Porcelain marks of the Königliche Porzellan Manufaktur. No. **1039** is found on dolls' heads. These marks date from approximately 1837-70.

**1033.** Tinted china head with brown hair and blue eyes, made by Königliche Porzellan Manufaktur, has "K.P.M." mark. *Courtesy of Marion Holt; photograph by Winnie Langley.*

**Konti, J.** 1923–25. Vienna. Made dolls.

**Kotter, Theodore F.** 1923–24. Hollis, N.Y. Was issued a U.S. design patent for a two-part rag doll representing a mammy wearing an apron and bandanna.

**Kraatz, W.** 1844. Berlin. Made wax dolls' heads, wax arms and legs, as well as whole wax dolls in glass cases, which were shown at the Berlin Exhibition.

**Kradle Babe.** 1925. Name for infant doll produced by *Domec Toys Inc.*

**Kraemer & Van Elsberg.** 1913–14. Cologne, Germany. Obtained two German patents for making eyes for dolls of celluloid, papier-mâché, metal, and other materials.

**Kraepelin, Emma.** 1893. Stockholm, Sweden. Made dressed dolls, and exhibited them at the Chicago World's Fair.

**Krahmer, Carl.** 1918. Frankenhausen, Thür. Made dolls.

**Krampe, Otto.** 1902–3. Schalksmühle, Westf. Doll manufacturer. Registered *Dornröschen* (Sleeping Beauty) as a trademark in Germany for sleeping dolls. He obtained U.S. and German patents for dolls' eyes that could be locked asleep or awake by a small knob at the back of the head under the hair of the doll.

**Kratky, Adolf.** 1895. Köppelsdorf, Thür. Made dolls.

**Kratz-Boussac, Henri Othon.** 1892–1910. Paris. In 1892 obtained a French patent for making one-piece dolls' heads in celluloid.

1910: Registered *La Parisienne* in France as a trademark for dolls. This mark was advertised in 1911 by a *Société Anonyme*.

**Kraus & Schöner, Inc.** 1925. Nürnberg, Bavaria. Handled dolls.

**Krause, Josef.** 1909. Zittau, Saxony. Made dolls.

**Krause, Otto.** 1908–14. Neustadt near Coburg, Thür. Manufactured and exported various kinds of dressed and undressed dolls. *M. Hirsch* was his distributor in London.

**Krauss, Gebrüder (Bros.).** 1863–1921. Eisfeld. Made and exported dolls. *Gottschalk* was their distributor in Paris and *Henry S. Benjamin* was their distributor in London.

1863–91: Advertised dolls of papier-mâché, wood, and other materials.

1907–11: Advertised dressed dolls.

**Krauss, Herman.** 1925. Rodach near Coburg, Thür. Made papier-mâché dolls.

**Krauss, Samuel.** 1853–73. Rodach near Coburg, Thür. Made papier-mâché dolls with movable heads. He displayed his dolls at the New York Exhibition in 1853 and at Vienna in 1873. *Le Montréer* distributed his dolls in Paris.

**Krebs, Rich.** 1918. Oberneubrunn, Thür. Manufactured dolls.

**Krebs, Stengel, & Levy.** 1915. New York City. All were formerly with *Steinfeld Bros.* Handled dolls and used the slogan *Kwick Selling Lines*.

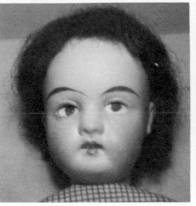

**1040A & B.** Bisque socket head on the left made by Gebrüder Krauss has open mouth with four upper teeth molded with the head, and a nostril area without red dots; the eyes are not original. Mark: Ill. **1042**. H. of socket head, 2½ inches. The bisque socket head on the right was possibly made by Gebrüder Krauss; it has heavy black eyelid lines, two-tone nostril area, closed mouth; the outlining and shading of the mouth all suggest decorative techniques often found on dolls from France. Mark: Ill. **1041**. H. 16 inches. *Coleman Collection* and *Courtesy of Eleanor Jean Carter.*

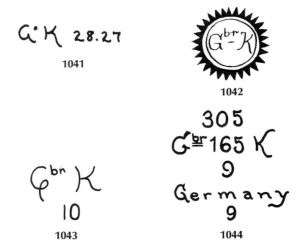

**1041–1044.** Marks that might stand for Gebrüder Krauss, Gebrüder Knoch, or Gebrüder Kuhnlenz. Mark No. **1042** is definitely a Gebrüder Krauss mark found on dolls.

**Kreimeyer, Albert.** 1919. Hannover, Prussia. Secured a German patent for sleeping eyes in dolls' heads.

**Kreutzer, Georg.** 1918–25. Unterlind and Sonneberg, Thür. Manufactured dressed dolls and babies.

**Kreyssig, Otto.** 1900–1909. Berlin. Made dolls.

**Kriege, Johannes.** 1904–5. Magdeburg, Germany. Produced and distributed dolls of various kinds; registered *Das Süsse Trudelchen* (The Sweet Little Dancer) as a trademark in Germany.

**Kris Kringle Kid Co.** 1924–25. Jersey City, N.J. They registered, as a trademark in U.S. for dolls, "Kris Kringle Kid," which was written with a single oversized *K* serving as the first letter for all three words.

**Krohn, Alexandre.** 1882–90. Paris. Distributed dolls and bébés to shops in Paris and Russia; used the trademark of a lion lying down with a doll between its front paws.

**Krönen.** Ca. 1820. Name for a type of wooden doll; found in old Sonneberg ledgers.

Ca. 1840: All-wooden dolls of the turned skittle type, with brimmed "hat," shown in German catalogs.

**Krönen Puppe (Crown Doll).** 1914–25+. Trademark registered by *Kestner* in Germany for dolls. This name appears on the crown without the streamers.

**Krueger, Richard G.** 1917. New York City. Made hand-painted rag dolls named *Bedtime,* which were 10 inches tall. Also made *Miss Liberty,* a celluloid doll dressed in silk, 10 inches tall.

**Krumm, Erich.** 1915. Neustadt near Coburg, Thür. Manufactured dolls.

**Kruse, Käthe (née Simon).** Ca. 1910–25+. Bad Kösen, Silesia, and Charlottenburg, Prussia. Made artistic dolls. In 1907, she made her first rag doll out of a towel, then spent three years perfecting it. PLAYTHINGS gave the following descriptions of the Käthe Kruse dolls in the December, 1910, January, 1911, and April, 1911 issues:

"Mrs. Kruse, the wife of a well-known Berlin sculptor, has taken out a patent for the manufacture of artistic dolls. These dolls are a combination of plastic faces and stuffed models, and are extremely well done. They excited great interest at an exhibition of dolls recently held in Berlin. The bodies are stuffed with wadding, the limbs being all movable and the whole result looks not at all like an ordinary doll, but something characteristically out of the common. The various faces have been designed from life by artists. . . . The inventor intends to bring out 'Bambini,' especially those of Lucia [sic] Della Robbia."

". . . Mrs. Prof. Kruse cut and stuffed dolls for four years, until they were satisfactory and suitable to be shown to the great public. And now she has made the great venture.

"The Kruse doll is perhaps more true to nature than any seen before, yet it is not a character doll. And it may be that this means progress in the direction of refinement and culture. The character doll shows a little too much of mannerism, a little overdrawing of traits of character. . . .

"Regarding the appearance of this doll, the following announcement is made: The muslin for the head having been correctly cut out, the reverse side is chemically treated. It is then sewed together and the empty space filled with wadding. In the same way, but without the use of chemicals, the lifelike body is made. Mrs. Kruse copies the head from a bambino of the Renaissance period, and her own children are models for the bodies. Here mother-love guides the hand. The muslin is good for painting—the features are painted in. Then they are sprayed with fixative, and the doll is washable."

". . . These dolls have now arrived on this side of the water, and orders may be placed for 1911 delivery.

**1045.** Käthe Kruse rag doll with the trade name "Karlchen," shown in 1922 German Art Exhibit in Newark, N.J. Contemporary picture. *Courtesy of the Newark Museum, Newark, N.J.*

The dolls are jointed throughout and are distinctly not of the ordinary run, being Art dolls with a capital 'A' in every respect. These dolls, only one of which is on display in this country as these lines are being written, have muslin heads beautifully hand painted in oil. The real child-like expression is brought out in a charming manner, and the effect produced is similar to that which one sees in an expensive oil painting—the most beautiful effect being gained when the object is placed a short distance off. Naturally, these dolls are more expensive than regulation dolls of the same size, but they certainly will make an appeal to high class trade which has a leaning toward the artistic."

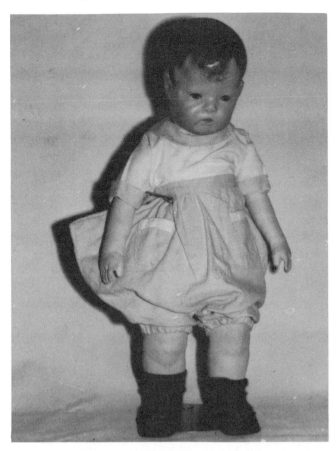

**1046A & B.** Boy and girl cloth dolls made by Käthe Kruse. Boy, dressed in original rompers, has "9774" on the sole of his foot; girl (shown without her dress) has "10116" on the sole of her foot. Stamped Käthe Kruse signature appears in purple ink on the other feet. H. 17 inches. *Courtesy of Dorothy Annunziato & Jessica Norman.*

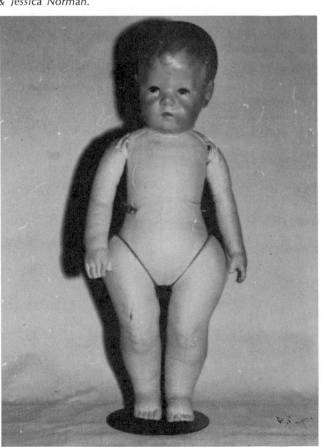

*Käthe Kruse.*
9771
**1047**

*Käthe Kruse*
81971

*Made in Germany*

**1048**

**1047 & 1048.** Käthe Kruse marks found on dolls.

1912: Exhibited dolls in Berlin.

1913: F. A. O. *Schwarz* advertised Käthe Kruse 18-inch doll for $10.00 undressed and $13.50 to $16.50 dressed.

1914: Dolls advertised as made of waterproof material.

1916: Obtained U.S. and German patents for stuffed dolls' bodies made of wire on which wire coils were wound; the coils were omitted at the joints. Flexible spine and neck wire coils were made thin. The framework was covered either by winding threads or by a rubber covering, to form the fleshy parts of the figure. The resulting bodies could take almost any desired position. There were *Kathrinchen,* a Dutch girl; *Lütt Martin; Fritz; Christinchen;* and *Michel;* price was $15.00 each.

1920–22: Obtained two more German patents for wire-body joints. The *Toddler* came out in 1922, and *Schlenkerchen* was registered in Germany as a trademark for this doll.

1923: Registered as a trademark in Germany a double *K* with the first one reversed, and the name "Käthe Kruse."

1925: Advertised *The Little Dreamer,* a life-sized baby doll.

The name "Käthe Kruse" usually appears stamped on the sole of one foot, a number being stamped in a different color of ink on the sole of the other foot. It seems likely that the lower numbers indicate older dolls, but that has not been proved as yet.

Among the various names Käthe Kruse gave her dolls were Wera, Wilhelminchen, Fanny, Emmy, Rumpumpel, Männe, Bärbel, Rudi, Babu, Erika, Bettina, Ursel, Olga, Pumpernella, Erna, Pepi, Friedel, Kathel, Willi, Ullrich, Peter, Robert, Trudila, Hilde, Beate, Henriette, Conrad, Hermann, Max, Liesel, Hans, and Karlchen; the last-named was exhibited in America in 1922 (see Ill. 1045).

**Krutkewitsch, Elvira.** 1923. Weimar, Germany. Secured a German patent for producing dolls' heads.

**Ku Tee (Ku-Tee).** 1919. Trade name for a washable cloth doll with hand-painted face and jointed limbs; made by *Hausman & Zatulove*.

**1049.** "Ku Tee" mark of Hausman & Zatulove.

**Kubelka, Josef.** 1884–1909. Vienna. His estate was granted a German patent in 1910; manufactured dolls and dolls' heads.

1884: Obtained Austrian, French, and German patents for making an indentation in the scalp of a doll's head made of a hard material such as porcelain, earthenware, papier-mâché, composition, or rubber; into this indentation wax (or a similar material) was poured, and hair was inserted into the wax. The same patent was obtained in England in 1887 and in the U.S. in 1889.

1909: Josef Kubelka & Theodor Friedmann obtained a German patent for securing natural or artificial hair in the pulp scalp of a doll.

1910: The same patent as the one in the previous year was obtained by the estate of Josef Kubelka.

**Kübler, E., & Co.** 1924. Berlin. Registered *Vetter Nick* as a trademark in Germany for rubber dolls.

**Kuddle Kiddies.** 1922. Trade name for dolls made by *Century Doll Co.*

**Kuddles.** 1915–17. Trademark registered in U.S. by *Jane Gray Co.* The name was usually stenciled on the rag doll. Dolls were made by Jane Gray Co., which advertised hand-painted heads and bodies stuffed with a filler softer than cotton, guaranteed never to lump, and light in weight. The dolls came as a pair, brother and sister, and wore removable rompers or dress of pink, tan, or blue checked gingham. Sizes 12 and 14 inches. Introduced Sarah Jane Veal of Georgia, the originator of Georgia Kuddles.

**Kuhles, Franz.** 1909–25+. Ohrdruf, Thür. Manufactured and exported, porcelain dolls. His establishment was called "Ohrdrufer Puppen und Spielwaren Fabrik."

**Kühn, Ernst.** 1925. Catterfeld, Thür. Manufactured dolls.

**Kühn & Grüning.** 1925. Catterfeld, Thür. Manufactured dolls.

**Kühn & Wagner.** 1923–25. Fürth, Bavaria. Manufactured and exported dolls.

**Kuhnert & Egli.** See **Greiner & Co.**

**Kühnlenz, Gebrüder.** 1909. Kronach, Bavaria. Porcelain factory. They made porcelain dolls of various kinds; specialized in dolls' heads. Note that initials were "G. K."

**1050A & B.** Bisque socket head and shoulder plate. The crown of the head is covered with wax, into which strands of hair have been inserted as described in the 1884 patent of Josef Kubelka. Jointed wooden body is covered with kid. Mark: Ill. **1051.** H. 17 inches. *Courtesy of Sylvia Brockmon.*

**1051.** Mark found on Joseph Kubelka dolls.

**Kummer, K. W.** 1844. Berlin. Won a silver medal for the papier-mâché dolls that he displayed at the Berlin Exhibition.

**Kundy, Franz.** See **Catterfelder Puppenfabrik.**

**Kunnin-Kids.** 1921–23. Trademark registered in U.S. by *Ontario Textile Co.;* usually affixed to doll with a label.

**Kunstgewerbliche Werkstätte.** 1922. Dachau, Germany. Registered *Elfi-Kiesling-Puppe* as a trademark in Germany for artistic dolls.

**Kuntz, Lazarus Albert, & Rosenthal, Alfred Abraham.** 1895. Berlin. Obtained a British patent for molding celluloid dolls' heads, which were generally applied to leather bodies. They stated that previously the head had been wider than the neck, and the breast wider than the head; therefore the neck became wrinkled or the breast was only partially formed, and the celluloid was of unequal thickness in its walls.

**Kupid.** 1919. *Newbisc* line of dolls made by *New Toy Co.;* two hundred numbers, dressed in sixty styles.

**Küsel, Herm.** 1897–1912. Coburg, Thür. Manufactured dolls.

**Kutie.** 1915–16. Trademark registered in U.S. by *Nellie Day* for dolls.

**Kutie Kid.** 1919–20. Made by *F. J. Schenk Co.* Advertised in 1919 by *Louis Wolf & Co.* as having painted hair and features; size 14½ inches, price $1.00 and up.

1920: Advertised by *Seamless Toy Corp.* as made of wood-pulp composition; sizes 14 and 15 inches; came with wig for $18.50 doz. wholesale.

**Kutie-Kiddies.** 1916. All-bisque bent-limb babies distributed by *Montgomery Ward & Co.* Wore lace-trimmed nightdress. Sizes 8½, 10, and 12 inches, price 92¢ to $1.55.

**Kutie Kins.** 1915. Line of felt-cloth dolls made by *A. W. Hanington & Co.* There were twelve subjects, as follows: Indian, Puss-in-Boots, Little Bo-Peep, Dutch Girl, Dutch Boy, Soldier Boy, Cupid, Japanese Boy, *Dolly Dimple,* Cowboy, Red Riding Hood, and Tom the Piper's Son. They had *Drayton*-type faces, and were advertised as hand-painted; size 10 inches, price 10¢.

**Kuzara, Mme. Elizabeth.** 1923. New York City. Wife of the Bohemian inventor, Joseph Kuzara. She made portrait dolls representing Bolshevist leaders, Kazan tribesmen, Cossacks, Slovak women, and Café Characters of Prague. She had made dolls for years, but these were her first commercial attempts.

**Kwacky-Wack.** 1912. Trademark registered by *Eisenmann & Co.* in Britain for dolls.

**Kweenie.** 1919–20. Trademark registered in U.S. by *Republic Doll & Toy Corp.* for dolls.

**Kwick Selling Lines.** 1915. Slogan of *Krebs, Stengel & Levy.*

# L

**La Belle.** 1916. Trade name used by *Kämmer & Reinhardt;* a paper label found on a bent-limb baby doll has this name. (See also **Baby Belle.**)

**La Cellulosine.** 1925. Trade name for celluloid dolls distributed by *J. Helft.*

**La Fée au Gui; La Fée au Trèfle; La Fée aux Trèfles; La Fée Bonheur.** 1909. Four trademarks registered by *Mme. E. Cayette* in France for dolls.

**La France.** 1895–98. Trademark used by *E. Pelletier* for dressed and undressed jointed bébés.

**La Francia.** 1917–19. Paris. A charity organization and the trade name for the dolls that they made; the dolls were distributed by *Grey & Grey.* The organization was founded to help the workers of France, war widows, wives of disabled soldiers, and the like. The faces were hand-painted and could be washed only with a sponge; otherwise the paint would come off. The bodies were made of scientifically stiffened material and were stuffed; they were advertised as being anatomically correct, and were tinted flesh color and shaded. All the dolls were dressed in handmade clothing. They represented boys, girls, peasants, workers, babies, and clowns. Each doll came with an outfit or layette and cost up to $7.00.

**La Georgienne.** Name found incised on dolls' heads made by *Lanternier.*

**La Madelon.** 1919–21. Trademark registered in France by *Alfred François Xavier Martin* and used for dolls and bébés made at the *Manufacture des Bébés & Poupées.* They advertised dressed and undressed *bébés incassables,* unbreakable heads and dolls.

**La Mignonne.** 1919–21. Trademark registered in France by *Les Arts du Papier, Ltd.* They advertised dolls, bébés, and *mignonettes,* all in "unbreakable" porcelanite.

**La Négress Blonde.** 1924. Trademark registered in France by *Au Perroquet Cie.*

**La Parisette.** 1919. Trademark registered in France by *Widow Coquillet* for dolls.

**La Parisienne.** 1910–12. Trademark registered in France by *Henri Othon Kratz-Boussac* and used for bébés manufactured by a *société anonyme.*

**La Parisienne.** 1920–25+. Trade name for dolls in a box made by *M. Eveno.*

**La Patricienne.** 1906–8. Advertised by E. Daspres, successor in Maison *Jules Steiner,* as a doll for all the world.

**La Petite.** 1910–12. Dressed dolls with bisque turning heads, advertised by *Butler Bros.* Came in sizes 9½, 11½, and 12½ inches.

**La Petite Caresse.** 1923. Trademark registered in Britain by Chad Valley Co., successors of *Johnson Bros. Ltd.*

**La Plastolite.** See **Plastolite.**

**La Poupée de France.** 1916. Trademark registered in France by *Louis Gautier.*

**La Poupée des Alliés.** 1916. Trademark registered in France by *Mme. Perrin.*

**La Poupée Française.** 1914. Trademark registered in France by *Marius Cornet* for various kinds of dolls.

**La Poupée Lina.** 1923. Trademark registered in France by *Maurice Mariage.*

**La Poupée Merveilleuse.** 1871–75. Trade name used by *Chaufour.* This name should not be confused with the later *Poupée Merveilleuse.*

**La Poupée Nicette.** 1924. Trademark registered in France by *Gaston Perrimond* for fabric dolls.

**La Prialytine.** See **Prialytine.**

**La Vénus.** 1923–25+. Trademark registered in France by *Adrien Carvaillo* for a rag doll and advertised by him in Paris Directories.

**La Vrai Parisienne.** 1916. Trademark registered in France by *Henry Perier.*

**Labat, Mme.** 1925+. Paris. Repaired dolls.

**Labry-Fegaud.** 1869–72. Paris. Made dolls.

**Lackenmacher Co., The.** 1922. New York City. Imported dolls.

**Lacmann, Jacob.** 1860–83, Philadelphia, Pa.; 1884–87, Philipine Lacmann, successor. Manufactured dolls' bodies. Jacob Lacmann was granted U.S. patents in 1871 for improvements in making doll fingers and in 1874 for improved methods of making hands and feet for dolls over a papier-mâché core. He witnessed the will of *Ludwig Greiner* in 1872, which indicates that these two famous doll makers were friends and explains the fact that many dolls with Lacmann marked bodies of heavy cotton material had Greiner marked heads of papier-mâché. Fine bisque heads with cork pates and paperweight eyes as well as *Cuno & Otto Dressel* marked heads have also been found on Lacmann bodies. By 1876 Jacob Lacmann's son, J. P. Alfred Lacmann, had joined the firm, which was then known as J. Lacmann and Son, and they advertised doll materials as well as doll bodies. At the

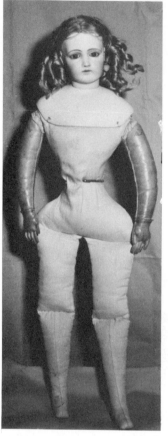
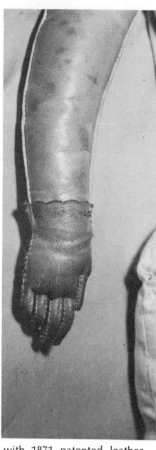

**1052A & B.** Lacmann cloth body with 1871 patented leather hands and arms. Lacmann's stamped mark is on the upper arm. Bisque socket head and shoulder plate, closed mouth, stationary eyes, cork pate, cloth feet. *Photograph by Winnie Langley.*

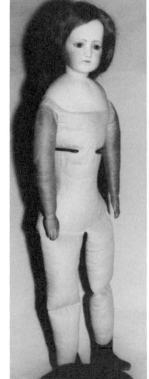

**1053A & B.** Lacmann body with hand patented in 1874—these hands are brown cloth over molded composition; blue leather booted feet are also over composition. Lacmann's mark (Ill. **1055**) is stamped on top of both arms and on the back of both legs; the seat is stamped size "8." Bisque swivel head on bisque shoulder plate, cork pate, applied and pierced ears. H. 27 inches. *Coleman Collection.*

**1054.** Four sizes of bodies made by Lacmann, with papier-mâché heads made by Ludwig Greiner. These bodies are made according to the 1874 patent; all except the smallest size have cloth covering the hands. The smallest doll has yellow shoes; the next one red shoes, and the two largest ones, blue shoes. *Courtesy of Winnie Langley; photograph by Winnie Langley.*

**1055.** Mark used on bodies made by Jacob Lacmann.

1876 Philadelphia Exhibition, Lacmann showed his products. The last entry found for J. Lacmann & Son was in 1883, when they were still making doll bodies.

**Lacouchy, D.** 1863–82. Paris. Was listed as a toymaker in 1863. In 1864 he was granted a French patent for improvements in the making of dolls. Between 1867 and 1873, Lacouchy made dressed kid-body dolls, doll clothes, and patented metal dolls. By 1877 he was listed as making kid-body dolls of fine and ordinary quality, dressed and undressed dolls.

**Lacourtille.** 1771–ca. 1840. Paris. Porcelain factory. No data have been found indicating whether china dolls'

heads were made here. However, its mark is very similar to the Meissen crossed swords, and should be distinguished from that mark.

**Laddie Boy.** 1915. Character doll made by *German Novelty Co.*

**Lady Acrobat.** Ca. 1905+. Wooden, rubber-jointed *Humpty Dumpty Circus* doll made by *Schoenhut.* Sizes 6 and 8 inches. The larger size also came with bisque head, molded hair, and painted features.

**Lady Blanche.** 1899. Doll distributed by YOUTH'S COMPANION. Came with bisque head, long curly-hair wig, jointed neck, shoulders, elbows, hips, and knees; wore satin dress, feather-trimmed hat, and shoes, stockings, and underwear. Size 15 inches; price $1.25.

**Lady Circus Rider.** Ca. 1905. Wooden *Humpty Dumpty Circus* doll made by *Schoenhut;* rubber jointed. Sizes 6 and 8 inches. The larger size also came with bisque head, molded hair, and painted features.

**1056A & B.** Lady Circus Rider made by Schoenhut has bisque head with painted and molded features; open-closed mouth, and teeth; jointed wooden body; dress is felt with gold braid. H. 8¼ inches. *Coleman Collection.*

**Lady Diana Manners.** 1924. *Celebrity Doll* originated by *Margaret Vale,* designed and made by *Jane Gray.* The doll represented Lady Diana Manners in the play THE MIRACLE by Morris Gest and Max Reinhardt. The doll had a hand-painted face and bore a tag with a facsimile autograph of Lady Diana Manners.

**Lady Dolls.** Before the 19th century, most dolls were called "babies," but since ladies and children dressed somewhat the same during those days, the dolls probably served for both. Catalogs and existing dolls suggest that during the first half of the 19th century there were lady dolls with heads made of papier-mâché or porcelain, with elaborate coiffures. Wax and wooden dolls appear to have served as ladies or as children, depending on the wishes of their owner.

The 1860's and 1870's were the golden era of the French lady dolls with their elegant clothes. The "French" bisque heads, which were new at that time, popularized this type of doll, whether they were made in France, Germany, Austria, or elsewhere. Collectors call these dolls "French Fashion" or "Parisienne" because many of them were dressed in the high style of Paris. Around 1876, *Strasburger, Pfeiffer & Co.* advertised French kid dressed dolls with "silk dresses made up in the latest Paris style," bisque turning heads, natural hair, glass eyes, earrings, and necklace; sizes 13, 16, 17, 17½, 18, and 19 inches; prices $1.50 to $40.00. In 1879, EHRICHS' FASHION QUARTERLY advertised "Dressed French Dolls" with bisque turning heads, real hair, and full-jointed kid bodies; prices were $2.75 to $25.00. The 1860's and 1870's were also the period of the so-called "Parian" or "Dresden" lady dolls with elaborate molded hairdos. By the 1880's, the lady dolls began to be supplanted by the new *Bébés Incassables* or baby dolls.

LADY DOLLS

**1057A & B.** Fashionable lady with bisque head, cobalt blue eyes, gusset-jointed kid body. H. 15 inches. *Coleman Collection.*

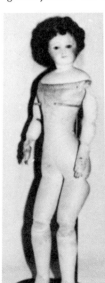

**1058A & B.** Pair of similarly dressed lady dolls with bisque shoulder heads, glass eyes, closed mouths, cloth bodies, kid arms. Dresses are of blue silk trimmed with ecru lace and dark velvet bands. Heights 16 and 18 inches. *Courtesy of the Chester County Historical Society.*

A few lady dolls continued to be made each year, with an upsurge in their popularity a few years before World War I.

1907: PLAYTHINGS reported that the conventional doll baby in France was being deposed by a "society woman of great elegance whose face is as oval and delicate

**1060A, B, & C.** Bride with bisque head, cloth body, composition limbs, probably ca. 1910. Contemporary white satin bridal gown. Head is marked "72" in green and incised lazy "0" and "5." H. 12 inches. H. of shoulder head, 4 inches. (See color photograph **C14.**) *Coleman Collection.*

**1059.** Lady doll made by Terrène; bisque head and hands. Mark: Ill. **1620.** H. 18 inches, *Courtesy of Eunice Althouse.*

as her predecessor's was round and chubby. Her slim bejewelled fingers have celluloid nails shaped like almonds and carefully manicured. Her eyes and lips are artistically 'touched up.' Her hair, teeth and other fascinations are in part detachable. She is well provided with rouge, powder, paddings and every requisite of fashionable beauty."

1910: Paris dolls costing $150 each were described as having "faces and figures modeled after fashionable feminine contours." LADIES' HOME JOURNAL, November 15, 1910, pictured a doll that looks like the *Gibson Girl* made by *Kestner*. It was noted in this year that the ratio of adult dolls increased with the age of the child, children under five usually preferring baby dolls.

1911: Lady dolls were very popular. They started with a line of Paris dolls dressed by Paris modistes, representing women twenty-five to thirty years old. These dolls were 24 inches high. Then smaller sizes were introduced and were made both in Germany and France. The German lady dolls were less expensive than the

French ones; at first they were $15.00 and up, but competition soon drove some of them down to $1.50. PLAYTHINGS, June, 1911, described some of these "Dolls of High Degree" as follows: "The latest styles from Paris are now presented in the doll world by means of the highest grade bisque dolls possible to manufacture . . . both equally attractive as display dolls and as dolls for sale to wealthy customers.

"Forty and fifty dollars is no unusual price to pay for dolls such as these; in fact the retail prices of some of them go far above these figures as the best of everything enters into their manufacture. Evening toilettes are presented besides the most elaborate of indoor and afternoon attire and the nobbiest effects in tailor made creations."

1912: European manufacturers brought out four *doll-faced dolls* with features changed slightly so that they

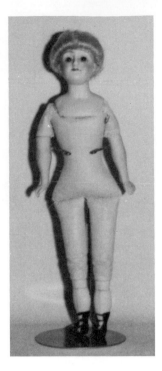

**1061.** Bisque shoulder head on a cloth body has bisque lower limbs; glass eyes and wig. Doll resembles the type sometimes called "Gibson Girl" by collectors. Head marked: "10/0 // made in Germany." H. 10 inches. H. of shoulder head, 2¾ inches. *Courtesy of Virginia Dilliplane.*

# PLAYTHINGS

# DOLLS OF HIGH DEGREE

### Patricians in the Doll Market that Command High Prices

**1062.** Ladies of high fashion, 1911. These dolls, in *Playthings Magazine,* appear to have bisque heads, jointed composition bodies, and elaborate clothes. *Courtesy of McCready Publishing Co.*

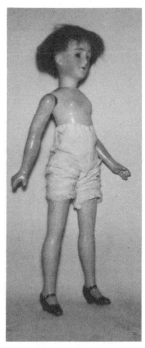

**1063A, B, & C.** Armand Marseille lady doll with bisque head and composition body, sleeping glass eyes, closed mouth. Head is marked "Germany // M. H. // A. 30 M." H. 9 inches. *Courtesy of Ollie Leavister.*

represented an eighteen-year-old girl, with a body molded accordingly.

1913: Imported dolls with the features and figures of girls eighteen to twenty-one years old. F. A. O. *Schwarz* advertised dolls with bisque heads having lady faces, jointed composition adult bodies, and dressed in a chemise. Sizes 16 and 26 inches; prices $2.75 to $6.50. (See color photographs C13, C14.)

**Laffitte, André.** 1917. Paris. Registered *Vita* as a trademark in France for dolls' heads and artificial eyes.

**Lafosse.** See **Steiner, Jules Nicholas.**

**Lake, Vincent.** See **Metal Doll Co.**

**Lakenmacher Co.** 1923. New York City. Used the trademark "L" for dolls.

**Lamagnère, Théophile.** 1882–1900. Paris. Made bébés of all kinds, including jointed *bébés incassables* with heads of carved wood; both dressed and undressed bébés. The carved wooden-head bébés were advertised in 1885.

1900: Was awarded a bronze medal for his dolls at the Paris Exposition.

**Lambert, André.** 1924. Paris. Registered *Zina* as a trademark in France for doll articles.

**Lambert, F.** Before 1897, Hamburg, Germany; 1897, Adolf Runge, successor. Manufactured dolls.

**Lambert, Leopold.** 1888–1923. Paris. Made and exported mechanical dolls and dolls in glass cases. He used "L. B." for his mark.

1888: He won a silver medal at the Barcelona Exhibition.

1889: He was Hors Concours for his display at the Paris Exposition.

1893: Showed dolls at the Chicago Exposition.

1904: Displayed his mechanical dolls with music at the St. Louis Exhibition.

It should be noted that the widow Lafosse, who was head of the *Jules Steiner* firm from 1893 to 1898, had the maiden name of Lambert.

**Lambert, Mlle. Cécile.** See **Rozier, Edmée.**

**Lambert, Thomas Bennett.** 1902. Chicago, Ill. Obtained a British patent for a phonograph doll.

**Lambert & Samhammer.** 1873–79. Sonneberg, Thür. Displayed dolls at the 1873 Vienna Exhibition and at the 1879 Sydney Exhibition. In Sydney, they received commendation for their dolls and dolls' heads. It is possible that Samhammer or at least a relative of his was the *Philipp Samhammer*, who was a doll maker of Sonneberg.

**Lamorlette, Mme.** 1839–46. Paris. Made dolls.

**Lamousse, Mme.** 1870–82. Paris. Made dolls.

**Lamplough, Henry.** 1916–25+. London. Obtained a British patent in 1916 for dolls made of cardboard or a similar material, having a surface of cotton fabric coated with a celluloid varnish. The color was applied to the dolls with a rubber stamp.

1924: Advertised unbreakable dolls and dolls' heads.

**1064.** Mark used by Leopold Lambert.     L. B.

**Lander, Hilda Gertrude.** See **Cowhan, Hilda.**

**Landfear, Elsie Dinsmore.** 1924–25. Jersey City, N.J. Obtained a U.S. design patent for a rag doll that resembled the Scarecrow of Oz. She registered the trademark in U.S. for the *Kris Kringle Kid Co.*

**Landon, Ann Dixie.** 1923. Piedmont, Calif. Was issued two U.S. design patents for rag dolls with long limbs; one represented Topsy and one represented Little Eva.

**Landsberger, Adolf, Firm.** 1907–9. Magdeburg, Saxony. Doll manufacturer. Registered in Germany "A L B" as a trademark.

**Landshut, Hermann & Co.** 1894–98. Waltershausen, Thür. A steam factory where dolls and doll parts were manufactured; dolls were exported also. They registered in Germany as a trademark the picture of a ball-jointed doll carrying a banner with the word *Linon* on it. This mark was stamped in red on the sole of the foot. A doll has been found with this mark on the sole of one foot, and on the sole of the other foot is 66543, the German patent number for the single-piece body patented by *Adolf Ascher* in 1892. The bisque head of the doll is marked with the number-alphabet size series of *Kestner.*

**1065.** Landshut's walking doll with body patented in 1892 by Ascher. Marks on soles of feet: Ill. **1066** and "DRP // 66543 // 1½." The bisque head has Kestner markings (see Ill. **976**), size C–7. H. 16 inches. *Coleman Collection.*

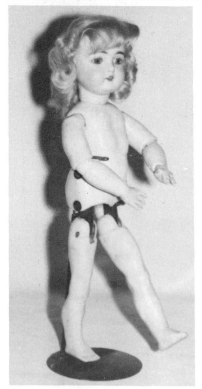

**1066**

**1066.** Landshut mark, generally found stamped in red on the soles of dolls' feet.

**Lanée.** 1885. Paris. Made dolls.

**Lang.** Before 1851–53. The heirs of Georg Lang of Oberammergau, Bavaria, displayed carved wooden dolls at the 1851 London Exhibition. No doubt one of these was the Erben G. Lange of Oberammergau who showed wooden dolls at the 1853 New York Exhibition and won a bronze medal.

**Lang.** 1869. Paris. Made dolls and dolls' heads of rubber.

**Lang, Emile.** 1915. France. Was granted a French patent for a doll's head made partly with adhesive linen.

**Lang & Co.** 1865–69. London. Made dolls of India rubber and gutta-percha.

1868: London Directory states that Lang & Co. made dolls with India rubber faces.

1869: Lang advertised rubber dolls and rubber dolls' heads in the Paris Directory.

**Langbein, Fritz.** 1918–25+. Neustadt near Coburg, Thür. Made *Täuflinge.*

**Langbein, Georg.** 1915–25+. Neustadt near Coburg, Thür. Manufactured jointed dolls, character babies, stuffed dolls, and dressed dolls.

**Langbein, M.** 1909. Wildenheid near Sonneberg, Thür. Made dolls' bodies.

**Langbein, Oscar.** 1908–25+. Sonneberg, Thür. Manufactured and exported dressed dolls.

**Langbein, Witwe (Widow) Carl.** 1895. Neustadt near Coburg, Thür. Made little or baby dolls.

**Lange, Alfred.** 1923. Friedrichroda, Thür. Registered in Germany the trademark *May Blossom* for dolls.

**Langer, Theob.** 1909. Breslau, Silesia. Manufactured dolls.

**Langfelder, Homma & Hayward, Inc.** 1922–25+. New York City. Distributors of Japanese and German dolls. Frederick Langfelder of New York City applied for a U.S. design patent in July, 1917, for a doll with eyes looking to the side; its feet were together, and it was dressed in a bathing suit. A diamond-shaped label with the word *Dolly* was on its stomach. The patent was granted in October, 1917, and Langfelder assigned his patent rights to *Morimura Bros.* All-bisque dolls, made in Japan, resemble the patent drawing, even to the paper sticker with the word "Dolly" on it. They have the same type of molded bathing suit, but the feet are apart and the lips are fuller. They came in sizes 3½ and 5½ inches.

By January, 1922, Langfelder, Homma & Hayward had taken over the Miscellaneous Import Department of Morimura Bros., which included their doll business. Langfelder, Homma & Hayward handled both German dolls and Japanese dolls. In 1922 they advertised: from Germany—Character Dolls, *Kidaline* Dolls, and Fully Jointed Dolls; from Japan—Bisque Dolls, Celluloid Dolls, and China Limb Dolls, which retailed for 5¢, 10¢, and 25¢. In 1924 and 1925 they also advertised rubber dolls. Their 1924 advertisement pictured the typical Japanese all-bisque type of doll. In 1925 their advertisement in

PLAYTHINGS claimed that Japan then led the world in the manufacture of bisque dolls.

**Langguth, Rud & Co.** 1925. Hüttensteinach, Thür. Manufactured dolls.

**Langholz, Eichelmann, Johanna.** 1900. Berlin. Manufactured dolls.

**Langrock, Joseph H.** 1921–22. New York City. Was issued a U.S. patent for a walking stuffed doll with legs that pivoted freely by means of a bar passed through multiple links that were formed of loops.

**Langrock Bros. Co.** 1916–17. Brooklyn, N.Y. Manufactured felt character dolls, which they named *El-Be-Co* dolls.

**Lanning, Frank.** See **Harvard Garment Co.**

**Lanternier, A., & Cie.** 1855–1925+. Limoges, France. Made decorated porcelain. The directories do not mention doll making, but bisque dolls' heads have been found with the mark of this company. A. Lanternier, Jr., learned the pottery business in England under Wedgwood. Lanternier dolls' heads have been found with *Favorite, La Georgienne, Lorraine,* and various other names on them. In 1915 and 1916, this was one of the three French companies selected by *Sèvres* for assistance in the manufacture of porcelain dolls' heads.

**Lany, William P. Dun.** 1917–18. Chicago, Ill. Obtained U.S. patent, which he assigned to *Sears, Roebuck & Co.* The patent pertained to the rotative movement of the joints of dolls made of hardened plastic material.

**Lanzendorf, Emil.** 1908. Nürnberg, Bavaria. Manufactured dolls.

**Laporte, Vve. (Widow).** See **Bouloch & LaPorte.**

**Lapp, F. W.** 1919. New York City. Copyrighted a cherub-type doll named *Evaline.*

**Laquionie & Cie.** 1919. Registered three trademarks in France for dolls together with the Société des Grands Magasins du *Printemps*. These trademarks were *Joli Guy, Muguette,* and *Rosette.*

**Lardot-Praquin.** 1867–82. Largny near Soissons, France. Made dolls that were sold in boxes.

**Large Dolls.** Dolls 36 inches or more in size were made for displays, for carnivals, or for premiums.

**Larsen, Howard R.** 1921–22. Milwaukee, Wis. Registered as a trademark in U.S. *Jiggle-Wiggle,* which was stamped directly on the doll.

**Larsen, Julius.** 1921. Copenhagen, Denmark. Obtained a German patent for movable eyes in dolls' heads.

**1067 & 1068.** Lanternier's marks found on dolls.

1067                              1068

**Laskey, Milton.** 1888. Malden, Mass. Obtained U.S. patent for a walking doll; assigned half of his rights to *George M. Cutter.*

**Lassie Doll.** 1921. Made by *Mutual Doll Co.* A jointed character doll of wood-pulp composition, designed by *Joseph L. Kallus,* distributed by *Borgfeldt.* Doll had painted or sleeping eyes and was 18 inches tall.

**Laughing Boy.** 1911. Copyrighted by *Louis Amberg & Son,* designed by *Jeno Juszko.* Doll had laughing eyes and mouth with teeth showing, chubby face, hair in bangs that were broken in the middle.

**Laughing Marietta.** 1912–14. Resembled *Naughty Marietta* dolls with molded ribbons in their hair; had composition head and hands on stuffed body. Laughing Marietta was probably made by *Louis Amberg & Son,* since it appeared with other Amberg dolls. It wore a print dress; size 12 inches; price 50¢.

**Laughing Sonny Boy.** Ca. 1920. Composition-headed doll made by the *Putnam David Smith* family.

**Laumaunier, Charles.** 1882. Handled dolls; used the initials "C. L."

**Launay, J.** See **Jomin, Mme. A.**

**Laure, Daniel.** See **Martinville & Salel Co.**

**Laurens, Vve. (Widow), & Dugourjal, Jeune (Jr.).** 1856–58. Paris. Made dolls with pink kid bodies and dolls dressed in French or foreign costumes.

**Laurette Taylor.** 1924. A *Celebrity Doll* originated by *Margaret Vale,* designed and made by *Jane Gray.* The doll represented Laurette Taylor as Jenny Wreay in Metro's HAPPINESS. It had a hand-painted face and bore a tag with a facsimile autograph of Laurette Taylor.

**Laurie.** 1912. Made by *Elektra Toy & Novelty Co.* Represented the character in LITTLE WOMEN. Dressed in school clothes; mate for *Amy.*

**Lauth-Sand, Mme.** 1916. Paris. Made rag dolls.

**Lavallée-Peronne, Mme.** See **Peronne, Mlle.**

**Lawn Baby.** 1911. Character doll; came dressed in short white slip.

**Lawrence & Co.** 1889–93. Boston, Mass., Philadelphia, Pa., and New York City. Cloth printers and distributors; made calico rag dolls designed by *Celia and Charity Smith,* as well as rag dolls patented by *Ida Gutsell* in 1893.

**Lawton Manufacturing Co.** 1923–25. London. Made dolls.

**Lazarski, Mme. T.** World War I era–1925+. Paris. Made luxury dolls in cloth, kid, and wax, and character felt dolls. Mlle. Fiszerowna made dolls in same *Ateliers Artistiques.*

1925: Used the trademarks *Mascotte* and *Bébés Marcheurs,* which she claimed were registered. Both of these names had once been used by the *Jules Nicholas Steiner* firm. She also made dolls for cotillions and dances, and dolls for publicity. Her dolls were shown at Paris Salon

National des Beaux-Arts; Musée des Arts Décoratifs; Salon des Humoristes; and l'Exposition Inter des Arts Décoratifs. In 1925, they were also shown in movies in France and abroad by Pathé-Journal, Gaumont, Aubert, Eclair, and Fox-Film.

**Le Baby.** 1898. Trade name of a bébé handled by *Wertheimer.*

**Le Bambin.** 1890–98. *E. Denamur's* House of Bambin made and distributed jointed bébés; 1892 advertisement stated that the dolls had the highest notches on the legs, and the best articulation.

**Le Bébé.** 1914. Trademark registered in France by *Marius Rocher* and used for clothes and accessories for dolls and bébés.

**Le Bey, Mme.** 1925. Paris. Doll maker.

**Le Coquet Bébé.** 1910. Trademark registered in France by Société *Gebaulet Frères.*

**Le Dormeur.** 1885. A patented bébé made by *Bru.* Its eyelids opened and closed. The bisque heads were manufactured at Montreuil-sous-Bois.

**Le Favori.** See **Bébé le Favori.**

**Le Grand, Ruth A.** 1922–23. Wilkes-Barre, Pa. Obtained U.S. design patent for a yarn doll with a Chinese queue, slanting eyes, and other oriental features.

**Le Jouet Artistique.** 1919. Words included on a trademark registered in France by *Fernand Calmon Hirschler & Paul Moise Hirschler.* Trademark also had the initials "F. P. H." on it.

**Le Joujou Pneu.** 1925. Trademark registered in France by *Paul Lucien Zierl* for rubber baby dolls.

**Le Magasin des Enfants.** Paris. Name stamped on foot of a French lady doll with kid body and bisque head marked on the shoulder with the "F. G." in a scroll mark, believed to belong to *Gaultier.* Name found stamped on the chest of a kid-body lady doll.

**Le Maire.** 1829–52. Paris. Made kid dolls. A kid body on a lady doll is labeled "Mons. Guillard & Le Maire// Rémond, Succr."

**Le Montréer (Montréer).** 1867–1921. Paris. Distributors of dolls.

1867: Y. Le Montréer was agent for doll makers in Sonneberg, Nürnberg, Fürth, Saxony, Württemberg, etc. His stock included porcelain goods from Lauscha and guaranteed talking bébés which sold from $5.00 doz. and up.

1895: Le Montréer Frères (Bros.) were wholesale dealers.

1913: Mme. Le Montréer, née Henriette Joseph, registered *Le Trottin* as a trademark in France.

1914: Mons. D. Le Montréer registered *Le Victorieux* as a trademark in France for dolls and bébés.

1919–21: D. Le Montréer was director of the *Comptoir de la Fantasie* and was using Le Victorieux as a trademark. He advertised dolls and *bébés incassables,* both dressed and undressed.

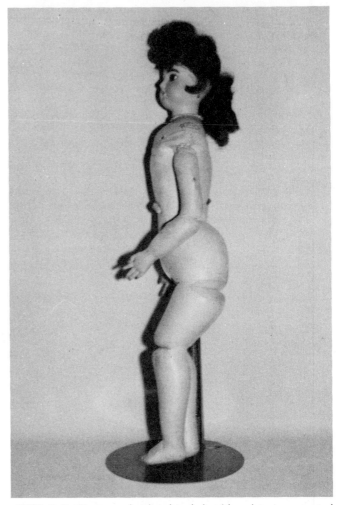

**1069A & B.** Bisque socket head and shoulder plate on gusseted kid body. Mark on head: Ill. **625.** Stamp on body: Ill. **1070.** This doll was probably sold at Le Magasin des Enfants. H. 18½ inches. *Courtesy of Virginia Dilliplane.*

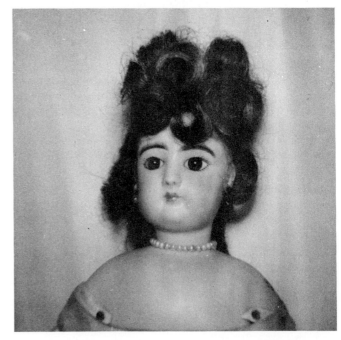

POUPÉE
AU MAGASIN DES ENFANTS
PASSAGE DE L'OPERA
PARIS

**1070.** "Magasin des Enfants," name found stamped on kid bodies.

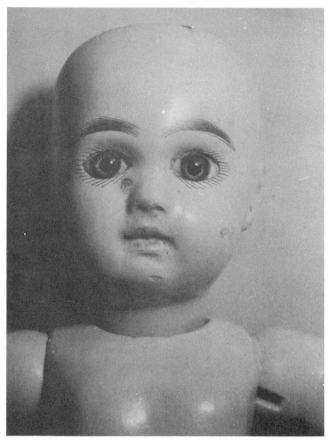

**1073.** Negro "Le Parisien" made by the Jules Steiner firm. She has a bisque head, pierced ears, glass eyes, and jointed composition body. Mark: Ill. **1074.** *Courtesy of Margaret Whitton; photograph by Winnie Langley.*

**1071.** All composition, ball-jointed doll. Head mark: Ill. **1072.** Body is marked "Jumeau." Doll has blue paperweight-type eyes. It is possible that the letters "L. M." stand for Le Montréer. *Courtesy of Margaret Whitton; photograph by Winnie Langley.*

# LM 6

**1072.** "L. M." may stand for Le Montréer, but it is not certain.

**Le Papillon.** 1921. Trademark registered in France by the *Société Française de Fabrication de Bébés et Jouets.*

**Le Parisien (Bébé le Parisien).** 1892–1908. Trademark registered in France by Amédée Onesime Lafosse, successor of *Jules Nicholas Steiner,* and used also by his successors, for dolls and bébés.

1898: Name used for a line of dolls, made in five categories: ordinary, with sleeping eyes, with jointed wrists, walking, or talking. Bisque head marked "Le Parisien // Paris // . . . A—14" is found on a 27-inch doll.

A 5
LE PARISIEN
Bᵀᴱ S G D G
A 5
**1074**

A3
Le PARISIEN
S.G.D.G.
**1075**

**1074 & 1075.** "Le Parisien" marks found on dolls made by Jules Steiner firm.

**Le Petit Chérubin.** 1888. Trademark registered in France by *Frédéric Remignard* for *bébés incassables.*

**Le Petit Français.** 1888–1906. Trademark registered in France by *François Emile Marseille* in 1888 and by *Claude Valéry Bonnal* in 1904. This trademark was used for jointed *bébés incassables.*

**Le Petit Parisien.** 1889. Trademark registered in France by *Jules Nicholas Steiner* for bébés. Dolls have been found stamped in blue ink on the body, "Le Petit Parisien // Bébé Steiner // Medaille d'Or // Paris 1889." The usual mark is with the words "Le Petit Parisien" on a flag held by a doll. Stickers with this mark are found on the bodies of bébés.

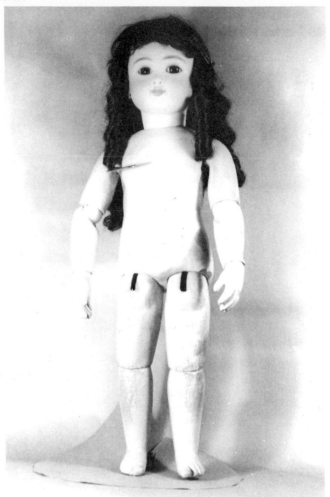

**1076.** Bisque head, cork pate, pierced ears, ball-jointed composition body. Head marked: "J. Steiner, B^te. S.G.D.G., Paris, FI^RE A 17." Body marked: "LE PETIT PARISIEN, BEBE STEINER, MEDAILLE D'OR, PARIS, 1889." H. 24½ inches. *Courtesy of Hazel Ulseth.*

**1077.** Le Petit Parisien, Bébé Steiner, has bisque head, composition body. Marked on the head: "J. Steiner, B^te. S.G.D.G., Paris." Marked on the body: Ill. 1079. Big toe is separate from other toes, a detail typical of Steiner. H. 24½ inches. *Courtesy of Hazel Ulseth.*

**1078.** Le Petit Parisien, a Bébé Steiner, marked on the bisque head "Steiner // Paris // B^te A 10," and on the hip of the jointed composition body as in Ill. 1079. H. 17 inches. *Courtesy of the International Doll Library Foundation.*

1078

**1079.** "Le Petit Parisien" mark used on Steiner dolls.

**Le Phénix.** See **Bébé Phénix;** also **Phénix Baby.**

**Le Préferé Bébé.** 1898. Trade name used by *A. Gobert.*

**Le Premier Pas.** See **Bébé Premier Pas.**

**Le Prince, Ange.** 1924. Paris. Registered *Scaramouche* as a trademark in France for mascot dolls.

**Le Radieux.** 1904. Trademark registered in France by *Claude Valéry Bonnal.*

**Le Ravissant.** 1904–8. Paris. Trade name used by *H. Cuvillier* or Cuvillier-Ferry, for bébés of various types.

**Le Rêve Bébé.** 1911. Trademark registered in France by *Société La Parisienne.*

**Le Saint.** 1921–25+. Paris. Advertised *Magic Dolls.*

**Le Séduisant.** 1898–1920. Trademark used in France in 1898 by *Ad. Bouchet,* then registered in 1903 and again in 1920 by *Société Française de Fabrication de Bébés et Jouets.* Mark was used for *bébés incassables.*

**Le Select.** 1899. Trademark registered in France by *Verdier & Cie.*

**Le Spécial.** 1904. Trademark registered in France by *Claude Valéry Bonnal.*

**Le Splendide.** See **Splendide Bébé.**

**Le Teteur.** See **Bébé Teteur.**

**Le Trottin.** 1913. Trademark registered in France by *Mme. Le Montréer.*

**Le Victorieux.** 1914–21. Trademark registered in France by *D. Le Montréer.*

1919–21: D. Le Montréer was director of *Comptoir de la Fantasie,* which used "Le Victorieux" as a trademark for dressed and undressed dolls.

**Le Vrai Modèle.** 1910. Trade name for a jointed *bébé incassable* made by *F. Ch. Rivaillon.*

**Leader Dolls.** 1922. Trade name used by *Reisman, Barron & Co.*

**Leader Toy & Novelty Co.** 1923–24. New York City. Made "Leader" dolls' heads; some came with moving eyes. Sizes were from 2 to 7 inches.

**Leather Arms.** Arms of leather have been used on many types of dolls, but especially on those with cloth and/or leather bodies. Although white or tan leather was most often used, occasionally red, blue, or other colors are found. Waxed dolls during the early 19th century often had three-fingered leather hands. In 1865, *Blakeslee* obtained a U.S. patent for a leather hand made of two pieces of unsplit leather glued together. Leather arms were made in accordance with his 1871 U.S. patent by *Jacob Lacmann. Strasburger, Pfeiffer & Co.* advertised, in 1876, sawdust-stuffed dolls' bodies with leather arms and either leather hands or china hands. Later, composition arms superseded leather ones, and by the time of World War I, leather arms were seldom used.

**Leather Dolls.** Since leather is an animal skin, it is eminently suitable for covering dolls, and it has long been

**1080.** All-kid doll, pin jointed at the shoulders and hips, has brown painted hair and eyes; contemporary blue knit outfit is embroidered in red and white. *Photograph by Winnie Langley.*

popular, especially kid, for dolls' bodies. Split leather is more pliable and usually makes a finer doll than unsplit leather.

1866: *Pierre Clément* patented a leather doll in France, and in the same year *Franklin Darrow* was issued a U.S. patent for a doll's head of leather.

1882: *Jules Voirin* patented leather dolls' heads in France.

1903: *Gussie D. Decker* patented an all-leather doll in the U.S.

1912: Emma Gleason patented a leather doll's head in the U.S., and as the *Gleason Doll Co.,* she made dolls with leather heads and muslin bodies.

1917: *Clark H. Downey* patented in U.S. a doll with a chamois face.

(See also **Kid Bodies.**)

**Leather Pasteboard.** 1904. *Gebrüder Süssenguth* advertised dolls made of stamped leather pasteboard.

**Lebas, Mme.** 1842. Paris. Made papier-mâché dolls.

**Lebel, Mme. (née Stapfer, Rachel).** 1916. Paris. Registered in France as a trademark *Patria,* for dressed dolls.

**Leblond, J. D.** 1853. Paris. Displayed India rubber mannikins at the 1853 New York Exhibition and won a bronze medal for them.

**Lebon.** 1863–82. Limoges, France. Became the successor to a Monsieur Chevrot (see *Bru*) in 1863. And by 1873 Lebon & Cie. of Limoges was manufacturing porcelain toys, some of which were for export. By 1882, Lebon had been succeeded by Léon Barjaud de la Fond & Cie.

They continued making porcelain toys, with some for export.

**Lechartier & Paul.** 1878–80. Paris. Made dressed and undressed dolls for export.

**Lechertier, Barbe & Co.** 1868. Paris. Were granted a French patent. Their invention dealt with a new means of articulating the joints and different parts of a papier-mâché (body) doll by means of elastic placed inside the body. (See also **Lechartier.**)

**Lechleitner, Aloys.** 1860–1925+. Berlin. Manufactured dolls.

**Lecomte (Leconte) & Alliot.** 1866–1900. Paris. Were issued a French patent in 1866 for a feeding doll with a reservoir that could be emptied. The doll was to be called *Marie Jeanne.* In 1888, E. LeConte, a maker of mechanical novelties, was granted a French patent for a doll in a carriage or wheelchair that moved by clockwork. This mechanical doll was to be called "Le Petit Bébé." Although there is a slight variation in the spelling of the name, it is possible that these two were either the same man or relatives, as their innovations were in the same category and they also gave a name to their inventions, a rare occurrence in patent specifications. H. LeConte & Co. won a bronze medal for their doll exhibit at the 1900 Paris Exposition; they used the mark "L. C."

**Leda.** 1917. Trademark registered in Britain by *Thomas Charles Salisbury* for dolls.

**Lee, Benjamin F.** 1821–70. New York City. Prior to 1850 he was listed as a merchant, but in 1850 rubber goods are mentioned specifically. Charles Goodyear, inventor of vulcanized soft rubber or *caoutchouc,* began to manufacture rubber toys as early as 1839, and he stated in his 1855 book, GUM ELASTIC, that the manufacture of rubber dolls in the United States was licensed to B. F. Lee.

**Lee, David Thorpe.** 1866. Birmingham, England. Obtained an English patent for a ball-jointed doll strung with either metal or rubber.

**Lee, Thomas.** 1857. London. Made dolls.

**Lefebvre, Alexandre, & Cie.** 1863–1921. Paris. In the 20th century, the factory was at Lagny, Seine-et-Marne. Made dolls and doll parts.

1869: According to a statement made fifty years later by his son, the father Lefebvre invented the *bébé incassable* or indestructible jointed bébé. However, patents secured by *Bru, Lee, Lechertier,* and others tend to refute this statement.

1878: The Maison Lefebvre's exhibit at the Paris Exposition was of papier-mâché toys.

1890: They were advertising molded papier-mâché toys and indestructible jointed bébés.

1900: The display of Alexandre Lefebvre received an Honorable Mention citation at the Paris Exposition.

1906: The firm was known as A. Lefebvre & Cie. They advertised rubber for doll joints.

1912: The *Bébés A. L.* were advertised. These had papier-mâché bodies and unbreakable heads that were washable. Their new patented joints were designed to sit and kneel. They came in sizes 10 to 28 inches.

1921: Registered Bébé A. L. as a trademark in France. New Bébé A. L. was awarded a gold medal; also advertised *poupards.*

**Lefèvre.** 1864–67. Paris. Made dolls. This may be a spelling variant of *Lefebvre.*

**Legendre, Mme.** 1864–65. Made dolls.

**Legrip, Mme.** 1833. Paris. Doll maker.

**Legros.** 1864–66, Paris; 1867–85, Vve. (Widow) Legros made dolls.

**Legs, Elongated.** 1921–22. Four design patents were issued—to *Dorothy Read, François Vathé, Edson Card,* and *William Blaydes*—for dolls with elongated legs.

**Leh, Hans.** 1890–1925+. Coburg, Thür. Manufactured dolls; specialized in dressed dolls. Used "L" as a mark.

**Lehmann, Ernst Paul.** 1881–1925+. Brandenburg, Prussia; later Nürnberg, Bavaria. Made mechanical dolls of tin.

1904: Obtained patent in Britain for a walking doll with an oscillating movement.

**Leick, Agnes (née Holy).** 1920. Grevenmacher, Luxembourg. Obtained a German patent for a doll with sleeping eyes.

**Leipold, Charles Wilson.** 1867–68. New York City. Listed in directories as a machinist, but his name and address are found on a doll's body.

**Leistner, Lor.** 1915–25+. Neustadt near Coburg, Thür. Manufactured dressed dolls.

**Lejean.** See **Villain, J.**

**Lejeune, E. A.** 1878–80. Paris. Showed rubber toys in the Paris Exposition of 1878. In the 1880 exhibition at Melbourne, his display of dolls and bébés was awarded a bronze medal. The Lejeune agent at Melbourne was E. Gay, Lamaille & Co. of Paris, London, and Melbourne.

**Lejeune, Louis-Aimé.** 1915. Saint Maur-des-Fosses, France. Registered in France as a trademark a picture of a pair of wings, to be used for dolls, especially dolls' heads and limbs.

**Leland, Hubert E.** 1924. New York City. Registered in U.S. *Hell'N-Maria* as a trademark for dolls. He also obtained a U.S. design patent for this doll.

**Leleu, Mlle.** 1885. Paris. Made dolls.

**Lelièvre, Mlle. Yvonne.** 1922. Registered *Lisette* as a trademark in France for fabric dolls.

**Lelouet, Mme.** 1876–78. Paris. Made dolls.

**Lemaître.** 1864–65. Paris. Made dolls.

**1081.** C. W. Leipold mark on the cloth chest of a doll (see Ill. **1082**). Untinted bisque head with gold-trimmed molded collar and tie. *Photograph by Winnie Langley.*

**1082.** Mark used on Charles Leipold's dolls.

**Lemoine, A.** See **Huret.**

**Lemonnier.** 1866. Paris. Obtained a French patent for dolls, joints, and busts.

**Lenci.** 1920–25+. Trademark registered in Britain in 1922 and in the U.S. in 1924, used since 1920, by *Enrico Scavini.* "Lenci" was the pet name of Elena Konig di Scavini, wife of Enrico Scavini.

1923: Advertised as popular with children from 5 to

**1083.** Two Lenci dolls of pressed felt with painted features and original clothes. The label on the dress reads "Lenci // Made in Italy." H. 17½ inches. *Courtesy of the Western Reserve Historical Society.*

105. "Every Lenci Doll is made in Italy by Italian Artists and is an individual work of art." Advertisement showed eight little girls, all with curly hair and all with eyes glancing to the side.

**Lenore, Mme., Art Doll Co.** 1924. New York City. Assignee of U.S. design patent rights of Lenore Bubenheim.

**Lenox Inc.** 1906–25+. Trenton, N.J. Walter Scott Lenox became a potter as soon as he left school, and in 1889 he entered into partnership with Jonathan Coxon, Sr., to form the Ceramic Art Co. In 1894, Lenox acquired the interests of his partner and operated alone until the Lenox company was formed in 1906. The sculptor and ceramist for Lenox was Isaac Broome, a native of Canada, who trained at the Pennsylvania Academy of Fine Arts. Broome received medals for his ceramic work at the 1876 Philadelphia Exhibition and the 1878 Paris Exposition. During World War I, when bisque dolls' heads could not be imported from Germany, Lenox made a few bisque dolls' heads for *EFFanBEE.* A head size #20 has been found on a 20-inch doll. The Lenox bisque heads were used on wood-flour composition bodies, with arms and legs of turned wood; dolls were commercially dressed in clothes typical of about 1920. One of these dolls wore a pin with a blue bird and the words "EFFanBEE Dolls" in red and white on a gold ground.

**Leonie.** 1912. Name of a doll copyrighted by *Elizabeth Lesser;* doll represented a young woman.

1084. Bisque head produced by Lenox on a trial basis for EFFanBEE during the World War I era. Mark: Ill. 1085. *Coleman Collection.*

1085. Lenox mark found on dolls' heads.

*Lenox Effanbee 16*

**Lepape, Georges.** 1916. Paris. Made dolls with wooden heads.

**L'Epine.** 1890. Secured a French patent for improvements in making dolls' heads and other parts of dolls.

**Leprestre, Mme.** 1846–52. Paris. Made dolls.

**Lerch, Philip.** 1858–ca. 1875. Philadelphia, Pa. Made toys. From 1866 through 1870 he appeared as a maker of dolls' heads. In 1867, Conrad Lang joined Lerch and the firm became known as Lerch & Co. Lerch has not been found listed in the Philadelphia Directories with Klag, but dolls' heads that appear to be of around the 1870's have been found bearing the paper label "Lerch and Klag// Manufacturers// Philadelphia, Pa." One of these dolls has convex eyeballs with painted eyes having the pupil in the center of the blue iris. The shoulder head is 7½ inches on a doll 25 inches tall.

**Lerch Kunstwerkstätten.** 1924. Berlin. Made *Art Dolls'* heads.

**Leroux, Vve. (Widow).** 1889–90. Paris. Made dolls.

**Leroy.** 1842–47. Paris. Made papier-mâché dolls.

**Les Arts du Papier.** 1919–25+. Paris. Made dolls, dolls' heads, and *mignonettes* of a composition called *porcelanite;* used trademarks *La Mignonne* for dolls and "A. P." for dolls' heads.

**Les Bébés de France Cie.** 1919–21. Paris. Made plastic bébés and dolls, among them a line bearing the slogan ". . . et si je tombe, je ne casse pas" (. . . and if I fall, I will not break). Company used the initials "B. F."

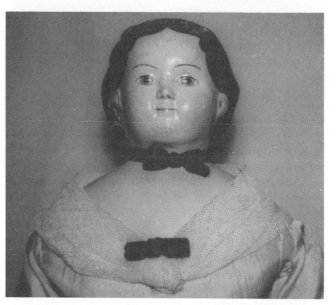

1086. Composition head made by Lerch has molded and painted features, blue eyes. Mark: Ill. 1088. H. 24 inches. H. of shoulder head, 6½ inches. *Courtesy of Mary Roberson.*

1087. Lerch composition head with molded and painted features; ears show. *Courtesy of Frances Walker; photograph by Winnie Langley.*

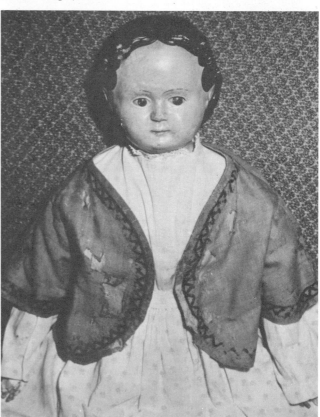

1088. Label found on dolls made by Philip Lerch.

*Lerch & Co.* MANUFACTURERS No. 7.

**Les Deux Gosses.** 1925. Trademark registered in France by Mlle. *Louise Adrienne Mabit.*

**Les Parisiennes à la Mode.** 1890's. Trade name used by *Ad. Bouchet.*

1912–14: Trade name used by *Brunswick & Cie.* for dolls.

**Les Poupées de France.** 1919–21. Trademark registered in France by *Edmond Lévi,* who had two factories for manufacturing plastic jointed bébés; some of these were dressed and some undressed.

**Les Poupées Parisiennes.** 1920. Trademark registered in France by Messrs. *Gaston Manuel* and E. de Stoecklin.

**Les Poupettes.** 1920. Trademark registered in France by Messrs. *Gaston Manuel* and E. de Stoecklin.

**Les Victorieuses.** 1919. Trademark registered in France by *Mme. Consuélo Fould.*

**Leschhorn, Rudolf.** 1925. Sonneberg, Thür. Manufactured dolls.

**Leschorn, L.** 1909. Frankfurt am Main, Hesse-Nassau. Manufactured dolls.

**Lesser, Elizabeth.** 1911–17. New York City. Copyrighted the following dolls: 1911, *Mary Elizabeth;* 1912, *Sister to Mary Elizabeth, Leonie,* and *Isabel;* 1913, *A Young American;* 1914, *1914 Girl;* 1915, *War Baby;* 1917, *Red Cross Nurse.* Mary Elizabeth, a girl of eight years, copyrighted in 1911, was probably the doll on which Elizabeth Lesser sued *Borgfeldt* for infringement in 1911. She lost her case because she did not submit copies of the alleged infringement.

**Lessieux & Soeur (Sister).** 1871–75, Paris; 1876–82. Louis Lessieux. Made dolls.

**Letort.** 1849. Paris. Obtained a French patent for detachable feet and heads on dolls.

**Leuchtkäfer (Lightning Bug).** 1921–22. Trademark registered in Germany by *Ann Kraemer* (née Ricke) for *Art Dolls.*

**Leuthäuser, R.** 1895. Rauenstein, Thür. Manufactured wax dolls.

**Leuthäusser, H.** 1909. Meschenbach, Thür. Manufactured dolls.

**Leutheuser, Richard.** 1894–1925+. Sonneberg, Thür. Manufactured and exported dolls.

1900: Was one of the Grand Prize winners at the Paris Exposition.

1904: Exhibited dolls at the St. Louis Exposition.

**Leven, H. Josef.** 1918–25+. Sonneberg, Thür. Manufactured dolls, especially leather dolls. Leven started with Hugo *Dressel* in 1891, and by 1918 had his own factory where he made leather dolls.

1925: Advertised dolls' heads, dolls' bodies, dressed dolls, felt dolls, leather dolls, fabric dolls, *Mama Dolls,* character dolls, and baby dolls.

**Leven & Sprenger.** 1896–1925+. Sonneberg, Thür. Manufactured dolls, especially leather dolls.

**Leverd & Cie.** 1869. Obtained a French patent for an improvement in making jointed dolls.

**Lévi, Edmond.** 1919–21. Paris. Registered *Les Poupées de France* as a trademark in France. Lévi had two factories, one in Neuilly-sur-Seine, near Paris, and the other in Paris. He manufactured jointed plastic bébés and sold them dressed and undressed.

**Levi, Joseph, & Son.** Before 1881, London; 1881, S. & H. Levi. Imported dolls.

**Levine, Jacob.** 1917. Philadelphia, Pa. Made dolls.

**Levine, Louis.** 1902–15. Patentee of a mold for making dolls' heads by a pressing process. By 1915 the *Joseph Roth Manufacturing Co.* of New York City was using this patented process.

**Lévy.** 1906–8. Paris. Manufactured rubber dolls.

**Lévy, Albert.** 1917–21. Paris. Registered *Tanagra* as a trademark in France in 1917 and in Germany in 1921. He manufactured dolls.

**Lévy, Pierre, & Cie.** 1919. Paris. Registered in France *Bébé Bijou* as a trademark.

**Lewis, Elizabeth Harrison.** 1916. White Sulphur Springs, W. Va. Was issued a U.S. design patent for an Indian girl doll dressed in buckskin.

**Leydel, Mme.** 1829–52. Paris. Made dolls.

**L'Heureux, Louis.** 1905. Paris. Registered in France "L'Heureux" as a trademark for dolls.

**Lhuillier, Vve. (Widow), & Barbanchou.** 1885. Paris. Made dolls.

**Liane.** Name on some of the dolls made by *J. Verlingue.* The body of one of these dolls is marked "Modern Bazar, Nice."

**Liberty.** 1918. Trademark registered in France by *Georges de Roussy de Sales.*

**Liberty & Co.** 1906–25+. London. Registered "Liberty" as a trademark in Britain for *Art Dolls* of fabric.

**Liberty Belle.** 1918. Wood-pulp composition doll made by the *Federal Doll Manufacturing Co.;* dressed in red, white, and blue silk.

**Liberty Boy.** 1917–18. Trademark registered in U.S. by the *Ideal Novelty & Toy Co.* for an all-composition doll with the molded uniform of an American soldier; jointed at shoulders, hips, and neck. The doll wore an army-type felt hat with cord.

1089. "Liane" mark used by J. Verlingue.

**1090A & B.** All-composition "Liberty Boy" made by Ideal, 1917/18; jointed at neck, shoulders, and hips; molded clothes except for the felt hat. Mark: Ill. **868.** H. 12 inches. *Coleman Collection.*

**Liberty Doll Co., The.** 1918–22. U.S. Made "unbreakable" dolls' heads, especially for export to South America.

**Lichterfeld, M.** 1914–20. Berlin. Agent for doll manufacturers.

**L'Idéal.** 1906. Trademark registered in France by *Mlle. Blanche Fouillot.*

**Lieb, R.** 1909–18. Wildenheid near Sonneberg, Thür. Made dolls' bodies.

**Liebermann, Carl.** 1909. Bettelhecken, Thür. Made dolls and *Täuflinge.*

**Liebermann, Chr.** 1909–12. Coburg, Thür. Made dolls.

**Liebermann, Ernst.** 1894–1925+. Neustadt near Coburg, Thür. Made and exported ball-jointed dolls and character babies. He used *Eli* and *Violett* as trademarks.

**Liebermann, Georg Nicol, & Liebermann, Louis.** 1902–9. Sonneberg, Thür. Obtained French and German patents for a doll with a moving mouthpiece, which was put into motion by the pressure of a lever in the back of the neck. Another German patent was obtained in 1909 whereby the eyes were attached to the sound and mouthpiece mechanism. These heads appear to be the ones with an area cut down in the forehead.

**Lieberuth, A., & Co.** 1915–20. Sonneberg, Thür. Manufactured dolls.

**Liebner, Zsigmond.** 1920's+. Budapest. "Uncle Liebner" was the most famous Hungarian toy dealer of his time; he handled dolls.

**Liedel, G.** 1855. Hildburghausen, Thür. Displayed papier-mâché dolls at the Paris Exposition. He might have made the dolls marked "G. L. Superior."

**Liedel, Theodor.** 1894. Sonneberg, Thür. Was granted a German patent for a sucking doll.

**Liège.** See **Bébé Liège.**

**Liège Dolls.** Liège, Belgium, has been celebrated for its dolls for hundreds of years. Many of the early ones were dressed in diminutive steel suits of armor. Dolls were also dressed to represent folklore characters or religious characters.

**Lien, Carl (Karl).** 1895–1925+. Neustadt near Coburg, Thür. Manufactured little or baby dolls. In the 20th century, he manufactured jointed dolls.

**Liesel.** 1916. Trade name for *Art Dolls* handled by *Strobel & Wilken.* These dolls resembled the *Käthe Kruse* dolls, and had painted hair and eyes. Their faces were called "waterproof," and they were dressed in Swiss costumes.

**Life.** 1924. Doll designed by *Julio Kilenyi,* copyrighted by *Jessie McCutcheon Raleigh.*

**Life Like Doll (Baby).** 1917–23. A *Mama Doll* that could walk and talk, patented by *Georgene Averill* in U.S. in 1918; one of the *Madame Hendren* line of dolls. (See also **Lyf-Lyk Baby.**)

**Life Like Faces.** 1906–9. Trademark for *Babyland Rag* dolls made by *Horsman* with "Life Like Faces."

1906: Line introduced with an infant doll in long clothes.

1907: Line included a *Topsy Turvy* doll with one head smiling and one head crying, dressed as a baby; price $8.50 doz. wholesale.

1908: Advertised thirty-four styles of Life Like Faces.

1909: Line included *Cy,* price $1.00; *Golf Boy* and *Golf Girl,* price $1.25 each; *Bo-peep,* price $1.25; *Sunbonnet Sue,* price $1.00.

**Life Like Line.** 1924. Line of dolls made by *American Stuffed Novelty Co.,* included *Trilby,* size 16 inches.

**Life Size Doll.** 1899–1912. Patented in U.S. by *Edgar G. Newell;* a drawing of the doll was registered as a trademark in the U.S. by Edgar G. Newell. Rag doll made by *Art Fabric Mills.* The doll was described in the patent papers as a rag doll, the size of an infant or child of two or three years of age; had printed front and back sections and tapering foot sections. The patent date,

**1091.** Mark of Life Like Line made by American Stuffed Novelty Co.

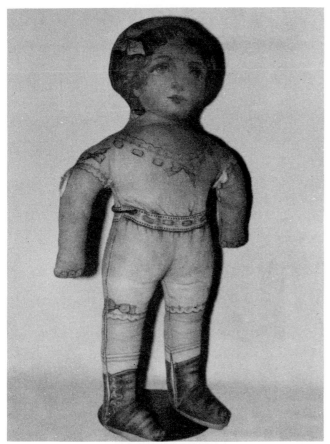

**1092A & B.** "Life Size Doll," a lithographed cloth cutout doll marked on the side of each foot, "Pat. Feb. 13, 1900," Edgar Newell's patent date. Blue ribbon and bows in the hair. H. 25 inches. *Courtesy of Eunice Althouse.*

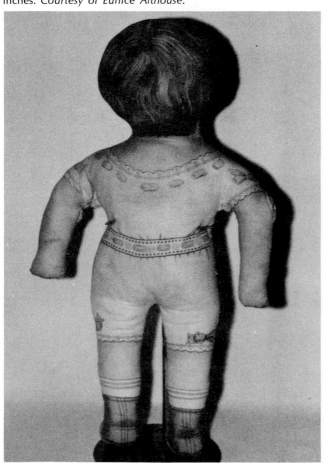

February 13, 1900, usually appears on the foot. These dolls were made 30 inches tall so that they could wear baby's cast-off clothes. The advertisement in LADIES' HOME JOURNAL, 1900, read, "This doll is an exact reproduction of a hand-painted French creation, done on extra heavy sateen, that will not tear. In oil colors that will not crock. The workmanship is perfect, the color effects the very finest.

"The doll is intended to be stuffed with cotton or other suitable material. It is this Century's model of the old-fashioned 'Rag Doll' that Grandma used to make. . . . "Dollie has Golden Hair, Rosy Cheeks, Brown Eyes, Kid Color Body, Red Stockings and Black Shoes and . . . if a piece of heavy cardboard is inserted in the soles, a perfect shoe is formed, enabling the doll to stand erect."

The 30-inch size cost 50¢, and the 20-inch size cost 25¢.

1908: *Selchow & Righter,* sole selling agents, advertised that the improved Life Size Doll was printed by lithographic process in eight colors on heavy standard drill cloth; sizes and prices were the same as in 1900.

1910: *Elms & Sellon* became distributors as well as Selchow & Righter; the dolls came in sizes 9 to 30 inches.

1912: Selchow & Righter still advertised the 20-inch size in six colors for 25¢ and the 30-inch size in eight colors for 50¢.

**Lignumfibro.** 1915–16. A new material for making dolls' heads and dolls' bodies invented by Mr. Fraenkel and used by *New Toy Manufacturing Co.* A 25-inch doll made of lignumfibro weighed less than three pounds. The manufacturers claimed that it was washable, unbreakable, and would not peel.

1915: All-lignumfibro dolls, 25¢ and up; lignumfibro head on stuffed body, 7 inches, 25¢ up.

1916: Baby dolls of lignumfibro came in sizes 11, 15½, 24, and 28 inches; price 50¢ to $2.00.

**Likeness Dolls.** 1924. Dolls made by a young officer for a New York shop run by a Russian woman. The faces were of hand-painted papier-mâché and could be either one's own likeness or that of a famous person. There was a Likeness Doll of Gloria Swanson. Bodies were stuffed. It took about ten days to make an order. The price was $15.00 for an approximate likeness or $100 for a likeness that approached a work of sculpture.

**Lili.** 1918. Trademark registered in France by *Mme. Poulbot.*

**Lilienthal, Michel.** 1922. Paris. Registered in France *Miss Dancing* as a trademark for dolls.

**Liliput.** 1894–1905. Trademark registered in U.S. by *Edmund Ulrich Steiner.*

1905: *Samstag & Hilder* advertised Liliput sitting dolls, which sold for 10¢, 15¢, 19¢, and 25¢.

**Liliput.** 1902. Trademark registered in Germany by *Carl Geyer.*

**Lillian Gish.** 1924. *Celebrity Doll* originated by *Margaret Vale*, designed and made by *Jane Gray*. The doll represented Lillian Gish as The White Sister in Metro's THE WHITE SISTER. It had a hand-painted face and bore a tag with a facsimile autograph of Lillian Gish.

**Lillian Russell.** 1903. Portrait doll reproduced by *Hamburger & Co.* from a familiar picture of Lillian Russell.

**Lillian Russell.** 1910. Miss Russell ordered a French doll maker to reproduce her in doll form as she appeared in WILDFIRE.

**Lilliput.** 1914. Name used for dolls by *Robert Heymann*.

**Lilliputian Dolls.** 1881–82. Distributed by *Millikin & Lawley;* small or miniature dressed dolls; eight sizes; price 6¢ to 37¢.

**Lilly.** 1913. Doll made by *Borgfeldt;* mate to *Willie*.

**Lily Tiso.** 1919. Doll copyrighted by *Guglielmo Voccia*.

**Limbach Porzellanfabrik.** 1772–1925 +. Limbach near Alsbach, Thür. Porcelain factory founded by Gotthelf *Greiner*.

1891: Advertised jointed dolls and *bathing children.*

1893: Showed dolls at the Chicago Exposition.

1919: Registered in Germany "Limbach Puppen" as their trademark for dolls.

**Limber Lou.** 1921. Doll made by *Trion Toy Co.*

**Lincoln Import Sales Co.** 1922. New York City. Imported dolls.

**Lindau, Carl Friedrich.** 1897. Hamburg, Germany. Manufactured dolls.

**L'Indestructible.** 1895. Trade name used by *Ad. Bouchet* for a jointed bébé with its head and hands made of a plastic material that he claimed looked like porcelain but lacked its fragility.

**Lindner, Edm.** 1851. Sonneberg, Thür. Distributor. At the London Exhibition he showed a *Täufling.*

**Lindner, Johannes Christoph.** 1863–1902. Sonneberg, Thür. A Johannes Christoph Lindner was living in Sonneberg in 1830. Johannes Christoph Lindner appears in German Directories from 1863 through 1902 as a doll maker. He displayed dolls at the 1873 Vienna Exhibition, the 1880 Melbourne Exhibition, and the 1893 Chicago Exhibition. From 1873 through 1882 he had a branch in Paris, and in 1882 was represented by *Le Montréer.* In 1875 he also had a London branch.

1881: Advertised *Täuflinge* and dressed dolls.

1884: Advertised, for export, dolls, babies of every kind and description, and clowns with cymbals.

1900: Lindner was one of the Grand Prize group at the Paris Exposition.

**Lindner, Louis, & Söhne.** 1863–1914, Sonneberg, Thür.; 1910+, subsidiary of *Gebrüder Bing* of Nürnberg. Manufactured dolls. In the 1860's Lindner was represented in

**1093.** Limbach bisque head, glass eyes, jointed composition body. Mark: Ill. **1094.** *Courtesy of Florence McCarter.*

The prices given for dolls are those for which the dolls were originally offered for sale. They are *not* today's prices.

Paris by *Gottschalk* and in 1873 by *Heppet Brodbeck.* Louis Lindner & Son displayed dolls at the 1873 Vienna Exhibition, the 1880 Melbourne Exhibition, the 1893 Chicago Exhibition, the 1900 Paris Exposition (where he was one of the Grand Prize winners), and the 1904 St. Louis Exhibition.

1911: Advertised various kind of dolls, including kid-bodied dolls, jointed composition dolls, and bent-limb baby dolls. A picture of some of their dolls suggests that they may have used heads made by *Gebrüder Heubach.* (See Ill. 1099.)

1914: Advertised dressed and undressed dolls of every description.

MADE IN GERMANY

**1094**

**1095**

**1096**      **1097**      **1098**

**1094–1098.** Marks of Limbach Porzellanfabrik. Nos. **1094** and **1095** have been found on dolls.

**Lindsay, Robert G.** 1916–17. New York City. Registered in U.S. *Buddy Bud* as a trademark for dolls. A single oversized *B* served as the first letter for both words in the mark—with the "uddy" directly above the "ud."

**Lindt Chocolate Co.** 1925+. New York City. Advertised enameled wooden walking dolls in two sizes for $36.00 and $72.00 a gross.

**Linen Paste.** 1902. Material of an unbreakable doll's face handled by *Nerlich & Co.* The doll came with painted features, glass eyes, flowing front hair, and excelsior-stuffed body. The 17½-inch size with fancy dress was priced at $8.40 doz. wholesale; 20-inch size with muslin dress was priced at $6.00 doz. wholesale.

**1099.** Advertisement of Louis Lindner & Sons in *Playthings*, January, 1911. Note that only one doll has a kid body, which was probably going out of fashion, and only one has a bent-limb baby body, which had not attained full popularity yet. The character baby head was still used on a fully jointed body. Gebrüder Heubach made character dolls' heads closely resembling some of these dolls. *Courtesy of McCready Publishing Co.*

**Linington, C. M.** 1866–94. Distributed dolls. In 1894, he advertised jointed "French" bisque dolls, kid-body dolls, baby dolls, patent nondestructible (composition) dolls, china-limb dolls, Japanese dolls, and Eskimo dolls.

**Linon.** 1894–95. French word for "linen," registered in Germany by *Hermann Landshut* for dolls and parts of dolls. Name appears on a stamp showing a banner carried by a jointed composition doll. The mark is usually found stamped in red on the soles of the feet of dolls. (See Ills. 1065, 1066.)

**Linon Bébé.** See **Bébé Linon.**

**L'Intrépide Bébé.** 1893–1921. Trademark registered in 1893 in France by *Roullet & E. Decamps* for dolls and bébés. From 1900–1902, the name was used for mechanical walking bébés.

## L'INTRÉPIDE BÉBÉ

**1100.** "L'Intrépide Bébé" mark used by Roullet & Decamps.

**Lion Tamer.** Ca. 1905. *Humpty Dumpty Circus* doll made by *Schoenhut;* all wood with rubber joints; sizes 6 and 8 inches.

**Lion's Claw.** 1914. Name and picture registered as a trademark in Britain by *Ethel Elizabeth Mary McCubbin* for dolls.

**Lipfert, Bernard.** Before 1912, Thür. 1912–25+, New York City. The Lipfert family had been connected with making dolls for four generations. When Bernard Lipfert first came to America, he worked as a doll painter for *Aetna Doll & Toy Co.;* then he designed many dolls for *Horsman* and *Ideal Novelty & Toy Co.,* including (for Horsman) *Mike* copyrighted 1916, *Blink* copyrighted 1916, *Little Peterkin* copyrighted 1918, and *Tynie Baby* copyrighted 1924. *Sucker Thumb Baby* (Suck-A-Thumb) and many others were designed for Ideal Novelty & Toy Co. After 1925, he designed Patsy, Shirley Temple, and the Dionne Quintuplet dolls.

**Lips.** See **Mouth; Moving Lips.**

**Lips, Movable.** *Heinrich Graeser* obtained a German patent in 1890 for a movable bottom lip, and *James S. Graham* (1921–24) secured a U.S. patent for lips that moved.

**Lisette.** 1922. Trademark registered in France by *Mlle. Yvonne Lelièvre.*

**Lisk, S., & Bro.** 1922–23. New York City. Manufactured and imported dolls from France, Germany, and Japan.

**Lisner, Rosa.** See **Dressed Doll Manufacturing Co.**

**Lithoid.** 1900–1901. Trademark registered in Germany by *Nöckler & Tittel* for material to be used for making dolls' heads.

**Little Admiral.** 1901. Character boy-doll dressed in costume of a naval officer, with gold epaulets, cocked hat, sword, and sword belt; price $2.25 doz. wholesale.

**Little Annie Rooney (Gamine).** 1925+: *Cameo Doll Co.* made wood-pulp composition versions; 1925+: small all-bisque versions made in Germany; 1925+: distributed by *Borgfeldt.* Borgfeldt registered "Little Annie Rooney" as a trademark in England in 1925 and in the U.S. and Germany in 1926, but said they had used it since 1925. In 1926, the doll was copyrighted by Jack Collins; the names of the artists were Jack Collins and *Joseph Kallus* on the copyright, which used the name "Gamine," but the description fit "Little Annie Rooney." The doll represented a character drawn by Jack Collins and played in the movies by Mary Pickford. In 1925, Joseph Kallus applied for a U.S. patent, which was granted in 1926, pertaining to making the legs equidistant when bent at the hip joint. The patent was used on an all-composition version of the doll. All-bisque version came in 3- and 4-inch sizes; had molded dress and shoes, yarn plaited hair, and felt hat; dress was in red or green plaid. The doll was jointed at the shoulders. For the mark inscribed on the skirt, see Ill. 1102.

**1101.** All-bisque "Little Annie Rooney" copyrighted by Jack Collins and Joseph Kallus. Her molded clothes consist of yellow shoes, green skirt, black jacket. She wears a red felt hat and has a strip of yellow wool hair across the front of her head that hangs down in two braids. Mark: Ill. **1102.** H. 4½ inches. *Coleman Collection.*

*Germany.*
**LITTLE ANNIE ROONEY**
**REG. U.S. PAT. OFF**
**COPR. BY JACK COLLINS**

**1102.** Mark on bisque version of Little Annie Rooney.

**Little Aristocrat.** 1893. Bisque-headed doll distributed by *Butler Bros*. Came with glass eyes, open mouth with teeth, elaborate lace-trimmed dress, straw hat, bronze shoes. Size 21 inches was priced $2.37 each wholesale.

**Little Beauty.** See **My Little Beauty.**

**Little Beauty.** 1910. Distributed by *Butler Bros*. Came with bisque head, sleeping eyes, teeth, and wig; was jointed at neck, shoulders, elbows, hips, and knees; size 8¼ inches.

**Little Beauty.** 1919. Doll copyrighted by *Nicola Bisaccia*. It had painted eyes glancing to the side; was jointed at the shoulders and feet were apart. Hair was molded. Doll was dressed in silk and net.

**Little Billy.** 1912. Designed by *Helen Trowbridge*, copyrighted by *Horsman*.

**Little Bo-Peep.** 1912. Trade name used by *Louis Amberg & Son* for dolls.

**Little Bo-Peep.** 1925. *A Story Book Doll* manufactured by *Sol Bergfeld & Son* and distributed by *Borgfeldt*. Doll had composition head and was 15 inches tall.

**Little Boy Blue.** 1911. Character doll with composition head and cloth body made by *Louis Amberg & Son*. From 1912–14, the doll appears to have been a subscription premium; size 12 inches, price 50¢ dressed.

**Little Boy Blue.** 1913. Bisque-headed doll made by *Franz Schmidt*, who used the trademark *Tausendschönchen*; handled in U.S. by *Tip Top Toy Co.* It was a bent-limb baby boy with molded and streaked hair, blue eyes, and two upper teeth. The hands were not in two different positions, as was usual for character babies at that time.

**Little Boy Blue.** 1921. Made by *Jane Gray Co.*; price $10.50 doz. wholesale.

**Little Bright Eyes.** 1896–99. Doll distributed by YOUTH'S COMPANION. Came with bisque head, long curly hair, kid body jointed at shoulders, elbows, hips, and knees; shoes and stockings; 15 inches tall; price $1.15 in 1896 and $1.00 in 1899, including paper patterns for trousseau.

**Little Bright Eyes.** 1911–12. Trademark registered in U.S. and in Germany by *Borgfeldt* for dolls with round faces, round eyes glancing to the side, and stuffed bodies.

**Little Brother.** 1911. Made by *Louis Amberg & Son*. Came with composition head, smiling features; pink sateen, cork-stuffed body; was dressed in rompers; mate to *Little Sister*.

**Little Brother.** 1918. Made by *Jessie McCutcheon Raleigh*, distributed by *Butler Bros*. Doll wore striped galatea suit; 13½ inches tall; price $2.75.

**Little Buck.** 1919. Indian-type doll made by *J. R. Miranda & Co.* Came with painted features and dressed in an Indian blanket.

**Little Cherub.** 1915. Made by *Louis Amberg & Son* and advertised as a "veritable angel." *Sears, Roebuck & Co.* distributed "Little Cherub Brand'" dolls about this time.

**Little Dorothy.** 1894. Doll distributed by YOUTH'S COMPANION. Came with bisque head and hands, sleeping eyes, teeth, kid body; wore shoes and stockings. The hair of the wig extended below the doll's waist. Size 14 inches tall; price $1.40, including paper patterns for trousseau.

**Little Dreamer, The.** 1925. Life-size baby doll made by *Käthe Kruse*.

**Little Emily.** 1924–25. Rag doll designed and made by *Madame Alexander*. It had a mask face with raised features, which were hand-painted by Madame Alexander. Came with wig of mohair imported from England; pink muslin body; size 14 inches, price $1.20.

**Little Ethel.** 1916. Distributed by *Montgomery Ward & Co.* Baby doll with jointed arms and legs, sleeping eyes; wore white lace-trimmed dress; size 18 inches, price $2.95.

**Little Fairy.** 1906. Cloth doll made by *Horsman*, to be cut out and stuffed; came in three sizes, priced 5¢, 10¢, 25¢.

**Little Fairy.** 1911–12. Made by *Louis Amberg & Son*. Came with composition head, cork-stuffed pink sateen body, and wore either an all-purple or all-blue dress and a bonnet with streamers.

**Little Hero.** 1918. Copyrighted by *Daniel Pollack*, designed by *Ernesto Peruggi*. A cherub-type doll with molded hair, eyes glancing to the side, bent arms jointed at shoulders; similar to *Little Nero*, but plumper.

**Little Hollander.** 1912. All-celluloid doll with brown and green clothing; price 50¢.

**Little Hussars.** 1901. Character boy dolls in Hussar uniform with sword and cap.

**Little Jimmy.** 1913–14. Character doll made by *Louis Wolf & Co.*; mate to *Irene*; price $1.00 and up.

**Little Johnny Jones.** 1913. Made by *Tip Top Toy Co.*, distributed by *Borgfeldt*. Came with composition head, hands, and legs; price 25¢.

**Little Kim.** 1920. Trademark registered in U.S. by *Notaseme Hosiery Co.* for dolls; label was printed on the boxes.

**Little Lord Fauntleroy.** 1911. Character boy doll made by *Louis Amberg & Son*. Had composition head and was dressed in black velvet Fauntleroy costume.

**Little Love Pirate.** 1919. Wood fiber doll made by *Progressive Toy Co.*

**Little Lucille.** 1919. Made by *Jessie McCutcheon Raleigh*.

**Little Mary Mix-Up.** 1919–24. Doll representing character drawn by R. M. Brinkerhoff for the NEW YORK EVENING WORLD; made by *Horsman & Aetna.*

1924: Came dressed in pink, blue, or lavender trimmed in white; price $1.69.

**Little Miss Happy.** 1919. Made by *Jessie McCutcheon Raleigh.* Story written about this doll and Santa Claus, in which the doll is the godchild of Santa Claus.

**Little Miss Muffet.** 1913. Doll with character face, jointed limbs; dressed in a hood and cloak.

**Little Miss Muffitt.** 1919–20. Trademark registered in U.S. by *Pacific Novelty Co.*

**Little Miss Sunshine.** 1913. Made by *Tip Top Toy Co.;* distributed by *Borgfeldt;* price $1.00.

**Little Mother Teaching Dolly to Walk.** 1920. Crying doll with voice in its head; made by *Ideal Novelty & Toy Co.*

**Little Nell.** 1924–25. Rag doll designed and made by *Madame Alexander.* It had a mask face with raised features, which were hand-painted by Madame Alexander. Came with wig of mohair imported from England; pink muslin body; size 14 inches; price $1.20.

**Little Nemo.** 1911–14. Line of dolls based on the Winsor McCay cartoons of this name.

1911: They were *Horsman Art Dolls* with *Can't Break 'Em* heads, cloth bodies, and molded hair. "Little Nemo" was dressed "in his best nightie."

1914: They were imported bisque dolls distributed by *Strobel & Wilken,* and included—besides Little Nemo— "Flip," "Imp," "Dr. Pill," and "Princess."

**Little Nero.** 1918. Copyrighted by *Daniel Pollack,* designed by *Ernesto Peruggi.* A cherub-type doll with molded hair, eyes looking straight ahead, bent arms jointed at the shoulders; similar to *Little Hero* but slimmer.

**Little Orphan Annie.** 1925. Doll represented character in Harold Gray's cartoon of this name; was made by the *Live Long Toy Co.*

**Little Patriot, The.** 1916. Trade name for doll distributed by *Montgomery Ward & Co.* Came with composition head and hands, curly mohair wig; was dressed in white. Size 17 inches, price $1.92.

**Little Pet.** 1908. Trademark registered in Britain by *Eisenmann & Co.* This might be a doll made of gauze over cardboard, which Eisenmann had patented in 1906.

**Little Peterkin.** 1918. Designed by *Bernard Lipfert,* copyrighted by *Horsman.* (See also **Peterkin.**)

**Little Playmate.** 1918. Made by *Jessie McCutcheon Raleigh,* distributed by *Butler Bros.* Size 13½ inches, price $3.35.

**Little Princess.** 1914–17. Made by *Ideal Novelty and Toy Co.* In 1914 the doll wore an opera cloak edged with fur.

**Little Princess.** 1918. Made by *Jessie McCutcheon Raleigh,* distributed by *Butler Bros.* Came with a wig. Size 18½ inches, $4.90.

**Little Princess.** 1919. Indian-type doll made by *J. R. Miranda & Co.* Had painted features; wore an Indian blanket; size 8 inches.

**Little Rascal.** 1915. Copyrighted by *Trion Toy Co.,* designed by *Ernesto Peruggi;* represented a child's head with hair parted on left side.

**Little Red Riding Hood.** 1881–82. Trade name of dressed dolls distributed by *Millikin & Lawley;* priced 37¢ to $10.50.

**Little Red Riding Hood.** 1893+. Cutout rag doll made by *Arnold Print Works,* designed and patented by *Celia M. Smith.* Printed cotton cloth was sold by the yard to be cut out and stuffed, several dolls to a yard. The doll was 16 inches tall. (See Ill. 1103.)

**Little Red Riding Hood.** 1911. Made by *Louis Amberg & Son;* came with composition head and cloth body.

**Little Red Riding Hood.** 1916. Molded-face rag doll wearing a red cloak and hood and white apron; distributed by *Montgomery Ward & Co.;* sizes 12 and 13½ inches; prices 35¢ and 59¢.

**Little Red Riding Hood.** 1923–24. Made by *Jeanette Doll Co.* The company claimed that 6,000 dolls were sold the first week they were on the market.

**Little Red Riding Hood.** 1925. A *Story Book Doll* manufactured by *Sol Bergfeld & Son;* distributed by *Borgfeldt.* It came with composition head; doll was 15 inches tall.

**Little Rogues, The.** 1912. Composition-head dolls made by the *Gund Manufacturing Co.*

**Little Rosebud.** 1912. *Minerva* metal head, curly wig, teeth, jointed kid body; size 15 inches; price $1.15.

**Little San Toy.** 1911. Designed by *Helen Trowbridge,* copyrighted by *Horsman.* This might be the doll that was marketed as the *Jap Rose Kid.*

**Little Shaver.** 1915. All-composition jointed character baby.

**Little Shavers.** 1919–20. Trademark registered in U.S. by *Elsie Shaver* for dolls.

**Little Sister.** 1911. Made by *Louis Amberg & Son.* Came with composition head, smiling features, cork-stuffed pink sateen body; dressed in blue and white with a sailor straw hat; mate to *Little Brother.* Size 14 inches, price $8.00 doz. wholesale.

**Little Sister.** 1914–16. Trademark registered in U.S. for rag dolls, by *Anne Maxwell.*

**Little Snookums.** 1909–10. Based on the cartoon THE NEWLYWEDS AND THEIR BABY. Baby in a crawling position on its knees was copyrighted by George McManus, and the name was registered as a trademark in Germany by *Max Fr. Schelhorn* for dolls and parts of dolls.

**1103.** "Little Red Riding Hood," rag cutout doll produced by the Arnold Print Works ca. 1892. H. 17 inches. *Photograph by Winnie Langley.*

**Little Stranger.** 1912. Made by *Louis Amberg & Son.*

**Little Suffragist.** 1914. Made by *Lilian E. Whitteker.*

**Little Sunshine.** 1913. Girl doll made by *Horsman.*

**Little Sunshine.** 1922–23. Trademark registered in Britain and in Germany by *Franz Kundy* for the *Catterfelder Puppenfabrik.*

**Little Sweetheart.** 1902–23. Trademark registered in Germany in 1902 and in U.S. in 1905 by Max Illfelder for *B. Illfelder & Co.* It was renewed in 1923.

**Little Sweetheart.** 1913–15. Composition-head baby doll made by *Louis Amberg & Son.* Came in sizes 16 inches to life size; prices 50¢ to $1.00.

**Little Viola.** 1895. Doll distributed by YOUTH'S COMPANION. Came with bisque head and long curly hair; kid body jointed at shoulder, elbow, hip, and knee. Size 15 inches, price $1.15 including paper patterns for trousseau.

**Little Walter.** 1912. Made by *EFFanBEE;* wore a breech-clout and safety pin.

**1104.** Llacer's mark found on sticker attached to dolls.

**Littlefield, Dorothy W.** 1922–23. Springfield, N.Y. Obtained a U.S. design patent for a yarn doll.

**Live Long Toys.** 1923–25+. Chicago, Ill. Made the *Gasoline Alley dolls* and *Little Orphan Annie,* all representing cartoon characters. They obtained design patents for *Skeezix, Uncle Walt,* and *Mrs. Blossom.*

1925: Made flower doll series designed by *Penny Ross.*

**Livetoy.** 1921. Line of dolls made by *R. C. Neighbour & Co.*

**Llacer, E.** Ca. 1925. Madrid. His gold sticker found on the clothes of an oriental infant doll with bisque head, which resembles *Ellar,* and a cloth body. The squeak box for the doll was made in Barcelona, Spain.

**Lloyd Manufacturing Co.** 1917–24. Woodcliffe or West New York, N.J. In 1924, merged with *The Art Metal Works* to form Voices Inc. of Newark, N.J.

1917: Secured a British patent for a talking *Mama Doll* made so that when the bellows were compressed, the doll's arms were elevated.

1921: *Horsman* used Lloyd voices in their Mama Dolls.

1922: Obtained patent in Britain for **Mama and Papa** voices combined in one talking mechanism. Lloyd voices used exclusively by *Averill* and Horsman.

1924: Burt Edward Lloyd registered "Lloyd's" as a trademark in Britain.

**Lloyd, Mlle.** 1916. Paris. Made rag dolls.

**Löbl & Brod.** 1899. Vienna. Manufactured and exported dolls and dolls' heads.

**Lochridge, Eleanor A.** 1922–23. Long Beach, Calif. Was issued a U.S. design patent for a rag doll dressed in a striped bathing suit and bathing cap.

**Loebel, Widmann & Co.** See **Maiden Toy Co.**

**Loewenberg, Henry, & Granier, Emile.** 1865. New York City. Loewenberg, and Emile Granier of Paris, were issued a British patent for a composition doll's head. The ingredients included four pounds of glue, three ounces of nutall and similar substances, eight ounces of glycerine, and one pound of acid.

**Löffler, Ig.** 1899. Vienna. Manufactured dolls and dolls' heads.

**Löffler & Dill.** 1887, London; 1891–1925+, Sonneberg, Thür. Manufactured dolls, especially dressed dolls.

1900: One of the group of Grand Prize winners at the Paris Exposition.

**Loiseau.** 1863–64. Paris. Made dolls.

**Lomax, Fannie.** 1904. Philadelphia, Pa. Made dolls.

**Lombard Leather Co.** 1919. Salem, Mass. Made kid dolls.

**Lombra, Chester,** 1912–13. Meriden, Conn. Obtained a U.S. patent for a multi-faced cloth doll. Several faces were connected at the neck so that they could be turned down and hidden under the clothing of the doll when not in use. A bandeau of celluloid or similar material across the top of the head held the face in place.

**London Belle.** 1895–98. One of the "D.P." line of dolls made by *Hamburger & Co.*, distributed by *W. A. Cissna & Co.* These dolls had bisque heads, blue eyes, long curly patent wigs, teeth, jointed arms; were dressed in "Empire style" with lace shoulder frill, high puffed sleeves, and embroidered skirt. Size 18½ inches, price $13.50 doz. wholesale.

**London Doll Market.** German agents, prior to World War I, made this the largest doll market in the world. After the war the supremacy seems to have passed to New York City. *Jumeau* and many French firms also had agents in London.

**London Rag Dolls.** Ca. 1865–1905. These dolls are best described by Clara L. Mateaux in THE WONDERLAND OF WORK (1884): "Then comes that thoroughly English invention, the rag doll, with its soft, pinky-white face and wondering blue eyes. She comes to perfection from the London maker's establishment; and here I may notice that there are a number of rag doll manufacturers in London alone. . . .

"As I have already mentioned, the well-known rag doll is essentially an English production that has risen into being only of late years, for our grandmothers knew her not. . . . For, whatever may be thought about the matter, the rag doll is not made of rags. Its face is a kind of wax mask, over which a piece of muslin has been stretched. It will very soon leak, or melt, if hugged too tightly. These faces have, as a rule, no back head belonging to them, but are fastened to a sort of skull, which is part and parcel of the body, made of calico and stuffed with sawdust just as that is. These limp, blue-eyed babies are always arrayed in neat, tidy little night-caps, the lace of which fits lightly round the soft features, and the bodies are arrayed in infant's robe and red merino hood to match the cap."

1876: HARPER'S BAZAR reported: "The English rag dolls are most prized, because they cannot be broken, and a child has not strength enough to tear them; they cost from 40¢ up to $10.00 each."

1879: *Ehrichs'* FASHION QUARTERLY advertised "London Rag Baby Dolls with muslin covered wax faces, prettily painted, with hair. Can be thrown about without damage or risk to furniture.

**1105.** "London Rag Baby," made of muslin drawn over a wax mask, has painted features; body and back of head are made of cloth; original clothes. H. 17½ inches. *Courtesy of the International Doll Library Foundation.*

"Neatly dressed in long figured slips, lace trimmed, with hood to match. Length 14½ inches . . . $0.25." Similar dolls came in sizes 17, 20, and 22 inches and cost up to 85¢.

There is some evidence that wax faces covered with material were also made in Germany in the 19th century.

**Lonz, Anni.** 1923–24. Coblenz, Germany. Producer and distributor of dolls, registered *Alah* as a trademark.

**Loofah.** 1917–18. A material used for dolls' bodies.

**Lopez, G.** 1921. Paris. Made and distributed dolls.

**Lopez, Moree Fawk.** 1921–22. Was issued a U.S. design patent for a rag doll.

**Lopto and Lopto Radlaufspiel.** 1924. Trademarks registered by *Thüringer Puppen und Spielwaren Export Co.* for dolls.

**Lord Kitchener.** Before 1917. Portrait doll of composition with molded mustache; it was dressed in a khaki British army uniform.

**Lord Plushbottom.** Ca. 1925. All-bisque doll representing the cartoon character of this name; had swivel neck and molded clothes.

**Lord Roberts.** Ca. 1900. Portrait doll with wax head and limbs. Had inserted hair, eyebrows, eyelashes, mustache, and goatee; blue glass eyes; hair-filled body. Doll was dressed in redcoat uniform with medals and high black leather boots. Size 18 inches.

**Lord Roberts' Memorial Workshops.** 1917–19. Disabled soldiers and sailors made dolls at these shops.

**1106.** All-bisque doll with "Lord Plushbottom" incised on the upper back; swivel neck, molded and painted features and clothes; including blue suit, gray hat, red tie, and cane. H. 3½ inches. *Courtesy of Dorothy Annunziato.*

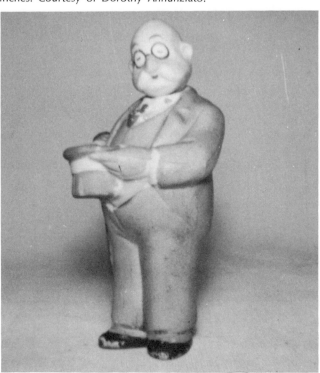

**Lorenz & Deutesfeld.** 1897. Hamburg, Germany. Manufactured dolls.

**Lori.** Bisque baby heads with molded hair have been reported as bearing this name. These dolls were made by *S. & Co.*

**Lorraine.** Name incised on bisque heads by *A. Lanternier & Cie.*

**Lotiron, Francis.** 1855. Paris. Made dolls.

**Lotze, O. H.** 1902. Hartford, Conn. Repaired dolls.

**Loudouze, Mlle. Geneviève.** 1925. Paris. Registered in France *Ninon* as a trademark.

**Louis, Mme.** 1867–70. Paris. Made dolls.

**Louit, Mme. (née De Montaigut, Jeanne).** 1916. Bordeaux, France. Registered in France *Poupées Gauloises* as a trademark for dolls.

**Louvre.** A large Paris department store that sold dolls in the early part of the 20th century. A doll bearing a price tag of the Louvre was also marked "B. L.," which may stand for *Bébé Louvre.*

**Love Me.** 1919. Copyrighted by *Fine Doll Manufacturing Co.;* designed by *Ernesto Peruggi.* This was a cherub-type doll with a ribbon in its molded bobbed hair; had bent arms, molded dress, shoes, and socks; legs were apart.

**Lovums.** Trade name for doll made by *EFFanBEE.* It carried the patent #1283558, which was a patent obtained by *Elmer J. Read* in 1918 for a jointed doll's body with the rounded neck fitting into the socket in the head. This same number was used on the Patsy dolls also made by EFFanBEE after 1925.

**Löwenstein, L.** 1909–18. Berlin. Made dolls and dolls' clothes.

**Löwenthal & Co.** 1836–97. Hamburg, Germany. Displayed papier-mâché dolls' heads and dolls at the 1844 Berlin Exhibition. The lacquered papier-mâché dolls' heads had curly or flat hairdos; many of them had glass eyes and glass teeth. They represented men and women of many nationalities, among them Turks, Chinese, and Scots. A woman doll from this factory, which could be dressed and undressed, sold for $28.00; it was described as "very pleasing." The factory employed between two hundred and three hundred people. At the London Exhibition of 1851, Löwenthal displayed dolls' heads both in wax and in papier-mâché. As late as 1897, James Löwenthal of Hamburg was listed as a doll maker.

J. E. masbon sc

LORRAINE

No

A. L. E. Cⁱᵉ

LIMOGES

**1107.** "Lorraine" mark of Lanternier.

**Lucas.** See **Bornoz, Léon.**

**Lucien Fils (Son).** 1862–84. Paris. Made dolls.

**Lucky Bill.** 1909. Doll made by Hahn & *Amberg* with Teddy Bear type of body. This was the first known copyrighted dolls' head in the U.S. It was copyrighted by Louis Amberg.

**Lucky Little Devil.** 1919. Copyrighted by *Gordon F. Gillespie,* designed by *Ceseare Paoli.*

**Ludd, Mme.** 1885. Paris. Made dolls.

**Lüders, F.** 1897. Hamburg, Germany. Manufactured dolls.

**Ludet, Mme.** 1864–90. Paris. Made dressed dolls. Used heads from Germany in the 1860's.

**Ludwig, Charles.** 1891. Hamburg, Germany. Made bathing dolls.

**Ludwig, Oskar.** 1897–1916. Gehren, Thür. Manufactured rag dolls, especially dolls of wool.

**Luge, A., & Co.** 1880–1925+. Sonneberg, Thür. Manufacturers and exporters; had branches in London and Paris. Specialized in dolls dressed in foreign costumes.

1884: Listed as Aug. Luge in directory.

1893: Displayed dolls at the Chicago Exposition.

1900: One of the Grand Prize winners at the Paris Exposition.

1904: Displayed dolls at the St. Louis Exhibition.

1911: Had the same London address as *Insam & Prinoth.*

1912: Registered *Pat-A-Cake Baby* as a trademark in Germany.

**Luge, Ferdinand.** 1881–1923. Sonneberg, Thür. Manufactured and exported dolls.

**Lullaby Baby.** 1924–25+. Represented a week-old infant; made by *Averill Manufacturing Co.,* who registered this name as a trademark in U.S. This was one of the *Madame Hendren* dolls. The head was of composition with painted hair and painted or sleeping eyes, slightly dimpled chubby cheeks. The baby body was cotton filled. Wore long baby dress of sheer material. Doll carried an identifying tag and came in three sizes; price $1.00 and up.

**Lulu.** 1916. Trademark registered in Britain by John Green Hamley of *Hamley Bros.*

**Lund, George.** 1924. Scarsdale, N.Y. Obtained a U.S. design patent for a boy doll dressed as a clown; doll has wide-open mouth showing teeth.

**L'Unique.** 1904. Trademark registered in France by *Claude Valéry Bonnal.*

**L'Universel.** 1892–98. Line of bébés made by *Jullien, Jne.* These *bébés incassables* had teeth, moving eyes, and limbs of hollow wood. They could walk and talk, and were dressed in various grades of clothes from inexpensive to luxurious.

**Lupton, Edward J.** 1922–24. Cleveland, Ohio. Was issued a U.S. design patent for a stockinet doll with eyes glancing to the side; doll was dressed in a sweater and stocking cap.

**Luster Trim.** Trim with a metallic luster derived from copper, platinum, and other metals was used to decorate porcelain dolls, especially on their shoes and fancy hairdos.

**Lutecia Baby.** 1915. Trademark registered in France by *J. César Koch* for dolls made in Paris.

**1108A & B.** Untinted bisque head with molded snood, feather, and tassel trimmed with luster decorations. Note the similarity in eye painting to the doll in Ill. **1109.** H. 20 inches. *Coleman Collection.*

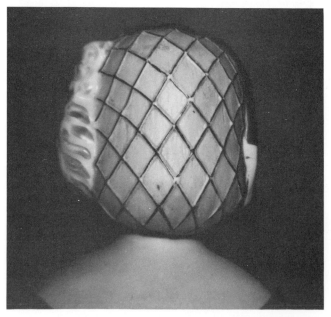

**1109A & B.** Luster-trim coronet on untinted bisque head, which has molded features, earrings, and ribbon tassel behind the ear. Note the comb marks in the elaborate hairdo, and the heavy black outline of the upper eyelids. Cloth body. H. 15 inches. *Coleman Collection.*

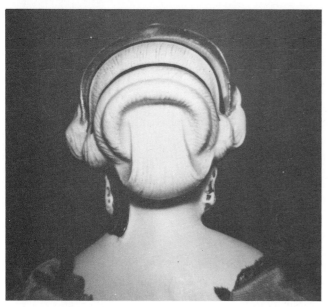

**Lutetia.** 1924. Trademark registered in France by Mlle. *Aline de Brzeska* for dolls.

**Luthard, A.** 1909–18. Bettelhecken, Thür. Made dolls and *Täuflinge.*

**Luthardt, Eg. Mich.** 1868–1925+. Steinach, Thür. Made and exported dolls with kid bodies; also, in the 1920's, made dolls with imitation kid bodies. Some of the dolls walked and talked and were dressed.

1911: Advertised jointed doll bodies of all kinds.

**Lutin.** Means "goblin." Was used as a name on dolls'

heads made by *J. Verlingue.* Krause made the clothes for some of these "Lutin" dolls.

**Lütt Martin.** 1916. Trade name of doll made by *Käthe Kruse;* price $15.00.

**Lutz, Fritz.** 1912–25+. Sonneberg, Thür. Manufactured and exported dolls and dolls' bodies.

1913: Registered in Germany as a trademark *Jing-Go-Ring Doll.*

**Lutz, Georg.** 1893. Sonneberg, Thür. Manufactured dolls.

**Lützelberger, Arno, & Co.** 1923–25. Also known as the Thüringer Spielwaren-Fabrik; made and exported dolls with composition heads.

1923: Registered in Germany *Ai-Ai* as a trademark.

**Lützelberger, Hermann.** 1895–1925+. Sonneberg, Thür. Manufactured dolls.

1900: One of the Grand Prize winning group at the Paris Exposition.

1904: Displayed dolls at the St. Louis Exhibition.

**Lützelberger, J. N.** 1873–1909. Sonneberg, Thür. Manufactured and exported dressed and undressed dolls.

1873: Showed dolls at the Vienna Exhibition.

1900: One of the Grand Prize group at the Paris Exposition.

1904: Displayed dolls at the St. Louis Exhibition.

**Luzie Lovem.** 1920–22. Trademark registered in U.S. by *Louisiana M. Davis.* In the actual mark, a single very large *L* served as the first letter for both words—the "uzie" appearing at the top with "ovem" placed directly underneath.

**Lyf-Lyk Baby.** 1917–25+. Trademark registered in U.S. by *Averill Manufacturing Co.* in 1925, but used since 1917. The name appears to have been spelled *Life Like* prior to 1924, when the doll could wag its head, had a stuffed cotton body, and came in several sizes.

**Lynd, William John.** 1886. Yreka, Calif. Obtained a U.S. patent for a speaking and singing doll, which operated by having a speaking tube inserted in the doll's head.

**Lyon, Etta.** 1913–14. Montclair, N.J. Registered *Tottie* as a trademark in U.S. for dolls.

**Lyon, Helena A.** 1921–22. Toledo, Ohio. Was granted a U.S. design patent for a rag doll with eyes glancing to the side.

**Lyon, Joseph, & Co.** 1862. New York City. One of the companies that made the *Autoperipatetikos* doll patented

**1110.** "Lutin" mark used by J. Verlingue.

in 1862 by *Enoch Rice Morrison*. The Lyon name appears on an original box in the Museum of the City of New York.

**Lyon Doll Co.** 1917–22. New York City. Made several lines of dolls, including the "Lyon Doll" dressed in "pussy willow" silk taffeta in white, pink, or blue; and all-composition dolls with or without wigs, and with straight or curved legs, no rubber being used for joining together.

**Lyro.** 1925. Name in a six-pointed star, registered as a trademark in Germany by *Franz Volpert*, producer and distributor of dolls.

**Lyxhayr.** 1911. Chemically treated vegetable fiber used for stuffing dolls; practically noninflammable; patented by W. A. Dickinson.

# M

**M. & A. Doll Co.** 1918–22. New York City. Made dolls.

**Ma Belle Marianne.** 1919. Made by *Trion Toy Co.*; had moving eyes.

**Ma Jolie.** 1917. Trademark registered in France by *Max Henri Marie de la Ramée* for unbreakable, noninflammable, washable dolls and dolls' heads.

**Ma Poupette.** 1925. Trade name used by *Edouard Merville* for dolls.

**Maar.** Name incised on some of the bisque heads made by *Armand Marseille*.

Made in Germany.
ArmandMarseille
256
A 3/0 M
Maar
**1111**

**1112**

**1111.** "Maar" mark on Armand Marseille dolls.

**1112.** Mark used by Ma. E. Maar of Mönchröden.

**Maar, E., & Sohn.** 1917–25+. Mönchröden near Coburg, Thür. Used the contraction "Emaso." Specialized in making jointed and nonjointed babies. Some bisque heads made by *Armand Marseille* have *Maar* on them; it is not known whether there was a connection. (See III. 522.)

**Maar, Oskar.** 1925. Mönchröden near Coburg, Thür. Specialized in dressed dolls.

Germany
Mabel

**1113.** "Mabel" mark used on dolls of Armand Marseille.

**Maaser, Robert.** 1918–25+. Sonneberg, Thür. Made dolls.

**Maaske, Wilhelm, & Gottschalk, Richard.** 1896. Berlin. Obtained a German patent for movable eyes in a doll's head.

**Mabel.** Name incised on some bisque heads made by *Armand Marseille*.

**Mabel.** 1905–14, and possibly earlier. China dolls' heads made with this name in gold letters on the chest. This type was produced by *Hertwig & Co.* and *Closter Veilsdorf*.

**Mabel.** 1916. Trade name used by *Ideal Novelty & Toy Co.*

**Mabit, Mlle. Louise Adrienne.** 1925. Paris. Registered in France two trademarks, *Janus* for dolls' heads, and *Les Deux Gosses* for dolls.

**Macazaga & Idarramendi, A.** 1878. Valladolid, Spain. Displayed dressed dolls at the Paris Exposition.

**MacDonald, Margaret.** 1921. Was issued a U.S. design patent for a rag doll with eyes glancing to the side.

**Mace, Dr. Jules.** 1913. Marseille, France. Obtained a German patent for moving eyes in a doll's head.

**Mace, L. H., & Co.** 1880's–1916. New York City. Imported and distributed dolls. *Edmund Ulrich Steiner* worked for them in the 1880's.

1910: Advertised dolls of "every kind," including jointed and kid dolls, dressed and undressed dolls, and rubber dolls; price for jointed doll was $1.00.

1911: Advertised *Mace Laura* line of dolls.

**Mace Laura.** 1911. Line of dolls handled by *L. H. Mace & Co.*; included jointed dolls, kid dolls, china dolls, celluloid dolls, and dressed dolls.

**Machet, Mme.** 1862–63. Paris. Made dolls.

**Madam Hendren.** See **Madame Hendren.**

**Madame Alexander.** See **Alexander, Madame.**

**Madame Butterfly.** 1913. Trademark registered in Germany by the *Max Handwerck* firm.

**Madame Georgene, Inc.** 1920–25+. *James Paul Averill* was the president; they handled dolls as wholesalers and as retailers. In 1924, *Borgfeldt* distributed Madame Georgene dolls.

1922: Advertised that they were the originators and designers of *Wonder Mama Dolls*. "They walk, they talk, they dance"; included *Mistress Bubbles, Master Bubbles, Billy Boy,* and *Betty*.

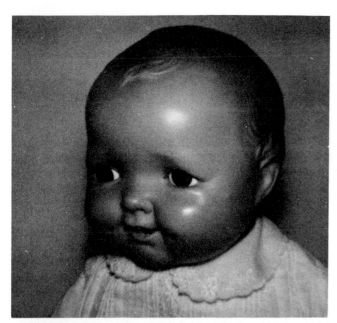

**1114.** Celluloid flanged-neck head, marked "Madam Hendren on the back of the neck, has molded hair, open-closed mouth with two lower teeth. Hands are celluloid; cloth body has bent legs. Mark: Ill. **1115.** H. 18 inches. *Courtesy of Dorothy Annunziato.*

**1115.** "Madam Hendren" mark used by Averill Manufacturing Co.

## MADAM HENDREN

1923: Registered "Wonder" as a trademark in U.S. used since 1920.

**Madame (Madam) Hendren.** 1915–25+. Line of dolls manufactured in U.S. by *Averill Manufacturing Co.* and in Canada by *Brophey Doll Co.*

1915: Advertised by Averill as including Dutch Boy (later called *Neutrality Jim*), Dutch Girl (later called *Gretchen*), cowboys and cowgirls, Indian chiefs and Indian maids; original creations dressed in wool felt; featured in Saks & Co. Christmas windows.

1916: *Preparedness Kids* and Soldier Boys added to the line; Dutch dolls came with long or short wigs, in various sizes; price $1.00 to $6.00. Line included *Turtle Brand* celluloid dolls.

1917: Advertised 150 numbers; new dolls included Easter dolls with wigs and Irish dolls for St. Patrick's Day.

1918: Advertised *Life Like Dolls, David,* and *Baby Darling;* these appear to have had bisque heads and moving eyes, and to have been fully jointed; came in three sizes. Also with composition heads, hands, and forearms, painted features and hair; chubby bodies stuffed with cotton; sizes 17, 20, and 24 inches; price $34.00 to $81.75 doz. wholesale.

1919: Advertised dolls with bisque heads; these may have been the dolls made by the *American Bisque Doll Co.* under license of Georgene Averill.

1920: Advertised romper doll filled with cotton and crying doll with wig; 12 inches tall, price $15.00 doz. wholesale.

1921: Advertised dolls that walked, talked, and slept; four hundred numbers of soft cuddling dolls known as Softanlite with cardboard tag affixed that read: "Genuine // 'Madame Hendren' // Softanlite Doll // (voice patented) // To operate voice, hold doll //in position lying on back // then turn completely over. // Made in U.S.A." Lloyd's patented voices were used in these dolls.

1922: Registered in U.S. by the *Averill Manufacturing Co.* the words "Talking and Walking Doll" and the picture of a doll as a trademark. This trademark was on a medallion attached to the doll by chain, wire, or string, and had been used since 1921. They advertised two hundred numbers, including *Dolly Reckord,* which recited and sang. Prices of Madame Hendren dolls were $1.00 and up.

1924: Advertised *Lullabye Baby,* a week-old infant, and the *Dolly Dingle Dolls* designed by *Grace G. Drayton.* These included Dolly Dingle, *Chocolate Drop, Happy Cry, Sis,* and *Mah Jongg Kid;* price $1.00 and up.

**Made First in America (First Made in America).** 1915–16. Slogan of the *Composition Novelty Co.,* used for dolls.

**Made in America Manufacturing Co.** 1915. New York City. Made line of thirty boy, girl, and baby dolls plus a line of eight numbers, 32 inches tall.

**Made in Holland Dolls.** 1920. Name used by *Rikkers Bros. Ltd.* for dolls with bisque heads, dressed in Dutch costumes. Germany was having trouble trying to sell dolls with bisque heads in America at that time, and they may have used a Dutch firm as an intermediary.

**Madelon.** See **La Madelon.**

**Maden, James Henry.** 1893–94. Manchester, England. Obtained two British patents, one with *W. H. Nuttall* for celluloid dolls, and the other for dolls' dresses with pictures such as portraits, views, etc., printed on them.

**Madonna.** 1919. Indian-type doll made by *J. R. Miranda & Co.* Came with painted features, clothed in an Indian blanket; 12 inches tall.

**Maelzel, Johannes (Jean).** 1808–27. Vienna and Paris. Invented various musical automata.

1823: Exhibited in Paris dolls that said "Mama" and "Papa" when their hands were touched.

1824: Obtained French patent for a talking doll that pronounced, by the play of its arms, the words "Papa" and "Mama." Max von Boehn, in DOLLS AND PUPPETS, says that Maelzel obtained a French patent in 1827 for a doll that said "Papa" and "Mama" when it was squeezed. No such patent has been discovered, and it is possible that Von Boehn confused the date of the similar 1824 patent.

**Mafuka.** 1925. Trademark registered in Germany by *O. Scheyer & Co.* for dolls.

**Magali.** 1925. Paris. Felt *Art Dolls* made by *Etablissements D. Giotti.*

**Magasin des Enfants.** Passage de l'Opéra, Paris. Mark on a kid body with bisque shoulder head and forearms. The head is a turned bald head.

**Maggie and Jiggs.** 1924. Pair of all-wood jointed dolls made by *Schoenhut,* distributed by *Borgfeldt,* who registered "Bringing Up Father" as a trademark in U.S.

**Magic Bébé.** 1911. Trademark registered in France by *Société La Parisienne.*

**Magic Dolls.** 1925. Trade name used by *Le Saint.*

**Magic Novelty Co.** 1919–20. West Hoboken, N.J. Registered *Chicin* as a trademark in U.S. for dolls.

**Magit.** 1925. Felt *Art Dolls* made in France.

**Maguy.** 1925. Trade name for cloth *Art Dolls* made by *Boccheciampe.*

**Magyar Asszonyok x Nemzeti Szövetsége (National League of Hungarian Women).** 1909–25+. Budapest. Made dolls in Hungarian costumes.

**Magyar Ruggyantaárugyár Rt.** Ca. 1925. Budapest. Made rubber and celluloid dolls.

**Mah-Jongg Sales Co.** 1923–24. San Francisco, Calif. Controlled by *Averill Manufacturing Co.*

1923: Registered "Mah-Jongg" in U.S. as a trademark for dolls.

1924: Registered "Mah-Jongg Kid" in U.S. as a trademark for dolls. These were advertised by Averill Manufacturing Co. as one of their *Madame Hendren* line designed by *Grace G. Drayton;* price $1.00 and up.

**Mahler, A. & F.** 1921. Handled dolls' eyes in U.S.

**Mahler Bros.** 1906. New York City. Advertised jointed dolls with bisque heads.

**Mahlknecht, Christian.** 1896. St. Ulrich, Grödner Tal. Distributed wooden dolls. (See Ill. 717.)

**Maid of Mystery.** 1920. Trade name for doll made by *Moss Novelty Manufacturing Co.* Came with wig and ball-jointed body made of a secret material that was not composition, wood pulp, celluloid, fabric, or metal.

**Maiden Toy Co.** 1915–17. New York City. In 1917, the factory was out of operation for six months because of the illness of the manager; then the company consolidated with Loebel, Widmann & Co. to form the Maiden America Toy Manufacturing Co., which was in business at least until 1919.

1915: Produced Maiden America dolls, for which a trademark was registered in U.S. by *Katherine Silverman.* These dolls came with a painted hair topknot, jointed arms, feet together; wore a red, white, and blue ribbon around their bodies; 5½ inches and five larger sizes; price 25¢ and up. Advertised as "The National Doll."

1918: Maiden America dolls distributed by *Riemann, Seabrey Co.* and *Tip Top Toy Co.*

1919: Used initials "M. A. T." for character dolls.

**Maier, Imanuel.** 1921. Plochingen, Germany. Obtained a German patent for holding parts of a hollow body together with a six-pronged staple.

**Mailing Dolls.** 1917. Leather or fabric dolls made by *Moore & Gibson Corp.*

**Maintenant.** 1885. Paris. Produced bébés and dressed dolls.

**Maire.** See **Le Maire.**

**Maire, Mme.** 1829. Paris. Handled dolls.

**Maison Bleue.** See **A la Maison Bleue.**

**Maison Deschamps.** See **Deschamps.**

**Maison du Petit Saint-Thomas.** 1886–91. Paris. Distributed dressed dolls, chiefly ones made in Paris. Most of these were bébés, priced from less than 50¢ to $17.00.

**Majestic.** 1894–1914. Registered as a trademark in U.S. for dolls by *Edmund Ulrich Steiner;* dolls were distributed by *Samstag & Hilder, Louis Wolf & Co.,* and *Sears, Roebuck & Co.*

1901: Sears advertised Majestic dolls as having ball-jointed composition bodies with jointed wrists, eyelashes, sleeping eyes, open mouth, teeth, human hair sewn wigs; dressed in chemise; sizes 18, 23½, and 25 inches; price $1.85 to $4.25. *Kämmer & Reinhardt* applied for the registration of *Majestic Dolls* as a trademark in Germany.

1903: Sears's advertisement similar to that in 1901 except that the sizes were 18½, 21, 24, 27, and 30 inches; prices $1.85 to $5.00.

**1116.** Bisque head with the "Majestic" trademark of Edmund Steiner has glass sleeping eyes, eyelashes, open mouth with two teeth. Ball-jointed body is composition. Mark on head: Ill. **1117,** except that the size is 6 instead of 2. H. 19 inches. *Courtesy of May Maurer.*

**1117.** "Majestic" mark of Edmund Steiner, found on dolls.

*Majestic 2 Reg'd*

1905: Majestic Model advertised by Samstag & Hilder as having American faces, jointed and kid bodies, dressed and undressed; dressed dolls priced at $1.00 and up.

1906: Majestic line of kid-bodied jointed and dressed dolls.

1910: Louis Wolf & Co. distributed Edmund Steiner's patented walking and sitting doll.

1914: Louis Wolf & Co. advertised character dolls in the Majestic line.

**Majestic Doll.** 1901–2. Trademark registered in Germany by *Kämmer & Reinhardt* for dolls and dolls' heads.

**Majestic Doll Co.** 1918–20. New York City. Manufactured dolls, distributed by *Riemann, Seabrey Co.;* dolls came with moving eyes.

**Mak-a-Dol.** 1922–23. Trademark registered in U.S. by *Georgene Averill* for dolls and dolls' outfits.

**Makathi, Gustav.** 1900. Berlin. Manufactured dolls.

**Mal' Auto de Ma Poupée.** See **Mal'Oto de Ma Poupée.**

**Malavarca, Eduardo.** 1919–20. Newark, N.J. Assigned his rights in the U.S. design patent for the Karo Princess Indian doll to *American Ocarina & Toy Co.*

**Mallet, Beatrice.** 1925. Paris. Made dolls exclusively for *Société Française de Fabrication de Bébés et Jouets.*

**Mally, Joseph Robert, & Co.** 1891–99. London. Fancy goods manufacturer; obtained two British patents, one in 1891 for dolls' clothing and the other in 1896 for sleeping eyes in wax dolls' faces.

**Malone, Miss Josephine L.** 1920. Chicago, Ill. Made rag dolls that she named *Hinky Doodle Family Rag Doll* and *Auntie Jo's Own Rag Babies.*

**Mal'Oto de Ma Poupée and Mal'Auto de Ma Poupée.** 1913: Trademarks registered in France by *Charles Rouard.*

**Maltese Dolls.** 1867. Wax dolls exhibited by *C. Polito* and *E. Zammit* at Paris Exposition.

**Maltête, Charles.** 1892–95. Paris. Made bébés that turned their heads and said "Mama." He displayed dolls at the Chicago Exposition in 1893.

**Mälzer.** 1897–1907. Ilmenau, Thür. Made dolls.

**Ma-Ma.** 1914–15. Line of boy dolls dressed in white bear plush; said "Mama" when the body was pushed in and out.

**Ma-Ma Doll.** 1919. Advertised by *Louis Wolf & Co.;* price $1.00 to $5.00.

**Mama Doll, The.** 1914. Doll with metal head advertised by *Samstag & Hilder;* said "Mama." Size 9 inches; price $8.50 doz. wholesale.

**1118A & B.** Typical "Mama Doll," short plump shape with swinging legs, has a voice box in the soft cloth body. Bisque shoulder head with sleeping eyes, wig; composition lower limbs; original clothes. Mark: Ill. **935.** H. 18 inches. H. of shoulder head, 7 inches. *Courtesy of Dorothy Annunziato.*

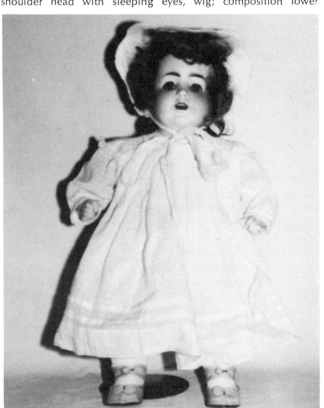

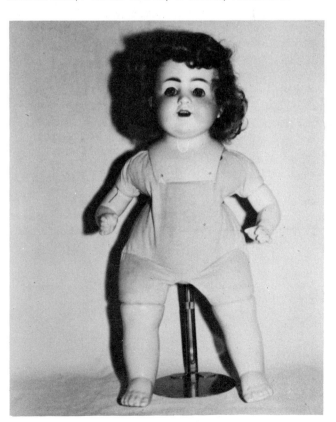

**Mama Dolls.** 1918–25+. Dolls with voices allegedly saying "Mama" date back several centuries, but the term "American Mama Doll" refers specifically to a doll that says "Mama," and has a soft body and swinging legs that simulate walking. This type of doll was patented by *Georgene Averill* in 1918. By 1919, *Louis Amberg & Son, Louis Wolf & Co.,* and *Gerling Toy Co.* were also advertising Mama dolls. Although Amberg claimed that he had patented a Mama voice as early as 1906, the principal makers of Mama voices, which usually operated with reeds and bellows, were Leo Grubman, *B. E. Lloyd* and *Louis V. Aronson,* who made the Ronson voices. Mama dolls usually had flange necks, composition heads, composition forearms, and soft chubby bodies.

**Mama I'm Awake Baby.** 1919. Advertised by *Louis Amberg & Son* as a doll that cried for its Mama when it awakened.

**Mama's Angel Child.** 1914. Trademark registered in U.S. by *Borgfeldt* for dolls.

**Mama's Angel Child.** 1919. Advertised as a new doll made by *Jessie McCutcheon Raleigh.*

**Mamma's Darling.** 1914. Imported, smiling doll.

**Mammy Jinny.** 1920. All-cloth doll made by *Jessie McCutcheon Raleigh;* 18 inches tall.

**Mammy Nurse.** 1905–21. *Chase* stockinet doll representing character in Joel Chandler Harris' books.

**Mancel.** 1871–74. Paris. Made dolls.

**Mangolin.** 1907. Trade name used by *Louis Wolf & Co.* for unbreakable dolls.

**Manhattan Doll Co.** 1890–1922. New York City. Discontinued business after U.S. entered the war in 1917, and resumed after peace in 1918; importers and jobbers; handled various types of dolls.

1918: Advertised 1,800 dolls in discontinued styles, fully jointed, sleeping eyes, human hair wigs; sizes 18, 20, 22, 24, and 26 inches; prices $24.00 to $48.00 doz. wholesale; cash only.

1919: Advertised imported dolls with bisque heads, composition bodies, fully jointed, and bent-leg baby dolls. Came with sleeping eyes, real hair; dressed in chemise; sizes 12, 15, 18, 20, 24, 26, and 30 inches; price $6.00 to $35.00 retail, with 25 to 35 percent discount given to dealers. Also advertised walking doll made in America of wood and composition; no mechanism; 28 inches tall; price $10.00 to $40.00 depending on the type of wig and clothes; $40.00 version came with gown and millinery created by real artists.

**Manhattan Toys & Dolls Manufacturing Co.** 1919–20. New York City. Made dolls' heads and all-composition dolls in various styles and sizes on hot presses. Copyrighted *Kewpies Model* and *Beauty Kist,* both designed by *Ernesto Peruggi.*

**Manikin Dolls.** 1920. Name used by *Horsman* for

"French" little girl models, dressed in silks. These dolls were play dolls, and were pictured on the cover of PLAYTHINGS magazine.

**Manji, Hattori.** 1893. Tokyo, Japan. Displayed dolls at the Chicago Exposition.

**Mannheimer Gummi-Gutta-Percha und Asbest-Fabrik.** 1907–11. Mannheim, Germany. Made and exported dolls.

**Manning, Joseph Alexander.** See **Non-Breakable Doll Co.**

**Manos.** 1916. Trademark registered in France by *Mlle. M. Fauche* for dolls.

**Mansert, August.** 1908–25+. Sonneberg, Thür. Made and exported dressed dolls.

**Mansfield, Etta.** 1917. New York City. Registered *Gollywog* as a trademark in U.S. for dolls; mark affixed to doll by a woven label.

**Manuel, Gaston, & de Stoecklin, E.** 1920. Paris. Registered in France *Poupées de Paris, Les Poupées Parisiennes,* and *Les Poupettes* as trademarks for dolls.

**Manufacture des Bébés & Poupées.** 1920–21. Paris. Factory at Levallois, Seine. Made *bébés incassables,* "unbreakable" heads and dolls, both dressed and undressed. Used *La Madelon* as a trademark. La Madelon registered in France by Alfred François Xavier Martin in 1919.

**Manufacture of Bisque Heads.** In general, bisque doll heads were made in the same manner as other bisque products. The earlier bisque heads are more likely to have been pressed than poured. Bisque may be either tinted or untinted; the latter is often called "Parian" by collectors, and may be either soft paste or hard paste porcelain. Although bisque bald-head dolls are often considered early, no documentary data have been found for them prior to the 1870's. Contemporary accounts of the methods of making bisque dolls' heads can best tell the story.

1884: "If you examine the craniums you will find a patch of cork hiding a bit of lead. When the baby tumbles it is brought by the law of gravitation on the back of its head, and is taken up unhurt."—THE WONDERLAND OF WORK, Clara Mateaux.

The method of making bisque heads in the *Jumeau* factory was described in a booklet published by J. Cusset in 1885: The longer the Kaolin mixture was left to macerate in water, the finer was the resultant bisque. After the water was drained away, the paste was of a dough-like consistency and was kneaded and rolled between cylinders. The thickness depended on the size of the heads—larger heads were thicker than small ones. The rolled-out paste was cut into squares approximating the size of the two-part plaster cast and carefully pressed into it. New molds were required for about every fifty heads.

After the paste had hardened sufficiently to hold its shape, the heads were removed; eye sockets were cut out and the paste around the eyes was thinned down to ensure more perfect fit of the glass eyes. Ears were

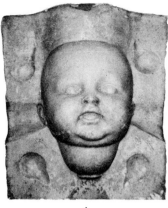
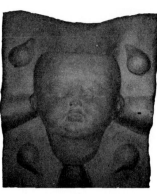

A              B

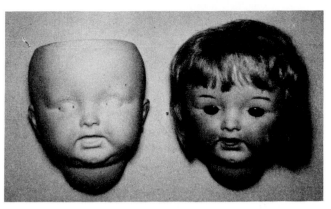

C

**1119A, B, & C.** Left to right: front half of the master mold, front half of the pouring mold, head that has been fired but not painted, finished head. These plaster molds and bisque heads were made by Ernst Reinhardt ca. 1920. Mark: Ill. **55.** *Coleman Collection.*

**1120.** Plaster model on left and bisque head on right. The bisque head is tinted pink and has been fired once, but needs painting and finishing. The model for the bisque head would have been larger and would have shrunk when fired. These were made by Ernst Reinhardt ca. 1920. *Coleman Collection.*

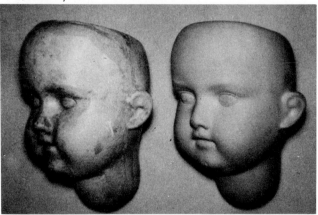

applied to the larger heads. Next the heads were placed on trays and fired in very hot, wood-burning ovens for about twenty-seven hours. After cooling, they were polished with sandpaper to a fine smoothness.

Mineral pigments were used for the coloring of the heads. Two coats of pale pink were applied all over the head and neck. Then the cheeks, lips, nostrils, eyebrows, and eyelashes were all painted before a second firing for seven hours at a lower temperature, which ensured the permanence of the painted decoration.

Eyes were set with wax and then plaster was spread over the back so that the eyes could not move. A piece of cork was fitted into the top of the head, and the wig was attached to the cork.

It should be noted that these heads made by Jumeau were pressed; the following description, a few years later, shows that Jumeau made poured heads.

Ca. 1894: "The making of the head approaches an art . . .

"We enter first the shops of sculpture and molding where artists sculpture, in plaster, faces of all sizes and expressions . . .

"The model heads are molded, and the impressions from these molds are taken with a paste of porcelain clay of a wonderful purity, filtered, strained, washed; the strainer in the last operation resembles a silk tissue. It is made to run through some taps into a mold, which it fills. The walls retain a certain thickness of the slip, which will become porcelain. The rest is emptied at the end of a few minutes into a tub.

"When this casting is finished, the heads come out of the molds, and are placed in the round terra-cotta trays called 'gazettes,' which are piled near the muffle-furnace; these piles present the aspect of great trunks of shining trees. After baking, these white masks have the lightness, transparency, and the fineness of grain of the most valuable porcelain.

"They pass then to the cutting out, which consists of making holes for the eyes, which were blank as in ordinary busts. Artificial eyes . . . are inserted into these holes . . ." (Some modern makers of ceramic dolls question whether Claretie could have seen the eyes cut out before rather than after baking.)

"These heads thus finished are covered with the freshest colors of youth, painted, daubed with rose; there are, in the painting shop, workwomen who make eyelashes all their lives, and others eyebrows, others lips, others rosy cheeks. A certain practice and some sureness of hand is necessary, especially for the eyelashes, which have equal and parallel strokes. . . .

"What still remains? It is necessary to put the doll's head on her shoulders, supply her with a cork pate, and to fasten the wig with little nails."—LES JOUETS by Léo Claretie, 1894; translation published 1965 by Dorothy S. Coleman in THE AGE OF DOLLS.

1897: ". . . plaster of Paris casts are made, and these are employed as moulds. They are used fifty times, and then destroyed, new ones being substituted.

A

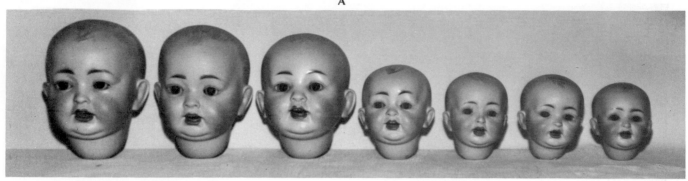

**1121A, B, & C.** The group of seven heads made in Germany at one factory are all model #151. From left to right their size numbers are: 10, 8½, 7, 2, 1, 0, 2/0; their heights are: 5½, 5, 4½, 3½, 3¼, 3, 2¾ inches. The difference in appearance is due to the individuality of the decorator. The three larger heads have four teeth; the smaller ones, only two. Four heads have brown eyes and three have blue. The heads were wrapped in "bogus" paper and packed according to size, either in individual boxes stuffed with excelsior or in boxes holding several heads. No. 151/7 was given a box of its own. *Courtesy of Eleanor Jean Carter.*

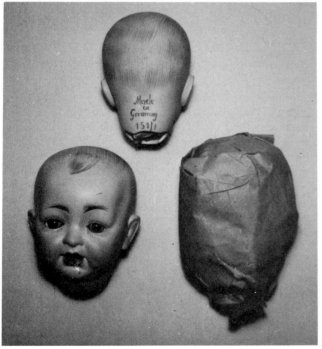

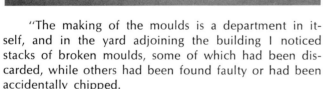

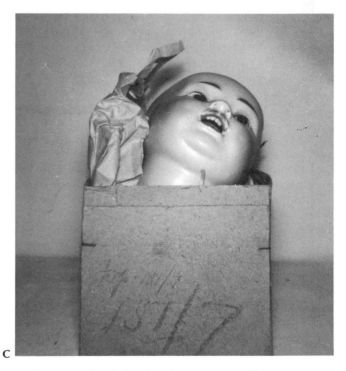

B          C

"The making of the moulds is a department in itself, and in the yard adjoining the building I noticed stacks of broken moulds, some of which had been discarded, while others had been found faulty or had been accidentally chipped.

"The dolls' heads are made of 'biscuit' which is a kind of composition composed of lime and various kinds of earth, mixed and stamped underfoot until it becomes a substance known as 'Kaolin.' This is put in water in large vats furnished with taps. . . . It is left in water several days, the longer it remains the finer being the porcelain; it is then again and again washed, filtered, and strained until it is of dazzling purity and whiteness." (The casting process is similar to that described by Claretie in the immediately preceding excerpt.)

"After the heads are turned out of the mould, they are conveyed into the cutting-room, where women workers cut the holes for the eyes . . . The next stage, if the heads are large ones, is the fixing on of the ears (in the small class these are moulded with the heads); and then comes the baking, for which process the heads are carefully placed so as not to touch each other on a round tray, or kind of sieve, called a 'gazette,' which holds about three dozen heads.

"As soon as the gazettes are filled, they are stacked in immense ovens or furnaces, the largest of them holding 2500 heads at one time, and these are then baked for a space of forty-eight hours.

"When the baking is over the gazettes are taken out and their contents left to cool . . . They are now packed into large baskets and carried into an adjoining room . . .

"The worker, seating herself before a basket, carefully rubs and polishes each head with sandpaper until

**1122A & B.** Bisque head with large crown hole. Many dolls have the top and/or back of the head cut off. Nearly half the head has been sliced off this doll and the eyes are stationary. Head marked "B 12 F." H. 27 inches. *Courtesy of Helen Jo Payne.*

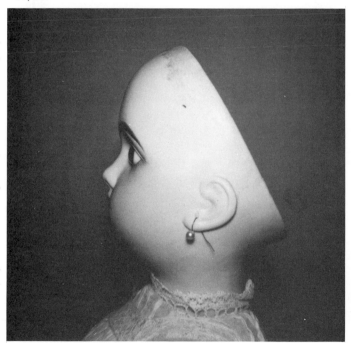

it is perfectly smooth . . . they are replaced in the basket, and taken to the colouring and decorating department. . . .

"The pallid, almost transparent, mask here receives the first flat layer of flesh tints, and two washes of pale pink paint—the colours used are mineral—are evenly laid over the face and neck.

"When dry they are passed on to the next room, where, under the hands of skillful artists, the faces assume the expression and almost the reality of life, and the pale porcelain image is transformed into a chubby, laughing child by touching the cheeks and nostrils with red, colouring the lips a deeper tint and parting them to show the little teeth; light eyelashes, delicate and even, are put in, and arched eyebrows, a little darker in colour. . . .

"The heads are again baked for seven hours to fix the colours, but the ovens are kept at a much lower temperature than was necessary for the Kaolin."—"A Village of Dollmakers," by Mons. Dinorben Griffith, PEARSON'S MAGAZINE, July, 1897.

"Several houses [Rabery, Bru, Pintel, and Eden-Bébé] . . . about 1900 became absorbed in the Bébé Jumeau, the one house that manufactured entire dolls. All the other houses had bought porcelain heads and glass eyes from Germany."—GAZETTE DES BEAUX ARTS, Dec., 1916.

The bisque dolls' heads described so far were made in the Jumeau factory. The next account describes the methods employed in the *Kestner* factory located in Ohrdruf, Thüringia.

1906: "First an expert modeler makes a head of clay, and from this a number of plaster moulds are made. Into these moulds is poured a thick liquid porcelain, the preparation of which requires especial care and experience. After standing for about ten minutes, the liquid begins to harden next the moulds, and the superfluous part is poured off. After another fifteen minutes the head is hard enough to remove from the mould,

**1123A & B.** Pressed bisque head with braided hair style. After the head was removed from the mold, comb marks were made over the line of juncture. Back shoulder is marked "13 D," probably size and/or mold number. H. 19 inches. H. of shoulder head, 5 inches. *Coleman Collection.*

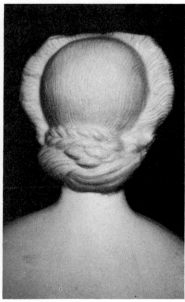

**1124A & B.** Poured bisque head with molded yoke, collar and tie glazed; painted features, untinted bisque. H. 14½ inches. H. of shoulder head, 3¾ inches. *Coleman Collection.*

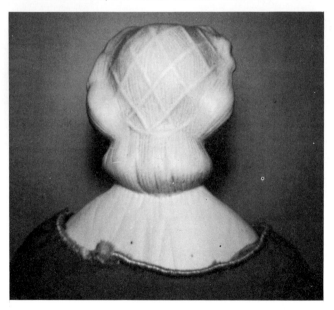

which is in two pieces that have simply to be separated. The seams on the doll head caused by the fitting together of the two parts of the mould are then smoothed down, and eyes and mouth openings are cut out and sometimes teeth set in. When the heads are thoroughly dried they are put in Chamotte vessels and upon porcelain supports pass into a large round kiln, where they are fired in white heat.

"When placed in the hands of skilled artists for finishing up they are simply dull white porcelain. A flesh color is deftly applied, and when this is dry, cheeks, lips, eyelashes and brows are painted in.

"The heads are then again fired to burn the colors in.

"After the colors are burned in, the heads are ready for eyes and hair. The former are inserted to stay open with cement, or for sleeping dolls they are connected with a balancing weight. A cardboard cap is inserted on the top to which the wig is to be affixed."—PLAYTHINGS, April, 1906.

The method of making bisque heads in "the largest house of all" in France—the *Société Française de Bébés et Jouets*—is given next:

1907: "The heads are molded of a finer paste, the chief ingredient of which is kaolin; and even after they have left the molds they pass through many processes on their way to perfection. One girl cuts the eye-sockets; another touches the cheeks with rouge; a third blackens the eyebrows; and so the head journeys down the long table and ends in an oven where it is baked into unbreakable consistency. It comes from the furnace eyeless and, of course, hairless. There is a hole in the top of the skull into which a cork is driven, and the wig is fastened with tacks to the cork."—PLAYTHINGS, January, 1907.

Although the above head is described as "unbreakable," it appears to be bisque since it is made of kaolin; the French referred to their bisque head dolls as *bébés incassables* (literally, "unbreakable babies"). Kaolin is the principal ingredient of porcelain, and bisque is unglazed porcelain.

1911: See **Manufacture of Waltershausen Dolls.**

1920: "Coal must be used to fire doll heads. Coal prices fabulous and scarce in Germany."—PLAYTHINGS, July, 1920.

Bisque heads were sometimes decorated with glossy paint, which gave them a partially glazed appearance.

**Manufacture of Celluloid (Pyroxylin) Dolls.** Celluloid is one of the earliest man-made plastics. It is a hard, elastic compound made by subjecting guncotton (pyroxylin), mixed with camphor and other substances, to hydraulic pressure. Pyroxylin is cellulose in the form of cotton or other vegetable fibers steeped in nitric and sulphuric acid and then washed.

1880: "Dolls' heads made of celluloid, when molded, have a glazed or glassy look . . . To remove this gloss I use a fine pumice-stone or some similar powder, and this powder rubbed over the face and neck takes off the polish . . . if the eyebrows and other lines indicating hair have been put on, as they usually are, before the powder is used, these hair-lines will be rubbed off by the attrition of the powder; or if these lines are put on after the surface has been abraded, they will show rough and uneven, and be liable in handling the dolls to be worn off. I therefore take a sharp-pointed knife, and, holding it usually at an oblique angle from the face, make fine incisions in the surface in the places for these hair-lines, and into the incisions I work a coloring of the shade required, which becomes fixed in the incisions."—United States Patent No. 235,933, granted to William B. Carpenter, 1880.

1906: "Celluloid doll heads at the *Kestner* factory are manufactured by a special process fully protected by patents . . . When brought from the moulds smooth and shiny they are worked in such a manner they acquire a dull, lifelike flesh tint vastly different from the usual glossy appearance of the celluloid heads coated with aniline colors, which after a short time fade and give the head a dead expression. The Kestner heads will stand exposure to strong light, and can scarcely be distinguished from the finest bisque head."—PLAYTHINGS, April, 1906.

1908: "Three years ago [1905] saw the advent of the celluloid beauty which graces the stores today. She is of correct mould and proportion, is beautifully painted by Italian girls, who are brought to Germany especially for this work . . .

"Two steel forms, moulded with great care to give just the proper proportions, represent, one the front half of the doll, the other the back. Sheets of celluloid are cut out and laid one in each of these steel moulds, and then the two are firmly locked together. There is an opening at the top of the steel forms, which is connected by a long tube to a tank of compressed air. The compressed air is heated and forces its way into the steel moulds, pressing the celluloid against the sides of the model and shaping the body of the doll. Thirty seconds suffices for this compressed air treatment; the forms are unlocked and the sides of the doll retain their required shape. They are cemented together with a special preparation of ether, and hand-painted by the Italian girls, to whom such work seems but second nature."—From an article by Maurice Walker of *Hamburger & Co.* in PLAYTHINGS, February, 1908.

**Manufacture of China Dolls.** The china used for dolls is a glazed, translucent porcelain. It can be either hard paste or soft paste, but most dolls are hard paste. They are made of a kaolin and feldspar mixture with a feldsparic glaze. Some dolls are glazed both inside and outside, but most are glazed only on the outside. A larger proportion of glazed china than bisque dolls' heads are pressed. This may be because china heads were popular at an earlier date. Pressed heads, recognizable by the roughness and unevenness on the inside, often have portions that are very thin, and in some cases they are reinforced with plaster.

Bisque and china heads were often made from the same mold, and many factories made both—e.g., *Kestner, Kling.* When the heads were fired and lost their moisture, they shrank, and then could serve as models for smaller-size heads. For this reason, the smaller heads lacked some of the detail found on larger heads. The decorative techniques and colors varied from factory to factory. Heads that apparently have the same hairdo will often differ markedly in details of decoration. Some heads, believed to be early, have a pink tinting, but all pink-tinted china heads are not necessarily early.

1884: "China dolls are more exclusively the product of a factory. After being modelled by hand, they are baked in a great oven for a week. During this time the utmost care and watchfulness are required. The tenders are never permitted to sleep. A draught of air will produce

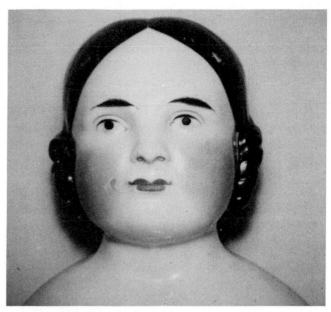

1125. Pressed china head. The doll has two-toned eyebrows, black on brown, and circular nostril. H. 25 inches. H. of shoulder head, 6½ inches. *Courtesy of Alberta Darby.*

disastrous results. A single oven contains 5,000 dolls, and thirty ovens are often full at once in one factory. At the end of the week the dolls come out in all conditions. About one in five is perfect. After baking, the dolls are painted and glazed. The imperfect ones are separated by themselves and sold to 'fairs' and 'cheap-John' concerns, which dispose of them to people who infest such places. One German factory has been running about one hundred and thirty years, and has produced about one billion dolls."—HARPER'S BAZAR, November 22, 1884.

**Manufacture of Cloth (Soft) Bodies.** Many cloth bodies were made at home from scraps of material, but even in the early 19th century there were also commercial cloth bodies. The popular one-piece cloth bodies found on wax over papier-mâché-headed dolls were made for the most part before Victoria came to the throne (see Ill. 1126). These bodies had a seam up the back and gussets at the side to form the waist and hips. The single seam up the inside of the legs, down the middle of the top and bottom of each foot causes the feet to toe in. These dolls had very long legs and relatively small heads. The sewed hips, knees, etc., which permitted dolls to bend at these joints were later innovations, and by 1860 a commercial body was patented that enabled dolls to sit down. *Sarah Robinson* and *Martha Wellington*, both in 1883, patented improvements in making cloth bodies that increased the naturalness of their articulation.

1875: "The legs, either of pot or cotton, have to be filled with moss or sawdust, and the same process is gone through with the body and arms, the task being intrusted to a number of young women."—"The Wax Doll Manufacture," from LITTLE BOUQUET, MONTHLY MAGAZINE, June, 1875.

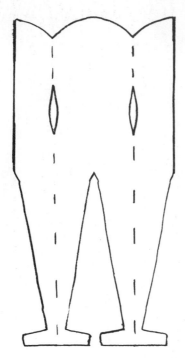

**1126.** Pattern showing how the one-piece cloth bodies were constructed. These bodies were used for the early wax-over-papier-mâché heads. The simplicity of the pattern helped to hold down the price, but made a rather pigeon-toed doll. (See Ill. **364.**)

**1127.** "Homemade" patchwork cloth body. The patches at the knees act as joints; the arms are made from leather gloves. Chest is padded to meet the outside line of the china shoulders. H. 24 inches. H. of shoulder head, 6¼ inches. *Coleman Collection.*

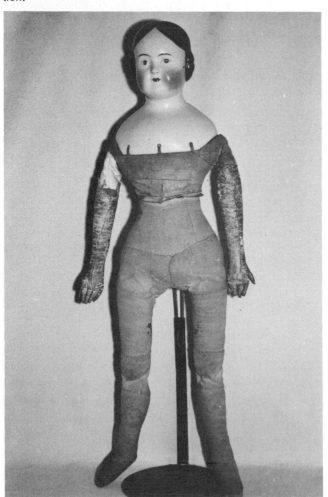

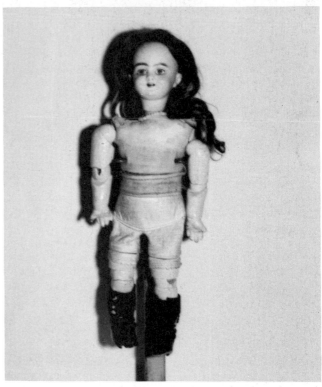

**1128.** Cloth upper torso and waist belt; kid lower torso and upper legs; wood and composition arms and legs; swivel joints with wire springs around a wooden core at neck and waist; flat piece of metal nailed on top of wooden core. Bisque head, Simon & Halbig mold #1059. H. 11 inches. *Courtesy of Lester & Alice Grinnings.*

1877: "The manufacturer gives out so many yards of cotton, and he knows to an inch how much material each dozen dolls will require, according to their size. The body-maker takes it home, and accomplishes the work in the following manner: One person cuts out the body for the doll, another sews it, a third rams in the sawdust, a fourth makes the joints, and in this way a family will produce many dozen in a week. The payment of this work is by the piece.

"The arms form another branch of this manufacture, upon which certain persons are almost exclusively employed. Except for the very commonest class of dolls, the arms are made of kid below the elbow, and cotton above; and in every case there is an attempt at fingers, although their number may not always be correct. The price paid for these arms complete is incredibly small. The work-woman furnishes the kid, cotton, and sawdust, and for large arms about six inches long receives 6½ pence for a dozen pair or thirteen cents in American money."—HARPER'S BAZAR, August 18, 1877.

1885: "The doll bodies were made of muslin, which was stuffed with hair and sawdust. The upper part of the arm was made of muslin, while the lower part was made of two pieces of leather, stitched together to represent fingers. The finger stitching was guided by small sticks about the size of match sticks, which were inserted in the leather. The arms were stuffed with sawdust, and at the shoulder joints some cattle hair was used to keep the sawdust from coming out. . . .

"In 1885 *Mr. Goldsmith* invented the corset body doll, which was the same as the ordinary stuffed doll. A piece of red or blue cambric, with rickrack on the edge, was sewed on the body."—PLAYTHINGS, December, 1908.

1893: "Doll bodies, as everybody knows, are usually made of calico stuffed with sawdust. . . . One of these bodymakers obtains so many yards of calico from a master, and, buying her own sawdust, makes the material into dolls. As she is usually helped by her children, she makes many dozens every week. Arms are made by other women."—CHATTERBOX, 1893.

*The Columbian Doll* of the early 1890's was made of firm muslin. First the muslin bag was filled loosely with fine excelsior; then cotton was placed between the muslin and the excelsior to give a smooth surface. The cotton was inserted by means of wooden sticks of various sizes and shapes, made in a carriage shop especially for this purpose out of wooden wheel spokes. The arms and legs were stuffed entirely of cotton, also by the use of these prodding sticks. The fingers and toes were indicated by appropriate stitches through the muslin cloth and cotton. To strengthen and stiffen the material, a sizing of starch and glue was applied and allowed to dry completely before the limbs were painted a flesh color.

1903: "The bodies of the dolls are merely stuffed sacks with extensions upon which the arms and legs can be sewed."—PLAYTHINGS, May, 1903.

1912: There are two contemporary descriptions of the making of pink sateen bodies in America; the first is for *Amberg* dolls and the second for *Horsman* dolls.

"After the patterns are made they are then passed on to the Cutting Department. One of the cutters . . . who stood at his work with a razor-edge cutting knife, having a blade about eighteen inches in length. This moved rapidly up and down on his grooved cutting table over ninety-six [sic] pieces of pink fabric which he deftly cut unto [sic] oddly shaped pieces, that later would be sewed into bodies, arms and legs. From the cutting room the pieces go into the Operating Department where long rows of young women, sitting at power machines, sew up the arms, legs and bodies separately. Next the arms and legs go to the Cork-Stuffing Department . . . and are carefully filled with a fine cork shoved in through funnels and tightly pounded.

"The arms and legs are then severally finished off by having the ends sewed up. When finished, a steel pin protected by a heavy cardboard disc and tin washer is put at the tops of each and then the jointers get in their work. The arms and legs are joined to the body by means of a steel pin which is riveted over card board and cast discs inside of the body, thereupon the headless

doll is turned over to a corps of men who stuff the trunk of the body similarly to the way they stuff the arms and legs with a fine cork."—PLAYTHINGS, May, 1912.

"Taking up the various operations which enter into the construction of the legs, arms, bodies and dresses, it should be stated that the first operation, that of cutting, is done by machinery, which follows the outlines of large steel dies constructed in the forms desired to produce hundreds of pieces of fabric for the legs, arms and bodies. This insures the perfect fitting of the various pieces which enter into the construction of the dresses and a proper and uniform size for legs, arms and bodies."—PLAYTHINGS, June, 1912.

1917: "The cloth for the bodies of the dolls comes to the factory in bales. Guided by a pattern laid off on the top of a pile of cloth 6 in. high, an operator cuts literally thousands of pairs of legs, arms and bodies at one time by means of a motor-driven knife . . . The parts are then sewed into closed shapes for the arms, legs and bodies on . . . motor-driven sewing machines which operate at the rate of 4,000 stitches per minute. . . .

"The cloth parts are then ready to go to the special sawdust-ramming machine. Sawdust is fed into hoppers at the top of this unique piece of equipment. When the operator has placed one of the little cloth sacks, fashioned perhaps to simulate an arm, over the spindle beneath the hopper, he . . . sets in rotation an augur-shaped tool inside the spindle. This feeds the sawdust into the cloth arm. At the same time a cam moves the rotating augur rapidly up and down so that it tamps the sawdust into the cloth as it feeds it."—PLAYTHINGS, February, 1917.

Doll bodies are stuffed with many things besides the sawdust, cotton, cork, moss, and hair mentioned above. Cotton batting is frequently found, especially in 20th-century doll bodies. Wool and cotton fabrics, silk floss, sand, excelsior, chopped hay, straw, flock, cork-dust as well as ground cork, milkweed, cattail fluff, seaweed, hemp, bran, wood flour, kapok, and even plaster have been found in bodies. It should be noted that often more than one kind of material was used for stuffing a doll.

Many patents have been granted for improvements in the construction of dolls' bodies. There was a continual effort to make the cloth body more realistic in shape and articulation. The culmination of these efforts brought forth the fully jointed, laminated cloth bodies and the all cloth body manufactured by the *Utley Company* in 1917. The latter was an exact copy of the ball-jointed composition-body doll. (See also **Cloth Bodies.**)

**Manufacture of Composition Bodies.** These bodies could be made of almost any type of composition, although papier-mâché seems to have been one of the most popular types. Beginning in the 1850's, dolls were made with bodies that combined cloth and composition. There was cloth at the upper arms and legs for articulation; the chest part of the torso was also cloth and usually contained a squeak box. No records of the fully jointed composition body have been found prior to the 1860's. In 1868, *Lechertier, Barbe & Cie.* obtained a French patent for a papier-mâché body with elastic for articulation of the joints.

1885: J. Cusset described the manufacture of the papier-mâché bodies in the *Jumeau* factory. They were made of gray paper and had front and back portions glued together and the socket applied for ball-jointed articulation. The parts of the body were painted white, sanded, and four more coats of paint plus a coat of varnish were applied. When dry, the body was strung with elastic and metal hooks, and the head was screwed into place so that it could turn.

Two other descriptions of the making of Jumeau bodies are as follows:

1894: ". . . they mold bodies of every size in heavy matrices of steel . . . The torso is formed from a single piece and is without seams. The workmen stuff the hollows with old paper moistened in the paste, in a way to secure an even thickness on the inner surface. When they open the matrix they unfasten from it an object in relief, which is a body . . . with the grayish green color of old paper. . . .

"The limbs are molded in other matrices, from which they come in the same dirty green color. . . . The hands are stamped apart in a very complicated machine, from which they emerge the color of flax-meal. . . .

"In the interior of the body a cross-piece of wood has been stuck to which are hooked the copper tendons of all the members. . . . Each extremity of the limb is provided with its ball and hook . . ."—LES JOUETS by Claretie, *op. cit.*

1897: ". . . the bodies were made all in one piece; this work in the factory is undertaken by women apprentices, who, when they are thoroughly proficient, have the work supplied to them in their own homes. Every worker has her specialty, some making bodies only, while others devote their attention to legs, and others again to the manufacture of arms.

"Into them [the molds] pieces of greyish brown paper moistened with paste, according to the thickness required for the various parts, are carefully fitted and rammed, so that every little indentation and hollow is carefully followed. . . .

"When all the different parts are carefully modelled, they are put on hurdles to dry, this taking from twenty-four to forty-eight hours, or even longer according to the season.

"The hands are made of a composite of ten different kinds of material, which, when mixed, is put into a special machine, and at every turn of its piston a little hand drops out of it. . . .

"When all of the brown paper members are dry they are sent into the painting rooms . . . When dry [after their first wash] the bodies are rubbed with pumice stone to smooth down and remove any unevenness of the painted surface. Then all . . . receive five successive coats of a beautiful rose tint and one of varnish.

"Inside the bust of the doll there is a piece of wood . . . and on this all the copper tendons of the limbs are hooked, and on this also presently the head will be fastened. A piece of elastic is attached to the legs, passed up the body where it is tied to the bar of wood, and the hands and arms are fastened in the same way."—PEARSON'S MAGAZINE, July, 1897, *op. cit.*

The methods employed in the manufacture of composition dolls' bodies by *Kestner* in Waltershausen is similar to those used in the Jumeau factory, as can be seen by the following:

1906: "The jointed dolls require hollow moulds, the pieces being made in two parts of paper pulp, which are fastened together and provided with the necessary sockets for the ball joints. After this a flesh color is poured over them and they are put on sticks to dry before being varnished. The finished bodies and legs are turned over to joiners, who fasten heads, arms and legs together by means of rubber cords and hooks in the bodies."—PLAYTHINGS, April, 1906.

The next description applies to "the largest house of all" in France, which must be the *Société Française de Bébés et Jouets.*

1907: ". . . workmen knead up into a dingy paste old cardboard; even old gloves, old rags, and gum tragacanth. . . . In an adjoining room the paste is poured into molds for the busts, the arms, the legs of dolls innumerable. There is a special machine for stamping out the hands . . . the steady stream of queer, little hands that fall ceaselessly from the iron monster . . .

". . . scores of women sat . . . fastening the arms and legs to the little green bodies with copper wires—the factory turns out two hundred thousand of these doll-fragments every day."—PLAYTHINGS, January, 1907.

1911: See **Manufacture of Waltershausen Dolls.**

World War I permitted America to come into the doll-manufacturing business and to compete with France and Germany. A description of the manufacturing process in the EFFanBEE (*Fleischaker & Baum*) factory in New York where 10,000 dolls a day were produced is given below.

1920: "There were several artists at work in the room . . . and round about on shelves were hundreds of casts of all manner of doll parts—heads, bodies, hands, feet and what not, in all sizes and shapes. It reminded me more of an art museum . . . the young man [Italian] was just starting operations on a lump of clay which was beginning to show signs of evoluting into the trunk or body of a doll. It was certainly interesting to watch him slice and pat his clay into the semblance of a graceful little figure . . .

"'This body,' [he said] 'will be an exact reproduction in clay of the drawing I have here. The drawing was made by a celebrated artist and is, as you see, shown from three different views or angles. When my model is finished it will be cast in plaster of Paris and from the plaster the dies will be made . . .'

"There were forty of these [hot presses] ranged against the walls of the great floor, in the middle of which a huge automatic mixing machine rumbled and groaned as it turned over and over on its axis.

"Baum conducted us to the middle of the floor and pointed out to us a pile of something that looked like wet sand that had just been removed from the mixer. 'That,' he said, 'is the first step in the making of a doll. We place a quantity of pulp into this receptacle and mix it with chemical binders so that it will hold together when put into the presses. If these chemicals were not there, the pulp would crumble like dust when it is pressed. After it is well mixed, the men take it in buckets to their machines and here you see it pressed into its first recognizable shape.' . . .

"The presses were fitted with upper and nether bronze dies, each of which were about sixteen by twenty-four inches on the surface and nearly four inches thick. . . .

"The upper dies are made to fit into the lower ones in such a manner that when a layer of the sandlike pulp was packed on top of the lower set it leaves a proper thickness for the particular part that is to be stamped into shape. . . . A long lever at the side of the machine when pressed down by the operator brought the two dies together, like the jaws of a giant animal, and from between came the hissing and sputtering of the damp pulp as the flame-heated dies baked it dry.

" 'It takes about six minutes to bake a setting,' explained Baum, 'and when one setting is removed from the press another is put in at once. Each part of the doll is made in halves and these halves are then set together for the next process . . . each [press] makes a complete part, such as the front and back . . . of a body, or upper or lower leg.' . . . all the parts were brown in color when they came out of the press . . .

"Halfway towards the grinding wheels they stopped a few minutes to watch the 'stickers' at work glueing the front and back halves of doll parts together which had been deliverd to them from the hot presses. . . .

"Deftly they [the grinders] applied the seamed edges of the parts to the abrasive wheels and ground off the rough edges . . . As each tray of parts was finished it was . . . taken to the filling department where any small roughness that still appeared on the parts was examined and every little depression or unsightly crevice filled with a prepared composition and the entire piece treated to a thorough rubbing with cloth and fine sandpaper. . . .

"The contents of a dozen copper caldrons like those employed in great hotels for cooking soups and broths were being stirred by men with paddles while around each caldron were steam coils to keep the liquid warm. The beautiful flesh colored mixture which they stirred is made up of harmless pigments and ingredients chief among which is glycerine . . . It is used to give the doll its skin and is called 'dip' because the parts are dipped into it instead of its being applied with a brush like paint, and then placed on racks to harden. . . .

"Then they are again passed to polishers, who rub them down with fine emery cloth, so that every detail and feature is smooth. Next comes the trimmer, who cuts off along the edges all the ends of the 'dip' which in its fluid state ran off during and after dipping.

". . . half a dozen stalwart men were operating several cold press machines. When the trade was in its infancy, these had been used for making doll heads and doll hands, but now doll hands alone are made on them.

"A mass of dark gray composition, for all the world in shape like a prepared baking of bread dough, lay on the work bench before each man. In making the hands, a small portion of the dough is taken from the mass and rolled out in the shape of a band about four inches wide and twelve inches long. This is laid on the face of the bronze die, and bronze cores placed. Another strip of the dough is placed on top, and the remainder or top part of the die superimposed to complete the whole piece. The set is then placed into the levered cold press and subjected to a heavy pressure.

"It takes about seventy-two hours for the hardening or seasoning to be completed, after the hands have been pressed into shape, before they can be dipped. . . .

"Each machine is capable of turning out from three to six pairs of hands about every three minutes, according to size."—PLAYTHINGS, April, May, June, July, August, and September, 1920.

In the October, 1920, issue of PLAYTHINGS, DuPont, makers of dry enamel for spraying dolls, made the claim that though some doll manufacturers used paint, enamel had the advantage of drying more perfectly.

**Manufacture of Composition Heads.** The methods employed in the manufacture of composition heads are similar to those used for composition bodies. The first (1892), second (1903), fourth (1908), and fifth (1912) of the descriptions that follow here apply to *Can't Break 'Em* heads made by *Hoffmann* and *Aetna*. The third excerpt (1906) applies to *Kestner;* the sixth (1913) covers German factories.

1892: The patent papers of Solomon Hoffmann describe the manufacture of Can't Break 'Em dolls as follows:

"These ingredients are compounded in substantially the following proportions: one hundred parts of glue and twenty-five parts each of glycerine, zinc oxide, and Japanese wax. These ingredients are mixed with a suitable quantity of water and are heated until they are thoroughly commingled and assume a liquid state. At this stage a suitable pigment may be added, ground, however, exceedingly fine. After the mixture has attained, for instance, about 75 Fahrenheit, it is poured into suitable molds or a mold to produce a doll's head, for instance, and after the poured material has become set and hardened it is smoothed or polished by the use of any approved tools—for example, sand or emery paper.

"In the manufacture of dolls' heads and limbs it is desired that the molded article should have a finish-coating, and this coating is produced by immersing the head or the limb in a bath composed of glue, glycerine, zinc oxide, Japanese wax, and a color to produce flesh-tint. After this coating has properly dried, the eyelashes, eyebrows, mouth, and nostrils are painted upon the face,

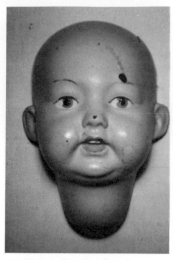

**1129A & B.** Wood pulp composition head made by the hot press method. Picture on the left shows the outside of the front half; the one at the right shows the inside of the front half. H. of socket head, 5 inches. *Coleman Collection.*

if a doll's head is being made, and the cheeks are colored properly. Finally, to prevent the possibility of the colors rubbing or running, the cast head is immersed in a thin collodion bath—that is to say, collodion of commerce thinned with ether."

1903: "A peculiar composition is poured hot into a mold to form the heads, arms or feet. [After the heads have cooled and been smoothed with sandpaper] the eyes which are specially imported from Europe are then inserted through the neck into the sockets. Other operators thereupon paint in the eyebrows and hair and tint the cheeks."—PLAYTHINGS, May, 1903.

1906: "Practically the same process [as for composition bodies] is followed out in making the so-called patent head of paper pulp. After these are dried they are given to artists, who paint in eyes, eyebrows, hair, mouth, and color the cheeks true to life. A coat of dull varnish as a finishing touch is added."—PLAYTHINGS, April, 1906 (Kestner).

1908: "The chemical ingredients of this mass and particularly the manner of combining them, remains to the present day, a secret of the Hoffmann family. One of its members personally does the mysterious trick in the laboratory and then the mass is brought out and boiled in large kettles. When the proper liquid state and temperature are attained, the molds (of plaster paris or metal), are filled with the composition. They are then turned upside down and placed on top of the kettle. Enough of the material adheres to the walls of the mold to reproduce a doll's head, leg or arm, and still the article remains hollow and sufficiently light.

"After drying over night, the molds are opened . . . in a few days when the atmosphere has absorbed all moisture . . . the articles become as hard as rock.

"The next stage in the manufacture is the removal of all seams which remain on the contour and show where the parts of the mold had come together. This and the smoothing away of all imperfections is done by sharp knives and sandpaper. When this operation is completed the parts receive their flesh color coat. This flesh color paint is composed, to a great extent, of the same ingredients as the composition and consequently is likewise unbreakable. Moreover, the paint, being heated, combines with the mass underneath and the two practically form one substance and forever preclude the possibility of 'chipping' or 'cracking' of the paint.* The heads are dried by being placed on specially made boards with long nails projecting in regular rows a few inches apart. Placed 'head down,' on the points of these nails. . . .

"Each face comes out of the mold with two indentations, showing where the eyes are to be placed. Guided by these markings a skilled workman inserts a strong pointed tool and cuts out two appropriate slits. Into these slits the eyes are placed from the hollow head, and then fastened by means of a few drops of hot liquid composition.

"Our face still wants eyelashes, eyebrows, lips and nostrils. Some very delicate brushes in the hands of an experienced artist soon supply these shortcomings and the head of our doll is complete.

". . . the heads are pasted on by a good strong gelatine glue and the doll is finished by the addition of flowing hair, or hair parted in the middle or on one side, or hair hanging in beautiful long curls."—PLAYTHINGS, July, 1908.

1912: "From the composition room the hot liquid mass is taken to the casters who pour it into the molds, the originals of which have been prepared by sculptors famous for their work in child subjects.

"After this, the heads . . . go through a hardening process in the short space of twenty-four hours.

"They are then . . . polished by lathes operated by machines and where all rough spots are removed by hand.

"After this polishing process they are dipped into urns containing the desired flesh tints, being smoothed by the hand application of paint brushes.

"Following this treatment the heads are taken to the art department where the latest appliances known in this branch of manufacturing are used to apply the complexion tints which blend true to life.

"After the machinery has done all in its power the heads are turned over to skilled artists who finish up the operation commenced by the machinery and paint in the eyes, redden the lips, sharpen the eyebrows, etc."—PLAYTHINGS, June, 1912.

1913: "The making of the composition dolls as seen in the German factories is an interesting process . . . First, there is the kneading room, where a big mixing trough is set up, and in this all sorts of rag-bag materials are to be found—old gloves, rags, bits of cardboard, etc., and gum tragacanth. This mixture is kneaded by hand to the consistency of a paste, heated and carried into the mold

---

* Time has proved this statement to be erroneous.

room. There it is dipped up by women and poured into the patterns, which are set up in rows. The molds are put away until they are cold enough to handle, when a workman, by dexterous movement of his hands, separates the leaden sides, and the doll's head is revealed. The polisher then trims off the ragged seams and sends the heads to another room, where the holes for the eyes are cut out. This is an extremely delicate task, as all the sockets must be of uniform size.

"The heads are next painted, waxed or glazed, depending upon the character of the material from which they are made . . . the heads must have rosy cheeks, red lips and dark or light eyebrows, as the color of the eyes used may require." —PLAYTHINGS, September, 1913.

The next two descriptions are both of the manufacture of composition dolls' heads in America.

1917: "When the heads are removed from the molds and the seams and rough places have been smoothed with sandpaper, they weigh about 6 ounces each. They are then loaded on racks and placed in a 49.2-kw. electric oven for a forty-five-minute bake. During this period the oven temperature . . . is maintained at 300 degrees Fahr. At the end of that time 2 ounces of moisture is evaporated from each head. From an average bake, which is 650 heads, about 8 gallons of water is removed. To accomplish this drying process without the electric heat formerly required from three to four days.

"When this first bake is finished the doors are partly opened and the oven is allowed to operate for fifteen minutes in this manner while the heads cool. Quick chilling would crack the composition. Then the heads are given a coat of glue sizing, which dries in three or four minutes and permits the first coat of enamel to be applied. On an air-dried head it takes about two days for glue sizing to dry because of the moisture in the casting, but with the electric process the first coat of enamel can be applied at once, and the heads can be taken to a second oven . . . Here they are again baked for forty-five minutes, but at a temperature of 200 degrees Fahr. They are then removed from oven No. 2, given another coat of enamel and placed in oven No. 3 [with] a temperature of 150 degrees Fahr. for forty-five minutes. The uniform forty-five minute interval has been selected for all ovens to keep the heads moving in uniform routine. . . . These ovens when loaded full at each bake can turn out 10,000 doll heads a day. The factory production will now average about 8,000 per day.

"From the ovens the heads are taken to a hand-finishing department, where girls operating air brushes spray colors on the castings to imitate hair and cheeks. The lips and eyes are painted by hand."—PLAYTHINGS, February, 1917.

The making of the EFFanBEE composition dolls' heads is very similar to the processes used in making their composition bodies, but there are some additional details:

1920: "A half finished model of a doll's head in some kind of white clay was perched on the work bench before him [an artist]. He gave it a rub of this thumb here and there and with some small instruments . . .

added minute bits of clay where they were needed to round out the features, or he scraped a bit off where it was not needed. . . .

"The chief [artist] carefully removed the new clay head from its little pedestal and oiled it carefully all over with a small feather brush. Bringing a pan he dumped into it a quantity of white plaster of Paris and mixed it with water to a stiff paste. When all was ready he poured the mass into a small square box about four inches deep and six inches in length and width. Before it 'set' or began to harden he carefully lifted the oiled clay head and pressed it gently and firmly face down into the soft plaster and let it stand. . . .

"Our artist was ready for the next operation again in about half an hour . . .

"He produced his little pot of oil again and dipping his feather brush into it oiled the smooth edge of the plaster that extended to the sides of the box and prepared a second box of plaster exactly like the first. When this was done he picked up the first box from which the back half of the head now protruded and turning it over without removing it from the box, pressed the back of the head just as gently as he had done in the first place with the face half, into the second box.

"It took another half hour or so for the second half to harden and as the edges had been oiled the two halves came apart easily when the hardening was complete . . . when the clay head was removed . . . [they saw] how clean and perfect the negative mold looked . . . additional models [could be made] from the casts which was simply a reversal of the formula just gone through. When the model is intended for direct die making, he told them, the clay model is made directly of plaster. . . .

" 'When we first began the manufacture of sleeping eye dolls,' he said, 'we found it necessary to cut the eye openings by hand. It was a slow and tedious performance . . . This is now done by an automatic eye cutting device.'

"He pointed out a machine and seated himself before it, pressing the pedal with his foot a few times to demonstrate the manner in which it was worked. Two steel cutting dies, their edges shaped to represent the curve of the upper and lower lid of the eye, are set side by side in the machine and are so arranged that when power is applied to the pedal these dies move downward and exactly meet the indications for the eyes on the head of the doll, which the operator places in position to receive them. With one clip, both apertures are punched. When the head is removed from the machine, the thickness of the head substance does not permit the placing of the eyes sufficiently close to the surface to make them look natural. The inside of the head is therefore applied to what is known as a 'phrasing machine,' which shaves it down from the inside of the lids, thinning them to natural proportions. . . .

"When the thinning process is finished, an expert, with . . . a fine file, carefully finishes the edges of the eyelids."—PLAYTHINGS, April, May, June, July, August, and September, 1920.

Methods of manufacture changed and improved through the years. PLAYTHINGS said in 1920: There were "many instances, not so many years ago when the doll expert would actually taste his product in order to see if he had arrived at the proper flour mixture."—PLAYTHINGS, July, 1920.

Unlike ceramic slip, which forms a coating in a mold and leaves a residue that can be poured off, composition often must be pressed into molds or between dies. This was generally accomplished at first by cold presses consisting of the exterior mold or die and an interior collapsible mold. The hot liquid composition, usually a glue and flour mixture, was poured into the exterior mold and then the collapsible mold was inserted and pressure applied so that the composition became the desired thickness. When it had cooled and hardened sufficiently to hold its shape, the collapsible mold was pulled out piece by piece. Heads cast in this manner can usually be identified by looking at the inside, which does not have complete seams but often a circular impression at the top of the head and six to ten vertical striations on the inside of the neck and head.

Around the time of World War I, the cold-press method was superseded by the hot-press method, which usually was applied to wood pulp composition. For a description of the operation of hot presses, see the **Manufacture of Composition Bodies,** where the making of EFFanBEE bodies in 1920 is described. Composition heads made by hot presses are nearly always in two parts with a conspicuous vertical seam all the way around the inside of the head.

Cold-press heads often had a coating applied to them that tends to peel off with age. The paint on hot-press heads is more likely to flake off. The wood-pulp composition is often darker in color than the glue and flour composition. The ingredients and methods of making composition varied with the individual manufacturer, which makes it difficult to generalize. Recognition of the structural difference between composition heads made in cold presses and those made in hot presses can enable the collector to approximate the age of a doll. Most cold-press composition heads were made prior to World War I, and most hot press ones were made during or after World War I.

In 1924, PLAYTHINGS carried the statement. "In these days practically all of our dolls are made by the 'hot' process. To insure perfect workmanship, cool or at least moderate temperature is required. Thus many hot days are eliminated from work."
(See also **Manufacture of Papier-Mâché Heads.**)

**Manufacture of Dolls.** As late as 1884, HARPER'S BAZAR said: "The friendly hand of the retail store-keeper unites the head and the body of the doll, and sends her out to be becomingly clothed." In a few cases, a doll could be made entirely by one manufacturer; or as many as twenty-five factories might be required to produce a single doll. According to CHATTERBOX in 1893, "In Sonneberg it takes eighty persons to make a doll . . . Doll-making is pretty much the same in essentials all

the world over; but in Germany labor is subdivided as much as possible."

The making of an individual doll part often provided the entire industry of a given place; sometimes the various parts of a doll were even produced in different countries. In 1894 Claretie in France wrote, "Formerly, the manufacturer of dolls had recourse to specialists: he had only to put together the different parts going into the making of the doll and to look for markets for the sale of his work; today all that has changed; many still do thus, but it is to the detriment of their house, for in order to do well and to succeed in selling much it will be necessary to unite fabrication."

The making of dolls in the homes continued in Germany long after large factories had taken over most of the French production. However, bisque and china parts were necessarily made in large factories. Thüringia supplied nearly 80 percent of the world production of dolls up until World War I. There more and more specialization took place with the passing years. Often, a factory that assembled dolls would make only one kind of doll in one size, and another factory would make the same type of doll in another size.

Most of the large American and British commission houses had their own doll factories in Germany, but when a popular doll swept the market, it would take the entire output of many factories to produce it. Dolls were often designed in America by representatives of the importing houses and then made up in European factories. Several of the best-known doll lines were absolutely controlled in America and could not even be purchased in Europe. This explains the fact that a distributor's name or initials are often found on a doll's head as well as (or instead of) the name of the factory that actually made it. In 1921 an advertisement stated: "You furnish the dies and we will make *your* dolls."

PLAYTHINGS, January, 1914 (p. 152), quoted the London TIMES: "The toymaker is an artist, and in art, as in nature, development is a condition of existence . . . For it is not children who buy toys; it is their elders who buy toys for them; and it is the elders, not the sequent generations of children, who find it tedious to meet the same toys year after year. 'The Market,' no less than the artists' need for development, demands ever new toys. The rhythm of progress is now an accepted law, and nowhere is it more evident than in art. A style reaches perfection; thenceforward it must decline . . . and a new path must be chosen."

The rise and fall in the making of wooden dolls was discussed by Ruth and R.C. Mathes in DOLL COLLECTORS MANUAL (1964). There is also ample evidence of similar trends in other types of dolls. As each new successful type of doll appeared on the market, other makers tried to imitate it and competition grew—until one day the type would be superseded by an entirely different type of doll, and thereafter it would decline in artistic merit as cheaper models were produced, until finally it virtually disappeared.

Doll collectors usually refer to the maker of a doll

as indicated by the name, initial, or symbol on the head. It should be recognized that this can represent the designer or the producer or the distributor. Except in a few cases, the markings on a doll give only part of its identification and history.

**Manufacture of Eyes.** Glass eyes are the principal type used, although many eyes are simply painted on the material of the head. The painting of eyes is a tedious operation that requires artistic accuracy. The iris was made intaglio or concave in some dolls, especially those produced by *Gebrüder Heubach,* and in some other dolls the eyeball was molded convex. Decalcomania film was used by *Schoenhut* in 1919. It was applied to the wooden eyeball, smoothed into position with a camel's-hair brush, and then varnished to protect the surface.

Birmingham, England, claims the honor of first producing glass dolls' eyes, but most glass eyes for dolls were made in Germany or France. Prior to World War I, three-fourths of all the glass dolls' eyes in the world were made in Lauscha, Germany. Most of the descriptions of making glass eyes pertain to the beautiful French glass eyes resembling paperweights, which were made in the *Jumeau* factory. (See **Eye Materials.**)

1885: J. Cusset described the making of glass eyes in the Jumeau factory. Working over a gas jet, girls formed a stick of black glass into a pupil, and around this, blue or brown glass into the iris. Fine rays of slightly twisted white glass were worked into the iris to give the "paperweight" appearance. White enamel, shaped like an eyeball, was gouged out in the center of one side and the iris inserted. Clear melted glass was spread over this to give the eye brilliance, and after cooling, the eye was fired again for several hours to make it unbreakable.

About 1894: "One enters a dark room, all hung with dark material, as at the photographer's. Here and there blue flames shine and whistle loudly. They are the blowpipes. Each of the workwomen has her own; one notices only figures bent over and strangely lighted up by the jets of flame. Here is one of them who is beginning her eye; let us watch her make it. She delicately holds in each hand a fragile stick of white enamel, the two ends of which she plunges into the fire of her blast apparatus. With an agile movement of her fingers . . . she turns the stick which melts, spreads out, widens, and becomes round under the skillful direction of the other stick. With astonishing skill and agility, she plunges her work into the fire, draws it back, presents it again to the flame as she has need of a substance softer or more resistant. The ball is rounded, is lengthened at the two corners, like an almond; and there is the white eye. Then she picks up another stick of colored enamel, which she handles with sureness, which melts and attaches itself to the center of the pupil. There is the finished eye . . . The cornea is of bluish-white . . . The iris appears in the depths of the pupil through watery transparency which gives the illusion of a real eye."—LES JOUETS by Léo Claretie, 1894; translation by Dorothy S. Coleman in THE AGE OF DOLLS, 1965.

1904: Here is a brief description of glass dolls' eyes made in Thüringia: "These lustrous orbs are carefully blown over gas as hot as goes to the manufacture of the finest Bohemian glass."

1907: French glass eyes were still made in the same way. "In order to see it [making of the eyes] you go down a stone stair case into a cellar and into complete blackness. You stand there in the dark and wonder. Suddenly you see points of flame here and there—the bluish flame of a blowpipe. Then you discover that behind each flame is a girl in a linen blouse; and her share of life is to stand there in the darkness, day after day, modelling dolls' eyes out of milky-white glass and blowing into them the tiny pupils of brown or blue."—PLAYTHINGS, January, 1907.

1912: In Germany "the manufacturing is done in dark cellars. Violet coloring is said to be the most difficult to make."—PLAYTHINGS, July, 1912.

**Manufacture of Gutta-Percha Dolls.** Gutta-percha differs from rubber both as a material and in the method of its use in manufacturing dolls. The patent papers of *Richard A. Brooman* of London in 1848 provide the following description: ". . . there has been recently imported from the East Indies a natural resin or resin-like substance or mastic not previously known or used in the arts and manufactures called gutta-percha . . . It may be so softened by immersion in hot water or by exposure to steam or hot air as to be capable without further treatment of being kneaded or molded or rolled out or pressed into any desired shape. . . . In some . . . properties, namely its adhesive and water and air repellent properties, gutta-percha resembles caoutchouc but it is advantageously distinguished from it in its freedom from stickiness when dry, in its not being so affected by atmospheric heat or by unctuous oils, in its being workable by means of hot water alone, and in its being fibrous . . .

"To prepare gutta-percha for application to manufacturing purposes it is first freed from the foreign matters with which it is usually found intermixed in the state in which it is imported, by repeated washings . . .

"When it is desired to give to the mass of gutta-percha a greater degree of elasticity than is natural to it, I mix up and incorporate with it while it is going through the kneading machine either a portion of caoutchouc or a portion of sulphur, or portions of both caoutchouc and sulphur. . . . The gutta-percha takes up the other materials readily and the whole are at the end of the process thoroughly amalgamated.

"Should it be desired to give any color to the mass of gutta-percha to render it the better adapted to the purposes to which it is to be applied, the requisite pigment or coloring matter is introduced in the same way as the sulphur and also in small quantities at a time. The color penetrates every part of the mass and becomes perfectly amalgamated and identified with it.

"The gutta-percha may be also improved in smoothness by incorporating with it some pulverized French or Turkey chalk or other soft powder, adding it in the same way as the sulphur or colors. I take the gutta-percha of any of the varieties before described, that is to say either plain or sulphurized or colored, and rasp it down to a powder. I then apply it in this state to the taking of casts or busts, cornices and other works of art in round or curved forms . . . When casts of busts, etc., are to be taken, the mold is filled with the grains or powder of the gutta-percha and then heated till the gutta-percha becomes reduced to a mass sufficiently ductile to be pressed into all parts of the mold."—United States Patent 5,592, Brooman, May 23, 1848.

In 1884, Clara Mateaux in THE WONDERLAND OF WORK explained: "Gutta-percha requires merely to be soaked in hot water and moulded, so the paste is rolled out in big sheets, which are warmed, pressed in moulds, and dropped into cold water; then the toys fall out."

**Manufacture of Kid Bodies.** The fine French kid bodies were generally made by splitting the leather so that it was more pliable. HARPER'S BAZAR in 1884 said:

**1130.** Kid body with hand-sewn seams up the middle of the back and front. The papier-mâché head has a band painted in color around the edge of the shoulder plate. Hair style suggests the 1830's. The joining of the wooden limbs to the kid body is covered with notched paper. *Courtesy of Marion Holt; photograph by Winnie Langley.*

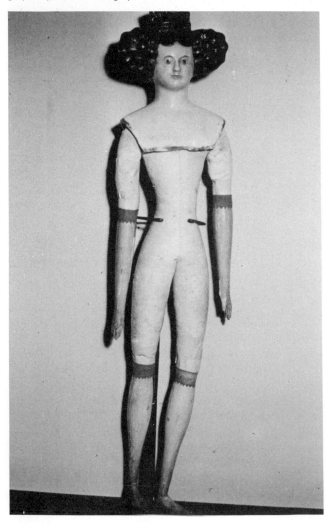

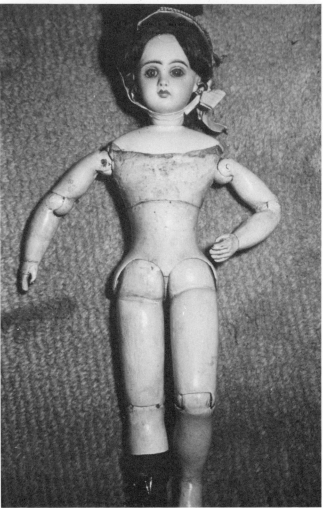

A

**1131A & B.** Kid has been pressed to form this doll and give it a smooth, tight-fitting surface. Note the seam up the back of the legs. Compare Ill. **392.** These dolls may have been made in accordance with Pierre Clément's 1866 patent. *Photograph by Winnie Langley.*

"The bodies of the dolls are made in a factory quite unlike those in which the heads and busts are formed. Good seamstresses are employed, for the sewing-machine here is useless. Everything must be done by hand. The so-called 'French-body,' of comparatively recent invention, has joints in its limbs, or divisions that do duty as such, and are so durable that little girls have been known to get tired of them. The bodies are variously filled, but horsehair is, perhaps, the best and most popular article for the purpose. Sawdust was once almost exclusively used; but many of us are old enough to remember the result of 'that' process of filling. The doll, growing aged and infirm, and her seams opening, could readily be tracked to her hiding-place . . . by the trail she left after her." It is interesting to find that in 1885 *Jumeau* was still using sawdust to fill his kid-body dolls.

In the early years of the 20th century, skins came

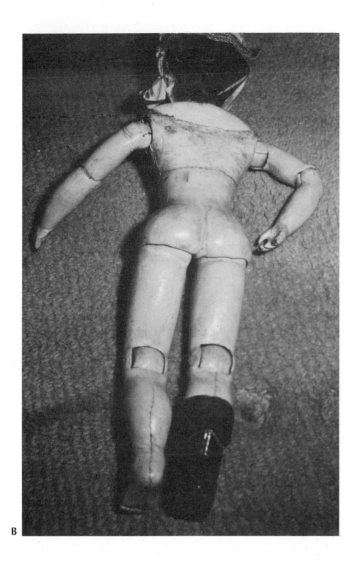

B

from Australia and were tanned in Germany and England. When wool prices were high and skins plentiful, kid-body dolls were cheaper.

In April, 1906, PLAYTHINGS carried a description of the manufacture of kid bodies by *Kestner:* "In making kid dolls, the sheepskins while moist are first tightly stretched on long tables, in order to get their full surface. The skins are then given to experienced cutters, who cut by tin patterns the bodies, arms and legs and these are subsequently deftly sewed together on machines. Stuffers then fill the bodies thus sewed together with sawdust, cork or hair." (See also **Kid Bodies.**)

**Manufacture of Leather Heads.** The flexibility of leather or rawhide makes it suitable for shaping into the configuration of a doll's head. The patent papers for *Lucretia Sallee* in 1865 and *Frank Darrow* in 1866 described the following methods for making these heads.

"A matrix is first to be made out of plaster-of-paris, and usually in two sections. In making a doll's head, the matrix may be in two sections or parts—one answering to the face and front and the other to the back of the head. The leather which is to form the outer coating or surface of the doll's head is next cut to fit to the size of the several sections or parts of the matrix, and then soaked in water until it is sufficiently soft and pliable. It is then laid within the several matrices and pressed and forced into them so as to conform fully to all the lines and curves therein. The leather should be laid with its smooth or finished surface to the walls of the matrices. It is then to be pressed and rubbed with a yarn ball, or a sponge or other suitable absorbing material, which will absorb or soak up the surplus water from the leather without displacing any part of its configurations in the matrices. A small portion of glue is next dissolved in vinegar and the solution is thickened with plaster-of-paris until the mass is of a proper or usual consistency, when it is immediately poured upon the leather in sufficient quantity to hold the leather in shape after it is removed from the matrix. The forms thus molded are next taken out from their matrices and united at their edges by lapping one edge over the other, and the joint cemented by the cement aforesaid . . . The cement or composition should be in sufficient thickness to form a body or support for the leather or other material which forms the outer covering of the toy. The said covering is then painted and varnished to suit the fancy and taste of the maker."—United States Patent 46,270, Sallee, February 7, 1865. (See Ills. 447, 1418.)

"The rawhide is first cured in the usual way. It is then cut into blanks of suitable size for the purpose desired. Then take a box of concentrated lye (about one pound, usually found in stores for sale), put it into about two gallons of water, then place said blanks in a suitable apparatus into which steam made from said composition or liquid may enter, and thereby saturate or steam said blanks, when they may be taken therefrom, one at a time, and introduced to the die and press, and pressed into the desired form or shape. When taken therefrom it will be hard and perfectly retain its shape or form into which it has been pressed while in its flexible or elastic state."—United States Patent 54,301, Darrow, May 1, 1866. (See also **Kid Heads.**)

**Manufacture of Papier-mâché Heads.** Winnie Langley has discovered an 1840 booklet, published by Dr. Fr. Retto in Leipzig and Quedlinburg, that describes the method of making papier-mâché dolls' heads. First a model was made; then molds were fired and varnished. The papier-mâché was prepared and pressed into the molds. When dry, it was smoothed and the two parts were trimmed and put together with cabinetmakers' glue. Limewater and ground colors were added and allowed to dry. The eyes, lips, and hair were painted; then a coat of varnish was added, and while the cheeks were still sticky they were painted with fine carmine or Florentine lacquer.

Ludwig Greiner, in his patent of 1858, described how he made his papier-mâché dolls' heads.

1858: "One pound of white paper, when cooked, is beat fine, and then the water is pressed out, so as to leave it moist. To this is added one pound of dry Spanish whiting, one pound of rye flour, and one ounce of glue. This is worked until it is well mixed. Then it is rolled out with a roller to the required thinness. After it is cut into pieces required for the mold it is molded. Wherever there is a part projecting out—for instance the nose—it must be filled with linen or muslin. This linen or muslin must be well saturated with a paste, which consists of rye-flour, Spanish whiting, and glue. After the heads are molded, each head consisting of two parts, they are left to get about half dry. Then they are put into the mold again and the parts well saturated with the paste. At the same time the linen or muslin is cut up into pieces to match the parts, and is also saturated with this paste and pressed on the inside of the parts. Then they are left to dry again as before. Then these parts are put together with the same composition as the head is made from. After this, when they are perfectly dry, a strip of the linen or muslin saturated with paste is laid inside of the head where the parts were put together, and a piece is also put over each shoulder and extending over the breast outside. Then they are painted with oil-paint, so that children may not suck off the paint."—United States Patent 19,770.

1874: Olive Thorne described the making of a papier-mâché doll's head prepared for waxing: "From a lump of soft clay, a man has cut and shaped a doll's head and neck . . . When the model is finished, the modeler makes lines on it, with colored crayons, as a guide to the next workman, who is called a molder.

"When the pattern, or model, is ready, there must be made a mold, in which to shape the paper pulp from the kettle. This is made by the molder. He takes the pretty clay model, when it is dry and hard, and lays it face up, in a dish of wet clay, pressing the clay into every corner up to the colored line which the modeler made. This being done, he builds a wall of clay around the mass, coming up some inches higher all around than the face of the model, which is left uncovered. The whole looks like a box half full of clay, with a face looking out of it . . . one man holding the clay walls together, while the other one pours over the face some melted sulphur which he has taken from the stove. Sometimes plaster of Paris is used instead of sulphur, but it is not thought to be so good.

"The mold is not done yet. The clay was put on merely to protect that part of the head while the rest was molded. When the sulphur is cold, the box is turned over, and the clay taken away, leaving . . . her face buried in sulphur . . .

"Clay walls are again built up, and more sulphur is poured in to make a mold for the back of her head. . . .

"Now the mold is finished and we must go back to our paper pulp, which we left boiling you know. When soft and ready for use, the water is squeezed out, and other things added—some powdered clay to make it stiff, and a little glue to make it sticky. These are worked up together till the mass is about like dough, and indeed it is made into loaves . . .

"The man with the rolling-pin is rolling out the paper dough—papier-mâché it is called . . . He makes it a little thicker than pie crust, and then cuts it into pieces the right size for use, making a pile of them, with flour or powdered clay between to prevent their sticking together.

"The man next to him is pressing one of these thin cakes of papier dough into the molds of Dolly's head, and the third man is making it fit more nicely into every crack and corner of the mold, with a tool of some sort, so that it will be a perfect copy of the original model.

". . . When the man has carefully fitted the sheet of dough into every part of the mold, he pares off the edges with a knife as you see a cook cut the crust from a pie plate, lifts the half head out of the mold, and lays it on the table to dry a little. When dry enough it is again pressed in the mold to give it a more perfect shape, and then is dried for the last time. The two halves being finished, they are glued together, and . . . take an upright position on the shelf, where she stands till she is hard and dry, looking more like stiff gray cardboard than anything else.

". . . Her next journey is to the eye-setter. A rough doctor he is, and the first thing he does is to cut off the top of her head, by running a sharp knife around it, and knocking the piece out with a hammer.

"What for? Merely to put in her eyes, my dear; and a curious operation it is too. If they are immovable eyes, like a common doll's, they would be simply glued in; but in a young lady of . . . pretensions, who meekly shuts her eyes when her mamma lays her down, there is much to be done.

"In the first place, the eyes themselves, life-like as possible, have been carefully made of glass, in a large factory which turns out nothing but eyes. These the eye-setter now fastens to a piece of curved wire with a ball of lead on the end. It is the weight of this lead which makes her eyes close when her head goes down. Then the workman, with a sharp knife, cuts a hole for each eye, and goes on to put them in . . . there is plaster to hold them in place, and support the cheeks; a cork, or sponge, to keep the lead from hitting her chin; pieces of wood to prevent her head from being easily crushed . . .

"When everything is in, the cut-off slice of her head is glued on again . . .

"Now the inside is finished, the next thing is to put on her lovely complexion.

"First must be removed any roughness, such as bits of glue at the seams of her head.

". . . [Women file] the roughness off, and [give] it a coat of ruddy flesh-colored paint, from the top of the head to the ends of the shoulders. Dolls who have hair made of the same material as their heads, like bisque and china dolls, have the hair varnished black, but [if she] has real hair, she is colored alike all over." After this, the head was dipped in "boiling clear white beeswax."—ST. NICHOLAS, February, 1875.

Herman Reinhardt, son of *Ernst Reinhardt,* of Sonneberg says that in the first decade of the 20th century papier-mâché dolls' heads were pressed by hand into sulphur molds and rubbed with kerosene.

(See also **Manufacture of Composition Heads; Papier-Mâché Dolls.**)

**Manufacture of Rag (Fabric) Heads.** The simplest and most common rag dolls' heads are made of two pieces of cloth sewed together and stuffed. Improved patterns were devised to give a spherical shape to the head and finally to provide features. The nose and ears have been made by various ingenious methods, such as the seam down the center of the face found on *Steiff* dolls. Stiffened material was molded into shape by heated pressure, as shown in the 1868 patent of *George H. Hawkins* and the 1873 patent of *Izannah Walker,* which are described as follows:

"I use as a stock of material for the manufacture of the heads buckram, muslin, or any cloth produced by weaving, felting, or other process, and saturated or dressed with starch, size, or any glutinous matter, and which, being moistened when required for use, is pressed while damp, between the dies, which, being heated, will dry the cloth and press it into the required shape at one and the same operation, and the drying of the glutinous matter will enable the cloth to retain the configuration given by the dies.

"The two parts of the head, after being thus formed, are adjusted together by lapping one part a short distance over the other, the lapped surfaces being properly moistened, and then pressed together by means of an inner and outer tool or tools, properly heated, and so constructed and arranged that one tool may be inserted within the head to form a bearing at the inner surface of the lap, while the other bears or presses against the exterior surface of the same. The pressure of these heated tools on the lapped surfaces, while moist, will form a close and tight seam."—United States Patent 81,999, Hawkins, September 8, 1868.

"In the construction of my doll I usually employ a press of ordinary construction, provided with upper and lower dies, of suitable shape, to form the front and back of the face, neck, and chest, and sometimes the body of the doll. In the dies I place several thicknesses of cotton or other cheap cloth, treated with glue or paste, so that they will adhere together and hold the shape impressed upon them by the dies. When these cloth forms are dry a layer of cotton batting or other soft filling is carefully laid over them, covering the whole or the head and neck portions only, as may be desirable, and then, in turn, covered with an external layer of stockinet or similar webbing. The latter is then fastened to the features of the cloth forms by stitches or paste, and they are then placed again in the press. After they are taken from the press the forms are filled with hair, cotton, or other stuffing, and a piece of wood having been centrally and longitudinally laid between the two for stiffening, they are tightly pressed together and secured by sewing, pasting, or gluing their edges to each other. The finishing is then done by painting the face and other parts neatly with oil-paint."—United States Patent 144,373, Walker, November 4, 1873. (See Ills. 785, 1653.)

To provide the face with sculptural form, fabric was sometimes stretched over various hard substances, notably in the *London Rag* dolls of the 19th century and the portrait dolls of the 1920's. Clara Mateaux, in THE WONDERLAND OF WORK in 1884, described the London Rag doll as follows:

"Its face is a kind of wax mask, over which a piece of muslin has been stretched. It will very soon leak, or melt, if hugged too tightly. These faces have, as a rule, no back head belonging to them, but are fastened to a sort of skull . . . made of calico and stuffed with sawdust."

In the 1920's, stockinet material was stretched over a plaster portrait model to form the doll's head. The features of rag doll faces are painted, embroidered, or appliquéd. Eyes are also made of beads, buttons, or glass inserted in the eye sockets.

**Manufacture of Rubber Dolls.** *Charles Goodyear's* discovery of the vulcanizing process for rubber made possible the manufacture of rubber dolls. After 1851, dolls' heads were made of hard rubber as well as soft rubber. Clara Mateaux, in THE WONDERLAND OF WORK in 1884, described the making of rubber dolls:

"This man uses a mould . . . of iron, and in two pieces, dividing the doll from side to side. These two sides are laid on the table, and he takes up two sheets of the prepared putty-like stuff, and lays them inside the moulds, poking and pulling it to make them fill the ins and outs of the hollow moulds; then he claps the two halves one on the other, and screws them tightly together, passing on and repeating the operation until he has filled some hundred of iron cases, in the same manner, which is soon done by his experienced hands. The next proceeding is to place them all in a vulcanizing bath; this is a large closed vessel filled with sulphur and other things, where he leaves them to cook for some hours according to the size and sort of toy they contain. When he considers them ready, he comes and turns them all out of their iron cases, and we see a set of dolls' heads, dolls . . . all complete, except for a little finishing-up and trimming round the edges where the joining of the moulds has left a seam; they are quite soft and elastic now, the balls can be squeezed and the dolls doubled up: a little paint is all that is required to make them presentable to young customers."

Sometimes gutta-percha and other materials were added to the rubber.

**Manufacture of Waltershausen Dolls.** 1911. August Trinius traveled through Thüringia and wrote a book about what he saw there. The following is a translation of part of his account: "On the northern part of the Thüringian woods, next to the famous resort, Friedrichroda, Waltershausen is situated. In the Napoleonic era *Johannes Daniel Kestner* founded the doll-making industry in Walterhausen with his wooden *Täuflinge.* This was the beginning of an industry that eventually included the mountain villages in a great circle around Waltershausen, which made dolls that are sent to every part of the world. The wooden Täuflinge grew into dolls with porcelain heads, bodies made of mohair fabric or the finest sheepskin, tailored and sewn. They are stuffed with ground cork, deer hairs, or sawdust. Mass production then demanded a simple and cheaper method of manufacture. Wet papier-mâché is used for making dolls' bodies, hands, and legs. After coming from the presses, the bodies have to be finished carefully. The children help their parents in this work. On warm days they can be seen everywhere, in the gardens, on the streets, working diligently. A grandmother sits under a tree with a boy and girl beside her, all sanding dolls' hands. The parts of the bodies are then painted and varnished. The dolls are strung with elastic, and every joint is movable. The joints are pressed during the production of the body.

"The better dolls are not pressed but molded. That is a branch of the doll industry that flourishes especially in the forest villages around Waltershausen. Mashed and softened pasteboard, plaster, dough of old black bread, and glue are made into a pulp and applied in layers into molds of plaster or stone until the body is readied by drying in the windows or outside the houses on tables or benches. On Saturday the villagers take their heavy loads to the factories in town. An important person in the factory is the modeller, who is humorously called 'the Mother of the Factory.' He has to be not only an artist but a man of experience also. It is not enough for him to create new designs for dolls, but he must have regard for the tastes of the buyers in different countries. A special doll worker puts the eyes into the dolls' heads; they are the best-paid workers, especially if they furnish the dolls with lashes made from human hair. No wonder, since the doll gets the right expression through its eyes. The dolls' heads are purchased from the numerous porcelain factories in Thüringia. The eyes come for the most part from Lauscha, Sonneberg, or other eye manufacturing centers. Waltershausen now has several eye-blowers who are not only skilled in blowing dolls' eyes but make human eyes perfectly too. Not only the eyes are put into ready-bought bisque heads, but the hair is added to the heads also. That is an industry in itself, practised mostly by women and children. There are not many families where tressing and hairdressing is not practised. The hairs of the angora goat are boiled, curled and tressed. This part is done by skilled hands and the hair is arranged on wooden heads in every possible coiffure. These wigs are then glued on the dolls' heads. Human hair is also used for wigs. It is natural that the tailoring and sewing of chemises and dresses for dolls is a job employing many women and girls. When all parts of the doll are ready, the assembling begins; the parts are joined together, and in the packing rooms the dolls are furnished with wigs and dressed in chemises or dresses, then packed in cardboard boxes. Every doll factory either produces cardboard boxes or acquires them from another factory in the town."

(The above information and translation was graciously provided by Mme. Eva Moskovszky Horváth of Budapest, Hungary, from an old German magazine that had belonged to her grandfather.)

**Manufacture of Wax Heads.** During the last quarter of the 19th century there were numerous articles written on the methods of making wax dolls' heads. The following are a sample of these.

1875: "Real dolls of wax are made thus: the boiling wax is poured into a plaster-mould; it adheres to the sides as it becomes cold, and when the mould is taken apart there is the beautiful wax-head, but simply a shell, and of course very weak. The head is cast complete, and only a small opening is left in the crown of the head. Then a workman takes the wax shell and very carefully lines it throughout with a kind of soft paste about the thickness of cardboard, which soon hardens and gives the head its strength and durability.

"After this process the head is placed over a hot furnace, the wax is permitted to melt to a slight degree, whereupon it is dusted with powder made of potato meal and alabaster, to give it a delicate flesh tint. In another room the head is provided with a pair of eyes . . .

"Another very skilled workman then receives the head, and finishes off the front appearance of the eyes, scooping off all the wax and affixing the lids.

"Then lashes have to be affixed, and then the little lady has to be provided with teeth, which are put in by skilled workmen one by one. A still more interesting study is the hairdressing room in a doll factory. All the dolls that come into this room are complete as far as their heads: there they are quite bald."—LITTLE BOUQUET, MONTHLY MAGAZINE, June, 1875.

1884: "The doll of pure wax is fit only to be put under a glass case, but its manufacture is an art far higher than ordinary doll-making, and approaching sculpture in its detail and finish. The mould is sometimes made of metal, but more ordinarily of wood or clay. The boiling wax is poured into it, the mould being first moistened with a non-adhesive substance, which enables the artist to take the cast out without leaving any portion of it sticking to the sides. But is this a doll's head? Assuredly it does not look much like one. To the unpractised eye it has the appearance of a lump of soft moist wax; but the lines are all there, and the skillful hand of the artist soon makes them apparent. But even then much has to be done to the bald head and colorless face before the doll is ready."—HARPER'S BAZAR, November 22, 1884.

1893: "The dolls made in England, which are known all over the world, are mostly of the better class—those with pretty wax faces . . . The first step is the making of the head. A quantity of East Indian wax is melted, and when it is near the boiling point some red coloring matter (rouge) is stirred in. Hollow moulds are then placed in rows, the part which forms the crown of the head being downwards, after which the maker takes a

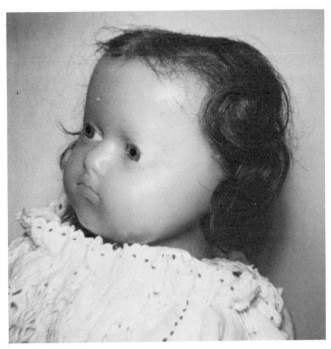

**1132.** Double poured wax head with the hair inserted in groups; blown glass eyes. This type was made by Pierotti. H. 22 inches. *Coleman Collection.*

canful of the melted wax and pours it into the moulds. When he has filled about a dozen, he returns to the first one, and pours back into the can whatever of the wax remains fluid. If he did not do this, the head would, of course, be solid. He serves the second mould in the same way, and so on with the rest.

"In a short time the heads can be removed from the moulds—a very simple matter, as the latter are in three pieces. Then they go to a man who puts in the eyes. He takes a knife and cuts out holes for the sockets, and, for small dolls, warms the little glass eyes over a gas jet and sticks them in the holes, securing them by running a little melted wax into the skull. But in the case of large dolls wax is run over the eyes, and the eyebrows and eyelids are afterwards carefully modelled with little tools.

"Next the head is trimmed and cleaned and rubbed over with violet powder. After this the cheeks are tinted with rouge, to make them look rosy, and the lips and nostrils touched up with vermilion, and then the article is taken in hand by a woman, who puts in the hair."—CHATTERBOX, 1893.

**Manufacture of Waxed Heads.** Many different materials were waxed for dolls' heads, but papier-mâché was used most frequently. The waxing of a papier-mâché head in 1874 and of a plaster head in 1884 are described:

1874: ". . . A frightful looking object she is, too, with color enough for a boiled lobster.

"When she has received her color, and got dry . . . she proceeds to the next operator, who is the waxer.

"In the kettle is boiling clear white beeswax, and

into it . . . Miss Dolly has been dipped, and is being held up to drain. If she had been intended for a cheap doll, she would have received but one dip, but being destined to belong to the aristocracy of the doll world, she received several dips, each one giving her a thin coat of wax, and toning down her flaming complexion into the delicate pink you see. The reason she was painted so red . . . is that she may have the proper tint when the wax is on.

"And now comes the next process, which is coloring her face . . .

"In this room is a long table with several workmen, each of whom does only one thing. The first one paints Miss Dolly's lips, and sets her down on the other side of him. The next one takes her up and puts on her eyebrows. The third colors her cheeks. The fourth pencils her eyelashes, and so she goes down the table, growing prettier at every step."—ST. NICHOLAS, February, 1875.

1884: "The manufacturers of Paris produce the finest wax dolls. It requires almost consummate skill to make these toys. Each workman has models at home, and buys materials for manufacture. The skeleton is constructed out of lime and plaster of Paris, and. the eyes, nose, mouth, and ears cut with a knife. The figure, being ready, is dipped in hot wax and dried. It then goes to the painter for features, then to the hair-dresser for a wig, and finally to the work-girls to be dressed. The money value of the doll depends upon its coating of wax; the thinly coated ones usually crack in cold weather. The wax formerly was produced through the agency of the bee, but a substitute is beginning to be found in ozocerite, or wax made from the residue of petroleum."—HARPER'S BAZAR, November 22, 1884.

It should be observed that pure beeswax was used in 1874, but in 1884 ozocerite or paraffin was beginning to be used. Sometimes the two were combined. The presence of beeswax can usually be detected by the odor.

**Manufacture of Wigs.** There are numerous records on the methods of making wigs, of which the following are samples:

1874: "Now Rosabel has a regular wig, made of real hair on a foundation of lace, and glued on, but many of the dolls in the factory have locks made of fine wool, which looks like real hair. This wool is braided up tight, and boiled to make it stay wavy. It is curled over a glass tube, and glued to the head curl by curl, whether long or short."—ST. NICHOLAS, February, 1875.

1893: "As to the materials used, the hair is mohair, manufactured by an English firm, and it is made into wigs at Munich by girls who are paid about 10 pence a dozen."—CHATTERBOX, 1893.

1894: "The dolls have magnificent wigs . . . They are sometimes made of real hair; these are then truly expensive wigs. Others are made of Thibet (hair of the Tibetan goat).

"Bundles of Thibet are brought in. Small locks of this are rolled on wooden curling pins surrounded with paper and boiled, then dried in a closet heated by gas. When the curling pins are taken out the hair is at once curly and cannot be uncurled.

"They pass then to the stitchers who sew them in rows put close together on the skull caps of cloth with curls in front and plaits behind. That makes lovely wigs which are nailed on the cork pates of the dolls."—LES JOUETS by Léo Claretie, 1894 (Jumeau Wigs).

1897: "The best wigs are made of real hair from Brittany and Italy, the latter being much the coarser . . .

"The common wigs are usually made of the hair of the Thibet goat, which is prepared and dyed in England. The hair is put into curl-papers, then boiled for two hours, and dried in a hot oven for four hours; but it is all the better if kept for six months before being used.

"Hair thus treated will never get out of curl. It is woven to fit the dolls' heads, or the sewers prick it in close rows on to cloth caps, after which the wigs are fastened on with tiny nails, the cork brains being, fortunately, perfectly impervious to pain." — PEARSON'S MAGAZINE, July, 1897 (Jumeau Wigs).

In 1903, PLAYTHINGS mentioned a patent process whereby both the smell and the danger of attack by moths were eliminated for real human hair wigs.

As late as 1907, PLAYTHINGS recorded that French dolls still had their wigs fastened with tacks to cork pates, but in 1922 the magazine said, "On the higher class dolls real human hair is used. Skilled women glue the hair on the heads in such a way that it appears to be really growing." This description pertained to dolls made by the *Société Française de Fabrication de Bébés et Jouets*.

**Manufacture of Wooden Dolls.** Alice Early, in ENGLISH DOLLS, EFFIGIES AND PUPPETS, reports a court case of 1733 involving a London turner who made wooden "babies" (dolls) turned on a lathe. The faces were painted and some of the dolls were dressed by his wife. A 1781 Sonneberg document describes doll bodies as turned and embossed with dough.

Margaret Howitt wrote an article entitled "A Tribe of Toymakers," which was published in 1875 in LEISURE HOUR. This describes the making of wooden dolls as follows: "I am writing from St. Ulrich—Ortiseit as native people call it.

". . . [A woman puts] dabs of vermilion on a multitude of farthing dolls. Tomorrow she will add the rosy lips, the red shoes and white stockings; the day after the black eyes, eyebrows and hair, all forming the distinctive features which these literal 'babes in the wood' must possess. She tells us Herr Purger gives her the dolls to paint. He pays her a farthing a dozen out of which she buys the paint and size. If she could work at home (she sells fruit at the hotel door too) she could paint several hundred dozen a week, but with her stall she never manages more than half the number . . . her father carves horses and dolls; her mother and sister

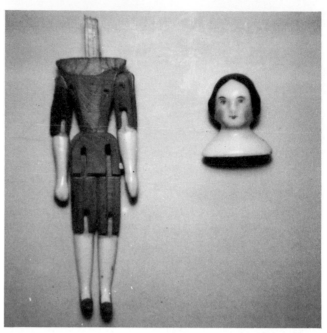

**1133.** Wooden, peg jointed body with china limbs and head secured on a dowel. H. 3⅝ inches. H. of shoulder head, ⅞ inches. *Courtesy of Flora Gill Jacobs.*

paint [them] . . . When in the last century and beginning of this in order to secure a ready sale for his toys and wood work, a maker would start forth with a whole boothful packed on his back, he usually directed his steps towards Italy and Spain as the countries in which he could most readily make himself understood. The trade was known in the seventeenth century, as there are figures in the little church of St. Anthony at St. Ulrich carved in 1682 . . . Johannes Demetz of Sovaut in St. Ulrich has generally received the credit of originating the trade. He began in 1703 to carve simple wooden frames for figures of saints and children's toys were made . . .

"Peter Wellponer who at the end of the last [18th] century reached Mexico with his toys, and other Grödners a little later on settling in New York and Philadelphia [carried their products with them].

"Some pedlars who visited Germany perceived the advantage of a variety of toys, made purchases in Bohemia and Saxony and especially at Oberammergau and Berchtesgaden in Bavaria, whither they at first sent their own to be painted until an enterprising Grödner (Franz Runggaldier) undertook this branch of industry at home and provided the pedlars with painted wares . . .

"Formerly it was merely the men who made the carved work, the women made lace. When machine made lace competed, women started to handle chisel and gouge equally with men . . .

"[A] one-eyed old lady carves little men and women. Probably her father and grandfather also carved such figures, but let us hope not quite such clumsy peasants with one-sided faces and bodies all askew. [They] cost one penny apiece . . .

"The village of St. Christina [is] noted for its lay figures and everywhere the carvers, male and female, were busy. It is especially so in winter when the Grödners carved dolls and other toys by the million, a family often sitting until late into the night round the 'panüc' as the low solid worktable is called . . .

"Great packing cases large enough to contain a cottage piano [stand] ready for the wagoner before the door of some wholesale exporter . . . On Saturday afternoons men, women, boys and girls bring the weeks work either in trucks or on their backs in baskets.

"The system of trade has in the course of this century entirely changed. The wood carver no longer traffics for himself but works for one of the eight or ten principal dealers, chiefly settled in St. Ulrich, who make weekly payments for the goods delivered and manage the foreign trade. The late Herr Purger greatly improved the trade by bringing good models to be copied from Munich and other centers of the art. The Grödner left to himself is not inclined to keep up with the age . . .

"The two principal toy warehouses, those of Herr Purger and Herr Insam . . . Wareroom after wareroom filled with piled-up bins of quadrupeds and bipeds chiefly in white wood . . . Here are billions of wooden dolls, flung down helter-skelter, paid for by Herr Insam at five farthings the dozen . . . Nearly all of these myriads of dolls are for Great Britain. Those larger dolls' heads, it is true, are destined for Amsterdam, but they merely rest there to receive bodies and the title of Dutch dolls, after which they resume their journey to become aunts and mothers to the lesser dolls which have already crossed the British Channel."

The early Sonneberg ledgers of around 1820 record the wooden "Tyroler" doll, which suggests that some of the dolls carved in the Grödner Tal may have been painted and finished in Thüringia as well as Bavaria.

In 1796 *Anton Wilhelm Schoenhut* was making wooden dolls in Germany, and 115 years later his grandson was making all-wood dolls in America. The hands and feet of these dolls were made of hardwood, and the doll was painted with enamel oil colors.

**Manufacture Parisienne de Bébés.** 1906. Factory in Paris; advertised factory patterns for dolls.

**Manus, A.** 1900. Berlin. Manufactured dolls.

**Manuzmann, Karl.** 1923–24. Ochenbruck near Nürnberg, Bavaria. Registered *Mimosa* as a trademark in Germany for dolls.

**Marais.** 1843–81. Paris and Montreuil-sous-Bois. Manufactured dolls.

1881: This was the only entry under Doll Factories listed in a Montreuil-sous-Bois directory.

**Marbais-Villain. See Villain, J.**

**Marcat, Mme.** 1904. France. Displayed wool and rubber dolls at the St. Louis Exposition.

**Marcel.** 1885. Paris. Made dolls.

**Marceline.** 1910–11. Trademark registered in U.S. by *A. Steinhardt & Bro.* for a doll representing the Hippodrome clown of this name. The head of the doll, copyrighted by A. Steinhardt & Bro., was designed by Stesfano Moraim and made of composition. The doll was dressed in ill-fitting evening clothes copied from those worn by Marceline on the stage; price $1.50.

**Marchal, Ed.** 1863+, Paris; toymaker; 1871–81, Marchal & Buffard (Bouffard). Made dolls at the shop known as *Aux Bébés Sages.*

1873: Displayed mechanical dolls at the Vienna Exhibition and won a Medal of Merit.

**Marchand-Duchaume, Mme.** 1871–75. Paris. Made dolls.

**Marcheix, Charles.** 1881–82. Paris. Doll manufacturer. Advertised jointed dolls, in fanciful costumes of silk or wool, knitted or crocheted.

**Marcheur. See Bébé Marcheur.**

**Marcoux, Charles.** 1920–23. Montreuil-sous-Bois, Seine. Registered Marcoux across a pennant as a trademark in France for porcelain heads. Also known as *Société Française des Bébés* or Société Française des Bébés Marcoux; made porcelain heads for dolls.

**Marc-Schnür, Maria. See Maré-Schur, Marie.**

**Marcus, Samuel.** 1917–24. Brooklyn, N.Y. Patented several inventions for dolls.

1918: Obtained U.S. patent for dolls' eyes made with a hemispherical celluloid shell as the exterior of the eye; an inner hemispherical metal plate fitted within the celluloid shell; at the rear of this metal shell was a plate providing means for connecting the eye with the end portion of the bridge. This patent number, 1,252,469, and date, January 8, 1918, are marked on the eyes used in some bisque heads made by *Fulper Pottery Co.* Eyes of this type were used extensively in America right after World War I when glass eyes were difficult to obtain.

1924: Secured U.S. patent for sounding device for dolls operated by a plunger, valves, and reeds.

**Marcuse, Day & Co., Ltd.** 1920–22. London. Made dolls.

**Maré-Schur, Marie (Marc-Schnür, Maria).** 1909–18. Munich. Created *Art Dolls.* Won distinction for doll display in the Munich Exhibition.

**Margaret Vale's Celebrity Creation. See Vale, Margaret.**

**Margie.** 1921. Trade name for cork-stuffed doll made by *EFFanBEE.*

**Margot.** 1913. Doll representing a chorus girl, made by *Elektra Toy & Novelty Co.*

**Margot, P. J. (F.) (Mme.).** 1862–78. Paris. Made dressed dolls of kid and linen. It is not known whether "P. J.," "P. F.," and Madame were all the same person or whether there were several Margots.

**Marguerite.** 1891. Doll distributed by YOUTH'S COMPANION. Came with bisque head, glass eyes, flowing hair wig in *Rembrandt* style; ball-jointed composition body with joints at neck, elbows, shoulders, hips, and knees; completely dressed including a trimmed hat; price $1.65.

**Marguerite.** 1902–3. Trademark registered in U.S. and in Germany by *Hamburger & Co.* It is possible that these were the bonnet-type dolls of this same name.

**Marguerite.** 1924–25. Cloth doll's head made by *Bernard Ravca*; represented character in FAUST. This was the first doll or doll's head made by Ravca.

**Marguerite Dolls.** 1901. Bisque-head dolls with fancy headdresses, such as the *Butterfly, Clover Leaf,* and Flower designs. These dolls were on cloth bodies with ceramic limbs.

**Mariage, Maurice.** 1923. Registered *La Poupée Lina* as a trademark in France for dolls.

**Marie.** 1862–70. Paris. Made dolls.

**Marie.** 1909–11. Mold #101, made by *Kämmer & Reinhardt,* distributed by *Strobel & Wilken* and *Borgfeldt.* This was one of the early character dolls in the *Royal* line, and was a mate to *Peter.* Came with jointed composition body and glass or painted eyes. Named for girl who posed for model.

**Marie & Bouquerel.** 1863–65. Paris. Distributor and exporter of Paris and German toys; specialized in cloth dolls of all kinds.

**Marie Doll.** 1911. Represented a girl of sixteen; made by *Louis Amberg & Son.*

**Marie Jeanne.** 1866. Name of a feeding doll patented by *Lecomte & Alliot.*

**Marienkäfer (Ladybug).** 1925. Trademark used by *Hermsdorfer Celluloid Warenfabrik* for celluloid dolls.

**Marigold.** 1924. Trademark registered in Britain by *Gross & Schild* for dolls.

**Marion.** 1912. Trade name for doll with composition head made by *Gund Manufacturing Co.*

**Marion.** See **Pet Name.**

**Marion, The.** 1924. Trademark registered in Britain by *Marn & Jondorf* for dolls.

**Marion & Co.** 1916–17. London. Made dolls.

**Marionette.** 1921. Trademark registered in Germany by *Mylius Sperschneider.*

**Marjorie.** 1918. Doll made by *Jessie McCutcheon Raleigh,* distributed by *Butler Bros.* Came with white lawn dress and baby hat. Size 11½ inches; price $2.40.

**Markmann, Sigismund.** 1909. Berlin. Made dolls. In the late 1920's there was a Wilhelm Markmann handling dolls in Berlin.

**Marks.** Marks can be found on nearly all parts of dolls and in many different forms. The most likely place for marks is on the back of the head or shoulder. Other likely places are inside the head or on the soles of the feet. Some of the more unusual places where marks have been found are on the upper arm, upper leg, top of the pate, voice box, eyeball, and eye weight. Marks can be incised, raised, pressed, stamped, printed, written, embroidered, etc.; they can be affixed directly to the doll or put on a label, sticker, tag, or ribbon. Marks are not necessarily identical for dolls of the same maker or distributor. There is usually some slight variation in marks on bisque heads. Marks on printed labels or tags are more likely to be identical.

Numbers usually refer to size and/or mold type. A four-digit number might represent a date or only a mold number. Care should be taken to differentiate between a zero and the letter "O." For example, "R O D" means the zero size of a *Rabery & Delphieu* doll. Confusion sometimes arises in reading O, C, and G. The beginning and ending of inscriptions are sometimes incomplete. Usually small sizes are indicated by a slash line or a fraction with a zero denominator—the higher the numerator, the smaller the doll.

Letters too are sometimes used to indicate size or mold type. The initials frequently include the place of manufacture as well as the maker. For example, "A W W" stands for *Adolf Wislizenus* of Waltershausen. Sometimes the first two letters in a name are used, as, for example, *IGODI* for *Johannes Gotthilf Dietrich.* This example also illustrates the fact that "I" and "J" are interchangeable in most European languages. "Co" on the end of a word usually stands for "Company"—"Einco" is the abbreviation of *Eisenmann & Co.*

The name or initials marked on dolls usually represent the owner of the model. This can be the designer, the manufacturer, or the distributor. PLAYTHINGS, January, 1915, explained: "A buyer can, by purchasing the die or dies (having it made to order), control the sale of any doll or dolls and, if desired, can have the name of the house printed on the doll head. The dolls will remain at the factory and dolls will be delivered as ordered."

In some cases, a mark represents several companies, such as *Otto Gans* and A. M. *(Armand Marseille)* on a single head. Some decorators put their initials on porcelain dolls' heads, and some German dolls made by cottagers were signed. These two groups of initials or names would be difficult to trace. Many initials on dolls stand for "patented" or "registered" in various languages. Often doll makers were confused themselves as to whether they had obtained patents, copyrights, or trademarks, and this information marked on the doll may not always agree with government records.

As indicated under *Imports, Dolls,* the name of the country of origin or its absence does have specific implications, but does not necessarily show whether the doll was or was not made before 1891.

Special attributes such as "washable" or its equivalent in other languages, the name of the stuffing material, and so on are sometimes found marked on dolls.

Besides numbers and letters, symbols are often used

as marks, and in the Index symbols are identified by shape—stars, anchors, and many others.

**Marks & Knoring Co.** 1915–17. Boston, Mass. Made dolls with celluloid faces and dolls with "long voices"; prices 10¢, 25¢, and 50¢.

**Marks Bros. Co.** 1918–25+. Boston, Mass. Made and imported celluloid shoulder and socket type dolls' heads.

1918: Advertised celluloid shoulder heads, sizes 5 and 6 inches.

1919: Advertised celluloid socket and shoulder heads, crying dolls, and rag dolls.

1920: Advertised dolls with celluloid heads, kidolene bodies, composition arms and legs; sizes 15, 18, and 22 inches.

1921: Advertised shoulder and socket celluloid heads with stationary or sleeping eyes; came in seven sizes. Cork-stuffed rag dolls with celluloid faces came in three sizes. Also, only American line of celluloid-head dolls stuffed with silk floss; dressed by *Katherine Rauser;* came in sizes 12, 14, 16, and 19 inches; 19-inch doll weighed 12 ounces.

```
MADE IN
U.S.A.
MARKS
BROTHERS CO
BOSTON
½
```

**1134.** Mark on dolls produced by Marks Bros.

**Marloth, Richard.** 1898. Dresden, Saxony. Made dolls.

**Marn & Jondorf.** 1924. London. Registered *The Marion* as a trademark in Britain for dolls. (See **Marx & Jondorf.**)

**Marottes.** According to a French dictionary of 1778, this word was defined as a stick with a doll's head at one end and a fancy hat. Among other names for this type of doll are *Folly Head,* "Whirling Musical Doll," and "Musical Rattle." French ones were made by *Dehais, Jullien, Rabery & Delphieu,* etc. In Germany they were called "Schwenker." (See **Franz Schmidt, Ed Kahn, G. Zinner.**)

1913: Marottes called "Columbine" and "Harlequin" played Viennese or German melodies and were advertised as gifts for "the littlest one."

**Marque, A.** Inscribed on dolls with bisque heads and composition bodies that appear to be French. Most of the faces are similar and appear to be of the character type, which suggests a 20th-century doll, probably early because of pierced ears. In 1916, Mons. Marque made a head for a Paris store.

**Marque Déposée.** French term for registered mark.

**Marquisette.** 1923. Trademark registered in France by *Charles Marie Paul Noël* for dolls.

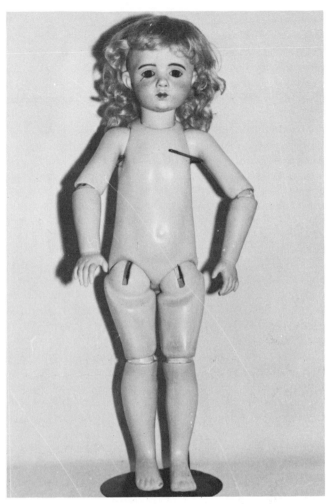

**1135A & B.** *A* Marque bisque head with glass eyes. Note the broken lines used for the painted upper lashes. The pierced ears stick out from the head. The doll has a slender neck and pointed chin. Mark: Ill. **1136.** Composition body has bisque elbow ball, forearms, and hands. H. 22 inches. *Courtesy of Sylvia Brockmon.*

*a Marque*

**1136.** Mark found on A. Marque dolls' heads.

**Marsch, H.** 1909. Berlin. Made dolls.

**Marseille, Armand.** 1865–1925+. Köppelsdorf, Thür. Armand Marseille established a porcelain factory in Köppelsdorf in 1865, according to Jervis' A BOOK OF POTTERY MARKS. Tradition says that he came from Riga, Russia. In Germany, Armand, his son, and his grandson were also known as Herman, but the surname suggests that either the family did not originate in Russia or they changed their name. German Directories list Armand Marseille as a maker of porcelain doll heads in the 1890's. It is believed that one of the heads marked 1894 was purchased ca. 1895. Armand Marseille made the following doll heads as well as many others: *Florodora* for *Borgfeldt* in 1901; *Baby Betty*, 1912; *Duchess*, 1914; *My Dream Baby*, 1924; *Columbia*, and probably *Queen Louise*. *Louis Wolf & Co., Louis Amberg & Son, Foulds & Freure, Arranbee, Otto Gans*, and many others used Armand Marseille dolls' heads.

1904: Armand Marseille, Jr., visited America and spent eight months studying business methods. He also displayed dolls at the St. Louis Exposition and won a Grand Prize. They produced dolls of various grades and artistic merit. The popularity of the Armand Marseille heads is attested by the fact that a greater number of their bisque heads are found on dolls than of any other identifiable manufacturer. Most of their heads are marked with a mold number: #370 for shoulder heads and #390 for socket heads seem to be the two most frequently found; they are known to have been made from the 1890's up until 1925 and after. Numbers such as 1894, 1900, 1908, and so on could represent the year in which the model was first used, but this has not been proved.

1914: Armand Marseille appears to have made the 975 line for Louis Wolf.

1915: Foulds & Freure advertised their 390 line. During World War I, the American market was cut off and the heads were stored in warehouses.

1919: Dolls with some of these German A. M. heads were sold at auction in the Astor Theater, New York. A PLAYTHINGS reporter purchased a #240 A. M. doll for $2.10, but anti-German riots prevented the completion of the auction. Several years later, the strong feeling had abated and Armand Marseille dolls' heads reappeared on the American market.

1924–25: Several bisque infant heads were produced, including My Dream Baby, mold #341 with closed mouth and #351 with open mouth, and *Amberg's New Born Babe*.

## ARMAND MARSEILLE DOLLS

A

B

C

**1137A, B, & C.** Bisque shoulder heads, mold #370, the most frequently found A. M. shoulder head. Mark: Ill. **1158.** Head on the left is size 5; has body of kid with composition forearms and lower legs. Head on the right is size 6. Heights of dolls, 23 inches and 25 inches. respectively. Heights of shoulder heads, 6 inches. and 6½ inches. respectively. *Courtesy of Hildred Brinkley.*

1139

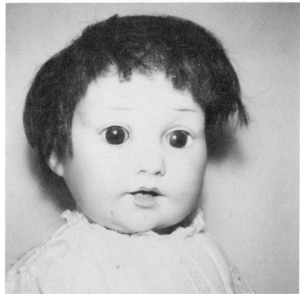
1140

**1138.** Bisque socket head, mold #390, the most frequently found A. M. socket head, resembles the #370 shoulder heads. The 390's were made from around the turn of the century into the 1930's. They had sleeping glass eyes, open mouth with teeth; were on jointed composition bodies. Doll pictured wears her original Volendam costume. Mark: Ill. **1161.** H. 9 inches *Coleman Collection.*

**1139.** Character bisque head with sleeping eyes, closed mouth, is on a jointed composition adult-type body. Mark: Ill: **1164.** H. 15 inches. *Courtesy of Virginia Dilliplane.*

**1140.** "G. B." bisque head, probably made for a distributor with the initials "G. B."; George Borgfeldt is a possibility. Doll has sleeping glass eyes, open mouth with two lower teeth; bent-limb composition baby body. Mark: Ill. **1176.** *Courtesy of Theodora Gearhart.*

**1141.** Character bisque head with glass eyes, open-closed mouth, dimples; on a bent-limb composition body. Mark: Ill. **1166.** H. 17 inches. Resembles Ill. **1142.** *Courtesy of Eunice Althouse.*

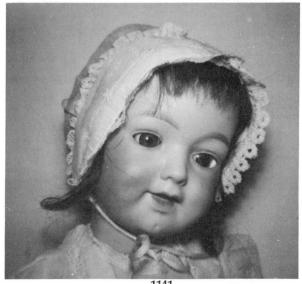
1141

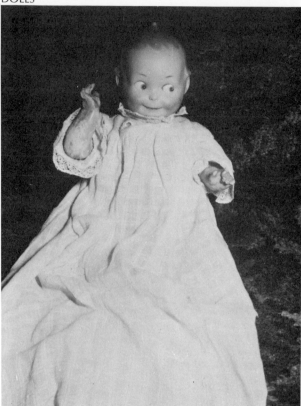

**1142.** Talking bisque-head character doll. The head has a hole cut out for the voice mechanism; glass eyes. Marked: "A. M.// 800." *Courtesy of Margaret Whitton; photograph by Winnie Langley.*

**1144.** Bisque character head with molded and painted features, including a topknot and roguish eyes. Head is marked "G.B.// A. M. 3-04." Composition body. (See Ills. **1140, 1145** for other "G.B." dolls.) *Courtesy of Fidelia Lence; photograph by Winnie Langley.*

**1143.** Character bisque head with intaglio eyes, closed mouth, red wig. Doll is dressed as a boy in a navy blue suit. *Courtesy of Margaret Whitton; photograph by Winnie Langley.*

**1145.** "G. B." bisque head with glass eyes; bent-limb composition body. Mark: Ill. **229.** *Courtesy of Margaret Whitton; photograph by Winnie Langley.*

**1146.** Bisque character head with glass eyes and closed mouth; composition body. Mark: Ill. **1165.** *Courtesy of Maurine Popp; photograph by Winnie Langley.*

**1147.** Crying infant, bisque head with blue glass eyes, made by Armand Marseille. *Courtesy of Margaret Whitton; photograph by Winnie Langley.*

**1148.** Bisque head with glass eyes glancing to the side, small closed pursed mouth; composition body jointed at neck, shoulders, and hips. Mark: Ill: **1150.** H. 10 inches. *Courtesy of Ollie Leavister.*

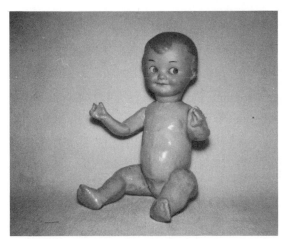

**1149A & B.** Bisque head with molded and painted hair, intaglio eyes glancing to the side, closed mouth; on a bent-limb composition body. Armand Marseille model #322, size 6/0. H. 8½ inches. *Courtesy of Dorothy Annunziato.*

**1150–1176.** Marks found on dolls' heads made by Armand Marseille. Marks Nos. **1173** and **1174** are those of the Köppelsdorfer Porzellanfabrik, the proprietors of which were Armand Marseille and Ernst Heubach.

Germany
310
A 8/0 M
1150

Germany
323
A 6/0 M
1151

A.M.
Germany.
341 /1K.
1152

A M
Germany
341/3K
1153

A.M.
Germany
341./5/0X. K
1154

A.M.
Germany.
347/0 J.
1155

A M
Germany
351. /4K
1156

A. M.
Germany.
353.12/0 K
1157

Armand Marseille
Germany.
370
A 6 M
1158

Armand Marseille
Germany
390
A 11/0 M
1159

Made in Germany.
Armand Marseille
390
A 9 M
1160

Armand Marseille
Germany.
390.
A 12/0X M.
1161

Made in Germany
Armand Marseille
390
D.R.G.M 2 ½
A. 11/0 M.
1162

Armand Marseille
390 n
D.R.G.M 216
A 6/0 M
1163

Armand Marseille
Germany
401
A 5/0 M
1164

Germany
550
A 3 M
D.R.G.M
1165

590
A. 5 M.
Germany
D.R.G.M.
1166

Germany.
971
A 5 M
D.R.G.M 267/1
1167

Armand Marseille
A · 975 M
Germany
1168

Armand Marseille
Germany
990
A 9/0 M
1169

1894
A.M. 0 D.E.P.
Made in Germany
1170

3200
AM 8/0 DEP
1171

3700
AM 2/0 D.E.P.
made in Germany
1172

Made in Germany
dep. 5/2/0
1173

A M
1174

Made in Germany
A 4 M
Z
1175

Germany
G. 329
A. 1. M.
D.R.G.M. 267/1
1176

**Marseille, François Emile.** 1888. Maisons Alfort, France. Registered *Le Petit Français* as a trademark for jointed *bébés incassables*.

**Mar-Sell-Ene.** 1911. Clown doll made by the *Nonbreakable Toy Co.*

**Marsh.** 1865–1913. London. William Marsh was listed as a doll maker in 1865. From 1878 until 1894, Charles Marsh was listed as a maker of wax dolls and wax over papier-mâché dolls; Charles's wife, Mrs. Mary Ann Marsh, was listed as repairing dolls from 1895 until 1910. From 1911 to 1913, Miss Jessie Marsh at the same address was listed as in the doll business.

**1177.** Poured wax-head doll manufactured by Charles Marsh; blue glass eyes, poured wax arms, original cream-colored dress. For blue-green stamp on the chest, see Ill. **1178.** *Courtesy of Marion Holt; photograph by Winnie Langley.*

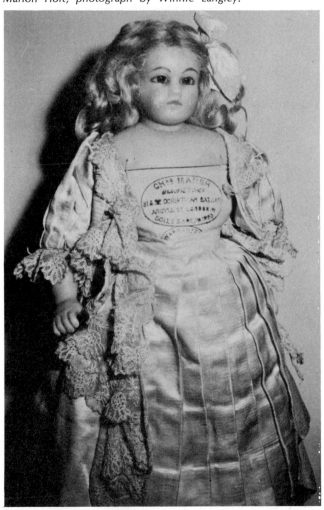

**1178**

**1179**

**1180**

**1178–1180.** Marks found on bodies of Marsh wax dolls.

**Martelet, Jeune (Jr.).** 1829–36. Paris. Made molds for dolls.

**Martha Washington.** 1906. Novelty doll with white hair arranged in the fashion of 1776.

**Martin, A.** 1874–76. Paris. Made dressed dolls and trousseaux.

**Martin, Alfred François Xavier.** See **Manufacture des Bébés & Poupées.**

**Martin, Benoit.** 1863. Paris. Obtained a patent for using swivel joints on a doll. One of these dolls is pictured by Luella Hart as the cover of her COMPLETE FRENCH DOLL DIRECTORY—a doll with a bisque head, swivel neck, wooden body with swivel waist, metal hands and wrists. On the chest is a brass plate with "Breveté SGDG. // Martin // Paris" on it.

**Martin, Dexter, & Martin, Frank D.** See **Jointed Doll Co.**

**Martin, Elsa.** 1909. Eppendorf, Saxony. Made wooden dolls.

**Martin, Ernst, & Rippel, Henry C.** 1881–83. New York City. Made wax dolls and wax dolls' heads. In 1883 they were joined by *Carl Wiegand,* and the firm was known as the *National Doll & Novelty Co.*

**Martin, Fernand (Seraphin).** 1880–1909. Paris. Specialized in mechanical toys, especially dolls. He obtained three British patents and one German and one French for walking dolls. One of his dolls walked by itself and sold for only 5¢ or 6¢. He exhibited dolls in Chicago in 1893, in Paris in 1900, where he won a bronze medal, and in St. Louis in 1904. PLAYTHINGS, June, 1909, reported that he had won thirty-seven gold and silver medals as well as the Legion of Honor and seven foreign medals.

**Martin, Hermann.** 1925. Hildburghausen, Thür. Made dolls.

**Martin & Runyon.** 1862–65. London. Made *Autoperipatetikos* dolls patented by *Enoch Rice Morrison.* A doll's box found in England bears the statement that H. Martin was the sole agent for Autoperipatetikos dolls.

**Martinville & Salel Co.** 1924. France. Obtained a French patent with Daniel Laure for a talking doll with a phonograph in its body.

**Maruei-Oki Doll Co.** 1925. Kyoto, Japan. Made dolls.

**Marvel.** 1905–10. Mark used by *Butler Bros.* on line of kid-body dolls made by *Kestner.* The mark was on the chest beneath the crown and streamers of the Kestner mark.

**Marvel Mama Dolls.** 1923. Made by *Century Doll Co.* Came with lined wigs, sleeping eyes, composition arms and legs, cotton-stuffed bodies.

**Marx & Jondorf.** 1925. Sonneberg, Thür. Made dolls. (See **Marn & Jondorf.**)

**Mary.** Ca. 1908. Wooden doll made by *Schoenhut* to go in "Mary Had a Little Lamb" set.

**Mary, Mme.** 1925. Paris. Made dolls.

**Mary Alice.** 1910–1911. Trademark registered in U.S. by *Lena Scurlock* for a portrait doll representing Mary Alice Chipps.

**Mary and Her Garden.** 1925. *Story Book Doll,* manufactured by *Sol Bergfeld & Son,* distributed by *Borgfeldt.* Came with composition head; 15 inches tall.

**Mary and Her Little Lamb.** 1925. *Story Book Doll,* manufactured by *Sol Bergfeld & Son,* distributed by *Borgfeldt.* Came with composition head; 15 inches tall.

**Mary Ann.** 1923. Walking doll made by *EFFanBEE.* Came with blue sleeping eyes, Mama voice, soft stuffed body. A button pinned to its dress had the word "EFFanBEE" on it; 20 inches tall, price $7.50.

**Mary Carroll.** 1924. *Celebrity Doll* originated by *Margaret Vale,* designed and made by *Jane Gray.* The doll represented Mary Carroll as Mamie Potter in Richard L. Herndon's THE POTTERS. It had a hand-painted face and bore a tag with a facsimile autograph of Mary Carroll.

**Mary Elizabeth.** 1911–15. Doll representing a child of eight years, copyrighted by *Elizabeth Lesser.* She sued *Borgfeldt* for infringement of this doll, but lost her case when she failed to submit copies of the alleged infringement.

**Mary Had a Lamb.** 1919. Doll made by *Jessie McCutcheon Raleigh;* came in two sizes.

**Mary Ha-Ha.** 1910. Doll produced by Hahn & *Amberg.*

**Mary Hay.** 1924. *Celebrity Doll* originated by *Margaret Vale,* designed and made by *Jane Gray.* The doll represented Mary Hay as Mary Jane in Arthur Hammerstein's MARY JANE McKANE. It had a hand-painted face and bore a tag with a facsimile autograph of Mary Hay.

**Mary Jane.** 1917. Fully jointed, all-composition character doll made by *EFFanBEE.* Came with sleeping eyes, real hair curls; wore a chemise and bore a round EFFanBEE tag.

**Mary Nash.** 1924. *Celebrity Doll* originated by *Margaret Vale,* designed and made by *Jane Gray.* The doll represented Mary Nash as "The Lady" in A. H. Wood's THE LADY. It had a hand-painted face and bore a tag with a facsimile autograph of Mary Nash.

**Mary Pickford Doll.** 1922. PLAYTHINGS, July, 1922, stated that Mary Pickford had opened a factory in Los Angeles to make these dolls based on a likeness of her by the Scandinavian artist Christian von Schneidau, which had been chosen in a competition with seven other artists. It was estimated that it would take $500,000 to develop the facilities necessary to manufacture the doll.

**Mary Quite Contrary.** 1919. Doll made by *Jessie McCutcheon Raleigh.*

**Mascot.** 1912. Doll made by *Horsman,* resembled a *Campbell Kid.* Came with *Can't Break 'Em* head and molded hair; wore college-type clothes.

**Mascotte.** See **Bébé Mascotte.**

**Mascotte.** 1925. Trade name used for dolls by *Mme. T. Lazarski.*

**Mascotte Boudoir.** 1922. Trademark registered in U.S. by *Joseph Meer Inc.* and affixed on the doll with a label.

**Mask Face Dolls.** These dolls usually have the back half of the head made of cloth or some material different from the more rigid face portion. The *London Rag Dolls* had wax masks that were covered with muslin, and the back of the head was covered by a cap. Many of the celluloid dolls had mask faces. *Albert Brückner, Charles Reese, Charles Bloom,* and others obtained U.S. patents for mask face dolls.

**Mason, Henry Hubbard.** 1878–93. Springfield, Vt. He became a partner in D. M. Smith & Co. in 1852. About 1879, the D. M. Smith Co. began to make jointed wooden dolls. Probably Mason was the member of this firm who was most interested in manufacturing dolls.

1881: Mason and Luke Taylor obtained a U.S. patent for an improvement in the construction of a doll's head and neck joint. This head was made of molded "plastic" (actually, composition) over a wooden base. One type was the so-called witch or wizard doll. According to a descendant, the bodies of these dolls were made of poplar wood, turned on a lathe. The arms and legs were of rock maple or beech. The feet and hands were of lead or pewter, except for a few early dolls that had wooden-spoon hands. Earlier dolls had wooden pins to fasten the hip joints, but later ones had steel screws. A few china or papier-mâché heads may have been tried before the composition ones were used. The composition was a doughy paste of glue, rosin, plaster of Paris, etc., molded in two-part molds. The feet were painted blue usually, and the head and shoulders were dipped in flesh-colored paint, except for the Negro dolls. Only size 12 inches was reported. No proof has yet come to light of a connection between the Mason dolls and those of the *Jointed Doll Co.*, other than the great similarity of construction. The Mason and Taylor dolls appear to have been made on the premises of D. M. Smith & Co.

Around 1885, Mason may have severed connections with D. M. Smith & Co., for in that year both D. M. Smith & Co. and H. H. Mason were listed as makers of jointed dolls. Smith was not listed under "Dolls" after 1886, but Mason continued with a doll listing through 1893.

**Maspeth Doll Manufacturing Co.** 1920. Maspeth, N.Y. Made moving eye dolls' heads.

**Masse Holz.** 1890's. A composition used by *Emil Paufler & Co.* to make "unbreakable" dolls' heads.

**Massiot.** Before 1906, Paris. In 1906, A. François was the successor. Made dolls.

**Masson, A. M.** 1921–23. U.S. Made dolls' hair.

**Massoneau, Mlle.** 1866. Paris. Made dolls.

**Master Bubbles.** 1922. Designed by *Mme. Georgene Averill,* manufactured and distributed by *Paul Averill, Inc.* They advertised that the doll walked, talked, and danced. Came with blond or tosca ringlet wig; cotton crepe rompers with figures appliquéd on front, and cotton crepe bonnet; 25½ and 28 inches tall; mate to *Mistress Bubbles.*

**Master Sam.** 1917. One of the *Uncle Sam Kids* made by *Horsman,* based on a patented design. Dressed in red, white, and blue; mate to *Miss Sam.*

**Mastercraft Babies.** 1918. Produced by *Century Doll Co.*

**Mastercraft Doll Co.** 1922–24. New York City. Made fabric dolls.

1922: Advertised "Mastercraft" dolls as well as *Flo Vel* with velvet faces, and *Rembrandt* dolls with hand-painted, waterproof, and washable fabric faces.

**Mathieu, Jérôme.** 1871–75. Paris. Made dolls.

**Mathoff Manufacturing Co.** 1923. U.S. Made dolls.

**Matlock Patent Washable Dolls.** 1907–12. Distributed by *Butler Bros.* The name "Matlock" may come from the mineral, Matlockite, found in Matlock, Derbyshire, England.

1907: Came with glass eyes, mohair curly wig; wore a kimono. Size 12 inches cost $2.10 doz. wholesale.

1910: Came with painted features, side-part curly wig; wore a chemise. Sizes 11, 16, 23¾, and 31½ inches; price 92¢ to $8.35 doz. wholesale.

**Matsubashi, Masazo.** 1900. Japan. Won Honorable Mention for his display of dolls at the Paris Exposition.

**Matthes, E. W., Firm.** 1909–25+. Berlin. Manufactured, distributed, and exported dolls and doll parts.

1913: Registered *Ursula* as a trademark in Germany.

1916: Registered *Friedel* as a trademark in Germany.

**Mauger.** 1860's–1870's. Charenton and Montreuil-sous-Bois, Seine. According to Janet Johl in THE FASCINATING STORY OF DOLLS, Mauger made bisque-head dolls in the factory that was bought by *Jumeau.*

**Maujean.** 1866–74. Paris. Made dolls.

**Maurer, Arthur.** 1923. Coburg, Thür. Manufactured dolls.

**Maurice Chevalier.** 1924–25. Cloth doll's head made by *Bernard Ravca;* represented the actor of the same name.

**Maurisse.** 1849–51. Paris. Made dolls.

**Mauroner, J. B.** 1896. St. Ulrich, Grödner Tal. Distributed wooden dolls.

**Maus, Widow Edith (née Westphal).** 1925. Brunswick, Germany. Specialized in jointed dolls; registered in Germany two trademarks, *Strampelchen* and a drawing of a mouse, for dolls and dressed dolls.

**Mausi (Mousie).** 1908. Trademark registered in Germany by *Robert Carl* for dolls and doll parts.

**Mawaphil Dolls.** 1923. Line of dolls with twenty-six numbers. Made in Atlanta, Ga., distributed by *Riemann, Seabrey Co.* Dolls were handmade and hand-painted; came with soft bodies; priced 50¢ to $2.50.

**Max.** 1907+. Wooden circus doll made by *Schoenhut;* 7½ inches tall. Represented the earlier comic character of this name. Many Germans made Max and *Moritz* dolls.

**Max, Carl & Co.** 1897–1914. Neustadt near Coburg, Thür. Manufactured and exported dolls, including *Tauflinge.* H. E. Eskart & Co. was their London agent.

**Maxwell, Anne.** 1914–16. Bayside, N.Y. Registered *Little Sister* as a trademark in U.S. to be used for rag dolls.

1915: Was granted a U.S. patent for a rag doll with plaitable hair, which was an integral part of the doll's head fabric.

**Maxwell, Bert Randolph.** 1918. Fairbury, Ill. Obtained U.S. design patent for a doll with bald head, goatee, and spectacles.

**May, Albert.** See **May & Lindner.**

**May, Otto.** 1912. Chemnitz, Germany. Doll manufacturer. Registered *Katz im Sack* as a trademark in Germany.

**May & Lindner.** Before 1891–Gotha, Germany. The successor was Albert May, and his successor was *Heinrich Graeser,* who in 1891 made bisque dolls' heads, bathing dolls, jointed dolls, etc.

**May Blossom.** 1922–23. Picture of a doll's head amid blossoms registered as a trademark in Britain in 1922 by *Dennis, Malley & Co.,* importers and exporters. The same picture registered as a trademark in Germany in 1923 by *Alfred Lange,* manufacturer and exporter of dolls.

**May Fair.** See **Mayfair Gifts & Playthings Inc.**

**May Frères (Bros.) Cie.** 1890–97. Paris. Also known as May & Bertin and May Fils (Sons). Appears to have merged with the *Jules Nicholas Steiner* firm after 1897.

1890: Registered *Bébé Mascotte* as a trademark in France; obtained French patent for metallic mountings for bébés.

1892: Advertised Bébé Mascotte as a jointed doll that could take all positions of the human body, including kneeling; joints were made of wood. The address of this company was at 5 rue Beranger, the *Gesland* address.

1901: Bébé Mascotte was advertised by the Steiner firm.

**May Queen.** 1910. Advertised by *Butler Bros.* Came with bisque head, sleeping eyes, hair eyelashes, side-part wig. Clothes could be removed. Size 20 inches, price $2.00.

**Maya.** 1925. Trademark registered in Germany by *Geschwister Heinrich's Kunstlerpuppen* (Brother Henry's Art Dolls). The dolls advertised as *Art Dolls.*

**Maybelle.** 1920–22. One of the *Bell Brand* line of dolls made by Bell Toy Co.; distributed by *Sears, Roebuck & Co.* Came with bisque heads, sleeping glass eyes, hair eyelashes, sewed mohair wigs, fully jointed bodies with jointed wrists. Wore lawn chemise. Sizes 24½ and 26½ inches; price $4.98 to $5.89. Prior to World War I, Sears advertised "Maybelle Jointed Dolls."

**Mayer, Fels.** 1890. Milan, Italy. Manufactured dolls.

**Mayfair, Gifts & Playthings Inc., The.** 1921. New York City. Produced little "May Fair" rag dolls 26 inches tall; they weighed eight ounces; price $37.00 doz. wholesale; also walking *Mama Doll,* price $100.00 doz. wholesale; in a fine dress, $25.00 each retail.

**Mayland-Ruter.** 1867–70. Paris. Made dolls.

**Mayorga, J.** 1878. Guatemala. Displayed dolls in native costumes at the Paris Exposition.

**Maytime Girl.** 1919. Cherub-type doll made by *New Toy Co.*

**Mäzel-Tov.** 1919–20. In a six-pointed star, trademark registered in Germany by *Joseph David Cronau* for dolls.

**McAboy, Mary (Mrs. F. E.).** 1913+. Missoula, Montana. Made dried-apple Indian dolls commercially. One day, recalling that her mother had made apple-faced Indian

**1181A & B.** Indian portrait doll made by Mary McAboy has composition head, painted eyes, wig, cloth body, wooden legs, original clothes. H. 14 inches. *Coleman Collection.*

dolls wrapped in blankets and sold at church socials, Mrs. McAboy made a whole Indian village, which was displayed in a grocery store. This quickly sold, and she made many more villages. Finally, in 1913, she began to produce these dried-apple Indian dolls commercially under the trademark *Skookum,* which is Siwash for "Bully Good." The trademark was registered in 1919, but had been used since 1913. In 1913 she applied for design patents for a squaw and a brave doll. These patents were granted in 1914. As the popularity of these dolls grew, it required a factory to produce them. They were made by the *H. H. Tammen Co.* of Denver, Colorado, and Los Angeles, California, as early as 1916, but still under the direction of Mary McAboy. Nearly every Indian tribe was represented—Pueblo, Sioux, Apache, Chippewa, and others.

PLAYTHINGS, February, 1922, described the use made of these dolls by the Public Library of Newark, N.J., as an example of their use in many other places: "If, for another example, the dolls of our western Indians are to be studied, Miss Kendall has a pair, Mr. and Mrs. Skookum, with faces made of dried-apples and the bodies fashioned from an oblong stick of wood. Think of the new world such a study opens up to a child. These dried apple-faced dolls have every wrinkle and decoration worn by the Indian and are unique pieces of work."

As business increased, the faces were made out of composition as well as dried apples, and later were made entirely of composition. The indestructible composition faces were painted and lined to look lifelike. Each doll was wrapped in an Indian blanket.

**McAlister, Claire.** 1924–25. San Francisco, Calif. Was issued a design patent for a ball-jointed type of doll with a queue; the doll wore Chinese clothes.

**McCandlish, Edward Gerstell.** 1924. Takoma Park, Md. Secured two U.S. design patents for cherub-type dolls, one of them dressed and one undressed.

**McCann, George Frederick.** 1922–23. Jersey City, N.J. Was granted a U.S. design patent for a doll representing a flapper with bobbed hair. The doll wore a short dress, plaid coat, necktie and collar, and striped stockings.

**McChesney, Lillian.** 1922–23. Honolulu, Hawaii. Was issued a U.S. design patent for a little-girl doll with eyes glancing to the side. Doll was dressed in a short dress with short sleeves, and had a large hat tied under her chin.

**McClay, Harry.** 1917. Philadelphia, Pa. Made dolls.

**McClurg, A. C., & Co.** 1909–16. Chicago, Ill. In 1913, known as McClurg & Keen. Doll jobber and distributor.

1911: Advertised imported baby dolls with beads around their necks.

1913: Distributed *Yankee Dolls* made by *Mitred Box Co.*

1916: Advertised *Kewpies, Happifats, Kestner,* and other dolls. Most of the dolls were handled by *Borgfeldt.*

**McConnell, Mary E. D.** 1916–17. New York City. Was issued a U.S. design patent for a rag doll with a long nose and the seam down the center of the face.

**McCowan, Emily.** 1922–23. New York City. Was granted a U.S. design patent for a rag doll wearing a cloche-type hat.

**McCrosky Bros.** 1920–22. Oakland, Calif. Registered *Rock-A-Bye-Dolly* as a trademark in U.S. for dolls.

**McCubbin, Ethel Elizabeth Mary.** 1914. London. Registered in Britain a picture of a lion's claw in a circle as a trademark for dolls.

**McElroy, Daniel S.** 1893–94. New York City. Obtained U.S. patent for a doll whose head and leg could be moved by moving its arm.

**McEnery, Charles T.** 1921. San Francisco, Calif. Secured a U.S. design patent for a doll.

**McMillan, Adelaide.** 1915. Workington, England. Obtained a British patent for a cork-filled rag doll; head and torso were made of four pieces, arms of two pieces each.

**Mead, Madge Lansing.** See **Mother's Congress Doll Co.**

**Meakin & Ridgeway.** 1919–21. New York City. Sole U.S. and Canadian agent for British dolls, including dolls with "china" heads, composition, kidette, and stockinet character dolls. Represented *Speights Ltd., Nottingham Toy Industry Ltd., Shanklin Toy Industry Ltd.,* and others.

**Mechanical Rubber Co.** 1915–17. Cleveland, Ohio. Made *Shield Brand* white rubber dolls, including an Uncle Sam, Sailor, Clown, and boys, girls, and baby dolls. By 1918, the firm became part of the United States Rubber Co., which used the Shield Brand "M" mark.

**Mechtold, George, & Co.** 1894–1915. Oberlind near Sonneberg, Thür., and Fürth, Bavaria. Manufactured and exported dolls.

1894: Obtained a German patent with Thomas Chillingworth for a ball-jointed doll with a hinged opening in the back of the torso for access to a clothes storage compartment inside the body.

**Medaille d'Or, 1878.** See **Jumeau.**

**Medaille d'Or Paris, 1889.** See **Steiner, Jules Nicholas.**

**Meder, K.** 1918. Eisfeld, Thür. Made dressed dolls.

**Meech, Herbert John.** 1865–91. London. Made wax and/ or composition dolls. He was doll maker to the Royal Family by royal appointment.

**Meer, Joseph, Inc.** 1922. Registered *Mascotte Boudoir* as a trademark in U.S., to be affixed to dolls with a label.

**Meffert & Co.** See **Catterfelder Puppenfabrik.**

**Meg.** 1923–25. Rag doll designed and made by *Madame Alexander.* It had a mask face with raised features, which were hand-painted by Madame Alexander. Came with wig of mohair imported from England; pink muslin body; size 14 inches; price $1.20.

**Megrot, Mlle.** 1871–79. Paris. Made dolls.

**Meier, A., Co.** 1892. Yokohama, China [*sic*]. Registered a trademark with dragons and leaves, in Germany, for dolls and other things.

**Meier, Harry W.** 1905–14. Baltimore, Md. Secured two U.S. patents for elastic devices for stringing dolls. The 1906 patent was for a one-piece branched elastic with hooks that attached to staples on the extremities of the dolls. These appear to have been the *Dolly Dimples* One Piece Doll Elastics, for which *Strobel & Wilken Co.* were

**1182A & B.** Poured wax doll with brown hair, blue glass eyes; has two red stamps of Herbert John Meech on the hips. Mark: Ill. **1183.** *Photographs by Winnie Langley.*

**1183.** Mark of H. J. Meech found on bodies of wax dolls.

sole selling agents. In 1914, Harry W. Meier & Co. obtained a U.S. patent for making the elastic cord separate for the arms because they had the greatest wear. In 1918, the patent rights and machinery were sold to *Braitling*.

**Mein Augenstern.** 1914. Used for two trademarks registered in Germany by *P. R. Zierow* for dolls; one of the trademarks also pictured a six-pointed star in an eye.

**Mein Gluckskind (My Lucky Child).** 1919. Trademark registered in Germany by *A. Wislizenus* firm for dolls. Trademark contains the initials "A. W. W."

**Mein Goldherz (My Golden Heart).** 1904. Trademark registered in Germany by *Bruno Schmidt* for dolls. Trademark contains the initials "B. S. W."

**Mein Kleiner Schlingel (My Little Rascal).** 1922–25. Trademark registered in Germany by *Bauer & Richter* for dolls.

**Mein Kleines (My Little Ones).** 1911. Trademark registered in Germany by *Kämmer & Reinhardt* for dolls and doll parts.

**Mein Liebling (My Darling).** 1901–25+. Four trademarks of various designs registered in Germany by *Kämmer & Reinhardt* in 1902, 1903, and 1905. There were also two English versions, *My Darling,* registered in 1906 and 1920 in Germany. These trademarks were used for dolls and doll parts and continued in use after 1925. (See also **My Darling** and color photograph C20.)

**Mein Sonnenschein (My Sunshine).** 1910. Trademark registered in Germany by *Catterfelder Puppenfabrik* for dolls and doll parts.

**Mein Stern (My Star).** 1923. Trademark registered in Germany by *Henriette Dunker* for dolls. Trademark contains the initials "M. H. A. D."

**Mein Stolz (My Pride).** 1925. Trademark used by *Koenig & Wernicke* for jointed dolls, bent-limb babies, and doll parts.

**Meine Einzige (My Only One).** 1910–25. Trademark registered in Germany by *Kley & Hahn* for ball-jointed dolls, character dolls, and leather dolls. Words are in a six-pointed star.

**Meisel, Aloys.** 1862–83. New York City. Distributed toys, especially imported German, French, and English dolls.

1878: Aloys Meisel of Brooklyn registered a trademark in U.S. to be used on toys.

1882–83: He was sole agent for the *National Doll & Novelty Co.* of New York City.

**Meissen.** 1710–1925+. Meissen, Saxony. The first European porcelain factory was established here. This was also known in the early 18th century as *Königliche Porzellan Manufaktur*, a name later used by the Royal State factory at Berlin. The crossed swords Meissen marks have been found on dolls' heads, but many imitations of these have been used by other porcelain factories. In some cases, original molds passed into other hands and were fraudulently used. Actual forgeries were made by Weise of Dresden. The word "Meissen" is the mark of the modern firm of Teichert. The authentification of a true Meissen product requires a skilled expert.

DOLLS WITH MEISSEN MARKS

**1185A, B, & C.** Front and two side views of flesh-tinted china head with Meissen mark on head and arms. Molded earrings; dark brown hair. *Photographs by Winnie Langley.*

**1184A & B.** Flesh-colored china head with Meissen mark and "756//2 pap" on it. Brown streaked hair with green ribbon entwined in the braid; part of ear shows. *Courtesy of Mrs. Charles Axelrod; photographs by Winnie Langley.*

MEISSEN

**1186.** Flesh-tinted china head with Meissen mark has blue eyes, reddish-brown streaked hair. *Courtesy of Margaret Whitton; photograph by Winnie Langley.*

**1187–1191.** Porcelain marks of the Meissen factory. It is not certain that all marks resembling these found on dolls indicate a Meissen origin.

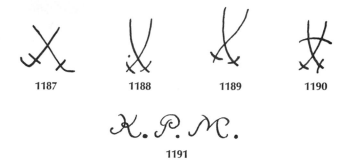

1187    1188    1189    1190

*K. P. M.*

1191

**Melba.** 1915–20. Mark of Mayer & Sherratt, England; used on bisque heads. Some had wigs; others were molded. They were generally shoulder heads on kid bodies.

**Meldram, Minnie M.** 1919–20. New York City. Registered *Soxie* as a trademark in U.S. for dolls; also obtained a U.S. design patent for a yarn doll.

**Melhuish, Edwin.** 1870. London. Made dolls.

**Menco Importing Co.** 1922. New York City. Imported dolls and advertised jointed dolls, kidoline dolls, bisque babies, and *Mama Dolls.*

**Menn, L.** 1873–75. Paris. Made dolls.

**Menoreau, A.** 1879. Paris. Made dressed and undressed dolls.

**Merle, M. A.** 1878. Paris. Displayed dolls called *Mignonnes* at the Paris Exposition.

**Mermaid Doll & Toy Co.** 1921–25. New York City. Made "Mermaid" *Mama Dolls.*

**Merrie Marie.** 1900+. Rag doll based on the patent of *Edgar G. Newell,* came in so-called "life size"; 24 inches.

**Merrill, Elizabeth Eunice.** 1917. Los Angeles, Calif. Was issued a U.S. design patent for a nurse doll with eyes glancing to the side.

**Merry Max.** 1913. Doll copyrighted by *Horsman,* designed by *Laura Gardin* (Mrs. Fraser). It represented a baldheaded, laughing child.

**Merry Miss.** 1916. Doll with composition head and hands, cork-stuffed body; distributed by *Montgomery Ward & Co.* Size 13¾ inches, price 92¢.

**Merry Widow (Die Lustige Witwe).** 1908–11. Line of dolls made in Germany under the personal supervision of *Edmund Ulrich Steiner;* the trademark was registered in Germany by Max *Illfelder* for dolls and dolls' heads. Merry Widow dolls came in three styles, with a boy and girl for each style and blondes and brunettes for each style. Those in style #1 were Viennese dolls in national costume. Dolls in style #2 were dressed in widow's weeds. Style #3 dolls were fanciful representations dressed in laces and ruffles.

1911: Advertised as having sleep eyes and being completely costumed; size 16 inches, price $1.00.

**1192.** "Merry Widow Doll" as advertised by Samstag & Hilder Bros. in *Playthings* in 1908. *Courtesy of McCready Publishing Co.*

Merry Widow
Doll
Registered

**Merry Widow.** 1919. Wigged cherub-type doll made by *New Toy Co.*

**Merveilleux.** See **Bébé Merveilleux.**

**Merville, Edouard.** 1925. Paris. Made dolls named *Ma Poupette.*

**Mesa.** Ca. 1919. Bisque dolls' heads made in New Jersey by *Ernst Reinhardt.*

**Mess, H.** 1465. Nürnberg, Bavaria. Made dolls, according to Max Von Boehn.

**Messing.** 1914–15. Georgenthal, Gotha. Manufactured dolls.

**Metal & Wood Toy Manufacturing Co.** 1922. Budapest, Hungary. Made artistic wooden toys and dolls, distributed in U.S. by *Roth, Baitz & Lipsitz.*

**Metal Doll Co.** 1902–3. Pleasantville, N.J. Made *All Steel Dolls* invented by Vincent Lake.

**Metal Dolls.** 1863–1925+. Made chiefly in France and U.S.

1863: *D. Lacouchy* of Paris advertised metal dolls.

1885: *Mons. Decré* patented metal bébés.

1876–1901: *William Rose, Kimball C. Atwood,* and *Robert Purvis,* all of the U.S., obtained patents for metal dolls.

Ca. 1903: All-steel dolls were made in Pleasantville, N.J. by the *Metal Doll Co.*

1919–23: Metal dolls were made all over the world. In the U.S., there were the *Atlas Doll & Toy Co., Giebeler-Falk, Morris Gerberg,* and *Charles Cábana. Mme. Buisson* obtained a French patent for an enameled metal doll. *Natale Antenori* in Rome made dolls of separate pieces of leaf metal soldered together. *A. Bucherer* of Switzerland obtained a German patent for a metal ball-jointed doll, and *H. Huck* of Germany made a similar type of doll.

**Metal Hands.** Used on *Huret* dolls, dolls made by the *Jointed Doll Co.,* the *Co-operative Doll Co., New England Doll Co., Giebeler-Falk,* and others. Dolls with bisque heads marked "P. + D." usually have metal hands. (See **Petit & Dumontier.**)

**Metal Heads.** 1861–1925+. Metal heads were made earlier and in greater numbers than entire metal dolls. Often metal limbs were used with metal heads. In 1861, *René Poulin* secured a French patent for copper or zinc dolls' heads and limbs. Later dolls' heads were also made of brass, pewter, tin, lead, and aluminum. In 1876, *Lucien Vervelle* obtained a French patent for metal heads.

Although some metal heads were made in U.S. and France, the majority were made in Germany. *Joseph Schön* of Germany patented metal dolls' heads in Germany, Britain, and U.S. in 1886/7, and in 1888 *Bushow and Beck* won a prize for metal dolls' heads at the Brussels Exposition. Around 1902, *Alfred Heller* began to make *Diana* metal heads, and in 1904 *Karl Standfuss* made *Juno* metal heads. By 1904, Sonneberg exported metal-head dolls to England, France, and U.S. Most of the large

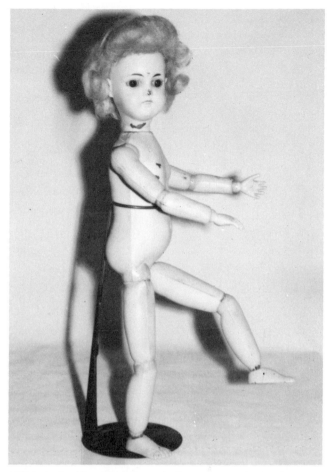

**1193A & B.** All-steel doll made by Metal Doll Co. has glass eyes. Interchangeable wigs are attached to the head by means of three snaps. Doll has open-closed mouth with teeth; spring joints at neck, shoulder, elbow, wrist, hip, knee, and ankle. Mark: Ill. **1194.** H. 17½ inches. *Coleman Collection.*

**1194.** Mark found on body of dolls by Metal Doll Co.

PATENTS PENDING
MADE BY
METAL DOLL CO.,
Pleasantville, N.J.

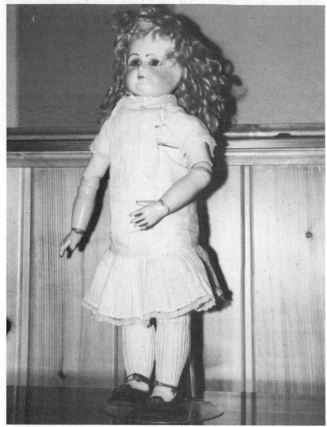

**1195.** Doll with metal hands, bisque head, glass eyes, closed mouth; ball-jointed composition body. Head mark: Ill. **1196.** H. 23 inches. *Courtesy of the International Doll Library Foundation.*

**1196.** Mark found on the heads of some dolls with metal hands; these may have been made by Petit & Dumontier.

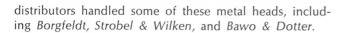

P+D

**1197.** Metal heads of molded and painted pewter on wooden bodies. Doll at the left has black hair, molded pink ribbon around her neck, and pierced ears. Doll at the right has pink flowers in her hair; is peg jointed at the shoulders and elbows. *Courtesy of Gladyse Hilsdorf; photograph by Winnie Langley.*

distributors handled some of these metal heads, including *Borgfeldt, Strobel & Wilken,* and *Bawo & Dotter.*

1914: The *Art Metal Works* of New Jersey made dolls with metal heads. After the war, *Atlas Doll & Toy Co., Amor Metal Toy Stamping Co.,* and *Giebeler-Falk,* all of the U.S., made dolls with metal heads and some with metal limbs also.

**Métayer, A.** 1860's. Tours, France. This name and address found on a paper label inside a china head with a waterfall type of hairdo. (See Ills. 1199, 1200.)

**Metro Doll Co.** 1921. New York City. *Joseph L. Kallus,* proprietor. Company was in existence only a few months and never actually made dolls. It was an interim company between the dissolution of the *Mutual Doll Co.* and the

establishment of the *Cameo Doll Co.* Metro Doll Co. did advertise *Bo-Fair* and *Dollie.*

**Metropolitan India Rubber & Vulcanite Co.** 1870. London. Made rubber dolls.

**Mettais, Jules.** See **Steiner, Jules Nicholas.**

**Mettefeu, D.** 1921. Paris. Made dolls.

**Metz & Ahlckes.** 1895, Hannover, Prussia. Made dressed dolls.

**Metzels.** Before 1918. Ibenhain, Thür. In 1918, the successor was Erich. Manufactured dolls.

**Metzler, Gebrüder (Bros.), & Ortloff.** 1864–1925+. Ilmenau, Thür. Porcelain factory that made dolls' heads. Had agents in Hamburg, Germany, and London.

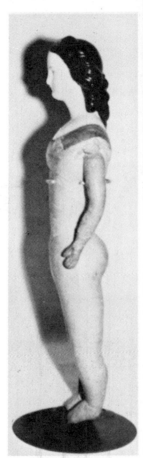

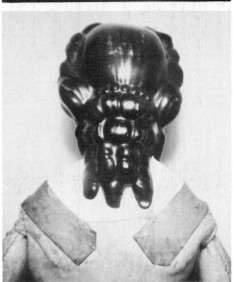

**1198.** Metal-head doll with flange neck on cloth body; sleeping metal eyes; composition arms and legs; original pink baby clothes. Original blue and white heart-shaped tag reads "Guaranteed // Metal Head // Unbreakable." H. 14 inches. *Courtesy of Eleanor Jean Carter.*

**Metzler, Richard (Sr. & Jr.).** 1893–1925+. Sonneberg, Thür. Manufactured dolls.

**Metzner, Albin.** 1909–12. Sonneberg, Thür. Made and exported dolls.

**Metzner, Edmund.** 1915–25+. Sonneberg, Thür. Manufactured and exported dolls' bodies especially of leather, stuffed dolls, dolls' heads, jointed character babies, and dressed jointed dolls.

**Mexican Dolls.** Both wax and carved wooden dolls were made in Mexico, but they were used more for religious purposes than for play. Around 1913, *Isabel Belaunsaran* wound silk thread around wire frameworks to make dolls less than an inch tall. The dolls had hair, features, and clothes.

**1199A, B, & C.** China head with waterfall hairdo, painted features, on leather lady-shaped body. For paper label inside head, see Ill. **1200.** H. 14 inches. H. of shoulder head, 4½ inches. *Coleman Collection.*

**1200.** Paper label found inside the head of a doll handled by A. Métayer.

**1201 & 1202.** Porcelain marks on dolls of Gebrüder Metzler & Ortloff.

Made in Germany
Metzler
890
E 8 M

1201             1202

**Meyer, C. Wilhelm.** 1907–18. Leipzig, Saxony. Doll manufacturer. Obtained German and British patents for making a doll's body with hinged joints, which were covered with a tricot material. He stated that heretofore the joints on articulated bodies had been visible. The description of these tricot-covered bodies fits those sold by *Gesland* in Paris.

**Meyer, Carl.** 1900–21. Sonneberg, Thür. Manufactured and exported dressed dolls of various types.

1900: One of the group of Grand Prize winners at the Paris Exposition.

**Meyer, David, & Bros.** 1921–25. New York City. Handled doll-makers' supplies, including wood flour.

**Meyer, L.** 1924–25. London. Imported dolls.

**Meyer, Louis, & Ring, Carl.** 1892. Bohemia, Austria. Obtained a German patent for a doll's head with moving eyelids.

**Mi-Baby.** 1924–25. A baby of the *Madame Hendren* line made by *Averill Manufacturing Corp.*, which registered "Mi-Baby" as a trademark in U.S. for dolls; trademark was affixed by a tag.

**Miblue.** 1925. Celluloid girl baby made by *Rheinische Gummi & Celluloid Fabrik Co.*

**Mibs.** 1921–23. A "Phyllis May" doll, designed by *Hazel Drukker,* made by *Louis Amberg & Son.*

1921: Price 10¢ and up. These were probably the all-bisque variety.

**1203.** All-bisque doll, made by Louis Amberg & Son, has molded features, blonde hair, green shoes, and pink socks. Bisque is pink-tinted throughout. Rubber jointed at shoulders. For incised mark on upper back, see Ill. **1204.** H. 3 inches. *Coleman Collection.*

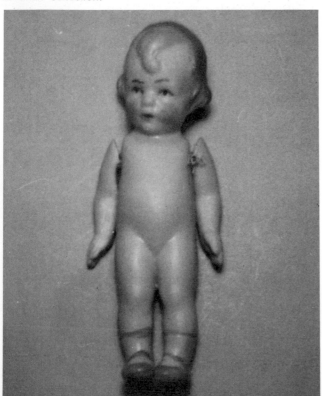

© LA&S 1921 Germany

**1204.** Mark on the back of an all-bisque version of "Mibs."

1922: Bore tag that read, "Please love me, I'm Mibs." Came with composition head and legs, molded hair, and painted eyes and features; cork-stuffed body; wore a lace-trimmed white lawn dress. Size 16 inches; price $1.79.

1923: Bore ribbon that read, "Please love me, I'm Mibs"; said "Mama"; prices 15¢ to $3.00.

**Michaelis, A., & Co.** 1895–1918. Rauenstein, Thür., and London. Manufactured and exported dolls.

1895: Made wax dolls.

1907–11: Advertised papier-mâché dolls.

1911: Registered *Michel* and the picture of a man smoking a pipe as a trademark in Germany for dolls.

**Michaelis, Hugo, & Co.** 1891. Rauenstein, Thür. Porcelain manufacturer.

**Michaelis, J. F. O.** 1892–95. Paris. Exporter; represented *G. Schmey* of Sonneberg and *William Dehler* of Neustadt. Advertised wax dolls, jointed bébés both dressed and undressed, and unbreakable dolls.

**Michaelis, M., & Co.** 1914–23. Berlin. Exported dolls.

**Michel.** 1911. Trademark registered in Germany by *A. Michaelis & Co.* for dolls.

**Michel.** 1916. Name of boy doll made by *Käthe Kruse;* wore a stocking cap; price $15.00.

**Michel, Eduard.** 1891. Ilmenau, Thür. Exported dolls' heads and *Täuflinge.*

**Michel, Hermann.** 1924–25. Berlin. Exported dolls.

**Michtom, Morris.** See **Ideal Novelty & Toy Co.**

**Mickey.** 1920. Hand-painted rag doll filled with sanitary floss; made by *Bandeau Sales Co.;* distributed by *Louis Wolf & Co.* Came in one size, 12 inches; price $1.50.

**Middie.** 1917. Sailor doll made by *Horsman.*

**Middy Boy and Middy Girl.** 1912. Wore blue and white sailor-type clothes; made by *Louis Amberg & Son.*

**Middy Girl, The.** 1913. Composition-head doll made by *Ideal Novelty & Toy Co.*

**Midolly.** 1919. Line of dolls made by *New Toy Co.*

**Mignon.** 1918–20. Used in two trademarks registered by *Felix Arena* for dolls and dolls' heads. The second trademark was registered with *Michel Lafond.*

**Mignonettes.** 1875–1925+. Name applied to small dolls of various types in France.

1875: Advertised as having *nankeen* bodies.

**1205.** "Mignon" mark used on dolls by Felix Arena.

1878: Advertised as being "in porcelain, in bisque, dressed and undressed." Porcelain mignonettes were called "*Bathers*" and were probably all-porcelain. Jullien appears to have been the only French doll manufacturer who made these at the time of the 1878 Paris Exposition, but they had been imported earlier and dressed in France.

1886: Jointed, dressed mignonettes with glass eyes were priced at 19¢ to 48¢.

**Mignonne.** See **La Mignonne.**

**Mignonnes.** 1878. Name of dolls displayed by *M. A. Merle* at Paris Exposition.

**Mihon.** 1861–63. Paris. Made kid dolls.

**Mike.** 1911. Name of doll manufactured by *Seligman & Braun.*

**Mike.** 1915–16. Made by *Horsman* and representing one of the *Gene Carr Kids* in the "Lady Bountiful" cartoon series published in the New York WORLD.

1916: Horsman copyrighted the doll, naming the artist as *Bernard Lipfert* and describing the doll as a "boy laughing with his eyes open."

**Mildred Mine (Mildred).** 1911–12. Copyrighted and made by *Louis Amberg & Son;* designed by *Jeno Juszko.* Doll represented a little girl of kindergarten age with a serious expression; her hair, straight at the sides, had a pompadour in the center, which was pulled back and tied at the top with a big hair bow. She came dressed in a lavender dress.

**Military Costume Dolls.** Through the years, dolls dressed in military costumes have been popular. Their colorful uniforms appeal to both boys and girls, men and women. The greatest number of military costume dolls were made during or soon after large-scale wars, but even in peacetimes many dolls were dressed as soldiers or sailors.

Dolls of various types and materials were dressed in military uniforms. Some all-bisque and some rubber dolls came with molded uniforms; luxury dolls came with elaborate military costumes that duplicated exactly—even to medals and insignia—the uniforms they portrayed. Sometimes collectors may fail to recognize the uniforms on their dolls, or even that they are dressed in uniforms,

because of the tremendous variety, which encompassed nearly all countries and periods as well as numerous ranks and services, and both full dress and fatigue outfits.

In the First Empire period, French catalogs showed boy dolls wearing clothes of the Revolutionary period. In the U.S., a china-headed doll with a painted mustache was dressed as a Union general of the Civil War, to represent General Audrey W. Arlington. (See Ill. 377.) Dolls in the 1860's and 1870's were often dressed as Vivandières (Ill. 404).

1877: *Ehrich Bros.* advertised walking dolls costumed as "an American General in full uniform—or a warlike Turk, with a Scimitar in his hand, going for the Russians." This doll was 9½ inches tall; price $3.00.

1890's: Some of the *Brownies* were costumed as soldiers and sailors. By the turn of the century, dolls were being dressed as *Rough Riders, Admiral Dewey,* and *Admiral Sampson.*

1906–7: *Butler Bros.* advertised dolls with bisque heads and arms, glass eyes, wigs, dressed in army or navy full dress or fatigue uniforms for Russian, American, German, or French soldiers. These costumes came in assorted colors and had braid, buttons, and the like. Size of these dolls was 6 inches; price 85¢ doz. wholesale. At this same time Butler Bros. also advertised dolls with bisque turning heads, glass eyes, and jointed limbs, dressed as Japanese soldiers in gray flannel uniforms with white leggings, gilt buttons, leather belts, nickeled buckles and side arms. These came in three styles of uniforms, size 8¾ inches, price $2.25 doz. wholesale.

1909: Many companies made dolls portraying Commander (Lt.) *Peary. Steiff* brought out dolls named *Private Murphy, Private Sharkey,* and *Sgt. Kelly.*

1912: Butler Bros. were still advertising dolls with bisque heads dressed as soldiers of the Boer War. They also advertised all-bisque dolls with molded sailor suits, size 4⅛ inches with jointed arms, price 42¢ doz. wholesale; size 5½ inches with jointed arms and legs, price 78¢ doz. wholesale. Butler Bros. advertised dolls with celluloid heads, painted hair and features, cloth bodies, dressed in bright-colored felt uniforms of various types. The dolls came with caps, patent leather belts, and cartridge belts; size 7 inches, price 89¢ doz. wholesale. *Ideal Novelty & Toy Co.* made *Captain Jinks* dolls.

1914–15: The outbreak of World War I brought a flood of military costume dolls. Even *Kewpies* wore military helmets and belts. There were *Tipperary Tommy* and *Tommy Atkins* dolls. *Sears, Roebuck & Co.* advertised a Soldier Boy in khaki uniform and hat; he had a composition head and arms, painted eyes and hair, cloth body; size 16½ inches, price 98¢.

1917–18: After the U.S. entered the war, nearly all dolls were dressed in military or patriotic costumes, including *Red Cross Nurses. Horsman* made *Rookie,* a soldier boy, and *Middie,* a sailor boy. Ideal Novelty & Toy Co. made *Liberty Boy* (see Ill. 1090). *Lelia Fellom* made a rag doll depicting a U.S. soldier on one side and a sailor on the other side. Butler Bros. advertised Soldier Boy dolls in khaki suits, size 13 inches, price $4.20 doz. wholesale, and size 17½ inches, $8.25 doz. wholesale. Sailor Boy dolls were dressed in navy blue lawn sailor suits with stitched bias trim and sailor hats to match; size 16½ inches, price $7.20 doz. wholesale.

Later, bisque-head dolls were still frequently dressed in military costumes. Several of them made in Italy wore the colorful uniforms of the Swiss Guard at the Vatican or the redcoat uniform of the British Guards.

**Milk Maid.** Ca. 1908. Wooden doll made by *Schoenhut;* mate to *Farmer.*

**Mille, G.,** See **Doleac, L., & Cie.**

**Miller, Frank L., Jr.** 1921. Chattanooga, Tenn. Was issued a U.S. design patent for a boy doll dressed in a sailor suit.

**Miller, Wesley.** 1874–75. New York City. Was granted U.S. patent for a hollow flexible rubber doll with a wire frame. He assigned his patent rights to *Joseph Banigan.*

**Miller Rubber Co.** 1923. Akron, Ohio. Assignee, by *Ralph Riley,* of a U.S. design patent for a clown doll.

**Millière, Maurice.** 1925. Paris. Creator of doll named *La Parisienne,* which was made by *Carlier, Fournelle & Gibon.*

**Millikin & Lawley.** 1881–82. London. Distributed dolls of various types, priced from 6¢ to $52.50. They advertised dolls like the one shown in Ill. 384 with porcelain head and limbs on cloth body. These came in eight sizes; price, dressed, 38¢ to $5.25.

**Milliners' Model Dolls.** Some collectors give this name to dolls with papier-mâché heads, kid bodies, and wooden limbs without articulation. Eleanor St. George appears to have been the first to use the term for this type of doll, but without historical basis. The following evidence suggests that there were milliners' dolls, but whether they resembled the type sometimes called "Milliners' Models" is doubtful.

1768: "A coxcomb, a fop, a dainty milk-sop
　　　Who essenced and dizzened from bottom to top,
　　　Looks just like a doll for a milliner's shop."
This verse was written before the "Milliners' Model" type of doll was made.

1840: Advertisement from THE LADIES GAZETTE OF FASHION, London, listed "Milliners' Dolls and band boxes."

1843: *Cochet & Verdey* made dolls in papier-mâché and kid bodies, as well as heads, for milliners and hairdressers.

1847: *Jean Pierre Soret* obtained a French patent for making papier-mâché heads for bébés and for modistes' (milliners') model dolls. The patent papers stated that French products of this sort had been inferior to similar German products.

**Million, Isabel.** 1911+. Knoxville, Tennessee. Made dried-apple dolls depicting Tennessee mountaineers. She also made other types of dried-apple dolls, including Indians, Japanese, Colonial dames, etc., but they were never as popular as the mountain folk—the colored mammy carrying a baby, grandpa, grandma, great-aunt Jemima, Uncle Toby, and a host of others. Each doll had a name, and was dressed by Isabel Million as well as being made by her out of apples, cotton, and wire. These dolls were sent all over the world.

**Million Dollar Doll.** 1919. Cherub-type doll made by *S. Kirsch & Co.*

**Mills, Helen Dorothy.** 1923–25. Eagle Rock, Calif. Was issued a U.S. design patent for a ball-jointed doll with wig; doll was dressed in a long ruffly costume with pantalets showing.

**Mills, Sarah.** 1901. Philadelphia, Pa. Made dolls.

**Mimi.** 1920. Cherub-type doll copyrighted by *Venetian Art & Novelty Co.;* designed by *Carlo Romanelli.*

**Mimi.** 1920. Doll copyrighted by *Jeanne I. Orsini.* A 9¼-inch copyright model had bobbed straight hair with bangs and a ribbon bow on the left side. The doll represented a baby girl with mouth shaped as if to say "Sh-h!" Doll's fingers extended out straight. A 5-inch all-bisque version with paper sticker on its stomach had jointed shoulders and hips, wig, and molded slippers and stockings.

**Mimi.** 1922–23. Trademark registered in Germany by *Borgfeldt* for dolls of various types, excluding rubber dolls.

**Mimosa.** 1923–24. Trademark registered in Germany by *Karl Manuzmann* for dolls.

**Miner, Edith M.** 1912. Colville, Wash. Was granted a U.S. design patent for a rag doll of a geometrical-patterned fabric.

**Minerva.** 1894–1925+. Trademark registered in U.S. by *A. Vischer & Co.* for metal dolls' heads; trademark registered in Germany by *Buschow & Beck* for dressed and undressed dolls, dolls' heads, and parts of dolls. Buschow & Beck advertised that they used this name for metal and celluloid heads and babies that they made. Alfred Vischer & Co.; *Borgfeldt, Louis Wolf & Co., Otto Graefe,* and many others distributed Minerva heads and dolls in the U.S. This type of head appears to have been patented by *Joseph Schön* in 1886/7.

1900: *Sears, Roebuck & Co.* advertised six sizes of molded heads; sizes 3 to 5 inches, price 19¢ to 55¢. Sizes 3⅞ to 6¼ inches, with open mouth, teeth, sleeping glass eyes, and sewed wigs, were priced up to $1.50. Another advertisement showed a Minerva head with the word "Patent" across the chest.

1901: Sears, Roebuck & Co. advertised that Minerva heads were made of sheet brass (other types of metal appear to have been used later). Sizes and prices varied only slightly from those of 1900.

**1206A & B.** "Minerva" metal head and an all-celluloid doll made by Buschow & Beck. Both dolls have painted eyes and are marked with a Minerva "helmet." The metal head has molded hair; some paint is chipped off the face. For chest mark see Ill. **1207.** H. of shoulder head, 3¼ inches. H. all-celluloid doll, 4 inches. *Head in Coleman Collection. Doll courtesy of Dorothy Annunziato.*

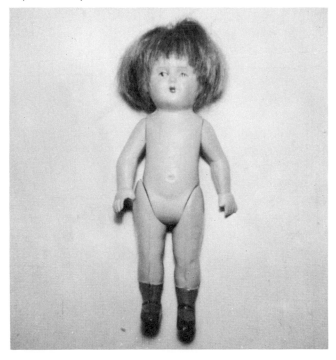

**1207.** Mark found on Minerva metal dolls' heads.

1904: Sears, Roebuck & Co. advertised Minerva heads on pink silesia bodies, hair-stuffed, as a new item; size 11½ inches, 25¢; 21 inches, 95¢.

1907: *Butler Bros.* was advertising Minerva heads of brass. These were coated with a "new process combination celluloid washable enamel," which was not advertised prior to 1906; sizes 2¾ to 6¾ inches; price 89¢ to $4.25 doz. wholesale.

1912: Minerva heads used on *Weeping Dolls* that cried real tears.

Ca. 1913: Advertised as of flexible sheet metal, which made the bust adjustable to any size doll's body. Came with washable flesh enamel color; painted hair and eyes. Size 2⅝ inches, 84¢ doz. wholesale; with glass eyes and painted hair in six sizes, 3 to 5¾ inches, price $1.20 to $4.10 doz. wholesale. With glued curly wig, open mouth, seven sizes, 3¾ to 6⅛ inches, $2.10 to $7.50 doz. wholesale.

1922: Sears, Roebuck & Co. advertised these dolls with painted hair and painted eyes, four sizes, 3¼ to 5⅛ inches, 19¢ to 49¢. With painted hair, fixed glass eyes, 6 and 6¼ inches, 79¢ and 98¢. With mohair wigs, sleeping eyes, open lips, and teeth, sizes 3¾ to 6½ inches, 98¢ to $1.95. Also *Wearwell Brand* and *Knockout Grade*, which had Minerva metal heads on silesia bodies with carved wood forearms and hands. The Knockout dolls were without wigs.

**Ming Toy.** 1919. Doll representing Fay Bainter in EAST IS WEST; made by the *Taiyo Trading Co.*

1920: A walking version of the same doll was made.

**Miniature Dolls.** See **Dolls' House Dolls.**

**Minnehaha.** 1911. Indian girl doll made by *Louis Amberg & Son;* came with composition head and cloth body.

**Minner, Herwin.** 1909–21. Gehren, Thür. Manufactured wool dolls.

**Miranda, J. R., & Co.** 1919. Oregon City, Ore. Made fourteen types of Indian dolls, including *Chief Buck, Squaw, Papoose,* and so on. They had painted features; were clothed in Indian blankets; sizes 7 to 14 inches, price $7.50 to $15.00 doz. wholesale.

**Mirette.** Name incised on bisque character head with open mouth, teeth, sleeping eyes; found on a marked *Jumeau* ball-jointed body. Size "12" is 29 inches tall; may not be original body.

**Misaki, Seijiro.** 1900. Japan. Won a silver medal for his doll display at the Paris Exposition.

**Mischievous Pippen.** 1910. Doll representing a child; copyrighted by *Horsman,* designed by *Helen Trowbridge.*

**Miss America.** 1917. Made by *Standard Doll Co.;* 16 inches tall.

**Miss Broadway.** 1912–13. Smiling little girl doll copyrighted by *Louis Amberg & Son,* designed by *Jeno Juszko.*

**1208.** Bisque head marked "Mirette," size "12" and "10731" just below the crown. Has sleeping eyes, open mouth with teeth, ball-jointed composition body with Jumeau mark. H. 29 inches. *Courtesy of Betty Lou Weicksel.*

Came with wavy hair falling over the left eye, three plaits around the back of the head, and showing combs in the coils; "bisc" finish composition head. Size 13 inches, price $1.00.

**Miss Campbell.** 1914. Chubby little girl doll made by *Horsman;* wore a party frock with a "Dutch" neck.

**Miss Charming.** See **EeGee Doll.**

**Miss Chicago.** 1921. Dolls made by *Katherine Rauser.*

**Miss Colonial.** 1918. Made by *Colonial Toy Manufacturing Co.*

**Miss Columbia.** 1920. Made by *Columbia Doll & Toy Co.*

**Miss Coquette.** 1912. Made by *EFFanBEE;* had eyes glancing to the side; price 50¢ to $3.50.

**Miss Dancing.** 1922. Trademark registered in France by *Michel Lilienthal.*

**Miss Dollie Daisie Dimple.** 1889. An English toy company provided her with a trunk full of clothes.

**Miss Firefly.** 1913. Doll represented a mischievous little girl; made by *Tip Top Toy Co.*

**Miss Frisco.** 1920. Doll copyrighted by *Grace A. Wilken;* had a dimple in her chin, heavy curved upper eyelashes and short lower eyelashes.

**Miss Happy.** 1919. Doll made by *Jessie McCutcheon Raleigh.* Came with moving eyes and was 22½ inches tall; price $7.50 to $10.00. A story was written about this doll.

**Miss Janet.** 1914. Girl doll made by *Horsman.*

**Miss Josephine.** 1919. One of the *Jay Bee* line made by *J. Bouton & Co.*

**Miss Liberty.** 1917. Celluloid doll made by *Richard G. Krueger.* It wore a silk dress; size 10 inches, price $18.00 doz. wholesale.

**Miss Mabel.** 1916. Baby doll in white dress trimmed with lace; distributed by *Montgomery Ward & Co.* Size 15 inches, price $1.25.

**Miss Malto Rice.** See **My Name Is Miss Malto Rice.**

**Miss Millionaire.** 1910–13. Trademark registered in Germany by *Butler Bros.* The mark was usually affixed to the chest of the doll with an elliptical sticker, on which appeared the words "Miss Millionaire" over a crown and crossed olive branches. A similar mark, but with the name *Superba* instead of "Miss Millionaire," was used by *Louis Wolf & Co.* "Miss Millionaire" was used for bisque-headed dolls with sleeping eyes, hair eyelashes, and usually hair eyebrows, side-part sewed curly wigs, kid bodies with rivet hip joints, and bisque hands; sizes 18½, 20½, 24½, and 27½ inches.

**Miss Mischief.** 1911. *Horsman Art Doll* advertised as "Can't make her eyes behave" (flirting-eyed type). Came with *Can't Break 'Em* head, cloth body, *Rembrandt*-style wig; blue and white dress.

**Miss Muffet.** 1909. *Art Fabric* doll produced by *Selchow & Righter;* came in sheets 20 by 27 inches for cutting out and stuffing.

**Miss Mysto.** 1910. Rag doll with celluloid face. Sizes 10 and 18 inches; price 25¢ and 50¢.

**Miss Najo.** 1917. Line of dolls made by *National Joint Limb Doll Co.* Came with sleeping eyes, human hair or mohair wig. There were seven sizes of girl dolls, 12 to 26 inches; four sizes of baby dolls, 12 to 19 inches; four sizes of standing baby dolls, up to 22 inches tall.

**Miss Rainshine.** 1922. Made by *Ideal Novelty & Toy Co.;* cried when it closed its eyes and called "Mama" when it opened its eyes.

**Miss Rosebud.** 1881–82. Trade name of doll distributed by *Millikin & Lawley;* came dressed in silk ball gown; price $10.50 to $55.00.

**Miss Rosy Cheeks.** See **Rosy.**

**Miss Sam.** 1917. One of the *Uncle Sam Kids* made by *Horsman,* who obtained a design patent for this doll. It was dressed in red, white, and blue with three stars on the yoke of the dress; skirt was made with stripes. Mate to *Master Sam.*

**Miss Simplicity.** 1912. Represented a Quaker girl; made by *Louis Amberg & Son.* Doll was dressed in blue or gray gown and bonnet. A Quaker boy was made to go with her.

**Miss Sunshine.** 1916–18. Made by *Jessie McCutcheon Raleigh,* distributed by *Montgomery Ward & Co.* and *Butler Bros.* Came with composition head and cork-stuffed body; size 13 inches.

**Miss Sunshine.** 1918. All-rubber girl with molded clothes made by *Faultless Rubber Co.;* came in red and tan.

**Miss Traveler.** 1916–18. Made by *Jessie McCutcheon Raleigh;* distributed by *Butler Bros.* Came with wig and corded white coat and hat; size 18½ inches, price $5.75.

**Miss U. S. A.** One of the *Yankee Doodle Kids* of *Madame Hendren,* made by *Averill Manufacturing Co.* Mate to *Uncle Sam Jr.* Price $8.50 doz. wholesale.

**Miss Viola.** 1910. Advertised by *Geo. H. Bowman Co.* A doll's body marked "Miss Viola" has been found with a head marked "G. & S." (probably *Gutmann & Schiffnie*). *Hamburger* registered *Viola* as a trademark.

**Missionary Ragbabies.** Ca. 1885–1910. Rag dolls made by *Mrs. Thomas K. Beecher* out of old silk jersey underwear.

**Misska.** 1920. Rag doll made by the *Art Toy Manufacturing Co.*

**Mistah Sunshine.** 1923–24. Trademark registered by *Schoen & Yondorf* Co. in U.S.; the doll came in bright colored felt.

**Mistinguette.** 1924–25. Cloth doll's head made by *Bernard Ravca.*

**Mistress Bubbles.** 1922. Designed by *Mme. Georgene Averill,* manufactured and distributed by *Paul Averill, Inc.* Advertisements claimed that the doll walked, talked, and danced. Came with blonde or tosca ringlet wig; wore cotton crepe dress with appliquéd figures, bloomers, and bonnet to match; 25½ and 28 inches tall. Mate to *Master Bubbles.*

**Mistress Mary.** 1913. Doll with black hair made by *Tip Top Toy Co.,* distributed by *Borgfeldt.*

**Mit Dem Goldreif (With the Golden Bloom).** 1923. Trademark registered in Germany by *Ilse Müller* for *Art Dolls* of fabric.

**Mitchell, Edgar.** 1917. Philadelphia, Pa. Made dolls.

**Mitred Box Co.** 1911–17. New York City, and in 1917, Long Island City; manufactured dolls that were distributed by *McClurg & Keen.*

1911–12: Registered *Yankee* as a trademark in U.S.

1912: Advertised bent-limb baby doll, dressed in kimono, 12 inches tall; dressed boy doll 13 inches tall; fully jointed dolls, sizes 18, 20, and 22 inches.

**Mittlestaedt (Mittelstaedt), E., Inc.** 1921–22. New York City. Imported dolls' hair.

**Mitzi.** 1913. Dutch girl made by *Elektra Toy & Novelty Co.;* mate to *Fritzi.*

**Mitzi.** 1922. Trademark registered in U.S. by *Rees Davis Toy Co.;* stamped on dolls.

**Mitzi.** 1924. *Celebrity Doll* originated by *Margaret Valc,* designed and made by *Jane Gray.* The doll represented Mitzi as Minnie in Henry W. Savage's LOLLIPOP. It had a hand-painted face and bore a tag with a facsimile autograph of Mitzi.

**Miyako Boeki Goshi Kaisha.** 1921–25. Kyoto, Japan. Manufactured dolls.

**Mlle. Babette.** 1919–20. Made by *Buddie Toy & Novelty Co.* and *Katherine A. Rauser.* Had closing eyes, sewed wig, and was fully jointed.

1919: Sizes 18 to 24 inches.

1920: Sizes 20, 24, and 26 inches.

**Mlle. Mah Jong.** 1924. Copyrighted by *Clara P. Ongawa.* The name is "Mlle." on the copyright card but on the picture of the model sent in for copyright, it is "Mme."

**Mme.** See **Madame;** also **Mlle.**

**MOA.** See **Arnold, Max Oscar.**

**Mobi.** 1921. Trademark registered in Germany by *Hermann Schiemer.*

**Mochidzuki, M. Nishinotoin Uonotana.** 1920–21. Kyoto, Japan. Manufactured dolls.

**Model.** 1900–1907. Trade name of a line of patent washable dolls made in Europe for *Butler Bros.* Came with painted teeth, glass eyes, *Rembrandt* hair; sizes 17, 19½, 24, 26, 29, 33, and 35 inches; price $2.00 to $8.75 doz. wholesale.

**Model Doll Co.** 1920. Brooklyn, N.Y. Made dolls, including a 16-inch girl doll.

**Modèle Bébé.** See **Bébé Modèle.**

**Models.** Numbers marked on dolls often refer to the model. PLAYTHINGS, in 1904, stated that the design room of a Sonneberg factory contained from 12,000 to 18,000 designs.

**Models (Leicester) Ltd.** 1919. Loughborough, Leicester. Doll manufacturers. Registered *Bringlee Doll* as a trademark in Britain for unbreakable dolls.

**Modern Toy Co.** 1914–25+. Brooklyn, N.Y. Made unbreakable character dolls.

1914: Advertised seventy-five subjects—boys, girls, and babies.

1915: Made *College Boy, Petite Polly,* and *Co-Ed.*

1916: Advertised *Babbitt at Your Service, Cleanser Boy;* size 15 inches; price $1.00.

1923: Used Ronson voices in their dolls; price $1.00.

1924–25: Produced *Buttercup.*

**Modèrne Bébé.** See **Bébé Modèrne.**

**Modestes.** 1919. Trademark registered in France by

*Georges de Roussy de Sales* for movable eyes for dolls.

**Moehling, M. J.** 1870–1925+, Aich near Karlsbad, Bohemia; ca. 1900–1925, successor was A. C. J. Anger. Porcelain factory that used the initials "A & M." (See Austrian doll in Ill. 56, which bears the "A & M" mark.)

**Mohawk Novelty Co.** 1923. New York City. Imported dolls.

**Mohler, Vernie H.** 1921. Indianapolis, Ind. Was issued a U.S. design patent for a doll's head.

**Moko.** 1910–25+. Registered in Germany and Britain by *Kohnstam & Co.*, as part of a trademark.

**Molds.** For porcelain dolls' heads, molds were of two types, the master mold and the pouring mold. The master mold design often belonged to large companies, such as *Borgfeldt*, rather than to the porcelain factory. The pouring mold was made from the master mold. The first heads made in a pouring mold were usually more sharply delineated than later ones, and by the time about fifty heads had been made from a pouring mold it had to be discarded and another one made from the master. Molds can have two or more parts, depending on design. Metal molds were used for making dolls' heads in many types of materials. A collapsible mold was used in making some of the early American composition heads.

Certain companies specialized in just the production of molds. Among these were Simar, later Simar & Flantin, who made molds in Paris from 1829 to 1855. In the U.S. there were S. G. Ecker Co. (1915–25); Anton Kunst (1920–25); Manhattan Modeling & Chasing Co. (1921); J. E. Steinmeier (1903–23), who claimed to have originated hot press baking dies and that he was the largest maker of doll dies in the U.S.; Louis Wittenberg (1916–21), who made hot or cold press dies and molds; Harry Erdos & Co. (1923–25), who made dies, molds, and presses; and Alex Rein & Co. (1925), who made molds and dies.

**Molet, Er.** 1885. Paris. Manufactured dolls.

**Möller, August, & Sohn.** 1923–25. Georgenthal, Thür. Manufactured and exported dolls and dolls' heads. Specialized in dolls' and baby dolls' heads of their own design; "tarnished" (not shiny) celluloid socket and shoulder heads and celluloid baby dolls; also handled wigs of mohair and real hair as well as doll parts for supplying doll hospitals.

**Möller, F. H., & Co.** 1918. Möhrenbach, Thür. Made dolls and *Täuflinge;* specialized in wool and plush dolls.

**Möller, Georg.** 1911–25+. Sonneberg, Thür. Specialized in manufacturing felt and velvet dolls.

**Möller, Prof. A.** 1893–1910. Director of the Sonneberg Industrial School, which taught the design and manufacturing of dolls. Students learned how to design dolls from examples of well-known works of art. Prof. Möller was in charge of the Sonneberg doll exhibits at the Chicago, Paris, St. Louis, and Brussels International ex-

positions. These exhibits won top honors at most, if not all, these expositions.

**Möller, R.** 1900. Sonneberg, Thür. One of the group of Grand Prize winners for dolls at the Paris Exposition.

**Molloy, David J., Co.** 1915. U.S. Manufactured dolls.

**Molly-O.** 1916. Doll with composition head and a white bow of ribbon attached to the molded hair. Made by *Horsman*, distributed by *Montgomery Ward & Co.;* size 15½ inches, price $1.45.

**Mölter, Heinrich.** 1914–18. Sonneberg, Thür. Manufactured dolls.

**Momijiya Ning Yo-Ten Ltd.** 1923–25 Fukuoka, Japan. Exported dolls.

**Momo.** 1918. Trademark registered in France by *Mme. Poulbot.*

**Mon Bébé.** 1900. Trade name for a *bébé incassable* (unbreakable) made by *Myer & Charnault.*

**Mon Trésor.** 1914. Trademark registered in France by *Henri Rostal* for dolls and bébés.

**Mona Lisa.** 1914. Trademark registered in France by *Gutmann & Schiffnie.*

**Moncaster, Matthew, & Hollingshead, George.** 1919. England. Secured a French patent for the movement of dolls' eyes.

**Monroe, Ansil W.** 1875. N.J. Was granted a U.S. patent for a hard rubber doll with a round neck that was attached to the torso with elastic cord. The hard rubber head was to have an angora wig.

**Montanari, Mme. Augusta.** 1851–64, London; 1855–84, Richard Montanari, her son; she died in 1864.

1851: Mme. Montanari won a prize medal for wax dolls at the London Exhibition; the report of the jury read: "Display of this Exhibitor is the most remarkable and beautiful collection of toys in the Great Exhibition. It is a series of dolls representing all ages, from infancy to womanhood, arranged in several family groups . . . The dolls have hair, eyelashes, and eyelids separately inserted in wax . . . a variety of expressions are given to the figures in regard to the ages and stations which they are intended to represent. The dolls are adapted for children of the wealthy rather than general sale, undressed dolls sell from 10 shillings to 105 shillings [about $2.50 to $26.00], dressed dolls are much more expensive. In a small case adjoining the wax dolls are displayed several rag dolls which are very remarkable productions, considering the material of which they are made. They consist entirely of textile fabrics, and the dolls are well adapted for the nursery, are reasonable in price, varying from 6 shillings 6 pence to 30 shillings [about $1.60 to $7.50] per doll including dresses." The official catalog, besides listing Augusta Montanari, also listed Napoleon Montanari at the same address.

1855: At the Paris Exposition, Mme. Montanari showed dressed wax dolls and claimed that the wax would resist

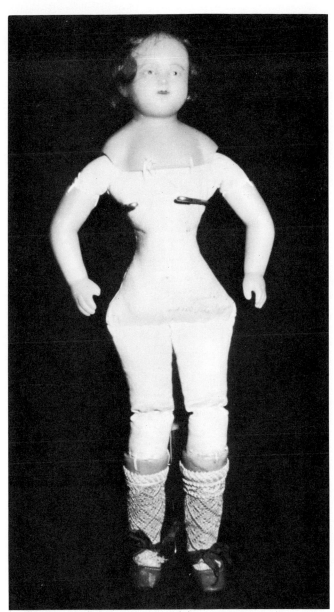

**1209.** Montanari poured wax doll, with wax head, arms, and legs; hair is inserted in small groups; glass eyes. Body marked on lower torso as shown in Ill. **1210.** *Photograph by Winnie Langley.*

*Montanari Manufacturer. 251 Regent St. and 180 Soho Bazaar*

**1210**

*Montanari 180 Soho Bazaar London*

**1211**

*Montanari*

**1212**

**1210–1212.** Marks on Montanari dolls.

the temperature of hot countries and being washed with alkaline water. Also at this exposition, Richard Montanari showed dressed dolls of linen.

1862: Only Augusta Montanari displayed dolls at the London Exhibition, and the catalog lists for her "model wax dolls with all modern improvements, model rag dolls."

1878: At the Paris Exposition, Richard Montanari of London appears to have been the only doll maker from England, but C. Montanari of Paris also exhibited dolls and Indian figures.

**Montgomery Ward & Co.** 1887–1925+. Chicago, Ill. Distributors. Sold *Goldsmith's* patent Corset Bodies; handled dolls made by *Kestner, Buschow & Beck, Louis Amberg & Son, Horsman, Schoenhut,* and others.

**Montréer.** See **Le Montréer.**

**Montreuil Bébé.** 1917. Trademark registered in France by *Edmond Hieulle.*

**Montreuil-sous-Bois.** Place near Paris where many potteries that made dolls were located. Bisque dolls' heads marked "Montreuil Sous Bois, France, D. L." have been reported. (See **Hieulle;** also Ill. 1730.)

**Moore & Gibson Corp.** 1917. U.S. Advertised that they manufactured *Bedtime* dolls, *Carriage Dolls, Floating Dolls, Balsam Dolls,* and *Mailing Dolls;* made of leather, imitation leather, fabrics, etc.; price 15¢ to $3.00.

**Moo-V-Doll Manufacturing Co.** 1919–20. Bridgeport, Conn. Assignee of a U.S. doll patent by Michael John Duff, also of Bridgeport. The patent is for a multi-face doll with a head of a shell of composition on which there are five faces with only five eyes, since each eye appears with two adjacent faces. The faces are turned by hand and topped with a wig. The head has a raised mark: "M.V.D. Co." On the cloth body is the mark: "Patent May 18, 1920."

**Moppietopp.** 1914. Trademark registered in U.S. by *David Wolf.*

**Moraim, Stesfano.** See **Marceline.**

**Moran Doll Manufacturing Co.** 1919–21. San Francisco and Los Angeles, Calif., and Kansas City, Mo. Successor Western Doll Co. of Los Angeles. Made dolls that were copyrighted by Mrs. May B. Moran.

1919: May Moran copyrighted *Blynke,* a cherub-type doll designed by A. Brymcardi and *Julius Benvenuti.*

1920: May Moran copyrighted Blinkie Doll with one eye almost closed, and *Bobette,* a cherub-type doll with open mouth and teeth, eyes glancing to the side, and real hair. Julius Benvenuti secured a U.S. design patent for a winking cherub type. The Western Doll Co. advertised Blynkie Doll, *Cry Blynkie,* and *Wee Wee;* these were composition dolls and came dressed and undressed. The company was also known as Jones-Moran Doll Manufacturing Co. at one time.

1921: May Moran registered in the U.S. "Wee Wee" as

a trademark for dolls; name was molded on base of doll.

**Morgenroth, A.** 1909–18. Hönbach, Thür. Made dolls' bodies.

**Morgenroth, Otto, Firm.** 1905–20. Sonneberg, Thür. Doll maker and exporter; registered in Germany *American Queen* as a trademark.

**Morimura Bros.** 1915–22. New York City. Name of a large Japanese import house. The members of the firm were subjects of the Emperor of Japan. During World War I and shortly thereafter, they also engaged in the production and distribution of dolls. About the beginning of 1922, their Miscellaneous Import Department, which handled the dolls, was taken over by *Langfelder, Homma & Hayward Inc.* In April, 1916, Morimura Bros. registered as their trademark *Queue San Baby,* which they had used since October, 1915. They stated that it was used by the firm in commerce among the several states of the United States. In November, 1915, *Hikozo Araki* of Brooklyn, New York, had applied for a design patent for a doll that portrayed Queue San Baby. The application stated that the patent was to be assigned to Morimura Bros. On February 29, 1916, the patent was granted for three and a half years. Thus, this doll was designed by a United States resident, produced by a New York firm, and distributed only in the United States. However, the dolls were actually made in Japan, as shown by two articles in PLAYTHINGS: (1) October, 1917: "At the outbreak of the European War there was consternation in the ranks of the dealers who had been supplying Miss Young America with her dolls, as Germany had been producing most of the dolls used . . . then came the surprise when Japan began the manufacture of dolls. A leading Japanese importing house promptly took the matter up. Experts were engaged, who knew just what was wanted, and were sent to Japan with instructions to build a factory for the manufacture of dolls.

"This was no easy matter as many natural obstacles had to be overcome. One of the most difficult of these was the modeling so as to catch the true European expression. In spite of the fact that the original model was before him, the Japanese artisan, true to the natural instinct of his race, persisted in getting a little of the Asiatic expression in the features. After infinite patience, a characteristic trait in the Japanese, a perfect reproduction was secured.

"Then the glass eyes had to be made. Again perseverance triumphed. The proper elastic to connect the joints had to be secured; then the proper material to make the body so that it would be durable.

"In spite of all the care that was taken, the first product did not turn out well, and heavy losses were entailed by those backing the enterprise. All the wiseacres joined in the chorus 'We told you so,' 'It can't be done,' etc. The Japanese, however, refused to be discouraged. They went at the problem with renewed vigor. Profiting by past experiences, the first mistakes were eliminated and success rewarded their persistent efforts. At last a doll was produced which has attracted considerable attention."

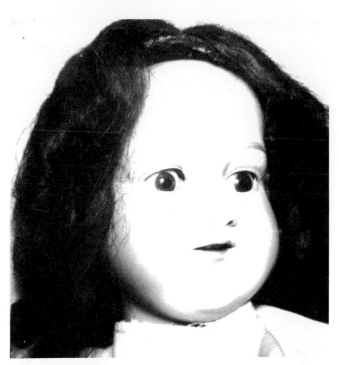

**1213.** Bisque head, made in Japan for Morimura Bros. during World War I period, has open mouth with teeth. Mark: Ill. **1215** plus numbers "1" and "3." *Coleman Collection.*

(2) September, 1919: "Since European goods were shut out, no other country in the world had been able to produce a bisque head doll until Morimura Bros. after long and hard effort presented their wonderful line three years ago [1916]. Since the advent of this line, the entire factory output has been sold usually the year previous to delivery date." (The success of these American-Japanese dolls is verified by a notice that Morimura Bros. would be unable to accept orders for their 1917 line of dolls after February 15, 1917.)

In July, 1917, Frederick Langfelder of New York City, a United States citizen, applied for a United States design patent for a doll with eyes looking to the side and dressed in a bathing suit. The Morimura Bros. firm was the assignee and the patent was granted in October, 1917, for a period of seven years.

Morimura Bros. also handled dolls made completely in America. In 1918 they took the entire output of the *Bester Doll Manufacturing Co.* of Bloomfield, N.J. These "Bester Dolls" were fully ball-jointed dolls made in sizes 16, 18, 20, 22, 24, and 26 inches. They were made with and without eyelashes and were dressed by *Katherine Rauser.*

Immediately after the war, in December, 1918, PLAYTHINGS carried a full-page advertisement for Morimura Bros. that stated: "Japanese Dolls and Toys on Import.//The Famous 'Baby Ella' Character Dolls// Bisque Head French Glass Moving Eyes with or without eyelashes. With and without wigs (Mohair and Natural Hair), 16 to 57 centimeters. [6½ to 23 inches] // *JOINTED DOLLS,* 23 to 54 centimeters [9 to 21½ inches]

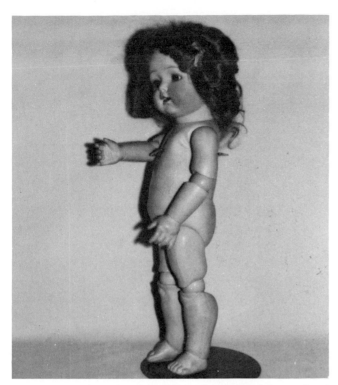

**1214A & B.** Doll produced by Morimura Bros. with bisque head made in Japan, blue sleeping eyes, open mouth with two upper teeth, composition toddler-type body. Mark on head: Ill. **1215.** H. 19 inches. *Courtesy of Jessica Norman.*

**1215 & 1216.** Marks used by Morimura Bros. on dolls.

1215             1216

with or without Eyelashes. Natural Hair Wigs. //'KIDO-LYN' Kid body Dolls. Hip Jointed, Jointed Arms. Hip and Knee Jointed. //BISQUE BABIES of all descriptions. //FULL LINE OF HEADS FOR JOINTED DOLLS. With or without Wigs. With or without Eyelashes.'' It appears that Morimura had been able to obtain some glass eyes from France for their bisque heads. They advertised ''French'' glass eyes for several years. The ''Kidolyn'' body dolls were made with the *Ne Plus Ultra* type of pin joint at the hips. The bisque babies were made with bent limbs and with wigs or so-called *bald heads*.

In PLAYTHINGS, September, 1919, Morimura Bros. advertised: '' 'Baby Ella,' 'Baby Rose,' 'My Darling,' 'First Prize Baby' //Bisque Dolls, Full Jointed, Kidaline Body, Baby Dolls. // Long curled wigs of natural hair, mohair wigs. //Dolls with bald heads. //Standing Character Dolls with Buster Brown and Sailor Suits. //China Limb Dolls, repeating our 1919 line. //Celluloid Dolls, Straight limb and celluloid character babies in all sizes. //Our 'Dolly Doll' in the bathing suit.'' These same dolls were advertised in 1920, plus *My Sweetheart, Baby O'Mine,* and *Nankeen* Dolls, which were probably the China Limb Dolls with china heads and china limbs on nankeen (cotton) bodies. Morimura Bros. referred to their dolls as ''M.B.'' dolls in 1921, which suggests that these initials were widely recognized by the trade then. They continued to advertise bisque, celluloid, and china limb dolls as well as Kidaline body dolls in 1921.

German dolls had returned to the American market in quantity by 1922, and before January, 1922, Morimura Bros.' Miscellaneous Import Department, which handled their dolls, was taken over by Langfelder, Homma & Hayward Inc. of New York City, who handled both Japanese and German dolls. Morimura Bros. continued as a Japanese Import House, but no record has been found of their handling dolls after 1922.

The Morimura all-bisque dolls labeled *Baby Darling* on stickers on the stomach may have been the My Darling dolls advertised in 1919 and 1920. ''My Darling'' was a trademark of Kämmer & Reinhardt, a circumstance that may have been responsible for the alteration in name.

**Morin, L.** 1921. Paris. Specialized in making articulated *poupards*.

**Moritz.** 1907+. Trade name for wooden doll made by *Schoenhut* for their circus; size 7½ inches. Represents the earlier comic character of this name. (See **Max.**)

**Moroder, Gebrüder (Bros.).** 1873–96. St. Ulrich, Grödner Tal. Distributed wooden dolls. Displayed wooden dolls at the 1873 Vienna and 1878 Paris Expositions.

**Morrell, Charles.** 1878–1925+. London. At the same address Mrs. Jane Arundel Morrell operated a doll warehouse.

1878: Advertised dressed and undressed dolls.

1879–84: Charles Morrell imported, exported, and distributed dolls, among them *Pierotti* wax dolls.

1894: Sold imports from France, Germany, and Austria; exported dolls to all parts of the world.

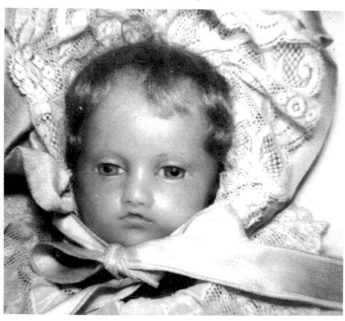

**1217A & B.** Wax-headed infant doll distributed by Morrell, possibly made by Pierotti. The doll has poured wax lower limbs as well as head; glass eyes, inserted hair and eyebrows; original clothes. Mark on torso, "H. W. Morrell // Dolls, Toys, & Games // 50 Burlington Arcade London." H. 20 inches. *Courtesy of the Newark Museum, Newark, N.J.*

**1218 & 1219.** Marks found on dolls of Charles Morrell.

1903: Advertised French and German dolls, including dressed dolls.

H. W. Morrell also handled wax dolls in the Burlington Arcade.

**Morrell, Frank, & Morrell, Richard.** 1922. London. Distributed dolls.

**Morrell, Horace W.** 1870. London. On the chest of one of his dolls with wax head and limbs, a blue elliptical sticker has been found that reads: "FROM // H. W. MORRELL'S // 50 // BURLINGTON ARCADE // LONDON // DRESSED DOLLS // IN EVERY VARIETY FROM 1/- TO 40/-." (25¢ to $10.00.)

**Morrison, Enoch Rice.** 1862+. New York City. Obtained a U.S. patent for a walking doll that he named *Autoperipatetikos*. The heads for these dolls have been found in various materials such as china, rag, and papier-mâché. *D. S. Cohen* and *Joseph Lyon & Co.*, both of New York City, and *Martin & Runyon* of London made these dolls in accordance with this patent.

**Morse, Ozias.** See **Checkeni.**

**Mortyn, James Leicester.** 1860–79. London. Made dolls.

**Moss.** 1860–85. Paris. Made dressed dolls of various kinds.

**Moss Novelty Manufacturing Co.** Made a doll of a secret formula, and named it *Maid of Mystery.*

**Most, G. H.** 1852–73. Paris. Was allegedly successor of Mlle. *Benoist,* but the name "Benoist" continued to appear in directories. Most made and distributed dolls.

1852: Advertised dolls' heads made in Germany.

1860: Was issued a French patent for dolls.

1867–73: Advertised dolls' heads of German composition, porcelain dolls' heads and arms, *nankeen* body dolls, talking bébés, and the latest novelties for dolls.

**Mother Goose.** 1916–17. Trademark registered in U.S. by

Samuel Gabriel & Co. It was on the *Hug-Me-Tight* dolls designed by *Grace Drayton* and advertised by *Bently-Franklin Co.* and *Colonial Toy Manufacturing Co.* They included Little Bo-Peep, Mary and Her Lamb, Curly Locks, and so on. Came in sizes 10½ to 11 inches; price 50¢.

**Mother Hubbard.** 1901. Dressed rag doll distributed by *Montgomery Ward & Co.*

**Mothercraft.** 1917–25. Trademark registered in U.S. by *May Bliss Dickinson;* used for dolls and dolls' clothing.

**Mothereau.** 1880–96. Paris. Made *Bébé Mothereau* and used the trademark "B.M."

1880: Alexandre Célestin E. Mothereau, Aîné (Sr.), was granted a French patent for improvements in a bébé's body so that it would remain in any position in which it was placed. Patent papers show a ball-jointed body.

1882: Mothereau and Bayeaux (Bayeux) obtained a French patent for stringing a jointed bébé. A. Bayeux (Bayeaux) and F. Mothereau were listed as doll makers in Paris.

1884: Advertised that he made jointed bébés on the Mothereau system, patented in France and abroad.

1892–95: Advertised the patented *Bébé Mothereau* as "The true Parisien, winner of a silver medal and of a bronze medal." (See Ill. 154.)

**Mothers' Congress Doll Co.** 1900–1911. Philadelphia, Pa. Made rag dolls in accordance with the U.S. patent of 1900 obtained by Madge Lansing Mead. The pattern for these dolls contained seven pieces, to be put together to produce rounded contours; the head was made from a single piece. The patent date, November 6, 1900, and the name *Baby Stuart* has been found on some of these dolls.

**Mother's Darling.** 1918. Made by *Jessie McCutcheon Raleigh,* distributed by *Butler Bros.* Came with painted hair and bent limbs; wore a long dress of lawn and a bonnet. Sizes 12½ and 18 inches; prices $4.00 and $5.25.

**Mothers Darling.** 1910. Trademark registered in Britain and Germany by *M. Kohnstam & Co.;* name is found on a picture of a nursing bottle for a doll.

**Motor Follies.** 1925. Trademark registered in U.S. by *Frank M. Phelps,* for dolls.

**Motschmann, Carl.** 1918–25+. Neustadt near Coburg, Thür. Made jointed dolls and babies.

**Motschmann, Ch.** 1855–1860's. Sonneberg, Thür. The Japanese bébés shown at the 1855 Paris Exposition by *Fr. Greffier* seem to have inspired Motschmann, who probably was the Sonneberg manufacturer who brought home and improved the oriental doll (according to PLAYTHINGS, February, 1908). Jo Elizabeth Gerken discovered a doll with head of wax over papier-mâché, on a cloth torso with composition pelvis, in the Landesmuseum of Brunswick, and on the cloth part of its leg was an oval stamp with the words "Patent 29 April //

**1220.** Mothers' Congress rag doll designed by Madge Lansing Mead and patented in 1900. Has blonde hair with blue ribbon in the hair. Mark: Ill. **1221.** *Courtesy of Winnie Langley; photograph by Winnie Langley.*

**1221.** Mark on rag doll made by Mothers' Congress Doll Co.

1857 // Ch. Motschmann // Sonneberg." This type of doll was made in Japan as well as in Germany.

**Motschmann & Hüffner, P.** 1879–97. Sonneberg, Thür. Made dolls.

1879: Commended for their doll display at the Sydney Exhibition.

1886: They obtained a French patent for doll improvements.

1897: Advertised *Täuflinge* and dressed dolls.

## MOTSCHMANN-TYPE DOLLS

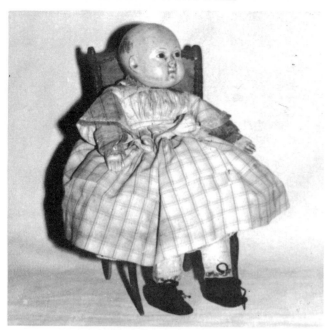

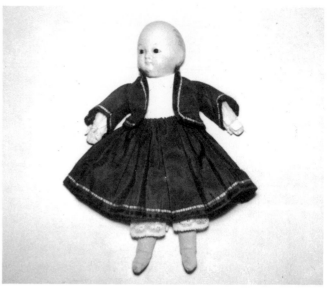

**1223.** Motschmann-type composition and twill cloth doll has wavy vertical wisps of hair painted at the sides, horizontal ones at back of the head. Contemporary clothing. H. 8 inches. *Courtesy of Alberta Darby.*

**1222A & B.** Papier-mâché head has hair indicated by painted vertical corkscrew curls; glass eyes. Limbs are wood and twill cloth; composition hands, feet, and pelvic section; floating joints. Contemporary clothing. H. 15 inches. *Courtesy of Helen Jo Payne.*

A     1224     B

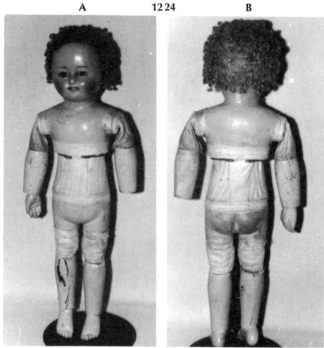

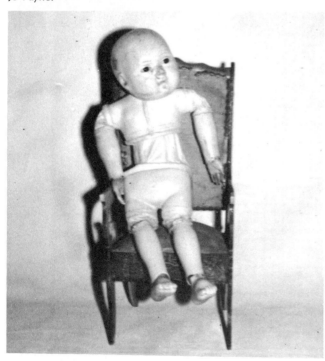

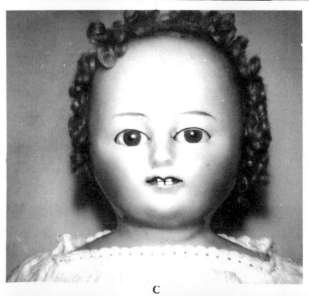

**1224A, B, & C.** Waxed-over-composition head with sleeping blue glass eyes, open mouth with two upper and two lower bamboo teeth. The wax does not extend over the shoulders and chest. Composition pelvic area, arms, and legs with floating joints. H. 19 inches. *Coleman Collection.*

C

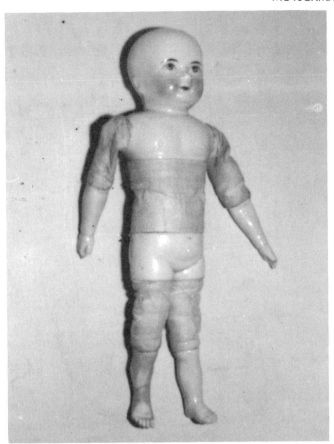

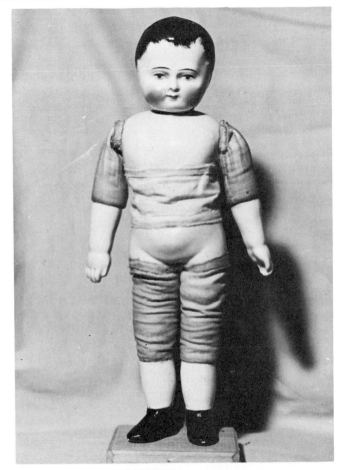

**1225A & B.** China and cloth doll of the Motschmann type, representing a baby doll. Bald china head; painted eyes; molded features, including breasts. H. 10½ inches. H. of shoulder head, 3¾ inches. *Courtesy of the International Doll Library Foundation.*

1226

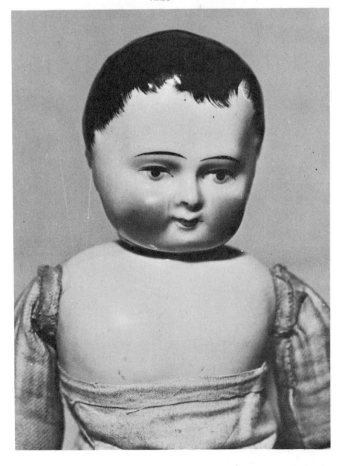

**1226A & B.** Doll with china and cloth parts similar to the doll patented by Motschmann in 1857. Has swivel neck, painted hair with brush marks, painted shoes. H. 12 inches. *Courtesy of Laura Treskow.*

MOTSCHMANN-TYPE DOLLS

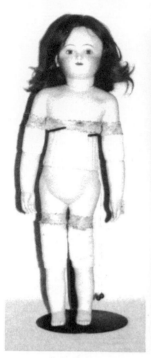

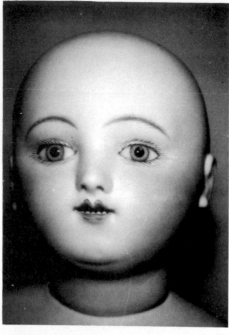

**1227A & B.** Bisque and cotton twill doll of the Motschmann type. Has leather bands over the joinings of the various parts of the body; cork pate, glass eyes, open mouth with many upper and lower teeth; pull-strings for the crying mechanism, which is marked "Steiner." H. 19 inches. *Courtesy of Mary Roberson.*

**1228.** All-wood doll except for the cotton twill in the waist area to cover the squeak box, and on upper legs for flexibility. Glass eyes, wisps of painted hair, swivel neck; ball joints at shoulders and elbows. H. 13¼ inches. *Coleman Collection.*

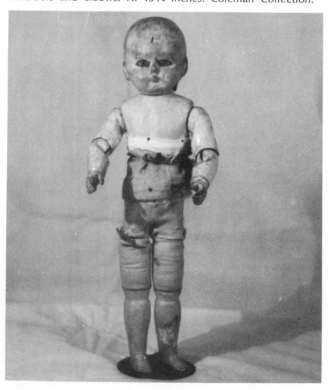

The prices given for dolls are those for which the dolls were originally offered for sale. They are *not* today's prices.

**1229.** Mark found on bodies of dolls made under patent of Ch. Motschmann.

**Moulage, J. & B.** 1925. Paris. Produced bébés and *poupards.*

**Mourgues, P.** 1909. Berlin. Manufactured dolls.

**Mousley, Geo. E.** 1923. Philadelphia, Pa. Manufactured G. E. M. brand dolls.

**Mouths.** Around the middle of the 19th century, a few composition and a few wax-over-papier-mâché doll heads were made with mouths that had an opening. Later, ceramic dolls with open mouths were made, but most of the early china and bisque dolls have closed mouths. Often the parted lips have no opening, but there is a white or pink area showing between them. This type of mouth is usually referred to as an open-closed mouth. Some of the early china heads as well as bisque heads have this type of mouth. Later bisque heads with open-closed mouths had the tongue and teeth molded, and though the mouth had the appearance of being open, there was no hole in it.

Closed mouths—with the lips together—are often found on French dolls, but not always. Many German dolls, especially early ones, also have closed mouths. A dark red lip line sometimes indicates where the lips meet. The top and bottom of the lips are also sometimes outlined with darker red lines. These darker lines are often found on heads having considerable detail in decoration. This primarily applies to bisque heads.

Many dolls were made with an opening into the head, parted lips, and teeth, at the end of the 19th and in the 20th centuries. These open mouths increased the expense of manufacture, but their popularity made them so prevalent that closed-mouth dolls, from 1890 on, are harder for collectors to find today and therefore bring higher prices than open-mouth dolls. This is not true for all-bisque and very small dolls, which usually have closed mouths, nor for non-bisque dolls.

**Moving Lips.** Ca. 1870–1925+. Dolls with moving mouth, especially the lower jaw, have been made and patented over a long period. Among the patents for these dolls were: 1890, *Heinrich Graeser;* 1902, *Georg Liebermann;* 1924, *James S. Graham.* In 1912 a "Moving Mouth Doll" with bisque head was advertised. When it was shaken to and fro, the tongue and the teeth of the lower jaw would move. The doll wore a pink costume; price $1.00.

**Möwes, J. E., Jr.** 1844. Berlin. Displayed wax dolls in costumes at the Berlin Exhibition.

**Mr. Bailey, The Boss.** Ca. 1925. All-bisque doll representing the character of this name in the "Smitty" cartoons. Came with molded clothes, swivel head; size 3⅜ inches.

**Mr. Common People.** 1911. Doll made by *Schoenhut;* based on the cartoons by Herbert Johnson in THE NORTH AMERICAN.

**Mr. Twee Deedle.** See **Twee Deedle.**

**Mrs. (Auntie) Blossom.** 1924–25+. Design patent for the doll was issued to *Frank O. King,* who also registered the name as a trademark in the U.S. for dolls. The name was to be a printed impression on the doll. The dolls were made by the *Live Long Toy Co.;* the idea of putting Frank King's figures into doll form was conceived and executed by *Mrs. William A. Benoliel.* Stuffed oil-cloth dolls marked "—King—//MRS. BLOSSOM//PAT. APPLIED FOR" represent Mrs. Blossom in coat, hat, and gloves; size 17 inches.

**Muffles.** 1910. Trademark registered in Germany by the *Max Fr. Schelhorn* firm for dolls.

**Mugsey.** 1911. A newsboy character doll made by *A. Steinhardt & Bro.*

**Muguette.** 1919. Trademark registered in France by *Messrs. Laquoinie & Cie.* Société des *Grands Magasins du Printemps.*

**Muhl, Georg.** 1925. Nürnberg, Bavaria. Specialized in stuffed cloth dolls and dolls' clothes.

**Mülhäuser, O.** 1915–20. Sonneberg, Thür. Manufactured dolls.

**Muller, A.** 1879. Paris. Made dolls and bébés.

**Müller, Adolph.** 1909. Sonneberg, Thür. Distributed and exported dolls.

**Müller, Albert.** 1918–25. Nossen, Saxony. Manufactured dolls.

**Müller, Andrew (Andreas).** 1894–1923. Sonneberg, Thür. In 1923, a successor had taken over the Andrew Müller firm and moved to Coburg, Thür. Made and exported jointed dolls and dolls' bodies with waxed and cast wax heads, but not heads of porcelain.

1230. All-bisque doll representing the cartoon character "Mr. Bailey, the Boss" and so marked on the upper back. Painted features and clothes; swivel neck. Mr. Bailey wears a gray coat, green and white checked vest, black tie, red pants. H. 3⅜ inches. *Courtesy of Dorothy Annunziato.*

1231. All-bisque doll with "Auntie Blossom" incised on the upper back. Has swivel neck, molded and painted features and clothes; wears pink dress, blue beads and earrings, high-heeled black pumps. H. 3⅜ inches. *Courtesy of Dorothy Annunziato.*

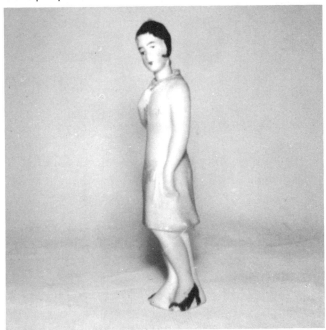

**1232.** Trademark of Andrew Müller.

1896: Registered a crown over crossed poles as a trademark in Germany.

1923: Specialized in jointed stuffed dolls.

**Müller, B.** 1918. Wildenheid near Sonneberg, Thür. Made dolls' bodies.

**Müller, B. Chr., & Mälzer (Mätzer).** 1895–1907. Ilmenau, Thür. Manufactured dolls.

**Müller, Bernhard.** 1895. Köppelsdorf, Thür. Made dolls' bodies.

**Müller, C. A., & Co.** 1851. Oberleutensdorf, Bohemia. Was cited with an Honorable Mention for their papier-mâché dolls at the London Exhibition.

**Müller, C. G. (J.), & Sohn.** 1863–93. Sonneberg, Thür. Manufactured dolls.

1873: Displayed dolls at the Vienna Exhibition.

**Müller, Carl.** 1895–1925+. Sonneberg, Thür. Also known as the Sonneberger Porzellanfabrik. Manufactured dolls.

**Müller, F.** 1909–18. Brattendorf, Thür. Made dolls.

**Müller, Franz.** 1905–18. Sonneberg, Thür. Manufactured dolls.

**Müller, Friedrich.** Ca. 1810. Sonneberg, Thür. Allegedly learned how to make papier-mâché dolls from a French soldier. The plastic mass was pressed into shape by molds and not molded individually as before. Thus, dolls were produced almost mechanically, the cost was considerably reduced, and the great Sonneberg doll industry founded.

**Müller, Friedrich Wilhelm.** 1909. Berlin. Made dolls.

**Müller, H.** 1909. Wildenheid near Sonneberg, Thür. Made dolls' bodies.

**Müller, H.** 1924. Was issued a British patent for glass eyes to be used on fabric dolls.

**Müller, Heinrich.** 1921–23. Nürnberg, Bav. Obtained two German patents for making moving heads on dolls.

**Müller, Helene (née Buttner).** 1905. Schalkau, Thür. Secured British patent for an improved method of making eyelashes for dolls. Claimed that up until then eyelashes had been made by gumming hairs to the eyelids singly. Her invention used hairs attached to a strip or hoop of elastic material, which was glued to the eyelids or eyeballs. Eyelashes could be made by clipping the edges of ordinary birds' feathers and splitting the quill; then the parts were cut to suitable shape and glued to the eyelids. True hair eyelashes were made by pushing one hair after another through a strip and securing it to strip with wax or glue.

**Müller, Ilse (née Jeserich).** 1923. Berlin. Registered *Mit dem Goldreif* (with the Golden Bloom) as a trademark in Germany for *Art Dolls*.

**Müller, J. F., & Strassburger (Strasburger).** 1863–93. Sonneberg, Thür. Manufactured dolls. *Gottschalk* represented them in Paris in the 1860's.

1873: Displayed dolls at the Vienna Exhibition.

1880: Exhibited dolls at the Melbourne Exhibition. It is possible that this firm made the composition heads marked "M. & S., *Superior*."

**Müller, K.** Wildenheid near Sonneberg, Thür. Made dolls' bodies.

**Müller, Karl, & Co.** Before 1924–25, Sonneberg, Thür.; 1925, known as Müller & Liebermann, at Effelder near Sonneberg. Specialized in dolls and baby dolls, dressed and undressed. Their trademark included the initials "K M Co." They made dolls named *Elie* and *Babys*.

**Müller, L.** 1909. Wildenheid near Sonneberg, Thür. Made dolls' bodies.

**Müller, Louis.** 1918–25+. Neustadt near Coburg, Thür. Made *Täuflinge*.

**Müller, Max.** 1909–18. Wallendorf, Thür. Manufactured dolls.

**Müller, Otto.** 1902. Sonneberg, Thür. Was granted a German patent for jointed dolls.

**Muller, Pierre.** 1924. Levallois, Seine. Registered in France *Olympia* as a trademark for dolls.

**1233A.** "Olympia" bisque socket head, made in France by Pierre Muller ca. 1924, has brown glass sleeping eyes, open mouth with teeth, cardboard pate under the wig of auburn hair. Mark: "Olympia" in script. *Courtesy of Eleanor Jean Carter.*

**1233B.** "Olympia" mark found on dolls of Pierre Muller.

**Muller, T. U.** 1867. Detroit, Mich. Made dolls' heads of cassia, a type of tree or shrub.

**Müller, Wilhelm G.** Before 1900–1925+. Sonneberg, Thür. Created and manufactured character babies, fully jointed dolls, and novelty dolls. *Louis Wolf & Co.* distributed his dolls.

**Müller, Witwe (Widow).** 1918. Wildenheid near Sonneberg, Thür. Made dolls' bodies.

**Muller & Delattre.** 1900. France. Won a bronze medal for their doll display at the Paris Exposition.

**Müller & Fröbel.** 1900–1921. Sonneberg, Thür. Manufactured dolls.

1900: One of the Grand Prize winning group at the Paris Exposition.

1904: Displayed dolls at the St. Louis Exhibition.

**Muller Frères (Bros.).** 1873–82. Paris. Distributed German dolls and bébés.

**Müller-Sarne, Julia (née Müller).** 1922. Dresden. Registered in Germany a trademark including the initials "J. S. M." and used for dolls and dolls' clothes.

**Multi-eyes.** 1912–16. *Ernst Reinhardt* obtained a U.S. patent in 1914, *John M. Dickson* obtained a U.S. patent in 1912, and *E. S. A. Perks* obtained a British patent in 1916 for dolls with several pairs of interchangeable eyes.

**Multi-face Dolls.** 1866–1925+. As early as 1866, *Dominico Checkeni* obtained a U.S. patent for a four-faced doll in which the head rotated on a horizontal axis. Later dolls usually rotated on a vertical axis.

1867: Both *Nicholas Joliet* and *Leon Casimir Bru* obtained French patents for two-faced dolls with head that rotated on a vertical axis.

1872: *Gabriel Benda* patented in France a doll whose face could be lifted off and another face with a different expression put in its place.

1874: *Gerarbon* obtained a French patent for a doll whose face could be changed to show different expressions.

1880–81: *Fritz Bartenstein* obtained German and U.S. patents for a two-faced doll with one laughing and one crying face, revolving on a vertical axis.

There were probably German patents also in the 1860's and 1870's but little data has been found as yet for this period in the German States. During the 1880's and 1890's, interest in multi-face dolls seems to have waned, and not returned until around 1900.

1898: *Peter Eadie, Jr.,* obtained a French patent for a three-faced doll.

1903: PLAYTHINGS had several references to two- or three-faced dolls with faces revolving on a pivot. They came as white and Negro, or with various expressions.

1904–5: *Carl Bergner* obtained patents in Britain and Germany for multi-faced dolls. A large number of the multi-face dolls found by collectors are marked "C. B."

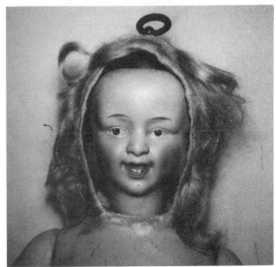

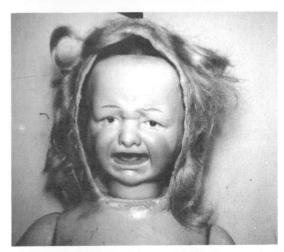

**1234A, B, & C.** Three-faced bisque head: sleeping, laughing, and crying. The laughing face resembles the face on dolls advertised by Louis Lindner in 1911 (see Ill. **1099**). This may be a Carl Bergner doll. The bent-limb baby body is marked on the back as shown in Ill. **179**. H. 13 inches. *Courtesy of Sylvia Brockmon.*

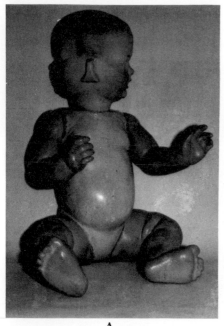

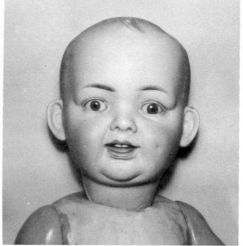

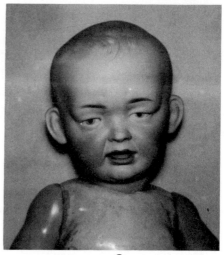

**1235A, B, & C.** Two-faced bisque-head baby. The smiling face with glass eyes is marked "12" on the neck; the frowning face with painted eyes is marked "56" on the neck. Both faces have open-closed mouths. Bent-limb baby body is composition. H. 19½ inches. *Coleman Collection.*

A                                        B                                        C

Most of these have three faces, and some are on bent-limb baby bodies, which suggests that they were made in the early 20th century. The character-type faces also seem to indicate this era. Other multi-face dolls include *Amberg's The Girl with the Curl; Ideal's Baby Bi-Face, Surprise Baby,* and *Soozie Smiles.*

Multi-face dolls were made in nearly all types of material: papier-mâché, wax, bisque, rubber, and rag. One of the oldest types was a rag doll with a different face on each side. These were made in the 20th century, as well as centuries ago when they were called "Moggy" in England and used as shop signs for rag merchants. In 1913 a multi-face rag doll was made with four lithographed faces; the face was folded into place and held by a bonnet and bandeau while the unused three faces were concealed under the yoke of the dress.

1920: A doll with five faces was patented and made by the *Moo-V-Doll Manufacturing Co.*

**Multi-head Dolls.** 1849–1925+. These were of two types; either the head could be removed and another one screwed in its place or similarly attached, or the doll had two heads, one of which was concealed by clothing. The *Topsy Turvy* rag dolls were examples of this type.

1849: *Le Tort* patented a doll with detachable heads in France.

1895: *Ad. Bouchet* advertised a doll with interchangeable heads.

1899: *Dewitt Bouton* obtained a U.S. patent for a multi-head doll.

1901: A reversible doll with a Negro baby at one end and a white baby at the other end.

MULTI-HEAD DOLLS

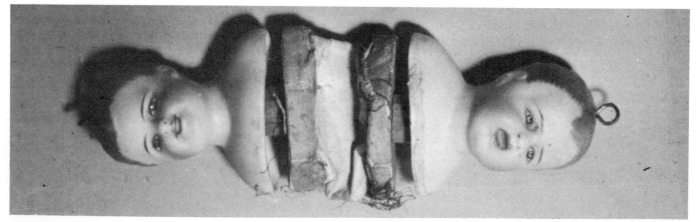

**1236.** Two heads of bisque, one smiling and one crying, have painted features and hair, brush marks at the hairline. Both heads have open-closed mouths. *Courtesy of Margaret Whitton; photograph by Winnie Langley.*

A

B

C

**1237A, B, C, & D.** Two topsy-turvy rag dolls with a girl at one end and a Negro Mammy at the other end. The doll shown full-length has molded faces, probably made by Brückner; original red and white dress. Only the two heads of the other doll are shown. These have flat lithographed faces in brown tones on sateen; cheeks and eyes are hand-tinted with water colors; original checked gingham clothes. H. 13½ inches. *Courtesy of Frances Walker; photograph by Winnie Langley. Courtesy of the Chester County Historical Society.*

D

**1238.** Doll with five interchangeable celluloid heads that could be screwed into place on the body. One head has a wig, the others molded hair; one head has glass eyes, the others painted eyes. Doll wears a pink dress. *Courtesy of Gladyse Hilsdorf; photograph by Winnie Langley.*

1905: *Ida Young* was issued a U.S. patent for detachable dolls' heads.

1909: *Mlle. Eugénie Faugier* obtained a French patent for a multi-head doll.

1912: Doll body was sold with half a dozen heads. *Five-in-One* doll was all celluloid and had five screw-on heads.

1915: *Helen Sancier* was granted a U.S. patent for a two-headed doll.

1920: Rag doll made by *EFFanBEE,* called *Reversible.*

1921: *David Wiener* obtained a U.S. patent for a multi-head doll. The *Famlee Dolls,* based on the Wiener patent, came on the market.

1924: *Lulu Myers* was issued a U.S. patent for multi-head dolls.

**Multi-Part Interchangeable.** 1919. Dolls advertised by *Brunswick.*

**Multiplication and Addition Doll.** 1913. Imported doll with china head and cloth body with multiplication and addition problems printed on it.

**Mumm.** 1923–24. Trademark registered in Germany by *Thüringer Kunstler Wollpuppen Fabrik Inc.* for *Art Dolls* of wool, character dolls, and stuffed dolls.

**Mummy Dolls.** See **Frozen Charlottes.**

**Munich Art Dolls.** 1909–12. *Marion Kaulitz* made dolls that were called by this name. She registered in Germany as a trademark a picture that included the words "Münchner Künstler Kaulitzpuppen." These dolls were shown in the French Doll Shop of *Gimbel Bros.*

1912: Some of these dolls were shown at a German Art Exhibit at the Newark, N.J., Museum.

**Munich Expressionist School.** See **Sachs, Hermann.**

**Munn, John Bently.** 1863. Montclair, N.J. Secured a British patent for an automatic walking doll. Joseph Alvin Munn and Jonathan Davis Cobb were his London agents.

**Munnier (Munier), Vve. (Widow).** 1834–52. Paris. Made dolls.

**Munson, Craig D.** 1925. Wallingford, Conn. Obtained three U.S. design patents for character-type dolls, which he assigned to the *International Silver Co.*

**Munster, Gebrüder.** Germany. Name found on a sticker on a doll. The head of this doll bears the initials of *Adolf Wislizenus.*

**Muntzner & Schneider.** 1920. Coburg, Thür. Manufactured dolls.

**Munyard, A. R.** 1923. London. Obtained British patent for a doll that would change its facial expression by rocking it or by moving its legs or laying it on its right side.

**1239A & B.** Munnier doll with wax-over-papier-mâché head and lower limbs; glass wire-pull sleeping eyes; open mouth with two upper and two lower teeth. The torso of papier-mâché covered with cloth contains the kicking and turning mechanism. Mark: Ill. **1240.** H. 20½ inches. *Courtesy of the Newark Museum, Newark, N. J.*

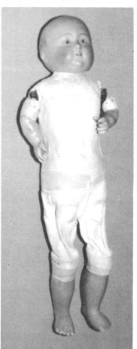

**1240.** Mark used on bodies of dolls produced by Widow Munnier.

**Munzberg, A.** 1923–25. Prague. (Praha), Czechoslovakia. Made dolls.

**Munzer, Alfred.** After 1921–25. New York City. After 1921, advertised *Sannitoy Mama Dolls* that walked, talked, and slept.

**Münzer, Aug.** 1895–1918. Breslau, Silesia. Manufactured dolls.

**Münzer & Schneider Inc.** 1909–18. Unterweid and Oberweid, Thür. Made dolls.

**Musée Pédagogique (Musée des Poupées).** See **Koenig, Mlle. Marie.**

**Muslin Bodies.** After 1845–1925+. *Kestner* made dolls with muslin bodies after 1845. *Charles F. Braitling* made muslin bodies of Dwight Anchor brand muslin. He made muslin bodies as late as 1916.

1917: *Foulds & Freure* advertised muslin dolls' bodies.

**Mutual Doll Company.** 1919–21. New York City. President *Joseph L. Kallus;* made composition dolls of a wood pulp, rosin, and starch mixture in a hot press. The dolls, distributed by *Borgfeldt,* included *Kewpies,* 1919–21; *Baby Bundie,* 1919–21; *Bo-Fair,* 1920–21; *Lassie,* 1921.

**Mutual Hair Goods Co. Inc.** 1921–25. New York City and Pachaug, Conn. Made wigs for dolls.

**My Annemarie.** 1923. Trademark registered in Germany for dolls made by *Wilhelm Follender.*

**My Beauty.** 1919–24. Trademark registered in U.S. by *M. Silverman & Son.*

**My Belle Marianne.** 1919. Made by *Trion Toy Co.*

**My Best Friend.** 1911–12. Doll copyrighted by *Louis Amberg & Son.* It had a baby face with heavy hair in a wave in front.

**My Cherub.** 1912–25. Doll made by *Arthur Schoenau,* who registered the name as a trademark in Germany.

**My Companion.** 1910–15. Line of dressed dolls distributed by *Louis Wolf & Co.,* who registered the name as a trademark in the U.S.

**My Darling.** 1906–25+. Line of jointed dolls made by *Kämmer & Reinhardt.* (See also **Mein Liebling;** color photograph **C20.**)

1906: "My Darling" registered as a trademark in Britain by Kämmer & Reinhardt.

1922: *John Bing Co.,* sole New York agent, advertised "My Darling" line of Kämmer & Reinhardt and *Heinrich Handwerck.*

**My Darling.** 1919–20. *Morimura Bros.,* New York City. Bisque doll or bisque doll's head made in Japan. (See also **Baby Darling.**)

**My Dearie.** 1908–22. Line of dolls handled by *Borgfeldt;* name registered as a trademark in U.S. by Borgfeldt.

**My Dream Baby.** 1924–25+. Trademark registered in U.S. by *Arranbee Doll Co.* for an infant doll. The bisque heads were made by *Armand Marseille* in both flange

**1241.** "My Darling," character doll with bisque head made by Simon & Halbig for Kämmer & Reinhardt, has glass sleeping eyes and closed mouth. Head is on a ball-jointed composition body. Doll wears original lace and lawn dress and bonnet. Mark: "K [star] R, S. & H., 117/A." H. 20½ inches. (See color photograph **C24.**) *Courtesy of the International Doll Library Foundation.*

**1242A & B.** "My Dream Baby" has bisque head made by Armand Marseille for Arranbee, in competition with the Bye-Lo Baby; glass sleeping eyes; composition baby body. Mark: Ill. **1153** plus "15/OX—K." H. 8½ inches. *Courtesy of Alberta Darby.*

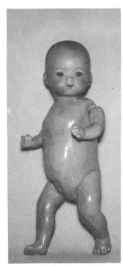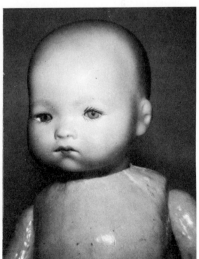

neck and socket neck types. The doll came with rubber or composition hands and glass moving eyes. There were three sizes, priced $1.25 and up. These dolls were in competition with the *Bye-Lo Baby,* and later were sometimes called "Dream Baby." Arranbee advertised five sizes of imported bisque heads. The mold number for socket heads is 341; 351 is also found.

**My Fairy.** 1922. Trademark registered in Germany by *Seyfarth & Reinhardt.*

**My Favorite.** 1916–18. Doll made by *Jessie McCutcheon Raleigh,* distributed by *Butler Bros.* It wore a colored lawn dress; size 11½ inches, price $2.50.

**My Girlie.** 1912–22. Trademark registered in Germany by *Borgfeldt* in 1912. Borgfeldt registered the name in U.S. as a trademark in 1922, stating that it had been in interstate or international use since 1913. "My Girlie" was incised on bisque socket heads with dolly-type faces.

**My Honey.** 1921–24. Trademark registered in Germany by *Edward Römhild.*

1923: Trademark registered in U.S. by *Konroe Merchants,* importers and sole distributors of "My Honey" dolls, which came with bisque heads, *roguish* sleeping eyes; sizes 9, 10½, 12, and 13½ inches.

**My Little Beauty.** 1903–5. Dressed dolls advertised by *Samstag & Hilder Bros.*

**My Lucky Child.** See **Mein Glückskind.**

**My Name Is Miss Malto Rice.** Found around the waist of a rag doll, written in red letters. The date of this doll is unknown and could have been after 1925.

**My Pearl.** 1921. Dressed and undressed dolls made by *Hermann Steiner;* trademark registered in Britain by an agent for Steiner.

**My Playmate.** 1903–21. Trademark registered in Germany by *Borgfeldt* in 1903.

1908: Advertised in PLAYTHINGS as a doll representing a child with a sober pensive face, "a most natural face." A baby doll with *Simon & Halbig* and *Kämmer & Reinhardt* marks has been found with the "My Playmate" label. According to a Kämmer & Reinhardt publication, they had only one mold prior to 1909 and did not make character dolls as early as 1908. This suggests that My Playmate could have been made by various factories in various molds. It was usually on a composition body.

1921: Borgfeldt registered the name as a trademark in the U.S. and stated that it had been used in America since 1907.

**My Sweetheart.** Name appears on the head of a doll with the initials "B. J. & Co.," which probably stand for *B. Illfelder & Co.,* who registered *Little Sweetheart* as a trademark in Germany in 1902 and in U.S. in 1905, and advertised *Sweetheart* dolls in 1910.

**My Sweetheart.** 1920. *Morimura Bros.* New York City. Doll made in Japan.

**Myer & Charnault.** 1900. Paris; factory at Montreuil-sous-Bois. Made *bébés incassables,* which they named *Mon Bébé.*

**Myers, Chas.** 1923–25. Dansville, Ill. Manufactured dolls.

**Myers, Lulu A.** 1922–24. Bailey, Colo. Obtained U.S. patent for doll with head, arms, and legs that were removable and could be interchanged.

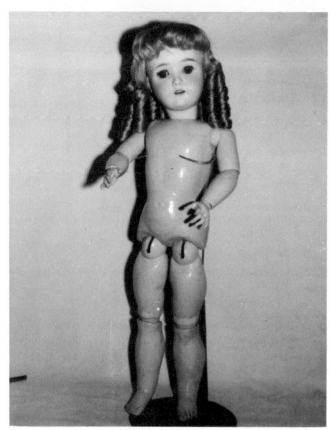

**1243A & B.** "My Girlie" doll produced by Borgfeldt: bisque head with blue sleeping eyes; hair eyelashes, also upper and lower painted lashes; open mouth with four upper teeth; wood and composition ball-jointed body. Mark: Ill. **1244.** H. 24 inches. *Courtesy of Dorothy Annunziato.*

**1244.** "My Girlie" mark used by Borgfeldt on doll's heads.

My Girlie
III
Germany

I O I
I I
My SWEETHEART
B. J. & Co.

**1245.** "My Sweetheart" mark found on dolls probably handled by B. Illfelder & Co.

**Myltyl.** 1911. Doll representing a character in the stage show BLUE BIRD; price $1.00.

**Myonettes.** 1917. Bisque dolls imported from France by *Grey & Grey Ltd.*

**Mystère.** 1920–25+. Trademark registered in France by *Belleville & Co.* for dolls, dolls' heads, dolls with movable eyes, dolls' heads with movable eyes, and a mechanism for dolls' movable eyes.

1925: Poupée "Mystère" advertised by the Société Française des Yeux.

# N

**N. V. Sales Co.** 1924. New York City. Manufactured dolls.

**Nadaud, Mlle. A.** 1878–90's. Paris. Handled dolls.

1878: Displayed dolls in the Paris Exposition.

Ca. 1890: Handled jointed composition-bodied dolls, some of which had bisque heads made by *Simon & Halbig*, especially their mold #1079, with patented eyelashes. A doll with the Nadaud stamp on its hip has a paper sticker on its back as shown in Ill. 1246.

**1246.** Mark found on dolls of Mlle. Nadaud.

**Nagai & Co.** 1917–18. New York City. Handled bisque dolls from Japan.

1917: Advertised dolls of various sizes and styles, including ones with movable eyes and mohair wigs in sizes 12 and 14 inches.

1918: Listed as a doll manufacturer.

**Nagel, C. (née Andrews).** 1897. Hamburg, Germany. Manufactured dolls.

**Nain Bleu.** See **Au Nain Bleu.**

**Najo.** 1917–18. Trademark registered in U.S. by *National Joint-Limb Doll Co.* for dolls with papier-mâché bodies.

**Names.** A few dolls had their names marked on them; these were generally porcelain dolls. Or they had tags or labels with their names, many of which have been lost through the years. However, the vast majority of dolls prior to the 20th century were unnamed. Even the word "doll" is relatively new; in earlier times, they were known as "babies," "little ladies," "fashion babies," or "pandoras." The creators of dolls often gave them trade names, which were sometimes registered as trademarks; names were used for lines and/or individual dolls.

The use of trade names was part of the identification and emphasis on character dolls. In 1910, PLAYTHINGS reported that names caught the memory and helped both dealer and distributor. They listed the following names with their characteristics: Gladys—laughing doll, Phyllis—stylish doll, Dorothy—dreamy doll, Peggy—chubby doll, Jeannette—French doll, Madeline—titian-haired beauty, Mary—one adored by everyone. But the connotations of names change down through the years.

Collectors sometimes name dolls, and these names get into print, but they usually have no historical significance. Names given by collectors often compound confusion because the same name may be given to several dolls of different types and history, a thing that is also occasionally done by makers.

**Nancy.** 1924. *Mama*-type doll with composition head and arms, soft body. She wore a crepe dress and bloomers; 24 inches tall; price $3.45.

**Nancy Ann.** 1923. *Mama*-type doll with blue sleeping eyes, made by *EFFanBEE*. A button pinned on the dress had the word EFFanBEE on it. Size 23 inches, price $10.00.

**Nancy C.** 1918. Made by *Jessie McCutcheon Raleigh,* distributed by *Butler Bros.* Wore a white lawn dress. Size 11½ inches with curly mohair wig cost $2.45; 13½-inch size with painted hair cost $2.85.

**Nancy Jane.** 1922. Made by *Ideal Novelty & Toy Co.* The doll was marked "Lead Me Home // For I am a // Walking Doll." She could wink and blink and was 13 inches tall.

**Nancy Lee.** 1912. Made by *Horsman.* Came with composition head and soft body; wore a costume copied from the yachting clothes of a European princess.

**Naneau, Hippolyte.** 1905. Registered *Gentil Bébé* as a trademark in France.

**Nankeen (Nankin or Nanking) Dolls.** 1884–1911, and probably longer. Had commercially made cotton cloth bodies. This type of doll was made in Germany, France, America, and elsewhere.

1884: "Nankeen China Dolls," with china heads, advertised as coming in sizes 5, 5½, 6, 6½, 7½, 8½, 9½, 10, and 11 inches; price 35¢ to $1.50 doz. wholesale.

**Nansen.** 1912. Doll dressed to portray the famous Norwegian Arctic explorer of this name; distributed by

*Butler Bros.* The doll had a bisque head and glass eyes. Size, 8½ inches; price, $2.08 doz. wholesale.

**Nash, Mrs. Watson Hill.** 1893. Jamaica, W.I. Displayed cashew dolls at the Chicago Exposition.

**Nathan, F.** 1925. Paris. Handled cloth dolls ready to stuff.

**National Doll, The.** See **Maiden Toy Co.**

**National Doll & Novelty Co.** 1882–83. New York City. Also known as *Wiegand, Martin & Rippel.* Made papier-mâché and/or waxed dolls.

**National Doll Co.** 1923–25. New York City. Claimed that they sold 50,000 moving-eye dolls, as well as many other dolls.

**National Joint-Limb Doll Co.** 1917–22. New York City. Made dolls with papier-mâché bodies, and registered *NAJO* as a trademark in U.S.

1917: Advertised girl dolls and baby dolls with sleeping eyes and human hair wigs with curls that could be washed and combed; also mohair wigs; body, head, and limbs all made by hand of papier-mâché, manufactured in U.S. from American raw materials; finished in a flat washable enamel; dressed in chemise. *Miss Najo* girl dolls came in seven sizes from 12 to 26 inches; bent-leg baby dolls came in four sizes, 12 to 19 inches; a standing baby came in four sizes up to 22 inches.

1918: Advertised that their dolls were the only joint-limb dolls made in America that were an exact replica of the *Kestner* dolls; had improved enamel finish and reinforced eye sockets. Girl dolls came in sizes 18, 20, 22, 24, and 26 inches; price $36.00 to $66.00 doz. wholesale. Standing baby came in sizes 17, 20, and 22 inches; price $33.00 to $45.00 doz. wholesale. The prices in 1918 were considerably less than in 1917. For example, the 26-inch girl doll dropped from $96.00 to $66.00 doz. wholesale.

**National Manufacturing Co.** 1921–22. West Hoboken, N.J. Made *Sunshine* and *Bess Darling*, sleeping dolls.

**Natural Doll Co.** 1915–25+. New York City. Made dolls' heads.

**Nature Arms and Legs.** 1909–25+. Bent limbs used on infant dolls. (See also **Next to Nature.**)

**Nature Babies.** 1912. Trade name used by *Horsman* for dolls modeled from life, including *Suck-a-Thumb, Gold Medal Prize Baby, Baby Bobby,* and *Baby Peterkin.*

**Nature Children.** 1921–22. Trade name used by *Louis Amberg & Son* for cuddly, crying, walking, sitting, and talking dolls that came in four sizes and sixteen styles; price $8.00 doz. and up.

**Nature Shaped.** Ca. 1920–25+. Name of composition bodies with the kneecap molded on the lower leg, and the joint above the knee, so that the dolls could wear the short dresses of the 1920's.

**Naughty.** 1919–25. Trademark registered in Germany and Britain in 1920 and in U.S. in 1922 by *Kämmer & Reinhardt.*

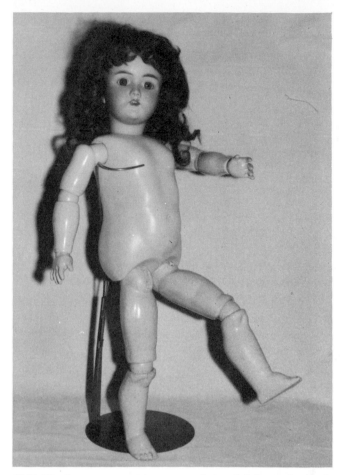

1247. The heavy composition torso of this doll bears the mark of the National Joint-Limb Doll Co. The bisque head, made by Simon & Halbig for H. Handwerck, and the limbs are probably not original. Mark on head: Ill. **768.** Mark on body: Ill. **1248.** H. 26 inches. *Courtesy of Dorothy Annunziato.*

**1248.** Mark of National Joint-Limb Doll Co.

1925: *Bing* was New York agent for the Naughty Dolly, which would not sleep on its left side, and was made by Kämmer & Reinhardt. (See also **Der Unart.**)

**Naughty Marietta.** 1912. Trade name for a *coquette*-type doll made by *Fleischaker & Baum.* Because of a doll with the same name by *Ideal Novelty & Toy Co., EFFanBEE* changed the name of this doll to *Miss Coquette.* It came in various sizes.

**Naughty Marietta.** 1912. Trade name for a *coquette*-type doll made by *Ideal Novelty & Toy Co.*

**Ne Plus Ultra Patent Joint.** Ca. 1883–1925+. *Sarah Robinson* patented this type of joint in the U.S. in 1883, when it was used for the hip, knee, and elbow. It was later partially superseded by the *Universal Joint*, patented in 1896, which was the reverse in structure and was used especially for knee joints. The Ne Plus Ultra Patent Joint, also called rivet hip joint or swivel joint, continued to be used for the hips.

**Neble, Arnold.** 1919–20. Weehawken, N.J. Was issued a U.S. design patent for a doll's head representing a lady with eyes looking down.

**Nedco.** See **New England Doll Co.**

**Needle Molding.** On cloth dolls, the features are frequently "molded" into three-dimensional form by stitching done with a needle.

**Negel, C. (née Andrews).** 1909–18. Hamburg, Germany. Made dolls.

**Negro Dolls.** These have been made in Europe and America for many years. They were especially popular right after the American Civil War and again in the 1890's, when dolls of all races were being shown extensively. The earliest French advertisement found, as yet, for a Negro bébé was in 1892 by *Danel & Cie.* Some of the Negro dolls were simply painted dark; others had the black pigment mixed in the slip of the bisque and also had Negroid features. Negro dolls were made in practically all the materials that were used for Caucasian dolls. (See color photographs C9, C24.)

NEGRO DOLLS

**1249A & B.** Doll with molded Negro features and hair. Black papier-mâché head, black wooden arms and legs, stiff kid body of the type made especially in the 1830's and 1840's. Original calico print dress and white apron. H. 6 inches. H. of shoulder head, 1½ inches. *Courtesy of the Museum of the City of New York.*

**1250A & B.** Negro bisque socket head. Lips are an orange-pink color; head and jointed composition body are black; coarse straight-hair wig. Mark on head: Ill. **1253.** H. 22 inches. *Courtesy of Lester & Alice Grinnings.*

NEGRO DOLLS

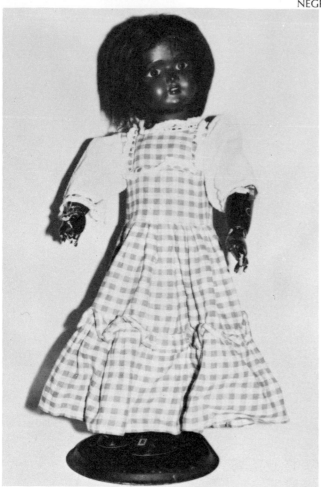

**1252.** Negro bisque head, glass eyes, open mouth with two rows of teeth; pierced ears; vivid multi-colored aboriginal garments. *Photograph by Winnie Langley.*

**1251A & B.** Negro bisque head on jointed composition body; doll-face type with coarse black straight-hair wig. Head mark: Ill. **1254.** H. 19 inches. *Courtesy of Lester & Alice Grinnings.*

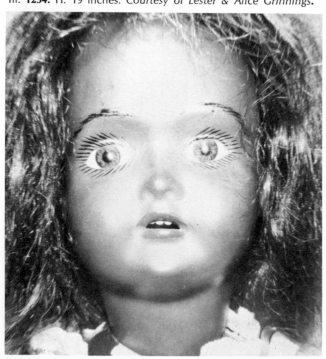

1253                                    1254

**1253 & 1254.** Marks found on Negro dolls.

**Negro Dude.** Ca. 1904. Wooden circus doll made by *Schoenhut.*

**Neighbour, R. C., & Co.** 1921. London and Lewisham, England. Used "Neto" as a trademark; manufactured *Livetoy* series of dolls.

**Neissner, A. C.** 1907–25+. Vienna. Manufactured dolls.

**Nekarda, Mabel Drake.** 1911. New York City. Registered *Votes-For-Women* and *Suffragette Kid* in U.S. as trademarks for dolls.

**Nelke, August.** 1895–1915. Coburg, Thür. Manufactured dolls, including dressed dolls.

**1255.** Mark used by Nelke Corp.

**Nelke, Chr.** 1909. Waltershausen, Thür. Made dolls.

**Nelke Corp.** 1917–25+. Philadelphia, Pa. Made dolls out of a single piece of circular knitted fabric, produced by Elk Knitting Mills Co. In 1917 these makers of knit underwear donated some of their material to make dolls for a charity bazaar. The dolls were so successful that the company decided to make dolls commercially, with hand-painted faces. Water colors would not last and oil paint was hard to work and sometimes poisonous. Finally, in 1920, they found a paint in bright colors that was non-poisonous, waterproof, permanent, and could not be sucked off. The doll was stuffed with a light fabric from Java that would float in water and dry quickly. There were no buttons or pins; the dolls bore a ribbon label.

1918: "Nelke Dollies" came dressed in rompers and were 12 inches tall.

1921: Advertised Nelke Boy and Nelke Clown, which came in two sizes.

1922: Advertised 11-inch size for 69¢.

1923: *Davis & Voetsch* were the distributors; the *Cop* and the *Imp* were new models. Nelke Corp. started to use *Diggeldy Dan* as a trademark in U.S.

1924: Registered Diggeldy Dan as a trademark in U.S. A rag cherub-type came in two sizes for 50¢ and $1.00. Boys, girls, cops, clowns, Indians, and sailors came in sizes 12, 14, and 18 inches, price $1.00 to $2.50.

1925: Registered "Nelke" as a trademark in the U.S.

**Nell, Harry.** 1899–1900. Philadelphia, Pa. Made dolls.

**Nellfoy & Co.** 1917–21. London, Made dolls.

1917: *Jessica Borthwick* registered "Nellfoy" as a trademark in Britain for dolls and dolls' dresses.

**Nellie Bly.** 1914. One of the *Trundle Bed Triplets,* brightly colored, stuffed with cork; 8½ inches high.

**Nellie Sunshine.** 1918. Doll copyrighted by *Jeanne I. Orsini,* represented a girl about five years old.

**Nemela, O.** 1909. Breslau, Silesia. Made dolls.

**Nemo.** 1910. Worsted doll distributed by *Butler Bros.* Came with painted features, wool hair, bead eyes, sitting body, and voice. Wore a flannel harlequin costume with felt hat. Size 10½ inches, price $2.10 doz. wholesale.

**Nemo.** See **Little Nemo.**

**Nenco.** 1915–16. Trademark registered in U.S. by *New Era Novelty Co.*

1916: "Nenco Babies" came with or without wigs; in four sizes; price $1.00 and up.

**Nénette.** 1918. Trademark registered in France by *Mme. Poulbot.*

**Nerlich & Co.** 1902–3. Toronto, Canada. Distributed dolls. Gave the trade 50 percent discount plus 5 percent off the list price for cash. Advertised *Handwerck* dolls, lithographed face-rag dolls, metal dolls, *Kestner* kid-body dolls with bisque heads, china-limb dolls, solid china babies, Negro dolls with all-black bodies, all-bisque babies, and many others. Dolls with washable paste (composition) head with glass eyes, paste limbs, flowing hair, and hay-stuffed bodies came in sizes 9½, 13, 15½, 18, 21, 25, and 29 inches; price 80¢ to $8.00 doz. wholesale.

**Nest, William.** 1852. London. Made dolls.

**Neto.** See **Neighbour.**

**Nettie Knit.** 1918. Undressed doll with knitting needles and wool made by *Gund Manufacturing Co.*

**Neubart, Heinrich.** 1893–94. Charlottenburg, Prussia. Was issued a German patent for a stuffed rag doll.

**Neuberger, Daniel.** 17th century. Augsburg, Bavaria. Made wax dolls that, according to Joachim Von Sandrart, were as hard as stone and so marvelously colored that they seemed alive.

**Neuberger, R.** 1897. Fürth, Bavaria. Manufactured dolls.

**Neubronner, Gustav.** 1851–1918. Frankenthal, Bavaria. Manufactured and exported dolls, especially dressed dolls.

1851: Displayed six elegantly dressed children's dolls at the London Exhibition.

**Neugebauer, Heinrich.** 1907–25+. Hüttensteinach near Sonneberg, Thür. Manufactured dolls.

**Neuhauser, B.** 1897. Hamburg, Germany. Manufactured dolls.

**Neumann, R.** 1891. Berlin. Exported dolls.

**Neumann & Marx.** 1906–11. Factories at Oyannax and Chauffry, France; part of the *Société Industrielle de Celluloid.* Used the initials "N. & M."; mark was the side view of the bust of a lion with wings and a dragon's tail. Advertised a new method of making celluloid dolls.

**Neutrality Jim.** 1916. One of the *Madame Hendren* line made by *Averill Manufacturing Co.* Came dressed as a Dutch boy, in various sizes, price $1.00 to $3.50.

**Neverbreak.** 1910. Line of character dolls produced by *A. Steinhardt & Bro.*

**Nevvabrake.** 1916. Pressed composition with a "bisc-like" finish made by *Art Doll & Toy Co.* Over one hundred characters were advertised. Price 50¢, $1.00, and up.

**New Born (Nuborn) Babe.** 1914–25+. Designed by *Jeno Juszko,* made by *Louis Amberg & Son.* The doll represented a two-day-old infant, modeled from life. Head had half-closed eyes, flattened nose, sunken chin, full cheeks, faunlike ears, and general "new-born" features, according to the copyright papers.

1914: Copyrighted by *Louis Amberg* and advertised that the "Novel conception of this infant makes it at once an

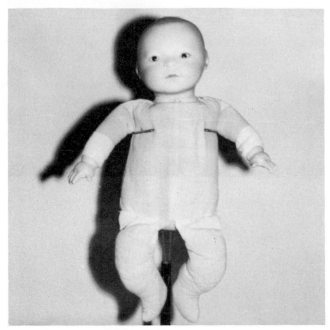

**1256A & B.** New Born Babe, copyrighted by Louis Amberg & Son in 1914. Bisque head was modeled by Jeno Juszko from a three-day-old infant. Note the pointed ears reminiscent of the Billiken. Doll has glass sleeping eyes, flange neck on a cloth body, composition hands. Head mark: Ill. **1257.** Body stamp: Ill. **1258.** H. 16 inches. *Coleman Collection.*

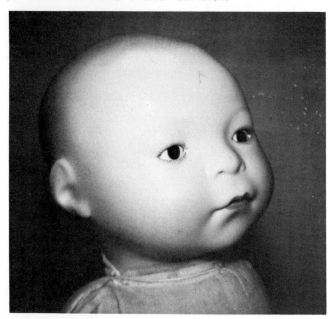

**1257 & 1258.** Marks found on New Born Babe dolls made by Amberg.

ⓒ L.A. & S. 1914
#G 45520
Germany #4

**HEADS COPYRIGHTED BY
LOUIS AMBERG & SON**

appealing and irresistibly sweet character." The copyright number, G. 45520, and date, 1914, appear on the back of many of the heads of these dolls. Among the numbers that appear on various versions are 371,886; 241 (RA.); 240 *(Hermann Steiner).* This seems to have been the first doll representing a tiny infant molded from life.

1925: Advertised as being made with either bisque or composition heads. The bisque heads were made by *Armand Marseille* and came in five sizes; price $2.00 and up. The composition heads came in three sizes with or without moving eyes; price $13.50 doz. wholesale. Amberg advertised that they were prosecuting infringements.

**New Born Baby.** 1925+. Copyrighted by B. E. Fleischaker of *EFFanBEE,* designed by *Ernesto Peruggi.* Copyright described doll as having head and neck of a newborn baby, broad head, fat cheeks, and wide-open eyes.

**New Doll Co.** 1913–15. New York City. Manufactured dolls.

**New Eccles Rubber Works Ltd.** 1921. London, Made rubber dolls.

**New England Doll Co. (Nedco).** 1919–21. Holyoke, Mass. In 1921, the American Tissue Mills was the successor. Made fully jointed dolls with socket heads and ball joints of a laminated cloth. A similar type had been made earlier by the *Utley Co.*

1921: Both Nedco and the American Tissue Mills names were used. They advertised papier-mâché heads and bodies, wooden arms and legs, and aluminum hands.

**New Era Novelty Co. (Nenco).** 1914–16. Newark, N.J. Made fully jointed unbreakable character dolls.

1915: Registered two trademarks in U.S.; one was the *Yama Yama Doll,* and the other was the *Nenco S'Kooter Kid.* They advertised *Our Baby* with jointed composition body, molded hair, and painted eyes, which came in four sizes. Their products were made entirely in their own factory, since they had terminated connection with the *Politzer Toy Manufacturing Co.* during 1915.

1916: Advertised Nenco Babies in four sizes; price $1.00 and up. (See Ill. 1731.)

**New Era Toy & Novelty Co.** 1921. Newark, N.J. Made cherub-type dolls, among them *Kimball* girl and Kimball boy; price $6.00 doz. wholesale. Also the *Flirt* and *Cherie* in sizes 14 and 16 inches; price $8.75 and $10.00 doz. wholesale.

**New Market Trading Co.** 1923. New York City. Handled imported bisque dolls. These came in sizes 16, 18, 20, 23, 24, 25, 27, and 29 inches; price $7.50 to $25.00 doz. wholesale.

**New Toy Co. (New Toy Manufacturing Co.).** Before 1912–21. New York City. The factory was in Newark, N.J. A large doll manufacturing company; they specialized in character dolls, and used the trade name "Nutoi."

**1259.** Mark used by New Toy Co.

1912: Advertised fifty items, including *Coquette* with a blue ribbon in her hair of the same material as her head; she was dressed in a blue kimono or white lawn frock; country boy and girl; sailor boy and girl; school boy and girl. Dolls came in four sizes, 10 to 16 inches tall; price 25¢ to $1.00.

1913: Advertised unbreakable character dolls with composition legs, arms, and hands, cork-stuffed bodies with joints inside the body.

1914: Made German, English, French, and Russian soldier dolls, price $1.00.

1915: Started to use *Lignumfibro,* a new material for dolls' heads and bodies invented by Mr. Fraenkel. Max *Bing* was the distributor.

1916: Registered Lignumfibro as a trademark in U.S.

1917: Advertised that they were America's largest doll maker and employed four hundred people. They produced 106 styles, all-composition or with soft bodies, infants or character dolls, in a material that would not chip or crack; came with or without wigs. Their $1.00 line of cork-stuffed dolls had inside joints.

1918: Advertised Nutoi and *Newbisc, The World's Doll.* Newbisc all-composition came in eleven sizes. There were hundreds of stuffed doll numbers with wigs and moving eyes. The all-composition babies were 14 inches tall. The factory employed 525 people.

1919: Completed a new factory that allegedly was the "largest doll factory in the world." They had claimed that their old factory was the largest in the U.S. devoted entirely to the manufacture of dolls. They expected to double their output from $1,000,000 to $2,000,000. The entire output of the new factory was sold by August, 1919. Among their dolls were *Midolly, Bride,* Bridesmaid, *Maytime Girl, Merry Widow,* and *Peggy.* There were eight sizes of Newbisc dolls; some of their dolls were made with steel spring joints.

1920: Registered Nutoi as a trademark in U.S. Advertised *Phyllis May,* a doll representing the character made famous by *Miss Hazel Drukker* in the NEW YORK EVENING MAIL; also advertised a walking doll with composition head and body, curly human hair wig; size 24 inches.

**New York Doll Co.** 1921–24. New York City. Manufactured dolls and dolls' heads.

**New York Merchandise Co.** 1920–24. New York City. Registered *Pearlie* as a trademark in U.S. for dolls.

**New York Rubber Co.** 1851–1917. New York City. Made rubber dolls under the *Goodyear* patent of 1851.

1854: Secured U.S. patent for improving rubber products.

1876: Showed dolls at the Philadelphia Exhibition.

1897: Advertised all-rubber dolls with knitted worsted dresses. Came as girls, boys, and babies, both white and Negro; sizes 4½, 5½, 6, 7¼, 8¼, 9, 9½, and 12 inches; price $1.60 to $18.00 doz. wholesale.

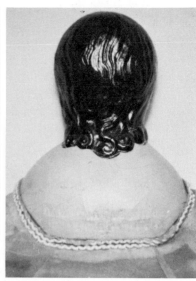

**1260A & B.** New York Rubber Co. doll with rubber head, painted features and hair, lower lashes only; cloth body, limbs covered with silk. Contemporary clothes include green organdy bodice, pantalettes that show. Mark: Ill. **1261.** H. 13½ inches. *Courtesy of the International Doll Library Foundation.*

**1261.** Mark on dolls of the New York Rubber Co.

### NEW YORK RUBBER CO.
### GOODYEAR'S PAT. 444

**New York Stationery & Envelope Co.** 1884–86. New York City. Assignee of a U.S. design patent for dolls by *Edward S. Peck.*

**New York Stuffed Toy Co.** 1924. New York City. Produced dolls.

**Newark India Rubber Manufacturing Co.** 1849–53+. Newark, N.J. Made rubber toys and, after 1853, made dolls, according to McClintock, TOYS IN AMERICA.

**Newbisc, The World's Doll.** 1918–20. Trade name used by the *New Toy Co.* in 1918 for a line of dolls. Registered as a trademark in U.S. in 1920, but had been used in interstate or international trade since 1919. The name was impressed in the composition or on bands attached to the doll or on printed labels on the packages. Dolls came in eleven sizes in 1918 and eight sizes in 1919. The 1919 line included *Kupid,* bent-leg babies and straight-leg babies, and steel spring jointed dolls.

**Newell, Edgar G.** See **Art Fabric Mills.**

**Newly Wed Kid.** Ca. 1907. Rag doll made by *Art Fabric Mills.*

**1262.** "Newbisc" mark used by the New Toy Co. for dolls.

**Newman, Alexander Morris.** 1906. Berlin. Obtained a British patent for a phonographic doll that was supposed to be an improvement over the *Edison* doll.

**Next to Nature.** Term used for bent-limb jointed *baby bodies.* (See also **Nature Arms and Legs.**)

**Next-to-Nature.** 1918. Baby dolls made by *Colonial Toy Manufacturing Co.* They came with moving eyes, mohair wig, open mouth, spring-jointed composition body with bent limbs; sizes 14, 16½, 18, 24, and 26 inches; price $28.80 to $72.00 doz. wholesale. The two largest sizes were made especially for displaying babies' garments. There was also a painted-eye version 18 inches tall, $27.00 doz. wholesale.

**Niagara Lithographing Co.** Early 20th century. Buffalo, N.Y. Made *Sunny Jim* muslin cutout dolls which were lithographed in colors.

**Nibsie.** 1924. Doll made by *Louis Amberg & Son*; resembled *Mibs.*

**Nibur Novelty Co.** 1923–25. New York City. Made dolls' heads.

**Nicette.** See **La Poupée Nicette.**

**Nicholson, Andrew.** 1869. Brooklyn, N.Y. Obtained a U.S. patent for a walking doll.

**Nicholson, Eberhardt P.** 1916–17. New York City. Was issued a U.S. patent for stringing dolls by means of metal rods, chains, and leaf springs.

**Nifty.** 1923. Trademark registered in France by *Borgfeldt.*

**Nimble Twinklers.** 1915. Stockinet dolls, reminiscent of *Palmer Cox's Brownies;* price 35¢.

**975 Line.** 1914–15. Medium-priced character babies, produced by *Louis Wolf & Co.,* bisque heads manufactured by *Armand Marseille.*

**1914 Girl.** 1914. Doll copyrighted by *Elizabeth Lesser;* wore an "up-to-date costume."

**Ning-Po.** 1917–19. China. Carved idols until he became a Christian; then he carved wooden dolls' heads for the *Door of Hope Mission.*

**Ni-Ni.** 1911. Trademark registered in Britain by John Green *Hamley* for dolls.

**Nini.** 1918. Trademark registered in France by *Mme. Poulbot.*

**Nini, La Princesse.** 1918. Trademark registered in France by *Mme. Poulbot.*

**Nini Kaspa.** 1912. Trademark registered in France by *Julius Bernhold* for unbreakable jointed bébés.

**Ninon.** 1923. Trademark registered in France by *Société Bonin et Lefort* for dolls and dolls' heads.

**Ninon.** 1925. Trademark registered in France by *Mlle. Geneviève Loudouze* for dolls.

**Nippon Novelty Co.** 1921. Manufactured dolls.

**Niquet & Bouchet.** 1889. France. Won a silver medal at the Paris Exposition for their India rubber dolls dressed in woolen jerseys.

**Nishikawa.** 1900. Won Honorable Mention for dolls at the Paris Exposition.

**Nister, E.** 1925. Nürnberg, Bavaria. Produced dolls.

**Nobbikid.** 1914–15. Trademark registered in Germany and in U.S. by *Borgfeldt.*

**No-Break (No-Brake).** 1909–12. Life-size rag doll patented by *Edward Tinkham Gibson* in U.S.; distributed by *Elms & Sellon.* The doll was advertised as printed in "oil colors" on durable cloth, jointed so that it could sit down. The dress design formed part of the sack that held the stuffing. Came in sizes 9 to 30 inches.

**Nöckler & Tittel.** 1892–1925+. Schneeberg, Saxony. Manufactured dolls and dolls' heads.

1898: Advertised dressed dolls for export, with unbreakable heads; dressed in costumes of all countries.

1901: Registered two trademarks, *Lithoid* and *Gummoid,* in Germany for dressed and undressed dolls and dolls' heads.

1909: Advertised dressed and undressed dolls, especially dolls in provincial costume.

1924: Advertised dolls, dolls' heads and parts.

**Noël.** 1878. Paris. Made dolls.

**Noël, Charles Marie Paul.** 1923. Saint-Etienne, France. Registered *Marquisette* as a trademark in France for dolls.

**Non-Breakable Doll Co.** 1912–16. Pawtucket, R.I. Obtained two U.S., two German, and one French patent; all pertained to eyes of dolls. They claimed to have patented an indestructible eye. Other patents pertained to the movement of eyes, both from side to side and opening and closing.

1915: Registered *Jam Kiddo* on a blue and white shield as a trademark in U.S. They advertised thirty-seven types of dolls, including Jam Kiddos, *Clownee, Toddles,* and *Red Riding Hood.*

**Nonbreakable Toy Co.** 1911–12. New York City. Advertised a clown doll named *Mar-sell-ene* and the *Kandy Twins* with eyes glancing to the side.

**Non-Breakable Toy Co.** 1916, Milwaukee, Wis.; 1917, Muskegon, Mich. Made *Capo* unbreakable dolls. Capo was short for Joseph Capuano, a pioneer in making unbreakable dolls.

1916: Advertised that they made over 8,000 dolls a day. The dolls weighed 3½ pounds or less and were 24 to 36 inches long.

1917: Advertised that they made about 3,000 dolls a day.

**Nonn & Sohn.** 1907–23. Liegnitz, Germany. Manufactured dolls.

**Nono.** 1925+. Doll made by *Harva Cie.*

**Nonpareil.** Name found on late 19th-century papier-mâché dolls' heads, usually with the initials "W A H," that were distributed by *R. Ridley & Sons.* (See Ill. 429.)

**Nonpareil.** 1912. Line of unbreakable character dolls handled by *W. C. Horn Bros. & Co.*

**Nonpareil Toy & Novelty Co.** 1920. U.S. made dolls, which were distributed by *Riemann, Seabrey Co.*

**Noodt, August, & Co.** See **Dittmer & Matz.**

**Nordicus Inc.** 1921–24. Hamburg, Germany. Manufactured and exported dolls; used the trade name *Golconda.*

**Nordschild, Leo.** 1923–24. Berlin. Producer and distributor of dolls. Registered *Bella Puppen* with the picture of two little girls as a trademark in Germany, for dolls and dolls' heads.

**Norexi.** 1925. Trade name used by *Julius Hofer* for dolls.

**Norgate, M. B.** 1918. Was issued a British patent for attaching a doll's head to a wooden block concealed in the upper portion of a stuffed body, to enable the head to turn easily.

**Noris.** 1905. Trademark registered in Germany by *Carl Debes & Sohn,* distributors of dolls.

**Norsk, Husflidsforening.** 1893. Christiania (Oslo), Norway. Displayed dolls at Chicago Exposition.

**North Pole.** 1910. *Eskimo Dolls* distributed by *Butler Bros.* Came with celluloid faces, painted features, and voices. Brown plush bodies were jointed at shoulders and hips. Dolls wore white felt mitts and boots. Size 9½ inches, price $2.00 doz. wholesale.

**Northmann, A.** 1897. Hamburg, Germany. Manufactured dolls.

**Northport Novelty Co.** 1913. Northport, N.Y. Registered *Flintex* as a trademark in U.S. for dolls.

**Northwestern Consolidated Milling Co.** See **Ceresota.**

**Norwalk, Albert B.** 1918–19. New York City. Obtained two U.S. patents for nun dolls in different habits.

**Norwegian Dolls.** See **Norsk, Husflidsforening; Olson, Kristian.**

**Norwood, Edwin P.** 1923–24. Chicago, Ill. Secured a U.S. design patent for a clown doll.

**Nostrils.** Two red dots usually indicated the nostrils on dolls (two light dots on Negro dolls). These were frequently omitted on the smaller early papier-mâché or china heads and on some dolls of composition or bisque after World War I. Many French dolls, except in very small sizes, have a two-tone area in each nostril, composed of a darker red dot in the middle of a lighter reddish area. Some of the finer and larger china or bisque heads have a circle, ellipse, or straight line in red to indicate the nostril. A few papier-mâché and a few ceramic dolls have pierced nostrils. Dolls made in Japan are more likely to have pierced nostrils than those made elsewhere. *Heubach* of Köpplesdorf, *Franz Schmidt,* and *Alt, Beck & Gottschalck* made some dolls with pierced nostrils.

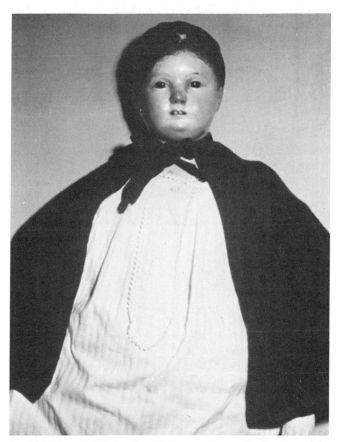

**1263.** Papier-mâché head with pierced nostrils, open mouth with teeth, glass eyes, painted black hair suggesting a baby or little boy. *Courtesy of Winnie Langley; photograph by Winnie Langley.*

**Notaseme Hosiery Co.** 1920–21. Philadelphia, Pa. Registered two trademarks in U.S.: *Little Kim* and *Binkie Doll.* Both were affixed with printed labels on the boxes or packages.

**Nöthlich & Falk, Otto Richard.** 1862. Neustadt near Coburg, Thür. Won a prize medal for papier-mâché dolls that they displayed at the London Exhibition.

**Nottingham Toy Industry Ltd.** 1919. Nottingham, Nottinghamshire. *Meakin & Ridgeway* were sole U.S. and Canadian distributors for Nottingham dolls.

**Noufflard, Mlle. Berthe.** 1916. Paris. Made dolls. *Sèvres* accepted one of her models.

**Novelty Doll Co.** 1925. Auburn, N.Y. Registered *Jack & Jill* as a trademark in U.S.

**Novelty Doll Co.** 1925. New York City. Copyrighted *Rock-a-By Baby,* designed by *Ernesto Peruggi.*

**Nuborn Babe.** See **New Born Babe.**

**Nude Dolls.** See **Frozen Charlotte.** (Undressed dolls usually wore a chemise and were not nude.)

**Nudoll Manufacturing Co.** 1920, Boston, Mass.; 1921, Samuel Orkin-Nudoll Manufacturing Co., also in Newark, N.J. Made kid-bodied dolls and cloth-bodied dolls, including baby dolls. Full-jointed kid dolls came with moving eyes, wigs, wooden arms, composition hands and lower legs; sizes 14, 16, 18, and 22 inches. Cork-stuffed, inside-jointed dolls cost $1.00.

**Nugent.** 1900–1901. U.S. Distributed various types of dolls, including those with bisque, composition, rag, or *Minerva* metal heads.

**Numbers.** Many dolls' heads bear numbers. Some of these represent the size, some represent the mold number, and occasionally there are numbers that represent dates, patent numbers, and so on. The size numbers on small heads are often in the form of fractions. In 1924, a doll hospital advertised that they could fit any head by simply comparing numbers. (See also **Marks.**)

**Nunn, George Laurence.** 1921, Liverpool, Lancashire; 1924, Nunn & Smeed. Manufactured dolls.

1921: Obtained British patent for a walking doll with spring hinges at the knee joint.

1924: Registered *Colonel Bogey* as a trademark in Britain for dolls.

**Nürnburg Fille.** See **Dutch Dolls.**

**Nürnberger Metall & Lackterwaarenfabrik.** 1908. Nürnberg, Bavaria. Formerly with *Gebrüder Bing;* obtained a German patent for production of rag dolls.

**Nurse.** 1918. All-rubber doll with molded clothes, made by *Faultless Rubber Co.* Came in red and tan.

**1265.** Doll with china head and arms. Head is marked with the crosshatching to form diamonds found on Nymphenburg ceramics. This mark was used in the 18th and 19th centuries. H. 14 inches. *Courtesy of Ruth & R. C. Mathes.*

**1264.** Dolls with hickory-nut heads, exhibited at the 1865 Sanitary Fair held in Chicago. *Courtesy of The Smithsonian Institution.*

**1266.** Nymphenburg mark found on dolls' heads.

**Nursing Doll.** See **Feeding Doll.**

**Nutoi.** See **New Toy Co.**

**Nuts.** Nuts have long been used for making dolls—hazelnuts, walnuts, and many other types. In 1893 *Mrs. Watson Hill Nash* displayed cashew nut dolls at the Chicago Exposition.

**Nuttall, William Henry, & Maden, James Henry.** 1893. Manchester, Lancashire. Obtained a British patent for making celluloid dolls molded from hot sheets of celluloid in a plastic state.

**Nye, Bessie Mills.** 1924. Arvada, Calif. Was issued a U.S. design patent for a rotund little girl doll.

**Nymphenburg.** 1761–1925+. Nymphenburg near Munich, Bavaria. (The state porcelain factory of Bavaria.) Its marks have been found on dolls, but as in the case of *Meissen,* there is a need to check the authenticity of products having the Nymphenburg marks. When the Frankenthal factory near Mannheim, Bavaria, closed in 1799, part of its molds were removed to Nymphenburg.

# O

**O You Kid (O-U-Kid).** 1914. Bisque doll representing a standing child, designed by *Fred Kolb,* copyrighted by *Borgfeldt.* Came dressed in nightie. (See **Oh You Kid.**)

**Obrect, Frances.** 1919–20. Flint, Mich. Secured a U.S. design patent for a *Sammy Sandman* doll.

**Obry.** 1871–73. Paris. Made dolls.

**Ocarino & Toy Co.** See **American Ocarina & Toy Co.**

**Oettel, Wilhelm.** 1895. Greiz, Thür. Manufactured dolls.

**Offenbacher, H., & Co.** 1920–24. Nürnberg, Bavaria. Exported and distributed stuffed dolls.

1921: Registered a trademark with the initials "O Co." in Germany.

**Offenbacher, S., & Co.** 1923–25. London. Handled dolls.

**Offene Handelsgesellschaft Moritz Pappe.** 1907–18. Liegnitz, Germany. Doll manufacturer. Registered in Germany a seven-pointed star in a circle as a trademark.

**Ogilwy, Robert.** 1843–60. London. In 1852, George

Teather joined Ogilwy to form the firm Ogilwy & Teather, but by 1856 each was working separately. Ogilwy made composition and waxed composition dolls.

**Oh You Kid.** Ca. 1914. All-bisque doll with embossed hair, arms against sides and without joints, chubby body; size 5¾ inches, price $1.75 doz. wholesale. (See **O You Kid;** also **O-U-Kids.**)

**Ohlhaver, Gebrüder.** 1918–25+. Sonneberg, Thür., and Hamburg, Germany. Manufactured *Revalo* line of dolls. Bent-limb babies and standing babies came clothed in dresses or chemises.

**Ohrdrufer Puppen & Spielwarenfabrik.** See **Kuhles, Franz.**

**Okada, Keitaro.** 1900. Haraki-Kin, Japan. Won a bronze medal for his display of dolls at the Paris Exposition.

**Olaf.** 1909. Trade name for German boy made by *Margarete Steiff;* 11, 13½, and 17 inches high.

**Old Angeline.** 1915. Doll copyrighted by *Mary Frances Woods.* Represented an Indian and came dressed with bright skirt, blanket wrapped around the shoulders, and a handkerchief on the head.

**Old Glory.** 1900–1907. Trademark registered in Germany by *A. Wislizenus* for jointed dolls; trademark registered in U.S. by *Hamburger & Co.* A doll marked "Old Glory" and "A W" on the body has a bisque head made by *Simon & Halbig.*

1907: *Bawo & Dotter* advertised Old Glory jointed dolls with "A1 heads of Simon & Halbig make."

1267. "Old Glory" mark used on dolls made by A. Wislizenus.

**Old Glory Kids.** 1916. Boy and girl dolls dressed in red, white, and blue; made by *Ideal Novelty & Toy Co.*

**Old Rip.** Early 20th-century character doll with bisque head representing Rip Van Winkle; probably made in Germany.

**Olie-Ke-Wob.** 1919–20. Trademark registered in U.S. by *Elsie Shaver* for dolls. Name stamped in ink on the package.

**Oliver Twist.** 1914. Boy doll made by *Louis Amberg & Son.*

**Oliver Twist.** 1924–25+. Rag doll designed and made by *Madame Alexander.* It had a mask face with raised features, which were hand-painted by Madame Alexander. Came with wig of mohair imported from England; pink muslin body. Size 14 inches; price $1.20.

**Olivier, Fernand Paulin.** 1920. Mézières, France. Registered *A la Clinique des Poupées* as a trademark in France.

**Ollier.** 1919–20. Montreuil, Seine. Manufactured dolls, *bébés, poupards,* and *mignonettes.* Used the initials "O. F."

**1268.** Old Rip, a bisque-head character doll with glass eyes, designed and dressed to represent Rip Van Winkle. Original black coat, brown trousers, and hat. Mark: Ill. **1269.** *Courtesy of Margaret Whitton; photograph by Winnie Langley.*

*Old Rip
9/0*

**1269.** "Old Rip" mark found on dolls.

**Olsen, Herbert Villiam Bodenhoff.** 1923. Copenhagen. Obtained a German patent for a doll with mechanism for producing tears.

**Olson, Kristian.** 1893. Telemarken, Norway. Displayed dolls at the Chicago Exposition.

**Olympia.** 1924. Trademark registered in France by *Pierre Muller* for dolls. The Olympia mark, written in script, is found on bisque heads with open mouth and teeth; also on ball-jointed composition bodies, often in large sizes. (See Ill. 1233.)

**Olympia Puppenconfection.** 1923–25. Vienna. Listed in directory as a doll manufacturer.

**O'Neill, Rose (Mrs. Rose O'Neill Wilson).** 1909–25+. A native of Wilkes-Barre, Pa., who lived much of her life at Bonniebrook, Day, Mo., she was a famous artist and designed the *Kewpie* doll, one of the most popular dolls ever created. Her first published drawing of Kewpies was in the December, 1909, LADIES' HOME JOURNAL. Ac-

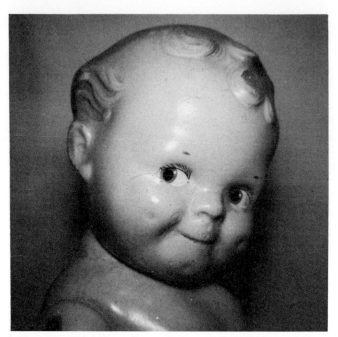

**1270.** Rose O'Neill's all-composition "Scootles," made by Cameo Doll Co., has molded and painted features. H. 12 inches. *Courtesy of Mary Roberson.*

*Rose ©
O'Neill*

**1271.** Rose O'Neill's mark on the sole of "Scootles" foot.

cording to Rowena Ruggles, the biographer of Rose O'Neill, by 1910 Rose had made a rag Kewpie that she was trying to perfect and had taken to Germany several times. (The rag *Dolly Dollykins* and *Bobby Bobbykins* had appeared on the market in 1909.) At the request of *Fred Kolb* of *Borgfeldt*, Rose designed the Kewpie doll in 1912 and went to Germany to supervise its manufacture by *Kestner*.

1913: She obtained design patents for a standing and for a sitting Kewpie; she copyrighted the Kewpie doll and registered "Kewpie" as a trademark in the U.S. Many of her Kewpie characters were made into doll forms.

1925: Rose O'Neill designed the *Scootles* doll, which represented the character of that name created by her.

**Ongawa, Clara P.** 1924. New York City. Copyrighted *Mme. Mah Jong,* a Chinese-type doll. The copyright card has "Mme.," and the picture of the doll with the card has "Mlle."

**Onondaga Indian Wigwam Co.** 1905–17. Syracuse, N.Y. Made dolls.

1917: Known as the Wigwam Co.; advertised unbreakable dolls that would not peel or crack and costumes secured by buttons and not pins.

**Ontario Textile Co.** 1921–23. Chicago, Ill. Registered in U.S. *Kunnin-Kids* as a trademark to be affixed by a label on a doll.

**Oo-Gug-Luk.** 1915. Copyrighted by *Louis Amberg & Son;* designed by *Jeno Juszko.* The doll's head was described as a true-to-life model of a Zulu, properly painted and with rings in ears and nose and a tuft of hair on the head.

**Oppenheimer, Maurice F.** 1913. Designed *Racketty Packetty Kiddy,* made and copyrighted by *Steinfeld Bros.*

**Oracle Doll.** See **Fortune Telling Doll.**

**Ordenstein, Richard.** 1913. London. Registered *Ragtime Kids* as a trademark in Britain for dolls.

**Oriental.** 1919. Name of doll copyrighted by *Guglielmo Voccia.*

**Original Condition.** This is a term used by doll collectors for dolls with all original parts. The value of a doll is considerably decreased when parts of it are not original or when the clothes have been replaced.

Most dictionary definitions of "original" agree with the following: "of or belonging to the beginning or first stage of existence of a thing." Therefore, when the term "original condition" is applied to a doll, it does not mean that the doll is in mint condition. A doll in mint condition is one that has been preserved tightly wrapped in its original box or container, and has never been played with by anyone. If a doll has all its parts, as originally made, with no substitutions or alterations, it can be designated as in "original condition" even though it may have lost a few strands of hair, its body may be a bit faded, or it may show a few similar evidences of the ravages of time.

Collectors who remove an old body because it does not please their particular taste should preserve the original body so that it can be passed on to the next collector. Bodies are an important part of a doll and sometimes help in dating it. A study of bodies at various dates and for various types of dolls is necessary so that a collector can recognize a replaced body. Fabric or kid bodies were seldom sewed by machine, nor did they have any but the simplest joints, prior to 1860.

Collectors of the early part of the 20th century often had little reverence for original bodies or original clothes; hence, dolls that have not passed through the hands of many collectors are more likely to be found in original condition. The authors purchased a china-headed doll from a collector of the 1920's and 1930's. This doll had strange plaster feet that were obviously new. It was assumed that the original feet had been broken and these were crude replacements, but examination showed that under the plaster there were perfect original china legs. These apparently had not suited the taste of the collector. Fortunately, however, they had not been destroyed and the doll could be returned to its original condition.

Collectors sometimes find a head on one type of body, and assume that all such heads were on that type of body—but this is not necessarily true. Heads and bodies were frequently sold separately, a circumstance that led to wide variation. China heads can be found on original bodies with bisque limbs, and bisque heads on original bodies with china limbs. *Lacmann* used heads on his cloth bodies of the same type as those found on gusseted kid bodies. Character baby heads were sometimes put on regular ball-jointed bodies, sometimes on bent-limb baby bodies or other types. (See Ill. 1099.)

It is very difficult to be certain that a doll wears its original clothes, and, of course, not all dolls were dressed when originally purchased. The clothes made for the doll when it was new would constitute its original clothes. Clothes that are obviously commercially made and are sewed onto the doll are likely to be original. If the clothes are contemporary with the age of the doll, and if they also fit its contours, they may be original. And if they are original, the material will be old; the stitches will probably be fine if hand done, and the fastening should be of tapes, old buttons, or long hooks with sewed thread eyes. The clothes are likely to represent the area from which the doll came; for example, a Paris doll would have fine fashionable clothes, but a doll from the American Midwest would be more likely to wear a sunbonnet and sturdy attire. The original clothes on an old doll may not suit the taste of a collector, who is naturally privileged to redress the doll, but *the original clothes should be kept.* Many of the turned bisque-head dolls were originally dressed in long baby dresses, though collectors often prefer to dress these dolls as children or even ladies. Many dolls were originally dressed in provincial costumes representing different countries. Unfortunately, collectors sometimes do not value these foreign costumes and prefer redressing the dolls even if this means destroying the original condition. When clothes are in tatters and it is impossible to preserve them even by sewing the tatters to a net base, it is generally desirable to reproduce the clothes as closely as possible and to keep a record of the date and amount of replacement.

Original condition is a function not only of age but also of the practices of the owners of dolls. Early china heads on original bodies are rarer than the even earlier molded papier-mâché heads on kid bodies. Collectors find 19th-century lady dolls in original clothes far more frequently than they find 20th-century *Schoenhut* dolls in original clothes.

**Original Rolf Berlich Puppe.** 1923. Trademark registered in Germany by *Rudolf Sauberlich,* for Rolf Berlich dolls and dolls' clothes.

**Original Rose Hein Puppen.** 1925. Trademark registered in Germany by *Therese Heininger.*

**Original Toy Co.** 1915–24. New York City. Made *Oteecee* character dolls.

**Orkin, Samuel—Nudoll Manufacturing Co.** See **Nudoll Manufacturing Co.**

**Ormond Dolls.** 1925. Advertised by *D. H. Wagner & Sohn;* included Pirouette, Pirola, Pipa, and Pitty.

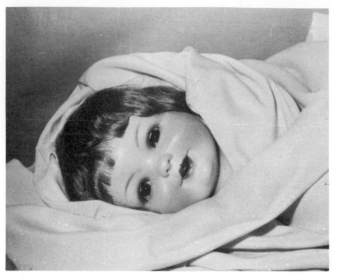

**1272.** Doll's head designed by Jeanne I. Orsini has sleeping eyes and wig. Mark: Ill. **1274.** *Courtesy of Margaret Whitton; photograph by Winnie Langley.*

**Orsini, Jeanne I.** 1916–25+. New York City. Designed dolls' house size character dolls. Nearly all her dolls were smiling except *Tummyache,* which was crying.

1916: Copyrighted *Dodo* and Tummyache.

1918: Copyrighted *Fifi* and *Nellie Sunshine.*

1919: Copyrighted *Uncle Sam.*

1920: Copyrighted *Didi, Mimi,* and *Zizi.* Thelma Bateman reports a small all-bisque *Vivi* doll with "J.I.O." on the shoulder and a round label saying, "VIVI // Reg. U. S. Pat. // Office Copr. 1920 // Orsini // Pat. app. for." This doll had a wig, character face and hands, and molded shoes.

**Orszagos Magyar Háziipari Szövetség (National Hungarian House Industry League).** Ca. 1925. Budapest. Workshop in Hungary; made dolls in Hungarian costumes. Shops in Vienna, Berlin, etc.

**Orthey, Charles, & Orthey, Mme. (née Guilminot, Jeanne).** 1921. France. Obtained a French patent for a doll with head of linen, leather, or other material; the features were outlined with colored threads.

**Ortlepp, Lewis.** See **Kling, Christian Friedrich.**

**Orwell Art Industries.** Before 1908. Dublin, Ireland. Made character dolls with unbreakable faces of a "secret composition material." The faces were painted and washable. Laura Starr had three of these dolls in her collection; one was an aged peasant woman and the others were young colleens.

**Osborne, John Joseph.** 1924–25. New York City. Manufacturer. Registered in U.S. and Britain *Totem Tom Tom* as a trademark for dolls.

**Oscher, Bertha.** 1919. Designed *Impie,* which was copyrighted by the *Ben-Arthur Studios.*

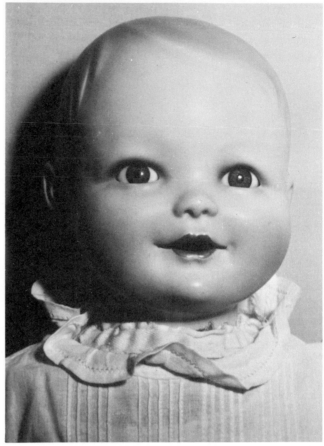

**1273.** Jeanne I. Orsini designed the bisque head of this doll. It has molded hair and glass eyes, and is marked "J. J. Orsini //1429 //2." *Photograph by Winnie Langley.*

Copr. By
J.J. Orsini
Germany
1430/4

**1274**

Copr. By
J.J. Orsini
Germany

**1275**

J.J. O. © 1919
47

**1276**

**1274–1276.** Marks found on dolls designed by Jeanne I. Orsini.

**Oschmann, Ernst.** 1925. Finisterbergen, Thür. Made jointed dolls, standing and sitting babies, all in handmade quality. Came in sizes 11 inches and up.

**Oteecee.** 1915–24. Brand name used by *Original Toy Co.* for their character dolls.

**Otsy-Totsy Dolls.** 1922–23. Trademark registered in U.S. by *Mayotto Browne.*

**Ott.** 1413. Nürnberg, Bavaria. Made dolls.

**Otto, Ferdinand.** 1914–20. Coburg, Thür. Manufactured dolls.

**Otto, Rudolf.** 1909. Sonneberg, Thür. Distributed and exported dolls.

**Otto Doll Supply Co.** 1917. New York City. Manufactured dolls.

**Ouachée.** See **Guillard, François;** also **Au Nain Bleu.**

**Ouenon.** 1861–62. Paris. Made dolls.

**O-U-Kids.** 1918. Composition cherub-type dolls made by *Gem Toy Co.* (See **O You Kid.**)

**Our Ann.** Name reported as found on a circular green label on the chest of a kid-body doll having a bisque head, mold #370, made by *Armand Marseille.* The label also has the initials "P. D. G. Co." and "Germany."

**Our Baby.** 1910. Copyrighted by Hahn & *Amberg.* Came with white or Negro coloring, velvet body, long infant dress; sizes 18 and 23 inches; prices $8.50 and $15.00 doz. wholesale.

**Our Baby.** 1913. Made by *Horsman* from a head designed by an American sculptor and exhibited at the National Academy of Design in New York City. Several styles of this number were offered. Came with long or short dresses.

**Our Baby.** 1915. Bent-limb baby made by *New Era Novelty Co.*

**Our Daisy.** 1903. Dolls handled by *Samstag & Hilder Bros.*

**Our Fairy.** 1914. Character doll produced by *Louis Wolf & Co.*

**Our Gang.** 1925. Dolls representing the Hal Roach comedy group, made by *Schoen & Yondorf Co.*

**Our Pet.** 1915. Trade name for doll made by *Ideal Novelty & Toy Co.*

**Our Pet.** 1921–22. Trademark registered in U.S. by *A. Strauss & Co.*

**Our Pride Kidette.** 1914. Trade name for a kid-bodied doll handled by *Strobel & Wilken.*

**Our Shop.** 1922–25+. Hungary. Made *Art Dolls.*

**Our Soldier Boys.** 1893 or soon thereafter. Designed by *Celia M. Smith,* made by *Arnold Print Works.* Several cutout dolls printed on cotton cloth, which sold for 12¢ to 20¢ a yard.

**Ourine, G.** 1925+. Paris. Made *Art Dolls.*

**Outdoor Baby.** 1918. Doll with composition head and hands, painted features, open mouth with pacifier, mohair wig; cork-stuffed body had concealed hip and shoulder joints; 18 inches tall; $33.00 doz. wholesale.

**Ouvré, Mme. Vera.** 1916. Paris. Made rag dolls.

**Overholt, Miles.** 1921–22. Los Angeles, Calif. Obtained U.S., French, and British patents for a rag doll with detachable limbs that were in the shape of smaller dolls. The two dolls that made the arms of the big doll had hands painted on the backs of their heads; their feet fastened with hooks and eyes to the shoulders of the large doll. The four small leg dolls were fastened, with their arms raised, two to the hips of the big doll and two to the legs of the upper small dolls. In the French patent this doll was called a "Gigogne."

**1277A & B.** Our Fairy, all-bisque doll with glass eyes, wig, open-closed mouth with teeth, movable arms. Ca. 1914. Mark on head: Ill. **1278.** Sticker on body: Ill. **1279.** H. 9 inches. *Courtesy of Dorothy Annunziato.*

**1278 & 1279.** Marks used on "Our Fairy" dolls. No. **1278** is on the head and No. **1279** is a sticker on the body.

**1280.** "Our Pet" mark used by A. Strauss & Co.

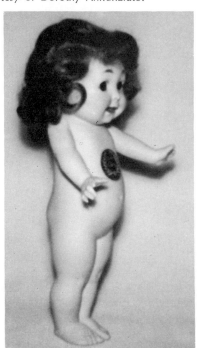
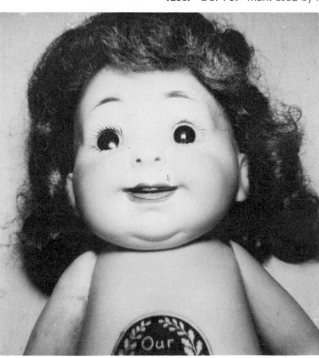

222
2 2
1278

1279

*Our Pet Germany 2/0*
1280

**Owenee Novelty Co.** 1922. Brooklyn, N.Y. Made walking and talking *Mama Dolls* with cotton cloth mask faces and cotton-stuffed bodies; 26-inch size, cost $1.98. Also made dolls with composition heads and hands, 26 inches tall, as well as dolls with hand-painted faces, 21 inches tall.

**Owens-Kreiser Co.** 1912–24. New York City. Distributed dolls made by *Gund Manufacturing Co., American Toy & Manufacturing Co.,* and others.

**Oz Doll & Toy Manufacturing Co.** 1924. Los Angeles, Calif. Made dolls.

**Ozocerite.** 1884–1925+. A wax made from residue of petroleum and used for making dolls; tended to supplant beeswax, but was sometimes mixed with it.

# P

**P. & M. Doll Co.** 1918–25+. New York City. Made P. & M. dolls' heads for dolls with painted or moving eyes, as well as arms and legs for dolls. Heads came in six sizes. Salvatore Paganello, native of Italy, founded this company.

**P. G. & Atlantic Toy Manufacturing Co.** 1922–24. New York City. P. G. Stuffed Toy Manufacturing Co. and *Atlantic Toy Manufacturing Co.* consolidated in 1922 and made walking and talking dolls; price $1.00 and up.

**Pacific Coast Doll Manufacturing Co.** 1918. Seattle, Wash. Made dolls designed by the Parisian sculptor, *Paul Beygrau.*

**Pacific Doll Manufacturing Co.** 1921. U.S. manufactured dolls.

**Pacific Novelty Co.** 1916–20. New York City. Manufactured dolls, especially baby dolls.

1920: Registered in U.S. *Little Miss Muffit* as a trademark.

**Pacini & Berni.** 1919. Chicago, Ill. Advertised glossy finish and dull finish dolls, including *Dearie Doll,* a standing doll 14 inches tall; price $3.50 doz. wholesale.

**Pacot, Mme.** 1829. Paris. Handled dolls.

**Paderewski, Mme.** 1915. Paris. Opened doll factory to aid Polish refugees, who made and dressed the dolls that were sold for their benefit. *Jedrick,* a Polish sculptor, designed the dolls; Michele, a Polish artist, painted their faces. The dolls had hard stuffed bodies and were dressed in Polish provincial costumes.

**Paillard.** See **Borreau, J.**

**Pain.** 1871–75. Paris. Made dolls.

**Paints.** Prior to the 18th century, dolls were colored with poisonous bismuth paints. Later, the faces were colored with white lead paint, which also was poisonous. By 1904, these paints were prohibited by law and only zinc oxide or similar harmless colors could be used.

**Paladin Baby.** 1903–12. Trademark registered in Germany by *Carl Hartmann* for dressed dolls.

**Palais Royal.** 1889–90. Trademark registered in U.S. by Rosa Lisner for *Dressed Doll Manufacturing Co.* The labels were to be applied by sewing or pasting one to each article.

**Pan.** 1887. Trademark registered in France by *Henri Delcroix* for doll's heads. It was to be stamped on the heads.

**1281.** "Pan" mark used by Henri Delcroix.      **PAN**

**Pa-na-ma.** 1915. Copyrighted by the *Trion Toy Co.;* designed by *Adolph Cohen.* The doll wore a straw hat and a white suit. Across the chest was a ribbon bearing the name "Pa-na-ma."

**Panama Kid, The.** 1915. Brown-skinned doll made by *Horsman;* represented "The boy that dug the ditch."

**Pandora.** The name given to early fashion dolls. They were called "Great Pandoras" or "Small Pandoras," depending on their size. In the World War I era, a doll named "Pandora" after the early fashion dolls was sold for the benefit of Belgian refugees. It had bisque head and arms and was dressed by famous Paris dressmakers.

**Pandore.** 1915. Trademark registered in France by *Mlle. Valentine Thomson.*

**Pannier.** 1872–92. Paris. Made dolls and bébés. Mons. Pannier was issued a French patent in 1872 for a bébé or doll with a metal frame and joints.

1873: Mme. Blanche Pannier of the Paris Maison de la Pannier was awarded a medal of cooperation for her display at the Vienna Exhibition. She also won recognition there as one of the four representatives of the Maison P. F. *Jumeau.* The Paris Directories listed her as a maker of wigs, hats, and clothes for dolls.

1877: Both Pannier and *Rauch* were listed at 140, rue du Temple.

1878: Mme. Pannier showed dolls' hats at the Paris Exposition and received a medal.

1881–82: Charles Pannier was listed under Dolls in the Paris Directories.

1883: There was a medal-winning Pannier display at the Amsterdam Exhibition.

1885–90: The Pannier advertisement stated that they made bébés, dolls, *mignonettes,* and *marottes,* and referred to medals won at Vienna, Paris, and Amsterdam.

1892: Mme. Pannier was listed as making bébés and dolls; Pannier Frères (Bros.) engaged in the porcelain business.

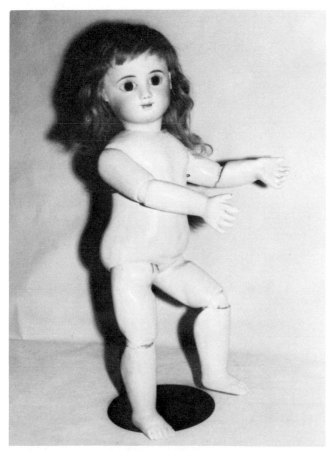

1282A & B. Bisque-head doll made by Pannier has glass eyes, pierced ears, closed mouth, and a jointed composition body resembling those made by Jumeau. Mark on head: Ill. 1283. Mark on sole of foot: Ill. 1284. H. 22 inches. *Coleman Collection.*

C 9 P.                    *Mme. Pannier*

1283                                      1284

1283 & 1284. Pannier marks used on dolls. No. 1283 is on the head, and No. 1284 is on the sole of the foot.

**Pannier, Achille.** 1874. Paris. Specialized in making dolls' dresses, shoes, hats, wigs, and similar items.

**Pansy Doll.** 1910–22. Trademark registered in U.S. and Germany by *Borgfeldt.*

**Pansy Kid.** Ca. 1914. Handled by *Sears, Roebuck & Co.*

## PANSY
## IV
## Germany

1285. "Pansy Kid" mark used by Sears, Roebuck & Co.

**Panzer, Rosa.** 1909–18. Nürnberg, Bavaria. Made dolls.

**Pápa.** 1811+. Hungary. An earthenware factory. Their price lists included dolls 16 inches high, according to data supplied by Eva Horváth. Dolls were the most expensive item made by this factory, which produced a cream-colored earthenware.

## PAPA

1286. Mark used by Pápa Pottery.

**Papa and Mama Dolls.** 1922. Made by *Ideal Novelty & Toy Co.*

**Papa and Mamma Talking Dolls.** 1906–12. Distributed by *Butler Bros.* Dolls had two cords attached to a bellows; when one cord was pulled, the doll said "Papa"; when the other cord was pulled, it said "Mamma." With bisque heads: 1906, sizes $14\frac{1}{2}$ and $16\frac{3}{4}$ inches; 1907, sizes $14\frac{1}{2}$ and $17\frac{1}{2}$ inches; 1910, sizes $13\frac{1}{2}$ and 18 inches. With patent washable (composition) heads: 1906, sizes $16\frac{1}{4}$, $18\frac{1}{2}$, and $21\frac{1}{2}$ inches; 1907, sizes $16\frac{1}{4}$, $18\frac{1}{2}$, and $27\frac{1}{4}$ inches; 1910–12, sizes 16 and 17 inches. (See also **Talking Dolls.**)

**Paperweight Eyes.** Term used by some collectors for blown glass eyes with depth and detail similar to that found in fine paperweights.

**Papier-mâché Dolls.** A type of composition; papier-mâché is defined in a late 19th-century dictionary as "a tough plastic material made from paper pulp containing an admixture of size, paste, oil, resin or other substances or from sheets of paper glued and pressed to-gether." The wood or rag fibers in paper give papier-mâché its tensile strength. To paper pulp are added paste or

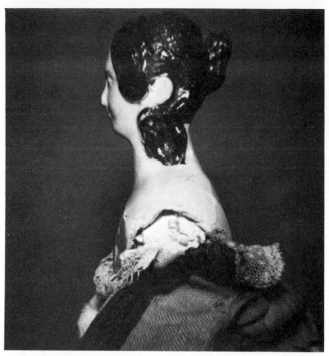

**1288.** Papier-mâché head has molded hair looped behind the ear and falling to the shoulders on the side, with a braided bun in back. Body is kid; limbs wood, with colored paper bands at the junctures. H. 11½ inches. *Coleman Collection.*

**1287.** Papier-mâché head with black pupil-less eyes, bamboo teeth, painted black hair with brush marks. Nail holes show how the wig was attached. The body is pink kid. Contemporary clothes include needlepoint slippers. H. 29 inches. *Courtesy of Helen Jo Payne.*

The prices given for dolls are those for which the dolls were originally offered for sale. They are *not* today's prices.

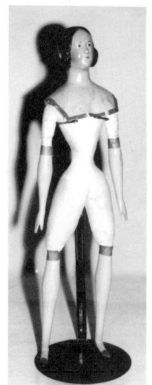

**1289A, B, & C.** Papier-mâché head with molded and painted hair in braids around the ears, a braided bun in back, and two looped braids under the bun. Molded breastplate is outlined in red. Note the similarity to those shown in Ill. **1290.** Painted slippers are green; red paper covers the juncture of the wooden limbs and the kid body. H. 20 inches. *Coleman Collection.*

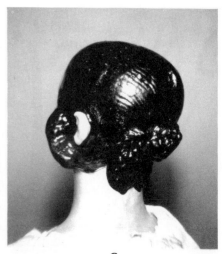

A                                               B                                               C

glue for adhesion and clay or flour for stiffness and solidity, plus the necessary chemicals. The word "papier-mâché" is used in English, French, and German. The French "carton-pâte" and the German "holz-masse" both seem to be variant terms for "papier-mâché."

One of the earliest references to papier-mâché dolls occurs in HISTOIRE DES JOUETS ET JEUX D'ENFANTS by Fournier. Here it was claimed that from the time of Francis I of France (ca. 1540), doll makers always used a mixture of clays, paper, and plaster called "carton-pierre" (literally, "stone pasteboard"). Moreover, according to D'Allemagne, Philibert Delorme said in 1550 that "carton-pâte" (pasteboard dough or papier-mâché) was poured into molds for dolls.

In the 18th century, the German communities of Nürnberg, Rodach, Sonneberg, and Neustadt, as well as towns in France, made papier-mâché toys. As late as the beginning of the 19th century, small pieces of paper, sand, and glue were kneaded together by hand; then the papier-mâché dolls were molded and finished individually by the maker. Shortly before 1810, it was discovered that papier-mâché dolls could be mass-produced in molds by a pressure process. This process was alleged to have been introduced into Sonneberg from

**1290.** Page from a Swiss catalog showing German dolls; dated between 1845 and 1860. Although unidentified, these dolls appear to have papier-mâché heads, kid bodies, and wooden lower limbs, similar to those shown in Ill. **1289.** *Courtesy of Marg. Weber-Beck from Franz Carl Weber, Zurich.*

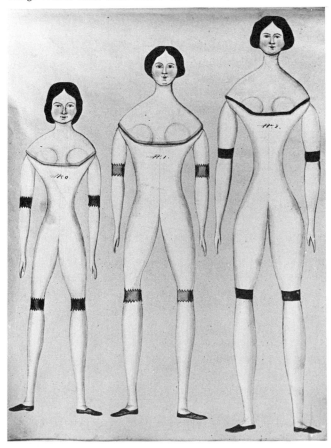

**1291.** Doll with papier-mâché head, painted features, kid body, turned wooden lower limbs with painted green slippers. Dressed in contemporary black wool suit. H. 15½ inches. *Courtesy of The Smithsonian Institution.*

Paris around 1807, and thus to have laid the foundation for the great German doll industry. By 1820, papier-mâché heads were used extensively on a new style of kid body with wooden limbs, which collectors often call "milliner's model" or "coiffure dolls." At Berlin in 1844, many of the dolls were made of papier-mâché. Mons. Natalis Rondot wrote about the 1851 London Exhibition: "Most dolls' heads are of papier-mâché, Saxony furnishes them." Thus, by the mid-19th century, papier-mâché dolls had reached their height of popularity.

Clara Mateaux, in THE WONDERLAND OF WORK (1884), explained: "There are several kinds of this material [papier-mâché], the simplest of which is that invented about a hundred years ago. It consists of sheets of paper laid one on another, and pasted firmly together upon a model of the thing to be imitated. Another kind is produced by mixing up a thick paper pulp and pressing it between moulds, or sometimes it is a compound of coarse fibres and some sort of clay, kneaded together with size until it forms a paste, which is rolled out into sheets by steam pressure.

"We also often meet with dolls and other toys of 'carton-pierre' which is a kind of plaster consisting of paper pulp, whiting, and glue, worked together and pressed in moulds, backed by coarse paper, and dried by steam."

In 1858, *Ludwig Greiner's* patent for a doll's head, called for white paper, Spanish whiting, rye flour, glue, and paste reinforced with linen or muslin. In 1869, G. F. Goetze patented an improved compound for "petrified papier-mâché" made of paper pulp, glue, turpentine, oil, flour, and whiting. Around 1870, papier-mâché began to be used for jointed dolls' bodies, a type that continued to be popular well into the 20th century. Meanwhile, ceramic heads and those of other types of composition gained popularity over papier-mâché heads. (See also **Manufacture of Papier-Mâché Heads.**)

**Papoose.** 1919. Indian-type doll made by *J. R. Miranda & Co.* Came with painted features and clad in a blanket; 7 inches tall.

**Papooski.** 1916. Trademark registered in Britain for dolls by a barrister (lawyer).

**Pappe, Moritz.** See **Offene Handelsgesellschaft Moritz Pappe.**

**Par Excellence.** 1906–10. Kid-body dolls made by *Kestner.* They had bisque heads and were all kid from the neck to the soles of feet. They were a better grade and more expensive than the *Marvel* brand. Both brands of bodies were distributed by *Butler Bros.* Par Excellence bodies were stuffed with sawdust and cork in equal amounts. These dolls had patent joints at shoulder, elbow, hip, and knee with nickel rivets; crown and streamer sticker on chest; bisque lower arms. The bisque head had sleeping glass eyes, teeth, and a curly sewed wig.

1906: Came in sizes 15, 17, 19, 21, 23½, and 26 inches.

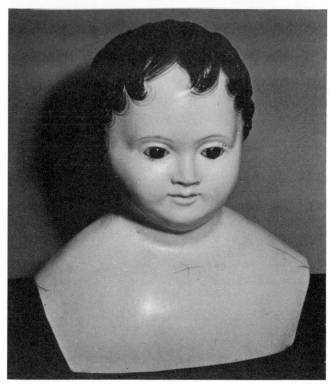

**1292.** Papier-mâché head with glass pupil-less eyes, molded and painted hair. H. of shoulder head, 11 inches. This head may have been intended for display rather than for use on a play doll. *Courtesy of Marion Holt; photograph by Winnie Langley.*

1907–10: Came in sizes 14¾, 17, 18, 19, 20, 21, 22, 23½, 24½, and 26 inches; price 75¢ to $4.75. In 1910, dolls in sizes 18 to 26 inches also came with hair eyebrows and eyelashes.

**Paradis Bébé.** 1911. Trademark registered in France by the *Société La Parisienne.*

**Paradis des Enfants.** See **Au Paradis des Enfants.**

**Paramount Rubber Consolidated, Inc.** 1923–24. Little Falls, N.J. Assignee of two U.S. design patents by *Domenic Zappia.* The designs were for an Indian girl and for a clown.

**Parcel Post Babies, The.** See **Featherweight Babies.**

**Parent, Charles Louis.** 1871–72. Le Havre, Seine-Maritime. Obtained French and U.S. patents for a ball-jointed doll strung with rubber elastic. The head and waist swiveled on a complete ball; the wrist, elbow, shoulder, hip, knee, and ankle joints had the lower member rounded at the top so that it fit into the cavity of the adjoining socket.

**Parfait-Bébé//Paris.** 1917. Trademark registered in France by *Edmond Hieulle.*

**Parfait Bébé//Paris//Manufacture Française//de Poupées et Jouets.** 1917. Trademark registered in France by *Mme. Aline Crosier.*

**Parian (Parian Bisque).** This material is defined in a late 19th-century dictionary as "a hard, fine, half-vitreous porcelain resembling Carrara marble: used for objects of art and ornaments." "Parian" is a generic term that may refer to either hard paste or soft paste porcelain.

1856: *John Ridgeway* at the *Cauldon Potteries* advertised Parian products. Parian originated in England.

1858: *Goss & Co.* established in Staffordshire for the production of Parian and "Ivory" porcelain busts.

1870: HARPER'S BAZAR described Christmas dolls: "There are bisque and Parian dolls, blond beauties always, of pink, flesh-like hue, with round blue eyes, dimpled cheeks, rosy lips, real yellow hair, and plump, natural limbs."

Collectors sometimes call untinted bisque dolls "Parian."

**Paris, Bébé de.** See **Bébé de Paris.**

**Paris Bébé.** 1889–1911. Created as a doll and registered in France as a trademark by *Danel & Cie.* in 1889. The Eiffel Tower mark was usually found on the bodies of these dolls.

1890: Advertised as a French bébé with patented joints having concealed or no rubber.

1911: Trademark registered in France by *Société Française de Fabrication de Bébés et Jouets.*

**Parisiana, Bébé.** See **Bébé Parisiana.**

**Parisien, Bébé le.** See **Le Parisien.**

**Parisienne, The.** 1923–24. Also known as the "Smoking Cigarette Girl," popular in America and Paris.

1924: Advertised by *Konroe Merchants* as having a cigarette in her mouth; had a bobbed hair wig and wearing trousers and high heels; 25 inches tall.

**Parisienne de Cellulosine Cie.** 1921. Factory at Oyonnax; salesrooms in Paris. Made celluloid dolls and dolls of noninflammable material.

**Parisienne Heads.** 1892. Advertised by J. Cros, successor of *Bonnafé;* they also advertised kid-bodied dolls.

**Parisiennes.** 1885. Name used by *Jumeau* for dolls with kid bodies. The heads were of the same type as the Jumeau bébés; only the bodies were different.

**Parisiennes à la Mode.** See **Les Parisiennes à la Mode.**

**Parlant, Bébé.** See **Bébé Parlant.**

**Parquet.** 1888. Obtained a French patent for making heads of dolls and bébés of blown glass and then decorating them.

**Parsons-Jackson Co.** 1910–19. Cleveland, Ohio. In 1918, it was Parsons & Parsons Co.; in 1918 and 1919, the location was New York City. Before they placed their dolls on the market in 1910, it took the company eight years to develop and produce them from the material called *Biskoline,* which resembled celluloid.

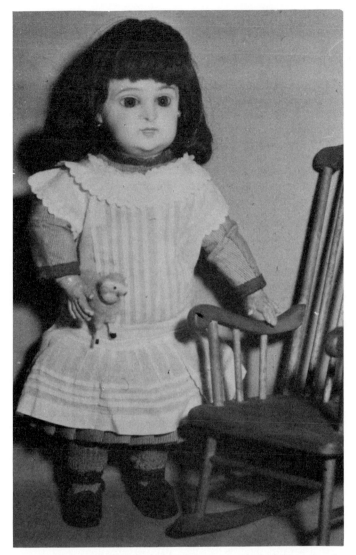

1293. "Paris Bébé" doll with Eiffel Tower mark, bisque head, glass eyes, jointed composition body. Mark: Ill. **1294.** *Photograph by Winnie Langley.*

1294 & 1295. "Paris Bébé" marks found on dolls.

PARIS-BEBE
Breveté
1294

TÊTE DÉPOSÉ
PARIS BEBE
1295

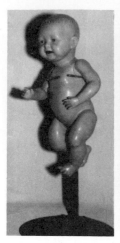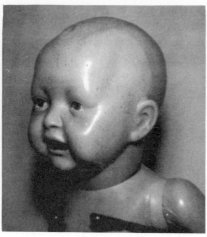

**1296A & B.** All-Biskoline doll made by Parsons-Jackson Co. has painted and molded hair and eyes, bent-limb baby body with steel spring joints. There is a raised stork mark on the back of the head and on the upper back, which also has "Trade Mark // Parsons-Jackson Co. // Cleveland, Ohio." H. 10½ inches. *Coleman Collection.*

**1297 & 1298.** Marks found on Parsons-Jackson dolls. No. **1297** is used on the heads, and **1298** on the bodies.

PARSONS-JACKSON CO.
CLEVELAND, OHIO.

1297                    1298

1912: Advertised *Biskoline Nature Dolls* or *Stork Brand Dolls* made of a non-absorbent material that would float in water. Bodies were held together with oil-tempered steel springs. Dolls came with molded hair and bent-limb bodies; wore rompers. Sizes 10½, 13, and 14 inches; price $1.50 to $2.50.

1913: Registered three trademarks in U.S. They were "K K K," "Biskoline," and the drawing of a stork. Used the slogan *Kant Krack.* Advertised fifty-six styles and sizes, including fully jointed straight-limb dolls as well as bent-limb babies. All were made of Biskoline, guaranteed for one year not to crack, peel, break, chip, or have the color wear off. The ball-jointed styles were dressed in rompers. A few models had molded shoes and socks, but most of them had bare feet.

1914–15: Assignee of two U.S. patents for stringing hollow-jointed bent-limb baby-type bodies with metal springs. Patents were issued to Frederick W. Parsons.

**Pasquet, Vve. (Widow).** 1873. Paris. Made dolls.

**Paste Heads.** Another name for composition heads.

**Pat-a-Cake Baby.** 1912. Trademark registered in Germany by *A. Luge & Co.*

**Pat-Biddy.** 1920. Trademark registered in U.S. by the *Faultless Rubber Co.*

**Patchell, James.** 1905. Philadelphia, Pa. Made dolls.

**Pate.** Term for the covering for the large hole found in the top of many dolls' heads. The wig is generally attached to the pate. French pates are usually cork, except on the dolls of *Jules Steiner.* Other pates are made of composition—frequently, merely cardboard. *Kestner* used plaster in his composition pates.

**Patent Indestructible.** See **Composition.**

**Patent Washable Dolls.** 1880's+. Name applied to certain composition dolls that were said to be washable, though children proved otherwise. They probably could be wiped gently with a damp cloth. They were made in a wide range of sizes, and were neither the least nor the most expensive dolls. Sometimes these dolls were also called Bisque Finish Dolls. Among the patent washable dolls advertised by *Butler Bros.* between 1906 and 1910 were the *Matlock* and Favorite Name dolls. The latter wore slips with girls' names embroidered on them—Mary, Emma, Edith, Ruth, Mabel, and Pauline, to name a few—and came in various sizes from 18 to 35½ inches.

**Patents.** Regular patents can be obtained for the materials of which a doll is composed, the articulation and assembling of the body, and for special functions such as sleeping, walking, and talking. The term of protection of these patents in the U.S. is seventeen years from the date of issue. There is also a special group called "design patents," which cover the design of a doll and are granted for terms of three and one-half, seven, or fourteen years. The first regular U.S. doll patent was obtained by *Ludwig Greiner* in 1858, and the first U.S. design patent for a doll was obtained by *Edward Peck* in 1886.

The U.S. Patent Office defines a patent as "A grant issued by the United States Government giving an inventor the right to exclude all others from making, using, or selling his invention within the United States, its territories and possessions. . . . A patent may be granted to the inventor or discoverer of any new and useful process, machine, manufacture, or composition of matter, or any new and useful improvement thereof . . . or on any new, original, and ornamental design for an article of manufacture. . . .

"A valid patent may not be obtained if the invention was in public use or on sale in this country for more than one year prior to the filing of your patent application. Your own use and sale of the invention for more than a year before your application is filed will bar your right to a patent just as effectively as though this use and sale had been done by someone else. [1836–70: There was no period of grace at this time, and the patent application had to be made before the product was put on the market. 1870–1939: Two years were allowed instead of the one year that has been in the law since 1939. Thus, before 1870, patented dolls could not legally be made prior to their patent application date; since then, they could legally be made only one year or two before the patent date. In most foreign countries, publication of an invention before the date of the application will bar the right to a patent, according to the U.S. Patent Office.] . . . A foreign citizen may obtain a U.S. patent under exactly the same conditions as a United States citizen . . .

"The application must be signed, sworn to, and filed in the Patent Office in the name of the true inventor. This is the person who furnishes the ideas, not the employer or the person who furnishes the money . . . The inventor . . . may sell all or any part of his interest in the patent application or patent to anyone by a properly worded assignment. The application must be filed in the Patent Office as the invention of the true inventor, however, and not as the invention of the person who has purchased the invention from him.

"The United States patent protects your invention only in this country. If you wish to protect your invention in foreign countries, you must file an application in the Patent Office of each such country within the time permitted by law. This may be quite expensive, both because of the cost of filing and prosecuting the individual patent applications, and because of the fact that most foreign countries require payment of taxes to maintain the patents in force." In 1912 PLAYTHINGS listed the following charges:

| Countries | Regular Patents (per year) | Design Patents | |
|---|---|---|---|
| Austria | $105 | 3 years | $42 |
| France | 96 | 5 years | 40 |
| Germany | 113 | 6 years | 47 |
| Great Britain | 82 | 5 years | 37 |
| Italy | 102 | 2 years | 45 |
| Russia | 142 | 10 years | 50 |

In France, fifteen years is the usual term for patents.

Patent dates and/or numbers often appear on dolls, and with this information the collector can obtain a copy of the patent papers for a particular doll. Studying these will give him valuable information about the history of the doll. Some collectors claim that certain dolls were produced several years before their patent date, but a study of the patent law shows this to be legally impossible.

Many British and French patents were secured by patent agents who represented the patentee, especially when the inventor lived in another country. The abridgements of the British patents frequently give only the name of the agent and not the name of the patentee or inventor. Therefore, it is best to consult the complete patent rather than to rely on indexes and abridgements, if accurate information is desired.

"Pat." or "pat'd" usually stand for "patent" or "patented" in America and Britain. "Breveté" or "Bté." are the French for "patented." With "Breveté" the initials "S.G.D.G." often appear. These stand for "sans garantic du gouvernement" (without guarantee of the government). "Deutsches Reichs Gebrauchs Muster" or

"D.R.G.M." indicates a German registered design or patent. In German, there is also "Gesetzlich geschützt" or "ges. gesch." for "registered" or "patented." Doll makers were sometimes confused as to whether they had a patent, a copyright, or just what it was. Often they gave a patent number that was in reality the number of a design patent or a copyright number; the reverse can sometimes be true too.

**Pat-o-Pat.** 1925. Infant doll that clapped its hands; made by *EFFanBEE*.

**Patria.** 1916. Trademark registered in France by *Mme. Lebel*.

**Patricienne, La.** See **La Patricienne.**

**Patten, J. N.** 1878–79. North Springfield, Vt. Listed as a maker of dolls in 1878; joined the *Jointed Doll Co.* by 1879.

**Patten, Zeboin C., Jr.** 1909–10. Chattanooga, Tenn. Registered *Velvokin* as a trademark in U.S. for dolls.

**Patty-Cake.** 1918–25+. Trademark registered in U.S.; used for rag baby dolls by *Horsman*.

**Patty-Cake.** 1925. Made by *Louis Amberg & Son*; *New Born Babe* type of infant that jingled and cried, slept, and walked. Advertisement read: "To see my hands clap, pull jingle bell." Price $2.00 and $2.50.

**Paufler, Emil, & Co.** 1876–1907. Schneeberg, Saxony. Made and exported jointed and dressed dolls.

1890's: Advertised unbreakable dolls' heads of *Masse Holz* and dressed and undressed jointed dolls.

**Paul.** 1912. Doll with composition head, eyes glancing to the side; made by *Tip Top Toy Co.* Sizes 9, 12½, and 15½ inches; price 25¢ to $1.00. Mate for *Virginia*.

**Paul, J.** 1889–90. Paris. Distributed dolls from Saxony.

**Paul Revere Pottery.** 1912–15, Boston, Mass.; 1915–25+, Brighton, Mass. Made bisque dolls' heads, probably during the World War I period. They were usually socket heads, some with closed mouth and some with open mouth; the heads were made for wigs. The pottery also made all-bisque dolls and porcelain sleeping eyes to be used in their heads. They used the initials "P. R. P." Various decorators' marks are found on the heads. "B I" was used by Edith Brown. "C 2" and "L R+" were also used.

**Paulina.** 1889–90. Doll distributed by YOUTH'S COMPANION. Came with bisque head, glass eyes, flowing hair in *Rembrandt* style wig; ball-jointed composition body with joints at neck, shoulders, elbows, hips, and knees. Paulina was completely dressed, including a trimmed hat. Price $1.65.

**Pauline.** 1905–14, and possibly earlier. China dolls' heads were made with "Pauline" in gold letters on the chest. This type was produced by *Hertwig & Co.* and *Closter Veilsdorf*.

**Pauline.** 1916. Distributed by *Montgomery Ward & Co.* A baby doll with a pacifier; 13½ inches tall; price $1.55.

**1299.** Bisque head manufactured by the Paul Revere Pottery has a closed mouth. Glass eyes and wig are not original. Mark on socket head: Ill. **1300.** Circumference of head, 7 inches. *Coleman Collection.*

**1300.** Mark found on dolls made by Paul Revere Pottery.

P·R·P
110·2

**Paxie.** 1918–19. Trademark registered in U.S. by *Martha St. Claire Wingert.*

**Paxie Ann.** 1922. Trademark registered in U.S. by *Martha St. Claire Wingert.*

**Payen.** 1865–85. Paris. Made dolls.

**Payne, John Edward.** 1849. London. Was granted a British patent for molding a doll out of gutta-percha combined with rubber.

**Peach.** 1914–15. Trade name for bisque dolls handled by *Strobel & Wilken.*

**Peachy Pets.** 1919. Fully jointed character dolls made by *Colonial Toy Manufacturing Co.*

**Peacock.** 1862. London. Exhibited wax and composition dolls in the London Exhibition. He advertised that he always had a stock of 1,000 dolls, both dressed and undressed. These included all kinds of composition dolls and wax dolls; among the latter were those made by the *Pierottis.* Peacock's prices were $5.00 to $25.00 for each doll, wholesale. These prices were probably for the fine wax dolls. An *Autoperipatetikos* doll with untinted bisque head has been reported as marked "J. Peacock."

**Peacock, William, & Sons.** 1903–11. London. Exported and distributed dolls.

**1301.** Mark used by Peacock.

From
**PEACOCK'S**
The Beaming Nurse
525 NEW OXFORD ST.
corner of Bloomsbury St.
LONDON, W.C.

**Peakies.** 1915. Trademark registered in U.S. by *Borgfeldt.*

**Péan.** 1862–90. Paris. Laurent Marie René Péan was granted an Austrian and a British patent for a doll whose movements were initiated by compressed air. Péan Frères (Bros.), successors of Laurent Péan, had displays in 1885 at Antwerp and in 1889 at Paris; they were Hors Concours at both exhibitions.

1890: Advertised that they manufactured, at their factory in Criel, Oise, toys in metal and cardboard as well as in porcelain and faïence. They also carried dolls' furnishings. Péan Frères was the number-one company in the *Chambre Syndicale de Fabricants de Jouets Français;* their mark was "P. F."

**Pearlie.** 1920–24. Trademark registered in U.S. by *New York Merchandise Co.* for dolls.

**Peary.** 1909. *Borgfeldt, Theo. H. Gary & Co., Horsman,* and *Strobel & Wilken* produced dolls representing Commander (Lieutenant) Peary.

**Peasant Children.** 1917. Character dolls made by *Horsman.*

**Peasant Doll.** 1915. *Zuza Walovich* secured a U.S. design patent for a Slavonian peasant doll.

**Peasant Dolls.** 1924–25+. *Bernard Ravca* made cloth dolls representing peasants in various French provinces. The stockinet faces and hands of these dolls were not treated chemically, as were those of his later dolls. The peasants wore wooden sabots and were autographed by Bernard Ravca.

**Pecher, M.** Ca. 1899. Vienna. Manufactured dolls and dolls' heads.

**Peck, Deon E.** See **Darrow Manufacturing Co.**

**Peck, Edward S.** 1884–86. Brooklyn, N.Y. Obtained a U.S. design patent for a rag Santa Claus doll, which he assigned to the *New York Stationery & Envelope Co.*

**Peck, Mrs. Lucy.** 1891–1921. London. Made, distributed and repaired dolls, especially wax dolls. Her establishment was known as "The Doll's Home" from at least 1901–21.

1902: Made wax dolls with real hair inserted.

**Peck, William E., & Co.** 1911. London agent for *Horsman.*

**Peebo Doll.** 1922. Trademark registered in Britain by *Arthur Graham.*

**Peek-a-Boo.** 1911. Trademark registered in Britain by *Bernard Home Thomson.*

**Peek-a-Boo.** 1913–15. All-composition dolls of *Can't Break 'Em* material made by *Horsman;* designed by *Grace G. Drayton.* These dolls had been called *Gee-Gee* when they first came out.

1913: Came in three styles of boys and girls; boys wore one-piece striped bathing suit or summer suit and were barefoot; girls were in polka dot dresses and barefoot. The eyes glanced to the side. Head, limbs, and lower torso were of composition; upper torso of cloth; legs and lower torso in one piece. Doll was 7½ inches tall.

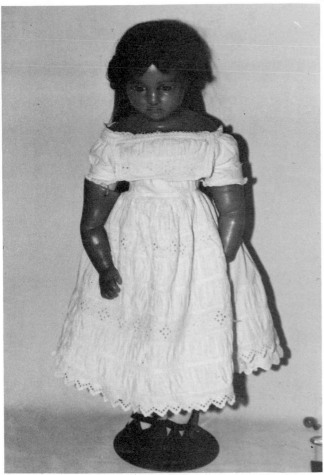

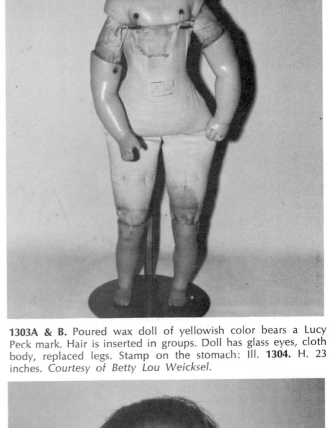

**1302A & B.** Poured, darkened-color wax doll made by Lucy Peck; glass eyes; cloth body. Mark stamped on the stomach: Ill. **1304.** H. 30 inches. *Courtesy of Betty Lou Weicksel.*

**1303A & B.** Poured wax doll of yellowish color bears a Lucy Peck mark. Hair is inserted in groups. Doll has glass eyes, cloth body, replaced legs. Stamp on the stomach: Ill. **1304.** H. 23 inches. *Courtesy of Betty Lou Weicksel.*

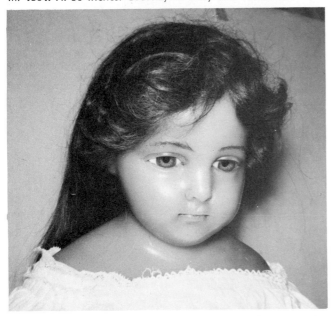

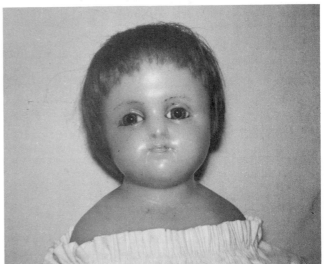

**1304–1307.** Marks found on the bodies of dolls handled by Lucy Peck.

FROM
Mrs. PECK
THE DOLL'S HOME
131. REGENT STREET
—W—

1304

FROM
MRS. PECK
THE DOLL'S HOUSE
131 REGENT STREET
—W—

1305

DOLLS AND TOYS OF ALL DESCRIPTION REPAIRED
MRS. LUCY PECK
THE DOLL'S HOUSE
131 REGENT ST LONDON
—W—

1306

DOLLS AND TOYS OF ALL ✱ DESCRIPTIONS REPAIRED ✱
MRS PECK
THE DOLL'S HOME
131 Regent Street
LONDON, W

1307

1915: Dolls were clad in ribbons instead of bathing suits.

**Peek-a-Boo.** 1925. Infant doll made by *Acme Toy Manufacturing Co.;* distributed by *Kaufman Levenson & Co.*

**Peeps.** 1918–20. A 12-inch doll made by *Jessie McCutcheon Raleigh.* Nancy Cox McCormack wrote a story about these dolls, which helped to sell thousands of them.

**Peerless Doll Co.** 1917–18. New York City. Made composition boy, girl, and baby dolls.

**Peerless Doll Heads Co.** 1921. New York City. Made "unbreakable" composition heads with moving eyes.

1921: Advertised "You furnish the dies and we'll make YOUR dolls."

**Peero.** 1913–14. Trademark registered in U.S. by *Borgfeldt.*

**Peg O'My Heart.** 1914. Trade name for doll made by *Louis Amberg & Son.*

**Peg Wooden Dolls.** See **Dutch Dolls.**

**Pegard, F.** 1833–47. Paris. Made dolls.

1833: Advertised dolls of pink kid and other types of dolls.

**Peggy.** 1919. Cherub-type doll made by *New Toy Co.;* came with a wig.

**Peggy.** 1920. Copyrighted by *Venetian Art & Novelty Co.;* designed by *Aida Pierini.* A cherub-type doll with molded hair.

**Peggy.** 1920. Walking doll made by *Averill Manufacturing Co.* Came with composition arms and legs, and dressed in gingham; 26 inches tall.

**Peggy Doll, The.** 1920–21. Trademark registered in U.S. by *Marian F. Gardineer.*

**Pelletier, E. (L).** Before 1890–1900. Marseille, France. Made and exported bébés.

1895: Advertised that he had won a Diploma of Honor or a gold medal for his jointed bébés fifteen times. He used the trademark *La France* for dressed and undressed jointed bébés.

1898: Specialized in making bébés with heads of wood.

1900: Paris agent was M. Cartier.

**Peloubet, Francis W.** 1884–86. Newark, N.J. Obtained U.S. patent for a spring-activated, clockwork walking doll. The doll lifted feet, balanced, and rocked on two horizontal rods at the front and back of each foot.

**Peltz.** 1891. Schneeberg, Saxony. Made dressed dolls.

**Penn Stuffed Toy Co.** 1924–25+. New York City. Manufactured dolls.

**Penny Ross.** See **Ross, Penny.**

**Penny Woodens.** See **Dutch Dolls.**

**Pensky, Alfred.** 1925+. Coburg, Thür. Manufactured miniature dolls.

**Pepper-Mint Kids.** 1921. Soft dolls made by *The Giftoy Co.;* designed by *Gertrude Stacy.*

# PERFECT

**1308.** Mark of Perfect Toy Manufacturing Co.

**Perfect Toy Manufacturing Co.** 1919–25+. New York City. Made "Perfect" dolls of wood-fiber composition.

1919: Used the trade name *Baby Betty* for a doll that came in various sizes.

**Perfection Doll Co.** 1916–23. Long Island City and Manhattan, N.Y. Manufactured "Perfection" sanitary dolls; distributed by *Louis Wolf & Co.*

1916: Price was 25¢ to $5.00.

1918–23: Price was 50¢ to $5.00.

**Perfumed Doll.** See **Baby Butterfly.**

**Perier, Henry.** 1916. Paris. Registered two trademarks in France for dolls—*La Vraie Parisienne* and "M. P." in a circle.

**Perks, E. S. A.** 1916. Middlesex, England. Obtained two British patents for dolls whose facial expression could be altered, one of them by having two interchangeable pairs of eyes.

**Perks, R. M.** 1924. Chislehurst, Kent. Registered *Dolfam* as a trademark in Britain.

**Permolin Products Co.** 1918. Brooklyn, N.Y. Made dolls to which they gave the trade name *Trulie Good.* Advertised dolls made of new composition without glue and half the weight of other dolls.

**Peronne, Mlle.** 1864–65. Paris. Married in 1865 and appeared as Mme. Lavallée-Peronne through 1884. She specialized in dolls' trousseaux at her shop, *A la Poupée de Nuremberg.* A kid-covered wooden-bodied lady doll has a label on its chest reading: A LA POUPEE DE NU-REMBERG // 21 rue de Choiseul // LAVALLEE-PERONNE // Trousseaux complets // Reparations [Repairs] // Paris.

**Perreau Fils.** See **Guillard.**

**Perrimond, Gaston.** 1924. Nice. Registered in France, *La Poupée Nicette* as a trademark.

**Perrin, Mme.** 1916. Paris. Registered in France *La Poupée des Allies.*

**Perth Amboy.** Ca. 1920. Name found on bisque heads made by *Ernst Reinhardt* in Perth Amboy, N.J.

**Peruggi, Ernesto.** 1915–25+. Italian citizen residing in New York City; designed dolls.

1915: Designed *Little Rascal, Georgy-Porgy, Toodles, Chubby, Sunshine, Happy, Pettish Polly,* and *Smiles,* all for *Trion Toy Co.*

1918: Designed *Little Hero* and *Little Nero* for *Daniel Pollack.*

1919: Designed Toodles for the *American Bisque Doll Co.;* designed *Kewpies Model* for the *Manhattan Toys*

*& Dolls Manufacturing Co.;* designed *Love Me* for the *Fine Doll Manufacturing Co.*

1920: Copyrighted two dolls, one described as a "Sweet sitting baby" and the other as a "Little boy dressed." He designed *Beauty Kist* for the Manhattan Toys & Dolls Manufacturing Co.

1923: Designed *Baby Grumpy* for *Hugo Baum.*

1925: Designed *New Born Baby* for *EFFanBEE;* designed *Rock-a-by Baby* for *Novelty Doll Co.*

**Pet Name.** 1905–25+. Trade name for china heads with names molded and painted in gold across the chest; they were distributed by *Butler Bros.,* who owned the molds for the heads. The dolls had wavy hair, a third of them blonde, the rest black-haired. A collar and bow was also molded with the head. Butler Bros. advertised *Marion, Agnes, Helen, Bertha, Dorothy,* and *Ethel.* These heads are believed to have been made by *Hertwig & Co.* and/or *Closter Veilsdorf.* The heads came in ten sizes, ranging in height from 3$\frac{1}{8}$ to 6$\frac{5}{8}$ inches; price was 35¢ to $3.00 doz. wholesale. These heads were also sold on "A B C" Body Educational Dolls by Butler Bros. The "A B C" line of bodies were of printed cloth with letters, illustrations, and names on them. The dolls with Pet Name heads and "A B C" bodies had china limbs and came in sizes 7$\frac{1}{4}$, 8, 8$\frac{1}{2}$, 10$\frac{1}{4}$, 11, 12, 13, 14, 16, 17$\frac{1}{2}$, 19$\frac{1}{2}$, and 21 inches; priced at 37¢ to $3.95 doz. wholesale.

**1309.** Pet Name china head as advertised by Butler Bros. in the early 20th century. This doll has blonde hair. "Bertha" appears in raised gold letters on the front of the shoulders, and "Patent App'd For// Germany" is impressed on the back of the shoulders. Cloth body is printed with nursery characters. H. 9$\frac{3}{4}$ inches. H. of shoulder head, 3 inches. *Coleman Collection.*

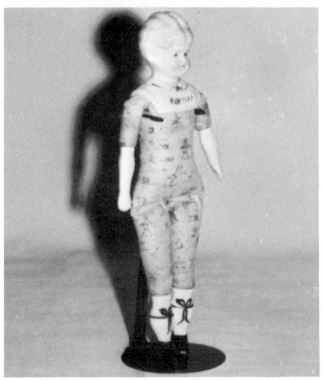

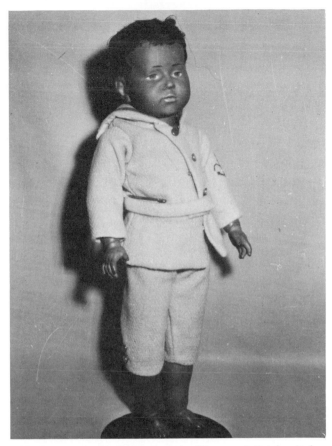

**1310.** Peter or mold #101, made by Kämmer & Reinhardt, has brown bisque head, black hair, painted eyes, brown composition body. *Courtesy of Marion Holt; photograph by Winnie Langley.*

**Peter.** 1909–11. Model #101, made by *Kämmer & Reinhardt* in their *Royal* line; distributed by *Strobel & Wilken* and *Borgfeldt.* One of the early character dolls, it was a mate to *Marie.* Came with jointed composition body, glass eyes or painted eyes. It was named for the boy who posed for the model.

**Peter.** 1924. One of the *Baby Grumpy* line made by *EFFanBEE.*

**Peter Pan.** See **Peter Pan Play Dolls.**

**Peter Pan.** 1913. Doll copyrighted by *Horsman;* designed by *Laura Gardin.*

**Peter Pan.** 1925. Made by *Goodyear Toy Co.* Came with composition head and arms, soft body of Duveteen with stuffed legs. Price $12.00 doz. wholesale. Mate to *Wendy.*

**Peter Pan Doll.** 1924. One of the *Jay Bee* line of *J. Bouton.* Doll represented Marilyn Miller, the star of Barrie's play PETER PAN. Every detail, even to the combing of the hair, was followed; height 10 inches.

**Peter Pan Play Dolls.** 1907–8. Trademark registered in the U.S. by *Samstag & Hilder.* The first three words in the trademark (all beginning with *P*) were written one under the other with a single oversize *P* serving as the first letter for all of them. The "Peter Pan" line of char-

# Peter Pan Doll
### Registered

**1311.** "Captain Hook" in Peter Pan line of dolls as advertised by Samstag & Hilder Bros. in 1908. *Courtesy of McCready Publishing Co.*

acter dolls was made in Germany under the personal direction of *Edmund Ulrich Steiner.* The "Pirates" were included in this line.

**Peterhänsel, Albert.** 1921–25+. Köppelsdorf, Thür. Made dressed dolls for export.

**Peterkin.** 1910–19. Line of dolls made by *Horsman.*

1910: Copyrighted by Horsman, designed by *Helen Trowbridge.* Had a *"bald head"* (without wig), closed mouth, and dimple in the chin.

1914: Horsman's advertisement of 1918 claimed the Peterkin heads were copyrighted in 1914. In that year (1914), Horsman had copyrighted *Drowsy Dick, Helen, Baby Rosebud, Phoebe,* and *Polly,* all designed by Helen Trowbridge.

1915: Peterkin line of dolls included Tommy Peterkin, Betsey Peterkin, and Willie Peterkin, all made with *Can't Break 'Em* heads. Peterkin, a child of toddling age, had a smile and wore pajamas.

1918: Made in all-*Adtocolite* form, jointed only at the

shoulders, with legs apart; came dressed and undressed. *Bernard Lipfert* designed *Little Peterkin* for Horsman.

Ca. 1919: All-bisque Peterkin made by *Fulper Pottery Co.;* has molded features; was jointed at shoulders; legs were apart. Size 11 inches. This doll resembles the illustrations of Peterkin in the 1915 edition of "Peterkin and the Little Grey Hare" in THE WONDER CLOCK OR FOUR AND TWENTY MARVELOUS TALES by Howard Pyle, which was first published in 1887.

**Peters, Heinrich.** 1878–1925+. Hannover, Prussia. His establishment was known as "Puppen-Peters"; manufactured and handled dressed dolls and repaired dolls.

**Petersen, C. L., Widow.** 1897, Hamburg, Germany. Manufactured dolls.

**Petiekin.** 1921–23. Trademark registered in U.S. by the Misses *Tebbets.*

**Petit, Jacob.** 1830–62. Fontainbleau, Seine-et-Marne, and a branch at Belleville near Paris. Made hard paste porcelain dolls' heads. The Fontainebleau factory was also known as Petit & Mardochée. In an effort to compete with the German dolls' heads of porcelain that were appearing on the French market, Jacob Petit obtained a French patent in 1843 for making heads of porcelain.

1853: Obtained a British patent for an improvement in the manufacture of porcelain.

**1312.** "Peterkin," all-bisque doll designed by Helen Trowbridge, made by Fulper Pottery Co., ca. 1919. H. 11 inches. *Courtesy of the Newark Museum, Newark, N.J.*

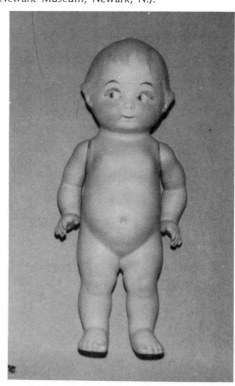

From 1863 to 1881, Fred Petit and Widow Petit were listed in Paris Directories as toymakers, but at a different address from that given earlier for Jacob Petit.

**Petit & Dumontier.** 1878–90. Paris. Made "unbreakable" dolls and bébés with articulated hands. It is not known whether this company made the dolls marked "P. D.," which usually had metal hands and bisque heads with cork pates. (See color photograph C20.)

**Petit Français, Le.**  See **Le Petit Français.**

**Petit Noël, Au.**  See **Au Petit Noël.**

**Petit Parisien.**  See **Le Petit Parisien.**

**Petitcollin.** 1914–25+. Factories at Lilas, Seine; Etain, Meuse; and a shop in Paris. Made celluloid dolls and bébés. Used the head of an eagle as a trademark (Tête d'Aigle).

**Petite.** 1923–25+. Trademark registered in U.S. by *American Character Doll Co.* for composition character babies.

1923: Came in sizes 13 to 26 inches.

1924: New 28-inch doll dressed in taffeta.

1925: Advertised *Walkie, Talkie, Sleepie*, price $1.50; *Teenie Weenie*, a *Bye-Lo* type of infant, and one hundred other numbers, price $1.00 to $25.00.

(See also **Baby Petite.**)

**Petite Caresse, La.**  See **La Petite Caresse.**

**Petite Française.** Name found on some of the bisque dolls' heads made by *J. Verlingue.* (See Ill. 1089.)

**Petite Polly.** 1915. Character doll made by the *Modern Toy Co.*

**Petitmangin.** 1865–82. Paris. Made dolls.

**Petri & Blum.** 1915–16. Handled imported dolls and American unbreakable character babies. Advertised *American Baby* with jointed composition head and body.

**Petsch, Hermann.** 1909–18. Halle, Saxony. Operated the *Hallesche Puppenklinik,* where dolls were made.

**Petseymurphy.** 1919. Trademark registered in Britain by *John Vincent* for dolls.

**Pettish Polly.** 1915. Copyrighted by *Trion Toy Co.* Girl's head with bangs over the forehead, designed by *Ernesto Peruggi.*

**Pettish Polly.** 1918. Distributed by *Gray & Dudley Co.* Came with composition head and hands, stuffed body and legs; wore waist, skirt, and striped stockings; 13-inch size cost 44¢.

**Petzold, Dora (née Krappe).** 1920–25+. Berlin. Produced and distributed dolls.

1920: Registered *Dora Petzold* as a trademark in Germany.

PAR BREVET

1314                                    1315

**1313A & B.** Pink-tinted china head made by Jacob Petit has painted blue eyes. Reddish-blonde hair is molded around the exposed ears. Note the eight sewholes. Mark: Ill. **1314.** *Courtesy of Gladyse Hilsdorf; photographs by Winnie Langley.*

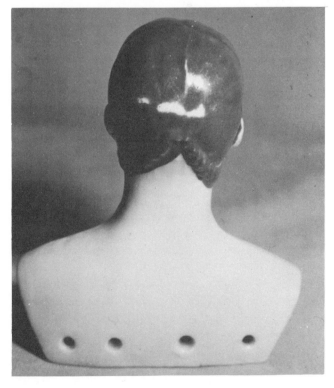

**1314.** Jacob Petit's mark found on dolls' heads.

**1315.** "Petite" mark used by American Character Doll Co.

1924: Registered "D P" with a girl in a circle as a trademark in Germany.

**Pfarr, Wilhelm.** 1904. Germany. Displayed dolls at the St. Louis Exhibition.

**Pfautz & Co.** 1920–22. Stettin, Germany. Claimed to be Worldwide Distributing Co.

1920: Registered *Welta* (world) as a trademark in Germany for dolls.

1922: Richard Pfautz was issued a patent in Germany for a moving doll.

**Pfeffer, Genevieve.** 1917–20. San Jose, Calif. Registered *Splash Me* as a trademark in U.S. for dolls. Obtained four U.S. design patents; one was probably used for *Com-A-Long* dolls by *Borgfeldt*.

**Pfeiffer, Emil, Firm.** 1894–1925+. Vienna. Made dolls; used Armand Marseille bisque heads, including "1894."

1897: Advertised bisque, composition, and washable dolls and dolls' heads.

1906: Was issued a trademark in Germany consisting of the figure of the Pied Piper ("Pfeiffer" means "Piper.")

1907: Registered in Germany the name "Pfeiffer" as a trademark.

1908: Registered in Germany *Tipple-Topple* as a trademark.

1916: Registered five trademarks in Germany, all containing the initials "E P" intertwined and either the words "Tipple Topple" or "Bébé."

1917: Registered in Germany *Huberta* and *Fritz* as two trademarks.

1922: Registered two trademarks in Germany: *Puppen-Pfeiffer*, and the picture of a little girl and dog.

1923: Registered three trademarks in Germany, all with the "E P" intertwined initials; two of these trademarks bore the word *Hubsy,* and the third, *Hubsy Clown.*

**Pfeiffer, Gebrüder (Bros.).** 1924–25+. Köppelsdorf, Thür. Manufactured dolls and used *Hanka* as a trademark.

**Pfeuffer, L.** 1909–18. Nürnberg, Bavaria. Manufactured wooden dolls.

**Pharoah.** 1923. Soft doll made by *Averill Manufacturing Co.*

**Phelps, Frank M.** 1925. Usk, Wash. Registered *Motor Follies* as a trademark in U.S. for dolls.

**Phénix-Baby.** 1899. Trademark registered in France by Jules Mettais, successor of *Jules Nicholas Steiner.* (See also **Bébé Phénix.**)

**Philadelphia Baby.** See **Sheppard, J. B., & Co.**

**Philadelphia Toy Co.** 1905. Philadelphia, Pa. Made dolls.

**Philips, Margaret B.** 1916–17. Port Allegany, Pa. Registered *Polly Preparedness Patriotic Person* as a trademark in U.S. The words in the trademark were written one under the other—sharing a single oversized *P* as their first

letter. Also obtained a design patent for Polly Preparedness, a girl doll dressed in stars and stripes.

**Phillips, Mary W.** 1919–20. Atlanta, Ga. Was issued a design patent for a rag doll.

**Phoebe.** 1914. Copyrighted by *Horsman,* designed by *Helen Trowbridge.* The doll represented a child with her hair parted on the left side.

**Phoenix Doll Co.** 1921–24. New York City. Manufactured composition character dolls; some were the 16-inch cherub type.

**Phoenix Quick.** 1924. Trademark registered in Germany by *Harburger Gummiwaren-Fabrik Phoenix Co.* for rubber dolls.

**Phonograph Dolls.** 1878–1925+. Among the many makers of phonograph dolls were *Edison, Stransky Frères, Max Oscar Arnold, Jenny Lind Doll Co., Jumeau, Giebeler Falk, Martinville & Salel Co., Samuel Haskell,* and *Averill Manufacturing Co.*

**Phonographe Bébé.** See **Bébé Phonographe.**

**Photo Doll.** 1920–22. Trademark registered in U.S. by *Baron Henry Scotford.*

**Photographic Faces.** 1905–9. *Dreamland Doll Co.* claimed to have originated this type of doll; they were followed by other companies who also produced dolls with photographic faces, such as the *Happyland* line, *Cinderella, Playtime, Babyland,* and *American Beauty.*

**Phyllis Doll.** 1923. Trademark registered in Germany for dolls and doll parts by *Schmidt & Rüchter.*

**Phyllis May.** 1919–21. Trademark registered by *Hazel Drukker Co.* for dolls representing the character in the NEW YORK EVENING MAIL by the author Hazel Drukker. These dolls were made by the *New Toy Co.* The trademark was affixed to the doll by means of a printed label. *Louis Amberg & Son* made *Mibs,* a "Phyllis May" doll.

**Pichot, Etablissement G.** 1925. Suresnes, Seine. Made dolls.

**Pickaninny.** 1893+. Cutout rag doll made by *Arnold Print Works;* designed by *Mrs. Celia M. Smith.*

**Pickaninny Baby.** 1925. Negro infant doll made by *The Toy Shop.*

**Pickanninies.** 1921. Cloth dolls made by *Martha Chase,* based on the characters in the books by Joel Chandler Harris. (See color photograph C9.)

**Pierini, Aida.** 1920. Designed the *Peggy* doll.

**Pierotti.** 1780–1925+. London. Dominic Pierotti came to England about 1780. According to family tradition, he made wax dolls, as did his son Enrico (Henry), who allegedly made solid wax dolls' heads with imbedded hair.

1847: The London Directory listed Henry Pierotti as a maker of both wax dolls and composition dolls. John Dominic Pierotti was listed as a maker of plaster figures, but in later directories he was listed as a maker of dolls.

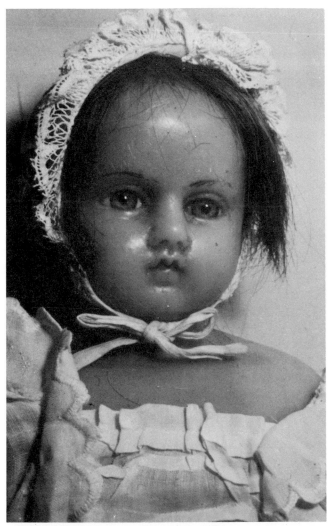

**1316.** Pierotti poured wax head with inserted hair, blue glass eyes. Mark on head: Ill. **1318.** *Courtesy of Margaret Whitton; photograph by Winnie Langley.*

**1317 & 1318.** Marks found on dolls made by Pierotti.

Pierotti                 Pierotti
**1317**                   **1318**

1862: Henry Pierotti displayed "wax model dolls with inserted hair, dolls and wax figures" at the London Exhibition. Celui Pierotti from the same address displayed "foreign and English toys."

The name "H. Pierroti" has been found on the back of wax dolls' heads. Pierotti wax dolls had hairs inserted either singly or several at a time, depending on the quality of the doll. The women of the family are believed to have made dolls' bodies, which were stuffed with cow hair. Among the better Pierotti dolls there were double- and even triple-poured wax ones. Many well-known doll companies of London handled Pierotti dolls, including *Aldis, Aldred, Cremer, Hamley, Morrell,* and *Peacock.* The grandchildren of Henry Pierotti carried on the business after 1925.

**Pierrot.** 1911. Trademark for a clown character doll made by **A. Steinhardt & Bro.**

**Pierrot and Pierrette.** 1925. Two 20-inch dolls made by the *American Stuffed Noverty Co.*

**Pietsch, Karl.** 1897–1925+. Neustadt near Coburg, Thür. Manufactured dolls and used "K P N" as a trademark.

1923: Advertised dressed and undressed dolls, baby dolls, double-jointed dolls, and sitting and standing dolls.

**Pigo.** See **Puppenindustrie Gotha.**

**Pilefer.** 1918. Trademark registered in France by *Mme. Poulbot.*

**Pillar Dolls.** See **Frozen Charlottes.**

**Pillowette Dolls.** 1913. Imported into U.S. These were dressed rag dolls with a formed face. When the head was pressed down, the doll cried.

**Pilzer Toy & Novelty Co.** 1921–24. New York City. Manufactured dolls.

**Pin Personalities.** 1922. Trademark registered in U.S. by *Cora L. Scovel.*

**Pinafore.** 1920–21. Trademark registered in U.S. by *Horsman* for dolls.

**Pinaut & Engelhard.** 1874. Paris. Distributors of dolls made by *J. C. Lindner.*

**Pineau.** 1881–82. Paris. Made dolls. (See also **Pnèau.**)

**Pink Lady.** 1919. Trade name for doll made by *Jessie McCutcheon Raleigh.*

**Pink Linen Dolls.** 1902–3. Had pink linen cloth bodies; larger sizes came with rivet jointed hips. The 10½-inch and 13-inch sizes came with painted features and hair, composition arms, and black cloth shoes; price 90¢ and $1.60 doz. wholesale. Sizes 15 and 19 inches came with bisque heads and arms, wigs with flowing hair; price $4.50 and $8.00 doz. wholesale.

**Pinka-Boo.** 1921. Trademark registered in Britain by *Polmar Perfumery Co.* for dolls.

**Pinky.** 1925. Made by *Madame Alexander;* inspired by a painting by Sir Joshua Reynolds.

**Pinky Winky Products Co.** 1922–24. Made Pinky Winky dolls with *fiberloid* faces based on patent of *Mabel H. Slater* and created by *Mme. Georgene Averill.* The doll rolled its eyes and said "Mama." Was dressed in pink and white voile; 19 inches high, price about $3.75. Mabel H. Slater registered "Pinky Winky Idol Eyes" as a trademark in U.S.

**Pintel, M., Jr.** 1913, Paris; 1921, Pintel Fils. Manufactured stuffed rag dolls.

1913: Registered in France a red, white, and blue ribbon as a trademark for rag dolls.

1921: Pintel was the secretary of the *Chambre Syndicale des Fabricants de Jouets Français.*

**Pintel & Godchaux.** 1890–99. Had a steam factory at

Montreuil. They are believed later to have joined the *Société Française de Fabrication de Bébés et Jouets.*

1890: Henri Pintel obtained a French patent for making jointed composition dolls. The patent was for diagonal hip joints, which up to then had functioned with elastic, the ends of which were fixed by dipping them in glue.

1892–5: Advertised jointed and patented *Bébé Charmant;* price 30¢ doz. and up wholesale. These dolls were jointed at the hips and shoulders.

1893: Displayed dolls at the Chicago Exposition.

**Pipe Clay.** 1862. Material used for dolls' heads and/or arms; mentioned in French patent issued to *Mme. Hortense V. Souty.*

**Piramonie.** 1915. France. Designed dolls, among them a Negro boy.

**Pistor, August.** 1912–20. Sonneberg, Thür. Manufactured dolls.

**Pistor, L.** 1909. Sonneberg, Thür. Manufactured dolls.

**Pitfield, William.** 1875–94. London. Made wax dolls.

**Pitti-Bum.** 1921–22. Trademark registered in Germany by *Bing* for dolls.

**Pitti-Sing.** 1893+. Cutout rag doll made by *Arnold Print Works,* designed by *Celia M. Smith.*

**Pizzonia & Iessi.** 1921–22. New York City. Made dolls.

**Plangon (Plagon).** Classical Greek term for dolls.

**Plaster (Plaster of Paris).** 17th cent.–1925+. A book of 1619 refers to the plaster doll of a workman's child—that the doll would break the first time it fell to the ground. An 1819 French patent mentioned articulated plaster figures.

Ca. 1840: *Andreas Voit* made heavy plaster dolls' heads.

1853: Mons. *Richard* obtained a French patent for making dolls' heads of plaster plus other ingredients.

1919: Cheap plaster dolls were exported from Germany. *Ella Smith* used plaster of Paris for the ears on her rag dolls.

**1319A & B.** Molded and painted plaster head on a turned wooden peg jointed body. H. 5½ inches. *Courtesy of the Newark Museum, Newark, N.J.*

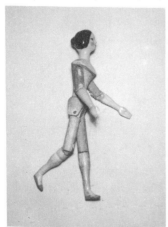
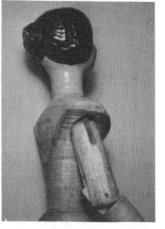

**1320.** Molded baby made of a plaster type of substance. H. 1½ inches. *Courtesy of Flora Gill Jacobs.*

**Plastic Dolls.** Before 1925, the term "plastic" applied to dolls made of pliable materials that could be molded. A few dolls were called "plastic" even in the 19th century.

**Plastolite.** 1917. Trademark registered in France by *J. Roger Gault* for a plastic paste and articles molded from this paste, such as the head and/or body of a doll.

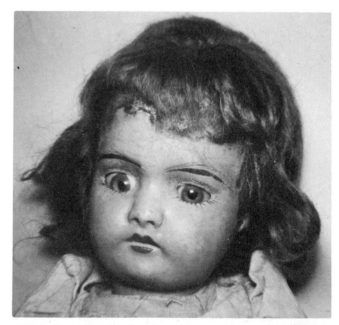

**1321.** Doll made entirely of Plastolite, a plaster-type composition, has glass eyes and ball-jointed body. Made ca. 1917. Mark on the back of the body: Ill. **1322.** *Courtesy of Eleanor Jean Carter.*

**1322.** Mark found on Plastolite doll.

6
La plastolite
paris
france

**Plattner, Hans, & Co.** 1924. Stuttgart, Baden-Württemberg. Made dolls.

**Playmate.** See **My Playmate.**

**Playmate.** 1918. Line of soft stuffed dolls handled by *Borgfeldt*. Came in a variety of styles with painted features. There were nurses, soldiers, sailors, infants, etc.

**Playmates.** 1922. Boy and girl dolls with composition heads and arms, painted eyes and hair; stuffed body and legs; jointed at hips and shoulders. They were distributed by *Sears, Roebuck & Co*. Size 13½ inches, price 95¢ a pair.

**Playtime.** 1906–8. Trademark registered in U.S. by Junius P. Bowden of *Rouech-Bowden Co.*, who made dolls with photographic faces. Dolls were distributed by *Louis Wolf & Co*. Advertisement claimed that the back of the head of these dolls was made in a special way. Dolls came dressed and undressed in a variety of sizes and prices.

**Pleasantville All Steel Dolls.** See **All Steel Dolls.**

**Please and Thank-You.** 1920–22. Trademark registered in U.S. by *Katherine Fisher*.

**Plément, Vincent.** 1885–90. Paris. Made dolls.

**Plessner, Julius.** 1907–20. Coburg, Thür. Manufactured dolls.

**Plichon, A.** 1875–76. Paris. Advertised *nankeen* dolls, dolls' heads of porcelain, and German bébés.

**Plombe in der Hand (Seal on the Hand).** 1923. Trademark registered in Germany by *Rudolf Säuberlich* and Rolf Berlich. A seal appears to have been placed on the cloth hand of the doll.

**Plumb, Henry.** 1865–68. London. Made gutta-percha dolls.

**Pnèau.** 1879. Paris. A doll maker at the doll shop *Au Petit Noël*. (See also **Pineau.**)

**Pocahontas.** 1911. *Art Doll* made by *Horsman*, representing an Indian girl with copper-colored complexion. Came with *Can't Break 'Em* head, molded hair, round eyes, cloth body; wore red and yellow dress and a vertical feather at the back of the head.

**Pointed Torso.** Many dolls were made with the bottom of the torso ending in a point. A horizontal hole usually extended through the pointed part of the torso to permit the attachment and articulation of the legs. Around 1800, wooden dolls were made in this manner. (See Ill. 1704.) Later, this type of body was made in all-bisque. (See Ill. 1323.) In the 20th century, composition, cloth, celluloid, and ceramic bodies were all made in this fashion.

**Poiret, Paul.** 1910. Paris. Originator of the hobble skirt; also started the fad of fashionable women carrying dolls. Dolls gowned by Paquin and Mme. Lanvin, 30 inches tall, cost from $80.00 to $200 each.

**Pola.** 1923. Trademark registered in Germany by *Thüringer Puppen-Industrie* for jointed dolls and dolls of rubber and other materials.

**Polack, Max.** 1902. Waltershausen, Thür. Registered *Polait* as a trademark in Germany for dolls and doll parts.

**Polait.** 1902. Trademark registered in Germany by *Max Polack* for dolls and doll parts.

**Policeman.** 1892. One of the *Brownies* designed by *Palmer Cox*.

**Polichinelle (Punchinello or Punch).** 17th century–1925+. France, Italy, England, and elsewhere. Clown doll based on the puppet Punch. This was one of the most popular doll forms for several centuries, if one judges by the numbers of them shown in contemporary pictures. They were made in all types of material—wood, bisque, papier-mâché, wax, and others. The customary face had a large nose and mouth and a projecting chin. The doll was humped-back and had a protruding stomach. It usually wore a wide ruff around the neck, short trousers, and a cap with from one to three points. *Gebrüder Heubach, Dehais, Doléac,* and *Jumeau* are all known to have made Polichinelles. Some of those made by Jumeau wore skirts and had the lovely Jumeau face but the characteristically shaped body and ruff. The German counterpart was "Kasper."

**Poli-Moli.** 1923–24. Trademark registered in Germany by *S. Weil, Jr.*, for rubber dolls.

**Polish Refugee Dolls.** 1918. Made for the benefit of Polish girls in Warsaw and exhibited in the Galleries of the Art Alliance. (See also **Mme. Paderewski.**)

**Polito, C.** 1867. Malta. Displayed wax figures at the Paris Exposition.

**1323.** All-bisque Polichinelle with molded clothes in blue, green, and pink. A Polichinelle with similar-type joints was patented by Gebrüder Heubach in 1880. H. 4 inches. *Coleman Collection.*

**Politzer Toy Manufacturing Co.** 1914 15. Manufactured and distributed dolls. Probably connected with Max Politzer, who prior to 1912 had been with *New Toy Co.,* but in 1912 went with *Tip Top Toy Co.*

1915: Politzer terminated his connection with *New Era Novelty Co.*

**Pollack, Daniel.** 1918. New York City. Copyrighted *Little Hero* and *Little Nero,* both designed by *Ernesto Peruggi.*

**Pollak & Samuel.** 1897. Joachimsthal, Bohemia. Manufactured jointed dolls. (See also **Samuel & Söhne.**)

**Pollard, E., & Co.** 1923. Obtained a British patent for improving the joints of dolls.

**Polly.** 1914–22. Copyrighted by *Horsman* in 1914; designed by *Helen Trowbridge.* Doll represented a laughing child with the hair parted on the left side.

1922: Horsman sued the *Gem Toy Co.* for infringement of the copyright on Polly, but the case was dismissed because Horsman had failed to deposit two copies with the copyright office, and had put only his initials on the doll.

**Polly.** 1918. Made by *Jessie McCutcheon Raleigh,* distributed by *Butler Bros.* Doll wore a wig and was 18½ inches tall; price $5.40.

**Polly.** 1920. Walking doll made by *Averill Manufacturing Co.* Came with composition arms and legs, wore a gingham dress and apron.

**Polly Pig-Tails.** 1910. Distributed by *Strawbridge & Clothier.* It was a rag doll similar to *Dolly Dollykins.* Wore two pigtails and plaid rompers.

**Polly Preparedness Patriotic Person.** 1916–17. Trademark registered in U.S. by *Margaret Philips.* The words in the mark were written one under the other, sharing a single oversized *P* as first letter.

**Polly Prim.** 1924. Trademark registered in U.S. by the *Rice-Stix Dry Goods Co.*

**Polly Prue.** 1912. Girl doll dressed in striped double-breasted coat and hat; made by *Horsman.*

**Polly Wise.** 1921. Doll made by *Horsman.*

**Pollyanna.** Ca. 1920. Composition-headed doll made by the *Putnam D. Smith* family.

**Pollyanna.** 1922. Made by *Schoen Toy Manufacturing Co.*

**Pollyanna, The Glad Doll.** 1916–17. Made by *Louis Amberg & Son* by special arrangement with the Pollyanna Glad Co. and special permission of the star of the theatrical production, Patricia Collinge.

**Pollyanna Co.** 1922–25. Chicago, Ill. Manufactured dolls, including *Teenie Pollyanna.*

**Polmar Perfumery Co.** 1921. London. Registered in Britain *I'Mere* and *Pinka-Boo* as two trademarks.

**Polynesian Dolls.** 20th century. Represented Polynesians. The dolls were usually made in Europe.

**Pomarantz, A. F., & Sons.** 1925. London. Imported dolls.

**Pomona.** 1918. Trademark registered in Britain by *M. V. Wheelhouse & Louise Jacobs.*

**1324.** Doll representing a Polynesian or Melanesian, probably from Fiji, has bisque head that is bald except for a tuft of hair. Note the size of the mouth, and the golden rings through ears and nose and around the ankle. Bent-limb composition baby body; original clothes and ornaments. *Courtesy of Margaret Whitton; photograph by Winnie Langley.*

**Poncet, Vve. (Widow), & Poncet, Mlle.** 1860–70. Paris. Made dolls.

1860: Secured a French patent for making dolls of breadcrumbs.

**Pond, F. L.** 1875. Winchester, Conn. Made dolls' bodies.

**Pontio, Maurice.** 1916. France. Obtained a French patent for a substance imitating porcelain, to be used for making dolls.

**Pooksie.** 1914. Trademark registered in Britain by John Green *Hamley,* for dolls.

**Poole, Edward.** 1854–65. London. Made wax dolls and composition dolls.

**Poole, John R.** 1843–60. London. Made wooden dolls. L. Poole was listed at the same address from 1852 to 1855, also making wooden dolls.

**Poole, William.** 1852–55. London. Made wax dolls and composition dolls.

**Pop Eyes.** 1916. Trade name for doll made by *Horsman*

and distributed by *Montgomery Ward & Co.* Made of composition with jointed shoulders and hips; 14-inch size cost $1.42.

**Popelin, Mlle. Marie.** 1884–89. Paris. Made dolls.

**Popineau.** 1855–70. Paris. At the same address as *Mlle. Gaudinot,* with whom Popineau apparently merged in 1866. They made dolls with rose kid bodies, and advertised fine and "half fine" dolls. They sent dolls to the provinces.

**Poppa-Momma Doll.** 1922–24. Made by *Ideal Novelty & Toy Co.* The doll had two different voices—an explosive "Poppa" when laid forward and, when laid backward, a gentler "Momma" as the air came out more slowly. Advertisements claimed that the doll could sit, walk, cry, talk, smile, wink, and blink.

**Poppe, Aug.** 1844–55. Coburg, Thür. Made dolls.

1844: Displayed papier-mâché, earthenware, and mechanical dolls at the Berlin Exhibition. One of his dolls "represented the famous ballet dancer of the 1830's and 1840's, Fanny Elsler [Elssler]. Other mechanical dolls represented a Tyrolean marksman with bows and arrows and enchanting clowns."

1854: Won a prize medal for his dolls at the Munich Exhibition.

1855: Displayed papier-mâché dolls at the Paris Exposition.

**Popper (Poppe), W. M.** 1895–98. Neustadt near Coburg, Thür. Made dolls, including dressed dolls.

**Poppy.** 1919. Doll made by *Jessie McCutcheon Raleigh.*

**Poppy.** 1925. Made of art leather by *Live Long Toys;* designed by *Penny Ross.* One of a flower doll series.

**Poppy Dolls.** 1912. Trademark registered in Germany by *Cuno & Otto Dressel* for stuffed dolls.

**Porcelain Dolls.** See **Bisque** (for unglazed porcelain); **China Head Dolls** (for glazed porcelain).

**Porcelainette.** 1920. Material used by *Beck Manufacturing Co.* to make "nonbreakable" dolls' heads .

**Porcelainite.** 1920. Material used by *Les Arts du Papier* to make *La Mignonne,* an unbreakable *mignonette* doll.

**Porter, Adelaide M.** 1920. Greenwich, Conn. Assigned her U.S. design patent for a yarn doll to *Huyler's Inc.*

**Porter, Ralph.** 1905. London. Made dolls.

**Portrait Dolls.** Throughout the ages, dolls portraying real people have been made, as well as dolls imaginatively portraying fictional or fairy-tale folk. Royalty and personages of the theatre have been especially popular subjects. Often a doll's similarity to the subject has been largely in its clothes and hair. A large number of dolls were made to resemble real people. The ubiquitous *Doll-Face Dolls* supposedly resembled Lillian Russell. The Industrial School in Sonneberg taught future designers of dolls to copy famous works of art. Occasionally well-to-do individuals posed for their own portraits in doll form. This was a fad in 1921.

1325. "Poppy Doll" with bisque shoulder head with flocked hair, glass eyes, cloth body, composition forearms; handled by Cuno & Otto Dressel in 1912. Mark stamped on the stomach: Ill. **1326.** H. 12½ inches. *Courtesy of Vaal Stark; photograph by John Schoonmaker.*

1326. Mark used on "Poppy Dolls" of Cuno & Otto Dressel.

**Porzellanfabrik Burggrub.** See **Schoenau & Hoffmeister.**

**Porzellanfabrik Kloster (Closter) Veilsdorf.** See **Closter Veilsdorf Porzellanfabrik.**

**Porzellanfabrik Limbach.** See **Limbach Porzellanfabrik.**

**Porzellanfabrik Veilsdorf.** See **Closter Veilsdorf.**

**Porzellanfabrik von Alt.** See **Alt, Beck & Gottschalck.**

**Possin.** 1839–43. Paris. Made dressed dolls.

**Potiers (Potier), Georges.** 1867–82. Paris. Made dolls.

1867: Won a silver medal for his doll display at the Paris Exposition.

1878: Awarded a gold medal at the Paris Exposition.

1880: Won a certificate of merit at the Melbourne Exhibition.

1882: Used the trademark "D. S."

**Potteries Toy Co.** 20th century. Staffordshire. Assembled the doll parts made by *Goss & Co.* These dolls usually had bisque heads and cloth-stuffed bodies.

**Pottery Dolls.** 19th century. Made in many places, including *Pápa* factory in Hungary, *Riehm* factory in Ilmenau (Thür.), and factories in Pennsylvania and the Ohio River Valley, where evidence has been found of the manufacture of various types of pottery heads for dolls. (See Ill. 500.)

**Pottier, F.** See **Belton.**

**Poulbot, Francisque.** 1913. Paris. Registered in France *Un Poulbot* and *Une Poulbotte* as two trademarks.

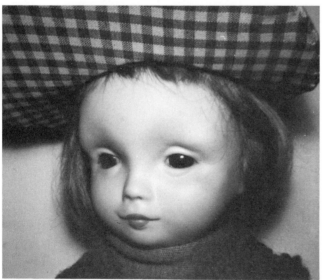

**1327.** Poulbot doll made by Société Française de Fabrication de Bébés et Jouets has stationary glass eyes, closed mouth, jointed body of composition and wood. Mark: Ill. **1328.** H. 17 inches. *Courtesy of Bess Goldfinger.*

**1328.** Mark found on Poulbot dolls.

S. F. B. J.
239
PARIS
Poulbot

**Poulbot, Mme.** 1918. Paris. Registered seventeen trademarks in France. They were Le Petit Lardon; *Sac de Terre; Pilefer; Coco; Coco L'Infernal brise-tout; Sansonnet; Nini; Nini La Princesse;* Moutchou, Moutchou La Mouche; *Lili;* Rintintin; *Nénette; Baba; Fanfois; Zizine; Momo.*

**Poulin, René.** 1861. Paris. Was issued a French patent for making dolls' heads and limbs of rolled or beaten copper or zinc, with or without enamel eyes. The metal was to be painted. This was probably the beginning of metal dolls' heads.

**"Poupard" Art.** 1919–21. Trademark registered in France by *Henri Bellet* for papier-mâché poupards.

**Poupards.** Dolls without legs, generally babies in swaddling clothes. Early ones were usually of papier-mâché or wood. They were often crude, and contemporaries noted their cheapness and ugliness. The report of the jury at the 1878 Paris Exposition said, "The once-common doll in papier-mâché and the old-fashioned poupard, although it is true that these articles had a very modest price, are now forsaken because people prefer others that are better made and not very much more expensive."

1914: Prof. Marchand, in a lecture at the Sorbonne, said, "Poupard lost his ugliness and became something of a hero."

There appears to have been a revival of the poupard in the 20th century. The *Société Française de Fabrication de Bébés et Jouets* and many individual companies made poupards. There were poupards with jointed arms and heads, talking poupards, and various others.

**Poupée de Nuremberg.** See **A la Poupée de Nuremberg.**

**Poupée Française.** 1894. French doll patented by *Toulouse* in France. Wire was imbedded in the paste, and after the paste hardened, formed the joints of the doll.

**Poupée Merveilleuse.** 1900. Trademark registered in France by Jules Mettais, successor of *Jules Steiner,* for dolls and bébés.

**Poupée Mystère.** 1925. Trade name used for dolls by the *Société de Paris.*

**Poupée Parisiana.** 1905. Trademark registered in France by *Société Anonyme de Comptoir General de la Bimbeloterie.*

**Poupée Sanver's.** 1908. Trademark registered in France by *Mme. Demarest.*

**Poupées de Paris.** 1920. Trademark registered in France by *Messrs. Gaston Manuel & E. de Stoecklin.*

**Poupées Gauloises.** 1916. Trademark registered in France by *Mme. Louit.*

**Poupées Genres.** 1855. Name given by *Françoise Greffier* to his dolls.

**Poupées Ninon.** 1925+. Name of the products of the doll factory at Frépillon, Seine-et-Oise.

**Poupées Raynal.** 1924–25+. Trademark registered in U.S. by *Yves de Villers & Co.*

**1329.** Poupard with papier-mâché head and painted features has a wooden stick running through the body and terminating in a handle for turning the head. Represents a baby dressed in swaddling clothes. H. 4½ inches. *Courtesy of The Smithsonian Institution.*

**1330.** "Poupée Merveilleuse" mark used by Jules Steiner firm.

## POUPÉE MERVEILLEUSE

**Poupées Verité.** 1915. Trademark registered in France by *Mlle. Gabrielle Verita.*

**Poupécs-Mignonettes.** 1914. Name used by *André Gault* for dressed and undressed dolls.

**Poupon Parisiana.** 1905. Trademark registered in France by *Société Anonyme de Comptoir General de la Bimbeloterie.*

**Pouting Tots (Pouting Baby Boy and Pouting Baby Girl).** 1914–15. Trade name for dolls made by *Louis Amberg & Son.*

1915: Name was given as "Pouty Pets," and the dolls were produced in new sizes and costumes.

**Pouty Pets.** See **Pouting Tots.**

**Prechtl, Edward.** Before 1902–18. Kreis and Brunswick, Brunswick. Manufactured dolls. His early dolls were cloth ones.

**Prehay, Mme.** See **Pretay, Mme.**

**Prelle, Carl.** 1912. Munich. Secured German patent for improving the ball joints on dolls.

**Premier Pas, Bébé.** See **Bébé Premier Pas.**

**Preparedness Doll Co.** 1917. New York City. Manufactured dolls with composition heads and stuffed bodies.

**Preparedness Kid.** 1916. One of the *Madame Hendren* line manufactured by *Averill Manufacturing Co.* Dolls were dressed as soldiers, in khaki cloth with leather belt and holster; 12½ inches high; price $1.25.

**Preshus.** 1917–18. Trademark registered in U.S. by *Borgfeldt.*

**President McKinley.** Ca. 1900. Composition portrait doll representing William McKinley, made by *Cuno & Otto Dressel;* 15½ inches tall.

**Pressner, M., & Co.** 1923–25. New York City. Manufactured and imported dolls.

**Pretay (Prehay), Mme.** 1862–66. Paris. Made dolls.

**Pretty Baby.** 1916. Distributed by *Montgomery Ward & Co.* Came with composition head and hands, glass eyes, curly wig, jointed at shoulder and hips; 16½ inches high; price $3.95.

**Pretty Peggy.** 1908. Line of dressed dolls with jointed composition bodies, handled by *Borgfeldt.*

**Pretty Peggy.** 1925. Doll with composition head and limbs, sleeping eyes, wig, cotton stuffed body; handled by *Louis Wolf & Co.* Size 30 inches, price $5.00.

**Pretty Polly.** 1919–20. Celluloid "bisque finish" doll made by *Seamless Toy Corp.;* came with wig, and was jointed at shoulders and hips; legs bent and crossed.

**Preusser & Co.** 1925+. Oelsnitz, Germany. Made dressed dolls.

**Preussing & Wilson.** 1914–20. Neustadt near Coburg, Thür., and Berlin. Manufactured and exported dolls.

1914: Registered a picture of a landscape as a trademark in Germany.

**Prialytine.** Name found on dolls' heads made of a type of composition.

**Price, Lenora.** 1917–18. Davenport, Okla. Was issued a U.S. patent for a waterproof doll made of a light material, such as sheeting. The face was covered with a white shellac and placed in a mold to dry. The hair and features were supplied with a waterproof paint. The limbs could be moved to "any desired" position.

**Prices, Original.** 1700–1925. In general, the price of a doll was divided evenly into three parts—that of the head, the body, and the wig—each accounting for about one third of the total. Often, the clothes were far more expensive than the doll itself.

1700: A wax baby with movable eyes and crying mechanism cost about $1.25 in England.

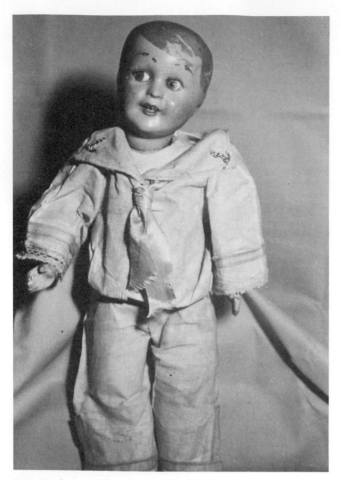

**1331.** Prialytine doll: painted blond hair, blue glass eyes, contemporary sailor suit. Mark: Ill. **1332.** *Photograph by Winnie Langley.*

**1332.** "Prialytine," name on composition dolls' heads.

La Prialytine

Paris

O - B

1733: Turned wooden dolls cost 62¢ doz. wholesale.

1759: George Washington paid approximately $2.50 for a fashionable wax baby for his four-year-old stepdaughter.

1844: Papier-mâché, wax, and wooden dolls shown at the Berlin Exhibition cost from 12¢ to 85¢.

1854: Dolls with porcelain heads shown at the Munich Exhibition cost from $1.90 to $3.40.

1869: The smallest bisque heads cost $3.50; the prices ranged up to $10.00. A 12-inch doll with jointed limbs and a bisque head sold undressed for $15.00. China and wax dolls were cheaper.

1874: Infant dolls with wardrobe cost $5.00. Dolls with waxed heads and limbs, wigs, and cotton bodies sold for $2.00 and up. Wax dolls ranged from $1.25 to $5.50, according to fineness even more than size. Bisque dolls with wigs cost $1.35 to $4.00. The heads alone were 65¢ to $2.50, and the jointed kid bodies ready for the heads cost $1.85 to $2.85.

1886: *Ridley's* advertised china-limb dolls with china

heads for 5¢ to 50¢. Dolls with composition bodies, bisque heads, and wigs, dressed in a chemise, cost $1.57 to $10.75. The similar kid-bodied dolls with bisque heads cost about half as much for comparable sizes. Dressed dolls cost up to $30.00.

1895: Wanamaker's advertised *Jumeau* dolls with bisque heads and composition bodies, size 13 inches, $12.00 with flaxen hair, and $13.00 with human hair. Bisque-head, composition-bodied German dolls cost 50¢ to $9.00.

1903: Dolls could be bought for a penny, though large toy shops sold dolls priced as high as $300.

1919: The cheapest French dolls cost $20.00, according to PLAYTHINGS magazine.

1924: Marshall Field & Co. advertised dolls with bisque heads and composition bodies for 95¢ to $4.50. Dolls with kid bodies cost about the same as those with composition bodies.

**Prices of Dolls.** Demand and supply are perhaps the major factors that usually determine the price of any collectible. In the case of antique dolls, the demand seems to far outweigh the supply. Billions of dolls were produced through the years. But billions of children played with them, and so it is easy to understand that the majority of dolls—loved though they were in their day—were eventually worn out or broken, forgotten, and finally discarded. However, fortunately for collectors, there were children who loved their dolls enough to take excellent care of them; and, of course, some children were permitted only to gaze at their beautiful dolls on rare occasions, and before long these "untouchables" were carefully stored away for posterity.

Emotional attachment to dolls has also aided their preservation. A doll that grandmother loved as a little girl somehow seemed to be part of the family, and so was preserved long after other objects with less sentimental implications had been disposed of. Most dolls over a century old have already found their way into museums or private collections. The supply is therefore limited, and the price of such dolls seriously affected. In the case of more recent dolls, the price seems to depend more on the type of doll that is in current demand than on the supply. A doll that is popular with collectors even though it is relatively plentiful often commands a far higher price than a rare and unidentified type of doll. The higher priced popular dolls tend to be pulled out of hiding in attics, whereas unusual dolls may be overlooked.

Original prices for dolls have little relationship to current prices. For example, a molded-hair *Schoenhut* doll could be produced cheaper than one with a wig, but the latter was more popular, and therefore more of them were produced. Today, the molded-hair Schoenhut doll commands a higher price because it is scarcer and deemed more artistic by collectors. For the same reasons, dolls with closed mouths are priced higher than those with open mouths.

Besides demand and supply, many other factors affect the price of dolls:

## 1. Artistic Beauty

Taste is a personal matter, and so the appeal of a particular doll to a prospective buyer is an influential factor. Collectors of dolls more often buy with their hearts than their heads. But taste can change, and so does the demand for various types of dolls. However, a doll with inherent artistic beauty will always be in demand.

## 2. Documentation

Few dolls come with authentic documentation. Family legends as to the age and/or origin of dolls are often erroneous. The marks on dolls do help to identify them and give clues as to their age and history. For this reason, a marked doll usually commands a much higher price than a similar type of doll without any marks. The type of mark is also most important. A marked *Bru* doll sells for many times the price of a marked *Armand Marseille* doll. A completely unmarked doll that resembled the Bru would be priced higher than the marked Armand Marseille doll. Many dolls have marks that are as yet meaningless to doll collectors. When these marks have been identified and information published about them, both demand for them and prices will increase.

## 3. Workmanship

Two dolls with exactly the same type of head, from similar molds, may be priced differently because of the workmanship. The grade of the china, the decorating skill, and the techniques used all affect the price. For example, brush marks and detail around the eyes, nose, and mouth all produce a finer and more expensive head. One of the chief reasons for the high price of dolls made in France is their exquisite workmanship—the beautiful glass eyes, the fine kid bodies, and so on.

## 4. Originality and Condition

Dolls of any type in mint condition are the most expensive of their particular type. The price drops according to the amount of damage and wear. A poorly mended doll is less desirable than one left as originally made. It is often difficult to determine whether the body and clothes are actually original. A large proportion of dolls exchanged heads or body parts even when they were fairly new, and most dolls have had several changes of clothing. Many dolls were dressed only in chemises when first purchased, and were advertised as undressed dolls. A doll with head, body, and clothes all labeled, or in its original box, would command a far higher price than otherwise. If an old doll has head, body, and clothes all of the same period, it is more valuable than one with modern parts and clothes. Carefully mended parts and clothes are more valuable than replacements.

The actual monetary value of dolls depends on all the factors discussed above, as well as others, such as age, height, uniqueness, association with a famous person, and so on. The prices of dolls vary tremendously, but in general they fall more or less into the following groups:

*Very expensive* (these would be in fine condition):
   Some of the French bébés such as unusual Brus and "AT's"
   Authenticated *Meissen, Königliche Porzellan Manufaktur, Sèvres,* etc.
   Rare wooden dolls of the 18th century and earlier

*Expensive:*
   Dolls named above in the more common types, or in less than fine condition. Also, the dolls below in fine condition:
   Marked French bébés with closed mouth and stationary eyes
   French lady dolls, sometimes called fashion dolls
   China-headed dolls with very unusual hairdos
   Very large *Frozen Charlottes*
   Early marked rubber dolls, such as *Goodyear, India Rubber Comb Co.,* etc.
   Early 19th-century wooden dolls over 7 inches tall
   Labeled poured wax dolls with inserted hair
      (except the late *Hamley* marked ones)
   *Bartenstein* wax dolls
   Other rare dolls such as some of the German character dolls
   Very fine papier-mâché-headed dolls, *Izannah Walker* dolls, etc.

*Medium priced:*
   Dolls named above in the more common types or in less than fine condition. The dolls below in fine condition:
   Most other 19th-century dolls except in small sizes
   Unmarked or German bisque dolls except in the small sizes
   China-headed dolls other than the wavy, lowbrow type, or small sizes of the earlier types
   Schoenhut wooden dolls
   Some metal-headed dolls such as *All Steel Dolls* and *Giebeler-Falk*
   Early *Käthe Kruse,* early *Chase Stockinet,* and other artistic fabric dolls

*Inexpensive* (fewer and fewer of these are available each year, especially in fine condition):
   Some of the common German small all-bisque or all-celluloid dolls
   Some of the poorer grades of German dolls with bisque or composition heads; cloth, kid, or composition bodies, in small sizes
   Most of the 20th-century composition dolls, especially the unidentified ones
   Most of the dolls made in Japan in the 20th century
   Some of the 20th-century rag dolls
   Wavy, lowbrow-hairdo china-headed dolls, except in large sizes; very small sizes of other common-type china dolls, including Frozen Charlottes

**Prieur, C.** 1890, Paris; 1895–98, successor was A. Ayrand. Handled bébés and dolls, French and foreign.

**Prieur, L.** 1859–1925+. Paris. Made dolls and doll parts; claimed that they were the oldest house of this kind in France.

1900: Advertised articles for dolls.

1912: Made dressed and undressed bébés and *mignonettes.*

1914: Advertised that they manufactured bébés, heads of all kinds, hair and Thibet wigs, and doll parts.

1921: Advertised bébés and doll articles, heads of all sorts, hair and mohair wigs, and doll parts.

1925: Advertised bébés and articles for bébés.

**Prieur, Miss Marie.** 1917–18. London. Made dolls.

**Primadonna.** 1919. Phonograph doll made by *Giebeler-Falk*. Had aluminum head and body, real hair wig; crown of the head was hinged and lifted toward the front; horn and turntable were located in the head and the mechanism was in the body; crank in back of doll. Doll came in two sizes, 25 and 30 inches tall, with records 3½ or 4 inches in diameter, which were placed on the turntable in the head to make the doll sing or talk.

**Primrose.** 1922. Trademark registered in Germany by the *Waltershauser Doll Factory* for dolls, dolls' heads, dolls' bodies, dolls' limbs, dolls' clothes, and dolls' wigs.

**Primula.** 1923. Trademark registered in Germany by *Thüringer Puppen & Spielwaren Export Co.*

**Prince, M., & Son.** 1922. New York City. Handled imported and domestic dolls.

**Princess.** 1897–1908. Trademark registered by *Borgfeldt* in Germany. This was probably the Princess doll advertised in 1901 as having a bisque head, open mouth and teeth, sleeping eyes, jointed composition body with jointed wrists; size 19½ inches, price $1.98.

1908: Dressed dolls with jointed composition bodies.

**Princess.** 1904. Line of jointed dressed dolls made by *E. A. Runnells & Co.*

**Princess.** 1925. Composition character doll with stuffed body made by the *American Unbreakable Doll Corp.*

**Princess Angeline.** 1917–20. Portrait doll of the only daughter of the Indian chief, Seattle, made by *Georgene Averill*. She had once lived in Oregon and had seen members of the Indian tribes that she portrayed. Doll had a composition face.

**Princess Doll, The.** 1905–25+. Trademark registered in U.S. by *Strawbridge & Clothier*.

**Princess Eulalia.** 1893. Distributed by *Butler Bros.* Came with French bisque head, eyes that opened and closed; dressed in satin and wool with an elaborate lace hat, blue stockings, and bronze shoes; 39 inches tall, price $18.75.

**Princess Helen.** 1916. Distributed by *Montgomery Ward & Co.* Came with composition head "imitation" bobbed wig, and dress; 16-inch size cost $1.25.

**Prinoth, Chn., & Co.** 1880–90. Nürnberg, Bavaria, and Paris. Made dolls of various types.

1880-84: Advertised wax dolls, *nankeen* dolls, and bathing dolls.

1885–90: Advertised dressed dolls and *bébés incassables*, as well as the types advertised earlier.

**Prinoth, Ferdinand.** 1896. St. Ulrich, Grödner Tal. Distributed wooden dolls. (See also **Insam & Prinoth.**)

**Prinsard, E.** 1919–21, Paris; 1925, Mme. Prinsard. Handled and repaired dolls; specialized in wigs.

1919–20: Advertised dolls' wigs of real hair.

1921: Advertised dolls, bébés, porcelain dolls' heads, "unbreakable" dolls' heads, and wigs of real hair.

**1333A & B.** Bisque "Princess" head has glass sleeping eyes and open mouth with teeth; ball-jointed body is composition. Original dress. Mark on head: Ill. **1334.** H. 23 inches. *Courtesy of Dorothy Annunziato.*

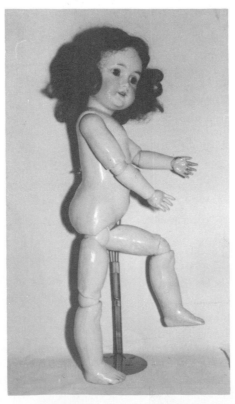

**1334.** "Princess" mark found on Borgfeldt dolls.

Princess
1
Germany

1925: Repaired dolls and bébés of various makes; handled "unbreakable" heads, character heads, and real hair wigs.

**Printemps, Grand Magasins du.** 1887–1925+. Paris store for which Messrs. *Laquionie & Cie.* registered in France *Juli Guy, Rosette,* and *Muguette* as trademarks. In 1887, advertised *Bébé Jumeau* and *Bébé Printemps.*

**Prinzessin Wunderhold.** 1912. Trade name used by *Arthur Schoenau.*

**Priscilla.** 1919. Doll made by *Jessie McCutcheon Raleigh.*

**Private Murphy.** 1909. U.S. soldier doll made by *Steiff;* it wore a khaki uniform without equipment.

**Private Sharkey.** 1909. Trade name for doll made by *Steiff;* wore khaki uniform with full equipment.

**Prize Baby.** 1913–24. Trademark registered in Germany and U.S. by *Borgfeldt.* This may have been the "Prize Baby" doll advertised in 1914 with composition head and hands and cloth baby body, which came in sizes 11, 14½, 17, 18½, and 21 inches; price 59¢ to $3.95.

**Prize Baby.** 1915. Doll made by *Ideal Novelty & Toy Co.* This may have been the Prize Baby distributed by *Montgomery Ward & Co.* that had a composition head, short bobbed mohair wig, a pacifier to go into the open mouth, and a cork-stuffed body. Size 14 inches, cost $1.70.

**Prize Baby.** 1919. Made by *Tip Top Toy Co.* Doll came in two sizes.

**Prize Winner Baby.** 1924. Made by *Royal Toy Manufacturing Co.*

**Procbázková, Marie.** 1921. Prague, Czechoslovakia. Made dolls.

**Prodige, Bébé.** See **Bébé Prodige.**

**Production.** Even allowing for some advertising exaggeration, the production figures for dolls stagger the imagination. Many companies claimed to have been *the* largest manufacturer, but figures seldom support their boast. Production information was given only sporadically, and not necessarily by the largest companies. The following figures are approximations, and in some cases may represent capacity rather than actual output, but they do give an indication of the vast size of the doll industry through the years:

1844: 360,000 dolls' heads, *Voit & Fleischmann*

1871: 1,000,000 wax dolls, *Edwards*

1881: 85,000 bébés, *Jumeau*

1883: 115,000 bébés, Jumeau

1884: 220,000 bébés, Jumeau

HARPER'S BAZAR reported that a German factory, in operation for about 130 years (1884 – 130 = 1754) had produced about a billion china dolls; a single oven contained 5,000 dolls, and thirty ovens were often full at one time.

1886: 205,000 bébés, *Falck-Roussell*

1887: 425,000 bébés, Falck-Roussell

1888: 555,000 bébés, Falck-Roussell
   1,120,000 bébés, *Grandjean*

1889: 643,000 bébés, Falck-Roussell
   1,170,000 bébés, Grandjean

1897: 3,000,000 bébés, Jumeau

1903: 2,000,000 porcelain dolls made in Sonneberg, plus many times that number of porcelain heads;
   20,000,000 papier-mâché dolls' heads made in Sonneberg;
   16,000 walking dolls in one order given to Louis *Amberg,* Brill & Co.

1907: 4,500,000 dolls, *Société Française de Fabrication de Bébés et Jouets*

1908: nearly 8,000 rag dolls, *Ella Smith*

1912: 5,000,000 dolls, Société Française de Fabrication de Bébés et Jouets
   1,000,000 dolls, *Horsman*

1915: 2,000,000 dolls' heads, *Independent Doll Co.*

1916: 1,000,000 dolls, *Trion Toy Co.*
   1,000,000 dolls, *Non-Breakable Toy Co.*

1920: 3,000,000 dolls, *EFFanBEE*
   2,600,000 dolls, *Reisman, Barron & Co.*
   1,500,000 dolls, *Danville Doll Co.*

1921: 6,000,000 dolls, Société Française de Fabrication de Bébés et Jouets

1922: 7,000,000 dolls, Société Française de Fabrication de Bébés et Jouets
   1,500,000 dolls, Reisman, Barron & Co.

1923: 1,600,000 dolls, *Regal Doll Manufacturing Co.*
   5,000,000 *Mama Dolls* sold in U.S., plus big foreign demand

1925: 1,500,000 dolls, Reisman, Barron & Co.

In December, 1903, PLAYTHINGS reported the "usual doll famine this year as in so many years past. Popular priced dolls entirely exhausted long before the holidays."

**Progressive Agency of New Jersey.** 1922–23. Newark, N.J. Showroom in New York City. Sole U.S. distributor of *Revalo* jointed dolls.

**Progressive Toy Co.** 1917–24. New York City. Manufactured dolls.

1917: Used trade name *Admiration* for their fully jointed wood-fiber dolls and babies; came with painted hair or wigs.

1918: Admiration Babies came in sizes 14 and 16 inches.

1919: Used trade names *Sweetie, Sweetness,* and *Little Love Pirate* for their wood-fiber dolls.

1920: Admiration and Sweetness dolls had bisque heads and came in four sizes.

1921: Advertised new line of genuine bisque heads with sleeping glass eyes, sewed wigs, fully jointed and baby bodies; sizes 14, 16, 20, and 24 inches.

1921: Dolls distributed by *Riemann, Seabrey Co.*

Admiration Babies had bent-limb baby bodies.

*Dimples, Eversweets,* Sweetness, and Sweetie were trade names for fully jointed dolls with bisque heads.

1923: Advertised *Chatterbox,* Admiration dolls, cotton-floss-stuffed walking dolls, and all-composition dolls that could walk and talk.

**Propper, W. M.** 1897. Prague, Bohemia. Manufactured dolls.

**Prosopotrope.** See **Checkeni, Dominico.**

**Prowodnik Co.** 1908–11. Riga, Russia. Warehouses in Paris, Vienna, Berlin, Shanghai, Hong Kong, Warsaw, Moscow, Samarkand, etc. Listed in British Directory under Dolls. Also known as Russian-French India Rubber, Gutta Percha and Telegraph Works.

**Prudhomme, R.** 1921. Paris. Manufactured rubber bébés.

**Puddin Head.** 1923. *Gene Byrnes* obtained two copyrights for *Borgfeldt* based on the fat boy in the *Reg'lar Fellers* cartoon. One of the "fat boy" heads had a hat and the other was without the hat.

**Pudgie (Pudgy Baby).** 1915. Doll with chubby cheeks and "laughing" eyes, made by *Louis Amberg & Son.*

**Pudgie.** 1919. Cherub-type doll of wood fiber made by *Tip Top Toy Co.* Came with or without human hair wig; size 13 inches.

**Pujol e Hijo, Jaime.** 1893. Barcelona, Spain. Displayed cardboard dolls at the Chicago World's Fair.

**Pullmann Doll Co.** 1917. Chicago, Ill. Made character dolls, price 25¢ to $2.00.

**Pulvermacher, Albert.** 1890–91. Sonneberg, Thür. Manufactured low-priced dolls. Obtained German, British, and U.S. patents for making spring-jointed dolls with spiral springs and pins; claimed that before then rubber cord had been used for dolls' joints.

**Pulvermacher & Westram, Albin.** 1895–1925+. Sonneberg, Thür. Manufactured and exported dolls.

1895: Specialized in dressed wax dolls. (See also **Pulvermacher, Albert.**)

**Pumice Stone.** 1862. *Mme. Hortense Vincent Souty* obtained a French patent for a jointed doll body made of painted pumice stone.

**Punch.** See **Pollichinelle.**

**Punch & Judy.** 1901. Rag doll made by *Textile Blueing Co.* Came in sateen painted with "oil" colors; intended to be stuffed with cotton. Size 27 inches, price 50¢ a pair.

**Punfield, Frederick William.** 1922–25+. London. Wholesale doll maker; sole British agent for *Rheinische Gummi & Celluloid Fabrik Co.*

**Pupil-less Eyes.** These are a relatively simple two-part type of eyes with a white eyeball and merely a dark circle in the center to represent both pupil and iris. Before 1850, most dolls with glass eyes had this type. After about 1870, these eyes were used largely on small and/or inexpensive dolls.

**Puppe der Zukunft (Doll of the Future).** 1904. Trademark registered in Germany by *Gebrüder Süssenguth.*

**Puppen.** German word for "dolls."

**Puppenfabrik Lichtenfels.** 1904. Lichtenfels, Bavaria. Specialized in jointed dolls.

**Puppenfabrik Thüringia.** See **Friedrichroda Puppenfabrik.**

**Puppenindustrie Gotha.** 1924. Gotha, Germany. Produced and distributed dolls; used the initials "P i G o"; obtained a German patent for half-hollow dolls' bodies.

**Puppen-Peters.** See **Peters, Heinrich.**

**Puppenpfeiffer (Whistler Dolls).** 1922. Trademark registered in Germany by *Emil Pfeiffer* firm.

**Purger, J. B.** 1851–96. St. Ulrich, Grödner Tal. Handled wooden dolls.

1851: Displayed carved wooden dolls at the London Exhibition.

**1335.** Type of all-wood, peg-jointed doll handled by Purger in the Grödner Tal in the 19th century. H. 11 inches. *Courtesy of the Newark Museum, Newark, N.J.*

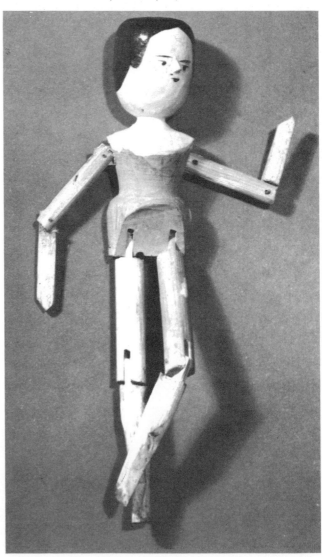

By 1875: He had died, but the firm carried on.

**Purvis, Robert C.** 1901. Laurel Springs, N.J. Obtained U.S. patent for a doll of sheet metal with metallic spring ball-and-socket joints. Assigned his rights to *Bernhard Wilmsen*.

**Pusmo.** Ca. 1400. Padua, Italy. Legendary person who allegedly took carved dolls to the court of Charles VI in France. These dolls were made to represent the empresses and other famous women of the Roman Empire, based on their likenesses as shown in statues and on coins. One of the dolls that particularly took the King's fancy represented the Empress Poppea. According to legend, the French word "Poupée" had its origin in this Poppea doll. Princess Clementine of Belgium claimed to have the original Poppea doll in her collection.

**Puspi.** 1925+. Trademark registered in Germany by the *H. Wordtmann* firm, which produced and distributed dolls.

**Putnam, Grace Storey, Mrs.** 1922–25+. Teacher in the Art Department of Mills College, Oakland, Calif. Designed *Bye-Lo Baby* doll for *Borgfeldt*. In 1922, she obtained a copyright for Bye-Lo, which was described as "doll's head, life-size modeled from a baby three days old—eyes slightly narrowed, mouth closed, fat rolls at back of neck, neck constructed to fit a socket." She was issued two copyrights in 1923 and two more in 1925, all for the Bye-Lo Baby. The Bye-Lo, as first produced by Borgfeldt in 1923 or 1924, had a flange neck instead of being made for a socket neck. Grace Putnam designed seven sizes of the soft cloth bodies with bent legs that allowed the feet to turn inward. The very earliest Bye-Lo Babies had cloth bodies designed by *Georgene Averill*, who was working for Borgfeldt at that time. The celluloid hands found on Bye-Los were a stock item and not modeled for the Bye-Lo.

When Grace Putnam copyrighted her model in 1922, she was not under contract with Borgfeldt, but was put under contract soon thereafter and remained under contract for at least twenty years. During this time Bye-Los were made of all-bisque, composition heads, wax heads, etc. She also designed several other dolls' heads after 1925.

**Pye, David W.** 1919. Red Bank, N.J. Assignee of a U.S. patent by *Margaret B. Spear* for a two-piece rag doll.

**Pyralin.** 1922. Made by *Du Pont* and described as follows: plastic as sculptor's clay; could be blown, molded, stamped, or machined; painted, embossed, engraved, or printed upon. This material appears to have been used for dolls.

**Pyroxylin.** 1914. Name used by *Société Industrielle de Celluloid,* which claimed they were the largest manufacturers in the world of pyroxylin raw material. *Alfred Burke* was sole agent in U.S. for French pyroxylin dolls and bébés.

**Pyroxylin Compounds.** 1914–15. Name given to material used for their dolls by *Rheinische Gummi & Celluloid*

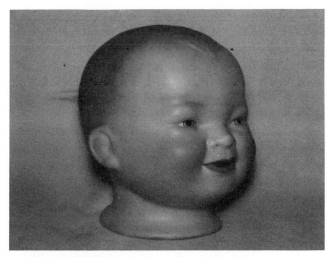

**1336.** Bisque head designed by Grace S. Putnam has painted features, open-closed mouth with molded tongue. Mark: Ill. **1337.** This head was probably made after 1925. *Courtesy of Lester & Alice Grinnings.*

**1337 & 1338.** Marks used on dolls designed by Grace Putnam.

> Copr. by
> Grace S Putnam
> Germany
> 1415/48
>
> 1337

> Copr. by.
> Grace S. Putnam
> MADE IN GERMANY
>
> 1338

*Fabrik Co.* when they registered their turtle trademark in the U.S. in 1915.

1914: New numbers in the *Jubilee* line of *Strobel & Wilken* character dolls had pyroxylin heads; some of these apparently had bodies covered with rubberoid.

# Q

**Quackenbush, E. & G.** 1915–17. New York City. Registered *Tiny Tots* as a trademark in U.S. for dolls made of a combination of rubber and cloth. Besides Tiny Tots, they made washable *Tubbies*.

**Quaker Doll Co.** 1915–18. Philadelphia, Pa. Made "Quaker Quality" character dolls.

QUA<sub>KER</sub>LITY

*1339.* Mark used by Quaker Doll Co.

1917: Advertised fifty models of dolls and dolls' heads.

**Qualitoy Co.** 1919. Newark, N.J. Made "Dolls of Quality" with composition or soft bodies.

**Quality Bilt.** 1918. Line of American dolls handled by *Century Doll Co.* Came with moving glass eyes, curly ringlet or plain hair wigs; 24 inches tall.

**Queen Anne Doll.** Georgian period. At the 1913 London's Annual Doll Show organized by the "London EVENING NEWS," there were 60,000 dolls sold or given away, for charity. According to PLAYTHINGS, January, 1914, among the dolls was "a Queen Anne doll, made and dressed by Princess Augusta, daughter of George III; as well as many other dolls of the Georgian and early Victorian eras."

**Queen Louise.** 1910. Trademark registered in U.S. by *Louis Wolf & Co.* Some of the bisque heads marked "Queen Louise" were probably made by *Armand Marseille.*

**Queen of Toyland, The.** 1925. Trade name for dolls made by Regal Doll Manufacturing Co., successor of *German American Doll Co.*

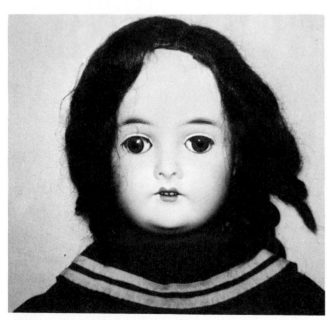

*1340.* "Queen Louise," bisque socket head with glass sleeping eyes, hair eyelashes, open mouth with teeth, produced by Louis Wolf & Co. ca. 1910. Mark on head: "30 // Germany // Queen Louise." H. of socket head, 6 inches. *Coleman Collection.*

*1341 & 1342.* "Queen Louise" marks of Louis Wolf & Co.

Germany
Queen Louise

Germany
Queen Louise
9

1341            1342

**Queen Quality.** 1903. Trade name for dolls with kid bodies advertised by *E. A. Runnells & Co.*

**Queen Quality.** 1910. Trademark registered in Germany by *A. Wislizenus* for jointed dolls and doll parts.

**Queue San Baby.** 1915–22. Line of dolls produced by *Morimura Bros.* They also used this name as their trademark beginning in October, 1915. The trademark was registered in 1916, at which time they stated that it was usually a printed label applied to the boxes or receptacles containing the dolls. Probably it was at a later date that the label was applied directly on the stomach of the doll, as it is often found.

Several different versions of Queue San Baby have been found. The Queue San Baby doll as designed by *Hikozo Araki* in 1915 and shown in Ill. 1343 was patented in 1916 for 3½ years and assigned to Morimura Bros. Few of the dolls marked "Queue San Baby" have been found with a country of origin marked on them. Their boxes were probably marked "made in Japan." Dolls that closely resemble this one but are marked "made in Germany" were either German imitations, or perhaps were made in Germany for *Langfelder, Homma & Hayward,* who acquired Morimura's doll business around 1922.

1917: *Baltimore Bargain House* advertised all-bisque Queue San Babies 4½ inches tall for 85¢ doz. wholesale.

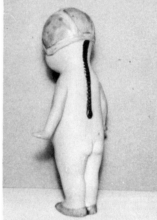

*1343A & B.* "Queue San Baby," all-bisque doll with molded cap, queue, and slippers, jointed at shoulders; was produced by Morimura Bros. ca. 1916. Sticker on chest: Ill. *1344.* H. 4½ inches. *Coleman Collection.*

*1344.* Mark on sticker found on "Queue San Baby."

**Quivy, H.** 1878–79. Paris. Made dolls.
1878: Displayed dressed and undressed dolls at the Paris Exposition.

RABERY & DELPHIEU DOLLS

**A**

# R

**R. B. & L. Manufacturing Co.** See **Roth, Baitz & Lipsitz, Inc.**

**R. F. Novelty Co.** 1919. St. Louis, Mo. Made *Baby Love*, a paper doll in the round, which could stand alone and had movable head and limbs. It was handmade and hand-painted.

**Rabery & Delphieu.** 1856–98, Paris; 1898–99, Genty was successor; 1899–1925+, firm became part of the *Société Française de Fabrication de Bébés et Jouets.*

1856: Jean Delphieu was granted a French patent for the use of pink cloth instead of pink kid for dolls' bodies.

1875: Delphieu advertised kid, linen, and other dolls, with swivel or stationary heads.

1876: Rabery & Delphieu advertised all kinds of jointed dolls, kid dolls, white or pink linen dolls, with bisque heads, swivel or stationary. Also a large variety of *marottes.*

1878: Alexandre Rabery and A. Delphieu exhibited dressed and undressed dolls at the Paris Exposition.

1879: Advertised jointed dolls of all kinds, some with white and some with pink kid bodies; some dressed and some undressed. Dolls had bisque heads. Also sold marottes.

1881: Advertised dolls with wooden bodies and white or pink kid bodies, either rigid or jointed, as well as indestructible jointed bébés or bébés with wooden bodies. Dolls came dressed or undressed. Also sold marottes.

1883: Won a silver medal for dolls at the Amsterdam Exhibition.

1889: Alexandre Rabery was awarded a silver medal at the Paris Exposition.

1890: A. Rabery was using the mark "R. D." for talking bébés and indestructible jointed bébés.

1893: Alexandre Rabery was granted a French patent for a walking talking doll, and he exhibited dolls at the Chicago World's Fair.

1898: Genty advertised talking bébés, walking bébés, with sleeping eyes and the trademarks *Bébé de Paris* and "R. D."

**B**

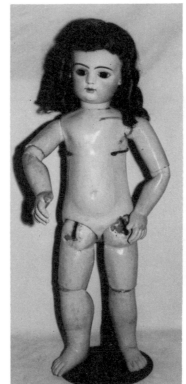

**C**

**1345A, B, & C.** Bisque-headed doll made by Rabery & Delphieu with stationary glass eyes, closed mouth, jointed composition body. Mark: Ill. **1348.** H. 28 inches. *Coleman Collection.*

**1346.** Doll with bisque head marked "R.D." for Rabery & Delphieu has glass eyes, jointed composition body. *Courtesy of Frances Walker; photograph by Winnie Langley.*

**1347.** Both body and head of this doll have marks of Rabery & Delphieu. The bisque head, marked "R.D.," has glass eyes, closed mouth. The jointed composition body is stamped with the mark shown in Ill. **165.** *Courtesy of Frances Walker; photograph by Winnie Langley.*

## R.4.D         R ⅝ D
### 1348                    1349

**1348 & 1349.** Marks of Rabery & Delphieu found on dolls.

*Roullet & Decamps* also used the initials "R. D.," but they made mechanical dolls primarily. The nonmechanical dolls marked "R. D." were probably made by Rabery & Delphieu.

**Rachel.** 1923–25. Doll representing character in *Frank King's* cartoon GASOLINE ALLEY, made by *Live Long Toy Co.* The idea for the doll was conceived and executed by *Mrs. William A. Benoliel.*

1924: Trademark registered in U.S. by Frank O. King; it was affixed to doll by a printed impression.

**Racker (Rascal).** 1919. Trademark registered in Germany by *Gans & Seyfarth* for dolls' heads.

**Racketty Packetty Kiddies (Kiddy).** 1913–15. Trademark registered in U.S. by *Steinfeld Bros.* Dolls represented the characters in the book of this name written by Frances Hodgson Burnett in 1906; they were designed by *Maurice F. Oppenheimer* and copyrighted by Steinfeld Bros. in 1913. The dolls were a family of eight "unbreakable" character dolls with movable heads and removable clothes; size 18 inches; price $3.00.

**1350.** "Rachel," all-bisque doll representing Frank O. King's character of this name; ca. 1925. Swivel neck; molded and painted clothes include an orange blouse, green skirt, and white apron. H. 3½ inches. *Courtesy of Dorothy Annunziato.*

**Rader & Nennstiel.** 1891. Sonneberg, Thür. Manufactured and exported dolls.

**Radick, Mary E.** 1915. White Plains, N.Y. Was granted a U.S. patent for a multi-face doll with one smiling and one crying face. The wig was pivotally connected to the dolls' head at the apex by a pin.

**Radium-Gummiwerke Inc.** 1922. Cologne, Germany. Produced rubber dolls and obtained a German patent for them.

**Raffaeli, E.** 1900–1912. Paris. Handled dolls' heads, wigs, dolls' clothes, and other items.

**Rag Bag Dolls.** 1908. Elaborately dressed dolls, made in France.

**Rag Dolls.** Rag dolls have been found in ancient Egyptian tombs. Old Greek and Roman rag dolls are preserved today in the British Museum. Down through the ages, rag dolls have been made in the home. They had the advantages of being soft and possible to construct of readily available material. However, homespun cloth was precious to our ancestors, and was probably used for dolls only by the more affluent people. Wooden dolls were usually not only less expensive but also the more popular type. Frequently, old rag dolls have heads of several layers of cloth—evidence of the fact that when a face became worn, a new one was put over it. Since early rag dolls were generally homemade, they differed according to the ingenuity and artistic skill of the individual who made them. In the days before sewing machines, they were all hand-sewn.

Articles in PLAYTHINGS, January, 1907, and September, 1926, describe this type of old doll as follows:

"It did not have any joints, and its stockings and shoes were already on, the shoes being outlined from the ink bottle and filled in with the same material.

"The face was not artistic, the nose being a straight streak, the mouth another streak at right angles to the nose. The eyes were little buttons from the button bag, and there were eyebrows made by making the pen spread up and down on the cloth above the eye. There was a petticoat, a pink calico or gingham dress and a pinafore apron, all of which were fastened on securely. . . . Hair she had none. Sometimes the dog and the little Mother had a tussle for her, and then, as neither would let go and something had to give, it was usually a stitch, and there were bits of cotton, or sawdust, or curled hair to gather up, together with the shedding of a few tears by her owner."

"Old rag dolls were treasured heirlooms of many New England homes. Of all sizes, and attired in many sorts of quaint costumes, they had some points in common. Their faces were invariably flat, their hands were stiff and rigid, their toes turned out in a most alarming manner. Sometimes they had black button eyes; frequently their prim faces were painted with beet and fruit juices; occasionally eyes, nose and mouth were embroidered. For hair they wore toupees of yarn or hemp or wisps of real hair. Their garments were full-

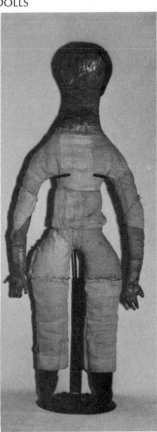

**1351A & B.** Homemade, hand-sewn rag doll with featureless face of oil-painted muslin. The type of face and the shape of the cap suggest that it may have been made by a member of a Pennsylvania religious group. Original dress. H. 20 inches. *Courtesy of Sylvia Brockmon.*

skirted gowns of sprigged muslins or prints and they often wore sunbonnets of the same materials as their dresses. In one New Hampshire family still lives an old rag doll who for over 80 years has pleased its daughters. True, she has become somewhat the worse for wear, but her blemished features have been renewed by the simple expedient of recovering her face with a piece of fresh cloth."

Commercial rag dolls appeared extensively in the second half of the 19th century. At the London Exhibition, *Mme. Montanari* displayed rag dolls "entirely of textile fabric," according to the report of the jury. The London Rag Doll achieved popularity especially in the 1870's and 1880's. However, this was not a true rag doll as it was made of muslin over a wax mask. The combination of wax and cloth was also used in America; *Rebecca Johnson* obtained a U.S. patent in 1887 for a cloth doll dipped in wax. Many earlier U.S. patents had been issued for combining various materials with cloth to stiffen and strengthen it. Among them were patents issued to *Ludwig Greiner, George Hawkins,* and *Izannah Walker.*

In 1886, *Edward S. Peck* obtained a U.S. design patent for a printed cutout rag doll. There followed many improvements on this type, notably those made

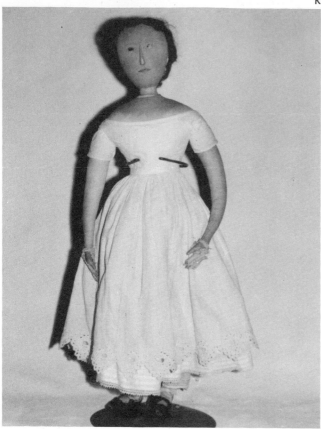

**1352A & B.** Homemade rag doll of cotton percale has embroidered features, open mouth with teeth, and needle-molded nose. The hair is sewed to the head. Doll wears a corset lacing up the back, white dress, and silk knit gloves. H. 25 inches. *Courtesy of Helen Jo Payne.*

**1353A & B.** Rag doll with stockinet face and hands, made in Newark, N.J. by Phoebe Wilson ca. 1878, who named her "Rag Nellie." Head has painted features, beads for eyes, and braided human-hair wig. Original blue dress. H. 14 inches. *Courtesy of the Newark Museum, Newark, N.J.*

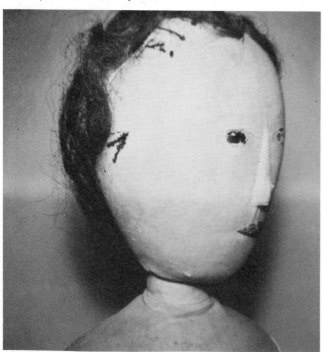

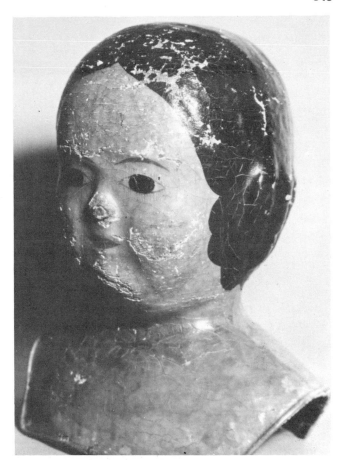

**1354A & B.** Head of cloth is reinforced with wire around the shoulder edge. Doll has painted and molded features and hair, and wears contemporary brown print dress. *Courtesy of Maurine Popp; photographs by Winnie Langley.*

**1355.** Stockinet-cloth head with metal around the edge has painted and molded hair and features. Note the vertical eyelashes. The round face and short neck suggest a baby. *Courtesy of Winnie Langley; photograph by Winnie Langley.*

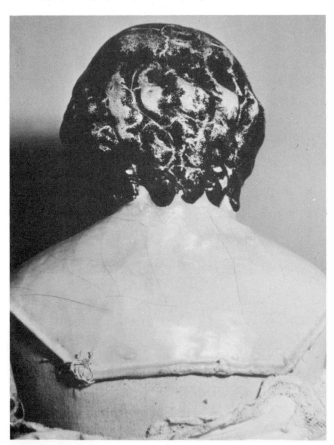

by *Charity Smith, Ida Gutsell,* and *Edgar Newell.* Following the success of the *Emma Adams' Columbian* doll, there were several U.S. patents for making rag dolls, including those obtained by *Madge Mead,* 1900; *Brückner,* 1901; and *Ella Smith,* 1905. In 1906, dolls with faces made from photographs of children appeared on the market. *Dreamland Doll Co.* claimed that they originated this type.

There were many American patentees of rag dolls in the early 20th century. Among them were *Edward Gibson, Charles Sackman, Anne Maxwell, Lenora Price, Lita and Bessie Shinn,* and *Charlotte Glossbrenner.*

Commercial rag dolls were primarily a product of America and England, but Europe also produced cloth dolls. Over a long period, possibly the entire 19th century, completely hand-sewn dolls with embroidered features were made by the people of Southern Russia. These dolls usually appear in pairs, a man and a woman. The man doll wears white clothes, including white leather boots. Dolls especially notable for their artistry were made in Germany by *Margarete Steiff* and *Käthe Kruse.* The *Scavinis* made artistic fabric dolls in Italy, which were imitated in many countries. Many cutout rag dolls were used for advertising purposes. (See Ill. 289.)

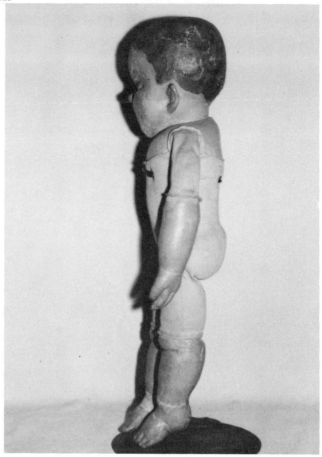

**1356A & B.** Rag doll that resembles the Columbian Dolls. The head is painted with oils. There are seams across the top of the head and down the center back of the head; sew lines indicate fingers and toes. Marked on head: "65" in blue and "343" in red. H. 15 inches. *Courtesy of Lester & Alice Grinnings.*

**1357A & B.** Stockinet rag doll, painted with oils and needle molded. Has seams across the top of the head and down the center of the back of the head. Limbs also are painted with oils and needle molded. H. 22 inches. *Courtesy of Lester & Alice Grinnings.*

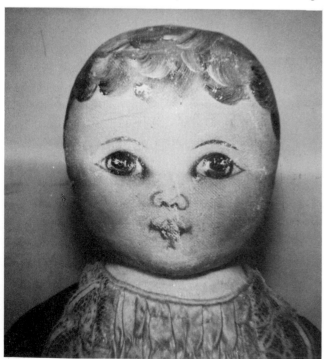

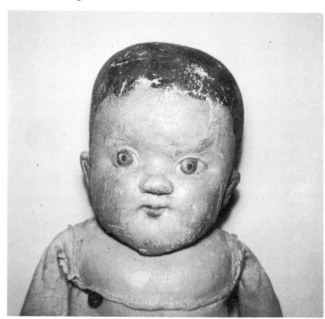

**Raggedy Ann.** 1915–25+. Trademark registered in 1915 by *John B. Gruelle*. Design patent issued to John B. Gruelle in 1915 for a rag doll with the label on the doll. Allegedly, he copied the doll from one that had belonged to his mother. The doll as originally designed differed in appearance from later versions of Raggedy Ann.

**Rags Bud.** 1921. Rag doll made by *Sophia E. Delavan;* price $12.50 doz. wholesale.

**Ragtime Kids.** 1913. Trademark registered in Britain by *Richard Ordenstein.*

**Rainbow Dolls.** 1915–16. Made by *Louis Amberg & Son.*

**Rakusei Gangu Kabushiki Kaisha.** 1921–25. Kyoto, Japan. Manufactured dolls.

**Rakuyesha, Yanaginobanba Gojo.** 1920. Kyoto, Japan. Manufactured dolls.

**Raleigh, Jessie McCutcheon.** 1916–20. Chicago, Ill. Made *Art Dolls.* After making the "Good Fairy" statuette in 1915, she turned to making dolls. First she obtained the services of the research departments of several large universities to produce a good composition material out of which the dolls could be made. *Emory Seidel* and other sculptors designed faces for the dolls representing "beautiful" children. The dolls were jointed, light in weight, and hand-painted. Jessie Raleigh's early dolls, distributed by *Butler Bros.,* came dressed or undressed. Sizes 11½ and 18½ inches; price $1.80 to $5.75.

1917: Copyrighted *Uncle Sam.*

1918: Advertised *Peeps,* the Fairy Doll, who had a story written about her.

1919: Made dolls with composition breastplate (shoulder) heads, painted features, moving eyes, human hair wigs, cork-stuffed bodies. Dolls had individual wardrobes that were made by home workers. Featured *Miss Happy,* who had a story written about her. Advertised twenty-six new dolls, including, *Mary Had a Lamb, Daisy Anna, Rosemary, Priscilla, Tiny Tot, Goldilocks,* Peeps, *Mama's Angel Child,* Red Riding Hood, *Mary-Quite-Contrary,* Big Mary, *Doll-O'-My-Heart, Poppy,* Little Sherry (a baby doll), *Lucille, Dorothy,* Rabbit Lady, and *Pink Lady.* Her dolls sold as far away as Australia.

1920: Advertised Peeps, Goldilocks, birthday dolls dressed suitably for each month, life-size baby doll, *Stair-Step Family* of three composition dolls, 18-inch dolls of all-cloth or of composition and cloth; also rag dolls named *Sam* and *Shoe Button Sue.*

**Ramel, Société Ch., & Cie.** 1916. Registered two trademarks in France, *J'Habille Mes Soldats* and *J'Habille Mes Poupées,* for papier-mâché dolls.

**Ramon Navarro.** 1924. *Celebrity Doll* originated by *Margaret Vale,* designed and made by *Jane Gray.* The doll represented Ramon Navarro as Scaramouche in Metro's movie SCARAMOUCHE. It had a hand-painted face and bore a tag with a facsimile autograph of Ramon Navarro.

**Ramspeck & Schnell.** 1909. Frankfurt am Main, Hesse-Nassau. Manufactured dolls.

**Ransom, Sidney.** 1924. Birmingham, Warwick. Doll manufacturer. Registered *Sabo* as a trademark in Britain for dolls made wholly or partly of celluloid.

**Rascal, The.** See **Der Schelm.**

**Rastus Baby.** 1910. Negro doll made by *Horsman.* Dressed in rompers; price $9.00 doz. wholesale.

**Rattle Head.** 1905. Advertised by *Butler Bros.* The ordinary china head was filled with small china balls that rattled when doll was moved. Came on cloth body with china limbs; 8 inches tall; 35¢ doz. wholesale.

**Rätz, Karl.** 1918. Schwarzdorf, Thür. Made dolls.

**Rau, G. F.** 1844. Oberlind near Sonneberg, Thür. Displayed little figures of papier-mâché, such as little Swiss maidens, at the Berlin Exhibition.

**Rauch, J.** 1889. Paris. Made dolls.

**Rauch, P.** 1862–90, Paris; 1867–90, P. Rauch Aîné (Sr.). Made dolls.

1878: Showed woolen dolls at the Paris Exposition.

**Rauch & Schelhorn.** 1923–25. Sonneberg, Thür. Manufactured dolls.

**Rauenstein.** See **Greiner, Fr. Chr., & Söhne.**

**Rauscher, G.** 1909–18. Wildenheid near Sonneberg, Thür. Made dolls' bodies.

**Rauscher, Th.** 1909. Hönbach, Thür. Made dolls' heads.

**Rauser, Mrs. Katherine A.** 1904–25+. Chicago, Ill. Designed and made clothes for dolls as well as making dolls. She started her business with one sewing machine.

1916: Made *Calvert Tot,* distributed by *A. S. Ferguson;* began to use *Dolly Modiste* as a trademark.

1917: Listed in directories as a doll manufacturer as well as a doll outfitter; registered in U.S. "Dolly Modiste" as a trademark; appointed couturière for *Schoenhut* dolls. She made outfits with buttons and buttonholes for the *American Toy & Doll Manufacturing Co.*

1919: Had factory with departments for pattern cutting, designing, making, and assembling; plus fifty home workers. Mrs. Rauser herself designed all of the deluxe line of dolls' garments. Clothes were made mostly of washable fabrics and could be buttoned and unbuttoned. Expensive dolls cost over $100. The dress of one doll had 450 French knots alone. Mrs. Rauser supplied clothes for *Horsman, Morimura Bros., Schoenhut,* and other doll manufacturers all over America and England. Among her dolls was *Mlle. Babette,* a fully jointed doll made by the *Buddie Toy & Novelty Co.;* sizes 18 to 24 inches.

1920: New factory for dressed dolls. Mlle. Babette came in sizes 20, 24, and 26 inches.

1921: Advertised *Miss Chicago* line of dolls. Dressed dolls for *Sophia Delavan* and *Marks Bros.*

**1358.** Some of the first rag dolls made by Bernard Ravca, ca. 1925. The group was called "Modiste's Atelier" (Milliner's Shop). Note that most of the dolls represent young women, not the elderly people for which Ravca later became famous. Heights ca. 16 inches. *Courtesy of Bernard Ravca.*

**Ravca, Bernard.** 1924–25+. Paris. Made dolls' heads of cloth with stockinet faces. Among his earliest ones were dolls representing *Marguerite* in FAUST, *Maurice Chevalier,* and *Mistinguette*. His first heads depicted young people. The dolls in the Modiste's Atelier were portraits of young girl types. His early *Peasant Dolls* did not have their faces and hands treated chemically as were those of his later dolls. He used the slogan "Real People Dolls."

**Ravisé, E.** 1925+. Paris. Made dolls and used "E. R." as a mark.

**Rawacj, S.** 1920–23. Coburg, Thür. Manufactured dolls.

**Ray, Jean.** 1925+. Paris. Made dolls exclusively for the *Société Française de Fabrication de Bébés et Jouets.*

**Rayburn, Townsend Co.** 1924–25. London. Made dolls.

**Raynal.** 1925+. Paris. Made felt and cloth dolls, advertised as a "new kind"; they were dressed in various costumes.

**Read, Dorothy.** 1921. Fort Smith, Ark. Obtained U.S. design patent for a long-legged doll.

**Read, Elmer J.** 1918. Rutherford, N.J. Obtained U.S. patent #1,283,558 for a method of making movable limbs and manufacturing jointed dolls. The number of this patent is often found on "Patsy," *Lovums,* and other dolls made by *EFFanBEE*. These dolls were made after 1925.

The 1918 patent was an improvement of a 1917 U.S. patent.

**Reader, Helen Vincent.** 1922–24. Roosevelt, Wash. Registered *Gooky Girl* as a trademark in U.S.; mark stamped on dolls.

**Real People Dolls.** Slogan used by *Bernard Ravca.*

**Really Truly.** 1914. Trademark registered in U.S. by *Mary R. Thomas* for character dolls. (Not to be confused with "Reely Trooly" one-dimensional dolls.)

**Reber, Louis.** 1918. Sonneberg, Thür. Made dolls with leather bodies.

**Rechsteiner.** 1840–42. Germany and Switzerland. Made talking dolls.

**Recknagel, Phil., & Co.** 1888–91. Eisfeld, Thür. Made and exported dolls.

1888: Displayed dolls at the Melbourne Exhibition.

**Recknagel, Th.** 1886–1925+. Alexandrinenthal near Oeslau, Thür. Hard paste porcelain factory. The mark of this factory appears on bisque-headed dolls. One of these is a 14-inch doll with closed mouth. Many dolls have the letters "R A" on their bisque heads. It is possible that Recknagel used only the initials without the crossed nails on some of his dolls' heads. (See Ill. 211.)

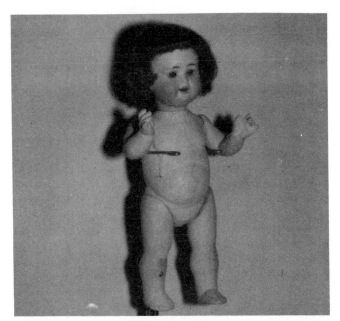

**1359A & B.** Bisque head marked "R A," which might stand for Th. Recknagel, who used these initials. Doll has sleeping blue eyes, open mouth with two upper teeth, two holes on either side of the head just below the crown, composition body with straight legs and curved arms. Mark: Ill. **1360.** H. 11 inches. *Courtesy of Dorothy Annunziato.*

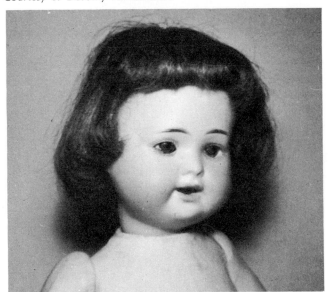

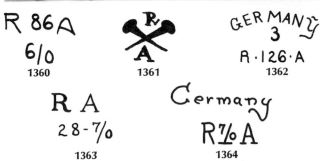

| | | |
|---|---|---|
| R 86 A | ⚔ | GERMANY |
| 6/0 | | 3 |
| | | R·126·A |
| **1360** | **1361** | **1362** |
| R A | Germany | |
| 28-7/0 | R7/0A | |
| **1363** | **1364** | |

**1360–1364.** Marks found on dolls that may have been made by Th. Recknagel of Alexandrinenthal. No. **1361** is definitely his mark, but the others are still questionable.

1898: Advertised that their specialty was fine bisque heads. Factory had over two hundred employees.

**Réclame, Bébé.** See **Bébé Réclame.**

**Records.** It is wise to keep uniform records on each doll in a collection; these can be elaborately detailed descriptions or brief identifications. The catalog notes should be kept either on file cards or in a loose-leaf notebook and in numerical order, with the identical number attached to the doll in some uniform but unobtrusive place —i.e., all numbered tags on the upper thigh. Following the identifying number comes the description: head material first, then body material, material of limbs, type of clothes (make sure those dolls with wardrobes have a complete listing), height, and approximate age. Next come the source of purchase and the price paid or the name of the donor and the estimated value; also the year in which the object was acquired. Any additional information such as a documented history, restoration, the listing of garments, references, and so on can be placed on the reverse of the record sheet. If a picture is available, it should be attached for easy identification. In any case, the records should contain an identifying number, photograph or description, and approximate value. A cross reference by the type of head can also be helpful. If an object is eliminated from the collection, draw a red line through the sheet but do not discard it. Do not use the number again.

**Red Cross Nurse.** 1917. Doll copyrighted by *Elizabeth Lesser* in U.S.

**Red Cross Nurse.** 1917–18. Doll designed by *Madame Alexander;* distributed by Maurice Alexander. It had a composition head and cloth body, and was dressed as a nurse.

**Red Cross Nurse.** 1918. Doll with composition head and hands, stuffed body; distributed by *Grey & Dudley.* Came dressed in white as a nurse; 15½ inches tall; price 80¢.

**Red Cross Nurse.** 1918–19. Cut out rag doll, 16 inches tall; price 10¢.

**Red Riding Hood.** See **Little Red Riding Hood.**

**Red Riding Hood.** 1901. Dressed doll with bisque head; carried a basket. Size 13 inches, price $9.00 doz. wholesale.

**Red Riding Hood.** 1907–10. A *Dolly Varden* dressed rag doll distributed by *Butler Bros.* Came with painted linen face, stubby arms, stuffed body. Size 14 inches; price $2.10 doz. wholesale.

**Red Riding Hood.** 1909. Muslin cut out doll made by *Saalfield;* 17½ by 18 inches; price 20¢.

**Red Riding Hood.** 1915. Made by *Non-Breakable Doll Co.* with "indestructible" sleeping eyes.

**Red Riding Hood.** 1917. Distributed by *Baltimore Bargain House.* Came with celluloid face; fully jointed. Size 9¾ inches, $1.20 doz. wholesale.

**Red Riding Hood.** 1918. Made by *K & K Toy Co.* Came with composition head and hands, painted features, jointed at hips and shoulders. Wore lawn dress, red hood and cape. Size 15 inches, $9.60 doz. wholesale.

**Redfern, G. F., & Co.** 1910–20. London agents for *Société Française de Fabrication de Bébés et Jouets, Sussfeld & Cie.,* and *Kämmer & Reinhardt.*

1920: Registered *Naughty* as a trademark in Britain for Kämmer & Reinhardt.

**Redó, Ignac.** Ca. 1925. Budapest. Made celluloid dolls and toys; forty-five to sixty-five workers.

**Rees, Leon.** 1912–23. London. Patented and distributed dolls.

1912: Obtained a British patent and two U.S. patents for making dolls with round faces and eyes that could be moved from side to side. His U.S. patents were assigned to *Monroe M. Schwarzschild.* These appear to have been the *Hug-Me Kiddies,* distributed by *Samstag & Hilder.*

1914–15: Obtained British and U.S. patents for attaching a rag doll's neck with elastic cord to a hemispherical cup in a stuffed body, so that the head would turn.

1923: Registered in Britain *Heather Belle* as a trademark.

**Rees Davis Toy Co.** 1922. Chicago, Ill. Registered in U.S. *Mitzi* as a trademark. The name was stamped on the dolls.

**Reese, Charles N.** 1920–25. Wilmette, Ill. Secured U.S. patent for a stuffed doll with a lower jaw pivotally mounted and operated by a lever at the back of the head. Hands and feet were of rubber, made so that the thumb and forefinger could be separated sufficiently to hold articles. Pieces of celluloid were inserted in the top of the finger to simulate nails.

**Reeves, Loula S.** 1915–18. Warren, Ohio. Obtained a U.S. patent for improvement in head and limb joints on stuffed dolls. A number of layers of fabric were cemented together on opposite sides of metal disks through which bolts were placed for a pivotal connection.

**Reeves, Ruth.** 1921. Designed peasant costumes with batik decorations, for dolls. *Marie Vassilief* made a caricature portrait doll of Miss Ruth Reeves.

**Regal Doll Manufacturing Co.** See **German American Doll Co.**

**Reg'lar Fellers.** 1922–23. Trademark registered in Germany by *Borgfeldt,* and used for dolls representing characters created by *Gene Byrnes.*

**Regulation China Limb Dolls.** 1893–1907. Name used for dolls with china heads having wavy hairdos that came down over the forehead and were generally fairly flat in the back. One third of these dolls were blondes, the others brunettes. Sizes 7½ to 17 inches; price 4¢ to 20¢. (See also **China Limb Dolls.**)

**Rehbock & Loewenthal.** 1914. Fürth, Bavaria. Registered in France *Chéri Bébé* as a trademark.

**Rehm, Carl.** 1895. Neustadt near Coburg, Thür. Manufactured dolls' bodies of kid.

**Rehm, Theod.** 1895–1909. Neustadt near Coburg, Thür. Manufactured little or baby dolls.

**Reich, A.** 1909–15. Coburg, Thür. In 1915, A. Reich, Jr., was the successor. Manufactured dolls.

**Reich, Goldmann & Co.** 1890–1925+. Offenbach, Germany. Made celluloid dolls, especially babies.

**Reichel, Joseph L.** 1913. Maple Lake, Minn. Obtained a patent in Germany for cutout dolls' faces.

**Reichmann, Lazarus.** 1877. New York City. Secured a U.S. patent for a doll's head. The shell of the head was to be made of beeswax, paraffin, and turpentine, with an inner supporting layer of sawdust, glue, and a suitable paste such as flour paste. The doll's head was to be given a real hair wig.

**Reidel, F., Jr.** 1909–10. Liegnitz, Germany. Manufactured dolls.

**Reidmeister.** 1860. Paris. Obtained French patent for doll with metal ball joints (appear to have been used with kid bodies), and head and lower arms of porcelain.

**Reinecke, Otto.** 1878–1925+. Hof-Moschendorf, Bavaria. His hard paste porcelain factory used "P M" marks (see Ills. 1371 and 1372) similar to those found on dolls. The "P M" stood for Porzellanfabrik Moschendorf. (See also **Grete.**)

**Reinhardt, C. F.** 1923. Coburg and Sonneberg, Thür. Manufactured dolls and babies; advertised trade collections for from 1,000 to 10,000 marks.

**Reinhardt, Ernst.** Born 1875 in a small hamlet near Hildburghausen, Thür. His family do not know of any relationship to the Reinhardts of Waltershausen. By his early twenties, Reinhardt was head of his own doll assembling plant. In addition to his regular employees, he had persons on nearby farms who worked at home making doll parts for him during the winter season. Laura Reinhardt, his wife, designed the doll clothes from a book with colored plates of German provincial costumes entitled DEUTSCHE VOLKSTRACHTEN by Albert Kretschmer, and helped with the dressing of the dolls. These were miniature dolls about 4 inches tall; they included Negroes and Orientals as well as provincial dolls. They were jointed at shoulders and hips only. The Reinhardt children helped to assemble them for two pfennigs a dozen (¼ cent).

In 1906 Reinhardt obtained a German patent pertaining to a mechanism for sleeping eyes. It suggested the use of celluloid, and the eyes made by Reinhardt in America were of stamped celluloid and closely followed the patent specifications. Reinhardt worked with *Armand Marseille* in order to learn the methods of making bisque doll heads, shortly before coming to America about 1909.

The Reinhardts settled in north Philadelphia, where they established a small doll factory and produced dolls with experimental bisque (translucent porcelain) heads. Steel dies were used for the papier-mâché bodies, and parts of the limbs were made of wood turned on a lathe. Laura Reinhardt, as dressmaker and milliner for the dolls,

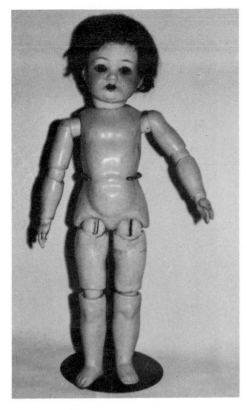

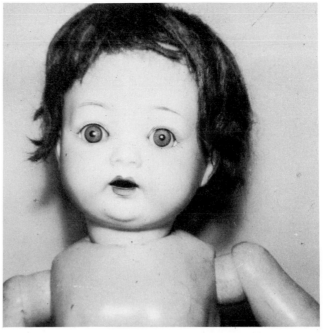

**PM
23
Germany
2**

1367

**P M
828
0**

1368

**1365A & B.** Bisque head with the mark of Otto Reinecke has sleeping eyes, open mouth with two teeth. Composition body has joint above the knee, a characteristic of dolls in the 1920's. Mark: Ill. **1367.** H. 15 inches. *Courtesy of Eleanor Jean Carter.*

**1366.** Bisque head that may have been made by Otto Reinecke. Molded hair including the blue ribbon, intaglio eyes, molded teeth, composition body. Mark on head: Ill. **1368.** *Photograph by Winnie Langley.*

**P M
914.
Germany
1**

1369

**P.M.
23
Germany.
2**

1370

**P M**

1371

**P M**

1372

**1367–1372.** Marks Nos. **1371** and **1372** were used by Otto Reinecke; similar marks (Nos. **1367, 1368, 1369,** and **1370**) are found on dolls' heads.

**1373–1377.** Ernst Reinhardt's marks found on bisque heads.

**R**

1373

**ER**

1374

**U S A
E R**

1375

**H 3
Reinhardt
East Liverpool
Ohio**

1376

**Made in U.S.A.
E. R.
Pat. ⊕ Sep.
19   14
Reinhardt**

1377

helped to fill the orders. Ernst Reinhardt, citizen of the U.S., applied for a U.S. patent in December, 1913, which was granted in 1914. The object of the patent was "to provide for the ready changing of both the eyes and hair of the doll whereby, when the eyes are changed . . . the wig can be readily detached and replaced by another when it is desired to change the color of the hair . . . to harmonize with the eyes, and . . . to provide simple and efficient means whereby the pivoted eyes may be readily locked in position when desired."

In 1916 Reinhardt, hoping to expand his production of bisque doll heads, moved his family to East Liverpool, Ohio, where he established a porcelain factory under the name *Bisc Novelty Manufacturing Co.* Every month from June through November, 1917, PLAYTHINGS carried a large advertisement that read, "Bisc Novelty Manufacturing Company, East Liverpool, Ohio, E. Reinhardt, Bisc Doll Heads, made in U.S.A., Genuine Bisc Doll Heads with Moving Eyes," and showed pictures of these dolls' heads.

Despite a tremendous number of orders, the Bisc Novelty Manufacturing Co. was short-lived because doll heads were a nonessential product and the natural gas required for their production was needed for war purposes. Reluctantly, the Reinhardts moved to Irvington, New Jersey, and the Mesa Munitions Plant. By the end of the war Reinhardt was again producing bisque heads. These were made in Irvington, Perth Amboy, and Metuchen. Doll heads marked *Mesa* and *Perth Amboy* were made between 1918 and 1922. The return of inexpensive German bisque doll heads in large quantities by 1922 put an end to Reinhardt's business.

Ernst Reinhardt created his models and made his own molds. He made both socket- and shoulder-type heads, with molded hair or wigs, and with sleep eyes or painted eyes. He also made bisque arms. Although experimental bisque dolls had been made much earlier in the U.S., Reinhardt appears to have been the first to produce porcelain bisque dolls' heads in America commercially, and entirely with domestic clays. (See Ill. 54.)

**Reinhardt, Georg.** 1891. Naumburg, Germany. Manufactured wool dolls.

**Reinhardt, Max.** 1895–1909. Neustadt near Coburg, Thür. Made dolls, including small dolls.

**Reisenweber, Adolf.** 1922. Sonneberg, Thür. European representative of *The Doll & Toy Manufacturer's Assoc.;* his New York distributor was *Roth, Baitz & Lipsitz, Inc.* Made walking and talking dolls.

**Reisenweber, Christoph.** 1918–25. Steinach, Thür. Specialized in dressed "stiff jointed" dolls.

**Reisenweber, Emil.** 1909–18. Steinach, Thür. Made dolls.

**Reisenweber & Zitzmann.** 1909. Steinach, Thür. Made dolls.

**Reisman, Barron Co.** 1916–25+. New York City. Made and distributed dolls and dolls' heads.

1916: Made character dolls, especially boys in college colors, priced at 50¢ and $1.00.

1919: Advertised 125 styles, including composition dolls, character dolls, dolls with wigs, and knitted cloth dolls; sizes 10 to 30 inches; price 25¢ to $3.00.

1920: Made 50,000 dolls' heads a week; 1,000 a day came from one of their hot presses; specialized in $1.00 dolls.

1921: Made 150 models; sizes 11 to 30 inches; prices 25¢ to $100.00.

1922: Advertised that they were the largest manufacturer of 25¢ to $1.00 dolls; made 30,000 dolls a week in three hundred styles, including The *Dolly Twins,* the *Leader* line of dolls, walking dolls, crying dolls, and wigged dolls.

1923: Advertised that they were the largest factory producing inexpensive dolls; made over one and a half million dolls a year.

1925: Manufactured and/or distributed complete dolls; three hundred styles, including *Mama Dolls* and an infant doll named *Just Born,* which came in sizes 15, 17, and 21 inches for $1.00, $2.00, and $3.00.

**Reismann, Paul.** 1925. Scheibe, in Schwarzburg, Rudolstadt, Thür. Made dolls.

**Rejall, Johannes.** 1922. Weisser Hirsch near Dresden, Saxony. Obtained a German patent for a wire-jointed doll; registered *Trutzi* as a trademark in Germany.

**Rejard.** 1836–52, Paris; 1866–70, Widow Rejard. Made dolls.

**Reliable Doll & Toy Manufacturing Co.** 1923–24. New York City. Manufactured dolls.

**Reliable Toy Co.** 1920–25+. Toronto, Canada. Started to make *Mama Dolls* in 1922.

**Reliance Novelty Co.** 1913–17. New York City. Manufactured dolls.

1913: Made "unbreakable" character dolls; size 13 inches cost 25¢.

1916: Made stuffed dolls in various sizes and styles; price 25¢ and up.

1917: Made Army Dolls, Navy Dolls, and Red Cross Nurses priced at 25¢ to $1.00. Also made *Dolly Drake,* which represented the girl in the Drake Bros. cake advertisement; price $1.00.

**Rembrandt.** 1922. Trade name of dolls made by *Master-Craft Doll Co.* These dolls were hand-painted, with washable fabric faces and big dimples in the cheeks. They were advertised as having the appearance of "carefully made portraits," and they walked and talked.

**Rembrandt Hair.** Late 1870's–1925+. Style of hairdo that remained popular for many years. The hair was cut in bangs across the forehead, fell straight around the sides and back of the head, then curled before it reached the shoulders.

**Remignard, Frédéric.** 1884–90. Paris. Made dolls, *bébés incassables* and *mignonettes.*

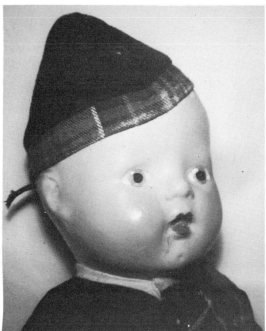

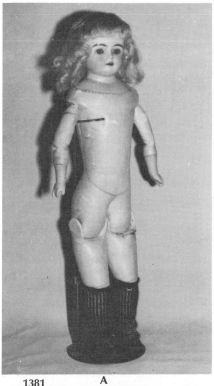

**1378A & B.** Composition doll made by Reliable Toy Co. with painted features and hair; jointed at shoulders and hips. Original Scottish costume. This doll may have been made after 1925. Mark: Ill. **1379.** H. 12½ inches. *Coleman Collection.*

**1381**                          **A**

**1379 & 1380.** Marks found on dolls of the Reliable Toy Co.

RELIABLE
MADE IN
CANADA
**1379**

RELIABLE
MADE IN CANADA
**1380**

**1381A & B.** Rembrandt style blonde wig on bisque shoulder head with sleeping glass eyes, open mouth with teeth; kid body with Ne Plus Ultra hip joints; bisque lower arms. H. 19 inches. *Courtesy of Edna Greehy.*

**B**

1888: Registered in France *Le Petit Chérubin* as a trademark for bébés made in Paris.

**Rémond.** See **Guillard.**

**Remy.** 1876–80. Paris. Made dolls.

**Renault & Bon-Dufour.** 1921. Paris. Manufactured *poupards* of "unbreakable" composition.

**Renders.** See **Guépratte.**

**Renninger, Charles.** 1891. London. Imported and distributed dolls made by *Metzler & Ortloff.*

**Renou.** See **Dehais.**

**Rentsch, E. H.** 1909–18. Altona am Elbe, Schleswig-Holstein. Manufactured dolls' heads.

**Renwick, Anna C.** 1914–15. Flushing, N.Y. Registered in U.S. *Corker* as a trademark for dolls.

**Repairing Dolls.** See **Custodianship of Dolls.**

**Replacements.** See **Original Condition.**

**Reproductions and Copies.** Throughout the ages many makers of dolls have copied other dolls or made copies of works of art in doll form. A popular type of doll might be copied over and over by various manufacturers. *George Hawkins* in the 1860's copied a beautiful untinted bisque head. His rag reproduction followed almost every detail of the original. (See Ills. 785 and 786.)

China heads of similar styles were made by numerous factories; for example, the popular china head with snood and bows on each side appears with various faces and decorative techniques. (See Ills. 329 and 330.) Even though the *Kewpie* and *New Born Babe* were protected by copyright, there were numerous imitators.

It is always easy to copy a successful doll, and collectors must distinguish between contemporary copies and modern reproductions. Dolls were produced in such vast quantities that most of them were, more or less, copies. However, since they were hand-painted, the individual craftsman's skill is usually discernible. Old dolls can generally be identified by the slight imperfections as well as the artistic skill. Mechanical aids were seldom available, and pink-tinted china heads did not have the same shade of pink over the entire face and neck as is usually found on reproductions. Also, bits of kiln dirt are frequently found in old porcelain heads. The artists who painted old dolls often spent a lifetime just painting eyes or mouths, and thus acquired great skill that is impossible to duplicate by hand in modern days.

Examination and study of many old dolls is the only way to distinguish an antique from a reproduction, and even then this can be a difficult task. The more valuable the doll, the greater is the incentive to reproduce it.

**Republic Doll & Toy Corp.** 1919–21. New York City. Made wood fiber composition dolls.

1919: Made a cherub-type doll in twenty styles; doll was named *Smiles.*

1920: Registered in U.S. *Kweenie* as a trademark. This name had been used for dolls in 1919. Smiles was made in sizes 12½ and 14½ inches. Also made *Bubbles,* a bent-limb baby with or without a wig.

**Restignat, Mme. (née Filliol).** 1868–72. Paris. Made dolls' bodies and dressed dolls as well as making trousseaux of all kinds.

1869: Obtained a French patent for a jointed cork doll's body, with a head that could turn completely around.

**Reta.** 1885. Doll distributed by YOUTH'S COMPANION. Came with "French bisque" head, shoulder plate, and hands; blue glass eyes, long blonde wig in *Rembrandt Hair* style; had swivel neck and jointed kid body. Wore lace stockings and velveteen slippers with bows. Size 13 inches; price $1.25.

**Retoux, Mme. (née Koppe, Catherine Laurence Louise).** 1889. Was granted a French patent for a jointed composition bébé with a spring inside the torso that allowed the bébé to be heightened or shortened.

**Reupke & Co.** 1924. Sonneberg, Thür. Made and exported dolls.

**Revalo.** 1921–25+. Line of dolls made by *Gebrüder Ohlhaver;* sole U.S. distributor was *Progressive Agency.* Line included ball-jointed dolls, bent-limb babies, and toddlers in either chemises or in dresses.

**Reversible.** See **Topsy Turvy.**

**Reversible.** 1920. Name given to two-headed rag doll by *EFFanBEE,* price $18.00 doz. wholesale.

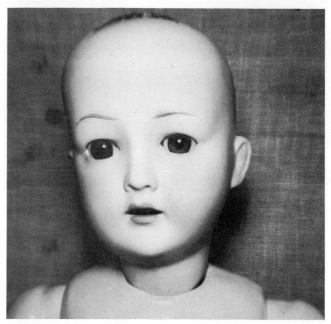

**1382.** Revalo doll has bisque head with sleeping glass eyes, hair eyelashes, vertically painted lower lashes. Mark: Ill. **1383.** H. 18 inches. *Courtesy of Hildred Brinkley.*

**1383 & 1384.** "Revalo" marks used on dolls of Gebrüder Ohlhaver.

Revalo
4
1383

Revalo
Germany
3
1384

**Revill, W. E.** 1917. Obtained British patent for mounting dolls' eyes.

**Rex Doll Company.** 1916–18. New York City. President, *Joseph L. Kallus.* Made composition dolls of a wood pulp, rosin, and starch mixture in a hot press. The dolls, distributed by *Borgfeldt,* included *Kewpies,* 1916–18; *Baby Bundie,* 1918.

**Rex Kid.** 1914. Character baby with composition head, excelsior-stuffed body; size 10½ inches, 29¢. Distributed by *T. Eaton Co.*

**Rezek, M.** 1921–25+. Prague, Czechoslovakia. Made dolls.

**Rheinische Gummi und Celluloid Fabrik Co.** 1873–1925+. Mannheim-Neckarau, Bavaria. Offices in London, Paris, Berlin, and Vienna. Made rubber and celluloid dolls.

1889: Began to use the turtle mark (*Schildkröte*), which represented the long life and durability of their products.

1897: Advertised rubber goods; *Bensinger & Co.* also used the turtle mark and were probably distributors.

1899: Registered turtle as a trademark in Germany, for dolls made of pyroxylin compounds. They obtained a German patent for dolls' heads with molded hairdos.

1902: Made celluloid dolls.

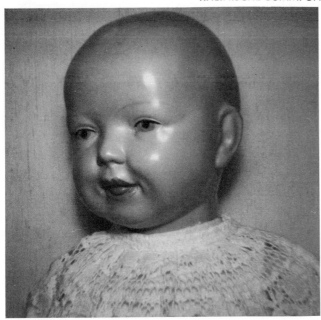

**1385.** Celluloid head with painted hair and features, marked with turtle and No. "30"; bent-limb composition body. H. 13 inches. *Courtesy of Theodora Gearhart.*

**1386.** Celluloid shoulder head marked with turtle mark and "Germany // 10 // 1928." Has sleeping eyes, open mouth with teeth; cloth body; original provincial costume. H. 13 inches. *Courtesy of The Smithsonian Institution.*

**1387A & B.** All-celluloid Negro doll with glass eyes, molded and painted hair under a kinky wig, Negroid features. Turtle marks of Rheinische Gummi und Celluloid Fabrik Co. on head and body. This doll was probably made after 1925. Head: "32/34." Body: "T 34." H. 13 inches. *Courtesy of Dorothy Annunziato.*

1386

**1388 & 1389.** Marks used by Rheinische Gummi und Celluloid Fabrik Co.

1388

SCHUTZ MARKE

1389

1905: Obtained German patent for inserting glass eyes in dolls' heads of celluloid.

1907: Manufactured celluloid dolls in Speyer, Bavaria.

1911: Raw celluloid for dolls, etc., was made in 150 colors.

1914: Registered their turtle as a trademark in France and Great Britain.

1915: Registered their turtle trademark in the U.S. for dolls made of pyroxylin compounds; mark was stamped on dolls and/or printed on labels of packages.

1922: Sole British agent was *Frederic William Punfield.*

They made celluloid dolls for *J. D. Kestner, Jr.* from Kestner molds having both the Kestner mark and the turtle on them. Celluloid dolls have been found with both the turtle and the mark of *Kämmer & Reinhardt.* Celluloid arms marked with a turtle are on a doll with a bisque head made by *Kling.* Some all-celluloid dolls are marked with the turtle. Some of the dolls in the *Madame Hendren* line of dolls have celluloid heads marked with the turtle.

Celluloid heads of various types have been found—painted eyes or glass eyes, sleeping eyes and flirting eyes, as well as stationary eyes; molded hair or wigs. Sizes from 3 to 25 inches.

**Rhodes, Dickson & Miller.** 1920–21. Seattle, Wash.

**Rice-Stix Dry Goods Co.** 1924–25+. St. Louis, Mo. Registered in U.S. *Polly Prim* as a trademark.

**Rich, William.** 1853–81. London. Made wax dolls. As an artist in wax, he was a member of the Berlin Repository.

1862: Displayed model wax and rag dolls at the London Exhibition.

**Richard.** 1853. Paris. Obtained a French patent for a type of composition made of a malleable paste of lime, plaster, stearic wax, tallow, and whiting. Doll heads made of this composition were known as *Buste Richard.* Richard claimed that his dolls' heads were superior to and more durable and cheaper than those formerly imported from Germany.

**Richardson, Charles E.** 1922–24. Syracuse, N.Y. Obtained U.S. patent for a talking or singing doll with a phonograph under the rear of a bustled skirt; handle and needle parts projected out in back.

**Richardson, Frank C. A.** 1910. Springfield, Mass. Obtained U.S. design patent for rag doll named *Teddy's Nig.*

**Richet.** 1881–90. Paris. Made dolls.

**Richter, C. G.** 1816–1914. Grünhainichen, Saxony. Made wooden dolls. Agents in Hamburg, Rotterdam, Barcelona, and Leipzig.

**Richter, Friedrich Adolph & Co. (Richter, F. Ad., & Cie.).** 1900–22. Rudolstadt, Thür. Manufactured dolls, especially mechanical ones.

1900: Was issued a British patent for mechanical dolls with music and motion.

1902: Used trade name *Aurora* for kid-bodied dolls.

1907: Registered in Germany a five-pointed star with a tail on it as a trademark for dolls.

**Richter, Robert.** 1921–23. Waltershausen, Thür. Obtained a German patent in 1921 with *Alfred Schroeder* for stringing dolls, and in 1923 another German patent for a drinking doll with a bottle and alimentary tract; body of the doll was bent-limb type.

**Ridgeway.** Ca. 1800–1925+. Cauldon, Staffordshire. This pottery made dolls at some time. Job Ridgeway founded the pottery at the end of the 18th century. His sons, John and William Ridgeway, carried it on. Their products were marked "J. Ridgeway" or "J. R."

1856: John Ridgeway of Cauldon was listed in the Birmingham Directory as a "Parian Manufacturer." After he retired in 1859, Messrs. Brown-Westhead and Moore took over the company and used the initials "B. W. M. & Co." for their mark as late as the first decade of the 20th century. For some years this firm was known as *Cauldon Potteries.* Fragments of dolls' heads have been discovered on the Cauldon premises, but the marks that were used on these dolls' heads have not been identified. Cauldon Potteries took over the pottery of *S. Hancock & Sons,* also known as Corona Potteries, some of whose wares from 1891 on were marked "S. H. & S." S. Hancock & Sons (Cauldon) are known to have made dolls and used the trademark "Corona" in the 1930's. According to a manager of Coalport China Ltd., "Corona" dolls were "made in several sizes and decorated in natural and black, and supplied either with fixed or movable eyes."

**Riding Hood Bud.** 1919. Novelty *Art Doll* made by *EFFanBEE;* dressed in cotton cloth costume.

**Ridley, R., & Sons.** 1886–88. U.S. Distributed dolls. (See Ill. 429.)

**Riedeler, A.** 1895–1925+. Königsee, Thür. Porcelain factory. Made dolls; 1925, also known as Riedeler & Bernhardt. Used "A R I" as a mark.

**Riehm, Robert.** 1897. Ilmenau, Thür. Made earthenware dolls.

**1390.** Ridley's mark found on dolls.

**1391.** Mark used by porcelain factory of A. Riedeler.

**Riemann, Seabrey Co.** 1912–24. New York City. Factory agent and distributor of dolls. George Riemann, Jr., president, started in 1880 with *Althof Bergmann & Co.* About 1886, he went with *Bawo & Dotter.*

1918: Distributed products of *Majestic Doll Co., Maiden America Dolls,* and *Baby Marion* of the *Emkay Manufacturing Co.*

1920: Sole agent for *Trion Toy Co.;* agent for *Non Pareil Toy & Novelty Co.*

1921: Agent for Trion, *Trego, Regal, Progressive Toy Co.,* and *Kampes.*

1923: Advertised *Mawaphil Dolls.*

**Rijard.** See **Rejard.**

**Rikkers Bros., Ltd.** 1920. New York City. Advertised *Made in Holland* dolls with bisque heads, moving eyes, jointed limbs and dressed in Dutch costumes.

**Riley, Ralph.** 1922–23. Akron, Ohio. Obtained a U.S. design patent for a rubber clown doll, which he assigned to the *Miller Rubber Co.*

**Ring, H., & Co.** 1886–1925+. Brieg, Silesia. Manufactured dolls.

1886: Obtained a German patent for an improved method of stuffing dolls' bodies.

1889: Was issued two German patents for an improved mechanism in the movement of dolls' heads.

1897: Secured a French patent for closing the eyes of bébés and dolls.

**Ring am Ohr (Ring on Ear).** 1908. Trademark registered in Germany by *Margarete Steiff.*

**Ring Master.** Ca. 1905. *Humpty Dumpty Circus* doll made by *Schoenhut.* It came with either wooden or bisque head, wooden body, in sizes 6 and 8 inches excluding the hat.

**Ringel, Charles.** 1918. New York City. Was issued a U.S. design patent for a cherub-type doll.

**Rip Van Winkle.** See **Old Rip.**

**Rischel, A., & Co.** 1893–1900. Berlin. Manufactured dressed dolls and dolls' outfits.

**Rite Specialty Co.** 1916–17. New York City. Registered in U.S. *Happy Rite Family* as a trademark.

**Ritter & Schmidt.** 1895. Ohrdruf, Thür. Porcelain factory that made dolls' heads, bathing dolls, and figurines. Factory was steam operated. They also exported their products.

**Rivaillon, F., Ch.** 1910. Paris. Factory at Montreuil-sous-Bois made jointed bébés, including Bébé *Le Vrai Modèle* and *Bébé Caro.*

**Rivet Hip Joints.** See **Ne Plus Ultra Joints.**

**Rizza, Giovanni.** 1920–21. Milan, Italy. Manufactured and exported dolls.

**Robbie Reefer.** 1912–13. Doll made by *Horsman* with a composition head and stuffed body. It was dressed in red reefer coat and white sailor hat and represented a boy of school age.

**Robert, André François Emile.** 1858. Paris. Obtained a French patent for a crying rubber doll and a British patent for molding vulcanized rubber dolls. Articulated wooden or metal limbs were inserted so the doll could bend. A belt covered the junction of torso and limbs.

**Robert, Samuel.** 1921–25. New York City. Did business as *Konroe Merchants.*

1923: Registered in U.S. *My Honey* as a trademark.

1925: Assignee of a U.S. design patent for a doll in pajamas, with a cigarette, by *Samuel Haskell.*

**Roberts Bros. (Harry Owen Roberts & John Owen Roberts).** 1903–25+. Gloucester and London, England. Made dolls, especially stockinet dolls.

1903: Procured a British patent for a doll on wheels.

**Robins.** 1843–1901. London. Until 1858, Joseph Robins made composition dolls; from 1859–84, William Robins made composition dolls at the same address; in 1887, Mrs. Harriet Robins made dolls at a different address; 1899–1901, Willie Robins made dolls at another address.

**Robinson, Sarah C.** 1883. Chicago, Ill. Obtained a U.S. patent for dolls' joints. These were to be used on bodies of cloth or leather stuffed with bran, sawdust, or hair. They consisted of a socket and lug joint, the connection being maintained by cords or threads drawn tightly and sewed through washers, buttons, or stiffened material on the outside of the lugs.

**Robinson Crusoe Doll.** 1897. Doll had bisque head with glass eyes, jointed body covered with colored fur; represented Robinson Crusoe. Came in sizes 11 and 14 inches; price $12.00 and $17.00 doz. wholesale. Similar dolls with white fur called *Eskimo Dolls.*

**Roch, J.** 1860–64. Paris. Made dressed dolls and fashion dolls (poupées de modes) for export.

**Rocharde, Ed.** Mid-19th century. Two dolls' heads signed "Ed. Rocharde" are pictured in Fawcett's DOLLS, A NEW GUIDE FOR COLLECTORS. One of these is an early china head with long curls; the other is a bisque head with glass eyes. E. Rocharde has not been found in Paris directories, but the "Breveté" and "S. G. D. G." found on the dolls' heads suggest that he was French.

**Rocher, Marius.** 1914. Paris. Registered *Le Bébé* as a trademark in France for bébés, dolls, and their clothes.

**Rocholl, A.** 1903–8. Manufactured rag dolls that were distributed by *A. S. Ferguson & Co.*

**Rochut, L.** 1885. Paris. Imported wax dolls.

**Rock, Berthold.** 1895–1918. Eisfeld, Thür. Manufactured jointed dolls.

**Rock & Graner.** 1851–79. Biberach, Württemberg. Won

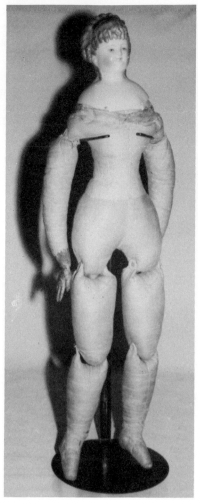

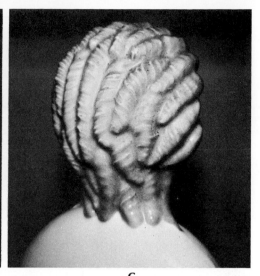

B

C

A

**1392A, B, & C.** Cloth body has joints patented by Sarah Robinson in 1883. The lugs of the joints at the shoulders, hips, and knees pivot on buttons. Leather hands with separated fingers. China head has café-au-lait colored spill-curl hairdo of the same period as the body. H. 22 inches. H. of shoulder head, 4³/₄ inches. *Coleman Collection.*

**1393.** Ed. Rocharde mark found on dolls' heads.

the following awards at expositions for their mechanical and papier-mâché dolls: 1851, London, prize medal; 1853, New York, Honorable Mention; 1854, Munich, Honorable Mention; 1855, Paris, silver medal; 1862, London, prize medal; 1873, Vienna, award unknown; 1879, Sidney, commendation. Charles Mittler & Echardt were their London agents in 1862.

**Rock-a-By Baby.** 1925. Copyrighted by *Novelty Doll Co.;* designed by *Ernesto Peruggi.* Copyright model had movable arms and was a full-figure baby doll.

**Rock-a-Bye Baby.** 1920–23. One of the *Madame Hendren* line of dolls made by *Averill Manufacturing Co.,* distributed by *Sears, Roebuck & Co.* Came with composition head, sleeping eyes, mohair wig, stuffed cotton body. Advertisement claimed that it could walk and talk, had three separate voices, and it cried until rocked to sleep. When it opened its eyes, it cried "Mama."

1921: Size 18 inches cost $11.50, including a cardboard cradle.

1922: Sizes 16, 18, and 20 inches; price $6.45, $7.65, and $9.89.

**Rock-a-Bye-Dolly.** 1920–22. Trademark registered in U.S. by *McCrosky Bros.*

**Rockwell, Grace Corry.** See **Corry, Grace.**

**Rodaer Puppen und Spielwarenfabrik.** See **Bauer & Richter.**

**Roeder, Anton.** 1924. Germany. Exported dolls.

**Roemer & Rodnick.** 1920. New York City. Manufactured dolls.

**Rogers, Henry S.** 1853. New York City. Displayed a variety of dressed wax and rag dolls at the New York Exhibition and was cited with an Honorable Mention.

**Rogers, Marguerite.** 1915–18. Lexington, Mass. Copyrighted *Schnitzel* and *Buddy.*

**Roggatz, L.** 1870–74. Paris. Made dolls.

**Rogner, Hermann.** 1924. Nürnberg, Bavaria. Branch factory in Sonneberg, Thür. Made and exported dolls.

**Roguish Eyes.** Eyes that glance to the side; also called *Goo Goo* Eyes, *Goggle* Eyes, and Eccentric Eyes. Occasionally found throughout the centuries—for example, the cloth-headed *Autoperipatetikos* dolls often had eyes painted so that they glanced to the side. This type of eyes was especially popular in the *Grace G. Drayton* and *Rose O'Neill* eras, as evidenced by *Dolly Dollykins, Campbell Kids, Kewpies, Hug-Me-Kiddies, Scootles,* et al.

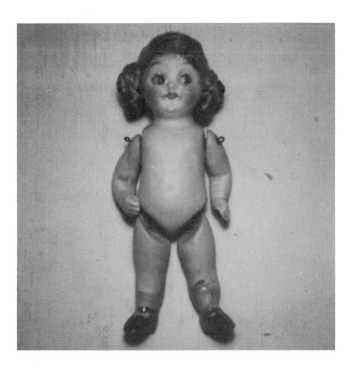

ROHMER DOLLS

**1394.** All-bisque doll with roguish glass eyes has her original wig with braids over the ears. Jointed at hips and shoulders; molded shoes and socks. Mark: "333.8 // Made in Germany." H. 3½ inches. *Courtesy of May Maurer.*

**Rohmer.** 1857–80. Paris. Mlle. Marie Antoinette Léontine Rohmer obtained two French patents in 1857. One was for articulated joints for kid bodies, and the other was for arms of gutta-percha or rubber for stuffed dolls, either jointed or not jointed.

1858: Mlle. Rohmer obtained another French patent, this one for a new kind of doll's head with a cord running through the head and down into the body to facilitate the turning of the head in any direction, and to hold the head to the body. This invention was to be used on dolls with bodies of kid, cloth, and gutta-percha.

1859–63: Mlle. Rohmer advertised patented jointed dolls.

1866–80: Maison Rohmer sold jointed kid-body dolls and bébés and dressed dolls. In 1867 they displayed dolls and jointed bébés at the Paris Exposition. Knee joints found on some Rohmer dolls are very similar to the *Universal Joints* patented by *Charles Fausel* in 1896 in the U.S.

> The prices given for dolls are those for which the dolls were originally offered for sale. They are *not* today's prices.

**1395A, B, & C.** Rohmer doll with china head and arms on a kid body. The limb portions have wood under the kid. On the stomach is the oval Rohmer stamp and two typical eyelet holes beneath the mark. Doll has swivel neck, glass eyes, and knee joint of a type often found on Rohmer dolls. Contemporary dress. Mark: Ill. **1399.** H. 17 inches. H. of shoulder head, 4 inches. *Courtesy of Sylvia Brockmon.*

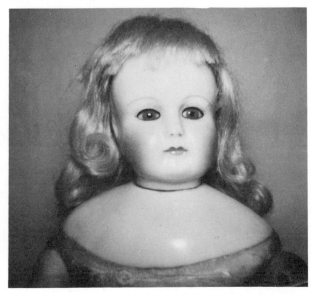

**1396.** Three dolls with china heads and arms; two of them also have china legs. All three have swivel necks and glass eyes, and the Rohmer mark on the front of the kid body. *Courtesy of Marion Holt; photograph by Winnie Langley.*

ROHMER DOLLS

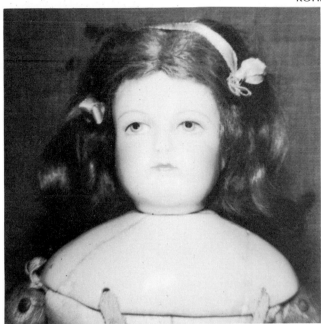

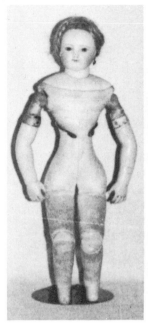

**1397A & B.** Rohmer marked body with china head, swivel neck, and painted features, including the eyes. Kid and wooden body has the typical Rohmer knee joint. Mark: Ill. **1399.** H. 15½ inches. H. of shoulder head, 4 inches. *Courtesy of Hildred Brinkley.*

**1398A & B.** Rohmer marked kid body with arms made partly of gutta-percha. This body has gusseted kid joints; there are no eyelet holes, but the mark is the same as found on the other bodies. Doll has a bisque socket-type head that also differs from the others pictured. The eyes are painted. Mark: Ill. **1399.** H. 15½ inches. H. of shoulder head, 4½ inches. *Courtesy of Mary Roberson.*

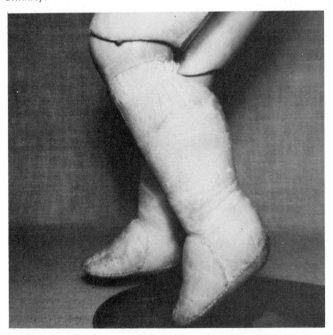

**1399.** Rohmer mark found on kid bodies.

**Roig, Mme.** 1916. Paris. Made "Bébé Gallia."

**Roithner, Hugo, & Co.** 1871–1925+. Schweidnitz, Silesia. Made wooden dolls.

**Rolf Berlich Puppe.** See **Säuberlich, Rudolf.**

**Rollinson Dolls.** 1916–17. These dolls were originated and designed by Gertrude F. Rollinson, and manufactured by *Utley Co.* Mrs. Rollinson conceived the idea of making rag dolls for crippled children in hospitals. The regular flat-face, painted features distressed her, and so she ex-

perimented until she had made three-dimensional noses, cheeks, eyes, and other features on stockinet dolls. The various dolls were modeled from life. Some had real hair and some had painted hair. The wigs came in long curls, short curls, and Buster Brown style. Girls were dressed in white dresses trimmed with colors and white bloomers; boys were dressed in suits; babies wore white dresses with lace trim, baby shirts, and flannel Gertrudes. Dolls came in sizes 14 to 28 inches.

**Romanelli, Carlo.** 1920. Los Angeles, Calif. Designed *Mimi,* a doll copyrighted by *Venetian Art & Novelty Co.*

**Römhild, Edward.** 1921–22. Sonneberg, Thür. Registered in Germany *My Honey* as a trademark for dolls and dolls' clothing.

**Rommer, Isaac A.** See **Ideal Novelty & Toy Co.**

**Romper Boy.** 1920. Made by *American Bisque Doll Co.*

**Romper Boy.** 1921. Rag doll with bobbing head, designed by *Grace Corry* and made by *Century Doll Co.*

**Rompy Ann.** 1921. Doll with composition limbs and soft body made by *DeLuxe Doll & Toy Co.*

**Roof, W.** 1918. Berlin. Made dolls.

**Rookie.** 1917. Doll made by *Horsman* and dressed as a soldier.

**Rookwood Pottery.** 1880–25+. Cincinnati, Ohio. Made a few dolls' heads, probably during the World War I period.

**Rörstrand Porcelain Factory.** 1726–1925+. Sweden. Made dolls' heads, arms, and legs. Mark generally is a red "R" under the glaze, inside the head. Other initials probably refer to the model and/or the initials of the decorator.

1868: Their catalog advertised dolls' heads, arms, and legs.

Ca. 1900: Dolls' heads were poured; earlier ones were pressed.

**Rosalind.** 1914. Cloth doll printed in colors, made by *Independent Toy Works;* 14-inch size cost 10¢.

**Roscamp-Puppen-Fantasien.** 1925. Trademark registered in Germany by Katarina Roscamp.

**Rosch.** See **Schneider, Robert.**

**Rose.** 1919. Trade name for doll made by *Federal Doll Manufacturing Co.* Rose came with composition head, breastplate, and arms; cork-stuffed body with legs jointed inside the body.

**Rose, Elizabeth.** 1922–24. Des Moines, Iowa. Obtained a U.S. design patent for a rag doll.

**Rose, William W.** 1866–74. New York City. Secured a British patent in 1866 for metal and wooden dolls, which could assume different poses if the pieces were re-arranged. In 1874, he took out another British patent for improvements over his first one.

**Rose Marie.** 1925+. Made by *EFFanBEE.* Had hair eyelashes; teeth, tongue; stuffed torso had long slim legs. Doll was advertised as a new slender line because children were tiring of clumsy stuffed bodies.

**Rose Percy.** Poured wax doll, made ca. 1862. Straw-colored hair was inserted in groups. Doll had blue glass eyes, no grommets on arms, which were wax to above the elbow; wax feet, cloth body, trousseau of clothes (including items from Tiffany), and ermine furs. Her clothes were made by hand at Mrs. Ogden Hoffman's "fashionable school." In 1864, Rose was raffled at the Sanitary Commission Bazaar in New York City for $1,200 to raise money for Union soldiers. She was knocked down to Dr. Peters, and remained in his family until she came to the American Red Cross and helped to raise money during World War I.

| 1400 | 1401 |

**1400 & 1401.** Marks used by Rookwood Pottery.

**Rosebud.** 1902–15. Registered in Germany as a trademark by Max Illfelder for a line of jointed dolls. These dolls were later distributed by *B. Illfelder & Co.* Some of the bisque heads were made by *Armand Marseille.*

**ROSEBUD**
**A 3/0 M**

**1402.** "Rosebud" mark used by Illfelder for dolls.

**Rosebud.** Ca. 1910–12. Velvet-body doll made by *Louis Amberg & Son.*

**Rosebud Babies.** 1920. Dolls made by *Horsman.*

**Rosel, Hermann.** 1921. Nürnberg, Bavaria. Obtained a German patent for a doll with a rubber body.

**Rosemarie.** 1923–25+. Trademark registered in U.S. by *Borgfeldt;* name was shown with a face on a rose.

**Rosemary.** 1918–19. Trade name of a doll made by *Jessie McCutcheon Raleigh,* distributed by *Butler Bros.* Sizes 11½ and 13½ inches; prices $2.40 and $3.10.

**Rosemary.** 1925. *Mama Doll* with composition head, shoulder plate, arms and legs, cloth torso, made by *EFFanBEE.* Wore gold heart necklace and button with the words "EFFanBEE Durable Doll" on it; marked on shoulder plate: "Walk, Talk, Sleep." Size 18 inches, price $5.00.

**1403.** "Rosemary," composition shoulder head on cloth and composition body like that of "Baby Dainty." Original dress and pin. Mark: Ill. **1404.** H. 18 inches. *Courtesy of May Wenzel.*

**1404.** Mark used on "Rosemary" dolls made by EFFanBEE.

**Rosenberg, Ignac.** Ca. 1925. Budapest. Made dolls' heads including wax heads.

**Rosenstein, Henry Co.** 1907–21. New York City. Doll jobbers; distributed *Zaiden* dolls.

**Rosenstein, M. R., Jr.** 1901. Stadt Kassel, Hesse. *Casseler Puppenfabrik;* specialized in jointed dolls and dressed dolls.

**Rosenthal, Adolph.** 1909. Berlin. Made dolls.

**Rosenthal, David.** 1911. New York City. Obtained two U.S. patents for a boy dressed in plaid rompers and a girl in pajamas.

**Rosette.** 1919. Trademark registered in France by Messrs. *Laquionie & Cie.,* Société des Grands Magasins du *Printemps.*

**Ross, Penny.** 1925. Designed *Poppy,* one of a flower doll series for *Live Long Toys.*

**Rossignol, Charles.** 1878–1900. Paris. Made walking dolls and other mechanical dolls.

1888: Obtained a French patent for a walking doll.

**1405.** Mark of Charles Rossignol. **C R**

**Rostaing, Charles Silvester.** 1859. Citizen of U.S. residing in Dresden, Saxony; secured a British patent for a compound of gutta-percha with mineral coloring and vegetable substances such as gums, tannin, and essential oils, to make dolls' heads.

**Rostal, Henri.** 1914. Paris. Used initials "H. R." and registered in France *Mon Trésor* and *Bébé Mon Trésor* as trademarks for dolls, bébés, and their trousseaux.

**Rosy (Miss Rosy Cheeks).** 1925. Made by *Ideal Novelty & Toy Co.* Had sleeping eyes, could walk and say "Mama," wore organdy dress and bonnet; size 13 inches.

**Rosy-Posy.** 1917–18. Trademark registered in U.S. by *Elektra Toy & Novelty Co.;* used generally as a printed label on the doll.

**Roth, Baitz & Lipsitz, Inc. (R. B. & L. Manufacturing Co.).** 1922–25+. New York City. Manufactured, imported, and distributed dolls. European office: *Adolf Reisenweber,* Sonneberg, Thür. Factory representative of the *Doll & Toy Manufacturers' Association* (Der Verband) of Sonneberg; sole American agent for Adolf Reisenweber, *Hermann Steiner, August Herpich, Albert Steiner, Carl Hartmann, Hermann Brandner, Carl Arm,* and *Louis Hess.*

1923: Their own *Mama Dolls* came with painted eyes and molded hair or wigs; sizes 12, 16, 19, 22, and 27 inches.

1925: Advertised bisque-headed infants that looked like *My Dream Baby;* doll was named *Baby Sister* and had Ronson criers. Price $1.50, $2.50, and $3.50.

**Roth, John H., & Co.** 1921. Peoria, Ill. Importers and jobbers. Handled dolls made by *Ideal Novelty & Toy Co.*

**Roth, Joseph, Manufacturing Co.** 1915–22. New York City. Made dolls' heads by a patented pressed process by *Lewis Levine.*

1915: Advertised "Exclusive dolls to all buyers who pay the cost price of making the steel dies used for the dolls which are desired. Thus a buyer can by having a die (or dies) made to order, control the sale of any doll and have the name of his house printed on the doll head. Dolls will remain at factory and be delivered as ordered." Made *Beauty Doll* and all-composition baby dolls.

**Roth, Louis.** 1895–1909. Sonneberg, Thür. Specialized in making wooden dolls, dressed dolls, and jointed dolls.

**Roth Novelty Co.** 1912. U.S. Manufactured dolls.

**Rothenberger & Froeber (Froeger).** 1896. Sonneberg, Thür. Manufactured dolls.

**Rothschild, Sigmund I.** 1917–20. New York City. Registered in U.S. *S I R* as a trademark for dolls, to which it was applied by a printed label.

**Rouaud, Charles.** 1913–21. Paris. Made dressed dolls and trousseaux for dolls.

1913: Registered in France *Mal'Oto de ma Poupée* and *Mal'Auto de ma Poupée* as trademarks.

**Rouech, Bowden Co.** 1906–08. Detroit, Mich. Made *Playtime* dolls with photographic faces, distributed by *Louis Wolf & Co.* Edward E. Rouech secured a U.S. patent for a rag doll, which he assigned to *Charles J. Horton.* Face portion of doll was to be made of fine soft cloth, such as mercerized cotton or silk, so that features could be printed thereon by a photographic process. The body and back of the head were to be made of coarser material and stuffed with sawdust, bran, excelsior, or cotton batting. Junius P. Bowden registered in U.S. "Playtime" as a trademark.

**Rough Rider.** 1901. Dolls dressed in cowboy hat, leggings, linen khaki uniform with pockets, buttons, and belt; also had blanket roll and canteen. Price 25¢.

**Rough Rider.** 1909. All-bisque dolls, 8 inches high, price 50¢.

**Rouillard.** 1920–21. Paris. Manufactured dolls of various types, including dolls with bisque heads, jointed dolls, dressed dolls, *mignonettes,* and others.

**Roulez & Simon, P.** Before 1847, Paris; 1847–55, successor was P. Simon. Handled German and French dolls and porcelain dolls heads.

**Roullet & Decamps.** 1865–1910, Paris; 1910–21, successor was Decamps Vve. (Widow) & Fils (Sons). Made walking dolls and other types of mechanical dolls. Jean Roullet founded the firm, and his daughter married Mons. Decamps.

1867: Roullet was awarded a bronze medal for his display at the Paris Exposition.

1878: J. Roullet won a silver medal for his mechanical dolls at the Paris Exposition.

1890: Advertised walking dolls that imitated natural movements.

1892: Roullet & Decamps were issued a French patent for a clockwork walking doll with jointed wrists.

1893: Société Roullet & E. Decamps obtained a French patent for a nonmechanical walking doll. They registered in France *L'Intrépide Bébé* as a trademark. Displayed dolls at the Chicago Exhibition.

1895–98: Advertised walking doll with patented mechanism named *L'Intrépide Bébé*.

1900: Won a silver medal for their exhibit at the Paris Exposition.

1906: Won a Grand Prize for their display at the Milan and Paris exhibitions.

1907: Won a Grand Prize at the Paris Exposition.

1908: Won Grand Prizes at the Paris Exposition and at the London Exhibition. E. Decamps' son-in-law became head of the firm.

1909: Won a Grand Prize at the Paris Exhibition.

1910: Won a Grand Prize at the Brussels Exhibition.

1914: Advertised mechanical toys with music.

1921: Advertised L'Intrépide Bébé.

*Jumeau* and *Simon & Halbig* marked heads have been found on walking and mechanical dolls with an "R. D." mark. Dolls marked "E. D." are often identified as made by Ernst Decamps. This may be correct, but the fact should not be overlooked that in Paris *E. Denamur, E. Daspres* (*Jules Steiner*); *E. Douillet* (*Jumeau*), and *E. Dumont* were also making dolls and bébés in the second half of the 19th century. Moreover, Ernst Decamps was the junior member of the firm Roullet & Decamps that used the mark "R. D." (See also **Rabery & Delphieu**.)

**R. D.**
1406

1407

**1406 & 1407.** Marks found on dolls made by Roullet & Decamps. These are usually mechanical dolls.

**Rousselot, Jean Baptiste Alexis.** 1845–52. Paris. Made dolls.

1845: Obtained a French patent for a mechanical doll that raised and lowered its arms. It had a hollow cardboard body, a German head with enamel eyes and teeth, and the arms were of kid with wire supports in them. There were no legs—the torso was set on wheels. A copper key wound the spring that activated the mechanism.

**Rowland, Janet Burd.** 1916. Yonkers, N.Y. Obtained U.S. patent for a rag doll with molded face and jointed arms and legs.

**Roy.** 1839–47. Paris. Made dressed dolls. In 1857, at another Paris address, a Roy obtained a French patent for a doll.

**Royal.** 1898. Trade name used by *W. A. Cissna* for a doll with "French bisque" head, blue eyes, teeth, curly woven wig, double-sewed kid body with bust trimmed at the edge. Size 24½ inches, price $1.20.

**Royal.** 1902–11, and perhaps later. Trademark registered in U.S. in 1903 by *Strobel & Wilken* for a line of dolls made by *Kämmer & Reinhardt*.

1903: *Samstag & Hilder Bros.* also used the trade name "Royal" for dressed and undressed walking dolls.

1908: Strobel & Wilken, distributors, advertised *Flirt*, a doll made by Kämmer & Reinhardt in their Royal line. It had eyes that would move sideways as well as sleeping.

1911: Line of character dolls that included *Hans, Peter, Marie, Gretchen*, and *Annie*. These dolls were named for the children who posed for them, and were distributed by Stobel & Wilken and *Borgfeldt*. (See Ill. 955.)

**Royal Baby Bunting.** See **Royal Toy Manufacturing Co.**

**Royal Copenhagen Manufactory.** 1772–1925+. Denmark. According to Estrid Faurholt, in A BOOK OF DOLLS AND DOLL HOUSES, dolls' heads were made by this factory from 1844 to 1884 in twelve models and various sizes. Most of these heads had molded hair with a center part and a bun in the back, the hair generally being brown in color. A 4-inch head came with six sewholes.

**Royal Toy Manufacturing Co.** 1914–25+. New York City. Made and imported Royal Doll line.

1914: Royal line included wigged character heads on kid bodies with pyroxylin arms and legs.

1921: Advertised walking, talking, and sleeping dolls.

1924: Used the slogan "A Doll of the Better Kind"; advertised *Prize Winner Baby* and fifty numbers of walking dolls.

1925: Advertised Royal Baby Bunting, an infant doll of the *Bye-Lo* type.

**Roze Doll.** 1919–20. Trademark registered in U.S. by *Federal Doll Manufacturing Co.* Came with composition head, shoulder plate and arms. The composition arms were attached with rubber elastic to the composition shoulder plate.

**1408A & B.** China head made by Royal Copenhagen and marked as in Ill. **1409.** *Courtesy of Frances Walker; photographs by Winnie Langley.*

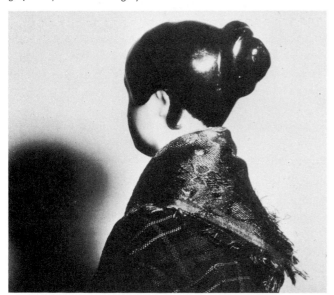

**1409–1411.** Marks of Royal Copenhagen Manufactory. No. **1409** is found on dolls' heads.

1409  1410  1411

**1412.** Mark used by Royal Toy Manufacturing Co.

**Rozier, Edmee.** 1921. Paris. Business name of *Mlle. Cecile Lambert,* who registered in France *Babet* as a trademark for dolls.

**Rozmann, Mlle.** 1916. Paris. Made rag dolls.

**Rubbadubdub.** 1921. Trademark used by *J. G. Franklin & Sons* for rubber dolls.

**Rubber Doll Factory.** 1881. Asnières-sur-Oise, France. Made rubber dolls.

**Rubber Dolls.** Rubber was used for dolls for centuries, but it was not until the *Goodyear* discovery of vulcanizing rubber, so that it would hold its shape, that it became an important material for producing commercial dolls. India rubber or *caoutchouc* was mixed with various other materials, even including gutta-percha. Coloring matter was added, and then the dolls were vulcanized (heated). Some of the early manufacturers of rubber dolls, beside Goodyear, were *Benjamin F. Lee, New York Rubber Co., India Rubber Comb Co., Newark India Rubber Co.,* and *Metropolitan India Rubber & Vulcanite Co. John Edward Payne* was making rubber and gutta-percha dolls in 1849, and by 1865 *Lang & Co.* were doing the same. From 1852 to 1864, *Jean L. H. Arnaud* obtained several patents for covering wooden bodies with vulcanized rubber. In 1875, both *Ansil W. Monroe* and *Wesley Miller* obtained patents for making rubber dolls. In the late 1870's, *Bru, Jules Steiner,* and *Derolland* were all making rubber dolls or bébés in France. Bru advertised rubber bébés as late as 1898. Firms in Germany, Austria, Hungary, and other European countries also made rubber dolls, as did U.S. firms. Sometimes the entire doll was of rubber; sometimes it was only the head, and in a few cases it was only the hands. This was especially true in 1925.

1897: New York Rubber Co. made boy and girl rubber dolls, which were distributed by *John D. Zernitz.* These all-rubber dolls were dressed in knitted worsted clothes.

1901: All-rubber dolls were distributed by *Montgomery Ward & Co.* They wore worsted hat and dress, came in sizes 7, 8½, 9, and 12 inches; price 20¢ to 70¢.

1910: All-rubber dolls were distributed by *Butler Bros.* They came with painted features, embossed shoes and stockings, knitted worsted dress and hat; sizes 4½, 7½, 8, 9½, and 10 inches; price 78¢ to $4.25 doz. wholesale.

*Mechanical Rubber Co.* and *Faultless Rubber Co.* both made rubber dolls in America during World War I.

**Rubberoid.** 1914. Material used to cover a new line of dolls' bodies, with pyroxylin heads.

**Rubin, Wilhelm.** 1897–1907. Prague, Bohemia. Manufactured dolls.

**Rudolph, J.** 1924. Brooklyn, N.Y. Handled dolls.

**Rudolph, Max.** 1908–25+. Waltershausen, Thür. Specialized in the manufacture of mohair and real hair wigs; also made dolls and babies.

1921: Obtained a German patent for the production of hair tresses.

RUBBER DOLLS

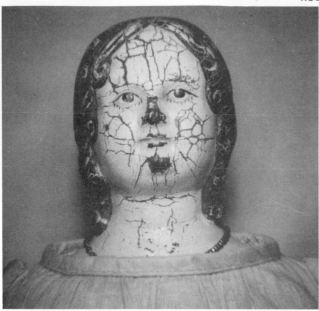

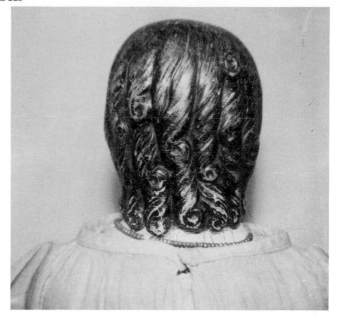

**1413A & B.** Rubber head—black rubber shows under the glossy paint. Note that there are only lower lashes. Painted features;

cloth body. H. 16½ inches. *Courtesy of the International Doll Library Foundation.*

**1414.** Rubber head with molded black hair and eyes; only lower lashes are painted. Doll wears pink dress and gray cloak. *Courtesy of Fidelia Lence; photograph by Winnie Langley.*

**Rudolph, Otto.** 1895. Sonneberg, Thür. Manufactured dolls.

**Rueckert & Co.** 1893. Germany. Displayed dolls at the Chicago World's Fair.

**Rufaut, Mme.** 1852–90. Paris. Made dressed dolls. In the decade between 1880 and 1890, she made bébés and dressed dolls.

**Rügemer, Hans.** 1905–6. Wurzburg, Germany. Obtained two patents in Germany for jointed dolls.

**Rüger, A.** 1909–18. Sonneberg, Thür. Made dolls.

**Rüger, Max.** 1925. Sonneberg, Thür. Manufactured dolls.

**Rungaldier, J. Antoine.** 1843–90. Paris. Made and distributed dolls. He appears to have been joined by Foucault from 1885–90.

1843: Advertised French and German toys, dolls with springs, kid-body dolls, and dressed dolls.

1873: Made dressed dolls of various types.

1879: Advertised dolls and bébés, both dressed and undressed.

1885: Rungaldier & Foucault advertised dolls and bébés.

1889: Displayed dolls at the Paris Exposition.

1890: Advertised wholesale French and foreign toys.

**Runnells, E. A., & Co.** 1903–21. Boston, Mass., and New York City. *Gust. Ehrlicher* was their European partner. Imported, manufactured, and distributed dolls.

A

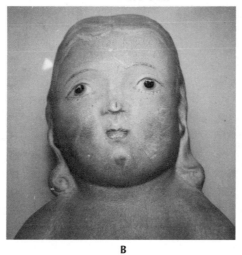

B

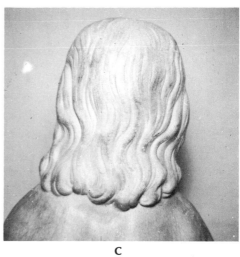

C

**1415A, B, & C.** Sand-colored rubber shoulder head has painted and molded features; turquoise-blue eyes with lower lashes only. Cloth body; leather arms to the shoulders. Original clothes include the blue wool challis dress with black velvet trim. H. 17½ inches. *Coleman Collection.*

**1416A & B.** All-rubber doll made of blonde molded rubber; molded black slippers with red rosettes and white socks. The original crocheted cap (not shown) was sewed through the head. Note the whistle airhole in the back of the head. H. 10¾ inches. *Courtesy of Mary Seward; photographs by Winnie Langley.*

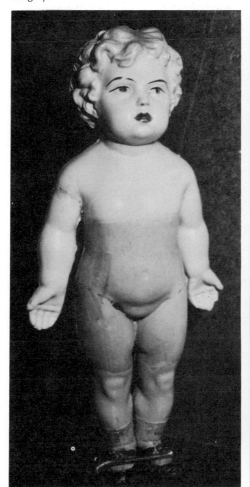

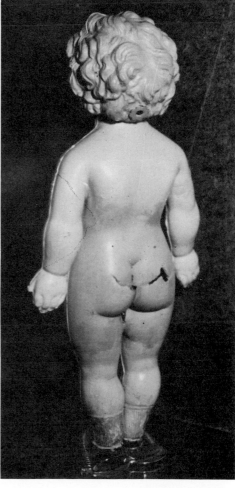

1903: Advertised *Globe Babies* (jointed dolls), *Queen Quality* (kid-bodied dolls), and patented self-feeding dolls.

1904: *Hahnesand & Heiman* were their New York agents; advertised *Princess* line of jointed and dressed dolls.

1918: Handled the *Dandyline Dolls,* produced by a Belgian doll factory.

**Rüping, Paul.** 1892–97. Coburg, Thür. Manufactured and exported various types of dolls, including dressed dolls, ball-jointed dolls, and *Täuflinge.*

**Ruprecht (Knecht Ruprecht).** Name of dolls representing St. Nicholas or his helpers.

**Rushton Co.** 1924. New York City. Made dolls.

**Russian Boy.** 1912. Made by *Ideal Novelty & Toy Co.*

**Russian Dolls.** In Russia, dolls have been made in rag and wood for at least several centuries. Fine cloth dolls were made in Southern Russia as a cottage craft. They had embroidered features and were entirely handmade. They usually came as a pair, man and woman, rather small in size; the man wore white leather boots.

Russian dolls in national costume were exhibited in London in 1862 by *C. Dorpat Han.* By 1865, according to tradition, *Armand Marseille* had come from Riga to Germany. In 1898 a wax Russian doll, obtained some time previously in Moscow, was described as having a quantity of real hair and wearing pointed red shoes and an embroidered dress.

Prior to World War I, wooden dolls were made in Sergiyevo; dolls with heads of unglazed pottery were allegedly made by Russian orphans. Russian dolls were fashionable in Europe in 1912, but the last Russian dolls for some time came to America in 1916. After the Russian Revolution, some of the refugees in Austria made dolls with painted muslin heads, some of which were dressed as cossacks. (See color photograph C5.)

**Russian Princess.** 1893. Distributed by *Butler Bros.* The doll had bisque head and hands, jointed body, stationary blue glass eyes, open mouth with teeth; was dressed in red plush coat and bonnet, black stockings, and bronze shoes. Height 29 inches, price $7.20.

**Russian-French India Rubber, Gutta-Percha Telegraph Works.** See **Prowodnik Co.**

**Ruth.** Ca. 1900. Name incised on the back of a bisque shoulder head with sleeping glass eyes, single-line eyebrows over slightly molded area, open mouth and teeth, and wig. The gusseted kid body had bisque forearms and cotton lower legs with drop-stitch knit stockings; size 12½ inches.

**1417.** "Ruth" mark found on bisque heads.

This is probably similar to the "Ruth" doll advertised by *W. A. Cissna* in 1898, which had a bisque head, teeth, woven wig, kid body, drop-stitch knit stockings. Size was 18½ inches; price $6.25 doz. wholesale.

**Ruth, Baby.** See **Baby Ruth.**

**Ruth Reeves.** See **Reeves, Ruth.**

# S

**S. & Co.** Early 20th century. Germany. Initials found stamped in green on bisque-head character babies. (See Ill. 452.)

**S. K. Novelty Co.** See **Kirsch, S., & Co.**

**Saalfield Publishing Co.** 1907–25+. Akron, Ohio. Made lithographed muslin cutout rag dolls.

1907: Made muslin dolls inspired by the drawings of Kate Greenaway; printed in four colors; size 17 inches, price 25¢.

1908: Muslin dolls printed in five colors included Aunt Dinah, Santa Claus, Delft Girl, and Papoose—all 5 inches tall for 5¢; Baby Boy and Baby Girl in outdoor costumes with *Drayton*-type faces, size 12 by 15 inches, price 10¢; Japanese Kimono Doll and *Little Red Riding Hood,* size 17½ by 18 inches, price 20¢.

1909: Continued to make the muslin cutout rag dolls named above, and added as new ones *Goldenlocks, Baby Blue Eyes, Dottie Dimple,* and *Topsy Turvy.*

1914: Goldenlocks was their featured rag doll.

1918: Made *Dolly Dear.*

**Sabo.** 1924. Trademark registered in Britain by *Sidney Ransom* for dolls made wholly or partly of celluloid.

**Sac de Terre.** 1918. Trademark registered in France by *Mme. Poulbot.*

**Sacajawea.** 1915. Portrait doll copyrighted by *Mary Frances Woods;* came with composition head, handkerchief on head, bright skirt, and blanket. The copyright model was 14 inches tall.

**Sachs, Filip.** 1902. Kalisz, Poland. Manufactured dolls.

**Sachs, Hermann.** 1922. Munich, Bavaria. Dolls made by Herr Sachs and his pupils in the Munich Expressionist School were displayed at the Rochester Exhibition.

**Sachs, Max.** 1923. Charlottenburg, Prussia. Doll manufacturer. Registered in Germany *Graziella Puppen* as a trademark for wax dolls and stuffed dolls.

**Sachsenwaeger, H. M.** 1908. Sonneberg, Thür. Made various kinds of dressed dolls.

**Sackman, Lillian.** 1907–8. New York City. Obtained U.S. patent for a rag doll with limbs and head made separately from the body and jointed to it by a coupling consisting of two disks and a pin, which enabled the head and limbs to move. A face was painted on both sides of the head, with a third face under the molded form face, which could be shown by unstitching the molded face.

1908: These dolls were manufactured by *Bruin Manufacturing Co.* under the trade name of *Wide Awake Rag Dolls.*

**Sackman Bros. Co.** 1909–11. Brooklyn, N.Y. Made stuffed velvet dolls, one of which was *Daisy Dolly,* 12 inches tall, price 25¢.

1911: Charles Sackman obtained a U.S. patent for a rag doll made with seams on the outside, and outlined in colors into which the pattern of the doll would merge.

**Sadin, Arthur.** 1916. Paris. Registered in France *Favori-Bébé* as a trademark.

**Sailor.** 1892+. One of the *Palmer Cox* cloth *Brownies.* The word "Valiant" appeared on his cap.

**Sailor Boy.** 1915. One of the *Jam Kiddos* made by the *Non-Breakable Doll Co.;* had molded hair; cost $1.00.

**Sailor Boy.** 1918. All-rubber doll with molded clothes, made by *Faultless Rubber Co.* Came in red or tan.

**Sailor Dolls.** See **Military Costume Dolls.**

**Sailor Dolls.** 1909. Shown at a toy show. There were five styles; each style came as a boy or as a girl. Dolls had various colored hair; wore sailor costumes in shades of blue and white; boys wore duck trousers.

**Sailor Lass and Sailor Boy and Sailor Girl.** 1918. Distributed by *Gray & Dudley Co.* Came with composition heads and hands, stuffed bodies and legs; dressed in sailor costumes. Lass was 13½ inches for 44¢; boy was 13 inches for 44¢; girl was 14 inches for 75¢.

**St. Patrick.** 1922. Doll dressed in green, made by *Averill Manufacturing Co.*

**Sakuda, Magobei.** 1900. Japan. Won a bronze medal at the Paris Exposition for his dolls.

**Sala, Louis.** Ca. 1870–1907. Chicago, Ill. Handled dolls; probably one of the oldest toymen in Chicago.

**Sales, N. V., Co.** 1924. New York City. Advertised a French flapper doll made of Creole composition. Came with bobbed hair wig, a cigarette in its mouth; wore a mannish suit with trousers, high-heeled shoes, and bead necklace. Dressed in felt; came in six colors. Also handled Negro *Mama Dolls* with unbreakable heads, hands, and legs.

**Salisbury, Thomas Charles.** 1917. Cardiff, Wales. Registered in Britain *Leda* as a trademark for dolls.

**Sallee, Lucretia F.** 1865. Decatur, Ill. Secured a U.S.

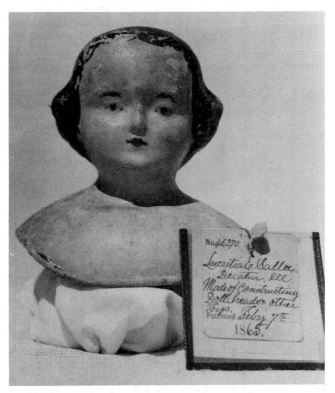

**1418.** Original patent application model submitted by Lucretia E. Sallee in 1865. H. of shoulder head, 7 inches. *Courtesy of Ruth & R. C. Mathes.*

patent for constructing dolls' heads with leather as an outer covering and a compound of glue, vinegar, and plaster of Paris as an inner support, molded so that the head would hold its shape.

**Salomon, L.** See **Israël, L.**

**Salvation Army Lass.** 1921. Doll made by *EFFanBEE* under special arrangement with Commander Evangeline C. Booth; had blonde bobbed wig with bangs; price $2.95.

**Sam.** 1920. Rag doll made by *Jessie McCutcheon Raleigh.* Size 15 inches, price $1.50. Mate to *Shoe Button Sue.*

**Sambo.** 1910. Character doll made by Hahn & *Amberg.* This was a Negro version of *Samson,* and resembled the *Baby* of *Kämmer & Reinhardt.* It had an "unbreakable and washable" composition head, velvet plush body, and was dressed in rompers that buttoned on. Sizes 10, 12, and 15 inches; the two larger sizes came with "unbreakable" hands; price $4.20 to $13.20 doz. wholesale.

**Sametz, Louis.** 1918–24. New York City. Listed in directories as a toy importer and jobber. Luella Hart, in TOY TRADER, May, 1954, stated that in 1945 Louis Sametz wrote that they discontinued making celluloid dolls about 1923 in Westport, Conn. Most of their products showed the Indian-head trademark (see Ill. 280), except for the celluloid *Kewpies* they made, which carried *Rose O'Neill's* mark. Around 1924 they made celluloid *Bye-Lo Babies.* The above information is from Luella Hart. No record has been found in Westport Directories of any Sametz. (See **Irokese Trading Corp.**)

**Samhammer, Philipp (Philip), & Co.** 1888–1915. Sonneberg, Thür. Manufactured dolls. F. Ellinghaus was his London agent during some of the period, but Philip Samhammer himself was frequently listed in London Directories.

1888: Obtained British patent for applying movable eyes to a rag doll. Doll was to contain bellows or squeaker for a voice; legs covered with knitted hose and feet with buckled shoes.

1893: Exhibited dolls and doll bodies at the Chicago World's Fair.

1900: One of the Grand Prize winners at the Paris Exposition.

1904: Displayed dolls at the St. Louis Exhibition.

1905: Listed in London as handling "Dolls of every description, dressed and undressed."

**Sam-Me.** 1917–20. Trademark registered in U.S. by *Hawkins & Stubblefield* for dolls.

**Sammy Sandman.** 1919–20. Design for this doll patented by *Frances Obrect* in U.S.

**Sammy Sock.** 1915. Painted-face rag doll made by *Strat Manufacturing Co.*

**Samson.** 1910–12. Doll made by Hahn & *Amberg* in competition with *Baby* (#100) made by *Kämmer & Reinhardt*. *Amberg* claimed that it was the first complete jointed doll ever made in the United States. It was made of washable composition, strung with wire springs, and was advertised as "Samson, Uncle Sam's Firstborn." The bent-limb composition baby body was not a success, and by 1912 nothing remained of it but broken molds. The head, which resembled "Baby," was used on stuffed bodies and called *Dolly Strong* in the white version and *Sambo* in the Negro version.

1910: Samson came in sizes 12 and 15 inches; price $8.50 and $13.50 doz. wholesale.

**Samson, Henry W.** 1922–24. Tonkawa, Okla. Secured a U.S. design patent for a doll with striped trousers and a striped conical hat.

**Samstag & Hilder Bros.** 1894–1920. New York City; branch in Chicago, Ill.; foreign offices in Sonneberg, Nürnberg, Berlin, Paris, London, Vienna, and Kobe. Manufacturers and importers of dolls. About 1903 *Edmund Ulrich Steiner* left *Strobel & Wilken* and took over the management of the doll department of Samstag & Hilder, where he remained for six years and produced his *Human Face Doll, Majestic, Liliput,* and others.

1903: Advertised that they obtained toys from cities, towns, and villages in France, Germany, Switzerland, and Austria. They handled *Duchess* kid-body dolls and Duchess jointed dolls, *Our Daisy* dolls, *My Little Beauty* dressed dolls with removable clothes, and *Royal* walking dolls that were dressed and undressed.

1904: Advertised dolls with bisque heads and arms, curly hair wigs, jointed kid bodies; price 10¢ to $2.00.

1905: Began to use trademark *Colonial Doll*. Advertised *Majestic* dolls with American faces on kid or jointed composition bodies; came undressed or dressed for $1.00. Also, there were Liliput sitting dolls, Daisy dolls, Little Beauty dolls, patent walking and sitting dolls with new features, controlled by Samstag & Hilder, as well as *Mama* and *Papa* dolls that spoke at the touch and without strings to be pulled.

1907: Began to use trademark *Peter Pan Play Dolls*. Edmund Ulrich Steiner won a court case upholding the patent on his walking doll. Samstag & Hilder were the sole selling agents for this doll. They advertised *Steiff* dolls.

1908: Advertised patent walking dolls, kid-body dolls, dolls with imitation kid bodies, rag dolls, china dolls, celluloid dolls, dolls' heads of bisque or of celluloid, and wigs.

1910: Obtained a U.S. design patent for a novelty doll.

1912: Registered *Hug Me Kiddies in U.S.* as a trademark. Advertised *Goggle Eye dolls, Double Face dolls,* character dolls with American Baby faces, dressed as American children.

1913: Advertised the *Parcel Post Babies,* a line of very light dolls.

1914: Advertised *Whistling Jim;* in a picture he looks like the whistling boy made by *Gebrüder Heubach*. Their representative in Sonneberg was the Burgomaster, and he helped to arrange for the transportation of dolls through Rotterdam, Amsterdam, and other neutral ports in Italy, Denmark, and Sweden. (See Ill. 1680.)

1920: Advertised *Baby Cuddles* and Colonial Quality dolls.

**Samuel & Söhne.** 1907–25+. Joachimstal, Bohemia (Czechoslovakia). Manufactured jointed dolls.

**Samulon, J.** 1893–1925+. Dresden, Saxony. Manufactured and exported dolls; specialized in dolls' house dolls. New York agent was Gary-Grautoff Co.

**Sancier, Helen A.** 1914–15. Edgewater, N.J. Obtained a U.S. patent for a two-headed doll. At center of the doll's body there was a transverse metal tube that formed a fulcrum about which the two heads rotated. The legs extended beyond the body on either side, and connected with the transverse tube. The shoes were weighted to preserve the equilibrium of the doll. The two heads and two pairs of arms were articulated, as would be the case in high-grade jointed dolls. Doll was dressed by providing separate waist portions, and the skirts were slit at each side over the legs so that the outer skirt of one costume formed the underskirt of the other costume.

**Sander, Karl (Carl).** 1909–24. Sonneberg, Thür. Made dolls.

**Sanders, George W.** See **Jointed Doll Co.**

**Sandy.** 1924. Rag doll made by *Federal Doll Manufacturing Co.* It would stand in any desired pose; sold for $1.00.

**Sani-Doll.** 1916–18. Made by *Famous Doll Studio,* which advertised that doll was modeled by well-known sculptor. Came in nineteen designs, sixteen sizes; price 50¢ to $6.00.

**Sanigenic.** 1917. Trademark registered in U.S. by *Utley Co.* It was to be applied with a rubber stamp on the cloth covering of the dolls' bodies.

**Sanitary Baby.** 1915–16. Made by *Ideal Novelty & Toy Co.* Came with glass eyes or painted eyes; had a body of imitation kid; sizes 16 and 25 inches.

**Sanitrion.** 1916–18. Trade name for dolls made by the *Trion Toy Co.* Dolls had composition heads, bodies made of loofah, and wore long dresses. They were distributed by *Butler Bros.*

1918: Size 8 inches cost $2.10, and size 10 inches cost $4.00 doz wholesale.

**Sannitoy.** 1924. Trademark of *Alfred Munzer,* used for *Mama Dolls.*

**Sanoner, Jos., Sohn.** 1896. St. Ulrich, Grödner Tal. Distributed wooden dolls.

**Sans Rival.** 1925+. Trade name used by *Mme. de Kasparek* for the *Art Dolls* that she made.

**Sansonnet.** 1918. Trademark registered in France by *Mme. Poulbot.*

**Santa.** 1900–1910. Jointed composition-body doll with bisque head made by *Hamburger & Co.*

1900: Trademark registered in U.S.

1901: Trademark registered in Germany.

1903: Doll came with a center-part curly wig; wore a chemise and a paper tag on its wrist; came in various sizes.

1904: One of the dolls in the Hamburger & Co. display at the St. Louis Exhibition, which won a grand prize.

1910: Advertised by Geo. H. Bowman Co., who may have assumed some of the property of Hamburger & Co. after they went bankrupt.

**Santa Claus.** 1884–86. Two-piece rag doll for which a U.S. design patent was obtained by *Edward Peck.* This doll was the inspiration for the rag dolls later made by *Celia and Charity Smith.* Santa Claus was 15 inches tall.

**Santa Claus.** 1916–17. *Alice Cassidy* obtained a U.S. design patent for a doll dressed as Santa Claus.

**Santy.** Ca. 1860. Produced wax-over-composition-head dolls with hair wigs, glass eyes, stuffed bodies. A 32-inch doll in Bethnal Green Museum is marked on the stomach as shown in Ill. 1422.

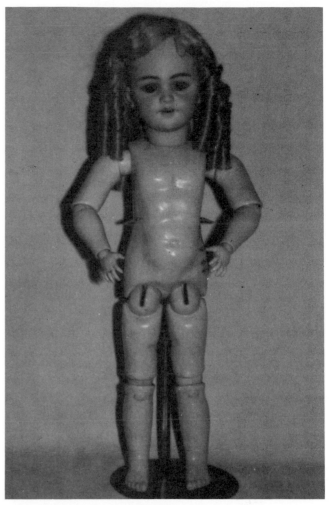

**1419A & B.** "Santa," a Hamburger & Co. doll with bisque head made by Simon & Halbig, has sleeping glass eyes, new wig, open mouth with four teeth, ball-jointed composition body. Mark on head: Ill. **1420.** H. 24 inches. *Courtesy of Dorothy Annunziato.*

S H 1249 DEP.
Germany
12
SANTA

1420

S&H 1249
DEP.
Germany
SANTA.

1421

**1420 & 1421.** "Santa" marks used for dolls by Hamburger & Co.

**1422.** "Santy" mark found on waxed dolls.

**Sardeau, Miss Hélène.** 1921–24. Native of Belgium; resided in Palm Beach, Fla., in winter and in New York City
the rest of the year. She and her sister Mathilde Kane and
Hélène Silberfeld of Belgium registered in U.S. *Ki-Ki* as
a trademark for dolls. Miss Sardeau and her sister combined the work of sculptor, painter, and modiste in making these portrait dolls. At the first sitting, Miss Hélène
molded the head. A plaster cast was made of this and
covered smoothly with stockinet, which was stitched at
the back of the neck. The doll was painted at later
sittings, and a wig of wool or goat's hair was matched
to the sitter's hair. Four or five sittings were required for
a head four inches in length. Miss Mathilde made the
bodies of cotton and muslin and dressed the dolls. All
except children had long, lanky bodies about three feet
tall. It was popular for mothers to have their children reproduced as dolls. Among the famous people of whom
Miss Sardeau made portrait dolls were Lenore Ulric,
Richard Bennett, Maria Jeritza, Rudolph Valentino, and
Mrs. William Randolph Hearst.

**Sarrasani's Circus.** See **Steiff, Margarete.**

**Sassy Sue.** 1911. Doll copyrighted by *Louis Amberg &
Son.* It was the head of a little girl, with mischievous
eyes, chubby smile, dimple, molded hair with center part.
The composition head had two holes in the hair, one
over each ear, for two detachable bows of taffeta ribbon.
Doll came with cork-stuffed pink sateen body, and cost
$8.00 doz. wholesale with cloth arms and $8.50 doz.
wholesale with composition arms.

**Sattler, Max.** 1895–1909. Neustadt near Coburg, Thür.
Manufactured little or baby dolls.

**Säuberlich, Rudolf, & Berlich, Rolf.** 1923. Charlottenburg,
Prussia. Made and distributed dolls and dolls' clothing.
Registered four trademarks in Germany: *Plombe in der
Hand* (Seal on the Hand), *Original Rolf Berlich Puppe,*
"Rolf Berlich Puppen Charlottenburg" in a circle, and a
picture of a doll's cloth hand with a tag attached to the
little finger.

**Sauer, August.** 1907–25+. Sonneberg, Thür. Manufactured dolls.

**Sauerteig, Johannes.** 1888–1925+. Sonneberg, Thür.
Made dolls of various kinds.

1888: With Lorenz Heinrich Friedrich Lutz, obtained a
British patent for a combination doll and music box,
which was operated by a crank handle connected with
the jointed arm of the doll.

**Saugnier, Mme., & Avard.** 1848–52. Paris. Made dolls.

**Sawdust.** Many dolls were stuffed entirely with sawdust;
others were stuffed with combinations of sawdust and
various materials such as cork, cotton, or hair. *Kestner's*
fine-grade kid bodies were stuffed with half sawdust and
half cork. Sawdust was also one of the ingredients used
for making some composition bodies and/or heads.

1868: *Brasseur* and Chevallier obtained a French patent
for making dolls' bodies or parts of bodies of a composition consisting of sawdust, glue, and other ingredients.

In the 20th century: Sawdust stuffing was superseded by
other materials for the most part, and wood flour took
its place in the manufacture of composition.

**Sayco.** See **Schoen & Yondorf Co.**

**Scailliet.** 1834–52. Paris. Made dolls.

**Scandinavian Dolls.** *Royal Copenhagen* produced china
heads. *Mlle. Brix* and *Herbert Olsen* also made dolls in
Denmark; *Kristian Olson* and *Husflidsforening Norsk* of
Norway produced dolls; *Emma Kraeplin* of Sweden made
dolls. In 1898, a doll collector commented that three out
of four Scandinavian dolls had china (or bisque) heads;
the fourth had a leather head. Nearly all Scandinavian
dolls represented peasant types.

**Scantlebury, Elizabeth C.** 1920. Brooklyn, N.Y. Designed
costume dolls. The round wax faces of her dolls were
tinted to the complexion of the countries that they
represented, and their hair was arranged according to
the national coiffures. Many of her dolls were placed in
schools, colleges, and libraries. It was claimed that her
geographical and educational dolls were known "all over
the world." She dressed dolls in period costumes ranging from the 14th to the 20th centuries. One doll was
dressed in a blue plaid silk dress that was an exact copy
of a real 1848 wedding dress. She studied data in
museums to make authentic reproductions of geographical costumes. She made a number of artistic baby dolls
also.

**Scaramouche.** 1924. Trademark registered in France by
*Ange Le Prince* for mascot dolls.

**Scatterday, Evalyn R.** 1921. Columbus, Ohio. Secured a
U.S. design patent for a boy doll with circular eyes,
dressed in patched overalls.

**Scavini, Enrico & Signora Elena Konig di.** 1920–25+.
Turin, Italy. Made fabric dolls; used the trademark *Lenci,*
a pet name of Signora Scavini.

1920: Sole U.S. distributor was *Ernst & Hermann* of New
York City. The dolls were made by Italian craftsmen in
fifty original designs, including Indians, cowboys, trapper
or voyageur, Negro minstrel, Chinese men, policemen,
soldiers, peasants, fishermen, milkmaids, Pierrots, Harle-
quins, and others. The Scavinis advertised that each doll
was designed by an artist. They were made of felt; had
no seam on the face, which was in one molded piece,
handpainted. Genuine hair was used on the dolls representing children and babies. The bodies were made so
that arms and legs could be placed in various positions.
When the dolls were shown at the Leipzig Fair, a German

newspaper wrote glowingly of them and ended with the phrase "to the secret envy of a good many Germans."

1921: Secured a British patent for dolls. Advertised one hundred models of character dolls.

1922: Name "Lenci" registered in Britain as a trademark. They had representatives in London, New York, Paris, and Leipzig.

1923: Advertisement suggested: "Develop artistic tendencies in your children, buy a Lenci doll." Each doll was handmade in the Lenci studio; many of them retailed for less than $10.00; came in sizes 5 to 45 inches. Two sales people in a New York store sold over $2,500 worth of Lenci dolls in one week. The trade name *Fad-Ette* was advertised by their New York agent, *Charles Ernst*.

1924: "Lenci" registered as a trademark in U.S., but had been used since 1920.

### LENCI DOLLS
#### Made by Scavini
Listings in an undated catalog

| Catalog No. | Size Inches | Name of Dolls or Description |
|---|---|---|
| 109 | 22 | Most popular child doll |
| 110 | 18 | Next most popular child doll |
| 111 | 13 | Other children dolls |
| 149 | 16 | |
| 159 | 16 | |
| 160 | | Baby in carriage |
| 165/1 | 29½ | Mara |
| 165/2 | 29½ | Gretchen |
| 165/3 | 29½ | Susie |
| 165/4 | 26½ | Columbina |
| 165/5 | 29½ | Bergère |
| 165/6 | 29½ | Miss Sweet Flower |
| 165/u | 29½ | Contessa Maffei |
| 178 | 17 | Fat girl |
| 180 | 40 | |
| 186 | 40 | Russian boy |
| 187 | 40 | Russian girl |
| 188 | 23 | Dschang-Go |
| 188/A | 23 | Li Tia Guai |
| 189 | 23 | Butterfly |
| 190 | 12 | Fukuruko |
| 250 | 29½ | Mimi |
| 251 | 23 | Hu Sun |
| 252 | 20 | Maria Teresa |
| 253 | 20 | Mozart |
| 255 | 23 | Tsau Guo Giu |
| 256 | 29½ | Musette |
| 257 | 31½ | Katinka |
| 258 | 28 | Teen-age girl |
| 260 | 31 | Sam |
| 261 | 31 | Kufi |
| 262 | 10 | Madonna and Child |
| 263 | 28 | Raquel Meller |
| 264 | 13 | |
| 300 | 17½ | Young children dolls (see Ill. 1083) |
| 350 | 20 | Older girl doll |

165/1 through 165/u: Adult dolls

188 through 190: Oriental dolls

260, 261: Negro children

All except Nos. 165/6, 178, 252, 253, and 350 have eyes glancing to the side.

**Schachne, Albert.** 1909. Nürnberg, Bavaria. Obtained a German patent for a doll that cried real tears when a rubber ball that was concealed in its body was pressed.

**Schade, Hugo.** See **Kling.**

**Schaefer, Otto.** 1909. Berlin. Made dolls.

**Schafft, G.** 1863–74. Waltershausen, Thür. Made papier-mâché dolls; after 1874 merged with *Wislizenus*.

**Schaitberger, Carl.** 1896–1925+. Sonneberg, Thür. Manufactured dolls and specialized in assortment boxes.

1900: One of the group of Grand Prize winners at the Paris Exposition.

**Schalk (Rogue).** 1919. Trademark registered in Germany by *Gans & Seyfarth* for dolls' heads.

**Schanne.** 1842–95. Paris. First it was N. Schanne or Schanne, Sr.; later, A. Schanne took over the business.

1867: A. Schanne exhibited dolls at the Paris Exposition.

**Scharf, H.** 1909–25+. Berlin. Made dolls and dolls' clothes.

**Scharff.** 1909–18. Altenbergen, Thür. Made wooden dolls.

**Scheibe & Burre.** 1924. Berlin. Designed and made dolls' heads and parts.

**Scheler, A.** 1909. Wildenheid near Sonneburg, Thür. Manufactured dolls.

**Schelhorn (Schellhorn), August.** 1897–1925+. Sonneberg, Thür. Successors of August Schelhorn were Handel & Grempel in Neustadt near Coburg, Thür., at least from 1909 on. They manufactured and exported dressed and undressed dolls.

**Schelhorn (Schellhorn), Daniel, Söhne.** 1891. Germany. Made dressed dolls with porcelain heads.

**Schelhorn, Fritz.** 1924. Sonneberg, Thür. Made dolls.

**Schelhorn (Schellhorn), Heinrich.** 1909–21. Sonneberg, Thür. Manufactured dolls with leather bodies.

**Schelhorn, Max Fr., Firm.** 1907–20. Sonneberg, Thür. Manufactured and exported dolls and parts of dolls. Made dolls that were distributed by *Samstag & Hilder*.

1907: Registered in Germany *Fluffy Ruffles* as a trademark.

1910: Registered in Germany three trademarks: *Snookums, Little Snookums // The Newlywed's Baby,* and *Muffles.*

1914: Registered in Germany the *Base Ball Fan* as a trademark for dolls and doll parts.

**Scherf, Georg.** 1908–10. Sonneberg, Thür. Manufactured dolls.

1908: Obtained U.S., German, and British patents for the use of a knee pan of wood or paper pulp in the stuffed thigh of leather or rag dolls. A cord was fastened above the knee pan and down to the sole of the foot. Scherf

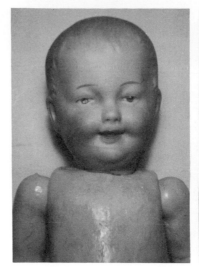

1424A & B. Two-faced baby doll made by Max Schelhorn; socket bisque head has one face laughing and one face crying, molded hair, intaglio eyes. (Body not original.) Ca. 1910. H. 7½ inches. *Courtesy of Lester & Alice Grinnings.*

1423A & B. Steiner Majestic walking doll with bisque head made by Max Schelhorn; doll turns its head as it walks. Has glass eyes, open mouth with four upper teeth, lamb's wool wig. Head marked as shown in Ill. 1425, except that the number is "32" instead of "S370." A similar doll was marked "Majestic // 5/0 // Germany // Reg'd." Original blue and white suit. H. 12½ inches. *Courtesy of Edna Greehy.*

S 370

1425. Mark found on dolls of Max Fr. Schelhorn.

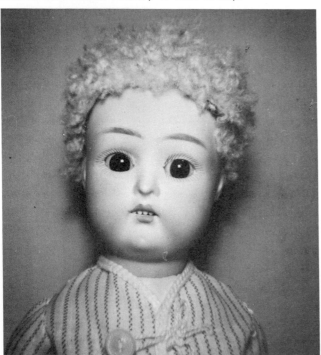

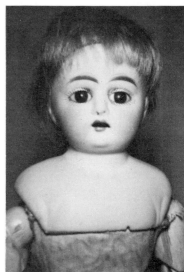

1426A & B. Bisque shoulder head on the type of body patented by Stephan Schilling in 1884. Ball-jointed wooden arms are connected by elastic through the excelsior-stuffed cloth body. Lower legs are of composition, as are the hands. Note the reinforcement strip at the knee joint, a feature also shown on the patent drawings. Horseshoe mark appears under "Made in Germany" and over "Dep. 5/3/0" on back of shoulder. H. 10½ inches. *Coleman Collection.*

1427. Mark used by Stephan Schilling on dolls.

commented that heretofore the legs of leather or rag dolls had been connected to the thighs by hinged or screw joints.

1910: Secured a U.S. patent for improving dolls' eyes so that they would remain either open or closed regardless of the position of the doll.

**Scherf, Peter.** 1890–1925+. Sonneberg, Thür. The widow of Peter Scherf was head of the firm at least from 1895–1909. Made and exported inexpensive bisque-headed dolls.

1890: Obtained a patent for improving dolls.

1916: Registered in Germany the *Fairy Kid* as a trademark.

**Scherzer, Richard.** 1897–1925+. Sonneberg, Thür. In 1915 only, the firm was known as R. Scherzer & Fischer. Manufactured dolls and used *Herzlieb* (Sweetheart) as a trademark.

**Scheyer, O., & Co.** 1925. Nürnberg, Bavaria. Registered in Germany *Mafuka* as a trademark for dolls.

**Schiemer, Hermann.** 1921–22. Nürnberg, Bavaria. Produced dolls.

1921: Registered in Germany *Mobi* as a trademark for dolls.

1922: Obtained a German patent for a doll with a ball joint at the waist so that the doll could bend in any desired direction.

**Schierholz, C. G., & Sohn.** 1817+. Plaue, Thür. Made hard-paste porcelain. Their marks were pairs of crossed parallel lines.

**Schierloh, Conrad.** Before 1897, Hamburg, Germany; by 1897, Moritz Zöppel was successor. Manufactured dolls.

**Schikowsky, R.** 1900. Berlin. Made dolls.

**Schildkröte.** 1889–1925+. Trademark of the *Rheinische Gummi & Celluloid Fabrik Co.;* a German word meaning either turtle or tortoise.

**Schiller, Société René, & Cie.** 1918. Paris. Registered in France *Yerri et Suzel* as a trademark for dolls dressed in provincial costumes of Alsace or Lorraine.

**Schilling.** 1884–1925+, Sonneberg, Thür.; 1884, Stephan Max Ferdinand Schilling; 1889–1920, Ferdinand M. Schilling; 1925, Max Schilling & Zitzmann. Manufactured dolls.

1884: Obtained U.S. patent for ball-and-socket arm joints for porcelain, wooden, or papier-mâché arms on cloth, linen, or leather dolls' bodies, with tube through the shoulders for elastic.

1889: Secured a German patent for a doll that talked as it walked.

1893: Displayed dolls and dolls' heads at the Chicago World's Fair. Applied for their trademark of a winged angel head over the word "deponirt" (deponiert).

1895: Registered in Germany their winged angel head trademark for dolls and dolls' heads of papier-mâché, paper, wood, and rubber; advertised dressed dolls. Their trademark with the words "Bisquitfaçon // Waschbar" has been found on dolls having bisque heads and kid bodies.

1900: One of the group of Grand Prize winners at the Paris Exposition.

1903: Registered in Germany their winged angel head plus several other figures as a trademark for dolls' heads of papier-mâché, paper, wood, and rubber.

1904: Displayed dolls at the St. Louis Exhibition.

1909: Advertised kid-body dolls.

1910: Dolls distributed by *Louis Wolf & Co.* Their dolls at the Seattle Exhibition were described as "from the master hands of Schilling who produces only dolls of quality."

**Schilling, P. M.** 1911. Sonneberg, Thür. Made wooden shoulder joints for *Baby-Gelenkpuppen*.

**Schindel & Co.** 1863–74. Waltershausen, Thür. Manufactured papier-mâché dolls. (See also **Wiesenthal, Schindel & Kallenberg.**)

**Schindhelm, B.** 1909–18. Bettelhecken, Thür. Made dolls and *Täuflinge*.

**Schindhelm, Fr.** 1918. Bettelhecken, Thür. Made dolls and *Täuflinge*.

**Schindhelm, Johannes.** 1895–1918. Neufang, Thür. Manufactured jointed dolls.

**Schindhelm & Knauer.** 1921–25. Sonneberg, Thür. Produced miniature dressed dolls and dolls in trunks with their trousseaux.

**Schlaggenwald.** 1793–1925+. Bohemia. Hard paste porcelain factory; had several early connections with Thüringia. Their first arcanist was from Hildburghausen.

1800: Luise *Greiner*, widow of Johannes Andreas Greiner, director of the Gera Porzellanfabrik, purchased the Schlaggenwald factory.

1803: Dr. Johannes Georg Lippert married Miss Friederike Greiner and became director of the factory.

1808: Václav Haas joined Lippert, and the firm became Lippert & Haas.

Ca. 1867: Firm became Haas & Czjzek.

By the 1830's, they made fine porcelain figures, but it is not known when they made dolls' heads. The "S" mark impressed on the several dolls' heads owned by Mrs. Eva M. Horváth was used from 1830 to 1870. The initials "L & H" were also used during this period. Mrs. Horváth's four Schlaggenwald china heads appear to date around the middle of the 19th century. Three of them are bald with black pates; the fourth has unglazed blonde hair with a hairdo of the early 1850's. Unusual characteristics of some of these china heads are the three separate upper eyelashes painted on the part of the eyelids toward the nose, and the lower eyelid painted in

**1428–1432.** Porcelain marks of Schlaggenwald. Marks Nos. **1429, 1430, 1431,** and **1432** are found on dolls' heads.

| | | |
|---|---|---|
| 1428 | 1429 | 1430 |
| | 1431 | 1432 |

red. The pupil of the eye has a white highlight. The heads came in various sizes. A 5-inch shoulder head has an oval face, mohair wig, long neck, and six sewholes; it is on a kid body.

**Schlenkerchen (Little Dawdler).** 1922. Trademark registered in Germany by *Käthe Kruse.* Probably used for *The Toddler.*

**Schlesinger Bros.** 1924. New York City. Displayed dolls at the Toy Fair. Leo Schlesinger & Co. of New York City made mechanical toys from 1875 to at least 1916. They won awards at 19th-century international exhibitions.

**Schletter, Hugo.** 1897. Vienna. Manufactured dolls and dolls' heads.

**Schlisler, Mme. Jeanne (née Dumay).** 1924. Paris. Registered in France *Ti-Koun* as a trademark for dolls.

**Schlopsnies, Albert.** 1909–10. Munich, Germany. Secured a German patent for jointed dolls and marionettes. (See also **Steiff, Fräulein Margarete.**)

**Schloss, Adolphe, Fils & Cie.** 1924–25. Paris. Registered in U.S. and in France *Berthoyette* as a trademark for dolls.

**Schlotthauer & Heuss.** Made dolls similar to the *Steiff* dolls; by 1926, Schlotthauer dolls were in the Sonneberg Museum.

**Schlutter, Willy.** 1920. Mannheim Neckarau, Bavaria. Obtained a German patent for making flat disk joints on celluloid dolls. It should be remembered that *Rheinische Gummi & Celluloid Fabrik Co.* was located in Mannheim.

**Schmalfuss, C. M.** 1890–1925+. Charlottenburg, near Berlin. Also known as the Berliner Puppenfabrik. Made dressed dolls and doll articles.

**Schmetzer, Louis.** 1875–76. Of Chicago, Ill., but residing in Rothenburg, Bavaria. Obtained a British patent for a jointed wooden doll. Later he secured both French and British patents for clothing for the doll made so that it would hide the joints.

**Schmey, Gustavus.** 1853–1925+. Sonneberg, Thür.; branches and/or representatives in London, Paris, New York, Coburg; by 1895 the firm was known as successors of G. Schmey. Made and exported dolls.

1895: Advertised jointed bébés, dressed and undressed; wax dolls and composition dolls.

1900: One of the Grand Prize winning group at the Paris Exposition.

1903: Advertised jointed composition dolls, kid-body dolls, and dressed dolls.

1904: Displayed dolls at the St. Louis Exposition.

1925: Advertised unbreakable dressed dolls and walking *Mama Dolls.*

**Schmidt, A.** Ca. 1900. Waltershausen, Thür. Porcelain factory; used intertwined initials "A S."

**Schmidt, Anna.** 1918. Dresden, Saxony. Made dolls.

**Schmidt, August.** 1909. Wilsdruff, Saxony. Made dolls' bodies and heads.

### BRUNO SCHMIDT DOLLS

**1433.** Bruno Schmidt's bisque-headed doll with molded and painted features, strawberry blonde wig, composition body, marked "B S W" in a heart and "529." *Courtesy of Margaret Whitton; photograph by Winnie Langley.*

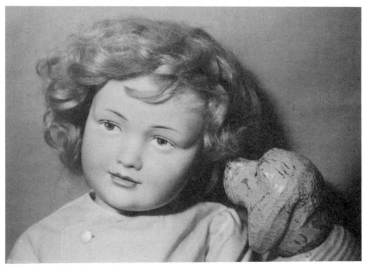

**1434.** Pair of bisque heads with same mold number, "2094," made by Bruno Schmidt. The heads have solid crowns with painted hair, glass eyes, and open mouths. Mark: Ill. **1438.** Smaller head is size 2. *Courtesy of Eleanor Jean Carter.*

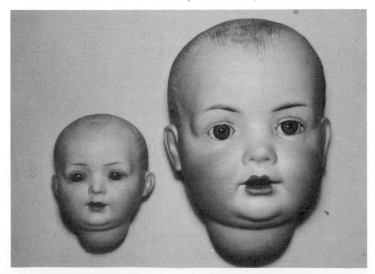

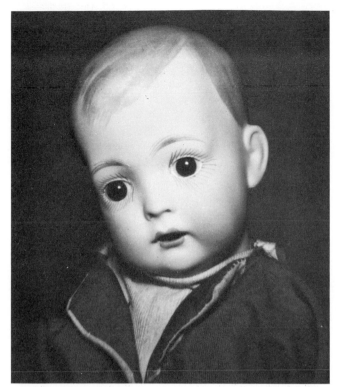

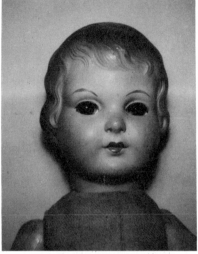

**1435.** Bruno Schmidt boy with bisque socket head, molded and painted hair parted on the side, glass eyes with long painted eyelashes not generally found on Schmidt dolls, open mouth. Mark: Ill. **1439.** H. 13½ inches. *Coleman Collection.*

**1436A & B.** Celluloid head made by Bruno Schmidt with painted features. Cloth body; original Dutch clothes. In Holland both little boys and little girls wore skirts. Note the similarity to the bisque head in Ill. **1435.** Mark on head: Ill. **1440.** H. 11 inches. *Courtesy of Edith Meggers.*

**1437A & B.** Celluloid socket head on cloth body; wooden ball-jointed arms. Bruno Schmidt heart mark on head numbered "H/33." H. 13 inches. *Courtesy of Jessica Norman.*

**1438**        **1439**        **1440**

**1438–1440.** Bruno Schmidt's marks found on dolls.

**Schmidt, Bruno.** 1900–1925+. Waltershausen, Thür. Manufactured and distributed dolls of various kinds, including dolls with porcelain heads, papier-mâché dolls, and celluloid dolls.

1904: Registered in Germany *Mein Goldherz* (My Golden Heart) and a heart with the letters "B. S.//W." in it as trademarks.

1908: Registered in Germany as a trademark a heart inside another heart.

1910: Registered in Germany *Herz* (Heart) as a trademark.

1915: Registered in Germany as a trademark a heart-shaped mark.

**Schmidt, C. A.** 1897–1915. Lichte near Wallendorf, Thür. Manufactured dolls and porcelain; also a china painter.

**Schmidt, Carl (Karl).** 1907–15. Waltershausen, Thür. Made dolls' heads for export.

**Schmidt, Eduard.** 1904–25. Coburg, Thür. Made dolls.

1925: Advertised that their "Sico" walking doll was the only soft stuffed doll that really walked. Registered in Germany *Sicora* as a trademark for dolls.

**Schmidt, Franz, & Co.** 1890–1925+. Georgenthal near Waltershausen, Thür. Made undressed jointed dolls and doll parts, and exported them.

1891: Obtained a British patent for sleeping eyes made so that the upper lids moved further and faster than the lower lids.

1895: Advertised ball-jointed dolls; stiff-jointed dolls; wooden doll heads; composition doll heads; bisque doll heads, arms, legs, and bodies, with swivel heads; wigs, shoes, and stockings; heads on handles (*marottes*).

1899: Obtained a German patent for dolls' joints made with three hemispherical cups, one inside the other.

1902: Registered in Germany the trademark "F. S. & Co." with a doll between crossed hammers. It should be noted the Schmitt of Paris also used crossed hammers as a trademark, but otherwise their marks were totally different.

1909: Registered in Germany *Cellulobrin* as a trademark for dolls' heads and parts of dolls. Factory also known at Puppenfabrik-Georgenthal.

1910: Registered in Germany *Tausendschönchen* (daisy) as a trademark for dolls, dolls' heads, and other parts of dolls.

1911: Advertised ball-jointed dolls.

1913: Advertised bisque-head baby doll under trade name *Little Boy Blue*.

1918: Described as a steam factory.

**Schmidt, H.** 1909–12. Coburg, Thür. Made dolls.

**Schmidt, H. Otto.** 1924. Leipzig, Germany. Made dolls.

**Schmidt, Oscar (Oskar) Julius.** 1887–1909. Sonneberg, Thür. Manufactured dolls.

1887: Secured a British patent for making dolls of glazed pasteboard prepared from wood and known to the trade as "leather-board." The body, head, etc., were shaped in two-part molds, then glued or pressed together with a layer of clay added to fill interstices, after which the doll was varnished or waxed.

1893: Displayed dolls at the Chicago Exposition.

**Schmidt, Paul, Firm.** 1921–25. Sonneberg, Thür. Made dolls of various kinds, including baby dolls.

1922: Registered in Germany "P Sch" in an oval as a trademark.

1923: Registered in Germany as a trademark the letters

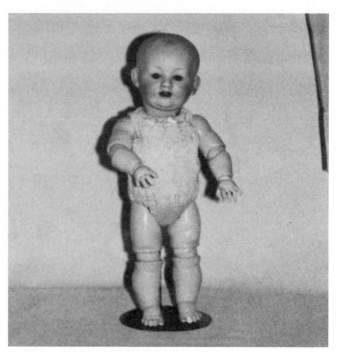

**1441A & B.** Franz Schmidt baby, mold #1272, with painted hair, pierced nostrils, open mouth with retractable tongue that falls back into the head when the eyes close. Toddler-type composition body. Mark on head: Ill. **1443.** H. 14 inches. *Courtesy of Mary Roberson.*

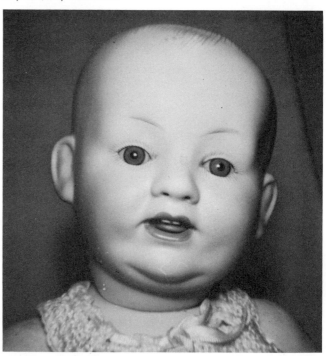

"P S" in a circle under a radiant sun and over a six-pointed star.

**Schmidt, Peter.** 1880–90. Philadelphia, Pa. Manufactured doll bodies and doll materials.

**Schmidt, Reinhold.** 1909–18. Oberlind in 1909 and Sonneberg in 1918, both in Thür. Made dolls with kid bodies.

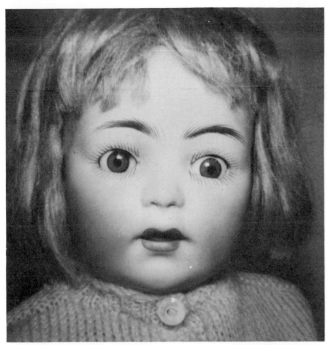

**1442.** Bisque-headed doll #1295 made by Franz Schmidt has sleeping eyes, both painted and hair upper eyelashes, pierced nostrils, two teeth, jointed composition toddler-type body. Mark: Ill. **1444.** H. 13 inches. *Courtesy of Mary Roberson.*

F.S. & Co
1272/357 ₴
Deponiert

**1443**

1295
F.S. & Co
Made in
Germany
30

**1444**

F S & Co.
1271/32x
DEPONIERT

**1445**

**1443–1445.** Marks found on dolls made by Franz Schmidt & Co.

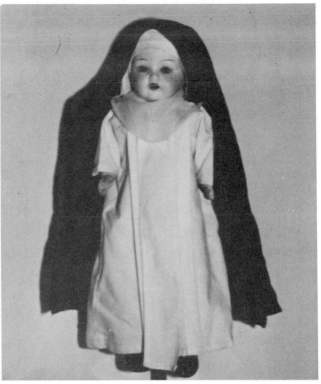

**1446.** Doll dressed as a Sister of Charity. Bisque shoulder head bears the P. Sch. mark believed to stand for Paul Schmidt. Doll has sleeping glass eyes, cloth body, composition limbs. Mark: Ill. **1447.** H. 15 inches. H. of shoulder head, 4½ inches. *Courtesy of Jessica Norman.*

P. Sch.
Germany.
O

**1447**

P. Sch.

**1448**

**1447 & 1448.** Marks used by Paul Schmidt on dolls.

**Schmidt, Richard.** 1895–1911. London. Importer and distributor of dolls; succeeded by Carl Strube in 1897.

**Schmidt & Rüchter.** 1923. Gräfenroda, Thür. Registered *Phyllis Doll* in Germany as a trademark.

**Schmidt & Steffen.** 1922. Berlin. Obtained a German patent for a doll dressed as a man.

**Schminansky, Hermann.** 1888. Berlin, Secured a British patent for making dolls' heads and limbs of metal cast in two parts and connected by a soldered joint. The main portion of the head was formed by pouring molten tin, zinc, or other material into a mold of proper shape. The cap was formed by dipping a polished metal mold into molten tin, a thin layer of which solidified on the mold; the cap was then soldered to the main part.

**Schmitt.** 1863–91. Paris. In 1863, dealt with wholesale toys. By 1867, the firm was listed as makers of children's toys.

1877: Schmitt & Fils (Sons), Maurice and Charles, were granted a French patent for decorating porcelain shoulder heads for dolls and bébés. This was an improved method that would permit any desired shades and colors to be given to a bisque head.

1878: Schmitt & Fils were awarded a silver medal at the Paris Exposition for their dolls and bébés.

1879: They were issued another French patent for jointed all-bisque bébés.

1883: Obtained a patent for a layer of wax to be applied to bisque doll and bébé heads after they had left the kilns. It was believed this would improve their appearance and make the dolls more durable. Waxed-over-composition heads are found on marked Schmitt bodies.

French patents granted to the Schmitt firm were: 1885, eye movement in dolls; 1887, doll improvements; and 1891, a new method for making dolls' heads. In 1885 they also obtained a patent in Germany for moving eyes by a knob at the back of the head. Their factory at this time was located at Nogent-sur-Marne, Seine. From 1879 to 1890, Schmitt & Fils (Sons), doll makers, advertised as their specialty an indestructible jointed bébé called *Bébé Schmitt*. This was exported as well as being sold on the domestic market. It should be noted that "Schmitt" was generally spelled "Schmidt" in Germany, and that *Franz Schmidt* in 1902 registered a trademark in Germany having crossed hammers similar to those found on French Schmitt dolls. (See Ills. 166, 167, 1675; also color photograph C16.)

SCHMITT FRENCH DOLLS

**1449.** Schmitt doll with bisque head, stationary eyes, lamb's wool wig, open-closed mouth with five teeth, composition body, original clothes. Mark on head and on bottom of torso: Ill. **1452.** H. 30½ inches. *Courtesy of Helen Jo Payne.*

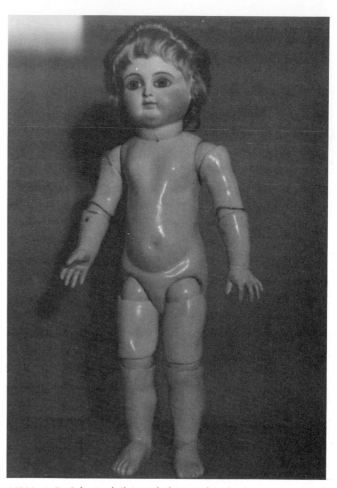

**1450A & B.** Schmitt bébé with bisque head, glass eyes, closed mouth, composition body. Mark: Ill. **1452.** H. 22½ inches. *Courtesy of Hazel Ulseth.*

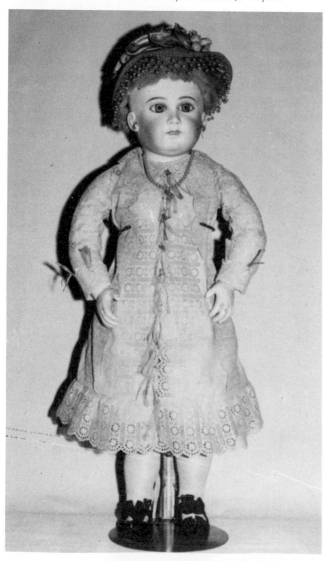

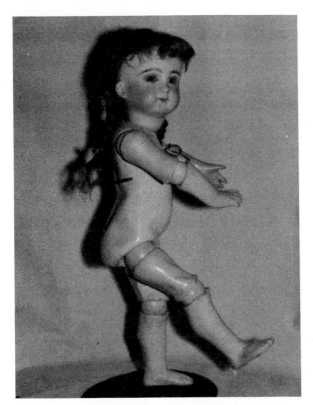

**1451.** Bébé made by Schmitt Fils has bisque head, stationary glass eyes, closed mouth, composition body. Note the length of the feet and the gauntlet-shaped arms, as well as the flat bottom of the torso. Mark on head and torso bottom: Ill. **1452.** H. 16 inches. (See color photograph **C16.**) *Coleman Collection.*

**1452.** Mark used by Schmitt of France on both heads and bodies.

**Schmitt, D.** 1918. Nürnberg, Bavaria. Distributed dolls.

**Schmitz, P. H.** 1893. Paris. Registered in France *Bébé Moderne* as a trademark. This trademark was renewed in 1903 by the *Société Française de Fabrication de Bébés et Jouets.*

**Schmuckler, Heinrich.** 1891–1925+. Liegnitz, Silesia. Doll factory known also as Erste Schlesische Puppenfabrik. (First Silesian Doll Factory); had agents in Berlin, Hamburg, Nürnberg, and New York City.

1895: Specialized in wool dolls and dolls' house dolls, especially for export.

1902: Factory had two hundred employees.

1921: Registered in Germany *Hesli* on the profile of a rabbit as a trademark for dressed dolls.

1923: Specialized in rag dolls and miniature dolls.

1925: German Manufacturers Association represented the firm in New York City. They made dolls' house dolls, rag babies, celluloid dolls, and standing dolls.

**Schnabel, Gebrüder (Bros.).** 1923–25. Neustadt near Coburg, Thür. Made various kinds of dressed dolls.

**Schnabel, Witwe (Widow) Mart.** 1918. Neustadt near Coburg, Thür. Made dressed dolls.

**Schneck, F. J., Co.** 1919–20. New York City. Made *Kutie Kid.*

**Schneegass, Louis, & Co.** 1909–23. Waltershausen, Thür. Manufactured dolls.

1910: Obtained British patent for stamping out at the same time the eye sockets, the mouth, and the hole in the skull for the wig, as the halves of the hollow dolls' heads were molded. Likewise, ball-and-socket jointed bodies were to be made in two halves with stamped-out lugs and pressed sockets. Colored paper was to be used to obviate the use of surface color, which would destroy the sharp outlines obtained by stamping out the items. Finally, an acid bath was to be used to harden and make the members rigid; then, if necessary, they could be sprayed with color.

1911: Obtained a German patent with *Carl Geffers* for improvements in making dolls.

1923: Was issued another German patent for making a doll's body with hollow parts.

**Schneewittchen (Snow White).** 1910–25+. Trademark registered in Germany by *Kley & Hahn* for dolls with ball joints and dolls with kid bodies.

**Schneider.** 1858–96. Paris. 1885–96, Schneider Fils (Sons). Produced and exported dolls and dolls' bodies.

1865–73: Specialized in dolls, porcelain dolls' heads, and dolls' bodies of rose kid and cloth.

1879–90: Advertised jointed dolls and kid bodies in rose and white.

1888: Benoist Schneider, Jr., registered in France an elliptical trademark with the letters "S.F." in it, which must have stood for Schneider Fils. Benoist Schneider, Jr., was listed in directories from 1888 to 1896, except for 1895, when C. Marchal was listed as a successor.

**1453.** Trademark used by Schneider Fils for dolls.

**Schneider, Franz.** 1915–25+. Sonneberg, Thür. Manufactured dolls.

**Schneider, Johannes Georg.** 1895. Lauscha, Thür. Porcelain factory that specialized in dolls' heads.

**Schneider, Otto.** 1918. Sonneberg, Thür. Made dolls.

**Schneider, Robert.** 1909–25+. Sonneberg and Coburg, Thür. Made dolls.

1925: Registered in Germany a trademark with the initials "Rosch//co" on it.

**1454.** Robert Schneider's trademark for dolls.

**Schneider, Rudolf.** 1914–25+. Sonneberg, Thür. Manufactured dolls and dolls' heads of wood and of papier-mâché.

1914: Registered in Germany a trademark with the following words on it: Bébé//tout en bois//entièrement articulé." (Baby//all in wood//entirely articulated.)

**Schneider & Hettich.** 1908–20. Sonneberg, Thür. Manufactured and exported dressed dolls.

**Schnepff, Albert.** 1904–18. Coburg, Thür. Made dolls and doll articles.

1904: Obtained a German patent for a movable doll's head.

1906: Secured a supplement to their 1904 patent in Germany, for heads with moving countenances.

**Schnickel-Fritz.** 1911. Trademark registered in U.S. by *A. Schoenhut* Co. for an all-wood doll with molded hair, open-closed mouth, and teeth; body was fully jointed with springs. Doll was dressed as a baby.

**Schnitzel.** 1915. Doll with the head of a man; had large eyes and large mouth. Copyrighted by *Marguerite Rogers* in U.S.

**Schoen, Michael.** 1919–21. New York City and France. Obtained U.S., French, and British patents for a doll's bust composed of front and rear sections joined along a median line; body parts were usually cast in molds, and were made of a plastic pulp or doughlike batch of wood flour and like ingredients. The dies simulated human form, including head, hair, neck, breast, shoulders, and back, except for the ends of the shoulders. The arms were rotatable into different angular positions and would remain in the desired adjustment; body was stuffed cloth. This patent is reminiscent of the 1884 *Schilling* patent, except that the arms are here connected by springs instead of elastic.

Michael Schoen registered in U.S. in 1920 *Roze Doll* as a trademark for *Federal Doll Manufacturing Co.*

1921: Secured a U.S. design patent for a girl doll dressed in a cape and hood.

**Schoen & Sarkady.** 1912–14. New York City. Manufactured stuffed dolls with American-made composition heads.

1913: Advertised *Hansel, Gretel,* and baby dolls.

1914: Opened a new factory in New Jersey.

**Schoen & Yondorf Co.** 1907(?)–1925+. New York City. Made dolls under the trade name "Sayco."

1922: Ignatz Schoen, formerly with *Schoen Toy Manufacturing Co.*, and Myer Yondorf were partners, and advertised dolls that could walk and talk.

1924: Registered in U.S. the following trademarks, all reported used since 1923: "My Bunny Boy," "Teddy in Boots," "Sayco," *Mistah Sunshine,* and *Jiggles the Clown.* It should be noted that in 1951 Schoen & Yondorf stated in PLAYTHINGS, "Millions and millions of little girls have loved their Sayco dolls since 1907." (See **Trademarks** for possible explanation of this seeming inconsistency.) The new doll in 1924 was the topsy-turvy doll called *Hell'n Maria* or Miss Helen Maria. The other dolls came with composition or cloth legs.

1925: Advertised the Hal Roach *Our Gang* dolls representing Mary, Jackie, Farina, Fatty, and Freckles. They also made some rag dolls with *Drayton*-type faces and some mechanical dolls, including a Creeping Baby and Dancing Katharina.

**Schoen Toy Manufacturing Co.** 1917–22. Manufactured composition dolls and stuffed-body dolls.

1917: Advertised all-composition babies with bent limbs and stuffed-body doll with wigs; price $1.00 and up.

1922: Advertised walking and talking dolls and *Polly-anna.* Ignatz Schoen left the firm to go with *Schoen & Yondorf Co.*

**Schoenau.** See **Schönau.**

**Schoenau, Gebrüder.** 1865–1925+. Hüttensteinach (North Köppelsdorf), Thür. Hard paste porcelain factory. After World War I, they were joined with *Swaine & Co.* For marks, see Ills. 1732, 1733, 1734, 1735, and 1736.

**Schoenau & Hoffmeister.** 1901–25+. Burggrub near Kronach, Bavaria. Also known as Porzellanfabrik Burggrub. A porcelain factory that specialized in dolls' heads and dolls. Their mark is often found on dolls dressed in provincial costumes. The "S H" in their mark (See Ill. 1460) should not be confused with the "S.H." for the better-known Simon & Halbig firm. Schoenau & Hoffmeister used 1906, 1909, 1916, and 1923 (among others) as numbers on their dolls. They may represent the years in which dolls were first produced from these various molds.

**Schoenemann, William C.** 1907. Philadelphia, Pa. Imported dolls.

**Schoenhut, A., & Co.** 1872–1925+. Philadelphia, Pa. Made wooden toys and dolls; distributed by *Strasburger, Pfeiffer & Co., Borgfeldt,* and *A. S. Ferguson.* According to family tradition, Albert Schoenhut's grandfather, Anton, had been a carver of wooden dolls in Württemberg at the end of the 18th century and was succeeded in the business by Albert's father, Frederick Schoenhut. Albert was born around 1850, and came to America when he was seventeen years old. After working for others for a few years, he established his own toy factory in 1872; his first order was from Strasburger, Pfeiffer & Co.

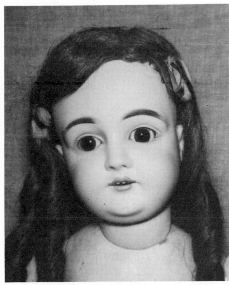

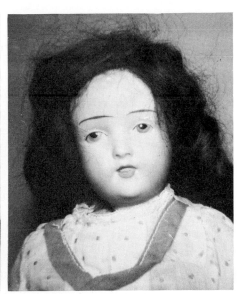

**1455**                 **1456**               **1457**

**1455.** Bisque head made by Schoenau & Hoffmeister, mold #4500, has glass eyes and open mouth with teeth. The ball-jointed composition body is of the Ascher type. Mark: Ill. **1460,** plus an "X" incised on the rear of the crown and "40" stamped in red on the sole of the foot. H. 15½ inches. *Courtesy of Hildred Brinkley.*

**1456.** Schoenau & Hoffmeister bisque-head doll with glass eyes, both hair and painted upper eyelashes, open mouth with

teeth, jointed composition body. Mark on head: Ill. **1461,** except for the addition "½ // Germany." H. 17½ inches. *Courtesy of Alberta Darby.*

**1457.** Schoenau & Hoffmeister bisque head with painted eyes and closed mouth; body is composition. Compare this head with the one in Ill. **1456,** which has the same mold number. Mark: Ill. **1461,** except for size "9/0." H. 12½ inches. *Courtesy of Ollie Leavister.*

**1458A & B.** Oriental bisque head made by Schoenau & Hoffmeister; the bisque is tinted yellow. Glass eyes, open mouth with four teeth; ball-jointed composition body. Mark: "4900 // S. P B H. // 6." The "PB" is in a five-pointed star. H. 12 inches. *Courtesy of Ollie Leavister.*

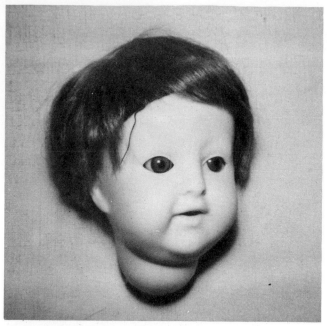

**1459.** Untinted, unpainted bisque head made by Schoenau & Hoffmeister. Porcelain heads were sometimes sold in the white to be decorated by the purchaser. All-white heads were also used for clowns occasionally. Mark: "Porzellanfabrik-Burggrub // 169 // 8/0 // Germany." H. of socket head, 3 inches. *Coleman Collection.*

### SCHOENAU & HOFFMEISTER DOLLS

**1460–1467.** Marks found on dolls made by Schoenau & Hoffmeister at their Porzellanfabrik Burggrub.

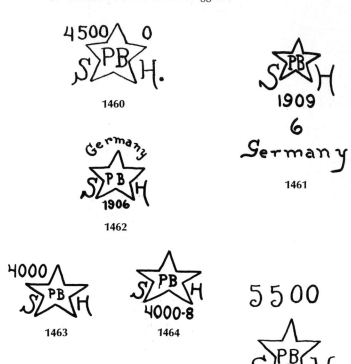

PORZELLAN
FABRIK
BURGGRUB
169
A/0
Germany
1466

Porzellanfabrik-Burggrub
769
8/0
Germany
1467

Probably the first dolls made by Schoenhut were the circus clowns for the *Humpty Dumpty Circus*. These were patented in U.S., Germany, and Britain in 1903, and the Humpty Dumpty Circus was copyrighted in 1903 also. More dolls were added to the circus, namely the *Ring-Master, Lion Tamer, Gent Acrobat, Lady Acrobat,* and *Lady Circus Rider.* These three men were the same doll except for their dress, as were the two women, and were made with either wooden or bisque heads. There were also a *Chinaman, Hobo,* and *Negro Dude.* In 1907 *Max* and *Moritz,* two German boys, were introduced, followed by a *Farmer* and *Milkmaid* in a farm set and *Mary* in a Mary Had a Little Lamb set. The Rolly-Dollys were patented in 1908, made in many different designs in at least five sizes. Another Schoenhut toy, a 53-piece set named "Teddy's Adventures in Africa," was brought out with several new dolls, including a portrait doll of *Teddy Roosevelt.* This was the first spring-jointed doll made by Schoenhut.

In 1909 Albert Schoenhut filed the application for his swivel, spring-jointed dolls, but the patent was not granted until 1911. At the beginning of 1911 imported character dolls constructed entirely of wood were being sold in America, and on May 1, 1911, Schoenhut's sample dolls and price lists were ready for the toy trade. These "All-Wood Perfection Art Dolls," as they were labeled, were all-wood painted in enamel oil colors. Their solid wood heads came either with molded hair (sometimes they were referred to as carved heads; they were carved and then finished by molding under pressure) or with mohair wigs in various colors. They wore two-piece costumes in the latest fashions for boys and girls; one boy wore a gray baseball costume. The feet were made of hardwood with two holes in the soles to enable the doll to stand and pose readily. Among the first molded-hair types was a baby named *Tootsie Wootsie* and a toddler named *Schnickel-Fritz* with a toothy smile. The first advertisements stated that all the dolls were 16 inches

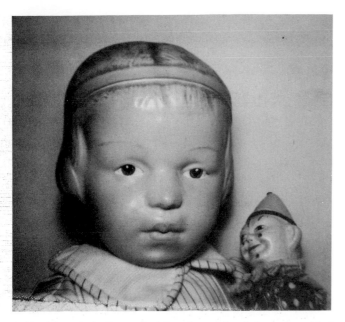

**1468.** Schoenhut all-wood girl with molded hair and molded blue ribbon around head and tied in a small bow in back. Decal mark on upper back: Ill. **1476.** H. 16 inches. *Courtesy of Alberta Darby.*

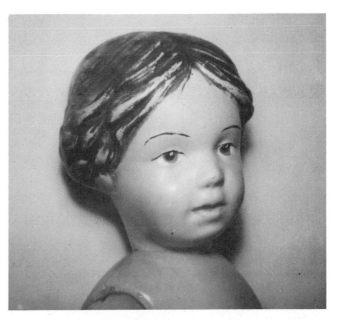

**1469A & B.** All-wood doll by Schoenhut has molded hair with molded pink bow on the back of the head. Mark impressed on upper back of the body: Ill. **1477.** H. 14 inches. *Courtesy of Alberta Darby.*

tall, but later versions of Tootsie Wootsie and Schnickel-Fritz were 15 inches tall. In December, 1911, Schoenhut advertised *Mr. Common People,* a doll based on cartoons by Herbert Johnson. Companies in Germany, England, and France as well as the U.S. all purchased these dolls as soon as they appeared on the market.

1912: Many new models were added, including the molded head with bun on top (#102), the molded head with a ribbon around it, the head with a molded bonnet, and more of those with bobbed hair and short boyish hair. The dolls were sold with only union suits, but costumes especially made for them could be bought separately by dealers. All the dolls were dressed as children or babies, and there were almost as many boys as girls. Dolls came in four sizes, 14, 16, 19, and 21 inches. The price in April was $1.50 and up, but in June it was $2.00 and up. *Montgomery Ward & Co.* advertised Schoenhut dressed dolls with mohair wigs; sizes 14, 16, and 19 inches, price $2.98 to $4.00. Albert Schoenhut died in 1912 and was succeeded by his six sons: Harry E., Gustav A., Theodore C., Albert F., William G., and Otto F.

1913: Infant dolls with curved limbs called "natural arms and legs" appeared for the first time. Harry Edison Schoenhut obtained a copyright on a baby's head from which the infant doll head was modeled. This head carries the copyright symbol ©. Adolph Graziana, an Italian sculptor who had copyrighted numerous statues of children, and a Mr. Leslie had been the artists for the earlier

character dolls, but Harry E. Schoenhut himself was the artist for the infant doll. These infant dolls first came out with molded hair, but a few months later they appeared with a Dutch-style bobbed wig. The new-type heads were put on fully jointed toddler bodies, as well as on bent-limb bodies. They came in two sizes for each type of body. The Schoenhut Character Art dolls were slightly reminiscent of the earlier *Marion Kaulitz* and *Käthe Kruse* art dolls.

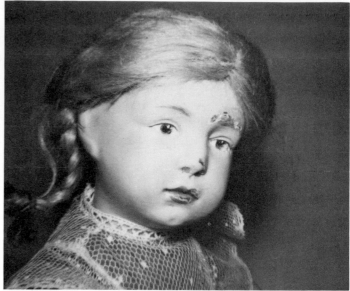

**1470A & B.** Schoenhut all-wood girl with character face, original blonde wig, and original red shoes. H. 16 inches. *Courtesy of Alberta Darby.*

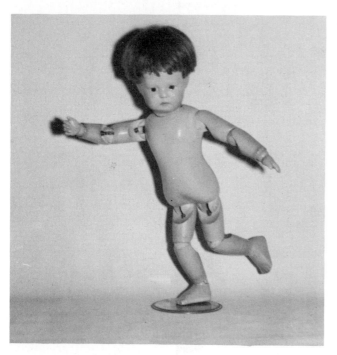

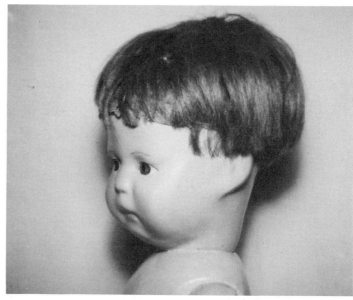

**1471A & B.** Copyrighted head on all-wood Schoenhut doll with metal spring joints. Green decal mark on head: Ill. **1478.** Mark on upper back of body: Ill. **1476.** H. 11 inches. *Courtesy of Alberta Darby.*

1915: The *Doll Face* dolls were introduced; they had stationary eyes of "imitation glass," and curly or bobbed mohair wigs. Came dressed in union suits, with shoes, stockings, and a stand. Dresses for the dolls were made in Schoenhut's own factory, where they also made the mohair wigs in two colors, blonde and tosca. These dolls were made in sizes 14, 16, 19 (19½), and 21 inches and cost $32.00, $38.00, $48.00, and $56.00 doz. wholesale.

By 1915, the model with the center part and molded bun on top of its head had been replaced by a model with center part and a molded ribbon bow on the back of the head, and was given the same number (102). The molded ribbons were painted pink or blue. About 20 percent of the character dolls were boys, far fewer than earlier. These dolls were advertised as 14 (14½), 16 (16½), 19, and 21 inches tall. The molded head dolls

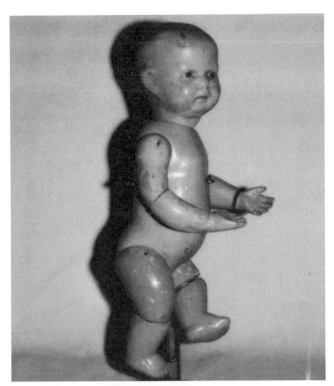

**1472.** Bent-limb all-wood baby made by Schoenhut with copyrighted head. Dowel joinings used at elbow and knee of bent limbs. Note the slight separation on the far leg. Head mark: Ill. **1478.** H. 13 inches. *Courtesy of the International Doll Library Foundation.*

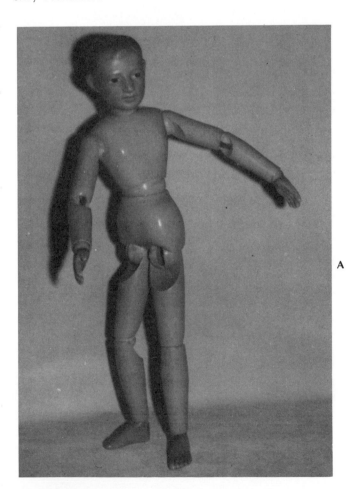

A

cost $24.00 to $45.00 doz. wholesale, those with wigs cost $28.00 to $56.00 doz. wholesale. For the 19-inch size, those with bobbed wigs cost $42.00 doz. wholesale and those with curls cost $48.00 doz. wholesale. A series of older boys usually dressed as athletes—football, baseball, basketball players, etc.—19 inches tall, with jointed waists appeared about this time; they were sometimes called "manikins."

The copyrighted babies came 9 and 11 inches sitting, with bent limbs, and 14 and 17 inches standing, fully jointed. Both the arms and legs of the bent limbs were made with two pieces of wood fitted together at the bend. The 9-inch bent-limb baby cost $28.00 doz. with painted hair and $33.00 doz. wholesale with bobbed wig.

B

**1473A & B.** Schoenhut "Manikin" doll, all wood, completely jointed even to the swivel waist; steel spring joints. Original football outfit includes helmet, nose guard, and football. Ca. 1915. H. 19 inches. (See color photograph **C1.**) Dressed doll: *Courtesy of The Smithsonian Institution.* Undressed doll: *Courtesy of Ollie Leavister.*

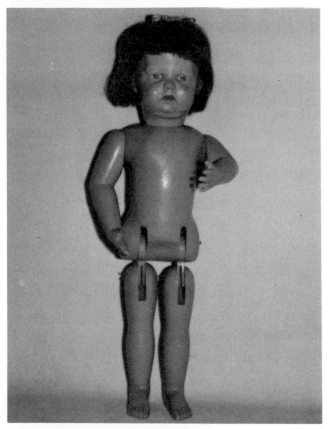

**1474.** Walkable Schoenhut wooden doll with copyrighted head, ca. 1919. Mark on head: Ill. **1478.** Mark on body: Ill. **1477.** H. 16 inches. *Courtesy of Alberta Darby.*

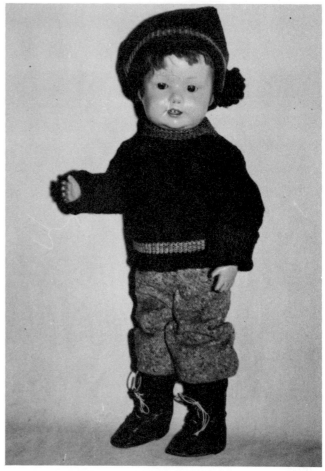

**1475A & B.** Schoenhut all-wood doll with sleeping decal eyes, open mouth with metal teeth. Mark on head: Ill. **1478.** Mark on upper back of body: Ill. **1476.** H. 16 inches. *Courtesy of Alberta Darby.*

1916: Schoenhut enlarged the factory and raised the prices of the dolls.

1917: Appointed Mrs. *Katherine A. Rauser* as couturière for their dolls.

1919: Walkable Doll put on the market May 1. It had a copyrighted baby head. Did not have the customary holes in the soles of its feet, but the soles of its shoes were made at a slight angle to facilitate walking. Came in sizes 11, 14, and 17 inches.

1920: William G. Schoenhut obtained a U.S. patent for making dolls' eyes with a decalcomania film.

1921: Harry E. Schoenhut procured two U.S. patents for movable eyes, which were used chiefly in the copyrighted baby heads and the "Doll Face" heads.

1922: Most of the dolls wore wigs; the two larger sizes in the molded hair dolls seem to have been discontinued, leaving only sizes 14 and 16 inches. The same models as appeared in 1912 were continued, except for the change in 102 noted in 1915. The walking dolls were still made in sizes 11, 14, and 17 inches and cost $34.00 to to $84.50 doz. wholesale. The bent-limb babies with mohair wigs and moving eyes, sizes 13 and 15 inches, cost $64.00 and $80.00 doz. wholesale respectively.

1924: Schoenhut brought out a cheaper line of dolls called Bass-Wood Elastic Dolls, which were jointed with rubber elastic instead of the metal springs. They also brought out new stuffed dolls with Mama voices; these had cloth bodies, wooden heads and hands. The heads were hollowed out as much as possible to make them light in weight; they were copyrighted baby heads with mohair wigs and came in two sizes, 14 and 16 inches. (In 1927 they cost $48.00 and $66.00 doz. wholesale.) The *Bringing Up Father* wooden dolls trademarked by Borgfeldt in 1924 may have been *Maggie and Jiggs* made by Schoenhut.

1925: This was probably the year in which Schoenhut brought out their infant head in wood that closely resembled the *Bye-Lo Baby*.

Catalogs for Schoenhut dolls were published as late as 1930, and they were still advertising the molded head and wigged all-wood dolls, but they were also advertising an all-composition doll made of wood flour. These dolls were 13 inches tall, had molded hair, and sold for $30.00 doz. wholesale. They were jointed at the neck, shoulder, and hips.

After 1911 Schoenhut gave his dolls numbers rather than names, but to facilitate telegraphic orders he also used code words, all beginning with the letter D. For example, the molded cap doll, #106, was coded as "Deadly"; one of the boy dolls was coded as "Dearn."

**Schöffl & Co.** 1922. Berlin. Registered in Germany *Hafraco-Puppe* as a trademark for dolls, especially *Art Dolls*.

**Scholz, Paul.** 1866–73. Vienna. Made papier-mâché dolls.

**Schön, Joseph.** 1886–87. Reichenbach, Silesia. Obtained British, German, and U.S. patents for making dolls' heads of pressed sheet metal in two or more parts, then riveting or soldering them together and coating them with enamel (thus making unbreakable heads). (See also **Bushow & Beck.**)

**Schönau, Arthur.** 1884–1925+. Sonneberg, Thür. Formerly (1882) Bauersachs & Henninger. Manufactured and exported dressed and undressed dolls.

1900: Displayed dolls at the Paris Exposition.

1904: Exhibited dolls at the St. Louis Exposition.

1912: Advertised *Prinzessin Wunderhold, My Cherub, Carmencita*, jointed dolls, and babies of all kinds.

1913: Registered in Germany *Bébé Carmecita* as a trademark for a line of dolls.

1925: Registered in Germany *My Cherub* as a trademark for jointed dolls and babies.

**Schönau, Gebrüder, Swaine & Co.** 1854–97. Köppelsdorf and Hüttensteinach, Thür. Porcelain factory.

**Schönau, Günther.** 1882. Hüttensteinach, Thür. Made dolls.

**Schönhut, W. Fr.** 1890. Hermannstadt Siebenbürgen, Austria. Secured a German patent for the articulation of dolls' bodies.

**1476–1478.** Schoenhut marks. No. **1476** is a decal found on bodies; No. **1477** is impressed on bodies, and No. **1478** is on heads.

**School Boy and School Girl.** 1911. Manufactured by *Seligman & Braun*; price $8.00 doz. wholesale.

**School Boy and School Girl.** 1911–12. Also known as "School Boy with Cap"; made by *Louis Amberg & Son*. Came with composition heads and hands, pink sateen cork-stuffed bodies. Represented a typical American school boy (girl) about eight years old. Boy had various shades of hair and a red or blue cap. Size 22 inches high, price $2.00.

**School Boy and School Girl.** 1911–13. *Horsman Art Dolls* taken from life, representing an average boy (girl) seen on the way to school. Had *Can't Break 'Em* heads, molded hair on the boy, *Rembrandt* style wig on the girl; cloth bodies. The boy wore knickerbockers, shirt, and tie; girl wore a school frock and large blue straw hat.

**School Girl.** 1918. Made by *Jessie McCutcheon Raleigh*; distributed by *Butler Bros*. Wore pink or blue lawn frock and a flannel cape and hood. Size 11½ inches, price $2.60.

**Schools.** There were schools for designing and making dolls in both Sonneberg and Paris. The *Sonneberg Industrial School* (School of Industry), founded in 1851, was subsidized by the state; it functioned for many years. The Paris School of Design and Art Applied to Industry taught the design of dolls in the 1920's.

**Schott, Hermann.** 1918–25+. Schalkau, Thür. Manufactured dolls.

**Schranz & Bieber Co.** 1920. Jersey City, N.J. Made dolls; used the trademark *Esanbe*.

**Schregel & Buckholz (Buchholz).** 1891–97. Berlin. Exported dolls.

**Schreppel, Victor.** 1921. Neustadt near Coburg, Thür. Manufactured and exported dressed dolls.

**Schreyer & Co.** 1923–25+. Nürnberg, Bavaria. Made character dolls of fabric and other materials. Used the trademark *Shuco*. George Borgfeldt and Louis Wolf & Co. distributed their dolls.

**1479.** Trademark used by Schreyer & Co.

**Schrieber, Max.** 1924. Nürnberg, Bavaria. Made dolls.

**Schroeder, Alfred.** 1921–25+. Waltershausen, Thür. Made jointed dolls. In 1921, with *Robert Richter,* he obtained a German patent for stringing dolls with movable heads. A wire attached to a rod or piece of wood across the chest of the doll came up through the neck, and through the two holes in the back of the head, hooking over from the inside to the outside of the head. This patent may explain some of the holes found in the back of the bisque heads.

**Schröter, M.** 1909–20. Coburg, Thür. Made dolls.

**Schubart, Alfred.** 1923–25. Sonneberg, Thür. Manufactured dolls.

**Schubert, Eduard.** 1918–25+. Sonneberg, Thür. Made jointed dolls.

**Schubert, H.** 1891–1925+. Berlin. Manufactured and exported dolls and doll articles.

**Schuetzmeister & Quendt.** 1893–98. Boilstadt, Thür. Showed dolls and dolls' heads at the Chicago Exposition.

**Schultz, Frederick B.** 1892–1917. New York City. Obtained several U.S. patents for stringing dolls.

1893: Springs arranged in the body of the doll were connected by swivels with chains, for holding the parts together.

1894: Improvement in the 1893 patent so that the articulated members could be readily turned without danger of breaking or dislocating the jointed parts.

1917: His third patent was for elastic bands going through the legs or arms and body, with button-like fasteners on the outside of arms and legs. The fasteners had shanks that were hooked over elastic loops. The head hook went over the elastic arm loop. [This method of stringing dolls was often used on pointed torso dolls.]

**Schultze, Carl E.** 1903. New York City. Secured a U.S. design patent for a rag doll that represented his drawings of *Foxy Grandpa.* (See color photograph C7.)

**Schünemann, L.** 1876–1909. Madgeburg, Saxony. Manufactured dolls.

1876: Displayed dressed dolls at the Philadelphia Exhibition and was commended for the fineness and variety of their dresses and their good workmanship.

1891: L. Schünemann listed as successor of L. Hawelka.

**Schurg, Carl.** 1895. Ernstthal near Unterneubrunn, Thür. Made dolls.

**Schürr, Frau Marc.** Ca. 1920. Germany. Designed and made character *Art Dolls.*

**Schutz Marke (Schutzmarke).** German for *Trademark.*

**Schwab, Samuel Michael, Jr.** 1893. New York City. Obtained British and U.S. patents for rag dolls made of two pieces of printed cloth sewed together and stuffed. His patents followed by a few months the more famous patent of Charity Smith, sister-in-law of *Celia Smith.*

**Schwartz, Jos.** 1865–1903. New York City and Brooklyn, N.Y. Made dolls' outfits and distributed dolls. In 1903 Mrs. M. Schwartz was the senior member of the firm.

**Schwartz, Sig., Co.** 1917–22. New York City. Manufactured dolls.

1917: Registered in U.S. *Tynie-Tots* as a trademark.

1919: Advertised *Water Babies* that could float.

1920: Advertised *Joy-Toies* with celluloid heads and cloth bodies. Secured U.S. design patent for a rag doll with circular head and eyes glancing to the side.

**Schwarz.** 1848–1925+. Baltimore, Md.; Boston, Mass.; Philadelphia, Pa.; and New York City. Four Schwarz brothers came from Herford, Germany, to the U.S., and each opened a large toy store: Henry, the eldest, in Baltimore, Richard in Boston, Gustav A. in Philadelphia, and Frederick (F.A.O) in New York City.

The 1903 obituary of Henry Schwarz said: "More than 50 years ago when he started in business only children of wealthy parents had toys that were bought in stores. Doubtful if there was another store in the country devoted to sale of toys. Even dolls sold in very limited quantities. It was a time of home made playthings. Mother made rag dolls while father whittled rude toys with a knife. The German toy trade had already grown to large proportions but in this country, toys from Germany were comparatively unknown. . . . The four brothers controlled the principal cities in the East and were able to buy in large quantities and to control many lines: They dealt almost exclusively in toys of German manufacture. Henry Schwarz was the first man to use a live Santa Claus."

Frederick A. O. Schwarz registered in U.S. his bell and clapper trademark in 1898, which had been used in commerce, especially with England, since 1881.

1913: F.A.O. Schwarz advertised *Babyland Rag Dolls,* an indication that they handled not only German dolls but also American dolls by that time.

1480. G. Schwarz mark found on dolls.

**Schwarz, Frau A.** 1909. Dresden, Saxony. Made dolls.

**Schwarz, Josef.** 1899. Vienna. Made dolls and dolls' heads.

**Schwarzkopf & Fröber.** 1895–1925+. Sonneberg, Thür. Manufactured and exported dolls.

**Schwarzkopf Toy Co.** Before 1904. Baltimore, Md. Charles W. Schwarzkopf, president of this company, went with *Samstag & Hilder* in 1904 and with *Strobel & Wilken* in 1905.

**Schwarzschild, Monroe M.** 1912. New York City. He was

assignee of two U.S. design patents for dolls' heads by *Leon Rees* of London. These heads are believed to have been used on the *Hug Me Kiddies* distributed by *Samstag & Hilder*.

**Schweim, E.** 1893. Charlottenburg near Berlin. Manufactured dolls.

**Schwenk, Emil.** 1922–25+. Mönchröden near Coburg, Thür. Specialized in making small dolls.

**1481.** Mark for dolls of Emil Schwenk.

**Schwerdtfeger & Co.** 1920–25+. Rosswein, Saxony. Manufactured felt dolls.

**Schwerin, S.** 1918–24. Breslau, Silesia. Produced and distributed dolls.

1924: Successors of S. Schwerin registered in Germany a trademark with the word *Hedi* on it.

**Schwickart, Herman.** 1908. New York City. Obtained U.S. patent for sleeping doll's eyes that were removable from the head.

**Schwimmer & Rakovsky.** 1925. Vienna. Made dolls.

**Sckuhr, Günther, Firm.** 1923–25+. Hamburg, Germany. Distributors of dolls.

1924: Registered in Germany *Sckuhrex* as a trademark for dolls.

**Sckuhrex.** 1923–24. Trademark registered in Germany by *Günther Sckuhr Firm* for dolls.

**Scoll, Jacob.** 1923–25. Evanston, Ill. Secured a U.S. design patent for a jointed wooden doll with cylindrical head and torso.

**Scootles.** 1925+. Designed by *Rose O'Neill* (Mrs. Rose O'Neill Wilson); *Joseph Kallus* assisted in the modeling of this doll, as he had of the *Kewpie*. Produced and distributed by *Borgfeldt*. The first Scootles were bisque, manufactured in Germany, and came in three sizes, according to THE ONE ROSE by Rowena Ruggles.

**Scotch Boy.** 1881–82. Trade name of boy doll dressed in Scottish kilt, distributed by *Millikin & Lawley*; price 88¢ to $10.50.

**Scotch Bud Golf Beauty.** 1921. Rag doll made by *Delavan*; price $18.00 doz. wholesale.

**Scotch Highlander.** 1917. Made by the *Standard Doll Co.*; 16 inches high.

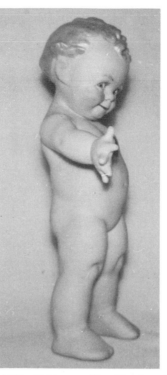

**1482.** All-bisque "Scootles," painted features, moving arms, label on stomach. Mark on foot: Ill. **1484.** H. 8 inches. *Courtesy of Jessica Norman.*

**1483A & B.** All-composition "Scootles," designed by Rose O'Neill, made by Cameo Doll Co. Has molded and painted features, movable head, arms, and legs. This was probably made in the 1930's. H. 15 inches. *Courtesy of Jessica Norman.*

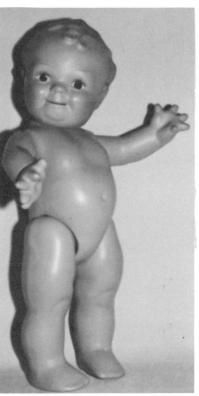

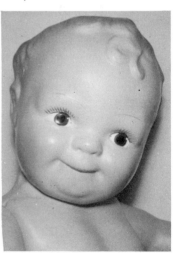

*Scootles*

**1484.** Mark found on "Scootles" doll designed by Rose O'Neill.

**Scotford, Baron Henry.** 1920–22. Atlantic City, N.J. Registered *Photo Doll* in U.S. as a trademark.

**Scott, Frank M.** 1893. Brooklyn, N.Y. With Abner F. Seymour, obtained a U.S. patent for manufacturing dolls' heads of celluloid or other plastic material. The patent papers stated that heads had usually been formed on sand cores, which were removed after baking. The patent proposed to mold the head in two sections, a front and a back. The die and mold were shaped to give the desired configuration. Finally, the two sections were cemented together.

**Scott, William.** 1856. London, Made gutta-percha dolls.

**Scovil, Cora L.** 1922. New York City. Registered *Pin Personalities* in U.S. as a trademark for dolls.

**Screw-Jointed Doll.** One of these was shown in an exhibit ca. 1924. Another one in a present-day collection has arms that move on a screw. It has a bisque head of the type found on lady dolls of the 1870's. The body is cloth over wood; doll is only 11 inches high.

**Scurlock, Lena M.** 1909–11. Kansas City, Mo. Registered in U.S. the words *Mary Alice* and a portrait of Mary Alice Chipps as a trademark for dolls designed to represent this once famous baby.

**Sea Baby // J. T. Kingsley Tarpey.** 1915. Trademark registered in Britain by *Jessie Toler Kingsley Tarpey* for dolls.

**Seam Down Center of Face.** Among the makers of dolls of this kind of construction were *Steiff, Mary McConnell,* and *Marguerite Kaeselau.*

**Seamless Rubber Co.** 1921–23. New Haven, Conn. Registered *Hula Maidens* in U.S. as trademark for dolls.

**Seamless Toy Corp.** 1918–20. New York City. Made all-composition dolls of wood fiber.

1918: Advertised that their dolls were the "lightest weight dolls in the world." Came jointed and with wigs.

1919: Advertised *American Beauty* and *Pretty Polly.*

1920: Advertised walking dolls, *Willie Walker;* jointed composition dolls, Pretty Polly and *Kutie Kid* cotton-stuffed dolls, novelty dolls, socket or shoulder heads with any style of wig and with or without moving eyes. They featured a fully jointed all-composition doll with "enamel bisque finish, guaranteed against cracking or peeling"; came with sleeping eyes, human hair wig, and a white lawn slip; size 21 inches. Their cotton-stuffed baby doll was dressed in white lawn and organdy; size 24 inches.

**Searl, Leon A.** 1914. New York City. Was issued a U.S. design patent for a bisque doll with a large tummy and a *Drayton*-type face.

**Sears, Roebuck & Co.** 1888–1925+. Chicago, Ill. Distributed dolls. In the 20th century one of their exclusive doll lines was *Dainty Dorothy.*

1918: Assignee of U.S. patent for doll joints by *William P. Dun Lany.*

**Sechseck im Ohr (Hexagon in Ear).** 1908. Trademark registered in Germany by *Steiff.*

**Seco.** See **Strauss & Eckhardt Co.**

**Sedard, Eugène.** 1919. Sceaux near Paris. Made dolls and toys of wood and other materials. Registered in France a trademark with the words "Paris Jouets" and "Toujours du Nouveau" and the initials "R-S" on it.

**Séduisant.** See **Le Séduisant.**

**Seeber, Friedrich.** 1891–1912. Vienna. Handled dolls and dolls' heads. In 1891 he was listed as an agent of *Fischer, Naumann & Co.*

**Seeber, Max.** 1922. Suhl, Thür. Secured a German patent for improving the production of dolls and doll parts.

**Seelemann, Fritz.** 1894–1911. Sonneberg, Thür. Made and exported various kinds of dressed dolls.

**Seelig, W.** 1925. London. Registered in Britain *Everrest* as a trademark for dolls.

**Segmented Doll.** The name used in the trade for dolls with many separate segments joined together, such as a ball-jointed doll.

**Sehm.** 1869–1925+. Guben, Brandenburg (Prussia). Made dolls, especially dressed dolls. The factory seems to have been founded by Mathilde Sehm, who was still in charge in 1891; Walter Sehm was in charge from 1897 to 1902, and M. Sehm from 1907 to 1925+.

1907: Advertised jointed bisque dolls and celluloid dolls.

1925: Dressed dolls' house dolls, dressed standing and sitting babies, dressed celluloid dolls, dolls' bodies with voices, and celluloid heads were advertised.

**Seidel, Emory.** 1917. Sculptor who designed faces for *Jessie McCutcheon Raleigh* dolls.

**Seidel, Erhard.** 1923–25. Sonneberg, Thür. Manufactured dressed and undressed dolls.

**Seifert, Eduard Friedrich.** 1891–1920. Eisfeld, Thür. Manufactured and exported dolls; specialized in Harlequin dolls in the 1890's.

1906: Obtained a German patent for a doll with a special facial expression.

**Seifert, Emil.** 1895. Neustadt near Coburg. Manufactured dolls' bodies of kid.

**Seifert, Erich.** 1921. Eisfeld, Thür. Manufactured dolls.

**Seifert, Max.** 1902–25+. Eisfeld, Thür. Manufactured dolls.

**Seifert, Wilhelm.** 1918. Eisfeld, Thür. Made jointed dolls.

**Seigenberg, Leo J.** 1923, Los Angeles, Calif. Together with Harry B. Sher, registered *Tut's "Mummie"* in U.S. as a trademark for dolls. The trademark was to be applied as a printed label on the doll.

**Selchow & Righter.** 1867–1923. New York City. In 1867, E. G. Selchow purchased the toy and doll manufacturing firm of A. B. Swift; a few years later, J. H. Righter became a partner, and the firm was known as E. G. Selchow & Co. until 1883, when it became Selchow & Righter Co., doll jobbers. They used the initials "S & R" in the 1920's.

1900+: Handled the dolls patented by *Edgar Newell,* such as *Merrie Marie.*

1903: Advertised a variety of printed dolls to be cut out and stuffed; price 75¢ for a dozen sheets.

1907: Advertised dolls printed on cloth in fast colors, to be cut out and stuffed; price 5¢, 10¢, and 25¢.

1908: Sole agents for the *Art Fabric Mills.*

1909: Handled dolls made by *Arnold Print Works.* Their Art Fabric Mills dolls were 20 by 27 inches; they included *Tom Thumb, Miss Muffet, Tiny Tim, Dolly Dimple, Boy Blue,* and *Bo Peep.*

1911: Successors to Art Fabric Mills. Advertised *Life Size Dolls,* dressed dolls, jointed dolls, kid-body dolls, celluloid dolls, character dolls, stuffed dolls, crying babies, and doll patterns.

1914: Advertised both imported and domestic dolls, including character babies, with wigs or painted hair.

1916: Advertised that they believed they were the only concern at the time with a stock of imported dolls. These imported dolls were dressed and jointed; price $13.50 to $48.00 doz. wholesale.

1919: Advertised "finest grade imported dolls"; with bisque heads, wigs, moving eyes, eyelashes, wooden bodies, shoes, and stockings; sizes 12, 14, 16, 18, 21, 23, and 25 inches; price $1.50 to $5.50 each.

**Select.** 1923. Trademark registered in France by Société *Bonin et Lefort* for dolls.

**Self Sell Doll Co.** 1924. Brooklyn, N.Y. Made dolls.

**Seligman & Braun.** 1911–13. Hoboken, N.J. Made stuffed and unbreakable dolls.

1911: Advertised that they were the sole manufacturers of American automatically talking, stuffed dolls. Dolls included *Mike, Bridget, School Boy and School Girl,* and Indians, price $4.00 to $24.00.

1912: Made dolls named *Joy* and *Gloom.*

**Selzen.** 1844. Hannover, Prussia. Displayed dolls' bodies at the Berlin Exhibition.

**Semm, Wilhelm.** 1909–18. Hannover, Prussia. Manufactured dolls.

**Senkeisen, Carl.** 1891. Fürth, Bavaria. Manufactured dolls.

**Senkeisen (Sinkeisen), Gebrüder.** 1907–12. Coburg, Thür. Manufactured dolls.

**Senner and Sennerin.** 1911. Line of dolls made by *Steiff;* dolls could stand by themselves; represented Tyrolean singers dressed in herders' costumes.

**Sentimentale.** 1919. Doll copyrighted by *Guglielmo Voccia.*

**Seonblum, Maurice.** 1921–24. France. Obtained two French patents for improving the movement in various directions of dolls' eyes.

**September Morn.** 1914. Trademark registered in U.S. by *Borgfeldt.* It was for an all-bisque doll based on a *Drayton* drawing, and was jointed at shoulders and hips.

**Seraphin.** 1923. Trademark registered in France by *Francis Thieck* and *Jean Born & Co.* for dolls.

**Sergeant Kelly.** See **Sgt. Kelly.**

**Sergel, Wilhelm.** 1916. Waltershausen, Thür. Manufactured dolls.

**Serre & Schneider.** 1864–80. Paris. Made jointed dolls, kid-body dolls, and porcelain heads. In 1904, J. du Serre showed jointed bébés at the St. Louis Exhibition.

**Severn & Long Co.** 1924. New York City. Handled dolls.

**Sèvres (Manufacture Nationale de Sèvres).** 1738–1925+. First at Vincennes, which adjoins Montreuil-sous-Bois, where many doll factories were located; in 1756 the factory was moved to the town of Sèvres, which provided its present name. This is the state porcelain factory, which includes laboratories for studies of the best technical processes. Commercial dolls in series were never made at Sèvres, but French doll companies have used the fa-

**1485.** Sèvres china head with blue painted eyes, reddish-brown wig, and painted eyebrows. *Courtesy of Gladyse Hilsdorf; photograph by Winnie Langley.*

cilities of Sèvres to improve their products. It is believed that the Sèvres artist *Carrier-Belleuse* designed some *Jumeau* bébés. The official United States Report of the 1889 Paris Exposition described the Jumeau doll as follows: "These are French dolls unmistakably. The heads are Sèvres porcelain painted by real artists."

Monsieur Bauduy, director of the Manufacture Nationale de Sèvres, wrote on November 5, 1962: "At this time, 1915–1916, the benefactors of our counsel were the houses of Verlingue at Boulogne-sur-Mer, Lanternier at Limoges, and Coiffe, Couty & Co. at Limoges. . . . Our archives . . . record that a small number of doll heads, modeled after certain heads of children of the 18th and 19th centuries, were made in our workshop in 1917/18 as experiments. It was a question then of creating a 'French doll's head' in opposition to the 'German doll's head' that had inundated the European market before the war of 1914–1918.

"These models, sent to the Museum of Decorative Arts in Paris in 1918, have been kept there, after having been on display in an Exposition of French Art at the Pavillion of Marsan in Paris in 1918." The heads of these dolls were of Sèvres hard paste porcelain covered with a glaze. The eyes, eyebrows, and eyelashes were painted; the cheeks and lips were lightly tinted. The dolls were gowned by famous couturières such as Lanvin. Included was a baby in long dress. The accession date is 1916.

**Seyfarth & Reinhardt.** 1906–25+. Waltershausen, Thür. Manufactured and exported dolls; used bisque heads made by *Ernst Heubach.*

1922: Registered in Germany two trademarks for dolls and doll parts, namely *Elfe* and *My Fairy.*

1923: Registered in Germany "SuR" as a trademark for dolls. Obtained a German patent for improvements in jointed dolls.

1925: Advertised fully jointed dolls, character babies, sitting and standing babies, walking *Mama Dolls,* stuffed Mama baby dolls with porcelain or composition heads.

**Seyfried, Albert.** 1880–83. Philadelphia, Pa. Manufactured dolls' bodies.

**Sgt. Kelly.** 1909. Trade name of a doll made by *Steiff.* Came dressed as a U.S. soldier, in a blue uniform.

**Shanklin Toy Industry Ltd.** 1919. Shanklin, Isle of Wight, Britain. Made dolls that were distributed by *Meakin & Ridgeway* in New York City.

**Sharkey.** See **Private Sharkey.**

**1486 & 1487.** Seyfarth & Reinhardt's marks for dolls.

**Shaver, Elsie.** 1919–20. New York City. Registered two trademarks in U.S., namely *Little Shaver,* to be affixed to the doll with a printed label, and *Olie-Ke-Wob,* to be stamped on the package. She also obtained five design patents in U.S., which appear to be for fabric dolls representing boys, a baby, and a lady.

**Shaw, Eulalia M.** 1920–21. Los Angeles, Calif. Was issued a U.S. design patent for a rag doll.

**Shaw, H. W.** 1920–22. New York City. Manufactured dolls.

**Shaw, Signe Beatrice.** 1923–24. Seattle, Wash. Secured a U.S. design patent for a stockinet doll.

**Shearer, Lillian J.** 1917–18. Denver, Colo. Obtained U.S. patent for a stockinet doll's head made by saturating two layers of stockinet material with a paste of starch and salt. One layer was pressed onto the mold; two strips of muslin formed the chin, and the outer layer of stockinet was molded over it. When dry, both the interior and exterior surfaces were painted. There were four or five coats on the exterior. For stiffening, the inner surface was coated with paraffin and stuffed with cotton. The pivotal joints at limb connections with the body were made with a cotter pin and wooden disk. Loops of yarn served as hair.

**SHEbee.** See **HEbee-SHEbee.**

**Sheen, Alfred, & Wenzel, George.** 1920. Breslau, Silesia. Two Art Academy students who created dolls of plaited straw.

**Shepard, Harry J.** 1919–20. New York City. Was issued a U.S. design patent for a ball-jointed character doll dressed in rags.

**Sheppard, J. B., & Co.** Philadelphia, Pa. Distributed a rag doll with painted features; sizes 18 to 22 inches. These dolls were known as "Sheppard Dolls" or "Philadelphia Babies." This company was in existence at least from 1860 to 1935; it is not known when nor for how long they sold these dolls.

**Sherman, S.** 1920–22. New York City. Manufactured dolls.

**Shield Brand.** 1915–17. Trade name of white rubber dolls made by *Mechanical Rubber Co.*

**Shilling-Patterson, Inga.** 1924–25. Washington, D.C. Registered in U.S. *Inga* as a trademark for dolls.

**Shimizu, Katsuzo.** 1900–25+. Kyoto, Japan. Manufactured dolls.

1900: Won a bronze medal for dolls at the Paris Exposition.

**Shimmikins.** 1920–22. Trademark registered in U.S. by *George F. Berkander.*

**Shinn, Lita, & Shinn, Bessie.** 1916–20. Muskogee, Okla. These sisters obtained a U.S. patent for a hand-painted rag doll. The doll, as described in the patent, was 18 inches tall; the back of the head was circular and 2½

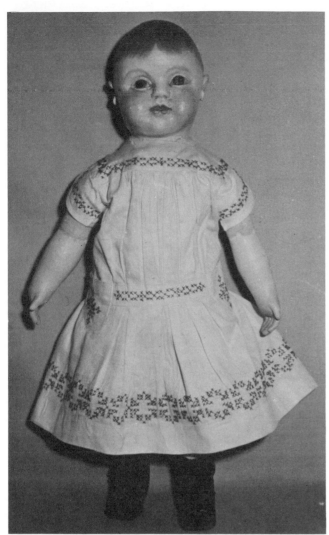

**1488.** Rag doll handled by Sheppard in the early 20th century; painted features and blonde hair. Original white dress has red cross-stitch embroidery; black shoes. *Photograph by Winnie Langley.*

*Patented Shinn Sisters*

**1489.** Mark found on Lita and Bertha Shinn dolls.

inches in diameter, but other sizes could have been made. The doll was of cotton fabric chemically treated to render it washable and waterproof. Each face was an original hand-painted one, with a glazed finish to the eyes, hair, and mouth. The head had a reinforcing neckpiece and a flexible back portion. The doll was stuffed with cotton, and the seams were whip-stitched together. The toes were indicated by stitching, and toenails were painted on the fabric. Dolls made by the Shinn sisters have been found with their name marked on the soles of the feet, but without the painted and stitched toes.

**Shoe Button Sue.** 1920. Rag doll made by *Jessie Mc-Cutcheon Raleigh;* mate to Sam; size 15 inches, price $1.50.

**Shortland, J. W.** 1918. Obtained British patent for eyes that moved in any direction and had movable eyelids.

**Shuco.** See **Schreyer & Co.**

**Shulman & Sons.** 1906–24. New York City. Importers and jobbers; advertised bisque dolls' heads, rubber dolls, and other items. Used slogan "The House of Service."

**1490.** Mark used by Shulman & Sons for dolls.

**Shults, Herbert Otto.** 1918–20. Chicago, Ill. Registered in U.S. a monogram-type trademark for dolls.

**Shy Girl.** 1920. Copyrighted by *Guglielmo Voccia.*

**Shynall Rag Doll Co.** 1913. London. Made dolls.

**Sibley, Lindsay & Curr Co.** 1914. Rochester, N.Y. Advertised *Waltershausen* dolls with eyelashes; sizes 28, 29, 30, and 34 inches.

**Sichert, K.** 1909. Sonneberg. Thür. Made dolls.

**Sichling, Heinrich.** 1876. Nürnberg, Bavaria. Showed dolls at the Philadelphia Exhibition. His dolls, designed for the wholesale trade, were commended for their fine finish, cheapness, and variety.

**Sico.** See **Schmidt, Eduard.**

**Sicoid.** See **Sociètè Industrielle de Celluloid.**

**Sicoïne.** 1919–20. Trade name used by *Société Industrielle de Celluloid* for a noninflammable material for dolls and doll parts. A doll's head with the raised mark "Sicoïne//S^{ie} A//France//2/0" has been found. This socket head has black pupil-less glass eyes and a closed mouth. It is 2¼ inches high. The material resembles a heavy plastic.

**Sicora.** 1925. Trademark registered in Germany by *Eduard Schmidt* for dolls.

**Sieben, Henry.** 1917. Kansas City, Mo. Registered in U.S. *Snow White* as a trademark for dolls.

**Siebeneicher, August.** 1891–1921. Eisfeld, Thür. Rudolph Förster was successor from 1902–21. Produced dressed dolls, wax dolls, *nankeen* dolls, and jointed dolls.

**Siegel, August.** 1895–1921. Neufang and Sonneberg, Thür. Manufactured dolls, especially kid-body dolls.

**Siegel, Ernst.** 1909. Neustadt near Coburg, Thür. Made dolls.

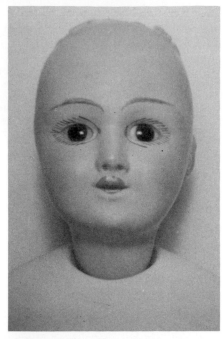

1491A. "Sicoïne" socket head made by Société Industrielle de Celluloid in France ca. 1920. The shoulder plate is spurious. Raised mark: Ill. **1491B.** H. of head only, 2¼ inches. *Courtesy of Eleanor Jean Carter.*

**1491B.** "Sicoïne" mark found on celluloid dolls.

**1492.** "Siegfried," name found on infant's head.

Siegfried
made in Germany
9

**Siegfried.** Name found on the bisque head of an infant-type doll similar to *Bye-Lo-Baby.*

**Siewert, Klara.** Ca. 1920. Germany. Designed and made character *Art Dolls.*

**Silberfeld, Hélène.** 1921–23. New York City. Citizen of Belgium; was issued a U.S. design patent for a long-limbed flapper doll with bobbed straight hair and wearing short plaid skirt, white blouse, and tam. (See also **Sardeau, Hélène.**)

**Silesia Doll Bodies.** 1901. Advertised by *Montgomery Ward & Co.* These were flesh-colored cloth stuffed with wool; had bisque forearms and hands. A cut shows a double row of stitching down the front and a circlet at the knee with a double row of stitching.

**Silly Sally.** 1921. Trade name for one of the *Chase* stockinet rag dolls.

**Silver Doll & Toy Manufacturing Co.** 1923–24. New York City. Made "Silver" dolls' heads for *Mama Dolls* in all popular sizes.

**Silver Doll Co.** 1924. U.S. Handled dolls that sold from 10¢ to $1.00.

**Silverman, Carl.** 1913–25+. New York City. Worked for *B. Illfelder* from 1896–1913. Imported and distributed dolls.

1914: Advertised *Blue Ribbon* jointed dolls, bisque character babies, kid-body dolls, "unbreakable" dolls, dolls' heads, and celluloid dolls. He imported dolls from Sonneberg, Nürnberg, Berlin, Paris, London, and Vienna.

1925: Handled Blue Ribbon dolls, *Lehmann's* mechanical toys, and German dolls that he advertised as notable for quality and diversity.

**Silverman, Katherine.** 1915. Chicago, Ill. Also did business in New York City. Obtained a U.S. copyright, a design patent, and registered in U.S. "Maiden America" as a trademark for a doll to be made by the *Maiden Toy Co.*

**Silverman, M., & Son.** 1919–24. Philadelphia, Pa. Registered in U.S. three trademarks for dolls, using *My Beauty* and the initials "SMS" intertwined.

**Simmons, Bessie A.** 1915–16. Oklahoma City, Okla. Registered in U.S. *Grosmutter* as a trademark for dolls.

**Simon, G.** 1867. Hildburghausen, Thür. Displayed dolls at the Paris Exposition.

**Simon, Gebrüder L. H.** 1907–11. Coburg, Thür. Made and exported dolls.

**Simon, L. H., Gebrüder (Bros.).** 1895–1920. Coburg, Thür. Manufactured and exported dolls of various kinds, including dressed and undressed dolls. They had a London office until 1914.

**Simon, Max.** 1913–25+. Coburg, Thür. Manufactured dolls. In 1913 he had a London office.

**Simon, N.** Ca. 1900. Berlin. Made dolls' bodies.

**Simon, P.** See **Roulez & P. Simon.**

**Simon, Wilhelm, & Co.** 1846–1910. Hildburghausen, Thür. A porcelain factory; manufactured dolls.

**Simon & Halbig.** Ca. 1870's–1925+. Gräfenhain near Ohrdruf, Thür. A porcelain factory that specialized in dolls' heads. They also made all-bisque dolls, celluloid and composition dolls' heads. Early documentation for Simon & Halbig is very elusive. No proof has been found of a connection with *P. Simon* of Paris who handled German porcelain heads. Some of the Simon & Halbig heads are of untinted bisque with molded hairdos that suggest the 1870's or baldhead lady types that were also popular then. These are shoulder heads with the mark on the front of the shoulder (see Ill. 1528); the number varies with the size. The *Edison* dolls had bisque heads made by two factories in Germany, but all the Edison dolls examined thus far have "S. H." heads. These Edison heads were made as early as 1889, and they provide the first documented date found as yet for Simon & Halbig heads. Simon & Halbig were described by Edison as a "large maker" of bisque heads in 1889.

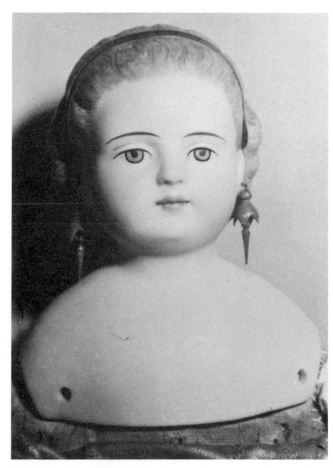

1493. German nurse made by Simon & Halbig has bisque shoulder head and arms, cloth body, molded and painted hair and features, pierced ears. Nurse holds a china "Frozen Charlotte" baby dressed in long clothes. All clothes original. Mark on front shoulder: "S 4 H." H. 15 inches. *Courtesy of The Smithsonian Institution.*

1494. Simon & Halbig bisque shoulder head with molded blonde hair, brush marks around the face, black painted band across the top of the head and curls in back, painted eyes, closed mouth, pierced ears. Mark on front shoulder: "S 7 H." *Photograph by Winnie Langley.*

**1495A & B.** Doll with bisque head, arms, and legs; shoulder head has glass eyes, blonde wig, closed mouth; arms are bent at the elbows. Cloth body. Head marked on shoulder "S 3/0 H" for Simon & Halbig. H. 7½ inches. *Courtesy of Kit Robbins.*

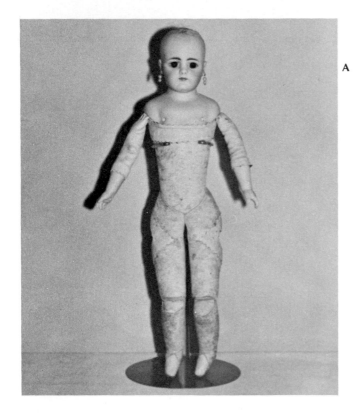

A

**1496A & B.** Bisque Simon & Halbig shoulder head with solid crown, glass eyes, wig, pierced ears. Gusset-jointed kid body has lower arms of bisque. Mark: Ill. **1532.** H. 13 inches. *Courtesy of Ollie Leavister.*

B

Simon & Halbig obtained numerous patents for dolls' eyes.

1890: They were issued two German patents for movable eyes. The first one was for manually moving eyelids with eyelashes by means of a wire with a loop at the end; the wire extended through the back of the doll's head. To close the eyes, the wire was pushed up; it was pulled down, to open them. Later in 1890, a similar patent was

obtained for a wire with a handle at the back of the neck under the hair to manipulate the eyeballs to the right or left.

1891 and 1893: Obtained supplemental German patents to improve eye movements.

1895: Carl Halbig was listed as the owner; this suggests that Simon had either died or retired. Halbig advertised dolls' heads and *bathing children.*

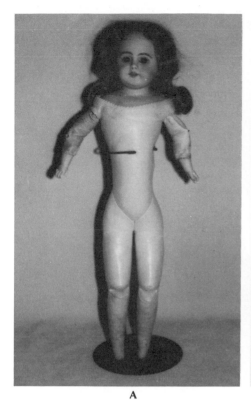

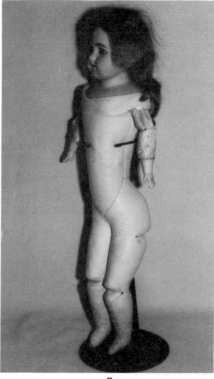

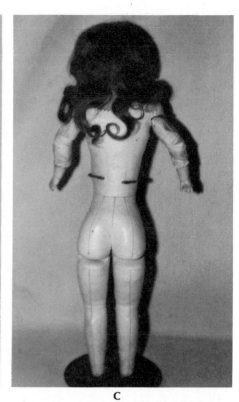

A                                    B                                    C

**1497A, B, C, & D.** Simon & Halbig bisque shoulder head has brown glass eyes, wig, pierced ears, open mouth with teeth. Gusset- or double-jointed kid body; bisque lower arms. Note the scalloped edge of the kid around the neck. This doll is known to have been in existence in the 1880's. Marked on back shoulder: "S 8 H 1010. DEP." H. 21 inches. *Coleman Collection.*

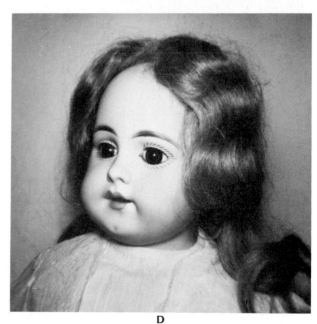

D

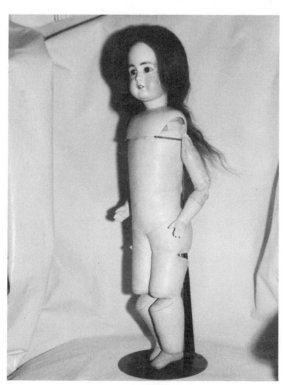

1498

**1498.** Simon & Halbig bisque swivel head and bisque shoulder plate; brown glass eyes, wig, open crown, pierced ears, open mouth with one lower and two upper teeth (all teeth square in shape). Gusset-jointed kid body has bisque lower arms. Mark on back of head: Ill. **1520.** Mark on back of shoulder plate: Ill. **1521.** H. 22 inches. *Coleman Collection.*

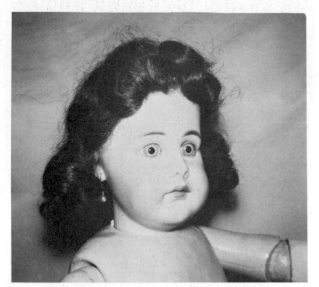

**1499.** Bisque head made by Simon & Halbig from the same mold, #949, as the head shown in Ill. **1498.** This head does not have a shoulder plate and is on a jointed composition body. It has a bisque crown under the wig, with holes through which elastic was run for tying the head to the body. Stationary blue glass eyes, closed mouth, pierced ears. Size 14. H. 25½ inches. *Courtesy of Hildred Brinkley.*

**1500.** Bisque-head doll with glass sleeping eyes, open mouth with teeth, hair wig arranged in two braids, ball-jointed composition body (wrists not jointed). Doll wears original costume of Bern, Switzerland, with stomacher trimmed with a beaded design and metal disks and chains. Head with Simon & Halbig mark: "1079–2 // DEP. // S H // Germany." H. 11½ inches. *Coleman Collection.*

**1501.** Bisque head made by Simon & Halbig with sleeping glass eyes, open mouth with teeth. Composition body has molded shoes. Original costume of Bern, Switzerland, similar to but not as elaborate as the costume shown in Ill. **1500.** Mark: Ill. **1522.** H. 7 inches. *Courtesy of Jessica Norman.*

1903: Obtained French and German patents for moving eyes.

1905: Carl Halbig secured a U.S. patent for eye movement, both to open and shut the eyes as well as to move them to left and right; all movements were effected by a single weight. Simon & Halbig, manufacturers of dolls' heads and all-bisque dolls, registered "S & H" as their trademark in Germany. This was shortly after *Schoenau & Hoffmeister* began to use "S H" also on dolls' heads. It seems logical that Simon & Halbig heads without the ampersand were made before this date.

1907: *Bawo & Dotter* advertised "Best quality goods with A 1 heads: Simon & Halbig make."

1914: Obtained another German patent for moving eyeballs. Registered in Germany the trademark of a picture of a seated figure. They described themselves as being a porcelain factory that made dolls' heads, chinaware, toys, celluloid, and woodenware.

Simon & Halbig heads were used by many doll makers, including *Kämmer & Reinhardt, Heinrich Handwerck, C. M. Bergmann, Cuno & Otto Dressel* (mold #1349 and *Jutta*), *Bawo & Dotter, Hamburger & Co. (Old Glory), Fleischmann & Blödel (Eden Bébé* and Simon & Halbig found on doll's head), *Gimbel Bros.* (mold #550) and "G. B.," which might stand for *George Borgfeldt.*

**1502.** Simon & Halbig doll dressed in original Scottish outfit. Bisque head has brown glass sleeping eyes, blonde wig, open mouth with four teeth, pierced ears. Jointed composition body. Mark: "S & H 1079 // 5½ // DEP." H. 14½ inches. *Courtesy of The Smithsonian Institution.*

Simon & Halbig heads have been found on bodies marked *Wislizenus, Eekhoff, Jumeau, Roullet & Decamps, Nadaud, Au Nain Bleu,* and on swimming "Ondine" dolls made by a member of the Martin family in the 20th century.

Most of the heads have a number that identifies the mold, except for the very early Simon & Halbig heads, the heads with names incised on them, and some of the heads with the names of other makers on them. The earliest socket-head number found to date seems to be 719. Numbers ending in "9" are found most frequently— among them 719, 739, 759, 909, 939, 949, 1009, 1039, 1059, 1079, 1129, 1159, 1199, 1249, 1269, 1279, 1299, 1329, 1349. About one third of the heads bear the number 1079, a popular dolly-faced version that was used for many years. Heads with 1039 are found on Jumeau bodies and have the *Wimpern* mark. The number 1249 was used on the *Santa* line of dolls, which were first made in 1900. Socket heads were sometimes used on bisque shoulder plates, but the plates usually had a different mold number from that found on the head—e.g., the head of mold #949 is frequently found on shoulder plate #941. Head #1199 has Burmese features.

Contemporaneously a line of shoulder heads without swivel necks was also made by Simon & Halbig; the line included mold numbers 950, 970, 1010, 1040, 1080, 1160, 1250, 1260. It is known that the 1010 head was made as early as the 1880's. The 1160 was advertised as late as 1916 with rococo or Louis XIV style of wigs. It came in various small sizes, including 1¼ and 2 inches.

Most of the Kämmer & Reinhardt character heads were made by Simon & Halbig, and carry both initials or names. Similar types of character heads made by Simon & Halbig carry mold numbers ranging from 120 to 600 but without the Kämmer & Reinhardt mark. These dolls were probably made after 1909.

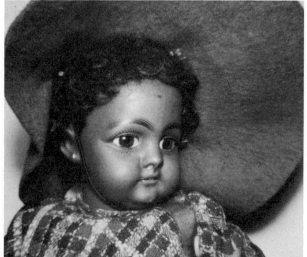

**1503.** Brown bisque head with short curly black-haired wig, brown glass eyes, open mouth with teeth. The nose dots are light-colored instead of the usual red. Brown composition body. Simon & Halbig head marked: "S & H 759 DEP." H. 15 inches. *Courtesy of Mary Dawson.*

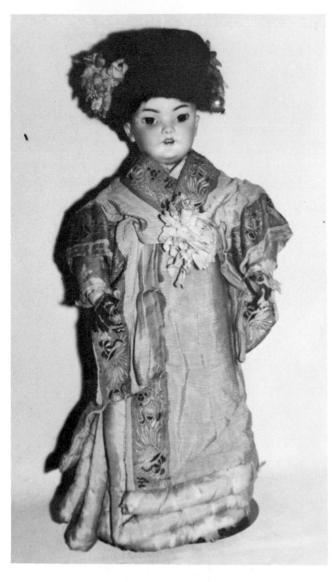

**1504.** Simon & Halbig Japanese bisque-headed doll. Glass almond-shaped eyes with openings slit on the diagonal. The decorated wig is original. Ball-jointed tan-colored composition body; original costume. Compare this head with the one in Ill. **1505.** Mark: "S H 1129 // Germany // DEP. // 9." H. 23 inches. *Courtesy of Eunice Althouse.*

Simon & Halbig used various methods of incising their name and/or initials on dolls' heads—for example, S H 8; S 8 H; S & H 8; Simon & Halbig; Halbig; Simon & Halbig with "S & H" below it, and still other ways. The same mold number may be found with various styles of marking initials or names.

Most Simon & Halbig heads carry a size number as well as a mold number. Those made for Kämmer & Reinhardt seem to represent the height of the doll in centimeters. The heads marked "Heinrich Handwerck" and "Simon & Halbig" appear to follow an entirely different pattern. Sizes 2½ and 3 have been found on 21-inch dolls, size 5 on a 28-inch doll, and size 6½ on a 31-inch doll. Some of the Simon & Halbig size patterns seem to follow those used by Jumeau and other French manufacturers. Apparently the size mark was determined by the doll maker who purchased the head from Simon & Halbig. One series with character faces has a roman numeral size mark; these are definitely character faces, but have pierced ears, which suggests an early date for character dolls. (See Ill. 1514.)

Many dolls with bodies made and distributed by various French doll companies have Simon & Halbig heads, as noted above. Unfortunately, records have not been found as yet showing how long the French used Simon & Halbig heads for their dolls. It is known that Simon & Halbig made bisque heads of the early type found on lady dolls. (See color photographs C19, C20, C24.)

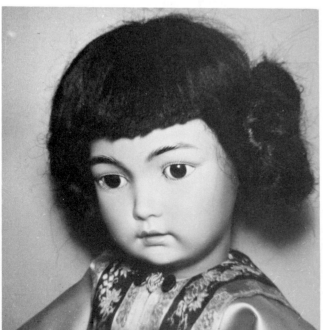

**1505.** Oriental flesh-tinted bisque head made by Simon & Halbig, model #1329, size 8. Has brown glass sleeping eyes, molded eyebrows, open mouth with four teeth, black mohair wig. Ball-jointed composition body. Note the differences from the head shown in Ill. **1504.** H. 21 inches. *Courtesy of Ollie Leavister.*

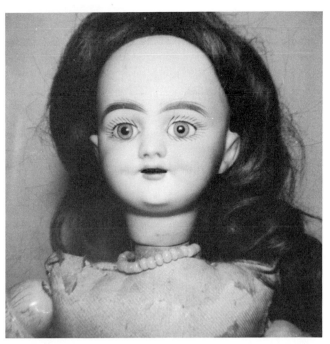

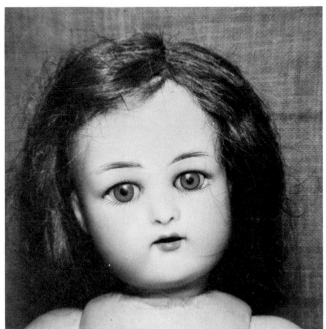

**1506.** Simon & Halbig bisque head marked "S H 1059 DEP. // 2." Blue glass eyes, open mouth with four upper teeth; flat neck joint; unusual body of cloth, kid, wood, and composition. H. 11 inches. *Courtesy of Lester & Alice Grinnings.*

**1508.** Simon & Halbig bisque head with character face, blue glass eyes, open mouth with teeth; wig. Bent-limb composition baby body. Mark: Ill. **1524.** H. 10 inches. *Courtesy of May Maurer.*

**1507A & B.** Unusual sleeping-eyed doll head made by Simon & Halbig. The eye mechanism is controlled by pull strings at the nape of the neck. The doll has glass eyes, wig, pierced ears, bisque socket head on ball-jointed composition body. Mark: Ill. **1523.** H. 13 inches. *Courtesy of Dorothy Annunziato.*

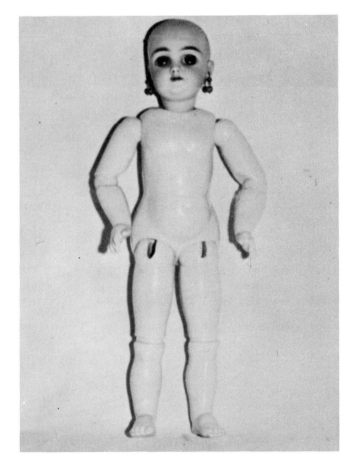

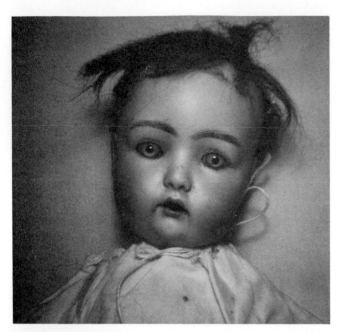

**1509.** Doll produced by Simon & Halbig, Kämmer & Reinhardt, and Cuno & Otto Dressel, as indicated by the marks on head and body (see Ills. **956** and **488**). Bisque head with sleeping eyes, wig, open mouth with four porcelain teeth; composition body. H. 12½ inches. *Courtesy of Hildred Brinkley.*

**1511.** Simon & Halbig bisque head with rococo style wig, cloth body with bisque lower limbs. Mark: Ill. **1525.** H. 11 inches. H. of shoulder head, 2½ inches. *Courtesy of Jessica Norman.*

**1510.** Doll made by Kämmer & Reinhardt using a Simon & Halbig bisque head with blue glass eyes, molded eyebrows, open mouth with teeth. Body is ball-jointed composition. Original dress. Doll is dated by The Smithsonian Institution as about 1900. H. 28 inches. *Courtesy of The Smithsonian Institution.*

1513

1514

**1512.** Bisque shoulder head, made by Simon & Halbig from mold #1160, has the wig arranged in the rococo style usually found on this model; stationary glass eyes. The cloth body has bisque limbs, molded ribbed stockings, and high boots with heels. Original silk dress. H. 8¼ inches. *Courtesy of The Smithsonian Institution.*

**1513.** Bisque head made by Simon & Halbig has smiling countenance, glass eyes, wig. Head marked: "S & H // 1388." *Courtesy of Margaret Whitton; photograph by Winnie Langley.*

**1514.** Doll with bisque head marked "SIMON & HALBIG // S & H // IV." Pensive character face, glass eyes, wig, closed mouth. Body is jointed composition. A smaller but similar doll is marked with "II," which suggested that the Roman numeral "IV" may be a size mark. H. 17 inches. *Coleman Collection.*

**1515.** Bisque socket head marked "SIMON & HALBIG // G B // A" has brown glass sleeping eyes, hair upper eyelashes, painted lower lashes, open mouth with four teeth and tongue. The "G B" may stand for George Borgfeldt, and the "A" for the size. Mark: Ill. **1526.** H. of socket head, 5½ inches. *Courtesy of Dorothy Annunziato.*

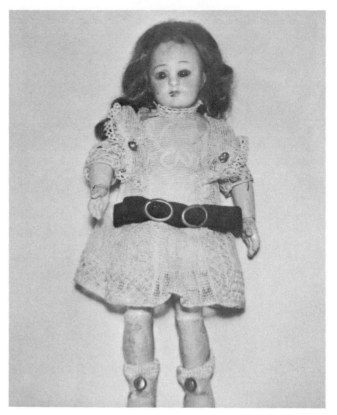

**1516.** Simon & Halbig bisque head with glass eyes and wig is on a jointed composition body. Doll wears her original chemise of sized gauze and lace. Mark: Ill. **1527.** *Courtesy of Jessica Norman.*

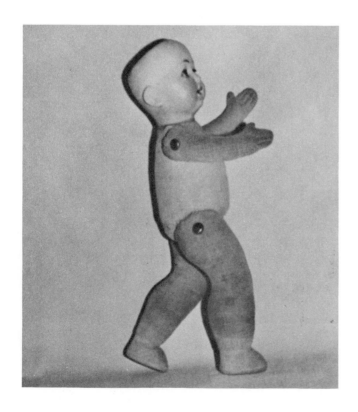

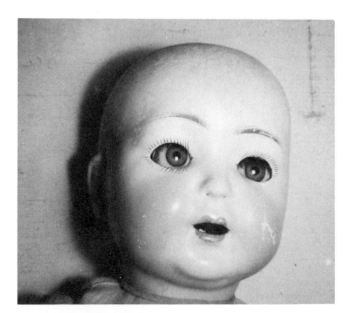

**1517A & B.** Plaster composition socket head marked "SIMON & HALBIG // 1616 // Made in Germany." Pink muslin torso and pink velvet limbs. H. 12 inches. *Courtesy of Edna J. Greehy.*

**1518.** Negro bisque socket head made by Simon & Halbig has glass eyes, open mouth with two teeth, pierced ears; on a jointed composition body. Doll is dressed in contemporary clothes. Head is marked "S5H 739 DEP." The 739 mold number is usually found on Negro dolls. H. 13¼ inches. *Courtesy of The Smithsonian Institution.*

**1519–1538.** Marks found on dolls with heads made by Simon & Halbig. No. **1519** is the trademark of Simon & Halbig.

S & H
**1519**

S 11 H
949
**1520**

S 10 H 941
**1521**

HALBIG
K ✡ R
Germany
17
**1522**

S H 1039
4 DEP
**1523**

1299
SIMON & HALBIG
3½
**1524**

S & H
1160 - 2/0
**1525**

SIMON & HALBIG
G B

A
**1526**

1008
SIMON & HALBIG
S & H
Germany
3/0
**1527**

S 8 H
**1528**

S 11 H 719 DEP
**1529**

S 14 H
949
**1530**

S 13 H
949
**1531**

S H 3½
950
**1532**

St
S & H 1009
**1533**

S H 1069 DEP
2
**1534**

1079-2
DEP
S H
Germany
**1535**

SIMON & HALBIG
**1536**

C.M. BERGMANN
SIMON & HALBIG
13½
**1537**

S & H
WSK 4/0
**1538**

**Simonin-Cuny.** 1900. Paris. Advertised bébés of all kinds, dressed and undressed, including bébés with composition heads.

**Simonne, F.** 1847–78. Paris. Made dolls and from 1863 on; also made dressed bébés. Kid-body lady dolls with bisque heads have been found with the turquoise blue ink stamp of Simonne on their chest.

1867: Won Honorable Mention for his display of mechanical dolls at the Paris Exposition.

1878: Showed dolls and bébés at the Paris Exposition. A *Jumeau* bébé with body marked "Medaille d'Or" also has a Simonne label, which suggests that he was in business after 1878. (See color photograph C24.)

**1539.** Lady doll handled by Simonne has bisque turning head and shoulder plate, glass eyes, kid body with bisque arms. Mark stamped on body: Ill. **1541.** *Courtesy of Gladyse Hilsdorf; photograph by Winnie Langley.*

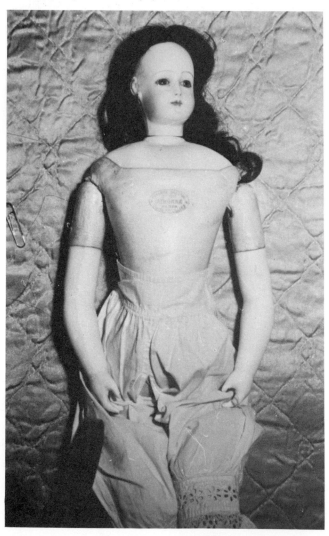

1540 A

1540 B

**Simonot, Claude Joseph.** 1892–93. Paris. Obtained patents in France, Germany, Britain, U.S., Austria, Italy, and Spain for a doll that could walk, without clockwork mechanism, and turn its head as it walked. He assigned his patent rights to *Fleischmann & Blödel* of Fürth.

**Simplex Stuffed Toy Manufacturing Co.** 1925. New York City. Manufactured *Eagle Brand Dolls* under the supervision of Mrs. *Joseph G. Kaempfer*. Their dolls, with sleeping eyes and hair lashes, cost $39.00 doz. wholesale; dolls representing a week-old infant cost $15.00 doz. wholesale.

**Simpson, Robert, Co.** 1918. Toronto, Canada. Distributed dolls.

**Simpson-Crawford Co.** 1906. New York City. Advertised 10,000 German dolls with dresses for 25¢ to $3.50 each, and dolls' heads of bisque, metal, or celluloid for 50¢.

**Sindall, Frederick.** 1895–1905. London. Made rag dolls and exported them.

**Singer Bros.** 1921. New York City. Distributed dolls.

**Singleton, James N. G.** 1911. Orlando, Fla. Registered in U.S. *Sixth Race* as a trademark for dolls.

**SIR.** 1919–20. Trademark registered in U.S. by *Sigmund I. Rothschild,* to be affixed to dolls with a printed label.

**1540A, B, & C.** Bisque head "13" on doll with Simonne sticker in blue (see Ill. **1541**). Stamped in blue on the body is "JUMEAU // MEDAILLE D'OR // PARIS." These unmarked "long-faced" heads are often found on Jumeau bodies. The knee ball is attached to the upper part of the leg rather than the lower part, as is usual. The big toe is separated. Original clothes consist of turquoise blue silk brocade dress trimmed with ecru lace and gray-blue ribbon tabs in tiers down the front; dust ruffle, long slip, half slip, and split drawers. Shoes are marked with "T" in a square. H. 26 inches. (See color photograph **C24**.) *Courtesy of Lester & Alice Grinnings.*

C

**Siren.** 1898. Trade name for a dressed doll with bisque head and open mouth; distributed by *W. A. Cissna & Co.* Size 18 inches, price $6.50.

**Siruguet.** 1829. Paris. Handled dolls.

**Sis.** 1924. One of the *Madame Hendren* line of dolls made by *Averill Manufacturing Co.* and registered in U.S. as a trademark by them. It was advertised as being covered by a *Grace G. Drayton* copyright; price $1.00 and up.

**Sis Hopkins.** 1911–12. Made by *Louis Amberg & Son* with consent of Rose Melville, the actress who had played the part of Sis Hopkins for thirteen years. The first plastic model was copyrighted in 1911 by Louis Amberg & Son. Then, in 1912, they copyrighted it again, naming the artist as *Jeno Juszko*. It was described as "Head of laughing child with hair combed back and two braids emanating from sides of head, front comb, ribbons, eyes coquettishly to one side and teeth clearly showing."

1912: Came in two styles, one with the tongue sticking out and the other with upper and lower teeth showing in a broad grin; movable head with eyes to side; ribbons in pigtails; cork-filled pink sateen body with or without composition arms. Doll was dressed in pink and white or blue and white checked gingham dress with yellow edging at the bottom of the skirt; plaid stockings.

**Sischo, Kittie F.** 1922–23. Santa Monica, Calif. Registered in U.S. *Tumblin' Tim* as a trademark for dolls.

**Sister.** 1912. Composition-headed doll made by *Gund Manufacturing Co.*

**Sister, Model No. 4.** 1911. Copyrighted by *Louis Amberg & Son;* came with big ribbon bow on the left front of the head.

**Sister to Mary Elizabeth.** 1912. Copyrighted by *Elizabeth Lesser.* Copyright model was of wax.

**Sixth Race.** 1911. Trademark registered in U.S. by *James Singleton.*

**1541.** Simonne mark found on bodies.

## SIS HOPKINS

**1542.** "Sis Hopkins" mark used by Louis Amberg.

**Sizes.** Dolls vary in size from tiny ones of less than a half-inch to those larger than life-size. Dolls 30 inches in height or more are usually called "Show Dolls." These may be used for either display purposes or play. Sizes are generally denoted by numbers, but in a few cases are indicated by letters. The number patterns often vary considerably even for the same company. For example, *Lacmann's* bodies with the same number are not necessarily the same size. Jumeau heads with the same number are not always on dolls of the same size. There must have been different series, but sufficient samples have not yet been studied to identify these. In 1924 a doll hospital advertised: "We can fit any head by simply comparing numbers." Either they were overly boastful, or the series were a function of time and changes took place only over a long period. (See **Jumeau, Kestner,** and **Simon & Halbig** for further information on size series.)

During most of the 19th century, the head was often relatively small compared with the height of the body —with some exceptions, especially for *Frozen Charlottes* and *Motschmann*-type dolls. This characteristic may have been due to the fact that heads were usually of costlier material than bodies. Infant dolls were often dressed in extremely long dresses. Around 1900 the trend changed, and the tendency was to make the head too large, proportionately. PLAYTHINGS in 1913 reported: "We used to get dolls with enormous heads and tiny bodies, real baby dolls were the worst offenders. It is still noticeable in some character dolls. Latest models show improvement."

Since ceramic heads skrink when fired, the smaller sizes often were made from molds taken from the next larger size; this accounts for the loss of detail as the head was reduced in size. However, this practice was not always followed in the better-grade dolls. In 1907 PLAYTHINGS described the making of baby faces: "Separate models must be used for each size as it will not do to enlarge or diminish from the same model to produce larger or smaller heads."

**Skating Charlotte.** 1915–16. Trademark in U.S. by *Borgfeldt.*

**Skeezix.** 1922–25+. One of the *Gasoline Alley* dolls created by *Frank O. King* and produced by *Live Long Toys.* Skeezix came as a baby and as a little boy. The name was registered in U.S. as a trademark, and a U.S. design patent was obtained for the doll. It came in several materials; all-bisque versions were 2¾ inches, 6½ inches, and probably other sizes; the rag doll made of oilcloth was marked "—King—//SKEEZIX//REG. U.S. PAT. OFF.//PAT. APPLIED FOR"; size was 13½ inches.

**Skeleton Process.** 1911. Patent process used by *Ideal Novelty & Toy Co.* to make composition character dolls.

**Skinney.** 1915. Trade name for doll made by *Horsman;* it represented the character of that name in Gene Carr's LADY BOUNTIFUL cartoon series published in the NEW YORK WORLD.

**Skipper, The.** 1922–23. Trademark registered in Germany by *Borgfeldt* of Berlin, for dolls.

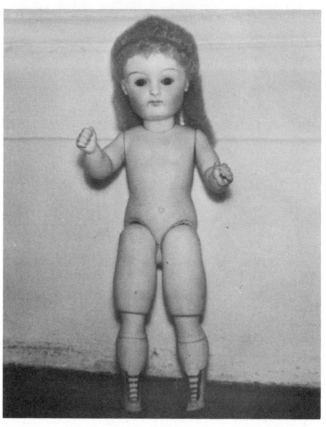

**1543A & B.** All-bisque doll of a fairly large size with various types of joints, lambs' wool wig, brown glass sleeping eyes, closed mouth, bent arms with clenched right fist, molded pink boots. No marks. H. 8½ inches. *Courtesy of Kit Robbins.*

**Skittle Dolls.** 1735–1925+. Crude, turned wooden dolls shaped like skittles; made in Sonneberg, Thür, and elsewhere.

**Skookum.** 1913–25+. Trademark registered in U.S. by *Mary McAboy* for Indian dolls; name was affixed to the soles of the feet with paper stickers. The word "Skookum" is Siwash for "Bully Good." These dolls had either

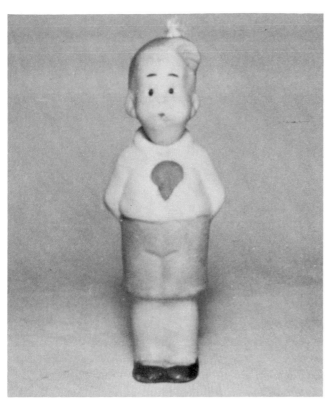

1544. "Skeezix" as a boy—all-bisque doll representing Frank O. King's character of this name. He has a swivel neck; molded and painted clothes include green pants and red tie. H. 2¾ inches. *Courtesy of Dorothy Annunziato.*

1545. Skittle-shaped wooden doll with hemp arms. H. 10 inches. *Courtesy of the International Doll Library Foundation.*

1546A & B. "Skookum," Indian portrait-type doll designed and patented by Mary McAboy. The doll has bronze-colored composition head and wears a colorful Indian blanket and feather headdress. H. 15½ inches. *Coleman Collection.*

dried-apple faces or composition faces, and the bodies were built up from an oblong stick of wood and covered with an Indian blanket. They were designed by Mary McAboy, who obtained design patents for a Brave and a Squaw. *H. H. Tammen Co.* manufactured the dolls. They were also handled by the *Arrow Novelty Co.* The dolls represented real Indians of various tribes as seen on the reservations; they were used for educational work in the Newark, N.J., schools.

1916: Came in two sizes, price 75¢ and $1.25.

**Skookum, The Bully Kiddo.** 1916–17. Copyrighted by *Louis Amberg & Son,* who made this doll under exclusive license from the Northwest Fruit Exchange, national advertisers of Skookum apples. Doll resembled their Indianhead trademark.

**S'kooter Kid.** 1915. Trademark registered in U.S. by *New Era Novelty Co.*

**Slater, Mabel (née Hunt).** 1921–25. New York City. Obtained patents for dolls that were produced by the *Pinky Winky Products Co.*

1922: Was issued a German patent for a doll's head with moving eyes.

1923: Was granted a U.S. patent for a smoking doll; inflammable material was placed in the neck, and smoke escaped through openings of the eyes, nose, and mouth.

1924: Registered "Pinky Winky Idol Eyes" as a trademark in U.S. Obtained a German patent for a doll's head and a British patent for a doll of sheet rubber. The Pinky Winky dolls had fiberloid faces.

1925: Obtained U.S. patent for a doll's eye with an iris that could be shifted in position.

**Sleeping Beauty.** 1903. Name of a patented doll that would keep its eyes open or closed in any position, the change being effected by means of a small button at the back of the head.

**Sleeping Beauty.** 1917–18. Doll made by *Ideal Novelty & Toy Co.*, who advertised that the doll had patented moving eyes that would not stick.

**Sleeping Beauty.** See **Dornroschen.**

**Sleeping Eyes.** 1700–1925+. Dolls had sleeping eyes that opened and closed, at least as early as 1700. Many of the early 19th century dolls had eyes that were manipulated from the outside. Counterweight sleeping eyes appear to have been used in the first half of the 19th century, but did not grow to great popularity until the end of the century. The greatest number of patents for dolls relate to the movement of the eyes. *Simon & Halbig* obtained many patents for eyes. In 1905, *Louis Amberg & Son* advertised that by means of a button arrangement the eyes could be made to open or close in any position. Several manufacturers made sleeping eyes with the lids moving while the eyeball remained stationary.

**Slip Casting.** Ca. 1860–1925+. Potter's clay in the liquid state is poured into molds for slip casting; after it begins to harden on the edge, the remainder is poured off. This method was not used generally until the latter part of the 19th century. Prior to that time, the clay was rolled thin and pressed by hand into the molds, a method practically superseded by slip casting in the 20th century.

**Slivers.** 1915. Trade name for a clown doll.

**Sloan & Co.** 1916–18. Liverpool, England. Made dressed felt dolls.

**Slumber Toys.** 1919–20. Trademark registered in U.S. by *Josephine Janes Co.* for dolls; name was to be affixed to the doll with tags or stamped on the doll.

**Smiles.** 1915. Copyrighted by *Trion Toy Co.*, designed by *Ernesto Peruggi*. Doll had laughing young child's head.

**Smiles.** 1919–20. Trade name of a wood-fiber composition doll made by *Republic Doll & Toy Corp.* It was a cherub type, made in twenty styles, came with or without a wig; sizes $12\frac{1}{2}$ and $14\frac{1}{2}$ inches.

**Smiling Doll.** 1909. Line of dolls with "new" type of composition for heads, or in the lower-priced dolls, bisque heads. Each doll's head was molded and hand-painted. Advertised as representing types of children that one sees and admires every day; natural-looking dolls in every size and dress, representing all ages.

**Smiling Doll.** 1911. Character doll with composition head, molded hair in Buster Brown style. Face modeled from that of a six-year-old girl.

**Smiling Dolls.** These dolls were made in bisque and in china, probably around the 1870's. They were generally lady dolls. The bisque heads are marked with letters that seem to indicate size; for example, an "E" is 15 inches tall and a "K" is $22\frac{1}{2}$ inches tall. (See Ill. 194.) Around 1900 and thereafter, some of the character and multi-face dolls wore smiles.

**Smiling Sue.** 1910. A *Neverbreak* doll made by *A. Steinhardt & Bro.* The composition head resembled *Baby* (model #100) of *Kämmer & Reinhardt*. It had a jointed, satin baby body and wore a shirt trimmed with lace and ribbons. A ribbon across the chest read: "Smiling, Smiling, Baby Sue,//There is no other just like you." The price of the doll was $8.50 doz. wholesale. Mate to *Honey Boy.*

**Smith, Anna.** 1900–17. Philadelphia, Pa.; 1913–17 called A. Smith & Co. Made dolls.

**Smith, Celia and Charity.** 1889–1911+. Ithaca, N.Y. Mrs. William Hazlitt Smith (Celia) and Miss Charity Smith were sisters-in-law; Charity was the artist and Celia had the original ideas for making rag dolls.

1889: They designed a two-piece doll of calico with outspread arms, painted hair and features, and a chemise. *Lawrence & Co.* produced these dolls as cutout dolls

**1547.** Rag doll patented by Charity Smith in 1893 has printed features, underclothes, and gold-colored necklace; blonde hair, brown eyes, and red trim on the underclothes. *Courtesy of Mabel Quick; photograph by Winnie Langley.*

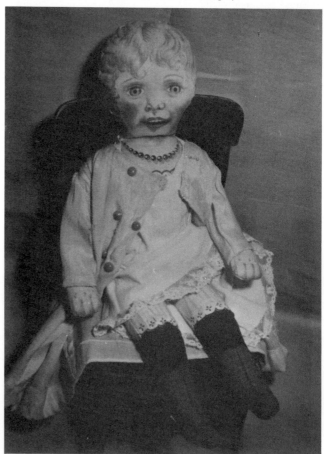

sold commercially by the yard; their popularity soon brought many imitators.

1892: Celia Smith obtained a design patent for the figure of a cat made with three pieces so that it would stand erect. The calico cat was later immortalized by Eugene Field's poem "The Duel."

1893: The 1892 design patent was used for several dolls —first, *Pickaninny;* then *Little Red Riding Hood;* followed by *Pitti-Sing* and later by others. These dolls were printed in color on cotton cloth by the *Arnold Print Works.* They were to be stuffed, and pasteboard was to be inserted in the bottom to make them stand erect. The large dolls cost 10¢ each, or dolls could be purchased by the yard, several dolls to a yard depending on the size of the doll. These dolls were distributed by *Selchow and Righter* of New York City well into the 20th century. Meanwhile, in 1893 Charity Smith obtained patents in the U.S. and Britain for a jointed rag doll made of two pieces but with dart seams to provide shape and articulation. This doll was jointed so that it could sit on a chair. The body could be made separately and used with a china head if desired. These dolls were also produced by the Arnold Print Works and distributed by Selchow and Righter.

1911: *Elms & Sellon,* distributors, advertised, "New this season, 15 inch jointed cloth doll, latest thing." The picture with this advertisement is identical to that used in the 1890's advertisements for the Charity Smith jointed rag doll named *Dollie.* The seventeen years of Miss Smith's patent would just have expired, and apparently others had hastened to copy her rag doll.

**Smith, Edward.** Ca. 1880's. London. Handled wax dolls.

**1548.** Mark used on the body of wax dolls of Edward Smith.

**Smith, Ella.** 1904–24. Roanoke, Ala. Mrs. S. S. Smith (née Gauntt, Ella Louise) made and designed rag dolls that she called "Alabama Indestructible Dolls." These came in white or Negro versions.

1904: Displayed dolls at the St. Louis Exposition.

1905: Obtained a U.S. patent in which she described her doll as follows:

"I make the body or trunk, the arms, hands, legs and feet of stuffed fabric and apply over the feet and hands and as high up on the legs and arms as desirable one or more coats of flesh-colored and preferably waterproof paint. The head, face, neck and bust are also fabric-covered, and the neck or bust is secured to the

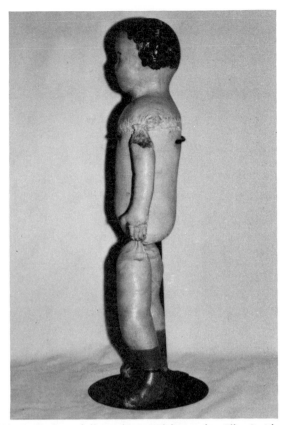

**1549A & B.** Rag doll made in Alabama by Ella Smith and painted with oils has white dots on both sides of the pupils, black lip line, black nose dots. Mark on stomach: Ill. **1550.** H. 22½ inches. *Courtesy of Lester & Alice Grinnings.*

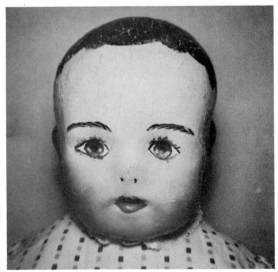

PAT. NOV. 9, 1912
**NO. 2**
ELLA SMITH DOLL CO.

**1550.** Mark on body of rag dolls made by Ella Smith.

trunk by suitable stitching. The outer fabric of the face covers and conforms to the curvature of a backing molded to conform to the contour of the human face. The fabric of the head is stitched up and stretched over a stuffed head portion forming a continuation of the stuffed body, and as a means for making the head rigid a rod or stick may be inserted through the head and passed down a suitable distance into the trunk or body.

" . . . if desired, the doll may be provided with a wig. I prefer, however, to produce the appearance of hair by paint applied directly to the fabric of the head, since the paint acts both to stiffen the fabric, and . . . to to render the head waterproof. The ears are preferably made of stuffed fabric and sewed to the side of the head, after which they are painted."

1907: Displayed dolls at Southeastern Fair in Atlanta, Ga., and at Jamestown Exposition.

1908: Nearly 8,000 of these dolls were made.

1919: Obtained a U.S. patent for making the ears of "a plastic composition such as plaster of Paris" and stapling the ear to the head instead of sewing it.

1921: Was issued a German patent for making dolls' heads and doll parts.

1924: Obtained three U.S. patents. One was for a sanitary covering with an opening down the back, which fastened with snaps. This covering for the doll could be removed for cleaning. Ears were provided on the cover so that they would fit over the ears of the doll itself. The second patent was a pattern for a doll's body that would give proper proportions and suitable curves to the trunk, head, arms, and legs. The ears were an integral part of the head. The arms were constructed so that they could not easily be torn off of the body. The head and shoulders were stiffened by use of a small cylinder of wood or other suitable material. The doll was stitched up the back. The third patent was for a mold and a method of doll construction. A two-piece head was formed from a four-piece mold. The mold had a front, two sides, and back and was made of babbitt or other suitable metal. The head was made by placing a layer of fabric, such as stockinet, then a layer of plastic, another layer of fabric, and another layer of plastic, in the mold; after the material had hardened, it was removed from the mold and sewed or stapled together.

**Smith, Joachim.** 1763. London. Modeled wax portraits in miniature.

**Smith, Mildred K.** 1923–24. Scottsdale, Ariz. Obtained a U.S. design patent for a cherub-type doll with large wings and hair streaming backward and upward. She assigned half of her rights to Lillian Wilhelm Robertson.

**Smith, Mr. & Mrs. Putnam David.** 1913–22. Santa Cruz, Calif. Assisted by their daughter, Margaret Smith, they designed and made dolls. These dolls are often referred to as P.D. Smith or Mabel P. Smith dolls. Most of them were of a wood-pulp composition; some have eyes that move from side to side as well as sleep. Some of the baby dolls have cloth bodies. *Baby Beautiful, Pollyanna,* and *Laughing Sonny Boy* were among the dolls made by this family. The dolls were artistic but expensive.

1918: Margaret W. Smith obtained a copyright for "Clara," a figurine of a Red Cross nurse.

1919: Mabel P. Smith designed "Duck Me," a figurine of a child in a bathing suit, copyrighted by Lloyd W. Stetson. Margaret W. Smith designed "Doughboy's Doughgirl," a figurine of a girl with doughnuts in her hands, copyrighted by Lloyd W. Stetson.

1922: Margaret Smith designed two oriental figurines and an oriental head, which may have been used on a doll; these were copyrighted by *Carmalete Waldo Webb.* The head was named *Yat Quong.*

**Smith, Sampson.** 1846–20th century. Longton, Staffordshire. China toy manufacturer; used the mark "S S" intertwined from 1846–58 and "S.S. Ltd." from 1860 on. During the 19th century, his figures were formed by hand-pressing bats of clay into molds; in the 20th century casting was done with slip.

**Smith Doll & Toy Co., Ltd.** 1919. Dunnville, Ont. Made dolls and advertised that their dolls were sent all over the world.

**Smock Doll Co.** 1918. East Orange, N.J. Employed ten persons to make dolls.

**Snookums.** 1909–10. Trademark registered in Germany by *Max Fr. Schelhorn.*

**Snookums.** Ca. 1910. Made by *Horsman.* Had a *Can't Break 'Em* composition head representing the baby of this name as drawn in cartoons; molded open-closed mouth with a single tooth, molded hair, plush body.

**Snookums.** 1919. Composition cherub-type doll made by *American Ocarina & Toy Co.*

**Snow White.** 1917–18. Trademark registered in U.S. by *Henry Sieben.* These dolls were made by the *American Toy & Manufacturing Co.,* who advertised that the dolls were modeled by one of America's foremost sculptors from the character played by Marguerite Clark in the movies.

**Snowbird.** 1917. Doll with composition head, made by *Colonial Toy Manufacturing Co.;* came dressed in parka type of garment.

**Snowball.** 1915. One of the Gene Carr Kids from the "Lady Bountiful" series in the NEW YORK WORLD. These dolls were probably made by *Horsman.*

**Snowball, Mrs. S.** 1855. London. Made wax dolls.

**Snuggles.** 1917. Trademark registered in U.S. by *Best & Co.* for dolls of various materials.

**Société.** French word for society, company, or firm, in its commercial senses; a "société anonyme" is a joint-stock company. "Compagnie" (abbreviated "Cie.") is another commonly used term. "Société" is frequently used when several firms merge—for example, the *Société*

*Française de Fabrication de Bébés et Jouets,* or the *Société Steiner.*

**Société Anonyme.** 1910–12. Paris. Manufactured bébés. Their capital was $200,000 and they used the trademarks *La Parisienne* and *Eureka.* (See also **Société.**)

**Société Anonyme de Comptoir General de la Bimbeloterie.** 1905. Paris. Registered in France as their trademarks *Poupon Parisiana, Poupée Parisiana,* and *Bébé Parisiana.* The *Société Française de Fabrication de Bébés et Jouets* had registered "Bébé Parisiana" in France in 1902.

**Société Anonyme pour le Commerce et l'Industrie.** 1921. Paris. Advertised *poupards.*

**Société au Bébé Rose.** 1910. Registered in France *Au Bébé Rose* as a trademark.

**Société Bernheim & Kahn.** See **Bernheim & Kahn.**

**Société Binder & Cie.** See **Binder & Cie.**

**Société Bonin & Lefort.** See **Bonin & Lefort.**

**Société de l'Ancienne Faïencerie.** See **Verlingue, J.**

**Société de Paris (Française).** 1925+. Paris. Used the trade names, *Poupée Mystère* and *Yeux Expression.*

**Société Fouquet & Douville.** See **Fouquet & Douville.**

**Société Française de Fabrication de Bébés & Jouets.** 1899–1925+. Paris, and Montreuil-sous-Bois, France. An anonymous Société known to have included *Jumeau, Bru, Fleischmann & Blödel, Rabery & Delphieu,* and *Pintel & Godchaux* probably from the beginning of the Société. By 1903, *P. H. Schmitz* and *Ad. Bouchet;* by 1904, *Jullien;* and by 1911, *Danel & Cie.* had also joined the Société. Nearly all the "S.F.B.J." dolls had bisque heads on jointed composition bodies, but a few are found with composition heads. Most of their dolls are numbered. Probably the two most frequently found numbers are "60" and "301," both of which have the dolly-type faces. Character faces are also frequently found and were made in a wide range of models; these seem to have been numbered from at least 203 to 252. A few low numbers such as 24 and 52 have also been reported. These dolls come with wigs generally, but a few have molded hair, especially those that resemble boys. Glass eyes predominate but painted eyes are also found. Some of the eye sockets are cut out more circular than is usual, and the pupils then look upward leaving some of the white of the eye at the bottom.

1900: A member of the jury and displayed dolls at the Paris Exposition.

1901: Obtained a French patent for talking dolls.

1904: Secured a French patent for improving their sleeping eyes.

1905: Obtained three French patents—one for a kiss-throwing doll; one for a new mechanism in the legs of a jointed doll; and one for a bébé's head with improvement in the sleeping eyes. Registered a trademark in France with the initials "S.F.B.J."

DOLLS OF SOCIETE FRANCAISE DE FABRICATION DE BEBES ET JOUETS

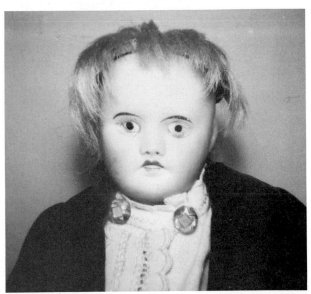

**1551A, B, & C.** Two dolls made by the Société Française de Fabrication de Bébés et Jouets from their mold "60." Doll shown in close-up has painted eyes, open-closed mouth with teeth. The doll pictured full-length has glass eyes and open mouth, and the painting of her features is done more artistically, thus making her a more attractive doll. Both have jointed composition bodies. Doll in close-up is marked "23 // YP // S.F.B.J. // Paris // 10/0." H. 13 inches. *Courtesy of Ollie Leavister.* Other doll is marked as in Ill. **1559.** H. 19½ inches. *Coleman Collection.*

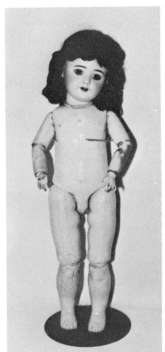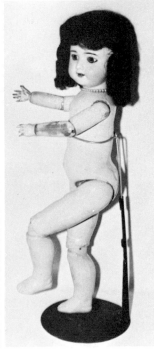

1909: Were issued a French patent for a doll that would "talk" in any position in which it might be held.

1910: Registered in Britain their trademark "S.F.B.J." Listed in British Directory, with *Henry S. Benjamin* as

**1552.** A Martinique version of the Société Française de Fabrication de Bébés et Jouets doll with head "60." This is another variation of the heads shown in Ill. **1551.** Has glass eyes; composition body. Mark: Ill. **1638,** except for "60" instead of "301." H. 10½ inches. *Courtesy of May Maurer.*

their agent. They advertised dressed and undressed dolls.

1911: Registered in France as trademarks *Bébé Prodige, Bébé Jumeau,* and *Bébé Français.*

1912: Advertised 5,000,000 dolls a year produced at their Vincennes factory; dolls not dressed there but sent to Paris, where several hundred girls, some of them fashion experts, dressed the dolls in the latest styles. Prizes were offered each year for improvements. Women all over the world competed in designing clothes—one reason why French dolls were dressed so exquisitely.

1913: Registered in France *Bébé Triomphe* as a trademark.

1918: Obtained a French patent for a type of composition used for putting moving eyes into dolls' heads of porcelain or other material.

1920: Registered in France as trademarks *Bébé Parisiana, Bébé Moderne, Le Séduisant,* and *Bébé Parfait.*

1921: Registered in France two trademarks: *Le Papillon* and a drawing of a bee, which was to be used for dolls, wigs, shoes, and clothes. They had a full-page advertisement in PLAYTHINGS and stated that *Arthur Geoffroy* was their sole agent in U.S. They advertised *Bébé Jumeau, Bébé Bru, Eden Bébé,* dressed dolls, character dolls, walking dolls, and jointed dolls; price 25¢ to $50.00. They produced 6,000,000 dolls.

1922: Had 2,800 employees; used 2,000 models, including many types of character dolls. Chocolate-hued and mulatto dolls, manufactured in large quantities, were popular in France and in the French Colonies. Many of their dolls were sold in South America and Australia, but

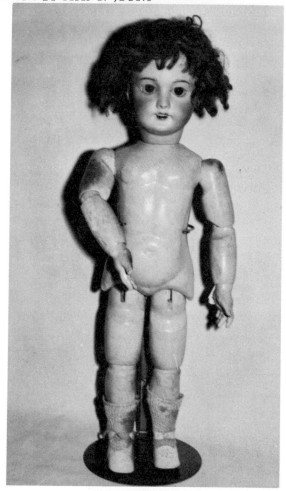

**1553A & B.** Société Française de Fabrication de Bébés et Jouets doll with head "301," molded eyebrows. Mark on head: Ill. **1560.** Red, white, and blue sticker on back of body: Ill. **1561.** H. 21½ inches. *Courtesy of Mary Seward.*

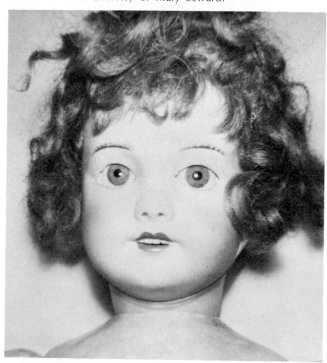

DOLLS OF SOCIETE FRANCAISE DE FABRICATION DE BEBES ET JOUETS

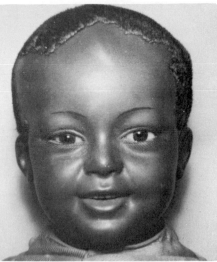

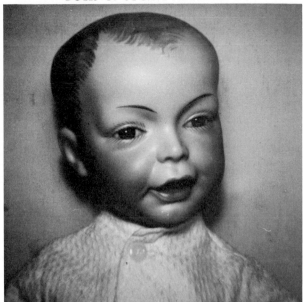

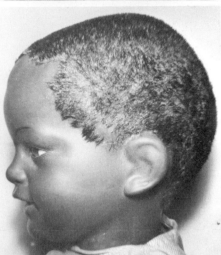

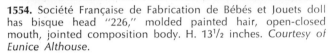

**1554.** Société Française de Fabrication de Bébés et Jouets doll has bisque head "226," molded painted hair, open-closed mouth, jointed composition body. H. 13½ inches. *Courtesy of Eunice Althouse.*

**1556.** Doll of the Société Française de Fabrication de Bébés et Jouets with bisque head, glass eyes, upper teeth, composition body. *Courtesy of Margaret Whitton; photograph by Winnie Langley.*

**1555A, B, & C.** Negro doll of the Société Française de Fabrication de Bébés et Jouets with bisque head "227," size "6"; skin wig, six molded upper teeth, lips an orange-red color. The eyes smile as well as the mouth. Dark-colored jointed composition body. Mark: Ill. **1562.** H. 16½ inches. (See color photograph **C24.**) *Courtesy of Lester & Alice Grinnings.*

**1557.** Société Française de Fabrication de Bébés et Jouets doll with bisque head, brown hair, blue eyes, open-closed mouth with teeth, jointed composition body. *Courtesy of Margaret Whitton; photograph by Winnie Langley.*

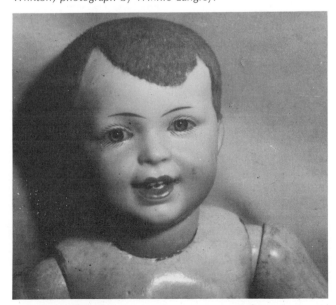

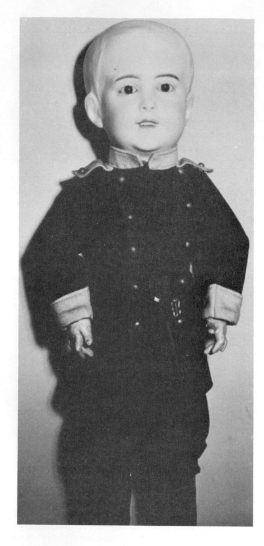

**1558.** Société Française de Fabrication de Bébés et Jouets bisque-head doll with molded hair in a boyish style, glass eyes, dressed in a navy blue suit with brass buttons. *Courtesy of Margaret Whitton; photograph by Winnie Langley.*

**1559–1570.** Marks of the Société Française de Fabrication de Bébés et Jouets. Marks Nos. **1569** and **1570** are registered trademarks; the other marks are found on dolls.

S. F. B. J.
60
PARIS
1559

25
FRANCE
S F B J
301
PARIS
8
1560

FABRICATION FRANÇAISE
SFBJ
PARIS
1561

S. F. B. J.
2 2 7
PARIS
6
1562

S. F. B. J
2 36
PARIS
1563

S. F. B. J.
2L9
PARIS
1564

S. F. B. J.
2 4 7
PARIS
1565

FRANCE
S. F. B. J.
3 0 1
PARIS
2/0
1566

R
S. F. B. J.
PARIS
10
1567

DÉPOSÉ
S.F.B.J.
1568

S
F
B
J
1569

LE SÉDUISANT
1570

Americans seemed to prefer German dolls. *Mme. Bonneaud* was chief fashion designer. One of their deluxe dolls walked, nodded her head, and threw kisses. It had chestnut brown hair, wore a black gown of the latest fashion, loose and flowing; size 24 inches.

1924: Obtained a French patent for a talking bébé; the talking apparatus was fitted into the body, and the sound was amplified.

1925: Advertised that they had eight factories; made dressed and undressed bébés including Bébé Jumeau, Bébé Bru, Eden Bébé, and poupards, both silent and talking. The Parisian dolls of *Jean Ray* and of *Béatrice*

*Mallet* were handled exclusively by the S.F.B.J. They used the *Unis France* mark with the numbers 71 and 149 in their advertisement. (See color photograph C24.)

**Société Française de Jouets & de Caoutchouc Bébés.** 1914. Factory was at Bezons, Seine-et-Oise. Made rubber bébés.

**Société Française des Bébés.** 1921–23. Paris. Factory was at Montreuil, Seine. Made porcelain heads and used the trademark *Marcoux.*

**Société Gerbaulet Frères.** See **Gerbaulet Frères.**

**Société Industrielle de Celluloid.** 1902–25+. Paris. Made celluloid dolls and used the trade name "Sicoid."

*Neumann & Marx* were associated with this Société; *H. S. Benjamin* was their London agent and *Alfred Burke* was their sole U.S. representative.

1909: Obtained a German patent for a swimming doll.

1910: Secured a British patent for a floating doll of hollow celluloid.

1912: Advertised "Sicoid" as a noninflammable material for dolls.

1913: Won a gold medal at the Leipzig Exposition for their drinking baby.

1914: Advertised that they were the largest manufacturers in the world of Pyroxylin raw material. They made babies and dolls; their babies were made up to life size and were with or without hair. They also made dolls' heads, arms, and legs. They used the "N & M" mark, which had belonged to Neumann & Marx.

1919: Advertised new noninflammable materials called "Sicoid" and "Sicoine," permanent creations for dolls, as well as celluloid dolls, dolls' heads, and parts. Capital of $800,000.

1921: Had five factories in France; made celluloid and "Sicoid" dolls.

1924: Obtained a German patent for joints for dolls.

1925: Seven factories in France; a capital of $2,400,000.

**Société Industrielle des Téléphones.** 1900. Factories at Rattier and Menier, France. Made rubber bébés.

**Société la Parisienne.** 1911. Paris. Registered in France as trademarks *Bébé Eureka, Bébé le Rêve, Paradis Bébé, Magic Bébé, Bébé Stella,* and *Bébé Lux.*

**Société les Arts du Papier.** See **Les Arts du Papier.**

**Société Steiner.** See **Steiner, Jules.**

**Société Treude & Metz.** See **Treude & Metz.**

**Société Vallée & Schultz.** See **Vallée & Schultz.**

**Socolu.** 1925. Trademark used by *Sonnenfeld & Co.*

**Softanlite Dolls.** See **Madame Hendren.**

**Soldier.** 1892. One of the *Brownies,* designed by *Palmer Cox.*

**Soldier.** 1916. One of the *Capo* line of dolls made by the *Non-Breakable Toy Co.;* size 30 inches.

**Soldier Boy.** 1914. Made by *Louis Amberg & Son;* doll carried a toy pistol.

**Soldier's Baby.** 1914. Trademark registered in Britain by *Elizabeth Boase,* doll manufacturer.

**Soldier Dolls.** See **Military Costume Dolls.**

**Solid China Babies.** See **Frozen Charlotte;** also **Bathing Dolls.**

**Sollmann, Emil.** 1918–25+. Neustadt near Coburg, Thür. Made *Täuflinge.*

**Sommer, Jacques Adolphe.** 1886. Paris. Registered in France a tiny trademark of two concentric circles with some lettering inside them.

**Sommereisen.** 1898. Obtained a French patent for hollow doll's head of aluminum.

**Sommerick, Benno.** 1924. Nürnberg, Bavaria. Made dolls.

**Sommers, E. L.** 1921–22. U.S. Manufactured dolls.

**Son Brothers & Co.** 1919. San Francisco, Calif. Imported dolls and dolls' heads from Japan.

**Sonie.** 1918. Made by *Jessie McCutcheon Raleigh,* distributed by *Butler Bros.* Doll wore a lawn blouse and chambray pants; size 13½ inches, price $2.90.

**Sonneberg, Thür.** Before 1700–1925+. Doll center of the world. First made turned wooden dolls of wood from the Thüringian forests. Early Sonneberg ledgers record *Tyroler* wooden dolls as a type of doll. It seems likely that wooden dolls made in the Tyrol were sent to Sonneberg, perhaps for painting and finishing before distribution. About 1807, the mass production of papier-mâché heads for dolls began in Sonneberg.

The brilliant period of Sonneberg dolls began around 1850, and soon after this jointed dolls became popular. Dolls were made of wood, wax, china, bisque, papier-mâché, and other compositions. Except for the porcelain dolls, most of the others were designed and made in homes, then sold to dealers and exporters. They were sent all over the world, to every civilized country. In 1882, a Frenchman wrote of the Sonneberg dolls: "Bébés in chemise, in papier-mâché, in porcelain are not less distinguished by their originality, their elegance and the novelty of their forms than by the excessive moderateness of their prices." Each worker had a specific task, one person would paint eyes on dolls of only one type and one size; another person would paint just the mouths on the same dolls. Kaolin and lignite, used in making bisque dolls' heads, were imported from Bohemia, as were some of the blown glass eyes. Some mohair for wigs came from England.

In 1903, a design room of a Sonneberg factory contained from 12,000 to 18,000 designs. Two million dolls of one variety alone were made. China factories turned out twenty million dolls' heads (china and bisque heads) a year. The number of papier-mâché heads was much larger because they were cheaper and more in demand. World War I seems to have had little effect in Sonneberg; by 1922, the manufacturers there had orders for years in advance.

**Sonneberg Industrial School.** 1851–1925+. A school devoted to the education of modelers, designers, and manufacturers of dolls. PLAYTHINGS in 1909 had an article on this school, which stated that students from America, Austria, Russia, England, and Roumania had all attended it, some at their government's expense. The students drew from antique and modern busts, figures, and from nature. They modeled from casts of parts of the human frame, masks, heads, busts, and figures. Afterward came the preparation of industrial models in clay, wax, and plastilina. In some cases, special orders for such work were given to the school. Wood carving included heads, legs, and bodies, as well as turning dolls' legs, joints, etc. Special study was made of the reproduction in quantity of dolls' heads and papier-mâché articles.

**Sonneberger Porzellanfabrik.** See **Müller, Carl.**

**Sonnenfeld & Co.** 1925. Made dressed dolls and dolls with sleeping eyes. Used the trademark *Socolu*.

**Sonntag, Hermann.** See **Thiele, Anna.**

**Sonny.** 1920. Walking doll with composition head, arms, and legs; made by *Averill Manufacturing Co.* Came dressed in rompers and sunbonnet; size 26 inches.

**Soozie Smiles.** 1923–24. Trademark registered in U.S. by *Ideal Novelty & Toy Co.* for a two-faced doll with one face smiling and one face crying. The trademark was to be affixed to the doll with a printed label; this was a large square tag pinned to the front of Soozie's checked rompers. The London DAILY GRAPHIC reported that Soozie Smiles made the Queen laugh.

1924: Advertised as having eyes that rolled as well as slept, winked, and blinked. She even cried real tears and called "Mama." Soozie walked and had a variety of costumes. A "Soozie Smiles Junior" was also made.

**Soret, Jean Pierre.** 1847. Paris. Was granted a French patent for making papier-mâché heads for bébés and for modistes' (milliners') model dolls. The patent papers stated that up to this time French products of this sort had been inferior to similar German products.

**Sörgel, Heinrich.** 1897. Hamburg, Germany. Wholesale doll manufacturer.

**Sourtiat.** 1862. Paris. Made dolls.

**Souty, Mme. Hortense Vincent.** 1862. Obtained a French patent for a jointed doll's body of pumice stone covered with glue and several layers of oil paint. The head and arms of the doll could be made of China, bisque, or pipe clay.

**Soxie.** 1919–20. Trademark registered in U.S. by *Minnie M. Meldram* for dolls.

**Span.** 1911–12. Copyrighted by *Louis Amberg & Son,* designed by *Jeno Juszko.* Doll had composition head of a Dutch girl with a round chubby face, hair parted in middle and rounded over the temples, large eyes glancing to the side; cork-stuffed pink sateen body; was dressed in a striped gingham frock with green suspenders, Dutch shoes. Mate to *Spic;* represented figure in the advertisements of a metal polish.

**Spanish Dolls.** These dolls were largely imported ones before World War I, but in 1915 Spain began to make dolls of wax, papier-mâché, and china; many were dressed in national costumes. Among the 19th-century doll makers in Spain were *Macazaga & Idarramendi, Ybo Esparza,* and *Jaime Pujol e Hijo. José Florido* made dolls after World War I. In 1920, the Canary Islanders were famous for their rag dolls, made by women. These dolls had flat faces, enormous feet, and embroidered dresses. In 1921 Spain exported dolls to Germany.

**Spear, Margaret B.** 1919. New York City. Was granted a U.S. design patent for a two-piece rag doll with a farmer on one side and his wife on the other side. She assigned her patent to *David W. Pye.*

**Spear & Bergmann, J. C.** 1882. Sonneberg, Thür. Made dolls.

**Spearmint Kid.** 1915. Advertised by *Baker & Bennett Co.* Came with "Wrigley" eyes, a voice; price 50¢.

**Spearmint Kiddo.** 1912–13. Copyrighted by *Louis Amberg & Son,* designed by *Jeno Juszko.* The copyright described the doll as having "Wrigley" eyes, smiling face, naïve expression, teeth showing, long straight hair parted in the middle, dress trimmed with mint leaves.

1913: Advertised as having new bisque finish, "Wrigley" eyes, arrows on dress, and mint leaves around head; size 13 inches, price $1.00.

**Special.** 1893. Trade name used by *Butler Bros.* for some of their "washable" composition-headed dolls.

**Special.** Name found on bisque heads made by *Adolf Wislizenus.* Other companies may also have made dolls' heads marked "Special." (See **Spezial;** also **Dolly Princess.**)

**Speights Ltd.** 1913–24. London; factory at Dewsbury, Yorkshire. Manufactured composition dolls, dolls' hair, and wigs.

1917: Registered in Britain *Kidette* as a trademark for children's dolls.

**Speir, Emil.** 1893–1902. Berlin. Manufactured and exported dolls and dolls' bodies.

**Sperrhake, Arno.** 1891–1921. Eisenberg, Thür. Manufactured and exported jointed dolls, dressed dolls, and dolls for dolls' houses.

**Sperschneider, Mylius.** 1921–25. Sonneberg, Thür. Made ball-jointed dolls, bent-limb and standing babies.

1921: Registered in Germany a trademark that included the word *Marionette* and the initials, "M S S" in two superimposed five-pointed stars.

**Speyer, Carl.** 1899–1909. Made dolls. His London representative was *Martin Hirsch.*

1571. "Special" mark used by Adolf Wislizenus on dolls.

1572 & 1573. "Spezial" marks found on dolls. No. 1572 used on Charles Bergmann dolls. No. 1573, maker unknown.

**Spezial.** Mark used by *Charles M. Bergmann* on bisque head of a composition-bodied doll.

**Spic.** 1911–12. Copyrighted by *Louis Amberg & Son*, designed by *Jeno Juszko*. Came with composition head of a Dutch boy with big blue eyes looking downward, high eyebrows, hair pulled out at the sides; cork-stuffed pink sateen body; dressed in red trousers and Dutch shoes. Mate to *Span*. Represented figure in the advertisements of a metal polish.

**Spielberg, A., & Kline S.** 1914. Had doll factory in New York City with branches in Pittsburgh, Pa., and Cleveland, Ohio.

**Spindler, Georg.** 1900–10. Germany. Won Grand Prizes at Paris and Brussels expositions for his dolls.

**Splashme.** 1918–20. Trademark registered in U.S. by *Genevieve Pfeffer* for dolls. These may have been figurines rather than play dolls; they were distributed by *Borgfeldt*.

**Splendide Bébé.** 1893–1900. Trademark registered in France by *Cosman Frères* for jointed dolls and bébés, "ordinary" dolls, and clowns.

1893: Advertisement for the Splendide Bébé, "Notre Bébé-Prime" (our finest bébé), by Mons. Abel Goubaud of Paris read as follows: "This bébé is 20 inches high with a beautiful bisque head, wig of silky blonde hair.

"It is entirely articulated; at the shoulders, at the elbows, at the knees and at the wrists. It will hold all the attitudes of a child.

"It is dressed in an elegant chemise trimmed with lace and ribbons . . . the price is $1.60."

## *Splendide Bébé*

**1574.** "Splendide Bébé" mark used by Cosman Frères.

**Spratt, Miss H.** 1881. London. Made dolls at the same address as *Thomas Betts*.

**Spring, Auguste.** 1918. Berlin. Manufactured dolls.

**Spring, W.** 1900–1909. Berlin. Manufactured dolls.

**Springer, Edward H.** 1920–21. Santa Monica, Calif. Was granted a U.S. design patent for a doll's head.

**Spring-jointed Bodies.** 1892–1925+. Spring joints were used by many doll manufacturers, including *Frederick B. Schultz, Metal Doll Co., Schoenhut, Parsons-Jackson, Kämmer & Reinhardt,* and *Catterfelder Puppenfabrik.*

**Springsteen, Robert E.** 1883. Indianapolis, Ind. Made dolls. He was the assignee of the wire skeleton doll patented by *Lucinda Wishard*.

**Squaw.** 1919. Indian-type character doll made by *J. R. Miranda & Co.* Came dressed in an Indian blanket; size 12 inches.

**Squier, Bernice, & Squier, Blanche.** 1920. Battle Creek, Mich. Obtained a U.S. design patent for a doll of yarn.

**Stacy, Gertrude.** 1921. Designed the *Pepper-Mint Kids, Amphibious Clown, Bully Boy Brewster,* and *Sunbonnet Jane* for the *Giftoy Co.*

**Stahl, Carl.** 1902–23. Berlin. Manufactured and exported dolls.

**Stair-Step Family.** 1920. Three composition dolls made by *Jessie McCutcheon Raleigh;* came in sizes 5, 7, and 9 inches.

**Stallard & Co.** 1905. London. Registered in Britain *Kismi* as a trademark for toy dolls.

**Standard Doll Co.** 1917. New York City. Made an "800" line of 16-inch dolls and a "100" line of 14-inch dolls. Among the 16-inch dolls were *Scotch Highlander, Uncle Sam, Miss America,* and *French Zouave*.

**Standard Products Co.** 1923–24. New York City. Made composition dolls, including Negro dolls; price $11.50 to $25.00 doz. wholesale.

**Standard Specialty Co.** 1915–16. New York City. Made and distributed American dolls, including the *Flicks Kids*.

**Standard Toy Manufacturing Co.** 1917. U.S. Advertised baby, boy, and girl character dolls, and *Yama* dolls. Price 25¢ to $2.00.

**Standard Warenvertreib.** 1924. Berlin. Distributed dolls.

**Standfuss, Karl (Carl).** 1904–25+. Deuben near Dresden, Saxony. Made metal and celluloid dolls, dolls' heads, and parts. His trademark was *Juno*.

1909: Was granted two German patents for jointed bathing dolls (probably of celluloid).

1910: Obtained a German patent for improving the manufacture of dolls.

1925: Advertised that he was the sole manufacturer of celluloid *Kewpies* and celluloid *Bye-Lo Babies*. He made flirting dolls, celluloid dolls, dolls' heads, and babies, as well as the Juno metal dolls' heads.

**Star.** See **Star Manufacturing Co.**

**Star Brand.** See **Star Toy & Novelty Co.**

**Star Doll & Toy Co.** 1915–25+. New York City. Manufactured dolls.

1924: Advertised *Mama Dolls* for $1.00 and up.

**Star Manufacturing Co.** 1887–1925+. London; factory at Cubitt Town, England. Manufactured and exported dolls, especially composition dolls. Their trademark was a six-pointed star with the word "Star" in it.

**Star Toy & Novelty Co.** 1914–19. New York City. Made Star Brand "unbreakable" character dolls.

1915–16: Advertised the *Yama Kid*.

1917: Advertised Hawaiian Hula Hula dolls wearing "shredded wheat skirts."

**Starckjohann, C., & Co.** 1897. Hamburg, Germany. Manufactured dolls.

**Starfish Hands.** After 1910, some hands were made with

the fingers apart, resembling a starfish. This type of hand is found on *cherub-type dolls* such as *Kewpies*.

**State Charities Aid Association.** 1914–16. New York City. Registered in U.S. as a trademark *Daddy Long-Legs Doll;* they manufactured and sold these dolls for the benefit of their children's department.

**Statham, Samuel Edmond.** 1893. Manchester, England. Manufacturer. Was granted a British patent for manufacturing seamless vulcanized rubber dolls.

**Stauch, Carl.** 1895. Neustadt near Coburg, Thür. Made little or baby dolls.

**Stauch, Chr.** 1909. Neustadt near Coburg, Thür. Made dolls.

**Steel Doll.** See **All Steel Doll.**

**Steidtmann, E., & Co.** 1891–1902. Geringswalde, Saxony. Manufactured dolls.

**Steiff, Fräulein Margarete.** 1877–1925+. Giengen, Württemberg. After her death in 1909, the factory was operated by her nephews. They made dolls of felt, plush, and velvet. Dolls were characterized by a seam down the middle of the face, and identified by a metal button in the ear, except for very early dolls.

Margarete Steiff began by making animals from waste pieces of felt provided by a nearby large felt factory. Dolls with felt heads were first made in 1894. Later, she advertised that hers was the first factory that made soft stuffed character dolls.

1903: Steiff had establishments in Berlin, Hamburg, Leipzig, London, Paris, Amsterdam, and Florence.

1904: Won a Grand prize for the Steiff display at the St. Louis Exposition. It included Teddy Bears, which Morris Michtom had apparently first designed in 1902.

1905: Registered in Germany *Knopf im Ohr* (Button in Ear) as a trademark for cloth jointed dolls, which were both produced and distributed.

1907: Registered in Germany "Steiff" as a trademark for cloth jointed dolls. Registered in France "Bouton dans l'oreille" as a trademark for dolls.

1908: Had 2,000 employees in the factory, and yet Margarete Steiff claimed that she personally examined every doll made there. It was also stated that though the doll's faces had originally been made of felt, they now used specially made plush and velvet. Yet this very year Franz Steiff, one of her nephews, obtained a U.S. patent for heads made of molded felt. Registered in U.S. "Steiff" as a trademark; it had been used since 1907. Registered in Germany the following seven trademarks: "Steiff's Prima Spielwaren" (First Class Toys); "Steiff's chemisch reine Spielwaren" (chemically clean Toys); "Steiff Original"; *Sechseck im Ohr; Ring am Ohr.* The last two were "Hexagon in the ear" written in Russian and in another language. Steiff dolls were distributed in U.S. by *Samstag & Hilder.*

1909: Registered in Germany *Billy Doll* as a trademark. Registered in U.S. "Knopf im Ohr" as a trademark, which

**1575A & B.** Felt doll with Steiff mark represents a Heidelberg University student. Has dueling scars on his cheek, painted mustache, real hair under the cap, button eyes, seam down the middle of the face. He is dressed in original clothes. H. 16 inches. *Courtesy of Dorothy Annunziato.*

**1576.** Steiff officer with felt head, painted sideburns, original clothes. Blue felt uniform is trimmed in red and has brass buttons. Note his military bearing. H. 21 inches. *Courtesy of Jessica Norman.*

**1577.** Steiff mark used for dolls.

B outon dans l'oreille

had been used since 1905. Advertised three U.S. soldier dolls, namely, *Sgt. Kelly, Private Sharkey,* and *Private Murphy;* plus four dolls of other nations—*Hubertus, Alida, Olaf,* and *Anthony.* (See Ill. 39.)

1910: Won a Grand Prize at the Brussels Exhibition.

1911: Registered in France "Steiff" as a trademark. Advertised new items in the felt character-doll line, including a Chinaman, an Irish footman, clowns, a German in brown togs, including knee breeches, leather leggings, and tan shoes, a Polish workingman, a blond-haired Dutch pair in wooden shoes (man wore yellow coat and black knee breeches; woman wore red and blue garments); an Indian warrior; *Strubelpeter; Senner and Sennerin.* These dolls could stand upright without support, owing to their large shoes and the balance of their bodies; sizes up to 18 inches.

1913–15: *Borgfeldt* was sole distributor in U.S.

1921–22: Registered in Germany a drawing of an arm as a trademark.

Date unknown: Produced a group named *Sarrasani's Circus,* designed by cartoonist A. Schlopsnies.

**Stein, H.** 1923–25. Prague (Praha), Czechoslovakia. Made dolls.

**Steinbruck, Nobacket Co.** 1882. Waltershausen, Thür. Made papier-mâché dolls.

**Steiner, A.** 1925. Steinach, Thür. Made dolls.

**Steiner, Albert.** 1922. Sonneberg, Thür. Made dressed dolls. New York agent was *Roth, Baitz & Lipsitz.*

**Steiner, Albin.** 1913–14. Sonneberg, Thür. Obtained a U.S. patent for a crying doll that emitted a long slow cry. He assigned this patent to *Borgfeldt.* Together with Oskar Liebermann and Carl Scharfenberg, Albin Steiner also obtained a German patent for a toy doll.

**Steiner, Albin.** 1924. Köppelsdorf, Thür. Made baby dolls.

**Steiner, Chr. Fr. Albert.** 1909–18. Schalkau, Thür. Exported dolls.

**Steiner, Edmund Ulrich.** 1864–1916. Sonneberg, Thür., and New York City. Produced and distributed dolls. His obituary stated that he was born in 1858, but an article written in 1904 when he was alive to give information stated that he had started in the toy business in 1864. His father manufactured high-grade dolls, which were one of the first prominent lines to be marketed in the U.S. His brother Albert was also well known in the doll business. Edmund Steiner came to America as a young man, and later crossed the Atlantic eighty-four times in his career. He worked for *Horsman,* then for *L. H. Mace & Co.,* next for *Strobel & Wilken,* and then for *Louis Wolf & Co.* In the early 1890's he joined Curman in the firm Curman & Steiner, importers and jobbers. With the dissolution of this firm, Steiner returned to become manager of Strobel & Wilken's doll department. About 1901 he became manager of the doll department of *Samstag & Hilder,* a position he held for six years. Then for eight years he rejoined Louis Wolf & Co. Around 1915, with the curtailment of imports from Germany, he joined a glass company. He died in 1916.

1901: Began work on his *Human Face Doll.*

1902: Obtained a patent for his walking and sitting doll; when led by the hand, it would move its feet forward alternately and successively. The doll could also sit erect. Registered in U.S. and Germany the trademark *Majestic,* which had been used since 1894. Registered in U.S. the trademark *Liliput* in a scroll with an eagle, which had also been used since 1894.

1903: Registered in Germany *Daisy* as a trademark for dolls.

1907: Won a court case upholding his patent for the walking and sitting doll.

EDMUND ULRICH STEINER DOLLS

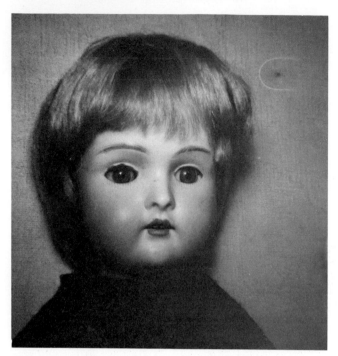

**1578.** "Majestic" bisque head bearing the trademark of Edmund Ulrich Steiner. Has glass sleeping eyes, pierced ears, open mouth, and two teeth. Mark Ill. **1117.** H. of socket head only, 3½ inches. *Coleman Collection.*

**1579.** Bisque head produced for Edmund Ulrich Steiner has glass sleeping eyes, open mouth, and teeth. Kid body has bisque lower arms. Mark: Ill. **1581.** H. 18 inches. H. of shoulder head only, 4½ inches. *Courtesy of Dorothy Annunziato.*

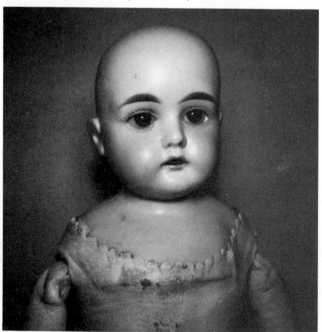

Steiner's Patent
Walking & Sitting
Dolls

**1580.** Edmund Ulrich Steiner's walking doll as advertised by Samstag & Hilder Bros. in 1908. *Courtesy of McCready Publishing Co.*

**1581.** Mark used on dolls of Edmund Ulrich Steiner.

**Steiner, Hermann.** 1921–25+. Sonneberg and Neustadt near Coburg, Thür. Made dolls.

1921: Registered in Britain *My Pearl* as a trademark for dressed and undressed dolls. London agent was *Boult, Wade & Tennant.* Made porcelain dolls' heads.

1922: Sole distributor in U.S. was *Roth, Baitz & Lipsitz,* who advertised that Hermann Steiner made *Waltershausen Dolls.* This appears to refer to the grade of the dolls rather than their place of origin.

1925: Made character babies and standing dolls; specialized in newborn babies. Had a porcelain factory that made dolls' heads of various types.

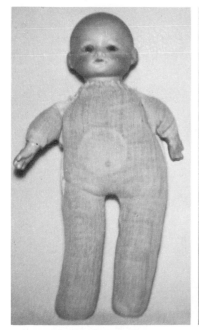

**1582A & B.** Infant doll made by Hermann Steiner with sleeping glass eyes, two-piece cloth body, composition hands, squeak box. Head mark: Ill. **1584.** H. 9 inches. *Coleman Collection.*

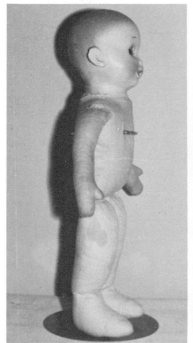

**1583A & B.** Composition head with flange neck made by Hermann Steiner. Eyes have unattached disks for pupils, which move by gravity within the eyeball. Body is cloth. Mark: Ill. **1585.** H. 12½ inches. (This doll may have been made after 1925.) *Courtesy of Ollie Leavister.*

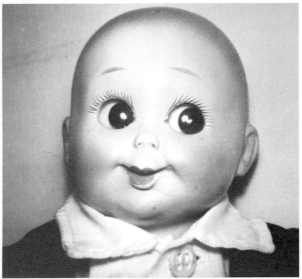

HERMANN STEINER DOLLS

15
ℋ
Germany
240

**1584**

DRGM 95464
ℋ
Germany
947

**1585**

Herm Steiner
ℋ
Germany

**1586**

128
Herm Steiner
ℋ

**1587**

**1584–1587.** Hermann Steiner marks found on **dolls.**

**Steiner, Jules Nicholas.** 1855–91, Paris; also known as Société Steiner; 1892, Amédée Lafosse; 1893–98, Widow Lafosse, née Lambert, the successor; had also taken over the doll business of *Henri Alexandre;* 1899–1901, Jules Mettais, successor, acquired the *May Frères* doll business; 1906–8, Edmond Daspres was the successor with a factory at Montreuil-sous-Bois. Many Steiner dolls have the name *Bourgoin* on them. This name has been found on dolls with the 1880 patented type of eyes, as well as on many other types. It frequently appears with "Ste.," which probably stands for "Société" or Steiner Cie. In 1862 Steiner obtained a French patent for an automatic talking bébé, and in 1863 a French patent for a mechanical doll. From 1864 through 1873 Steiner advertised that he specialized in patented talking, mechanical, and jointed dolls and bébés. At the 1878 Paris Exposition, Steiner showed

JULES NICHOLAS STEINER DOLLS

**1588A, B, & C.** Two walking Jules Steiner dolls with bisque heads and lower arms. The walking mechanism is contained in a pressed cardboard skirt. Several dolls of this type have been found with Steiner sales slips allegedly made out to "Mr. Jumeau." Apparently the writer was unaware of the fact that in French it would be M. Jumeau, not "Mr." *Courtesy of Winnie Langley* and *Margaret Whitton; photographs by Winnie Langley.*

The prices given for dolls are those for which the dolls were originally offered for sale. They are *not* today's prices.

JULES NICHOLAS STEINER DOLLS

A       B

**1589A & B.** Crying Jules Steiner doll. When wound, the doll kicks and the head turns from side to side. The bisque head has glass eyes and an open mouth with numerous upper and lower teeth, which are typical of certain Steiner dolls. These dolls have no mark on the heads, but the mechanism has a Steiner mark. H. 19½ inches. *Courtesy of the Newark Museum, Newark, N.J.*

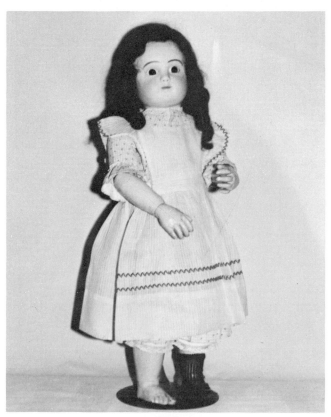

1590

mechanical talking bébés. Like *Bru,* Steiner received a silver medal for his exhibit, about which the jury, in its official report, wrote: "We must not forget to cite the talking bébé. The manufacturer who is almost the only one in France to produce this toy has turned out bébés perfectly made and amazingly lifelike.

"We notice also, among the products of this manufacturer of dolls and bébés, some made chiefly of rubber. We are persuaded that there would be in this case a great improvement if they were able to apply hard rubber to a certain extent and thus produce dolls having the advantage of being solid." Steiner continued his efforts to improve his dolls, and his applications for patents poured in.

1880: Obtained both French and German patents for moving eyes in dolls and bébés, which he claimed were an improvement over the counterweights that had been used up to that date. Wire-eyed Steiner dolls were based on this patent.

1881: There was another French patent for improving doll eyes.

1884: Was granted a French patent for a method of molding dolls and bébés out of pasteboard by the use of compressed air.

**1590.** Wire-eyed Jules Steiner doll with a wire handle at the crown of her head behind the ear. This opens and closes the eyes, which are marked "Steiner // 6 // B^te· S.G.D.G." The glass pupil and iris are set into an opaque white eyeball. Note the separate big toe, a Steiner characteristic. H. 28½ inches. *Courtesy of Helen Jo Payne.*

JULES NICHOLAS STEINER DOLLS

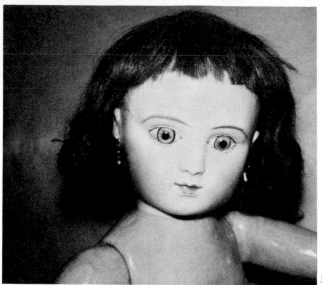

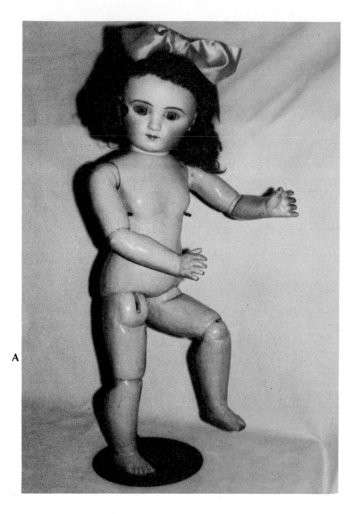

B   A

**1591A & B.** Jules Steiner bébé with bisque head, glass eyes, pierced ears, jointed composition body. Mark: Ill. **1593.** H. 28 inches. *Coleman Collection.*

1592

1889: Obtained a patent for improving porcelain and bisque heads for indestructible jointed bébés and dolls. At the Paris Exhibition Steiner received a gold medal for his exhibit, which "followed in the same lines as M. Jumeau." Steiner registered as a French trademark the girl with a banner, and the words *Le Petit Parisien.*

1890: At the Paris Exposition Steiner received the Diplôme d'Honneur. His advertisement in the Paris Directory stated that he was the inventor of the Bébé in France. But this claim might be questioned because *Soret* of Paris mentioned bébés in his 1847 French patent, and *Fr. Alph. Greffier* from Nantes, France, had exhibited bébés in the 1855 Paris Exposition, the year in which the Steiner firm was founded. In 1890 Steiner advertised "'Mama' and 'Papa' talking dolls, mechanical dolls, indestructible jointed bébés with eyes that move when it pleases and jointed wrists. All these bébés are put together with excellent articulation, lightness and incomparable build. It is impossible to confound them with dolls of German make." The last patent found for Steiner was in 1890, when he obtained a French patent for walking dolls with clockwork mechanism, which he named *Bébé Premier Pas* (Baby First Step) and *Bébé Marcheur.*

**1592.** Jules Steiner bébé with bisque head, glass eyes, jointed composition body. Head marked "STEINER, PARIS, F1$^{AE}$ A13." H. 20½ inches. *Courtesy of Hazel Ulseth.*

1891: The last record found for an exhibit by Steiner was that of the Paris Exposition, where he was honored with Hors Concours as a member of the jury. Unlike the case of Bru, nearly all the awards and honors seem to have come to the Steiner firm while the founder, Jules Nicholas Steiner, was in charge.

1892: Amédée Lafosse had succeeded as the head of the Steiner firm. He advertised in the Paris Directory that the firm owned twenty-four patents and made five categories of indestructible bébés, talking and ordinary, sleeping eyes, jointed wrists, mechanical and walking. These bébés had heavy bisque heads (called "unbreakable") and were named Le Parisien and "Premier Pas." The factory was at 60 rue d'Avron, Paris. Lafosse registered the trademark "Le Parisien" in 1892. In the same year, he obtained a French patent on talking bellows for dolls. Lafosse appears to have died shortly after becoming head of the Steiner firm, for in 1893 it was the Widow Lafosse who obtained a French patent for a walky-talky doll.

1894: Widow Lafosse was granted a French patent for a walking doll with a head that moved. By 1895, she was using the French trademark Bébé Phénix. This trade name had been used by Henri Alexandre in 1890, and by his successor, Tourrel, in 1892, which suggests that Widow Lafosse may have taken over the Alexandre business.

1897: Widow Lafosse obtained another French patent for a kiss-throwing and talking doll, and the following year she was granted yet another French patent for improving dolls' heads and limbs. At this time she advertised that the Steiner firm owned thirty patents.

1899: Jules Mettais succeeded the Widow Lafosse. He used the trade names "Le Parisien," "Le Phénix," Liège, and Poupée Merveilleuse. These names were registered by Jules Mettais as trademarks in France in 1899, as "Phénix Bébé," "Bébé Liège," and "Poupée Merveilleuse."

1900: The directory advertisement still stated that the Steiner firm made five categories of indestructible jointed bébés, and described the dolls as ordinary, speaking, sleep eyes, jointed wrists, and mechanical. They also advertised Negro and mulatto bébés, and that the factory was still located on rue d'Avron. Jules Mettais won a silver medal for his exhibit at the 1900 Paris Exposition.

1901: Mettais registered the trademark Bébé Modèle in France. He used the trade name Mascotte, which indicated that the Steiner firm had probably obtained this

from their neighbor, May Frères (Brothers). (Both companies had been located on rue Saintonge.)

1904: Edmond Daspres had a doll and bébé factory at Montreuil-sous-Bois, where many porcelain doll factories were located. Since he had the initials "E. D.," he may have made some of the bisque-headed dolls marked "E. D."

1906: E. Daspres was listed in the Paris Directory as head of the Steiner firm.

1908: He advertised La Patricienne, described as a "worldly doll."

Steiner dolls seldom have the characteristic cork pates found on French dolls; their pates are usually made of pressed cardboard. Betty Lou Weicksel has observed that some of the closed-mouth Steiner dolls have their upper eyelashes painted as a dot and dash, with the dot at the eyelid line. A purple wash seems often to have been applied under the paint, and is especially noticeable around the joints; some of the pates are also purple.

The name "Bourgoin" is found on many Steiner marked heads, especially those with the "A" and "C" marks, which appear to relate to mold series. Besides the "A" and "C" series, which occur most frequently, a "D," "FA," and "FC" (or "FG") series have also been reported. The mechanical Steiners and those with many teeth seldom have the Steiner name on their heads, but have it on the mechanism within the doll.

According to a small sample of marked Steiner dolls, the size markings seem to be somewhat as follows:

| Size No. | Height (in Inches) |
|----------|--------------------|
| 3/0      | 9                  |
| 2/0      | 11                 |
| 0        | 13                 |
| 1        | 16                 |
| 3        | 20                 |
| 5        | 24                 |
| 6        | 28                 |

Steiner dolls have been reported from 8½ to 38 inches tall.

**Steiner, Louis.** 1909–24. Sonneberg, Thür. Obtained several patents for dolls. (See Ill. 534.)

1910: He was granted a U.S. patent for eyebrows of hair strips or fur eyebrows, which he assigned to Borgfeldt.

1593–1598. Marks used for dolls by Jules Nicholas Steiner and his successors. No. 1594 is a Mettais mark; No. 1598 is a Lafosse mark.

STEINER B^TE S.G.D.G. S^TE C.6 BOURGOIN
1593

J. STEINER
S^TE S.G.D.G.
PARIS
F^IRE A II
1595

MARQUE DE FABRIQUE
1594

STEINER
.S.G.D.G.
PARIS
A II
1596

S^TE F ³⁄₀
1597

BÉBÉ "LE PARISIEN"
MEDAILLE D'OR
PARIS
1598

1924: Secured a German patent for a Mama voice.

**Steiner, Nicol.** 1915–20. Neustadt near Coburg, Thür. Manufactured dressed dolls.

**Steiner, R.** 1918. Neufang, Thür. Made dolls.

**Steiner, Rudolph.** 1889–1914 (?). Sonneberg, Thür. Produced dolls.

1889–90: Obtained British and U.S. patents for a nursing doll; the liquid was siphoned from a bottle, through the doll's mouth, and into a hidden receptacle under the doll. The patent suggests a ball-jointed composition body, but there is some indication that he may have made all-wood dolls also.

**Steiner, Victor.** 1903–25+. Sonneberg, Thür. Manufactured walking *Mama Dolls,* jointed dolls, and baby dolls.

**Steiner, Willi.** 1925+. Freiburg, Bavaria. Manufactured *Bussi* rag dolls.

**Steinfeld Bros.** 1898–1917. New York City. Manufactured and imported dolls.

1913: Copyrighted *Racketty Packetty Kiddy,* a doll designed by *Maurice F. Oppenheimer,* based on a character in the book of the same name written by Frances Hodgson Burnett. "Racketty Packetty Kiddies" was registered in U.S. as a trademark in 1915, but used since 1913.

1914: Racketty Packetty Kiddies advertised as unbreakable character dolls with movable heads; clothes could be removed. Came in a family of eight. Size 18 inches, price $3.00.

**Steinhardt, A., & Bro.** 1910–12. New York City. Imported and manufactured dolls.

1910: Advertised *Neverbreak* character dolls, *Smiling Sue* and *Honey Boy.*

1911: Registered in U.S. as trademarks *Marceline* and *Twee Deedle.* Copyrighted the Marceline doll, designed by Stefano Moraim. Advertised the following character dolls: *Mr. Twee Deedle,* Marceline, *Pierrot, Columbine, Mugsey, Buttons, Dutch-He* and *Dutch-She, Wilhewin,* and *Jockey.*

**Steinhauser, A., & Co.** 1891. Erfurt, Germany. Advertised that they were the most important woolen doll factory in Germany. Employed two hundred people. The dolls, all handmade, were exported to England, Belgium, Holland, Russia, France, Spain, Portugal, Austria, Roumania, Turkey, and other countries. They used the initials "A. St." in a triangle as their mark.

**Steinman-Beyencenet, Maurice.** 1923. London. Registered in Britain as a trademark *Wob-Li-Gob* for dolls.

**Steinmann Toy Manufacturing Co.** 1924. New York City. Made dolls.

**Stella.** 1903–9. Trade name for a rag doll made by *Horsman.* Advertised as a new patent shaped face with pretty features, a good profile; was dressed, including a bonnet. Size 13 inches, priced 25¢. It came in styles No. H/O and No. 00.

**Stella.** 1920. Trademark registered in Germany by *J. Stellmacher* for dolls.

**Stellmacher, J., Firm.** 1920. Steinheid, Germany. Registered in Germany *Stella* as a trademark for dolls.

**Stempfle & Vogel.** 1923–25+. Sonneberg, Thür. Manufactured dolls.

**Stern, Bertha S.** 1902–13. Philadelphia, Pa. B. Stern & Co. was successor in 1913. Made dolls.

**Steuber, Daniel.** 1879–88. Philadelphia, Pa. Made dolls' bodies and handled materials for dolls.

**Steuber, Mary.** 1878. Philadelphia, Pa. Patented in U.S. a commercial doll's leg, made by sewing the stocking to the leg and the boot to the stocking, before sewing up the back seam, so that there was only one thickness of material, thus obviating the making of a foot and leg and then making separate stockings and separate boots. Dolls with the type of legs patented by Mary Steuber usually are found with cloth bodies and china, bisque, or papier-mâché heads. Numerous commercial bodies appear to have followed this patent; either Mary Steuber granted licenses to other manufacturers, or many companies copied the idea after the patent expired.

**1599.** Cloth body with legs of the type designed by Mary Steuber, leather arms, and china head with molded bow in front center of the curls. H. 16 inches. H. of head only, 5 inches. *Coleman Collection.*

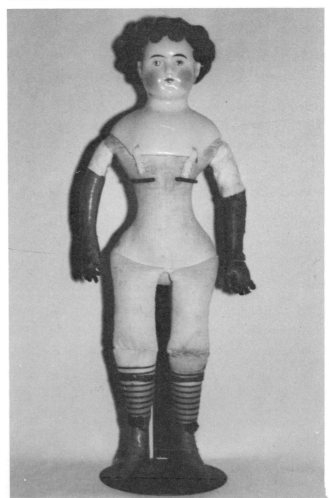

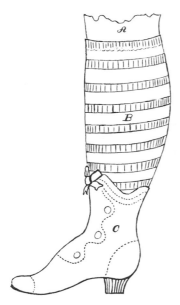

**1600.** Leg patented in 1878 by Mary Steuber. "A" is the leg portion, "B" is the stocking portion, "C" is the shoe portion. These are joined, but are not superimposed. *Patent Drawing.*

**Stevens, Abbie B.** 1919. Atlanta, Ga. Registered in U.S. *Georgia Peaches Home Grown,* written in a peach, and used as a trademark for dolls.

**Stevens, Annie L.** 1911–13. Fresno, Calif. Was granted a U.S. patent for a rag doll. The head was composed of a face section, two side sections that also formed the front of the neck, and two back sections that formed the back of the neck as well. The ears were made of two pieces, which were inserted between the face and the side sections and joined with them.

**Stiefel, Wilhelm.** 1901. Berlin. Obtained a German patent for hollow composition bodies for dolls, especially walking dolls.

**Stier, Gustav.** 1895–1920. Sonneberg, Thür. Manufactured and exported dolls, including wax dolls.

1900: One of the group of Grand Prize winners at the Paris Exposition.

**Stier, Heinrich.** 1852. Sonneberg, Thür. PLAYTHINGS Magazine in 1909 credited a Herr Stier with having invented the sleeping eye operated by lead weight, for dolls.

**Stiff, Walter & E.** 1881–97. London. Made and exported wax dolls and wax figures.

**Stiff-jointed Dolls.** The limbs of these dolls moved only backward and forward.

**Stockinet Dolls.** Among those who made stockinet dolls were *Martha Wellington, Martha Chase, Lillian J. Shearer,* and *Roberts Bros.*

**Stokes, Jane Gray.** 1915–23. New York City. Produced dolls under the name *Jane Gray Co.*

1916: Obtained a U.S. design patent for a rag doll with

an hourglass shape, made with a full skirt and a wide hat.

1917: Registered in U.S. *Kuddles* as a trademark for dolls; it had been used since 1915.

1923: Registered in U.S. as a trademark for dolls *Jazz Hound,* used since 1922.

**Stollwerch, Gebrüder.** 1906. Cologne, Germany. Registered in Germany as a trademark for dolls a star above three crowns.

**Stone Bisque.** 1890's–1900's. A nontranslucent type of bisque; often used for bonnet dolls or for inexpensive dolls.

**Stoneware.** Both brown and gray stoneware dolls' heads have been found. They generally have molded features and hair. Some were probably produced in the upper Ohio River pottery area.

**Storage.** Frequently, a sizable collection of dolls cannot all be put on display at one time because of the space limitations of the display area. Thus, it is often necessary to provide satisfactory storage areas for the dolls not being displayed. Possible places include chests of drawers, trunks, or sturdy boxes of suitable size. Wherever dolls are stored, the space should be large enough so that no overcrowding is necessary. Containers should be lined with newspaper, to discourage moths, but the dolls themselves should be individually wrapped in clean cloth of adequate size or in several layers of tissue paper.

A cardboard tube placed over the head of a wax or waxed doll will prevent any damage that might result from having the wrapping touch the wax. If a doll has ceramic lower limbs, a wooden bead or spool strung between the limbs will prevent them from knocking together and breaking. A doll with sleeping eyes should be stored face downward in a prone position. Before storing a doll, make certain it is free of any insects, and at regular intervals during storage add a moth preventive. Drawers or containers should each be labeled as to contents, and when the contents are changed, the labels should be corrected. (See **Custodianship of Dolls;** also **Display.**)

**Storch, Inc.** 1925. Breslau, Silesia. Manufactured dolls.

**Storch Bros.** 1835+. Cincinnati, Ohio. Imported and distributed dolls.

**Stork Brand Dolls.** 1910–13. *Parsons-Jackson Co.* Registered in U.S. a picture of a stork as a trademark. Among the other doll-making companies that used a stork as a trademark were *Louis Amberg & Son, Paul Hausmeister & Co.,* and *Jacob Jung.*

**Story Book Dolls.** 1925. Copyrighted by *Sol Bergfeld & Son,* manufacturers; distributed by *Borgfeldt.* They had composition heads, were 15 inches tall, and included the following: *Little Red Riding Hood, Little Bo-Peep, Mary and Her Garden, Goldey Locks, Babes in the Woods, Jack and Jill, Tom and the Pig,* and *Mary and Her Little Lamb.*

**Stöter, Otto.** 1906. Cologne, Germany. Obtained a German patent for putting eyes in dolls' heads.

**Stoupuv.** 1921–23. Prague (Praha), Czechoslovakia. Made dolls.

**Strampelchen (Little Kicker).** 1925. Trademark registered in Germany by Widow *Edith Maus* for dolls, including dressed dolls. Advertised as "large dolls and small prices."

**Strandfee (Sea Nymph).** 1923. Trademark registered in Germany by *D. Eberwein & Co.*, doll makers.

**Stransky Frères.** 1892. Paris. Advertised a talking, singing phonograph doll.

**Strasburger, Alfred.** 1924. New York City. Obtained a U.S. design patent for a Japanese-type doll with its blouse printed with mah-jongg symbols.

**Strasburger, Isidore.** 1863–66. Paris. Made dolls' bodies of cloth and of kid; also made dolls' clothes.

**Strasburger, Pfeiffer & Co.** 1851–81. New York City. Produced, imported, and distributed dolls, including dolls made by *New York Rubber Co.* Oscar Strasburger was joined by Edward Nuhn in 1858.

1871: George F. Pfeiffer and George Fritz joined the firm, which became known as Strasburger, Fritz and Pfeiffer. Fritz and Pfeiffer lived in Europe at the time. They registered in the U.S. their triangular-shaped trademark, which they had used since 1869.

1872: Firm was known as Strasburger & Pfeiffer. They supplied data on dolls for the Christmas issue of HARPER'S BAZAR.

1876: Won a prize medal at the Philadelphia Exhibition for their display. Among the dolls advertised in their catalog were:

Rubber Babies with rubber string, boys and girls, dressed and undressed, painted and not painted; sizes 3, 3¼, 3½, 4¼, 4½, 5, 5¼, 5½, 6½, and 7¼ inches; price $1.00 to $6.00 doz. wholesale.

China Babies or Bathing dolls, all-china, glazed, with black hair, in "common" or in "superior" quality; or with yellow hair and painted comb; fourteen sizes from 1 to 6½ inches; price 8¢ to $2.75 doz. wholesale.

China babies also came with black hair and gilt boots, or black hair and painted boots, or black hair and painted shirt, or Negro babies; some of the Negro babies had turbans and some had colored shirts.

Bisque Babies or Bathing dolls came with molded blonde hair, barefeet, in fourteen sizes from 1 to 6½ inches; price 9¢ to $2.50 doz. wholesale.
Also came with gilt boots or painted boots, with fixed arms or movable arms, with black molded hair as well as blonde. Dolls with natural hair came in sizes 3 to 8 inches; price $1.75 to $9.00.

Bisque Boys with light hair came in sizes 4, 4½, and 5½ inches; price $1.50 to $2.25 doz. wholesale.

China Limb Dolls with china head, feet, and arms on cloth bodies; came in ordinary quality, better quality, very fine quality with jointed body that would sit upright, and extra fine quality with stitched bodies and painted bisque boots; sizes 2 to 30

**1602.** Mark used by Strasburger, Pfeiffer & Co.

**1601.** Glazed china Bathing Doll (Frozen Charlotte) with black hair and gilded boots as advertised by Strasburger & Pfeiffer in 1876. H. 3¾ inches. This was the largest size in which this type of doll was advertised. *Coleman Collection.*

inches; the fine-quality dolls came only in sizes 11 to 23 inches; price 38¢ to $13.50 doz. wholesale. The price variation was more a function of size than of quality.

China Limb dolls with natural hair came in fifteen sizes, 6 to 21 inches tall; price $2.00 to $13.50 doz. wholesale.

Bisque Limb dolls with fixed heads came with painted hair and painted boots or gilt boots; the hair was blonde, and sometimes had a blue band in it; sizes 6 to 21 inches; price 75¢ to $9.00 doz. wholesale.

Bisque Limb dolls with moving heads and natural hair, fixed glass eyes; bisque limbs had painted shoes and stockings, came in two grades; sizes 11 to 22½ inches; price $9.00 to $30.00 doz. wholesale.

Wax Dolls, with molded hair; came with assorted colored bands in hair; wooden limbs or wax limbs, or wooden arms with wax legs; steady eyes or moving eyes; painted feet or painted shoes; sizes 10 to 30½ inches; price $1.00 to $13.50 with shirt.

Wax Dolls with natural hair; came with wooden limbs or wax limbs; with steady eyes or moving eyes; with painted feet or painted shoes; sizes 10 to 27 inches; price $1.25 to $24.00 doz. wholesale.

Finest Quality Wax Dolls; long flowing hair, moving eyes, fine feet with gaiters and stockings; embroidered shirt and drawers; sizes 13½ to 28 inches; price $1.50 to $4.50 each.

Model Wax Dolls with human hair in assorted headdresses; steady or moving eyes, wax limbs; linen embroidered shirt; sizes 13½ to 34 inches; price $2.50 to $15.00 each.

French Kid Dolls with bisque moving heads, natural hair; kid jointed bodies, and either kid limbs or bisque hands; eleven sizes; price $2.00 to $12.00 each. Dressed French Kid Dolls cost as much as $40.00 each.

Patent Dolls; heads, arms, and feet made of Indestructible Material (composition); came with painted hair or natural hair; with painted eyes or steady glass eyes; sizes 12 to 24 inches; price $4.00 to $33.00 doz. wholesale.

Rag Dolls with wax faces, covered closely with fine gauze; advertised that "water or heat has no effect on this improvement"; came with Red Riding Hoods, white hoods, or fancy hoods and embroidered long dresses; several sizes; price up to $3.75 each.

Worsted Dolls, knit of wool yarn; came in assorted colors; some with elastics, some crying; sizes $6\frac{1}{2}$ to 17 inches; price $3.50 to $24.00 doz. wholesale.

Doll Bodies; came stuffed with sawdust and with leather arms; hair stuffed, with leather arms having open or closed fingers, or with leather arms and china hands.

China Doll Heads, with plain or fancy black hair, some with gilt combs; eighteen sizes from $2\frac{3}{4}$ to $8\frac{3}{4}$ inches; price 63¢ to $15.00 doz. wholesale.

Glazed Boys' Heads with gilt and colored neckties; sizes 4 to $6\frac{1}{4}$ inches; price $2.00 to $7.00 doz. wholesale.

Bisque Doll Heads; came with light painted hair or natural hair; boys and girls; painted eyes or glass eyes; ears pierced or not pierced; breast plain or fancy; sizes $2\frac{1}{4}$ to $6\frac{1}{2}$; price $1.75 to $10.50 doz. wholesale. The ones with natural hair and glass eyes were the most expensive; next came the ones with light painted hair with black band, earrings, and fancy painted breasts.

Patent Doll Heads, "indestructible" (composition); came with painted eyes and assorted colors of hair; sixteen sizes, $2\frac{1}{4}$ to $13\frac{1}{2}$ inches; price $1.00 to $36.00 doz. wholesale.

(The above is from the catalog; courtesy of Flora Jacobs.)

1881: George Borgfeldt and Joseph and Marcel Kahle left Strasburger & Pfeiffer to establish *Geo. Borgfeldt & Co.*

**Strasburger Puppen Manufaktur.** 1899–1903. Strasbourg, Alsace & Lorraine. R. Kahn, proprietor. Made dolls.

**Strassburger, R.** 1909–18. Sonneberg, Thür. Made leather dolls.

**Strasser.** 1924–25+. Registered in Germany as a trademark for dolls and babies by *Hedwig Maria Huldschinsky* (née Strasser). These were lifelike *Art Dolls* made with movable and washable heads, suitable for the tropics. Advertised as the doll with the "human face"; distributed in America by *Louis Wolf & Co.*

**Strat Manufacturing Co.** 1915. U.S. Made rag doll that they named *Sammy Sock.*

**Strathmann & Joachim.** 1882. Sonneberg, Thür. Manufactured dolls.

**Straube, W.** See **Kling, C. F., & Co.**

**Strauss, Adolph, & Co.** 1857–1925+. New York City.

Known as "Asco" (see Ill. 50). In 1923, the successor was Strauss-Eckhardt Co. or "Seco." They were importers and distributors of dolls. Evidence suggests that they may not have handled dolls until 1912, when they advertised "out of the ordinary" dolls for 5¢, 10¢, and 25¢.

1914: Advertised kid jointed dolls and dressed character dolls.

1922: Registered in U.S. *Our Pet* as a trademark for dolls, to be affixed with printed labels to doll or package. Max Eckhardt was a firm member, but the company was still known as Strauss & Co. Advertised dressed dolls, jointed dolls, and *Kidlyn* dolls of Sonneberg and of Nürnberg make.

1923: Began to use the trademark (in an ellipse) "The House of // SECO // Service."

1924: Advertised imported dolls, *Mama Dolls,* jointed dolls, *Kidoline* dolls, and character dolls.

1925: Registered in U.S. as a trademark (in an ellipse) "The House of // SECO // Service."

**Straw, Plaited.** 1920. *Alfred Sheen & George Wenzel* created dolls of plaited straw.

**Strawbridge & Clothier.** 1905–25+. Philadelphia, Pa. Distributed dolls.

1906: Registered in U.S. as trademarks *Princess Doll* and *Baby Helen,* both trademarks having been used since 1905. The Princess Doll trademark was for commerce, especially with France.

1910: Exclusive wholesale distributor of *Dolly Dollykins, Bobby Bobbykins,* and other rag dolls.

**Street, James A., & Wantland, Edward F.** 1921–23. Los Angeles, Calif. Obtained U.S. patent for a doll's body with a heart-shaped picture mounting at the heart spot.

**Strehl Mar.** 1912. Zuckelhausen near Leipzig, Saxony. Was issued a German patent for a talking doll.

**Streng, A.** 1909–18. Köppelsdorf, Thür. Made dolls.

**Strobel, Heinrich, & Son.** 1902–20. Fürth, Bavaria. Exported dolls.

**Strobel & Wilken Co.** 1864–1925+. Cincinnati, Ohio, and New York City. Imported, produced, and distributed dolls. The firm was founded in 1849 by the Strobels of Cincinnati, manufacturers of leather goods. In 1864 George Wilken joined the business, and they began to handle toys. After the Civil War, when European trade was resumed, they imported dolls.

1875: Displayed their products at the Cincinnati Exhibition.

1886: Opened a branch in New York City, which grew rapidly until it became the main office.

1895: Began to use their trademark *American Beauty,* probably for rag dolls.

1897: Used "S W & Co. // Carlsbad" as a mark, according to Jervis in his BOOK OF POTTERY MARKS. This mark was probably used on ceramic products made in

**1603A & B.** Strobel & Wilken doll with bisque head, dark pupil-less eyes, composition body, and original Jordanian bride costume with dowry coins on hat and necklace. Mark on head: Ill. **1604.** H. 9 inches. *Courtesy of Jessica Norman.*

**1604–1606.** Marks of Strobel & Wilken used on dolls.

Karlsbad, Bohemia, for Strobel & Wilken.

1902: Registered in U.S. their trademark "American Beauty."

1903: Registered in U.S. *Royal* as a trademark for dolls. Began to sell *Diana* metal dolls' heads made by *Alfred Heller.*

1905: Advertised "American Beauty" dolls, *Darling* dolls, *Wonderland* and *American Fashion* dressed dolls, Royal, *Waldorf,* and *Jubilee* jointed dolls, and a new line called *Kanwashem.* They had a new line of bisque head dolls that they controlled; new construction kid bodies; a "strong line" of bisque babies and dressed dolls of all nations.

1906: Their "American Beauty" rag dolls had colored photographic faces.

1908: Acquired a new warehouse in Sonneberg, Thür. The novelty in their "Royal" (*Kämmer & Reinhardt* line) was the *Flirt* with eyes that moved from side to side as well as opening and closing. These dolls came in various sizes and many styles of wigs.

1909: Advertised "Royal," *Handwerck,* and "Jubilee" dolls. Jubilee was an import line of "smiling babies" with jointed composition arms and jointed wrists, baby bonnets, and long dresses. They also advertised the "581" line of models produced from life. Their picture shows a bent-limb baby body, the first of this type found as yet. The head of this baby resembles the Kämmer & Reinhardt *Baby* (model 100). It has the character baby type of hands.

Commander *Peary* and Dr. *Cook* were advertised as character dolls.

1910: Advertised "Baby" and other character dolls made by Kämmer & Reinhardt. (See Ill. 941.)

1911: Distributors for dolls made by *Ideal Novelty & Toy Co.* and by *Kaempff.*

1913: Advertised new *Aluminia* dolls' heads.

1914: Registered in U.S. *Brighto* as a trademark for dolls. Advertised, besides "Brighto," *Arabesque, Our Pride Kidette, Peach,* and the *Nemo* series.

1915: Advertised *Susie's Sister* line of character dolls and *Tootsie,* a new line of character babies. They still advertised the three Standard Brands, namely, Royal, Jubilee and Handwerck; but they introduced some Japanese lines.

1916: Distributed *Zaiden* dolls and the *Utley Co.'s* new *Rollinson* dolls. Advertised the *American Art Dolls,* which included *Ulrich, Buddy,* and *Faith.*

1917: Advertised *Cuddlekins.*

1918: Distributed *Snow White* dolls made by *American Toy & Manufacturing* Co.

1921: Advertised "1158" line of hand-painted terry-cloth dolls.

1924: Still advertising Arabesque, Jubilee, and American Beauty lines.

**Strube, Carl.** See **Schmidt, Richard.**

**Strubelpeter.** 1911. New line of dolls made by *Steiff;* came with blonde tousled hair and long, claw-like fingernails. The doll represented a youth in a famous German fairy tale who refused to have his hair or fingernails cut.

**Strunz, Wilhelm.** 1909. Nürnberg, Bavaria. Was granted a German patent for a rag doll.

**Struss, Wilhelm.** 1924. Hamburg, Germany. Made dolls.

**Stuffed Dolls.** This type of dolls was made from ancient times, but patents for them began around 1860. Among the patentees were *Fischer, Naumann & Co., Sarah Robinson, Wolf Flechter, Elizabeth Bell, Albert J. Gleason, Alice Harding Butler, Benjamin Goldenberg, Käthe Kruse, Loula S. Reeves, Georgene Averill, Lenora Price, Michael Schoen, Elizabeth Barry, Joseph Langrock,* and *Charles N. Reese.*

**Stuffing for Dolls.** See **Manufacture of Cloth Bodies; Manufacture of Kid Bodies.**

**Stutson, Thomas E.** See **Wolf, Louis, & Co.**

**Success.** 1898. Trade name of a doll with "French bisque" head and kid body, distributed by *W. A. Cissna.* Came with woven wig, open mouth and teeth, scalloped edge around bust; size 21¼ inches, price $8.90 doz. wholesale.

**Suchetzky, Elise (née Schmidt).** 1919. Berlin. Distributed dolls; registered in Germany *Esy* as a trademark.

**Sucker Thumb (Suck-a-Thumb).** 1912–13. Trade name for a baby doll made by *Horsman.* It came with a composition head, having the appearance of a three- or four-week-old infant, which was described in PLAYTHINGS as having a "heavy jowl, baggy jaw and smudgy nose." The soft body was of pink or flesh-colored sateen, stuffed with cork. It was dressed in a long white slip. Price $8.50 doz. wholesale.

**Sucker Thumb Baby.** 1924–25. Made by *Ideal Novelty & Toy Co.* There was a tiny hole in the dolls' puckered mouth, which could just hold the thumb of the little hand that was rubber to the wrist.

**Suffa, K.** 1909. Hönbach, Thür. Made dolls' heads.

**Suffa, R.** 1909. Hönbach, Thür. Made dolls' heads.

**Suffering Suffragette.** 1912. Trade name for a doll that walked by means of a metal rod in each foot; price 50¢.

**Suffragette Kid.** 1911. Trademark registered in U.S. by *Mabel D. Nekarda,* to be affixed to the clothes of the doll.

**Suffragina.** 1914. Described as the *Votes for Women* doll; advertised as washable, unbreakable, and sunproof. Made by *Elektra Toy & Novelty Co.*

**Sugar Baby.** *Mama* type of baby made by *EFFanBEE;* came with molded composition head, brown sleeping eyes, open mouth and teeth, cloth body with composition limbs. Marked "Sugar Baby."

**Sultana.** 1893. Trade name for bisque-headed doll distributed by *Butler Bros.* Size 21 inches, price dressed $3.45.

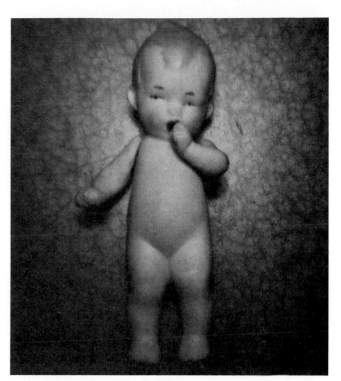

**1607.** All-bisque version of a "Sucker-Thumb" doll has molded features and hair, including a topknot; open circular mouth into which the thumb of the bent-arm hand will readily go. Doll is jointed at the shoulders. Size 3 inches. *Courtesy of Eleanor Jean Carter.*

## EFFANBEE
## SUGAR BABY

**1608.** "Sugar Baby" mark used on EFFanBEE dolls.

**Summer Girl.** 1918. Made by *Jessie McCutcheon Raleigh,* distributed by *Butler Bros.* Size 13½ inches, price $3.90.

**Sumner, Hermann Gove.** See **Butterfield, Louis M.**

**Sun Bonnet Sue and Sun Bonnet Ann.** 1919–20. Made by *Sunny-Twin Dolly Co.;* designed and patented by Mrs. *Patricia Carey.* These jointed celluloid baby dolls wore handmade and embroidered clothing. Sue was dressed in blue and was the mate to *Sunny Boy Blue.* Ann was dressed in pink and was the mate to Sunny Boy Dan. Came in two sizes, price $13.50 and $45.00 doz. wholesale.

**Sunbonnet Dolls.** 1910–11. Boy and girl dolls with character faces; boy was dressed in rompers. Price 25¢, 50¢, and $1.00.

**Sunbonnet Girl.** 1911. One of the *Horsman Art Dolls,* modeled from life. Had *Can't Break 'Em* head, molded hair, cloth body; was dressed in pinafore and sunbonnet. This was one of twenty dolls sold in a sample line for $16.50 (for the entire sample).

**Sunbonnet Jane.** 1921. A soft doll designed by *Gertrude Stacy* and made by the *Giftoy Co.*

**Sunbonnet Sal.** 1912–14. Girl doll made by *Horsman*; came with composition head, cork-stuffed pink or flesh-colored sateen body; dressed in blue-checked gingham dress, white apron, and a sunbonnet.

**Sunbonnet Sue.** 1850's. Name given to a doll with wax face, cloth body stuffed with sawdust. Her monogram initials were embroidered on her stockings.

**Sunbonnet Sue.** 1909. Made by *Horsman* with *Life Like Face*; price $1.00.

**Suner.** 1920. Trademark registered in Britain by *Hewitt Bros., Willow Pottery,* for dolls.

**Sunny Boy Blue and Sunny Boy Dan.** 1919–20. Made by *Sunny-Twin Dolly Co.,* designed and patented by Mrs. *Patricia Carey.* These jointed celluloid baby dolls wore handmade and embroidered clothing. Boy Blue was dressed in blue and was the mate to *Sun Bonnet Sue.* Dan was dressed in pink and was the mate to Sun Bonnet Ann. Two sizes, price $13.50 and $45.00 doz. wholesale.

**Sunny Jim.** Ca. 1905. Rag doll and also a plaster figure, based on the character originated by Minny Maude Hanff; probably designed by W. W. Denslow, who illustrated THE WIZARD OF OZ. The cutout rag dolls came with "Force" cereal box tops. They were lithographed in colors on muslin; size 18 inches. Dolls also made later.

**Sunny Jim.** 1909. Made by Hahn & *Amberg*; came with a Teddy Bear type of "fur" body.

**Sunny Jim.** 1910. Distributed by *Butler Bros.*; came with composition head. When doll was pressed, the mouth opened and a bellows sounded a voice. Price, dressed, $2.00 doz. wholesale.

**Sunny Jim.** 1914. Doll made by *Ideal Novelty & Toy Co.*

**Sunny Orange Blossom.** 1924–25. Made by *Louis Amberg & Son,* designed and patented by *Otto Ernst Denivelle.* She had a composition head with molded orange-shaped cap trimmed with imitation orange blossoms; painted eyes, toddler-type cloth body with composition limbs. Doll was dressed all in orange, with its name on a ribbon across the chest. Mark on the yoke read: "©//L. A. & S.—1924." Doll made the sound of an orange when squeezed; 14 inches tall.

**Sunny-Twin Dolly Co.** 1919–20. Los Angeles, Calif. Made "Sunny Twin dolls." Had agents in New York. *Patricia Carey* obtained a U.S. design patent for dolls that she assigned to *Leslie Clark Brintnall,* who registered in U.S. "Sunny-Twin" as a trademark for dolls. These jointed celluloid baby dolls were named *Sun Bonnet Sue, Sunny Boy Blue,* Sun Bonnet Ann, and Sunny Boy Dan.

**Sunshine.** 1913. Bust of a child copyrighted by *Horsman,* designed by *Helen Trowbridge,* distributed by F. A. O. Schwarz. Came with *Can't Break 'Em* composition head; size 16 inches; price $2.50.

**Sunshine.** 1915. Girl's head with ribbon in hair. Copyrighted by *Trion Toy Co.;* designed by *Ernesto Peruggi.*

**Sunshine.** 1921–22. Sleeping doll made by *National Manufacturing Co.;* size over 12 inches.

**Sunshine Brand Dolls.** Ca. 1914–22. Distributed by *Sears, Roebuck & Co.*

1922: Came with bisque head and forearms, sleeping glass eyes, hair eyelashes, mohair wigs; kid bodies had riveted joints at hips and knees. Sizes 16, 18, 21, 23, and 25 inches; price $2.45 to $5.89.

**Sunshine Girl.** 1912. Trademark registered in Britain by *Bing* for dolls.

**Sunshine Girl.** 1913. Described as an American-type girl with the face of a shy Quaker; came with composition head, blue eyes, red-gold hair; dressed in pink, blue, or yellow.

**Sunshine Kid.** 1912. Trademark registered in Britain by *Bing* for dolls.

**Sunshine Kids.** 1915–16. Trademark registered in U.S. by *Indestructo Specialties Co.* for dolls.

**Superba.** 1904–15. Trade name for a line of kid-body dolls handled by *Louis Wolf & Co.* These dolls had bisque heads and forearms, sleeping eyes, real hair eyelashes, curly mohair wigs, and composition legs. The bodies were stuffed with cork and sawdust in equal amounts, and were nickel rivet jointed at shoulders, elbows, hips, and knees. Sizes 14½, 16¼, 17¼, 18¼, and 21¼ inches; price 79¢ to $2.25. The name was affixed to the chest of the doll with a blue elliptical paper sticker on which was the word "Superba" over a crown and crossed olive branches. (See also **Miss Millionaire.**)

**Superior.** 1850's–90's. Name found on composition heads. A composition head exhibited by *Cuno & Otto Dressel* at the New Orleans Exhibition in 1884 has the *Holz Masse* mark on the outside and on the inside a triangular paper label with the words "Indestructible Heads//Superior" and Dressel's Holz Masse trademark between these words. Dressel exhibited heads with molded hair and wigged heads; the inside of the heads was covered with a coarse gauze material and painted pink. The outside of the heads had a finish that was almost bisque-like (See Ill. 481.)

Composition heads with "M & S, Superior" and with "G L, Superior" have been found. (See Ills. 423 and 425.) Both these appear with the number "2015." The "M & S, Superior" also is found with the number "4515." The number variation appears to indicate a difference in mold. Kimport reports a composition head with painted brown eyes and black sausage curls that bears the label "A. F. & C., Superior, 2015, Made in Germany." It is most likely that "A. F. & C." stands for *A. Fleischmann & Cramer* of Sonneberg. The Dressels were also of Sonneberg, and intermarried with the Fleischmanns.

The Dressels assembled and distributed dolls with

parts made by other firms. It seems possible that the "M & S" may stand for *Müller (J. F.) & Strassburger* also of Sonneberg. They were important enough to be displaying dolls at the international exhibitions around the time when these "M & S" dolls would have been made. Both blonde and brunette molded hair dolls have been found with "M & S. Superior" mark. The "G L., Superior" dolls may have been made by *G. Liedel* of Hildburghausen near Sonneberg, who displayed composition dolls at the 1855 Paris Exposition.

Socket-head composition dolls with sleeping eyes, open mouth, and teeth have been found marked "M & S." These heads are also painted pink on the inside and have a smooth bisque-like finish, but otherwise are much cruder than the early heads. (See Ill. 427.)

**Superior.** 1898. Trade name given to a doll with a "washable," "indestructible" composition head by *W. A. Cissna & Co.* It had a wig; body was stuffed. Size 17½ inches, price 25¢.

**Superior Bébé.** See **Bébé Superior.**

**Superior Doll Manufacturing Co.** 1915–22. New York City. Made all-composition dolls. David *Zaiden*, president of this company, was a chemist who in 1906 had produced composition dolls' heads.

1915: Advertised doll faces verging on character faces, moving eyes, hair eyelashes, teeth, moving tongue, real hair wigs of various colors, jointed composition bodies, some fully jointed that could stand alone. Nine sizes, 14 to 29 inches; price $1.00 and up.

**Supplies for Doll Makers.** In addition to eyes, voices, wigs, and molds, which are discussed elsewhere, many firms specialized in producing other supplies for doll makers. Among these were:

*Elastic for stringing dolls:*
    *Dolly Dimples Doll Elastic;* sold by *Strobel & Wilken* and *Charles Braitling*
    La Fleche Frères & Cie., Paris
    A. Laurent & Co., London and Paris
    Oreste-Martin, Manchester and Paris

*Enamels, varnishes, etc.:*
    Celluloid Zapon Co., New York City
    *Du Pont,* Wilmington, Del.

*Springs for dolls:*
    Bridgeport Spring & Wire Works, Devon, Conn.

*Stuffing materials:*
    American Sea Grass Co.
    Atlantic Excelsior Manufacturing Co.
    Boston Excelsior Co., New York City

*Wood flour:*
    David Meyer & Bros., New York City
    Schmalz Dairy Farm, Hoboken, N.J.

**SuR.** See **Seyfarth & Reinhardt.**

**Surprise Baby.** 1923. Two-faced doll made by *Ideal Novelty & Toy Co.* Came with two voices. One face

smiled and said "Mama"; when the other face was turned to the front, it cried real tears.

**Surprise Doll.** 1867–72. Two patents were obtained by the *Bru's* in France for "Surprise" dolls. One was by Leon Casimir Bru for a doll with a turning head and two faces; the head could be turned without disarranging the wig. The other patent was secured by Madame Bru in 1872 for a doll with a musical apparatus in its body that would play tunes.

**Susie's Sister.** 1915. Line of character dolls distributed by *Strobel & Wilken;* came with "unbreakable" heads that were hand-painted and resembled expensive European *Art Dolls;* jointed arms and legs. Size 17 inches; price $2.00.

**Süssenguth, Christian, Jün.** 1895–1909. Neustadt near Coburg, Thür. Made dolls and dolls' bodies.

1898: Obtained British patent for a jointed dolls' body made of paper, cardboard, or leather board; covered with stiffened fabric or leather; parts joined by hinges or rivet connections and riveted or sewed at the edges. The head and forearms could be made of porcelain, wood, wax, composition, or the same material as the body.

**Süssenguth, Gebrüder.** 1899–1925+. Neustadt near Coburg, Thür. Made dolls of various kinds.

1899: Registered in Germany *Dewey Doll* as a trademark.

1904: Registered in Germany the initials "G S" and the words *Puppe der Zukunft* (Doll of the Future) as a trademark for dolls; the factory stamped these dolls out of "leather pasteboard."

**Süssenguth, Hans.** 1918–25+. Sonneberg, Thür. Manufactured dolls.

**Süssenguth, Reinhold & Co.** 1895–98. Neustadt near Coburg, Thür. Manufactured dressed dolls and *tauflinge.*

**Sussfeld & Cie.** 1917. Paris. Doll distributors. Registered in France and in Britain *Clio Bébé* and *Thalie Bébé* as trademarks for dolls. Their London agents were *G. F. Redfern & Co.*

**Suzaine, Mme.** 1863–73. Paris. Handled dolls and made trousseaux for them.

**Suzel.** See **Yerri et Suzel.**

**Swaine & Co.** 1854–1918. Hüttensteinach (North Köppelsdorf), Thür. Hard-paste porcelain factory. After World War I they joined *Gebrüder Schoenau* and became Gebrüder Schoenau, Swaine & Co.

**Swat Mulligan.** 1911. Baseball doll made by *Louis Amberg & Son.* Came with composition head, pink sateen cork-stuffed body; wore a baseball cap and carried a bat and ball; price $1.00.

**Sweater Boy.** 1917. Trade name for doll made by *Ideal Novelty & Toy Co.*

**Sweet Baby Doll Co.** 1918–22. New York City. Made dolls.

**Sweet Lavender.** 1915. Made by the *Non-Breakable Doll Co.* Doll came with molded hair; price $1.00.

**Sweet Marie.** 1900–1910. Rag doll based on the patent of *Edgar Newell.*

**Sweet Nell.** 1925. Trade name for dolls and babies made by *Hugo Wiegand.*

**Sweet Susan.** 1916. Baby doll in a long dress, distributed by *Montgomery Ward & Co.* Came with mohair wig and pacifier. Size 17½ inches, price $3.30.

**Sweetheart.** 1910–15. Line of jointed dolls handled by *B. Illfelder & Co.*

**Sweetheart.** 1915. Made by *Louis Amberg & Son.* Sizes 12 and 16 inches; price $4.00 and $8.00 doz. wholesale.

**Sweetheart.** 1919. Doll made by *Jessie McCutcheon Raleigh.*

**Sweetheart.** See **Little Sweetheart.**

**Sweetie.** 1916. All-composition doll with painted hair and eyes; body jointed at the shoulders; airbrush flesh finish. Wore one-piece bathing suit and cap to match. Size 13½ inches; price $17.00 doz. wholesale.

**Sweetie.** 1917–19. Trademark registered in U.S. by *Faultless Rubber Co.* for an all-rubber girl doll; nude body came in red or tan. Size 3¾ inches.

**1609.** "Sweetie," all-rubber doll made by Faultless Rubber Co. Mark on back: Ill. **540.** H. 3¾ inches. *Courtesy of Jessica Norman.*

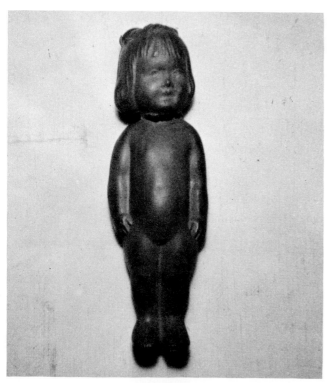

**Sweetie and Sweetness.** 1919–21. Pair of wood-fiber dolls made by *Progressive Toy Co.*

1921: Advertised as having new bisque heads on fully jointed bodies; sizes 14, 16, 20, and 24 inches.

**Sweetums.** 1925. Infant doll made by *Century Doll Co.*, who were getting their bisque heads from *Kestner* at this time. It was advertised as having sleeping eyes, sewed wig, crying voice. Made in two sizes. The model for "Sweetums" was purchased from a "world famous" sculptor.

**Swieka.** 1915. Russia. An artist who created portrait-type dolls; size 13½ inches.

**Swift, A. B.** See **Selchow & Righter.**

**Swiss Dolls.** These are generally hand-carved wooden dolls. They often have carved hair with a braid wound around the head; painted eyes and features. In 1921, the *Bücherer* firm obtained patents for a ball-jointed metal doll.

**Syer, Ernest.** 1919–22. London. Imported dolls.

**Symphony Chime Doll.** 1912. Had a composition head, and when doll was shaken, a chime sounded in its body. Price $1.00.

**1610.** All-wood doll made in Switzerland in the 20th century has carved hair with a braid around the head, carved and painted features. Body is carved, not turned. Doll is jointed at neck, shoulders, elbows, hips, and knees. H. 11½ inches. *Coleman Collection.*

# T

**T. & T. Toy Co.** 1924. New York City. Handled dolls.

**Tago.** 1925. Trade name for soft stuffed dolls made by *Paul Bühl & Tannewitz.*

**Taig.** See **Brotteig.**

**Taillandier, E. H.** 1925. Paris. Specialized in kid dolls' heads.

**Taiyo Trading Co.** 1919–21. New York City and Toronto, Canada. Combined the *Tajimi Co.* and *Takito, Ogawa & Co.* Imported and manufactured dolls.

1919: Advertised *Baby Lucy* and *Ming Toy.*

1920: Advertised *Geisha.*

**Tajimi Co.** 1917–18. New York City. Combined with *Takito, Ogawa & Co.* in 1919 to become *Taiyo Trading Co.* Imported dolls, especially the bisque-headed doll *Baby Lucy,* made in Japan.

**1611.** Mark used by Tajimi Co.

**Takito, Ogawa & Co.** 1918. New York City and Chicago, Ill. Combined with *Tajimi Co.* in 1919 to become *Taiyo Trading Co.* Imported dolls, especially jointed dolls.

**Talking Dolls.** Dolls that can talk have challenged man for centuries. The principal methods of making dolls talk are by pulling strings, exerting pressure on some part of the body, moving one or more of the limbs of the doll, or by changing its position. Bellows were used to produce sound at an early date, and in the 19th century reeds were placed in dolls' bodies and sound produced by blowing across them. The most realistic types of talking dolls were those that contained a phonograph. *Jean Maelzel* patented a talking doll in 1824 that operated when its arms were moved. *Théroude* claimed that he invented the talking doll. In the 1850's, the *Motschmann*-type dolls had "voices" that sounded when the head was pushed downward. *Jumeau* made talking bébés as early as 1865. At this date, the bébés would probably have had kid bodies. It is not known when Jumeau started to make his talking bébés with the two strings from a jointed composition body. This pull-string type of talking doll was made in the mid-19th century and was popular from the 1880's up to World War I. PLAYTHINGS in 1903 reported that "Modern Parisian dolls move lips and speak articulated sentences." These were probably phonograph dolls. They spoke in French and German. A

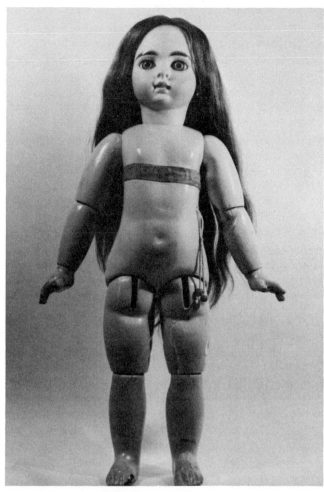

**1612.** Pull-string talking doll that says "Mama" and "Papa." The doll has bisque head, glass eyes, cork pate under its wig, pierced ears; composition body that has been cut open for insertion of voice box. Head marked "168." H. 24 inches. *Courtesy of Hazel Ulseth.*

French patent for dolls with moving lips was obtained as early as 1890. Another doll said one word when its right arm was raised and another word when the left arm was raised. In 1877 *William Harwood* made a talking doll in America.

1904: A doll would call "Mama" when it was picked up. It was silenced or regained its voice if a catch at the back of its head was moved.

1906: A new talking doll raised one leg to say "Mama" and the other leg to say "Papa."

1908: Doll would talk when rolled from side to side; formerly it had talked only when changed from a horizontal to a vertical position, or vice versa. Another doll said "Mama" when one foot was pressed and "Papa" when the other foot was pressed.

1909: A German patent pertained to a doll's head with automatic "voice" and movable mouthpiece with tongue and teeth, operated by the pressure of a lever at the back of the neck.

1916: Advertisements stated that the voices of dolls made a sound for a longer period than formerly.

1924: PLAYTHINGS reported that Paris dolls shouted when they were picked up. They spoke very good French, to the extent of four words, and also sang a bit of a French song. (See **Crying Dolls; Mama Dolls; Phonograph Dolls; Voices.**)

**Tam O'Shanter Doll.** 1893. Bonnet-type dolls with molded tams, distributed by *Butler Bros.* These dolls were advertised as "solid white china" and distinguished from "glazed china." They were probably what collectors call "stone bisque." They were jointed at the shoulders and came in sizes 2¼ and 7 inches. Price was 8¢ and 78¢ doz. wholesale.

**Tammen, H. H., Co.** 1916–20. New York City, Denver, Colo., and Los Angeles, Calif. Manufactured the *Skookum* character Indian dolls of dried apples or composition as designed by *Mary McAboy.*

**Tana.** Name incised on a bisque head made in Limoges, France. The character-doll head that bears this name has a closed mouth, painted eyes, and is bald.

**Tanagra.** 1917–25+. Trademark registered in France in 1917 and in Germany in 1921 by *Albert Levy.*

1921: "Tanagra" used as a trade name by a Paris Société with a factory at Montreuil-sous-Bois. They advertised dressed and undressed bébés of all kinds, and porcelain heads with stationary or sleeping eyes.

**Tanagrette.** 1921. Trademark registered in France by *Octave Durand.*

**Tango Tots.** 1914. Made by *Louis Amberg & Son.*

**Tante Lore (Aunt Lore).** 1916. Trademark registered in Germany by *Wohlegemuth & Lissner* for dolls.

**Tariff.** See **Imports.**

**Tarpey, Jessie Toler Kingsley.** 1915. London. Registered in Britain as a trademark *Sea Baby // J. T. Kingsley Tarpery.*

**Täuflinge.** A German word that, literally, refers to babies before they are christened. *Johannes Daniel Kestner* in the first decade of the 19th century made dolls with wooden bodies turned on a lathe, carved, and painted, which he called "Täuflinge." This name continued into the 20th century, to be used for Waltershausen babies. According to a descendant of the *Fleischmann* and *Cuno* and *Otto Dressel* families of Sonneberg, the word "Täuflinge" was used for dolls dressed in chemises. There seems to be no precise definition of the word, and its meaning probably changed with time and place. PLAYTHINGS, December 1, 1903, described a Täufling as a doll "half dressed with chemise, shoes and stockings." The DEUTSCHES SPIELWAREN ZEITUNG, January, 1926, described an 1880 doll as a "ball or double-jointed Täufling with bisque head and movable eyes." Max von Boehn, in 1932, wrote in DOLLS AND PUPPETS that the term Täufling "signifies a baby doll of flesh-coloured papier-mâché dipped in a wax solution . . . the dress is only a little chemise."

**Tausendschönchen (Daisy).** 1910–25+. Trademark registered in Germany by *Franz Schmidt & Co.;* used by *Tip Top Toy Co.*

**Tea Cup Dolls.** See **Frozen Charlottes.**

**Tears.** Some crying character dolls have tears molded on their faces, but the earliest record found so far of dolls that cried liquid tears was in 1909. These were the Weeping Dolls of *Schachne.* In 1923, several patents were obtained for dolls that would cry real tears, and *Ideal Novelty & Toy Co.* put out a two-faced doll with one face that cried real tears.

**Teather, George.** 1856. London. Made wax dolls. (See also **George Ogilwy.**)

**Tebbets, Marian Curry, & Tebbets, Miss.** 1921–23. Pittsburgh, Pa. Registered in U.S. *Petiekin* as a trademark for dolls; obtained a U.S. design patent for a baby doll in a long dress and a frilly bonnet.

**Teddy.** 1911. Copyrighted by *Horsman,* designed by *Helen Trowbridge.*

**Teddy Doll.** Ca. 1913. Came with composition head, painted features, soft stuffed body of blue, red, or gray baby-lamb cloth; jointed limbs and neck. Size 24½ inches, price 98¢.

**Teddy Jr.** 1910. Made by *A. Steinhardt & Bro.* Came with satin body, jointed arms and legs; wore gingham jumper and a ribbon across the chest reading: "The 'Neverbreak' Teddy Jr. is here too.// Just like Bess and Smiling Sue." Price $8.50 doz. wholesale.

**Teddy Roosevelt.** Ca. 1909. First spring-jointed doll made by *Schoenhut.* It was a wooden portrait doll jointed at the knees and hips so that it could sit on the Schoenhut horses.

**Teddy's Nig.** 1910. Name of a rag doll, the design of which was patented by *Frank C. A. Richardson.* Doll represented an African Negro and was made to commemorate Teddy Roosevelt's 1909–10 African hunting expedition. Doll was of fine black stockinet with shoe-button eyes, brass rings in nose and ears, ornamental metal bands around arms and legs, a bead necklace around neck. Design patent shows a grass skirt, but a doll with "leopardskin" loincloth has a label reading "Trade Mark —Teddy's Nig—June 7, 1910," the patent date, on the loincloth band. Size 14½ inches.

**Teddy-Turnover.** 1907. *Topsy Turvy* type of doll made by *Dreamland Doll Co.* Came with a brown or white rag doll at one end and a teddy bear at the other end. Size 12½ inches; price $1.00.

**Teen-age Girl Dolls.** During the 19th century, many of the girl dolls probably represented teen-agers, but no record of them, as such, has been found as yet.

1908: *Louis Wolf & Co.* advertised a "High school girl doll with modern coiffure."

1911: Young lady dolls with the faces of girls in their teens but dressed as adults took an important place among the character doll lines. *Louis Amberg & Son* produced dolls representing both sixteen- and eighteen-year-old girls. (See **College Kids.**)

**Teenie Pollyanna.** 1922. Cutout rag doll and its clothes, made by *Pollyanna Co.;* price $1.00 for doll and one outfit.

**Teenie Weenie.** 1921–22. Trademark registered in Germany by *Borgfeldt* for dolls.

**Teenie Weenie.** 1925. Trade name for a *Bye-Lo* type of infant doll in the *Petite* line made by the *American Character Doll Co.*

**Teeth.** Teeth were an added touch of realism during most of the 19th century, but open mouths and "pearly teeth" did not become popular until the end of the 19th century and early in the 20th. As can readily be seen from the pictures of dolls with teeth, these additions did not generally enhance the appearance of the dolls. Prior to 1850 both milk glass and bamboo were used for teeth, and they continued in use for some decades until they were finally supplanted by ceramic teeth. Porcelain teeth

were sometimes molded with the head and sometimes molded separately and inserted later. Possibly some of the earlier types of porcelain teeth are the square-topped ones found in *Simon & Halbig* heads, mold #949. These generally consisted of two upper teeth and a single tooth on the bottom, giving the doll a rather odd look. Upper teeth are more usual than lower ones or than both upper and lower. A brass head made in France had glass teeth. Besides bamboo, porcelain, and glass, teeth sometimes were made of metal or celluloid.

In 1913 PLAYTHINGS reported that a doll's mouth appeared to open and close because the lower teeth and tongue moved up and down when the doll was moved up and down. On some dolls with two rows of teeth, the lower ones swung back and the tongue took their place when the doll was put into a horizontal position. (See Ill. 1618; also **Mouth.**)

TEETH

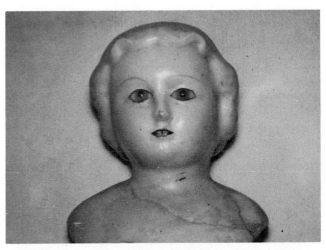

**1614.** Four milk glass teeth appear in this waxed composition head. The head has molded blonde hair and blue glass sleeping eyes. H. of shoulder head, 6 inches. *Coleman Collection.*

**1615.** Pink china head with upper and lower teeth. The doll has deeply molded eyes that are shadowed and have both upper and lower lashes; wig; china arms on a hand-sewn kid body. H. 14 inches. *Courtesy of Laura Treskow.*

**1613.** Papier-mâché head with black pupil-less glass eyes, open mouth with four bamboo teeth. Doll has a three-wheeled walking mechanism, and wears her original straw bonnet. Probably mid-19th century. H. 11 inches. *Courtesy of the Chester County Historical Society.*

**1616.** Two rows of teeth in the open mouth of a bisque shoulder-headed doll with glass eyes. Head is marked "E. B.," possibly for E. Barrois. *Courtesy of Marion Holt; photograph by Winnie Langley.*

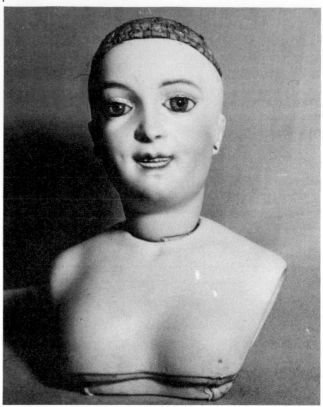

**1617.** Smiling mouth with two rows of teeth in a swivel-neck bisque head with pierced ears and cork pate. Shoulder plate is marked "Déposé R C." *Courtesy of Marion Holt; photograph by Winnie Langley.*

**1618A & B.** Moving teeth and tongue in a bisque head. When the doll is upright, the lower teeth are in position; when she is lying down and the eyes close, the lower teeth retract and a tongue takes their place. Head marked "Germany // 410 // 5/0." H. 10 inches. *Courtesy of Kit Robbins.*

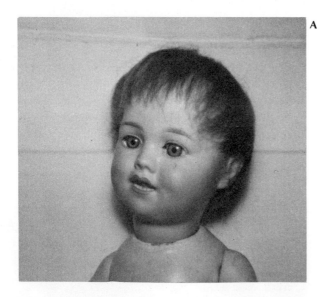

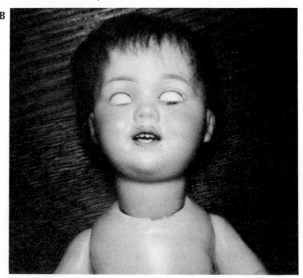

**Tempier.** 1843. Paris. Made dolls and dolls' trousseaux.

**Tennis Girl.** 1915. Trade name for a doll made by *Ideal Novelty & Toy Co.*

**Tentation.** See **A la Tentation.**

**Terminology.** Considerable confusion exists in the terminology used in the doll world. For one thing, the meaning of some words as well as their use has changed through the years. Originally, all dolls were called "babies," but later only children—and still later only infant—dolls were called "babies." The word "indestruct-ible" (*incassable* in French) usually referred to a doll with a composition body and/or head that could easily be broken by the rough treatment meted out by children. The international aspect of dolls has also sometimes made it necessary to use foreign terms because there is no English word with the same meaning—for example, the German *Täuflinge*. Other problems in doll terminology have arisen out of overzealous and not too truthful advertising—for instance, the use of the term gutta-percha for dolls of molasses and glue, or of wax for ceramic dolls.

American writers of the 20th century often collected data on dolls by sending out letters requesting information from collectors. As a result, the names given to various types of dolls by individual collectors then appeared in print and became part of doll terminology, often with no historical basis. As the number of collectors and books on dolls grew, these "personal" names became innumerable. Even more of a problem was the fact that the identical name often appeared in print representing entirely different types of dolls. Unfortunately the same thing occasionally occurred with trade names, as witnessed by the five *American Beauty* entries, the three *Mabel* entries, and others. The confusion has been compounded by the use of a multitude of names with no official basis, such as "Godey," a name applied by some collectors to dolls with any one of at least four different hairdos. Likewise the name "Queen Victoria" is often applied to various dolls of wax, china, bisque, or other materials simply because some people thought their dolls resembled portraits of Queen Victoria, but the dolls may have totally different appearances. These names, as well as countless others—Nellie Bly, Amelia Bloomer, Queen Charlotte, Jenny Lind, Adelina Patti, and Sammy, to name a few—are not included as entries. It can readily be seen that the hundreds of actual trade names that were used officially for dolls and are given as entries are more than sufficient, without inventing hundreds of other names based only on the whim of the owner and often duplicating names already in use.

Certain terms—such as *Biedermeier* for bald-headed china dolls, *Belton* for bald-headed bisque dolls, *Parian* for untinted bisque dolls, French *Fashion* for kid- (or wooden-) bodied lady dolls, *Milliners' Models* for dolls with papier-mâché heads, kid bodies, and wooden limbs—are technically inaccurate but are used so generally in the doll world that it is difficult for collectors to forego them, especially since no accurate substitute terms have as yet been devised. However, collectors should keep in mind that practically all so-called "Biedermeier" dolls were made after the Biedermeier period. "Belton" dolls were made after the death of the doll manufacturer named Belton. And very few "Parian" dolls were made of parian. England and America were the chief producers of parian, but most of the so-called parian dolls were made in Germany or Central Europe. Many so-called "French Fashion" dolls were made outside France and merely dressed there. Of such dolls

actually made in France, many were sold without a stitch of clothes, and very few were real fashion dolls. Jumeau referred to his kid-body dolls as "Parisiennes" in 1885, but these had the same type of heads as his bébés, and few of the lady dolls were made as late as this. There is no evidence that the term meant any more than a Paris origin. "Luxury Dolls" is another term that has been used for these dolls. There seems to be little doubt but that they were in the luxury class, especially those with trousseaux. However, wax dolls with inserted hair were probably the most expensive dolls of all, though nearly all fine dolls were priced so that only the well-to-do could afford them for their children. The term "Milliners' Model" apparently originated with Eleanor St. George, and, according to her own account, there seems to be no real basis for it other than that she liked the term.

The terminology used in this encyclopedia, although differing sometimes from current usage, is based on documentary sources. (See also **Names**.)

**Terra Cotta.** See **Earthen Dolls**.

**Terrène.** 1863–90. Paris. Was listed in directories as a hairdresser from 1863–73; then Widow Terrène, toymaker, was listed in Paris Directories at the same address from 1881–90. Terrène won medals at the expositions of 1867, 1868, 1872, 1873, and 1874, according to their advertisement. Dolls have been found with the body marked "J. Terrène, 10 rue de Marché-St. Honoré." This is the address listed in the directories. Most of these dolls are jointed so that they can walk; the torso is wood covered with kid; upper arms are metal, but heads and lower arms are bisque.

**Terror.** 1905. A character doll with composition head and cotton-stuffed cloth body, distributed by *Butler Bros.* Size 9½ inches, price $2.25 doz. wholesale.

**Tersch, M., Firm, Kunstwerkstätten.** 1920. Berlin. Registered in Germany the initials "T K B" written vertically, as a trademark for dolls and dolls' heads.

**Testard.** 1829–55. Paris. Several members of the family appear to have made dolls.

1842: Mlle. Testard made dressed dolls and dolls with rose or white kid bodies. She sold German dolls that would bend, dolls dressed in the latest fashion, and dolls with springs.

1843: Advertised dolls with rose or white kid bodies.

1849: Louis Testard won an Honorable Mention award at the Paris Exposition.

1855: He exhibited dolls at the Paris Exposition.

**Tête d'Aigle (Eagle's Head).** 1925. Trademark used by *Petitcollin* for celluloid dolls.

**Tête Mobile Bébé.** See **Bébé Tête Mobile**.

**Teteur Bébé.** See **Bébé Teteur**.

**Textile Blueing Co.** 1901. New York City. Made rag dolls, especially *Punch and Judy*.

**Thalheimer, Sylvain, & Cie.** 1900. Paris. Registered in

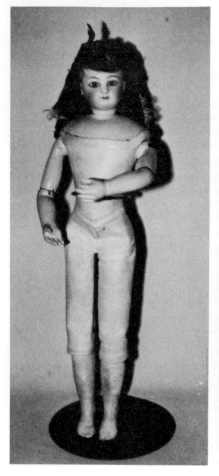

**1619A & B.** Terrène doll with bisque socket head on a shoulder plate. Kid body, with kid covering the metal knee joints; painted metal upper arms, bisque lower arms, wooden lower legs. Has original dress also labeled "Terrène." Mark (label on back of doll): Ill. **1620.** H. 18 inches. *Courtesy of Eunice Althouse.*

**1620.** Mark found on body of Terrène dolls.

France as a trademark *Bébé Tentation,* and produced dolls that won a silver medal.

**Thalie Bébé.** 1917. Trademark registered in France and Britain by *Sussfeld & Cie.*

**Théroude, Alexandre Nicholas.** 1842–95. Paris. Made dolls, especially mechanical dolls.

1843: Advertised that he made dolls with ordinary kid bodies and with jointed kid bodies, as well as mechanical dolls. His products were sent to the Provinces and abroad.

1849: Won a bronze medal for his dolls at the Paris Exposition.

1852: Was granted a French patent for a mechanism to be put inside a doll to give it sound and movement.

1855: Was awarded a silver medal at the Paris Exposition. Advertised mechanical toys, moderately priced, for export to compete with foreign products.

1856: Advertised that he was the inventor of talking dolls. (See **Talking Dolls.**)

1862: Won a prize medal at the London Exhibition.

1867: Was awarded a prize medal at the Paris Exposition.

1881: Théroude, Sr., and Jr., were listed in the Paris Directory.

1890: Théroude, Sr., obtained a French patent for a new type of jointed doll.

1890–95: Advertised automatons and mechanical toys for museums and displays.

**They Walk, They Talk, They Sleep.** 1923–25+. Slogan found on dolls made by *EFFanBEE.* Dolls that do none or only some of these things were still marked with this trademark.

**They Walk and They Talk.** 1922. Slogan found on dolls made by *EFFanBEE.*

**1621A, B, & C.** Walking mechanical doll made by A. Théroude. It has a composition head, pupil-less glass eyes, four upper and four lower bamboo teeth, kid arms. The arms as well as the head move when she walks. Feet rest on a three-wheeled platform, which includes a key-wind mechanism, marked as in Ill. **1622**. Original clothes. H. 16 inches. *Coleman Collection.*

**1622.** Mark used on Théroude mechanical dolls.

**Thieck, Francis, and Born, Jean, & Cie.** 1923. Paris Registered in France *Seraphin* as a trademark for dolls.

**Thiele, Anna.** 1885–1925+, Waltershausen, Thür. From 1913 to before 1920, Hermann Sonntag was the successor; from 1920 to 1925+, Gustav Thiele was successor. They manufactured dolls and dolls' wigs of hair and mohair.

**Thiele, Gustav.** 1911–14. Eppendorf, Saxony. Made dolls' heads, especially for export.

**Thiele, R.** 1909. Berlin. Made dolls.

**Thilen, Moritz.** 1852–78. Vienna. Made dressed dolls.

1873: Displayed dolls at the Vienna Exhibition.

1878: Showed his dolls at the Paris Exposition.

**Thoenissen, Heinrich, & Co.** 1925. Neustadt near Coburg, Thür. Manufactured dolls.

**Thomas, Mme.** 1876–77. Paris. Made dolls.

**Thomas, Mary R.** 1914. Boston, Mass. Registered in U.S. *Really Truly* as a trademark for character dolls.

**Thomas, Maurice.** 1925. Paris. Advertised that he made dolls for children and for parlors.

**Thomason, Henry.** 1870. London. Made dolls.

**Thompson, George N.** 1866. New Haven, Conn. Assignee of part of the multi-face doll patent obtained by *Dominico Checkeni* in the U.S.

**Thomson, Bernard Home.** 1911. London. Registered in Britain *Peek-A-Boo* as a trademark for dolls.

**Thomson, Mlle. Valentine.** 1915. Paris. Registered in France *Pandore* as a trademark for dolls.

**Thorpe, David Lee.** 1866. Birmingham, Warwick. Was issued a British patent for a ball-jointed doll. The doll was to be strung either with metal or rubber.

**Thorpe, Joseph.** 1856. London. Made wax dolls.

**390 Line.** 1915. Line of socket heads, advertised by *Foulds & Freure*. This was probably the *Armand Marseille* socket-head mold "390," which appears to have been made for a long time.

**Thueringer.** See **Thüringer**.

**Thuillier, A.** 1875–90. Paris. Made jointed dolls with wooden or kid bodies, as well as jointed composition bodies or *bébés incassables*. The dolls were sold either dressed or undressed. A. Thuillier seems to be a likely maker of the dolls marked "A. T.," although this has never been proved. "A. T." bisque heads have been found on wooden, on kid, and on composition bodies, which supports the Thuillier attribution. These dolls come in a wide range of sizes. Size 2 is generally 12 inches, and the dolls range up to at least size 14 at 29 inches.

**1623A, B, & C.** This doll may have come from the Thuillier establishment. It has a bisque socket head, glass eyes, pierced ears, cork pate, wig, and composition body. Head is marked "A. T." as shown in Ill. **1625**. H. 19 inches. *Courtesy of Hazel Ulseth.*

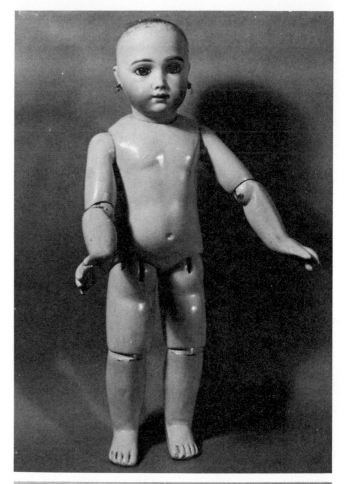

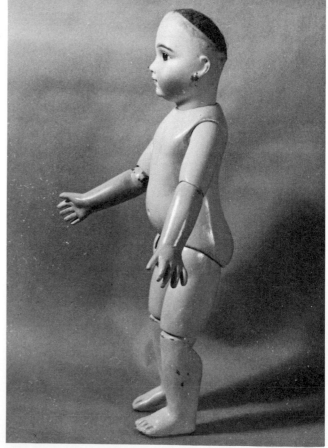

A

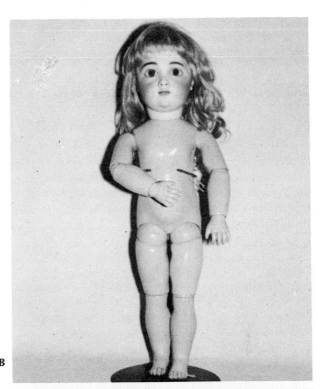

B

**1624A, B, & C.** "A. T." mark on the bisque head of this doll may indicate that it was a Thuillier product. It has glass eyes, pierced ears, closed mouth; ball-jointed turned wooden body. Doll wears original dress and cap of blue satin trimmed with lace and ribbon. Mark on head: Ill. **1626.** H. 19 inches. *Courtesy of Sylvia Brockmon.*

A 10 T
**1625**

AT · N° 8
**1626**

**1625 & 1626.** "A. T." marks found on dolls that were probably made by A. Thuillier.

C

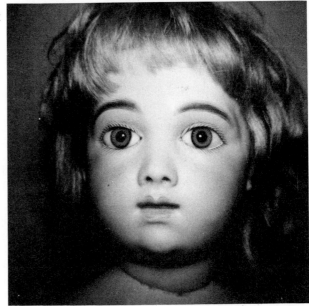

**Thumbs Up.** 1920. Trademark registered in France by John Green Hamley of *Hamley Bros.* for dolls.

**Thüringer Kunstler-Wollpuppen Fabrik.** 1923–24. Weimar, Thür. Produced and distributed stuffed character *Art Dolls* of wool.

1924: Registered in Germany *Mumm* as a trademark for dolls.

**Thüringer Puppen & Spielwarenexport Co.** 1923–24. Berlin. Distributed and exported dolls.

1923: Registered in Germany *Primula* as a trademark.

1924: Registered in Germany two trademarks, *Lopto* and *Lopto Radlaufspiel,* for dolls.

**Thüringer Puppenfabrik Cabarz Inc.** 1923–25+. Waltershausen, Thür. Manufactured dolls.

**Thüringer Puppen-Industrie, Inc.** 1922–23. Waltershausen, Thür. Manufactured dolls, including jointed dolls and rubber dolls.

1923: Registered four trademarks in Germany: one used the initials "T.P.I.W." with a drawing of a mask; two used the initials "T.P.I" plus the word "Waltershausen"; the fourth was the word *Pola.*

**Thüringer Spielwaren-Fabrik.** See **Lutzelberger, Arno.**

**Thüringer Stoffpuppen-Fabrik.** 1923–24. Bad Berta, Thür. Manufactured and distributed dolls, especially stuffed dolls.

1923: Registered in Germany as a trademark *Weimarpuppen//Weimarpuppchen.*

**Tiffany, Anson B.** 1856–65. Hartland, Conn. Manufactured dolls.

**Ti-Koun.** 1924. Trademark registered in France by *Mme. Jeanne Schlisler* for dolls.

**Tilson, William.** 1865. London. Made dolls.

**Tinet.** 1815–73. Montreuil-sous-Bois, Seine. Hard paste porcelain factory; may have made dolls' heads, since it was in a doll-making area. Tinet used as a mark two pairs of crossed swords with their points touching to form a diamond.

**Tinie Baby.** See **Tynie Baby.**

**Tinkler.** 1880's. London. A wax doll has been found with what appears to be "E. Tinkler" written on it. In 1881 John Tinkler handled merchandise for babies.

**Tiny Tads.** 1912–14. Boy and girl dolls with composition heads and hands believed to have been made by *Louis Amberg & Son*. These dolls were offered as subscription premiums in a group of dolls, most of which are known to have been made by Amberg. Tiny Tads had molded hair and cloth stuffed bodies jointed at neck, shoulder, and hips; eyes glanced to the side. Girl wore a print dress, and the boy wore rompers with striped stocking-legs. Size 12 inches, price 50¢.

**Tiny Tim.** 1909. Cutout rag doll made by *Art Fabric Mills;* distributed by *Selchow & Righter.* Came in a sheet 20 by 27 inches.

**Tiny Tim.** 1924. Tiny boy doll that said "Mama"; dressed in checked romper suit. Price $1.00.

**Tiny Tim.** 1924–25. Rag doll designed and made by *Madame Alexander.* It had a mask face with raised features, which were hand-painted by Madame Alexander. Came with wig of mohair imported from England; pink muslin body. Size 14 inches, price $1.20.

**Tiny Toddler.** 1913. Made by *Ideal Novelty & Toy Co.*

**Tiny Tot.** 1919–20. Baby doll made by *Jessie M. Raleigh;* came with moving eyes, bobbed mohair wig. Size 18 inches.

**Tiny Tots.** 1912. Advertised by *Borgfeldt* as being "unbreakable," which probably means made of composition. These may be the same as the "Tiny Tot" and "Tiny Tot's Brother," a pair of character dolls with composition head and hands, stuffed body; girl wore an apron over her frock and had a hair ribbon; boy was dressed in rompers. Sizes 10 and 16 inches. These dolls were advertised as premium dolls in the WOMAN'S WORLD, 1912.

**Tiny Tots.** 1913–14. Small dolls that could stand by themselves; made by *Louis Amberg & Son.* Price 65¢.

**Tiny Tots.** 1915–17. Trademark registered in U.S. by *E. & G. Quackenbush;* used for sanitary dolls. Mark was to be impressed on dolls or printed on labels. There were eighteen varieties of these dolls, which were made with a combination rubber and cloth material; most of them had baby-type heads.

**Tip Top Toy Co.** 1912–21. New York City. Established in 1912 by Max Politzer and *Joseph Kaempfer,* both formerly with *New Toy Co.* Later Politzer appears to have

been with *Politzer Toy Manufacturing Co. Borgfeldt* was associated with Tip Top Toy Co. and even gave them license to distribute *Kewpies* to the carnival trade.

1912: Made dolls with composition heads and eyes glancing to the side, named *Paul* and *Virginia.*

1913: Handled bisque-head dolls made by *Franz Schmidt;* these were the *Tausendschönchen* line of dolls headed by *Little Boy Blue.* Tip Top Toy Co. also handled the following American dolls: *Bertie* and *Gertie, Dottie Dimples, Cy from Siwash, Jim Thorpe, Miss Firefly, Little Johnny Jones, Little Miss Sunshine, Mistress Mary.*

1916–18: Advertised their Kewpies as having "genuine bisque finish," made in America under special license with Borgfeldt. Size of the Kewpie was 13 inches.

1918: Distributed *"Maiden America"* dolls.

1919: Advertised *"Tip Top Baby"* with bent limbs, sizes 18 to 24 inches; fully jointed kid-body dolls with sleeping eyes, in five sizes; *Prize Baby* and *Pudgie.*

1921: Advertised the mechanical "Shimmy Dolls" made by the *Zaiden Toy Works.*

**Tipperary Kid.** 1915. Trademark registered in U.S. by *John Dick* for dolls.

**Tipperary Mary.** 1914–15. Trademark registered in U.S. by *German Novelty Co.* for character dolls.

**Tipperary Tommy.** 1914–15. Trademark registered in U.S. by *German Novelty Co.* for character dolls.

**Tipple Topple.** 1908–16. Two trademarks registered in Germany by *Emil Pfeiffer* for dolls. In 1916 the initials "E P" were added to the words "Tipple Topple."

**Tischer, E.** 1909–18. Wildenheid near Sonneberg, Thür. Made dolls.

**Tiss Me.** 1919–20. Trade name for a doll with its face turned up and lips puckered for a kiss; eyes glancing to the side. *Carol Bonwit* secured a design patent in U.S. for just such a doll; it had joints at shoulders and the legs were together.

**Titsworth, Edith Dayton.** 1913–14. Greenwich, Conn. Obtained a U.S. design patent for a rag doll dressed as a clown, with eyes glancing to the side; the iris nearly covered the complete eye.

**Toddler, The.** 1922. Made by *Käthe Kruse.* It was on a skeleton framework; the "flesh" was cotton wool and gauze, covered with a "skin" of tricot material. Sizes 8 to 20 inches and also larger than life-size manikins. (See also **Schlenkerchen.**)

**Toddles.** 1912. Trademark registered in Britain by *Eisenmann & Co.*

**Toddles.** 1915. One of the *Jam Kiddos,* made by *Non-Breakable Doll Co.* Came with composition head, sleeping eyes, molded hair, price $1.00.

**Toddles.** 1921–22. Trademark registered in U.S. by *Atlas Doll Co.* The mark was molded into doll.

**Toddling Toodles.** 1925. A *Happiness Doll* produced by

*Louis Wolf & Co.* It could walk unassisted for 30 to 40 feet. Size 12 inches, price $30.00 doz. wholesale.

**Toggy.** 1923. Trademark registered in Britain by the *Atlantic Rubber Co.*

**Tom and the Pig.** 1925. *Story Book Doll* manufactured by *Sol Bergfeld & Son*, distributed by *Borgfeldt.* Came with composition head; size 15 inches.

**Tom Thumb.** 1909. *Art Fabric* doll made by *Selchow & Righter*—cutout rag doll on sheet 20 by 27 inches.

**Tom Thumb.** 1911. Child doll copyrighted by *Horsman*; designed by *Helen Trowbridge.*

**Tommie Jones.** 1913. American boy doll made by *Tip Top Toy Co.*, distributed by *Borgfeldt.*

**Tommy Atkins.** 1909. All-bisque doll in red suit; size 8 inches, price 50¢.

**Tommy Atkins.** 1914. Name given to soldier *Kewpie*, imported by *Borgfeldt.*

**Tommy Snooks.** 1921. Trade name for one of the stockinet rag dolls made by *Martha Chase*, a soft rag doll of heavy cotton cloth.

**Tommy Toodles.** 1903. Trade name for a doll advertised in PLAYTHINGS.

**Tommy Trim.** 1906. Cloth doll to be cut out and stuffed; produced by *Horsman.* Came in three sizes, price 5¢, 10¢, and 25¢.

**Tongues.** Seldom were tongues shown on dolls until the end of the 19th century. At first, they were molded with the head and made of the same material as the head. These were used mostly on character dolls. Later, they were made of various materials—felt, cardboard, celluloid, and others.

1912–15: Moving tongues were in evidence. One type protruded from the mouth and wagged whenever the doll was moved; a second type shook up and down when the doll was shaken; another type stuck out when the doll was upright and fell back into the mouth when the doll was laid prone; in still another type, the tongue replaced the teeth when the doll was placed horizontal.

**Toodles.** 1911–12. *Art Doll* representing a baby boy of toddler age, made by *Horsman.* Came with *Can't Break 'Em* composition head and hands, molded hair; cloth body, jointed at hips and shoulders. Doll was dressed in Carter's "smock and knickers," a familiar English style of clothing that had recently been adopted in U.S. for children. The yoke played a prominent part on the short dress worn over the bloomers. Size of the doll was 12 inches; price $1.00.

**Toodles.** 1915. Baby's head with mouth open copyrighted by the *Trion Toy Co.*, designed by *Ernesto Peruggi.*

**Toodles.** 1919. Standing doll copyrighted by *American Bisque Doll Co.*, designed by *Ernesto Peruggi.* Doll had eyes glancing to the side, bent arms, molded hair, and molded bathing suit.

**Tootsie.** 1905–6. Trademark registered in Germany by *Borgfeldt.*

**Tootsie.** 1911. *Art Doll* made by *Horsman* and described as a "Modish little lady." The doll had *Can't Break 'Em* composition head with molded hair and ribbon with a big bow on side of head; cloth body.

**Tootsie.** 1915. Line of new character babies advertised by *Strobel & Wilken.*

**Tootsie Boy and Tootsie Girl.** 1912. Character dolls with composition heads and hands and jointed knees; made by *Gund Manufacturing Co.* They represented school-age children. Girl wore frilly apron; boy wore shirt and pants. Price 25¢ to $2.00.

**Tootsie Wootsie.** 1911. Trademark registered in U.S. by *A. Schoenhut Co.* The name was used for an all-wooden doll, fully jointed with springs. It had molded short hair, a baby-type face, and was dressed as a baby.

**Tootsie Wootsie.** 1916. Made by *Elektra Toy & Novelty Co.* Priced with wig at $24.00 doz.; without wig, $21.00 doz. wholesale.

**Tootsy Wootsy.** 1909. Line of Indian rag dolls; included "Pocahontas" and "Big Chief." The two dolls plus a tent cost 75¢.

**Topsy.** 1893+. Trade name of rag doll designed by *Celia M. Smith*, made by *Arnold Print Works.* The printed cotton cloth was sold by the yard, to be cut out and stuffed. The doll represented a little Negro girl.

**Topsy.** 1900. Four-piece cutout type of rag doll made by the *Art Fabric Mills* in accordance with the U.S. patent of *Edgar Newell.* These dolls usually have the patent date "Feb. 13, 1900" on the sole of the foot.

**Topsy.** 1909. A doll with celluloid face made by *Horsman.* Size 14½ inches, price 25¢.

**Topsy.** 1910. Rag doll of the type later made famous by *Grace Drayton.* This was a Negro version of *Dolly Dollykins*; it came with four short, beribboned pigtails, plaid dress, and polka dot stockings.

**Topsy Turvy (Reversible).** These dolls had two heads, one at either end. The skirt hid one head while the other was on view. This type of doll was made with heads of various materials—ceramic, composition, celluloid, rag, and so on—but the most popular were probably the rag dolls with one head white and the other Negro. *Albert Brückner's* 1901 patent date is frequently found on the cloth faces of these dolls. The white end is a blonde wearing a blue checked dress; the Negro end has black hair and a red dress.

1907: *Teddy-Turnover*, made by the *Dreamland Doll Co.*, had a doll at one end and a Teddy Bear at the other end. Another popular rag doll had one head smiling and one head crying. This was a *Babyland Rag Doll* made by *Horsman.*

1909: *Saalfield's* muslin cutout doll had one head with a hat and one head without a hat.

**Torakiyo Sato.** 1893. Tokyo. Displayed dolls at the Chicago Exposition.

**Torres, Viuva.** 1898. Rio de Janeiro. Manufactured dolls.

**Totem Tom Tom.** 1924–25. Trademark registered in U.S. and in Britain by *John Joseph Osbourne* for dolls.

**Tottie.** 1913–14. Trademark registered in U.S. by *Etta Lyon;* to be affixed to doll or package with a printed label.

**Toulouse, V.** 1894–96. Paris. Obtained a French patent for a *Poupée Française,* a new type of jointed doll with the joints imbedded in the composition of the body. Two wires, one on each side of the body, which went up the arms, through the torso, and down the legs, were placed in the casting mold.

**Tour St.-Jacques.** 1893–94. Distributed dolls, including *Bébé Jumeau, Bébé Prodige, Eden Bébé.* Their dolls were dressed in a chemise; sold for 35¢ to $9.80. Bébés Jumeau came in ten sizes, from 15 to 30 inches.

**Touron & Simon.** Before 1882. France. Porcelain manufacturers. By 1882 they had joined *Coiffe.*

**Tourrel..** See **Alexandre, Henri.**

**Townsend, George.** 1856. Longton, Staffordshire. Made china toys and figures.

**Toy Joy Co.** 1918. U.S. Made dolls.

**Toy Shop, The.** 1922–25+. New York City. Manufactured dolls and used the initials "T.S."

1923: Made *Mama Dolls* and *Aunt Jemima.*

1924: Advertised Aunt Jemima and *U-Man Doll;* these were made of a new material and special process.

1925: Advertised Aunt Jemima; *Pickaninny Baby,* a Negro infant; *Jack* and *Jill.*

**1627.** Mark used for dolls by The Toy Shop.

**Toyland Doll Co.** 1906. Detroit, Mich. Advertised a doll with colored photographic face, jointed cotton cloth body, garments that fastened with hooks or buttons. Size 15 inches, price $1.10.

**Toyo Gangu Goshi Kaishi Mina.** 1923. Nagoya, Japan. Made dolls.

**Tozan, J.** 1915. A French artist who created dolls, including those representing Breton peasant girls. Size 14 inches.

**Trademarks.** In identifying dolls, trademarks are of great value. A trademark is defined as "a word, name, symbol, or device, or any combination of these, adopted and used by a manufacturer or merchant to identify his goods and distinguish them from those manufactured or sold by others." The first constitutional trademark registration act was passed in 1881. However, a trademark does not need to be registered. According to the U.S. Patent Office, "Trademark rights are protected

under common law, but registration results in material advantages to the trademark owner." The rights last for twenty years from the date of issue, and the registration may be renewed indefinitely as long as the mark is still in use in commerce. "A trademark may be assigned with the good will of the business with which it is used." The establishment of trademark rights is described by law as follows: "Rights in a trademark are established by adoption and actual use of the mark on goods moving in trade, and use ordinarily must continue if the rights are to be maintained. No rights exist until there has been actual use; and a trademark may not be registered until the goods bearing the mark have been sold or shipped in interstate, foreign or Territorial commerce . . . The mark must be applied in some manner to goods or their containers . . .

"A trademark may not be registered if it so resembles a mark previously registered in the Patent Office, or a mark or trade name previously used in the United States by another and not abandoned, as to be likely, when applied to the applicant's goods, to cause confusion, mistake or deception . . .

"Registration must be obtained in each country where protection is desired."

If a doll was trademarked, it must have been made and distributed more than just locally, whereas patented dolls may never have been produced commercially. The trademark of a doll may be put on a box, package, wrapper, label, tag, or ribbon rather than on the doll itself, but the copyright must appear directly on the doll.

When two (or more) U.S. firms handled dolls made by a European company having a registered trademark, they could both use this European trademark.

The United States and Puerto Rico were (in 1917) the only countries that required the use of a trademark before it could be registered. Germany, Norway, Sweden, Hungary, and many Latin American countries recognized only the first to register a trademark as the legal owner. Therefore, it was necessary for American manufacturers to register trademarks abroad or to run the risk of having their marks pirated. In many countries registration was the only thing that was recognized.

"Reg." stands for "registered" in the U.S. "Dep." stands for "déposé" in France or "deponirt" in Germany, both meaning "registered." On French trademarks are often found the words "marque déposée" meaning registered trademark." Both "Fabrikmarke" and "Schutz Marke" are used for "trademark" in German. "Eingetragen" ("eingetragene" or "eingetr.") and "deponirt" ("deponiert") are used for "registered" in German.

Very few trademarks were registered in any country prior to 1880. Trademarks are often reregistered in European countries after fifteen or twenty years.

**Tragacanth.** See **Gum Tragacanth.**

**Tragit-Delbosque.** See **Delbosque, Mlle.**

**Transogram Co.** 1919. New York City. Advertised a walking doll for 25¢.

**Trash.** 1914. Material used for making dolls. According

to an article in PLAYTHINGS, May, 1914, dolls were made by the children of the London slums out of matchboxes, tram [trolley] tickets, newspaper posters, and other waste items.

**Trautmann, Carl.** See **Catterfelder Puppenfabrik.**

**Trautwein, Erika.** 1919–20. Breslau, Silesia. Was granted a German patent for putting a doll's body together.

**Treat-Em-Rough Kiddie.** 1919–20. Doll was stamped brass from head to toe; made by *Art Metal Works.* It had molded and enameled features and hair and a spring-jointed body. Chiefly bent-limb babies were made.

1920: Advertised as the only metal doll that talked.

**Trebeck, Thomas Frederick.** 1851. London. Displayed dolls at the London Exhibition.

**Trebor.** Name on bisque heads probably made by *Otto Reinecke.*

**Tredoulat, Aîné (Sr.), & Malvesin, Aîné.** 1859. Paris. Were issued a French patent for durable rubber dolls' heads in various sizes and colors.

**Trego Doll Manufacturing Co.** 1918–21. New York City. Registered "Trego" in U.S. as a trademark, to be affixed with printed labels on dolls or packages.

1918: Their dolls had human hair wigs, sleeping eyes, ball-jointed limbs; sizes 21 and 25 inches.

1919: Advertised jointed-limb dolls; sizes 18, 22, and 26 inches.

1920: "Trego" dolls came with genuine bisque heads, human hair or mohair wigs in ringlet or long curl style, moving eyes, ball-jointed bodies including joints at wrist. Sizes were 19, 22, and 25 inches.

1921: Agent was *Riemann, Seabrey Co.*

**Tremblatt, Barney.** 1923. Minneapolis, Minn. Obtained U.S. design patent for a two-piece rag doll representing an Indian boy with large "feather" headdress.

**Trésor.** See **Mon Trésor.**

**Tresse.** 1906. Name used for groups of equal lengths of hair sewed onto a gauze cap in order to form a wig.

**Trestournel, M.** 1884. Paris. Made dolls and dressed bébés.

**Treude & Metz.** 1902–4. Laasphe, Westphalia. Made walking dolls that moved on wheels activated by springs. These dolls were based on German, French, British, and U.S. patents. *Paul Fuchs* obtained the patent in the U.S. and assigned his rights to Treude & Metz.

**Treuter, Oscar.** 1893. Germany. Displayed dolls at the Chicago Exposition.

**Trilby.** 1924–25. One of *Life Like Line* of rag dolls made by *American Stuffed Novelty Co.;* distributed by *Edwin A. Besser, Borgfeldt,* and *Louis Wolf & Co.* These dolls came in six styles, with cloth faces, hand-sewn "flapper" wigs, soft cotton-stuffed bodies; felt dress or suit and shoes; sizes 11, 16, and 19 inches.

**1628A & B.** "Trilby," a line of cloth dolls made by the American Stuffed Novelty Co., ca. 1924. Doll has painted features, curly mohair wig, cotton cloth head and body, original clothes with black felt pants; shoes lacking. The line was an American version of the Lenci dolls. H. 11 inches. *Coleman Collection.*

**Trinidad Dolls.** 1914. Made in Trinidad by coolie tailors, these dolls were dressed as East India coolie women or slaves. The ring in the nose signifies betrothal; red line in the center of the head, marriage.

**Trinks, Moritz.** 1897. Prague, Bohemia. Manufactured dolls.

**Triomphe, Bébé.** See **Bébé Triomphe.**

**Trion Toy Co.** 1915–21. Brooklyn, N.Y. Manufactured dolls.

1915: Copyrighted *Little Rascal, Georgy-Porgy, Toodles, Chubby, Sunshine, Happy, Pettish Polly,* and *Smiles,* all designed by *Ernesto Peruggi;* also copyrighted *Pa-na-ma* designed by *Adolph Cohen.*

1916: Advertised production of 25,000 a week; used the slogan "Dolls that Delight" and the trade name *Sanitrion* dolls.

1918: Advertised "moving eye dolls that move."

1919: Expected to market a half-million dolls, including *My Belle Marianne.*

1920–21: Sole distributor was *Riemann, Seabrey Co.* Dolls included *Limber Lou.*

**Triquet, Mme. Vve. (Widow).** Ca. 1900. Rouen, France. Handled dolls, especially ball-jointed composition-body dolls with bisque heads.

**Triumph Toy Co.** 1917. U.S. Made dolls.

**Trognitz, F., & Co.** 1844. Ohrdruf, Thür. Described as a new doll-making firm in 1844 and the only important papier-mâché factory in the Dukedom of Gotha at that time. (Sonneberg was in Saxe-Meiningen.) Trognitz displayed at the Berlin Exhibition a boy's head with glass eyes and a doll dressed as a Hungarian official.

**Trottie Truelife.** 1921. Doll advertised by *EFFanBEE* as looking "Just like a 2 year old." Came with cotton-stuffed body, floppy legs; wore either a gingham dress or rompers. Price $5.00.

**Trottin.** See **Le Trottin.**

**Trowbridge, Helen.** 1910–22. Upper Montclair, N.J. Designed dolls for *Horsman;* among these were the following:

1910: *Bobby, Mischievous Pippin,* and *Peterkin*

1911: *Chinkee, Tom Thumb, Fairy, Little San Toy, Teddy, Baby Bill, Janet, Betty,* and *Carl*

1912: *Little Billy*

1913: *Sunshine*

1914: *Helen, Phoebe, Baby Rosebud,* and *Polly*

1922: Helen Trowbridge was issued a design patent for a rag doll with yarn hair and eyes looking to the side. She assigned the patent rights to *Horsman.*

**Trulie Good.** 1918. Trade name for doll made by *Permolin Products Co.* They advertised that it was made of a new composition without glue and was half the weight of other dolls. It came with or without wig, and was jointed at shoulders, neck, and hips. Sizes 14 and 15 inches.

**Trundle Bed Tripletts.** 1914. Brightly colored dolls with

**1629.** Trion Toy Co.'s mark for dolls.

**1630.** Mark found on bodies handled by Mme. Vve. (Widow) Triquet.

bodies stuffed with cork. Size 8½ inches high and 5 inches wide.

**Trutzi.** 1922. Trademark registered in Germany by *Johannes Rejall.*

**Tub.** 1921–24. Trademark registered in U.S. by *Karmen Corp.* for washable sanitary rag dolls, designed by *Clara V. Havens.*

**Tubbies.** 1917. Sanitary dolls of a combination of rubber and cloth; made by *E. & G. Quakenbush.*

**Tubbins.** 1921. Made by *Virginia Havens* of one piece of cloth folded and tied with a single tape. They could be washed and ironed.

**Tuchmann, Victor, & Co.** 1891. Invicta Works, London. Manufactured dolls and registered in Britain as a trademark a picture of a boy and a girl with dolls and a toy boat.

**Tuchtfeldt, Ad.** 1897. Hamburg, Germany. Made rubber dolls.

**Tuco Doll.** 1917. Made by the *Utley Co.;* came with movable eyes, jointed arms and legs, in various sizes.

**Tum Tum.** 1922–23. Trademark registered in U.S. by *Fleming Doll Co.;* mark was printed on the containers.

**Tumblin' Tim.** 1922–23. Trademark registered in U.S. by *Kittie F. Sischo* and affixed by means of printed labels to doll or package.

**Tummyache.** 1916. Crying baby doll copyrighted by *Jeanne I. Orsini.*

**Tuphorn, Oswald.** Before 1925. Sonneberg (Grossbreitenbach), Thür. By 1925, the successors of Oswald Tuphorn had taken over. Manufactured baby dolls, rag dolls, felt dolls, clowns, and others.

**Turkish Dolls.** 1923. Reforms inaugurated by Mustapha Kemal, Pasha of Turkey, included a new interpretation of Mohammed's teachings as given in the Koran, to allow children to have dolls, which had been denied Moslem girls for hundreds of years.

**Turnbull, Charles Edward, & Co.** 1903–25+. London. Manufactured dolls.

**Turpin, Laura.** Ca. 1890–1920. Newtown, Ohio. Made rag dolls with hand-painted faces, which were family portraits. After her death, most of her dolls were given as a collection to the Cincinnati Art Museum.

**Turrin & De Zordo.** 1920. New York City. Manufactured dolls.

**Turtle Brand (Mark).** 1889–1925+. Registered in Germany, U.S., and Britain as a trademark for dolls or parts of dolls made of pyroxylin compounds (celluloid), by *Rheinische Gummi & Celluloid Fabrik Co.* Turtle Brand products were imported into U.S. by *Bawo & Dotter, Borgfeldt, Averill Manufacturing Co., Adam Bernhard,* and others. The "Turtle" mark is often found on celluloid hands and arms as well as on heads and entire dolls of celluloid.

**Tut Manufacturing Co.** 1923–24. Los Angeles, Calif. Registered in U.S. *Tu-Tankh-Amen Dolls* as a trademark.

**Tu-Tankh-Amen Dolls.** 1923–24. Trademark registered in U.S. by *Tut Manufacturing Co.* for dolls.

**Tut's Mummie.** 1923. Trademark registered in U.S. by *Seigenberg & Sher,* to be affixed to dolls by means of a printed label.

**Tuttle, George W.** 1853. New York City. Displayed dressed dolls at the New York Exhibition.

**Twee Deedle (Mr. Twee Deedle).** 1911. Trademark registered in U.S. by *A. Steinhardt & Bro.* and affixed to doll or package with a printed label. Doll represented character of the same name in the NEW YORK HERALD. It was made entirely of felt and wore green pants, yellow coat with red pompoms, and yellow shoes. Came in two sizes, price $1.00 and $1.50. Sometimes called "Mr. Twee Deedle."

**Twelvetrees, Charles.** 1925. Artist and creator of the "Twelvetrees Kids"; from these drawings he designed the HEbee—SHEbee dolls for *Horsman.*

**Twig Dolls.** See **Wooden Dolls.**

**Twilite Baby.** 1915. Trade name for doll made by *Louis Amberg & Son.*

**Twin Joy Doll Co.** 1925. New York City. Made dolls.

**Twinkie.** 1920. Trade name for a cherub-type doll made by *S. Kirsch & Co.* Size 7 inches.

**Two-in-One-Doll, The.** 1922. Two-headed doll with reversible skirt that covered one head at a time; made by *Wolf Doll Co.* Price $1.00.

**Two-in-One Dolls.** See **Topsy Turvy.**

**Twolip.** 1921. Trade name for doll made by *Highgrade Toy Manufacturing Co.*

**Ty Cobb.** 1911. Character doll representing the baseball hero of this name, made by *Ideal Novelty & Toy Co.* with their patented "Skeleton Process." Doll was advertised as "unbreakable and washable," which probably meant that it had a composition head.

**Tyltyl.** 1911. Doll represented one of the children in Maeterlinck's play THE BLUE BIRD; price $1.00.

**Tynie (Tinie) Baby.** 1924–25+. Infant doll copyrighted by *Horsman,* designed by *Bernard Lipfert.* Came with either bisque or composition head; had soft body and a "voice" box; some had rubber hands; wore a long dress. This was the Horsman version of the *Bye-Lo.*

**Tynie Tots' Tub and Carriage Toys.** 1922. Floating dolls, rubber coated and stuffed with kapok, made by a company that specialized in toys for babies.

**Tynie-Tots.** 1917. Registered in U.S. as a trademark by *Sig. Schwartz Co.*

**Tyroler.** Early 19th century. Trade name of a type of wooden doll, as found recorded in old Sonneberg ledgers.

1840: Name in German sample book for *skittle dolls.*

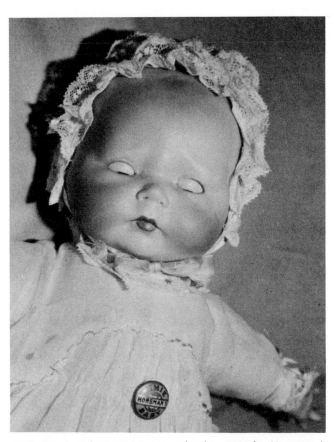

**1631.** "Tynie Baby" (Tinie) copyrighted in 1924 by Horsman in competition with the Bye-Lo Baby. This sleeping infant has a bisque head and glass eyes, and wears its original blue, black, and gold button. *Courtesy of Marie McCollom; photograph by Winnie Langley.*

# U

**U.S.A. Export Co.** 1924. Berlin. Handled dolls.

**U.S. Doll Co.** 1923–24. New York City. Made dolls' heads and arms.

**U.S. Dolls.** See **American Dolls.**

**U.S. Emblem.** 1905. Trade name for dolls distributed by *Butler Bros.* They had china heads and limbs. Two out of every three had black hair, and the remainder blonde hair. On the muslin bodies were printed, in red and blue, the U.S. coat of arms and the names of various states. Size 10¼ inches, price 65¢ doz. wholesale.

**U.S. Toy & Novelty Co.** 1919–20. New York City. Registered in U.S. *Wauketoi* as a trademark for a line of walking dolls.

**Uebler & Reck.** 1924. Nürnberg, Bavaria. Made dolls.

**Ulhenhuth, Henry, & Co.** 1876–90. Paris and later at Lagny, Seine-et-Oise. Manufactured dolls and bébés.

1876: Was awarded an Honorable Mention for their display at the Paris Exposition.

1878: Exhibited dressed and undressed articulated dolls of kid and bisque at the Paris Exposition.

1879: Was awarded a medal for their doll display at the Paris Exposition.

1886: Won a medal for their dolls at the Liverpool Exhibition.

1890: Made *bébés incassables,* which they called *Bébé Merveilleux.*

**Ulla Puppe.** 1921–25+. Trademark registered in Germany by Arthur *Gotthelf* for dolls and baby dolls.

**Ullmann, Alois.** 1923. Teplice Sanov (Teplitz-Schönau), Czechoslovakia. Made dolls.

**Ullrich, Ch. C. J.** 1889. Leipzig, Saxony. Obtained a German patent for a crying doll.

**Ulmcke, Carl C.** 1912–25+. New York City. Imported dolls.

**Ulrich.** 1916. American Art Doll representing a Dutch boy; advertised by *Strobel & Wilken* as being a lifelike character doll, waterproof and indestructible. It had painted hair and eyes and resembled the *Käthe Kruse* dolls.

**U-Man Doll.** 1924. Made by the *Toy Shop.* Advertisement claimed a special process was used and a material not previously used for making dolls.

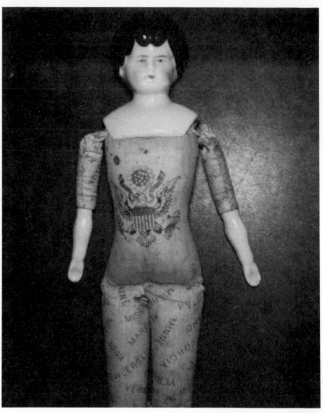

**1632.** "U. S. Emblem" doll handled by Butler Bros. in 1905; china head and limbs; muslin body with the names of states in blue and red. Emblem appears on the front of the torso. H. 10 inches. *Courtesy of the Museum of the City of New York.*

**1633.** Mark used by Henry Ulhenhuth & Co.

**Un Poulbot and Une Poulbotte.** 1913. Two trademarks registered in France by *Francisque Poulbot.*

**Unbreakable.** This term is applied to many dolls that are indeed breakable; it often refers to composition dolls.

**Uncle.** 1907. Trade name for rag doll made by *Art Fabric Mills.*

**Uncle Mose.** 1908–25+. Trademark registered in U.S. by *Aunt Jemima Mills Co.* for a rag doll representing an elderly Negro man.

**Uncle Sam.** 1892–97. One of the *Brownies* designed by *Palmer Cox.* These came as rag cutout dolls and as composition dolls with heads of undressed kid and of various other materials.

**Uncle Sam.** 1905. Advertised by *Butler Bros.* as one of the "All Nation Indestructible Dolls"; size 12 inches, price $4.25 doz. wholesale.

**Uncle Sam.** Prior to 1908, this doll was purchased in a New York wholesale house; it had a bisque head made by *Gebrüder Knoch.* (See Ill. 1029.)

**1634**

**1635A & B.** "Uncle Sam" with bisque head marked "S 1," gray hair and whiskers, molded eyebrows, glass eyes. Original clothes include a blue felt coat, white silk vest with blue stars, blue tie with red stars, red striped cotton trousers, gray spats, black shoes. H. 13 inches. *Courtesy of Sylvia Brockmon.*

A   B

**1634.** All-composition Brownie depicting Uncle Sam, designed by Palmer Cox. Has molded clothes—blue coat, red tie, white shirt, gold vest, red and white striped pants, black shoes. Note the painted, round bulbous eyes that glance down and to the side. A similar one was advertised in 1897. H. 5 inches. *Coleman Collection.*

**Uncle Sam.** 1916. A laughing Uncle Sam doll; it was copyrighted by *Jeanne I. Orsini.*

**Uncle Sam.** 1916. Designed by *Grace Drayton;* made by *Bently-Franklin Co.* as one of the cotton-stuffed *Hug-Me-Tight* line of rag dolls.

**Uncle Sam.** 1916. Made by *EFFanBEE;* price $1.00.

**Uncle Sam.** 1917. Advertised by the *Baltimore Bargain House* for premium and carnival use. Came with composition head and hands, jointed limbs, and dressed in appropriate costume. Size 36 inches, price $1.45.

**Uncle Sam.** 1917. Copyrighted by *Jessie M. Raleigh;* size 6 inches.

**Uncle Sam.** 1917. Trade name of doll made by *Standard Doll Co.;* size 16 inches.

**Uncle Sam Doll Corp.** 1920–22. Boonton, N.J., and New York City. Made dolls' heads.

**Uncle Sam Jr.** 1917. One of the *Yankee Doodle Kids* in the *Madame Hendren* line of the *Averill Manufacturing Co.* Mate to *Miss U.S.A.* Price $8.50 doz. wholesale.

**Uncle Sam Kids.** 1917. Dolls made by *Horsman;* included *Miss Sam* and *Master Sam,* both dressed in red, white, and blue.

**Uncle Walt.** 1923–25. One of the *Gasoline Alley* dolls created by *Frank O. King,* produced by *Mrs. William Benoliel* for the *Live Long Toy Co.* The doll was produced as an oilcloth two-piece stuffed doll with brown trousers, red shirt, and orange hair, size 27 inches, and also as an all-bisque doll 3½ inches tall. It is not known whether the Live Long Toy Co. made both types of dolls.

1923: "Uncle Walt" was registered as a trademark in U.S. by Frank O. King, the mark to be an impression on the doll.

**Undressed Doll.** 1903. Described in PLAYTHINGS as a doll clothed only in a chemise.

**Une Poulbotte.** See **Un Poulbot.**

**Uneeda Biscuit Boy (Uneeda Kid).** 1914–17. Trademark registered in U.S. by the *Ideal Novelty & Toy Co.* By special arrangement with the National Biscuit Co., Morris Michtom obtained a design patent in U.S. for this doll, which represented the figure on the Uneeda Biscuit box. The doll carried a miniature box of Uneeda Biscuits under its arm; it wore rompers; a coat and hat of yellow sateen, and high black boots. Sizes 16 and 24 inches; price $1.00 for 16-inch doll.

1916: Came also with jointed legs and had a mate named *Zu-Zu Kid.*

1917: Dolls named "Uneeda Kid" and "Uneeda Kid Jr."

**1636.** All-bisque version of "Uncle Walt" has swivel neck. Molded clothes include a yellow shirt, blue pants, red tie, and white cap. H. 3⅝ inches. *Courtesy of Dorothy Annunziato.*

**1637.** Doll marked "Unis France" and "301," probably made by Société Française de Fabrication de Bébés et Jouets; bisque head, glass eyes, composition body. Doll is dressed in original clothes as an Alsatian girl. Mark: Ill. **1638.** H. 12 inches. *Courtesy of May Maurer.*

**1638 & 1639.** Unis France marks used by the Société Française de Fabrication de Bébés et Jouets. Other firms may have. also used mark No. **1639.**

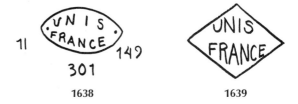

**Uneeda Doll Co.** 1917–25+. New York City. Made stuffed dolls, including *Mama Dolls*.

1920: Advertised that they were the only factory with a complete line of popular-priced dolls. Their dolls came with sleeping eyes or painted eyes, with wigs or painted heads; price 25¢ to $5.00.

1923: Advertised that they were the originators of the washable fabric face doll. (See *Martha Chase* and many others.) They had eight numbers in their *Cra-Doll* line, which had complete sewed heads and not masks.

1924: One of their newest dolls was *Baby Betty;* they also had moving-eyed dolls in sizes 14 to 28 inches and composition-leg dolls from 14 inches up.

1925: Dolls were priced 25¢ to $15.00.

**Unerreicht (Unrivaled).** 1911. Trademark of *Adolph Harrass* for jointed dolls.

**Unger.** 1880. Germany. Displayed dolls at the Melbourne Exhibition.

**Unger, Robert.** 1909–16. Waltershausen, Thür. Manufactured and exported dolls.

**Unique Novelty Doll Co.** 1925. New York City. Made dolls.

**Unis France.** Ca. 1922–25+. Some of the dolls made by the *Société Française de Fabrication de Bébés et Jouets*

(S.F.B.J.) bear the "Unis France" mark, usually with the numbers 71 and 149 on either side of the ellipse containing the words "Unis France." Luella Hart, in TOY TRADER, October, 1965, stated that "Unis" stood for "Union Nationale Inter-Syndicali" (sic), and that *Petitcollin* and other firms also belonged to this association.

**United Arts & Crafts Workers.** 1917. U.S. Made dolls.

**United States Rubber Co.** See **Mechanical Rubber Co.**

**Universal Doll Corp.** 1818–22. New York City. Manufactured dolls.

**Universal Joint.** 1895–25+. Patented in U.S. by *Charles Fausel* in 1895. The Universal Joint was used on kid or fabric bodies. This joint had three members held together by a bolt, which allowed the knuckle end to pivot within the concave area; at the same time, a swivel connection between the two parts of the knuckle permitted one of the members to rotate on the other member. (See Ill. 542.)

**Universel.** See **L'Universel.**

**Ursula.** 1913. Trademark registered in Germany by *F. W. Mathes* for dolls, doll parts, dolls' wigs, and so on.

**U-Shab-Ti.** 1923. Trade name for a doll dressed in Egyptian costume; doll was made by *Averill Manufacturing Co.*

**Usher, Ruth H.** 1920–21. Brooklyn, N.Y. Was granted a U.S. design patent for a rag doll.

**Utley Co.** 1916–19. Holyoke, Mass. They probably were succeeded in 1919 by the *New England Doll Co.* Made fabric dolls and dolls of "cloth papier-mâché." *Strobel & Wilken* and *Louis Wolf & Co.* distributed their dolls.

1916: Made stockinet character *Rollinson Dolls.*

1917: Registered in U.S. as a trademark *Sanigenic,* the name to be affixed to the cloth covering of the doll's body with a rubber stamp. Advertised *Tuco Doll* with jointed limbs and *Fabco Doll,* an all-fabric jointed doll.

1918: Advertised ball-jointed dolls made of cloth papier-mâché. They came with sleeping eyes, four styles of wigs, socket heads; bodies were flesh tinted, washable, and lightweight. Doll-face dolls were 14 to 26 inches; character dolls came 14 to 20 inches.

**Uwanta.** 1899. Trademark registered in U.S. by *Borgfeldt.*

# V

**Vacation Girl.** 1918. Made by *Jessie M. Raleigh,* distributed by *Butler Bros.* Came with wig; size 18½ inches, price $5.10.

**Vaccia, Guglielmo.** See **Voccia, Guglielmo.**

**Vale (Howe), Margaret F.** 1923–25+. Registered two trademarks in U.S.; one was "Margaret Vale's Celebrity Creations" and the other was *The Jolly Roger* and a picture of a ship. Margaret Vale, a niece of Woodrow Wilson, conceived the idea of having dolls represent famous personalities in dramatic successes, operas, and books. She selected the people, obtained rights from them, and then had *Jane Gray Co.* make dolls to represent the celebrities.

**Valentine Bud.** 1919. Trade name for a novelty *Art Doll* made by *EFFanBEE;* it wore a crepe-paper costume.

**Valet.** 1855–78. Paris. Made dolls, including mechanical dolls.

1855: Advertised dolls with movement, at reasonable prices.

**Vallée, Louis Albert Jules, & Schultz, Adolphe Louis Guillame.** 1893. Paris. Obtained French, German, and U.S. patents for a method of molding dolls' heads, especially those of celluloid, all in one piece by means of an expanding and contracting die and matrix.

**Valli Valli.** 1910. Portrait doll of Valli Valli as she appeared in THE DOLLAR PRINCESS. Doll could open and shut its eyes.

**Vamp Dolls.** 1922. Trade name for dolls from Paris; they came with long legs and shapely arms.

**Vampie.** 1919–21. Copyrighted twice by *Gordon F. Gillespie;* the first copyright named Edna Berg as the artist, and the second named J. L. Roop as the artist. The doll had exaggerated eyes and eyelashes. "Vampie" registered in U.S. as a trademark by Gordon F. Gillespie in 1921.

**Vamps.** 1920. Cherub-type doll made by *Duckme Doll Co.*

**Van Raalte, H. & A.** 1891. London. Imported dolls.

**Vangel, A. L.** 1879. Vienna. Was granted a German patent for a plastic substance to be used in the production of dolls' heads.

**Vanheems & Wheeler.** London. Distributed dolls made by the *Société Française de Fabrication de Bébés et Jouets.* (S.F.B.J.)

**Vanitie Doll.** 1921–22+. Made by *Mutual Doll Co.* in 1921 and by *Cameo Doll Co.* in 1922 and thereafter; distributed by *Borgfeldt.* This Spanish-style lady doll, designed and copyrighted by *Joseph L. Kallus,* was made of wood-pulp composition, especially for the amusement park trade.

**Vanity Fair Dolls.** 1901. These dolls had china head and limbs on a muslin body; the shoulder head had a molded gilt necklace that included an oval mirror as a pendant. The gilded part of the necklace was only the front; the gilding ended at the midpoint of the shoulders. Dolls came in sizes 7, 10, 13, and 16 inches, price 40¢ to $2.00 doz. wholesale.

**Vannier, Mme.** 1864. Paris. Made dressed dolls with trousseaux.

**Vantropol.** 1889. Paris. Made dolls.

**Vassar.** 1912. Trade name for a bisque-headed doll distributed by *Butler Bros.* It came with either blue or brown glass sleeping eyes, hair eyelashes, and curly wig, and was jointed at shoulders, elbows, and hips. Size 13 inches, price $4.50 doz. wholesale.

**Vassilief, Mme. Marie.** 1921. Paris. Widow of a Russian nobleman; made portrait dolls of famous people, including one of *Ruth Reeves,* the costume designer. These dolls were make of kid and stuffed with sawdust; size 24 inches. They were sold to the general public.

**Vater, Alfr.** 1918. Eisenberg, Thür. Made dolls.

**Vathé, François.** 1921. New York City. Was granted a U.S. design patent for a doll with a short body and very long jointless but flexible limbs.

**Veal, Sarah Jane.** See **Kuddles.**

**Vecque.** 1867–76. Paris. Made dolls.

**Velter, G.** See **Borreau.**

**Velvokin.** 1909–10. Trademark registered in U.S. by the *Chattanooga Medicine Co.* for dolls.

**Venetian Art & Novelty Co.** 1920. Los Angeles, Calif. Copyrighted two cherub-type dolls with joints at the shoulders and *starfish hands*. One doll, named *Peggy,* was designed by *Aida Pierini;* the other doll was named *Mimi* and designed by *Carlo Romanelli.*

**Vera.** 1892. Name of doll offered as a subscription premium by YOUTH'S COMPANION. It had bisque head and hands, brown glass eyes, teeth, long blonde curly hair, swivel neck, jointed shoulders and hips, half kid body. Size was 14 inches. Came with hammock and paper patterns.

**Verdainne (Verdavaine), H.** 1839–52. Paris. Made dressed dolls.

**Verdavainne, Alphonso.** 1847–72. Paris. Made leather bodies and dressed dolls.

**Verdieck, Carl.** 1918. Hamburg, Germany. Made dolls.

**Verdier & Gutmacher.** 1897–1902, Paris; 1899–1902, name was Verdier & Cie.; Etienne Rodolphe Verdier and Sylvain Gutmacher. Obtained French, German, British, and U.S. patents for making unbreakable dolls, especially dolls' heads. The description in the patent stated that several superimposed layers of cloth material, consisting of linen, jaconet, and a very fine fabric, were secured together with starch and compressed together to produce a thick, tight compound fabric. When dry, the fabric was cut into pieces of the required size, slightly moistened, and pressed into shape by means of stamps and matrices, the pressing form being heated after the insertion of the cloth. The pressing required three minutes. After that, the cuts for the eyes, mouth, etc., were made. The flanges were fixed together with glue or paste and strips of linen glued at the jointed parts inside the heads to impart more strength. The head was then coated with a flesh-colored mixture of sulfate of baryta and gelatin or a kaolin or chalk whitening. Then two coats of sizing were applied and the head painted in the usual manner by means of waterproof paints. To impart a varnish to the head, it was dipped in a bath of gelatin and water and immersed promptly in a mixture of formic aldehyde and water or chrome-alum, which allegedly rendered it washable even in boiling water.

1899: Verdier & Cie. used the initials "V. G." and registered in France four trademarks, namely: *Bébé le Select. V. G., Bébé Métropole. V. G., Bébé Monopole. V. G.,* and *Bébé Excelsior V. G.*

**Verger.** See **Dehais.**

**Verita, Mlle. Gabrielle.** 1915. Paris. Registered in France as a trademark the words *Poupées Verité* and the initials "G V." She made rag babies, boys and girls.

**1640.** Doll made by J. Verlingue and called "Petite Française," "Liane." For mark on the back of the bisque head (except for the bottom line) see Ill. **1089.** Composition body. Another doll with a similarly marked head has a body marked "Modern Bazar, Nice." H. 18½ inches. *Courtesy of Bess Goldfinger.*

**1641.** All-bisque doll made by J. Verlingue has the name "Liane" incised on the back of the head, sleeping glass eyes, neck joint protected with kid lining. Mark: Ill. **1089.** H. 6 inches. *Coleman Collection.*

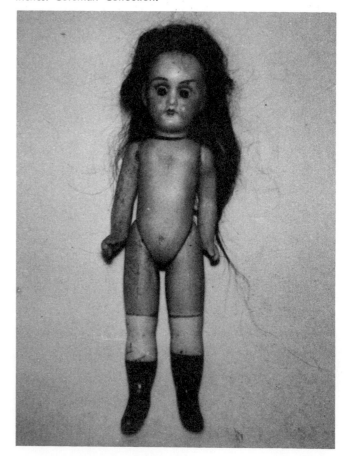

**Verlingue, J.** 1915–21. Boulogne-sur-Mer and Montreuil-sous-Bois, France. Made porcelain dolls' heads and *mignonettes*. He is believed to have used an anchor with the initials "J V" as a mark (see Ill. 1089).

1915–16: Verlingue was one of those who benefited from the counsel of *Sèvres,* in improving his products.

1919: Agent in Paris was Fournier-Blanquin. Verlingue was director of the Société de l'Anc. Faïencerie in Boulogne, as well as the owner of a factory at Montreuil-sous-Bois.

1921: He had a factory at Boulogne. His Paris address and telephone number were the same as those of *Gesland.*

**Vermeiren, Maison.** Before 1921, Paris; 1921, Humbert successor. Made dolls.

**Vermont Novelty Works. See Ellis, Britton & Eaton.**

**Verpillier, Emil, & Graves, Charles Watson.** 1892–98. Newark, N.J. Obtained one French, three U.S., and two German patents for improvements in the construction of ball joints for dolls.

1895: The ball-and-socket joint was combined with a hinge joint.

1898: Patent related to kid- or cloth-covered doll bodies, although it was applicable also to dolls with papier-mâché bodies. The arms and legs were of wood or papier-mâché, and the body was stuffed with sawdust, hair, or similar material. The patent provided for a skeleton frame within the body, tubular portions on the frame, and a ball joint connected with each tubular portion; the members of the doll were secured to these joints so that they were capable of a rotary movement about the longitudinal axis as well as a flexible movement in any plane different to the plane of rotation.

**Verry Fils.** 1865–73. Paris. Name found on kid-bodied lady doll. Verry Fils at the same address was listed in Paris Directories as a goldsmith and cutler.

**Vervelle, Lucien Alexis.** 1876. France. Was granted a French patent for dolls' heads of metal.

**Vesely, V.** 1908-12. Prague, Bohemia. Manufactured dolls.

**Vetter, Nicol.** 1898–1918. Wildenheid near Sonneberg, Thür, 1909–18, N. & R. Vetter. Made dolls' bodies.

**Vetter (Cousin) Nick.** 1924. Trademark registered in Germany by *E. Kübler & Co.* for rubber dolls.

**Vey & Kreiter.** 1873–74. Waltershausen, Thür. Made and exported talking and crying dolls.

**1642A & B.** Doll from the Verry Fils establishment, with bisque head and shoulder plate, glass eyes, closed mouth, kid gusseted body. Mark on body: Ill. **1643.** H. 15 inches. H. of shoulder head, 4 inches. *Courtesy of Eunice Althouse.*

**1643.** Verry Fils mark found on kid bodies.

1643

**Victoria Toy & Novelty Co.** 1910. U.S. Made dolls.

**Victorieux.** See **Le Victorieux.**

**Victory.** 1917. Trademark registered in Britain by *Henry Solomon Benjamin;* mark included a picture of Victory with wings.

**Victory Doll.** 1917–20. All-composition doll made by *Louis Amberg & Son* under the supervision of *Otto Denivelle.*

1918: Made in four sizes; came with sleeping eyes and wigs.

1919: Advertised as made in "innumerable styles"; came with hair eyelashes and "fool proof eyes"; eight sizes.

**Videlier (Vidalier).** 1829–82, Paris; 1865–82, *Brasseur-Videlier,* successors. Made dolls.

1861: Widow Videlier made dolls of various kinds, dressed and undressed dolls.

1865–82: Brasseur-Videlier made inexpensive dolls, luxury dolls, and jointed dolls; dressed and undressed dolls and dolls' trousseaux.

**Viel.** 1889. Paris. Made dolls.

**Vienna.** 1898. Trade name of a hinge-jointed kid-body doll advertised by *W. A. Cissna & Co.* It had a bisque head, teeth, curly blonde hair wig, kid body sewed with colored thread, hinge joint at hip, gusset joint at knee. Size 16 inches, price $6.75 doz. wholesale.

**Vierecke & Leutke.** 1902. Riga, Russia. Made dolls.

**Viktoria.** Name found on bisque heads made in Germany by *Julius Hering.* One of these dolls is reported to have an open mouth with two teeth, glass eyes, jointed composition body; size 13 inches. Another one of these dolls is 21 inches.

**Villard & Weill.** 1834–1923, Paris and Lunéville, France; 1890, Henri Villard was in charge of the Lunéville factory; 1914–23, the successors were called Société Anonyme des Anciens Etablissements Villard & Weill. Made dolls.

1878: Displayed dolls at the Paris Exposition.

1879: Showed dolls at the Sydney Exhibition.

1889: Won a gold medal at the Paris Exposition.

1900: Awarded a gold medal at the Paris Exposition.

1904: Won a Grand Prize at the St. Louis Exhibition.

1905: Displayed dolls at the Liège Exposition.

1914: Had a capital of 750,000 francs.

**Villiard, G.** Before 1890, Paris, factory at Lilas; 1890, Charles Villiard Fils was successor. Made supple rubber dolls with enamel eyes. Advertised that they invented the "true *bébé incassable.*"

**Vincent, John.** 1919. Weymouth, England. Registered in Britain *Petseymurphy* as a trademark for dolls.

**Viola.** 1902–4. Trademark registered in Germany by

1644. All-composition "Victory," doll made by Louis Amberg & Co. ca. 1918, has metal sleeping eyes, open mouth with teeth, ball-jointed composition body. Mark: Ill. **1645.** H. 16 inches. *Courtesy of Dorothy Annunziato.*

1645. "Victory Doll" mark used by Louis Amberg.

*Hamburger & Co.* and used for a line of jointed dolls with bisque heads. These were advertised as moderate-priced dolls with the bodies of a better grade than the heads and wigs. *Wislizenus* and *Gutmann & Schiffnie* may have participated in the production of some of these dolls.

**Viola Doll Co.** 1917–24. New York City. Manufactured dolls.

1918: Advertised fifty numbers, including sleeping-eyed dolls, with or without wigs, cork-stuffed bodies, sewn dresses, and dressed jointed celluloid dolls.

1923: Produced *Mama Dolls* with sleeping eyes.

**Violet.** See **Baby Violet.**

**Violet.** 1910–22. Line of dolls with *Minerva* metal heads on kid bodies, distributed by *Sears, Roebuck & Co.* The

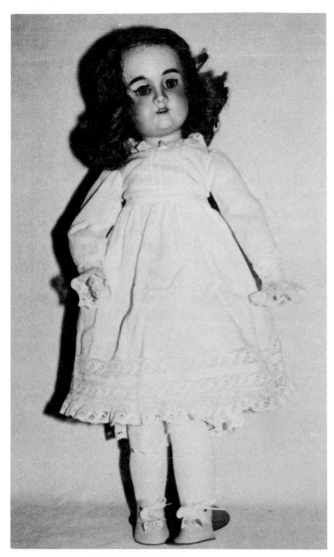

**1646.** "Viola"–name on bisque head made ca. 1903 for Hamburger & Co. Doll has sleeping glass eyes, open mouth and teeth, ball-jointed composition body, contemporary dress. Mark: Ill. **1647.** H. 20½ inches. *Courtesy of Dorothy Annunziato.*

**1647 & 1648.** "Viola" marks found on dolls handled by Hamburger & Co.

Made in Germany
Viola
H. & Co.
5.

1647

Made
in
Germany
8
Viola

1648

name was affixed to the chest of the dolls with a paper sticker reading "Violet, copyright 1910 by Sears, Roebuck & Co. Germany." One of these dolls has a size four Minerva head with stationary blue glass eyes, brown wig, open mouth, teeth, and tongue; white kid body has cambric legs below the knees and ceramic hands.

1916: Advertised as having white kid body with riveted joints at hips; curled sewed wig, moving eyelids. Came in sizes 16, 18, and 20 inches; price $1.19 to $1.98.

1922: Dolls had Minerva metal heads, sleeping eyes, sewed wigs, molded celluloid forearms and hands, imitation kid body with riveted joints at hips and knees. Sizes were 16, 18, 20, and 23½ inches; price $1.98 to $3.48.

**Violett.** Trademark of *Ernst Liebermann.*

**Violon, Mme. Jeanne.** 1924. La-Varenne-Saint-Hilaire, Seine. Registered in France *Jeannine* as a trademark for dolls.

**Virginia.** 1912. Made by *Tip Top Toy Co.* Came with composition head, eyes glancing to the side. Sizes 9, 12½, and 15½ inches, price 25¢, 50¢, and $1.00. Mate to *Paul.*

**Virginia Dare.** Ca. 1917. Baby doll made by *Averill Manufacturing Co.*

**Virnich.** 1874–25+. Cologne, Germany. B. H. Virnich, founder of the firm, was known as "The Doll King." In 1902 he was succeeded by his son, P. H. Virnich. They handled dolls.

**Vischer, Alfred, & Co.** 1894–1907. New York City. Importers and sole agents for *Minerva* metal heads.

1899: Advertised metal dolls' heads with molded hair and with wigs.

1901: Registered in U.S. "Minerva" as a trademark for metal dolls' heads.

1905: Advertised Minerva dolls' heads and *Knock About Dolls.*

**Vita.** 1917. Trademark registered in France by *André Laffitte* for dolls' heads and moving eyes to go into these heads.

**Vitu (Vittu), Mme.** 1870–93, Paris; 1890–93, A. Hesse, successor. Made dolls.

1893: Displayed dolls at the Chicago Exposition.

**Vivandière.** Dolls were sometimes dressed as Vivandières. Mons. Alexander Girard, in an article in PLAY-THINGS, 1903, referred to the Vivandière or nurse dolls as being typical of the War of 1870 period. The Vivandière shown in Ill. 404 appears to be earlier than 1870.

**Vivi.** 1920. All-bisque doll made by *Jeanne I. Orsini.* Some versions had painted eyes, and some had glass eyes and an open-closed mouth.

VIVI
REG. U.S. PAT. OFF.
CORP.- J.J. ORSINI
1920
PAT APPLIED FOR

**1649.** "Vivi" mark on dolls by Jeanne I. Orsini.

**Vivian.** 1908. Line of rag dolls made by *Bruin Manufacturing Co.;* included *Wide-Awake* rag dolls.

**Voccia (Vaccia), Guglielmo.** 1919–20. An Italian, living in New York City. He copyrighted several dolls in U.S.—namely, *Bella Veneziana, Clown, Sentimentale, Shy Girl, Keep Kool, I Love You, Lily Tiso,* and *Oriental.*

**Vogel, Fritz.** 1879–82. Sonneberg. Thür. Manufactured dolls and dolls' heads.

1879: Obtained two German patents for covering dolls' heads and joints with stretched leather. The second patent, an improvement over the first one, pertained especially to papier-mâché heads. He was commended for the "useful and cheap" toys that he showed at the Sydney Exhibition.

1880: Obtained French and German patents for improvements in making dolls' heads and jointed dolls with elastic skin as a cover.

1881: Was granted a German patent for a talking mechanism for dolls.

1882: Obtained a German patent for coating papier-mâché, *Xylolith,* or wood with paraffin or a paraffin mixture.

**Vogel, Gertrud (née Closs).** 1920. Dresden, Saxony. Registered in Germany her initials "G V" in a "C" as a trademark for dolls.

**Vogelsanger, Paul.** 1908–18. Munich, Bavaria. A sculptor who modeled the heads for the dolls made by *Marion Kaulitz.* He created *Art. Dolls,* which were shown in Munich in 1918.

**Vogt, A. Heinrich, & Co.** 1906–14. Paris. Exported dolls.

**Voices.** (See **Talking Dolls.**) Most of the "Voices" made in Germany were made in the Thüringian doll centers. H. Hölbe, *Albin Steiner,* Ed. Steiner, and *V. Steiner* made voices in Sonneberg. *Frickman & Lindner* and *Adolf Von der Wehd* made voices in Köppelsdorf. Th. Dobrich and A. Sauerteig made voices in Neufang.

Probably the largest maker of voices was called Voices Inc., located in Newark, N.J. This firm combined the *Art Metal Works,* which made Ronson voices under *Louis Anderson;* the Grubman Engineering & Manufacturing Co., which made Grubman voices; and the *Lloyd Manufacturing Co.,* which made Lloyd voices. These firms obtained fourteen U.S. patents for voices between 1915 and 1924. The court validated Louis Aronson's patents for *Mama Doll* voices in 1924, and referred to the making of Mama dolls as an art, saying, "To obtain simplicity is the highest trait of genius." Singer-Frisch Manufacturing Co. of Jersey City, N.J., made Frisch voices.

**Voight, Armin.** 1918. Herschdorf near Königsee, Thür. Made dolls.

**Voight, Bruno.** 1891. Olbernhau near Sonneberg, Thür. Obtained a German patent for a *fortune-telling doll.*

**Voight, Edwin.** 1902–9. Rodach near Coburg, Thür. Made dolls.

**1650.** Trademark used by Friedrich Voight.

**Voight, Friedrich.** 1879–1925+, Sonneberg, Thür.; 1918–25+, successors of Friedrich Voight. Made jointed and wooden dolls and wooden dolls' heads. Used *Frivona* as a trademark.

1911: Produced wooden, celluloid, and porcelain heads.

**Voigt, Gebrüder.** 1909. Eilmersdorf, Thür. Made wool dolls.

**Voirin, Jules.** 1882. Paris. Obtained a French patent for a "children's doll" with shoulder head in molded leather. He claimed that up to that time dolls' heads had been made of painted wood, papier-mâché, or enameled porcelain. (See also **Leather Dolls.**)

**Voit, Andreas.** 1835–55. Hildburghausen, Thür. Made papier-mâché dolls' heads as well as some heavy plaster heads that looked as if they were stamped out of clay.

1844: Won a bronze medal for his display of twelve single doll heads at the Berlin exhibition.

1855: Exhibited papier-mâché dolls' heads at the Paris Exposition.

**Voit & Fleischmann.** 1844. Nürnberg, Bavaria. Won a silver medal at the Berlin Exhibition for their dolls. They claimed that they made 360,000 dolls' heads a year.

**Völker, Carl.** 1909–18. Oberlind, Thür. Made dolls.

**Völker, Curt.** 1895. Orlamünde, Thür. Manufactured dolls.

**Völker, Karl (Carl).** 1908–25+. Sonneberg, Thür. Manufactured various kinds of jointed and dressed dolls, including baby dolls.

**Volkmann, A.** 1897–1918. Hamburg, Germany. Made and distributed dolls.

**Vollée, Mme.** 1921–25+. Paris. Made dolls and dolls' clothes.

**Vollmar, A.** 1909. Haselrieth, Thür. Made dolls.

**Volpert, Franz.** 1925. Charlottenburg, Prussia. Produced and distributed dolls; registered in Germany *Lyro* in a six-pointed star as a trademark for dolls.

**Volvox Inc.** 1911–12. Hamburg, Germany. Produced and distributed dolls; registered in Germany "Volvox" as a trademark for dolls driven by clockworks.

**Von Alt Porzellanfabrik.** See **Alt, Beck & Gottschalck.**

**Von Berg, Hermann.** See **Berg, Hermann.**

**Von Bihl, W. A.** 1909. Berlin. Wholesale doll manufacturer.

**Von der Wehd, Adolf.** 1925. Sonneberg and Köppelsdorf, Thür. Manufactured jointed dolls, dressed dolls, and undressed dolls as well as dolls' voices. He advertised one of his dolls: "Please raise my arm and I will say 'Mama.'"

**Von Erichsen, Paul.** 1880. Washington, D.C. Made dolls.

**Von Querfurth, Fr. Edle.** 1924. Berlin. Designed dolls.

**Von Zeddelmann, Oskar.** 1924. Berlin. Made wax dolls' heads and doll parts.

**Voogt et Navaro.** 1925. Paris. Handled dolls.

**Votes-For-Women.** 1911–15. Trademark registered in U.S. by *Mabel D. Nekarda;* mark was to be affixed to the dress or hat of the doll.

1915: *Ernst Karg* obtained a U.S. design patent for a doll wearing a ribbon on its chest reading "Votes-For-Women."

**Vuaquelin, M.** 1925. Paris. Made dolls.

**Vulquin, M., Jeune (Jr.).** 1877. Paris. At his shop named *A la Grande Duchesse,* formerly run by Jalibert, Vulquin made dressed dolls and dolls' trousseaux.

# W

**Wabbly.** Ca. 1922. Name for rag dolls that were a Paris craze. They were introduced into U.S. in about 1922. These dolls had hand-painted faces and cloth bodies with soft and supple arms and legs. Often they were dressed in rich materials to match their owners' clothes. Sizes up to 36 inches.

**Wacker, Albert.** Before 1925, Nürnberg, Bavaria; 1925+, successor was Bayersche Celluloid Warenfabrik. Made dolls. Used "W" in a circle as a mark.

**Wackerle, Prof. Joseph.** 1918. Munich, Bavaria. Created lifelike *Art Dolls,* which were shown in Munich Exhibition.

**Wada, Heibei.** 1900. Japan. Won a bronze medal for dolls at the Paris Exposition.

**Wade, Katherine W.** 1924. San Francisco, Calif. Was granted three U.S. design patents for dolls. The first one was for a bobbed-hair girl with a bow in her hair, flower-print dress, socks, and single-strap slippers.

**Wade Davis.** 1908–25+. Trademark registered in U.S. by *Aunt Jemima Mills Co.* for a cutout rag doll representing a Negro boy.

**Wages.** For work on dolls, the pay has always been much lower in Europe than in the U.S. In Paris in 1867, men received $1.00 a day and women less than 50¢ a day. In 1878 the Paris wage for men was $1.50 a day

and for women about 75¢ a day. In 1920 in the U.S., pieceworkers on dolls received $7.00 to $8.00 a day and eye painters received $12.00 to $14.00 a day.

**Wagner, Amalie.** 1897. Vienna. Manufactured dolls and dolls' heads.

**Wagner, D. H., & Sohn.** 1742–1925+. Grünhainichen, Saxony. In the 20th century, had branch factories in Sonneberg, Thür., and Nürnberg, Bavaria. Handled Sonneberg dolls of various kinds, especially rag dolls.

1879: Won first prize at the Sydney Exhibition and were commended for their "ingenious and well made toys."

1880: Had a display at the Melbourne Exhibition.

1881: Exhibited products at Porto Alegre, Brazil, Exposition.

1925: Advertised *Ormond* dolls.

**Wagner, Jean Wallace.** 1924–25. Bunola, Pa. Was issued a U.S. design patent for a rag doll representing a Negro boy with woolly hair; doll wore pants rolled up to the knees and carried an umbrella over his arm.

**Wagner & Zetzsche.** 1875–1925+. Ilmenau, Thür. Richard Wagner and Richard Zetzsche manufactured dolls,

**1651.** Wagner & Zetzsche doll with bisque head and hands. Mark is "W Z" intertwined; see Ill. **1652.** *Courtesy of Marian Pickup.*

dolls' heads, dolls' bodies, and dolls' shoes. When a kid body for a fashionable type of lady doll was being examined, under the shoulder plate a piece of blue paper was found on which were the "W & Z" initials of Wagner & Zetzsche. The multiple fancy initials resembled a decorative pattern at first glance.

1891: Advertised kid bodies, dolls' shoes, and doll articles.

1898: Manufactured and exported kid bodies and cloth bodies.

1909: Made and exported kid bodies, shoes, etc.

1912: Was granted a German patent for a jointed cloth-body doll.

1915: Registered in Germany *Harald* as a trademark for dolls and parts of dolls.

1918: Advertised dolls, dolls' bodies, dolls' heads, and shoes.

In 1933 they were still advertising pin-jointed kid bodies. According to Luella Hart's DIRECTORY OF GERMAN DOLLS, "Obletter," the name of a Munich store, was found on the soles of shoes worn by some dolls made by Wagner & Zetzsche.

**1652.** Mark found on dolls of Wagner & Zetzsche.

**Wakano, Soyemon.** 1900. Japan. Won a bronze medal for dolls at the Paris Exposition.

**Walch, G.** 1909–18. Unterweid, Thür. Made dolls.

**Waldorf.** 1905. Jointed doll handled by *Strobel & Wilken.*

**Walker, Izannah F.** 1873. Central Falls, R.I. Obtained a U.S. patent for making rag dolls. The patent stated: "In the dies I place several thicknesses of cotton or other cheap cloth, treated with glue or paste, so that they will adhere together and hold the shape impressed upon them by the dies. When these cloth forms are dry a layer of cotton batting or other soft filling is carefully laid over them, covering the whole or the head and neck portions only . . . and then in turn, covered with an external layer of stockinet or similar webbing. The latter is then fastened to the features of the cloth forms by stitches or paste, and they are then placed again in the press. After they are taken from the press the

IZANNAH WALKER DOLLS

**1653A & B.** Rag doll made by Izannah Walker has stockinet pressed head painted with oils, corkscrew painted curls, muslin body, original dress. H. 21 inches. *Courtesy of the International Doll Library Foundation.*

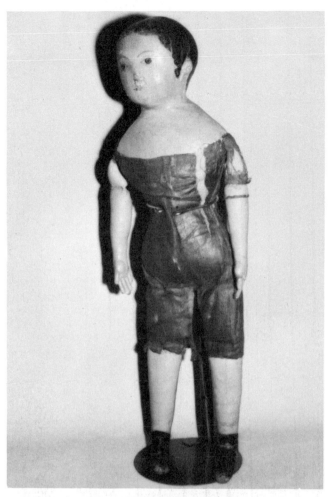

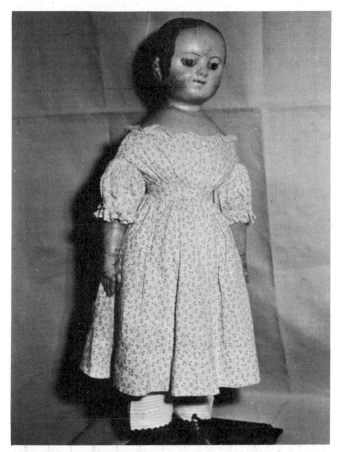

**1654A & B.** Izannah Walker doll: stockinet head, brown muslin body; features and hair painted in oils. H. 18½ inches. *Courtesy of the International Doll Library Foundation.*

**1655.** Izannah Walker rag doll wearing contemporary red and white print dress and red shoes. *Courtesy of Freda Hawkins; photograph by Winnie Langley.*

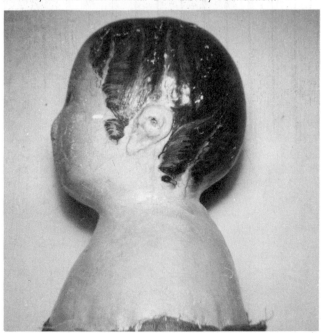

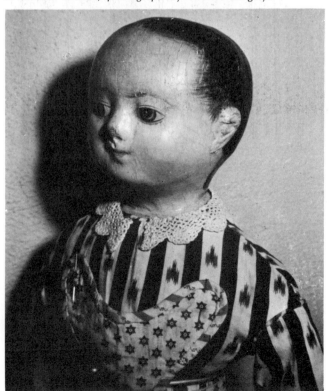

**1656.** Rag doll made by Izannah Walker wears red and brown figured dress with a brown and white print apron. *Courtesy of Frances Walker; photograph by Winnie Langley.*

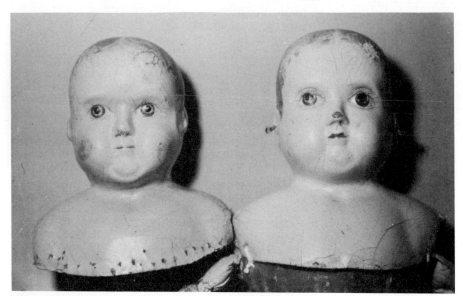

*Patented Nov. 4ᵀᴴ 1873*

**1658.** Mark found on Izannah Walker dolls.

**1657.** Pair of Izannah Walker heads with 1873 patent date marked on them. Note the earrings on the head at the right. *Courtesy of Winnie Langley; photograph by Winnie Langley.*

forms are filled with hair, cotton or other stuffing, and a piece of wood having been centrally and longitudinally laid between the two for stiffening, they are tightly pressed together and secured by sewing, pasting or gluing their edges to each other. The finishing is then done by painting the face and other parts neatly with oil-paint."

According to patent law, it would have been illegal for Izannah Walker to have made these dolls more than two years before her application date, which was June, 1873. Yet according to a statement made by Mrs. Sheldon of the Chase Doll Factory, in DOLL COLLECTORS OF AMERICA (1940), Izannah Walker made her rag dolls as early as around 1855. The dating of the Izannah Walker dolls prior to the 1873 patent date appears to be based on family tradition supplied by a great-niece of Izannah Walker. Johl, in YOUR DOLLS AND MINE, reports this family tradition and gives four different dates for the first Izannah Walker dolls: 1840 (p. 40), 1845 (p. 39), 1848 (p. 37), 1855 (p. 41). Two death dates for Izannah Walker are given: 1886 (p. 39) and 1888 (p. 37). Typographical errors could account for some of these differences, but certainly not all of them.

Izannah Walker dolls have been found in sizes 15, 17, 18½, 20, 21, and 24 inches. They come with painted hair, often with corkscrew-type curls and/or brush marks. Shoes are sometimes painted on the feet; otherwise the feet are bare. (See also **Manufacture of Rag Heads.**)

**Walker, Lida Kingsley.** 1925. St. Catharines, Ontario. Obtained two U.S. design patents for dolls. One doll was dressed in a coat and had a scarf around the neck, a pillbox hat, and high shoes; the other was a rag doll with stringy hair, bonnet untied, one shoe on and one bare foot.

**Walkie, Talkie, Sleepie.** 1925. One of the *Petite* line of dolls advertised by the *American Character Doll Co.*; price $1.50.

**Walking, Talking, Sleeping.** 1920's. Trademark found on dolls made by the *Ideal Novelty & Toy Co.*

**Walking Dolls.** Dolls that walk have been made for centuries. They were made in Germany in the 17th century and in Paris in 1737. Most of the walking dolls of the 19th century were propelled by a clockwork mechanism. In the 1860's, among the several patents for walking dolls the most famous was the *Autoperipatetikos* by *Enoch Rice Morrison*. In the 1880's, there were several patents by *F. M. Schilling, Peloubet,* and various others for walking dolls. The credit for the invention of a walking doll that turned its head as it walked and did not require a clockwork mechanism goes to *Claude Joseph Simonot* of Paris, who in 1892/3 registered his patent in seven countries and assigned his patent rights to *Fleischmann & Blödel*. Within a few years many other doll manufacturers patented and/or made similar walking dolls; among them were *Cosman Frères, Roullet & Decamps, Rabery & Delphieu,* Mme. *Lafosse, Hermann Landshut & Co.,* and *Ermund Ulrich Steiner*. At the turn of the century, walking dolls were still being made with wheels operated by a clockwork mechanism, as evidenced by the *Ferdinand Imhof* and *Oscar Arnold* patents and *Louis Amberg's* walking dolls. The introduction of the *Mama Doll* with swinging legs so that it could "walk" when properly held resulted in a spate of so-called walking dolls shortly after World War I (1918–22). Among the producers of these were *Averill*, Amberg, *Horsman, EFFanBEE, Ideal, Century, Elektra, New Toy Co.,* as well as many others less well-known. *Schoenhut* made his all-wood walking doll to compete with these others. Although patents on walking dolls are many, imitations seem to be even more numerous. One advantage of the patented walking dolls is that they help to date heads that are otherwise not documented.

**Walküre.** 1902–25+. Trademark registered in Germany by *Kley & Hahn.* This mark is usually found on bisque heads with jointed composition bodies. Often "Walküre" dolls were dressed in provincial costumes of various countries. (See color photograph C17.)

*Walkure*
*Germany*
*56*

1659. "Walküre" mark of Kley & Hahn, used for dolls.

**Wall, C.** 1855–85. Paris. Made dolls.

**Wallach & Co.** 1925. Vienna. Made dolls.

**Wall-Eyed Dolls.** 1912. Trade name for a special type of moving-eye doll that included *Jack* and *Jill.* The dolls were advertised as being the only American dolls with movable glass eyes. Their large, wide-apart eyes were painted to represent human eyes, and could be turned in any direction by the touch of a finger.

**Wally.** Name incised on bisque heads made by *Limbach Porzellanfabrik* (see Ill. 1095).

**Wally.** 1912. Trade name for a doll with a composition head, made by *Gund Manufacturing Co.*

**Walovich, Zuza.** 1915. Hawleyville, Conn. Was granted a U.S. design patent for a doll representing a Slavonian *Peasant.*

**Walpu.** 1925. Trademark registered in Germany by *Walterhauser Puppenfabrik* for dolls.

**Walsh, Delmar A.** 1922–24. Kansas City, Mo. Obtained U.S. design patent for clowns in checked costumes; one clown had the alphabet in the fabric checks, and the other had numbers in the checks.

**Walter.** 1910–11. Character boy doll made by *Kämmer & Reinhardt,* distributed by *Strobel & Wilken* and *Borgfeldt;* named for the boy who posed for the model. Doll usually came with bisque head and jointed composition body; one of the *Royal* line. (See Ill. 941.)

**Walter, Gebrüder.** 1923. Berlin. Made and exported dolls.

**Walter, Johannes.** 1908–12. Oeslau, Thür. Manufactured dressed dolls.

**Walter, R.** 1909–12. Coburg, Thür. Manufactured dolls.

**Walterhauser Puppenfabrik.** 1925. Sonneberg, Thür. Produced and distributed dolls; registered in Germany *Walpu* as a trademark. (See also **Waltershauser Puppenfabrik.**)

**Waltershausen Dolls.** This term usually means dolls made in Waltershausen, Thür., which was next to Sonneberg in importance as a doll center. The finest grades of dolls were made in Waltershausen, but all grades were made in Sonneberg. Sometimes "Waltershausen" appears to be used to refer to the fine grade of a doll regardless of its place of origin.

**Waltershauser Puppenfabrik.** 1922–25+, Waltershausen, Thür. Manufactured jointed dolls and babies.

1921: Registered in Germany the initials "W P" in a circle within a square, as a trademark.

1922: Registered in Germany *Primrose* as a trademark for dolls, dolls' heads, dolls' bodies, limbs, wigs, and clothes.

**Waltershauser Stoffspeilwarenfabrik.** 1925. Waltershausen, Thür. Made stuffed dolls.

**Walther, J., & Sohn.** 1924–25. Oeslau, Thür. Porcelain factory; made dolls' heads.

**Walther, O.** 1909. Pössneck, Thür. Manufactured dolls.

**Wanamaker's.** 1895–1925+. Philadelphia, Pa., and New York City. Imported and distributed dolls.

1895: Advertised *Jumeau,* German, *nankeen, English rag,* and many other types of dolls. Their Jumeau bébés were undressed and came in sizes 8, 9, 10, 12, and 13 inches, price $3.75 to $13.00. German dolls with jointed composition bodies cost up to $9.00.

1915: Wanamaker's sold 14-inch dolls dressed in Paris for $2.00 to $4.00.

**Wangenheim, N.** 1925. Freiburg, Saxony. Made dolls.

**Wannez & Rayer.** 1891. Paris. Handled *Bébé Loulou.*

**War Baby.** 1915. Name of standing doll copyrighted by *Elizabeth Lesser.*

**War Nurse.** 1917–21. Trademark registered in U.S. by *Sophia Delavan* for dolls.

**War Orphan.** 1917–21. Trademark registered in U.S. by *Sophia Delavan* for dolls.

**Ward, Samuel Henry.** 1918. London. Registered in Britain *Forget-Me-Not* as a trademark for dolls.

**Warnhöfer, K.** 1891–1909. Nürnberg, Bavaria. Manufactured fabric dressed dolls.

**Waschecht.** The German word meaning "washable," marked in black letters on the chest of composition-head dolls. However, the appearance of one of these dolls suggests that they were not really washable.

**Water Babies.** 1919–20. Trade name for dolls with celluloid heads and cloth bodies that could float; made by *Sig. Schwartz Co.*

**Waterbury Watch Co.** Early 20th century. Waterbury,

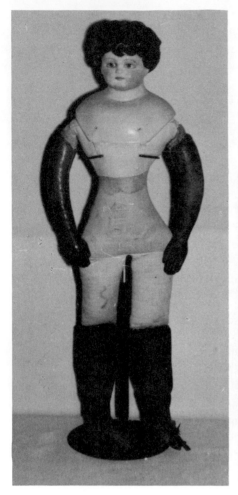

**1660A & B.** Molded composition head marked "Waschecht" (washable) in black on the chest. The inside of the head is marked "AO/50" in black ink. Hair and eyes are painted brown, lower lashes only; cloth body with leather arms. H. 25 inches. *Coleman Collection.*

Conn. Made an all-metal walking doll propelled by a clockwork mechanism, with key wind at the waist. Its large feet had a pair of rollers near the heels; size ca. 12 inches.

**Waterproof Cloth Bodies.** 1914–18. In 1914, bodies were imported into the U.S. made in the same style as kid bodies but of a waterproof material other than rubber.

1918: *Lenora Price* secured a U.S. patent for a waterproof cloth body.

**Watson, Florence Kyle.** 1923–24. Bluefield, W. Va. Was granted a U.S. design patent for a doll with jointed shoulders; doll had a large feather on top of its turban and a ruff around the bottom of its skirt.

**Wattilliaux, Charles Auguste.** 1891–96. Paris. Made and distributed dolls, including *Jeannette;* he used initials "W X."

**Wauketoi.** 1919–20. Trademark registered in U.S. by *U. S. Toy & Novelty Co.* for a line of walking dolls.

**Wax Dolls.** Ancient times–1925+. The early Romans made wax dolls, and dolls of wax continued to be made in Italy for centuries. Resin was added to the wax to give it stability and smoothness. *Daniel Neuberger* made wax dolls in the 17th century in Bavaria. Wax dolls were also made in England at an early date. Some of the dolls in Ann Sharp's doll house of ca. 1700 have wax heads,

and there is a record in 1700 of a wax baby with an invention to make it cry and to turn its eyes.

The Powell family in England, from 1748 until 1912, dressed dolls periodically in order to record the changes in clothes. The wax dolls in this collection probably were made in England. They give an excellent chronological record. The wax head on the 1748 doll is on a legless wooden body; this doll is 8 inches in size. The 1761 doll has a wax head on a cloth body; it is 14½ inches tall.

Wax dolls were made in France in the 18th century. An 18th-century wax doll purchased in Paris has hair eyelashes made on a strip and inserted in the wax; the hair was attached to the wax head with early two-piece pins. The eyes are beads of wax. The doll is dressed in a silk gown trimmed with gilt braid, worn over a satin quilted petticoat, as befitted a lady of rank. (See Ill. 1661.)

The luxury dolls of the mid-19th century were the fine wax dolls with inserted hair made by the *Pierottis,* the *Montanaris,* and others. Very rarely were hairs inserted singly; even inserting hair in small groups was an expensive process. At about this time Sonneberg was famous for its wax dolls. The wax heads were usually poured and reinforced with plaster or a composition; only occasionally were they solid wax. In the 1860's the English began to cover wax masks with muslin; dolls made in this way were called *London Rag Dolls.* In 1877

**1661.** Late 18th-century wax doll with modeled features. The eyelashes are inserted, but the wig is pinned onto the head. Wax limbs are on a torso of wire covered with fabric strips. Original dress has a train from the shoulders; a quilted silk petticoat. H. 7½ inches. *Coleman Collection.*

**1662A & B.** Doll with poured wax head and limbs, cloth body, hair inserted in groups, eyebrows and eyelash hair inserted, original red silk dress. H. 13 inches. *Courtesy of Bess Goldfinger.*

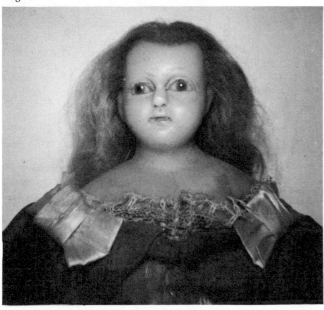

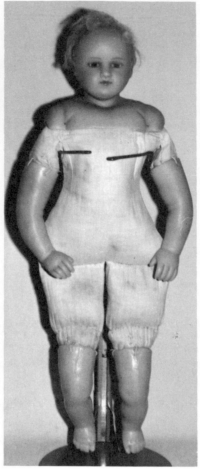

A                B

C

**1663A, B, C, & D.** Poured wax baby has hair on head and eyelashes inserted, glass eyes, hand-sewn linen body stuffed with fibers. Note the rolls of fat around the neck and the bent limbs. H. 24½ inches. *Courtesy of Eunice Althouse.*

**1664.** Poured wax head and poured torso to below the waist. The lower part of the body is machine-sewn cloth; wax limbs. Doll wears a wig. H. 17½ inches. *Courtesy of the Chester County Historical Society.*

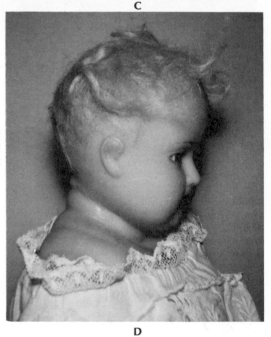

D

The prices given for dolls are those for which the dolls were originally offered for sale. They are *not* today's prices.

**1665.** Poured wax head and limbs; glass eyes; inserted hair. The modeling of the feet and hands includes dimples and nails. H. 18 inches. *Courtesy of the Museum of the City of New York.*

**1666.** All-wax baby with bent limbs, jointed at shoulders and hips; head is attached to torso; glass eyes; original gauze chemise and bonnet. H. 6 inches. *Courtesy of the Museum of the City of New York.*

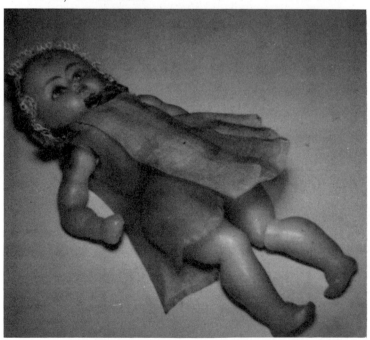

**1667A & B.** Poured beeswax doll with hair inserted in tiers about an eighth of an inch apart; three black combs across the top of the head. Doll has glass eyes, cloth body, wax limbs; original white silk dress, pink sash, and ribbons at shoulders and in hair. Part of 1881 Boston newspaper was found in her leg. H. 23 inches. (See color photograph **C22**.) *Courtesy of Lester & Alice Grinnings.*

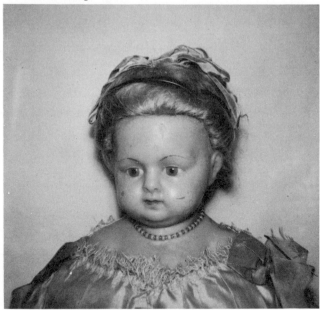

**1668.** Solid wax doll of a brown color has molded black hair in an elaborate hairdo; glass eyes. *Courtesy of Gladyse Hilsdorf; photograph by Winnie Langley.*

*Lazarus Reichmann* of New York City patented a process of strengthening a wax head by applying on the inside of it, with a brush, a mixture of sawdust, glue, and paste. His patent also mentioned the addition of turpentine to the wax to prevent cracking. But resins had been used for this purpose at a much earlier date.

Wax dolls, easily damaged by temperature changes and scratches, were expensive and seldom had a turning head or sleeping eyes. Dolls from Paris in 1876 Exhibition melted in summer heat. Their popularity began to wane in the 1870's, though they continued to be made in limited quantities. (See **Ehrich Bros.,** 1878.)

As late as 1909 the public widely misnamed bisque dolls as "wax" dolls, according to an article in PLAYTHINGS. This confusion in nomenclature lends uncertainty as to what were really wax dolls. Waxed-over-composition dolls were frequently referred to as "wax dolls." For example, in 1887 *Montgomery Ward & Co.* stated that they did not handle wax dolls, but they used the phrase "Imitation Wax Washable" in advertising a doll with a composition head.

Wax dolls and heads were advertised by the following firms: *Martin & Rippel,* 1881, New York City; *Herrera Y Hoyo,* 1893, Mexico; *Georg Hoffmann,* 1895, Rauenstein; *R. Leuthauser,* 1895, Rauenstein; *Andr. Müller,* 1895, Sonneberg; *G. Schmey,* 1895, Sonneberg; *Zeuch & Lausmann,* 1895, Sonneberg. By 1904 very few wax dolls were made in Sonneberg; England was the only country where their popularity continued. In London *Thomas Betts,* Mary *Marsh* and Jessie Marsh, *Mrs. Lucy Peck,* the Pierottis, and others continued to make wax dolls in the 20th

century. They were also made in Spain and in Ecuador. In Germany, *J. D. Kestner* made wax dolls, and *Kämmer & Reinhardt* made some of their *Mein Liebling* line of dolls in wax as well as in bisque and celluloid.

In 1920 wax dolls enjoyed popularity for the display of costumes, and similar purposes. *Elizabeth Scantlebury* of Brooklyn used dolls of wax for her historical and geographical costume dolls. A woman in Paris made dolls with heads and shoulders of carved and painted wax, and bodies of heavy wire twisted about with tissue paper. These dolls were dressed to individual order—in the latest Parisian styles or perhaps as court ladies of the time of Marie Antoinette, with white wig, elaborately curled and wreathed with rosebuds. In 1925 *Mme. T. Lazarski* of Paris made wax dolls that were displayed in French art galleries and used in French movies. (See also **Manufacture of Wax Dolls; Flossie, Mme.** See color photograph C22.)

**Waxed Dolls.** 19th century. Nearly every type of doll material has been covered with wax to improve its appearance or for other reasons. Wood, porcelain, rag, rubber, and metal, as well as many types of composition, have been coated with wax. According to legend, one day a doll maker in Sonneberg accidentally upset a caldron of heated wax over some of the papier-mâché heads that he was making. The first waxed heads made in Sonneberg are believed to have had molded hair. The wax and varnish were put on the prepared heads with a brush in a more or less crude and uneven manner. Later, the papier-mâché heads were dipped in wax; wigs, sleeping eyes, and other refinements followed. *J. D. Kestner* made dolls with wax-over-papier-mâché heads from about 1860 on.

Other countries also were making waxed dolls. In the U.S., *Rebecca Johnson* in 1887 obtained a patent for dipping a cloth doll's head in wax, and in 1890 *Philip Goldsmith* made wax-over-composition dolls' heads. In the 1880's *Josef Kubelka* of Vienna secured several patents for using wax on porcelain heads. Waxed dolls were made in Paris and in large quantities in England.

On the early waxed dolls, the features were painted on the faces before they were covered with wax; later, the features were painted on the wax itself Many of the waxed heads had molded hair. Hair inserted in a slit in the head appears to have preceded the general use of wigs. Although not as fragile as poured wax heads, waxed heads also suffered from changes in temperature and abrasions; and often small fingers would scrap off the wax, for children found it delightful to chew. Waxed rubber dolls were advertised in 1872 for small children. By 1900, waxed dolls had nearly disappeared. (See also **Manufacture of Waxed Dolls; Schmitt.** See color photograph C3.)

**Wear, Ira O.** 1908–9. Oberlin, Kans. Obtained a U.S. patent for sleeping eyes with movable lids over fixed eyeballs.

**Wearwell Brand.** 1922. Dolls with "white" metal *Minerva* heads, distributed by *Sears, Roebuck & Co.* They came

**1670.** Motschmann-type baby with wax-over-composition head, glass eyes, painted wisps of hair, wooden limbs with floating joints (twill material for cloth parts); pink paint on hands and arm. Wears original blue silk infant's gown and cap with white lace and net, blue ribbons. H. 15 inches. *Courtesy of the Museum of the City of New York.*

**1669A & B.** Pair of dolls with wax-over-composition heads on cloth bodies. Their glass eyes close when a wire is pulled at the hip. Original dresses. H. 19½ inches. *Courtesy of the Newark Museum, Newark, N.J.*

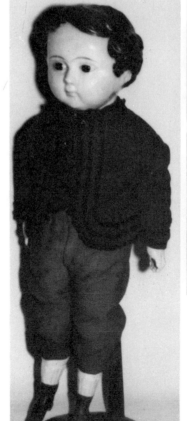

**1671A & B.** Boy doll with wax-over-composition head, pupil-less glass eyes, composition lower limbs and lower torso as found in Motschmann-type bodies. Upper torso contains a squeak box, which is activated by pushing the upper and lower sections of the body together. Original blue jacket and vest with brown trousers. H. 17½ inches. (See color photograph **C3.**) *Coleman Collection.*

WAXED DOLLS

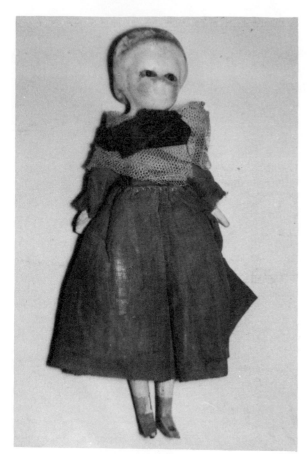

**1672.** Wax-over-composition head, glass eyes, molded hair; cloth torso, wooden limbs; squeak box; original dress of blue organdy, net fichu, and ribbon trim, pink painted boots. H. 7½ inches. *Courtesy of Lester & Alice Grinnings.*

**1673.** Pair of dolls with wax-over-composition heads, blue glass eyes, molded pompadour-style hair, cloth bodies, wooden limbs, orange painted high boots. Contemporary clothes. Boy, 11 inches. Girl, 9½ inches. *Coleman Collection.*

**1674.** Waxed wooden head of this doll has carved braided hair and pierced ears. *Courtesy of the Chester County Historical Society; photograph by Winnie Langley.*

**1675A & B.** Wax-over-composition head on a ball-jointed composition body. The body and face of this doll resemble those made by Schmitt & Fils. Spherical-shaped neck fits up into head socket. No mark on the doll, but a similar head is on a marked Schmitt body. H. 16 inches. *Courtesy of Lester & Alice Grinnings.*

with curly mohair wigs, fixed glass eyes, teeth; pink silesia cloth bodies and legs, stuffed with hair; carved wooden hands and forearms. Sizes were 15, 17, 20, and 22½ inches, price 85¢ to $1.65.

**Webb, Carmalete Waldo.** 1922. Los Angeles, Calif. Copyrighted three oriental figures or dolls designed by Margaret Smith, daughter of *Putnam D. Smith.*

**Webb, Florence.** 1916. Obtained a British patent for a doll's head, hands, and feet of leather. The head was molded over a buckram form, and the hands and feet were wired so that they were movable and could retain a given position.

**Webber, William Augustus.** 1882–84. Medford, Mass. Obtained U.S., British, German, French, Belgian, and Canadian patents for the "Webber Singing Doll." The British patent also included the names of George Bradford Kelly and Edward Lyman Rand, both of Boston, Mass., and John Leslie Given of Cambridge, Mass. The patent description read: ". . . a series of reeds and reed chambers, a raceway for a perforated music sheet, air passages leading from the raceway to the reeds, and mechanism for holding the perforated music sheet in close contact with and feeding it along the raceway." A month after Webber obtained his U.S. patent, John Leslie Given secured a U.S. patent for a similar doll with a perforated cylindrical drum in place of the perforated music sheet, and other improvements such as making the back of the doll rigid and activating the mechanism by pressing in the front. The doll was distributed by the Massachusetts Organ Co., Boston, Mass.

1882: Advertised that although thousands of these dolls were ready for the holiday trade, the supply was exhausted early in December. The doll was described as "Of the finest French make, with wax head, real hair, and finest eyes, and is no different in appearance from the best of imported dolls; but within its body is a most ingenious machine which when it is lightly pressed, causes the doll to sing one of the following airs: 'Home, Sweet Home,' 'Greenville,' 'I Want to be an Angel,' 'There is a Happy Land,' 'Bonnie Doon,' 'How Can I Leave Thee,' 'A B C Song,' 'America,' 'Thou, thou reign'st' (German), 'Frohe Botschaft' (German), 'Tell Aunt Rhoda,' 'Buy a Broom,' 'Yankee Doodle.' . . . We have two sizes. No. 1—22 inches high, wax head, real hair, fine eyes, and a very beautiful face—a strictly first-class French Doll. Price complete $2.75. No. 1½—same as No. 1, but eyes close when laid down. 50¢ extra. No. 2—30 inches high, extra fine wax head, real hair, and finest eyes. Price $5.00. No. 2½—same as No. 2, but with closing eyes. 75¢ extra. . . . An embroidered chemise . . . goes with each doll."

1883/4: Advertisement claimed: "The Doll has been improved in every way since last year. Instead of the stiff German body, as in all imported Dolls, our Doll has an AMERICAN MADE BODY with limber joints, so that it will sit easily and gracefully in any position. The arm is of Finest Kid with separate fingers. . . . The

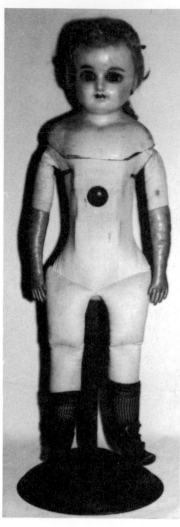

**1676.** Webber singing doll has wax-over-composition head. The cloth body is stamped vertically on the front: "I sing I want to be an Angel." Webber mark is stamped on the lower back (see Ill. **1677**), as well as "Patented in U. S. // Aug. 9, 1881 // Oct. 4, 1881 // April 25, 1882 // May 20, 1880." and "Belgium April 1, 1881 // France April 8, 1881 // Canada April 4, 1881 // Germany." Note the button on stomach, to make the doll sing. H. 22 inches. *Courtesy of Lester & Alice Grinnings.*

**1677.** Mark on the bodies of William Webber's Singing Dolls.

**1678.** Mark used for dolls by Weidemann Co.

Waxen Heads with long hair are of the best French and German make, made especially for this Doll, and they are as beautiful as life, long hair, beautiful eyes, and delicately tinted cheeks. . . .

"We can furnish 3 sizes: No 1, 22 inches high, price $2.75; No. 2, 24 inches high, larger head, price $3.25; No. 3, 26 inches high, our best Doll, price $4.00. . . . Fine Embroidered Chemise 25¢ extra. . . . Fine costumes for these dolls with under clothing lace trimmed, finely made $3.00 to $5.00 extra."

The following songs were offered in addition to those offered the preceding year: "Sweet Bye and Bye," "Coming Thro' the Rye," God Bless the Prince of Wales," "Grandfather's Clock," "Child's Song," "Last Rose of Summer," "Joyful Message" (German), "Old Folks at Home," "Pop Goes the Weasel," "So Many Stars" (German), "Sleep my Child" (German), "When I a Little Bird," "'Cradle's Empty," "God Save the Queen."

**Weber, Ernst.** 1918. Steinbach near Sonneberg, Thür. Made dolls' heads and dolls' bodies.

**Weber, Franz Carl.** 1881–1925+, Zurich; 1917+, also Geneva. Distributed dolls. The 1893 catalog advertised dressed and undressed dolls, *Täuflinge,* "little dolls for doll rooms," dolls' heads, and doll's bodies.

**Weber, Gebrüder.** 1893–94. Berlin. B. Weber, Willy Weber (sculptor), and Hans Weber (mechanician) obtained German and British patents for dolls that turned their heads from side to side and had movable eyes. These may have been display dolls.

**Webster, Stella N.** 1923–24. Los Angeles, Calif. Registered in U.S. *Birthday* as a trademark for dolls.

**Weckles & Co.** 1892. Hamburg, Germany. Registered in Germany a figure of an insect as a trademark for dolls.

**Wedel, M.** 1920. Coburg, Thür. Manufactured dolls.

**Wee Wee.** 1920–21. Trademark registered in U.S. by May B. Moran for the *Moran Doll Manufacturing Co.* Used for cherub-type composition dolls that came dressed and undressed.

**Weeping Doll.** 1911–12. Doll with a *Minerva* metal head that wept real tears when pressed and stopped when released. It had a cloth body, and in the back was a small sack that, when squeezed, caused a drop of water to fall from each eye. Size 12 inches, price $1.00. This doll was also available as a premium doll for YOUTH'S COMPANION. *Soozie Smiles* in 1924 wept real tears.

**Wegner, Hermann.** 1909–25+. Sonneberg, Thür. Made dolls.

**Wehncke, Ernst.** 1857–1925+. Hamburg, Germany. Made dolls; used a "W" in a circle as a trademark.

**Wehner, Wilhelm.** 1908–25+. Sonneberg, Thür. Made and exported dressed dolls.

**Weidemann Co.** 1922–23. New York City. Importers' and manufacturers' agent for European and American dolls.

**Weidmann, Carl.** 1900. Leipzig, Saxony. Was issued a German patent for dolls' bodies with metal parts.

**Weiersmuller, Willy.** 1925. Nürnberg, Bavaria. Manufactured cloth dolls.

**Weil, S., Jr.** 1923–24. Mannheim, Germany. Registered in Germany *Poli-Moli* as a trademark for rubber dolls.

**Weiller Manufacturing Co.** 1917. Dunkirk, N.Y. Made a line of muslin dolls lithographed in five colors; came in three styles with cork or sawdust stuffing; size 10 inches.

**Weimarpuppen // Weimarpuppchen.** 1923. Trademark registered in Germany by *Thüringer Stoffpuppen-Fabrik* for stuffed dolls.

**Weiner, Bessie.** 1899–1917. Philadelphia, Pa. Made dolls.

**Weiner, David.** See **Wiener, David.**

**Weinkammer, Gebrüder.** 1897–1902. Salzburg, Austria. Made wax dolls.

**Weinland, L.** 1909–18. Sonneberg, Thür. Made dolls.

**Weinshenker, J., & Co.** 1923–24. New York City. Made *Mama Dolls.*

**Weir, Robert H.** 1866–80. Cohoes, N.Y. and Philadelphia, Pa. In 1866, he obtained a U.S. patent for a walking doll.

1880: Was issued a U.S. patent for a method of working leather over a cast or relief to form a figure. Weir assigned this patent to *Samuel Goodman & Daniel Meyers,* both of Philadelphia, Pa.

**Weiss, Heinrich.** 1894–98. Sonneberg, Thür. Manufactured and exported dressed and undressed dolls.

1895: Registered in Germany as a trademark a drawing of a rearing horse held by a man.

**Weiss, J.** 1923–25. Vienna. Made dolls.

**Weiss, Jean.** Before 1911, Nürnberg, Bavaria; 1911, successors. Made rag dolls and dressed celluloid dolls.

**Weissbeck, Henry.** 1893. Llandudno, Wales. Obtained a British patent for dolls' eyes that rotated vertically; these eyes were used in wax or china heads.

**Well Made Doll Co.** 1919–25+. New York City. Handled "Well Made Dolls."

1919: Advertised dolls for 25¢ and up; a 14½-inch doll cost 50¢.

1924: Advertised *Mama Dolls* with composition legs; sizes 19, 21, and 24 inches.

**Wellington, Martha L.** 1883. Brookline, Mass. Obtained a U.S. patent for a rag or leather doll made with a wire frame for eyes, eyebrows, nose, mouth, and chin, to be covered with tubular stockinet and stuffed with cotton batting; oil colors were preferred for painting the doll.

**Wellmann, Gustav, Inc.** 1925+. Hannover, Hannover. Produced rubber dolls and registered in Germany *Fax* as a trademark for rubber dolls.

**Wellponer, Peter.** Late 18th century. Brought wooden dolls from the Grödner Tal to Mexico.

**Welsch, F.** 1925. Breslau, Silesia. Made dolls.

**Welsch & Co.** 1915–25+. Sonneberg, Thür. Manufactured dolls; used bisque heads produced by *Max Oscar Arnold.* The dolls were distributed by *John Bing Co.* in New York. The Welsch name often appears with "MOA" on dolls' heads.

1923: Made jointed and dressed dolls, which they carried in open sizes.

1925: Made dolls with socket heads on jointed composition bodies and dolls with shoulder heads on kid bodies. Advertised all-cloth dolls and dolls for dolls' houses. Sizes 2¼ to 7 inches.

**Welst, Agn. Grimmaisch.** 1909–18. Leipzig, Saxony. Manufactured dolls.

**Welta.** 1920. Trademark to be used for dolls; registered in Germany by *Pfautz & Co.;* also known at the Weltall (Worldwide)-Distributing Co.

**Welzel, Heinrich.** 1909. Friedenau, Prussia. Made dolls.

**Wendt, Theodor.** 1924. Hamburg, Germany. Exporter; registered in Germany the initials "T W" superimposed, as a trademark for dolls.

**Wendy.** 1925. Made by *Goodyear Toy Co.* Came with composition head and arms, soft body of Duveteen with stuffed legs; mate to *Peter Pan.* Price $12.00 doz. wholesale.

**Wenzel, A.** 1918–25+. Sonneberg, Thür. Made *Täuflinge.*

**Wenzel, Robert.** 1925+. Sonneberg, Thür. Made stiff-jointed dolls and dressed dolls.

**Werner, Bernh.** 1895. Neustadt near Coburg, Thür. Manufactured little or baby dolls.

**Wernicke, Paul.** 1924–25. Waltershausen, Thür. Doll maker; registered in Germany "Wernicke" as a trademark.

**Wertheimer.** 1898. Paris. Made dressed dolls including one called Bébé *Le Baby.*

**1679.** Welsch & Co.'s mark found on dolls.

**Western Art Leather Co.** 1917. Denver, Colo. Made stuffed dolls of leather; price $3.00 doz. wholesale.

**Western Doll & Toy Manufacturing Co.** 1918–19. Los Angeles, Calif. Assignee of a U.S. patent of *Romeo Caccialanza.*

**Western Doll Co.** See **Moran Doll Manufacturing Co.**

**Western Doll Manufacturing Co.** 1921. Chicago, Ill. Distributed dolls.

**Western Grocer Co.** 1923–24. Marshalltown, Iowa. Registered in U.S. *Jack Sprat* as a trademark to be affixed with a printed tag to a doll or the package containing doll.

**Weston, Samuel, & Weston, William James.** 1922. London. Were issued a German patent for dolls' eyeballs.

**Westwood, Ethel P.** 1923–25. New York City. Registered in U.S. *Dolly Jingles* as a trademark for dolls. She obtained two design patents, probably for rag dolls that had painted faces and were dressed as a boy or as a girl in sailor-type costumes.

**Weyh, Aug.** 1915–25+. Wildenheid near Sonneberg, Thür. Manufactured dolls.

**Weyh, M.** 1918. Wildenheid near Sonneberg, Thür. Made dolls.

**Weyh, Willy.** 1925. Sonneberg, Thür. Made dolls.

**Whatsamatter.** 1924. Trademark registered in U.S. by *Borgfeldt.*

**Wheeldon, Arthur Leonard.** 1913–18. London. Obtained two U.S. patents for stuffed rag dolls, which he assigned to *Dean's Rag Book Co.*

1915: Patent pertained to a sheet of fabric containing a printed doll to be cut out, together with a buckram backing to be pressed with hot or cold dies in order to form a molded face.

1918: Patent stated that whereas rag dolls were usually made with the front of the body, leg, and foot in one piece, the back of the body, leg, and foot in a second piece, and the soles of the feet each in other pieces, all to be sewed with the printing inside and then turned inside out, Wheeldon's new invention would eliminate the separate sole pieces and result in a foot easier to make and better shaped.

**Wheelhouse, James.** 1911–20. London. From 1919–20, William Wheelhouse was successor. Made dolls, including wax dolls.

**Wheelhouse, M. V., & Jacobs, Louise.** 1918–25. London. Registered *Pomona* in Britain as a trademark for toys.

1925: Miss M. Wheelhouse was listed as a doll maker.

**Wheelhouse, William, & Wheelhouse, Charles.** 1857–65. London. Made dolls.

**Whistling Jim.** 1913–14. Advertised by *Samstag & Hilder.* The picture in the advertisement resembled the whistling boy with a bisque head made by *Gebrüder Heubach.* This imported doll whistled when squeezed; came in three sizes; price 25¢, 50¢, and $1.00.

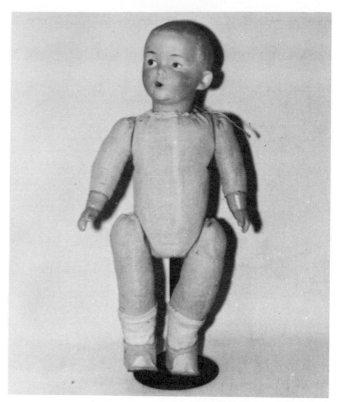

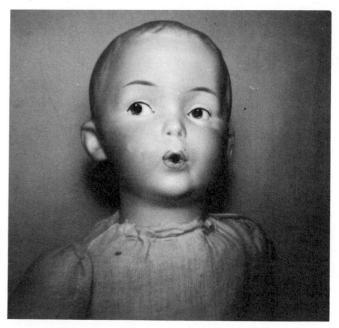

1680A & B. "Whistling Jim" has character bisque head with painted features, including intaglio eyes; pink cloth body with composition hands. Ca. 1913. Mark: "3, Germany," over Ill. **823,** over "3774." H. 12 inches. *Coleman Collection.*

**Whistling Joe.** 1913. Bisque-head doll with mouth puckered for whistling; when squeezed, the doll sounded two distinct notes.

**Whistling Willie.** 1914. A doll that whistled when squeezed; made by *Louis Amberg & Son.*

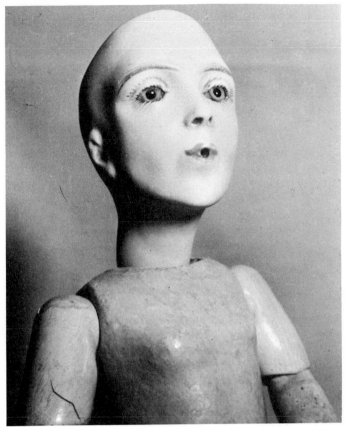

1681. "Whistling" bisque head closely resembles one made by the Société Française de Fabrication de Bébés et Jouets. *Courtesy of Margaret Whitton; photograph by Winnie Langley.*

**Whitehouse, John N.** 1913–25. New York City. Obtained two U.S. patents.

1913: Patent pertained to the movement of eyes, which were wall-eyed and became cross-eyed when the body was pressed.

1925: Patent for a head of molded material with concave eye openings reinforced with sheet metal.

**Whitely, Rena.** 1916. Designed Indian doll copyrighted by *Gordon F. Gillespie.*

**Whitlock, Edwin L., & Madison, James.** 1923–25. New York City. Were issued two U.S. design patents for dolls dressed in Chinese clothes; one doll was a man with drooping mustache and the other was a woman with her hair on top of her head.

**Whitteker, Lilian E.** 1914. Cincinnati, Ohio. Created and manufactured the *Little Suffragist,* an American Peace doll; price 25¢.

**Wichmann, Bärbel (née Emisch.)** 1922. Berlin. Doll manufacturer; registered in Germany *Bärbel-Puppe* as a trademark.

**Wickelpuppen.** 1840. German name for *poupards;* made partly of leather, faces have various expressions.

**Wicklein, Martin.** 1909. Köppelsdorf, Thür. Manufactured dolls.

**Wicks, Catherine (Kate) C.** 1893–1904. Philadelphia, Pa. In 1902, called Wicks Doll Bazaar Co. Made dolls' heads and bodies.

**Wicks, Henry (Harry).** 1853–65. London. Made composition dolls.

**Wicks, James.** 1853–54. London. Made composition dolls but not at the same address as *Henry Wicks.*

**Wide-Awake Doll.** 1913–14. Trademark registered in Germany by *Butler Bros.* for an all-bisque doll that was probably made in competition with *Kewpies.* The name is usually incised on the back of the doll, which had an open-closed mouth with two upper teeth, painted eyes glancing to the side, painted slippers, and socks. Doll was jointed at the shoulders. Sizes 4³/₄, 6¹/₄, and 8 inches; price 89¢ to $4.00 doz. wholesale.

**Wide-Awake Rag Doll.** 1908. One of the *Vivian* line of dolls made by *Bruin Manufacturing Co.* It was based on a U.S. patent by *Lillian Sackman,* and was made so that by turning the head and adjusting the cap an entirely new face appeared. Doll had jointed neck, shoulders, and hips; was stuffed with antiseptic cotton; various dresses. Clothes could be removed. Sizes 13, 15, and 17 inches.

1682. "Wide-Awake" all-bisque doll handled by Butler Bros., ca. 1914; has open-closed mouth with two upper teeth. Mark on back: Ill. **1683.** H. 5 inches. *Coleman Collection.*

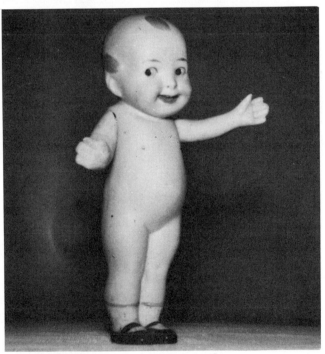

1683. "Wide-Awake" mark used on all-bisque dolls of Butler Bros.

THE
"WIDE-AWAKE"
DOLL
REGISTERED
GERMANY

**Widmer, Mme. Adèle.** 1861–70. Paris. Made and dressed dolls.

**Wiederseim, Grace (née Gebbie).** See **Drayton, Grace.**

**Wiegand, Carl.** 1876–83. New York City. Obtained a U.S. patent for a doll's head molded of two or more layers of fabric with an intermediate layer of paper. In 1881, was listed as a toymaker.

1882–83: Joined *Martin & Rippel,* manufacturers of wax dolls' heads, to form the *National Doll & Novelty Co.,* also known as Wiegand, Martin & Rippel.

**Wiegand, Hugo.** 1911–25+. Waltershausen, Thür. Manufactured dolls and dolls' bodies, especially character babies and ball-jointed dolls.

1919: Registered in Germany *Edelkind* as a trademark for dolls and dolls' bodies.

1925: Advertised *Sweet Nell* as a trademark.

**Wieland, C.** Before 1909–18, Berlin; 1909–18, successors. Made dolls.

**Wiener, August.** 1908–9. Köppelsdorf, Thür. Made porcelain dolls' heads.

**Wiener (Weiner), David.** 1918–25. New York City. Obtained U.S. patent in 1921, which stated that "unbreakable" heads were liable to breakage, and when a head broke the whole doll was thrown away, although new heads were not unavailable, because it was inconvenient to change heads. With his new patented head that screwed into the shoulders on a stuffed doll, a replacement was readily available in case of damage and it was also possible to have multiple heads for a doll. This patent was used for multiple heads made by *Chang-O-Doll Co.* and by *Berwick Co.* for *Famlee Dolls.*

1924–25: Was granted a U.S. patent for a stuffed doll with a detachable connection in the shoulder portion.

**Wiener, Ed.** 1918. Rauenstein, Thür. Made dolls.

**Wiener, Ferd.** 1915–20. Köppelsdorf, Thür. Manufactured dolls.

**Wiesenthal, Schindel & Kallenberg.** 1858–1925+. Waltershausen, Thür. Made wax dolls and baby dolls in bisque, china, papier-mâché, and other materials. The relationship to *Schindel & Co.* is not known.

1891: Advertised ball-jointed dolls.

1893: Displayed dolls at the Chicago Exhibition.

1918: Exported and made dolls.

**Wigs.** Wigs for dolls have been made for many years and in many countries. Human hair and mohair were the principal materials, but many other fibers have been used also. The British are especially famous for their mohair. Among the British wig manufacturers were Julius Ephraimson (1884+), Oreste-Martin (1892+), and A. Scoles (1917+). Some of the French wig makers were E. Auteroche (1873+), Pecclet (1890+), Richert & Peltier (1891+), Mme. Salmon (1895+), J. Villain (1898+), Richert (1900+), Maynard (1904+), E. Bossaut (1912+), and J. Caraël (1919+). Gustav Thiele (1885+), Max Ru-

**1684.** Original 1876 patent application model submitted by Carl Wiegand. H. of shoulder heads, 4 inches. *Courtesy of Ruth E. & R. C. Mathes.*

dolph (1908+), Martha Köllner (1911+), Gustav Schuchardt (1918+), Edwin Beck (1922+), and W. Zaake & Co. (1924+) made wigs in Germany. Masferrer F. Scr. Xifrè made wigs in Spain. Before World War I, *Charles Braitling* (1909+), David Dreher (1915+), *Sophia E. Delavan* (1916+), and S. Yagoda (1920+) made wigs in America. When World War I broke out and it was impossible to obtain wigs from abroad, scores of American firms began to manufacture them. Some of the more important companies were J. Follender (1917+), who supplied wigs for *Century Doll Co., Louis Wolf & Co.,* and *A. S. Ferguson;* Joseph Ruf (1921+) supplied "My Deary" mohair wigs for *Borgfeldt, Strobel & Wilken,* and Louis Wolf & Co. There were at least seven other manufacturers who started to make wigs around 1921: U.S. Doll Wig Co., E. Mittlestaedt, Unique Wig Manufacturers, Royal Wig Manufacturing Co., A. M. Masson, Rose Hieman Hair Co., and Guarantee Hair & Novelty Works.

The Delavan trademark on paper stickers has been found inside wigs. This trademark is a picture of a doll's head with long curls; around the picture in a circle is "American Wig" and under the circle "Made in Germany." (For further information on wigs, see **Hair, Materials for; Hair, Method of Affixing; Hair Style, Wigs.**)

**Wigs, Interchangeable.** Some of the 19th century doll heads have several small holes in the crown so that the wigs could be tied on and readily changed if desired. The all-metal *Steel Doll* made in Pleasantville, N.J., about 1903 had three holes below the rim of the crown, which matched three snaps in the several wigs with which the doll was supplied. The wigs simply snapped on and could easily be changed. *Carl Bergner* of Sonneberg in 1905 obtained a German patent for a doll head with interchangeable wigs. *Ernst Reinhardt* of Philadelphia, Pennsylvania, applied for a U.S. patent in 1913 whereby numerous small holes, just below the crown rim, would make it possible for a wig to be detached easily and replaced by another one when it was desired to change the color or style of the hair. (See also **Dallwig Distributing Co.**)

**Wigwam Co.** 1917–18. Doll factory at Syracuse, N.Y. Sole New York agent, *Baker & Bennett.* Made dolls with composition heads, which they advertised were guaranteed not to peel; cloth bodies.

1918: Advertised that their dolls had "bisque-like" finish. The head was rigidly nailed to the skeleton body, which had curved back and rounded tummy; arms and legs were firmly secured with spring tension joints. The body was stuffed around the wooden skeleton with ground cork, and the composition hands fastened so that the cork could not spill out; button-on clothes. A Boy Scout doll with painted hair and eyes, size 16 inches, was priced at $12.00 doz. wholesale. Dolls with wigs and sleeping eyes, size 18 inches, were priced $18.00 doz. wholesale.

**Wilckens, Witwe (Widow).** 1909. Hamburg, Germany. Made dolls.

**Wild, Lewis.** 1884–25+. London. Importer and agent for foreign manufacturers of dolls.

1884–91: Imported wax, composition, and china dolls. ("China" probably included bisque dolls, as was often the case in England.)

1921–25: Agent for dolls made in Canada and Germany.

**Wilhelm, Grete (née Hujber [Huiber]).** 1920. Vienna. Producer of dolls' heads; obtained a German patent for improving the method of making dolls' heads.

**Wilhewin.** 1911. Trade name for a character doll representing a baseball player; doll was made by *A. Steinhardt & Bro.*

**Wilken, Grace A.** 1920. San Francisco, Calif. Secured a copyright for a model of a doll with a dimple in its chin and heavy upper eyelashes, short lower eyelashes.

**Wilkins, F.** 1915. Obtained a British patent for improving the stringing of dolls.

**Williams, J. A., & Co.** 1923. Pittsburgh, Pa., and New York City. Importers and distributors of *Mama Dolls* and American-made dolls.

**Williams, Jennie.** 1923–25. Denver, Colo. Was granted a U.S. patent for a rag baby doll with a circular-shaped piece of silk for the face; painted hair and features. Doll had a seam down the center back of the body and from the small of the back on either side down the center of each leg.

**Willie Walker.** 1920. Walking doll made by *Seamless Toy Corp.* It had an all-composition body with a very long torso. Height of the doll was 21 inches.

**Willig, Albert.** 1895–1918. Giessübel, Thür. Manufactured dolls.

**Willow Pottery.** See **Hewitt Bros.**

**Willshur, Charles.** 1891–99. London. In 1899, the successor was Mrs. Henrietta Willshur. Made dolls' bodies.

**Willy.** 1913. Trade name of doll handled by *Borgfeldt;* mate to *Lilly.*

**Wilmsen, Bernhard.** 1895–1913. Philadelphia, Pa. Handled dolls and toys, especially Christmas decorations.

1901: Assignee of sheet metal doll patented by *Robert Purvis.* This doll resembled the *All Steel Doll.*

**Wilson, Margaret,** 1900–1901. Philadelphia, Pa. Made dolls.

**Wilson, Mrs. Rose O'Neill.** See **Rose O'Neill.**

**Wilson, Thomas Francis.** 1854–91. London. Made wax dolls. At the same address, 1856–65, George Isaac Wilson also made wax dolls.

**Wilson Bros. Ltd.** 1923–25. London. Made dolls.

**Wimmer, Carl.** 1923. Babenhausen, Hesse. Secured a German patent for improvements in stringing the joints on hollow-bodied dolls with elastic.

**Wimpern.** German word for "eyelashes." This word has been found on dolls with *Simon & Halbig* bisque heads, molds #1039 and #1079. It has also been found on dolls with *Au Nain Bleu* marks, *E. Chauvière* marks, and *Nadaud* marks, all three of which are French marks.

**1685.** "Wimpern" (eyelashes) mark found on dolls, especially those of Simon & Halbig.

**Wingert, Martha St. Clair.** 1918–23. Whittier, Calif. Registered two trademarks in U.S. for dolls; one was *Paxie* and the other for *Paxie Ann.*

1918: Was issued a U.S. design patent for a doll with eyes glancing to the side; doll wore a snowsuit.

1923: Obtained a U.S. design patent for a rag doll with hair braided in back; doll wore an apron over a print dress.

**Winkelmann, Helene.** 1909. Dresden, Saxony. Made dolls.

**Winkie.** 1919–20. Designed by *Jeno Juszko* for *Borgfeldt;* the name was registered in Britain and France as a trademark by Borgfeldt.

**Winking Dolls.** These were largely a product of the years between 1910 and the 1920's.

1914: Winking dolls were imported into U.S.; they came with one eye completely closed, the mouth turned up in a smile. Dolls were of two sizes, and dressed either as a boy or as a girl in red, white, and blue bathing suits.

1918: *Ideal Novelty & Toy Co.* made the eyes of their dolls so that they shut independently and thus could wink.

1919: *Benvenuti* designed *Blynke,* a winking doll.

1924: A Paris baby doll was advertised as having bonnet strings tied demurely under its rosy chin, but when the doll was picked up, it slowly winked.

**Winkler, Edmund.** 1915. Sonneberg, Thür. Manufactured dolls.

**Winkler, Ernst, Firm.** 1908–25+. Sonneberg, Thür. Made and exported dolls and doll parts; specialized in dressed dolls and miniature dolls.

1911: Registered in Germany a "W" in a circle within a seven-pointed star and the words *Gekleidete Puppe,* as a trademark.

1925: Registered in Germany "E W" in a circle within a seven-pointed star and the words "Winkler Puppe," as a trademark.

**Winkler, Friedrich Edmund.** 1895–1911. Sonneberg, Thür. Made and exported jointed dolls.

1899: Registered in Germany *Bébé Articulé* as a trademark for dolls.

1900: One of the group of Grand Prize winners at the Paris Exposition.

**Winnie Winters (Winter).** 1912. Imported doll with bisque head, sleeping eyes, wavy hair wig, body jointed at shoulders and hips; dressed in winter coat, hat, and muff; size 15 inches.

**Winter, Mrs. E. P.** 1922. St. Paul, Minn. Created dolls of wire and worsted, which were dressed as Colonial Dames, Golf Flappers, Hawaiians, and a Wedding Party. The dolls were not known to have been made for commercial use, since Mrs. Winter was a "Leader of Society."

**Winter Girl.** 1918. Made by *Jessie M. Raleigh,* distributed by *Butler Bros.* Wore a white flannel jacket and sports cap. Size 13½ inches, price $2.85.

**Winters & Reineke.** 1907. Philadelphia, Pa. Imported and distributed dolls. Louis L. Reineke, proprietor, had been in this business since 1880. They advertised *Steiff* dolls. Indian dolls, Eskimo dolls, and others.

**Wishard, Lucinda B. J.** 1883–84. Indianapolis, Ind. Obtained a U.S. patent for making a wire skeleton for dolls. Wire had been used previously to stiffen stuffed bodies, but her patent provided loops at the extremities for attaching outer portions and knots at joints for reinforcement and to permit greater ease in bending. The patent was assigned to *Harry E. Drew* and *Robert Springsteen.*

1884: Lucinda Wishard showed her dolls at the New Orleans Exposition.

**Wislizenus, Adolf.** 1851–1925+. Waltershausen, Thür. Made and exported dolls. Factory was founded in 1851 to make papier-mâché dolls. In 1873 the firm was represented by *Le Montréer* in Paris, and shortly thereafter they took over the *G. Schafft* doll-making firm.

1891: Advertised *Gobelin Dolls.*

1900: Started to use *Old Glory,* which they registered in Germany as a trademark for jointed dolls in 1902.

WISLIZENUS DOLLS

**1686.** Molded composition head made by Adolf Wislizenus. Mouth and eyebrows have striated painting; lower eyelashes only are painted. Mark, paper sticker on back: Ill. **1690.** H. of shoulder head, 6 inches. *Courtesy of Eunice Althouse.*

**1687.** Wislizenus composition head with painted gray-blue eyes, pierced ears, blonde wig; marked "A W // SaA 8." H. of shoulder head, 7 inches. *Collection of the late Sarge Kitterman; photograph by Winnie Langley.*

 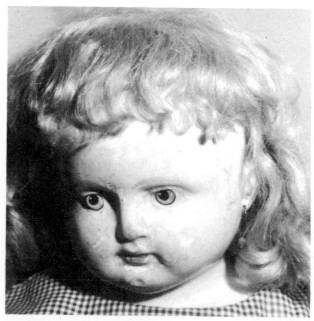

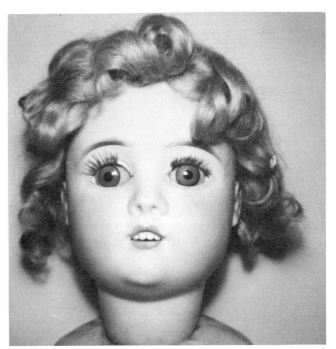

**1688.** Bisque-headed doll made by Wislizenus has glass sleeping eyes, painted eyelashes and hair eyelashes, open mouth with teeth; ball-jointed body is composition. Mark: Ill. **1691.** H. 24 inches. *Courtesy of Jessica Norman.*

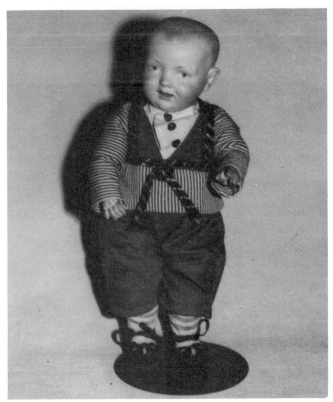

**1689A & B.** Character boy with bisque head; painted features, including molded teeth in open-closed mouth; jointed toddler-type composition body. Mark on head: Ill. **1694.** Mark stamped on body in purple: Ill. **1692.** H. 12 inches. *Courtesy of Alberta Darby.*

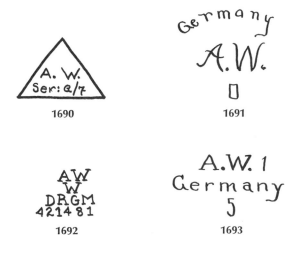

1690

1691

1692

1693

1694

**1690–1694.** Marks found on dolls made by Adolf Wislizenus. Note the double digits, "5" and "0," superimposed in Mark **1694.**

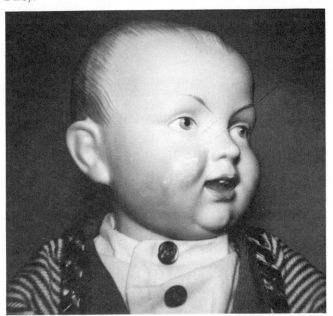

1901: Obtained two German patents for improvements in ball-jointed dolls.

1902: *Hamburger & Co.* registered in U.S. "Old Glory" as a trademark.

1925: Advertised jointed bisque dolls and character babies.

**Witch or Wizard.** 1881+ Patented in U.S. by *Mason & Taylor*. Doll, also known as Wizard, was made so that it could give the illusion of having its head severed. A character doll representing a witch has *Hexe* incised on the bisque head. This was a 20th-century doll.

**Witt, D.** 1885. Hamburg, Germany. Manufactured dolls.

**Witthauer, Carl Otto.** 1909–25+. Neustadt near Coburg, Thür. Manufactured dolls, especially dressed dolls; factory was called Deutsches Puppenheim.

**Witthauer, Christopher.** 1862–1909. Neustadt near Coburg, Thür. Manufactured and exported dolls.

1862: Displayed papier-mâché dolls at the London Exhibition.

**Witton, T. F.** 1855. London. Made dolls.

**Wittzack, Emil.** 1891–1914. Leipzig or Gotha, Germany. Made wool dolls.

1893: Displayed dolls at the Chicago Exposition.

**Wizard.** See **Witch.**

**Wob-Li-Gob.** Trademark registered in Britain by *Maurice Steinman-Beyencenet* for dolls.

**Wohlegemuth & Lissner.** 1916. Berlin. Registered in Germany *Tante Lore* (Aunt Lore) as a trademark for dolls which they distributed.

**Wohlleben, A. H.** 1921–25+. Baltimore, Md. Made dolls and advertised glass eyes for dolls.

**Wohlleben, H.** 1909–25+. Sonneberg, Thür.; 1923–25+ Wohlleben & Weyh, successors. Manufactured dolls.

**Wolbold, H.** 1881–83. Philadelphia, Pa. Handled doll articles, including dolls' shoes.

**Wölckner, Adolf.** 1909–18. Magdeburg, Saxony. Manufactured dolls.

**Wolcott, Henry Goodrich.** 1895–96. Fishkill, N.Y. Was granted a British patent for molding soft India rubber dolls.

**Wolf, David.** 1914. Registered in U.S. *Moppie Topp* as a trademark for dolls.

**Wolf, Hermann.** 1923. Nordhausen, Germany. Doll factory named Erste Nordhauser Spielwaren-Fabrik. He registered in Germany the picture of a wolf over the initials "H//W. E. N. Sp. F." as a trademark for dolls.

**Wolf, Julius J.** 1888–90. Cincinnati, Ohio. Obtained a U.S. patent for wax dolls' heads with imitation hair and glass eyes. He assigned half his rights to *Philip Goldsmith*.

**Wolf, Julius Hermann.** 1910. Leutmitz near Dresden, Saxony. Secured a German patent for improving ball joints for dolls.

**Wolf, Louis & Co.** 1870–1925+. Sonneberg, Thür., Boston, Mass., and New York City. Handled German and American dolls. In 1918 they claimed to have been established in 1860, but earlier records show them as having been established in 1870. They appeared in New York Directories as early as 1889. Many of the bisque dolls' heads that they used were made by *Armand Marseille*. They probably designed and assembled dolls as well as importing and distributing them.

1892: Began to use *Cinderella* as a trademark, but did not register it in U.S. until 1897.

1904: Displayed dolls at the St. Louis Exposition. They advertised *Bergmann* celebrated jointed dolls; *Superba* and *Columbia* kid-body dolls; *Young America* dressed dolls.

1905: Advertised dolls with celluloid and metal heads as well as bisque.

1906: New dolls advertised were *Featherweight* with kid bodies, celluloid heads, arms, and legs; "Cinderella" American rag dolls; *Minerva* metal-head Knockabout dolls, and *Playtime* dolls with photographic faces.

1907: Mentioned a factory in Sonneberg; advertised Bergmann, Columbia, Young America, Superba, Featherweight, and Minerva dolls as well as *Mangolin* "unbreakable" (composition) dolls.

1908: Advertised Bergmann jointed dolls in all sizes and Featherweight celluloid and kid dolls in all sizes; a new doll represented a high school girl with the latest coiffure.

1910: Registered in U.S. *Queen Louise* as a trademark. New dolls advertised were *Schilling* dolls; Knockabout dolls with celluloid heads; *E. U. Steiner's* patented walking and sitting doll; and *My Companion* dressed dolls.

1911: Registered in U.S. "My Companion" as a trademark for dolls; advertised *Excelsior* dolls.

1913: Advertised *Baby Irene* and *Little Jimmy*, character dolls modeled from life. (See **Knock About,** 1913.)

1914: Advertised *Our Fairy; Majestic; 975 line;* and *Baby Belle* made by Bergmann. Started to use *Chubby* as a trademark for the boy doll with a rotund tummy, eyes to the side, dressed in a union suit, for which a design patent was secured by Thomas E. Stutson, a member of the Louis Wolf firm.

1915: Registered in U.S. "Chubby" as a trademark; they used it for an all-bisque doll with movable arms. At the Chicago Toy Exhibit, they showed over seven hundred styles of foreign-made character dolls. Work, apparently stopped at the outbreak of the War, had resumed in the four toy factories they maintained in Sonneberg. They still advertised Excelsior, Superba, Columbia, Young America, Baby Belle, and the 975 line. They had a new Japanese department with bisque babies made in Japan.

1916: Advertised "L. W. & Co." dolls (character baby with bisque head mold "152" is marked "L. W. & Co."); *Perfection* dolls; Japanese dolls, and the new *Rollinson* dolls made by *Utley Co.*

1917: Sole agents for *Emkay Doll Manufacturing Co.*

1919: Advertised Japanese bisque dolls modeled after old German designs; jointed dolls; imitation kid dolls;

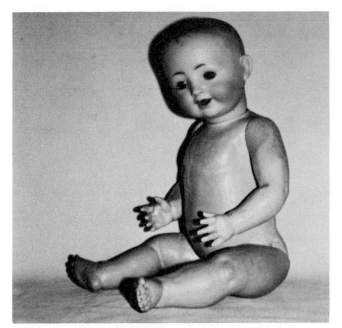

**1695A & B.** Bisque-headed baby doll made for Louis Wolf & Co. has painted hair, glass eyes, bisque tongue, bent-limb composition baby body. Note the two dot-dimples on the cheeks. Mark: Ill. **1697,** except for "48" instead of "18." H. 21 inches. *Courtesy of Jessica Norman.*

**1696.** Bisque-headed doll probably handled by Louis Wolf & Co.; glass eyes, open mouth and teeth, jointed composition body; dressed in original peasant costume. Mark: Ill. **1700.** H. 15½ inches. *Courtesy of May Maurer.*

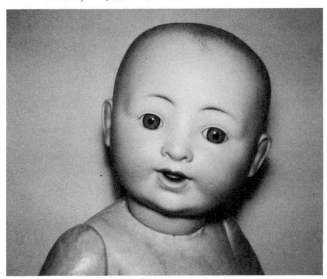

**1697–1700.** Marks on dolls handled by Louis Wolf & Co., except for No. **1700,** which may or may not belong to Louis Wolf.

composition dolls with celluloid enamel; *Mama Dolls* and *Kutie Kid;* dolls priced 50¢ to $5.00.

1920: Advertised *Mickey* dolls made by the *Bandeau Sales Co.*

1921: Advertised *Grunty Grunts and Smiley Smiles,* which was two dolls in one.

1923: Still advertising Perfection dolls and "L. W. & Co." dolls, as well as one hundred styles of Mama Dolls in twelve sizes, price $1.00 to $5.00.

1925: Imported dolls from England, France, Germany, Austria, and Czechoslovakia; agent for *Schreyer & Co.* (Shuco), *W. G. Müller, Seyfarth & Reinhardt, Strasser Dolls,* and *American Stuffed Novelty Co.* They also advertised *Pretty Peggy* and the *Happiness Doll* line, which included *Baby Sunshine,* and Lindstrom mechanical dolls.

**Wolf Doll Co.** 1905–25+. New York City. Made composition-headed character dolls.

1922: Registered in U.S. as a trademark *Hans Brinker// with the//Silver Skates,* to be affixed as a printed label on doll or package. Hans Brinker had composition head and hands. Size 15 inches, price $1.00. Wolf Doll Co.

also advertised the *Two-in-One Doll,* a topsy-turvy doll with reversible skirt that covered one of the two heads; price $1.00.

1925: Advertised *Mama Dolls* with Ronson voices.

**Wolff, Gebrüder.** 1912. Nürnberg, Bavaria. Nürnberger Celluloid Fabric; made celluloid dolls.

**Wolkoff, V.** 1920. Was issued a British patent for cloth dolls with flexible wire skeletons; the wires were not rigidly connected. Wires were inserted in each finger and thumb.

**Wollheim, Heinrich.** 1899. Dresden, Saxony. Obtained a British patent for dolls' heads stamped and embossed out of cardboard.

**Wolson Novelty Co.** 1925. New York City. Manufactured dolls.

**Wonder.** 1920–23. Trademark registered in U.S. by *Madame Georgene, Inc.,* for a line of *Mama Dolls* designed and created by *Mme. Georgene Averill.* It was advertised that they could walk, talk, and dance.

1921: Came in four sizes.

1922: Paul Averill was the sole manufacturer and distributor. The line included *Mistress Bubbles, Master Bubbles, Billy Boy,* and *Betty.* The "Wonder Dolls" or "Wonder Babies" were used in the musical comedy TANGERINE on Broadway and in five road companies. The doll appeared in the "Atta Baby" number with Miss Becky Cauble, Allen Kearns, and the chorus.

1923: *Borgfeldt* was the sole distributor.

**Wonder Baby, The.** 1913. Made by *Louis Amberg & Son.* New "Bisc" finish heads, which were advertised as unpeelable because they were undipped. Flesh-colored bodies were cork stuffed and steel jointed. Dolls wore lace trimmed dresses. Price 25¢ to $15.00.

**Wonderland.** 1905–15. Line of dressed dolls handled by *Strobel & Wilken.*

**Wonderland Toy Making Co.** 1923. London. Made dolls.

**Woo Chang.** 1898. Trade name for a Japanese-type doll distributed by *W. A. Cissna & Co.;* it had hair, a squeaker, and wore an oriental costume. Size 8 inches, price 15¢.

**Wood, Reuben.** 1868–69. Syracuse, N.Y. Listed in the Business Directory as manufacturing all kinds of toys and importing French, German, and English toys.

**Wood Pulp.** 1890–1925+. One of the principal ingredients in many types of composition used for making dolls. In 1890 *Colin* patented wood pulp bébés in France. It may have been used earlier elsewhere.

**Wood Toy Co.** 1920. New York City. Probably the manufacturer of *Dolly Walker,* which was patented and distributed by *Harry Coleman.*

**Wood-Bisk.** 1921. Trade name for composition material used by *Century Doll Co.* for dolls and dolls' heads.

**Wooden Dolls.** Dolls have been made of wood throughout recorded history—it was a convenient and inexpensive material. A wooden doll could be simply made from a forked twig, or it could be a highly carved work of art. Probably more homemade dolls were whittled of wood than were made of rags because cloth was far more valuable and difficult to obtain. An Egyptian doll has been found with a wooden head on a rag body.

In the 17th and 18th centuries, the four great wood-carving areas were the Grödner Tal in Austria, Sonneberg in Thüringia, and Oberammergau and Berchtesgaden in Bavaria. The doll industry in Sonneberg started largely because the Thüringian forests provided wood for the dolls. The guild would not let a turner paint his doll; bismuth painters did the decorating. A 1781 document states that the turned wooden dolls made in Neuenbau were embossed with dough by the Sonneberg embossers. Some of the old Sonneberg ledgers refer to wooden dolls as *Tyroler* dolls, which suggests that dolls made in the Grödner Tal (Tyrol) may have been decorated in Sonneberg as well as in Oberammergau and Berchtesgaden. The fact that early Grödner Tall dolls were sent to the last two places for painting was mentioned by Margaret Howitt in 1875. Kestner made wooden dolls in Waltershausen in the early 19th century. A Bavarian wooden doll of ca. 1840 has screw-type joints, but these are probably not typical.

Wooden dolls were also made in France and England. The English ones are perhaps the best documented of all. A doll probably made in England, mentioned in a 1548 British will, has a wooden head covered with plaster. A wooden doll believed to have been played with in Holyrood Palace in the late 17th century has a large head with painted eyes and with beauty spots painted on the face, large hands, and jointed legs; it is 15¾ inches in size. Wooden dolls were used in the Ann Sharp dolls' house of ca. 1700. There are 18th-century records of English turners making and painting dolls; apparently the British guilds were less strict than those on the Continent. These dolls usually had flat backs, and occasionally the bark of the tree was left on hidden parts of the body. A wooden doll with a swivel neck found in England is claimed to date back to the 18th century, and the Victoria and Albert Museum dates one of their all-wooden dolls as 1763; it has ball joints.

Most of the wooden dolls of the 18th century had the head and torso in one piece. Some had painted eyes, but as the century progressed, most of them had pupilless glass eyes; the eyebrows and eyelashes were painted with stylized dots. The English heads appear to have been proportionately larger than those made on the Continent. Sometimes the hands were cloth, and sometimes they were of wood. The torsos were either square or pointed; the latter type is believed to have been a later variation. In the early 19th century, dolls more frequently began to have colored irises and molded gesso faces rather than carved features.

Meanwhile, competition grew on the Continent with the production of the peg wooden or *Dutch Dolls.* These were completely articulated. The larger sizes had ball joints, and often swiveled at the waist, but the smaller sizes had simple peg joints. In the early 1800's the bust

**1701.** Turned wooden doll characteristic of those made in the 18th century. The head and chest are covered with gesso and then painted; the eyes are enameled glass, and small dots delineate the hair of the eyelashes and eyebrows; the wig is made of flax. Limbs are whittled. Original dress has wide panniers of the mid-18th century. *Courtesy of The Smithsonian Institution.*

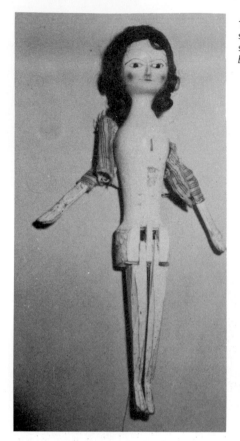

**1702.** All-wooden doll of the Georgian era, jointed at hips and shoulders, has black pupil-less glass eyes with characteristic stylized dots for eyelashes and eyebrows; hair wig. *Photograph by Winnie Langley.*

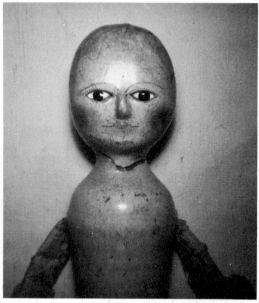

**1703A & B.** Wooden doll with cloth arms, probably 18th century. Stylized dots make the eyelashes and eyebrows around the glass eyes. The short legs and neck suggest that this doll may have represented a baby. H. 10½ inches. *Courtesy of the International Doll Library Foundation.*

**1704A & B.** Pointed torso with gesso-covered wooden head. The pupil-less enameled glass eyes have dots painted around them and at the top of the eyebrow line. There is a hole through the back of head for tying the wig, holes through shoulders and point for tying arms and legs, which were probably made of cloth. Note the characteristic straight back and the bark or veneer at the shoulder where paint has chipped away. H. 6¼ inches. *Coleman Collection.*

area was frequently carved and/or painted, the features were delicately carved and painted, and the hair carved in elaborate fashions. Only occasionally was the doll given a wig, as found on most of the English-type wooden dolls. Continental wooden dolls of this kind frequently had holes for earrings to be attached, and carved combs and coronets often decorated the heads. Spit curls were generally painted around the faces. This type of doll is well represented by the collection with which Victoria played before she was Queen. By the mid-19th century, these wooden dolls were becoming cruder, with less carving and often mere spherical heads. Heads of other materials such as china, wax, papier-mâché, and so on were also used on the peg jointed

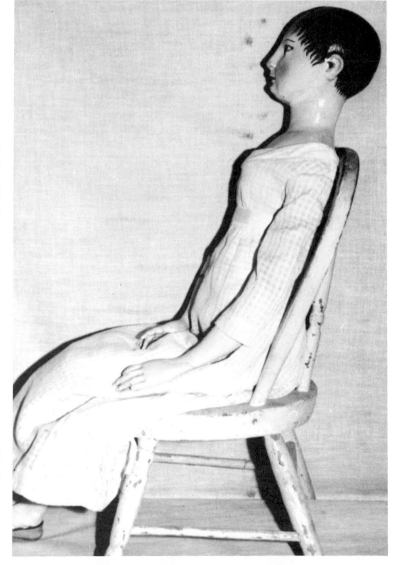

**1705A & B.** Wooden doll with face of gesso over wood, blue glass eyes, square-bottom torso, cloth arms with wooden hands. Note the very high forehead, the dots around the eyes and along the top of the eyebrows, the short space between nose and mouth, and the pink circles on the cheeks. Contemporary early 19th-century cambric dress; the pantaloons go down into red leather boots. H. 19½ inches. *Courtesy of the Chester County Historical Society.*

**1706.** Ball-jointed wooden doll with highly varnished paint over gesso, wind-blown painted hair of ca. 1805; carved ears; red painted slippers with black border at top; contemporary dress. H. 28½ inches. *Courtesy of the Chester County Historical Society.*

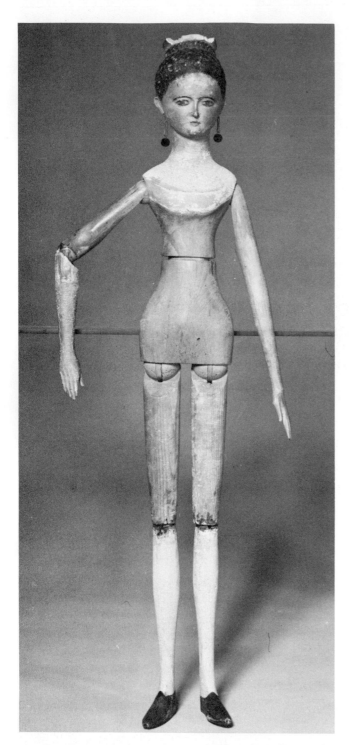 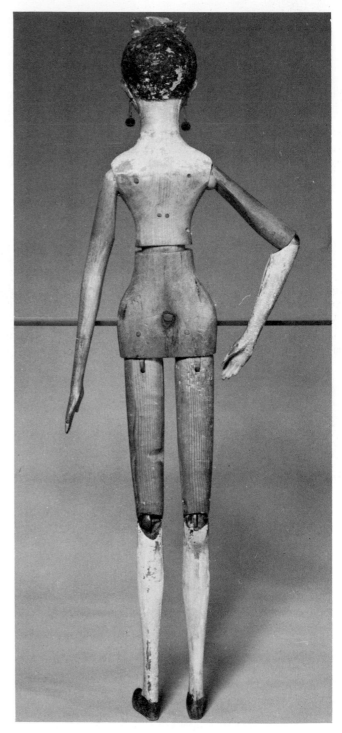

**1707A & B.** Ball-jointed wooden doll of ca. 1810 has carved hair with braid in front held by a gold tiara. Flowers and leaves are painted in colors on the chest section. Note the earrings, waist joint, and the replaced nonjointed arm. H. 34 inches. *Courtesy of The Smithsonian Institution.*

**1708A & B.** Wooden doll with ball joints, painted hair and features, gold tiara in the hair, dots around eyes and along the eyebrows, threaded pupils, protruding bosom for wearing Empire-type dresses, waist joint, red painted slippers with black line around the top. H. 22 inches. *Courtesy of the Chester County Historical Society.*

1709

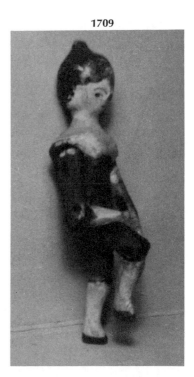

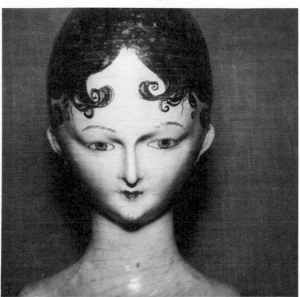

**1709.** Small peg-jointed wooden doll with early-type glossy painted features and gold tuck comb; wisps of gray hair around the face; painted red slippers. H. 1½ inches. *Coleman Collection.*

**1710.** Wooden doll with tuck comb and painted hair; ball joints at hips and shoulders and peg joints at elbows and knees. H. 12½ inches. *Courtesy of the Western Reserve Historical Society.*

**1711.** Peg-jointed wooden doll made in the Grödner Tal has highly varnished head with remnants of a tuck comb; painted gray hair below black on the top of the head. Slippers painted red. H. 3½ inches. *Coleman Collection.*

1710

1711

**1712.** All-wooden, peg-jointed dolls similar to those played with by Princess Victoria in the 1830's. Allegedly, these dolls were given to the English ambassador to Greece by the Greek people. They are dressed in colorful provincial costumes such as those worn by a Greek lady of Crete, an Albanian lady, and so on. *Photograph by Winnie Langley.*

**1713A & B.** Compare this peg-jointed wooden doll with those shown in the 1845 to 1860 Swiss catalog (Ill. **1714**). Note the painted curls under the black top of the head, and the cloth around the turned wooden waist. H. 7¼ inches. *Courtesy of the Newark Museum, Newark, N.J.*

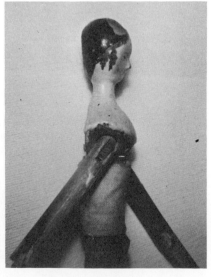

wooden bodies. In the second half of the 19th century, great developments occurred in doll making, but wood continued to be a popular material, especially in Germany, Bohemia, and other parts of Austria. English wooden dolls began to disappear from the records, perhaps because they may have fitted the German description of them as a "piece of painted wood, big and heavy." The American wooden dolls made by the *Cooperative Manufacturing Co.* were described as "some unnoticeable toys" when shown in the Vienna Exhibition in 1873.

In the early 20th century wooden dolls continued to be made largely in Germany. Some of the firms producing them were *Julius Dorst, Fleischmann & Cramer,* and *Zeuch & Lausmann.* Hand-carved, jointed all-wood dolls were made in Switzerland at this time.

1907: Hand-carved wooden dolls were imported into the U.S. from Holland.

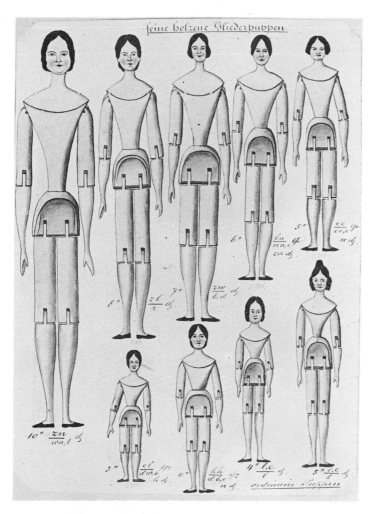

**1714.** "Fine jointed wooden dolls" in the top row and "Ordinary dolls" in the bottom row, as shown in a Swiss catalog of 1845 to 1860. These peg-jointed "Dutch" dolls appear to have gesso-covered heads. The heights are given in Zolls, which correspond to inches, and range from 3 to 10 inches. *Courtesy of Marg. Weber-Beck from Franz Carl Weber, Zurich.*

**1715.** Spherical-head, all-wooden dolls joined at shoulders and hips. Original clothes; the boy is in red velvet, the girl in red silk, both trimmed with gold braid. H. of both dolls, 2¼ inches. *Courtesy of Flora Gill Jacobs.*

**1716A, B, C, & D.** All-wooden doll with carved hair, ball-jointed body but no waist joint, painted red slippers. Her original clothes consist of a white silk dress with yellow ribbon pleated around the hem, a red brocade redingote, and embroidered long pantalettes from just above the knees. H. 23½ inches. *Courtesy of Alberta Darby.*

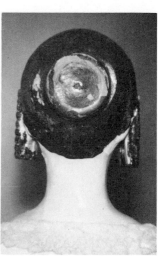

A                    B                    C                    D

**1717.** Wooden "Dutch" peg-jointed doll made in the Grödner Tal, probably late in the 19th century. Old clothes consist of lace mobcap, red wool shawl, and brown dress. H. 6½ inches. *Coleman Collection.*

**1718A & B.** Large-size wooden "Dutch" doll made in the Grödner Tal, probably late in the 19th century; has ball joints but is not jointed at waist; no gray hair is painted under the plain black top of the head; painted red slippers. H. 17 inches. *Coleman Collection.*

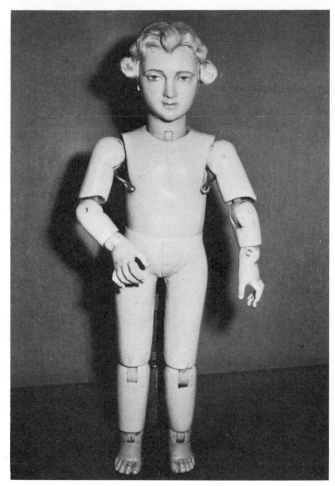

**1719.** All-wooden jointed doll with carved white hair. Doll probably represents a Marquis of the "Ancien Régime." Note the detail in hands and feet. H. 18¾ inches. *Courtesy of Margaret Whitton; photograph by Winnie Langley.*

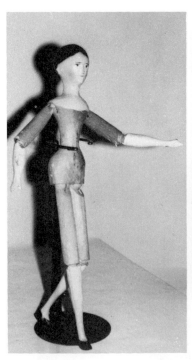

**1720.** "Wooden Ladies' Heads," as shown in a Swiss catalog of about 1845 to 1860. Note that all except the two smallest sizes have earrings. The letter fractions are a price code. *Courtesy of Marg. Weber-Beck from Franz Carl Weber, Zurich.*

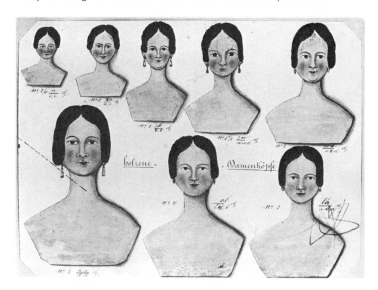

**1721.** Painted gesso over wood lady's head with black hair and blue eyes. Note the similarity to the heads shown in Swiss catalog (Ill. **1720**). *Collection of late Laura Sturges; photograph by Winnie Langley.*

**1722.** Carved wooden head with painted features. Compare with the wooden ladies' heads advertised in the Swiss catalog of 1845 to 1860 (Ill. **1720**). H. of head only, 2¼ inches. *Coleman Collection.*

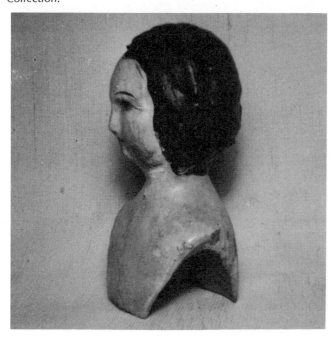

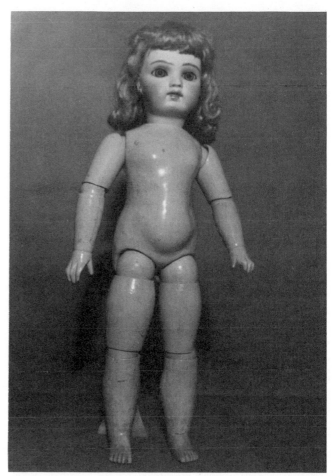

**1723.** All-wooden body with bisque head having a flat solid crown under the wig; carved hands and feet; ball-jointed body. Head marked: "10." H. 16 inches. *Courtesy of Hazel Ulseth.*

1909: *Schoenhut* filed application for his patented all-wood, spring-jointed doll.

1911: All-wood character dolls were made in Europe. They were advertised as being carefully constructed, even to toe and fingertips.

Various types of wood have been used for dolls: pine in the Grödner Tal; boxwood in France; oak in England; applewood in China *(Door of Hope)*; and basswood by Schoenhut. Many compositions used for making dolls have a wooden base, such as wood pulp and wood flour. (See color photograph C2.)

**Wooden Kate.** Ca. 1890's. Austria-Hungary. Name of a wooden folk art doll sold largely in markets. It had a plain face with a pug nose, black painted hair, a carved knot on the back of the head, long limbs.

**Woods, Mary Frances.** 1904–25+. Portland, Ore. Designed and made Indian dolls; each doll was handmade and had an individual expression. *Konstructo Co.* was

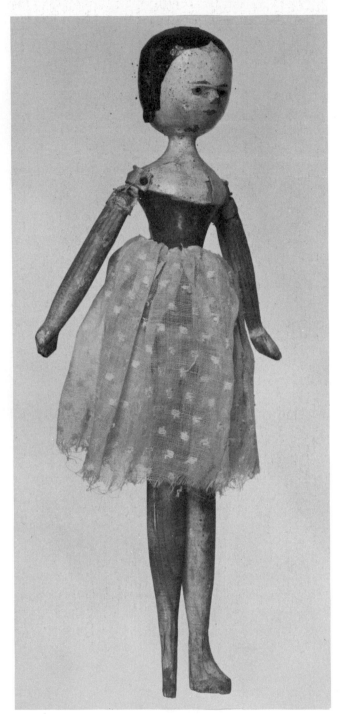

**1724.** Doll with carved hair, red painted torso, leather joints at shoulders and hips. Possibly the type known as a "Wooden Kate." *Courtesy of The Smithsonian Institution.*

the sole distributor. Mary Frances Woods obtained the following copyrights, some of which may have been for figurines rather than dolls:

1904: Chief Joseph; Princess Angeline; a squaw.

1915: Cigarette Friend, an Indian chief; Nez Percé Indian papoose fastened on an Indian cradle board,

wrapped in a blanket; Nez Percé squaw madonna with papoose on back, modeled of composition and painted, straight black hair, dressed in Indian blanket, size 14 inches; *Old Angeline; Sacajawea; Chief Wolf Robe;* and an Indian doll made of glue composition, flour, and paper for the head, with black hair, painted face, heavy cardboard body; this doll wore a hat and an Indian blanket, was 10 to 14 inches high. The last description may have applied to some of the other dolls also.

**Woodtex Co.** 1922–23. New York City. Made dolls' heads, arms, and legs in a range of sizes.

**Wool Dolls.** Name used for a type of doll made in Germany.

**Wordtmann, H.** 1897–25+, Hamburg, Germany; 1925, H. Wordtmann Firm. Manufactured and distributed dolls.

1925: Registered in Germany *Puspi* as a trademark for dolls.

**Work, Henry C.** 1873. Brooklyn, N.Y. Granted a U.S. patent for a walking doll.

**World Standard, The.** 1918–20. Slogan used by *Louis Amberg & Son,* found on bisque heads made by *Fulper Potteries.*

**Worldwide Distributing Co.** See **Pfautz & Co.**

**Worrell, Lola Carrier.** 1922–24. New York City. Proprietress of *Flapper Novelty Co.* Obtained a U.S. design patent for a rag doll with long limbs, a girl dressed in overalls and striped shirt, with a cap on the side of her bushy hair.

**Worthy Doll Manufacturing Co.** See **Eclipse Doll Manufacturing Co.**

**Wot-Zat.** 1915. Trademark registered in U.S. by *Thomas Hindle* for dolls; it was to be affixed on the doll with a printed label.

**Wright, Violette F.** 1924. Philadelphia, Pa. Was granted a U.S. design patent for a two-sided rag doll representing a Chinese man with queue; doll was dressed in plain garb on the smiling side and in striped garb on the downcast side.

**Wu Wu.** 1915. Trademark registered in Britain by John Green *Hamley* for dolls.

**Wunderlich, Ernst.** 1918. Ibenhain, Thür. Made dolls.

**Wurtz, Henry, & Newton, William Edward.** 1865–66. New York City. Obtained a British patent for an artificial material to be used in molding dolls and other toys for which vulcanized rubber, horn, ivory, bone, shell, or papier-mâché had previously been used. The material was made by heating an aqueous solution of glue or gelatin and chromic acid or an alkaline bichromate, and allowing the liquid to gelatinize before mixing it with sand, clay, or powder to give it hardness, or with chopped fiber such as cotton, hair, asbestos, etc., to give it strength and toughness. The sheets were rubbed with glycerine to prevent their becoming brittle; the product could be softened with steam.

**Wynne, Robert W.** 1915. Copyrighted in U.S. a doll grouping, which he named "Night Before Christmas."

**Wynne, William Richard.** 1895–97. London. Obtained a German patent for a feeding doll and a British patent for a bubble-blowing doll.

# X

**Xylolith.** 1882. Material for making dolls' heads, mentioned in a German patent obtained by *Fritz Vogel*.

# Y

**Yahma.** 1916. Trade name for a clown doll, one of the line of *Capo* dolls made by *Non-Breakable Toy Co.*; size 30 inches.

**Yale Novelty Co.** 1919–20. Leominster, Mass. Assignee of a U.S. design patent issued to *Frank F. Ernst & William H. Gorham*.

**Yama Boy.** 1917. Trade name for a doll made by *Berg Bros.* It had stuffed hands and feet, wore a striped clown's outfit; size 12 inches; price $2.25 doz. wholesale.

**Yama Doll.** 1917. Made by *Standard Toy Manufacturing Co.* Size 30 inches; price $2.00.

**Yama Kid.** 1915. Made by *Star Toy & Novelty Manufacturing Co.* Came dressed as a clown; sizes 19, 25, and 30 inches.

**Yama Yama.** 1915–16. Trademark registered by *New Era Novelty Co.*; dolls distributed by *Butler Bros.* Wore black and white striped clown costume. Made in four sizes, including 13½ and 30 inches.

**Yamagawa, Y.** 1878. Tokyo. Exhibited dolls at the Paris Exposition.

**Yamato Importing Co.** 1919–20. Chicago, Ill. Imported bisque dolls and dolls' heads from Japan. Advertised that they were the only genuine bisque dolls made in Japan, which seems rather unlikely.

**Yankee Doll.** 1911–13. Trademark registered in U.S. by *Mitred Box Co.* for a line of dolls; distributed by *McClurg & Keen.* Heads of rose-tinted composition; ball-jointed composition bodies with rubber cording and bent-limb baby bodies. The line included *doll-faced dolls,* character girl and boy dolls, and baby dolls. The dolls were advertised as having blue or brown sleeping eyes, which were unbreakable and could not fall out; wigs made by a wig maker with fourteen years' experience in Sonneberg; bodies so strong that a two hundred-pound man stood on a body without harming it. They came in several sizes, including a 15-inch doll for $1.00. One of the models was a *coquette*-type girl.

**Yankee Doodle.** 1912–13. Copyrighted by *Louis Amberg & Son;* designed by *Jeno Juszko.* It was described in the copyright as having a lively expression, bright eyes, wide-open mouth, stub nose, and comically modeled ears and hair. It was advertised as having a "bisc" finish and dressed in stars and stripes. Yankee Doodle was the mate to *Hail Columbia.* Size 15 inches, price $1.00.

**Yano & Joko.** 1920. New York City. Made celluloid dolls.

**Yarn Dolls.** 1890–1925+. They were especially popular in the 1920's, when there were numerous design patents that used yarn for making dolls.

**Yaseihara, Yazo.** 1900. Japan. Won a silver medal for his display of dolls at the Paris Exposition.

**Yat Quong.** 1922. Head of an oriental child copyrighted by *Carmalete Waldo Webb;* designed by Margaret Smith, daughter of *Putnam D. Smith.*

**Y-Do-I.** 1904–5. Trademark registered in U.S. by *Cole-Ackerman Co.* for dolls.

**Yellow Kid.** 1897. Distributed by *John D. Zernitz Co.* Represented the cartoon character of this name drawn by Richard Felton Outcault. In 1895, Outcault had originated colored comic sheets with the Yellow Kid as his hero. The doll was made of composition, jointed at the shoulders and hips; dressed in yellow tissue paper. Height 5 inches; price $1.90 doz. wholesale.

**Yerri & Gretel.** 1917. Size 8½ inches. Had eyes glancing to the side and were dressed in the costumes of Alsace-Lorraine. These dolls have been found in boxes with labels that suggest they were made by L'Oncle (Uncle) *Hansi* and distributed by *J. P. Gallais & Cie.* of Paris.

**Yerri & Suzel.** 1918. Trademark registered in France by *Société Réné Schiller & Cie.* for dolls dressed in costumes of Alsace or Lorraine.

**Yeux Expression, Société de.** 1925. Paris. Made dolls.

**Yol, Atelier Artistique.** 1925. Paris. Made dolls.

**Young, Ida.** 1903–5. Butte, Mont. Secured a U.S. patent for detachable dolls' heads. The neck was provided with a screw arrangement so that the head could be removed and another put in its place.

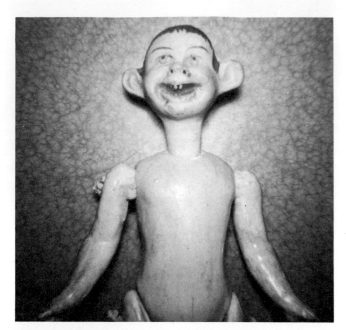

**1725.** The "Yellow Kid," as created by Frank Outcault. All-composition doll has painted and molded hair and features, open-closed mouth with upper teeth. H. 7 inches. *Courtesy of Eleanor Jean Carter.*

**Young America.** 1904–15. Line of dressed dolls handled by *Louis Wolf & Co.* All the designs and patterns for the clothes were made in the U.S. They represented the distinctive styles of American children, the intervening age between baby and grown-up dolls. Lace and spangles were replaced by simple frocks and pinafores.

**Young America.** 1913. Copyrighted by *Elizabeth Lesser.* Size 15 inches.

**Young-Nelson Studio.** 1921. U.S. Made dolls.

**Yukla.** 1894. Trade name for an Eskimo doll advertised in YOUTH'S COMPANION. It had a bisque head, body covered with white fur, and was jointed at neck, shoulders, and hips. Size 8 inches; price 30¢.

# Z

**Zacharias, Auguste.** 1918. Berlin. Manufactured dolls.

**Zaiden, David.** 1906–25+. A citizen of Russia, Zaiden lived in New York City and New Jersey. A chemist, he created and manufactured composition dolls.

1906: Produced an "unbreakable" (composition) doll's head made by a new process. It is interesting to note that *Kestner* started to make "Unbreakable" dolls' heads in 1906, and the first record of David Zaiden in

America is not until 1915 when he was president of the *Superior Doll Manufacturing Co.,* which advertised that they made "The real German Doll." It seems probable that, like *Solomon Hoffmann,* Zaiden must have come from Russia to the U.S. via Germany. By 1915, he had spent years making jointed composition bodies as well as composition heads.

1915: He changed from the Superior Doll Manufacturing Co. to the *Colonial Toy Manufacturing Co.* They described their "Zaiden" dolls as having every head uniform, with the eyes set in by machines that had a capacity of 430, in assorted sizes, every eight hours. Some of the heads had glass moving eyes with eyelashes, and some had painted eyes, teeth, and moving tongues, real hair wigs, usually with short hair. The composition bodies were made as bent-limb babies or as toddlers with pointed torso and ball-jointed knees; both styles had ball-jointed wrists. They claimed that the bodies were lighter in weight than the imported ones. David Zaiden had experimented for years to produce these bodies, which could not be made on regulation doll presses but had to have special ones, designed and built so that the body would not shrink and the two halves could be glued together.

1916: The word "Zaiden" was impressed on dolls made by the Colonial Toy Manufacturing Co. These dolls were distributed by *Borgfeldt, Strobel & Wilken,* and *Baker & Bennett Co.* The dolls were advertised as being the only "fully formed moving eyed doll" manufactured in America. They came in fourteen sizes with moving eyes and with or without wigs.

1919: David Zaiden was with the *H. & Z. Doll & Toy Co.,* which made composition dolls with moving eyes. He obtained a U.S. patent for sleeping eyes of glass, china, or celluloid made as a hemisphere instead of a globe; the lashes were secured to the outer edge of the lid with a buffer to prevent jarring. He claimed his method of construction was simpler and cheaper than preceding ones.

1921–23: David Zaiden was president of the Zaiden Toy Works in Newark, N.J. This company was connected with the *Tip Top Toy Co.* They made mechanical dolls patented by David Zaiden. Zaiden's dolls were distributed by *Louis Wolf & Co., Bankograph Co., M. L. Kahn & Co., I. Eisenstein & Co., Henry Rosenstein, Western Doll Manufacturing Co., Singer Bros., Fair Trading Co., Foulds & Freure,* and *James Bell Co.*

**Zammit, E.** 1867. Floriana, Malta. Displayed wax figures in national costume at the Paris Exposition.

**Zappia, Domenic.** 1923–24. Cleveland, Ohio. Assigned his rights for six design patents to *Paramount Rubber Consolidated Inc.* The designs included a *Clown,* a Dutch girl, a policeman, a sailor, an Indian girl, and an Indian with a large feather headdress.

**Zast, P. R.** 1920's. Poland. Made celluloid dolls. According to Luella Hart in TOY TRADER, May, 1954, celluloid-headed boy and girl dolls with painted eyes and molded bobbed hair, cloth bodies stuffed with sawdust, celluloid arms and hands, dressed in the Polish costumes of Krakow, have their heads marked with a triangle enclosing the initials, "A. S. K." Their shoulders are marked "P. R. Zast// [inverted triangle] Poland."

**Zeh, Eduard.** 1913. Germany. Was granted a French patent for a jointed doll with movements largely controlled by spiral springs.

**Zeh, F.** 1909. Sonneberg, Thür. Made dolls.

**Zeh, G.** 1895. Eisfeld, Thür. Made dolls.

**Zeh, K.** 1909. Sonneberg, Thür. Exported and distributed dolls.

**Zeh, Otto.** 1896–98. Eisfeld, Thür. Obtained a patent for coloring fired white porcelain without additional firing. This was done by dipping the porcelain in a paint solution of water color to which was added a little glue and glycerin. Then it was dipped into highly durable ground lac, which soaked into the coat of color and combined with it permanently on the surface of the porcelain. After the porcelain dried, a thin coat of nonsoluble dull lac or wax was applied.

**Zehner, Bernhard.** 1908–25+. Schalkau, Thür. Manufactured and exported dolls.

1908–14: Made dolls with cloth or "fur" bodies.

1911: Made dressed dolls, mostly 11 inches tall.

1920's: Specialized in dressed dolls, ball-jointed dolls, "stiff" dolls, baby dolls, *Mama Dolls,* and mechanical dolls.

**Zehner, Edmund Carl.** 1925. Schalkau, Thür. Manufactured dolls. Specialized in *"Waltershausen* double-jointed or stiff-jointed dolls" and walking dolls, with or without voices.

**Zeicherer.** 1918. Coburg, Thür. Made dolls.

**Zeidler, A.** 1909–18. Sonneberg, Thür. Made jointed dolls.

**Zeidler, Carl.** 1921–25+. Neustadt near Coburg, Thür. Manufactured dolls.

**Zeidler, Fritz.** 1909. Neustadt near Coburg, Thür. Made dolls.

**Zeidler, Moritz.** 1895–1909. Neustadt near Coburg, Thür. Manufactured little or baby dolls.

**Zeidler, Walter.** 1921–25+. Neustadt near Coburg, Thür. Manufactured dressed dolls, jointed dolls, and character babies.

**Zeigerer, Willy.** 1912–15. Coburg, Thür. Made dolls.

**Zellers-Stevens Inc.** 1921–23. New York City. Imported dolls.

**Zernitz, John D., Co.** 1897. Chicago, Ill. Doll jobber; imported and distributed dolls.

**Zeuch & Lausmann.** 1895–1925+. Sonneberg, Thür. Manufactured and distributed dressed and undressed dolls, *Täuflinge,* dolls' heads, and parts of dolls. Dolls

and doll parts made of papier-mâché, wood, wax, or metal.

1895: Registered in Germany a coat of arms as a trademark for dolls.

1900: One of the Grand Prize winners at the Paris Exposition.

1904: Displayed dolls at the St. Louis Exhibition.

1907: Advertised dressed, washable, and movable (jointed) dolls; medium-sized movable baby dolls; dolls' heads.

1909: Advertised dressed and jointed dolls, jointed *Täuflinge,* and dolls' heads.

**Zier, P. R.** 1902. Berlin. Manufactured and exported dolls.

**Zierl, Paul Lucien.** 1925. Coeuilly-Champigny-sur-Marne, Seine. Registered in France *Le Joujou Pneu* as a trademark for rubber baby dolls.

**Zierow, P. R.** 1897–1925+. Berlin. Manufactured and exported ball-jointed dolls and dolls' bodies.

1910: Registered in Germany as a trademark the superimposed initials "P Z" plus a picture of a ball-jointed doll.

1914: Registered in Germany two trademarks. One was *Mein Augenstern* (Star of My Eye), and the other was a drawing of an eye with a six-pointed star in the center of the pupil, "Puppen Zierow" above the eye, and "Mein Augenstern" below the eye.

**Zimmer, S. D.** 1909–13. Fürth, Bavaria. Made dolls.

**Zimmer, Walter.** 1909–13. London. Distributed dolls of *S. D. Zimmer* and *J. Franz.*

**Zina.** 1924–25+. Trademark registered in France by *André Lambert* for dolls and dolls' articles.

**Zinner, Adolf.** 1909–23. Schalkau, Thür. Manufactured dolls.

**Zinner, Gottlieb & Söhne.** 1898-1923. Schalkau, Thür. Manufactured dolls, especially mechanical dolls with music boxes, and *Marottes.*

**Zitzmann, Emil.** 1912–20. Steinach, Thür. Manufactured and distributed dolls and dolls' bodies, especially those with leather and cloth bodies.

1913: Registered in Germany an anchor with the letters "E Z" on either side of the shank.

**Zitzmann, Wilhelm.** 1925. Sonneberg, Thür. Made pasteboard limbs, etc., for dolls.

**1726.** Trademark used by Emil Zitzmann for dolls.

**Zizi.** 1920. Name copyrighted by *Jeanne I. Orsini.* Copy right model described as a girl with bobbed hair parted on the right side, wearing a ribbon all around the head, with two bows, one on each side; arms straight. Size 9¼ inches.

**Zizine.** 1918. Trademark registered in France by *Mme. Poulbot* for dolls.

**Zoch, Justus.** 1907–11. Dresden, Saxony. Made dolls.

**Zoppel, Moritz.** See **Schierloh, Conrad.**

**Zouaves.** 1875. Trade name for dolls representing soldiers, made by *Jullien.* (See also **French Zouave.**)

**Zulu Dolls.** 1897. Trade name used by *John D. Zernitz Co.* for dolls representing Zulus; they had painted eyes, curly hair, jointed bodies. Sizes 5 and 7¼ inches; price $1.50 to $2.50 doz. wholesale.

**Zurkuhl, Walter.** 1910–20. Sonneberg, Thür. Made dolls. Won Grand Prize at Brussels Exposition in 1910.

**Zu-Zu Kid.** 1916–17. Copyrighted and made by *Ideal Novelty & Toy Co.;* based on a design patent by Isaac Rommer. Doll represented the Zu-Zu trademark figure of the National Biscuit Co.'s ginger snaps. The doll was a girl, dressed as a clown in a suit of yellow sateen dotted with large and small brown stars. She carried a miniature package of Zu-Zu Ginger Snaps in her arm. Zu-Zu Kid was a mate to *Uneeda Kid.*

**Zylonite.** 1906–13. Material used for dolls and dolls' heads, which were distributed by *Butler Bros.* This was a hollow, plastic type of material, and the all-zylonite dolls were made so that they would float in an upright position in water.

1906: All-zylonite dolls came with painted hair and features; jointed shoulders. Sizes 3¾, 6, 8, and 11 inches; price 85¢ to $8.00 doz. wholesale.

1907: Sizes were the same as in 1906, except that sizes 12½ and 14½ inches were added; prices were reduced about 20 percent; the largest sizes cost $8.50 and $13.50 doz. wholesale.

1910: New sizes and new prices were advertised. All-zylonite dolls with painted hair and features, jointed at shoulders, now came in sizes 3, 4⅜, 5⅜, 6¼, 7⅛, 8¾, 10, and 12½ inches; price 45¢ to $7.60 doz. wholesale. In addition to the all-zylonite dolls, zylonite heads could be purchased. With painted hair and features, the heads were 3¼, 4⅛, and 5¼ inches; price was 87¢ to $3.50 doz. wholesale. The $3.50 heads had glass eyes. Other heads with glass eyes had side-part curly wigs; head sizes 4 and 5 inches cost $2.25 and $4.50 doz. wholesale.

1912: All-zylonite dolls with jointed shoulders were the same sizes as in 1910 and cost nearly the same. Butler Bros. added all-zylonite dolls with joints at shoulders and hips. These had molded shoes and socks. Came in sizes 8¼ and 11 inches; price was $4.20 and $7.50 doz. wholesale. The zylonite heads were the same sizes as in 1910, but moving eyes were a new feature in the 5-inch wigged head.

Ca. 1913: Bent-limb babies were advertised in all-zylonite; they had painted hair and features and came in sizes 5¼, 7¼, and 9⅛ inches; price was 95¢ to $3.90 doz. wholesale.

**1727.** Mark used for "Capo" line of dolls.

**1728.** Late "Furga" mark. Name "Furga," an earlier porcelain mark, found on dolls.

**1729.** Mark used by Hausman & Zatulove for dolls.

**1730.** "Montreuil" mark found on dolls, especially dolls representing men. This may be Hieulle's mark.

**1731.** Mark used by the New Era Novelty Co.

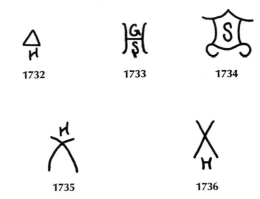

**1732–1736.** Marks used by Gebrüder Schoenau Porzellanfabrik in Hüttensteinach (Köppelsdorf-Nord).

**1737.** Mark used by Jacobs & Kassler, successors of Hitz, Jacobs & Kassler.

**1738.** Mark used by Otto Gans.

# SELECTED BIBLIOGRAPHY

The marks and labels on dolls themselves, or their containers, are the most important source of information.

## I. OFFICIAL SOURCES

**d'Allemagne, Henri René,** *Les Jouets à la World's Fair en 1904 à Saint Louis,* Paris, 1908.

British *Patent Specifications,* 1844 ff.

British *Trademarks,* 1878 ff.

**Calvin, Jeannette M.,** *International Trade in Toys,* U.S. Department of Commerce, Washington, D.C., Government Printing Office, 1926.

*Catalogue Général,* Exposition Universelle de 1867 à Paris, publié par la Commission Impériale.

*Catalogue Officiel,* de 1878 à Paris, publié par le Commissariat Général.

*Catalogue Officiel,* L'Exposition Universelle de 1855, Paris.

*Cincinnati Industrial Exposition Guide,* presentation copy, Sixth Cincinnati Industrial Exposition, 1875.

*Complete Official Catalog including the British and all Other Sections,* by Authority of the Imperial Commission, 1867 Paris Universal Exhibition (English version).

*Exposition de l'Industrie Française,* published by M. Challamel, 1844.

*France Commission Supérieure Rapports,* Exposition Universelle de Vienne en 1873, Paris, 1875.

French *Patents,* 1824 ff.

French *Trademarks,* 1885 ff.

German *Patents,* 1878 ff.

German *Trademarks,* 1875 ff.

**Hamelle, Henry,** *Rapport Général,* Exposition de Saint-Louis 1904, Comité Francais des Expositions à l'Etranger.

**Howe, Julia Ward,** *Report and Catalogue of the Woman's Department,* New Orleans, 1884, printed by Rand, Avery & Co., 1885.

*Illustrated Catalogue of Industrial Department,* International Exhibition of 1862, British Division, London.

*Liste des Récompenses, décernées aux Exposants,* Exposition Universelle et Internationale de Bruxelles en 1910, Imprimerie A. Lesigne.

*Liste des Récompenses,* Exposition Universelle de 1900 à Paris, Imprimerie Nationale, 1901.

*Official Catalog,* International Exposition, St. Louis, 1904, Exposition of the German Empire.

*Official Catalog of Exhibits,* Melbourne, 1880, Mason, Firth & M'Cutcheon.

*Official Catalogue,* Centennial International Exhibition, Melbourne, 1888, published by M. L. Hutchinson.

*Official Catalogue,* Sydney, 1879.

*Official Catalogue of Exhibits,* World's Columbian Exposition, Chicago, 1893, W. B. Conkey Co.

*Official Descriptive and Illustrated Catalogue,* including Reports of Juries. London, 1851, Spicer Bros., 3 vols.

*Reports of the United States Commission to the Universal Exposition of 1889 at Paris.* Washington, Government Printing Office, 1891.

**Richards, William C.,** ed. of Official Catalog, *A Day in the New York Crystal Palace,* G. P. Putnam & Co., 1853.

**Rossollin, M.,** *Rapport sur la Bimbeloterie,* Exposition Universelle Internationale de 1878 à Paris, 1880.

Royal Commission, *Official Catalogue of the British Section,* International Exhibition, St. Louis, 1904, printed by William Clowes & Sons, Ltd.

United States *Copyrights,* 1909 ff.

United States *Design Patents,* 1886 ff.

United States *Patents,* 1858 ff.

United States *Trademarks,* 1871 ff.

**Walker, Francis,** *Reports and Awards U.S. International Exhibition 1876,* Philadelphia, Government Printing Office, 1876.

*Welt Ausstellung 1873 in Wien* (Official General Catalog).

## II. DIRECTORIES

*Adressbuch der Sächsisch-Thüringischen Industrie,* Dresden, im Selbstverlag des Vereins, 1907, 1911.

*Almanach du Commerce de Paris,* Paris, Didot, 1811.

*Annuaire Général du Commerce (Annuaire-Almanach du Commerce),* Paris, Didot-Bottin, 1842 ff.

*Baltimore Directory,* R. J. Matchett, John W. Woods, et al., 1855 ff.

*Boston Directory,* Charles Stimpson, Sampson & Murdock, et al., 1855 ff.

*Bridgeport, Connecticut, Directory,* Price & Lee Co., 1872 ff.

*Brooklyn City and Business Directory,* Geo. T. Lain, 1870 ff.

*Business Directory of the City of Brooklyn,* Lain & Co., 1877 ff.

*Business Directory of New York City, Boston, Philadelphia, and Newark, N.J.,* Austin Publishing Co., 1889.

*Cincinnati, Ohio, Directory,* C. S. Williams, 1855 ff.

*Covington and Newport, Kentucky, Directory,* Williams & Co., 1866 ff.

*Deutsches Reichs Adressbuch,* Rudolf Mosse, ed., Verlag des Deutsches Reichs, Adressbuch G.m.b.H.

*Elmira, N.Y., Directory,* Andrew & W. Harry Boyd, 1871 ff.

*Exposition Universelle de Paris 1889,* Paris, Didot Bottin, 1890.

*Gopsill's Philadelphia Business Directory,* Gopsill, after 1907, merged with Boyds, 1870 ff.

*Handels und Gewerbekammer zu Sonneberg,* Sonneberg, 1893–1902.

*Jersey City & Hoboken Directory,* James & William Gopsill, Boyds, et al., 1856 ff.

Kelly, *Birmingham Post Office Directory,* 1856.

*Kelly's Birmingham Directory,* London, Kelly's Directories, Ltd., 1909.

*Kelly's Directory of Merchants, Manufacturers and Shippers,* London, Kelly's Directories, Ltd., 1877 ff.

*Leuchs Adressbuch,* Nürnberg, C. Leuchs & Co., 1895–1902 (75 vols.).

*Lowe's International Commercial Directory,* Florence, Lowe, 1916–17.

*Massachusetts Register and Business Directory,* George Adams, 1853 ff.

*Meiers Adressbuch der Exporteure und der Importeure,* Hamburg, Verlag von Meiers Adressbuch, 1903 ff.

Mortimer, Thomas, *The Universal Director* (London Directory), London, J. Coote, 1763.

*New England Business Directory,* George Adams, Sampson & Murdock, 1856 ff.

*New Jersey Business Directory,* Stacy B. Kirkbride, Jr., R. L. Polk & Co., 1850 ff.

*New York Directory*
  David Longworth, 1816 ff.
  John Doggett's, 1841 ff.
  Trow's Printing & Bookbinding Co., 1851 ff.
  H. Wilson, 1852 ff.
  W. Phillips', 1881 ff.

*Newark Directory,* Newark *Daily Advertiser,* B. T. Pierson, 1835 ff.

*Perry's Directory of Great Britain and Ireland, Etc.,* London, W. Perry & Co., Ltd., 1908 ff.

*Post Office London Directory,* London, B. Critchett, 1807 ff.

*Philadelphia Business Directory,* Gopsill, Boyd, et al., 1874 ff.

*Philadelphia Directory,* B. & T. Kite, Edward & John Biddle, et al., 1813 ff.

*Providence and R.I. Business Directory,* Sampson, Davenport & Co., 1866 ff.

*Providence Directory,* Carlile & Brown, H. H. Brown, 1826 ff.

*Trow's Business Directory of Boroughs of Brooklyn and Queens,* Trow Directory Printing and Bookbinding Co., 1880 ff.

*Vermont Business Directory,* Briggs Directory and Publishing Co., 1870 ff.

*Vermont State Business Directory*, Symond's, Wentworth & Co., 1870 ff.

*Walton's, The Vermont Directory*, various publishers, 1869 ff.

*Watkin's Commercial and General London Directory and Court Guide*, London, 1853–55.

*Who's Who in American Art*, Alice Coe McGlauflin, ed., Washington, D.C., The American Federation of Arts, 1935.

## III. CATALOGS*

Althof, Bergmann & Co., *Catalogue*, New York, 1874.

Baker & Bennett Co., *Dolls Catalogue*, New York, n.d. (ca. 1917).

Baltimore Bargain House, *Catalogue*, 1904 ff.

Best & Co., *Liliputian Bazaar*, New York, 1902 ff.

Butler Bros., *Wholesale Catalogue*, Chicago, 1886.

Cissna, W. A., & Co., *The Hustler*, Chicago, 1898.

Croft, William, & Sons, *Catalogue*, Toronto, 1907 ff.

Eaton, Timothy, Co., *Catalogue*, Toronto, 1887 ff.

Ehrich Bros., *Toy Price List*, New York, 1874 ff.

Ellis, Britton & Eaton, *Price List*, New York, Aug., 1869.

German-American Import Co., *Catalogue*, New York, 1925.

Gray & Dudley Co., *Catalogue*, Nashville, Tenn., 1918.

Jordan, Marsh & Co., *Catalogue*, Boston, 1897 ff.

Linington's, C. M., *Silent Salesman*, 1894.

Macy, R. H., & Co., *Catalogue*, New York, 1909 ff.

Maison du Petit Saint-Thomas, *Jouets, Etrennes*, Paris, 1886 ff.

Nerlich & Co., *Catalogue*, Toronto, 1902 ff.

Nugent's, *Catalogue*, 1900 ff.

O'Neill, H., & Co., *Catalogue*, New York, 1896 ff.

Schoenhut, A., Co., *Illustrations of Schoenhut's Marvelous Toys*, Philadelphia, n.d.

———, *Schoenhut Doll*, n.d.

———, *The "Schoenhut Doll" Catalogue, All-Wood Perfection Art Doll*, 1915.

Sears, Roebuck & Co., *Catalogue*, Chicago, 1894 ff.

Simpson, Robert, *Catalogue*, Toronto 1918.

Strasburger, Pfeiffer & Co., *Descriptive Catalogue*, New York, 1875 (included medal won in 1876).

Tour St.-Jacques, *Catalogue*, Paris, 1893 ff.

Wanamaker's, *Catalogue*, Philadelphia, 1895 ff.

Ward, Montgomery, & Co., *Catalogue*, Chicago, 1887 ff.

White, R. H., Co., *Catalogue*, Boston, 1884 ff.

Woodward & Lothrop, *Christmas Toys and Games*, Washington, D.C., 1911.

Zernitz, John D., *Toys For All*, Chicago, 1897.

## IV. GENERAL REFERENCE BOOKS

d'Allemagne, Henri René, *Histoire des Jouets*, Paris, 1903.

*American Made Dolls and Figurines*, Doll Collectors of America, Inc., Winchester, Mass., 1940.

*An A. M. Picture Book*, The Heart of Ohio Doll Club, n.d.

Angione, Genevieve, *All-Bisque and Half-Bisque Dolls*, Camden, N.J., Thomas Nelson & Sons (to be published 1969).

Bateman, Thelma, *Delightful Dolls, Antique and Otherwise*, Washington, D.C., Hobby House Press, 1966.

Bédelet, Amédée, *La Reine des Poupées*, trans. by Edith Bartholomew, Wichita, Kansas, Calico Print Shop, 1965.

von Boehn, Max, *Dolls and Puppets*, trans. by Josephine Nicoll, rev. ed., Boston, Charles T. Branford Co., 1956.

Christopher, Catherine, *The Complete Book of Doll Making and Collecting*, New York, Greystone Press, 1949.

Claretie, Léo, *Les Jouets, Histoire, Fabrication*, Paris Ancienne Maison Quantin, n.d. (ca. 1894).

Cole, Adeline P., *Notes on the Collection of Dolls and Figurines at the Wenham Museum*, Wenham Historical Association, 1951.

Cole, Ann Kilborn, *Touring Mary Merritt's Doll Museum*, Dan Weidner, 1963.

Coleman, Elizabeth A., *Dolls, Makers and Marks, Including Addenda*, Washington, D.C., Dorothy S. Coleman, 1966.

Coleman, Evelyn, Elizabeth, and Dorothy, *The Age of Dolls*, Washington, D.C., Dorothy S. Coleman, 1965.

Cunningham, Lucy and Herbst, Beth, *Styles for Dolls*, Wichita, Kansas, Calico Print Shop, 1963.

Daiken, Leslie, *Children's Toys Throughout the Ages*, London, B. T. Batsford, Ltd., 1963. Spring Books, 1965.

Deutschen Spielzeugmuseum Sonneberg, *Spielzeug*, Leipzig, Im Prisma Verlag, 1963.

*Doll Collectors Manual*, The Doll Collectors of America, Inc., Boston, 1949, 1956–57, 1964, 1967.

*Dolls*, Doll Collectors of America, Inc., Boston, Mass., 1946.

*Dolls*, Victoria and Albert Museum. London, Her Majesty's Stationery Office, 1960.

*Dolls from the Collections of the Members*, The Doll Collectors Guild, Helen Biggart, et al., eds., Brooklyn, N.Y., 1964.

*Dolls Through the Ages*, Exhibition Guide, London, July 8, 1954.

Early, Alice K., *English Dolls, Effigies and Puppets*, London, B. T. Batsford, Ltd., 1955.

Fawcett, Clara Hallard, *Dolls, A New Guide for Collectors*, Boston, Mass., Charles T. Branford Co., 1964.

———, *On Making, Mending and Dressing Dolls*, New York, H. L. Lindquist Publications, 1949.

*First Doll Exhibition*, The Doll Collectors of America, Inc., Winchester, Mass., May 21, 1938.

Fisher, Elizabeth Andrews, *Doll Stuff Again*, Middletown, Conn., Harold and Elizabeth Andrews Fisher, 1961.

Foley, Daniel, *Toys Through the Ages*, Philadelphia, Chilton Books, 1962.

Fournier, Edouard, *Histoire des Jouets et de jeux d'enfants*, Paris, 1889.

Fraser, Antonia, *Dolls*, New York, G. P. Putnam's Sons, 1963.

———, *A History of Toys*, Delacorte Press, 1966.

Freeman, Ruth, *American Dolls*, Watkins Glen, N.Y, Century House, 1952.

———, **and Larry**, *Cavalcade of Toys*, New York, Century House, 1942.

Fritzsch, Karl Ewald, and Bachmann, Manfred, *An Illustrated History of Toys*, trans. by Ruth Michaelis-Jena, London, Abbey Library, 1966.

Gerken, Jo Elizabeth, *Wonderful Dolls of Wax*, Lincoln, Nebraska, Doll Research Associates, 1964.

Gordon, Lesley, *A Pageant of Dolls*, New York, A. A. Wyn, Inc., 1949.

———, *Peepshow into Paradise*, New York, John de Graff, Inc., 1953.

Gröber, Karl, *Children's Toys of Bygone Days*, trans. by Philip Hereford. London, B. T. Batsford, Ltd., 1928.

———, *Das Puppenhaus*, Leipzig, n.d. Reprinted as *Die Puppenstadt*, Konigstein im Taunus: Verlag Karl Robert Langewiesche, n.d.

Grollier, Charles de, *Manuel de l'Amateur de Porcelaines*, Paris, 1914.

Hansmann, Claus, *Puppen aus Aller Welt*, Munich, F. Bruckmann, 1959.

Hart, Luella, *Complete French Doll Directory, 1801-1964*, Luella Hart, 1965.

———, *Directory of British Dolls*, Luella Hart, 1964.

———, *Directory of German Dolls, Trademarks*, 1875–1960, Luella Hart, 1964.

———, *Directory of United States Doll Trademarks*, 1888-1968. Luella Hart, 1968.

Hercík, Emanuel, *Folktoys, Les jouets populaires*, 2d edition, Prague, Orbis, 1952.

Hertz, Louis H., *The Handbook of Old American Toys*, Wethersfield, Conn., Mark Haber & Co., 1947.

Hillier, Mary, *Dolls and Doll Makers*, New York, G. P. Putnam's Sons, 1968.

———, *Pageant of Toys*, New York, Taplinger Publishing Co., Inc., 1965.

Holme, C. Geoffrey, *Children's Toys of Yesterday*, London, The Studio, Ltd., 1932.

---

*Some of these catalogs were made available to us through the graciousness of Eleanor Jean Carter, Dorothy Cook, Clara Fawcett, Flora Gill Jacobs, Marjorie M. Smith (publisher-editor of *Spinning Wheel* magazine), and Montgomery Ward & Co.

**Holton, Gladys Reid,** *A Monograph on Metal Head Dolls,* Penfield, N.Y., Genesee Valley Doll Collectors Club, n.d.

**Hooper, Elizabeth,** *Royal Dolls,* Baltimore, Md., 1938.

**Horine, Maude M.,** *Memories of Rose O'Neill,* Branson, Mo., 1950.

**Jackson, Mrs. F. Nevill,** *Toys of Other Days,* London, "Country Life" Library, 1908.

**Jacobs, Flora Gill,** *A History of Dolls' Houses,* New York, Charles Scribner's Sons, 1965.

————, **and Faurholt, Estrid,** *A Book of Dolls & Doll Houses,* Rutland, Vermont, Charles E. Tuttle Co., 1967.

Jenny Lind Doll Club of Southern Conn., Region 14, The United Federation of Doll Clubs, *Program Booklet for Regional Convention,* Hartford, Conn., April 27 & 28, 1968.

**Jervis, W. Percival,** *A Book of Pottery Marks,* Newark, N.J., 1897.

**Johl, Janet Pagter,** *The Fascinating Story of Dolls,* New York, H. L. Lindquist, 1941.

————, *More About Dolls,* New York, H. L. Lindquist, 1946.

————, *Still More About Dolls,* New York, H. L. Lindquist, 1950.

————, *Your Dolls and Mine,* New York, H. L. Lindquist, 1952.

**Johnson, Audrey,** *How to Repair and Dress Old Dolls,* Newton, Mass., Charles T. Branford Co., 1967.

**Kaut, Hubert,** *Alt-Wiener Spielzeugschachtel,* Vienna, Hans Deutsch, 1961.

**Kenny, D. J.,** *Illustrated Guide to Cincinnati,* St. Louis, Pacific Publishing Co., 1893.

**Ketterman, Marie,** *Two Hundred Years of Pennsylvania Dolls,* Plymouth Meeting, Pa., Mrs. C. Naaman Keyser, 1949.

**King, Edna Knowles,** *A Doll's Family Album,* Chicago, Albert Whitman & Co., 1937.

**Lehr, Margaret Marshall, and Follett, Margaret Pattie,** *A Scrapbook About Old Dolls,* Moorhead, Minn., Follett Studios, 1964.

————, *Speaking of Old Dolls,* Moorhead, Minn., Follett Studios, 1964.

*Lehrblätter für den Fachunterricht,* Berufsschule Neustadt bei Coburg, Coburg, Neue Presse. 1954.

**Leslie, Miss Eliza,** *American Girl's Book,* Boston, Munroe and Francis, 1831.

**Lesser, Frederike,** *Dolly's Dressmaker,* trans. by Madame de Chatelain, London, Joseph, Myers & Co., n.d. (Facsimile reproduction), Johannesburg, Mich., Barbara Bannister, 1961.

**Lewis, Mary E., and Dignam, Dorothy,** *The Marriage of Diamonds and Dolls,* New York, H. L. Lindquist, 1947.

**Low, Frances H.,** *Queen Victoria's Dolls,* London, George Newnes, Ltd., 1894.

**McClintock, Inez and Marshall,** *Toys in America.* Washington, D.C., 1961.

**Matéaux, Clara L.,** *The Wonderland of Work,* New York, Cassell & Co., 1884.

*Memoirs of a Doll,* by Itself, Philadelphia, American Sunday-School Union, 1854.

**Mills, Winifred H., and Dunn, Louise M.,** *The Story of Old Dolls and How to Make New Ones,* New York, Doubleday, Doran & Co., 1940.

**Noble, John,** *Dolls,* New York, Walker and Company, 1967.

*Notice sur la Fabrication des Bébés Jumeau,* Paris, J. Cusset, printer, 1885 (translated and published as *The Jumeau Doll Story* by Nina S. Davies, 1957).

**Pylkkänen, Riitta,** *Dockor och tennsoldater* (with English text), Helsingfors, Findlands Nationalmuseum, Bilderbok n:r 1, 1961.

**Rabecq-Maillard, M. M.,** *Histoire du Jouets,* Paris, Hachette, 1962.

**Remise, Jac, and Fondin, Jean,** *The Golden Age of Toys,* translated by D. B. Tubbs, Edita S. A. Lausanne, 1967.

**Robinson, Julia A.,** *Dolls, an Anthology,* Chicago, Albert Whitman & Co., 1938.

**Roh, Juliane,** *Altes Spielzeug,* Munich, F. Bruckmann, 1958.

**Ruggles, Rowena Godding,** *The One Rose,* Oakland, Calif., Rowena Godding Ruggles, 1964.

**Sacks, Israel, Inc.,** *Exhibition of Early American Dolls and Dolls' Furniture,* New York, April 30, 1934.

**St. George, Eleanor,** *Dolls of Three Centuries,* New York, Charles Scribner's Sons, 1951.

————, *The Dolls of Yesterday,* New York, Charles Scribner's Sons, 1948.

————, *Old Dolls,* New York, M. Barrows and Co., 1950.

*Santa Claus' Dolls,* ed. by Elisabeth Hoyt, Boston, W. A. Wilde Co., 1911.

**Sanua, Louise,** *Le Jouet,* Association Nationale d'Expansion Economique. Paris, 1917.

**Schoonmaker, Patricia N.,** *Research on Kämmer and Reinhardt Dolls,* Patricia N. Schoonmaker, 1965.

**Seeger and Guernsey,** *Cyclopaedia of the Manufactures and Products of the United States,* New York, Seeger and Guernsey Co., 1890, 1892, 1900.

**Selfridge, Madalaine, and Cooper, Marlowe,** *Dimples and Sawdust,* 1967.

**Sézan, Claude,** *Les Poupées Anciennes, Paris,* Les Editions Pittoresques, 1930.

**Singleton, Esther,** *Dolls,* New York, Payson & Clarke, Ltd., 1927.

*Souvenir Program,* Heart of Ohio Doll Club, Region 12, United Federation of Doll Clubs, April 26 and 27, 1968.

**Starr, Laura B.,** *The Doll Book,* New York, The Outing Publishing Co., 1908.

*Supplement to American Made Dolls and Figurines,* Doll Collectors of America, Inc., Boston, Mass., 1942.

**Symons, Harry L.,** *Playthings of Yesterday,* Toronto, The Ryerson Press, 1963.

*Toys and Games,* London Museum, London, Her Majesty's Stationery Office, 1959.

**Trimpey, Alice Kent,** *The Story of My Dolls,* Racine, Wisc. Whitman Publishing Co., 1935.

**Weaver, Mignonet M.,** *Mignonet's Doll Haven,* Oklahoma City, Okla., Mignonet M. Weaver, 1966.

**White, Gwen,** *A Book of Dolls,* New York, The Macmillan Co., 1956.

————, *Dolls of the World,* Newton Centre, Mass., Charles T. Branford Co., 1963.

————, *European and American Dolls,* New York, G. P. Putnam's Sons, 1966.

**von Wilckens, Leonie,** *Tageslauf im Puppenhaus,* Munich, Prestel Verlag, 1956.

**Wittkop-Ménardeau, Gabrielle,** *Von Puppen und Marionetten,* Zurich, Werner Classen Verlag, 1962.

## V. GENERAL REFERENCE PERIODICALS*

*Antiques Journal, The* (formerly *The American Antiques Journal*), Uniontown, Pa., 1945 ff.

*Children's Friend,* a monthly magazine devoted to the best interests of the young, West Chester, Pa., 1868–74.

*Delineator, The,* Butterick Publishing Co., New York, 1875–1937.

*Demorests Monthly Magazine,* later *Demorests Family Magazine,* New York, 1876 ff.

*Deutsche Spielwaren Zeitung,* Nürnberg, Bavaria, Meisenbach, 1909 ff. (later *Das Spielzeug,* Bamberg).

*Doll Collector, The,* Reed Printing and Publishing, Carlos Ind., 1964 ff.

*Doll News,* Official Publication of United Federation of Doll Clubs, Inc., 1953 ff.

*Doll Talk,* Independence, Mo., Kimport Dolls, 1937 ff.

*Doll's Dressmaker, The Magazine for Girls,* ed. Jennie Wren, pseud., New York City, Vols. 1–3 (1891–93).

*Godey's Lady's Book,* also called *Godey's Lady's Book and Ladies' American Magazine* and *Godey's Lady's Book and Magazine.* Philadelphia, 1830 ff.

*Harper's Bazar,* New York, Harper and Brothers, 1867 ff.

*Harper's Young People,* New York, Harper and Brothers, 1880 ff.

*Hearth and Home,* York Pettengill, Bates & Co., 1868–75.

*Hobbies,* Chicago, 1932 ff.; "Dollology," 1936 ff. Clara Fawcett, editor of "Dollology," 1952 ff.

*Ladies' Home Journal,* Curtis Publishing Co., Philadelphia, 1883 ff.

*Ladies' World, The,* McClure Publishing Co., New York, 1880 ff.

*Les Jouets et Jeux Anciens,* Bulletin Illustré de la Société des

---

*Various issues of contemporary periodicals often contain articles on dolls and premium lists that include dolls and/or advertisements of dolls. The listed periodicals represent only a fraction of those that contain such information.

Amateurs de Jouets et Jeux Anciens, Vols. I, II (1905–7).

*McCall's Magazine* (also called *Queen of Fashion,* 1894–97), New York, 1894 ff.

*McClure's Children's Annual,* New York, McClure, Phillips & Co., 1902 ff.

*Novelty News, The,* Chicago, The Novelty News Co., 1917 ff.

*Pansy, The,* Boston, D. Lothrop & Co., 1883 ff.

*People's Home Journal,* premium list, 1913–1914.

*Playthings.* New York, McCready Publishing Co., 1903 ff.

*Revue de la Mode,* Gazette de la Famille, Paris, A. Goubaud, 1892–94.

*Ridleys' Fashion Magazine,* New York, E. Ridley & Sons, 1886 ff.

*St. Nicholas,* Scribner and later Century Co., 1873 ff.

*Souvenir Programs,* United Federation of Doll Clubs: ed. by Eleanor McKeague, *et al.,* Twelfth Annual Convention, Aug., 1961; ed. by Kathryn Rozek, Thirteenth Annual Convention, Aug., 1962; ed. by Helen Trimble and Virginia Galloway, Fourteenth Annual Convention, Aug., 1963; ed. by Eunice Sheard, Fifteenth Annual Convention, Aug., 1964; ed. by Mrs. E. P. Carter, Sixteenth Annual Convention, Aug., 1965; ed. by Mrs. Paul H. Hubbard, Seventeenth Annual Convention, Aug., 1966; ed. by Maurine Popp, Eighteenth Annual Convention, Aug., 1967; ed. by Goodie Bennett, Nineteenth Annual Convention, Aug., 1968.

*Spinning Wheel,* Taneytown, Md., 1945 ff.

*Toy Trader, The,* Middletown, Conn., Elizabeth Andrews Fisher, 1948 ff.

*Toy World,* San Francisco, Pacific Publishing Co. 1928 ff. (merged with *Toys and Novelties,* 1936).

*Wide Awake Pleasure Book,* Boston, D. Lothrop & Co., 1875 ff. (later merged with *St. Nicholas*).

*Woman's Home Companion,* New York, Crowell Publishing Co., 1873 ff.

*Woman's World,* London, Cassell & Co., 1187 ff.

*Youth's Companion,* Boston, Perry Mason Co., 1874 ff.

## VI. ARTICLES OF SPECIAL INTEREST

*(Listed by author)*

**Cole, Ann Kilborn,** "Doll Legacy," *The Philadelphia Inquirer Magazine,* Dec. 6, 1956, p. 58.

**Espy, Hilda Cole,** "The Busy, Busy Life of a Doll Collector." *Woman's Day,* Vol. 28, No. 4 (Jan. 1965), pp. 23–35.

**Griffith, M. Dinorben,** "A Village of Dollmakers." *Pearson's Magazine,* Vol. IV, No. 19 (July, 1897).

**Munn, Marguerite,** "Dolls of Early Minnesota," *Gopher Historian,* Fall, 1958, pp. 24–6.

**Noble, John,** "The History of Dolls in Europe and America," *Woman's Day,* Vol. 28, No. 4 (Jan., 1965), p. 76.

**O'Brien, Robert,** "The Magic World of Dolls," *Reader's Digest,* Dec., 1964, pp. 146–53.

**Pryor, Samuel F.,** "The World of Dolls," *The National Geographic,* Vol. CXVI, No. 6 (Dec., 1959), pp. 817–31.

**Roe, F. Gordon,** "Christmas in Lilliput," *Antiques,* Dec., 1940.

*(Listed by title)*

"Doll Rarities in American Collections," *Antiques,* Vol. LXVII (Jan., 1955), pp. 60–1.

"Edison's Phonographic Doll," *Scientific American,* Vol. LXII, No. 17 (April 26, 1890), pp. 257, 263.

"Make-believe and Whimsey," *The Museum,* published by the Newark Museum, Vol. 7, No. 1, New Series, Winter, 1955.

"Making of Common Things, Dolls, The," *Chatterbox,* No. XXVII (1893), pp. 214–6.

"Wax Doll Manufacture, The," *Little Bouquet,* monthly magazine, June, 1875.

Figures given in italic type are illustration numbers, not page numbers. The letter C preceding a number refers to a color plate.

People are indexed by their surnames; dolls are indexed by full names. Page references for the names of partners, company officials, and the like, are to the *main* firm or company entry; references are not given for all other entries where such a name may be mentioned.

A text entry is duplicated in this index only when a large company produced more dolls than are listed in that company's text entry. The index attempts to give all the references for such companies. This index also assembles certain groups of dolls not listed by group in the alphabetical entries—dolls in specific costumes (Quaker, Scottish, etc.), for instance; dolls depicting motion-picture stars or dolls used in movies; and other categories.

Examine both the alphabetical text entries and the indexes for any particular item, since there are numerous variations in wording and/or spelling, and some lines and dolls are listed in a foreign language. See also Index of Marks.

# INDEX OF MARKS

The important parts of the marks shown in this book are listed here by category, as follows:

I. **Numerals,** both Arabic and Roman, except for obvious size numbers, or numbers representing dates or parts of addresses.

II. **Dates,** listed in chronological order. (Some of the numbers from 1894 to 1928 listed in Category I *may* actually represent dates.)

III. **Addresses** (except for the word "Germany," which appears in a great many marks).

IV. **Letters,** singly or with numerals. (Frequently, it was difficult to distinguish between a zero and an "O.") Included here are the Kestner letter and number size series (see page 353).

V. **Initials and abbreviations.** In this group, letters are frequently superimposed, reversed, and/or joined together. Also, initials are often separated by a size number. If this happens to be a zero, it can be mistaken as a middle initial. Some names, like "EFFanBEE," are spelled-out initials.

VI. **Names, words, and phrases** as they appear on dolls, with the given name, initial, or preposition first. (May sometimes overlap information in other categories, but valuable in deciphering hard-to-read marks.)

VII. **Symbols and shapes,** including the outlines of marks.

Similarities in marks are not necessarily proof of identity, since the same numeral or symbol may be found in the marks of more than one firm. Marks are difficult to read at best. There is variation in the capitalization of letters; "C" and "G" are easy to confuse; and numerals are often unclear. Thus, 3 and 8 are sometimes misread, as are 8 and 6, 1 and 7, 8 and 9, 4 and 9, and others. For example, the last digit in Ill. 588 is known from the patent papers to be "5," but on the doll itself it closely resembles a "6."

Index reference numerals in italics are to illustration numbers, not pages. Numerals combined with the letter "C" refer to color photographs.

## I. Numerals

| | | | |
|---|---|---|---|
| (lazy O), C14; 1060 | 28, 1041, 1363, 1440 | 100, 32, 37, 196, 342, 540, | 167, 361; 966, 980 |
| 00, 600 | 30, 73, 664, 937, 1063, 1340, | 582, 591, 604; 68-69, 100, 940 | 168, 991, 1612 |
| 09, 1431 | 1385, 1432 | 101, 342, 426, 493; 942, | 169, 1019, 1459, 1466-1467 |
| ½, 965, 1134, 1456 | 31, 972 | 1245, 1310 | 171, 355; 967, 981, 992 |
| 1, 113 | No. 31, 113, 222; 150 | 107, 342 | 180, 355 |
| No. 2, 93 | 32, 953, 1387, 1423 | 109, 213, 342; 765 | 186, 355 |
| II, 1514 | 34, 1387 | 110, 1300, 1694 | 186.5 1022 |
| 3-04, 1144 | 35 831 | 114, 264, 283, 284, 342; 822 | 187, 355 |
| No. 3, 329 | 36, 69, 956 | 115, 1694 | 189, 1022, 1025 |
| III, 1244 | 40, 1455 | 117, 944, 1241 | 190, 837 |
| No. 4, C6 | 42, 587 | 120, 571 | 191, 959 |
| IV, 1285, 1514 | 45, 934 | 122, 945, 953 | 192, 1029 |
| 5, 113 | 47, 1276 | 123, 1026 | 195, 355 |
| 5/3/0, 1426 | 48, 1337, 1695 | 126, 342; C19, C24; 588, | 196, 203 |
| No. 5, 329 | 50, 428, 1660 | 946-947, 1362 | 199, 1031 |
| No. 7, 1088 | 52, 585 | 128, 1587 | 200, 41, 1604, 1679 |
| No. 8, 1626 | 55, 957 | 129, 355 | 201, 275, 1030 |
| X, 1455 | 56, 935, 1235, 1659 | 137, 341 | 203, 585 |
| XI, 202 | 60, 585; 936, 1551-1552 | 139, 769 | 211, 352; 968, 982 |
| 12, 1235 | 62, 469 | 141, 961, 975 | 215, 993 |
| No. 12, 91 | 64, 811 | 146, 353 | 215, 993 |
| 13, 113 | 65, 949, 1356 | 148, 1022 | 216, 1163 |
| No. 13, 162 | 69, 772 | 149, 588, 626; 1638 | 227, C24; 1555, 1562 |
| 15, 203, 334 | 71, 588, 626; 1638 | 151, 1121 | 226, 1554 |
| 15/0, 834 | 72, C14; 1060 | 152, 654; 962, 976, 1698 | 231, 223; 539 |
| 16, 1085, 1417 | 77, 811 | 154, 318, 355; 577, 963, 977 | 232, 389 |
| 17, 1522 | 79, 773 | 156, 853 | 236, C24, 51, 1563 |
| 18, 1695, 1697 | 81, 984 | 158, 361; 1017 | 239, 1328 |
| 20, 1390 | 86, 1360 | 161, 462 | 240, 428, 472; 1584 |
| No. 22, 856, 862 | 89, 816, 1429 | 162, 964, 978 | 241, 472; 29, 969 |
| 23, C19; 1367, 1370, 1551 | 92, 21 | 164, 577, 989 | 243, 229, 970, 983 |
| 24, 585 | 93, 487 | 165, 1044 | 247, 1565 |
| 26, 984 | 95, 160 | 166, 990 | 248, 539 |
| 27, 1041 | 99, 774 | | |

## II. Dates

## III. Addresses

## IV. Letters

## V. Initials and Abbreviations

## VI. Names, Words, and Phrases

## VII. Symbols and Shapes